Long Island's

Prominent North Shore Families:

Their Estates and Their Country Homes

Volume II

Raymond E. and Judith A. Spinzia

VirtualBookworm

College Station, Texas

2006

Long Island's Prominent North Shore Families: Their Estates and Their Country Homes. Volume II, by Raymond E. and Judith A. Spinzia ISBN 1–58939–786–x.

Library of Congress Control Number: 2006926268

Published 2006 by Virtualbookworm.com Publishing Inc., P.O. Box 9949, College Station, TX 77842, US.

Manufactured in the United States of America

Table of Contents

Volume I

Acknowledgments. .   *v*

Introduction   *vii*

Maps of Long Island Estate Areas   *xiii*

Factors Applicable to Usage .   *xvi*

Surname Entries A – M   1

Volume II

Surname Entries N – Z   561

Appendices:

     Architects   897

     Civic Activists.   932

     Estate Names .   945

     Golf Course on former North Shore Estates .   975

     Hereditary Titles   976

     Landscape Architects .   977

     Maiden Names   1007

     Motion Pictures Filmed at North Shore Estates   1060

     Occupations   1066

     Rehabilitative Secondary Uses of Surviving Estate Houses   1102

     Statesmen and Diplomats Who Resided on Long Island's North Shore   1107

     Village Locations of Estates   1118

     America's First Age of Fortune: A Selected Bibliography   1133

     Selected Bibliographic References to Individual
     North Shore Estate Owners   1140

Biographical Sources Consulted   1193

Maps Consulted for Estate Locations   1194

Photographic and Map Credits   1195

Even though an individual may not have used Sr., Jr., I, II, etc., they have been added to the surnames in an attempt to designate relationships and alleviate confusion (the exception being President Theodore Roosevelt). In some instances, birth dates have been calculated using the age at the time of death as given in *The New York Times* obituary.

Estate ownership, as delineated by map sources, is not necessarily by individual but rather by a family's estate holdings, thereby giving a truer assessment of how a family's estate changed from 1927 through the Depression to the end of World War II.

Since the 1927 map used for Nassau County did not list acreage and the 1932 and 1946 maps occasionally omitted acreage, a definitive comparison of estate sizes has not been possible.

The same could be said for the estates in Suffolk County except that the maps used were from 1929, which only occasionally listed acreage, 1931, which did not list acreage, and from 1944 and occasionally 1946, which, like the Nassau County counterparts, occasionally omitted acreage.

The exact street address of some houses could not be determined due to the diminution of the estates by subdivision. In these cases, the road on which a major portion of the estate bordered has been recorded as the address. It should also be noted that some of the subsequent owners may not have lived in the estate's main house but rather in an outbuilding that had been converted into a residence. To aid in tracing the estate properties, these owners have been included in the hope that this will prove useful to future researchers.

Estate photographs in the Nassau County Museum Collection, in which photographs of many of the estates can be found and to which we have referred in this work are filed by village name. Unfortunately many of the village designations in the collection do not correspond to present-day village boundaries. In preparing these volumes, current (2006) village boundaries and street names have been used to locate the various estates. For this reason, there are discrepancies between the village names as used by the county and those included in these volumes. Therefore, it is necessary to refer to surname entries to determine in which village the Nassau County Museum's photographs have been filed.

The Spinzias

Nast, Conde (1874-1942)

Occupation(s):
publisher - president, *Vogue; House and Garden; Glamour; Vanity Fair;*
president, Conde Nast Publications, Inc.;
a founder and partner, Home Pattern Co.

attorney
capitalist - real estate - president, Park–Lexington Corp.

Marriage(s):
M/1 - 1902-1923 - Jeanne Clarisse Coudert (1879-1955)
M/2 - 1928 - Leslie Foster

Listed in *Long Island Society Register, 1929*: no
Address: Sands Point Road, Sands Point
Acreage / map sources: not on 1927 or 1946 maps
                                  15 acres / 1932 map
Name of estate: *Sandy Cay*
Year of construction: c. 1930
Style of architecture: Federal
Architect(s):   Ferruccio Vitale designed the
                                      swimming pool complex
                                      (for Nast)
Landscape architect(s):   Ferruccio Vitale, 1930 (for Nast)
Estate photographs can be found in the Nassau County Museum
    Collection filed under Sands Point/Nast.
House extant: no; demolished in 1954*
Historical notes:

pool complex, c. 1940

The house, originally named *Sandy Cay,* was built by Conde Nast.
Jeanne Clarisse Coudert Nast was the daughter of Charles R. Coudert of Manhattan. She subsequently married Jose Victor Onativia, Jr. of Manhattan.
Conde and Jeanne Coudert Nast's daughter Natica married Gerald Felix Warburg and resided at *Box Hill Farm* in Brookville. Their son Charles married Charlotte Babcock Brown and, subsequently, Juliet L. Houser.
Leslie Foster Nast subsequently married Rex Benson.
Conde and Leslie Foster Nast's daughter Leslie married Lord St. Just of Great Britain.
The estate was owned by Dorothy Schiff, Clarence Budington Kelland, and, subsequently, by Percy Uris, all of whom called it *Sandy Cay*.
*The house was destroyed by fire, but the two-story garage survived and has been converted into a residence.

Neelands, Thomas D., Jr. (1902-1972)

Occupation(s):
capitalist - founder, N. R. Airways (at Roosevelt Field);
chairman, finance committee, Robinson Aviation;
chairman, Capitol Airlines (which merged into United Airlines in 1960)
financier - founder, T. D. Neelands, Jr. & Co. (investment banking firm)
industrialist - chairman, finance committee, Proctor–Silex Corp.

Marriage(s):
Jennifer Stratton

Listed in *Long Island Society Register, 1929*: no
Address: Cornwells Beach Road, Sands Point
Acreage / map sources: not on 1927, 1932, or 1946 maps
Name of estate: *La Presqu' Ile*
Year of construction: 1924
Style of architecture: French Renaissance
Architect(s):   Thomas Harlan Ellett designed the service court which included
                                      a garage, guest house, and caretaker's cottage (for Cowl)

Landscape architect(s):
House extant: yes
Historical notes:

The house was built by Donald Hearn Cowl.
It was owned by Neelands, who called it *La Presqu' Ile*, and, subsequently, by Alexander Milton Lewyt.

Neff, Walter Perry

Occupation(s): financier - vice-president, Chemical Bank (formed in 1954 by the merger of
The Chemical Corn Exchange Bank and New York Trust Co.)
attorney

Marriage(s): Michele Diane Du Bois

Listed in *Long Island Society Register, 1929*: no
Address: Centre Island Road, Centre Island
Acreage / map sources: not on 1927, 1932, or 1946 maps
Name of estate:
Year of construction:
Style of architecture:
Architect(s):
Landscape architect(s):
House extant: unconfirmed
Historical notes:

The *Social Register New York, 1964* and the *Social Register, 1981* and *1999* list W. Perry and Michele D. Du Bois Neff as residing on Centre Island, while the *Social Register, 1983* lists the Neffs' address as Dogwood Lane, Mill Neck.
He was the son of Dr. and Mrs. Eugene Neff of Madison, WI.
Michele Diane Du Bois Neff was the daughter of Randall Milne Du Bois of Upper Brookville.

Neilson, Raymond Perry Rodgers, Sr. (1881-1964)

Occupation(s): artist*
educator - instructor, Art Students League;
instructor, National Academy of Design

Marriage(s): M/1 - 1906-1924 - Mary Stevenson Park
M/2 - 1940-1957 - Inglis Griswold (d. 1957)

Listed in *Long Island Society Register, 1929*: yes
Address: Bostwick Lane, Old Westbury
Acreage / map sources: on 1927 map (owned by Mrs. Park Neilson)
14 acres / 1932 map (owned by W. G. Park)
10 acres / 1946 map (owned by Dr. A. Park)
Name of estate:
Year of construction:
Style of architecture: 20th-century Eclectic
Architect(s): Algernon S. Bell designed the house (for Neilson)
McKim, Meade and White designed alterations (for W. G. Park)
Landscape architect(s):
House extant: yes
Historical notes:

The house was built by Raymond Perry Rodgers Neilson, Sr.
He was the son of Louis and Anne Perry Rodgers Neilson of Manhattan.
Mary Stevenson Park Neilson was the daughter of William Gray and Elizabeth Sweitzer Park, who resided at *Turnpike Cottage* in Old Westbury. Her brother Darragh Anderson Park, Sr. was married to Dorothy Hyde and, subsequently, Nona Gibbs McAdoo. He resided at *Hyde Park* in Old Brookville.
Inglis Griswold Neilson was the daughter of Matthew Griswold of Erie, PA, and a descendant of Governors Matthew Griswold and Roger Griswold of CT.
Neilson's son Raymond Perry Rodgers, Jr. married Margaret Kane Pensinger, the daughter of George H. Pensinger of Santa Barbara, CA.
*A portrait artist, who studied with William Merritt Chase and George B. Bridgman, Neilson received many awards for his paintings.
The estate was, subsequently, owned by William Gray Park, who called it *Turnpike Cottage*.

Netter, Dr. Frank H. (1906-1991)

Occupation(s):   physician
                                             educator
                                             artist -   medical illustrator* - *The Ciba Collection of Medical Illustrations* (13 volumes); *Atlas of Human Anatomy,* 1989

Marriage(s):   1956-1991 - Mary Vera Burrows (d. 1993)

Listed in *Long Island Society Register, 1929*: no
Address: Route 25A, Muttontown
Acreage / map sources: not on 1927, 1932, or 1946 maps
Name of estate:
Year of construction: c. 1913
Style of architecture: Georgian Revival
Architect(s):   Henry Otis Chapman designed the house (for G. Smith)
Landscape architect(s):   Charles Wellford Leavitt and Sons (for G. Smith)
House extant: yes
Historical notes:

     The house, originally named *Blythewood,* was built by George Smith.
     Alfred Cotton Bedford purchased the estate from Smith in 1923 and renamed it *Pemberton.*
     The estate was owned by Albert L. Hoffman, Sr., who renamed it *Radnor House*, and, subsequently, by Netter.
     *Netter drew over 4,000 illustrations of human anatomy, physiology, and pathology. He was the first to illustrate an open-heart operation and organ transplants. His 13-volume work *The Ciba Collection of Medical Illustrations* sold over 3 million copies and is used in medical schools throughout the world. For the 1939 Golden Gate Exposition, he created a seven-foot transparent woman that depicted the physical and sexual development of a woman including the development and birth of a baby. It was so realistic that, it was reported, that every 15 minutes it caused a viewer to faint. [*The New York Times* September 19, 1991, section D, p. 28.]
     Vera Burrows Netter was the daughter of Henry E. Burrows of Manhattan. She had previously been married to James D. Stetson.
     The estate was occupied by the Church for the Realization of God, and purchased in 1990 by developer, Alan Stam. In 1990, the house and five acres were for sale. The asking price was $3 million. The new (1990) house, built on the west side of the driveway, was also for sale in 1990 for $2 million.

Nicastro, Louis Joseph (b. 1928)

Occupation(s):   industrialist -   chairman, president, chief operating officer, WMS Industries (home and arcade video games, slot machine, and pinball game manufacturer); president - XCOR International, Inc.; chief executive, Iota Industries
                                             financier -   director and vice-president, Inland Credit Corp.; chairman of board, Serose Holding Co.

Marriage(s):   1950 - Rosalie Laura Vanson

Listed in *Long Island Society Register, 1929*: no
Address: Horse Shoe Road and Cleft Road, Mill Neck
Acreage / map sources: not on 1927, 1932, or 1946 maps
Name of estate:
Year of construction: 1922
Style of architecture: Italian Renaissance
Architect(s):   Guy Lowell designed the house (for A. V. Davis)
Landscape architect(s):   Ferruccio Vitale, 1922 (for A. V. Davis)
                                             Ellen Biddle Shipman (for A. V. Davis)
House extant: yes
Historical notes:

     The house was built by Arthur Vining Davis.
     The estate was, subsequently, owned by Nicastro.

Nicholas, Harry Ingersoll, II (1884-1961)

Occupation(s):   financier - stockbroker

Marriage(s):   1907-1961 - Dorothy Snow (1886-1969)
             - landscape architect
              writer - numerous articles on landscape design

Listed in *Long Island Society Register, 1929*: yes
Address: Jericho – Oyster Bay Road, Muttontown
Acreage / map sources: on 1927 map; 24 acres / 1932 map; 21 acres / 1946 map
Name of estate: *Rolling Hill Farm*
Year of construction:
Style of architecture:
Architect(s):
Landscape architect(s):
House extant: unconfirmed
Historical notes:

 Harry Ingersoll Nicholas II was the son of Harry Ingersoll and Alice M. Hollins Nicholas, Sr. of *Virginia Farm* in North Babylon. His sister Beatrice married Edward Nicoll Townsend, Jr. of Manhattan. His sister Reta married Uriel Atwood Murdock II and resided in Babylon. His sister Daisy married Grosvenor Nicholas and resided in Old Westbury. His sister Evelyn married Alexander Duncan Cameron Arnold, Sr. of West Islip and, subsequently, Joseph H. Stevenson of Hewlett. His sister Elsie married Alonzo Potter and resided at *Harbor House* in St. James.
 Dorothy Snow Nicholas was the daughter of Frederick A. and Mary Palen Snow who resided at *Gardenside* in Southampton. Her brother George, who resided in Syosset, married Carmel White and Carol Kobbe.
 The Nicholases' son Harry Ingersoll Nicholas III married Katherine F. Elkins and, subsequently, Josephine Lee Auchincloss, whose parents resided at *Builtover* in Roslyn Heights. Their son Frederick married Mary Sprague.

Nichols, Acosta, Sr. (1872-1945)

Occupation(s):   financier - partner, Spencer Trask and Co. (investment banking firm);
                 director, Bank of America;
           capitalist - director, Coahuila Coil Railway Co.;
                 real estate - director, Broadway Realty Co.;
                 director, Mercantile Properties Inc.
           industrialist - director, American Sugar Beet Co.;
                 director, Salamanca Sugar Co.;
                 director, Frisbie & Stanfield Knitting Co.;
                 director and treasurer, Mexican Coal & Coke Co.
Civic Activism: secretary, Community Service Society;
           *

Marriage(s):   1909-1945 - Elizabeth Abbott Lane (1872-1950)
             - Civic Activism: member of board, Society for the Prevention
                    of Cruelty to Children;
                  director, Town Hall, Inc., NYC

Listed in *Long Island Society Register, 1929*: yes
Address: Oyster Bay Cove Road, Oyster Bay Cove
Acreage / map sources: on 1927 map; no acreage given on 1932 map; 43 acres / 1946 map
Name of estate: *Wothiholme*
Year of construction:
Style of architecture:
Architect(s):
Landscape architect(s):
House extant: unconfirmed
Historical notes:

 *Acosta Nichols, Sr. was also director of the Nassau County chapter of the Boy Scouts of America and a member of the board of directors of the Theodore Roosevelt Memorial Association. He donated a complete laboratory building to the Long Island Biological Association.

Nichols, Francis Tilden, Sr.

Occupation(s):
Civic Activism:
president, local school board;
trustee, Village of Muttontown

Marriage(s):
1929 - Louise Thayer

Listed in *Long Island Society Register, 1929*: no
Address: Brookville Road, Muttontown
Acreage / map sources: not on 1927 map; 65 acres / 1932 map; 66 acres / 1946 map
Name of estate: *Bayberry Downs*
Year of construction: c. 1930
Style of architecture: French Manor
Architect(s): William E. Frenayne, Jr. designed the house (for F. T. Nichols, Sr.)
Landscape architect(s): Ferruccio Vitale (for F. T. Nichols, Sr.)
House extant: yes
Historical notes:

The house, originally named *Bayberry Downs,* was built by Francis Tilden Nichols, Sr.
He was the son of William Henry and Rose Tilden Nichols, Jr., who resided at *Applegarth* on Centre Island. His sister Marian married William Payson Viles and resided in Augusta, ME.
Louise Thayer Nichols was the daughter of Frank H. Thayer of Boston.
In 1953, the Nichols' twenty-two-year-old son, Francis Tilden Nichols, Jr., accidentally shot himself while hunting on the estate.
The estate was, subsequently, owned by Esmond Bradley Martin, Sr.

Nichols, George, Sr. (1878-1950)

Occupation(s): capitalist - partner, Minot, Hooper & Co. (cotton dealers)
Civic Activism: president, Cold Spring Harbor Whaling Museum

Marriage(s):
1917-1950 - Jane N. Morgan
- Civic Activism: trustee, Community Service Society (formed by merger
of Charity Organization Society and Association
for Improving the Condition of the Poor);
board member, Huntington Township Art League (now,
Art League of Long Island)*

Listed in *Long Island Society Register, 1929*: yes
Address: Lawrence Hill Road, Cold Spring Harbor
Acreage / map sources: not on 1929 map; on 1931 map
75 acres / 1944 and 1946 maps
Name of estate: *Uplands*
Year of construction: 1915
Style of architecture: Georgian Revival
Architect(s): Forster, Gade and Graham
Landscape architect(s):
House extant: yes
Historical notes:

front facade, 2004

The *Social Register, Summer 1950* lists George and Jane N Morgan Nichols [Sr.] as residing at *Uplands* in Cold Spring Harbor.
He was the son of John White Treadwell and Mary Blake Slocum Nichols, who resided at *The Kettles* in Cove Neck.
Jane N. Morgan Nichols was the daughter of John Pierpont and Jane Grew Morgan, Jr., who resided at *Matinecock Point* on East Island in Glen Cove.
The Nicholses' daughter Henrietta married Benjamin Barnes and, subsequently, August Meyer. Their son George married Nancy Taylor Kinks. Their daughter Jane married Walter Hines Page II. The Pages also resided on Lawrence Hill Road. *[See following entry for additional family information.]*
*The Huntington Township Art League was housed in the barn complex of the estate for awhile.
Part of the estate is now the Long Island Nature Conservancy's Uplands Farms Sanctuary.

Nichols, John White Treadwell (1852-1920)

Occupation(s):   capitalist - partner, Minot, Hooper & Co. (cotton dealers)

Marriage(s):   1876-1920 - Mary Blake Slocum (1854-1943)

Listed in *Long Island Society Register, 1929*: yes
Address: private road off Cove Neck Road, Cove Neck
Acreage / map sources: on 1927 map (owned by Mrs. J. W. Nichols)
                                      33 acres / 1932 and 1946 maps (owned by Mrs. J. W. Nichols)
Name of estate: *The Kettles*
Year of construction: c. 1903
Style of architecture: Dutch Colonial
Architect(s):   Minerva Nichols designed the house (for J. W. T. Nichols)
Landscape architect(s):
House extant: no; demolished by subsequent owner Charles Wang
Historical notes:

    The house, originally named *The Kettles,* was built by John White Treadwell Nichols.
    The *Long Island Society Register, 1929* lists Mary Blake Slocum Nichols as residing at *The Kettles* in Cove Neck.
She was the daughter of William Henry and Sarah Elizabeth Williams Slocum, who resided in Jamaica Plain, MA.
    The Nicholses' son, George Nichols, Sr., who resided at *Uplands* in Cold Spring Harbor, married Jane N. Morgan, the
daughter of John Pierpont and Jane Grew Morgan, Jr. of *Matinecock Point* on East Island in Glen Cove. Their daughter
Elizabeth married Edwin Pemberton Taylor, Jr. and resided at *White Oaks* in Oyster Bay Cove. Their daughter Susan
married Harold Trowbridge Pulsifer, the son of Nathan Trowbridge and Almira Houghton Valentine Pulsifer, and resided
at *Cooper's Bluff* in Cove Neck. Their son William married Isabel Bruce and resided at *Four Winds* in Laurel Hollow.
Their daughter Helen married Mansfield Esterbrook. Their son John married Cornelia Du Bois Floyd and resided in
Garden City and at the William Floyd estate in Mastic Beach. The latter house is open to the public under the auspices of
the National Park Service.
    [See previous entry for additional family information.]

Nichols, William Henry, Jr. (d. 1928)

Occupation(s):   industrialist - president, General Chemical Co.;
                                              chairman of board, Allied Chemical & Dye Corp.

Marriage(s):   Rose Tilden (d. 1943)

Listed in *Long Island Society Register, 1929*: yes
Address: Centre Island Road, Centre Island
Acreage / map sources: on 1927 map
                                        63 acres / 1932 and 1946 maps
Name of estate: *Applegarth*
Year of construction: 1892
Style of architecture: Elizabethan
Architect(s):   Renwick, Aspinwall and Owen designed the house
                                        (for Wetmore)
Landscape architect(s):
House extant: no; demolished c. 1940
Historical notes:

    The house, originally named *Applegarth,* was built by Charles Whitman Wetmore.
    The estate was, subsequently, owned by Nichols, who continued to call it *Applegarth.*
    The *Long Island Society Register, 1929* lists Rose Tilden Nichols as residing at *Applegarth* on Centre Island, while the
Social Register, Summer 1932 lists her as residing at *The Briar Patch* on Fishers Island and the *Social Register, Summer
1937* lists her residence as York Harbor, ME.
    She was the daughter of Samuel D. and Harriet Packwood Tilden.
    The Nicholses' son Francis Tilden Nichols, Sr. resided at *Bayberry Downs* in Muttontown. Their daughter Marian
married William Payson Viles, the son of Blaine B. Viles of Augusta, ME.

Nickerson, Hoffman (1888-1965)

Occupation(s):
politician - assemblyman, New York State Legislature, 1916
writer - *The Inquisition,* 1923;
        The Turning Point of Revolution, 1928;
        The American Rich, 1930;
        Can We Limit War, 1934;
        The Armed Horde, 1793-1939, 1940;
        Arms and Policy, 1945;
        The New Slavery, 1947;
        The Loss of Unity, 1961

Marriage(s):
M/1 - 1916 - Ruth Constance Comstock
M/2 - 1938-1965 - Jane Soames (1901-1988)
     - writer - *Short History of North Africa, from Pre-Roman*
        Times to the Present: Libya, Tunisia, Algeria,
        Morocco, 1961;
        Homage to Malthus, 1975;
        The English;
        The Coast of Barbary;
        Belloc, 1970 (editor);
        The Origins of the First World War
         (translated text from French);
        The Political and Social Doctrine of Fascism
         (translated text from Italian)

Listed in *Long Island Society Register, 1929*: yes
Address: West Shore Road, Mill Neck
Acreage / map sources: on 1927 map
                 41 acres / 1932 map
                 38 acres / 1946 map
Name of estate: *Monomoit*
Year of construction: 1895
Style of architecture: Dutch Colonial
Architect(s):
Landscape architect(s):
House extant: yes
Historical notes:

    The house, originally named *Steepways,* was built by Phillips Abbott.
    The estate was owned by Nickerson, who called it *Monomoit,* and, subsequently, by Mrs. Hollander.
    Hoffman Nickerson took part in General Pershing's pursuit of Pancho Villa into Mexico.
    Both the *Long Island Society Register, 1929* and the *Social Register, Summer 1937* list Hoffman and Ruth C. Comstock Nickerson as residing at *Monomoit,* West Shore Road, Oyster Bay [Mill Neck]. The *Social Register, Summer 1945* lists Ruth C. Comstock Nickerson as residing in Edgarton, MA, while the *Social Register, 1988* lists Ruth C. Comstock Nickerson's residence as 116 East 66th Street, NYC.
    The *Social Register New York, 1948* lists Hoffman and Jane Soames Nickerson as residing on West Shore Road, Oyster Bay [Mill Neck], while the *Social Register New York, 1965* lists them as residing on Cove Road, Oyster Bay. The *Social Register, 1988* lists Jane Soames Nickerson as residing on Dogwood Lane, Locust Valley.
    Who Was Who, 4:703, lists the name of Nickerson's estate as *Yellow Cote House* and the address as Oyster Bay.
    The Nickersons' son Eugene Hoffman Nickerson served as Nassau County Executive. He was married to Marie Louise Steiner.

Monomoit

Nitze, Paul Henry (1907-2004)

Occupation(s):	statesman - Secretary of Navy in Department of Defense, 1963-1967;
	Deputy Secretary of Defense, 1967-1969;
	United States Ambassador-at-Large, 1986
	diplomat - member, United States delegation to Strategic Arms
	Limitation Talks, 1969-1974;
	Chief United States delegate, International Nuclear Forces
	Talks, 1981-1984
	financier - member, Dillon Reed & Co. (investment banking firm)
Civic Activism:	a founder, Johns Hopkins School of Advanced International Studies,
	Washington, DC, 1943
Marriage(s):	M/1 - 1932-1987 - Phyllis Pratt (1912-1987)
	M/2 - Elizabeth Scott

Listed in *Long Island Society Register, 1929*: no
Address: Old Tappan Road, Glen Cove
Acreage / map sources: on 1927 map (owned by J. T. Pratt)
                                             49 acres / 1932 map (owned by R. B. Pratt)
                                             11 acres / 1946 map (owned by Nitze)
Name of estate: *The Farm House*
Year of construction: c. 1913
Style of architecture: Neo-Colonial
Architect(s):   Charles A. Platt designed the house (for J. T. Pratt, Jr.)
Landscape architect(s):
House extant: yes
Historical notes:

The house, originally named *The Farm House*, was built by John Teele Pratt, Jr.
The estate was, subsequently, owned by Nitze who continued to call it *The Farm House*.
Phyllis Pratt Nitze was the daughter of John Teele and Ruth Baker Sears Pratt, Sr., who resided at *Manor House* in Glen Cove. Her brother John Teele Pratt, Jr. resided at *Beechwood*, which was also located on Old Tappan Road in Glen Cove. Her sister Sally married James Jackson, Jr. and resided in MA. Her sister Virginia married Robert Helyer Thayer, Sr. and resided in Glen Cove.
The son of William Albert Nitze, Paul Henry Nitze was a recipient of the Presidential Medal of Freedom. In 2004, the Navy launched the destroyer *USS Nitze*, named in his honor.
Paul and Phyllis Nitze's son Albert married Ann Kendall Richards, the daughter of E. E. Richards of South Bend, IN, and Clearwater Beach, FL.
In 1995, the estate was owned by Dr. Lorenzo Sanesi, who called it *La Primavera*.

Niven, John Ballantine (1871-1954)

Occupation(s):	financier - founder, Touche, Niven and Co. (accounting firm)
Civic Activism:	mayor, Village of Mill Neck;
	treasurer, St. Andrew's Society of New York State
Marriage(s):	1905-1954 - Susan Wallace Ogden Gordon (d. 1968)

Listed in *Long Island Society Register, 1929*: yes
Address: Mill Hill Road, Mill Neck
Acreage / map sources: on 1927 map; no acreage given on 1932 map; 20 acres / 1946 map
Name of estate: *Rhuna Craig*
Year of construction: c. 1923-1928
Style of architecture: Tudor
Architect(s):   Francis A. Nelson designed the house (for Niven)
Landscape architect(s):
House extant: yes
Historical notes:

The house, originally named *Rhuna Craig*, was built by John Ballantine Niven.
The estate was, subsequently, owned by Leroi Close.

Nixon, Lewis (1861-1940)

Occupation(s):   naval architect*

industrialist -   president and director, United States Shipbuilding Co.;
                                  founder, Standard Motor Co.;
                                  founder and president, Lewis Nixon Shipyards;
                                  president, Nixon Nitration Works
politician -   chairman, New York State Democratic Convention, 1906
diplomat -   delegate, Fourth Pan-American Conference, 1910;
                              E. E. and M. P. on special mission to represent the
                              United States at Chilean Centenary, 1910

Civic Activism: president, board of directors, Webb Institute of Naval Architecture,
                              Glen Cove

Marriage(s):   M/1 - 1891-1937 - Sally Lewis Wood (d. 1937)
M/2 - 1938-1940 - Mary Doran Martin

Listed in *Long Island Society Register, 1929*: yes
Address: Barker's Point Road, Sands Point
Acreage / map sources: on 1927 map
                              not on 1932 or 1946 maps

Name of estate:
Year of construction:
Style of architecture:
Architect(s):
Landscape architect(s):
House extant: unconfirmed
Historical notes:

    The *Long Island Society Register, 1929* lists Lewis and Sally Lewis Wood Nixon as residing in Sands Point, while the *Social Register, Summer 1932* lists them as residing in Monmouth Beach, NJ.
    *Nixon designed the battleships *USS Oregon, USS Indiana,* and *USS Massachusetts,* and the cruiser *USS Chattanooga.*

Norris, James King (1893-1973)

Occupation(s):   industrialist -   chairman, Utica Drop Forge and Tool Corp.;
                                    president, Central Foundry Co.

Marriage(s):   Laura B. F. Lewis

Listed in *Long Island Society Register, 1929*: no
Address: Moore's Hill Road, Laurel Hollow
Acreage / map sources: not on 1927 or 1932 maps
                              7 acres / 1946 map
Name of estate: *The Acre*
Year of construction: c. 1937
Style of architecture:
Architect(s):
Landscape architect(s):
House extant: unconfirmed
Historical notes:

    The house, originally named *The Acre*, was built by James King Norris.
    The *Social Register, Summer 1950* lists James King and Laura B. F. Lewis Norris as residing at *The Acre* in East Norwich [Laurel Hollow].
    The Norrises' son William married Patricia Gates, whose father Thomas S. Gates of Devon, PA, was Secretary of the Navy and Secretary of Defense in President Dwight Eisenhower's administration.

Norton, Huntington (1878-1958)

Occupation(s):   financier - stockbroker

Marriage(s):   M/1 - 1906 - Marie Adele Montant
                                  M/2 - 1938-1958 - Helen Lambert (b. 1891)
                                      - capitalist - real estate - developer
                                        politician - assemblyman, Connecticut State Legislature
                                            from Town of Durham, 1953-1957

Listed in *Long Island Society Register, 1929*: yes
Address: East Main Street, Oyster Bay
Acreage / map sources: on c. 1922 map
                                  not on 1927, 1932, or 1946 maps
Name of estate: *Notley Hill*
Year of construction: 1919
Style of architecture: Long Island Farmhouse
Architect(s):   Peabody, Wilson and Brown designed the house (for H. Norton)
Landscape architect(s):
House extant: unconfirmed
Historical notes:

   The house, originally named *Notley Hill*, was built by Huntington Norton.
   He is listed in the February 1919 telephone directory at this address.
   The *Long Island Society Register, 1929* lists Huntington and Marie A. Montant Norton as residing at *Notley Hill* in Oyster Bay.
   She was the daughter of Augustus P. and Hanah M. Townsend Montant who resided at *Ramsbroke* in Oyster Bay.

Norton, Skeffington Sanxay, Jr. (1899-1977)

Occupation(s):   shipping - chairman, Norton, Lilly & Co. (cargo steamship company);
                                             director, Norton Line (foreign flag-carrier operating out of
                                                 eastern South American ports)
Civic Activism: advisor to War Shipping Board during World War II

Marriage(s):   1923 - Susan Scott

Listed in *Long Island Society Register, 1929*: yes
Address: Cedar Swamp Road, Brookville
Acreage / map sources: on 1927 map (owned by S. S. Norton)
                                  26 acres / 1932 map (owned by S. S. Norton)
                                  24 acres / 1946 map (owned by S. K. Norton)
Name of estate: *North Meadow Farm*
Year of construction:
Style of architecture:
Architect(s):
Landscape architect(s):
House extant: unconfirmed
Historical notes:

   The *Long Island Society Register, 1929* lists Skeffington Sanxay and Susan Scott Norton, Jr. as residing in Jericho [Brookville], while both the *Social Register, Summer 1932* and *1937* list their address as Cedar Swamp Road, Glen Head [Brookville]. The *Social Register New York, 1948* lists the Nortons' residence as Piping Rock Road, Locust Valley, while the *Social Register New York, 1976* lists them as residing at 35 Sutton Place, NYC.
   Susan Scott Norton was the daughter of Walter Scott of Pelham Manor, NY.
   The Nortons' son Skeffington Sanxay Norton III married Virginia Shirley Wendel, the daughter of Hugo Otto Wendel of Cincinnati, OH. Their daughter Janet married H. Edward Bilkey, Jr. Their daughter Ann married Clinton Gilbert, Jr. Their daughter Susan married William Stewart and resided in Old Westbury. She subsequently married James A. Thomas of Manhattan.
   [See following entry for additional family information.]

Norton, Skeffington Sanxay, Sr. (1869-1931)

Occupation(s):   shipping - partner and chairman, Norton, Lilly & Co. (cargo steamship
                                                     company)

Marriage(s):   1893-1931 - Susan Howard King (1872-1953)
                                        - Civic Activism: board member, Peoples Chorus of New York City;
                                                        chairman, Greenwich House Music School, NYC

Listed in *Long Island Society Register, 1929*: yes
Address: Cedar Swamp Road, Brookville
Acreage / map sources: on 1927 map (owned by S. S. Norton)
                                26 acres / 1932 map (owned by S. S. Norton)
                                24 acres / 1946 map (owned by S. K. Norton)
Name of estate: *North Meadow Farm*
Year of construction:
Style of architecture:
Architect(s):
Landscape architect(s):
House extant: unconfirmed
Historical notes:

   Skeffington Sanxay Norton, Sr.'s grandfather John Norton founded the firm of John Norton and Sons which became
Norton, Lilly & Co.
   Susan Howard King Norton was the daughter of General Horatio C. King.
   The Nortons' daughter Rose married Enos W. Curtin. Their daughter Ethel married Gordon Saltonstall Howe, Jr. of
Haverhill, MA. Their daughter Esther married George Soule and, subsequently, Baron Charles Philip von Wrangel of
Huebenthal, Russia.
   [See previous entry for additional family information.]

Noyes, David Chester, Sr. (1883-1954)

Occupation(s):   capitalist - real estate - director and secretary, Douglas L. Elliman Co.
                                                              (owned upper east-side apartment buildings
                                                               on Park Avenue);
                                                           director, several holding companies for
                                                              apartment buildings in The Bronx
                                financier - director and secretary, Douglas L. Elliman Brokerage Co.
                                                     (insurance brokerage firm)
Civic Activism: trustee, St. Luke's Home for Aged Women;
                                president, Washington Square Home

Marriage(s):   1916-1954 - Eva Mali (1894-1988)

Listed in *Long Island Society Register, 1929*: no
Address: Saw Mill Road, Cold Spring Harbor
Acreage / map sources: not on 1929 map; on 1931 map (owned by D. C. Noyes);
                                23 acres / 1944 and 1946 maps (name misspelled as Eva N. Noyes)
Name of estate: *Netherwood*
Year of construction: c. 1928
Style of architecture: French Provincial
Architect(s):   Noel and Miller designed the house (for D. C. Noyes, Sr.)
Landscape architect(s):
House extant: yes
Historical notes:

   The house, originally named *Netherwood,* was built by David Chester Noyes, Sr.
   Eva Mali Noyes' father Pierre Mali was a Manhattan merchant and Belgian Consul–General to the United States.
   The Noyeses' daughter Frances married Robert Duncan Elder, Jr. Their daughter Jean married Peter Takal. Their son
David Chester Noyes, Jr. married Elizabeth Bull, the daughter of Melville Bull of Manhattan, and resided in Cold Spring
Harbor and Lloyd Harbor.

Noyes, Winchester (1878-1954)

Occupation(s): shipping - president, J. H. Winchester & Co. (world-wide shipping agents and brokers)

Civic Activism: president, American Seamen's Friend Society; chairman of board, Seamen's House

Marriage(s): 1899-1954 - Helen Humpstone (1879-1956)

Listed in *Long Island Society Register, 1929*: yes
Address: off Laurel Hollow Road, Laurel Hollow
Acreage / map sources: not on 1927 map; 4 acres / 1932 map; 5 acres / 1946 map
Name of estate: *Tenacres*
Year of construction:
Style of architecture:
Architect(s):
Landscape architect(s):
House extant: unconfirmed
Historical notes:

Both the *Long Island Society Register, 1929* and the *Social Register, Summer 1951* list Winchester and Helen Humpstone Noyes as residing at *Tenacres* in Huntington [Laurel Hollow].

Helen Humpstone Noyes' brother Ernest married Violet Morse.

The Noyeses' daughter Mary married Seldon Chapin. Their daughter Hope married James Mulford Townsend, Jr.

Oakman, Walter George, Sr. (1845-1922)

Occupation(s): financier - chairman of board, Guaranty Trust Co.
capitalist - vice-president, Central Railroad of New Jersey;
president, Richmond & Virginia & Georgia Railroad Co.;
director, Brooklyn Heights Railroad Co.;
director, Brooklyn Rapid Transit Co.;
director, Buffalo, Rochester, & Pittsburgh Railway Co.;
real estate - director, Greeley Square Realty Co.
industrialist - director, Jefferson & Clearfield Coal & Iron Co.;
director, American Car & Foundry Co.

Marriage(s): 1879-1922 - Elizabeth Conkling (1856-1931)

Listed in *Long Island Society Register, 1929*: no
Address: Willis Avenue, Roslyn
Acreage / map sources: on 1906 map
not on 1927, 1932, or 1946 maps
Name of estate: *Oakdene*
Year of construction: c. 1900
Style of architecture: Colonial Revival
Architect(s): Grosvenor Atterbury designed the house (for Oakman)
Landscape architect(s):
House extant: no; demolished c. 1946*
Historical notes:

rear facade

The house, originally named *Oakdene*, was built by Walter George Oakman, Sr.

The Oakmans had previously resided in Islip.

Elizabeth Conkling Oakman was the daughter of United States Senator and boss of New York's Republican party machine Roscoe Conkling.

Walter George and Elizabeth Conkling Oakman, Sr.'s daughter Helen married Buchan M. Liddell and resided at *Ashford* in Ludlow, England. Their daughter Katharine married John Hammond. Their son George Walter Oakman, Jr. was severely wounded during World War II while serving with Britain's Coldstream Guard.

In 1912, Henry D. Walbridge purchased the estate and called it *Waldene*.

*The estate was, subsequently, owned by Samuel Rubel, who subdivided it for a housing development.

Oberlin, Abraham (b. 1921)

Occupation(s):   industrialist - co-founder with Meyer Osofsky, president, and chairman
                              of board, Aileen Inc. (women's apparel manufacturer)*

Marriage(s):

Listed in *Long Island Society Register, 1929*: no
Address: Overlook Road, Lattingtown
Acreage / map sources: not on 1927, 1932, or 1946 maps
Name of estate:
Year of construction: 1917
Style of architecture: Georgian Revival
Architect(s):   Rouse and Goldstone designed the original house (for Cozzens)
                              Roger Harrington Bullard designed the addition of two lateral wings,
                                 1929 (for Morgan)
Landscape architect(s):   Charles Wellford Leavitt and Sons (for Cozzens)
Estate photographs can be found in the Nassau County Museum Collection filed under Locust Valley/Cozzens.
House extant: yes
Historical notes:

   The house, originally named *Maple Knoll,* was built by
Issachar Cozzens III.
   The estate was owned by Henry Sturgis Morgan, Sr. and,
subsequently, by Oberlin.
   *In 1995 Oberlin retired from the company's
management.

front facade, 1920

O'Connor, John A. (1866-1953)

Occupation(s):   artist

Marriage(s):   Nathalie du Vivier

Listed in *Long Island Society Register, 1929*: yes
Address: East Main Street, Oyster Bay
Acreage / map sources: not on 1927 map
                              no acreage given on 1932 map
                              2 acres / 1946 map
Name of estate: *Sunnymede*
Year of construction: c. 1896
Style of architecture: Tudor
Architect(s):
Landscape architect(s):
House extant: no
Historical notes:

   The house, originally named *Sunnymede,* was built by Stanley Walker Dexter.
   The estate was, subsequently, owned by O'Connor, who continued to call it *Sunnymede*.
   The *Long Island Society Register, 1929* lists John A. and Nathalie du Vivier O'Connor as residing at *Sunnymede* in
Oyster Bay. The *Social Register, 1952* lists the O'Connors as residing in Oyster Bay.
   Nathalie du Vivier O'Connor was the daughter of Charles du Vivier of Manhattan. Her brother Edward married
Jacqueline Constance Delmonico.

O'Donohue, Charles A. (1859-1935)

Occupation(s):   financier -   director, Kings Country Trust Co.;
                                                              trustee, East River Savings Bank, NYC

Marriage(s):   Olive A. Scoville (d. 1951)

Listed in *Long Island Society Register, 1929*: yes
Address: East Shore Road, Huntington Bay
Acreage / map sources: not on 1929 map
                                        on 1931 map
                                        no acreage given on 1944 map

Name of estate:
Year of construction: c. 1917
Style of architecture: Georgian Revival
Architect(s):   Severance and Schumm designed the house
                                            (for O'Donohue)

Landscape architect(s):
House extant: yes
Historical notes:

front facade, 2004

    The house was built by Charles A. O'Donohue.
    Both the *Brooklyn Blue Book and Long Island Society Register, 1918* and *1921* list Charles A. and Olive A. Scoville O'Donohue as residing at *The Moorings* in Bay Shore. The *Long Island Society Register, 1929* lists the O'Donohues as residence as Shore Road, Huntington [Huntington Bay].
    The house is on The National Register of Historic Places.

Oeland, Isaac Raymond, Sr. (1862-1941)

Occupation(s):   attorney* - partner, Oeland and Kuhn
                                        industrialist - president, Palmetto Oil Co.

Marriage(s):   1885-1941 - Anne Withers

Listed in *Long Island Society Register, 1929*: yes
Address: Woodbury Road and Syosset – Woodbury Road, Woodbury
Acreage / map sources: on 1927 map
                                        no acreage given on 1932 map
                                        13 acres / 1946 map

Name of estate: *Larch*
Year of construction:
Style of architecture:
Architect(s):
Landscape architect(s):
House extant: unconfirmed
Historical notes:

    The *Long Island Society Register, 1929* lists Isaac Raymond and Annie [Anne] Withers Oeland [Sr.] as residing at *Larch* in Woodbury.
    *Isaac Raymond Oeland, Sr. was the attorney for the Brooklyn Rapid Transit Co. and the *Brooklyn Eagle*. As special assistant to the United States Attorney General, he prosecuted the World War I German spy Captain Franz von Rintelin.
    The Oelands' daughter Cathleen married William Henry Harrison Childs and, subsequently, Frederick Henry Grau, with whom she resided in Great Neck.

Oelsner, Edward Carl William, Sr. (1889-1973)

Occupation(s):   shipping -   founder, president, and chairman of board, United States Navigation*

Marriage(s):   Eva Pearl

Listed in *Long Island Society Register, 1929*: no
Address: Yacht Club Road, Centre Island
Acreage / map sources: not on 1927, 1932, or 1946 maps
Name of estate: *Seacroft*
Year of construction: c. 1906
Style of architecture: Spanish Colonial
Architect(s):   Frederick R. Hirsh designed the house (for S. T. Shaw, Sr.)
Landscape architect(s):
House extant: yes
Historical notes:

The house, originally named *The Sunnyside,* was built by Samuel T. Shaw, Sr.
The estate was, subsequently, owned by George Edgar Brightson, who called it *Harbor Point.*
In 1933, it was purchased by Oelsner, who called it *Seacroft.*
He was the son of Edward and Glenny Oelsner.
*Oelsner founded United States Navigation in 1911. It was one of the first shipping firms to establish regular independent cargo lines on a large scale using time-chartered ships.
The Oelsners' son John married Carroll Mentzendorff, the daughter of Carl W. Mentzendorff of Montclair, NJ. Their son Warren married Carol Arlyne Perkins, the daughter of Harrison Bennet Perkins of Madison, WI.
The estate was subsequently owned by the Oelsners' son Warren, who continued to call it *Seacroft.*
In 2000, the estate was still owned by the Oelsner family.

Seacroft

Oelsner, Warren James

Occupation(s):   shipping -   chairman and president, Oceanic Operations and West Indies Transport Line

Marriage(s):   1958 - Carol Arlyne Perkins

Listed in *Long Island Society Register, 1929*: no
Address: Yacht Club Road, Centre Island
Acreage / map sources: not on 1927, 1932, or 1946 maps
Name of estate: *Seacroft*
Year of construction: c. 1906
Style of architecture: Spanish Colonial
Architect(s):   Frederick R. Hirsh designed the house (for S. T. Shaw, Sr.)
Landscape architect(s):
House extant: yes
Historical notes:

The house, originally named *The Sunnyside,* was built by Samuel T. Shaw, Sr.
The estate was, subsequently, owned by George Edgar Brightson, who called it *Harbor Point.*
In 1933, it was purchased by Edward Carl William Oelsner, Sr., who called it *Seacroft.* The estate was subsequently owned by his son Warren James Oelsner, who continued to call it *Seacroft.*
The *Social Register, 1996* lists W. James and Carol Perkins Oelsner as residing at *Seacroft* on Centre Island.
She was the daughter of Harrison Bennet Perkins of Madison, WI.
In 1982 the Oelsners' daughter Carol married Anthony Kane Baker, whose parents George Fisher and Frances Drexel Munn Baker [III] resided at *Ventura Point* on Centre Island.
In 2000 the estate was still owned by the Oelsner family.

O'Hara, Thomas H.

Occupation(s):   financier -   stockbroker

Marriage(s):   Elizabeth *[unable to confirm maiden name]*

Listed in *Long Island Society Register, 1929*: no
Address: Kings Point Road, Kings Point
Acreage / map sources: on 1927 map
                               5 acres / 1932 map
                               not on 1946 map
Name of estate:
Year of construction: c. 1920s
Style of architecture: Tudor
Architect(s):   Julius Gregory designed
                                   the house (for O'Hara)
Landscape architect(s):
House extant: yes
Historical notes:

The house was built by Thomas H. O'Hara.

dining room, 1928

Ohl, John Phillips (1909-1994)

Occupation(s):   attorney -   partner, Cahill, Gordon, Reindel, and Ohl
Civic Activism: *

Marriage(s):   1923 - Lillian Margaret Thompson

Listed in *Long Island Society Register, 1929*: no
Address: Middle Neck Road, Sands Point
Acreage / map sources: not on 1927, 1932, or 1946 maps
Name of estate:
Year of construction: 1929
Style of architecture: Tudor
Architect(s):   Harrie Thomas Lindeberg designed the house
                                   (for D. M. Parker)
Landscape architect(s):
House extant: yes
Historical notes:

The house was built by Dale M. Parker.
In 1929, Parker defaulted on the mortgage. The house remained vacant until 1947 when it was purchased by Ohl.
*John Phillips Ohl helped draft the Revenue Act of 1934. During World War II he served as a "dollar-a-year man," drafting the World War II Excess Profits Tax and the five-year amortization of war plants. [*The New York Times* January 13, 1994, section D, p. 21.]
The Ohls' son Brian married Paula Bodi, the daughter of Harry A. Bodi, Jr.

O'Keeffe, Samuel

Occupation(s):

Marriage(s):   1923 - Constance Devereux Wilcox

Listed in *Long Island Society Register, 1929*: yes
Address: North Country Colony section (off Crescent Beach Road), Glen Cove
Acreage / map sources: 1927 map illegible
                                      not on 1932 or 1946 maps
Name of estate:
Year of construction: c. 1896-1900
Style of architecture: Shingle
Architect(s):   Charles Pierrepont Henry Gilbert designed the house
                                          (for Hoagland)*
Landscape architect(s):
House extant: yes
Historical notes:

   The house was built by Dr. Cornelius Nevius Hoagland. The estate was owned by George Patterson Tangeman, who called it *Green Acres*.
   It was later owned by Cornelius Hoagland Tangeman and, subsequently, by O'Keeffe.
   The *Long Island Society Register, 1929* lists Samuel and Constance Devereux Wilcox O'Keeffe as residing on Crescent Beach Road, Glen Cove.
   He was the son of Samuel J. O'Keeffe.
   Constance Devereux Wilcox O'Keeffe was the daughter of Harold Morton Wilcox of NYC. Her sister Marjory married John Jacob Atwater, Sr. and resided in Kings Point.
   The O'Keeffes' daughter Elizabeth married Donald R. Pierce, the son of Forrester W. Pierce of Roslyn.
   In 1929, O'Keeffe purchased a colonial homestead and thirty-five acres in New Cannan, CT, as his permanent residence. [*The New York Times* February 13, 1929, p. 41.]
   *It is unconfirmed as to whether or not the farm complex, designed by Gilbert, was ever built.

Olds, George Daniel, Jr. (1892-1976)

Occupation(s):   industrialist - assistant to president, Continental Oil Co.;
                                                        president, Petroleum Chemicals Co.;
                                                        director, Old Salt Seafood Co.;
                                                        director, Fall River Navigation Co.

Marriage(s):   1914 - Margaret H. Atwater

Listed in *Long Island Society Register, 1929*: yes
Address: Steamboat Road, Kings Point
Acreage / map sources: not on 1927 or 1946 maps
                                      3 acres / 1932 map
Name of estate:
Year of construction:
Style of architecture:
Architect(s):
Landscape architect(s):
House extant: unconfirmed
Historical notes:

   The *Long Island Society Register 1929* lists George D. and Margaret H. Atwater Olds, Jr. as residing on Steamboat Road, Great Neck [Kings Point].
   Their daughter Dr. Margaret Atwater Olds married Dr. Arthur Kazimier Cieslak of Cleveland, OH.

O'Neill, George Dorr, Sr. (b. 1926)

Occupation(s):   financier - member, Harris Upham and Co. (later, Smith, Barney, Harris,
                                                         Upham and Co.; Smith, Barney and Co.; now, Salomon
                                                         Smith Barney) (investment banking firm);
                                                      chairman, executive committee, Equity Corp.;
                                                      chairman, Meriwether Capital Corp.;
                                                      chairman, Chemstone Corp.

Marriage(s):   1949 - Abby Rockefeller Milton (b. 1928)

Listed in *Long Island Society Register, 1929*: no
Address: Sunset Road, Oyster Bay Cove
Acreage / map sources: not on 1927, 1932, or 1946 maps
Name of estate:
Year of construction:
Style of architecture:
Architect(s):
Landscape architect(s):
House extant: yes
Historical notes:

    George Dorr O'Neill, Sr. was the son of Grover and Catharine Gray Porter O'Neill, Sr., who resided at *Fleetwood* in Oyster Bay Cove.
    Abby Rockefeller Milton O'Neill is the great-granddaughter of John D. Rockefeller and the daughter of David and Abby Rockefeller Milton [later, Pardee; then, Mauze] who resided at *Laurel Hill* in Mill Neck.
    The O'Neills' daughter, also named Abby, married Charles Wells Caulkins, the son of John E. Caulkins of Grosse Pointe Farms in MI.

O'Neill, Grover, Sr. (1890-1972)

Occupation(s):   financier - member, Roosevelt and Son (investment banking firm);
                                                      founder and partner, Grover O'Neill & Co. (investment banking
                                                         firm and, later, a real estate brokerage firm);
                                                      director, Oyster Bay Trust Co.

Marriage(s):   1917-1972 - Catharine Gray Porter (1897-1992)
                                            - Civic Activism: *

Listed in *Long Island Society Register, 1929*: yes
Address: Cove Road, Oyster Bay Cove
Acreage / map sources: on 1927 map
                                            not on 1932 map
                                            44 acres / 1946 map
Name of estate: *Fleetwood*
Year of construction: c. 1907
Style of architecture: Elizabethan Revival
Architect(s):   A. Dunham Wheeler designed the house (for Sewell)**
Landscape architect(s):
House extant: yes
Historical notes:

    The house, originally named *Fleetwood,* was built by Robert Van Vorst Sewell.
    The estate was owned by O'Neill and, subsequently in 1957, by Eugene Du Bois. Both O'Neill and Du Bois continue to call it *Fleetwood.*
    *From 1942-1945, Catharine Gray Porter O'Neill was chairwoman of the Red Cross' apartment house division. As such, she supervised the fund-raising activities in more than five thousand Manhattan apartments. She was also a founder and member of the board of the Embroiders' Guild of America.
    The O'Neills' son George Dorr O'Neill, Sr. married Abby Rockefeller Milton. They also resided in Oyster Bay Cove.
    **A. Dunham Wheeler was the son of Candace Thurber Wheeler, a textile and interior designer, who with Louis Comfort Tiffany, Samuel Colman, and Lockwood de Forest founded L. C. Tiffany & Associated Artists.
    The interior of the house has murals and carvings of scenes of "Canterbury Tales" by Robert Van Vorst Sewell.

Ono, Yoko (b. 1933)

Occupation(s):   artist - conceptual artist
                               entertainers and associated professions -   singer

Marriage(s):   1969-1980 - John Lennon (1940-1980)
                                  - entertainers and associated professions -   singer; composer

Listed in *Long Island Society Register, 1929:* no
Address: Ridge Road, Laurel Hollow
Acreage / map sources: not on 1927, 1932, or 1946 maps
Name of estate:
Year of construction: c. 1911
Style of architecture: Shingle
Architect(s):
Landscape architect(s):
House extant: yes
Historical notes:

side / front facade, 2004

    The house, originally named *Cannon Hill,* was built by John Henry Jones Stewart.
    The estate was owned by Oliver B. James, Sr., who called it *Rocky Point,* John Gerdes, who called it *Cannonhill Point,* Henry Blackstone, Martin Dwyer, Jr., Ono [Lennon], and, subsequently, by Daniel Carroll de Roulet, Sr., who renamed it *Cannon Hill.*
    Blackstone converted the garage complex into a residence and has lived in the converted structure since he sold the estate to Dwyer.

O'Rourke, Innis, Sr. (1891-1972)

Occupation(s):   industrialist -   founder, Concrete Conduit Corp., Corona, Queens;
                                                 founder, Precast, Inc.
                               capitalist -   president, J. & I. O'Rourke (construction company)

Civic Activism: trustee, Village of Kings Point

Marriage(s):   M/1 - Augusta L. Travers
                               M/2 - 1949-1972 - Helen Silver (1895-1962)
                                  - Civic Activism: director, American Women's Voluntary Services
                                                     during World War II

Listed in *Long Island Society Register, 1929*: yes
Address: Kings Point Road and Ballantine Lane, Kings Point
Acreage / map sources: on 1927 map; 3 acres / 1932 map; 3 acres / 1946 map
Name of estate:
Year of construction: c. 1900
Style of architecture: Neo-Colonial
Architect(s):
Landscape architect(s):
House extant: yes
Historical notes:

    The house was built by John Francis O'Rourke, Sr.
    The estate was, subsequently, owned by his son Innis O'Rourke, Sr.
    Augusta L. Travers O'Rourke was the daughter of V. Paul Travers of Kings Point. Her sister Joan married Dr. Edward Markey Pullen of Manhattan. Her sister Antoinette married Leo Bernard Farrell.
    Innis and Augusta L. Travers O'Rourke, Sr.'s son Travers married Bette Ann Lund, the daughter of Roy Lund of Buffalo, NY. Ms. Lund's former husband Emmett Corrigan, Jr. had been killed in World War II. The O'Rourkes' son Innis O'Rourke, Jr. married Louise Fraser, the daughter of J. Frank Fraser of Flushing, NY.
    Helen Silver was the daughter of Edgar O. Silver of Llewellyn Park, West Orange, NJ. She had previously been married to Stephen M. Foster.
    Innis O'Rourke, Sr. and his second wife were residing on Frost Mill Road, Mill Neck, at the time of his death. [*The New York Times* September 17, 1972, p. 60.]

O'Rourke, John Francis, Sr. (1854-1934)

Occupation(s):   capitalist - president, O'Rourke Engineering & Construction Co.*
                                              engineer
                                              educator - professor of engineering, Cooper Union, NYC

Marriage(s):   1890-1934 - Katharine B. Innis (1862-1938)

Listed in *Long Island Society Register, 1929*: no
Address: Kings Point Road and Ballantine Lane, Kings Point
Acreage / map sources: on 1927 map; 3 acres / 1932 and 1946 maps
Name of estate:
Year of construction: c. 1900
Style of architecture: Neo-Colonial
Architect(s):
Landscape architect(s):
House extant: yes
Historical notes:

The house was built by John Francis O'Rourke, Sr.

The *Social Register New York, 1907* lists John F. and Katharine B. Innis O'Rourke [Sr.] as residing at 8 West 50th Street, NYC.

He was born in Tipperary, Ireland, and immigrated to the United States at the age of two with his parents.

Katharine B. Innis O'Rourke was the daughter of Aaron Innis, a manufacturer from Poughkeepsie, NY.

*O'Rourke's company built the Pennsylvania Railroad and Long Island Rail Road tunnels under the East River, NYC; the Bush Terminal, NYC; the foundation for the New York Stock Exchange Building, NYC; the foundation for the Equitable Building, NYC; and six subway tunnels in Manhattan and Brooklyn. [*The New York Times* July 30, 1934, p. 13.]

The estate was, subsequently, owned by their son Innis O'Rourke, Sr. The younger O'Rourke subsequently moved to Mill Neck and was residing in Mill Neck at the time of his death.

Osborn, Alexander Perry, Sr. (1884-1951)

Occupation(s):   attorney - partner, Beekman, Menken and Griscom
                                         capitalist - director, Western Pacific Railroad Corp.;
                                                         director, Denver & Rio Grande Western Railroad Co.
                                         financier - partner, Redmond and Co. (investment banking firm);
                                                          director, Industrial Finance Corp.
                                         industrialist - director, Standard Plate Glass Co.
Civic Activism: trustee, American Museum of Natural History, NYC

Marriage(s):   M/1 - 1915-1930 - Anne M. Steel
                               M/2 - 1933-1951 - Marie Cantrell (d. 1988)

Listed in *Long Island Society Register, 1929*: yes
Address: East Norwich Road, Brookville
Acreage / map sources: not on 1927, 1932, or 1946 maps
Name of estate: *Valley House*
Year of construction:
Style of architecture: Neo-Colonial
Architect(s):   Warren and Clark designed alterations (for Osborn)*
Landscape architect(s):
House extant: yes
Historical notes:

*The existing eighteenth-century farmhouse was renovated for Alexander Perry Osborn, Sr., who named it *Valley House.*

The *Long Island Society Register, 1929* lists Alexander Perry and Anne M. Steel Osborn [Sr.] as residing at *Valley House* on East Norwich Turnpike [Road], Roslyn [Brookville].

He was the son of Dr. Henry Fairfield and Mrs. Lucretia Thatcher Perry. His father was an eminent paleontologist.

Anne M. Steel Osborn subsequently married Edmound W. Nash and resided with him in Westport, CT.

Alexander and Anne Osborn's daughter Lucretia married William Henry McKleroy of Manhattan and Baltimore, MD.

Ottley, Gilbert (1907-1948)

Occupation(s):   financier -   partner, Gilbert and Rogers (stock brokerage firm)

Marriage(s):   1933-1948 - Gladys Howland Graham

Listed in *Long Island Society Register, 1929*: no
Address: Wolver Hollow Road, Upper Brookville
Acreage / map sources: not on 1927 or 1932 maps
                                        9 acres / 1946 map
Name of estate: *Wuff Woods*
Year of construction: c. 1920
Style of architecture: Federal
Architect(s):   Bradley Delehanty designed the house (for G. Ottley)
Landscape architect(s):
House extant: yes
Historical notes:

The house, originally named *Wuff Woods,* was built by Gilbert Ottley.
The *Social Register New York, 1948* lists Gilbert and Gladys H. Howland Graham Ottley as residing in Glen Cove.
He was the son of James Henry and Lucetta Banks Gilbert Ottley, Sr., who resided at *Oakleigh* in Glen Cove. His sister Martha married Van Devanter Crisp and resided at *Hillandale* in Upper Brookville.
Gladys Howland Graham Ottley was the daughter of Edward Howland and Gladys Smith Graham, who resided at *High Trees* in Oyster Bay. She subsequently married Paul Budd Magnuson, Jr.
The Ottleys' son Philip married Glenna Holleran, the daughter of F. Joseph Holleran of Greenwich, CT, and East Hampton. Their daughter Lela married Randall Winslow Hackett.

Ottley, James Henry, Sr. (1851-1922)

Occupation(s):   publisher -   owner and president, *McCalls Magazine*
                                        financier -   director, New Netherland Bank;
                                                      director, United States Life Insurance Co.

Marriage(s):   1900-1922 - Lucetta Banks Gilbert (1870-1953)
                                          - Civic Activism: board member, St. Luke's Home for Aged Women

Listed in *Long Island Society Register, 1929*: yes
Address: Crescent Beach Road, Glen Cove
Acreage / map sources: 1927 map illegible
                                        not on 1932 map
                                        9 acres / 1946 map
Name of estate: *Oakleigh*
Year of construction:
Style of architecture: Georgian Revival
Architect(s):   Howard Major designed c. 1915 alterations
                                            (for J. H. Ottley, Sr.)*
Landscape architect(s):
House extant: no; demolished c. 1950
Historical notes:

The house, originally named *Oakleigh,* was built by James Henry Ottley, Sr.
He was the son of Enoch and Frances Elizabeth Henry Ottley of Phelps, Ontario, Canada.
[See previous entry for additional family information.]
Both the *Long Island Society Register, 1929* and the *Social Register, Summer 1951* list Lucetta Banks Gilbert Ottley as residing at *Oakleigh* in Glen Cove.
*Ottley converted the Shingle-style house into a Georgian Revival.

581

Outerbridge, Samuel Roosevelt (1876-1953)

Occupation(s):	financier - investment banking
	shipping - partner, A. E. Outerbridge & Co.
	industrialist - director, Homasote Co. (wall board manufacturer)
Civic Activism:	trustee, Village of Centre Island
Marriage(s):	1906-1953 - Amie W. Willetts (1878-1956)

Listed in *Long Island Society Register, 1929*: yes

Address:	Centre Island Road, Centre Island
Acreage / map sources:	on 1927 map
	2 acres / 1932 map
	not on 1946 map
Name of estate:	
Year of construction:	
Style of architecture:	Neo-Colonial
Architect(s):	Electus D. Litchfield
Landscape architect(s):	
House extant: unconfirmed	
Historical notes:	

Both the *Long Island Society Register, 1929* and the *Social Register, Summer 1951* list Samuel Roosevelt and Amie Willets [Willetts] Outerbridge as residing on Centre Island.

He was the son of A. Emilius Outerbridge.

Amie W. Willetts Outerbridge was the daughter of Joseph C. and Emma C. Prentice Willetts. Her brother William married Christine Newhall Clark and resided at *Homewood* in Roslyn. Her sister Marion, who married Ernest Cuyler Brower and, subsequently, his brother George Ellsworth Brower, resided at *Locust Hill* in Roslyn.

The Outerbridges' son Joseph married Sarah Richmond, the daughter of L. Martin and Sarah Thacher Richmond, who resided at *Sunninghill* in Old Brookville. Their daughter Marion married Charles H. Welles III of Scranton, PA.

Page, Frank C. Bauman (1870-1938)

Occupation(s):	industrialist - chairman of board, E. W. Bliss Co. (heavy machinery and World War I munitions manufacturer); director, Boyleston Manufacturing Co.
Marriage(s):	1897-1938 - Henrietta Jackson (1874-1961)

Listed in *Long Island Society Register, 1929*: yes

Address:	Mill River Hollow Road, Upper Brookville
Acreage / map sources:	on 1927 map
	not on 1932 or 1946 maps
Name of estate:	*Elmcroft*
Year of construction:	c. 1917
Style of architecture:	Classical Revival
Architect(s):	Little and Browne designed the house (for F. C. B. Page)
Landscape architect(s):	A. Chandler Manning (for F. C. B. Page)
House extant: yes	
Historical notes:	

The house, originally named *Elmcroft*, was built by Frank C. Bauman Page.

The *Long Island Society Register, 1929* lists Frank C. Bauman and Henrietta Jackson Page as residing in East Norwich. The *Social Register, Summer 1932* lists the Pages as residing at *Elmcroft* in Oyster Bay [Upper Brookville], while the *Social Register New York, 1959* lists Henrietta Jackson Page's address as 210 East 68th Street, NYC.

The Pages' daughter Ruth married Franklin E. Burke, Jr.

The estate was owned by Nathan Lewis Miller, who called it *Norwich House,* and, subsequently, by the Soviet Mission to the United Nations.

A portion of the estate property is now part of the Mill River Club.

As of 2001 the Russian government still owned the house and remaining estate property.

Page, Arthur Wilson, II (1883-1960)

Occupation(s):   publisher -   vice-president, Doubleday, Page & Co.
                                    capitalist - vice-president, American Telephone & Telegraph Co.
                                    industrialist - director, Continental Oil Co.;
                                                    director, Westinghouse Electric Corp.
Civic Activism: trustee, Pierpont Morgan Library, NYC;
                                    trustee, Metropolitan Museum of Art, NYC;
                                    overseer, Harvard University, Cambridge, MA

Marriage(s):   1912-1960 - Mollie W. Hall (1886-1964)
                                      - Civic Activism: president, Army Relief Society, 1936-1946;
                                                         director, Girl Scouts of America;

Listed in *Long Island Society Register, 1929*: yes
Address: off West Mall Drive, West Hills
Acreage / map sources: not on 1929 map; no acreage given on 1931 map; 18 acres / 1944
Name of estate: *County Line Farm*
Year of construction:
Style of architecture:
Architect(s):   Delano and Aldrich designed the alterations (for Page)
Landscape architect(s):
House extant: unconfirmed
Historical notes:

   The house was purchased by Arthur Wilson Page.
   He was the son of Ambassador Walter Hines and Mrs. Alice Wilson Page Sr. of Garden City.
   Arthur Wilson and Mollie W. Hall Page II's daughter Mollie married Anderson Hewitt and resided in Stowe, VT.
Their son Arthur Wilson Page, Jr. [III] married Anita Peabody Hadden, the daughter of Hamilton and Anita L Peabody
Hadden, who resided at *Harbor Lights* in Cold Spring Harbor. Their son Walter inherited *County Line Farm*.

Page, Walter Hines, II (1915-1999)

Occupation(s):   financier -   president, and chairman, J. P. Morgan and Co. (investment banking);
                                                 president and chairman, Morgan Guaranty Trust
                                    industrialist - director, American Kennecott Copper Corp.;
Civic Activism: president, Cold Spring Harbor Whaling Museum;
                                    chairman, Cold Spring Harbor Laboratory Association

Marriage(s):   1942-1998 - Jane N. Nichols (d. 1998)
                                      - Civic Activism: trustee, Pierpont Morgan Library, NYC;
                                                         director, Nature Conservancy*

Listed in *Long Island Society Register, 1929*: no
Address: Lawrence Hill Road, Cold Spring Harbor
Acreage / map sources: not on 1927, 1932, or 1946 maps
Name of estate:
Year of construction: 1947
Style of architecture: Contemporary Ranch
Architect(s):   Delano and Aldrich designed
                                     the house (for Page)

Landscape architect(s):
House extant: yes
Historical notes:

side facade, 2004

   The house was built by Walter Hines Page II.
   Jane N. Nichols Page was the daughter of George and Jane N. Morgan Nichols, Sr., who resided at *Uplands* on
Lawrence Hill Road, Cold Spring Harbor.
   *The land she and her mother donated became Long Island Nature Conservancy's Uplands Farms Sanctuary.
   The Pages' son Mark married Laura Nields, the daughter of John and Laura Nields of West Hills. Their son Walter
Hines Page III married Susan Arlen. Their daughter Jane married Philip Ree Mallinson.
   [See previous sentry for additional family information.]

Paley, William S. (1901-1990)

Occupation(s):	capitalist - president, Columbia Broadcasting System (CBS), 1928-1946; chairman, Columbia Broadcasting System (CBS), 1946-1983
	publisher - co-chairman of board, *International Herald Tribune*
	financier - partner, Whitcom Investment Co.
	industrialist - founder and director, Genetics Instruments; vice-president and secretary, Congress Cigar Co.
Civic Activism:	president, Museum of Modern Art, NYC; founder, William S. Paley Foundation
Marriage(s):	M/1 - 1932-1947 - Dorothy Hart
	M/2 - 1947-1978 - Barbara Cushing (1915-1978)
	- journalist - fashion editor, *Vogue*
	Civic Activism: trustee, North Shore University Hospital, Manhasset; trustee, Museum of Broadcasting, NYC; trustee, William S. Paley Foundation; trustee, Greenpark Foundation; member, board of governors, Human Resources Center, Albertson (a rehabilitation and educational facility for the handicapped)

Listed in *Long Island Society Register, 1929:* no

Address:	Shelter Rock Road, North Hills
Acreage / map sources:	not on 1927 or 1932 maps
	82 acres / 1946 map
Name of estate:	*Kiluna Farm*
Year of construction:	c. 1910
Style of architecture:	Shingle Farmhouse
Architect(s):	Walker and Gillette designed the house (for Pulitzer)
	Charles A. Platt designed the swimming pool and bathhouse, 1913 (for Pulitzer)
	James W. O'Connor designed the tennis building (for Pulitzer)
Landscape architect(s):	Charles A. Platt designed the formal garden with circular lily pond, and pergola (for Pulitzer)

Estate photographs can be found in the Nassau County Museum Collection filed under Manhasset/Pulitzer.
House extant: no; demolished in 1990*
Historical notes:

The house, originally named *Kiluna Farm,* was built by Ralph Pulitzer, Sr.

In 1938 Paley, purchased the estate from Pulitzer for less than $200,000 and continued to call it *Kiluna Farm.*

Dorothy Hart Paley had previously been married to John Randolph Hearst, Sr., who was the son of William Randolph and Millicent Wilson Hearst. Mrs. William Randolph Hearst resided at *St. Joan* in Sands Point.

Barbara Cushing Paley had previously been married to Stanley Grafton Mortimer, Jr. Her sister Mary (Minnie) married William Vincent Astor and resided with him at *Cloverly Manor* in Sands Point. Mary subsequently married James Whitney Fosburgh. Her sister Betsey married James Roosevelt, the son of President Franklin Delano and Mrs. Anna Eleanor Roosevelt Roosevelt. James' brother Franklin Delano Roosevelt, Jr. married Ethel du Pont and resided in Woodbury. Betsey subsequently married John Hay Whitney, residing with him at *Greentree* in Manhasset.

In 1980, Paley sold the estate to developer Edward Klar for $6 million.

*In February 1990, the house and children's cottage were destroyed by arson.

Klar eventually built Stone Hill, a development of some ninety houses, on the estate grounds.

Mrs. Paley's dressing room, 1942

584

William S. Paley Estate, *Kiluna Farm*

dining room, 1942

entrance hall, 1942

east wing, 1942

guest bedroom, 1942

living room, 1942

Palmer, Carlton Humphreys (1891-1971)

Occupation(s):	industrialist - chairman of board, E. R. Squibb & Sons of Indiana (pharmaceutical manufacturer); director, Lentheric Inc.; director, Lentheric International Corp.
	capitalist - director, Long Island Rail Road
Civic Activism:	established Lowell M. Palmer Foundation (provided medical and biological research fellowships); trustee and benefactor, Long Island University*; director, National Society for the Prevention of Blindness; member, citizens advisory board, New York Public Library, NYC
Marriage(s):	M/1 - 1919 - Winthrop Bushnell (1899-1988) - writer - *Theatrical Dancing in America,* 1945; *The New Barbarian,* 1951; *Beat the Wind,* 1960 journalist - associate editor, *Dance News,* 1940-1950; associate editor, *Confrontation,* 1970 M/2 - 1942 - Antoinette Johnson - educator - professor of English literature, Long Island University M/3 - 1951-1971 - Winthrop Bushnell (1899-1988)

Listed in *Long Island Society Register, 1929*: no
Address: Centre Island Road, Centre Island
Acreage / map sources: not on 1927 or 1932 maps
26 acres / 1946 map
Name of estate: *Hearthstone*
Year of construction: c. 1914
Style of architecture: Elizabethan
Architect(s): Robert Williams Gibson designed the house, stables, farm complex, boathouse, and docks (for Bullock)
Landscape architect(s): Olmsted (for Bullock)
Fletcher Steele (for Bullock)
Estate photographs can be found in the Nassau County Museum Collection filed under Centre Island/Bullock
House extant: no; demolished c. 1990
Historical notes:

The house, originally named *Yeadon,* was built by George Bullock.

In 1936, Mrs. Bullock sold the estate which consisted of stables, garages, chauffeur's cottage, superintendent's house, greenhouse, boathouse, dock, and a thirty-room main house with nine bathrooms. [*The New York Times* April 2, 1936, p. 47.]

The estate was owned by Robert Barr Deans, Sr., who continue to call it *Yeadon,* and, subsequently, by Palmer, who called it *Hearthstone.*

Both the *Social Register, Summer 1932* and *1937* list Carlton H. and Winthrop Bushnell Palmer as residing at *Quasset Farm* in CT.

The *Social Register, Summer 1945* and *1950* list Carlton H. and Antoinette Johnson Palmer as residing at *Hearthstone* in Oyster Bay [Centre Island], while the *Social Register New York, 1952* lists only Carlton H. Palmer as residing on Centre Island.

The *Social Register, Summer 1954* lists him as having remarried Winthrop Bushnell Palmer and residing with her at *Hearthstone* in Centre Island, while the *Social Register, 1988* lists Winthrop Bushnell Palmer's address as Centre Island Road, Centre Island.

Carleton Humphreys Palmer was the son of Lowell Mason and Grace Humphreys Foote Palmer [Sr.]. His brother Lowell Mason Palmer, Jr. resided on Beverly Road in Kensington.

Winthrop Bushnell Palmer was the daughter of Ericsson F. Bushnell. Her sister Emilie married John Stuart Martin, who resided at *Fox Hollow* in Matinecock. Emilie subsequently married John Drant. The Bushnells were related to David Bushnell, who in 1773, while still a student at Yale College, built the first submarine to be used in warfare.

*Palmer School of Library and Information Services at C. W. Post Campus of Long Island University, Brookville, is named for Carlton Humphreys Palmer.

Park, Darragh Anderson, Sr. (1891-1953)

Occupation(s):

financier - partner, Parker and Co. (investment banking firm);
president, New York Empire Bank;
partner, vice-president, Manufacturers Trust Co.

Civic Activism:

treasurer, Society for the Prevention of Cruelty to Children;
general chairman, Travelers Aid Society's fund-raising campaigns,
1942, 1943, 1945;
chairman, men's division, Lighthouse For the Blind

Marriage(s):

M/1 - 1913-1939 - Dorothy Hyde (1891-1949)
M/2 - 1943-1953 - Nona Gibbs McAdoo (d. 1971)

Listed in *Long Island Society Register, 1929*: yes
Address: Simonson Road, Old Brookville
Acreage / map sources: on 1927 map; no acreage given on 1932 map; not on 1946 map
Name of estate: *Hyde Park*
Year of construction: c. 1920
Style of architecture: French Manor House
Architect(s): Peabody, Wilson and Brown designed the house (for D. A. Park, Sr.)
James W. O'Connor designed c. 1938 alterations (for A. S. Martin)
Landscape architect(s):
House extant: yes
Historical notes:

The house, originally named *Hyde Park,* was built by Darragh Anderson Park, Sr.

He was the son of William Gray and Elizabeth Sweitzer Park, who resided at *Turnpike Cottage* in Old Westbury. His sister Mary married Raymond Perry Rodgers Neilson, Sr. and resided in Old Westbury.

Dorothy Hyde Park was the daughter of Charles Livingston Hyde of Manhattan. She subsequently married Oliver Iselin.

Nona McAdoo Park's father William Gibbs McAdoo was Secretary of the Treasury in President Woodrow Wilson's administration. Her stepmother Eleanor Wilson McAdoo was the daughter of President Wilson.

Darragh and Dorothy Park, Sr.'s daughter Edith married Alastair Bradley Martin. The estate was, subsequently, owned by the Martins.

Park, William Gray (1848-1909)

Occupation(s):

industrialist - founder and chairman of board, Crucible Steel Co. of America;
owner, Leggett Spring & Axle Co.
financier - director, Mellon National Bank
capitalist - real estate*

Marriage(s):

1882-1909 - Elizabeth Sweitzer (1858-1949)

Listed in *Long Island Society Register, 1929*: yes
Address: Bostwick Lane, Old Westbury
Acreage / map sources: on 1927 map (owned by Mrs. Park Neilson)
14 acres / 1932 map (owned by W. G. Park)
10 acres / 1946 map (owned by Dr. A. Park)
Name of estate: *Turnpike Cottage*
Year of construction:
Style of architecture: 20th-century Eclectic
Architect(s): Algernon S. Bell designed the house (for Neilson)
McKim, Meade and White designed alterations (for W. G. Park)
Landscape architect(s):
House extant: unconfirmed
Historical notes:

The house was built by Raymond Perry Rodgers Neilson, Sr. Neilson was married to Mary Stevenson Park.

The estate was, subsequently, owned by William Gray Park, who called it *Turnpike Cottage.*

*William Gray Park built and owned, with his brother David, The Park Building, once the largest office building in Pittsburgh, PA. *[See previous entry for family information.]*

Parker, Dale M. (1892-1959)

Occupation(s):   capitalist -   secretary, Columbia Gas System
                                            attorney
                                            financier -   partner, Harriman Brothers (investment banking firm)

Marriage(s):

Listed in *Long Island Society Register, 1929*: no
Address: Middle Neck Road, Sands Point
Acreage / map sources: not on 1927, 1932, or 1946 maps
Name of estate:
Year of construction: 1929
Style of architecture: Tudor
Architect(s):   Harrie Thomas Lindeberg designed the house (for D. M. Parker)
Landscape architect(s):
House extant: yes
Historical notes:

    The house was built by Dale M. Parker.
    In 1929, Parker defaulted on the mortgage. The house remained vacant until 1947 when it was purchased by John Phillips Ohl.

Parker, John Alley

Occupation(s):   financier -   private investment banker

Marriage(s):   M/1 - 1892-1910 - Jane Hume (d. 1911)
                                            M/2 - 1911 - Edith Helen _____ (d. 1949)

Listed in *Long Island Society Register, 1929*: no
Address: Sands Point Road, Sands Point
Acreage / map sources: not on 1927, 1932, or 1946 maps
Name of estate: *Driftwoods*
Year of construction: c. 1912
Style of architecture: Spanish Colonial
Architect(s):   Addison Mizner designed the house (for J. A. Parker)
Landscape architect(s):
House extant: yes
Historical notes:

    The house, originally named *Driftwoods*, was built by John Alley Parker.
    Parker's estate consisted of thirty acres. [Joan Gay Kent, *Discovering Sands Point: Its History, Its People, Its Places* (Sands Point, NY: Village of Sands Point, 2000), p. 82.]
    Edith Helen Parker had previously been married to Samuel Dilliplane Ellis.
    John Alley and Jane Hume Parker's only son John married Edna Kellogg, a professional opera singer who performed with the Metropolitan Opera Company and Chicago Grand Opera Company.
    The estate was owned by Seymour Johnson, who continued to call it *Driftwoods,* and, subsequently, by Count Alexander Paulovitch De Leslie.

Parker, Lottie Blair (1858-1937)

Occupation(s):   entertainers and associated professions -   actress
writer - *Way Down East,* 1897 (play);
          Under Southern Skies, 1901 (play);
          Homespun, 1909 (novel);
          A War Correspondent (play);
          Lights of Home (play);
          The Redemption of Davis Corson
            (dramatization of the Charles Frederick Goss novel);
          White Roses (play)

Marriage(s):   1882-1921 - Harry Doel Parker (1859-1921)
          - entertainers and associated professions -   theatrical manager

Listed in *Long Island Society Register, 1929*: no
Address: East Shore Road, Great Neck
Acreage / map sources: on 1927 map (owned by Parker)
          not on 1932 or 1946 maps

Name of estate:
Year of construction:
Style of architecture: Victorian*
Architect(s):
Landscape architect(s):
House extant: no
Historical notes:

    From 1922 to 1929, Herbert Bayard Swope, Sr. rented the house from Lottie Blair Parker.
    *It was a three-story Victorian house with a wrap-around porch.
    The house was, subsequently, owned by Lee Rosenberg.

Parker, Robert Meade, Sr. (1865-1945)

Occupation(s):   industrialist -   president, Brooklyn Cooperage Co.;
            president, Pennsylvania Stave Co.;
            vice-president, American Sugar Refining Co.
          capitalist -   president, Butler County Railroad;
            president, Great Western Land Co.;
            real estate - director, Kearny Land Co.

Marriage(s):   1914-1945 - Rachel MacDougall (d. 1971)

Listed in *Long Island Society Register, 1929*: yes
Address: Forest Avenue, Glen Cove
Acreage / map sources: not on 1927 or 1932 maps
          9 acres / 1946 map

Name of estate: *Bonnieneuk*
Year of construction:
Style of architecture:
Architect(s):
Landscape architect(s):
House extant: unconfirmed
Historical notes:

    The *Long Island Society Register, 1929* lists Robert Meade and Rachel MacDougall Parker as residing at *Bonnieneuk*
on Forest Avenue, Glen Cove.
    He was the son of Cortlandt and Elizabeth Wolcott Stites Parker of Newark, NJ.
    The Parkers' daughter Rachel married Gaines Gwathmey, Jr.

Parker, Valentine Fraser

Occupation(s):   attorney

Marriage(s):   1953 - Judith Ann Rasmusson

Listed in *Long Island Society Register, 1929*: no
Address: Sidney Road, Huntington Bay
Acreage / map sources: not on 1929, 1931, or 1944 maps
Name of estate:
Year of construction: c. 1900
Style of architecture:
Architect(s):
Landscape architect(s):
House extant: unconfirmed
Historical notes:

The house was built by John Robb.
The estate was purchased by Stanley P. Jadwin in 1921 and, subsequently in 1966, by Parker.
Valentine Fraser Parker was the son of Cola G. Parker of Menasha, WI.
Judith Ann Rasmusson Parker was the daughter of Cameron S. and Augusta Young Rasmusson of Chicago, IL.

Patchin, Robert Halsey (1881-1955)

Occupation(s):   shipping - vice-president and director, W. R. Grace & Co.
                                       capitalist - a founder, Pan American Grace Airways (Panagra,
                                                     a joint venture with Pan American Airways)
                                     journalist - correspondent, *The Des Moines Leader;*
                                              correspondent, *The Washington Times;*
                                              correspondent, *New York Herald Tribune*
                      writer -   numerous articles
Civic Activism: member, board of appeals, Village of Roslyn Harbor

Marriage(s):   M/1 - 1904-1919 - Mary Custis Lee Carter (d. 1919)
                                     M/2 - 1924-1955 - Minga Pope (1868-1957)
                                       - artist - painter and sculptress
                                       writer -   *Gardens In and About Town*
                                       landscape architect

Listed in *Long Island Society Register, 1929*: yes
Address: Woodhollow Road and Long Island Expressway
                               South Service Road, East Hills
Acreage / map sources: not on 1927 map
                             5 acres / 1932 map
                             5 acres / 1946 map
Name of estate: *Firth House*
Year of construction:
Style of architecture:
Architect(s):
Landscape architect(s):
House extant: unconfirmed
Historical notes:

Both the *Long Island Society Register, 1929* and the *Social Register, Summer 1937* list Robert Halsey and Minga Pope Patchin as residing at *Firth House* in Old Westbury [East Hills], while the *Social Register, Summer 1945* and *1951* list the Patchins as residing at *Hawthorne House* in Roslyn [Roslyn Harbor].
   [See following entry for family information.]

Patchin, Robert Halsey (1881-1955)

Occupation(s):	shipping - vice-president and director, W. R. Grace & Co.
	capitalist - a founder, Pan American Grace Airways (Panagra, a joint venture with Pan American Airways)
	journalist - correspondent, *The Des Moines Leader;* correspondent, *The Washington Times;* correspondent, *New York Herald Tribune*
	writer - numerous articles
Civic Activism:	member, board of appeals, Village of Roslyn Harbor
Marriage(s):	M/1 - 1904-1919 - Mary Custis Lee Carter (d. 1919)
	M/2 - 1924-1955 - Minga Pope (1868-1957)
	- artist - painter and sculptress
	writer - *Gardens In and About Town*
	landscape architect

Listed in *Long Island Society Register, 1929*: yes
Address: Bryant Avenue, Roslyn Harbor
Acreage / map sources: not on 1927 map
                                10 acres / 1932 map
                                10 acres / 1946 map
Name of estate: *Hawthorne House*
Year of construction: c. 1920
Style of architecture: elements of English Country
Architect(s):
Landscape architect(s):
House extant: yes
Historical notes:

    The eleven-room house with six bedrooms and five-and-a-half bathrooms was originally a barn on the William Cullen Bryant estate *Cedarmere*.

    It was purchased by Patchin in 1920 from Bryant's granddaughter Minna Godwin Goddard and moved from its original location on Motts Cove Road South to its present location on Bryant Avenue.

    Both the *Long Island Society Register, 1929* and the *Social Register, Summer 1937* list Robert Halsey and Minga Pope Patchin as residing at *Firth House* in Old Westbury [East Hills], while the *Social Register, Summer 1945* and *1951* list the Patchins as residing at *Hawthorne House* in Roslyn [Roslyn Harbor].

    He was the son of Robert Azor and Calista Halsey Patchin of Des Moines, IA.

    Robert Halsey and Mary Custis Lee Carter Patchin's daughter Phyllis married Robert Soutter.

    Minga Pope Patchin was the daughter of John Pope and the sister of the internationally known architect John Russell Pope. She had previously been married to Harry H. Duryea and resided in Old Brookville. Her son Hendrik Vanderbilt Duryea married Pauline Chapin Bourne, the only daughter of Joseph Baker Bourne of Manhattan. [*The New York Times* April 5, 1924, p. 15.]

    The house, which was subsequently owned by Stanley Reed, Jr., was for sale in 2004. The asking price was $1.599 million; the annual taxes were $30,320.

front facade, 2004

Payson, Charles Shipman (1898-1985)

Occupation(s):	attorney
	capitalist - director, Automation Industries Inc.
	industrialist - director, Armco Steel;
	director, Vitro Corp.
Civic Activism:	donated $17 million to the Portland [ME] Museum of Art for the construction
	of its Charles Shipman Payson building;
	donated paintings valued at $6.4 million to the Portland [ME] Museum of Art;
	chairman, New York Chapter, National Service Fund of Disabled American
	Veterans
Marriage(s):	M/1 - 1924-1975 - Joan Whitney (1903-1975)
	- capitalist - owner, New York Mets (baseball team);
	minority stockholder, New York Giants (baseball team
	which became the San Francisco Giants)
	Civic Activism: director, New York Hospital, NYC;
	director, St. Mary's Hospital, West Palm Beach, FL;
	co-founder and director, North Shore Hospital (now,
	North Shore University Hospital), Manhasset;
	trustee, United Hospital Fund;
	trustee, Lighthouse for the Blind;
	trustee, Museum of Modern Art, NYC;
	trustee, Metropolitan Museum of Art, NYC
	M/2 - 1977-1985 - Virginia Kraft (b. 1920)
	- journalist - editor, *Sports Illustrated*

Listed in *Long Island Society Register, 1929*: yes
Address: Shelter Rock Road, Manhasset
Acreage / map sources: not listed separately on 1927, 1932, or 1946 maps
Name of estate:
Year of construction: 1924
Style of architecture: Federal
Architect(s): Delano and Aldrich designed the house (for Payson)
Builder: E. W. Howell Co.
Landscape architect(s):
House extant: yes
Historical notes:

The house was built by Charles Shipman Payson.
Both the *Long Island Society Register, 1929* and the *Social Register, Summer 1975* list Charles Shipman and Joan Whitney Payson as residing in Manhasset.
Born in Portland, ME, he was the son of Herbert and Sally Carroll Brown Shipman.
Joan Whitney Payson was the daughter of William Payne and Helen Hay Whitney, who resided at *Greentree* in Manhasset. Her brother, John Hay Whitney also resided at *Greentree*.
Charles Shipman and Joan Whitney Payson's daughter Lorinda married Vincent de Roulet and resided in North Hills. Their other daughters both reside in Europe, Lady Weidenfeld resides in London and Payne Middleton resides in Rome. Their son John was killed, at the age of eighteen, at the Battle of the Bulge during World War II.
The estate is now owned by the Unitarian Church.
Virginia Kraft Payson, subsequently, resided at the former John Scott Browning, Sr. Sands Point estate *Kidd's Rocks,* which she called *Lands End.*

front facade, 1998

Peabody, Charles Augustus, Jr. (1849-1931)

Occupation(s):   financier -   president, Mutual Life Insurance Co.;
                                            director, City Bank Farmers Trust Co.;
                                            director, National City Bank;
                                            trustee for the estate of John Jacob Astor.
              attorney -   partner, Peabody, Baker and Peabody
              capitalist -   director, Illinois Central Railroad Co.;
                                            director, Union Pacific Railroad Co.;
                                            director, Central of Georgia Railroad Co.

Marriage(s):   Charlotte Damon

Listed in *Long Island Society Register, 1929*: yes
Address: Saw Mill Road and Harbor Road, Cold Spring Harbor
Acreage / map sources: no acreage given on 1929 map; on 1931 map; not on 1944 map
Name of estate:
Year of construction: 1910-1912
Style of architecture: Tudor
Architect(s):   Grosvenor Atterbury designed the house (for C. A. Peabody, Jr.)
Landscape architect(s):
House extant: no; demolished in 1978
Historical notes:

    The house was built by Charles Augustus Peabody, Jr.
    The Peabodys' son Julian married Celestine Hitchcock and resided at *Pound Hollow Farm* in Old Westbury. Their daughter Anita married Hamilton Hadden, Sr. and resided at *Harbour Lights* in Cold Spring Harbor. Their son John married Mary C. Bishop and resided at *Sedgemere* in St. James.
    The estate was, subsequently, owned by Arnold P. Hadden.

Peabody, Julian Livingston, Jr.

Occupation(s):   attorney -   member, LeBoeuf, Lamb, Leiby, and MacRae

Marriage(s):   M/1 - 1938 - Celia Randolph Robinson (1908-1989)
                            M/2 - 1968 - Grace Eddy (1930-1990)
                                 - artist*

Listed in *Long Island Society Register, 1929*: no
Address: West Hills Road, West Hills
Acreage / map sources: not on 1929, 1931, or 1944 maps
Name of estate:
Year of construction:
Style of architecture:
Architect(s):
Landscape architect(s):   Ellen Biddle Shipman, 1941 (for W. H. Jackson)
House extant: unconfirmed
Historical notes:

    In 1944, Peabody purchased the twenty-eight-acre estate of William H. Jackson. The estate included a fifteen-room main residence, stable, garage, superintendent's cottage, chauffeur's cottage, and greenhouse. He also purchased an adjoining twelve acres from Sarah Sammis. [*The New York Times* November 22, 1944, p. 32.]
    Peabody was the son of Julian Livingston and Celestine Hitchcock Peabody, Sr., who resided at *Pound Hollow Farm* in Old Westbury. His sister Daphne married Edward Eugene Murray and resided in Old Westbury.
    Celia Randolph Robinson Peabody was the daughter of John Randolph and Mary Fletcher Metcalf Robinson, who resided in Brookville. Her sister Mary married John C. West of Providence, RI. *[See following entry for additional family information.]*
    Julian Livingston and Celia Randolph Robinson Peabody, Jr.'s daughter Patricia married James Murphy Davies and resided in Ketchum, ID.
    Grace Eddy was the daughter of Randolph L. Eddy of Manhattan. She had previously been married to Charles F. Willis II.
    *One of her large abstract oil paintings hangs in the National Museum for Women in the Arts in Washington, DC.

Peabody, Julian Livingston, Sr. (1881-1935)

Occupation(s):   architect -   partner, Peabody, Wilson and Brown
[See Architects appendix for list of Long Island North Shore commissions.]

Marriage(s):   1913-1935 - Celestine E. Hitchcock (d. 1935)

Listed in *Long Island Society Register, 1929*: yes
Address: Powell Lane, Old Westbury
Acreage / map sources: on 1927 map; 21 acres / 1932 and 1946 maps
Name of estate: *Pound Hollow Farm*
Year of construction: c. 1910
Style of architecture: Long Island Farmhouse
Architect(s):   Julian Livingston Peabody, Sr. of Peabody, Wilson and Brown
          designed his own house
Landscape architect(s):   Ellen Biddle Shipman, 1924 (for J. L. Peabody, Sr.)
House extant: yes
Historical notes:

The house, originally named *Pound Hollow Farm,* was built by Julian Livingston Peabody, Sr.

The *Long Island Society Register, 1929* lists the name of Peabody's estate as *Pound Hollow Farm.*

He was the son of Charles Augustus and Charlotte Damon Peabody, Jr., who resided in Cold Spring Harbor. His sister Anita married Hamilton Hadden, Sr. and resided at *Dogwood* in Jericho and, subsequently, at *Harbour Lights* in Cold Spring Harbor. His brother John married Mary C. Bishop and resided at *Sedgemere* in St. James.

Celestine Hitchcock Peabody was the daughter of Thomas and Louise Eustis Hitchcock, Sr., who resided at *Broad Hollow Farm* in Old Westbury. Her sister Helen married James Averell Clark. They also resided in Old Westbury. Her brother Francis married Mary Atwell of Manhasset. Her brother Thomas Hitchcock, Jr. married Margaret Mellon and resided in Sands Point. After his death Margaret purchased the Hitchcock family's Old Westbury estate *Broad Hollow Farm.*

The Peabodys both died when the liner *Mohawk,* on which they were passengers, sank during a voyage to Guatemala.
[See previous entry for additional family information.]

Peck, Fremont Carson, Sr. (1898-1990)

Occupation(s):   publisher - *The Brooklyn Daily Times;*
          The Brooklyn Times–Union;
          The Standard Union
          merchant - director, F. W. Woolworth Co.
Civic Activism: trustee, Carson C. Peck Hospital, Brooklyn (which merged with
          Methodist Hospital)

Marriage(s):   M/1 - 1921-1969 - Mary Isabel Foster (d. 1969)
          M/2 - 1970-1989 - Elizabeth F. Gleason (d. 1989)

Listed in *Long Island Society Register, 1929*: yes
Address: Piping Rock Road and Frost Pond Road, Old Brookville
Acreage / map sources: not on 1927 map; no acreage given on 1932 map; 36 acres / 1946 map
Name of estate:
Year of construction: c. 1929
Style of architecture: French Chateau
Architect(s):   Benjamin W. Morris designed the house (for F. C. Peck, Sr.)
Landscape architect(s):   Armistead Fitzhugh (for F. C. Peck, Sr.)
House extant: yes
Historical notes:

The house was built by Fremont Carson Peck, Sr.

The *Long Island Society Register, 1929* lists Fremont Carson and Isabel Foster Peck [Sr.] as residing in Locust Valley [Old Brookville].

He was the son of Carson C. and Clara Sargent Peck, who resided in Brooklyn.

The estate was, subsequently, owned by James Abercrombie Burden III, who called it *Woodside.*

Peck, Thomas Bloodgood, II (1875-1958)

Occupation(s):	financier - insurance
Marriage(s):	M/1 - 1904-1919 - Elinor Parke Custis Lewis
	M/2 - 1921-1958 - Agnetta Floris (1881-1971)

Listed in *Long Island Society Register, 1929*: yes
Address: Split Rock Road, Syosset
Acreage / map sources: not on 1927 map; no acreage given on 1932 map; 3 acres / 1946 map
Name of estate: *The Shack*
Year of construction:
Style of architecture:
Architect(s):
Landscape architect(s):
House extant: unconfirmed
Historical notes:

    Both the *Long Island Society Register, 1929* and the *Social Register, Summer 1937* list Thomas Bloodgood and Agnetta Floris Peck [II] as residing at *The Shack* in Syosset, while the *Social Register New York, 1951* and *1957* list the Pecks as residing at 601 East 20th Street, NYC. Agnetta Floris Peck was residing on Whitter Boulevard, Bethesda, MD, at the time of her death.
    She was the daughter of Joseph Floris.
    Elinor Parke Custis Lewis Peck was the daughter of Edward Parke Custis Lewis of *Castle Point* in Hoboken, NJ. She was the great-granddaughter of Nellie Custis, the adopted daughter of President George Washington. [*The New York Times* June 17, 1904, p. 9.]
    Peck's son Thomas Bloodgood Peck III was United States Vice-Consul to Singapore.

Pell, Clarence Cecil, Jr. (1912-1998)

Occupation(s):	financier - founder, Air Transport Insurance, SA (an airline self-insurance firm)
Marriage(s):	M/1 - 1936-1941 - Eve Mortimer
	M/2 - 1959-1998 - Francesca L. Hinckley

Listed in *Long Island Society Register, 1929*: yes
Address: Jericho Turnpike, Old Westbury
Acreage / map sources: on 1927 map (owned by C. C. Pell)
                                   19 acres / 1932 and 1946 maps (owned by C. C. Pell)
Name of estate:
Year of construction: c. 1920
Style of architecture: Colonial Revival
Architect(s):
Landscape architect(s):
House extant: yes
Historical notes:

    The house was built by Howland Haggerty Pell, Sr.
    The estate was owned by Clarence Cecil Pell, Sr., and, subsequently, by his son Clarence Cecil Pell, Jr.
    The *Long Island Society Register, 1929* lists Clarence C. Pell, Jr. as residing with his parents in Westbury [Old Westbury].
    Eve Mortimer Pell was the daughter of Stanley Grafton Mortimer of Tuxedo Park, NY. She subsequently married Lewis Cass Ledyard III of Oyster Bay Cove.
    Clarence and Eve Mortimer Pell's daughter Eve married Herbert Paul McLauglin, Jr. of Lake Forest, IL. Their son Clarence Cecil Pell III married Jane Elizabeth Gurnee, the daughter of Mark S. Gurnee of Silver Springs, MD.
    The *Social Register New York, 1975* lists Clarence C. and Francesca L. Hinckley Pell [Jr.] as residing on Jericho Turnpike, Old Westbury.
    He won the national racquet tennis doubles championship eight times from 1937 to 1959. In 1958, he also won the national racquet tennis singles championship.
    The Pells were descendants of Sir John Pell, Lord of the Manor of Pelham and owner of much of what is now Westchester County. [*The New York Times* May 14, 1998, section B, p. 10.]

Pell, Clarence Cecil, Sr. (1885-1964)

Occupation(s):   financier - stockbroker

Marriage(s):   M/1 - Madeline Borland (d. 1949)
                                  M/2 - Susan Wesselhoeft

Listed in *Long Island Society Register, 1929*: yes
Address: Jericho Turnpike, Old Westbury
Acreage / map sources: on 1927 map (owned by C. C. Pell)
                                  19 acres / 1932 and 1946 maps (owned by C. C. Pell)

Name of estate:
Year of construction: c. 1920
Style of architecture: Colonial Revival
Architect(s):
Landscape architect(s):
House extant: yes
Historical notes:

The house was built by Howland Haggerty Pell, Sr.
The estate was owned by Clarence Cecil Pell, Sr., and, subsequently, by his son Clarence Cecil Pell, Jr.
The *Long Island Society Register, 1929* lists Clarence C. and Madeline Borland Pell [Sr.] as residing on Jericho Turnpike, Westbury [Old Westbury].
He was United States racquet singles champion twelve times between 1915 and 1933. He and Stanley G. Mortimer won the racquet doubles championship nine times.
[See previous entry for additional information.]

Pell, Howland Haggerty, Sr. (1872-1949)

Occupation(s):   financier - a founder and partner, S. H. P. Pell and Co. (stock brokerage firm);
                                              a founder and partner, Pell and White (stock brokerage firm);
                                              member, Carden, Green and Co. (stock brokerage firm)

Marriage(s):   M/1 - 1895-1919 - Mary Wilson Willets
                                  M/2 - 1919 - Margaret Greeley

Listed in *Long Island Society Register, 1929*: no
Address: Jericho Turnpike, Old Westbury
Acreage / map sources: on 1927 map (owned by C. C. Pell)
                                  19 acres / 1932 and 1946 maps (owned by C. C. Pell)

Name of estate:
Year of construction: c. 1920
Style of architecture: Colonial Revival
Architect(s):
Landscape architect(s):
House extant: yes
Historical notes:

front facade, c. 1914

The house was built by Howland Haggerty Pell, Sr.
He was the son of John Howland and Caroline E. Hyatt Pell of Manhattan. His brother Theodore Roosevelt Pell resided at *Wampage* in Sands Point.
The estate was, subsequently, owned by Clarence Cecil Pell, Sr. and then by his son Clarence Cecil Pell, Jr.
Howland Haggerty and Mary Wilson Willets Pell's daughter Mary married W. Gillette Bird, the son of Harrison Kerr Bird of Manhattan. Pell's son Howland Haggerty Pell Jr. married Grace Milburn, the daughter of Ralph Milburn and, subsequently, Madeleine F. Harding.
The Pells traced their ancestry to Sir John Pell, Lord of the Manor of Pelham and owner of much of what is now Westchester County. [*The New York Times* May 14, 1998, section B, p. 10.]

Pell, John Howland Gibbs (1904-1987)

Occupation(s):	financier - a founder and partner, John H. Pell and Co. (investment banking firm); trustee, Dime Savings Bank of New York (now, The Dime)
	educator - chancellor, Long Island University, 1962-1964
	publisher - director, Macmillan, Inc.
	writer - *Life of Ethan Allen,* 1929; articles on history and finance
Civic Activism:	owned and restored historic Fort Ticonderoga, Ticonderoga, NY; president, Fort Ticonderoga Association; member, Commissioner of Education's Commission of New York State Museums; member, Interstate Commission on Lake Champlain Basin
Marriage(s):	1929-1987 - Pyma Daphne Tilton

Listed in *Long Island Society Register, 1929*: no
Address: Centre Island Road, Centre Island
Acreage / map sources: not on 1927, 1932, or 1946 maps
Name of estate: *Pelican Point*
Year of construction:
Style of architecture:
Architect(s):
Landscape architect(s):
House extant: unconfirmed
Historical notes:

Born in Southampton, LI, John Howland Gibbs Pell was the son of Stephen Hyatt Pelham and Sarah Gibbs Thompson Pell.

Pyma Daphne Tilton Pell was the great-granddaughter of John Bigelow, who was the United States Minister to France in President Abraham Lincoln's administration.

The Pells' daughter Sarah married Edwin C. Dunning and, subsequently, Hubert R. Hudson.

Pell, Theodore Roosevelt (1878-1967)

Occupation(s):	capitalist - real estate - president, Pell & Tibbitts (Sands Point real estate firm)
Civic Activism:	board member, Museum of the City of New York; secretary, St. Nicholas Society; vice president, Colonial Lords of Manors in America
Marriage(s):	1903-1965 - Florence Cramp (d. 1965)

Listed in *Long Island Society Register, 1929*: yes
Address: Prospect Lane, Sands Point
Acreage / map sources: on 1927 map
not on 1932 or 1946 maps
Name of estate: *Wampage*
Year of construction:
Style of architecture:
Architect(s):
Landscape architect(s):
House extant: unconfirmed
Historical notes:

Wampage

Theodore Roosevelt Pell was the son of John Howland and Caroline Hyatt Pell of Manhattan. His brother Howland Haggerty Pell, Sr. resided in Old Westbury.

Florence Cramp Pell was the daughter of Edwin S. Cramp of Philadelphia, PA.

Theodore Roosevelt Pell was United States men's indoor singles tennis champion in 1907, 1909, and 1911 and indoor doubles tennis champion in 1905, 1909, 1911, and 1912. He was a member of the United States Olympic team in 1912 and was inducted into the National Lawn Tennis Hall of Fame in 1966.

President Theodore Roosevelt's mother Martha was Pell's godmother.

Pennington, Hall Pleasants (1889-1942)

Occupation(s):	architect - partner, Pennington, Lewis and Mills
	[See Architects appendix for list of Long Island North Shore commissions.]
Civic Activism:	designed hospitals for the American Red Cross during World War I
Marriage(s):	M/1 - 1914 - Alice Damrosch
	M/2 - 1931-1942 - Rose de Montauzan

Listed in *Long Island Society Register, 1929*: no

Address:	Chicken Valley Road and Valley Road, Matinecock
Acreage / map sources:	not on 1927 map; no acreage given on 1932 map; 3 acres / 1946 map
Name of estate:	
Year of construction:	c. 1929
Style of architecture:	Classical Revival
Architect(s):	Hall Pleasants Pennington designed his own house
Landscape architect(s):	
House extant: yes	
Historical notes:	

The house was built by the architect Hall Peasants Pennington, as his own residence.

He was the son of Josias Pennington of Baltimore, MD.

Alice Damrosch Pennington was the daughter of Dr. Walter Johannes and Mrs. Margaret Blaine Damrosch, who resided at *Monday House* in Upper Brookville. She subsequently married Dudley Francis Wolfe of Boston, MA, and, then, Herman S. Kiaer.

Rose de Montauzan Pennington was the daughter of Camille de Montauzan of Lyons, France. She had previously been married to Henry Bartol Register of Philadelphia, PA.

The estate was, subsequently, owned by Joseph L. Merrrill, who called it *Chanticleer*.

Pennoyer, Paul Geddes, Sr. (1890-1971)

Occupation(s):	attorney - partner, A. Iselin and Co.
	diplomat - representative, United Nations San Francisco Conference, 1945;
	statesman - member, Secretariat State–War–Navy Committee, 1945
Civic Activism:	trustee, Pierpont Morgan Library, NYC;
	member, board of governors, New York Hospital, NYC
Marriage(s):	1917-1971 - Frances Tracy Morgan (1897-1989)
	- Civic Activism: a founder, Greenvale School, Greenvale

Listed in *Long Island Society Register, 1929*: yes

Address:	Duck Pond Road, Glen Cove
Acreage / map sources:	on 1927 map; no acreage given on 1932 map; 74 acres / 1946 map
Name of estate:	*Round Bush*
Year of construction:	c. 1917
Style of architecture:	Tudor
Architect(s):	Roger Harrington Bullard designed the house (for Pennoyer)
Landscape architect(s):	Olmsted, 1926 (for Pennoyer)
House extant: no*	
Historical notes:	

The house, originally named *Round Bush,* was built by Paul Geddes Pennoyer, Sr.

Frances Tracy Morgan was the daughter of John Pierpont and Jane Grew Morgan, Jr., who resided at *Matinecock Point* on East Island in Glen Cove. Her sister Jane married George Nichols, Sr. and resided at *Uplands* in Cold Spring Harbor. Her brother Henry Sturgis Morgan, Sr. resided in Lattingtown, at *Beacon Farm* in Asharoken, and on Eaton's Neck. Her brother Junius Spencer Morgan resided at *Apple Trees* in Matinecock and at *Salutation* in Glen Cove.

The Pennoyers' daughter Frances married August Hamilton Schilling and resided in Woodside, CA. Their daughter Virginia married Norman B. Livermore, Jr. and resided in San Rafael, CA. Their daughter Katherine married Eugene E. O'Donnell and resided in Marlboro, MA. Their daughter Jessie married Frank V. Snyder and resided in Greenwich, CT. Their son Robert married Victoria L. Parsons and resided in Manhattan. Their son Paul Geddes Pennoyer, Jr. married Cecily Henderson and resided at *The Stable* on Duck Pond Road in Glen Cove.

*The estate is now a housing development named Matinecock Woods.

Perin, Charles Page (1861-1937)

Occupation(s):   industrialist - general manager and president, blast furnaces collieries in
                                                  Virginia and Kentucky for Carnegie Steel;
                                      director, Stonega Coke and Coal Co.;
                                      president, Embree Iron Co.;
                                      director, American Pig Iron Storage Warrant Co.;
                                      director, American Road Machinery Co.
                    writer - *Mission en Siberie*, 1901 (published in France)

Marriage(s):   M/1 - 1887-1914 - Keokee Monroe Henderson (d. 1914)
                                M/2 - Jeannette Bean
                                M/3 - 1925-1937 - Katharine Sharp

Listed in *Long Island Society Register, 1929*: yes
Address: Centre Island Road, Centre Island
Acreage / map sources: on 1927 map (owned by K. S. Hoyt)
                                6 acres / 1946 map (owned by K. H. Perin)
                                not on 1932 map
Name of estate:
Year of construction:
Style of architecture:
Architect(s):
Landscape architect(s):
House extant: unconfirmed
Historical notes:

    Charles Page Perin was a pioneer in the development and manufacture of pure iron by electrolysis.
    He was the son of Dr. Glover Perin.
    Katharine Sharp Perin had previously been married to Colgate Hoyt, Sr. and resided at *Eastover* on Centre Island.

Perine, William DeNyse Nichols (d. 1932)

Occupation(s):   financier - member, J. P. Morgan and Co. (now, J. P. Morgan
                                      Chase) (investment banking firm)

Marriage(s):   Mary Bennett (d. 1932)

Listed in *Long Island Society Register, 1929*: no
Address: Horse Shoe Road, Mill Neck
Acreage / map sources: not on 1927 or 1946 maps
                                no acreage given on 1932 map
Name of estate: *Windermere House*
Year of construction: c. 1930
Style of architecture: Federal
Architect(s):
Landscape architect(s):
House extant: yes
Historical notes:

    The house, originally named *Windermere House,* was built by William DeNyse Nichols Perine.
    The *Brooklyn Blue Book, 1930* lists William DeNyse Nichols and Mae [Mary] Bennett Perine as residing at *Windermere House* in Mill Neck.

Windermere House

Peters, William Richmond (1850-1931)

Occupation(s):   shipping -   founder and president, Peters, White & Co.
                                                  (chemical importers)
                              financier -   a founder, Columbia Trust Co.;
                                                    director, Atlantic Mutual Insurance Co.
                              industrialist - director, Mutual Chemical Co.;
                                                  director, Phosphate Mining Co.

Civic Activism: president, The Sheltering Arms, Manhattan (child care
                                                institution founded by his father in 1864)

Marriage(s):   1879 - Helen Heister

Listed in *Long Island Society Register, 1929*: yes
Address: West Shore Road, Mill Neck
Acreage / map sources: on 1906 map (owned by William R. Peters)
                                on 1927 map (name misspelled as William H. Peters)
                                no acreage given on 1932 map (name misspelled as William H. Peters)
                                68 acres / 1946 map (owned by T. and I. Peters)
Name of estate: *Hawirt*
Year of construction: c. 1904
Style of architecture: Colonial Revival
Architect(s):   Erick Kensett Rossiter designed the house (for W. R. Peters)
                                Bradley Delehanty designed 1940 alterations (for Marsh)

Landscape architect(s):
House extant: yes
Historical notes:

    The house, originally named *Hawirt*, was built by William Richmond Peters.

    The *Long Island Society Register, 1929* lists William R. and Helen Heister Peters as residing at *Hawirt* on West Shore Drive [Road] in Oyster Bay [Mill Neck].

    He was the son of Thomas McClure Peters.

    Helen Heister Peters was the daughter of Henry Anton Heister.

    William Richmond and Helen Heister Peters' daughters remained unmarried. Their son Thomas McClure Peters II married Marion Hood Post, the daughter of William Stone Post of Manhattan and Bernardsville, NJ. She was the granddaughter of Confederate Army General John Bell Hood.

    The estate was inherited by the Peterses' children Thomas, Isabel, and Alice. [*The New York Times* December 1, 1932, p. 14.]

    In 1939, John Bigelow Marsh, Sr. purchased the estate, which he called *Nyrmah*, from Thomas and Isabel Peters. Subsequently, it was owned by Alfred Gwynne Vanderbilt II.

    In 2000, the twenty-five-room, 13,000-square-foot house, six-car garage, guest house, and 15.9 acres were for sale. The asking price was $8.5 million; the annual taxes were $48,122.

West Shore Road, Mill Neck,
c. 1915

Petrova, Olga (c. 1884-1977)*

Occupation(s):	entertainers and associated professions - actress
	radio commentator for radio station WKRS
	writer - *The Black Virgin* (collection of short stories);
	Butter With My Bread (autobiography), 1942;
	numerous verse and satirical fiction contributions to magazines;
	dramatist - authored and starred in: *Daughter of Destiny;*
	The Orchid Lady; Bridges Burned;
	More Truth Than Poetry;
	authored and played in: *The White Peacock,* 1921;
	Hurricane; What Do We Know

Marriage(s):	M/1 - Dr. John Dillon Stewart (d. 1938)
	- physician
	M/2 - 1939 - Louis Willoughby
	- entertainers and associated professions - British actor

Listed in *Long Island Society Register, 1929*: yes
Address: Kings Point Road, Kings Point
Acreage / map sources: on 1927 map; not on 1932 or 1946 maps
Name of estate:
Year of construction:
Style of architecture:
Architect(s):
Landscape architect(s):
House extant: unconfirmed
Historical notes:

  *Mme. Olga Petrova is listed in several sources with differing birth dates.
  She was the author of several motion pictures in which she appeared.
  The estate was purchased by Walter Percy Chrysler, Sr. Irritated by the public beach next to his Kings Point estate, *Forker House,* Chrysler offered the Petrova estate plus $85,000 to the village for the public beach. When the village refused, he offered the property plus $15,000 in cash and he further offered to build two swimming pools, a bath house, and a pier. He even offered to assume any defective title liability and to take over the village's lease on that part of the park owned by the village. When his offers were refused, Chrysler gave the former Petrova estate to his son Jack. [Vincent Curcio, *Chrysler: The Life and Times of an Automotive Genius* (New York; Oxford University Press, 2000), p. 455.]

Pettinos, Charles E. (d. 1951)

Occupation(s):	industrialist - founder and president, Charles E. Pettinos & Co.
	(graphite firm)*

Marriage(s):	Joy Chapman

Listed in *Long Island Society Register, 1929*: yes
Address: South Centre Island Road, Centre Island
Acreage / map sources: on 1927 map; not on 1932 or 1946 maps
Name of estate: *Thatch Cottage*
Year of construction: c. 1920
Style of architecture: French Norman
Architect(s): Mrs. John E. McLeran designed the house (for Pettinos)
Landscape architect(s):
House extant: yes
Historical notes:

  The house, originally named *Thatch Cottage,* was built by Charles E. Pettinos.
  *Pettinos was known as "The Graphite King."
  Charles E. and Joy Chapman Pettinos' daughter Eleanor married Richard Allmand Blow, the son of George Preston Blow of Chicago, IL.
  The estate was owned in 1928 by Sherman M. Fairchild and, subsequently, by William Erhard Weiss, Jr.

Phelps, Ansel (1871-1950)

Occupation(s):   financier - stockbroker

Marriage(s):   1905-1950 - Georgiana L. Wilmerding (1871-1961)
- Civic Activism: director, Theodore Roosevelt Memorial Association

Listed in *Long Island Society Register, 1929*: yes
Address: Centre Island Road, Centre Island
Acreage / map sources: on 1927 map
4 acres / 1932 map
not on 1946 map
Name of estate: *Brick Yard Point*
Year of construction:
Style of architecture:
Architect(s):
Landscape architect(s):
House extant: unconfirmed
Historical notes:

    Both the *Long Island Society Register, 1929* and the *Social Register, Summer 1932* list Ansel and Georgiana L. Wilmerding Phelps as residing at *Brick Yard Point* on Centre Island.
    He was the son of Charles Henry and Mary Booth Phelps of Summit, NJ.
    Georgiana L. Wilmerding Phelps was the daughter of John Christopher Wilmerding.

Philips, William Pyle (1882-1950)

Occupation(s):   attorney - partner, Byrne and Cutcheon
financier - partner, J. & W. Seligman and Co. (investment banking firm)
capitalist - director, United Artists Theater Circuit, Inc.;
director, Twentieth Century-Fox Film Corp.;
director, Columbia Gas & Electric Corp.;
director, Park Sheraton Hotel, NYC
industrialist - director, Sinclair Oil Corp.;
director, Helena Rubinstein, Inc.;
director, Cuba Cane Sugar Corp.;
director, Pierce-Arrow Motor Car Co.
Civic Activism: trustee, Haverford, College, Haverford, PA

Marriage(s):

Listed in *Long Island Society Register, 1929*: yes
Address: Piping Rock Road and Frost Pond Road, Old Brookville
Acreage / map sources: on 1927 map
not on 1932 or 1946 maps

Name of estate:
Year of construction:
Style of architecture:
Architect(s):
Landscape architect(s):
House extant: unconfirmed
Historical notes:

    The *Long Island Society Register, 1929* lists William P, Philips as residing in Locust Valley [Old Brookville], while the *Social Register New York, 1933* and *1948* list him as residing at 200 West 56th Street, NYC.
    He was the son of George M. Philips of West Chester, PA.
    The estate was, subsequently, owned by C. Merrill Chapin, Jr.

Phillips, Ellis Laurimore, Sr. (1873-1959)

Occupation(s):   capitalist - a founder and president, Long Island Lighting Co., 1912-1937;
                              financier - president, Eastern Seaboard Securities

Civic Activism: established Ellis L. Phillips Foundation, which donated an electrical
                                 engineering building to Cornell University, Ithaca, NY

Marriage(s):   1919-1959 - Kathryn F. Sisson (1879-1970)
                                 - educator - dean of women, Chadron State Teachers' College, Chadron, NE,
                                    1913-1915;
                                       dean of women, Ohio Wesleyan University, Delaware, OH,
                                       1915-1919;
                                       a founder and president, National Association of Dean of Women
                                 writer - *A Room in the World,* 1964

Listed in *Long Island Society Register, 1929*: yes
Address: Bayview Road, Plandome Manor
Acreage / map sources: on 1927 map; not on 1932 or 1949 maps
Name of estate: *Laurimon*
Year of construction: c. 1926
Style of architecture: Tudor
Architect(s):
Landscape architect(s):   Ruth Dean (for Phillips)
Estate photographs can be found in the Nassau County Museum Collection filed under Plandome/Phillips.
House extant: yes
Historical notes:

   The house, originally named *Laurimon,* was built by Ellis Laurimore Phillips, Sr.
   The Phillipses' son Ellis Laurimore Phillips, Jr. married Marion Grumman of Plandome Manor.

Phipps, Henry, Jr. (1839-1930)

Occupation(s):   industrialist - partner, Andrew J. Carnegie;
                                 partner, Bidwell & Phipps (agents for Du Pont Powder Co.);
                                 partner, Kloman & Phipps (iron mill)

Civic Activism: built psychiatric clinic at Johns Hopkins Hospital, Baltimore, MD;
                              gave $1 million to New York City for sanitary tenement housing;
                              bequeathed over $7 million to various charities

Marriage(s):   1872-1930 - Anne Childs Shaffer (1850-1959)

Listed in *Long Island Society Register, 1929*: yes
Address: 345 Lakeville Road, Lake Success
Acreage / map sources: on 1927 map
                              93 acres / 1932 map
                              112 acres / 1946 map
Name of estate: *Bonnie Blink*
Year of construction: c. 1916-1918
Style of architecture: Federal
Architect(s):   Horace Trumbauer designed the house
                                 (for H. Phipps, Jr.)
Landscape architect(s):   Olmsted, 1915-1916 (for H. Phipps, Jr.)
House extant: yes
Historical notes:

front facade, 1998

   The house, originally named *Bonnie Blink,* was built by Henry Phipps, Jr.
   The Phippses' daughter Helen married Bradley Martin and resided at *Knole* in Old Westbury. Their daughter Amy
married Frederick E. Guest and resided at *Roslyn Manor* in Brookville. All of their sons resided in Old Westbury as well:
Henry Carnegie Phipps at *Spring Hill*; Howard Phipps, Sr. at *Erchless*; and John Shaffer Phipps at *Westbury House.*
   In 1949, the Phipps family donated nine acres to the Great Neck School District. At the same time, the district
purchased an additional 106 acres of the estate. The house serves as the administrative headquarters of the school district
and is now called the Phipps Administration Building. In 1966, an extension was added to the house by the district.

Phipps, Henry Carnegie (1879-1953)

Occupation(s):   capitalist - real estate - built apartments at Sutton Place, NYC;
Civic Activism: director, Society of Phipps Houses (non-profit organization that built
middle income housing for Bellevue and New York Hospital as
well as apartments in Sunnyside, Queens, and in The Bronx)

Marriage(s):   1907-1953 - Gladys Mills (1884-1970)

Listed in *Long Island Society Register, 1929*: yes
Address: Garvan – Whitney – Phipps Road, Old Westbury
Acreage / map sources: on 1927 map (owned by H. C. Phipps)
180 acres / 1932 map (owned by Gladys Phipps)
165 acres / 1946 map (owned by Gladys Phipps)
Name of estate: *Spring Hill*
Year of construction: c. 1902
Style of architecture: Italian Renaissance
Architect(s):   John Russell Pope designed the
house (for Stow)
Horace Trumbauer designed 1918
alterations (for H. C. Phipps)
Landscape architect(s):   Olmsted, 1915-1916 (for H. C. Phipps)

red ballroom, c. 1955

Estate photographs can be found in the Nassau County Museum
   Collection filed under Old Westbury/ Phipps.
House extant: no; demolished in 1970s
Historical notes:

The house was built by William L. Stow.
The estate was owned by George Crocker and, subsequently, by Phipps, who called it *Spring Hill.*
Henry Carnegie Phipps was the son of Henry and Anne Shaffer Phipps, Jr., who resided at *Bonnie Blink* in Lake Success. *[See other Phipps family entries for additional information.]*
Gladys Mills Phipps was the sister of Ogden Livingston Mills, who resided in Woodbury. Her sister Beatrice married Bernard Arthur William Patrick Hastings Forbes, the Earl of Granard.
The Phippses' son Ogden Phipps resided in Old Westbury. Their daughter Sonia married Herbert Farrell, Jr. of Sandusky, OH, and, subsequently, Count Hans Christoph Scherr–Thoss of Dobrau, Silesia. Their daughter Barbara married Stuart S. Janney, Jr. of Baltimore, MD. Their daughter Audrey married Philip D. Holden of Manhattan.
The Phippses' Westbury stables were known as Wheatley Stable. They bred the thoroughbred champion *Seabiscuit.*

Phipps, Howard, Jr. (b. 1934)

Occupation(s):   financier - trustee, Bessemer Securities Corp.
Civic Activism: president, New York Zoological Society, NYC

Marriage(s):   1956 - Mary N. Stone
         - Civic Activism: president, Girl Scout Council of Greater New York

Listed in *Long Island Society Register, 1929*: no
Address: Post Road, Old Westbury
Acreage / map sources: on 1927 map (owned by Howard Phipps)
123 acres / 1932 and 1946 maps (owned by Howard Phipps)
Name of estate: *Erchless*
Year of construction: c. 1935
Style of architecture: Colonial Revival
Architect(s):   Adams and Prentice designed the house (for H. Phipps, Sr.)
Landscape architect(s):
House extant: yes
Historical notes:

The house, originally named *Erchless*, was built by Howard Phipps, Sr.
The estate was, subsequently, owned by Howard Phipps, Jr., who continued call it *Erchless.*
[See following entry for family information.]

Phipps, Howard, Jr. (b. 1934)

Occupation(s):   financier - trustee, Bessemer Securities Corp. [Phipps' family
financial trust, now open to public investment]*

Civic Activism: president, New York Zoological Society, NYC

Marriage(s):   1956 - Mary N. Stone
                                         - Civic Activism: president, Girl Scout Council of Greater New York

Listed in *Long Island Society Register, 1929*: no
Address: Post Road, Old Westbury
Acreage / map sources: not on 1927, 1932, or 1946 maps
Name of estate: *Little Erchless*
Year of construction:
Style of architecture:
Architect(s):
Landscape architect(s):
House extant: unconfirmed
Historical notes:

   *Howard Phipps Jr.'s inheritance was worth $430 million. ["Forbes 400 List," 1996.] He was the son of Howard and Harriet Dyer Price Phipps, Sr.
   Mary N. Stone Phipps was the daughter of James K. Stone of La Anna, PA.
   The Phippses' son George married Kristina Ann Emanuels, the daughter of Kenneth J. Emanuels of Sacramento, CA. Their son Howard Phipps III married Terry Beesley, the daughter of J. Alan Beesley, the UN Ambassador from Canada. Their daughter Martha married Walter L. Maguire of Madison, CT.
   [See following entry for additional family information.]

Phipps, Howard, Sr. (1881-1981)

Occupation(s):   capitalist - real estate - president, Society of Phipps Houses (non-profit
organization that built middle income housing for Bellevue
and New York Hospital as well as apartments in Sunnyside,
Queens, and in The Bronx)

Marriage(s):   1931-1981 - Harriet Dyer Price (1901-1981)*
                                         - Civic Activism: president (for thirty-one years), Girl Scout Council
of Greater New York

Listed in *Long Island Society Register, 1929*: no
Address: Post Road, Old Westbury
Acreage / map sources: on 1927 map (owned by Howard Phipps)
                                         123 acres / 1932 and 1946 maps (owned by Howard Phipps)
Name of estate: *Erchless*
Year of construction: c. 1935
Style of architecture: Colonial Revival
Architect(s):   Adams and Prentice designed the house (for H. Phipps, Sr.)
Landscape architect(s):
House extant: yes
Historical notes:

   The house, originally named *Erchless*, was built by Howard Phipps, Sr.
   He was the son of Henry and Anne Childs Shaffer Phipps, Jr., who resided at *Bonnie Blink* in Lake Success. His brother Henry Carnegie Phipps resided at *Spring Hill* in Old Westbury. His brother John Shaffer Phipps resided at *Westbury House* in Old Westbury. His sister Helen married Bradley Martin and resided at *Knole*, also in Old Westbury. His sister Amy married Frederick E. Guest and resided at *Roslyn Manor* in Brookville.
   *Harriet Price Phipps' mother and Juliette Gordon Low, the founder of the Girl Scouts of America in 1912, were very close friends. Harriet called Ms. Low her "Aunt Daisy."
   Harriet's brother Theodore Hazeltine Price, Jr. resided at *Ben Robyn Farm* in West Hills.
   [See previous entry for additional family information.]
   The estate was, subsequently, owned by the Phippses' son Howard Phipps, Jr.

Phipps, John Shaffer (1874-1958)

Occupation(s):	attorney
	industrialist - director, U. S. Steel Corp.(which became U S X);
	director, International Paper Co.
	shipping - director, Grace Steamship Line
	financier - director, Guaranty Trust Co.
	capitalist - real estate - developer in Florida*
Civic Activism:	established a foundation for the establishment of Westbury Gardens
	and the preservation of Mrs. Phipps' gardens:
	**
Marriage(s):	1903-1957 - Margarita Celia Grace (1876-1957)

Listed in *Long Island Society Register, 1929*: yes
Address: 71 Old Westbury Road, Old Westbury
Acreage / map sources: on 1927 map; 317 acres / 1932 map; 294 acres / 1946 map
Name of estate: *Westbury House*
Year of construction: 1905-1907
Style of architecture: Georgian Revival
Architect(s):   George Abraham Crawley designed the house (for J. S. Phipps)
                                             Horace Trumbauer designed alterations (for J. S. Phipps)
                                             Paul R. Smith designed the swimming pool (for J. S. Phipps)
Landscape architect(s):   George Abraham Crawley designed the polo field, 1905;
                                             tennis courts, 1906; rose garden, 1907; the walled garden
                                             with lattice work and corner pavilions, 1907 (for J. S. Phipps)
                                             Jacques Greber (for J. S. Phipps)
                                             Olmsted (for J. S. Phipps)
Estate photographs can be found in the Nassau County Museum Collection filed under Old Westbury/Phipps
     and also under Westbury/Phipps.
House extant: yes
Historical notes:

     The house, originally named *Westbury House,* was built by John Shaffer Phipps.
     Both the *Long Island Society Register, 1929* and the *Social Register New York, 1957* list John S. and Margarita Celia
Grace Phipps as residing at *Westbury House* in Westbury [Old Westbury].
     He was the son of Henry and Anne Childs Shaffer Phipps, Jr., who resided at *Bonnie Blink* in Lake Success. His
brother Howard Phipps, Sr. resided at *Erchless* in Old Westbury. His brother Henry Carnegie Phipps resided at *Spring
Hill* in Old Westbury. His sister Helen married Bradley Martin and resided at *Knole,* also in Old Westbury. His sister
Amy married Frederick E. Guest and resided at *Roslyn Manor* in Brookville.
     Margarita Celia Grace Phipps was the daughter of Michael Paul and Margarita A. Mason Grace. Her father was one of
the founders of the Grace Steamship Line.
     John Shaffer and Margarita Celia Grace Phipps' daughter Margaret married James Gordon Douglas II and,
subsequently, Etienne Boegner. She resides at *Orchard Hill* in Old Westbury. Mrs. Boegner inherited *Westbury House*
and the furnishings. She contributed the furnishings to "Old Westbury Gardens," which, through the foundation
established by her father, maintains the remaining property, the house, and her mother's gardens as a non-profit public
property. Mrs. Boegner is still active in the preservation of the estate.
     Their son Michael married Muriel Lane. He was residing in Palm Beach, FL, at the time of his death. Their son Hubert
married Carla Gordon and, subsequently, Lady Phoebe Pleydell–Bouverie. He resided near Marshall, VA. Their son John
married Elinor Klapp and was residing at *Ayavalla Plantation* in Tallahassee, FL, at the time of his death.
     *Phipps advanced large sums of money to Florida banks during Florida's 1927 land devaluation crisis.
     **On several occasions Phipps loaned his yachts to the
American Museum of Natural History as well as to other
institutions for scientific expeditions. During World War II, the
estate hosted children from Great Britain. [Peggie Phipps
Boegner and Richard Gachot, *Halcyon Days: An American
Family Through Three Generations* (New York: Harry N.
Abrams, Inc.), The house, which is on the National Register of
Historic Places, is open to the public. It is now known as
Westbury Gardens.

side facade, c. 1915

Phipps, Ogden (1908-2002)

Occupation(s):
financier - partner, Smith, Barney and Co. (investment banking firm)
chairman, Bessemer Securities Corp. [Phipps' family financial trust]
industrialist - director, International Paper Co.;
director, Seaboard Oil Co.;
director, Cerro De Pasco Copper Corp.;
director, United States Leather Co.

Marriage(s):
M/1 - 1930-1935 - Ruth Pruyn (1907-1994)
- Civic Activism: chairman of board, Field Foundation
M/2 - 1937-1987 - Lillian Stokes Bostwick (1906-1987)
- Civic Activism: chairman, Saratoga Performing Arts Center
board member, Metropolitan Opera Association, NYC;
director, Visiting Nurse Association of New York

Listed in *Long Island Society Register, 1929*: no
Address: Garvan – Whitney – Phipps Road, Old Westbury
Acreage / map sources: on 1927 map; 180 acres / 1932 map; 16 acres / 1946 map
Name of estate:
Year of construction:
Style of architecture:
Architect(s): Delano and Aldrich designed alterations (for O. Phipps)
Landscape architect(s):
House extant: unconfirmed
Historical notes:

Ogden Phipps was the son of Henry Carnegie and Gladys Mills Phipps, who resided at *Spring Hill* in Old Westbury. His sister Barbara married Stuart L. Janney, Jr. of Baltimore, MD. His sister Sonia married Herbert Farrell, Jr. and, subsequently, Count Hans Christoph Scherr–Thoss of Dobrau, Silesia. His sister Audrey married Philip D. Holden.

Ogden and Ruth Pruyn Phipps' 31-year-old son Henry Ogden Phipps "was [allegedly] an addict who died of acute poisoning from a stimulant" in a suite he was renting at the Hamilton Hotel in NYC.

Ruth Pruyn married Marshall Field III in 1936 and resided at *Caumsett* in Lloyd Harbor. *[See surname entry for Marshall Field III for additional family information.]*

Lillian Stokes Bostwick Phipps' brothers Albert C. Bostwick II and George Herbert Bostwick, Sr., also resided in Old Westbury as did their uncle Frederick Ambrose Clark, who resided at *Broad Hollow House*. Lillian had previously been married to Robert Vandenburgh McKim and resided with him in Old Westbury. The McKims' daughter Florence married Nelson Doubleday, Jr., whose parents resided at *Barberrys* in Mill Neck.

Physioc, Joseph Allen, Sr. (1865-1951)

Occupation(s):
artist
entertainers and associated professions - set designer - Metropolitan Opera;
Broadway plays

Marriage(s):
Jessica Eskridge (1861-1948)
- entertainers and associated professions -
actress;
singer - soprano, Brooklyn Opera Co.

Listed in *Long Island Society Register, 1929*: no
Address: Bayville Avenue, Bayville
Acreage / map sources: on c. 1922 map; not on 1927, 1932, or 1946 maps
Name of estate: *Cedar Cliff*
Year of construction: c. 1895
Style of architecture: Shingle
Architect(s):
Landscape architect(s):
House extant: no; demolished c. 1950
Historical notes:

The house, originally named *Cedar Cliff*, was built by Joseph Allen Physioc, Sr.

Pickett, John Olen, Jr.

Occupation(s):   capitalist - partner, New York Islanders Hockey Team, since 1988
                                                              real estate - Florida properties

Marriage(s):   Marilyn D. Seaman

Listed in *Long Island Society Register, 1929*: no
Address: Glen Cove – Oyster Bay Road, Matinecock
Acreage / map sources: not on 1927, 1932, or 1946 maps
Name of estate:
Year of construction: 1926
Style of architecture: Dutch Colonial
Architect(s):   Bradley Delehanty designed the house (for P. A. S. Franklin, Sr.)
Landscape architect(s):
House extant: yes
Historical notes:

   The house, originally named *Royston*, was built by Philip Albright Small Franklin, Sr.
   The estate was, subsequently, owned by Pickett.
   Marilyn D. Seaman Pickett was the daughter of Alfred Jarvis Seaman, Jr., who served as mayor of Upper Brookville.
She subsequently married William Irving Hollingsworth III.
   The Picketts' son John Olen Pickett III married Alexandra Hersey Hamm, the daughter of William H. Hamm III.

Pierce, Winslow Shelby, Jr.* (1894-1950)

Occupation(s):   inventor - invented improvements in split-bearing structure, bearing
                                                              supports, precision pivots, measuring devices, and
                                                              miniature ball bearings
                                       industrialist - founder and president, Split Ball-Bearing Corp.;
                                                              founder and president, Miniature Precision Bearing Corp.

Marriage(s):   Mary Dobbin Brush

Listed in *Long Island Society Register, 1929*: yes
Address: Bayville Avenue, Bayville
Acreage / map sources: on c.1920 map; not on 1927 map; no acreage given on 1932 or 1946 maps
Name of estate: *Dunstable*
Year of construction: 1903
Style of architecture: Eclectic Jacobean
Architect(s):   Babb, Cook and Willard designed the original house (for W. S. Pierce II)
                                       Delano and Aldrich designed 1926 alterations (for H. Williams)
Builder: E. W. Howell Co.
Landscape architect(s):   Beatrix Jones Farrand designed the willow garden, tiered rock wall garden with
                                                  Chinese lattice fencing, and a pool garden, 1928-1929 (for H. Williams)
                                       Olmsted, 1933 (for H. Williams)
Estate photographs can be found in the Nassau County Museum Collection filed under Bayville/Pierce.
House extant: no; demolished in 1968*
Historical notes:

   The eighty-room house, originally named *Dunstable*, was built by Winslow Shelby Pierce II. Winslow Shelby Pierce,
Jr. resided on his parent's estate.
   *Although listed in the *Social Register* and his obituary as "Jr.," Winslow Shelby Pierce was, in reality, not a junior but
rather the third.
   Mary D. Brush Pierce subsequently married Grenville Clark [Sr.] and resided at *Outlet Farm* in Dublin, NH.
   [See following entry for additional family information.]
   In 1926, the estate was purchased by Harrison Williams for $750,000. Williams renamed the estate *Oak Point* and had
Delano and Aldrich design the alterations.
   Pierce bought adjoining property and built homes for himself and his family members.
   In the 1960s, Mona Strader Williams [von Bismarck] sold a portion of the estate property.
   *Von Bismarck demolished the house to reduce the estate's property taxes.

Pierce, Winslow Shelby, II (1857-1938)

Occupation(s): attorney - partner, Pierce and Greer;
personal attorney of George J. Gould
capitalist - chairman of the board, Union Pacific Railroad;
chairman of board, Western Maryland Railroad Co.;
chairman of board, Wabash Railroad Co.
financier - director, Equitable Trust Co.;
director, Chase National Bank of New York;
director, Glen Cove Bank;
president, Matinecock Bank, Locust Valley (which merged
into Norstar Bank)

Civic Activism: mayor, Village of Bayville, 1919-1929

Marriage(s): 1891-1937 - Grace Douglass Williams (d. 1937)

Listed in *Long Island Society Register, 1929*: yes
Address: Bayville Avenue, Bayville
Acreage / map sources: on c. 1922 map
not on 1927 map
no acreage given on 1932 or 1946 maps
Name of estate: *Dunstable*
Year of construction: 1903
Style of architecture: Eclectic Jacobean
Architect(s): Babb, Cook and Willard designed the original house
(for W. S. Pierce II)
Delano and Aldrich designed 1926 alterations (for H. Williams)
Builder: E. W. Howell Co.
Landscape architect(s): Beatrix Jones Farrand designed the willow garden, tiered rock
wall garden with Chinese lattice fencing, and a pool garden,
1928-1929 (for H. Williams)
Olmsted, 1933 (for H. Williams)
Estate photographs can be found in the Nassau County Museum Collection filed under Bayville/Pierce.
House extant: no; demolished in 1968
Historical notes:

The eighty-room house, originally named *Dunstable*, was built by Winslow Shelby Pierce II.
Both the *Long Island Society Register, 1929* and the *Social Register New York, 1933* list Winslow Shelby and Grace D.
Williams Pierce [II] as residing at *Dunstable* in Bayville.
He was born in Shelbyville, IN, the son of Dr. Winslow S. and Jane Hendricks Pierce [I]. His uncle Thomas A.
Hendricks was Vice-President of the United States in President Grover Cleveland's administration.
The Pierces' daughter Allison married Louis de Bebian Moore and resided at *Moorelands* in Oyster Bay Cove. Their
daughter Helen married Allen Lefferts and resided in Manhattan. Their daughter Grace married John Gordon Sandelands,
the Thirteenth Baron of Torpichen. Their son Winslow Shelby Pierce, Jr. [III] resided with his wife Mary at *Dunstable*.
In 1926, the estate was purchased by Harrison Williams for $750,000.
Pierce bought adjoining property and built homes for
himself and his family members.
In the 1960s, Mona Strader Williams [von Bismarck] sold a
portion of the estate property.
*Von Bismarck demolished the house to reduce the estate's
property taxes.

front facade, c. 1910

Pierson, Dr. Richard Norris, Sr. (1893-1976)

Occupation(s):	physician - director, American Hospital of Istanbul, Turkey
Civic Activism:	president, Planned Parenthood Federation of America; a founder, Birth Control League
Marriage(s):	1927-1976 - Frances Dorothy Stewart (d. 1993) - writer - *Uncle Louis and Laurelton Hall,* 1981*

Listed in *Long Island Society Register, 1929*: yes
Address: White Hill Road, Cold Spring Harbor
Acreage / map sources: not on 1929 or 1931 maps
                                                      10 acres / 1944 map
Name of estate: *Whitehill Place*
Year of construction:
Style of architecture:
Architect(s):
Landscape architect(s):
House extant: unconfirmed
Historical notes:

The *Long Island Society Register, 1929* lists Dr. Richard Norris and Mrs. Frances Dorothy Stewart Pierson [Sr.] as residing at 1060 Park Avenue, NYC, while the *Social Register, Summer 1932* lists the Piersons as residing at *Three Oaks* in Cold Spring Harbor. Both the *Social Register, Summer 1937* and the *Social Register New York, 1964* list the Piersons' residence as *Whitehill Place* in Cold Spring Harbor.

He was the son of Samuel Pierson of Stamford, CT.

Frances Dorothy Stewart Pierson was the daughter of William Adams Walker and Frances E. de Forest Stewart II, who resided at *Edgeover* in Cold Spring Harbor.

The Piersons' son Richard Norris Pierson, Jr. married Anne Bingham and resided in Tenafly, NJ. Their son Stephen married Anne H. Griggs and resided in Stamford, CT. Their son The Rev. Stewart Pierson married Julie G. Burger and resided in Pittsburgh, PA.

*Louis Comfort Tiffany's brother Burnett Young Tiffany's first wife was Emma N. Pierson.

Piquet, Dr. Samuel D. (1873-1961)

Occupation(s):	physician
Marriage(s):	1900-1961 - Laura E. Mann

Listed in *Long Island Society Register, 1929*: yes
Address: Jericho Turnpike near Piquet's Lane, Woodbury
Acreage / map sources: on 1927 map
                                                      40 acres / 1932 map
                                                      23 acres / 1946 map
Name of estate:
Year of construction:
Style of architecture:
Architect(s):
Landscape architect(s):
House extant: unconfirmed
Historical notes:

The *Long Island Society Register, 1929* lists Dr. Samuel D. and Mrs. Laura E. Mann Piquet as residing in Syosset [Woodbury].

He was a direct descendant of Dr. Louis Pasteur.

Piquet was residing on Peconic Bay Boulevard, Mattituck, at the time of his death.

Pirie, Samuel Carson, Sr. (1864-1938)

Occupation(s):	merchant - chairman of board, Carson, Pirie, Scott & Co. (one of Chicago's largest department stores)
	capitalist - president, Sea Cliff Water Co.; president, Wenalden Co.
	financier - director, Arex Indemnity Co.; director, Associated Reciprocal Exchanges

Marriage(s): 1899-1907 - Harriet Masters Lockwood (d. 1907)

Listed in *Long Island Society Register, 1929*: yes
Address: Prospect Avenue, Sea Cliff
Acreage / map sources: not on 1927, 1932, or 1946 maps
Name of estate:
Year of construction: c. 1929
Style of architecture: Georgian
Architect(s):
Landscape architect(s):
House extant: yes
Historical notes:

The house was built by Samuel Carson Pirie, Sr.
He was the son of John Thomas and Sarah Carson Pirie of Amby, IL.
The Piries' son Samuel Carson Pirie, Jr., married Jean Adams of Chicago, IL.
In 2000, the 6,000-square-foot house and two acres were for sale. The asking price was $1.8 million.

Plimpton, Francis Taylor Pearsons, Sr. (1900-1983)

Occupation(s):	attorney - associate, Root, Clark, Buckner and Ballantine; partner, Debevoise and Plimpton
	financier - trustee, Bowery Savings Bank
	writer - *As We Knew Adlai*, 1965
	diplomat - United States deputy-representative to the United Nations in the Kennedy and Lyndon B. Johnson administrations
Civic Activism:	chairman, Board of Ethics of City of New York; trustee, Phillips Exeter, Amherst, MA; trustee, Union Theological Seminary, NYC; overseer, Harvard University, Cambridge, MA; director, New York Philharmonic Society, NYC; trustee, Barnard College, NYC; board member, Metropolitan Museum of Art, NYC; a founder, Lawyers for Choice

Marriage(s): 1926-1983 - Pauline Ames

Listed in *Long Island Society Register, 1929*: no
Address: Chichester Road, West Hills
Acreage / map sources: not on 1929 or 1931 maps
27 acres / 1944 map
Name of estate: *Sweet Hollow*
Year of construction: c. 1938
Style of architecture: Colonial Revival
Architect(s):
Landscape architect(s):
House extant: yes
Historical notes:

rear facade

The Plimptons' daughter Sarah married Robert O. Paxton, the son of Matthew W. Paxton of Lexington, VA, and resides in Manhattan. Their son George, the noted writer and actor, married Freddy M. Espy and, subsequently, Sarah Whitehead Dudley. He maintained a home in Sagaponack until his death in 2003. Their son Francis Taylor Pearsons Plimpton, Jr. married Susan Wadsworth and resides at *Maltesa Farm* in Kingstown, RI.

Polk, Frank Lyon, Sr. (1871-1943)

Occupation(s):	politician - member, Civil Service Commission of New York, 1907-9; president, Civil Service Commission of New York, 1908-9
	attorney - counselor United States Department of State, 1915-19; partner, Davis, Polk, Wardwell, Gardiner, and Reed (which became Davis, Polk, Wardwell, Sunderland, and Kiendl)*
	statesman - Acting Secretary of State, 1918-19; Under Secretary of State, 1919-20
	diplomat - United States Plenipotentiary to negotiate peace, 1919; chairman, United States delegation to Paris Peace Conference, 1919
	capitalist - director, Erie Railroad Co.
	financier - director, United States Trust; director, Park Bank; trustee, Bowery Savings Bank; trustee, Mutual Life Insurance Co. of New York
	intelligence agent**
Civic Activism:	member of board, New York Board of Education; president, American Friends of Yugoslavia, Inc. vice-president, British War Relief Society; vice-president, Woodrow Wilson Foundation; vice-president, Church Pension Fund of Protestant Episcopal Church; trustee, Cathedral of St. John the Divine, NYC; president, board of trustees, New York Public Library, NYC; trustee, Manhattan Maternity and Orthopedic Hospital, NYC
Marriage(s):	1908-1943 - Elizabeth Sturgis Potter (1886-1960)

Listed in *Long Island Society Register, 1929*: yes
Address: Muttontown Road, Muttontown
Acreage / map sources: not on 1927 and 1946 maps; 20 acres / 1932 map
Name of estate:
Year of construction:
Style of architecture:
Architect(s):
Landscape architect(s):
House extant: unconfirmed
Historical notes:

Frank Lyon Polk, Sr., was the son of William Mecklenburg. and Ida A. Lyon Polk of NYC and a great-nephew of President James Knox Polk.

*Democratic candidate for President of the United States John William Davis, who resided at *Mattapan* in Lattingtown, was also a partner in the law firm.

**During World War I, Polk and his assistant Gordon Auchincloss, Sr., who resided in Glen Cove and at *Ronda* in Matinecock, were in charge of coordinating United States intelligence operations.

The *Long Island Society Register, 1929* lists Frank Lyon and Elizabeth Sturgis Potter Polk [Sr.] as residing in Lawrence while both the *Social Register, Summer 1932* and *1937* list the Polks as residing in Syosset [Muttontown]. The *Social Register New York, 1948* lists Elizabeth S. Potter Polk as residing at 817 Fifth Avenue, NYC, while the *Social Register New York, 1959* lists her residence as 3 East 71st Street, NYC.

The Polk's daughter Elizabeth married Raymond Richard Guest, Sr. who resided at *Roslyn Manor* in Brookville. Their daughter Alice married Winthrop Rutherfurd, Jr. and resided at *Stone House* in Allamuchy, NJ.

The Polks' sons married sisters; Frank Lyon Polk II married Katharine Hoppin Salvage and James Potter Polk, Sr. married Margaret Smith Salvage. Both of the Polks' daughters-in-law were the daughters of Sir Samuel Agar and Mary Katharine Richmond Salvage, who resided at *Rynwood* in Old Brookville.

Polk, Frank Lyon, II (1912-1952)

Occupation(s):   attorney -   member of his father's firm, Davis, Polk,
Wardwell, Sunderland and Kiendl

Marriage(s):   1934-1952 - Katharine Hoppin Salvage

Listed in *Long Island Society Register, 1929*: yes
Address: Muttontown Road, Muttontown
Acreage / map sources: not on 1927; 20 acres / 1932 map; not on 1946 map
Name of estate:
Year of construction:
Style of architecture:
Architect(s):
Landscape architect(s):
House extant: unconfirmed
Historical notes:

Frank Lyon Polk II was the son of Frank Lyon and Elizabeth Sturgis Potter Polk, Sr., who resided in Muttontown. *[See previous entry for additional family information.]*

Katharine Hoppin Salvage Polk was the daughter of Sir Samuel Agar and Mary Katharine Richmond Salvage, who resided at *Rynwood* in Old Brookville. She subsequently married John C. Wilmerding of Old Westbury. Katharine's sister Margaret married Frank Lyon Polk II's brother James Potter Polk, Sr., and, subsequently, Charles Champe Taliaferro III. Charles Champe and Margaret Smith Salvage Taliaferro III resided in Oyster Bay Cove, and, later, in Lattingtown.

The Polks' son Frank Lyon Polk III married Nancy H. Wear and resided in Glen Head. Their son Samuel married Anne Page Homer, the daughter of Charles Le Boutillier Homer of Wayne, PA. Their son William married LuAnn Smith, the daughter of The Rev. Eugene L. Smith of Closter, NJ, and resided in Groton, MA.

Polsinelli, Vincent (b. 1962)

Occupation(s):   financier -   vice-president, Madison Ins. Co. (heavy equipment insurer)
merchant -   president, Bocu Salon and Spa (largest LI salon-spa complex)
industrialist -   president, Atlas Concrete Co.
capitalist -   vice-president, Atlas Roll–Off Containers and Recycling Co.;
secretary and treasurer, Pro–Construction Co.

Marriage(s):   1989 - Maria Serrano (b. 1961)
- merchant - vice-president, Bocu Salon and Spa

Listed in *Long Island Society Register, 1929:* no
Address: Syosset – Cold Spring Harbor Road, Laurel Hollow
Acreage / map sources: not on 1927, 1932, or 1946 maps
Name of estate: *Jones Manor*
Year of construction: c. 1911
Style of architecture: Georgian Revival
Architect(s):
Landscape architect(s):
House extant: yes
Historical notes:

The house, originally named *Jones Manor*, was built by Mary Elizabeth Jones. After her death the house was owned by her son Arthur Eaton Jones.

Arthur's sister Rosalie was given the house, one hundred acres, and $65,000 in a court settlement in which she was accused by family members of mismanaging the financial affairs of their mother's trust.

The house was, subsequently, owned by Frank Deesposito, who converted it into a nursing home. Deesposito sold the house to Jerry and Robin Ake, who established Echo Home of Laurel Hollow. The house continued to be used as a healthcare facility until 2000.

The 25,000-square-foot house on four acres, was for sale in 2001. It is now a private residence, owned by Polsinelli, who is meticulously restoring it to include twelve bedrooms, ten bathrooms, a theater room, a billiard room, a library, and a great room. He has renamed it *Jones Manor*.

Pomeroy, Daniel Eleazer (1868-1965)

Occupation(s):   politician - vice-chairman, Republican National Committee,
             1928-1932, 1937-1940;
               eastern campaign manager for Herbert Hoover, 1928
            financier - vice-president, Bankers Trust Co.;
            industrialist - director, American Brake Shoe Co.;
               director, Bucyrus Erie Co.

Civic Activism: trustee, American Museum of Natural History, NYC*

Marriage(s):   M/1 - 1895-1930 - Frances Morse (d. 1930)
            M/2 - 1937-1964 - Trevania Dallas (d. 1964)

Listed in *Long Island Society Register, 1929*: no
Address: Mill River Hollow Road, Upper Brookville
Acreage / map sources: not on 1927, 1932, or 1946 maps
Name of estate:
Year of construction:
Style of architecture:
Architect(s):
Landscape architect(s): Olmsted (for Pomeroy)
House extant: unconfirmed
Historical notes:

  Daniel Eleazer Pomeroy was born in Troy, PA.
  *In 1926 he was a member of the George Eastman Expedition to British East Africa.
  Trevania Dallas was the daughter of Trevanion Dallas of Nashville, TN. She had previously been married to Hugh Blair–Smith.

Pool, Dr. Eugene Hillhouse (1874-1949)

Occupation(s):   physician - surgeon
            educator - professor of clinical surgery, Cornell University Medical College, NYC
            writer - numerous medical papers;
               Surgery of the Spleen, 1923 (co-authored with Dr. Ralph Stillman);
               Surgery at the New York Hospital One Hundred Years Ago, 1929
                (co-authored with Dr. Frank J. McGowan)
Civic Activism: treasurer, Children's Aid Society;
            treasurer, St. Paul's School

Marriage(s):   M/1 - 1904-1930 - Esther Phillips Hoppin
            M/2 - 1932 - Katharine Lanier Lawrance (1893-1936)
            M/2 - 1940 - Frances Saltonstall

Listed in *Long Island Society Register, 1929*: yes
Address: Ludlam Lane, Lattingtown
Acreage / map sources: on 1927 map; not on 1932 map; 4 acres / 1946 map
Name of estate:
Year of construction:
Style of architecture:
Architect(s):
Landscape architect(s):
House extant: unconfirmed
Historical notes:

  Dr. Eugene Hillhouse Pool was the son of John Hillhouse and Sophie Boggs Pool of NYC.
  Esther Phillips Hoppin Pool was the daughter of William Warner and Katherine Beekman Hoppin, Sr. of Manhattan.
  Katharine [Kitty] Lanier Lawrance had previously been married to William Averell Harriman and resided in Old Westbury. She subsequently married Stanley G. Mortimer.
  Frances Saltonstall Pool was the daughter of Philip Leverett Saltonstall of Boston, MA. She had previously been married to George von L. Meyer, Sr. Her sister Rose married William Chapman Potter and resided in Old Westbury.

Poor, Henry Varnum, Sr. (1880-1931)

Occupation(s):   attorney -   partner, Larken, Rathbone and Perry
    publisher -   chairman of board, Poor's Publishing Co.

Marriage(s):   1911 - Ruth Ashmore

Listed in *Long Island Society Register, 1929*: yes
Address: Syosset – Cold Spring Harbor Road, Cold Spring Harbor
Acreage / map sources: not on 1929, 1932, 1944, or 1946 maps
Name of estate:
Year of construction:
Style of architecture:
Architect(s):
Landscape architect(s):   Olmsted, 1887 (for Poor)
House extant: unconfirmed
Historical notes:

    The *Long Island Society Register, 1929* lists Henry V. and Ruth Ashmore Poor [Sr.] as residing on Syosset Road [Syosset-Cold Spring Harbor Road], Cold Spring Harbor.

Porter, Seton (1882-1953)

Occupation(s):   industrialist - a founder and chairman of board, National Distillers
    Products Corp.;
    chairman, American Sumatra Tobacco Corp.;
    chairman, W. A. Gilbey, Ltd.;
    chairman, Italian Swiss Colony Wine;
    president, General Precision Equipment Corp.;
    director, Republic Aviation Corp.
    capitalist - director, Twentieth Century–Fox Film Corp.;
    director, General Aniline & Film Corp.
Civic Activism: board member, Beekman–Downtown Hospital, NYC (which was formed
    by the merger of Beekman Street Hospital and Downtown Hospital);
    served on fund-raising boards, Greater New York Fund, American Red
    Cross, and United Service Organizations

Marriage(s):   1936-1953 - Frederica V. Berwind (d. 1954)
    - Civic Activism: *

Listed in *Long Island Society Register, 1929*: no
Address: Duck Pond Road and Wellington Road, Matinecock
Acreage / map sources: not on 1927, 1932, or 1946 maps
Name of estate: *Still House*
Year of construction: c. 1920
Style of architecture: Federal
Architect(s):   Bradley Delehanty designed the house (for Cravath)
Landscape architect(s):   Isabella Pendleton (for Cravath)
House extant: yes
Historical notes:

    The house, originally named *Still House,* was built by Paul Drennan Cravath. Two of his first three houses, *Veraton* [1] and *Veraton* [II], were destroyed by fire in 1908 and 1914 respectively. Cravath built *Veraton* [III] c. 1914. In c. 1920, after selling *Veraton* [III], he built *Still House*. Cravath resided at *Still House* until his death in 1940.
    In 1940, Baron Eugene de Rothschild purchased the estate.
    It was, subsequently, owned by Porter, who continued to call it *Still House.*
    Frederica Berwind Porter had previously been married to Henry Herman Harjes, who had resided in Oyster Bay Cove and who had died in 1926 as the result of a polo injury.
    *Mrs. Porter is credited with organizing and endowing the first privately funded military hospital in France during World War I. She remained at the front lines until the Armistice. [*The New York Times* June 14, 1954, p. 21.]
    Since 1976, the estate has been owned by Drs. Harold Willids and Shirley R. P. Andersen, Sr. In 1997, the Andersens put the house, still called *Still House,* up for sale. The asking price was $2.5 million.

Porter, William Henry (1861-1926)

Occupation(s):	financier - partner, J. P. Morgan and Co. (now, J. P. Morgan Chase) (investment banking firm);
	president, Chemical National Bank;
	director, Fifth Avenue Bank (now, Bank of New York);
	director, Title Guarantee & Trust Co.;
	director, Fidelity & Casualty Co.;
	director, Bankers Trust Co.;
	director, Royal Exchange Assurance of London;
	director, Mutual Life Insurance Co. of New York;
	director, Franklin Savings Bank, Franklin Square
Civic Activism:	president, New York Clearing House Association;
	treasurer, New York Chamber of Commerce;
	trustee, New York University, NYC;
	trustee, Middlebury College, Middlebury, VT*;
	commissioner, Palisades Interstate Park
Marriage(s):	1887 - Esther Jackson

Listed in *Long Island Society Register, 1929*: yes
Address: Lattingtown Road, Glen Cove
Acreage / map sources: on 1937 map
no acreage given on 1932 map
44 acres / 1946 map (owned by Bogheid Corp.)
Name of estate: *Bogheid*
Year of construction: c. 1906
Style of architecture: Neo-Dutch Colonial
Architect(s):
Landscape architect(s):
House extant: no; demolished c. 1930
Historical notes:

The original house was built by Donald Fairfax Bush, Sr.

The estate was, subsequently, purchased by Porter, who called it *Bogheid*.

He was the son of William Trowbridge and Martha Elizabeth Samson Porter of Middlebury, VT.

The *Long Island Society Register, 1929* lists Esther Jackson Porter as residing on Lattingtown Road, Glen Cove, while the *Social Register, Summer 1932* lists the name of her estate as *Bogheid*.

William Henry and Esther Jackson Porter's only son James was killed in the Meuse–Argonne fighting during World War I.

In c. 1937, the Porters' only daughter Helen Porter Pryibil built her house, also named *Bogheid*, on the property.

Pryibil left her house [her father's house had been demolished c. 1930] and ten acres to the City of Glen Cove. The city sold the house and six acres to Martin F. Carey. He renamed the estate *Cashelmare* which means house by the blue sea in Gaelic. The house is in the middle of the Glen Cove Municipal Park and Golf Course.

*Porter donated funds to Middlebury College to build a hospital and an athletic field, and to create an endowment fund.

rear facade

Post, Marjorie Merriweather (1887-1973)

Occupation(s):	industrialist - director, General Foods Corp.
Civic Activism:	woman's suffrage - member, suffragist delegation that consulted with
	President Wilson in 1917 on suffrage issue;
	equipped a 2,000 bed hospital in France during World War I
	vice-chairman, Emergency Unemployment Drive, NYC;
	vice-president, National Symphony Orchestra, Washington, DC;
	board member, Good Samaritan Hospital, NYC;
	member, arts education committee, National Cultural Center, Washington, DC

Marriage(s):
M/1 - 1905-1919 - Edward Bennett Close (1882-1955)
    - attorney
M/2 - 1920-1935 - Edward Francis Hutton (1877-1962)
    - financier - founder, E. F. Hutton and Co. (investment banking firm)
      industrialist - chairman of board, General Foods Corp.;
          chairman of board, Zonite Products Corp.;
          director, Chrysler Corp. (now, Daimler–Chrysler Corp.);
          director, The Coca–Cola Co.
     Civic Activism: founder, Freedoms Foundation
M/3 - 1935-1955 - Joseph Edward Davies (1876-1958)
    - attorney - partner, Davies, Richberg, Tyding and Landa
      diplomat - United States Ambassador to the Soviet Union, 1936-1938;
          United States Ambassador to Belgium and Diplomatic
          Minister to Luxembourg [concurrent posts], 1938-1939;
          advisor to President Wilson at Paris Peace Conference, 1918;
          advisor, rank of ambassador, Marshall–Stalin Conf., 1943;
          advisor, rank of ambassador, Potsdam Conference, 1945
      statesman - Special Assistant to Secretary of State in the FDR admin.
      politician - secretary, Democratic National Committee
M/4 - 1958-1964 - Herbert Arthur May (1892-1966)
    - industrialist - treasurer, Standard Gauge Steel Co.;
          assistant treasurer, Union Drawn Steel Co.;
          director, Westinghouse Air Brake Co.;
          vice-president, Safety Car Heating & Lighting Co
     financier - director, Mellon National Bank

Listed in *Long Island Society Register, 1929*: yes
Address: Route 25A, Brookville
Acreage / map sources: on 1927 map (owned by Edward F. Hutton)
      no acreage given on 1932 map (owned by E. F. Hutton)
      100 acres / 1946 map (named misspelled as M. Post Daves)
Name of estate: *Hillwood*
Year of construction: 1921
Style of architecture: Tudor
Architect(s):   Charles Mansfield Hart designed the house (for Post/Hutton)
Landscape architect(s):   Marian Coffin designed the magnolia walks and prepared
      extensive garden designs, 1922 (for Post/Hutton)
Estate photographs can be found in the Nassau County Museum Collection filed under Old Westbury/Hutton.
House extant: yes
Historical notes:

   The house, originally named *Warburton Hall*, was built by William Albert Prime, Sr. The estate was owned by Edward Francis and Marjorie Merriweather Post Hutton, who transformed Prime's Spanish-style house into their seventy-room Tudor style house *Hillwood*. The only room that remains of Prime's c. 1911 house is the Great Hall.
   Edward Bennett Close received the Medal of Honor during World War I.
   Joseph Edward Davies was the son of Edward and Rachel Paynter Davis of Watertown, WI.
   Edward Francis and Marjorie Merriweather Post Hutton's daughter Nedenia (aka Dina Merrill) married Stanley Maddox Rumbough, Jr. and resided in Old Brookville. Ms. Merrill subsequently married actor Cliff Robertson.
   In 1950, Long Island University purchased the house and 176 acres for approximately $200,000 for its C. W. Post Campus. The house is now used as administrative offices.

Marjorie Merriweather Post Estate, *Hillwood*

entrance court, 1924

great hall

side facade, 1992

formal garden, 1924

pergola, 1992

Postley, Sterling (1877-1928)

Occupation(s):   financier - partner, Hutton and Co. (investment banking firm)

Marriage(s):   M/1 - 1898-1911 - Ethel Cook
                              M/2 - 1911-1928 - Jeanne Buckley Martin

Listed in *Long Island Society Register, 1929*: yes
Address: Mill River Hollow Road, Upper Brookville
Acreage / map sources: on 1927 map; no acreage given on 1932 map; not on 1946 map
Name of estate: *Framewood*
Year of construction: c. 1918
Style of architecture: Tudor
Architect(s):   Hoppin and Koen designed the house (for Postley)
Landscape architect(s):   Hicks Nurseries supplied plantings (for Postley)
House extant: yes
Historical notes:

   The house, originally named *Framewood,* was built by Sterling Postley.
   The *Long Island Society Register, 1929* lists Jeanne Buckley Martin Postley as residing at *Framewood* on Mill River Road [Mill River Hollow Road], Oyster Bay [Upper Brookville], while the *Social Register New York, 1933* lists her address as 420 Park Avenue, NYC.
   Postley's son Clarence married Evelyn Taylor, the daughter of Augustus Taylor, Sr. of San Francisco, CA. His son Brooke married Elisa Fanoni, the daughter of Antonio Fanoni of Manhattan.
   The estate was, subsequently, owned by Flora Macdonald Bonney, who called it *Sunstar Hill.*
   In 2001, the forty-five-room house and 19.6 acres were for sale. The asking price was $17 million; the annual taxes were $49,000.

Potter, Clarkson (1880-1953)

Occupation(s):   financier - vice-president, William R. Compton Bond and Mortgage Co.;
                                       partner, Hayden, Stone and Co. (investment banking firm);
                                       director, Canal Bank & Trust Co.
                              capitalist - director, Waldorf–Astoria Hotel Corp.;
                                       director, American Railway Express Co.
                              industrialist - director, National Aviation Corp.
                              Civic Activism: director, Better Business Bureau of New York City;
                                       national director, War Loan Organization during World War I

Marriage(s):   1902-1953 - Amy Holland

Listed in *Long Island Society Register, 1929*: yes
Address: Cedar Swamp Road, Old Brookville
Acreage / map sources: not on 1927 or 1932 maps; 7 acres / 1946 map
Name of estate:
Year of construction:
Style of architecture: Colonial Revival
Architect(s):
Landscape architect(s):
House extant: unconfirmed
Historical notes:

   The *Long Island Society Register, 1929* lists the Potters as residing at *La Panoesta* in Southampton.
   Both the *Social Register New York, 1948* and *1953* list Clarkson and Amy Holland Potter as residing in Glen Head [Old Brookville], while the *Social Register New York, 1971* lists only Amy Holland Potter, then residing at 31 East 79th Street, NYC.
   Clarkson Potter was the son Henry S. and Margaret Lionberger Potter of St. Louis, MO.

front facade, 1949

Potter, Edward Clarkson, Sr. (1862-1951)

Occupation(s):	financier - founder, E. C. Potter & Co. (stock brokerage firm)
Marriage(s):	1885-1938 - Emily Blanche Havemeyer (1866-1938)

Listed in *Long Island Society Register, 1929*: yes
Address: Walnut Street, Glen Cove
Acreage / map sources: not on 1927, 1932, or 1946 maps
Name of estate:
Year of construction:
Style of architecture:
Architect(s):
Landscape architect(s):
House extant: unconfirmed
Historical notes:

Both the *Long Island Society Register, 1929* and the *Social Register, Summer 1937* list Edward Clarkson and Emily Havemeyer Potter [Sr.] as residing on Walnut Road, Glen Cove. The *Social Register New York, 1951* lists Edward Clarkson Potter [Sr.] as residing in Sarasota, FL.

He was the son of Edward Tuckerman and Julia Blatchford Potter.

Emily Blanche Havemeyer Potter was the daughter of Theodore Augustus and Emily deLoosey Havemeyer, Sr. Her sister Blanche married William Butler Duncan and resided at *Park Hill* in Sands Point. Her sister Marie married Perry Tiffany and resided in Old Westbury. Marie Havemeyer Tiffany subsequently married Henry Fletcher Godfrey, Sr. and continued to reside in Old Westbury. Her brother Frederick Christian Havemeyer IV resided in Old Brookville. Their brother Theodore Augustus Havemeyer II resided at *Cedar Hill* in Upper Brookville.

The Potters' daughter Mary married Richard Boyd Ayer, whose parents Dr. James Cook and Mrs. May Candee Hancock Ayer resided at *Shadowland* in Glen Cove.

Potter, Edwin A., Jr. (1877-1940)

Occupation(s):	financier -	vice-president, Guaranty Trust Co. of New York; president, Finance and Trading Corp.; president, Assets Realization Co.
	capitalist -	director, Chicago Fifth Avenue Coach Co.
	merchant -	director, McCrory Stores Corp.
	attorney	partner, Potter, Duer and Griswold
Marriage(s):	1915-1940 - Cora Prindeville	

Listed in *Long Island Society Register, 1929*: yes
Address: Parkside Drive and Roslyn Road, Roslyn Heights
Acreage / map sources: on 1927 map
                                                10 acres / 1932 map
                                                13 acres / 1946 map
Name of estate:
Year of construction:
Style of architecture:
Architect(s):
Landscape architect(s):
House extant: unconfirmed
Historical notes:

Both *Long Island Society Register, 1929* and *the Social Register New York, 1933* list Edwin A. and Cora Prindeville Potter, Jr. as residing in Roslyn [Roslyn Heights], while the *Social Register, Summer 1945* lists only Cora Prindeville Potter as residing in Roslyn [Roslyn Heights]. The *Social Register, Summer 1946* and the *Social Register New York, 1957* list her as residing in Old Westbury.

Edwin A. Potter, Jr. was the son of Edwin A. and Harriet Berry Potter [Sr.] of Chicago, IL. His brother William Chapman Potter resided in Old Westbury.

Potter, Dr. Gilbert

Occupation(s):   physician

Marriage(s):   Elizabeth Williams

Listed in *Long Island Society Register, 1929*: no
Address: 111 Wall Street, Huntington
Acreage / map sources: not on 1929, 1931, or 1944 maps
Name of estate:
Year of construction:
Style of architecture: Greek Revival
Architect(s):
Landscape architect(s):
House extant: no
Historical notes:

Potter, William Chapman (1874-1957)

Occupation(s):   industrialist - manager and engineer, Guggenheim Exploration Co., Mexico.;
                                                    president, Intercontinental Rubber Co.;
                                                    chairman of board, Kennecott Copper Corp.;
                                                    president, Braden Copper Co.;
                                                    vice-president, Chile Copper Co.;
                                                    director, Anaconda Co.;
                                                    director, Bethlehem Steel Corp.
                                   financier - chairman of board and president, Guaranty Trust Co.
                                                    of New York;
                                                director, Federal Reserve Bank of New York, 1937-1940
                                   capitalist - director, Atchinson, Topeka and Santa Fe Railroad;
                                                director, Columbia Gas and Electric Corp.;
                                                vice-president, Chile Exploration Co.;
                                                director, Interborough Rapid Transit Co.
Civic Activism: treasurer, Juilliard Musical Foundation

Marriage(s):   M/1 - 1902 - Caroline Morton
                                   M/2 - 1923-1946 - Rose Lee Saltonstall (1892-1946)
                                                - Civic Activism: active in committee to repeal Prohibition;
                                                                   chairman, Women's Republican Finance
                                                                       Committee of Nassau County;
                                                                   chairman, Citizen's Committee, National
                                                                       Federation for Planned Parenthood

Listed in *Long Island Society Register, 1929*: yes
Address: Wheatley Road, Old Westbury
Acreage / map sources: on 1927 map; 19 acres / 1932 map; 17 acres / 1946 map
Name of estate:
Year of construction:
Style of architecture:
Architect(s):
Landscape architect(s):
House extant: unconfirmed
Historical notes:

   The *Social Register, Summer 1950* lists William C. Potter as residing on Wheatley Road, Old Westbury.
   He was the son of Edwin A. and Harriet Berry Potter [Sr.] of Chicago, IL. His brother Edwin A. Potter, Jr. resided in Roslyn Heights.
   Caroline Morton Potter subsequently married Harry Frank Guggenheim and resided with him at *Falaise* in Sands Point.
   Rose Lee Saltonstall Potter was the daughter of Philip Leverett Saltonstall of Boston. Her sister Frances married Dr. Eugene Hillhouse Pool and resided in Lattingtown.

Powell, Francis E., Jr. (1900-1964)

Occupation(s):	industrialist - assistant to the vice-president, Socony–Mobil Oil Co.; assistant to the president, Mobil International Oil Co. capitalist - manager, Monrovia Port Management Co.

Civic Activism:	board member, Y.M.C.A. of Nassau and Suffolk Counties
	         (a coordinating board headquartered at the Glen Cove Y.M.C.A., which
	            is located in the former sports complex of the combined Pratt estates);
	president, Glen Cove Neighborhood Association

Marriage(s):	1927-1964 - Florence Gibb Pratt (1906-1965)

Listed in *Long Island Society Register, 1929*: yes

Address:	Lattingtown Road, Glen Cove
Acreage / map sources:	not on 1927 or 1932 maps; 31 acres / 1946 map
Name of estate:	*Rattling Spring*
Year of construction:	c. 1887
Style of architecture:	Colonial Revival
Architect(s):	Richard Morris Hunt designed the house and stables (for Coles)
Landscape architect(s):	Beatrix Jones Farrand designed the rose arbor water rill, and plantings, 1900 (for Chubb)

House extant: unconfirmed

Historical notes:

The house, originally named *Rolling Stone,* was built by Elizabeth Coles.

In 1898, Percy Chubb, Sr. purchased the estate and called it *Rattling Spring.*

The estate was, subsequently, owned by Powell, who continued to call it *Rattling Spring.*

Florence Gibb Pratt Powell was the daughter of Herbert Lee and Florence Gibb Pratt, Sr., who resided at *The Braes* in Glen Cove. Her brother Herbert Lee Pratt, Jr., resided at *Whitehall* in Mill Neck. Her sister Harriet married Lawrence Bell Van Ingen, Sr. and Donald Fairfax Bush, Jr. and resided at *Preference* in Lattingtown. Her sister Edith also resided in Lattingtown, marrying Allan McLane, Jr. and residing at *Home Wood* and subsequently marrying Howard Washburn Maxwell, Jr. Her brother Frederic Richardson Pratt resided at *Friendfield Farm* on Skunks Misery Road, Lattingtown, having, subsequently, acquired the McLane estate.

The Powells' daughters Virginia married Charles Steele Cheston, Jr. of Blue Bell, PA, and resided in Millis, MA. Their daughter Edith married Carleton Burr Rand and, subsequently, John A. Papps, with whom she resided in Surrey, England. Their daughter Anne married Richard Remson, Jr. of Garden City and Buck Falls, PA. The Remsens resided at *Cottage* in Buck Falls, PA.

One reference states that the house was demolished c. 1948, while *The New York Times* August 15, 1965, p. 83, lists Florence Gibb Pratt Powell as residing at *Rattling Spring* at the time of her death and both the *Social Register New York, 1948* and *1965* list the Powells as residing at *Rattling Spring* in Glen Cove.

Powell, John (1898-1966)

Occupation(s):	publisher - president, Powell Magazines, Inc. industrialist - president, John Powell & Co. (insecticide manufacturer)
Marriage(s):	Alice Lynch

Listed in *Long Island Society Register, 1929*: no

Address:	Crescent Beach Road, Glen Cove
Acreage / map sources:	1927 map illegible; not on 1932 or 1946 maps
Name of estate:	
Year of construction:	c. 1928-1930
Style of architecture:	Norman
Architect(s):	William Lawrence Bottomley designed the house (for L. V. Luckenbach, Sr.)
Landscape architect(s):	

House extant: yes

Historical notes:

The house was built by Lewis V. Luckenbach, Sr.

The estate was, subsequently, owned by Powell.

Pratt, Charles Millard (1855-1935)

Occupation(s):	capitalist - head of syndicate that controlled the Long Island Rail Road
	industrialist - secretary, director, and treasurer, Standard Oil Co.
	(which became Exxon Corp.);
	director, Pratt & Lambert (paint manufacturing firm);
	director, Self-Winding Clock Co.;
	director, Chelsea Fiber Mills
	financier - director, Union Mortgage Co.;
	partner, Charles Pratt and Co. [Pratt family investment firm]
Civic Activism:	president of board, Pratt Institute, Brooklyn;
	president of board, Adelphi Academy, Brooklyn (which became Adelphi
	University, Garden City);
	board member, Brooklyn Bureau of Charities;
	trustee, Vassar College, Poughkeepsie, NY, to which he donated $800,000
Marriage(s):	1884-1935 - Mary Seymour Morris (1857-1947)

Listed in *Long Island Society Register, 1929*: yes
Address: Dosoris Lane, Glen Cove
Acreage / map sources: on 1927 map; 131 acres / 1932 map; 74 acres / 1946 map
Name of estate: *Seamoor*
Year of construction: 1890
Style of architecture: Shingle
Architect(s): Lamb and Rich designed the house (for C. M. Pratt)
Landscape architect(s):
Estate photographs can be found in the Nassau County Museum Collection filed under Glen Cove/Pratt.
House extant: no; demolished in 1969
Historical notes:

The house, originally named *Seamoor*, was built by Charles Millard Pratt.

The *Long Island Society Register, 1929* lists Charles Millard and Mary Seymour Morris Pratt as residing at *Seamoor* in Glen Cove. Mary Seymour Morris Pratt was residing at the estate at the time of her death.

Charles Millard Pratt was the son of Charles and Lydia Richardson Pratt, who resided in Glen Cove. His brothers all resided in Glen Cove as well. Frederic Bayley Pratt married Caroline Ames Ladd and resided at *Poplar Hill*. George du Pont Pratt, Sr., who resided at *Killenworth*, married Helen Deming Sherman and, subsequently, Vera Amherst Hale. Harold Irving Pratt, Sr. married Harriet L. Barnes and resided at *Welwyn*. Herbert Lee Pratt, Sr. married Florence Balsdon Gibb and resided at *The Braes*. John Teele Pratt, Sr. married Ruth Baker Sears and resided at *Manor House*. Their sister Lydia married Frank Lusk Babbott, Sr. and also resided in Glen Cove. Their sister Helen married Ernest Blaney Dane and resided in Brookline, MA.

Mary Seymour Morris Pratt was the daughter of Governor Luzon B. Morris of Connecticut.

The Pratts' son Richardson Pratt, Sr. married Laura Cecila Parsons and resided at *Winthrop House* in Glen Cove. Their son Theodore Pratt, Sr., who resided at *Whispering Pines* in Lattingtown, married Laura Merrick and, subsequently, Pauline Maynard. Their daughter Katharine married Burton Parker Twitchell, the son of The Rev. Joseph H. Twitchell of Hartford, CT, and resided in New Haven, CT.

front facade

Pratt, Frederic Bayley (1865-1945)

Occupation(s):	attorney
	financier - partner, Charles Pratt and Co. [Pratt family investment firm]
	capitalist - real estate - president, Morris Building Co.
Civic Activism:	numerous organizations including chairmanship of Pratt Foundation
Marriage(s):	1889-1945 - Caroline Ames Ladd (1862-1946)

Listed in *Long Island Society Register, 1929*: yes

Address:	Dosoris Lane, Glen Cove
Acreage / map sources:	on 1927 map; not on 1932 map;
	35 acres / 1946 map
Name of estate:	*Poplar Hill* [I]
Year of construction:	1898
Style of architecture:	20th-century Eclectic
Architect(s):	Babb, Cook and Willard designed the house (for F. B. Pratt)

side facade

Landscape architect(s):
House extant: no; demolished in 1920s*
Historical notes:

The house, originally named *Poplar Hill,* was built by Frederic Bayley Pratt.

He was the son of Charles and Lydia Richardson Pratt, who resided in Glen Cove. His brothers all resided in Glen Cove as well. Charles Millard Pratt married Mary Seymour Morris and resided at *Seamoor.* George du Pont Pratt, Sr., who resided at *Killenworth,* married Helen Deming Sherman and, subsequently, Vera Amherst Hale. Harold Irving Pratt, Sr. married Harriet L. Barnes and resided at *Welwyn.* Herbert Lee Pratt, Sr. married Florence Balsdon Gibb and resided at *The Braes.* John Teele Pratt, Sr. married Ruth Baker Sears and resided at *Manor House.* Their sister Lydia married Frank Lusk Babbott, Sr. and also resided in Glen Cove. Their sister Helen married Ernest Blaney Dane and resided in Brookline, MA.

Frederic Bayley and Caroline Ladd Pratt's daughter Mary married Christian A. Herter, who became Secretary of State in President Dwight Eisenhower's administration. They resided at *The Creeks* in East Hampton. The Pratts' daughter Helen married Richard Stockton Emmet, Sr. and resided at *High Elms* in Glen Cove.

*Pratt demolished *Poplar Hill* [I] to build *Poplar Hill* [II].

Pratt, Frederic Bayley (1865-1945)

Occupation(s):	attorney
	financier - partner, Charles Pratt and Co. [Pratt family investment firm]
	capitalist - real estate - president, Morris Building Co.
Civic Activism:	numerous organizations including chairmanship of Pratt Foundation
Marriage(s):	1889-1945 - Caroline Ames Ladd (1862-1946)

Listed in *Long Island Society Register, 1929*: yes

Address:	Dosoris Lane, Glen Cove
Acreage / map sources:	on 1927 map; not on 1932 map; 35 acres / 1946 map
Name of estate:	*Poplar Hill* [II]
Year of construction:	1917-1924
Style of architecture:	Georgian Revival
Architect(s):	Charles A. Platt designed the house(for F. B. Pratt)
Landscape architect(s):	Martha Brooks Brown Hutcheson drew the plans for terraced garden (for F. B. Pratt)

Estate photographs can be found in the Nassau County
   Museum Collection filed under Glen Cove/Pratt.
House extant: yes
Historical notes:

The house, originally named *Poplar Hill*, was built by Frederic Bayley Pratt.

The house is now the Glengariff Nursing Home.

[See previous entry for family information.]

front facade, 2003

Frederic Bayley Pratt's house, Poplar Hill II, 1927

Pratt, Frederic Richardson (1908-1966)

Occupation(s): industrialist - general manager, marine transportation division
of Socony–Mobil Oil Corp.;
director, South Porto Rico Sugar Co.
financier - trustee, Williamsburg Savings Bank;
partner, Charles Pratt and Co. [Pratt family investment firm]

Civic Activism: president, Boys Club of New York;
board member, Webb Institute of Naval Architecture, Glen Cove;
president of board, Roosa School of Music, Brooklyn;
board member, Manhattan School of Music

Marriage(s): 1930-1966 - Pauline Dodge

Listed in *Long Island Society Register, 1929*: no
Address: Skunks Misery Road, Lattingtown
Acreage / map sources: not on 1927 map; 33 acres / 1932 and 1946 maps
Name of estate: *Friendfield Farm*
Year of construction: 1924
Style of architecture: Georgian Revival
Architect(s): Carrere and Hastings designed the house (for McLane)
Kimball and Husted designed the gatehouse and farm complex
(for McLane)
Landscape architect(s):
Estate photographs can be found in the Nassau County Museum Collection filed under Locust Valley/McLane.
House extant: yes
Historical notes:

The house, originally named *Home Wood*, was built by Allan McLane, Jr.

The estate was owned by McLane's brother-in-law Frederic Richardson Pratt, who renamed it *Friendfield Farm*, and, subsequently, by Adrian T. Bogart, Jr., who called it *Friend Field*.

The *Social Register, Summer 1937* lists Frederic R. and Pauline Dodge Pratt as residing at *Friendfield Farm* in Locust Valley [Lattingtown], while the *Social Register New York, 1965* lists the Pratts as residing on Skunks Misery Road, Locust Valley [Lattingtown]. The *Social Register New York, 1969* lists only Pauline Dodge Pratt as residing at the Lattingtown address.

He was the son of Herbert Lee and Florence Gibb Pratt, Sr., who resided at *The Braes* in Glen Cove. His brother Herbert Lee Pratt, Jr., resided at *Whitehall* in Mill Neck. His sister Harriet married Lawrence Bell Van Ingen, Sr. and Donald Fairfax Bush, Jr. and resided at *Preference* in Lattingtown. His sister Florence married Francis Edward Powell, Jr. and resided at *Rattling Spring* in Glen Cove. His sister Edith married Allan McLane, Jr. and resided at *Home Wood* in Lattingtown, until the property was acquired by her brother Frederic. Edith subsequently married Howard Washburn Maxwell, Jr., but continued to reside in Lattingtown.

Pauline Dodge Pratt subsequently married the landscape architect Richard Webel, of the architectural firm of Innocenti and Webel, and resided in Glen Head.

Frederic Richardson and Pauline Dodge Pratt's son Robert married Marguerite Davenport, the daughter of John Sidney Davenport III of Richmond, VA, and, subsequently, Vassilia Frances Shelton, the daughter of Wilson A. Shelton. Their son Arthur married Sally Laird Davis, the daughter of Laurence Laird Davis of Cincinnati, OH, and resided in Manhattan. Their daughter Pauline married Joseph Douglas Schwerin, the son of Joseph Schwerin of *Creswell Farm* in Forest, VA, and resided in Manhattan.

Pratt, George du Pont, Sr. (1869-1935)

Occupation(s):	financier - partner, Charles Pratt and Co. [Pratt family investment firm]
	capitalist - assistant to the president, Long Island Rail Road
Civic Activism:	vice-president and treasurer, Pratt Institute, Brooklyn;
	trustee, American Museum of Natural History, NYC;
	trustee, Metropolitan Museum of Art, NYC;
	New York State Commissioner of Conservation, 1915-1921;
	president, American Forestry Association;
	treasurer, national council, Boy Scouts of America;
	vice-president, American Federation of Arts;
	treasurer, American Association of Museums;
	woman's suffrage*
Marriage(s):	M/1 - 1897-1923 - Helen Deming Sherman (1869-1923)
	- Civic Activism: founder and supporter, Lincoln Settlement House, Glen Cove, a neighborhood social center
	woman's suffrage*
	M/2 - 1926-1935 - Vera Amherst Hale (d. 1978)

Listed in *Long Island Society Register, 1929*: yes

Address:	Dosoris Lane, Glen Cove
Acreage / map sources:	on 1927 map
	48 acres / 1932 map
	44 acres / 1946 map
Name of estate:	*Killenworth* [I]
Year of construction:	1897
Style of architecture:	Queen Anne
Architect(s):	William B. Tubby designed the house (for G. du P. Pratt, Sr.)
Landscape architect(s):	Olmsted, 1907-1909 (*Killenworth* [I]) (for G. du P. Pratt, Sr.)

House extant: no; demolished c. 1912
Historical notes:

The house, originally named *Killenworth,* was built by George du Pont Pratt, Sr.

Both the *Long Island Society Register, 1929* and the *Social Register, Summer 1932* list George du Pont and Vera A. Hale Pratt [Sr.] as residing at *Killenworth* in Glen Cove, while the *Social Register, Summer 1937* lists only Vera A. Hale Pratt as residing at *Killenworth.* The *Social Register, Summer 1945* lists Mrs. Pratt's residence as Skunks Misery Road, Locust Valley [Lattingtown]. The *Social Register, 1978* lists the name of her estate as *Broom Hill.*

George du Pont Pratt, Sr. was the son of Charles and Lydia Richardson Pratt, who resided in Glen Cove. His brothers all resided in Glen Cove as well. Charles Millard Pratt married Mary Seymour Morris and resided at *Seamoor.* Frederic Bayley Pratt married Caroline Ames Ladd and resided at *Poplar Hill.* Harold Irving Pratt, Sr. married Harriet L. Barnes and resided at *Welwyn.* Herbert Lee Pratt, Sr. married Florence Balsdon Gibb and resided at *The Braes.* John Teele Pratt, Sr. married Ruth Baker Sears and resided at *Manor House.* Their sister Lydia married Frank Lusk Babbott, Sr. and also resided in Glen Cove. Their sister Helen married Ernest Blaney Dane and resided in Brookline, MA.

Helen Deming Sherman Pratt was the daughter of John Taylor and Julia Champion Deming Sherman of Brooklyn.

George du Pont and Helen Deming Sherman Pratt's daughter Dorothy married Samuel Croft Register II and resided with him at *Demingcroft* in Glen Cove. He is the son of Albert Layton Register of Philadelphia, PA. Their son George du Pont Pratt, Jr. married Jane Abbott, the daughter of Henry H. and Florence Call Abbott who resided at *Briar Patch* in East Hampton.

*George du Pont and Helen Deming Sherman Pratt were major contributors to the New York State Suffrage Party.

Vera Amherst Hale Pratt was the daughter of William Amherst and Ellen Derbishire Hale of Montreal, Canada.

Pratt, George du Pont, Sr. (1869-1935)

Occupation(s):   financier - partner, Charles Pratt and Co. [Pratt family investment firm]
                                      capitalist - assistant to the president, Long Island Rail Road

Civic Activism: *[See preceding page for detailed list.]*

Marriage(s):   M/1 - 1897-1923 - Helen Deming Sherman (1869-1923)
                                 - Civic Activism: founder and supporter, Lincoln Settlement House,
                                          Glen Cove, a neighborhood social center:
                                                  *

                        M/2 - 1926-1935 - Vera Amherst Hale (d. 1978)

Listed in *Long Island Society Register, 1929*: yes
Address: Dosoris Lane, Glen Cove
Acreage / map sources: on 1927 map; 48 acres / 1932 map; 44 acres / 1946 map
Name of estate: *Killenworth* [II]
Year of construction: 1913
Style of architecture: Tudor
Architect(s):   Trowbridge and Ackerman designed the house (for G. du P. Pratt, Sr.)
Landscape architect(s):   Olmsted, 1907-1909 (*Killenworth* [I]) (for G. du P. Pratt, Sr.)
                                   James Leal Greenleaf designed gardens and landscaping, 1913
                                       (*Killenworth* [II]) (for G. du P. Pratt, Sr.)
                                   Beatrix Jones Farrand designed the garden with summerhouse and tennis
                                        court, 1914; 1928-1929 (*Killenworth* [II]) (for G. du P. Pratt, Sr.)
Estate photographs can be found in the Nassau County Museum Collection filed under Glen Cove/Pratt.
House extant: yes**
Historical notes:

   The house, originally named *Killenworth,* was built by George du
Pont Pratt, Sr.
   [See previous entry for family information.]
   *George du Pont and Helen Deming Sherman Pratt were major
contributors to the New York State Suffrage Party.
   **Killenworth* [II] was built on the same site as was *Killenworth* [I].
   The house, which is on The National Register of Historic Places, is
now the country home of the Russian delegation to the United Nations.

rear facade, 1934

Pratt, Harold Irving, Jr. (1904-1975)

Occupation(s):   attorney
                                  financier - assistant secretary, U. S. Trust Co. of New York;
                                            chairman of board, Wall Street Growth Fund;
                                            partner, Charles Pratt and Co. [Pratt family investment firm]

Marriage(s):   1929-1975 - Ellen Rice Hallowell

Listed in *Long Island Society Register, 1929*: no

Address: Crescent Beach Road, Glen Cove
Acreage / map sources: 1927 map illegible; no acreage given on 1932 map; 33 acres / 1946 map
Name of estate:
Year of construction:
Style of architecture:
Architect(s):
Landscape architect(s):
House extant: unconfirmed
Historical notes:

   The *Social Register, Summer 1932* lists the Pratts as residing on Crescent Beach Road, Glen Cove.
   [See following entry for additional family information.]

Pratt, Harold Irving, Sr. (1877-1939)

Occupation(s):
financier - trustee, Brooklyn Savings Bank;
                 chairman of board, North American Reassurance Co.;
                 partner, Charles Pratt and Co. [Pratt family investment firm]
capitalist - real estate - treasurer and director, Morris Building Co.
industrialist - director, Self-Winding Clock Co.

Civic Activism:
president of board, North Shore Community Hospital (now, North Shore
     University Hospital), Manhasset;
president of board, Brooklyn Hospital;
donated property for construction Glen Cove City Hall and Post Office;
donated property for Harriet Barnes Pratt Park, Glen Cove;
vice-president and treasurer, Pratt Institute, Brooklyn

Marriage(s):
1901-1939 - Harriet L. Barnes (1879-1969)
   - Civic Activism: trustee, New York Botanical Garden, The Bronx, NYC;
                     chairman, Greater New York Planting Committee;
                     chairman, City of Glen Cove Planning Board;
                     first president, Junior League of Brooklyn;
                     director, canteen program of Y.M.C.A. of Greater New
                        York during World War I;
                     director, Land Army of America (supplied women farm
                        workers during World War I);
                     member, redecorating committee, White House Green
                        Room, during the Coolidge administration;
                     director, New York City Defense Recreation Committee
                        during World War II

Listed in *Long Island Society Register, 1929*: yes
Address: 100 Crescent Beach Road, Glen Cove
Acreage / map sources: on 1927 map; 73 acres / 1932 map; not on 1946 map
Name of estate: *Welwyn*
Year of construction: c. 1906
Style of architecture: Georgian
Architect(s): Babb, Cook and Willard designed the house (for H. I Pratt, Sr.)
               Delano and Aldrich designed alterations (for H. I. Pratt, Sr.)*
Landscape architect(s): Olmsted, c. 1906-1936 (for H. I. Pratt, Sr.)
               Isabella Pendleton (for H. I. Pratt, Sr.)
               James Leal Greenleaf designed the gardens and and landscaping; west garden
                   plans were drawn by Martha Brooks Brown Hutcheson (for H. I. Pratt, Sr.)
Estate photographs can be found in the Nassau County Museum Collection filed under Glen Cove/Pratt.
House extant: yes
Historical notes:

    The house, originally named *Welwyn,* was built by Harold Irving Pratt, Sr.
    He was the son of Charles and Lydia Richardson Pratt, who resided in Glen Cove.
    [See other Pratt entries for additional family information.]
    Harriet L. Barnes Pratt was the daughter of John and Jane Barnes of Rockford, IL.
    Harold Irving and Harriet L. Barnes Pratt, Sr.'s daughter Eleanor married James Ramsey Hunt, Jr. and resided in Manhattan. Their daughter Barbara married David R. Wilmerding and resided in Berwyn, PA. Their son Harold Irving Pratt, Jr. married Ellen Rice Hallowell and resided in Glen Cove.
    *Delano and Aldrich's 1920s alterations transformed the eclectic 1906 house into a Georgian-styled structure.
    The estate is now Nassau County's Welwyn Preserve. The house, which is on The National Register of Historic Places, is The Holocaust Memorial and Educational Center of Nassau County.
    The Pratts donated their New York City house at 58 East 68th Street at Park Avenue to the Council on Foreign Relations.

rear facade, c. 1935

Harold Irving Pratt, Sr.'s house,
Welwyn, front facade, c. 1935

Pratt, Herbert Lee, Jr.

Occupation(s):   financier -   partner, Charles Pratt and Co. [Pratt family investment
                                                      firm]

Marriage(s):   1926 - Hope G. Winchester (d. 1979)

Listed in *Long Island Society Register, 1929*: yes
Address: off Cleft Road, Mill Neck
Acreage / map sources: not on 1927 map
                                    no acreage given on 1932 map
                                    23 acres / 1946 map
Name of estate: *Whitehall*
Year of construction: c. 1906
Style of architecture: Tudor
Architect(s):
Landscape architect(s):
House extant: unconfirmed
Historical notes:

   The house, originally named *Laurel Hill,* was built by Henry O'Brien.
   The estate was owned by Abby Rockefeller [Pardee] Mauze, who continued to call it *Laurel Hill*; Pratt, who renamed it *Whitehall*; and, subsequently, by William James Catacosinos, Sr.
   The *Long Island Society Register, 1929* lists Herbert L. and Hope G. Winchester Pratt, Jr. as residing in Glen Cove, while the *Social Register, Summer 1932* lists the Pratts' residence as *Whitehall* in Mill Neck. Both the *Social Register, Summer 1949* and the *Social Register New York, 1949* list them as residing on East Exeter Boulevard, Phoenix, AZ.
   Herbert Lee Pratt, Jr. was the son of Herbert Lee and Florence Gibb Pratt, Sr., who resided at *The Braes* in Glen Cove. His sister Harriet, who married Lawrence Bell Van Ingen, Sr. and Donald Fairfax Bush, Jr., resided at *Preference* in Lattingtown. His sister Florence married Francis Edward Powell, Jr. and resided at *Rattling Spring* in Glen Cove. His sister Edith resided in Lattingtown, marrying Allan McLane, Jr., and residing at *Home Wood* and subsequently marrying Howard Washburn Maxwell, Jr. His brother Frederic Richardson Pratt resided at *Friendfield Farm* on Skunks Misery Road, Lattingtown, having, subsequently, acquired the McLane estate.
   Hope G. Winchester Pratt was the daughter of Lycurgus Winchester. Her sister Curgie married J. Stewart Barney, Jr.

Pratt, Herbert Lee, Sr. (1871-1945)

Occupation(s): industrialist - president and chairman of the board, Standard Oil Co.
(which became Exxon Corp.);
director, American Can Co.
financier - president, Charles Pratt and Co. [Pratt family investment firm];
director, Bankers Trust Co.

Civic Activism: treasurer, Amherst College, Amherst, MA;
treasurer, Pratt Institute, Brooklyn;
treasurer, Metropolitan Museum of Art, NYC;
vice-chairman, American Wildlife Association

Marriage(s): 1897-1935 - Florence Balsdon Gibb (d. 1935)
- Civic Activism: woman's suffrage
member, Board of Regents, University of the State
of New York;
member, Board of Education, City of Glen Cove;
first woman president of board, Nassau Hospital
(now, Winthrop University Hospital), Mineola*

Listed in *Long Island Society Register, 1929*: yes
Address: Crescent Beach Road, Glen Cove
Acreage / map sources: on 1927 map; no acreage given on 1932 map; 116 acres / 1946 map
Name of estate: *The Braes*
Year of construction: c. 1902
Style of architecture: Georgian Revival
Architect(s): James Brite designed the house and 1912 alterations (for H. L Pratt, Sr.)
Landscape architect(s): James Leal Greenleaf designed two long pergolas, formal rose garden,
terraces, formal water garden, and central tier (for H. L. Pratt, Sr.)
Ellen Biddle Shipman and James Leal Greenleaf jointly designed
landscaping (for H. L. Pratt, Sr.)**
Isabella Pendleton later altered the terraced garden and added an iris
garden (for H. L. Pratt, Sr.)

Estate photographs can be found in the Nassau County
Museum Collection filed under Glen Cove/Pratt.
House extant: yes
Historical notes:

front facade, 1998

The house, originally named *The Braes,* was built by
Herbert Lee Pratt, Sr.

The *Long Island Society Register, 1929* lists Herbert Lee
and Florence Gibb Pratt [Sr.] as residing at *The Braes* in
Glen Cove, while the *Social Register, Summer 1937* lists
only Herbert Lee Pratt [Sr.] as residing at *The Braes.*

He was the son of Charles and Lydia Richardson Pratt,
who resided in Glen Cove. *[See other Pratt entries for
additional family information.]*

Florence Balsdon Gibb Pratt was the daughter of John and Harriet Balsdon Gibb who resided in Brooklyn and at
Afterglow in Bay Shore. Her brother Arthur married Emily Mathews and resided at *Gageboro* and *Iron Action* in Glen
Cove. Her brother Walter married Florence Althea Swan and resided at *Old Orchard* in Glen Cove. Her brother Lewis
married Anna Pinkerton and resided at *Cedarholme* in Bay Shore. Her sister Ada Louise married William Van Anden
Hester, Sr., and resided at *Willada Point* in Glen Cove.

Herbert Lee and Florence Balsdon Gibb Pratt, Sr.'s son Herbert Lee Pratt, Jr., resided at *Whitehall* in Mill Neck. Their
daughter Edith resided in Lattingtown, marrying Allan McLane, Jr. and residing at *Home Wood* and subsequently
marrying Howard Washburn Maxwell, Jr. Their son Frederic Richardson Pratt resided at *Friendfield Farm* on Skunks
Misery Road, Lattingtown, having, subsequently, acquired the McLane estate. Their daughter Harriet married Lawrence
Van Ingen, Sr. and, subsequently, Donald Fairfax Bush, Jr., both of whom resided at *Preference* in Lattingtown. Their
daughter Florence married Francis Edward Powell, Jr. and resided at *Rattling Spring* in Glen Cove.

*The Pratts' daughter Harriet Balsdon Pratt [Van Ingen] Bush was the first woman president of the board of trustees of
Roosevelt Hospital (which became St. Luke's–Roosevelt Hospital Center) in NYC.

**According to Shipman records, Shipman and Greenleaf worked together on estate's landscape design.

Since 1945, the estate has been Webb Institute of Naval Architecture.

Pratt, John Teele, Jr. (1903-1969)

Occupation(s):

industrialist - vice-president and director, Chromium Corp. of America;
vice-president and director, United Chromium Inc.;
director, Transcom Electronics Inc.

capitalist - vice-president and director, Chemical Treatment Co.;
real estate - director, Birmingham [Alabama] Realty Co.

financier - partner, Post and Flagg (stock brokerage firm);
partner, Harris Upham and Co. (later, Smith, Barney, Harris,
Upham and Co.; Smith, Barney and Co.; now, Salomon
Smith Barney) (investment banking firm);
trustee, United States Trust Co. of New York;
partner, Charles Pratt and Co. [Pratt family investment firm]

Civic Activism:

trustee, Pratt Institute, Brooklyn;
trustee, Huntington Library, San Marino, CA;
trustee, Museum of American Indian Foundation;
director, Nassau County Chapter of the American Red Cross;
board member, Community Hospital of Glen Cove;
trustee, American Indian–Heye Foundation;
trustee, Glen Cove Neighborhood Association

Marriage(s):

M/1 - 1924-1935 - Mary Christy Tiffany
M/2 - 1935-1969 - Elizabeth Woodward

Listed in *Long Island Society Register, 1929*: no
Address: Old Tappan Road, Glen Cove
Acreage / map sources: on 1927 map (owned by J. T. Pratt)
                            49 acres / 1932 map (owned by R. B. Pratt)
                            11 acres / 1946 map (owned by Nitze)
Name of estate: *The Farm House*
Year of construction: c. 1913
Style of architecture: Neo-Colonial
Architect(s):   Charles A. Platt designed the house (for J. T. Pratt, Jr.)
Landscape architect(s):
House extant: yes
Historical notes:

The house, originally named *The Farm House,* was built by John Teele Pratt, Jr.

The *Long Island Society Register, 1929* lists John Teele and Mary Christy Tiffany Pratt, Jr., as residing at *The Farm House* in Glen Cove.

Both the *Social Register, Summer 1937* and the *Social Register New York, 1969* list John T. and Elizabeth Woodward Pratt [Jr.] as residing in Glen Cove, while the *Social Register New York, 1972* lists only Elizabeth Woodward Pratt as residing on Old Tappan Road, Glen Cove.

Pratt was the son of John Teele and Ruth Sears Baker Pratt, Sr., who resided at *Manor House* in Glen Cove. His sister Virginia married Robert Helyer Thayer, Sr. and resided in Glen Cove. His sister Sally married James Jackson, Jr. and resided in Massachusetts. His sister Phyllis married Paul Henry Nitze and subsequently owned *The Farm House.* The Nitzes continued to call it *The Farm House.*

Mary Christy Tiffany Pratt was the daughter of George Shepley Tiffany of St. Louis, MO. She later married Harry Knight and, subsequently, William Gifford Nickerson. The Nickersons resided in New Boston, NH.

John Teele and Mary Christy Tiffany Pratt, Sr.'s son John Teele Pratt III married Jane Slocum Stone, the daughter of James Kays Stone of *Poke House* in LaAnna, PA. Their daughter Christy married Bayard C, Auchincloss and resided in Oklahoma City, OK. Their daughter Felicite married Kennett Love and resided in Princeton, NJ.

Elizabeth Woodward Pratt was the daughter of William and Elizabeth Ogden Cryder Woodward II, who resided at *Enfield Chase* in Brookville. She subsequently married Alexander C. Cushing and continued to reside in Glen Cove. Her brother William Woodward, Jr., resided at *The Playhouse* in Oyster Bay Cove.

In 1995, the estate was owned by Dr. Lorenzo Sanesi, who called it *La Primavera.*

side facade

Pratt, John Teele, Jr. (1903-1969)

Occupation(s):   industrialist - vice-president and director, Chromium Corp. of America;
                                                vice-president and director, United Chromium Inc.;
                                                director, Transcom Electronics Inc.
                           capitalist - vice-president and director, Chemical Treatment Co.;
                                                real estate - director, Birmingham [Alabama] Realty Co.
                           financier - partner, Post and Flagg (stock brokerage firm);
                                                partner, Harris Upham and Co. (later, Smith, Barney, Harris,
                                                      Upham and Co.; Smith, Barney and Co.; now, Salomon
                                                      Smith Barney) (investment banking firm);
                                                  trustee, United States Trust Co. of New York;
                                                  partner, Charles Pratt and Co. [Pratt family investment firm]

Civic Activism: trustee, Pratt Institute, Brooklyn;
                          trustee, Huntington Library, San Marino, CA;
                          trustee, Museum of American Indian Foundation;
                          director, Nassau County Chapter of the American Red Cross;
                          board member, Community Hospital of Glen Cove;
                          trustee, American Indian–Heye Foundation;
                          trustee, Glen Cove Neighborhood Association

Marriage(s):   M/1 - 1924-1935 - Mary Christy Tiffany
                          M/2 - 1935-1969 - Elizabeth Woodward

Listed in *Long Island Society Register, 1929*: yes
Address: Old Tappan Road, Glen Cove
Acreage / map sources: on 1927 map; not on 1932 map; 19 acres / 1946 map
Name of estate: *Beechwood*
Year of construction: 1934
Style of architecture: Federal
Architect(s):   William Platt designed the house (for J. T. Pratt, Jr.)
Builder: E. W. Howell Co.
Landscape architect(s):
House extant: yes
Historical notes:

     The house, originally named *Beechwood,* was built by John Teele Pratt, Jr.
     The *Long Island Society Register, 1929* lists John Teele and Mary Christy Tiffany Pratt, Jr., as residing at *The Farm House* in Glen Cove.
     Both the *Social Register, Summer 1937* and the *Social Register New York, 1969* list John T. and Elizabeth Woodward Pratt [Jr.] as residing in Glen Cove, while the *Social Register New York, 1972* lists only Elizabeth Woodward Pratt as residing on Old Tappan Road, Glen Cove.
     [See previous entry for family information.]
     In the early 1960s, the estate was owned by Keith Sutton.
     It was owned by the Russian Orthodox Church of the Ascension for a period of time.
     It is now called *Beechwood Manor* and is again a private residence.

front facade, 2003

Pratt, John Teele, Sr. (1873-1927)

Occupation(s):   attorney -   member, Carter, Ledyard and Milburn;
                                      founder, Fosburgh, Pratt and Osborn
                         financier - partner, Charles Pratt and Co. [Pratt family investment firm];
                                      director, International Acceptance Bank;
                                      partner, Grayson, M. P. Murphy and Co. (stock brokerage firm);
                                      director, The Thrift, Brooklyn (a banking firm);
                                      director, Finance and Trading Corp.
                         publisher - partner, *The New York Evening Post*

Civic Activism: chairman, National Budget Commission during World War I;
                         trustee, Pratt Institute, Brooklyn;
                         a founder, hospital in Warwick, NY, for people of moderate incomes;
                         associate director, United States Public Service Reserve during World War I;
                         major, American Red Cross during World War I

Marriage(s):   1903-1927 - Ruth Sears Baker (1877-1965)
                           - politician - member, United States Congress representing Manhattan's
                                           "Silk Stocking" District, 1928-1932*
                             Civic Activism: trustee, Wellesley College, Wellesley, MA;
                                              board member, Philharmonic Symphony Society, NYC;
                                              chairman, Fine Arts Foundation;
                                              president, Women's National Republican Club

Listed in *Long Island Society Register, 1929*: yes
Address: Dosoris Lane and Old Tappan Road, Glen Cove
Acreage / map sources: on 1927 map; not on 1932 map; 99 acres / 1946 map
Name of estate: *Manor House*
Year of construction: 1909-1915
Style of architecture: Georgian Revival
Architect(s):   Charles A. Platt designed the house, pavilion, playhouse, garage,
                            stables, laundry building, and farm complex (for J. T. Pratt, Sr.)
Landscape architect(s):   Charles A. Platt designed the formal gardens, reflecting pool,
                            garden pavilion, and landscaping (for J. T. Pratt, Sr.)

House extant: yes
Historical notes:

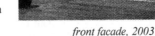

   The house, originally named *Manor House,* was built by John Teele
Pratt, Sr., at a cost of about $300,000.
   He was the son of Charles and Lydia Richardson Pratt, who resided
in Glen Cove. His brothers all resided in Glen Cove as well. Charles
Millard Pratt married Mary Seymour Morris and resided at *Seamoor.*
Frederic Bayley Pratt married Caroline Ames Ladd and resided at *Poplar
Hill* George du Pont Pratt, Sr., who resided at *Killenworth*, married Helen
Deming Sherman and, subsequently, Vera Amherst Hale. Harold Iriving
Pratt, Sr. married Harriet L. Barnes and resided at *Welwyn.* Herbert Lee

front facade, 2003

Pratt, Sr. married Florence Balsdon Gibb and resided at *The Braes*. Their sister Lydia married Frank Lusk Babbott, Sr.
and also resided in Glen Cove. Their sister Helen married Ernest Blaney Dane and resided in Brookline, MA.
   *Ruth Sears Baker Pratt was the first congresswoman from New York State. She was the daughter of Edwin Howard
and Carrie Virginia Richardson Baker of Ware, MA.
   Both the *Long Island Society Register, 1929* and the *Social Register, Summer 1965* list Ruth Sears Baker Pratt as
residing at *Manor House* in Glen Cove.
   John Teele and Ruth Sears Baker Pratt, Sr.'s daughter Virginia married Robert Helyer Thayer, Sr. and resided in Glen
Cove. Their son John Teele Pratt, Jr. resided at *The Farm House* and at *Beechwood,* both of which were in Glen Cove.
Their daughter Phyllis married Paul Henry Nitze and, subsequently, owned *The Farm House,* previously owned by her
brother. Their daughter Sally married James Jackson, Jr. and resided in Massachusetts.
   The house served as the summer White House for Herbert Hoover.
   The house, which is on The National Register of Historic Places, was subsequently owned by the Harrison Conference
Center of Glen Cove.
   The house was expanded and a swimming pool placed in the center of the formal gardens by the conference center.
   In 1998, the estate was sold to Doubletree Corporation, a subsidiary of the Memphis-based Promus Hotel Corporation.

Pratt, Richardson, Sr. (1894-1959)

Occupation(s):   financier - trustee, Brooklyn Savings Bank;
director, United States Trust Co.;
partner, Charles Pratt and Co. [Pratt family investment firm]

Civic Activism: chairman of board, Pratt Institute, Brooklyn;
president, Board of Education, City of Glen Cove;
trustee, Amherst College, Amherst, MA

Marriage(s):   1917-1959 - Laura Cecila Parsons (1894-1985)
- Civic Activism: a founder, Spence–Chapin Service to Families and Children

Listed in *Long Island Society Register, 1929*: yes
Address: Dosoris Lane, Glen Cove
Acreage / map sources: 1927 map illegible; not on 1932 or 1946 maps
Name of estate: *Winthrop House*
Year of construction:
Style of architecture:
Architect(s):
Landscape architect(s):   Olmsted (for R. Pratt, Sr.)
House extant: unconfirmed
Historical notes:

The *Long Island Society Register, 1929* lists Richardson and Laura Cecila Parsons Pratt [Sr.] as residing on Dosoris Lane, Glen Cove, while the *Social Register, Summer 1959* lists the Pratts as residing at *Winthrop House* on Dosoris Lane, Glen Cove. The *Social Register, 1985* lists Laura C. Parsons Pratt as continuing to reside in Glen Cove.

Richardson Pratt, Sr. was the son of Charles Millard and Mary Seymour Morris Pratt, who resided at *Seamoor* in Glen Cove. His brother Theodore Pratt, Sr. resided at *Whispering Pines* in Lattingtown.

The Pratts' son Richardson Pratt, Jr. married Mary Esterbrook Offutt, the daughter of Casper Yost Offutt of Omaha, NE. Their daughter Mary married Charles Minor Barringer and resided in Washington, DC.

Pratt, Theodore, Sr. (1897-1977)

Occupation(s):   financier - director, Chase Manhattan Bank;
director, Germanic Safe Deposit Co.;
partner, Charles Pratt and Co. [Pratt family investment firm]

Civic Activism: trustee, Pratt Institute, Brooklyn

Marriage(s):   M/1 - 1910-1925 - Laura Merrick
M/2 - 1930-1977 - Pauline Maynard (d. 1977)

Listed in *Long Island Society Register, 1929*: yes
Address: Old Tappan Road, Lattingtown
Acreage / map sources: on 1927 map; 15 acres / 1932 map; not on 1946 map
Name of estate: *Whispering Pines*
Year of construction: c. 1923
Style of architecture: Federal
Architect(s):   Trowbridge and Ackerman designed the house (for T. Pratt, Sr.)
Landscape architect(s):
House extant: yes
Historical notes:

The house, originally named *Whispering Pines,* was built by Theodore Pratt [Sr.].

He was the son of Charles Millard and Mary Seymour Morris Pratt, who resided at *Seamoor* in Glen Cove. His brother Richardson Pratt, Sr. resided at *Winthrop House* in Glen Cove.

Theodore and Laura Merrick Pratt, Sr.'s son Merrick married Marietta Boyle.

Pauline Maynard Pratt was the granddaughter of Horace Maynard, the Postmaster General in President Rutherford B. Hayes' administration. She subsequently married Gordon Sarre.

Theodore and Pauline Maynard Pratt, Sr.'s, daughter Mary married Corbine Braxton Valentine, Jr. of Richmond, VA.

The estate was owned by Everett W. King and purchased in 1973 from King by Walter Cook.

Pratt, Vera Amherst Hale (d. 1978)

Marriage(s):   1926-1935 - George du Pont Pratt, Sr. (1869-1935)
- financier - partner, Charles Pratt and Co. [Pratt family investment firm]
  capitalist - assistant to the president, Long Island Rail Road
  Civic Activism: trustee, American Museum of Natural History, NYC;
  trustee, Metropolitan Museum of Art, NYC;
  New York State Commissioner of Conservation, 1915-1921;
  treasurer, National Council, Boy Scouts of America;
  vice-president, American Federation of Arts;
  treasurer, American Association of Museums;
  woman's suffrage*

Listed in *Long Island Society Register, 1929*: yes
Address: Skunks Misery Road, Lattingtown
Acreage / map sources: not on 1927 or 1932 maps; 13 acres / 1946 map
Name of estate: *Broom Hill*
Year of construction:
Style of architecture:
Architect(s):
Landscape architect(s):
House extant: unconfirmed
Historical notes:

Both the *Long Island Society Register, 1929* and the *Social Register, Summer 1932* list George du Pont and Vera A. Hale Pratt [Sr.] as residing at *Killenworth* in Glen Cove. The *Social Register, 1978* lists the name of her Skunks Misery Road estate as *Broom Hill*.

Vera Amherst Hale Pratt was the daughter of William Amherst and Ellen Derbishire Hale of Montreal, Canada.

George du Pont Pratt, Sr. was the son of Charles and Lydia Richardson Pratt, who resided in Glen Cove.

*George du Pont and his first wife, Helen Deming Sherman Pratt, were major contributors to the New York State Suffrage Party. *[See surname entry for George du Pont Pratt, Sr. for complete list of civic activities.]*

Preston, Lewis Thompson, Sr. (1900-1937)

Occupation(s):

Marriage(s):   M/1 - 1925 - Priscilla Baldwin
- Civic Activism: chairman, Women's Committee, National Service
  Fund of Disabled American Veterans
  M/2 - 1930-1934 - Eppes Hawes

Listed in *Long Island Society Register, 1929*: yes
Address: Route 25A and Valentine's Lane, Old Brookville
Acreage / map sources: on 1927 map; not on 1932 or 1946 maps
Name of estate: *Longfields*
Year of construction: c. 1920
Style of architecture: French Renaissance
Architect(s):   Delano and Aldrich designed the house (for Watriss)
Landscape architect(s):
House extant: no
Historical notes:

The house was built by Frederick N. Watriss.

The estate was, subsequently, owned by Preston, who called it *Longfields*.

He was the son of Ralph Julius and Elizabeth Thompson Preston, who resided at *Ivy Hall* in Jericho. His brother William Payne Thompson Preston, Sr. also resided in Jericho.

Priscilla Baldwin Preston was the daughter of Joseph Clark Baldwin, Jr., who resided at *Shallow Brook Farm* in Mount Kisco, NY. Her sister Fanny married William Payne Thompson Preston, Sr. and resided at *Longfields* in Jericho. Fanny subsequently married Edwin Denison Morgan IV and resided at *Sycamore House* in Old Westbury.

Eppes Hawes Preston was the daughter of Senator Harry B. Hawes of Missouri. She subsequently married Lloyd Moore and resided in Old Brookville. She later married William Fahnestock, Jr. and LeRay Berdeau.

The estate is now the Dematteis Center for Cardiac Research and Education.

Preston, Ralph Julius (1864-1919)

Occupation(s):   attorney
Civic Activism: deputy Red Cross Commissioner for Europe during World War I

Marriage(s):   M/1 - 1894 - Elizabeth Thompson
                                        M/2 - Julia Graves

Listed in *Long Island Society Register, 1929*: no
Address: Jericho Turnpike and Kirby Lane, Jericho
Acreage / map sources: on 1927 map; no acreage given on 1932 map; not on 1946 map
Name of estate: *Ivy Hall*
Year of construction: c. 1904
Style of architecture: Federal
Architect(s):   Warren and Wetmore designed the house (for R. J. Preston)
Landscape architect(s):
Estate photographs can be found in the Nassau County Museum Collection filed under Jericho/Taylor.
House extant: no; demolished c. 1950
Historical notes:

    The house, originally named *Ivy Hall,* was built by Ralph Julius Preston.
    He was the son of Jerome and Hannah Preston.
    Elizabeth Thompson Preston was the daughter of William P. Thompson.
    Ralph Julius and Elizabeth Thompson Preston's son Lewis Thompson Preston, Sr. resided at *Longfields* in Old Brookville. Their son William Payne Thompson Preston, Sr. resided in Jericho.
    The estate was owned by James Blackstone Taylor, Sr. from 1906 to 1920, and, subsequently, by Elbert H. Gary, who continued to call it *Ivy Hall.*

Ivy Hall

Preston, William Payne Thompson, Sr. (1895-1961)

Occupation(s):   financier -   partner, G. M. P. Murphy and Co. (stock brokerage firm)

Marriage(s):   M/1 - 1920-1931 - Fanny Taylor Baldwin
                                          M/2 - 1932 - Doris Alford

Listed in *Long Island Society Register, 1929*: yes
Address: Jericho Turnpike, Jericho
Acreage / map sources: not on 1927, 1932, or 1946 maps
Name of estate: *Longfields*
Year of construction: 1910
Style of architecture: Federal
Architect(s):   Carrere and Hastings designed the house (for W. P. Thompson, Jr.)
Landscape architect(s):   Ellen Biddle Shipman designed the formal garden, lawns, flagstone
                                        terrace, and curved driveway (for W. P. T. Preston, Sr.)

House extant: no
Historical notes:

    The house, originally named *Longfields,* was built by William Payne Thompson, Jr.
    The estate was owned by William Payne Thompson Preston, Sr., who continued to call it *Longfields.*
    William Payne Thompson Preston, Sr. was the son of Ralph Julius and Elizabeth Thompson Preston, who resided at *Ivy Hall* in Jericho. His brother Lewis Thompson Preston, Sr. resided at *Longfields* in Old Brookville.
    Fanny Taylor Baldwin Preston was the daughter of Joseph Clark Baldwin, Jr., who resided at *Shallow Brook Farm* in Mount Kisco, NY. Her sister Priscilla married Lewis Thompson Preston Sr. and resided at *Longfields* in Old Brookville. In 1934, Fanny married Edwin Denison Morgan IV and resided with him at *Sycamore House* in Old Westbury.
    Doris Alford Preston was the daughter of M. Hendricks Alford.
    The estate was, subsequently, owned by Jack Isidor Straus, who renamed it *Green Pastures*.

Preston, William Payne Thompson, Sr. (1895-1961)

Occupation(s):   financier - partner, G. M. P. Murphy and Co. (stock brokerage firm)

Marriage(s):   M/1 - 1920-1931 - Fanny Taylor Baldwin
                                      M/2 - 1932 - Doris Alford

Listed in *Long Island Society Register, 1929*: yes
Address: Jericho Turnpike, Jericho
Acreage / map sources: not on 1927, 1932, or 1946 maps
Name of estate:
Year of construction: 1924
Style of architecture: Long Island Farmhouse
Architect(s):   Peabody, Wilson and Brown designed the house
                                      (for W. P. T. Preston, Sr.)

Landscape architect(s):
House extant: unconfirmed
Historical notes:

    The house was built by William Payne Thompson Preston, Sr.
[See previous entry for family information.]

Price, Theodore Hazeltine, Jr. (1905-1969)

Occupation(s):   attorney
                         financier - partner, Hicks, Price and Donaldson (stock brokerage firm);
                                     president, Price and Co. (stock brokerage firm);
                                     associate, Mitchell Hutchins and Co. (stock brokerage firm)
                       capitalist - real estate - director, Anahma Realty Co.

Marriage(s):   1935 - Nancy A. Heckscher

Listed in *Long Island Society Register, 1929*: no
Address: West Mall Drive, West Hills
Acreage / map sources: not on 1927, 1932, or 1946 maps
Name of estate: *Ben Robyn Farm*
Year of construction: c. 1910
Style of architecture: Colonial Revival with eclectic modifications
Architect(s):   Delano and Aldrich designed the studio (for Robbins)
Landscape architect(s):
House extant: yes
Historical notes:

    The house, originally named *Ben Robyn,* was built by Francis LeBaron Robbins, Jr.

    In the latter part of the 1940s, Robbins sold the estate to Price, who called it *Ben Robyn Farm.*

    He was the son of Theodore Hazeltine and Harriet Dyer, Price, Sr. of Manhattan. His sister Harriet married Howard Phipps, Sr. and resided at *Erchless* in Old Westbury. His sister Elizabeth married Archibald McMartin Richards and resided at *McMartin House* in Litchfield, CT.

    Nancy A. Heckscher Price was the daughter of Gustav Maurice and F. Louise Vanderhoef Heckscher, who resided at *Three Winds* in Old Westbury. Her brother August Heckscher II was New York City Commissioner of Parks. Her sister Frances married Philip Hofer and resided in NYC and at *Holly House* in Stamford, CT.

    Price sold off some of the estate's property before selling the house in the early 1970s to Arthur Ludwig.

    In 1985, upon Ludwig's death, his widow sold the house to David Belding, Sr.

    The ballroom had an orchestra loft and fifteen-foot ceilings. In the 1970s, the ballroom and a pool house were demolished. The pool, however, remains as an outdoor pool.

    Marble, taken from the floors of the Glen Cove estate of Joseph Raphael DeLamar, *Pembroke,* was used to face the fireplace in the living room.

    In 2001, the eighteen-room, 6,000-square-foot house on two acres was for sale by the Beldings. The asking price was $989,990; the annual taxes were $16,836.

Prime, William Albert, Sr. (1863-1936)

Occupation(s): capitalist - founder and director, National Dredging Co.;
director, Great Lakes Transit Co.;
director, Illinois Ship and Dredge Co.
financier - member, Charles E. & W. F. Peck (marine insurance
brokerage firm)
industrialist - director, Cuban Oil Co.;
director, Paso Robles Oil

Marriage(s): M/1 - 1887 - Marion Dutton
M/2 - 1903-1936 - Nina Cornelia Thompson (d. 1939)

Listed in *Long Island Society Register, 1929*: yes
Address: Route 25A, Brookville
Acreage / map sources: not on 1927, 1932, or 1946 maps
Name of estate: *Warburton Hall*
Year of construction: c. 1911
Style of architecture: Spanish
Architect(s): Addison Mizner designed the house (for Prime)
Landscape architect(s): Marian Coffin designed the magnolia walk and prepared
extensive garden designs, 1922 (for Post/Hutton)
House extant: no; demolished c. 1921
Historical notes:

The house, originally named *Warburton Hall,* was built by William Albert Prime, Sr.
The *Long Island Society Register, 1929* lists William A. and Nina C. Thompson Prime [Sr.] as residing in Greenvale [Brookville], while the *Social Register, Summer 1937* lists Nina C. Thompson Prime's residence as Clinton Avenue, Saratoga Springs, NY.
The estate was owned by Edward Francis and Marjorie Merriweather Post Hutton. They transformed Prime's Spanish-style house into their seventy-room Tudor style house *Hillwood.* The only room that remains of Prime's house is the Great Hall. *[See surname entry for Marjorie Merriweather Post.]*

Prince, Frederick Henry, Jr. (1886-1962)

Occupation(s): sportsman, huntsman, and gentleman farmer

Marriage(s): L. Virginia Mitchell (d. 1986)

Listed in *Long Island Society Register, 1929*: no
Address: Old Westbury Road, Old Westbury
Acreage / map sources: not on 1927 or 1932 maps
11 acres / 1946 map
Name of estate:
Year of construction:
Style of architecture:
Architect(s):
Landscape architect(s):
House extant: unconfirmed
Historical notes:

Both the *Social Register, Summer 1937* and the *Social Register New York, 1959* list Frederick H. and L. Virginia Mitchell Prince, Jr. as residing in Westbury [Old Westbury], while the *Social Register New York, 1972* lists only L. Virginia Mitchell Prince as residing in Old Westbury. The *Social Register New York, 1975* and the *Social Register, 1986* list Mrs. Prince's residence as Wheatley Road, Brookville.
Prince was a leader of Boston society. In 1914, he created a scandal by leaving Boston and becoming a railroad brakeman in Cincinnati. With the advent of World War I, he became one of the original thirty-seven members of the Lafayette Escadrille and was awarded the *Croix de Guerre* by the French government.

Proctor, Charles E. (1866-1950)

Occupation(s):   artist*

Marriage(s):   1901-1950 - Nina Gregory Jones

Listed in *Long Island Society Register, 1929*: yes
Address: Kings Point Road, Kings Point
Acreage / map sources: on 1927 map
                                  13 acres / 1932 map
                                  not on 1946 map
Name of estate: *Shadowlane*
Year of construction: 1914
Style of architecture: 20th-century Eclectic
Architect(s):   Little and Browne designed the house (for Proctor)
Landscape architect(s):
House extant: no; demolished c. 1960
Historical notes:

    The house, originally named *Shadowlane,* was built by Charles E. Proctor.
    He was the son of W. S. and Voulette Singer Proctor, and the grandson of Isaac Merrit Singer, the founder of the sewing machine manufacturing firm, I. M. Singer & Co.
    The *Long Island Society Register, 1929* lists Charles E. and Nina G. Jones Proctor as residing on Kings Point Road, Great Neck [Kings Point]. The *Social Register New York, 1948* lists the Proctors as residing in Mill Neck, while the *Social Register New York, 1963* lists only Nina G. Jones Proctor, then residing in Garden City.

    Nina Gregory Jones Proctor was the daughter of William Gregory Jones of Brooklyn.
    *Proctor was decorated by King Umberto of Italy for his paintings.

Shadowlane, c. 1914

Proctor, Charles E. (1866-1950)

Occupation(s):   artist*

Marriage(s):   1901-1950 - Nina Gregory Jones

Listed in *Long Island Society Register, 1929*: yes
Address: Mill Hill Road, Mill Neck
Acreage / map sources: not on 1927 map
                                  on 1932 map (owned by Mrs. Proctor)
                                  7 acres / 1946 map (owned by Nina G. Proctor)
Name of estate:
Year of construction:
Style of architecture:
Architect(s):
Landscape architect(s):
House extant: unconfirmed
Historical notes:

    Charles E. Proctor was the son of W. S. and Voulette Singer Proctor and the grandson of Isaac Merrit Singer, the founder of the sewing machine manufacturing firm, I. M. Singer & Co.
    [See previous entry for family information.]

Provost, Cornelius W. (1865-1954)

Occupation(s):   financier -   partner, Provost Brothers (stock brokerage firm)

Marriage(s):   M/1 - Alice L. Smith (d. 1924)
                                           M/2 - div. 1928 - Marietta Bailey (b. 1895)
                                               - entertainers and associated professions -   stage actress

Listed in *Long Island Society Register, 1929*: yes
Address: Route 25A and Mill River Road, Muttontown
Acreage / map sources: not on 1927, 1932, or 1946 maps
Name of estate: *Woodley*
Year of construction: c. 1912
Style of architecture: Colonial Revival
Architect(s):   Henry Otis Chapman designed the house (for Provost)
Landscape architect(s):
House extant: yes
Historical notes:

    The house, originally named *Woodley,* was built by Cornelius W. Provost.
    The *Brooklyn Blue Book and Long Island Society Register, 1918* and *1921* list Cornelius W. and Alice L. Smith Provost as residing at *Woodley* in Syosset [Muttontown].
    The *Long Island Society Register, 1929* lists Cornelius W. and Marietta Bailey Gates Provost as residing in Brookville.
    Both the *Social Register New York, 1933* and *1954* list Cornelius W. Provost's residence as the Metropolitan Club in Manhattan.
    Provost's son Lloyd married Elizabeth B. Peet and resided in Manhattan.
    The estate was owned by William Halsted Vander Poel, who called it *Woodstock,* and, subsequently, by Camille Jean Tuorto Amato, who called it *Woodstock Manor.*

Pruyn, Robert Dunbar (1879-1955)

Occupation(s):   financier -   stockbroker

Marriage(s):   1903-1943 - Betty Metcalf (1881-1943)

Listed in *Long Island Society Register, 1929*: yes
Address: Dosoris Lane, Glen Cove
Acreage / map sources: not on 1927 or 1946 maps
                                           no acreage given on 1932 map

Name of estate:
Year of construction:
Style of architecture: Neo-Colonial
Architect(s):
Landscape architect(s):
House extant: yes
Historical notes:

front facade, 2003

    The house was built by Robert Dunbar Pruyn with money and on land loaned to him by John Teele Pratt, Sr. Because of financial losses caused by the Depression, Pruyn realized that he would not be able to repay the loan and returned the estate to Pratt's widow Ruth Baker Pratt.
    The *Long Island Society Register, 1929* lists Robert D. and Betty Metcalf Pruyn as residing on Dosoris Lane, Glen Cove.
    The Pruyns were residing at *Linden Farm* in Syosset [Oyster Bay Cove] at the time of their deaths. [*The New York Times* October 16, 1943, p. 13 and December 19, 1955, p. 27.]
    Betty Metcalf Pruyn was the daughter of Frederick Wilder Metcalf of Erie, PA.
    The Pruyns' daughter Ruth was married to Ogden Phipps, who resided in Old Westbury, and, subsequently, to Marshall Field III, who resided at *Caumsett* in Lloyd Harbor. Their son Robert married Wilhelmina D. Balken and resided in Lomita, CA.
    The Glen Cove estate was taken over by the Pratt's daughter and son-in-law Robert Helyer and Virginia Pratt Thayer. The Thayers operated a small farm on the estate until 1945.
    In 1956, the estate was purchased by the Glen Cove School District for use as an administration building.

Pruyn, Robert Dunbar (1879-1955)

Occupation(s):   financier - stockbroker

Marriage(s):   1903-1943 - Betty Metcalf (1881-1943)

Listed in *Long Island Society Register, 1929*: yes
Address: Route 25A, Oyster Bay Cove
Acreage / map sources: not on 1927 or 1932 maps
                                  27 acres / c. 1939-1940 map (owned by R. D. Pruyn)
                                  28 acres / 1946 map (owned by Marshall Field)
Name of estate: *Linden Farm*
Year of construction:
Style of architecture:
Architect(s):
Landscape architect(s):
House extant: unconfirmed
Historical notes:

    The Pruyns were residing at *Linden Farm* in Syosset [Oyster Bay Cove] at the time of their deaths. [*The New York Times* December 19, 1955, p. 27 and October 16, 1943, p. 13.]
    [See previous entry for family information.]

Pryibil, Helen Porter (1897-1969)

Civic Activism: active in fund-raising for the Salvation Army

Marriage(s):   M/1 - 1917-1928 - Richard L. Davisson, Sr. (1891-1968)
                                      - attorney -   founder, Davisson, Manice, McCarty and Lockwood
                                  M/2 - 1928-1947 - Paul Pryibil (1898-1947)
                                      - financier - stockbroker

Listed in *Long Island Society Register, 1929*: yes
Address: Lattingtown Road, Glen Cove
Acreage / map sources: on 1927 map (owned by William H. Porter)
                                  no acreage given on 1932 map (owned by William H. Porter)
                                  44 acres / 1946 map (owned by Bogheid Corp.)
Name of estate: *Bogheid*
Year of construction: c. 1938
Style of architecture: French Manor House
Architect(s):   Delano and Aldrich designed the house (for Pryibil)
Landscape architect(s):   Olmsted (for Pryibil)
House extant: yes
Historical notes:

    Helen Porter Pryibil built the house, originally named *Bogheid,* on the property of her father's estate, which was also named *Bogheid.*
    The house contains sixty rooms, twelve bedrooms, seventeen fireplaces, indoor tennis court, bowling lanes, and a theater.
    Helen Porter Pryibil was the daughter of William Henry Porter of Glen Cove. After divorcing Davisson, she continued to reside at the Lattingtown Road, Glen Cove, address.
    Richard L. and Helen Porter Davisson's son William married Elsie Proctor Van Buren of Glendale, OH.
    Paul Pryibil had previously been married to Elois Schaefer. After marrying Helen, he too is listed as residing on Lattingtown Road, Glen Cove.
    Pryibil left her house [her father's house had been demolished c. 1930] and ten acres to the City of Glen Cove.
    The city sold the house and six acres to Martin F. Carey. He renamed the estate *Cashelmare* which means house by the blue sea in Gaelic. The house is in the middle of the Glen Cove Municipal Park and Golf Course and can be seen from Pryibil Beach.

rear facade, 2003

Pulitzer, Ralph, Sr. (1879-1939)

Occupation(s):   publisher - *New York World;*
                                                      president, Press Publishing Co.;
                                                      vice-president, Pulitzer Publishing Co.

Marriage(s):   M/1 - 1905-1924 - Frederica Vanderbilt Webb (1882-1949)
                                                  M/2 - 1928-1939 - Margaret K. Leech (1893-1974)
                                                      - writer - historian (American history); biographer; novelist

Listed in *Long Island Society Register, 1929:* yes
Address: Shelter Rock Road, North Hills
Acreage / map sources: on 1927 map; 153 acres / 1932 map; not on 1946 map
Name of estate: *Kiluna Farm*
Year of construction: 1910
Style of architecture: Shingle Farmhouse
Architect(s):   Walker and Gillette designed the house
                                             (for Pulitzer)

Kiluna farm, c. 1910

Charles A. Platt designed the swimming
     pool and bathhouse, 1913 (for Pulitzer)
James W. O'Connor designed the tennis
     building (for Pulitzer)
Landscape architect(s):   Charles A. Platt designed the garden with
                                     lily pond and pergola (for Pulitzer)

Estate photographs can be found in the Nassau County Museum Collection filed under Manhasset/Pulitzer.
House extant: no; demolished in 1990 after house and children's cottage were destroyed by arson
Historical notes:

    The house, originally named *Kiluna Farm,* was built by Ralph Pulitzer, Sr.
    He was the son of the publisher Joseph Pulitzer, for whom the Pulitzer Prize is named.
    Frederica Vanderbilt Webb Pulitzer was the daughter William Seward D. and Eliza ("Lila") Osgood Vanderbilt Webb, Sr. Her brother James Watson Webb, Sr. resided in Old Westbury and at *Woodbury House* in Syosset. Her brother William Seward D. Webb, Jr. resided in North Hills. Frederica subsequently married Cyril Hamlen Jones.
    In 1938, Pulitzer sold the estate to William S. Paley for less than $200,000. Paley continued to call it *Kiluna Farm.*
    In 1980, Paley sold the estate to developer Edward Klar for $6 million.
    Klar eventually built Stone Hill, a housing development of some ninety houses on the estate grounds.

Pulling, Thomas John Edward (1898-1991)

Occupation(s):   educator - founder and headmaster, Millbrook School in Duchess
                                                  County, NY
                              writer - *Random Reminiscences,* 1973
Civic Activism: chairman, Long Island Biological Association

Marriage(s):   1928-1979 - Lucy Leffingwell (1907-1979)

Listed in *Long Island Society Register, 1929:* no
Address: Yellowcote Road, Oyster Bay Cove
Acreage / map sources: on 1927 map (owned by R. C. Leffingwell)
                                         no acreage given on 1932 map (owned by Leffingwell)
                                         116 acres / 1946 map (owned by R. C. Leffingwell)
Name of estate: *Redcote*
Year of construction:
Style of architecture:
Architect(s):
Landscape architect(s):
House extant: unconfirmed
Historical notes:

    Thomas John Edward Pulling [aka Edward Pulling] was the son of T. J. Pulling who resided in Santa Barbara, CA.
    Lucy Leffingwell Pulling was the daughter of Russell Cornell and Lucy Hewitt Leffingwell, who resided at *Redcote* in Oyster Bay Cove. She inherited her parents' estate, which she continued to call *Redcote.*

Pulsifer, George Hale (1896-1957)

Occupation(s):   financier -   partner, Pulsifer and Hutner (investment banking firm);
                                                           partner, Hale Pulsifer (investment banking firm)

Marriage(s):   1936-1957 - Margaret A. Sparrow (d. 1961)

Listed in *Long Island Society Register, 1929*: no
Address: Duck Pond Road, Matinecock
Acreage / map sources: on 1927 map (owned by Sparrow)
                                        not on 1932 map
                                        21 acres / 1946 map (owned by M. Pulsifer)
Name of estate: *Killibeg*
Year of construction: 1912
Style of architecture: Tudor
Architect(s):   Howard Greenley designed the house (for Sparrow)
Landscape architect(s):
House extant: yes
Historical notes:

    The house, originally named *Killibeg,* was built by Edward Wheeler Sparrow.
    The estate was, subsequently, owned by the Sparrow's daughter Margaret and son-in-law George Hale Pulsifer, who continued to call it *Killibeg.*
    The Pulsifers' son Nathaniel married Holly Miller of Richmond, VA.
    In the 1960s, the house was owned by the Locust Valley School District.

Pulsifer, Harold Trowbridge (1886-1948)

Occupation(s):   publisher -   president, The Outlook Co. (publisher of *The Outlook Magazine*,
                                                           a poetry magazine of which he was managing editor, secretary,
                                                           and treasurer)
                                        writer -   poet - *Mothers and Men*, 1916; *Harvest of Time*, 1932;
                                                           Elegy for a House, 1935; *First Symphony*, 1935; *Rowen*, 1937

Civic Activism: president, Poetry Society of America;
                                        trustee, Roosevelt Memorial Association*

Marriage(s):   1924-1948 - Susan Farley Nichols (d. 1987)
                                           - Civic Activism: co-president, American Women's Committee to Release
                                                              Mercy Ships for European Children (a program to
                                                              bring British children to safety in other countries
                                                              during World War II)

Listed in *Long Island Society Register, 1929*: yes
Address: private road off Cove Neck Road, Cove Neck
Acreage / map sources: on 1927 map (owned by Mrs. J. W. Nichols)
                                        33 acres / 1932 and 1946 maps (owned by Mrs. J. N. Nichols)
Name of estate: *Cooper's Bluff*
Year of construction:
Style of architecture:
Architect(s):
Landscape architect(s)
House extant: yes
Historical notes:

    Harold Trowbridge Pulsifer was the son of Nathan Trowbridge and Almira Houghton Valentine Pulsifer, who resided at *Houghton Farm* in Mountainville, NY.
    *A life-long friend of President Theodore Roosevelt, Pulsifer's home was on property adjacent to that of the President.
    Susan Farley Nichols Pulsifer was the daughter of John White Treadwell and Mary Blake Slocum Nichols, who resided at *The Kettles* in Cove Neck. *[See surname entry for John White Treadwell Nichols for further family information.]*
    The Pulsifers' son Jonathan married Lois Nicoll Pratt, the daughter of Harold Edward Pratt.

Pyne, Percy Rivington, II (1882-1950)

Occupation(s):	financier - founder, Pyne, Kendall and Hollister;
	director, National City Bank;
	director, Empire Trust Co.;
	director, Farmers Loan & Trust Co.;
	director, Princeton Bank & Trust Co.
	capitalist - director, Delaware and Hudson Railroad Co.;
	director, United New Jersey Railroad Co.;
	director, Cayuga & Susquehanna Railroad Co.;
	director, Sheepshead Bay Speedway Corp.;
	director, Delaware Navigation Co.
Civic Activism:	assistant director and business manager, Council of National Defense and War Industries during World War I;
	first vice-chairman, National Americanization Committee;
	board member, Patterson School of NC;
	treasurer, Princeton University, Princeton, NJ;
	treasurer, St. Luke's Hospital (which became St. Luke's–Roosevelt Hospital Center), NYC;
	treasurer, Children's Aid Society;
	treasurer, Y.M.C.A. of Greater New York;
	treasurer, Perkiomen School;
	treasurer, Kipps Bay Boys Club;
	member, executive committee, Nassau County Chapter, Boy Scouts of America;
	treasurer, Diocesan Convention of Churches of New York
Marriage(s):	bachelor

Listed in *Long Island Society Register, 1929*: yes
Address: Mott's Cove Road, Roslyn Harbor
Acreage / map sources: on 1927 map
                                          69 acres / 1932 map
                                          not on 1946 map
Name of estate: *Rivington House*
Year of construction: c. 1925
Style of architecture: late Stuart Manor House
Architect(s):   Cross and Cross designed the house (for Pyne)
Landscape architect(s):   Beatrix Jones Farrand executed 185 drawings for the farm
                                          complex and gardens, including annual garden, swimming
                                          pool, fencing, trellis screening, weather vane, finials, pot
                                          stands, sundial and box plantings for forecourt, 1926-1929
                                          (for Pyne)
                                          James Leal Greenleaf (for Pyne)

Estate photographs can be found in the Nassau County Museum
    Collection filed under Roslyn/Pyne.
House extant: yes
Historical notes:

   The house, originally named *Rivington House*, was built by Percy
Rivington Pyne II.
   Both the *Long Island Society Register, 1929* and the *Social Register,
Summer 1937* list Percy R. Pyne II as residing at *Rivington House* in
Roslyn [Roslyn Harbor].

interior, 1929

Queen, Emmet (b. 1854)

Occupation(s):	industrialist - a founder, Guffey & Queen (oil company);
	president, Great Lakes Coal Co.
	capitalist - president, Western Allegheny Railroad Co.

Marriage(s):   1889 - Susan Morley

Listed in *Long Island Society Register, 1929*: no
Address: Crescent Beach Road, Glen Cove
Acreage / map sources: not on 1927, 1932, or 1946 maps
Name of estate:
Year of construction: 1899-1902
Style of architecture: Mediterranean Villa
Architect(s):   Charles Pierrepont Henry Gilbert

                                designed the 1899 house and
                                stables (for Humphreys);
                                designed the 1916 house
                                (for Woolworth)

Landscape architect(s):   Brinley and Holbrook (for Woolworth)   *rear / side facade*
House extant: no; demolished in 1916*
Historical notes:

    The first house on the site, built by Dr. Alexander Crombie Humphreys, was purchased by Queen in 1907.
    Emmet Queen was the son of John and Mary Evans Queen of Queenstown, PA.
    Susan Morley Queen was the daughter of James Morley of Johnston, PA.
    The Queens' daughter Philippa married Robert Clement of Rutland, VT.
    In 1914, Frank Winfield Woolworth purchased the estate from Queen and named it *Winfield Hall.*
    *The house, destroyed by fire, was replaced by the present house, built in 1916-1917 by Woolworth, which was also called *Winfield Hall.*
    In 1925, Charles Edward Francis McCann purchased the estate from the other Woolworth heirs for $395,000. The McCanns never resided at *Winfield Hall*; they resided at their Oyster Bay Cove estate *Sunken Orchard.*
    In 1929, the estate was purchased from McCann by Richard Samuel Reynolds, Sr.
    Reynolds sold the estate to Grace Downs School, a business school for girls.
    In 1976, a group of businessmen purchased the estate and leased it to Pall Corporation for a conference center.
    In 2003, the house, which is on The National Register of Historic Places, was for sale. The asking price was $20 million.[*Newsday* April 18, 2003, p. C2.]

Randall, Darley, Jr.

Occupation(s):   financier - banker

Marriage(s):   1926 - Grace Helen Talbot (1902-1971)
                                  - artist*

Listed in *Long Island Society Register, 1929*: yes
Address: Woodbury Road, Woodbury
Acreage / map sources: not on 1927 or 1932 maps; 16 acres / 1946 map
Name of estate: *Apple Trees*
Year of construction:
Style of architecture:
Architect(s):
Landscape architect(s):
House extant: unconfirmed
Historical notes:

    Grace Talbot Randall was the daughter of LeRoy Herrick Talbot and the granddaughter of Governor Thomas Talbot of Massachusetts.
    *In 1922, her sculpture was awarded a prize from the Architectural League of New York. In 1926, she was awarded a medal by the National Association of Women Artists.
    The Randalls' daughter Leslie married Gary Thomas Andrews, the son of Harold T. Andrews of Rockville Centre.
    Their son Darley Talbot Randall married Zene Adelia McAlpin Pyle, the daughter of Gordon Alpin Pyle.

Raquet, Walter

Occupation(s):   financier - managing director, Knight Securities (stock brokerage firm)

Marriage(s):   Denise *[unable to confirm maiden name]*

Listed in *Long Island Society Register, 1929*: no
Address: Lattingtown Road, Lattingtown
Acreage / map sources: not on 1927, 1932, or 1946 maps
Name of estate: *Lockjaw Ridge*
Year of construction: c. 1916-1917
Style of architecture: Elizabethan
Architect(s):   Theodate Pope Riddle of Lamb and Rich designed the house
                                    (for E. H. Gates)
                                James W. O'Connor designed the tennis court complex (for Sloane)
                                William Lawrence Bottomley designed 1935 alterations to the house
                                    (for Sloane)*
Landscape architect(s):   Ferruccio Vitale, 1917 (for E. H. Gates); later 1924 (for Sloane)
House extant: yes
Historical notes:

   The seventeen-room, 6,000-square-foot house, originally named *Dormer House,* was built by Elizabeth Hoagland Gates.
   In 1927, it was purchased by George Sloane, who called it *Brookmeade.*
   *In 1935, the east wing of the house was added.
   The third owner was Patrice Munsel, who called it *Lockjaw Ridge* mocking what was known as the "Locust Valley Lockjaw British accent."
   In 1980, Munsel sold the estate to Guillermo Vilas.
   In 1992, it was purchased by Raquet.
   Both Vilas and Raquet continued to call the estate *Lockjaw Ridge*.
   In 1999, the house and 4.07 acres were for sale. The asking price was $1.85 million; the annual taxes were $23,507.

Rathborne, Joseph Cornelius, II

Occupation(s):   industrialist - president, Joseph Rathborne Land and Lumber Co. [LA]

Marriage(s):   Georgia Winship (1884-1981)
                                    - Civic Activism: served with American Red Cross Motor Corps during WWI;
                                                trustee, Society for the Preservation of Long Island
                                                        Antiquities*

Listed in *Long Island Society Register, 1929*: yes
Address: Powell Lane and Jericho Turnpike, Old Westbury
Acreage / map sources: on 1927 map; 5 acres / 1932 and 1946 maps
Name of estate: *North Refuge*
Year of construction: c. 1938
Style of architecture: Georgian Revival
Architect(s):   William Lawrence Bottomley designed the house
                                    (for J. C. Rathborne II)
Landscape architect(s):
House extant: no
Historical notes:

   The house, originally named *North Refuge,* was built by Joseph Cornelius Rathborne II.
   *As director of the Society for the Preservation of Long Island Antiquities, Georgia Winship Rathborne took part in the restoration of the historic Thompson House in Setauket.
   The Rathbornes' daughter Kathleen married Harry A. Wilmerding and resided in Mill Neck.
   There is a G. W. Rathborne, presumably Georgia Winship Rathborne, listed on the 1932 and 1946 maps as owning twenty-five acres in 1932 and thirty-two acres in 1946 on Stone Hill Road [Long Island Expressway South Service Road], Old Westbury. *[We have been unable to determine if there was a residence on this property.]*

Redmond, Geraldyn Livingston, Sr. (1894-1930)

Occupation(s):

Marriage(s):   1918-1930 - Katharine E. Register (d. 1978)

Listed in *Long Island Society Register, 1929*: yes
Address: Wolver Hollow Road, Upper Brookville
Acreage / map sources: on 1927 map; not on 1932 or 1946 maps
Name of estate: *Gray House Farm*
Year of construction: c. 1924
Style of architecture: French Manor
Architect(s):   James W. O'Connor designed the
                           house (for G. L. Redmond, Sr.)
Landscape architect(s):   Robert Fowler
                           (for G. L. Redmond, Sr.)

House extant: yes
Historical notes:

stables, 1928

    The house, originally named *Gray House Farm,* was built by Geraldyn Livingston Redmond, Sr.
    He and his brother Roland, who resided at *White Elephant Farm* in Oyster Bay Cove, sons of Geraldyn and Estelle Livingston Redmond of Manhattan and Tivoli, NY, were direct descendants of First Lord of the Manor Robert Livingston, recipient of a 1673 land grant in New York from Queen Anne.
    Katharine E. Register Redmond was the daughter of Albert L. Register of Boston MA. Widowed while vacationing in Paris, she subsequently married Norman K. Toerge, Sr. and resided at *The Hitching Post* in Matinecock. Her sister Barbara married James Bogert Tailer, Jr. of Manhattan.
    The Redmonds' daughter Estelle married Cyrus Edson Manierre of Lake Forest, IL. Their son Geraldyn Livingston Redmond [Jr.], who resides in Glen Cove, married Anne Martin, the daughter of Henry Clifford and Elfrieda A. Weber Martin of Glen Cove, and, subsequently, Lida B. Schock.

Redmond, Roland Livingston (1892-1982)

Occupation(s):   attorney -   partner, Carter, Ledyard and Milburn
                         capitalist - director, Louisville & National Railway;
                                   director, Atlantic Coast Line Railway
Civic Activism: president (for seventeen years), Metropolitan Museum of Art, NYC;
                         trustee, Pierpont Morgan Library, NYC;
                         trustee, New York Public Library, NYC;
                         trustee, American Geographic Society;
                         *

Marriage(s):   M/1 - 1915 - Sara Delano
                         M/2 - 1957-1982 - Lydia P. Bodrero (formerly, Princess di San Faustino)

Listed in *Long Island Society Register, 1929*: yes
Address: Berry Hill Road and Redmond Lane, Oyster Bay Cove
Acreage / map sources: on 1927 map; no acreage given on 1932 map; 25 acres / 1946 map
Name of estate: *White Elephant Farm*
Year of construction:
Style of architecture:
Architect(s):
Landscape architect(s):
House extant: unconfirmed
Historical notes:

    Sara Delano Redmond was the daughter of Warren Delano of Tarrytown, NY, and a first cousin of FDR.
    Lydia P. Bodrero Redmond had previously been married to Valentine E. Macy, Jr., with whom she resided at *Wayside* in Southampton. *[See previous entry for additional family information.]*
    *During World War II Redmond constructed, at his own expense, a half-scale prototype of a cargo ship that could be immediately decommissioned upon its arrival in England and dismantled for the scrap iron.
    He also conceived the idea of arranging for the exhibit of Michelangelo's *Pieta* at New York's 1964 World Fair.

Reed, Lansing Parmelee (1882-1937)

Occupation(s):   attorney -   partner, Davis, Polk, Wardwell, Gardiner and Reed
capitalist -   director, International Telephone & Telegraph Co.
industrialist - director, Standard Brands

Civic Activism: trustee, New York Public Library, NYC;
trustee, Union Theological Seminary, NYC;
trustee, Miss Chapin's School;
trustee, Phillips Andover Academy;
board member, Y.M.C.A. of Greater New York

Marriage(s):   1911-1937 - Ruth Lawrence

Listed in *Long Island Society Register, 1929*: yes
Address: Snake Hill Road, Lloyd Harbor
Acreage / map sources: not on 1929 map; on 1931 map;
14 acres / 1944 and 1946 maps
Name of estate: *Windy Hill*
Year of construction: 1926-1927
Style of architecture: Georgian Revival
Architect(s):   Charles A. Platt designed the house, garage
    barn, and gardener's cottage (for Reed)

front facade, 2004

Landscape architect(s):   Ellen Biddle Shipman and Charles A. Platt jointly designed
    the formal gardens and terraces, 1925 (for Reed)

House extant: yes
Historical notes:

    The house, originally named *Windy Hill*, was built by Lansing Parmelee Reed.
    He was the son of The Rev. Edward Allen and Mrs. Mary Bliss Reed of NYC.
    Ruth Lawrence Reed was the daughter of The Rt. Rev. William Lawrence, Episcopal Bishop of Massachusetts.
    The Reeds' daughter Ruth married Samuel Hazard Gillespie, Jr. of Morristown, NJ, and resided in Cold Spring Harbor.
Their daughter Hester married Joseph Robinson Eggert, Jr. of Upper Montclair, NJ. Their daughter Julia married Arthur
Edward Palmer, Jr. of Morristown, NJ. Their daughter Mary married Roger B. Shephard of St. Paul, MN

Reeve–Merritt, Edward (1850-1931)

Occupation(s):   financier -   vice-president, Union Trust Co.

Marriage(s):   1890-1931 - Leila Roosevelt (1850-1934)

Listed in *Long Island Society Register, 1929*: yes
Address: Cove Neck Road, Cove Neck
Acreage / map sources: on c. 1922 map (owned by Reeve Merritt)
on 1927 map (owned by J. A. Roosevelt)
on 1932 map (owned by W. E. Roosevelt)
on 1946 map (owned by J. K. Roosevelt)
Name of estate: *Elfland*
Year of construction: c. 1900
Style of architecture:
Architect(s):
Landscape architect(s):
House extant: no
Historical notes:

    The *Long Island Society Register, 1929* lists Edward and Leila Roosevelt Reeve–Merritt as residing at *Elfland* on Cove
Neck Road, Oyster Bay [Cove Neck].
    He was the son of Edward and Mary Reeve Merritt. He chose to hyphenate his parental surnames.
    Leila Roosevelt Merritt was the daughter of James Alfred and Elizabeth Norris Emlen Roosevelt, who resided at
Yellowbanks in Cove Neck. She had previously been married to Montgomery Roosevelt Schuyler, the son of The Rev.
Montgomery and Mrs. Lydia Eliza Roosevelt Schuyler. Her brother William Emlen Roosevelt inherited the *Yellowbanks*
estate. He married Christine Griffin Kean, the daughter of John and Lucy Halstead Kean of Elizabeth, NJ. Her sister
Caroline married William Talman Moore, Jr. and resided at *Puente Vista* on Centre Island.

Regan, Thomas J. (1874-1959)

Occupation(s):   attorney - Whitney financial administrator*
                                              capitalist - real estate - president and director, Locustwood Estates Inc.;
                                                                 president and director, Straight Improvement Co.

Marriage(s):   1905-1940 - Aurora Sala (1882-1940)

Listed in *Long Island Society Register, 1929*: yes
Address: Wheatley Road, Old Westbury
Acreage / map sources: on 1927 map; not on 1932 or 1946 maps
Name of estate:
Year of construction: 1908
Style of architecture: Federal
Architect(s):
Landscape architect(s):
House extant: yes
Historical notes:

    Thomas J. Regan was the son of Bartholomew and Jane Higgins Regan of Boston, MA.
    *He was secretary of the Gertrude Whitney Trust and treasurer of the William C. Whitney Foundation.
    Aurora Sala Regan was the daughter of Juan and Amelia Chadrac Sala of NYC. She was a noted thoroughbred horsebreeder whose stable near Nashville, TN, had over one hundred horses at the time of her death.
    The Regans' daughter Jean married Rigan McKinney of New York and Cleveland, OH. She later married Lewis Mills Gibb, Jr. of *Cedarholme* in Bay Shore.

Remington, Franklin (1865-1955)

Occupation(s):   industrialist - founder, chairman of board, and president, Foundation
                                               Co. (an engineering and construction firm)*;
                                          chairman of board, Pratt Daniel Corp.;
                                          director, Aerotoc Co.;
                                          director, Thermax Engineering Co.
                        financier - director, Canadian Foreign Investment Corp.
                        writer - *Brawn and Brains* (autobiography)
Civic Activism: mayor, Village of Centre Island

Marriage(s):   1902-1947 - Maude Howard (1860-1947)

Listed in *Long Island Society Register, 1929*: yes
Address: Centre Island Road, Centre Island
Acreage / map sources: on 1927 map (owned by F. Remington)
                                          9 acres / 1932 map (owned by F. Remington)
                                          9 acres / 1946 map (owned by M. H. Remington)
Name of estate: *Driftwood*
Year of construction: 1911
Style of architecture: Georgian Revival
Architect(s):   Ewing and Chappell designed the house (for Remington)
Landscape architect(s):
House extant: no; demolished in 1990**
Historical notes

    The house, originally named *Driftwood*, was built by Franklin Remington.
    Born in Utica, NY, Franklin Remington was the son of Samuel R. and Flora Carver Remington. His grandfather was the inventor and manufacturer of the Remington rifle.
    *Franklin Remington's firm built foundations for the Woolworth, Singer, Bankers Trust, and municipal buildings in NYC. During World War I, his company built a total of 148 ships including 120 cargo ships and mine sweepers. When he retired in 1929, his company was the largest international engineering company in the world.
    The estate was, subsequently, owned by Drayton Cochran.
    **The house was demolished in 1990 but the estate's guest cottage, caretaker's cottage, and boathouse were restored.
    A ten-year-old house on 6.5 acres of the estate's property was for sale in 2000. The asking price was $4.9 million; the annual taxes were $53,000. [*Newsday* March 31, 2000.]

Franklin Remington's house, Driftwood

Rentschler, Gordon Sohn (1885-1948)

Occupation(s):	industrialist - president, Hooven, Owens & Rentschler Co. (manufacturers of heavy machinery);
	director, Niles–Bement–Pond Co.;
	director, General Machinery Corp.;
	director, General Sugar Co.;
	director, Cuban Dominican Sugar Corp.;
	director, Anaconda Copper Mining Co.;
	director, Corning Glass Works, Corning, NY;
	director, National Cash Register Co.
	financier - chairman of board, National City Bank;
	chairman of board, City Farmers Trust Co.;
	chairman of board, International Banking Corp.;
	director, Home Insurance Co.;
	director, Federal Insurance Co.
	capitalist - director, Union Pacific Railroad;
	director, Edison Co. of New York
Civic Activism:	trustee, Princeton University, Princeton, NJ;
	trustee, Massachusetts Institute of Technology, Cambridge, MA;
	trustee, Carnegie Institution of Washington (Cold Spring Harbor Laboratory was a division of CI, at that time);
	trustee, Ford Foundation;
	treasurer, National War Fund;
	treasurer, American Chinese Movement for Mass Education
Marriage(s):	1927-1948 - Mary S. Coolidge (d. 1988)

Listed in *Long Island Society Register, 1929*: yes
Address: Cedar Swamp Road and Pound Hollow Road, Old Brookville
Acreage / map sources: not on 1927, 1932, or 1946 maps
Name of estate: *Waveland*
Year of construction:
Style of architecture:
Architect(s):
Landscape architect(s):   Olmsted, 1929 (for G. S. Rentschler)
House extant: unconfirmed
Historical notes:

   The *Long Island Society Register, 1929* lists Gordon S. and Mary Coolidge Atkins Rentschler as residing at *Waveland* on Cedar Swamp Road, Glen Head, while the *Social Register, Summer 1946* lists the Rentschlers as residing on Duck Pond Road, Locust Valley [Matinecock]. The *Social Register, Summer 1949* lists Mrs. Rentschler as continuing to reside on Duck Pond Road, while the *Social Register, Summer 1955* lists her residence as Marion, MA.
   Gordon Sohn Rentschler was born near Hamilton, OH. He was the son of George A. and Phoebe Rentschler.
   Mary S. Coolidge Rentschler had previously been married to Atkins. She was residing at 770 Park Avenue, NYC, at the time of her death.
   In May 1951 the Rentschlers' daughter Phoebe married Louis L. Stanton and resided in Norwalk, CT.
   The estate was, subsequently, owned by Walbridge S. Taft, who continued to call it *Waveland*.

Rentschler, Gordon Sohn (1885-1948)

Occupation(s):	industrialist - president, Hooven, Owens & Rentschler Co. (manufacturers of heavy machinery);
	director, Niles–Bement–Pond Co.;
	director, Pratt & Whitney;
	director, General Machinery Corp.;
	director, General Sugar Co.;
	director, Cuban Dominican Sugar Corp.;
	director, Anaconda Copper Mining Co.;
	director, Corning Glass Works, Corning, NY;
	director, National Cash Register Co.
	financier - chairman of board, National City Bank;
	chairman of board, City Farmers Trust Co.;
	chairman of board, International Banking Corp.;
	director, Home Insurance Co.;
	director, Federal Insurance Co.
	capitalist - director, Union Pacific Railroad;
	director, Edison Co. of New York
Civic Activism:	trustee, Princeton University, Princeton, NJ;
	trustee, Massachusetts Institute of Technology, Cambridge, MA;
	trustee, Carnegie Institution of Washington (Cold Spring Harbor Laboratory was a division of CI, at that time);
	trustee, Ford Foundation;
	treasurer, National War Fund;
	treasurer, American Chinese Movement for Mass Education
Marriage(s):	1927-1948 - Mary S. Coolidge (d. 1988)

Listed in *Long Island Society Register, 1929*: yes

Address:	Duck Pond Road, Matinecock
Acreage / map sources:	not on 1927 or 1932 maps
	52 acres / 1946 map
Name of estate:	
Year of construction:	c. 1914
Style of architecture:	Georgian Revival
Architect(s):	Guy Lowell designed the house (for Cravath)
Landscape architect(s):	Guy Lowell (for Cravath)
	Olmsted designed the tree *allee* entrance and formal garden (for Cravath)

House extant: yes*
Historical notes:

   The house, originally named *Veraton* [III], was built by Paul Drennan Cravath, who built four houses on Long Island. The estate was, subsequently, owned by Rentschler.
   The *Social Register, Summer 1946* lists Gordon S. and Mary S. Coolidge Rentschler as residing on Duck Pond Road, Locust Valley [Matinecock], while the *Social Register, Summer 1949* lists Mary S. Coolidge Rentschler as residing on Duck Pond Road. The *Social Register, Summer 1955* lists her residence as Marion, MA.
   Gordon Sohn Rentschler was born near Hamilton, OH. He was the son of George A. and Phoebe Rentschler.
   Mary S. Coolidge Rentschler had previously been married to Atkins. She was residing at 770 Park Avenue, NYC, at the time of her death.
   In May 1951 the Rentschlers' daughter Phoebe married Louis L. Stanton and resided in Norwalk, CT.
   *The house has been extensively modified.

front facade

Reynolds, Jackson Eli (1873-1958)

Occupation(s): attorney
                financier - chairman of board, First National Bank of New York;
                            president, First Security Co.;
                            director, Prudential Insurance Co. of America;
                            director, Provident Loan Society of New York;
                            director, Federal Reserve Bank of New York
                industrialist - director, American Radiator and Standard Sanitary
                                        Corp.;
                                director, Lehigh & Wilkes–Barre Coal Co.;
                                director, National Biscuit Co.
                capitalist - director, New York Central Railroad;
                             director, Southern Pacific Railroad

Civic Activism: chairman, Committee for Organization of Banks for International
                        Settlements after World War I;
                 a founder, Maternity Center Association;
                 trustee, Charity Organization Society (which merged with Association
                        for Improving the Condition of the Poor to become Community
                        Service Society);
                 trustee, State Charities Aid Association;
                 member, Municipal Art Commission;
                 trustee and chairman of finance committee, Columbia University, NYC;
                 *

Marriage(s): 1903-1950 - Marion D. Taylor (1879-1950)
               - Civic Activism: a founder, Maternity Center Association

Listed in *Long Island Society Register, 1929*: yes
Address: Old Tappan Road, Lattingtown
Acreage / map sources: on 1927 map
                        no acreage given on 1932 or 1946 maps
Name of estate:
Year of construction: c. 1919
Style of architecture: Georgian Revival
Architect(s): Harrie Thomas Lindeberg designed the house
                (for J. E. Reynolds)
Landscape architect(s):
House extant: yes
Historical notes:

The house was built by Jackson Eli Reynolds.

Both the *Long Island Society Register, 1929* and the *Social Register, Summer 1937* list Jackson E. and Marion D. Taylor Reynolds as residing on Old Tappan Road, Locust Valley [Lattingtown]. The *Social Register New York, 1957* lists only Jackson E. Reynolds, then residing at 330 Park Avenue, NYC.

He was the son of James N. and Almira Giddings Reynolds of Woodstock, IL.

*There is a Jackson Eli Reynolds chair at Stanford University Law School.

The house, subsequently, became the rectory for St. John's Episcopal Church in Lattingtown.

It is now a private residence.

front facade, 2004

Reynolds, Richard Samuel, Sr. (1881-1955)

Occupation(s):   industrialist - vice-president, R. J. Reynolds Tobacco Co.;
                                              founder and president, United States Foil Co.;
                                              founder and president, Reynolds Alloys Co.;
  founder and president, Reynolds Corp.;
  director and largest stockholder, Eskimos Pie Corp.;
  director and largest stockholder, Robertshaw Thermostat
      (which became Robertshaw–Fulton);
  director, Reynolds Reduction Co.
inventor - devised a moisture-saving tin container that preserved tobacco
      better than cheesecloth bags;
  developed waterproof ammunition containers during World War I
writer - *Crucible: Poems,* 1950;
  War Enthroned and Other Poems, 1936;
  frequent contributor to the *North American Review;*
  The Marble King of Bristol, 1981 (posthumously published memoirs)
financier - founder, Reynolds and Co. (stock brokerage firm)

Civic Activism: trustee, Poetry Society of American and the English Speaking Union

Marriage(s):   1905-1955 - Julia Louise Parham

Listed in *Long Island Society Register, 1929*: no
Address: Crescent Beach Road, Glen Cove
Acreage / map sources: not on 1927 or 1932 maps
                                    16 acres / 1946 map
Name of estate: *Winfield Hall*
Year of construction: 1916-1917
Style of architecture: elements of Italian and French Renaissance
Architect(s):   Charles Pierrepont Henry Gilbert designed the 1899 house
                                    and stables (for Humphreys);
                                    designed the 1916 house (for Woolworth)
Landscape architect(s):   Brinley and Holbrook (for Woolworth)
Estate photographs can be found in the Nassau County Museum Collection filed under Glen Cove/Woolworth.
House extant: yes
Historical notes:

    The first house on the site, built by Dr. Alexander Crombie Humphreys, was purchased by Emmet Queen in 1907.
    In 1914, Frank Winfield Woolworth purchased the estate from Queen and named it *Winfield Hall.* In 1916, the house was destroyed by fire. The present house, built in 1916-1917 by Woolworth, was also called *Winfield Hall.*
    In 1925, Charles Edward Francis McCann purchased the estate from the other Woolworth heirs for $395,000. The McCanns never resided at *Winfield Hall*; they resided at their Oyster Bay Cove estate *Sunken Orchard.*
    In 1929, the estate was purchased from McCann by Reynolds.
    The *Social Register, Summer 1945* lists Richard S. and Julia L. Parham Reynolds [Sr.] as residing at *Winfield Hall* in Glen Cove, while the *Social Register, Summer 1946* lists the Reynolds as residing at *Slow Tide* in Glen Cove.
    [See following entry for family information.]
    In 1976, a group of businessmen purchased the estate and leased it to Pall Corporation, which uses it as a conference center.
    In 2003, the house which is on The National Register of Historic Places, was for sale. The asking price was $20 million. [*Newsday* April 18, 2003, p. C2.]

front facade, 1991

Reynolds, Richard Samuel, Sr. (1881-1955)

Occupation(s):	industrialist - vice-president, R. J. Reynolds Tobacco Co.;
	founder and president, United States Foil Co.;
	founder and president, Reynolds Alloys Co.;
	founder and president, Reynolds Corp.;
	director and largest stockholder, Eskimos Pie Corp.;
	director and largest stockholder, Robertshaw Thermostat
	(which became Robertshaw–Fulton);
	director, Reynolds Reduction Co.
	inventor - devised a moisture-saving tin container that preserved tobacco
	better than cheesecloth bags;
	developed waterproof ammunition containers during World War I
	writer - *Crucible: Poems,* 1950;
	War Enthroned and Other Poems, 1936;
	frequent contributor to the *North American Review;*
	The Marble King of Bristol, 1981 (posthumously published memoirs)
	financier - founder, Reynolds and Co. (stock brokerage firm)
Civic Activism:	trustee, Poetry Society of American and the English Speaking Union
Marriage(s):	1905-1955 - Julia Louise Parham

Listed in *Long Island Society Register, 1929*: no	
Address:	Cedar Lane, Glen Cove
Acreage / map sources:	not on 1927 or 1932 maps
	16 acres / 1946 map (former Woolworth estate)
Name of estate:	*Slow Tide*
Year of construction:	
Style of architecture:	Colonial Revival
Architect(s):	
Landscape architect(s):	
House extant: yes	
Historical notes:	

Both the *Social Register, Summer 1932* and *1945* list Richard S. and Julia L. Parham Reynolds [Sr.] as residing at *Winfield Hall* in Glen Cove, while the *Social Register, Summer 1946* lists the Reynolds as residing at *Slow Tide* in Glen Cove. The *Social Register, Summer 1955* lists the street address for *Slow Tide* as Cedar Lane, Glen Cove. The *Social Register, Summer 1962* lists only Julia L. Parham Reynolds as residing at *Slow Tide*, while the *Social Register, Summer 1963* and *1972* list Mrs. Reynold's residence as Lock Lane, Richmond, VA.

Born in Bristol, TN, Richard Samuel Reynolds, Sr. was the son of Abram David and Senah Ann Reynolds.

Julia Louise Parham Reynolds was from LaGrange, TN.

The Reynoldses' son Richard Samuel Reynolds, Jr. married Virginia Sargeant and resided in Richmond, VA. Their son William Gray Reynolds married Mary Spotwood Nicklas, the daughter of C. Aubrey Nicklas of Manhattan and Spring Lake, NJ. Their son David resided in Louisville, KY. Their son J. Louis Reynolds married Helen Fortescue, the daughter of Granville Roland and Grace Hubbard Bell Fortescue of *Wildholme* in Bayport. Helen's father was the illegitimate son of Robert Barnwell and Marion Theresa O'Shea Roosevelt, Sr. of *Lotos Lake* in Bayport.

front facade, 2003

Richards, Frederick L.

Occupation(s):   financier - stockbroker

Marriage(s):   1912-1936 - Hazel J. Bache

Listed in *Long Island Society Register, 1929*: yes
Address: Kings Point Road, Kings Point
Acreage / map sources: on 1927 map
                                     8 acres / 1932 map
                                     not on 1946 map
Name of estate: *Hazelmere*
Year of construction: c. 1910
Style of architecture: Georgian Revival
Architect(s):   William Adams designed the house (for F. L. Richards)
Landscape architect(s):   William Adams (for F. L. Richards)
House extant: yes
Historical notes:

    The house, originally named *Hazelmere*, was built by Frederick L. Richards.
    The *Long Island Society Register, 1929* lists Frederick L. and Hazel J. Bache Richards as residing at *Hazelmere* on Kings Point Road, Great Neck [Kings Point].
    Hazel J. Bache Richards was the daughter of Jules S. and Florence R. Scheftel Bache, who resided in NYC. After her divorce from Richards she married Frederick Beckman, who was more than twenty years her junior. [*The New York Times* December 10, 1936, p. 9.]
    The Richardses' daughter Barbara married Clarence W. Michel of Bellrose, Queens. Their daughter Dorothy married Walter Hirshon, the son of Charles Hirshon.
    In 1936, Frederick L. Richards was residing at 791 Park Avenue, NYC. [*The New York Times* December 10, 1936, p. 9.]

Richards, Ira, Jr. (1879-1961)

Occupation(s):   financier - a founder and partner, Richards & Heffernan
                                                 (stock brokerage firm);
                                                 partner, Carlisle, Mellick and Co.
                                                 (stock brokerage firm);
                                                 partner, Richards, Pell and Hume
                                                 (stock brokerage firm)

Marriage(s):   1913-1961 - Grace M. Meurer

Listed in *Long Island Society Register, 1929*: yes
Address: Locust Valley – Bayville Road, Lattingtown
Acreage / map sources: on 1927 map
                                     no acreage given on 1932 map
                                     9 acres / 1946 map
Name of estate:
Year of construction:
Style of architecture:
Architect(s):   Bradley Delehanty designed 1927 alterations
                                                 (for Ira Richards)
Landscape architect(s):
Estate photographs can be found in the Nassau County Collection filed under Locust Valley/Richards.
House extant: unconfirmed
Historical notes:

    The *Long Island Society Register, 1929* lists Ira and Grace M. Meurer Richards, Jr., as residing in Locust Valley [Lattingtown]. The *Social Register New York, 1959* lists the Richards as residing at 435 East 52nd Street, NYC.
    Grace M. Meurer Richards was the daughter of Jacob Meurer of Brooklyn and Belle Terre. She subsequently married Gordon Sarre and continued to reside in Manhattan.

Richmond, L. Martin (1881-1959)

Occupation(s):   financier - partner, Moore and Schley (stock brokerage firm);
                                          partner, Proctor and Borden (stock brokerage firm);
                                          partner, Blake Brothers and Co. (stock brokerage firm);
                                          partner, Richmond and Myles (stock brokerage firm);
                                          trustee, Manhattan Savings Bank;
                                          governor, New York Stock Exchange

Civic Activism: trustee, Home for Old Men and Aged Couples

Marriage(s):   Sarah Thacher (1888-1965)

Listed in *Long Island Society Register, 1929*: yes
Address: Cedar Swamp Road, Old Brookville
Acreage / map sources: on 1927 map; no acreage given on 1932 map; 15 acres / 1946
Name of estate: *Sunninghill*
Year of construction: c. 1928
Style of architecture: English Country
Architect(s):   Roger Harrington Bullard designed the house (for Richmond)
Landscape architect(s):   Ellen Biddle Shipman and Innocenti and Webel jointly
                                          designed the garden (for Richmond)

House extant: yes
Historical notes:

    The house, originally named *Sunninghill,* was built by L. Martin Richmond.

    Both the *Long Island Society Register, 1929* and the *Social Register, Summer 1932* list L. Martin and Sarah Thacher Richmond as residing at *Sunninghill* in Glen Head [Old Brookville], while the *Social Register, Summer 1937* lists the Richmonds as residing at *Up and Up Farm* in Bridgewater, VT.

    Born in Flushing, Queens, he was the son of David and Katharine Hoppin Richmond. His sister Mary married Sir Samuel Agar Salvage and resided at *Rynwood* in Old Brookville.

    The Richmonds' daughter Elizabeth married J. Lowell Pratt and resided in Manhattan. Their daughter Sarah married Joseph Willetts Outerbridge, the son of Samuel Roosevelt and Amie W. Willetts Outerbridge who resided on Centre Island.

Richter, Horace

Occupation(s):   industrialist - vice-president, United Mills Corp. (manufacturer
                                          of women's sleepwear)

Marriage(s):

Listed in *Long Island Society Register, 1929*: no
Address: Hoffstot Lane, Sands Point
Acreage / map sources: on 1927 map (owned by Mrs. M. D. Sloane)
                                        not on 1932 or 1946 map
Name of estate:
Year of construction: c. 1900
Style of architecture: Colonial Revival
Architect(s):
Landscape architect(s):
House extant: yes
Historical notes:

    The house, originally named *Kidd's Rocks,* was built by John Scott Browning, Sr.

    In 1921, Malcom Douglas Sloane purchased the house from Browning's widow. After Sloane's death, his widow Elinor Lee Sloane married Albert Delmont Smith and resided with him at the former Sloane Sands Point estate, which the Smiths called *Keewaydin.*

    In 1929, the Smiths sold the estate to Herbert Bayard Swope, Sr. and moved to *Mill Pond,* in Lloyd Harbor. Swope continued to call the former Sloane estate *Keewaydin.*

    In 1964, the estate was purchased from Swope's widow by Richter. It was purchased in 1968 by Irwin Hamilton Kramer. In 1983, Charles Shipman Payson purchased the estate and renamed it *Land's End.*

    In 2001, the house and fourteen acres were for sale by Mrs. Payson. The asking price was $50 million.

Rickert, Edward J. (1862-1935)

Occupation(s):   capitalist -   real estate - president, Rickert–Brown Realty Co.
                                                (which became Rickert–Finlay
                                                Realty Co.)*

Marriage(s):   Mona Lamorere

Listed in *Long Island Society Register, 1929*: no
Address: Kensington section, Great Neck
Acreage / map sources: not on 1927, 1932, or 1946 maps
Name of estate:
Year of construction: 1908
Style of architecture: Spanish Villa
Architect(s):   Charles Pierrepont Henry Gilbert designed the house
                                 (for Rickert)

Landscape architect(s):
House extant: no; demolished c. 1960
Historical notes:

side facade

The house was built by Edward J. Rickert.
*Rickert's company was a pioneer in the development of Bayside, Douglas Manor, and Great Neck. [*The New York Times* January 12, 1935, p. 15.]
The Rickerts' daughter Helen married William Ford Goulding of Manhattan.

Ricks, Jesse Jay (1879-1944)

Occupation(s):   industrialist - president and chairman of board, Union Carbide
                                   attorney -   partner, Meagher, Whitney, Ricks and Sullivan

Marriage(s):   1909-1944 - Sybil Hayward

Listed in *Long Island Society Register, 1929*: yes
Address: Middle Neck Road and Stonytown Road, Flower Hill
Acreage / map sources: on 1927 map; 131 acres / 1932 map; 128 acres / 1946 map
Name of estate:
Year of construction: c. 1927
Style of architecture: Tudor
Architect(s):   Frederick A. Godley designed the house (for Ricks)
Landscape architect(s):   Olmsted, 1926 (for Ricks)
                                 J. R. Marsh (for Ricks)
House extant: no; demolished in 1964
Historical notes:

The house was built by Jesse Jay Ricks.
The *Long Island Society Register, 1929* lists Jesse J. Ricks as residing in Plandome.
He was the son of James Benjamin and Pammie Letitia Geltmacher Ricks of Taylorville, IL
The Rickses' son James married Ethel Gertrude Secord, the daughter of Frederick L. Secord of Kokoma, IN. Their daughter Jane married Wilfred L. King, the son of J. Strickland King of Manhattan. Their son John married Elizabeth Ann Linkletter, the daughter of George Onderdonk Linkletter, Sr. of Manhasset.

Ricks, Jesse Jay (1879-1944)

Occupation(s):   industrialist -   president and chairman of board, Union Carbide
                        attorney -   partner, Meagher, Whitney, Ricks and Sullivan

Marriage(s):   1909-1944 - Sybil Hayward

Listed in *Long Island Society Register, 1929:* yes
Address: Brookside Drive, Plandome
Acreage / map sources: not on 1927, 1932, or 1946 maps
Name of estate:
Year of construction:
Style of architecture: Colonial Revival
Architect(s):
Landscape architect(s):
House extant: unconfirmed
Historical notes:

    The *Long Island Society Register, 1929* lists Jesse J. Ricks as residing in Plandome.
    [See previous entry for family information.]
    John Gerdes purchased the house from Ricks.

Ridder, Eric, Sr. (1918-1996)

Occupation(s):   publisher - *The Journal of Commerce;*
                                director, Seattle Times Co.;
                                director, Knight–Ridder Newspapers, Inc.;
                                business manager, *The St. Paul Dispatch* and
                                    The Pioneer Press
Civic Activism: trustee, South Street Seaport, NYC

Marriage(s):   M/1 - 1939-1954 - Ethelette French Tucker
                        M/2 - 1955-1991 - Florence Madeleine Graham (d. 1991)

Listed in *Long Island Society Regist*er, *1929*: no
Address: Feeks Lane, Lattingtown
Acreage / map sources: not on 1927, 1932, or 1946 maps
Name of estate:
Year of construction: c. 1906
Style of architecture: Federal
Architect(s):
Landscape architect(s):
House extant: unconfirmed
Historical notes:

front facade, 1994

    The house was built by H. W. Warner.
    The estate was owned by William McNair, who called it *Northway House,* and, subsequently, by his daughter Elvira McNair Fairchild, who also called it *Northway House.*
    The *Social Register, 1983* lists Eric and F. Madeleine Graham Ridder [Sr.] as residing on Feeks Lane, Locust Valley [Lattingtown]. The *Social Register, 1991* lists the Ridders as residing on Piping Rock Road, Locust Valley.
    Born in Hewlett, he was the son of Joseph E. and Hedwig Schneider Ridder.
    Eric Ridder, Sr. was a member of the American yachting team that won the gold medal at the 1952 Olympics. In 1964, he co-captained the yacht *Constellation* in its successful defense of the America's Cup.
    Florence Madeleine Graham Ridder was the daughter of Ephraim Walters Sterling and Florence Bridgham Graham of Pittsburgh, PA. She had previously been married to Julian Kean Roosevelt, who resided at *Bonnie Brae* on Centre Island.
    In 1997, the estate was owned by Steven Thurman. The house was then on 5.4 acres. The rest of the estate's property had been sold for a housing development.
    In 2000, the house and 5.4 acres were for sale. The asking price was $2.95 million; the annual taxes were $35,000.

Riggs, George (1894-1965)

Occupation(s): inventor - engineer - designed air to ground communication
  system for the armed forces

Marriage(s): Lucy Dunham Wheeler

Listed in *Long Island Society Register, 1929*: yes
Address: Luquer Road, Plandome Manor
Acreage / map sources: not on 1927, 1932, or 1946 maps
Name of estate:
Year of construction:
Style of architecture:
Architect(s):
Landscape architect(s):
House extant: unconfirmed
Historical notes:

Both the *Long Island Society Register, 1929* and the *Social Register New York, 1959* list George and Lucy D. Wheeler Riggs as residing on Luquer Road, Port Washington [Plandome Manor], while the *Social Register New York, 1963* lists them as residing on Dophin Green, Port Washington. The *Social Register New York, 1967* lists only Mrs. Riggs as residing at the Dophin Green address, while the *Social Register New York, 1969* lists her residence as Glenbrook Road, Stamford, CT.

Riggs was residing on Dolphin Green, Port Washington, at the time of his death. [*The New York Times* October 22, 1965, p. 43.]

Riggs, Glenn E., Sr. (1907-1975)

Occupation(s): entertainers and associated professions - actor;
  radio and television personality*

Marriage(s): M/1 - Elizabeth Ann Laird (b. 1913)
  M/2 - Lynn Tian

Listed in *Long Island Society Register, 1929*: no
Address: Bryant Avenue, Roslyn Harbor
Acreage / map sources: not on 1927, 1932, or 1946 maps
Name of estate: *Sycamore Lodge*
Year of construction: 1863
Style of architecture: Flemish / Gothic
Architect(s): Frederick S. Copley
Landscape architect(s): Olmsted, 1919-1923 (for Demarest)
House extant: yes
Historical notes:

The estate was inherited by Blanche Willis Emory and her husband William Helmsley Emory, Jr., who resided there from 1876 to 1917. The estate was named *Clifton* by the Emorys after the original Cairns' Roslyn Harbor home, which was also named *Clifton*.

In 1917, the estate was purchased by John M. Demarest, who renamed it *Sycamore Lodge*.

In 1932, Demarest gave the estate to his daughter Lucille Demarest Brion.

In 1950, it was purchased from Brion by Riggs.

*He was the announcer for numerous radio shows including *Jungle Jim, Lavender and New Lace, Boston Blackie, Mark Trail, My True Story, True or False, Vic and Sade,* and those starring Paul Whiteman and Bing Crosby. His television announcing credits included *The Philco Playhouse, Wide Wide World,* and *Omnibus.* He was also the announcer for the series of programs hosted by Bishop Fulton J. Sheen.

The Riggses' daughter Elizabeth married Samuel M. Strong III.

In 1957, the estate was purchased from Riggs by Frank Curry Fahnestock.

rear facade, 2004

659

Rinaldini, Luis Emilio (b. 1953)

Occupation(s):	architect - member, Johnson Burgee Architects, 1974-1978
	financier - member, Lazard, Freres & Co. (investment banking firm)
Marriage(s):	M/1 - 1974-1987 - Elaine Nash McHugh
	M/2 - 1987 - Julie Sayre Short

Listed in *Long Island Society Register, 1929*: no
Address: Post Road, Old Westbury
Acreage / map sources: not on 1927, 1932, or 1946 maps
Name of estate:
Year of construction: 1932
Style of architecture: Georgian
Architect(s):   Henry Renwick Sedgwick designed the house (for R. Winthrop II)
Landscape architect(s):
House extant: yes
Historical notes:

The house, originally named *Groton Place,* was built by Robert Winthrop II.
In 1997, Winthrop sold the house to Rinaldini and a portion of the estate's property for a housing development.

Ripley, Julien Ashton, Sr. (d. 1966)

Occupation(s):	capitalist - real estate - Manhattan properties
Civic Activism:	trustee, Village of Muttontown
Marriage(s):	1905 - Helen A. Bell

Listed in *Long Island Society Register, 1929*: yes
Address: Route 25A and Ripley's Lane, Muttontown
Acreage / map sources: on 1927 map; not on 1932 or 1946 maps
Name of estate: *Three Corners Farm*
Year of construction: c. 1910
Style of architecture: Georgian Revival
Architect(s):   Guy Lowell designed the house (for J. A. Ripley, Sr.)
Landscape architect(s):   Olmsted (for J. A. Ripley, Sr.)
                                              Lewis and Valentine (for J. A. Ripley, Sr.)
Estate photographs can be found in the Nassau County Museum Collection filed under East Norwich/Ripley.
House extant: yes
Historical notes:

The house, originally named *Three Corners Farm,* was built by Julien Ashton Ripley, Sr.

The *Long Island Society Register, 1929* lists Julien Ashton and Helen A. Bell Ripley [Sr.] as residing at *Three Corners Farm* in Oyster Bay [Muttontown]. The *Social Register, Summer 1932* lists the Ripleys as residing on West Shore Drive, Oyster Bay [Mill Neck], while the *Social Register, Summer 1937, the Social Register New York, 1948,* and the *Social Register New York, 1954* list the Ripleys' address as Remsen's Lane, Oyster Bay [Muttontown]. The *Social Register New York, 1956* and *1967* list Julien Ashton Ripley [Sr.] as continuing to reside on Remsen's Lane, Oyster Bay [Muttontown].

The Ripleys' son Dr. Julien Aston Ripley, Jr. was a professor of physical sciences at Stanford University, Dickinson College in Carlisle, PA, Wilkes College in Wilkes–Barre, PA, and Abadan Institute of Technology in Iran. [*The New York Times* June 28, 1974, p. 36.]

Helen A. Bell was the daughter of Charles Bell and a niece of Alexander Graham Bell. Her sister Grace resided at *Wildholme* in Bayport. Grace was married to Granville Roland Fortescue, the illegitimate son of Robert Barnwell Roosevelt, Sr. of *Lotos Lake* in Bayport. Grace Fortescue and her son-in-law Navy Lieutenant Thomas H. Massie were accused of manslaughter in the death of Joseph Kahahawi, a Hawaiian youth who had allegedly assaulted Lieutenant Massie's wife. [Harry W. Havemeyer, *East on the Great South Bay: Sayville and Bellport 1860-1960* (Mattituck, NY: Amereon House, 2001), pp. 37-46, 207-225; *The New York Times* April 30, 1932, pp. 1, 16.]

In 1929, the Ripley's sold *Three Corners Farm.* [*The New York Times* May 16, 1929, p. 56.]

It was owned by George Callendine Heck, Sr., who called it *Linwood,* and, subsequently in 1986, by Gregory Coleman.

Julian Aston Ripley, Sr.'s house, Three Corner Farm

Ripley, Lucy Fairfield Perkins (d. 1949)

Occupation(s):   artist -   sculptor;
                                        painter

Marriage(s):   1912 - Paul Morton Ripley
                              - industrialist - president, Brooklyn Cooperage Co.;
                                                 president, Phelps Dodge Corp.
                                  shipping - president, American Sugar Transit Corp.;
                                              traffic manager, American Sugar Refining Co.
                                  capitalist - real estate - president, Great Western Land Co.

Listed in *Long Island Society Register, 1929*: no
Address: Route 25A, Muttontown
Acreage / map sources: not on 1927 or 1932 maps
                                     19 acres / 1946 map

Name of estate:
Year of construction:
Style of architecture:
Architect(s):
Landscape architect(s):
House extant: unconfirmed
Historical notes:

   Lucy Fairfield Perkins Ripley was the daughter of Cyrus Maynard and Anna Payne Fairchild Perkins of Winona, MN.
   Ripley, who studied art at the Arts Students League in Paris, exhibited at the *Salon Les Tuilleres* in Paris, 1934; *Salon des Beaux Arts*, 1935; Paris Salon, 1935; Georgett Passedoit Galleries in NYC, 1936; Painters and Sculptors Gallery in NYC; and St. Honore in Paris.
   She was awarded the bronze medal in the St. Louis Exposition for her art work. In 1919, Ripley was awarded the Helen Barnet Prize of Women Painters and Sculptors Association.
   Paul Morton Ripley was the son of J. T. and Harriett T. Konant Ripley of Rock Island, IL.

Robbins, Francis LeBaron, Jr. (1884-1945)

Occupation(s):   attorney -   member, Winthrop, Stimson, Putnam and Roberts
Civic Activism: member, board of governors, Five Points House of Industry;
                                         vice-president, Citizens Committee of America

Marriage(s):   M/1 - 1910-1927 - Frances Cleveland Lamont
                                         M/2 - 1927-1942 - Anna Robenne (d. 1942)

Listed in *Long Island Society Register, 1929*: yes
Address: West Mall Drive, West Hills
Acreage / map sources: on 1927 map
                                         no acreage given on 1932 map
                                         on 1944 map
                                         98 acres / 1946 map
Name of estate: *Ben Robyn*
Year of construction: c. 1910
Style of architecture: Colonial Revival with eclectic modifications
Architect(s):   Delano and Aldrich designed the studio
                                         (for Robbins)

Landscape architect(s):
House extant: yes
Historical notes:

    The house, originally named *Ben Robyn*, was built by Francis LeBaron Robbins, Jr.

    The *Long Island Society Register, 1929* lists Francis LeBaron and Anna Robenne Robbins, Jr. as residing at *Ben Robyn* in Woodbury [West Hills].

    Born in Geneva, Switzerland, he was the son of Francis LeBaron and Lucy Morton Hartpence Robbins, Sr. His mother was the niece of Levi P. Morton, who was Governor of New York and Vice-President of the United States in President Benjamin Harrison's administration.

    Francis LeBaron and Frances Cleveland Lamont Robbins' daughter Elizabeth married Robert E. Montgomery.

    In the latter part of the 1940s, Robbins sold the estate to Theodore Hazeltine Price, Jr., who called it *Ben Robyn Farm*. Price sold off some of the estate's property before selling the house in the early 1970s to Arthur Ludwig.

    In 1985, upon Ludwig's death, his widow sold the house to David Belding, Sr.

    The ballroom had an orchestra loft and fifteen-foot ceilings. In the 1970s, the ballroom and a pool house were demolished. The pool, however, remains as an outdoor pool.

    Marble, taken from the floors of the Glen Cove estate of Joseph Raphael DeLamar, *Pembroke,* was used to face the fireplace in the living room. *Pembroke* was demolished by the construction firm for which Norman Ludwig, Arthur Ludwig's son, worked.

    In 2001, the eighteen-room, 6,000-square-foot house on two acres was for sale by the Beldings. The asking price was $989,990; the annual taxes were $16,836.

rear facade, 2004

Robertson, Charles Sammis (1905-1981)

Occupation: financier -   partner, Harris Upham and Co.; (investment banking firm)
Civic Activism: co-founder, with his wife Louise, Robertson Foundation*

Marriage(s):   M/1 - Marie Louise Hoffman (d. 1972)
                                  - Civic Activism: co-founder, with her husband,
                                                          Robertson Foundation*
                             M/2 - Jane Gent

Listed in *Long Island Society Register, 1929*: no
Address: Banburry Lane, Lloyd Harbor
Acreage / map sources: not on 1929 or 1931 maps
                             19 acres / 1944 and 1946 maps

Name of estate:
Year of construction: 1938
Style of architecture: Georgian Revival
Architect(s):   Mott B. Schmidt designed
                                the house and garage
                                (for C. S. Robertson)

Landscape architect(s):
House extant: yes
Historical notes:

front facade, 1998

The house was built by Charles Sammis Robertson.

Marie Louise Hoffman Robertson was heir to the Great Atlantic and Pacific Tea Company fortune.

*Charles Sammis and Marie Louise Hoffman Robertson donated $35 million to Princeton University through the Robertson Foundation. In 2002, unhappy with Princeton's administration, the Robertson family threatened to withdraw the endowment which had appreciated to $550 million. [*The New York Times* July 18, 2002, pp. B1 and B5.]

In 1976, Robertson donated the estate to Cold Spring Harbor Laboratory which now uses it as a conference center.

Robertson, Julian Hart, Jr.

Occupation(s):   financier -   president, Tiger Management Investment Fund*;
                                           vice-president and director, Kidder, Peabody and Co.
                                              (investment banking firm)
Civic Activism: a founder, Tiger Foundation which provides funds to NYC for social
                                services, job training, and youth development

Marriage(s):   1972 - Josephine Vance Tucker
                                 - industrialist - president, Tuckertown (manufacturer of decorative items)

Listed in *Long Island Society Register, 1929*: no
Address: Wheatley Road, Upper Brookville
Acreage / map sources: not on 1927, 1932, or 1946 maps
Name of estate:
Year of construction: c. 1928
Style of architecture: Georgian
Architect(s):   William Lawrence Bottomley designed the house (for Whitehouse)
Landscape architect(s):
House extant: yes
Historical notes:

The house, originally named *Broadwood*, was built by James Norman Whitehouse.

The estate was, subsequently, owned by Robertson.

*In 2000, Tiger Management Investment Fund, one of the largest hedge funds in the world with assets of $21 billion, was forced to liquidate due to financial losses. At the time of the liquidation, Robertson was one of the most powerful money managers on Wall Street.

Josephine Vance Tucker Robertson is the daughter of Robert Edwin Tucker of San Antonio, TX.

The Robertsons' son Julian Spencer Robertson married Sarah Winslow Collins, the daughter of Terence Winslow and Beth Collins of Washington, DC.

Robertson, Thomas Markoe (1878-1962)

Occupation(s):   architect - a founder, Sloan and Robertson

Marriage(s):   1924-1962 - Cordelia Drexel Biddle (1900-1984)
- writer - *My Philadelphia Father* (with Kyle Crichton)*
Civic Activism: board member, Boys Harbor, East Hampton;
director, Musicians Emergency Fund;
chairman, benefit committee, Southampton Hospital

Listed in *Long Island Society Register, 1929*: yes
Address: Bacon Road and Bass Pond Drive, Old Westbury
Acreage / map sources: on 1927 map; 15 acres / 1932 and 1946 maps
Name of estate: *Guinea Hollow Farm*
Year of construction:
Style of architecture:
Architect(s):
Landscape architect(s):
House extant: yes
Historical notes:

   Cordelia Drexel Biddle Robertson was the sister of Anthony J. Drexel Biddle, United States Ambassador to Spain. She had previously been married to Angier Duke and had two sons by that marriage: United States Ambassador Angier Biddle Duke, the United States Chief of Protocol, and Anthony D. Duke, who resided in East Hampton.
   *The biography of Col. Anthony J. Drexel Biddle, became the 1956 Broadway comedy *The Happiest Millionaire*.

Robins, Lydia DeLamater

Marriage(s):   John Robins

Listed in *Long Island Society Register, 1929*: no
Address: Bevin Road, Asharoken
Acreage / map sources: not on 1929, 1931, or 1944 maps
Name of estate: *The Robin's Nest*
Year of construction: 1856
Style of architecture: Long Island Farmhouse
Architect(s):   Harry Ellingwood Donnell
                    designed 1911 alterations
                    (for George Hazard Robinson)

Landscape architect(s):
House extant: yes
Historical notes:

front facade, 1929

   In 1862, Cornelius Henry DeLamater purchased *Walnut Farm House* from William Beebe, a farmer who had built the house. DeLamater resided in it until his house *Vermland* was completed in the latter part of 1862.
   In 1876, his daughter Lydia DeLamater Robins and her husband John moved into the house and renamed it *The Robin's Nest.*
   The house was extensively altered in 1876, 1882, 1883, and 1884.
   Upon the death of Cornelius Henry DeLamater's wife Ruth in 1894, the house was deeded to Lydia DeLamater Robins.
   In 1898, the estate was purchased by Lydia's brother-in-law George Hazard Robinson. From 1898-1902, Robinson's daughter Ruth Attmore Robinson Donnell and her husband Harry used the house as their summer home.
   In 1902, the estate became the summer home of Robinson's other daughter Laura Attmore Robinson Donnell and her husband William Ballon Donnell. After William died of appendicitis in 1905, Ruth continued to use the estate as her summer home.
   In 1911, George Hazard Robinson made extensive alterations to the house.
   Laura Attmore Robinson Donnell inherited the estate and in 1927 began to subdivide its property.
   In 1943, she transferred ownership to her son-in-law Frederick Sandblom, who further subdivided the property.
   In 1946, Sandblom sold the house to Marcel Emmanuel Vertes.
   In 1954, Vertes' estate sold the house to Lucille Borglum. The Borglums still owned the house in 1994.
[Edward A. T. Carr, Michael W. Carr, and Kari-Ann R. Carr, *Faded Laurels: The History of Eaton's Neck and Asharoken* (Interlaken, NY: Heart of the Lakes Publishing, 1994), pp. 128-31.]

Robinson, Miss Edith Attmore (1873-1959)

Marriage(s):   unmarried

Listed in *Long Island Society Register, 1929*: yes
Address: Bevin Road West, Asharoken
Acreage / map sources: 1000 acres / 1929 map
                                                on 1931 map
                                                not on 1944 map
Name of estate: *The Point*
Year of construction: 1876
Style of architecture: French Second Empire
Architect(s):   Harry Ellingwood Donnell designed 1899 house alterations,
                                                    the new boathouse, billiard house, greenhouse, guest cottage,
                                                    garage, and superintendent's house (for G. H. Robinson)
Landscape architect(s):
House extant: yes
Historical notes:

   The house, originally named *The Point,* built by George Hazard Robinson, looked like a smaller replica of Cornelius Henry DeLamater's house *Vermland.*
   By 1901 Robinson owned about seventy-five percent of Eaton's Neck. After his death in 1919 the estate was divided among his wife and children.
   The *Long Island Society Register, 1929* lists Edith Robinson as residing with her mother Sarah DeLamater Robinson on Eaton's Neck [Asharoken].
   After his wife's death, her part of the estate passed to their daughter Edith Attmore Robinson. In 1932, she lost the estate for unpaid taxes.
   In 1937, most of the remaining property was sold to Henry Sturgis Morgan, Sr.
   In 1938, the house was sold to Richard E. Bishop, who established a perfume factory on the estate grounds. Since the area was zoned residential the Village of Asharoken forced him to discontinue manufacturing perfume at the estate. Bishop sold off the estate's carriage house and boathouse.
   In 1963, it was purchased by Reed Law.
   In 1977, it was sold to John R. Miller III, who began an extensive restoration.
[Edward A. T. Carr, Michael W. Carr, and Kari-Ann R. Carr, *Faded Laurels: The History of Eaton's Neck and Asharoken* (Interlaken, NY: Heart of the Lakes Publishing, 1994), pp. 120-27.]

rear facade, 1993

Robinson, George Hazard (1847-1919)

Occupation(s):

industrialist - principle owner and vice-president, Gorham Silver Co.;
partner, DeLamater Iron Works (manufacturers of machinery
for gun turrets and engines of *USS Monitor)**;
director, American–LaFrance Fire Engine Co.;
director, Baeck Wall Paper Co.;
director, S. S. Hepworth Co.;
director, William A. Miles Co.

financier - president, Garfield National Bank;
trustee, Bowery Savings Bank;
director, Manhattan Life Insurance Co.

Marriage(s): 1869-1919 - Sarah DeLamater (1846-1929)

Listed in *Long Island Society Register, 1929*: yes
Address: Bevin Road, Asharoken
Acreage / map sources: 1000 acres / 1929 map
on 1931 map
not on 1944 map

Name of estate:
Year of construction: 1856
Style of architecture: Long Island Farmhouse
Architect(s): Harry Ellingwood Donnell designed 1911 alterations
(for G. H. Robinson)

Landscape architect(s):
House extant: yes
Historical notes:

In 1862, Cornelius Henry DeLamater purchased *Walnut Farm House* from William Beebe, a farmer who had built the house. DeLamater resided in it until his house *Vermland* was completed in the latter part of 1862.

In 1876, his daughter Lydia DeLamater Robins and her husband John moved into the house and renamed it *The Robin's Nest*.

The house was extensively altered in 1876, 1882, 1883, and 1884.

Upon the death of Cornelius Henry DeLamater's wife Ruth in 1894, the house was deeded to Lydia DeLamater Robins.

*DeLamater Iron Works was known as "The Asylum" since it was a place where visionaries and inventors met. After the building of the *USS Monitor* it became known as "The Cradle of the Modern Navy." Numerous artifacts from the *USS Monitor* including its red lantern, which was the last object seen of the *Monitor* as it sunk and, ironically, the first artifact retrieved, the ship's anchor, and the propeller are on display at the Mariners' Museum in Newport News, VA. Plans are in progress to retrieve the thirty-six ton engine and turret gun.

In 1898, the estate was purchased by Lydia's brother-in-law George Hazard Robinson. From 1898-1902, Robinson's daughter Ruth Attmore Robinson Donnell and her husband Harry used the house as their summer home.

The *Long Island Society Register, 1929* lists Sarah DeLamater Robinson as residing on Eaton's Neck, Northport [Asharoken].

In 1902, the estate became the summer home of Robinson's other daughter Laura Attmore Robinson Donnell and her husband William Ballon Donnell. After William died of appendicitis in 1905, Ruth continued to use the estate as her summer home.

In 1911, George Hazard Robinson made extensive alterations to the house. The DeLamaters, subsequently, owned an 1876 house at 3 Bevin Road, Asharoken, named *The Point*.

Laura Attmore Robinson Donnell inherited the estate and in 1927 began to subdivide its property.

In 1943, Laura transferred ownership to her son-in-law Frederick Sandblom, who further subdivided the property.

In 1946, Sandblom sold the house to Marcel Emmanuel Vertes.

In 1954, Vertes' estate sold the house to Lucille Borglum. The Borglums still owned the house in 1994.
[Edward A. T. Carr, Michael W. Carr, and Kari-Ann R. Carr, *Faded Laurels: The History of Eaton's Neck and Asharoken* (Interlaken, NY: Heart of the Lakes Publishing, 1994), pp. 128-31.]

Original Walnut Farm house is structure in rear; Robin's Nest is in the foreground, 1878

Robinson, George Hazard (1847-1919)

Occupation(s):   industrialist - principle owner and vice-president, Gorham Silver Co.;
                                partner, DeLamater Iron Works (manufacturers of
                                    machinery for gun turrets and engines of *USS Monitor)*;
                                director, American–LaFrance Fire Engine Co.;
                                director, Baeck Wall Paper Co.;
                                director, S. S. Hepworth Co.;
                                director, William A. Miles Co.
                  financier - president, Garfield National Bank;
                            trustee, Bowery Savings Bank;
                            director, Manhattan Life Insurance Co.

Marriage(s):   1869-1919 - Sarah DeLamater (1846-1929)

Listed in *Long Island Society Register, 1929*: yes
Address: Bevin Road West, Asharoken
Acreage / map sources: 1000 acres / 1929 map
                        on 1931 map
                        not on 1944 map
Name of estate: *The Point*
Year of construction: 1876
Style of architecture: French Second Empire
Architect(s):   Harry Ellingwood Donnell designed 1899 house alterations, the
                            new boathouse, billiard house, greenhouse, guest cottage,
                            garage, and superintendent's house (for G. H. Robinson)

Landscape architect(s):
House extant: yes
Historical notes:

   The house, originally named *The Point*, built by George Hazard Robinson, looked like a smaller replica of Cornelius Henry DeLamater's house *Vermland*.
   By 1901 Robinson owned about seventy-five percent of Eaton's Neck. After his death in 1919 the estate was divided among his wife and children.
   The *Long Island Society Register, 1929* lists Sarah DeLamater Robinson as residing on Eaton's Neck, Northport [Asharoken].
   After his wife's death, her part of the estate passed to an unmarried daughter Edith Attmore Robinson. In 1932, she lost the estate for unpaid taxes.
   In 1937, most of the remaining property was sold to Henry Sturgis Morgan, Sr.
   In 1938, the house was sold to Richard E. Bishop, who established a perfume factory on the estate grounds. Since the area was zoned residential the Village of Asharoken forced him to discontinue manufacturing perfume at the estate. Bishop sold off the estate's carriage house and boathouse.
   In 1963, it was purchased by Reed Law.
   In 1977, it was sold to John R. Miller III, who began an extensive restoration.
[Edward A. T. Carr, Michael W. Carr, and Kari-Ann R. Carr, *Faded Laurels: The History of Eaton's Neck and Asharoken* (Interlaken, NY: Heart of the Lakes Publishing, 1994), pp. 120-27.]

The Point, 1880

Robinson, John Randolph (1879-1973)

Occupation(s):   industrialist - representative, Harbison, Walker and Co., Pittsburgh, PA
                                                  (brick and refractory manufacturer)

Marriage(s):   Mary Fletcher Metcalf (d. 1962)

Listed in *Long Island Society Register, 1929*: yes
Address: Wheatley Road, Brookville
Acreage / map sources: not on 1927, 1932, or 1946 maps
Name of estate:
Year of construction: 1927-1928
Style of architecture: Georgian Revival
Architect(s):   William Lawrence Bottomley designed the house
                                         (for J. R. Robinson)

Landscape architect(s):
House extant: yes
Historical notes:

    John Randolph Robinson built the house after he sold his other estate to Philip Gossler.
    The estate was owned by Daniel Gleason Tenney, Sr., before becoming part of C. W. Post College of Long Island University.

Robinson, John Randolph (1879-1973)

Occupation(s):   industrialist - representative, Harbison, Walker and Co., Pittsburgh, PA
                                                  (brick and refractory manufacturer)

Marriage(s):   Mary Fletcher Metcalf (d. 1962)

Listed in *Long Island Society Register, 1929*: yes
Address: Wheatley Road, Brookville
Acreage / map sources: not on 1927, 1932, or 1946 maps
Name of estate:
Year of construction: c. 1917
Style of architecture: Georgian Revival
Architect(s):   John Russell Pope designed the original house (for J. R. Robinson);
                                         1920s alterations (for Gossler)
                                James W. O'Connor designed c. 1937 alterations (for Hutton)
Landscape architect(s):   Ellen Biddle Shipman designed the gardens, courtyards
                                         and terraces, c. 1925 (for Gossler); later garden designs,
                                         1942 (for Hutton)
Estate photographs can be found in the Nassau County Museum Collection filed under Wheatley Hills/Gossler.
House extant: yes
Historical notes:

    The house was built by John Randolph Robinson.
    Both the *Long Island Society Register, 1929* and the *Social Register New York, 1933* list J. Randolph and Mary F. Metcalf Robinson as residing in Westbury [Brookville], while the *Social Register, Summer 1937* lists only Mary F. Metcalf Robinson as residing in Westbury[Brookville]. The *Social Register New York, 1959* lists Mrs. Robinson's address as 485 Park Avenue, NYC.
    The Robinsons' daughter Celia married Julian Livingston Peabody, Jr. and resided in West Hills. Their daughter Mary married John C. West, the son of Thomas H. West of Providence, RI.
    The estate was purchased by Philip Green Gossler, Sr., who called it *Highfield*.
    Edward Francis Hutton purchased the estate after his divorce from Marjorie Merriweather Post, in 1935, and renamed it *Hutfield*.
    The estate is now part of C. W. Post College of Long Island University.

John Randolph Robinson's house, front facade, 1998

Robinson, Monroe Douglas (1887-1944)

Occupation(s):	diplomat - goodwill ambassador to Peru, espousing Pan-American friendship before the Good Neighbor Policy had crystallized
	restaurateur - president, Double R. Coffee House*
	journalist - correspondent, *The New York Times*
Civic Activism:	chairman, New York Office, War Finance Committee during World War II
Marriage(s):	1916-1925 - Dorothy May Jordan (1886-1976)
	- Civic Activism: board member, Philharmonic Symphony Orchestra, NYC; active supporter, Professional Children's School, Metropolitan Opera Association, New York City Ballet, and City Center of Music and Drama, NYC

Listed in *Long Island Society Register, 1929*: yes
Address: Jericho – Oyster Bay Road, Muttontown
Acreage / map sources: on c. 1922 map (owned by Monroe Robinson)
on 1927 map (name misspelled as E. C. Chadwick)
63 acres / 1932 map (owned by Dorothy Jordan Chadwick)
56 acres / 1946 map (owned by Dorothy Jordan Chadwick)

Name of estate:
Year of construction:
Style of architecture:
Architect(s):
Landscape architect(s):
House extant: unconfirmed
Historical notes:

    The *Long Island Society Register, 1929* lists Monroe Douglas and Dorothy M. Jordan Robinson as residing on Oyster Bay Road [Jericho – Oyster Bay Road], Syosset [Muttontown]. The *Social Register New York, 1933* lists only Monroe Douglas, then residing at the Racquet Club in NYC.

    He was the son of Douglas and Corinne Roosevelt Robinson, the cousin of President Franklin Delano Roosevelt, and the nephew of President Theodore Roosevelt. His mother was Theodore Roosevelt's sister.

    Dorothy May Jordan Robinson was the daughter of Eben D. Jordan and an heir to the Jordan, Marsh and Co. clothing retail stores fortune. After her divorce from Robinson, she continued to reside on the estate with her second husband Elbridge Gerry Chadwick.

    Monroe Douglas and Dorothy May Jordan Robinson's daughter Dorothy married Randolph Appleton Kidder, the son of Alfred Vincent Kidder, Sr.

    *The Robinson and Roosevelt families were the principal owners of The Double R. Coffee House chain of restaurants.

Robinson, Thomas Linton (1880-1940)

Occupation(s):   attorney - partner, Arrel, McVey and Robinson;
                   partner, Hine, Kennedy and Robinson
               financier - vice-president, American Exchange Bank of New York;
                   vice-president, Guaranty Trust Co. of New York;
                   president, Wick Brothers Trust Co.;
                   vice-president, Dollar Savings and Trust Co.;
                   director, Wheatley Hills National Bank
               industrialist - chairman of board and president, Republic Rubber Co.;
                     director, Aiken Mills (textile firm);
                     director, Anderson Cotton Mills (textile firm);
                     director, Langley Mills (textile firm)
Civic Activism: commissioner, American Red Cross during World War I;
               member, Dawes Commission, 1924;
               vice-chairman, Unemployment Commission, New York State;
               *

Marriage(s):   1907 - Ysable Bonnell

Listed in *Long Island Society Register, 1929*: yes
Address: Roslyn Road, East Williston
Acreage / map sources: on 1927 map
               22 acres / 1932 and 1946 maps
Name of estate: *Red Barns*
Year of construction:
Style of architecture: Modified Dutch Colonial
Architect(s):
Landscape architect(s):
Estate photographs can be found in the Nassau County Museum Collection filed under East Williston/Robinson.
House extant: unconfirmed
Historical notes:

 Both the *Long Island Society Register, 1929* and the *Social Register, Summer 1932* list Thomas L. and Ysable Bonnell Robinson as residing at *Red Barns* in East Williston, while the *Social Register New York, 1953* lists Mrs. Robinson as residing at *Red Barns*. The *Social Register New York, 1954* list her address as 327 East 58th Street, NYC.
 Born in Ravenna, OH, he was the son of George Foreman and Mary Gillis Robinson.
 *Thomas Linton Robinson was appointed deputy administrator of all finance codes under the National Recovery Administration, but resigned in 1934 because of illness.
 Ysable Bonnell Robinson's sister Elida Floyd Bonnell married William Clark Langley and resided in Old Westbury.
 The Robinson's daughter Laura married George Douglas Debevoise of Manhattan.

Edward Roesler, Jr.'s house,
front facade, 2004

Roesler, Edward, Jr. (1905-1987)

Occupation(s):   financier - partner, Laidlaw and Co. (later, Kuhn Brothers
                                                        and Laidlaw) (investment banking firm)

Marriage(s):   M/1 - 1931-1967 - Anne Smith Baker (d. 1967)
                                  M/2 - 1969-1987 - Frances E. Kerr

Listed in *Long Island Society Register, 1929*: no
Address: West Gate Boulevard, Plandome
Acreage / map sources: not on 1927, 1932, or 1946 maps
Name of estate:
Year of construction:
Style of architecture: Colonial Revival
Architect(s):
Landscape architect(s):
House extant: yes
Historical notes:

　　The *Social Register New York, 1948* lists Edward and Anne S. Baker Roesler [Jr.] as residing on West Gate Boulevard, Plandome.
　　He was the son of Edward and Jessie Onderdonk Laidlaw Roesler, Sr., who resided at *Augustina* in Kings Point.
　　Anne Smith Baker Roesler was the daughter of John C. Baker, Sr., who resided in Saddle Rock.
　　Edward and Anne Smith Baker Roesler's daughter Anne married David Grabow Slocum, the son of H. Turner Slocum of Glen Cove. Their daughter Jane married Charles DeBovoise Corcoran, the son of Francis L. Corcoran of Locust Valley.
　　The *Social Register New York, 1967* lists Edward Roesler [Jr.] as residing on Duck Pond Road, Glen Cove. The *Social Register New York, 1971* lists Edward and Frances E. Kerr Roesler [Jr.] as residing on Whisky Hill Road, Woodside, CA.
　　Frances E. Kerr Roesler was the daughter of Frank R. Kerr of Portland, OR. She had previously been married to Richard H. Marshall.

Roesler, Edward, Sr. (d. 1946)

Occupation(s):   financier - partner, Laidlaw and Co. (later, Kuhn Brothers
                                                        and Laidlaw) (investment banking firm)
                                                governor, New York Stock Exchange

Marriage(s):   1901-1946 - Jessie Onderdonk Laidlaw (1875-1962)

Listed in *Long Island Society Register, 1929*: yes
Address: Kings Point Road, Kings Point
Acreage / map sources: on 1927 map (name misspelled as A. Roessler)
                                  53 acres / 1932 and 1946 maps (name misspelled as A. Roessler)
Name of estate: *Augustina*
Year of construction:
Style of architecture:
Architect(s):
Landscape architect(s):
House extant: unconfirmed
Historical notes:

　　The *Social Register New York, 1932* lists the Roeslers as residing at *Augustina* in Kings Point. The *Social Register New York, 1948* lists Jessie O. Laidlaw Roesler as residing with her son Edward and daughter-in-law Anne S. Baker Roesler on Westgate Boulevard, Plandome. The *Social Register New York, 1953* lists her as residing on Grace Avenue, Great Neck [Great Neck Plaza]. She was residing on Grace Avenue, Great Neck [Great Neck Plaza], at the time of her death. [*The New York Times* March 15, 1962, p. 35.]
　　Jessie Onderdonk Laidlaw Roesler was the daughter of Henry Bell and Elizabeth Carter Onderdonk Laidlaw. Her sister Edith married Imlay Benet and, subsequently, Attilio Ferrucci, with whom she resided in Rome, Italy. Her sister Alice married Jessie Lynch Williams and resided in Carmel, CA. Her brother Elliot married Ethel Colton and resided in Plainfield, NJ. Her brother James married Harriet Wright Burton and resided at *Hazeldean* in Sands Point.

Roesler, Walter, Sr. (d. 1953)

Occupation(s):   financier -   Walter Roesler and Co. (stock brokerage firm)

Marriage(s):   Helen M. Lewis (1887-1965)

Listed in *Long Island Society Register, 1929*: yes
Address: Kings Point Road, Kings Point
Acreage / map sources: on 1927 map (name misspelled as A. Roessler)
                                  53 acres / 1932 and 1946 maps (name misspelled as A. Roessler)
Name of estate: *Tuckaway*
Year of construction:
Style of architecture:
Architect(s):
Landscape architect(s):
House extant: unconfirmed
Historical notes:

    The *Long Island Society Register, 1929* lists the summer address of Walter and Helen M. Lewis Roesler [Sr.] as *Pine Lane Farm* in Great Barrington, MA, while the *Social Register New York, 1933* lists only Walter Roesler [Sr.] as residing in Great Neck [Kings Point].
    Helen M. Lewis Roesler subsequently married Edward P. Renner and resided in Lakeville, CT.
    The Roeslers' daughter Gwynne married Sherman Brownell Yoost, Jr. of Quogue.

Rogers, Henry Alexander (1881-1941)

Occupation(s):   capitalist - real estate - vice-president, Douglas L. Elliman & Co.;
                                                    vice-president, Worthington Whitehouse Inc.;
                                                        president, Wheatley Hills Real Estate Corp.

Marriage(s):   Ada T. Belden

Listed in *Long Island Society Register, 1929*: yes
Address: Ryefield Road, Lattingtown
Acreage / map sources: on 1927 map
                                    no acreage given on 1932 map
                                    not on 1946 map
Name of estate: *Locust Lodge*
Year of construction:
Style of architecture:
Architect(s):
Landscape architect(s):
House extant: unconfirmed
Historical notes:

    The *Long Island Society Register, 1929* lists Henry Alexander and Ada T. Belden Rogers as residing on Church Lane, Locust Valley. The *Social Register, Summer 1937* lists the Rogers as residing at *Locust Lodge* in Locust Valley [Lattingtown]. The *Social Register New York, 1948* lists Mrs. Rogers residence as 40 East 54th Street, NYC, while the *Social Register New York, 1957* lists her address as 130 East 57th Street, NYC.
    Born in New Haven, CT, he was the son of Henry and Antoinette Anderson Rogers. The family of his maternal grandparents were founders of Storrs College of the University of Connecticut. [*The New York Times* October 31, 1941, p. 23.]

Roig, Harold Joseph (1885-1972)

Occupation(s):

attorney - member, Byrne and Cutcheon;
member, Ivins, Wolf and Hoguet

shipping - vice-chairman, secretary, and director, W. R. Grace & Co.;
director, Grace Line Inc.;
director, Panama Mail Steamship Co.;
director, Maritimas Mexicanas;
director, Corporacion Maritima Colombiana;
director, Grace & Co. Central America;
director, Grace & Co. Mexico

capitalist - director, Pan American Grace Airways (Panagra, a
joint venture with Pan American Airways);
director, Panama Agencies Co.

financier - president, Marine Midland Grace Trust Co. of New York;
director, Grace National Bank;
director, Grace Trust Co.;
director, Grace Brothers and Co. (London-based
investment banking firm);
member, New York Commodity Exchange;
member, New York Cotton Exchange;
member, New York Coffee Exchange;
member, New York Sugar Exchange;
member, Liverpool Cotton Exchange

industrialist - president and chairman of board, Naco Fertilizer Co.;
director, Cartavio Sugar Co., Peru;
director, Sedwick Machine Works;
director, International Machine Co.

educator - instructor in American history, Department of History,
Cornell University, Ithaca, NY

Civic Activism:
treasurer, Lenox Hill Hospital, NYC;
president and treasurer, Great Neck Preparatory School;
secretary, Nitrate Committee which regulated Chilean nitrate during
World War I;
trustee, Buckley Country Day School, North Hills;
trustee and judge - Village of Kings Point

Marriage(s):
1917-1972 - Henrietta B. Hayens

Listed in *Long Island Society Register, 1929*: no
Address: Kings Point Road, Kings Point
Acreage / map sources: not on 1927 map
4 acres / 1932 and 1946 maps

Name of estate:
Year of construction: c. 1920
Style of architecture: French Manor House
Architect(s):
Landscape architect(s):
House extant: yes
Historical notes:

The house was built by Harold Joseph Roig.
He was the son of Adolphus S. and Josephine
Cope Roig of Poughkeepsie, NY.

front facade

Roosevelt, Archibald Bulloch, Jr. (1918-1990)

Occupation(s):   financier -   vice-president and director, Chase Manhattan Bank
                                        intelligence agent - Middle East specialist, Central Intelligence Agency
                                        diplomat -   special assistant to U. S. Ambassador to the Court of St. James, 1962-1966;
                                                          special assistant to United States Ambassador to Spain, 1958;
                                                          consul, Istanbul, Turkey, 1951-1953
                                        writer - *For Lust of Knowing: Memoirs of an Intelligence Officer*, 1988

Marriage(s):   M/1 - 1940-1950 - Katherine Winthrop Tweed
                                        M/2 - 1950-1990 - Selwa Carman Showker* (Lebanese spelling is Shuqayr)
                                              - journalist - columnist, *Washington Evening Star*, 1954-1959; free-lance

Listed in *Long Island Society Register, 1929*: no
Address: Turkey Lane, Cold Spring Harbor
Acreage / map sources: not on 1929 map; on 1931 map (incorrectly listed as owned by Kermit Roosevelt); 9 acres / 1944 and 1946 maps (owned by A. B. Roosevelt)
Name of estate: *Turkey Lane House*
Year of construction:
Style of architecture:
Architect(s):
Landscape architect(s):
House extant: unconfirmed
Historical notes:

Archibald Bulloch Roosevelt, Jr. resided in the house owned by his father Archibald Bulloch Roosevelt, Sr. Katherine Winthrop Tweed Roosevelt subsequently married Dr. Robert Blackwood Robertson.
[See following entry for additional family information.]
Archibald Bulloch and Katherine Winthrop Tweed Roosevelt, Jr.'s son Tweed married Candace MacGuigan.
*Selwa Carman Showker Roosevelt was the Chief of Protocol in President Ronald Reagan's administration.

Roosevelt, Archibald Bulloch, Sr. (1894-1979)

Occupation(s):   financier -   president, Roosevelt and Weigold (stock brokerage firm)
                                        restaurateur - a founder, Brazilian Coffee Houses chain, NYC

Marriage(s):   1917-1971 - Grace Stackpole Lockwood (1893-1971)

Listed in *Long Island Society Register, 1929*: yes
Address: Turkey Lane, Cold Spring Harbor
Acreage / map sources: not on 1929 map; on 1931 map (incorrectly listed as owned by Kermit Roosevelt); 9 acres / 1944 and 1946 maps (owned by A. B. Roosevelt)
Name of estate: *Turkey Lane House*
Year of construction:
Style of architecture:
Architect(s):
Landscape architect(s):
House extant: unconfirmed
Historical notes:

Archibald Bulloch Roosevelt, Sr. was the son of President Theodore and Mrs. Edith Kermit Carow Roosevelt, who resided at *Sagamore Hill* in Cove Neck. His brother Kermit married Belle Wyatt Willard and resided at *Mohannes* in Cove Neck. His brother Theodore Roosevelt, Jr. married Eleanor Butler Alexander and resided at *Old Orchard*, also in Cove Neck. His sister Ethel married Dr. Richard Derby and resided at *Old Adam* in Oyster Bay. His brother Quentin was killed in World War I. His sister Alice married U. S. Senator Nicholas Longworth and resided in Washington, DC.

Grace Lockwood Roosevelt was fatally injured in an automobile accident with a school bus.

The Roosevelts' son Archibald Bulloch Roosevelt, Jr. resided with his parents. Their daughter Nancy married William Eldred Jackson II and resided at *Hurrahs Nest* and *Roosevelt Cottage* in Cold Spring Harbor. Their daughter Theodora married Thomas Keogh, Thomas O'Toole, and A. A. Rauschuss. The Rauchusses resided in Patterson, NC. Their daughter Edith married Alexander Gregory Barmine.

Roosevelt, Franklin Delano, Jr. (1914-1988)

Occupation(s):   attorney
                                         statesman - Under Secretary of Commerce during the Kennedy administration
                                         politician - member, United States Congress, from New York, 1949-1954
                                         merchant - owned *Fiat* automobile dealership

Civic Activism: chairman, Equal Employment Opportunity Commission during the Kennedy
                                             administration;
                                         member, President's Committee on Civil Rights, during the Truman and
                                         Kennedy administrations

Marriage(s):   M/1 - 1937-1949 - Ethel du Pont (1916-1965)
                                         M/2 - 1949-1970 - Suzanne Perrin (b. 1921)
                                         M/3 - 1970-1976 - Felicia Schiff Warburg
                                         M/4 - 1977-1981 - Patricia Luisa Oakes
                                         M/5 - 1984-1988 - Linda McKay Stevenson (b. 1939)

Listed in *Long Island Society Register, 1929:* no
Address: Plainview Road and Northern State Parkway, Woodbury
Acreage / map sources: not on 1927, 1932, or 1946 maps
Name of estate:
Year of construction:
Style of architecture:
Architect(s):
Landscape architect(s):
House extant: unconfirmed
Historical notes:

    The house was located adjacent to and south of the Ogden Livingston Mills estate. Franklin and Ethel du Pont Roosevelt, Jr. resided there with their sons Christopher and Franklin Delano Roosevelt III. [*The New York Times* January 30, 1952, p. 27.]

    Franklin Delano Roosevelt, Jr. was the third son of President Franklin Delano and Mrs. Anna Eleanor Roosevelt Roosevelt. The President's family home was in Hyde Park, NY. His mother was the daughter of Elliott and Anna Livingston Hall Roosevelt. Elliott was the brother of President Theodore Roosevelt. [Anna] Eleanor and Franklin were fifth cousins; her father Elliott was Franklin's godfather. Orphaned at the age of ten, Eleanor lived with her maternal grandmother Mary Livingston Ludlow Hall, spending several summers at the "old Richardson place" in Hempstead, which became the rectory of St. Ladislaus Church. [*Hempstead Sentinel* October 7, 1943, n. p.; E. H. Gwynne–Thomas, *The Presidential Families* [New York: Hippocrene Books, p. 348.]

    Franklin Delano Roosevelt, Jr.'s brother James married Betsey Cushing, who subsequently married John Hay Whitney and resided with him at *Greentree* in Manhasset; Romelle Schneider; and Gladys Irene Owens. His sister Anna married Curtis Dall; John Boettiger, who committed suicide in 1950 by jumping out the seventh floor window of a Manhattan apartment building; and James Halstead. His brother Elliott married Elizabeth Browning Donner; Ruth Josephine Googins; Faye Emerson, who subsequently married bandleader Skitch Henderson; Minnewa Bell; and Patricia Peabody Whitehead. His brother John married Anne Lindsay Clark and Irene Boyd McAlpin. [E. H. Gwynne–Thomas, pp. 329-350.]

    Franklin, a naval officer during World War II, was awarded the Silver Star for courageous action during the invasion of Sicily. He ran unsuccessfully for the governorship of New York and for the post of attorney general.

    Ethel du Pont Roosevelt was the daughter of Eugene du Pont of *Owl's Nest* in Centerville, DE, an outspoken critic of FDR, Sr. She subsequently married Benjamin S. Warren, Jr. and resided at Grosse Pointe Farms in Michigan. Ethel committed suicide in 1965.

    In 1941, the Roosevelts leased the Henry Pierson estate on Mill River Road in Upper Brookville. [*The New York Times* September 17, 1941, p. 40.]

    Franklin Delano and Ethel du Pont Roosevelt, Jr.'s son Christopher married Rosalind Havemeyer, the daughter of Horace and Rosalind Everdell Havemeyer, Jr., who resided in Dix Hills. Roosevelt's son Franklin Delano Roosevelt III married Grace R. Goodyear.

    Suzanne Perrin Roosevelt was the daughter of Lee James Perrin of Manhattan.

    Franklin Delano and Suzanne Perrin Roosevelt, Jr.'s daughter Nancy married Thomas Ellis Ireland.

    Felicia Schiff Warburg had previously been married to RCA president Robert Sarnoff. She was relative of *New York Post* publisher Dorothy Schiff, who resided at *Sandy Cay* in Sands Point and at *Old Fields* in East Norwich. [E. H. Gwynne–Thomas, pp. 349.]

Roosevelt, George Emlen, Sr. (1887-1963)

Occupation(s):	financier - partner, Roosevelt and Son (investment banking firm);
	director, Guaranty Trust Co.;
	director, Bank for Savings, NYC
	capitalist - director, Union Pacific Railway Co.
Civic Activism:	president of board, Chapin School;
	president of board, Roosevelt Hospital (founded by James Henry Roosevelt,
	which became St. Luke's–Roosevelt Hospital Center), NYC;
	vice-president, Indian Mountain School;
	treasurer, Relief Foundation;
	treasurer, New York Dispensary;
	treasurer, New York University
Marriage(s):	M/1 - 1914-1937 - Julia Morris Addison (1888-1937)
	M/2 - 1939-1963 - Mildred P. Cobb (d. 1979)

Listed in *Long Island Society Register, 1929*: yes

Address:	Cove Neck Road, Cove Neck
Acreage / map sources:	on 1927 map (owned by W. E. Roosevelt)
	149 acres / 1932 map (owned by W. E. Roosevelt)
	90 acres / 1946 map (owned by George E. Roosevelt)
Name of estate:	*Gracewood*
Year of construction:	1884
Style of architecture:	Shingle
Architect(s):	McKim, Mead and White designed the house (for Gracie)
	the wing, which includes a ballroom, was added in 1924

Landscape architect(s):
House extant: yes .
Historical notes:

The house, originally named *Gracewood,* was built by James King Gracie.

The estate was owned by George Emlen Roosevelt, Sr. and, subsequently in 1989, by Terry Choung. Both Roosevelt and Choung continued to call it *Gracewood.*

The *Long Island Society Register, 1929* lists George Emlen and Julia M. Addison Roosevelt [Sr.] as residing at *Gracewood* in Oyster Bay [Cove Neck].

He was the son of William Emlen and Christine Kean Roosevelt, who resided at *Yellowbanks* in Cove Neck. His brother Philip James Roosevelt, Sr. married Jean Schermerhorn Roosevelt, the daughter of John Ellis and Nannie Mitchell Vance Roosevelt who resided at *Meadow Croft* in Sayville. Philip and Jean Roosevelt resided at *Dolonar* in Cove Neck. His brother John Kean Roosevelt married Elise Annette Weinacht, the daughter of Edward and Helena Elise Hanbold Weinacht of Elizabeth, NJ, and resided in Glen Cove and at *Yellowbanks.* His sister Christine married James Etter Shelley, the son of Charles M. and Kathleen McConnell Shelley of Selma, AL. His sister Lucy, who died in her mid-20s, was unmarried.

Born in Fitchburg, MA, Julia Morris Addison Roosevelt was the daughter of The Rev. Charles Morris and Mrs. Ada Thayer Addison.

George Emlen and Julia Morris Addison Roosevelt, Sr.'s daughter Medora married Herbert Whiting, the son of Herbert Allison and Dorothy Stanley Whiting of Scituate, MA. Their daughter Margaret married Alessandro Mario Luigi Pietro Pallavicini, the son of Arrigo and Chiaro Draghi Pallavicini of Rome, Italy, and, subsequently, George Philip Kent the son of George Foster and Cecilia Kanaly Kent of Kansas. Their son George Emlen Roosevelt, Jr. married Nadine Unger and, subsequently, Marilyn Wood. Their son Julian Kean Roosevelt, who resided at *Bonnie Brae* on Centre Island, married Florence Madeleine Graham and, subsequently, Margaret Fay Schantz.

Mildred P. Cobb had previously been married to Dudley Bell Rich, Sr. The Richs' son Dudley Bell Rich, Jr. married Mary Adele Rogers, the daughter of George W. Rogers of Forest Hills, Queens.

Cove Neck Road, Cove Neck, c. 1915

Roosevelt, James Alfred (1825-1898)

Occupation(s):	financier - partner, Roosevelt and Son (investment banking firm); vice-president, Chemical National Bank; director, New York Insurance & Trust Co.; vice-president and treasurer, Bank for Savings, NYC
Civic Activism:	president, Roosevelt Hospital (founded by James Henry Roosevelt, which became St. Luke's–Roosevelt Hospital Center). NYC; trustee, Society for the Prevention of Cruelty to Children
Marriage(s):	1847-1898 - Elizabeth Norris Emlen (1825-1912)

Listed in *Long Island Society Register, 1929*: no
Address: Cove Neck Road, Cove Neck
Acreage / map sources: on 1927 map (owned by W. E. Roosevelt)
                            62 acres / 1932 and 1946 maps (owned by P. J. Roosevelt)
Name of estate: *Yellowbanks*
Year of construction: 1881
Style of architecture: Shingle
Architect(s):   Bruce Price designed the house (for J. A. Roosevelt)
Landscape architect(s):
House extant: yes
Historical notes:

   The house, originally named *Yellowbanks,* was built by James Alfred Roosevelt, the father of William Emlen Roosevelt and an uncle of President Theodore Roosevelt.
   Elizabeth Norris Emlen Roosevelt was the daughter of William Fishbourne and Mary Parker Norris Emlen of Philadelphia, PA.
   The Roosevelts' daughter Leila married Montgomery Roosevelt Schuyler, the son of The Rev. Montgomery and Mrs. Lydia Eliza Roosevelt Schuyler and, subsequently, Edward Reeve–Merritt and resided at *Elfland* in Cove Neck. Edward Reeve–Merritt was the son of Edward and Mary Reeve Merritt. Their daughter Caroline married William Talman Moore, Jr. and resided at *Puente Vista* on Centre Island. Their daughter Mary remained unmarried.
   The estate was, subsequently, owned by William Emlen Roosevelt, John Kean Roosevelt, and Oliver Russell Grace. All continued to call the estate *Yellowbanks.*
   The house is on The National Register of Historic Places.

Yellowbanks,
sketch by Lorraine Graves Grace

Roosevelt, John Kean (1890-1974)

Occupation(s):	civil engineer
	financier - partner, Roosevelt and Son (investment banking firm);
	director, Chemical Bank and Trust Co.
	capitalist - chairman of board, Elizabethtown Gas;
	director, Elizabethtown Water Co.;
	director, Hackensack Water Co.;
	vice-president, International Telephone & Telegraph Corp.
Marriage(s):	1916-1972 - Elise Annette Weinacht (1896-1972)

Listed in *Long Island Society Register, 1929*: yes
Address:	Cove Neck Road, Cove Neck
Acreage / map sources:	on 1927 map (owned by W. E. Roosevelt)
	62 acres / 1932 and 1946 maps (owned by P. J. Roosevelt)
Name of estate:	*Yellowbanks*
Year of construction:	1881
Style of architecture:	Shingle
Architect(s):	Bruce Price designed the house (for J. A. Roosevelt)
Landscape architect(s):	
House extant: yes	
Historical notes:	

The house, originally named *Yellowbanks*, was built by James Alfred Roosevelt.

The estate was, subsequently, owned by William Emlen Roosevelt, John Kean Roosevelt, and Oliver Russell Grace. All continued to call the estate *Yellowbanks*.

John Kean Roosevelt was the son of William Emlen and Christine Griffin Kean Roosevelt, who resided at *Yellowbanks* in Cove Neck. His brother George Emlen Roosevelt, Sr., who resided at *Gracewood* in Cove Neck, married Julia Morris Addison, the daughter of The Rev. Charles Morris and Mrs. Ada Thayer Addison, and, subsequently, Mildred P. Cobb. His brother Philip James Roosevelt, Sr. married Jean Schermerhorn Roosevelt, the daughter of John Ellis and Nannie Mitchell Vance Roosevelt who resided at *Meadow Croft* in Sayville. Philip and Jean Roosevelt resided at *Dolonar* in Cove Neck. His sister Christine married James Etter Shelley, the son of Charles M. and Kathleen McConnell Shelley of Selma, AL. His sister Lucy, who died in her mid-20s, was unmarried.

Elise Annette Weinacht Roosevelt was the daughter of Edward and Helena Elise Hanbold Weinacht of Elizabeth, NJ.

The Roosevelts' son William Emlen Roosevelt II married Arlene Marion King, the daughter of Rufus Gun King of Edmonds, WA. Their daughter Dorothea married James Sylvester Armentrout, Jr., the son of The Rev. James Sylvester and Mrs. Jane Churchill Gulick Armentrout, Sr., and resides in Amber, PA. Their son Peter married Marjorie Snyder, the daughter of Joseph Arthur and Barbara Bunting Snyder, and resides in Denver, CO. Their daughter Elizabeth Emlen Roosevelt resides at *The Bilge* on Cove Neck Road, Cove Neck. Her home is in the boatsman's cottage on her father's estate.

The house is on The National Register of Historic Places

Roosevelt, John Kean (1890-1974)

Occupation(s):	*[See previous entry for detailed list.]*
Marriage(s):	1916-1972 - Elise Annette Weinacht (1896-1972)

Listed in *Long Island Society Register, 1929*: yes
Address:	Meadow Spring Road, Glen Cove
Acreage / map sources:	not on 1927, 1932, or 1946 maps
Name of estate:	
Year of construction:	
Style of architecture:	
Architect(s):	
Landscape architect(s):	
House extant: unconfirmed	
Historical notes:	

The *Long Island Society Register, 1929* lists John Kean and Elsie [Elise] A. Weinacht Roosevelt as residing on Meadow Spring Road, Glen Cove. *[See previous entry for additional family information.]*

Roosevelt, Julian Kean (1924-1986)

Occupation(s):	capitalist - real estate - director, Broadway Improvement Co.
	financier - partner, Dick & Merle–Smith (investment banking firm);
	vice-president, Sterling Grace and Co. (investment banking firm);
	director, Fundamental Investors Inc.;
	director, Diversified Investment Fund Inc.;
	director, Westminster Fund Inc.;
	director, Diversified Growth Stock Fund, Inc.;
	director, Union Square Savings Bank;
	director, Roosevelt and Son (investment banking firm)
Civic Activism:	trustee, Father Bigelow Memorial Association;
	president, Centre Island Association;
	trustee, executive board, United States Olympic Committee;
	trustee, United States Coast Guard Academy, Groton, CT;
	trustee, State University of New York Maritime College, The Bronx, NYC
Marriage(s):	M/1 - 1946-1955 - Florence Madeleine Graham (1926-1991)
	M/2 - 1957-1986 - Margaret Fay Schantz (b. 1926)

Listed in *Long Island Society Register, 1929*: no
Address: Centre Island Road, Centre Island
Acreage / map sources: not on 1927, 1932, or 1946 maps
Name of estate: *Bonnie Brae*
Year of construction: c. 1955
Style of architecture: Georgian Revival
Architect(s):
Landscape architect(s):
House extant: yes
Historical notes:

   Who's Who in America, 1962-1963 lists *Bonnie Brae* as the name for Roosevelt's estate.
   The estate was previously owned by Archibald Waters MacLaren, who had also called it *Bonnie Brae*.
   Julian Kean Roosevelt was the son of George Emlen and Julia Addison Roosevelt, who resided at *Gracewood* in Cove Neck. His sister Medora married Herbert Whiting, the son of Herbert Allison and Dorothy Stanley Whiting of Scituate, MA. His sister Margaret married Alessandro Mario Luigi Pietro Pallavicini, the son of Arrigo and Chiaro Draghi Pallavicini of Rome, Italy, and, subsequently, George Philip Kent the son of George Foster and Cecilia Kanaly Kent of Kansas. His brother George Emlen Roosevelt, Jr. married Nadine Unger and, subsequently, Marilyn Wood.
   Florence Madeleine Graham Roosevelt was the daughter of Ephraim Walters Sterling and Florence Madeleine Bridgham Graham of Pittsburgh, PA. She subsequently married Eric Ridder, Sr., and resided in Lattingtown.
   Julian and Florence Graham Roosevelt's son George Emlen Roosevelt III married Sandra Lee O'Donnell.
   Margaret Fay Schantz Roosevelt was the daughter of Dr. Charles William and Mrs. Ruth Virginia Satterfield Schantz. She had previously been married to Donald William Scholle.
   Julian and Margaret Schantz Roosevelt's daughter Fay Satterfield Roosevelt married Julian Potter Fisher II, the son of Peter Rowe and Cary Randolph Fox Fisher.

oil painting of Bonnie Brae
by William Jonas, c. 1970

Roosevelt, Kermit, Sr. (1889-1943)

Occupation(s):

shipping - a founder and vice-president, United States Steamship Line;
secretary, American Ship & Commerce Corp.;
vice-president, Kerr Steamship Co.;
a founder, Roosevelt Steamship Co. (which was eventually merged
into the United States Steamship Line);
director and vice-president, International Mercantile Marine Co.

capitalist - director, New York Madison Square Garden Corp.;

restaurateur - co-founder, with brothers Theodore and Archibald, brother-in-law,
Dr. Richard Derby, and cousin Philip James Roosevelt, Sr.,
Brazilian Coffee Houses chain, NYC

writer - *War in the Garden of Eden*, 1919;
The Happy Hunting Ground, 1920;
Christman Week in Mowgli Land, 1926;
Cleared for Strange Ports, 1927;
co-authored with Theodore Roosevelt, Jr.:
East of the Sun and West of the Moon, 1926;
Trailing the Giant Panda, 1929

Marriage(s):

1914-1943 - Belle Wyatt Willard (1892-1968)
- Civic Activism: a founder, Young America Wants to Help (a junior
division of British War Relief during World War II);
active in Lenox Hill Neighborhood Association;
active in Lenox Hill Hospital, NYC

Listed in *Long Island Society Register, 1929*: yes

Address: Cove Neck Road, Cove Neck

Acreage / map sources: on 1927 map (owned by Roosevelt)
9 acres / 1932 map (owned by Mrs. K. Roosevelt)
9 acres / 1946 map (owned by Belle W. Roosevelt)

Name of estate: *Mohannes**

Year of construction: c. 1927

Style of architecture: Colonial Revival

Architect(s):

Landscape architect(s): Ellen Biddle Shipman (for K. Roosevelt, Sr.)

House extant: no; demolished c. 1950

Historical notes:

The house, originally named *Mohannes*, was built by Kermit Roosevelt, Sr.

The *Long Island Society Register, 1929* and the *Social Register, Summer 1937* list Kermit and Belle Wyatt Willard Roosevelt [Sr.] as residing at *Mohannes* on Cove Neck Road, Oyster Bay [Cove Neck], while the *Social Register, Summer 1954* lists only Belle W. Willard Roosevelt as residing at *Mohannes*. The *Social Register New York, 1967* lists Mrs. Roosevelt's residence as 9 Sutton Place, NYC.

Kermit Roosevelt, Sr. was the son of President Theodore and Mrs. Edith Kermit Carow Roosevelt, who resided at *Sagamore Hill* in Cove Neck. His brother Theodore Roosevelt, Jr. married Eleanor Butler Alexander and resided at *Old Orchard*, also in Cove Neck. His brother Archibald, who resided at *Turkey Lane House* in Cold Spring Harbor, married Grace Stackpole Lockwood. His sister Ethel married Dr. Richard Derby and resided at *Old Adam* in Oyster Bay. His brother Quentin was killed in World War I. His sister Alice married United States Senator Nicholas Longworth and resided in Washington, DC.

Born in Baltimore, MD, Belle Wyatt Willard Roosevelt was the daughter of Joseph Edward and Belle Layton Wyatt Willard. Her father served as United States Ambassador to Spain.

The Roosevelts' son Kermit Roosevelt, Jr. married Mary Lowe Gaddis. Their son Joseph married Nancy Cummings and, subsequently, Carol Adele Russell. Their twenty-eight-year-old son Dirck died in 1953 following surgery in England for an abscess. Their daughter Belle married John Gorham Palfrey, Jr.

*Mohannes is the second part of the name of the Indian Chief Sagamore Mohannes.

Roosevelt, Laura d'Oremieulx (1858-1945)

Civic Activism: president, New York Philharmonic Society, NYC

Marriage(s):   1883-1896 - Dr. James West Roosevelt (1858-1896)
                                       - physician

Listed in *Long Island Society Register, 1929*: yes
Address: Cove Neck Road, Cove Neck
Acreage / map sources: on 1927 map (owned by Mrs. J. W. Roosevelt)
                              4 acres / 1932 map (owned by Mrs. J. W. Roosevelt)
                              4 acres / 1946 map (owned by Mrs. J. W. Roosevelt)
Name of estate: *Waldeck*
Year of construction:
Style of architecture:
Architect(s):
Landscape architect(s):
House extant: unconfirmed
Historical notes:

The *Brooklyn Blue Book and Long Island Society Register, 1921* lists *Waldeck* as the name of Roosevelt's estate.

Laura d'Oremieulx Roosevelt was the daughter of Theophile M. and Laura Wolcott Gibbs d'Oremieulx. The Wolcotts were descendents of Oliver Wolcott, Sr., a signer of the Declaration of Independence. Oliver Wolcott, Jr. was Secretary of the Treasury in President George Washington's administration. Laura's paternal grandfather was Count Henry Jacques d'Oremieulx of France.

James West Roosevelt was the son of Silas Weir and Mary West Roosevelt and a first cousin of President Theodore Roosevelt, who resided at *Sagamore Hill* also in Cove Neck.

Their son Nicholas, who married Tirzah Maris Gates, served as United States Minister to Hungary before becoming assistant to the publisher of *The New York Times.* Their son Oliver, who resided on Roger Avenue in Woodmere married Grace Helen Temple Olmstead, the daughter of Chauncey Lockhardt Olmstead, and, subsequently, Mary De Verdery Akin, the daughter of John Wesley and Frances Trippe Johnson Akin of Atlanta, GA.

*Philip James Roosevelt, Jr. 's house,
front facade, 1945*

Roosevelt, Philip James, Jr. (1928-1998)

Occupation(s):	financier - president, The Roosevelt Investment Group, Inc., Oyster Bay
Civic Activism:	president, trustee, and member, executive committee, Theodore Roosevelt Association;
	trustee, The Holy Way Laymen's;
	trustee, National Bible Association;
	trustee, New York Diabetes Association;
	trustee, Youngs Memorial Cemetery, Oyster Bay
Marriage(s):	M/1 - 1952-1967 - Barbara Ellen Scott (b. 1928)
	M/2 - 1969 - Philippa Dayrell Buss (b. 1943)

Listed in *Long Island Society Register, 1929*: no
Address: East Main Street and Cove Neck Road, Cove Neck
Acreage / map sources: not on 1927, 1932, or 1946 maps
Name of estate:
Year of construction: 18th century
Style of architecture: Long Island Farmhouse
Architect(s):
Landscape architect(s):
Estate photographs can be found in the Nassau County Museum Collection filed under Oyster Bay/Young.
House extant: yes
Historical notes:

   Philip James Roosevelt, Jr. resided in the historic Thomas Youngs' House, to which many additions and alterations had been made since the 1700s.
   The *Social Register New York, 1964* lists Philip and Barbara Roosevelt as residing on Cove Neck Road, Oyster Bay.
   He was the son of Philip James and Jean Schermerhorn Roosevelt, Sr., who resided at *Dolonar* in Cove Neck. His sister Philippa married Benjamin E. Jeffries and resided in Boston, MA. His brother John Ellis Roosevelt II married Helen C. Sparrow and resided in Manhattan.
   Barbara Ellen Scott Roosevelt was the daughter of John Lennox Scott of Seattle, WA. She subsequently married Ormond deKay, Jr. and resided in Manhattan.
   Philip and Barbara Scott Roosevelt's son Philip James Roosevelt [III] married Vicki Beth Nadler and resided in Chappaqua, NY.
   Philippa Dayrell Roosevelt was the daughter of Robert Conygham and Patricia Joan Young Buss of Farnborough, England.
   In 1997, the house was purchased from Roosevelt by Charles B. Wang for approximately $2 million. Taxes on the eight-acre estate in 1997 were approximately $14,000.
   It is currently owned by Eric Best.

rear facade, 2004

Roosevelt, Philip James, Sr. (1892-1941)

Occupation(s):

financier - partner, Roosevelt and Son (investment banking firm);
director, Investors Management Co.;
trustee, Central Hanover Bank and Trust Co.;
director, Continental Insurance Co.

capitalist - director, Chicago, Milwaukee, & St. Paul Railroad;
treasurer and director, Broad Improvement Co.
(real estate holding firm);
director, Continental Reality Investment Co.;
director, Third Avenue Railway Co.

industrialist - director, Kent Coal Co.;
director, Rochester & Pittsburgh Coal & Iron Co.

restaurateur - co-founder, with cousins Theodore, Kermit and Archibald
Roosevelt and their brother-in-law, Dr. Richard Derby,
Brazilian Coffee Houses chain, NYC

Civic Activism:

trustee, Village of Cove Neck;
treasurer, Roosevelt Hospital (founded by James Henry Roosevelt, which
became St. Luke's-Roosevelt Hospital Center), NYC

Marriage(s):

1925-1941 - Jean Schermerhorn Roosevelt (1890-1984)

Listed in *Long Island Society Register, 1929*: yes

Address: off Cove Neck Road, Cove Neck

Acreage / map sources: on 1927 map (owned by W. E. Roosevelt)
62 acres / 1932 and 1946 maps (owned by P. J. Roosevelt)

Name of estate: *Dolonar*

Year of construction: 1928

Style of architecture: Georgian Revival

Architect(s): Hall Pleasants Pennington designed the house
(for P. J. Roosevelt, Sr.)

Landscape architect(s):

House extant: yes

Historical notes:

Philip James Roosevelt, Sr. built the house, originally named *Dolonar,* on land given to him by his father William Emlen Roosevelt.

He was the son of William Emlen and Christine Griffin Kean Roosevelt, who resided at *Yellowbanks*. His brother George Emlen Roosevelt, Sr., who resided at *Gracewood* in Cove Neck, married Julia Morris Addison, the daughter of The Rev. Charles Morris and Mrs. Ada Thayer Addison. and, subsequently, Mildred P. Cobb. His brother John Kean Roosevelt married Elise Annette Weinacht, the daughter of Edward and Helena Elise Hanbold Weinacht of Elizabeth, NJ, and resided in Glen Cove and at *Yellowbanks*. His sister Christine married James Etter Shelley, the son of Charles M. and Kathleen McConnell Shelley of Selma, AL. His sister Lucy, who died in her mid-20s, was unmarried.

Philip James Roosevelt, Sr. drowned when his dinghy capsized in Oyster Bay. His wife found his body on the beach near *Dolonar.*

Jean Schermerhorn Roosevelt was the daughter of John Ellis and Nannie Mitchell Vance Roosevelt, who resided at *Meadow Croft* in Sayville. She was Philip James Roosevelt, Sr.'s second cousin. Her sister Gladys married Fairman Rogers Dick and resided at *Apple Tree Hill* in Old Brookville.

The Roosevelts' son Philip James Roosevelt, Jr. married Barbara Ellen Scott, the daughter of John Lennox Scott of Seattle, WA, and, subsequently, Philippa Dayrell Buss, the daughter of Robert Conygham and Patricia Joan Young Buss of Farnborough, England. Their daughter Philippa married Benjamin E. Jeffries and resided in Boston, MA. Their son John Ellis Roosevelt II married Helen C. Sparrow and resided in Manhattan.

The estate was, subsequently, owned by Charles B. Wang, who remodeled the house.

Roosevelt Hospital, New York City

Roosevelt, Quentin II (1919-1948)

Occupation(s):   capitalist - vice-president, Chinese National Airline Corp.
intelligence agent - member, Central Intelligence Agency*

Marriage(s):   1944-1948 - Frances Blanche Webb (1917-1995)
- artist - book illustrator**
educator - assistant professor, Department of Fine Arts, C. W. Post
College of Long Island University, Brookville
intelligence agent - member, Central Intelligence Agency***
Civic Activism: trustee, Theodore Roosevelt Memorial Association;
trustee, Oyster Bay Historical Society

Listed in *Long Island Society Register, 1929*: no
Address: Cove Neck Road, Cove Neck
Acreage / map sources: not on 1927, 1932, or 1946 maps
Name of estate: *Sakunska*
Year of construction:
Style of architecture:
Architect(s):
Landscape architect(s):
House extant: yes
Historical notes:

    Quentin Roosevelt II, was the son of Theodore and Eleanor Butler Alexander Roosevelt, Jr., who resided at *Old Orchard* in Cove Neck.
    *He participated in hazardous air drops to Nationalist Chinese soldiers and died in a plane crash near Hong Kong.
    **As a courtroom artist, Frances, the daughter of Watt and Anna Wetmore Webb, sketched the Alger Hiss trial for the *New York Journal American*. [*Newsday* September 13, 1995, p. A39.] In 1962, she built an artist studio on the estate.
    ***Peter Collier and David Horowitz state, in their book, that Frances was also working for the CIA in 1948 when Quentin died in a plane crash. [*The Roosevelts: An American Saga* (New York: Simon & Schuster, 1994), p.449.] *[We have not been able to find corroborating support for this statement.]*
    When Frances died in 1995, Charles B. Wang purchased the 3.5-acre estate for $1.2 million.

Roosevelt, Theodore (1831-1878)

Occupation(s):   financier - partner, Roosevelt and Son (investment banking firm)
Civic Activism: member, Allotment Commission, which protected the interest of Union Soldiers;
New York State Commissioner of Public Charities;
trustee, Children's Aid Society;
a founder, Orthopedic Hospital, NYC;
a founder, Metropolitan Museum of Art, NYC;
a founder, Museum of Natural History, NYC

Marriage(s):   1853-1878 - Martha Bulloch (1836-1884)

Listed in *Long Island Society Register, 1929*: no
Address: East Main Street, Oyster Bay Cove
Acreage / map sources: not on 1927, 1932, or 1946 maps
Name of estate: *Tranquility**
Year of construction:
Style of architecture: Greek Revival
Architect(s):
Landscape architect(s):
House extant: no; demolished in mid-1930s
Historical notes:

front facade

    In 1876, Theodore Roosevelt, the father of President Theodore Roosevelt, rented the house from Otis D. Swan. Roosevelt called the estate *Tranquility.*
    He was the son of Cornelius Van Schaack and Margaret Barnhill Roosevelt.
    The house was, subsequently, owned by John Abeel Weekes, who continued to call it *Tranquility.*
    *This older spelling, using only a single l, was used by both Roosevelt and Weekes.

Roosevelt, Theodore (1858-1919)

Occupation(s):

politician - candidate for mayor of New York City, 1886;
president, New York City Police Board, 1895-1897;
Governor of New York State, 1899-1900
statesman - Assistant Secretary of the Navy in the McKinley
administration, 1897-1898;
Vice-President of the United States, 1901;
26th President of the United States, 1901-1909
writer - thirty-nine books, including an autobiography;
numerous articles and letters

Marriage(s):

M/1 - 1880-1884 - Alice Lee (1861-1884)
M/2 - 1886-1919 - Edith Kermit Carow (1861-1948)

Listed in *Long Island Society Register, 1929*: yes
Address: Sagamore Hill Road, Cove Neck
Acreage / map sources: on 1927 map; no acreage given on 1932 map; 86 acres / 1946 map
Name of estate: *Sagamore Hill*
Year of construction: 1884-1885
Style of architecture: Queen Anne/Shingle
Architect(s): Lamb and Rich designed the house (for T. Roosevelt)
Christopher Grant LaFarge designed north trophy room addition,
1905 (for T. Roosevelt)*
Landscape architect(s):
Estate photographs can be found in the Nassau County Museum Collection filed under Oyster Bay/Roosevelt.
House extant: yes
Historical notes:

The house, originally named *Sagamore Hill,* was built by Theodore Roosevelt.
Both the *Long Island Society Register, 1929* and the *Social Register New York, 1948* list Edith K. Carow Roosevelt as residing at *Sagamore Hill* in Cove Neck.
President Theodore Roosevelt was the son of Theodore and Martha Bulloch Roosevelt, who resided at *Tranquility* in Oyster Bay Cove.
Theodore and Alice Lee Roosevelt's daughter Alice married United States Senator Nicholas Longworth and resided in Washington, DC.
Theodore Roosevelt and Edith Kermit Carow Roosevelt's son Theodore Roosevelt, Jr. married Eleanor Butler Alexander and resided at *Old Orchard* in Cove Neck, on property adjacent to that of his parents. Their son Kermit Roosevelt, Sr. married Belle Wyatt Willard and resided at *Mohannes,* also in Cove Neck. Their son Archibald Bulloch Roosevelt, Sr., who resided at *Turkey Lane House* in Cold Spring Harbor, married Grace Stackpole Lockwood. Their daughter Ethel married Dr. Richard Derby and resided at *Old Adam* in Oyster Bay. The Roosevelt's youngest child, Quentin, was killed in World War I. Roosevelt Field in Garden City, which later became Roosevelt Field Shopping Center, was named in memory of Quentin.
The aircraft carrier *USS Theodore Roosevelt* is named in honor of President Roosevelt.
From 1901-1909, the estate served as "Teddy's" summer White House.
The estate is now a national historic park and is on The National Register of Historic Places.
*Christopher Grant LaFarge was the son of the famed stained-glass designer John LaFarge.

front facade, 1994

Roosevelt, Theodore, Jr. (1887-1944)

Occupation(s):	publisher - vice-president, Doubleday, Doran & Co., Garden City (became Doubleday & Co., Inc.)
	writer - *Average Americans,* 1919; *East of the Sun and West of the Moon,* 1926; *All in the Family,* 1929;
	co-authored with Kermit Roosevelt, Sr.:
	Trailing the Giant Panda, 1929; *Rank and File,* 1928
	military - general, Normandy invasion*
	statesman - Governor of Puerto Rico, 1929-1932;
	Assistant Secretary of the Navy in the Harding and Coolidge administrations, 1921-1924;
	Governor General of the Philippine Islands, 1932-1933
	politician - assemblyman, New York State Legislature, 1919-1920;
	unsuccessful Republican candidate for NYS governorship, 1924
	capitalist - chairman of board, American Express;
	restaurateur - a founder, Brazilian Coffee Houses chain, NYC
Civic Activism:	a founder, American Legion, 1919;
	president, National Health Council, 1935;
	chairman, United Council for Civilian Relief in China, 1938-1940;
	chairman, American Bureau for Medical Aid to China, 1940;
	vice-president, Boy Scouts of America;
	trustee, Field Museum of Natural History, Chicago, IL
Marriage(s):	1910-1944 - Eleanor Butler Alexander (1885-1960)
	- Civic Activism: woman's suffrage
	YMCA assistant director for leave areas in France for American troops, 1917-1918;
	worked to establish a living wage for Puerto Rican women, 1929-1931;
	organized first American Women's Committee for China Relief, 1937;
	director, American Red Cross Club in England, 1942**
	active in W.A.C. recruiting during World War II;
	president, Town Hall, Inc., NYC;
	trustee, Hofstra University, Hempstead;
	member, Girl Scout Council of Greater New York

Listed in *Long Island Society Register, 1929*: yes
Address:	Sagamore Hill Road, Cove Neck
Acreage / map sources:	not listed separately on 1927, 1932, or 1946 maps
Name of estate:	*Old Orchard*
Year of construction:	c. 1938
Style of architecture:	Georgian Revival
Architect(s):	William McMillan designed the house (for T. Roosevelt, Jr.)
Landscape architect(s):	
House extant: yes	
Historical notes:	

The house, originally named *Old Orchard*, was built by Theodore Roosevelt, Jr.
[See previous entry for family information.]
    *Theodore Roosevelt, Jr. received every United States military combat decoration including the Congressional Medal of Honor. He died of a heart attack shortly after participating in the Normandy landings during World War II.
    Eleanor Butler Alexander Roosevelt was the daughter of Henry Addison and Grace Green Alexander of NYC.
    **Eleanor was the recipient of the Medal of Freedom for her American Red Cross work during World War II.
    She was known by the Oyster Bay branch of the family as "Eleanor the Good."
    The Roosevelt's daughter Grace married William McMillan, Jr. Their son Theodore Roosevelt III, who served as Secretary of Commerce in the Commonwealth of Pennsylvania, married Alice Mason Babcock. Their son Cornelius Van Schaack Roosevelt II, who remained unmarried, was a member of the Central Intelligence Agency and resided in Washington, DC. Their son Quentin married Frances Blanche Webb and resided at *Sakunska*, also in Cove Neck.
    The estate is now part of a national historic park.

Roosevelt, William Emlen (1857-1930)

Occupation(s):
financier - partner, Roosevelt and Son (investment banking firm);
director, Chemical National Bank;
director, Central Hanover Bank & Trust Co.;
trustee, Union Square Savings Bank;
director, Fidelity and Casualty Co.;
director, Bank of New York & Trust Co.;
capitalist - real estate - president, Broadway Improvement Co.;
chairman of board, All-American Cables Co. (which merged
into International Telephone & Telegraph Co.);
director, International Telephone & Telegraph Co.;
director, Mobile & Ohio Railroad;
director, Third Avenue Railway

Civic Activism:
president and secretary, Roosevelt Hospital (founded by James Henry
Roosevelt, which became St. Luke's–Roosevelt Hospital Center),
NYC;
vice-president, New York Eye and Ear Infirmary, NYC;
trustee, Home for Incurables;
trustee, Burke Relief Foundation

Marriage(s):
1883-1930 - Christine Griffin Kean (1858-1936)
- Civic Activism: chairman, New York Eye and Ear Infirmary Women's
Auxiliary;
board member, Association for the Relief of Respectable
Aged and Indigent Females of the City of New York

Listed in *Long Island Society Register, 1929*: yes
Address: Cove Neck Road, Cove Neck
Acreage / map sources: on 1927 map (owned by W. E. Roosevelt)
62 acres / 1932 and 1946 maps (owned by P. J. Roosevelt)
Name of estate: *Yellowbanks*
Year of construction: 1881
Style of architecture: Shingle
Architect(s): Bruce Price designed the house (for J. A. Roosevelt)
Landscape architect(s):
House extant: yes
Historical notes:

The house, originally named *Yellowbanks*, was built by James Alfred Roosevelt.

The estate was, subsequently, owned by William Emlen Roosevelt, John Kean Roosevelt, and Oliver Russell Grace. All continued to call the estate *Yellowbanks*.

The *Long Island Society Register, 1929* lists William Emlen and Christine G. Kean Roosevelt as residing at *Yellowbanks* in Oyster Bay. The *Social Register, Summer 1932* lists Christine G. Kean Roosevelt as residing at *Yellow Banks* in Oyster Bay [Cove Neck].

William Emlen Roosevelt was the son of James Alfred and Elizabeth Norris Emlen Roosevelt, who also resided at *Yellowbanks*. His sister Leila married Edward Reeve–Merritt and resided at *Elfland* in Cove Neck. Her sister Caroline married William Talman Moore, Jr. and resided at *Puente Vista* on Centre Island.

Christine Griffin Kean Roosevelt was the daughter of John and Lucy Halstead Kean of Elizabeth, NJ.

The Roosevelts' son George Emlen Roosevelt, Sr., who resided at *Gracewood* in Cove Neck, married Julia Morris Addison, the daughter of The Rev. Charles Morris and Mrs. Ada Thayer Addison. and, subsequently, Mildred P. Cobb. Their son Philip James Roosevelt, Sr. married Jean Schermerhorn Roosevelt, the daughter of John Ellis and Nannie Mitchell Vance Roosevelt who resided at *Meadow Croft* in Sayville. Philip and Jean Roosevelt resided at *Dolonar* in Cove Neck. Their son John Kean Roosevelt married Elise Annette Weinacht, the daughter of Edward and Helena Elise Hanbold Weinacht of Elizabeth, NJ, and resided in Glen Cove and at *Yellowbanks*. Their daughter Christine married James Etter Shelley, the son of Charles M. and Kathleen McConnell Shelley of Selma, AL. Their daughter Lucy, who died in her mid-20s, was unmarried.

The house is on The National Register of Historic Places.

Rose, George, Jr. (1900-1934)

Occupation(s):   financier - member, McWilliam, Wainwright and Co.

Marriage(s):   1928-1932 - Jeannette T. Ross

Listed in *Long Island Society Register, 1929:* yes
Address: Lakeville Road and Marcus Avenue, Lake Success
Acreage / map sources: 1927 and 1932 maps illegible
                                        not on 1946 map
Name of estate: *Four Corners*
Year of construction:
Style of architecture:
Architect(s):
Landscape architect(s):
House extant: no
Historical notes:

   The *Long Island Society Register, 1929* lists George and Jeannette Ross Rose, Jr. as residing at Lakeville Road and Marcus Avenue, Great Neck [Lake Success]. The *Social Register, Summer 1932* lists the Roses as residing at *On The Way* in Westbury.
   He was the son of George and Josephine M. Maginnis Rose, Sr., who resided at *Overland House* in Old Westbury and *Overland Farm* in Glen Head. His brother Reginald married Bertha Benkard and resided in Upper Brookville. His sister Josephine married John William Mackay [III] and resided in Lattingtown and at *Happy House* in East Hills.
   Jeannette Ross Rose was the daughter of Edward Field Ross of Clinton, NY. She had previously been married to James P. Vogel of Tuxedo Park, NY.

Rose, George, Sr. (1872-1936)

Occupation(s):

Marriage(s):   Josephine M. Maginnis (d. 1957)

Listed in *Long Island Society Register, 1929*: yes
Address: Store Hill Road (Long Island Expressway North Service Road), Old Westbury
Acreage / map sources: on 1927 map (owned by Gen. Rose)
   not on 1932 or 1946 maps
Name of estate: *Overland House*
Year of construction: c. 1910
Style of architecture: English Neoclassical
Architect(s):   Hoppin and Koen designed the house (for G. Rose, Sr.)
Landscape architect(s):
House extant: no; demolished c. 1950
Historical notes:

   The house, originally named *Overland House,* was built by George Rose, Sr.
   The *Long Island Society Register, 1929* lists George and M. Josephine Maginnis Rose [Sr.] as residing at *Overland House* in Old Westbury.
   George Rose, Sr. died in Paris, France, while vacationing with his wife. He was the son of J. Benson Rose, a founder and first president of Royal Baking Powder Co.
   [See previous entry for additional family information.]
   The estate was subsequently owned by Harold Elster Talbott II, who renamed in *The Pillars.*

Overland House

Rose, George, Sr. (1872-1936)

Occupation(s):

Marriage(s):   Josephine M. Maginnis (d. 1957)

Listed in *Long Island Society Register, 1929*: yes
Address: Greenvale – Glen Cove – Cedar Swamp Road, Glen Head
Acreage / map sources: not on 1927 map; 40 acres / 1932 map; 36 acres / 1946 map
Name of estate: *Overland Farm*
Year of construction:
Style of architecture:
Architect(s):
Landscape architect(s):
House extant: unconfirmed
Historical notes:

 The *Social Register, Summer 1932* lists George and M. Josephine Maginnis Rose [Sr.] as residing at *Overland Farm* in Glen Head. The *Social Register, Summer 1950* lists Josephine M. Maginnis Rose as residing at *Overland Farm* in Glen Head.
 George Rose, Sr. died in Paris, France, while vacationing with his wife. He was the son of J. Benson Rose, a founder and first president of Royal Baking Powder Co.
 Josephine M. Maginnis Rose was the daughter of J. H. Maginnis of New Orleans, LA.
 The Roses' daughter Josephine married John William Mackay III and resided in Lattingtown and at *Happy House* in East Hills. Their son Reginald married Bertha Benkard and resided in Upper Brookville. Their son George Rose, Jr. married Jeannette T. Ross and resided at *Four Corners* in Lake Success and at *On The Way* in Westbury.

Rose, Reginald Perry (1903-1978)

Occupation(s):   financier -   partner, DeCoppet and Doremus (stock brokerage firm)
            capitalist -   theatrical producer

Marriage(s):   1926-1978 - Bertha Benkard (1906-1982)
           - Civic Activism: chairperson, committee that refurnished the principal
                    rooms in President Theodore Roosevelt's home
                    Sagamore Hill;
                  trustee, Henry Francis du Pont Museum;
                  trustee, New York Historical Society;
                  director, Museum of the City of New York

Listed in *Long Island Society Register, 1929*: yes
Address: Mill River Hollow Road, Upper Brookville
Acreage / map sources: not on 1927, 1932, or 1946 maps
Name of estate:
Year of construction: c. 1760
Style of architecture:
Architect(s):
Landscape architect(s):
House extant: unconfirmed
Historical notes:

 The *Social Register New York, 1975* lists Reginald P. and Bertha Benkard Rose as residing on Mill River Road, Oyster Bay [Upper Brookville].
 He was the son of George and Josephine Maginnis Rose, Sr., who resided in both Glen Head at *Overland Farm* and Old Westbury at *Overland House*. His sister Josephine was married to John William Mackay III and resided in Lattingtown and at *Happy House* in East Hills. His brother George Rose, Jr. married Jeannette T. Ross and resided at *Four Corners* in Lake Success and *On The Way* in Westbury.
 Bertha Benkard Rose was the daughter of Henry Horton and Bertha King Benkard, who resided in Garden City and, later, in Muttontown.
 The Roses' son R. Peter Rose also resided on Mill River Hollow Road, Upper Brookville. Their son George H. Rose resided on Bayville Road, Lattingtown.

Rosenberg, Lee (1878-1945)

Occupation(s):   financier - member, New York Stock Exchange;
                                                       member, New York Cotton Exchange;
                                                       member, New Orleans Cotton Exchange

Marriage(s): Pauline *[unable to confirm maiden name]*

Listed in *Long Island Society Register, 1929*: no
Address: East Shore Road, Great Neck
Acreage / map sources: not on 1927 map
9 acres / 1932 map (owned by Rosenberg)
7 acres / 1946 map (owned by Rosenberg)

Name of estate:
Year of construction:
Style of architecture: Victorian*
Architect(s):
Landscape architect(s):
House extant: no
Historical notes:

From 1922 to 1929, Herbert Bayard Swope, Sr. rented the house from Lottie Blair Parker.
*It was a three-story Victorian house with a wrap-around porch.
The house was, subsequently, owned by Rosenberg.

Rossiter, Arthur Wickes, Sr. (1874-1955)

Occupation(s): financier - member, J. W. Davis and Co. (stock brokerage firm)
Civic Activism: president of board, Hospital for Special Surgery, NYC

Marriage(s): M/1 - 1906-1926 - Alice Riggs Colgate (1877-1926)
M/2 - 1931-1953 - Ella Fuller Guthrie

Listed in *Long Island Society Register, 1929*: yes
Address: Crescent Beach Road, Glen Cove
Acreage / map sources: 1927 map illegible
not on 1932 map
7 acres / 1946 map

Name of estate: *Cedarcroft*
Year of construction: c. 1906
Style of architecture: Italian Renaissance
Architect(s): Albro and Lindeberg designed the house (for Rossiter)
Landscape architect(s):
House extant: yes
Historical notes:

The house, originally named *Cedarcroft*, was built by Arthur Wickes Rossiter, Sr.

The *Long Island Society Register, 1929* lists Arthur Wickes Rossiter [Sr.] as residing in Glen Cove, while the *Social Register, Summer 1932* lists Arthur Wickes and Ella F. Guthrie Rossiter [Sr.] as residing at *Cedarcroft* in Glen Cove. The *Social Register New York, 1972* lists only Ella F. Guthrie Rossiter as residing at *Cedarcroft* on Crescent Beach Road, Glen Cove.

Alice Riggs Colgate Rossiter was the daughter of Robert and Henrietta Craig Colgate.

Ella Fuller Guthrie Rossiter was the daughter of William Dameron and Ella Elizabeth Fuller Guthrie, who resided at *Meudon* in Lattingtown. She had previously been married to W. Eugene Kimball and resided in Glen Cove.

Arthur Wickes and Alice Riggs Colgate Rossiter, Sr.'s son Arthur Wickes Rossiter, Jr., who resided in Lloyd Harbor, married Mary Frances Allen, the daughter of Walter Cleveland Allen of Stamford, CT. Their daughter Henrietta married James Van Deventer and, subsequently, J. Dwight A. Francis, the son of Henry A. Francis of Pittsfield, MA.

The estate was, subsequently, owned by Bouvier Beale, Sr.

Rothschild, Baron Eugene de

Occupation(s):   financier - investment banker

Marriage(s):   M/1 - 1925-1946 - Katherine Wolff (1884-1946)
M/2 - 1952 - Jeanne Stuart
- entertainers and associated professions - actress

Listed in *Long Island Society Register, 1929*: no
Address: Duck Pond Road and Wellington Road, Matinecock
Acreage / map sources: not on 1927, 1932, or 1946 maps
Name of estate: *Still House*
Year of construction: c. 1920
Style of architecture: Federal
Architect(s):   Bradley Delehanty designed the house (for Cravath)
Landscape architect(s):   Isabella Pendleton (for Cravath)
House extant: yes
Historical notes:

    The house, originally named *Still House,* was built by Paul Drennan Cravath. Two of his first three houses, *Veraton* [1] and *Veraton* [II], were destroyed by fire in 1908 and 1914 respectively. Cravath built *Veraton* [III] c. 1914. In c. 1920, after selling *Veraton* [III], he built *Still House*. Cravath resided at *Still House* until his death in 1940.
    In 1940, Rothschild purchased *Still House*. The Baron and Baroness, the former Katherine Wolff of Philadelphia, PA, were residing at this address at the time of her death.
    Baroness Jeanne Stuart de Rothschild was the daughter of William John Stuart of London, England.
    During World War II, the Baron allowed patients from St. Albans Naval Hospital in Queens County the use of the house and its lands on weekends.
    The estate was, subsequently, owned by Seton Porter, who continued to call it *Still House*.
    Since 1976, the estate has been owned by Drs. Harold Willids and Shirley R. P. Andersen, Sr. In 1997, the Andersens put the house, still called *Still House,* up for sale. The asking price was $2.5 million; the annual taxes were about $30,000.

Rothschild, Baron Robert de (1880-1946)

Occupation(s):   financier - investment banker
Civic Activism: chairman, Jewish Refugee Committee in France, during World War II

Marriage(s):   Nellie Beer (1891-1949)

Listed in *Long Island Society Register, 1929*: no
Address: Hoffstot Lane, Sands Point
Acreage / map sources: not on 1927, 1932, or 1946 maps
Name of estate: *Belcaro*
Year of construction: c. 1910
Style of architecture: Italian Renaissance
Architect(s):   Mortimer Foster designed the house (for Hoffstot)
Landscape architect(s):
House extant: no; main house demolished in 1950s*
Historical notes:

    The twenty-nine-room house, originally named *Belcaro,* was built by Frank Norton Hoffstot.
    In 1941, the estate was owned by Rothschild, who continued to call it *Belcaro*.
    Baroness Nellie Beer de Rothschild was the daughter of Edmond and Alice Beer.
    During World War II the estate was used as an aircraft warning post.
    *In 1953, the caretaker's house was destroyed by fire.

Roulston, Thomas Henry, Sr. (1874-1949)

Occupation(s):
merchant - president, Thomas Roulston, Inc. (grocery store chain of seven hundred stores in Queens, Brooklyn, Nassau, and Suffolk Counties)

financier - trustee, Dime Savings Bank of Brooklyn (later, Dime Savings Bank of New York; now, The Dime);
trustee, Kings County Trust Co.

Marriage(s):
M/1 - 1902-1920 - Florence Davies (d. 1920)
M/2 - 1939-1949 - Marjorie Hillis (1890-1971)

- writer - *Live Alone and Like It*, 1936*; *Orchids on Your Budget*, 1937*; *Corned Beef and Caviar* (with Bertina Foltz); *Work Ends at Nightfall*, 1938* (poetic portraits); *New York, Fair or No Fair: A Guide for the Woman Vacationist*, 1939; *You Can Start All Over*, 1951*; *Keep Going and Like It*, 1967

journalist - executive editor, *Vogue*, 1932-1936;
editor, *Authors Guild Bulletin*

Listed in *Long Island Society Register, 1929*: yes
Address: Kane's Lane, Huntington Bay
Acreage / map sources: not on 1929 or 1944 maps; on 1931 map
Name of estate: *High Lindens*
Year of construction: c. 1850
Style of architecture: Eclectic Italianate
Architect(s):
Landscape architect(s):
Estate photographs can be found in the Nassau County Museum Collection filed under Huntington/Roulston.
House extant: yes
Historical notes:

Thomas Henry Roulston, Sr. purchased the John Patrick Kane house *Interbaien*.
The house is on the National Register of Historic Paces.
Live Alone and Like It, Orchids on Your Budget, and *Work Ends at Nightfall* deal with the lives of working women. *You Can Start All Over* can best be described as an empowerment how-to for women.

Rousmaniere, James Ayer (b. 1918)

Occupation(s):
financier - non-profit fund-raiser

Marriage(s):
1943 - Jessie Broadus Pierce (b. 1918)

Listed in *Long Island Society Register, 1929*: no
Address: Oyster Bay Cove Road, Oyster Bay Cove
Acreage / map sources: not on 1927 or 1932 maps
11 acres / 1946 map (owned by M. A. Rousmaniere)
Name of estate: *Bobbingsworth*
Year of construction:
Style of architecture: Long Island Farmhouse (Fleet family homestead)
Architect(s):
Landscape architect(s):
House extant: yes
Historical notes:

The estate, called *Bobbingsworth*, was owned by John E. Rousmaniere.
It was, subsequently, owned by his son James Ayer Rousmaniere, who continued to call it *Bobbingsworth*.
The *Social Register, Summer 1955* lists James A. and Jessie B. Pierce Rousmaniere as residing at *Bobbingsworth* in Oyster Bay [Oyster Bay Cove].
James Ayer Rousmaniere's sister Frances married Richard S. Storrs and resides in Cove Neck. His sister Mary married Albert H. Gordon and resided at *Halcyon* on Fishers Island.

Rousmaniere, John E. (1877-1944)

Occupation(s):   financier -   director, Grace National Bank
                                          attorney -   member, Ropes, Gray and Gorham, Boston, MA
                                          politician -   member, Massachusetts Legislature for two years
                                          industrialist -   president, Cabot Manufacturing Co. (textile manufacturer);
                                                                            director, American Woolen Co.;
                                                                            director, Tubize Rayon Co.;
                                                                            director, Cosmos Imperial Mills

Civic Activism: trustee, Village of Oyster Bay Cove

Marriage(s):   1910-1944 - Mary Farwell Ayer (1878-1954)

Listed in *Long Island Society Register, 1929*: no
Address: Oyster Bay Cove Road, Oyster Bay Cove
Acreage / map sources: not on 1927 or 1932 maps
                                            11 acres / 1946 map (owned by M. A. Rousmaniere)
Name of estate: *Bobbingsworth*
Year of construction:
Style of architecture: Long Island Farmhouse (Fleet family homestead)
Architect(s):
Landscape architect(s):
House extant: yes
Historical notes:

    Mrs. Rousmaniere's brother James resided at *Shadowland* in Glen Cove.

    The Rousmanieres' daughter Frances married Richard S. Storrs and resides in Cove Neck. Their daughter Mary married Albert H. Gordon and resided at *Halcyon* on Fisher's Island.

    The house was, subsequently, owned by the Rousmanieres' son James, who continued to call it *Bobbingsworth*.

Rouss, Peter Winchester (d. 1932)

Occupation(s):   merchant -   president, Charles Broadway Rouss, Inc.;
                                                      president, Acorn Stores, Inc.

Marriage(s):   Ellen Swan

Listed in *Long Island Society Register, 1929*: yes
Address: Bayville Avenue, Bayville
Acreage / map sources: on 1927 map
                                            not on 1932 or 1946 maps
Name of estate: *Callender House*
Year of construction: c. 1906
Style of architecture: Classical Revival
Architect(s):
Landscape architect(s):
Estate photographs can be found in the Nassau County
    Museum Collection filed under Bayville/Rouss.
House extant: yes
Historical notes:

front facade, c. 1920

    The house, originally named *Callender House*, was built by Peter Winchester Rouss.

    He was the son of Charles Baltzell Rouss.

    The Rouss' daughter Margaret married George J. Patterson and also resided in Bayville.

    In 1932, Robert Livingston Clarkson purchased the house and ten acres and continued to call it *Callender House*.

    In about 1958, the house was sold to the Medical Center Realty Corporation for $250,000.

    In 1961, after extensive changes, it became the Oyster Bay Hospital of Bayville.

    In 1972, it was purchased by a group of plastic surgeons who renamed it *The Renaissance* and used it as a health spa and alcoholic convalescent home for the wealthy.

    In 1980, it was purchased by the United Cerebral Palsy Association of Nassau County for use as an intermediate care facility

    It is now Jones Manor on the Sound, a nursing facility.

Rubel, Samuel

Occupation(s):   capitalist - Ebling Brewery;
                                        president, Rubel Corp. (coal deliverer; ice manufacturer and deliverer)

Marriage(s):   Dora Nachmowitz
                                         - Civic Activism: president, Brooklyn Women's Hospital

Listed in *Long Island Society Register, 1929*: no
Address: Willis Avenue, Roslyn
Acreage / map sources: not on 1927 or 1932 maps; 64 acres / 1946 map (owned by Rubel Corp.)
Name of estate:
Year of construction: c. 1900
Style of architecture: Colonial Revival
Architect(s):   Grosvenor Atterbury designed the house (for Oakman)
Landscape architect(s):
House extant: no; demolished c. 1946*
Historical notes:

   The thirty-two-room house, originally named *Oakdene,* was built by Walter George Oakman, Sr.
   In 1912, Henry D. Walbridge purchased the estate and called it *Waldene.*
   During a court case in which Rubel was accused of attempting to create a monopoly in Brooklyn's ice trade, he was fined for contempt of court and sentenced to ten days in jail. [*The New York Times* March 29, 1934, p. 5.]
   *The house was destroyed by fire. The estate's land was subdivided by Rubel for a housing development.

Rumbough, Stanley Maddox, Jr. (b. 1920)

Occupation(s):   industrialist - president, White Metal Manufacturing Co.;
                                        president, Metal Container Corp.;
                                        co-founder, Trinidad Flour Mills;
                                        co-founder and director, Jamaica Flour Mills
                                        capitalist - co-founder and chairman of board, Electric Engineering Ltd.
                                        financier - director, ABT Family of Funds, Inc.
                                        statesman - assistant to Secretary of Commerce in the Eisenhower administration.;
                                        White House assistant in the Eisenhower administration

Marriage(s):   M/1 - 1946-1966 - Nedenia M. Hutton (aka Dina Merrill) (b. 1926)
                                         - financier - director, E. F. Hutton and Co. (investment banking firm)
                                        entertainers and associated professions - actress
                                        industrialist - president, Amaranthe (cosmetic manufacturer)
                                        M/2 - 1967-1990 - Margaretha Wagstrom
                                         - free-lance portrait and commercial photographer
                                        M/3 - 1990 - Janna Herlow

Listed in *Long Island Society Register, 1929*: no
Address: Piping Rock Road, Old Brookville
Acreage / map sources: not on 1927, 1932, or 1946 maps
Name of estate:
Year of construction:
Style of architecture:
Architect(s):   Delano and Aldrich designed alterations (for Rumbough)
Landscape architect(s):
House extant: unconfirmed
Historical notes:

   Stanley Maddox Rumbough, Jr. was the son of Stanley and Elizabeth J. Colgate Rumbough, Sr., who resided at *Elston Oaks* in Lloyd Harbor. His sister Elizabeth married Duncan Van Norden and resided in Manhattan.
   Nedenia Hutton Rumbough was the daughter of Edward Francis and Marjorie Merriweather Post Hutton who resided at *Hillwood* in Brookville. She subsequently married the actor Cliff Robertson.
   Stanley Maddox and Nedenia M. Hutton Rumbough, Jr.'s twenty-three-year-old son David drowned in a boating mishap. Their daughter Nedenia married Charles Stiffer Craig of Birmingham, MI.
   Margaretha Wagstrom Rumbough was the daughter of Nils Erik Wagstrom of Ornskoldsvik, Sweden.

Rumsey, Charles Cary, Sr. (1879-1922)

Occupation(s):   artist - sculptor*

Marriage(s):   1910-1922 - Mary Harriman (1881-1934)
                                       - publisher - chain of Southern newspapers;
                                               co-founder, *Today*
                             Civic Activism: trustee, Barnard College;
                                              donated her husband's 22-foot-high bronze statue
                                               of Francisco Pizarro to be placed in front of the
                                               Government Palace in the *Plaza de Armas* in
                                               Lima, Peru;
                                  **

Listed in *Long Island Society Register, 1929*: yes
Address: Wheatley Road, Brookville
Acreage / map sources: on 1927 map; not on 1932 or 1946 maps
Name of estate:
Year of construction: c. 1910
Style of architecture: Dutch Colonial
Architect(s):   F. Burrall Hoffman, Jr. designed the house and the
                                   addition of dining room, second story sleeping
                                   porch, and southwest terraces and porches
                                   (for C. C. Rumsey, Sr.)
                                 Peabody, Wilson and Brown designed c. 1930 alterations
                                 (for Cutting)
Builder: E. W. Howell Co.
Landscape architect(s):   Morris and Rotch designed the terraced garden
                                 (for C. C. Rumsey, Sr.)

House extant: yes
Historical notes:

The house was built by Charles Cary Rumsey, Sr.

He was the son of Lawrence Dana and Jennie Cary Rumsey of Buffalo, NY.

Charles Rumsey, who was on his way home from polo practice was killed at the intersection of Jericho Turnpike and Tulip Avenue in Floral Park when the convertible automobile in which he was a passenger over-turned. [*The New York Times* September 22, 1922, pp. 1, 2.]

*His commissions included the hunt frieze on the Manhattan Bridge and the bronze statue of a bull which is located on Route 25A in Smithtown.

Both the *Long Island Society Register, 1929* and the *Social Register, Summer 1932* list Mary Harriman Rumsey as residing in Sands Point.

She was the daughter of Edward Henry and Mary Williamson Averell Harriman. Her brother William Averell Harriman had residences in Old Westbury and Sands Point.

**Mary Harriman Rumsey was a spokeswoman for consumer interests during the early days of the New Deal. In June 1933, Franklin Delano Roosevelt appointed her chairperson of the Consumers Advisory Board of the National Recovery Association. She was a founder of the Junior League for the promotion of settlement movements. Later renamed the Junior League of New York, it was from this beginning that the Junior League movement developed. She helped organize the Eastern Livestock Cooperative Marketing Association. During World War I, she supported the organizing of Community Councils. In 1929, she took part in the work of New York City's Emergency Exchange Association, a Depression-era barter system.

A memorial to Mary Harriman Rumsey, in New York City's Central Park, was designed by Gertrude Vanderbilt Whitney.

The Rumseys' son Charles Cary Rumsey, Jr. married Mary Meloney, a clerk in the Oyster Bay Town Hall. [*The New York Times* October 5, 1934, p. 27.] He later married Martha Zec, the daughter of Dr. Branko Zec of Beverly Hills, CA.

The estate was, subsequently, owned by Dr. Fulton Cutting.

rear facade

Rumsey, Mary Harriman (1881-1934)

Occupation(s):   publisher - chain of Southern newspapers;
                                                  co-founder, *Today*

Civic Activism: trustee, Barnard College;
                                                  donated her husband's 22-food-high bronze statue of Francisco Pizarro to be
                                                        placed in front of the Government Palace in the *Plaza de Armas* in Lima, Peru

Marriage(s):   1910-1922 - Charles Cary Rumsey, Sr. (1879-1922)
                                               - artist - sculptor

Listed in *Long Island Society Register, 1929*: yes
Address: Middle Neck Road, Sands Point
Acreage / map sources: on 1927 map; 5 acres / 1932 and 1946 maps
Name of estate:
Year of construction: c. 1929
Style of architecture: French Chateau
Architect(s):   McKim, Mead and White designed the house (for M. H. Rumsey)
Landscape architect(s):
Estate photographs can be found in the Nassau County Museum Collection filed under Sands Point/Rumsey.
House extant: yes
Historical notes:

    The house was built by Mary Harriman Rumsey on the property of the R. W. Thomas, Sr. estate.
    Both the *Long Island Society Register, 1929* and the *Social Register, Summer 1932* list Mary Harriman Rumsey as residing in Sands Point.
    Rumsey was forced to sell the estate due to the financial losses of her newspapers. [Rudy Abramson, *Spanning the Century: The Life of W. Averell Harriman, 1891-1986* (New York: William Morrow & Co., Inc., 1992), pp. 245-247.]
    [See previous entry for additional family information.]

front facade, 2004

Runyon, Clarkson, Jr. (1874-1945)

Occupation(s):   financier - partner, Carlisle, Mellick and Co. (stock brokerage firm)

Marriage(s):   1903-1945 - Jane Peterson Allen

Listed in *Long Island Society Register, 1929*: yes
Address: Duck Pond Road, Glen Cove
Acreage / map sources: not on 1927, 1932, or 1946 maps
Name of estate: *The Farm House*
Year of construction: 1917
Style of architecture: Eclectic Jacobean
Architect(s):   Mott B. Schmidt designed the house (for Runyon)
Landscape architect(s):   Olmstead, 1919 (for Runyon)
House extant: yes
Historical notes:

    The house, originally named *The Farm House,* was built by Clarkson Runyon, Jr.
    The *Long Island Society Register, 1929* lists Clarkson and Jane P. Allen Runyon as residing on Duck Pond Road, Glen Cove.
    He was the son of Clarkson and Laura Philipp Runyon, Sr. of New Brunswick, NJ.
    The Runyons' son Dr. Laurance Runyon resided in New Brunswick, NJ.

Rusch, Henry Arthur, Sr. (1869-1938)

Occupation(s):	financier - partner, Rusch and Co.
Marriage(s):	1904-1938 - Eda Florence Dolliver (1879-1976)

Listed in *Long Island Society Register, 1929*: yes
Address: Centre Island Road, Centre Island
Acreage / map sources: on 1927 map (owned by H. A. Rusch)
    15 acres / 1932 map (owned by H. A. Rusch)
    16 acres / 1946 map (owned by F. D. Rusch)
Name of estate: *June Acres*
Year of construction: c. 1908
Style of architecture: Spanish Renaissance
Architect(s):   J. Clinton Mackenzie designed the house (for Rusch)
Landscape architect(s):
House extant: yes
Historical notes:

    The house, originally named *June Acres,* was built by Henry Arthur Rusch, Sr.
    The *Long Island Society Register, 1929* lists Henry A. and Florence Dolliver Rusch [Sr.] as residing on Centre Island. The *Social Register, Summer 1937* lists the name of their estate as *June Acres*. The *Social Register, Summer 1975* lists Eda Florence Dolliver Rusch as continuing to reside at *June Acres.*
    Born in Long Branch, NJ, Arthur Rusch, Sr. was the son of Adolph and Cecilie Daeniker Rusch.
    Eda Florence Dolliver Rusch was residing at the estate at the time of her death.

Russell, Faris R. (1883-1968)

Occupation(s):	financier - vice-president, National Bank of Commerce; partner, White, Weld and Co. (investment banking firm) industrialist - chairman of board and president, Ward Baking Co.
Civic Activism:	mayor, Village of Mill Neck
Marriage(s):	1909-1954 - Mary Clayton Martin (1889-1954)

Listed in *Long Island Society Register, 1929*: yes
Address: Frost Mill Road, Mill Neck
Acreage / map sources: on 1927 map (owned by F. R. Russell)
    no acreage given on 1932 map (owned by Russell)
    8 acres / 1946 map (name misspelled as R. Clayton)
Name of estate: *Clayton*
Year of construction: 1921
Style of architecture: Eclectic French Farmhouse
Architect(s):
Landscape architect(s):
House extant: yes
Historical notes:

    The eleven-room, 3,000-square-foot house, originally named *Clayton,* was built by Faris R. Russell.
    The *Long Island Society Register, 1929* and the *Social Register, Summer 1937* list Faris R. and Mary C. Martin Russell as residing at *Clayton* in Mill Neck, while the *Social Register, Summer 1950* lists the Russells as residing at *Hameau* in Mill Neck. The *Social Register New York, 1967* lists only Faris R. Russell, then residing on Weir Lane, Locust Valley [Lattingtown].
    He was the son of The Rev. George Alexander and Mrs. Felicia Putnam Russell.
    Purportedly modeled after *L'Hameau,* a playhouse in Versailles, the house was extensively remodeled by subsequent owners. It is now situated on one acre across from a bird sanctuary.
    The house was for sale in 1999. The asking price was $649,000; the annual taxes were $4,200.

Rutherfurd, John M. L. (1888-1971)

Occupation(s):   capitalist -   real estate - active in development of Miami Beach, FL
Civic Activism: member, Bureau of Aeronautics during World War II*

Marriage(s):   M/1 - Wilfreda Mortimer
                                            M/2 - Florence Crozer
                                            M/3 - Katherine Chamber Herring

Listed in *Long Island Society Register, 1929*: yes
Address: Sands Point Road, Sands Point
Acreage / map sources: on 1927 map
                                not on 1932 or 1946 maps

Name of estate:
Year of construction:
Style of architecture:
Architect(s):
Landscape architect(s):
House extant: unconfirmed
Historical notes:

    The *Long Island Society Register, 1929* lists John M. L. and Florence Crozer Rutherfurd as residing on Sands Point Road, Port Washington [Sands Point].
    In 1938, Rutherfurd beat his own world speedboat record.
    *He was instrumental in establishing the Navy's war-time pre-flight training programs in colleges during World War II.
    Katherine Chamber Herring Rutherfurd was the daughter of Senator Clyde Herring of Iowa.
    Wilfreda Mortimer Rutherfurd was the daughter of Richard Mortimer of Tuxedo, NY.
    John M. L. and Wilfreda Mortimer Rutherfurd's son Jay was Assistant Chief of Protocol for the United States State Department.
    John M. L. and Florence Crozer Rutherfurd's son Edward C. married Patricia A. O'Shields.

Ryan, Byford (d. 1924)

Occupation(s):   entertainers and associated professions -   opera singer*

Marriage(s):   Marjorie S. Langley (1885-1973)
                                   - attorney
                                    educator -   instructor of Braille, Hunter College, NYC

Listed in *Long Island Society Register, 1929*: yes
Address: Locust Valley – Bayville Road, Lattingtown
Acreage / map sources: on 1927 map (owned by Mrs. Byford Ryan)
                                no acreage given on 1932 map (name misspelled as Mrs. Buford Bryan)
                                8 acres / 1946 map (owned by Ryan)

Name of estate:
Year of construction:
Style of architecture:
Architect(s):
Landscape architect(s):
House extant: unconfirmed
Historical notes:

    The *Long Island Society Register, 1929* and the *Social Register, Summer 1955* list Marjorie S. Langley Ryan as residing in Locust Valley [Lattingtown]. The *Social Register New York, 1956* lists her as residing at 2 East 70th Street, NYC, while the *Social Register New York, 1972* lists Mrs. Ryan's address as 160 Central Park South, NYC.
    *Byford Ryan was the leading tenor at the Komische Opera, Berlin, Germany.
    Marjorie S. Langley Ryan was the first woman to be licensed as a harbor pilot in New York Harbor. [*The New York Times* March 3, 1973, p. 34.]

Ryan, John Carlos (1899-1956)

Occupation(s):   capitalist - vice-president and assistant to general
manager, Montana Power Co.

Marriage(s):   1924 - Marjorie Close

Listed in *Long Island Society Register, 1929*: no
Address: Searingtown Road and Long Island Expressway, Roslyn Heights
Acreage / map sources: not listed separately on 1927, 1932, or 1946 maps
Name of estate:
Year of construction: c. 1926
Style of architecture: Tudor
Architect(s):   Chandler Stearns designed the house (for J. D. Ryan)
Landscape architect(s):   Noel Chamberlain prepared extensive landscape designs
                                    (for J. D. Ryan)

House extant: yes
Historical notes:

    John Dennis Ryan built the house for his son John Carlos Ryan on property adjacent to his own estate. After a heated dispute with his father, John Carlos Ryan refused to reside in the house and, indeed, never did.
    Marjorie Close Ryan was the daughter of James A. Close of Hancock, MI.
    The estate was. subsequently, owned by Grover A. Whalen, Sr.
    The house is now the clubhouse for the Renaissance Country Club.

Ryan, John Dennis (1864-1933)

Occupation(s):   industrialist - president and chairman, Anaconda Copper Mining Co.;
                                     managing director, Amalgamated Copper Co.;
                                     president and chairman, Chile Copper Co.;
                                     president, United Metals Selling Co.
                          capitalist -   president, Montana Power Co.
                          financier -   director, National City Bank of New York
                          statesman - second assistant to Secretary of War and director of air
                                     service in the Wilson administration
Civic Activism: director, aircraft production during World War I;
                          chairman, Aircraft Board during World War I;
                          director, air service during World War I;
                          member, War Council during World War I;
                          member, Central Committee of American Red Cross

Marriage(s):   1896 - Nettie M. Gardner

Listed in *Long Island Society Register, 1929*: yes
Address: Searingtown Road, North Hills
Acreage / map sources: on 1927 map; 150 acres / 1932 map; 145 acres / 1946 map
Name of estate: *Derrymore*
Year of construction: c. 1902-1903
Style of architecture: Georgian Revival
Architect(s):   McKim, Mead and White designed the house, stables,
                                     and outbuildings (for Canfield)
Landscape architect(s):   Olmsted, 1904-1906 (for Canfield)
Estate photographs can be found in the Nassau County Museum Collection filed under Roslyn/Ryan.
House extant: no; demolished c. 1940
Historical notes:

    The house, originally named *Cassleigh,* was built by Augustus Cass Canfield, who died in 1904.
    The widowed Josephine Houghteling Canfield married Frank Gray Griswold in 1907 and continue to reside on the estate until 1915.
    The estate was, subsequently, owned by John Dennis Ryan, who called it *Derrymore.*
    Ryan's father John C. Ryan was the discoverer of the Baltic copper field in Michigan and manager of the famous Hecla mine.

Ryle, Arthur, Sr. (1865-1934)

Occupation(s):	industrialist - president, Sauquoit Silk Manufacturing Co.
	financier - a founder, Paterson National Bank, Paterson, NJ
Marriage(s):	Caroline E. Fisher (d. 1952)

Listed in *Long Island Society Register, 1929*: yes
Address: Piping Rock Road, Matinecock
Acreage / map sources: on 1927 map; no acreage given on 1932 map; 13 acres / 1946 map
Name of estate: *Whileaway*
Year of construction:
Style of architecture:
Architect(s):
Landscape architect(s):
House extant: unconfirmed
Historical notes:

    The *Long Island Society Register, 1929* lists Arthur and Caroline E. Fisher Ryle [Sr.] as residing at *Whileaway* in Locust Valley [Lattingtown].
    He was the son of William and Mary E. Danforth Ryle of Paterson, NJ.
    At the time of her death, Caroline E. Fisher Ryle was residing at 101 East 72nd Street, NYC.
    The Ryles' son Arthur [Jr.] married Jane O. Fosdick, whose parents Clark and Lena H. Orne Fosdick resided in Woodmere. Jane O. Fosdick Ryle's grandfather Charles A. Childs resided in NYC and at *The Hedges* in Newport. RI.

Sage, Henry William, II (1872-1938)

Occupation(s):	industrialist - vice-president, Sage Land & Improvement Co
	(lumbering firm)
Civic Activism:	trustee, American Museum of Natural History, NYC*;
	served with American Red Cross during World War I;
	trustee, Village of Brookville;
	director, New York Society for Prevention of Cruelty to Children
Marriage(s):	1899-1938 - Marjorie Lowrie

Listed in *Long Island Society Register, 1929*: yes
Address: Cedar Swamp Road, Brookville
Acreage / map sources: on 1927 map; 80 acres / 1932 map; not on 1946 map
Name of estate:
Year of construction: c. 1911
Style of architecture: Tudor
Architect(s):   John Russell Pope designed the house (for V. G. F. Vanderbilt)
Landscape architect(s):   DuChene (for V. G. F. Vanderbilt)
House extant: no
Historical notes:

    The house was built by Virginia Graham Fair Vanderbilt.
    The estate was owned by Sage and, subsequently by Edouard LeRoux, who called it *Cottage Normandy*.
    The *Long Island Society Register, 1929* lists Henry W. and Marjorie Lowrie Sage [II] as residing on Cedar Swamp Road, Glen Cove [Brookville]. The *Social Register, 1937* lists the Sages as residing in Jericho. The Social Register *New York, 1948* lists Marjorie Lowrie Sage's residence as Main Street, Farmington, CT, while the Social Register *New York, 1959* lists Mrs. Sage as continuing to reside in Farmington, CT.
    Henry William Sage II was the son of William Henry and Jane Curtin Sage, Sr.
    The Sages' daughter Marjorie married W. Allston Flagg, Sr. and resided in Old Westbury. Their son Henry William Sage III married Eleanor Purviance. Their son DeWitt Sage married Betty Young Wickes, the daughter of Forman Wickes who resided at *Wickcliffe* in Brooklandville, MD.
    *The Sages donated their collection of East African Kidong Valley birds to the museum.

Saltzman, Arnold Asa (b. 1916)

Occupation(s):   industrialist - director, Dorma Manufacturing Corp.;
                                         chairman of board, Windsor Oil and Gas;
                                         president, Premier Knitting Co., Inc.;
                                         director, Seagrave Leather Corp.
                         capitalist - real estate - director, Dorving Realty Corp.;
                                         director, Newgate, Inc.;
                                         director, Premier Gallerie, Inc.;
                                         president and chairman of board, Vista Resources, Inc.
                         diplomat* - United States Ambassador to Czechoslovakia;
                                         United States Ambassador to Austria;
                                         United States Ambassador to Soviet Union;
                                         United States Ambassador to South America;
                                         United States Ambassador to Central America;
                                         chairman, National Committee on American Foreign Policy
                         writer - *National Growth and Development;*
                                         co-author, *Bending With the Winds: Kurt Walheim and the United Nations*

Civic Activism: advisor to Sargeant Shriver for Peace Corps;
                         executive director, Hope for Youth;
                         president, Coalition of Directors of Residential Treatment Alternatives for Youth;
                         vice-president of board, North Shore University Hospital, Manhasset;
                         vice-president of board, Maimonides Hospital, NYC;
                         trustee, Columbia University, NYC;
                         trustee, Hofstra University, Hempstead;
                         president, Nassau County Museum of Art, Roslyn Harbor;
                         member, acquisitions committee, Museum of Modern Art, NYC;
                         trustee, Baltimore Museum of Art, Baltimore, MD

Marriage(s):   1942 - Joan Roth
                           - Civic Activism: founder, Community Advocates, Inc. (non-profit agency
                                             for equal access for quality health and mental care
                                             for all citizens);
                                         president, Guide Dog Foundation of Smithtown;
                                         president, North Shore Child and Family Guidance
                                             Association, Roslyn Heights;
                                         vice-chairman, Long Island Community Foundation;

Listed in *Long Island Society Register, 1929:* no
Address: Shephard's Lane, Sands Point
Acreage / map sources: not on 1927, 1932, or 1946 maps
Name of estate:
Year of construction: 18th century
Style of architecture: Colonial
Architect(s):
Landscape architect(s):
House extant: no**
Historical notes:

   The house was built by Stephen Mott (1726-1813) on 225 acres which he had inherited from his father Adam Mott II. The house was, subsequently, inherited by various members of the Mott family until it was sold to William Lippincott. [Mary Feeney Vahey, *A Hidden History: Slavery, Abolition, and the Underground Railroad in Cow Neck and on Long Island* (Port Washington, NY: Cow Neck Peninsula Historical Society, 1998), p. 31.]
   The house was later owned by Max Lincoln Schuster, who called it *Cow Neck Farm.*
   In the 1980s, Schuster sold the property to Saltzman, who presently owns it.
   *Saltzman served as an United States ambassador in five administrations including those of Presidents Kennedy and Johnson. He received a Presidential commendation for his work on the International Nuclear Non-Proliferation Treaty.
   In 1993 Saltzman pleaded guilty to mail fraud and to a false claim that the Irving Tanning Company of Heartland, ME, had sustained a $610,000 loss. Saltzman's connection to the company was not readily discernible. [*The New York Times* September 4, 1993, p. 24.]
   **The house was destroyed by fire in 1980. The barn remains and has been converted into a residence.
   A cave on the estate may have been a stop on the "underground railroad." [Vahey, p. 31.]

Salvage, Sir Samuel Agar (1876-1946)

Occupation(s):	industrialist - chairman of the board, American Viscose Corp.*
Civic Activism:	a founder and president, British War Relief Society during World War II;
	trustee, St. Luke's Hospital (which became St. Luke's–Roosevelt Hospital Center), NYC;
	director, Seamen's Church Institute, NYC
Marriage(s):	1908-1946 - Lady Mary Katharine Richmond (d. 1964)
	- Civic Activism: a founder, North Shore Community Association; board member, Glen Cove Community Hospital; trustee, Village of Old Brookville

Listed in *Long Island Society Register, 1929*: yes

Address:	Cedar Swamp Road, Old Brookville
Acreage / map sources:	on 1927 map
	no acreage given on 1932 map
	75 acres / 1946 map
Name of estate:	*Rynwood*
Year of construction:	c. 1927
Style of architecture:	Elizabethan
Architect(s):	Roger Harrington Bullard designed the house (for Salvage)
Landscape architect(s):	Ellen Biddle Shipman the designed the courtyard service courtyard, terrace, three separate formal gardens, swimming pool, slated-roof dove-cote, tea house, tennis court, and several acres of surrounding fields, 1926 (for Salvage)**

Estate photographs can be found in the Nassau County Museum Collection filed under Glen Head/Salvage.

House extant: yes

Historical notes:

The house, originally named *Rynwood*, was built by Sir Samuel Agar Salvage who resided at the estate until his death.

The *Long Island Society Register, 1929* lists Samuel A. and M. Katharine Richmond Salvage as residing in Glen Head [Old Brookville].

*He was known as the "Father of the Rayon Industry in the United States." [*The New York Times* July 11, 1946, p. 23.]

Mary Katharine Richmond Salvage's brother L. Martin Richmond resided at *Sunninghall* in Old Brookville.

The Salvages' daughters married brothers; Katharine married Frank Lyon Polk II and Margaret married James Potter Polk, Sr. Both of the Salvages' sons-in-law were the sons of Frank Lyon and Elizabeth Sturgis Potter Polk, Sr. of Muttontown. Margaret, subsequently, married Charles Champe Taliaferro III and resided in Oyster Bay Cove, and, later, in Lattingtown. Katharine subsequently married John C. Wilmerding of Old Westbury.

In 1946, the estate was sold to Margaret Emerson, heiress to the Bromo–Seltzer fortune, who had changed her name back to Emerson, her maiden name, after several marriages.

In 1960, Frederick William Irving Lundy purchased the estate. He sold it in 1977.

In 1980, Banfi Vintners purchased the estate and restored it. The estate became their international headquarters.

**Banfi Vintners replaced the swimming pool with a reflecting pool because of a village ordinance requiring a safety fence around a swimming pool.

Emerson, Lundy, and Banfi Vintners continued to call the estate *Rynwood*.

side facade, 1992

*Sir Samuel Agar Salvage's
garden at Rynwood, 1992*

Samuels, John Stockwell, III (b. 1933)

Occupation(s):   industrialist - chairman of board, Carbomin International, Inc.
                                                attorney
                                                financier - chairman of board, Exchange Bank of Chicago
Civic Activism: chairman of board, City Center Music and Drama, NYC;
                                                  chairman of board, New York City Ballet;
                                                chairman of board, New York City Opera;
                                                director, Lincoln Center for the Performing Arts, NYC

Marriage(s):   1958 - Ellen Richards

Listed in *Long Island Society Register, 1929*: no
Address: Salutation Road, West Island, Glen Cove
Acreage / map sources: not on 1927, 1932, or 1946 maps
Name of estate: *Salutation*
Year of construction: 1929
Style of architecture: English Manor House
Architect(s):   Roger Harrington Bullard designed the house (for J. S. Morgan)
Landscape architect(s):   Olmsted, 1875 (for Dana)
                                                    [This was the earliest Olmsted commission in the North Shore estate area.]

House extant: yes
Historical notes:

    The former Charles Anderson Dana estate, *The Wings,* was owned by William Lamon Harkness, who incorporated part of the Dana house into his own house.

    Junius Spencer Morgan purchased the estate and in 1929 remodeled the house leaving only the servants wing of the Dana house. The former Dana/Harkness house became a guest house on the Morgan estate. Morgan built his own house and renamed the estate *Salutation.*

    In 1974, the estate was sold by the Morgans to Samuels.

    Samuels also owned the former Henry F. du Pont estate *Chestertown House*, in Southampton, which was subsequently purchased by Barry Trupin in 1979 for $700,000.

    Samuels was accused of alleged criminal fraud in an oil venture and imprisoned in a Bahrainian jail. After his release, he returned to the United States. [Steven Gaines, *Philistines at the Hedgerow: Passion and Property in the Hamptons* (Boston: Little, Brown & Co., 1998), p. 238.]

    In 1993, the house and 21.46 acres were for sale by order of the United States Bankruptcy Court for the Eastern District of New York. The minimum asking bid was $5.7 million.

Sanderson, Henry (1868-1934)

Occupation(s):   capitalist -   president, Morris Electrical Light Co.;
                                                     president, New York Transportation Co.;
                                                     president, Fifth Avenue Stage Co.*
                            financier -   partner, Sanderson and Brown (investment banking firm);
                                                     president, Union Trust Co.

Civic Activism: advisor to American Relief Association, 1919

Marriage(s):   M/1 - Beatrice Walter (d. 1921)
                                       M/2 - 1914 - Elizabeth Fairchild
                                       M/3 - 1930-1934 - Helen Rice

Listed in *Long Island Society Register, 1929*: no
Address: Planting Fields Road, Upper Brookville
Acreage / map sources: on 1927 map; not on 1932 or 1946 maps
Name of estate: *La Selva*
Year of construction: c. 1915-1916
Style of architecture: Mediterranean Villa
Architect(s):   Hunt and Hunt designed the
                                        house (for Sanderson)
Landscape architect(s):   Olmsted, 1925 (for Sanderson)

                                      Olmsted designed the swimming
                                      pool, 1928 (for Wheeler)
Estate photographs can be found in the Nassau County Museum
   Collection filed under Oyster Bay/Sanderson.
House extant: yes
Historical notes:

La Selva, 2004

    The house, originally named *La Selva,* was built by Henry Sanderson.
    He was the son of Edward Patterson and Elisa Crassous Sanderson of Titusville, PA.
    *The Fifth Avenue Stage Company installed the first mechanically operated stage on Manhattan's Fifth Avenue.
    Elizabeth Fairchild Sanderson was the daughter of Louis Howes Fairchild of New Orleans, LA. She had previously been married to _____ Howard.
    Helen Rice Sanderson was the daughter of J. Warren Rice of New Brunswick, NJ. She had previously been married to Dr. Robert Watts, Jr. and Townsend Morgan.
    Henry and Beatrice Walter Sanderson's son James married Dorothy Dickinson, the daughter of Albert G. Dickinson of Grand Rapids, MI.
    In 1928, the estate was sold to Frederick Seymour Wheeler, who called it *Delwood*. When Mrs. Wheeler died, she willed it to the Community Hospital of Glen Cove.
    In 1963, the estate was owned by St. Francis Center and is now a monastery.

Sands, Miss Anna (d. 1932)

Marriage(s):   unmarried

Listed in *Long Island Society Register, 1929*: yes
Address: Wolver Hollow Road, Upper Brookville
Acreage / map sources: on 1927 map; not on 1932 or 1946 maps
Name of estate:
Year of construction:
Style of architecture:
Architect(s):   Delano and Aldrich
Landscape architect(s):
House extant: unconfirmed
Historical notes:

    Anna Sands was the daughter of Samuel Stevens and Mary Emily Aymar Sands, Sr.
    Her brother Robert and sister Louise also remained unmarried. Her brother Samuel Stevens Sands, Jr. married Anne Harriman. Upon Samuel's death Anne married Lewis Morris Rutherfurd. He also died at an early age. She subsequently married William Kissam Vanderbilt, Sr. and resided with him at *Idlehour* in Oakdale. Her sister Katherine married Theodore Augustus Havemeyer II and resided at *Cedar Hill* in Upper Brookville.

Sanesi, Dr. Lorenzo

Occupation(s):   physician

Marriage(s):

Listed in *Long Island Society Register, 1929*: no
Address: Old Tappan Road, Glen Cove
Acreage / map sources: not on 1927, 1932, or 1946 maps
Name of estate: *La Primavera*
Year of construction: c. 1913
Style of architecture: Neo-Colonial
Architect(s):   Charles A. Platt designed the house (for J. T. Pratt, Jr.)
Landscape architect(s):
House extant: yes
Historical notes:

side facade

The house, originally named *The Farm House,* was built by John Teele Pratt, Jr.

In 1946, Paul Henry Nitze, who was married to John Teele Pratt, Jr.'s sister Phyllis, owned the estate. The Nitzes continued to call it *The Farm House.*

In 1995, the estate was owned by Sanesi, who called it *La Primavera.*

Satterlee, Dr. Henry Suydam, Sr. (1874-1967)

Occupation(s):   physician

Marriage(s):   M/1 - 1903-1933 - Ethel A. Whitney (1876-1958)
                               M/2 - 1933-1967 - Cecily I. Sheldon

Listed in *Long Island Society Register, 1929*: yes
Address: Cove Neck Road, Cove Neck
Acreage / map sources: on c. 1922 map (owned by E. Whitney)
                               on 1927 map (owned by F. C. Whitney)
                               not on 1932 or 1946 maps
Name of estate:
Year of construction:
Style of architecture:
Architect(s):
Landscape architect(s):
House extant: unconfirmed
Historical notes:

The *Long Island Society Register, 1929* lists Ethel A. Whitney Satterlee as residing in Cove Neck.

The *Social Register New York, 1959* lists Ethel A. Whitney Satterlee as residing at 108 East 82nd Street, NYC.

Dr. Henry Suydam Satterlee, Sr. was the son of Dr. Francis LeRoy and Mrs. Mary P. Gouverneur Satterlee, Sr. of Manhattan.

Ethel A. Whitney Satterlee was the daughter of Stanton Whitney.

Henry Suydam and Ethel A. Whitney Satterlee, Sr.'s son Henry Suydam Satterlee, Jr. married Asta Brandin, the daughter of Oscar E. Brandin of Pasadena, CA. Their son Stanton married Helen B. Wilmerding and resided in Stonington, CT.

The *Social Register New York, 1967* lists Dr. Henry Suydam and Mrs. Cecily I. Sheldon Satterlee [Sr.] as residing in Newport NH.

Cecily L. Shelton Satterlee had previously been married to John Clinton Work. The Works' daughter Cecily married Howard Slade II, the son of Winthrop Slade of Cambridge, MA. The younger Slades resided in Syosset.

Satterwhite, Dr. Preston Pope (1867-1948)

Occupation(s):   physician

Marriage(s):   1908-1927 - Florence C. Brokaw (d. 1927)

Listed in *Long Island Society Register, 1929*: yes
Address: West Shore Road, Kings Point
Acreage / map sources: on 1927 map; 48 acres / 1932 map; 40 acres / 1946 map
Name of estate: *Preston Hall*
Year of construction: c. 1900
Style of architecture: Federal
Architect(s):   Little and O'Connor designed the house (for J. E. Martin)
Landscape architect(s):   Olmsted, 1915-1917 (for Satterwhite)
                                        Lewis and Valentine designed the evergreen settings
Estate photographs can be found in the Nassau County Museum Collection filed under Great Neck/Satterwhite.
House extant: no; demolished c. 1932*
Historical notes:

   The house, originally named *Martin Hall,* was built by James E. Martin, Sr.
   In 1930, the estate was purchased for $610,000 by Satterwhite, who married Florence C. Brokaw after the death of her first husband James E. Martin, Sr. Satterwhite renamed the estate *Preston Hall.*
   The *Long Island Society Register, 1929* lists Dr. Preston Pope Satterwhite as residing at *Martin Hall* on West Shore Road, Great Neck [Kings Point]. The *Social Register, Summer 1937* lists Dr. Preston P. Satterwhite as residing at *Preston Hall* in Great Neck [Kings Point].
   Florence C. Brokaw Satterwhite's brother Clifford Vail Brokaw, Sr. resided at *Westways* on Centre Island and at *The Elms* in Glen Cove. Her brother William Gould Brokaw resided at *Nirvana* in Kings Point. Her sister Lilla married Harry Bramhall Gilbert, with whom she resided at *Sunshine* in Kings Point, and, later, Cyril Dugmore, with whom she resided at *The Gables* in Lattingtown. Their father, William Vail Brokaw, was one of the founders of Brokaw Brothers Clothing Co. The Brokaw name was changed from Broucard to Brokaw. [*The New York Times* March 20, 1939, p. 17.]
   *The house was gutted by fire destroying many art treasures and doing several million dollars' worth of damage. [*The New York Times* November 9, 1932, p. 21; December 28, 1948, p. 21.]

garden fountain, 1926

Savage, The Rev. Theodore Fiske (1885-1957)

Occupation(s):   clergy
                                        writer -   *The Presbyterian Church in New York City,* 1949

Marriage(s):   1913-1957 - May Halsted Terry

Listed in *Long Island Society Register, 1929*: no
Address: West Neck Road, Lloyd Harbor
Acreage / map sources: not on 1929 map; on 1931 map; 13 acres / 1944 map
Name of estate: *Seven Springs*
Year of construction:
Style of architecture:
Architect(s):
Landscape architect(s):
House extant: unconfirmed
Historical notes:

   Both the *Social Register, Summer 1932* and *1955* list The Rev. Theodore Fiske and Mrs. May H. Terry Savage as residing at *Seven Springs* in Lloyd Harbor, while the *Social Register, Summer 1958* lists May H. Terry Savage as residing in Minerva, NY.
   Born in Berkeley, CA, The Rev. Theodore Fiske Savage was the son of Charles A. and May Fiske Savage.

Schenck, Nicholas Michael (1880-1969)

Occupation(s): capitalist - president and chairman of board, Loew's Inc.
                                      (a holding company for MGM Studio);
                               director and president, Loew's Boston Theatres Co.;
                               partner, with his brother Joseph, Palisades Amusement Park,
                                      Fort Lee, NJ
                financier - president, Midland Investment Corp.

Marriage(s): 1927-1969 - Pansy Wilcox (d. 1988)
                        - Civic Activism: trustee, New York Infirmary, NYC

Listed in *Long Island Society Register, 1929*: no
Address: Harbor Road, Sands Point
Acreage / map sources: not on 1927 or 1932 maps; 21 acres / 1946 map
Name of estate:
Year of construction: c. 1903
Style of architecture: Modified Tudor
Architect(s):
Landscape architect(s):
House extant: yes
Historical notes:

The house, originally named *Park Hill,* was built by William Butler Duncan.
In 1922, the estate was purchased by William Vincent Astor.
It was, subsequently, owned by Schenck.
[See following entry for family information.]
Mrs. Schenck claimed the architect for the house was Delano and Aldrich while the Sotheby's sale brochure states that the architectural firm was Cram, Ferguson, and Goodhue. [Joan Gay Kent, *Discovering Sands Point: Its History, Its People, Its Places* (Sands Point, NY: Village of Sands Point, 2000), p. 143.] The house does not appear on the list of Long Island commissions found in the Delano and Aldrich office books in the Avery Architectural Archives, Columbia University. [Mark Alan Hewitt, *Domestic Portraits: The Early Long Island Houses of Delano and Aldrich* in *Long Island Architecture,* Joann P. Krieg, ed. (Interlaken, NY: Heart of the Lakes Publishing, 1991), p. 113.]

Schenck, Nicholas Michael (1880-1969)

Occupation(s): capitalist - president and chairman of board, Loew's Inc.
                                      (a holding company for MGM Studio);
                               director and president, Loew's Boston Theatres Co.;
                               partner, with his brother Joseph, Palisades Amusement
                                      Park, Fort Lee, NJ
                financier - president, Midland Investment Corp.

Marriage(s): 1927-1969 - Pansy Wilcox (d. 1988)
                        - Civic Activism: trustee, New York Infirmary, NYC

Listed in *Long Island Society Register, 1929*: no
Address: Grenwolde Drive, Kings Point
Acreage / map sources: not on 1927 and 1946 maps; no acreage given on 1932 map
Name of estate:
Year of construction:
Style of architecture:
Architect(s):
Landscape architect(s):
House extant: yes
Historical notes:

Schenck's daughter Marti Stevens was a supper club and theater singer. His daughter Mrs. Joanne Brandt resided in Southern Pines, NC. His daughter Nicola married the actor Helmut Dantine.

Schermerhorn, Alfred Coster (1896-1956)

Occupation(s):   financier - partner, Fahnestock and Co. (stock brokerage firm)
Civic Activism: trustee, Institute for the Education of the Blind;
                                    trustee, Museum of the City of New York;
                                    trustee, New York Society Library

Marriage(s):   1926-1937 - Ruth Fahnestock (b. 1908)

Listed in *Long Island Society Register, 1929*: yes
Address: Piping Rock Road, Matinecock
Acreage / map sources: not on 1927 or 1932 maps
                                    11 acres / 1946 map (owned by R. F. Schermerhorn)
Name of estate:
Year of construction: c. 1929
Style of architecture: Federal
Architect(s):   Leroy P. Ward designed the house (for Schermerhorn)
Landscape architect(s):
House extant: yes
Historical notes:

    The house was built by Alfred Coster Schermerhorn.
    The *Long Island Society Register, 1929* lists A. Coster and Ruth Fahnestock Schermerhorn as residing in Southampton, while the *Social Register New York, 1933* lists the Schermerhorns as residing in Locust Valley [Matinecock]. The *Social Register New York, 1956* lists A. Coster Schermerhorn's residence as 120 East 75th Street, NYC.
    He was the son of Alfred E. and Elizabeth Coster Schermerhorn of NYC.
    Ruth Fahnestock Schermerhorn was the daughter of Harris and Mabel Metcalf Fahnestock, who resided in Manhattan and Southampton. After her divorce from Schermerhorn, she married Marie Alfred Fouqueroux de Marigney.

Schieren, George Arthur, Sr. (1878-1944)

Occupation(s):   industrialist - president, Charles A. Schieren Co. (manufacturers
                                           of industrial leather belting);
                                           vice-president and general manager, Holsten Extract Co.
                                           (merged into Charles A. Schieren Co.)
               capitalist - real estate - president, Schieren Realty Corp.

Marriage(s):   1903-1944 - Blanche Mabelle Barker (1874-1950)

Listed in *Long Island Society Register, 1929*: yes
Address: East Shore Road, Kings Point
Acreage / map sources: on 1927 map
                                    no acreage given on 1932 or 1946 maps
Name of estate: *Beachleigh*
Year of construction: c. 1915
Style of architecture: Federal
Architect(s):   Aymar Embury II designed the house (for Schieren)
Landscape architect(s):   Ruth Dean (for Schieren)
House extant: yes
Historical notes:

    The house, originally named *Beachleigh,* was built by George Arthur Schieren, Sr.
    The *Brooklyn Blue Book and Long Island Society Register, 1918* and *1921* and the *Long Island Society Register, 1929* list George Arthur and Blanche M. Barker Schieren [Sr.] as residing on East Shore Road, Great Neck [Kings Point].
    He was the son of Charles A. and Marie Louise Bramm Schieren, who resided at *Mapleton* in Islip. George's father was the mayor of Brooklyn in 1894 and 1895, prior to its incorporation into New York City as a borough. George's brother Harrie married Alice Unkles and resided in Montclair, NJ.
    The estate was owned by Abi Kalimian after 1946.

Schiff, Dorothy (1903-1989)

Occupation(s):   publisher - *New York Post*
Civic Activism: member of board, Henry Street Settlement, NYC;
                                         member of board, Mt. Sinai Hospital, NYC;
                                         member of board, Woman's Trade Union League of New York;
                                         trustee, New York City Board of Child Welfare

Marriage(s):   M/1 - 1923 - Richard B. W. Hall
                                         M/2 - 1932-1943 - George Backer (1903-1974)
                                               - publisher - vice-president and director, *New York Post*
                                       M/3 - 1943 - Theodore O. Thackrey
                                               - publisher - co-publisher, *New York Post*
                                       M/4 - 1953-1965 - Rudolf Goldschmid Sonneborn (1898-1986)
                                               - industrialist - director, secretary, and treasurer,
                                                              Sonneborn Chemical & Refining Co.;
                                                         president, Sonneborn Assoc. Petroleum Corp.

Listed in *Long Island Society Register, 1929*: yes
Address: Route 25A, East Norwich
Acreage / map sources: on 1927 map (owned by Mortimer L. Schiff)
                                         no acreage given on 1932 map (owned by Mortimer L. Schiff)
                                         not on 1946 map
Name of estate: *Old Fields*
Year of construction: c. 1934
Style of architecture: Georgian Revival
Architect(s):   Treanor and Fatio designed the house (for D. Schiff)
Landscape architect(s):
House extant: yes
Historical notes:

   The house, originally named *Old Fields,* was built by Dorothy Schiff, while married to her second husband George Backer, on three hundred acres that Schiff had inherited from her father. It cost approximately $1 million to build in the depths of the Depression and was paid for solely from Dorothy's money. The construction firm that built the house was owned by George Backer's father, a Tammany figure who had become involved in New York City's building trades' scandal.
   The *Long Island Society Register, 1929* lists Richard B. W. and Dorothy Schiff Hall as residing at *Henderson House*, Merrick Road, Southampton.
   Dorothy Schiff was the daughter of Mortimer L. and Adele G. Neustadt Schiff, who resided at *Northwood* in Oyster Bay. Her brother John Mortimer Schiff also resided at *Northwood* in Oyster Bay.
   In 1940, Schiff sold the estate to Consuelo Vanderbilt Balsan for about one-tenth of what it had cost to build.
   Balsan sold the estate to Pine Hollow Country Club. The house and its grounds are now part of the club.

front facade, 1998

Schiff, Dorothy (1903-1989)

Occupation(s):   publisher - *New York Post*
Civic Activism: member of board, Henry Street Settlement, NYC;
                                  member of board, Mt. Sinai Hospital, NYC;
                                  member of board, Woman's Trade Union League of New York;
                                  trustee, New York City Board of Child Welfare

Marriage(s):   M/1 - 1923 - Richard B. W. Hall
                                  M/2 - 1932-1943 - George Backer (1903-1974)
                                        - publisher - vice-president and director, *New York Post*
                                  M/3 - 1943 - Theodore O. Thackrey
                                        - publisher - co-publisher, *New York Post*
                                  M/4 - 1953-1965 - Rudolf Goldschmid Sonneborn (1898-1986)
                                          - industrialist - director, secretary, and treasurer,
                                                        Sonneborn Chemical & Refining Co.;
                                                president, Sonneborn Assoc. Petroleum Corp.

Listed in *Long Island Society Register, 1929*: yes
Address: Sands Point Road, Sands Point
Acreage / map sources: not on 1927, 1932, or 1946 maps
Name of estate: *Sandy Cay*
Year of construction: c. 1930
Style of architecture: Federal
Architect(s):   Ferruccio Vitale designed the swimming
                                  pool complex (for Nast)
Builder: E. W. Howell Co.
Landscape architect(s):   Ferruccio Vitale, 1930 (for Nast)
Estate photographs can be found in the Nassau County Museum Collection filed under Sands Point/Nast.
House extant: no; demolished in 1954*
Historical notes:

    The house, originally named *Sandy Cay,* was built by Conde Nast.
    The estate was owned by Dorothy Schiff, who lived there with her third husband Theodore O. Thackrey. After marrying him in 1943, Schiff made him editor and co-publisher of the *New York Post*.
    [See previous entry for family information.]
    The estate was also owned by Clarence Budington Kelland and, subsequently, by Percy Uris.
    Schiff, Kelland, and Uris continued to call the estate *Sandy Cay.*
    *The house was destroyed by fire, but the two-story garage survived and has been converted into a residence. [Joan Gay Kent, *Discovering Sands Point: Its History, Its People, Its Places* (Sands Point, NY: Village of Sands Point, 2000), p. 122.]

grass steps leading to the house, c. 1940

Schiff, John Mortimer (1904-1987)

Occupation(s):	financier - partner, Kuhn, Loeb and Co. (investment banking firm): director, C. T. I. Financial Corp.; trustee, Provident Loan Society
	merchant - director, Great Atlantic and Pacific Tea Co.(A & P stores)
	industrialist - director, Tide Water Oil Co.; director, Westinghouse Electric Corp.; director, United States Rubber Co.
	capitalist - director, Salt Lake Railroad
Civic Activism:	president of board, Henry Street Settlement, NYC; a founder, president, and chairman of board, Visiting Nurse Service of New York
Marriage(s):	M/1 - 1934-1975 - Edith Brevoort Baker (1913-1975) - Civic Activism: trustee, Babies Hospital trustee, Hewitt School
	M/2 - 1976-1987 - Josephine L. Laimbeer (1913-2002) - entertainers and associated professions - actress* Civic Activism: president, The Society of the Memorial Sloane–Kettering Cancer Center, NYC; volunteer (for over 30 years), Memorial Sloane–Kettering Cancer Center, NYC; board member, The Long Island Alzheimer's Foundation; volunteer, Wildlife Conservation Society

Listed in *Long Island Society Register, 1929*: yes

Address:	Berry Hill Road, Oyster Bay
Acreage / map sources:	on 1927 map (owned by Mortimer L. Schiff) no acreage given on 1932 map (owned by Mortimer L. Schiff) 468 acres / 1946 map (owned by J. M. Schiff)
Name of estate:	*Northwood*
Year of construction:	c. 1905
Style of architecture:	Tudor
Architect(s):	Charles Pierrepont Henry Gilbert designed the house (for M. L. Schiff) Alfred Hopkins designed the farm complex, c. 1914 (for M. L. Schiff)
Landscape architect(s):	James Leal Greenleaf designed the gardens and landscaping (for M. L. Schiff)

Estate photographs can be found in the Nassau County Museum Collection filed under Oyster Bay/Schiff.
House extant: no; demolished c. 1948**
Historical notes:

John Mortimer Schiff was the son of Mortimer L. and Adele G. Neustadt Schiff, who resided at *Northwood* in Oyster Bay. His sister Dorothy resided in Sands Point and at *Old Fields* in East Norwich.

Edith Brevoort Baker Schiff was the daughter of George Fisher and Edith Brevoort Kane Baker II, who resided at *Vikings Cove* in Lattingtown.

John Mortimer and Edith Brevoort Baker Schiff's son Peter married Elizabeth B. Peters and resides in Cove Neck. Their son David married Martha E. Lawler and resides in Manhattan.

The *Social Register, 1987* lists John M. and Josephine L. Laimbeer Schiff as residing at *Northwood* on Berry Hill Road, Oyster Bay. The *Social Register, 1999* lists Josephine L. Laimbeer Schiff's residence as Piping Rock Road, Locust Valley.

*Josephine L. Laimbeer appeared in Cole Porter's 1929 musical *Fifty Million Frenchmen*, retiring from the stage in 1931 when she married John Randolph Fell. [*The New York Times* August 19, 2002, p. A13.] Fell was a partner in Lehman Brothers. The Fells' daughter Natalie married John Spencer and resides with him in Wainscott.

**After World War II, John Mortimer Schiff demolished his father's house and built a Norman-style house, but continued to use the name *Northwood*.

The estate's main gate and farm complex survive.

In 1992, portions of the Garver, Schiff, and Flagg estates were incorporated into Nassau County's Tiffany Creek Preserve.

Schiff, Mortimer L. (1877-1931)

Occupation(s):   financier - partner, Kuhn, Loeb and Co. (investment banking firm);
                                                    director, Chemical Bank and Trust Co. (a merger of The
                                                                Chemical Corn Bank and New York Trust Co.; it
                                                                became Chemical Bank in 1954);
                                                    director, Chemical Safe Deposit Co.;
                                  industrialist - director, Pacific Oil Co.
                                  capitalist - director, L. A. & Salt Lake Railroad;
                                                  director, Western Union Telegraph Co.

Civic Activism: -   trustee, Baron de Hirsch Fund;
                                  president, Jewish Board of Guardians;
                                  vice-president, Boy Scouts of America

Marriage(s):   1901-1931 - Adele G. Neustadt (1878-1931)

Listed in *Long Island Society Register, 1929*: yes
Address: Berry Hill Road, Oyster Bay
Acreage / map sources: on 1927 map (owned by Mortimer L. Schiff)
                                   no acreage given on 1932 map (owned by Mortimer L. Schiff)
                                   468 acres / 1946 map (owned by J. M. Schiff)
Name of estate: *Northwood*
Year of construction: c. 1905
Style of architecture: Tudor
Architect(s):   Charles Pierrepont Henry Gilbert designed the house
                                      (for M. L. Schiff)
                                  Alfred Hopkins designed the farm complex, c. 1914
                                      (for M. L. Schiff)
Landscape architect(s):   James Leal Greenleaf designed the gardens and landscaping
                                      (for M. L. Schiff)
Estate photographs can be found in the Nassau County Museum Collection filed under Oyster Bay/Schiff.
House extant: no; demolished c. 1948*
Historical notes:

The house, originally named *Northwood,* was built by Mortimer L. Schiff.
*When he died, he left one-third of the estate acreage, but no buildings, to his daughter Dorothy. Her brother John Mortimer Schiff razed *Northwood* after World War II and replaced it with a Norman-style house, which he continued to call *Northwood.*
[*See previous entry for additional family information.*]
The estate's main gate and farm complex survive.
In 1992, portions of the Garver, Schiff, and Flagg estates were incorporated into Nassau County's Tiffany Creek Preserve.

Northwood, c. 1910

Schmidlapp, Carl Jacob, Sr. (1888-1960)

Occupation(s):

financier - vice-president, Chase Manhattan Bank;
director, Continental Insurance Co.;
director, Union Trust Co.;
director, American Fire Insurance Co.

industrialist - director, Chicago Pneumatic Tool Co.;
director, Punta Alegre Sugar Corp.;
director, Fuel & Iron Corp.;
director, Fidelity Sugar Co.;
director, General Foods Corp.

Marriage(s):   1920-1960 - Frances Cooper (d. 1967)

Listed in *Long Island Society Register, 1929*: yes
Address: Frost Mill Road, Mill Neck
Acreage / map sources: on 1927 map; no acreage given on 1932 map; 81 acres / 1946 map
Name of estate: *Rumpus House*
Year of construction:
Style of architecture: Neo-Colonial
Architect(s):   Peabody, Wilson and Brown designed c. 1920 alterations
(for Schmidlapp)
Builder: E. W. Howell Co.
Landscape architect(s):   Ellen Biddle Shipman, mid-1920s (for Schmidlapp)
Ferruccio Vitale (for Schmidlapp)

House extant: yes
Historical notes:

front facade

The house, originally named *Rumpus House,* was built by Carl Jacob Schmidlapp, Sr.

Both the *Long Island Society Register, 1929* and the *Social Register, Summer 1962* list Carl J. and Frances Cooper Schmidlapp [Sr.] as residing in Mill Neck

He was the son of Jacob G. and Emily Balke Schmidlapp of Cincinnati, OH.

Schniewind, Henry, Jr. (1869-1962)

Occupation(s):   industrialist - founder and president, Susquehanna Silk Mills
(manufacturers of silk and rayon goods)

Marriage(s):   G. Helen D. Greeff

Listed in *Long Island Society Register, 1929*: yes
Address: Jackson Lane, Glen Cove
Acreage / map sources: 1927 map illegible; not on 1932 map; 8 acres / 1946 map
Name of estate: *Wyndhem*
Year of construction:
Style of architecture:
Architect(s):
Landscape architect(s):
House extant: unconfirmed
Historical notes:

Both the *Long Island Society Register, 1929* and the *Social Register, Summer 1937* list Henry and G. Helen D. Greeff Schniewind, Jr. as residing at *Wyndhem* in Glen Cove.

The Schniewinds' daughter Helen married Warren B. Pond. Their daughter Margaret married Julian Carr Stanley and resided in Lattingtown. Their daughter Emily married James Jackson Lee and resided on Muttontown Road. Their daughter Ethel married Hiram Edward Manville, Jr. and, subsequently, Sherman Pratt, the son of George du Pont Pratt, who resided at *Killenworth* in Glen Cove. Their son Henry Schniewind III married Helen Ball, the daughter of Wilbur L. Ball of Locust Valley. Helen Ball Schniewind's sister Marian married Francis Kendall Thayer, Jr., whose parents resided in Sands Point.

Schreiber, Dr. George, Jr. (1889-1962)

Occupation(s):   physician - dentist

Marriage(s):   Hallie Jaques

Listed in *Long Island Society Register, 1929*: yes
Address: Harbor Road, Port Washington
Acreage / map sources: not on 1927 map; 4 acres / 1932 and 1946 maps
Name of estate: *Harbor Acres*
Year of construction:
Style of architecture:
Architect(s):
Landscape architect(s):
House extant: unconfirmed
Historical notes:

The *Long Island Society Register, 1929* lists Dr. George and Mrs. Hallie Jaques Schreiber, Jr. as residing at *Harbor Acres* in Port Washington.

Schultze, Max H. (1888-1935)

Occupation(s):   financier - partner, Otto Heinze & Co. (stock brokerage firm);
                                               partner, Schultze and Eckstein (investment banking firm)

Marriage(s):   Elise *[unable to confirm maiden name]*

Listed in *Long Island Society Register, 1929*: yes
Address: Horse Hollow Road, Lattingtown
Acreage / map sources: not on 1927, 1932, or 1926 maps
Name of estate: *The Gables*
Year of construction: c. 1910
Style of architecture: Tudor
Architect(s):
Landscape architect(s):
House extant: no; demolished in early 1960s*
Historical notes:

The house, originally named *The Gables,* was built by Max H. Schultze.

The *Brooklyn Blue Book and Long Island Society Register, 1918* lists Mr. and Mrs. Max H. Schultze as residing at 280 Garfield Place, Brooklyn. The *Long Island Society Register, 1929* lists their residence as Town Path Road [Horse Hollow Road], Glen Cove [Lattingtown].

The estate was, subsequently, owned by Cyril Dugmore, who continued to call it *The Gables.*

The estate is owned by Locust Valley School District. The house was used for pre-kindergarten classes and served as an administrative building.

*The house was destroyed by fire.

The Gables, c. 1917

714

Schuster, Max Lincoln (1897-1970)

Occupation(s):

publisher - co-founder and publisher, Simon & Schuster, Inc.;
partner (with wife), M. Lincoln Schuster and Rae
Schuster Publishing & Research Associates;
a founder, *PM* magazine

writer - *Eyes on the World: A Photographic Record of History
in the Making,* 1935;
editor, *A Treasury of the World's Great Letters,* 1940

journalist - staff, United Press Associations [International];
correspondent, *Boston Evening Transcript*

Marriage(s):

Rae B. Haskell (1900-1976)
- landscape architect
publisher - partner (with husband), M. Lincoln Schuster and Rae
Schuster Publishing & Research Associates

Listed in *Long Island Society Register, 1929*: no
Address: Shephard's Lane, Sands Point
Acreage / map sources: not on 1927 or 1932 maps; 7 acres / 1946 map
Name of estate: *Cow Neck Farm*
Year of construction: 18th century
Style of architecture: Colonial
Architect(s):
Landscape architect(s):
House extant: no*
Historical notes:

The house was built by Stephen Mott (1726-1813) on 225 acres which he had inherited from his father Adam Mott II. The house was, subsequently, inherited by various members of the Mott family until it was sold to William Lippincott. [Mary Feeney Vahey, *A Hidden History: Slavery, Abolition, and the Underground Railroad in Cow Neck and on Long Island* (Port Washington, NY: Cow Neck Peninsula Historical Society, 1998), p. 31.]

The house was later owned by Schuster, who called it *Cow Neck Farm.*

Rae B. Haskell had previously been married to the landscape architect John Jacob Levison and resided in Sea Cliff.

*The house was destroyed by fire in 1980. The barn remains and has been converted into a residence.

In the 1980s, Schuster sold the property to Arnold Asa Saltzman.

A cave on the estate may have been a stop on the "underground railroad." [Vahey, p. 31.]

Schwab, Hermann C., II (1892-1934)

Occupation(s):   financier - member, Joseph Walker and Sons (stock brokerage firm)
Civic Activism: trustee, Chrystie Street House

Marriage(s):   1919-1934 - Ruth Baldwin Bliss

Listed in *Long Island Society Register, 1929*: yes
Address: Cedar Swamp Road and Chicken Valley Road, Old Brookville
Acreage / map sources: on 1927 map; no acreage given on 1932 map; not on 1946 map
Name of estate: *Chicken Valley Farm*
Year of construction:
Style of architecture:
Architect(s):
Landscape architect(s):
House extant: unconfirmed
Historical notes:

Both the *Long Island Society Register, 1929* and the *Social Register, Summer 1932* list Hermann C. and Ruth B. Bliss Schwab II as residing at *Chicken Valley Farm* in Glen Head [Old Brookville].

The *Social Register, Summer 1937* lists Ruth B. Bliss Schwab as having married The Rev. Lyman C. Bleecker and residing at the St. John's Episcopal Church Rectory in Cold Spring Harbor.

The Schwabs' son Hermann C. Schwab III married Lesley Hyde Ripley, the daughter of B. H. Ripley of Manhattan and Newport, RI.

Schwartz, Alexander Charles, Sr. (1895-1967)

Occupation(s):   financier - partner, Bache and Co. (investment banking firm)
capitalist - director, Desilu Productions;
director, Hotel Corporation of America;
director, Consolidated Electrodynamics Corp.;
director, Kermae Nuclear Fuels Corp.;
director, Pacific Uranium Mines Co.

Marriage(s):   1929 - Craigie McKay

Listed in *Long Island Society Register, 1929*: no
Address: Middle Neck Road, Sands Point
Acreage / map sources: on 1927 map (name misspelled as Bchwartz)
6 acres / 1932 map (name misspelled as J. Schwartz)
not on 1946 map

Name of estate:
Year of construction:
Style of architecture:
Architect(s):
Landscape architect(s):
House extant: unconfirmed
Historical notes:

Schwartz, Charles (1915-1969)

Occupation(s):   attorney - partner, Schwartz and Frohlich
capitalist - secretary, Columbia Pictures Corp.
writer - *The Law of Motion Pictures* (co-authored with Lewis Frohlich);
A Modern Interpretation of Judaism: Faith Through Reason, 1949
(co-authored with Bertie Grad Schwartz)

Marriage(s):   Bertie Grad (1901-1976)
- attorney - partner, Schwartz and Frohlich
writer - *A Modern Interpretation of Judaism: Faith Through Reason,* 1949 (co-authored with Charles Schwartz)
Civic Activism: first woman president, Jewish Book Council of the National Jewish Welfare Board;
vice-president, National Women's League for Conservative Judaism;
member, Task Force on Art and Literature in Jewish Life of the Federation of Jewish Philanthropies

Listed in *Long Island Society Register, 1929*: no
Address: Middle Neck Road, Sands Point
Acreage / map sources: on 1927 map (name misspelled as Bchwartz)
6 acres / 1932 map (name misspelled as J. Schwartz)
not on 1946 map

Name of estate:
Year of construction: c. 1910
Style of architecture: Georgian Revival
Architect(s):   Augustus N. Allen designed the house (for M. C. Fleischmann)
James W. O'Connor designed the stables (for M. C. Fleischmann)

Landscape architect(s):
House extant: yes
Historical notes:

The house, originally named *The Lindens,* was built by Max C. Fleischmann.
Fleischmann sold the estate to George Tuttle Brokaw for $250,000.
The estate was purchased by Schwartz and, subsequently in 1938, by Alfred Gwynne Vanderbilt II.

Scott, Donald, Sr. (1879-1967)

Occupation(s):   publisher -   director, *New York Evening Post;*
                                              director, Appleton–Century–Crofts Co.
                                educator -   professor of anthropology and archeology, Harvard
                                                University, Cambridge, MA;
                                              director, Peabody Museum of Archeology and Ethnology,
                                                Harvard University, Cambridge, MA

Marriage(s):   M/1 - 1908-1917 - Mary Channing Eustis (d. 1917)
                                M/1 - 1919-1967 - Mary Louise Smith

Listed in *Long Island Society Register, 1929*: yes
Address: Lloyd Lane, Lloyd Harbor
Acreage / map sources: no acreage given on 1929 map
                                on 1931 map
                                44 acres / 1944 map
Name of estate: *Whitewood*
Year of construction: 1912
Style of architecture:
Architect(s):
Landscape architect(s):
House extant: yes
Historical notes:

   The house, originally named *Whitewood,* was built by Donald Scott, Sr.
   Both the *Long Island Society Register, 1929* and the *Social Register, Summer 1937* list Donald and Mary L. Smith
Scott [Sr.] as residing at *Whitewood* in Huntington [Lloyd Harbor].
   The estate was purchased by Morris Hadley, who continued to call it *Whitewood.*
   It was, subsequently, owned by the Hadleys' son John Wood Blodgett Hadley, who called it *White Wood Point.*

Scott, Rufus W. (1874-1962)

Occupation(s):   industrialist - president and chairman of board, Tubize Rayon Corp.
                                                    (which merged into Celanese Corp. of America in 1946)
Marriage(s):   Daisy French Burt (d. 1963)

Listed in *Long Island Society Register, 1929*: yes
Address: Feeks Lane, Lattingtown
Acreage / map sources: not on 1927 or 1932 maps
                                20 acres / 1946 map
Name of estate: *Scottage*
Year of construction:
Style of architecture: Colonial Revival
Architect(s):   R. Barfoot King designed c. 1925 alterations (for R. W. Scott)
Landscape architect(s):   Noel Chamberlain, 1929 (for R. W. Scott)
Estate photographs can be found in the Nassau County Museum Collection filed under Locust Valley/Scott.
House extant: yes
Historical notes:

   The house, originally named *Scottage,* was built by Rufus W. Scott.
   The *Long Island Society Register, 1929* and the *Social Register, Summer 1962* list Rufus W. and Daisy French Burt
Scott as residing at *Beachlight* in Great Neck. *[unable to locate]*
   Scott commissioned Louise Tiffany Taylor, a descendant of Louis Comfort Tiffany, to decorate the interior of the
house.
   The estate was, subsequently, owned by Edmund Calvert Lynch, Jr., who renamed it *Floralyn.*

Scudder, Townsend, II (1865-1960)

Occupation(s):   attorney -   judge -   New York State Supreme Court
politician -   member, United States Congress, 1898-1899; 1903-1905,
representing New York 1st Congressional District;
vice-president, New York State Parks Commission

Marriage(s):   M/1 - 1891-1924 - Mary Dannat Thayer (d. 1924)
M/2 - 1928-1960 - Alice Booth McCutchen

Listed in *Long Island Society Register, 1929*: yes
Address: Glenwood Road and Glen Cove Avenue, Glen Head
Acreage / map sources: on 1927 map; no acreage given on 1932 map; not on 1946 map
Name of estate: *Robinhurst Farm*
Year of construction:
Style of architecture:
Architect(s):
Landscape architect(s):
House extant: unconfirmed
Historical notes:

    The *Long Island Society Register, 1929* lists Townsend and Alice Booth McCutchen Scudder [II] as residing at *Robinhurst Farm* in Glen Head, while the *Social Register, Summer 1932* lists the Scudders' residence as *Brynwood* on Round Hill Road, Greenwich, CT.
    Scudder's daughter Elizabeth married Wadleigh Capehart.

Sears, Joseph Hamblen (1865-1946)

Occupation(s):   journalist -   managing editor, *The Cosmopolitan Magazine;*
editor, *Harper's Young People* (later, *Harper's Round Table);*
editor, *Harper's Bazaar;*
editor, *Harper's Weekly*
publisher -   president, D. Appleton & Co.
writer -   *Governments of the World To-day,* 1895;
Fur and Feather Tales, 1897;
None But the Brave, 1902;
A Box of Matches, 1904

Marriage(s):   1891-1937 - Anna Wentworth Caldwell (1864-1937)
    - writer -   several short stories
Civic Activism: officer, National Women's Service
during World War I;
*

Listed in *Long Island Society Register, 1929*: yes
Address: Oyster Bay Cove Road, Oyster Bay Cove
Acreage / map sources: on 1927 map; no acreage given on 1932 map; 5 acres / 1946 map
Name of estate: *The Other House*
Year of construction:
Style of architecture:
Architect(s):
Landscape architect(s):
House extant: unconfirmed
Historical notes:

    The *Long Island Society Register, 1929* lists Joseph Hamblen and Anna Wentworth Caldwell Sears as residing at *The Other House* in Oyster Bay [Oyster Bay Cove], while the *Social Register New York, 1937* lists only Joseph Hamblen Sears as residing at *The Other House.*
    *Anna Wentworth Caldwell Sears was an anti-suffragist.

Seligman, Joseph Lionel, Sr. (1887-1944)

Occupation(s):	financier - member, J. W. Seligman and Co. (investment banking firm); vice-president, Bond & Goodwin (stock brokerage firm)

Marriage(s):   1911-1944 - Josephine Knowles

Listed in *Long Island Society Register, 1929*: yes
Address: Bryant Avenue, Roslyn Harbor
Acreage / map sources: on 1927 map; 8 acres / 1932 map; 14 acres / 1946 map
Name of estate: *Greenridge*
Year of construction: 1916
Style of architecture: Tudor
Architect(s):   Harold Victor Hartman designed the house (for A. Williams)
Landscape architect(s):
House extant: yes
Historical notes:

    The house, originally named *Greenridge,* was built by Arthur Williams.
    The estate was owned by Seligman, who continued to call it *Greenridge*, and, subsequently, by Mead L. Briggs.
    Both the *Long Island Society Register, 1929* and the *Social Register, Summer 1937* list Joseph L. and Josephine Knowles Seligman [Sr.] as residing at *Greenridge* in Roslyn [Roslyn Harbor]. The *Social Register New York, 1948* and the *Social Register, 1986* list Mrs. Seligman as residing at *Harborview* in Pensacola, FL.
    Joseph Lionel Seligman was the son of Isaac and Guta Loeb Seligman.
    The Seligmans' son Joseph L. Seligman, Jr. married Margaret Van Horne, the daughter of Loren Van Horne of San Francisco.

Senff, Gustavia A. Tapscott (d. 1927)

Marriage(s):   Charles H. Senff (1837-1911)
                    - industrialist - director, American Sugar Refining Co.

Listed in *Long Island Society Register, 1929*: no
Address: Muttontown Road, Muttontown
Acreage / map sources: on 1927 map; 274 acres / 1932 map; 271 acres / 1946 map
Name of estate:
Year of construction: c. 1907
Style of architecture: Italian Neo-Classical
Architect(s):   Hiss and Weeks designed the house (for C. I. Hudson, Sr.)
Landscape architect(s):   Ferruccio Vitale designed the formal Italianate sunken garden, descending gardens, pergola, catalpa walk, foot paths, bridle paths, brick terrace, and landscaping, 1906-1920 (for C. I. Hudson, Sr.)
Estate photographs can be found in the Nassau County Museum Collection filed under East Norwich/Hudson and also under Muttontown/Hudson/Senff/Zog.
House extant: no; demolished in 1959*
Historical notes:

    The house, originally named *Knollwood,* was built by Charles I. Hudson, Sr.
    After Hudson's death, the estate was owned by Gustavia Senff and, subsequently, by her nephew Charles Senff McVeigh, Sr.
    Gustavia A. Tapscott Senff was the daughter of William B. Tapscott of Richmond, VA.
    In 1951, King Zog I of Albania purchased the estate from McVeigh.
    In 1955, without ever occupying the house, King Zog sold it to Lansdell Kisner Christie. Zog sold the estate due to an unresolved property tax dispute with Nassau County.
    *Christie demolished the house. His widow sold the estate to Nassau County.
    It is now part of Nassau County's Muttontown Preserve.

rear facade, c. 1910

Sewell, Robert Van Vorst (1860-1924)

Occupation(s):   artist - painter and sculptor

Marriage(s):   L. A. Brewster

Listed in *Long Island Society Register, 1929*: no
Address: Cove Road, Oyster Bay Cove
Acreage / map sources: on c. 1922 map
                                   not on 1927, 1932, or 1946 maps
Name of estate: *Fleetwood*
Year of construction: c. 1907
Style of architecture: Elizabethan Revival
Architect(s):   A. Dunham Wheeler designed the house (for Sewell)*
Landscape architect(s):
House extant: yes
Historical notes:

    The house, originally named *Fleetwood*, was built by Robert Van Vorst Sewell.
    The *Brooklyn Blue Book and Long Island Society Register, 1921* lists Mr. and Mrs. Robert V. V. Sewell as residing on Cold Spring Road [Oyster Bay Cove Road], Oyster Bay [Oyster Bay Cove].
    The estate was owned by Grover O'Neill, Sr., and, subsequently in 1957, by Eugene Du Bois. Both O'Neill and Du Bois continued to call it *Fleetwood*.
    *A. Dunham Wheeler was the son of Candace Thurber Wheeler, a textile and interior designer, who with Louis Comfort Tiffany, Samuel Colman, and Lockwood de Forest founded L. C. Tiffany & Associated Artists.
    The interior of the house has murals and carvings of scenes of the "Canterbury Tales" by Sewell.

Fleetwood, c. 1907

Shaw, Robert Anderson (1870-1941)

Occupation(s):   attorney -   member, Phillips and Avery

Marriage(s):   1901-1941 - Myrtle Grace Wilhelm

Listed in *Long Island Society Register, 1929*: no
Address: North Colony section Glen Cove
Acreage / map sources: 1927 map illegible; not on 1932 or 1946 maps
Name of estate:
Year of construction: c. 1900-1902
Style of architecture: Tudor
Architect(s):   Charles Pierrepont Henry Gilbert designed the house
                                      (for R. A. Shaw)

Landscape architect(s):
House extant: no*
Historical notes:

    The house was built by Robert Anderson Shaw.
    Born in Marietta, OH, he was the son of Rodney Keene and Lovina Clark Shaw.
    The Shaws' daughter Elizabeth married Alexander Milton, Jr., the son of Alexander and Jeannie Milton, Sr. of Newark, NJ.
    *The gatehouse and gate are all that remain of the Shaw estate.

Shaw, Samuel T., Sr. (1861-1945)

Occupation(s):   capitalist -   real estate - co-owner with Simeon Ford, Grand
                                                  Union Hotel, NYC

Marriage(s):   M/1 - Joan Baird (d. 1913)
                                    M/2 - 1916-1940 - Amalia Dalumi (d. 1940)

Listed in *Long Island Society Register, 1929*: yes
Address: Yacht Club Road, Centre Island
Acreage / map sources: not on 1927, 1932, or 1946 maps
Name of estate: *The Sunnyside*
Year of construction: c. 1906
Style of architecture: Spanish Colonial
Architect(s):   Frederick R. Hirsh designed
                                  the house (for S. T. Shaw, Sr.)

Landscape architect(s):
House extant: yes
Historical notes:

The Sunnyside

    The house, originally named *The Sunnyside,* was built by Samuel T. Shaw, Sr.
    The *Long Island Society Register, 1929* lists Mr. and Mrs. Samuel T. Shaw [Sr.] as residing on Centre Island.
    He was the son of James E. and Julia A. Shaw.
    Samuel and Joan Shaw's son Samuel T. Shaw, Jr. married Simone Vanophen and resided in Plymouth, CA.
    The estate was, subsequently, owned by George Edgar Brightson, who called it *Harbor Point*.
    In 1933, it was purchased by Edward Carl William Oelsner, Sr., who called it *Seacroft*. The estate was subsequently owned by the Oelsners' son Warren James Oelsner, who continued to call it *Seacroft*. In 2000 the estate was still owned by the Oelsner family.

Shea, Edward Lane (1892-1963)

Occupation(s):   industrialist -   president, Tide Water Oil Co.;
                                         executive vice-president, Tide Water Associated Oil Co.;
                                       president and chairman of board, Ethyl Corp.
                         capitalist -   president, North American Co. (a utilities holding company)
                         director of numerous companies
Civic Activism: member of board, Memorial Hospital for Cancer and Allied Disease;
                         trustee, Presbyterian Hospital (now, Columbia–Presbyterian Medical
                                 Center), NYC;
                         director, John and Mary R. Markle Foundation

Marriage(s):   M/1 - 1926-1947 - Olive Field (1897-1947)
                                    M/2 - 1950-1963 - Mary Mathilde Johnston

Listed in *Long Island Society Register, 1929*: no
Address: Skunks Misery Road, Lattingtown
Acreage / map sources: not on 1927 or 1932 maps; 8 acres / 1946 map
Name of estate:
Year of construction: 1909
Style of architecture: Federal
Architect(s):   Severance and Schumm designed the house (for J. Anderson)
                          Bradley Delehanty designed c. 1930 alterations (for J. Anderson)
                          Frederick Ayer II and Bradley Delehanty designed c. 1938
                              alterations (for Shea)

Landscape architect(s):
House extant: yes
Historical notes:

    The house, originally named *Aberfeldy,* was built by John Anderson.
    The estate was, subsequently, owned by Shea.
    Olive Field Shea was the daughter of Cornelius James Field of Kew Gardens.
    Edward and Olive Shea's son Peter married Nancy Lee Stewart, the daughter of John Stewart of Palo Alto, CA.

Shearman, Lawrence Hobart (1866-1941)

Occupation(s):   shipping -   vice-president, W. R. Grace & Co.

Civic Activism: member, National Council of Defense Advisory Shipping
                                         Committee during World War I;
                             shipping advisor, General Headquarters of American Expeditionary
                                         Force in France during World War I

Marriage(s):   1891-1941 - Effie Beare

Listed in *Long Island Society Register, 1929*: yes

Address: I. U. Willets Road and Shelter Rock Road, North Hills

Acreage / map sources: on 1927 map
                               51 acres / 1932 map
                               not on 1946 map

Name of estate:

Year of construction: c. 1918

Style of architecture: Tudor

Architect(s):   James W. O'Connor designed
                               the house (for Shearman)

Landscape architect(s):   Paul Smith (for Shearman)

House extant: yes

Historical notes:

front facade, 2004

    The house was built by Lawrence Hobart Shearman.

    Born in Washington, DC, he was the son of William P. and Mary Washington James Shearman. His mother was a descendant of Lawrence Washington, the half-brother of President George Washington.

    The Shearmans' daughter Elise married Paul Niesley, the son of Charles M. Niesley of Manhasset.

    The estate was purchased in 1937 by Frederick Lunning for $200,000. [*The New York Times* February 6, 1938, p. 185.] Lunning called the estate *Northcourt*.

    It is now the Buckley Country Day School.

Sheehan, William Francis (1859-1917)

Occupation(s):   attorney -   partner, Hatch, Wingate and Sheehan
                               politician - assemblyman, New York State Legislature, 1885-1891;
                                          Speaker of the House, New York State Legislature 1891;
                                          Lieutenant Governor of New York State, 1892-1895
                               capitalist - director, Kings County Electric Light & Power Co.;
                                          director, Albany & Southern Railroad Co.;
                                          director, Louisville Lighting Co.;
                                          director, Western New York & Pennsylvania;
                                          director, Traction Co.

Marriage(s):   1889-1917 - Blanche Cecilia Nellany (b. 1868)

Listed in *Long Island Society Register, 1929*: no

Address: 41 Shelter Rock Road, North Hills

Acreage / map sources: not on 1927, 1932, or 1946 maps

Name of estate: *The Height*

Year of construction: pre-1916

Style of architecture: Federal

Architect(s):   Hoppin and Koen designed 1916 alterations (for Sheehan)

Landscape architect(s):

House extant: yes

Historical notes:

    The house was built by William Singer.

    In 1916, Sheehan purchased and remodeled the house, which he called *The Height*.

    The estate was owned by Robert George Elbert, who called it *Elbourne*, and, subsequently, by Joseph Peter Grace II, who renamed it *Gracewood*.

    The house is now a private clubhouse for a housing development called *Gracewood*.

Sheeline, Paul Cushing (1922-2003)

Occupation(s):	capitalist - president and chairman of board, Intercontinental Hotels; director, Pan American World Corp.; director, Resorts International
	financier - director, National Westminster Bank, USA
	attorney
Civic Activism:	member, Presidential Board of Advisors on Private Sector Initiative in the Reagan administration; director, Foreign Policy Association, 1981-1990; director, Scientists for Public Information, 1980-1991; chairman, American–Arab Association for Commerce and Industry, 1984-1986; trustee, St. Luke's–Roosevelt Hospital Center, NYC, 1983-1998; trustee, Battle of Normandy Foundation
Marriage(s):	M/1 - Harriet Moffat
	M/2 - Sandra Wahl

Listed in *Long Island Society Register, 1929:* no
Address: Southdown Road, Lloyd Harbor
Acreage / map sources: not on 1929, 1931, or 1944 maps
Name of estate:
Year of construction: c. 1790
Style of architecture: Long Island miller's cottage
Architect(s):   Polhemus and Coffin, 1929 alterations (for Gwynne)
Landscape architect(s):
House extant: yes
Historical notes:

In 1927, Gertrude Knowlton Wombwell gave *Mill Cove* to her daughter Mildred Van Schaick Gwynne.
In 1969, the Gwynne family donated a portion of their property for the creation of the Mill Cove Waterfowl Sanctuary.
Included in the gift was the c. 1790 Lefferts Mill, which is one of the few remaining tidal mills on Long Island.
The house was purchased in 1980 by Sheeline.

Shepard, Rutherford Mead (1875-1933)

Occupation(s):	financier - member, William Y. Connor & Co. (stock brokerage firm)
Marriage(s):	1907-1933 - Winifred Prentiss Kay (d. 1969)

Listed in *Long Island Society Register, 1929*: no
Address: Ridge Road, Glen Cove
Acreage / map sources: not on 1927, 1932, or 1946 maps
Name of estate:
Year of construction: c. 1894
Style of architecture: Dutch Colonial
Architect(s):   Little and Browne designed the house (for Fowler)
Landscape architect(s):
House extant: yes
Historical notes:

The house was built by George Fowler.
The estate was owned by Rudolph R. Loening, who called it *Glimpse Water,* and, subsequently, by Shepard.
He was the son of Augustus D. Shepard who resided at *The Gables* in Fanwood, NJ.
The *Social Register New York, 1933* lists Rutherford M. and Winifred P. Kay Shepard as residing at 333 East 68th Street, NYC. Mrs. Shepard was residing at the 68th Street address at the time of her death.
Winifred Prentiss Kay Shepard was the daughter of James Murray Kay of Brookline, MA.
William Rutherford Mead, of the architectural firm of McKim, Mead and White, was Shepard's uncle.

Sheridan, Frank J., Jr. (1885-1937)

Occupation(s):   advertising executive - partner, Shahan and Sheridan
                                                          (commercial and advertising
                                                          art firm)

Marriage(s):   Eleanor Grant

Listed in *Long Island Society Register, 1929*: yes
Address: Barker's Point Road, Sands Point
Acreage / map sources: on 1927 map
                                     not on 1932 or 1946 maps
Name of estate:
Year of construction:
Style of architecture:
Architect(s):
Landscape architect(s):
House extant: unconfirmed
Historical notes:

The *Long Island Society Register, 1929* lists Frank J. and Eleanor Grant Sheridan, Jr. as residing in Sands Point.

Sherman, Charles Austin, Sr. (1863-1950)

Occupation(s):   capitalist - president, Sherman & Sons (cotton goods importers)
Civic Activism: chairman of board, Navy Y.M.C.A.;
                                     trustee, Hyslop House

Marriage(s):   Leila Morse Willis

Listed in *Long Island Society Register, 1929*: yes
Address: Centre Island Road, Centre Island
Acreage / map sources: on 1927 map
                                     not on 1932 or 1946 maps
Name of estate: *Minnewawa*
Year of construction: c. 1900
Style of architecture: Shingle
Architect(s):
Landscape architect(s):
House extant: yes
Historical notes:

The house, originally named *Minnewawa*, was built by Charles Austin Sherman, Sr.

The *Long Island Society Register, 1929* lists Charles Austin and Leila Morse Willis Sherman [Sr.] as residing at *Minnewawa* in Oyster Bay [Centre Island].

Born in Brooklyn, he was the son of John Taylor and Julia Deming Sherman and was a descendant of Roger Sherman, a signer of the Declaration of Independence. His paternal grandfather's estate *Bloomingdale Farm* included what is now the site of the New York Public Library at Forty-second Street and Fifth Avenue in Manhattan. [*The New York Times* February 25, 1950, p. 17.]

The estate was, subsequently, owned by James David Mooney II.

Sherry, Louis (1856-1926)

Occupation(s):   restaurateur - founder and owner, Sherry's Restaurant,
                                        5th Ave. and 44th St., NYC

Marriage(s):   Marie Bertha *[unable to confirm maiden name]*

Listed in *Long Island Society Register, 1929*: no
Address: 260 Country Club Road, Manhasset
Acreage / map sources: not on 1927, 1932, or 1946 maps
Name of estate: *Sherryland*
Year of construction: c. 1915
Style of architecture: French Renaissance
Architect(s):   McKim, Mead and White designed alterations
Landscape architect(s):   Olmsted, 1924-1925 (for Munsey)
House extant: yes
Historical notes:

    The house, originally named *Sherryland,* was built by Louis Sherry.
    It was at Sherry's Restaurant that Cornelius Kingsley Garrison Billings, who resided at *Farnsworth* in Upper Brookville, gave his famous dinner on horseback in 1900.
    The estate was owned by Frank Andrew Munsey, who purchased it in 1922, and, subsequently, by Virginia Graham Fair Vanderbilt, who called it *Fairmont.*
    In 1938, the estate was sold to William Jaird Levitt, Sr., who built the Strathmore housing development on the estate property. [*The New York Times* January 16, 1938, section XII, p. 1.] The house, which is located in the Strathmore section of Manhasset, is now the Strathmore Vanderbilt Country Club of Manhasset.

front facade, 1998

Shipman, Julie Fay Bradley (1876-1971)

Civic Activism: chairman, Clean City Committee, NYC, 1934

Marriage(s):   M/1 - 1899-1930 - The Right Rev. Herbert Shipman (d. 1930)
- clergy - rector, Church of The Heavenly Rest, NYC;
                 suffragan bishop, Episcopal Diocese of New York, 1921-1930)*
M/2 - 1942-1971 - John Charles Fremont II
- military - captain, United States Navy;
                 supervisor, Harbor of New York for the War Department;
                 supervisor, Third Naval District during World War II;
                 member, Shipping Section, Supreme Economic Council 1919

Listed in *Long Island Society Register, 1929*: no
Address: Glenwood Road, Glen Head
Acreage / map sources: not on 1927, 1932, or 1946 maps
Name of estate: *Lynrose*
Year of construction: c. 1931
Style of architecture:
Architect(s):   William Lawrence Bottomley designed the house (for Shipman)
Landscape architect(s):   Warner and White (for Shipman)
Estate photographs can be found in the Nassau County Museum Collection filed under Roslyn/Shipman.
House extant: no
Historical notes:

    The house, originally named *Lynrose,* was built by Julie Fay Bradley Shipman.
    She was the daughter of Edson and Julia W. Williams Bradley, who resided at *Seaview Terrace* in Newport, RI.
    The Right Rev. Herbert Shipman was the son of The Rev. Jacob Shaw Shipman, rector of Christ Episcopal Church in Manhattan. His sister Gertrude married William Herbert Burr of New Canaan, CT. His sister Louisa married Henry Hubbard and resided in Manhattan.
    *Shipman, who is buried at the United States Military Academy at West Point, served as chaplain at the Academy; chaplain to the 104th Artillery during the Mexican War; and chaplain to the First Army Corps in France during WWI.
    John Charles Fremont II was the grandson of the explorer, soldier, and political leader John Charles Fremont. The elder Fremont was instrumental in liberating California from Mexico and was the Republican candidate for the presidency of the United States in the 1856 election.

Shonnard, Horatio Seymour, Sr. (1875-1946)

Occupation(s):   financier - stockbroker

Marriage(s):   M/1 - 1909-1928 - Elizabeth Joyce
                         M/2 - 1929 - Sophie Meldrim

Listed in *Long Island Society Register, 1929*: yes
Address: Main Street, Oyster Bay
Acreage / map sources: not on 1927, 1932, or 1946 maps
Name of estate: *Boscobel*
Year of construction: c. 1885
Style of architecture: Colonial Revival
Architect(s):   Donn Barber designed c. 1920s alterations on the house transforming
                 it from Queen Anne to Colonial Revival, the c. 1920s Tudor garage,
                 stables, and boathouse (for Shonnard)
           George Browne Post designed c. 1888 alterations to the house
                 (for Underhill)
Landscape architect(s):   Donn Barber designed the formal garden, c. 1920s (for Shonnard)
House extant: no; demolished in 1950s
Historical notes:

    The house was built by Francis T. Underhill.
    The estate was owned by Camille Weidenfeld and, subsequently, by Shonnard, who called it *Boscobel.*
    Sophie Meldrim Shonnard had previously been married to Edward H. Coy.

Shutt, Edwin Holmes, Jr. (1927-1994)

Occupation(s):   industrialist - chief executive officer, Tampax Inc. (now, Tambrands Corp.); vice-president, Procter & Gamble, Co.; president and chief executive, Clorox Co.

capitalist - director, Online Resources Corp.; director, BTC Diagnostics, Inc.

financier - director, First National Bank of Long Island

Civic Activism: member, arbitration panel, New York Stock Exchange; member, executive committee, San Francisco Bay Association, Boy Scouts of America; trustee, Oakland Museum Association, Oakland CA; trustee, Friends of the Arts; trustee, National Association of Women's Centers; member, advisory board, School of Business, University of California, Berkeley, CA

Marriage(s): 1953 - Mary Truesdale

Listed in *Long Island Society Register, 1929*: no
Address: Sunset Road, Oyster Bay Cove
Acreage / map sources: not on 1927, 1932, or 1946 maps
Name of estate:
Year of construction: c. 1939
Style of architecture: Federal
Architect(s): Bradley Delehanty designed the house (for J. K. Colgate, Sr.)

Landscape architect(s):
House extant: yes
Historical notes:

The house, originally named *Oaklea,* was built by John Kirtland Colgate, Sr.
The estate was, subsequently, owned by Shutt.
He was the son of Edwin Holmes and Louise Davenport Tebbetts Shutt, Sr. of St. Louis, MO.

Simpson, Robert H.

Occupation(s): financier - stockbroker

Marriage(s): M/1 - Alice Wood (d. 1947)
M/2 - Ethel Otis

Listed in *Long Island Society Register, 1929*: yes
Address: East Norwich Road and Brookville Road, Jericho
Acreage / map sources: on 1927 map
not on 1932 or 1946 maps
Name of estate: *Kinross*
Year of construction: c. 1920
Style of architecture:
Architect(s):
Landscape architect(s): Olmsted (for Simpson)
Charles Downing Lay (for Simpson)
House extant: unconfirmed
Historical notes:

The house, originally named *Kinross,* was built by Robert H. Simpson.
The *Long Island Society Register, 1929* lists Robert H. and Alice Wood Simpson as residing at *Kinross* in Jericho, while the *Social Register, Summer 1937* lists their residence as *Allways* in Mill Neck.
The *Social Register New York, 1951* lists Robert H. and Ethel Otis Simpson as residing at 40 East 83rd Street, NYC.
The estate was, subsequently, owned by Robert Grant, Jr.

Sinclair, Harry Ford, Sr. (1876-1956)

Occupation(s):　　　　　　　　industrialist - president, Sinclair Oil and Refining Corp.,
　　　　　　　　　　　　　　　　　　　　Sinclair Gulf Corp., and Sinclair Oil Corp.

Marriage(s):　　　　　　　　　1943-1956 - Elizabeth Farrell (1879-1964)
　　　　　　　　　　　　　　　　　- entertainers and associated professions - concert pianist

Listed in *Long Island Society Register, 1929*: yes
Address:　　　　　　　　　　　Bayview Avenue, Kings Point
Acreage / map sources:　　　　on 1927 map
　　　　　　　　　　　　　　　36 acres / 1932 map
　　　　　　　　　　　　　　　36 acres / 1946 map

Name of estate:
Year of construction:　　　　c. 1900
Style of architecture:　　　　Mediterranean Villa
Architect(s):　　　　　　　　Little and O'Connor designed the house
　　　　　　　　　　　　　　　　(for Gilbert)

Landscape architect(s):
House extant: no; demolished in 1970s*
Historical notes:

side facade, c. 1908

　　The house, originally named *Sunshine*, was built by Harry Bramhall Gilbert.
　　The estate was, subsequently, owned by Sinclair, who moved to Kings Point in 1918. Sinclair continued to reside at the estate after the Teapot Dome Scandal.
　　The *Long Island Society Register, 1929* lists H. F. Sinclair [Sr.] as residing on Bayview Avenue, Great Neck [Kings Point].
　　*The estate property was subdivided for a housing development.

Sizer, Robert Ryland, Sr. (1859-1925)

Occupation(s):　　　　　　　　merchant - president, Sizer & Co. (wholesale lumber)

Marriage(s):　　　　　　　　　Mary Theodora Thomsen (1866-1941)

Listed in *Long Island Society Register, 1929*: yes
Address:　　　　　　　　　　　North Plandome Road, Plandome Manor
Acreage / map sources:　　　　on 1927 map
　　　　　　　　　　　　　　　not on 1932 or 1946 maps

Name of estate:　　　　　　　*Norwood*
Year of construction:
Style of architecture:
Architect(s):
Landscape architect(s):
House extant: unconfirmed
Historical notes:

　　The *Long Island Society Register, 1929* lists Mary Theodora Thomsen Sizer as residing at *Norwood* on Shore Road [North Plandome Road], Port Washington [Plandome Manor].
　　Robert Ryland and Mary Theodora Thomsen Sizer, Sr.'s daughter Elizabeth married Samuel Vernon Mann, Jr. and resided in Kings Point. Their daughter Emmalena married David Duncan II, the son of William Butler and Blanche Havemeyer Duncan who resided at *Park Hill* in Sands Point.

Slade, John, Sr. (1866-1932)

Occupation(s):   financier -   partner, Simmons and Slade (stock brokerage firm)

Marriage(s):   M/1 - 1892 - Alice Bell
                                         M/2 - 1914-1932 - Edith B. Weekes (d. 1965)

Listed in *Long Island Society Register, 1929*: yes
Address: Mill River Hollow Road, Upper Brookville
Acreage / map sources: on 1927 map; not on 1932 or 1946 maps
Name of estate: *Underhill House*
Year of construction: c. 1800
Style of architecture: Modified Federal
Architect(s):   Alexander Mackintosh designed the house (for J. Slade, Sr.)
Landscape architect(s):
House extant: yes
Historical notes:

    The house, originally named *Underhill House,* was built by John Slade, Sr.
    The *Social Register New York, 1948* and *1965* list Edith B. Weekes Slade as residing at *Underhill House,* Mill River Road, Oyster Bay [Upper Brookville].
    John Slade, Sr.'s sister-in-law Josephine Bissell Roe Slade resided at *Pine Terrace* in Mill Neck.
    Edith B. Weekes Slade was the daughter of Arthur Delano and Lily Underhill Weekes, Sr. and a descendant of the Colonial Indian fighter Captain John Underhill. Her brother Arthur Delano Weekes, Jr. resided at *The Anchorage* in Oyster Bay Cove. Her brother Harold married Louisine Peters, with whom he resided at *Wereholme* in Islip, and, subsequently, Frances Stokes, with whom he resided at *Valentine Farm* in Old Brookville.

front facade

    John and Alice Bell Slade, Sr.'s son John Slade, Jr. married Bernadine Blount Gleeson, the daughter of Charles L. Gleeson of Scarsdale, NY.

Slade, John, Sr. (1866-1932)

Occupation(s):   financier -   partner, Simmons and Slade (stock brokerage firm)

Marriage(s):   M/1 - 1892 - Alice Bell
                                         M/2 - 1914-1932 - Edith B. Weekes (d. 1965)

Listed in *Long Island Society Register, 1929*: yes
Address: Berry Hill Road, Oyster Bay Cove
Acreage / map sources: not on 1927 or 1932 maps
                                         4 acres / 1946 map (named misspelled as L. N. Slade)
Name of estate: *Berry Hill Farm*
Year of construction:
Style of architecture:
Architect(s):
Landscape architect(s):
House extant: unconfirmed
Historical notes:

    The house, originally named *Berry Hill Farm,* was built by John Slade, Sr.
    Both the *Long Island Society Register, 1929* and the *Social Register, Summer 1932* list John and Edith B. Weekes Slade [Sr.] as residing at *Berry Hill Farm* in Oyster Bay [Oyster Bay Cove], while the *Social Register, Summer 1937* lists only Edith B. Weekes Slade as residing at *Berry Hill Farm.*
    [See previous entry for additional family information.]
    The estate was, subsequently, owned by Irvine E. T. Baehr, who called it *Piazzola.*

Slade, Josephine Bissell Roe (d. 1954)

Marriage(s):	1902 -1913 - Prescott Slade (1868-1913) - financier - member, Taylor, Smith and Hard (investment banking firm)

Listed in *Long Island Society Register, 1929*: no
Address: Horse Shoe Road, Mill Neck
Acreage / map sources: not on 1927 map
                                                 no acreage given on 1932 map
                                                 15 acres / 1946 map
Name of estate: *Pine Terrace*
Year of construction: c. 1929
Style of architecture: Dutch Colonial
Architect(s):   Chester A. Patterson designed the house
                                                    (for J. B. R. Slade)
Landscape architect(s):
House extant: yes
Historical notes:

The house, originally named *Pine Terrace,* was built by Josephine Bissell Roe Slade.
The *Social Register, Summer 1937* lists Josephine B. Roe Slade as residing in Mill Neck, while the *Social Register, Summer 1945* lists the name of the estate as *Pine Terrace.* The *Social Register New York, 1954* lists Josephine B. Roe Slade as residing at 1220 Park Avenue, NYC.
She was the daughter of General Charles Francis Roe.
Prescott Slade's brother John resided at *Berry Hill Farm* in Oyster Bay Cove and *Underhill House* in Upper Brookville.
The Slades were residing in Cedarhurst at the time of Prescott Slade's death.
The estate was, subsequently, owned by the Slades' daughter Katherine and son-in-law Henry Dennison Babcock, Sr.

Slater, Horatio Nelson, III (1893-1968)

Occupation(s):   industrialist - founder, Slater Manufacturing Co., Inc.
                                                    (manufacturers of rayon cloth);
                                                    president, S. Slater & Sons, Inc. (cotton mills)
Civic Activism: member, Industrial Advisory Board of the National Recovery
                                                    Administration*

Marriage(s):   1921-1968 - Martha Byers Lyon

Listed in *Long Island Society Register, 1929*: yes
Address: Duck Pond Road and Piping Rock Road, Matinecock
Acreage / map sources: on 1927 map
                                                 not on 1932 map
                                                 46 acres / 1946 map
Name of estate: *Ricochet*
Year of construction:
Style of architecture:
Architect(s):
Landscape architect(s):
House extant: unconfirmed
Historical notes:

The *Long Island Society Register, 1929* lists Horatio Nelson and Martha B. Lyon Slater [III] as residing at *Ricohet* on Duck Pond Road, Locust Valley [Matinecock]. The *Social Register, Summer 1966* lists Martha B. Lyon Slater as residing at *Holly House* on Duck Pond Road, Locust Valley [Matinecock].
*In 1933 he wrote the first code for textiles for the National Recovery Administration. [*The New York Times* May 2, 1968, p. 47.]
Horatio Nelson Slater III was the great-grandson of Samuel Slater, who was known as the "father of the cotton industry."

Sloan, Alfred Pritchard, Jr. (1875-1966)

Occupation(s):   industrialist - president, General Motors Corp.
Civic Activism: *

Marriage(s):   1898-1956 - Irene Jackson (d. 1956)
                                   - Civic Activism: *

Listed in *Long Island Society Register, 1929*: yes
Address: West Shore Road, Kings Point
Acreage / map sources: on 1927 map
                              21 acres / 1932 map
                              20 acres / 1946 map
Name of estate: *Snug Harbor*
Year of construction: c. 1916
Style of architecture: French Renaissance
Architect(s):   Walker and Gillette designed the house (for Aldrich)
Landscape architect(s):   Olmsted (for Aldrich)
House extant: yes
Historical notes:

    The house, originally named *Snug Harbor,* was built by Sherwood Aldrich.
    From 1927 to 1950, the estate was owned by Sloan, who continued to call it *Snug Harbor*. The *Social Register, Summer 1945* lists *Snug Harbor* as the name of Sloan's estate.
    *Since the Sloans never had children, their entire fortune was given to charity. They established the Alfred P. Sloan, Jr. Foundation with a gift of $305 million. [*The New York Times* February 18, 1966, p. 30.] Alfred P. Sloan bequeathed an additional $20 million to cancer research. [*The New York Times* February 2, 1966, p. 31.]
    Sloan's niece Elisabeth Pratt Sloan was married to John Holyoke Livingston and resided in Oyster Bay Cove.

Sloane, Charles Byron (1895-1955)

Occupation(s):   educator -   professor, Department of Chemistry, Seton Hall
                                       University, South Orange, NJ

Marriage(s):   M/1 - Dorothy Mitchell
                            M/2 - Eleanor McCormick

Listed in *Long Island Society Register, 1929:* yes
Address: Middle Neck Road, Sands Point
Acreage / map sources: on 1906 and 1927 maps (owned by C. W. Sloane)
                              29 acres / 1932 map (owned by N. B. Sloane)
                              not on 1946 map
Name of estate: *The Place*
Year of construction:
Style of architecture:
Architect(s):
Landscape architect(s):
House extant: yes
Historical notes:

    The *Long Island Society Register, 1929* lists Charles Byron Sloane as residing at *The Place* in Sands Point with his father Charles William Sloane.
    The *Social Register New York, 1933* lists C. Byron and Dorothy Mitchell Sloane as residing at *The Place* in Sands Point, while the *Social Register, Summer 1937* lists the Sloanes' residence only as Sands Point.
    [See following entry for additional family information.]
    The estate was, subsequently, owned by George Washington Vanderbilt IV, who built a new, Contemporary-style house in c. 1937.

Sloane, Charles William (1850-1929)

Occupation(s):   attorney

Marriage(s):   Nina Byron

Listed in *Long Island Society Register, 1929:* yes
Address: Middle Neck Road, Sands Point
Acreage / map sources: on 1906 and 1927 maps (owned by C. W. Sloane)
                                  29 acres / 1932 map (owned by N. B. Sloane)
                                  not on 1946 map
Name of estate: *The Place*
Year of construction:
Style of architecture:
Architect(s):
Landscape architect(s):
House extant: yes
Historical notes:

   The *Social Register New York, 1907* lists Charles William and Nina Byron Sloane as residing at *The Place* in Sands Point. The *Long Island Society Register, 1929* lists Charles William Sloane as continuing to reside at *The Place* in Sands Point and lists Charles Byron Sloane as residing at *The Place* with his father.

   The *Social Register New York, 1933* lists C. Byron and Dorothy Mitchell Sloane as residing at *The Place* in Sands Point, while the *Social Register, Summer 1937* lists the Sloanes' residence only as Sands Point.

   The Sloanes' son The Rev. Charles O'Connor Sloane, a Roman Catholic priest and as such unmarried, resided in Yonkers, NY. Their son Cyril resided in Patchogue. Their son Reginald resided in Elizabeth, NJ. Their daughter Christine married Godwin Ordway, Jr., a graduate of the United States Military Academy at West Point, and resided in Chevy Chase, MD. Godwin's father was a colonel in the Army and he was the grandson of General Ordway of Washington, DC.

   The estate was, subsequently, owned by George Washington Vanderbilt IV, who built a new, Contemporary-style house in c. 1937.

George Sloane's house, Brookmeade,
front facade, c. 1919

Sloane, George (1888-1946)

Occupation(s):   financier -   a founder, Sloane, Pell and Co. (stock brokerage firm);
                                           partner, C. E. Welles;
                                           partner, Rhodes and Co. (investment banking firm)

Civic Activism: chairman, Price Control Board of Fauquier County, VA, during
                                  World War II

Marriage(s):   M/1 - 1921-1929 - Isabel C. Dodge (d. 1962)
                                M/2 - 1930-1946 - Katherine Elizabeth Ingalls

Listed in *Long Island Society Register, 1929*:   yes
Address: Lattingtown Road, Lattingtown
Acreage / map sources: on 1927 map
                                  no acreage given on 1932 map
                                  14 acres / 1946 map
Name of estate: *Brookmeade*
Year of construction: c. 1916-1917
Style of architecture: Elizabethan
Architect(s):   Theodate Pope Riddle of Lamb and Rich designed the house
                                      (for E. H. Gates)
                                  James W. O'Connor designed the tennis court complex
                                      (for G. Sloane)
                                  William Lawrence Bottomley designed 1935 alterations
                                      to the house (for G. Sloane)*
Landscape architect(s):   Ferruccio Vitale, 1917 (for E. H. Gates);
                                  1924 (for G. Sloane)

House extant: yes
Historical notes:

     The seventeen-room, 6,000-square-foot house, originally named *Dormer House,* was built by Elizabeth Hoagland Gates.

     In 1927, the estate was purchased by Sloane, who called it *Brookmeade.*

     The *Long Island Social Register, 1929* lists George and Isabel C. Dodge Sloane as residing at *Brookmeade* in Locust Valley [Lattingtown], while the *Social Register, Summer 1932* lists only Isabel C. Dodge Sloane as residing at *Brookmeade.*

     Isabel C. Dodge Sloane was the daughter of John Dodge, one of the founders of Dodge Motor Company.

     The *Social Register New York, 1933* lists George and Katherine E. Ingalls Sloane as residing at *Whitehall Farm* in Warrenton, VA, while the *Social Register, Summer 1946* lists the Sloanes' residence as *The Spinney* in Pointe au Pic, Province of Quebec, Canada.

     Katherine Elizabeth Ingalls Sloane was the daughter of George H. Ingalls of Manhattan. She had previously been married to Carroll Booth Alker, who resided in Muttontown, Lattingtown, and at *Ca Va* in Old Brookville. After Sloane's death, she married Edwin Darius Graves, Jr. of Washington, DC.

     *In 1935, the east wing of the house was added.

     The third owner was opera singer Patrice Munsel, who called it *Lockjaw Ridge,* mocking what was known as the "Locust Valley Lockjaw British accent."

     In 1980, Munsel sold the estate to Guillermo Vilas.

     In 1992, it was purchased by Walter Raquet.

     Both Vilas and Raquet continued to call the estate *Lockjaw Ridge.*

     In 1999, the house and 4.07 acres were for sale. The asking price was $1.85 million; the annual taxes were $23,507.

Sloane, Malcolm Douglas (1885-1924)

Occupation(s):

Marriage(s):   1915-1924 - Elinor Lee (d. 1964)

Listed in *Long Island Society Register, 1929*: no
Address: Hoffstot Lane, Sands Point
Acreage / map sources: on 1927 map (owned by Mrs. M. D. Sloane); not on 1932 or 1946 map
Name of estate:
Year of construction: c. 1900
Style of architecture: Colonial Revival
Architect(s):
Landscape architect(s):
House extant: yes
Historical notes:

The house, originally named *Kidd's Rocks*, was built by John Scott Browning, Sr.
In 1921, Sloane purchased the estate from Browning's widow.
Malcolm Douglas Sloane was the son of William Douglas and Emily Thorn Vanderbilt Sloane, Sr. His grandfather William and great-uncle John founded the W. & J. Sloane Carpet Company. His sister Florence married James Abercrombie Burden, Jr. and resided at *Woodside* in Muttontown. After Sloane's death, his widow Elinor Lee Sloane married Albert Delmont Smith and resided with him at the former Sloane estate *Kidd's Rocks,* which the Smiths renamed *Keewaydin.*
Elinor Lee Sloane was the daughter of Charles H. Lee of Manhattan.
In 1929, the Smiths sold the estate to Herbert Bayard Swope, Sr. and moved to *Mill Pond,* in Lloyd Harbor. Swope continued to call the Sands Point estate *Keewaydin.*
In 1964, the estate was purchased by Horace Richter. It was purchased in 1968 by Irwin Hamilton Kramer. In 1983, Charles Shipman Payson purchased the estate and renamed it *Lands End.*
In 2001, the house and fourteen acres were for sale by Mrs. Payson. The asking price was $50 million. In 2003, the asking price had been reduced to $29.5 million.

Smith, Albert Delmont (1886-1962)

Occupation(s):   artist - specialized in portraits*
Civic Activism: director, Heckscher Art Museum, Huntington

Marriage(s):   1927-1962 - Elinor Lee (d. 1964)

Listed in *Long Island Society Register, 1929*: yes
Address: Hoffstot Lane, Sands Point
Acreage / map sources: on 1927 map (owned by Mrs. M. D. Sloane); not on 1932 or 1946 map
Name of estate: *Keewaydin*
Year of construction: c. 1900
Style of architecture: Colonial Revival
Architect(s):
Landscape architect(s):
House extant: yes
Historical notes:

After the death of Malcolm Douglas Sloane his widow Elinor Lee Sloane married Albert Delmont Smith and resided with him at the former Sloane estate *Kidd's Rocks* which they renamed *Keewaydin.*
The *Long Island Society Register, 1929* lists Albert D. and Elinor Lee Smith as residing at *Keewayden [Keewaydin]* in Port Washington [Sands Point].
The Smiths' son Peter married Mariana Mann, the daughter of L. O. V. Mann of Manhattan.
*Albert Delmont Smith's paintings are displayed in many American museums.
In 1929, the Smiths sold the estate to Herbert Bayard Swope, Sr. and moved to *Mill Pond* in Lloyd Harbor. The *Social Register, Summer 1932* lists the Smiths as residing at *Mill Pond* in Lloyd Harbor.
[*See previous entry for chronology of estate ownership.*]

Smith, Albert Delmont (1886-1962)

Occupation(s):   artist - specialized in portraits*
Civic Activism: director, Heckscher Art Museum, Huntington

Marriage(s):   1927-1962 - Elinor Lee (d. 1964)

Listed in *Long Island Society Register, 1929*: yes
Address: School Lane, Lloyd Harbor
Acreage / map sources: not on 1929 map; on 1931 map; 58 acres / 1944 map
Name of estate: *Mill Pond*
Year of construction:
Style of architecture:
Architect(s):
Landscape architect(s):
House extant: unconfirmed
Historical notes:

The *Long Island Society Register, 1929* lists Albert D. and Elinor Lee Smith as residing at *Keewayden [Keewaydin]* in Port Washington [Sands Point], while the *Social Register, Summer 1932* lists the Smiths as residing at *Mill Pond* in Lloyd Harbor.

Elinor Lee Smith had previously been married to Malcolm Douglas Sloane, who died in 1924. The Sloanes had resided at *Kidd's Rocks* in Sands Point. Elinor subsequently married Albert Delmont Smith. The Smiths continued to reside at the former Sloane estate changing its name to *Keewaydin*.

The Smiths' son Peter married Mariana Mann, the daughter of L. O. V. Mann of Manhattan.

*Albert Delmont Smith's paintings are displayed in many American museums.

Smith, Albert Edward, Sr. (1874-1958)

Occupation(s):   capitalist - partner and one of three founders (together with James Stuart Blackton and William T. Rock), Vitagraph Company of America (an early motion picture company headquartered in Bay Shore and Brooklyn)*

inventor - invented Vitagraph, one of the earliest successful motion picture projectors with non-flicker shutter and stop-motion photography;
invented ball and socket steering joint for automobiles;
invented electric gear shift for automobiles

writer - *Two Reels and a Crank*, 1952 (co-authored with Phil A. Koury)

Marriage(s):   M/1 - 1897 - Mary Elizabeth Arthur
                                          M/2 - 1912 - Hazel Neason
                                          M/3 - 1920 - Lucile Beatrice O'Hair

Listed in *Long Island Society Register, 1929*: no
Address: Centre Island Road, Centre Island
Acreage / map sources: on c. 1922 map; not on 1927, 1932, or 1946 maps
Name of estate:
Year of construction: c. 1899
Style of architecture: Tudor
Architect(s):   Renwick, Aspinwall and Owen designed the house (for Bullock)
Landscape architect(s):
House extant: unconfirmed
Historical notes:

The house, originally named *The Folly* [II], was built by George Bullock, who over the years owned several Long Island houses.

The estate was owned by Smith, by George Shaw Mahana, who called it *Birchlea,* and, subsequently, by Walter Stanley Gubelmann, who called it *Southerly.*

*In 1926, Vitagraph was absorbed into Warner Brothers. In 1948, The Motion Picture Academy of Arts and Sciences awarded Smith an Oscar for his pioneer work in the motion picture industry.

His partner James Stuart Blackton, Sr. resided at *Harbourwood* in Cove Neck.

Albert Edward Smith, Sr.'s house,
side / rear facade, 1899

Smith, Albert Lawrence, Sr. (1890-1934)

Occupation(s):	financier - partner, Edward B. Smith and Co. (investment banking firm);
	director, Western Savings Fund of Philadelphia;
	director, Industrial Finance Co.;
	director, Industrial Acceptance Corp.
	capitalist - real estate - chairman of board, Roosevelt Field, Inc., Garden City
	director, Buffalo & Susquehanna Railroad Corp.;
	director, Lehigh Valley Transit Co;
	director, Easton Consolidated Electric Co.
	industrialist - director, Giant Portland Cement Co.;
	director, East Sugar Loaf Coal Co.
Civic Activism:	director, Beekman Street Hospital, NYC (which combined with Downtown Hospital to become Beekman–Downtown Hospital)
Marriage(s):	M/1 - 1914-1924 - Virginia Norris Harrison (d. 1924)
	M/2 - 1923-1934 - Glee C. Jamison

Listed in *Long Island Society Register, 1929*: no
Address: Brookville Road, Brookville
Acreage / map sources: not on 1927 map; 70 acres / 1932 map; 65 acres / 1946 map
Name of estate: *Penllyn*
Year of construction: c. 1918
Style of architecture: Federal
Architect(s):   Alfred C. Bossom designed the house (for J. W. Harriman)
Landscape architect(s):   Olmsted, 1918-1928 (for J. W. Harriman)
House extant: no; demolished c. 1950
Historical notes:

    The house, originally named *Avondale Farms,* was built by Joseph Wright Harriman.
    The estate was, subsequently, owned by Smith, who renamed it *Penllyn.*
    The *Social Register, Summer 1932* lists Albert L. and Glee C. Jamison Smith [Sr.] as residing at *Penllyn* in Brookville.
The *Social Register New York, 1966* lists Mrs. Smith's address as 320 East 72nd Street, NYC.
    Albert Lawrence Smith, Sr. was the son of Edward B. and Laura Howell Jenks Smith of Philadelphia.

Smith, Earl Edward Tailer, Sr. (1903-1991)

Occupation(s):
financier - a founder and partner, Paige, Smith & Remick
(investment banking firm);
director, Bank of Palm Beach & Trust Co.
industrialist - director, United States Sugar Corp.;
director, Lionel Corp.;
director, C. F. and I. Steele Corp.
diplomat - United States Ambassador to Cuba, 1957-1959
politician - mayor, City of Miami, FL, 1971-1977
writer - *The Fourth Floor*

Marriage(s):
M/1 - 1926-1935 - Consuelo Vanderbilt (b. 1903)
M/2 - Mimi E. Richardson
M/3 - 1948-1965 - Florence Pritchett (1920-1965)
- journalist - her column "The Mood and the Food"
appeared in the Living Section of
The Journal American
entertainers and associated professions -
panelist on television show "Leave it to the Girls"
M/4 - 1968-1991 - Lesly Stockard Hickox

Listed in *Long Island Society Register, 1929*: yes
Address: House Drive, Sands Point
Acreage / map sources: on 1927 map (name misspelled as E. A. C. Smith)
18 acres / 1932 map (name misspelled as M. C. Smith)
not on 1946 map
Name of estate: *Iradell*
Year of construction:
Style of architecture:
Architect(s):
Landscape architect(s):
House extant: unconfirmed
Historical notes:

The *Social Register, Summer 1932* lists Earl E. T. and Consuelo Vanderbilt Smith as residing at *Iradell* in Sands Point. He was the son of Sydney J. and Fannie Bogert Tailer Smith.

Consuelo Vanderbilt Smith was the daughter of William Kissam and Virginia Graham Fair Vanderbilt, Jr., who resided at *Deepdale* in Lake Success prior to their divorce. She was named for her aunt Consuelo Vanderbilt (Spencer-Churchill, Duchess of Marlborough) Balsan, the daughter of William Kissam and Alva Erskine Smith Vanderbilt, Sr., who resided at *Idlehour* in Oakdale. After her divorce from Smith, Consuelo married Henry Gassaway Davis III in 1936 in the water off of Miami Beach aboard her father's yacht *Alva*. Davis had just recently been divorced from his second cousin, the former Grace Vanderbilt. Consuelo's third marriage, in 1941, was to William J. Warburton III and her fourth, to N. Clarkson Earl, Jr., who died in 1969.

The *Social Register, Summer 1937* lists Earl E. T. and Mimi E. Richardson Smith as residing at *The Towers* in Greenwich, CT.

Florence Pritchett Smith was the daughter of Samuel Mason Pritchett, a successful shoe manufacturer from Orange, NJ.

Earl Edward Tailer and Florence Pritchett Smith's son Earl Edward Tailer Smith, Jr. married Tatiana Gardner, the daughter of George Peabody Gardner of Brookline, MA.

Smith, George Campbell, Sr. (1858-1933)

Occupation(s):   publisher - vice-president, president, and treasurer,
                                                       Street and Smith Publications, Inc.
                                       ("dime novel" publisher)

Marriage(s):   Anne K. Schmertz

Listed in *Long Island Society Register, 1929*: yes
Address: Wellington Road, Matinecock
Acreage / map sources: on 1927 map
                              no acreage given on 1932 map
                              not on 1946 map
Name of estate:
Year of construction:
Style of architecture:
Architect(s):
Landscape architect(s):
House extant: unconfirmed
Historical notes:

    The *Long Island Society Register, 1929* lists George C. and Annie [Anne] K. Schmertz Smith [Sr.] as residing in Locust Valley [Matinecock].
    His brother Ormond Gerald Smith, who married Grace Hewitt Pellet, resided at *Stepping Stones* in Brookville and *Shoremonde* on Centre Island. They were the sons of Gerald Hewitt Smith.
    The Smiths' daughter Dorothy married Artemas Holmes and resided at *Holmestead Farm* in Old Brookville. Their daughter Anne married Wilmurt O. Swaine.

Smith, Herbert Ludlam, Sr. (1875-1927)

Occupation(s):   financier - partner, Smith and Lewis (stock brokerage firm);
                                                     vice-president and director, Garden City Bank

Marriage(s):   Marie Schoonmaker

Listed in *Long Island Society Register, 1929*: yes
Address: off South Centre Island Road, Centre Island
Acreage / map sources: on c. 1922 and 1927 maps
                              not on 1932 or 1946 maps
Name of estate: *Oliver's Point*
Year of construction: 1912
Style of architecture: Shingle
Architect(s):   Herbert R. Brewster designed the house (for H. L. Smith, Sr.)
                              Walker and Gillette designed 1930s alterations which eliminated
                                  the bays (for Baker)
Landscape architect(s):
House extant: no; demolished c. 1970
Historical notes:

    The house, originally named *Oliver's Point,* was built by Herbert Ludlam Smith [Sr.].
    He was the son of Isaac and Cornelia Ludlam Smith, who also resided on Centre Island.
    The *Brooklyn Blue Book and Long Island Society Register, 1918* lists Mr. and Mrs. Herbert Ludlam Smith [Sr.] as residing in Oyster Bay [Centre Island].
    In 1927, the Smiths were residing on Cathedral Avenue, Garden City.
    The *Long Island Society Register, 1929* lists Marie Schoonmaker Smith as residing on Second Street, Garden City.
    The estate was, subsequently, owned by William Francis Carey, Jr.
    During the Depression, the estate reverted back to the Smith family, who then sold it to George Fisher Baker III, who called it *Ventura Point.*

Smith, Howard Caswell, Sr. (1871-1965)

Occupation(s):	financier - trustee, Bank of New York;
	director, American National Fire Insurance Co.;
	director, Great American Insurance Co.;
	director, One Liberty Street Corp.;
	trustee, Franklin Savings Bank, Franklin Square
	industrialist - partner, Hathaway & Co.
	publisher - chairman of board, Appleton–Century–Crofts, Inc.
Civic Activism:	mayor, Village of Cove Neck;
	trustee, Theodore Roosevelt Memorial Association
Marriage(s):	M/1 - 1898 - Katherine Lyall Moen
	M/2 - 1919-1952 - Anna Barry Phelps (1877-1952)
	- Civic Activism: director, Red Cross canteen in England during World War I
	M/3 - 1954 -1965 - Mary Fitch Phelps

Listed in *Long Island Society Register, 1929*: yes
Address: private road off Cove Neck Road, Cove Neck
Acreage / map sources: on 1927 map; 21 acres / 1932 map; 24 acres / 1946 map
Name of estate: *Shoredge*
Year of construction: c. 1906
Style of architecture: Tudor
Architect(s):
Landscape architect(s):
House extant: no; demolished c. 1960
Historical notes:

The house, originally named *Shoredge*, was built by Howard Caswell Smith, Sr.
Howard Caswell and Katherine Lyall Moen Smith, Sr.'s son R. Moen Smith resided in Andover, MA. Their son St. Clair Moen Smith resided in Cleveland, OH. Their son Caswell Moen Smith served as mayor of Plandome.
Anna and Mary Phelps Smith were the daughters of George H. Phelps of Lakeville, CT.

Smith, Ormond Gerald (1860-1933)

Occupation(s):	publisher* - president, Street and Smith Publications Inc. ("dime novel" publisher);
	founder, *Ainslee's* magazine;
	founder, *Popular* magazine;
	founder, *People's Smith's* magazine;
	founder, *Top Notch* magazine;
	founder, *Picture Play* magazine
	capitalist - real estate - president, Ormorge Realty Co.
Marriage(s):	1899 - Grace Hewitt Pellet

Listed in *Long Island Society Register, 1929*: yes
Address: Cedar Swamp Road, Brookville
Acreage / map sources: not on 1927 map; 10 acres / 1932 and 1946 maps
Name of estate: *Stepping Stones*
Year of construction:
Style of architecture:
Architect(s):
Landscape architect(s):
House extant: unconfirmed
Historical notes:

Ormond Gerald Smith's brother George Campbell Smith, Sr. resided in Matinecock. They were the sons of Gerald Hewitt Smith.
*The first works of the American short story writer William Sidney Porter, who wrote under the pseudonym of O. Henry, appeared in Smith's magazines.

Smith, Ormond Gerald (1860-1933)

Occupation(s):   publisher* - *[See previous entry for list of publications.]*
                                     capitalist - real estate - president, Ormorge Realty Co.

Marriage(s):   1899 - Grace Hewitt Pellet

Listed in *Long Island Society Register, 1929*: yes
Address: Centre Island Road, Centre Island
Acreage / map sources: not on 1927, 1932, or 1946 maps
Name of estate: *Shoremonde*
Year of construction: c. 1910
Style of architecture: Federal
Architect(s):   Hoppin and Koen designed the house (for O. G. Smith)
Landscape architect(s):   Ralph Weinrichter (for O. G. Smith)
Estate photographs can be found in the Nassau County Museum Collection filed under Centre Island/Smith.
House extant: no; demolished c. 1940
Historical notes:

    The house, originally named *Shoremonde,* was built by Ormond Gerald Smith.
    His brother George Campbell Smith, Sr. resided in Matinecock.
    *The first works of the American short story writer William Sidney Porter, who wrote under the pseudonym of O. Henry, appeared in Smith's magazines.
    The estate was owned by John North Willys, who called it *Northcliff,* and, subsequently, by E. LeRoux.

front facade, c. 1910

Smith, Owen Telfair (b. 1937)

Occupation(s):   attorney
                                       politician - chairman, Nassau County Planning Committee;
                                              Deputy County Executive, Nassau County, 1980-1987
                                      restaurateur - partner, Milleridge Inn, Jericho;
                                              partner, Lauraine Murphy Restaurants, Manhasset
                                      writer - *Professional Corporations, 1973; Wage and Price Freeze, 1973; Fletchers Corporation Forms, 1974; Real Estate Forms of Organization, 1975*
                                      educator - chairman, Finance Department, C. W. Post College of Long Island University, Brookville

Marriage(s):   1985 - Bernadette Casey (b. 1943)

Listed in *Long Island Society Register, 1929*: no
Address: Ridge Road, Laurel Hollow
Acreage / map sources: not on 1927, 1932, or 1946 maps
Name of estate:
Year of construction: c. 1929
Style of architecture:
Architect(s):   Delano and Aldrich designed the house (for Duer)
Landscape architect(s):   Olmsted, 1929-1931 (for Duer)
House extant: yes
Historical notes:

    The house, originally named *Whispering Laurels,* was built by Beverly Duer.
    The estate was owned by William Rogers Deering, who called it *Roseneath.*
    Since 1988 it has been owned by Smith.
    Bernadette Casey Smith is the daughter of William Joseph and Sophia Kurz Casey, Jr., who resided at *Mayknoll* in Roslyn Harbor.

Smithers, Christopher Dunkin, Sr. (1865-1952)

Occupation(s): financier - a founder and partner with his brother, F. S. Smithers and Co.
(investment banking firm)
industrialist - director, IBM

Civic Activism: trustee, Village of Lattingtown

Marriage(s): 1902-1952 - Mabel Carew Brinkley (1880-1957)

Listed in *Long Island Society Register, 1929*: yes
Address: Overlook Road, Lattingtown
Acreage / map sources: on 1927 map; no acreage given on 1932 map; 20 acres / 1946 map
Name of estate: *Dunrobin*
Year of construction: c. 1900
Style of architecture: Colonial Revival
Architect(s): Bradford Lee Gilbert designed the house (for Baldwin)
Landscape architect(s):
House extant: no; demolished c. 1937
Historical notes:

The house was built by William H. Baldwin, Jr.
The estate was, subsequently, owned by Smithers, who called it *Dunrobin.*
The *Long Island Society Register, 1929* lists Christopher D. and Mabel C. Brinkley Smithers [Sr.] as residing at *Dunrobin* on Overlook Road, Glen Cove [Lattingtown], while the *Social Register New York, 1951* lists their residence as Delray Beach, FL.
His brother Francis S. Smithers resided at *Myhome* in Glen Cove.
The Smithers' son Robert Brinkley Smithers resided at *Longhur* in Mill Neck. In 1933 the Smithers' daughter Mabel married Edward Bonner Bowring.

Smithers, Francis S. (1848-1919)

Occupation(s): financier - a founder and partner with his brother, F. S. Smithers and Co.
(investment banking firm);
president, Bank of Montreal;
director, American Bank Note Co.
capitalist - director, Detroit Edison Co.;
director, United Railways of San Francisco

Marriage(s): M/1 - Louisa M. Bancroft (d. 1895)
M/2 - 1898-1919 - Mabel Stevens (1869-1952)

Listed in *Long Island Society Register, 1929*: yes
Address: Red Spring Lane, Glen Cove
Acreage / map sources: 1927 map illegible; not on 1932 or 1946 maps
Name of estate: *Myhome*
Year of construction:
Style of architecture: Colonial Revival
Architect(s):
Landscape architect(s): Ellen Biddle Shipman
(for F. S. Smithers)

House extant: unconfirmed
Historical notes:

rear facade, c. 1917

The *Long Island Society Register, 1929* lists Mabel Stevens Smithers as residing at *Myhome* on Red Springs Lane, Glen Cove.
Francis S. Smither's brother Christopher Dunkin Smithers, Sr. resided at *Dunrobin* in Lattingtown.

Smithers, Robert Brinkley (1907-1994)

Occupation(s):   financier -   member, Brown Brothers (investment banking firm);
                                                 partner, F. S. Smithers and Co. (investment banking firm)
Civic Activism: established the Christopher D. Smithers Foundation, 1952

Marriage(s):   M/1 - 1930-1983 - M. Gertrude Finucane (d. 1983)
                             M/2 - Adele *[unable to confirm maiden name]*

Listed in *Long Island Society Register, 1929*: no
Address: Oyster Bay Road, Mill Neck
Acreage / map sources: not on 1927, 1932, or 1946 maps
Name of estate:
Year of construction: c. 1914
Style of architecture: Cotswold
Architect(s):   Harrie Thomas Lindeberg designed the house
                              (for I. Brokaw)
Landscape architect(s):   Olmsted (for I. Brokaw)
House extant: yes
Historical notes:

    The house, originally named *Frost Mill Lodge,* was built by Irving Brokaw.
    In the 1960s, the estate was purchased by Robert Brinkley Smithers.
    [See previous entry for family information.]
    Smithers also resided at *Longhur* which adjoined this property.

Smithers, Robert Brinkley (1907-1994)

Occupation(s):   financier -   member, Brown Brothers (investment banking firm);
                                                 partner, F. S. Smithers and Co. (investment banking firm)
Civic Activism: *

Marriage(s):   M/1 - 1930-1983 - M. Gertrude Finucane (d. 1983)
                             M/2 - Adele *[unable to confirm maiden name]*

Listed in *Long Island Society Register, 1929*: no
Address: Oyster Bay Road, Mill Neck
Acreage / map sources: not on 1927, 1932, or 1946 maps
Name of estate: *Longhur*
Year of construction: c. 1926
Style of architecture: French Renaissance
Architect(s):   Walker and Gillette designed the house
                              (for I. Brokaw)
Landscape architect(s):   Marian Coffin, 1930 (for I. Brokaw)
House extant: yes
Historical notes:

    The house, originally named *Goose Point,* was built by Irving Brokaw.
    The estate was purchased by Smithers, who called in *Longhur.*
    The *Social Register, Summer 1961* lists Robert Brinkley and M. Gertrude Finucane Smithers as residing at *Longhur* in Locust Valley [Mill Neck].
    He was the son of Christopher Dunkin and Mabel Brinkley Smithers, Sr., who resided at *Dunrobin* in Lattingtown.
    *Robert Brinkley Smithers established the Christopher D. Smithers Foundation in 1952 to honor his father by donating $13.5 million to the foundation. Over the years he had donated an additional $27.9 million to anti-alcoholism programs. [*The New York Times* January 12, 1994, sec. B, p. 7.]

Smull, Jacob Barstow (1874-1962)

Occupation(s):   shipping -   vice-president, J. H. Winchester & Co. (steamship
                                                                brokerage firm)
                    financier -   chairman of board, Seaman's Bank of Savings, NYC;
                                                               director, Harriman National Bank (which became
                                                               National Bank & Trust Co.);
                                                               director, New York Life Insurance Co.

Civic Activism: appointed by President Harding to be president of United States
                                Shipping Board Emergency Fleet Corp.
                    treasurer, Y.M.C.A.;
                    treasurer, New York City Mission Society;
                    treasurer, Webb Institute of Naval Architecture, Glen Cove;
                    treasurer, Citizens Budget Committee;
                    treasurer, Village of Laurel Hollow

Marriage(s):   1911-1962 - Ethel Stilwell

Listed in *Long Island Society Register, 1929*: yes
Address: Moore's Hill Road and Ridge Road, Laurel Hollow
Acreage / map sources: on 1927 map
                                no acreage given on 1932 or 1946 maps

Name of estate: *Ridgelands*
Year of construction:
Style of architecture:
Architect(s):
Landscape architect(s):
House extant: unconfirmed
Historical notes:

    Both the *Long Island Society Register, 1929* and the *Social Register, Summer 1961* list J. Barstow and Ethel Stilwell Smull as residing at *Ridgelands* on Ridge Road, Syosset [Laurel Hollow].

Snow, George Palen (d. 1968)

Occupation(s):   attorney
                    financier -   vice-president, City Mortgage Co.

Marriage(s):   M/1 - 1926-1961 - Carmel White (1888-1961)
                                    - journalist - chairman, editorial board, *Harper's Bazaar*
                    M/2 - 1962-1968 - Carol Kobbe (d. 1976)

Listed in *Long Island Society Register, 1929*: yes
Address: Belvedere Drive, Syosset
Acreage / map sources: on 1927 map
                                  not on 1932 or 1946 maps

Name of estate:
Year of construction:
Style of architecture:
Architect(s):
Landscape architect(s):
Estate photographs can be found in the Nassau County Museum Collection filed under East Norwich/Snow.
House extant: unconfirmed
Historical notes:

    George Palen Snow was the son of Frederick A. and Mary Palen Snow, who resided at *Gardenside* in Southampton.
    Carol Kobbe Snow was the daughter of Gustave and Carolyn Wheeler Kobbe of Bay Shore. She had previously been married to Robert Woodward Morgan of *Meadow Road Farm* in East Islip.
    Theodore Ellis Stebbins II purchased land from George Palen Snow on which he built his own home. [*The New York Times* March 10, 1935, p. RE1.] Stebbins named his estate *White Oak Farm*.

Sobelman, Max

Occupation(s):   industrialist - vice president, Montrose Chemical Corp.

Marriage(s):

Listed in *Long Island Society Register, 1929*: no
Address: Red Spring Lane, Glen Cove
Acreage / map sources: 1927 map illegible
                                       not on 1932 or 1946 maps
Name of estate:
Year of construction: c. 1900
Style of architecture: Colonial Revival
Architect(s):
Landscape architect(s):
House extant: yes
Historical notes:

     The house was built by Edmund Wetmore.
     The estate was owned by John Nobel Stearns, Sr., who called it *The Cedars,* and, subsequently, by Sobelman.

Sousa, John Philip, Sr. (1854-1932)

Occupation(s):   entertainers and associated professions - composer;
                                                    entertainer

Marriage(s):   1879-1932 - Jane Middlesworth Bellis (d. 1944)

Listed in *Long Island Society Register, 1929*: yes
Address: Hicks Lane, Sands Point
Acreage / map sources: on 1927 map
                                       4 acres / 1932 map
                                       not on 1946 map
Name of estate: *Wildbank*
Year of construction: c. 1907
Style of architecture: Mediterranean
Architect(s):   Trowbridge and Ackerman
Landscape architect(s):
House extant: yes
Historical notes:

     The house was built by A. B. Trowbridge. It was purchased by Sousa in 1915 and remained in the Sousa family until 1965.
     The *Long Island Society Register, 1929* lists Mr. and Mrs. John Philip Sousa [Sr.] as residing in Port Washington [Sands Point].
     He was born in Washington, DC, the son of John Antonio and Maria Elisabeth Trinkhaus Sousa. The elder Sousa played the trombone in the United States Marine Band.
     Jane Middlesworth Bellis Sousa was the daughter of art and real estate dealer Henry Bellis. She was born in Philadelphia, PA.
     The estate was, subsequently, owned by Peter Hirsch, who continued to call it *Wildbank*.
     The house is on The National Register of Historic Places.

rear facade, 2004

Sparks, Sir Thomas Ashley (1877-1963)

Occupation(s):   shipping -   resident director, Cunard Steamship Co.

Marriage(s):   1900-1958 - Lady Mina Jane Roberts (d. 1958)
                                  - Civic Activism: *

Listed in *Long Island Society Register, 1929*: yes
Address: Route 25A and Berry Hill Road, Oyster Bay Cove
Acreage / map sources: on 1927 map; no acreage given on 1932 map; 290 acres / 1946 map
Name of estate: *Northaw*
Year of construction: c. 1900
Style of architecture: Georgian Revival
Architect(s):
Landscape architect(s):
House extant: no; demolished c. 1968 after it was destroyed by fire
Historical notes:

    The house was built by Henry Herman Harjes.
    The estate was, subsequently, owned by Sparks, who called it *Northaw*.
    *During the Depression, Lady Sparks organized a soup kitchen behind the Cunard Building in NYC, which averaged three hundred meals each day. She became known as "Lady Bountiful of the Waterfront."
    The Sparks' daughter Eleanor married Jordan Lawrence Mott IV and resided at *Bunker Hill* in Oyster Bay Cove. She subsequently married John Stuart Martin, with whom she resided at *Fox Hollow* in Matinecock, and Henry Pomeroy Davison II, with whom she resided at *Appledore* in Upper Brookville. Their daughter Amy married Van Duzer Burton, Sr. and resided with him at *Pink Coat Cottage* in Syosset. Amy subsequently married Edward William Boyd Sim, a captain in the British Royal Navy, who was killed in World War II, and, later, Frederick Timpson Seggerman of Manhattan.

Sparrow, Edward Wheeler (1846-1913)

Occupation(s):   financier -   president and founder, City National Bank of Lansing [MI]
                              capitalist -   real estate - extensive timber and mineral holdings in
                                                Michigan

Marriage(s):   M/1 - 1896-1899 - Helen Therese Grant (d. 1899)
               M/2 - 1903-1913 - Margaret Parish Beattie (1870-1958)
                        - Civic Activism: a founder, Studio Club of Y.W.C.A. of
                                          Greater New York;
                                    trustee, Peabody Home for Elderly Women

Listed in *Long Island Society Register, 1929*: yes
Address: Duck Pond Road, Matinecock
Acreage / map sources: on 1927 map (owned by Sparrow)
                          not on 1932 map
                        21 acres / 1946 map (owned by M. Pulsifer)
Name of estate: *Killibeg*
Year of construction: 1912
Style of architecture: Tudor
Architect(s):   Howard Greenley designed the house (for Sparrow)
Landscape architect(s):
House extant: yes
Historical notes:

    The house, originally named *Killibeg,* was built by Edward Wheeler Sparrow.
    The *Long Island Society Register, 1929* lists Margaret Parish Beattie Sparrow as residing at *Killibeg* in Locust Valley [Matinecock].
    The estate was, subsequently, owned by the Sparrows' daughter Margaret and son-in-law George Hale Pulsifer, who continued to call it *Killibeg*.
    In the 1960s, the house was owned by the Locust Valley School District.

Sperry, Edward G. (1891-1945)

Occupation(s):	inventor - designed ship stabilizers
	industrialist - treasurer, Sperry Gyroscope Co., Lake Success (which
	became Sperry Corp.; now, UNISYS);
	co-founder with his father, Sperry Products, Lake Success
	(manufacturers of rail-flaw detector and specialty
	military parts)
	capitalist - director, Brooklyn Union Gas Co.
	financier - director, South Brooklyn Savings Bank
Civic Activism:	board member, Brooklyn Hospital;
	board member, Greenwood Cemetery, Brooklyn;
	trustee, Village of Upper Brookville;
	member, board of zoning appeals, Village of Upper Brookville;
	trustee, Brooklyn and Queens Y.M.C.A.;
	trustee, Elmer A. Sperry Trust
Marriage(s):	Mary Elizabeth Garvin

Listed in *Long Island Society Register, 1929*: no

Address:	Wash Hollow Road and Mill River Hollow Road, Upper Brookville
Acreage / map sources:	not on 1927 or 1932 maps; 16 acres / 1946 map
Name of estate:	
Year of construction:	c. 1930
Style of architecture:	Federal
Architect(s):	Bradley Delehanty designed the house (for Damrosch)
Landscape architect(s):	
House extant: yes	
Historical notes:	

The house, originally named *Monday House,* was built by Dr. Walter Johannes Damrosch.
The estate was purchased in 1937 by Sperry and, subsequently, by Dr. Emilio Gabriel Collado II.
Sperry was the son of Elmer Ambrose Sperry, the founder of Sperry Gyroscope Co.

Spiegel, Jerry (b. 1930)

Occupation(s):	capitalist - real estate*
Marriage(s):	

Listed in *Long Island Society Register, 1929*: no

Address:	Jericho Turnpike and Plainview Road, Woodbury
Acreage / map sources:	not on 1927, 1932, or 1946 maps
Name of estate:	
Year of construction:	c. 1915
Style of architecture:	Federal
Architect(s):	John Russell Pope designed the house (for Mills)
Landscape architect(s):	
House extant: no	
Historical notes	

The house was built by Ogden Livingston Mills.
Andre Gromyko, who at the time was the head of the Soviet delegation to the United Nations, rented the house for a year. His young daughter was the cause of local amusement when she cut flowers from Mrs. Mills gardens and sold them on Jericho Turnpike. [*The New York Times* January 30, 1952, p. 27.]
In 1952, the 172-acre estate was sold to Spiegel.
*In 1981 Spiegel was the largest individual owner of commercial and industrial property on Long Island.
The estate is now Woodbury Country Club.

Spreckels, Claus August (1858-1946)

Occupation(s):   industrialist - general manager, Spreckels Sugar Refining Co.;
                                       general manager, Hawaii Commercial & Sugar Co.*;
                                       founder, president and chairman of board, Federal
                                            Sugar Refinery Co. of Yonkers

Marriage(s):   1883-1933 - Oroville Dore (d. 1933)

Listed in *Long Island Society Register, 1929*: no
Address: Shelter Rock Road, North Hills
Acreage / map sources: on c. 1922 map
                                        1927 map illegible
                                        not on 1932 or 1946 maps
Name of estate:
Year of construction:
Style of architecture:
Architect(s):
Landscape architect(s):
House extant: unconfirmed
Historical notes:

   *Claus August Spreckels was the son of Claus Spreckels, who was known as "The Sugar King." He and his brother Rudolph sued their father for control of the Hawaiian company and received an out-of-court settlement.

Stafford, Jennie K.

Occupation(s):   capitalist - real estate*

Marriage(s):   Robert Stafford (1847-1896)
                            - capitalist - real estate - partner, Stafford & Whittaker Hotels

Listed in *Long Island Society Register, 1929*: no
Address: Lloyd Lane, Lloyd Harbor
Acreage / map sources: not on 1927, 1932, or 1946 maps
Name of estate: *Broadwater*
Year of construction: c. 1902
Style of architecture: Spanish Renaissance Villa
Architect(s):   Lionel Moses designed the house (for Stafford)
Landscape architect(s):
House extant: yes
Historical notes:

   The house, originally named *Broadwater,* was built by Jennie K. Stafford.
   *Mrs. Stafford managed the Hotel Imperial on Broadway in NYC for twenty years after the death of her husband. The hotel was part of the chain of hotels co-founded by Robert Stafford.
   In August 1916, Mrs. Stafford married Samuel G. Murphy, a San Francisco banker. In December of the same year she sold the Hotel Imperial to J. Otto Stack and Robert W. Goelet. [*The New York Times* July 30, 1916, section I, p. 15 and December 12, 1916, p. 22.]
   The estate, was subsequently, owned by John B. Mulferrig.

side facade, c. 1902

Stanley–Brown, Joseph (1858-1941)

Occupation(s):   financier -   manager, railroad department, Fisk and Robinson (investment
                                                            banking firm)
                                    capitalist - assistant to president, Long Island Rail Road;
                                                            assistant secretary, Union Pacific & Southern Pacific Rail Road
                                    politician - private secretary to President Garfield*
Civic Activism: chairman, finance committee, National Academy of Sciences;
                                    editor, Proceedings of National Geological Society

Marriage(s):   1888-1941 - Mary ("Mollie") Garfield (1867-1947)

Listed in *Long Island Society Register, 1929*: no
Address: Harbor Road, Laurel Hollow
Acreage / map sources: not on 1927, 1932, or 1946 maps
Name of estate:
Year of construction: 1898
Style of architecture: Shingled Cottage Log Cabin
Architect(s):
Landscape architect(s):
House extant: yes
Historical notes:

The house was built by Joseph Stanley–Brown.

His paternal grandfather, whose surname was Stanley, became entangled in legal problems in Scotland and moved to the United States, changing his name to Brown. First Lady Lucretia Garfield insisted that Joseph should change his surname to Stanley–Brown if he wished to marry the Garfields' daughter Mary. Hence, the hyphenated Stanley–Brown. After President Garfield's assassination, Lucretia Garfield financed Joseph's university education. [E. H. Gwynne–Thomas. *The Presidential Families*. New York: Hippocrene Books, 1989, pp. 217-219.]

*A self-taught stenographer, Stanley–Brown was secretary to John Wesley Powell, the American geologist and explorer, who recommended Stanley–Brown to Garfield.

Mary Garfield was the daughter of President James Abram and First Lady Lucretia Rudolph Garfield. Mary's brother Harry married Belle Hartford Mason, the daughter of James Mason of Cleveland. Her brother James married Helen Newell of Chicago.

The Stanley–Browns are interred in Cleveland, OH, with President and First Lady Garfield in the presidential mausoleum.

The house was purchased by Frederic Beach Jennings in 1914, who called in *Laurel Break*. It was subsequently owned by his son Percy Hall Jennings, Sr., who continued to call it *Laurel Break*.

Stearns, John Noble, II (1864-1947)

Occupation(s):   industrialist - silk manufacturer

Marriage(s):   Helen W. Kemper

Listed in *Long Island Society Register, 1929*: yes
Address: Red Spring Lane, Glen Cove
Acreage / map sources: 1927 map illegible; not on 1932 or 1946 maps
Name of estate: *The Cedars*
Year of construction: 1900
Style of architecture: Colonial Revival
Architect(s):
Landscape architect(s)
House extant: yes
Historical notes:

The house was built by Edmund Wetmore.

The estate was owned by Stearns, who called it *The Cedars,* and, subsequently, by Max Sobelman.

John Noble Stearns II was the son of John Nobel and Alice Bloomer Stearns, Sr.

Helen W. Kemper Stearns had previously been married to _____ Ahles.

The Stearns' son John Noble Stearns III married Alice Cudahy of Chicago, IL, and resided in Old Brookville.

Stearns, John Noble, III (d. 1974)

Occupation(s):   industrialist - silk manufacturer*

Marriage(s):   1931-1974 - Alice Cudahy (d. 1986)

Listed in *Long Island Society Register, 1929*: yes
Address: Wheatley Road, Old Brookville
Acreage / map sources: not on 1927 or 1932 maps
                                    11 acres / 1946 map

Name of estate:
Year of construction: c. 1939
Style of architecture:
Architect(s):   James W. O'Connor designed the house
                                    (for J. N. Stearns III)
Landscape architect(s):   Innocenti and Webel (for J. N. Stearns III)
House extant: yes
Historical notes:

    The house was built by John Noble Stearns III.
    The *Social Register, Summer 1950* lists John Noble and Alice Cudahy Stearns [III] as residing on Wheatley Road, Glen Head [Old Brookville]. The *Social Register New York, 1972* lists the Stearns' residence as *Sandrift* on North Breakers Row, Palm Beach, FL.
    He was the son of John Noble and Helen Kemper Ahles Stearns II, who resided at *The Cedars* in Glen Cove.
    *Stearns was in business with his father. [*The New York Times* November 27, 1931, p. 26.]
    In 1923, he won the National Links Amateur Golf title. [*The New York Times* September 2, 1923, p. 20.]
    Alice Cudahy Stearns was the daughter of Edward A. Cudahy, Sr. of Chicago. IL. She had previously been married to Leander James McCormick of Chicago, IL. Her brother Edward A. Cudahy, Jr. married Margaret Carrey and, subsequently Eleanor P. Brush, the daughter of Dr. Murray Peabody Brush of California.

Stebbins, Theodore Ellis, Sr. (d. 1980)

Occupation(s):

Marriage(s):   1930-1980 - Mary Emma Flood (d. 1987)
                                  - artist - sculptress

Listed in *Long Island Society Register, 1929*: no
Address: Route 106, Syosset
Acreage / map sources: not on 1927 map
                                    24 acres / 1932 map (owned by Stebbins)
                                    34 acres / 1946 map (owned by M. E. Stebbins}
Name of estate: *White Oak Farm*
Year of construction: c. 1936
Style of architecture:
Architect(s):
Landscape architect(s):
House extant: unconfirmed
Historical notes:

    The house was built by Theodore Ellis Stebbins, Sr. on land purchased from George Palen Snow. [*The New York Times* March 10, 1935, p. RE1.] Stebbins named his estate *White Oak Farm*.
    The *Social Register, Summer 1937* lists the Stebbinses as residing in Woodside, CA. The *Social Register, Summer 1949* lists the Stebbinses ' residence as *White Oak Farm* in Syosset.
    He was the son of Theodore and Gertrude Ellis Stebbins of Manhattan.
    Mary Emma Flood Stebbins was the daughter of James Leary Flood and an heir to the Comstock silver fortune.
    The Stebbinses' daughter Jane married John Manning Greenleaf of Greenwich, CT. Their son Theodore Ellis Stebbins, Jr. married Alice Morgan of Chestnut Hill, PA. Their son James married Felicia Herzog, the daughter of Edwin H. Herzog of Lattingtown, and, subsequently, Cynthia Richards Rossbach.

Steele, Charles (1857-1939)

Occupation(s):   attorney - partner, Seward, Guthrie, Morawetz and Steele
            financier - partner, J. P. Morgan and Co. (investment banking firm);
                director, International Mercantile Marine Co.
            capitalist - director, Southern Railroad;
                director, Atchison, Topeka and Santa Fe Railroad
            industrialist - director, United States Steel Corp.;
                director, International Harvester

Marriage(s):   1885-1932 - Nannie French (d. 1932)

Listed in *Long Island Society Register, 1929*: yes
Address: Hitchcock Lane and Steele Hill Road, Old Westbury
Acreage / map sources: on 1927 map; 77 acres / 1932 and 1946 maps
Name of estate:
Year of construction: c. 1891
Style of architecture: Classical Revival
Architect(s):   James Brown Lord designed
            the house (for Lanier)
Landscape architect(s):
House extant: no; demolished c. 1950
Historical notes:

front facade

 The house was built by James Franklin Doughty Lanier.
 The estate was, subsequently, owned by Steele.
 It was Steele who, along with William Dameron Guthrie and Victor Morawetz, brought a case against the federal income tax to the United States Supreme Court and won. The tax was not reinstituted until 1913 when it was legalized by the passage of the Sixteenth Amendment to the Constitution.
 Steel's maternal great-grandfather Roger Nelson served as a brigadier general in the Revolutionary War, a member of Congress, and a judge in Maryland. His maternal grandfather John Nelson was a member of Congress, United States Minister to Naples, and United States Attorney General, 1843-1845.
 The Steeles' daughter Nancy married Devereux Milburn, Sr., and resided at *Sunridge Hall* in Old Westbury. Their daughter Kathryn married Francis Skiddy Von Stade, Sr., and also resided in Old Westbury.

Steers, James Rich, II (1898-1964)

Occupation(s):   capitalist - president, Steers Sand & Gravel Corp.;
                president, J. Rich Steers, Inc. (a construction firm)*

Marriage(s):   1924-1964 - Gwendoline Lamb

Listed in *Long Island Society Register, 1929*: yes
Address: West Neck Road, Lloyd Harbor
Acreage / map sources: not on 1929 map; on 1931 map; 13 acres / 1944 map
Name of estate:
Year of construction:
Style of architecture:
Architect(s):
Landscape architect(s):
House extant: unconfirmed
Historical notes:

 James Rich Steers II was the son of James Rich Steers, Sr., who resided at *Faircroft* in Port Chester, NY.
 Gwendoline Lamb Steers was the daughter of John Harries Lamb of Utica, NY.
 The Steerses' son James Rich Steers III married Judith Harvey, the daughter of Frederick Harvey of Nashville, TN. Their daughter Carol married Heber Blakeney Henry, Jr. of Clebourne, TX.
 *The construction company of which James Rich Steers II was president was involved in major projects throughout the world. Locally, it constructed the jet runway extensions at LaGuardia Airport.

Steers, James Rich, II (1898-1964)

Occupation(s):   capitalist -   president, Steers Sand and Gravel Corp.;
                                                   president, J. Rich Steers, Inc. (a construction and
                                                     engineering firm)*

Marriage(s):   1924-1964 - Gwendoline Lamb

Listed in *Long Island Society Register, 1929*: yes
Address: Wheatley Road, Brookville
Acreage / map sources: not on 1927, 1932, or 1946 maps
Name of estate: *Dogwood Hill*
Year of construction:
Style of architecture: French / Italian Country
Architect(s):
Landscape architect(s):
House extant: unconfirmed
Historical notes:

    The *Social Register New York, 1956* lists the Steers' residence as McCouns Lane, Oyster Bay [Oyster Bay Cove], while the *Social Register New York, 1959* lists the Steers as residing on Wheatley Road, Brookville. The *Social Register, 1981* lists Mrs. Steers as residing at *Dogwood Hill* in Brookville.
    [See previous entry for family information.]
    *The construction company of which James Rich Steers was president was involved in major projects throughout the world. Locally, it constructed the jet runway extensions at LaGuardia Airport.

rear facade, 1959

Stehli, Emil J. (1869-1945)

Occupation(s):   industrialist -   president, Stehli & Co. (silk manufacturers)

Marriage(s):   Marguerite J. Zweifel (d. 1959)

Listed in *Long Island Society Register, 1929*: yes
Address: Locust Valley – Bayville Road, Lattingtown
Acreage / map sources: on 1927 map
                                         no acreage given in 1932 map
                                         not on 1946 map
Name of estate: *Hawk Hill Place*
Year of construction: 1925
Style of architecture: Neo-Colonial
Architect(s):   Treanor and Fatio designed the house (for Stehli)
Landscape architect(s):
House extant: no; demolished c. 1960
Historical notes:

    The twenty-nine-room house, with eight bathrooms, originally named *Hawk Hill Place,* was built by Emil J. Stehli.
    The *Long Island Society Register, 1929* lists Emil J. and Marguerite J. Zweifel Stehli as residing at *Hawk Hill Place* in Locust Valley [Lattingtown].
    Marguerite J. Zweifel Stehli was residing in Summerville, NJ, at the time of her death.
    The estate was owned by the Stehlis' daughter Lilly and her husband Paul Hyde Bonner, Sr.
    Subsequently, it was owned by Winston Henry Hagen II, who called it *Fox Brae.*

Sterling, Duncan, Jr. (1907-1993)

Occupation(s):   financier - co-founder with Oliver R. Grace, Sterling, Grace and Co.
                                            (investment banking firm);
                                            partner, Van Wyck and Sterling (stock brokerage firm)

Civic Activism: mayor, Village of Bayville;
                               trustee, Browning School;
                               council member, C. W. Post College of Long Island University,
                                   Brookville

Marriage(s):   M/1 - 1933-1988 - Natalie B. Kountze (d. 1988)
                               M/2 - 1989-1993 - Elsie Benkard

Listed in *Long Island Society Register, 1929*: yes
Address: Schraeder Place, Bayville
Acreage / map sources: not on 1927, 1932, or 1946 maps
Name of estate:
Year of construction:
Style of architecture:
Architect(s):
Landscape architect(s):
House extant: unconfirmed
Historical notes:

    The *Long Island Society Register, 1929* lists Duncan Sterling Jr. as a minor residing with his parents in Oyster Bay. The *Social Register, Summer 1932* lists Duncan Sterling Jr. as a minor residing with his parents at *Keir Knoll* in Oyster Bay.
    The *Social Register, 1989* list Duncan Sterling [Jr.] as residing on Shrader [Schraeder] Place, Bayville.
    He was a vocal opponent of Robert Moses' proposed Bayville–to–Rye bridge.
    Duncan and Natalie B. Kountze Sterling, Jr.'s son Duncan Sterling III married Jean Spalding, the daughter of Jesse Spalding III of Manhattan.

Sterling, Dr. G.

Occupation(s):   physician

Marriage(s):

Listed in *Long Island Society Register, 1929*: no
Address: West Shore Road, Mill Neck
Acreage / map sources: not on 1927 map
                               no acreage given on 1932 map
                               9 acres / 1946 map
Name of estate:
Year of construction: c. 1906
Style of architecture: Shingle
Architect(s):
Landscape architect(s):
House extant: no; demolished c. 1964
Historical notes:

    The house was built by Hermann De Selding.
    The estate was owned by Mrs. William Martin and, subsequently, by Sterling.

Stern, Benjamin (1857-1933)

Occupation(s):   merchant - president, Stern's Brothers Department Store

Marriage(s):   1897-1933 - Madeline Schafer (d. 1933)

Listed in *Long Island Society Register, 1929*: yes
Address: Glenwood Road, Roslyn Harbor
Acreage / map sources: on 1927 map; 25 acres / 1932 map; not on 1946 map
Name of estate: *Claraben Court*
Year of construction: c. 1906 remodeling of the 1868-1872 house
Style of architecture: French Chateau
Architect(s):   Jacob Wrey Mould designed
         the 1868-1872 house
         (for Clapham)
Landscape architect(s):   DuChene designed elaborate
         formal gardens, walks,
         terraces, sunken garden
         cutting garden, rose garden,
         and woodlands (for Stern)

front facade

Estate photographs can be found in the Nassau County
   Museum Collection filed under Roslyn/Stern.
House extant: yes
Historical notes:

    The house, originally named *Stone House*, was built by Thomas Clapham. Because of financial problems, he never occupied the house but, instead, resided in a small cottage on the estate. After his death, the estate had several owners.
    In 1887, it was purchased by Ephram Hines for use as The Bryant School, a military school for boys.
    Then, it was owned by Dr. Valentine Mott.
    Stern purchased the estate and in 1906 remodeled the house into a French Chateau. He renamed it *Claraben Court*.
    He was the son of Meyer A. and Siphra Stern.
    Madeline Schafer Stern was the daughter of Simon Schafer of Manhattan.
    The estate was owned for a short time by Cartier.
    In 1943, it was purchased by Dr. Wendell Hughes, who renamed it *Wenlo*. In 1960, the house was severely damaged by fire. Hughes restored the house and removed some of the details from the Clapham and Stern eras.
    The house, which has mural recreations of the Sistine Chapel, and two acres were for sale in 1998 for $2.65 million.

Stern, Henry Root, Sr. (1882-1959)

Occupation(s):   attorney - partner, Mudge, Stern, Baldwin and Todd
         politician - permanent president, New York State Electoral College;
         treasurer, Nassau County and New York State Republican Party
         Committees
Civic Activism: chairman, New York State Board of Social Welfare in the Dewey administration;
         member, Nassau County Emergency Work Bureau, during the Depression;
         helped draft New York State's child labor law;
         trustee, Hofstra University, Hempstead

Marriage(s):   1909-1947 - Elsie Weston Lazarus (d. 1947)

Listed in *Long Island Society Register, 1929*: yes
Address: Old Court House Road, North Hills
Acreage / map sources: on 1927 map; 66 acres / 1932 map; 59 acres / 1946 map
Name of estate: *Penwood*
Year of construction:
Style of architecture:
Architect(s):
Landscape architect(s):
House extant: unconfirmed
Historical notes:

    The *Long Island Society Register, 1929* lists the Sterns as residing a *Penwood* in Manhasset [North Hills].

Stettinius, Edward Reilly, Jr. (1900-1949)

Occupation(s):	industrialist - vice-president in charge of industrial and public relations, General Motors Corp., 1931-1934; chairman of board, U. S. Steel Corp. (which became U S X), 1938; vice-president, General Aviation; director, General Electric Co.; director, North American Aviation, Inc.
	capitalist - director, Western Air Express Corp.; director, Eastern Air Lines; director, Transcontinental and Western Air, Inc.
	financier - director, Metropolitan Life Insurance Co.; director, Federal Reserve Bank of Richmond
	diplomat - chairman of United States delegation to the United Nations
	statesman - Under Secretary of State and Secretary of State in the Franklin Delano Roosevelt administration
	writer - *Lend-Lease: Weapon for Victory*, 1944; *Roosevelt and the Russians: The Yalta Conference*, 1949
Civic Activism:	chairman, War Resources Board, during World War II; member, Industrial Advisory Board, during World War II; director of priorities, Office of Production Management, during World War II; administrator, Lend-Lease Program, during World War II; member, advisory commission, Council of National Defense, during World War II; director, University of Virginia, Charlottesville, VA; director, Foreign Policy Association; director, Thomas Jefferson and Patrick Henry Memorial Foundations; member, governing board, central committee, American Red Cross
Marriage(s):	1926-1949 - Virginia Gordon Wallace

Listed in *Long Island Society Register, 1929*: yes
Address: Horse Hollow Road and Birch Hill Road, Lattingtown
Acreage / map sources: on 1927 map; no acreage given on 1932 map; 26 acres / 1946 map
Name of estate: *The Shelter*
Year of construction: c. 1905
Style of architecture: Shingle
Architect(s):
Landscape architect(s):
Estate photographs can be found in the Nassau County Museum Collection filed under Locust Valley/Stettinius.
House extant: no
Historical notes:

The house, originally named *The Hedges*, was built by Levi Candee Weir. It was subsequently owned by Edward Reilly Stettinius, Sr. and his son Edward Reilly Stettinius, Jr., both of whom called it *The Shelter*.

Edward Reilly Stettinius, Jr. also served in President Franklin Delano Roosevelt's administration as a member of the Industrial Advisory Board, director of priorities of the Office of Production Management, and administer of lend-lease.

His sister Isabel married John Bigelow Marsh, Sr. and resided at *Nyrmah* in Mill Neck. His sister Elizabeth married Juan Terry Trippe and resided in East Hampton.

The Stettiniuses' son Wallace married Mary Wingate Gray. Their son Joseph married Mary Ballou Handy, the daughter of Dr. Stafford Handy of Lynchburg, VA. Their son Edward Reilly Stettinius III, who married Nany Hall, died at the age of forty-one as a result of a hunting accident.

[See following entry for additional family information.]

garden and tea house, c. 1923

Stettinius, Edward Reilly, Sr. (1865-1925)

Occupation(s):   financier - partner, J. P. Morgan and Co. (now, J. P. Morgan Chase)
(investment banking firm)
industrialist - president, Diamond Match Co., 1909-1915;
treasurer and vice-president, Sterling Co. (machinery
manufacturers);
a founder, Sterling Consolidated Boiler Co. (which,
merged into Babcock & Wilcox Co.);
vice-president, Babcock & Wilcox Co.
statesman - Assistant Secretary of War in the Wilson administration

Marriage(s):   1894-1925 - Judith Carrington

Listed in *Long Island Society Register, 1929*: yes
Address: Horse Hollow Road and Birch Hill Road, Lattingtown
Acreage / map sources: on 1927 map; no acreage given on 1932 map; 26 acres / 1946 map
Name of estate: *The Shelter*
Year of construction: c. 1905
Style of architecture: Shingle
Architect(s):
Landscape architect(s):
Estate photographs can be found in the Nassau County Museum Collection filed under Locust Valley/Stettinius.
House extant: no
Historical notes:

    The house, originally named *The Hedges,* was built by Levi Candee Weir.
    It was, subsequently, owned by Stettinius and, then, by his son Edward Reilly Stettinius, Jr. The Stettiniuses both called the estate *The Shelter.*
    [See previous entry for family information.]

Stevens, Byam K., Jr.

Occupation(s):   financier - analyst, H. G. Wellington and Co. (formerly, Wellington
and Co.) (investment banking firm)
Civic Activism: mayor, Village of Muttontown

Marriage(s):   Priscilla Gilpin Lucas

Listed in *Long Island Society Register, 1929*: no
Address: Jericho Turnpike and Kirby Lane, Muttontown
Acreage / map sources: on 1927 map; no acreage given on 1932 map; 212 acres / 1946 map
Name of estate: *Kirby Hill*
Year of construction: c. 1900
Style of architecture: Georgian Revival
Architect(s):   Warren and Wetmore designed the house and stables (for J. S. Stevens)
Landscape architect(s):
Estate photographs can be found in the Nassau County Museum Collection filed under Jericho/Stevens.
House extant: yes
Historical notes:

    The house, originally named *Kirby Hall,* was built by Joseph Sampson Stevens.
    The estate was, subsequently, owned by Byam K. Stevens, Jr., who continued to call it *Kirby Hill.*
    Priscilla Gilpin Lucas Stevens was the daughter of Clinton M. Lucas.
    The Stevenses' daughter Priscilla married James Robert Polk, Jr. of Creve Coeur, MO.
    In 2000, Stevens sold the house and 110 acres. The house survives but the estate's property will be subdivided for a housing development.

front facade, c. 1903

Stevens, Charles Albert (1863-1895)

Occupation(s):

Marriage(s):   1891-1895 - Mary Madeline Brady (d. 1930)

Listed in *Long Island Society Register, 1929*: no
Address: Apple Green Drive, Old Westbury
Acreage / map sources: not on 1927, 1932, or 1946 maps
Name of estate: *Annandale*
Year of construction: c. 1896
Style of architecture: Shingle
Architect(s):   Walker and Gillette designed 1934
                               alterations (for W. G. Loew)
Landscape architect(s):   Olmsted (for W. G. Loew)
House extant: no; demolished in 1940s
Historical notes:

Annandale, c. 1910

    The house, originally named *Annandale,* was built by Charles Albert Stevens.
    He was the son of Edwin Augustus and Emily C. Lewis Stevens II, who resided at *Castle Point* on Stevens Point in Hoboken, NJ. His grandfather Edwin Augustus Stevens, Sr. established and endowed Steven Institute of Technology.
    Mary Madeline Brady Stevens was the daughter of New York State Supreme Court Judge John Rand and Mrs. Katherine Lydig Brady. She subsequently married British Major Charles Spencer Hall, with whom she resided at her Newport, RI, home, *The Pines,* and in Great Britain. She divorced Hall and, in 1908, married Herbert Melville Harriman. The Harrimans resided at *The Lanterns* in Jericho. The British court maintained that her 1907 Rhode Island divorce from Hall was invalid and adjudged that by marrying Harriman she became a bigamist. [*The New York Times* February 15, 1910, p. 1.]
    The estate was owned by Charles Tracy Barney and, subsequently, by William Goadby Loew, who called it *Loewmoor*.

Stevens, Joseph Sampson (1867-1935)

Occupation(s):   financier - director, Chemical National Bank

Marriage(s):   Clara Sherwood (d. 1925)

Listed in *Long Island Society Register, 1929*: yes
Address: Jericho Turnpike and Kirby Lane, Muttontown
Acreage / map sources: on 1927 map; no acreage given on 1932 map; 212 acres / 1946 map
Name of estate: *Kirby Hill*
Year of construction: c. 1900
Style of architecture: Georgian Revival
Architect(s):   Warren and Wetmore designed the house and stables (for J. S. Stevens)
Landscape architect(s):
Estate photographs can be found in the Nassau County Museum Collection filed under Jericho/Stevens.
House extant: yes
Historical notes:

    The house, originally named *Kirby Hall,* was built by Joseph Sampson Stevens.
    He was the son of Frederic William and Adele Livingston Sampson Stevens and great-grandson of Albert Gallatin, who was Secretary of Treasury in the administrations of Presidents Thomas Jefferson and James Madison. Stevens was a corporal in Troop K in Theodore Roosevelt's "Rough Riders." His mother was Duchess de Dino. His maternal grandparents resided at the Sampson mansion on Broadway and Bond Street in NYC.
    The estate was, subsequently, owned by Byam K. Stevens, Jr., who continued to call it *Kirby Hill.*
    In 2000, Stevens sold the house and 110 acres. The house survives but the estate's property is to be subdivided for a housing development.

rear facade, c. 1910

Stevenson, Malcolm, Sr. (1887-1953)

Occupation(s): industrialist - partner in Stevenson Brewery (with the advent of prohibition, the firm continued as a cold storage company)

Marriage(s): Maude Arden Kennedy (1893-1937)

Listed in *Long Island Society Register, 1929*: yes
Address: Jericho Turnpike, Old Westbury
Acreage / map sources: on 1927 map; 10 acres / 1932 and 1946 maps
Name of estate: *Two Maple Farm*
Year of construction: c. 1925
Style of architecture: Federal
Architect(s): Roger Harrington Bullard designed the house (for M. Stevenson, Sr.)

Landscape architect(s):
House extant: unconfirmed
Historical notes:

The house, originally named *Two Maple Farm,* was built by Malcolm Stevenson, Sr.
He was an internationally-known polo player.
His sister Florence married Thomas Le Boutillier II and also resided in Old Westbury.
Maude Arden Kennedy Stevenson had previously been married to Frederick Winston. After her divorce from Stevenson, she married S. Bryce Wing and resided at *Twin Oaks* in Old Westbury. She was the daughter of Mrs. H. Van Rensselaer Kennedy, who resided at *Three Oaks* in Hempstead.
The Stevensons' son Malcolm married Natica Gray Townsend, the daughter of Henry Townsend of Jericho.

Stewart, Cecil Parker (1881-1945)

Occupation(s): publisher - director, General Publishing Service Corp.
shipping - president, American Merchant Marine Steamship Corp.
capitalist - director, American Cable & Radio Corp.;
director, Commercial Mackay Corp.
director, International Utilities Corp.
industrialist - director, La Metropolitana Compania National de Seguros [Cuba];
director of numerous companies
Civic Activism: board member, Downtown Hospital, NYC (which combined with Beekman Street Hospital to become Beekman–Downtown Hospital)
mayor, Village of Centre Island

Marriage(s): M/1 - 1908-1924 - Reine Marie Tracy
M/2 - 1932 - Dorothy Kimball Wallace

Listed in *Long Island Society Register, 1929*: yes
Address: Centre Island Road, Centre Island
Acreage / map sources: on 1927 map (owned by C. P. Stewart)
7 acres / 1932 map (owned by C. P. Stewart)
not on 1946 map (owned by S. Cardelli)
Name of estate: *Orchard Cottage*
Year of construction:
Style of architecture:
Architect(s):
Landscape architect(s):
House extant: unconfirmed
Historical notes:

The *Long Island Society Register, 1929* lists Cecil Parker Stewart as residing at *Orchard Cottage* on Centre Island.
The estate was, subsequently, owned by the Stewarts' daughter Jacqueline and son-in-law Count Giovanni Guido Carlo Cardelli, who continued to call it *Orchard Cottage.*

Stewart, Glenn (1883-1957)

Occupation(s):   diplomat - First Secretary, United States Embassy, Vienna, Austria,
                                          in the Wilson administration;
                               Second Secretary, United States Embassy, Havana, Cuba,
                                          in the Wilson administration

Marriage(s):   M/1 - 1914 - Greta Hostetter
                                   M/2 - 1945-1957 - Jessie Maud Chardin (b. 1897)

Listed in *Long Island Society Register, 1929*: no
Address: Feeks Lane, Lattingtown
Acreage / map sources: on c. 1922 map
                               not on 1927, 1932, or 1946 maps

Name of estate:
Year of construction:
Style of architecture:
Architect(s):   Alfred Hopkins designed the farm complex
                               (for G. Stewart)
Landscape architect(s):   Ellen Biddle Shipman (for G. Stewart)
House extant: yes
Historical notes:

    Greta Hostetter Stewart was the daughter of Theodore and Allene Hostetter. Her mother, subsequently, married Anson Wood Burchard and resided with him at *Birchwood* in Lattingtown.

Stewart, John Henry Jones (1851-1926)

Occupation(s):   financier - vice-president, Atlantic Mutual Life Insurance Co.

Marriage(s):   Althea A. *[unable to confirm maiden name]*

Listed in *Long Island Society Register, 1929*: yes
Address: Ridge Road, Laurel Hollow
Acreage / map sources: on 1914 and c. 1922 maps
                               not on 1927, 1932, or 1946 maps
Name of estate: *Cannon Hill*
Year of construction: c. 1911
Style of architecture: Shingle
Architect(s):
Landscape architect(s):
House extant: yes
Historical notes:

    The house, originally named *Cannon Hill*, was built by John Henry Jones Stewart.

    The *Long Island Society Register, 1929* lists Althea A. Stewart as residing on Oyster Bay Road [Oyster Bay – Cove Road], Cold Spring Harbor [Oyster Bay Cove].

    The estate was owned by Oliver B. James, Sr., who called it *Rocky Point*, John Gerdes, who called it *Cannonhill Point*, by Henry Blackstone, Martin Dwyer, Jr., Yoko Ono [Lennon], and, subsequently, by Daniel Carroll de Roulet, Sr.

    The de Roulets renamed it *Cannon Hill.*

side / rear facade, 2004

Stewart, John Henry Jones (1851-1926)

Occupation(s):   financier - vice-president, Atlantic Mutual Life Insurance Co.

Marriage(s):   Althea *[unable to confirm maiden name]*

Listed in *Long Island Society Register, 1929:* yes
Address: Moore's Hill Road, Laurel Hollow
Acreage / map sources: not on 1927 or 1946 maps
                                      no acreage on 1932 map (owned by J. H. J. Stewart)
Name of estate:
Year of construction:
Style of architecture:
Architect(s):
Landscape architect(s)
House extant: yes
Historical notes:

    The house was built by John Henry Jones Stewart.
    While the exterior of the house was different from the house which Stewart had built on Ridge Road in Laurel Hollow, its floor plan was similar to the Ridge Road house.
    The *Long Island Society Register, 1929* lists Althea A. Stewart as residing on Oyster Bay Road [Oyster Bay – Cove Road], Cold Spring Harbor [Oyster Bay Cove].
    The estate was, subsequently, owned by Charles Edgar Ames.

Stewart, John K. (1869-1916)

Occupation(s):   industrialist - president, Stewart–Warner Speedometer Co.

Marriage(s):   Julia C. *[unable to confirm maiden name]* (d. 1917)

Listed in *Long Island Society Register, 1929*: no
Address: Mariner's Court, Centerport
Acreage / map sources: 1929 map illegible ; not on 1931 or 1946 maps
Name of estate:
Year of construction: c. 1890
Style of architecture: Queen Anne
Architect(s):
Landscape architect(s):
House extant: no; demolished in 1960*
Historical notes:

    The house was built by Austin Corbin.
    The estate was, subsequently, owned by Stewart. It was inherited by his daughter Marian, who was a minor at the time. She subsequently married Robert B. Honeyman, Jr. and resided with him at the estate. He was the son of Robert B. and Emilie Linderman Brodhead Honeyman, Sr., who resided in Brooklyn. Robert was the sole heir to the Bethlehem Coal Co. fortune. In 1940, the Honeymans moved their second residence to San Juan Capistrano, CA.
    Julia C. Stewart was residing in Aiken, SC, at the time of her death. [*The New York Times* August 15, 1917, p. 9.]
    Sergei Rachmaninoff rented the house during the summers of 1940 and 1941. He composed "Symphonic Dances" (called "Fantastic Dances") while staying in Centerport.
    During World War II the estate was subdivided for a housing development.
    *The house, which was extensively modified over the years, survived several fires before it was finally destroyed by fire.
    The remaining service buildings have been converted into private homes.

front facade, c. 1937

Stewart, William Adams Walker, II (1876-1960)

Occupation(s):   attorney -   founder, Sheldon and Stewart, 1906;
                                              founder, Stewart and Shearer, 1951;
                                            partner, Carter, Ledyard and Milburn
                            financier -   trustee, United States Trust Co. of New York;
                                            director, Commonwealth Insurance Co. of New York

Marriage(s):   M/1 - Frances E. de Forest (1879-1957)
                                  M/2 - Elizabeth S. Hoyt (d. 1984)

Listed in *Long Island Society Register, 1929*: yes
Address: Shore Road, Cold Spring Harbor
Acreage / map sources: not on 1929 map
                                  on 1931 map (owned by W. A. W. Stewart)
                                  7 acres / 1944 map (owned by Frances de F. Stewart)
Name of estate: *Edgeover*
Year of construction: c. 1937
Style of architecture:
Architect(s):   Grosvenor Atterbury designed the house (for W. A. W. Stewart II)
Landscape architect(s):   Olmsted, 1910-1912 (for W. A. W. Stewart II)
House extant: yes
Historical notes:

   The house, originally named *Edgeover,* was built by William Adams Walker Stewart II.
   His paternal grandfather John Aikman Stewart was Assistant Secretary of the Treasury in President Abraham Lincoln's administration. His sister Francis married Norman Thomas and resided in Cold Spring Harbor.
   Frances E. de Forest Stewart was the daughter of Robert Weeks and Emily Johnston de Forest, who resided at *Wawapek* in Cold Spring Harbor, as did her brother Johnston de Forest. Her sister Ethel married H. Rowland Vermilye, Sr. and resided at *Wood Winds* in Cold Spring Harbor. Her brother Henry Lockwood de Forest resided at *Meadowview*, also in Cold Spring Harbor.
   The Stewarts' daughter Frances married Dr. Richard Norris Pierson and resided at *Whitehill Place* in Cold Spring Harbor.
   In 1966 Elizabeth S. Hoyt Stewart married Stephen H. Philbin. The Philbins resided in Manhattan.
   Stewart's daughter Nancy married Edgar Hayden Curry, the son of Francis A. Curry.

Stillman, Irwin

Occupation(s):   capitalist -   real estate - president, Stillman Organization,
                                            Manhattan developer

Marriage(s):

Listed in *Long Island Society Register, 1929*: no
Address: Feeks Lane, Lattingtown
Acreage / map sources: not on 1927, 1932, or 1946 maps
Name of estate: *Hillcrest*
Year of construction:
Style of architecture:
Architect(s):
Landscape architect(s):
House extant: yes
Historical notes:

   In 1949, the estate was purchased by Mme. Chiang Kai-shek's brother-in-law Hsiang-hsi Kung and her sister Ailing Soong. Mme. Chiang Kai-shek resided at the estate from 1975 to 1993.
   In 1998, Kung's descendants sold the thirty-seven-acre estate for approximately $3 million to Irwin Stillman, who immediately put the entire estate up for sale for $6.5 million. The house and twelve acres could be purchased for $3.2 million and the farm complex on twelve acres was listed at $1.75 million. The balance of the estate's acreage was also available in six- and seven-acre parcels, each selling for $750,000.

Stimson, Henry Lewis (1867-1950)

Occupation(s):   attorney -   partner, Root and Clark;
                                                     partner, Winthrop and Stimson (later, Winthrop, Stimson, Putnam
                                                                 and Roberts)

statesman - Governor General of the Philippine Islands, 1927-1929
Secretary of War in the Taft, Franklin Delano Roosevelt, and
Truman administrations;
Secretary of State in the Hoover administration

diplomat - Special Representative of the President to Nicaragua, 1927;
chairman, United States delegation to London Naval Conference, 1930;
chairman, United States delegation to Disarmament Conference, 1932

writer - *My Vacations*, 1949

Marriage(s): 1893-1950 - Mabel Wellington White (1866-1955)

Listed in *Long Island Society Register, 1929*: yes
Address: Reservoir Road, West Hills
Acreage / map sources: no acreage given on 1929 map; on 1931 map; 147 acres / 1944 and 1946 maps
Name of estate: *Highold*
Year of construction: c. 1903
Style of architecture: Shingle
Architect(s):
Landscape architect(s):
House extant: no; demolished c. 1960
Historical notes:

    The house, originally named *Highold*, was built by Henry Lewis Stimson.
    He was the son of Lewis Atterbury and Candace Wheeler Stimson. His grandmother Candace Thurber Wheeler was a partner of Louis Comfort Tiffany, Samuel Colman, and Lockwood de Forest in L. C. Tiffany & Associated Artists.
    Stimson was residing at *Highold* at the time of his death.
    The estate was, subsequently, owned by the Boy Scouts of America.
    The estate's property is now Suffolk County's West Hills County Park.

Stoddard, Francis Russell, Jr. (1877-1957)

Occupation(s): attorney - member, Hamlin, Hubbell and Davis;
special deputy Attorney General, New York State

politician - assemblyman, New York State Legislature, 1912-1915;
chairman, New York State Prison Commission, 1921-1924

writer - *The Stoddard Family*, 1912; *War Time France*, 1918;
The Pilgrims, 1935*; *The History of Acquisition Cost in the
State of New York*, 1914; *The Truth About Pilgrims*, 1952*;
numerous articles

Marriage(s): 1909-1957 - Eleanor Sherburne Whipple

Listed in *Long Island Society Register, 1929*: no
Address: Harbor Road, Cold Spring Harbor
Acreage / map sources: not on 1929 map
on 1931 map (owned by Walter Whipple)
38 acres / 1944 map (owned by Francis Stoddard)
Name of estate: *Old Rectory*
Year of construction:
Style of architecture:
Architect(s):
Landscape architect(s):
House extant: unconfirmed
Historical notes:

    *Stoddard was able to trace his ancestry to ten colonists who came to Plymouth Colony on the Mayflower. He published scholarly research on the Pilgrims fathers and their descendants.

Stone, Charles Augustus, Sr. (1867-1941)

Occupation(s):	industrialist - founder, Stone and Webster, Inc. (an engineering firm)
	financier - director, Federal Reserve Bank of New York, 1919-23
Civic Activism:	member, executive committee, Massachusetts Institute of
	Technology, Cambridge, MA

Marriage(s):	1902-1940 - Mary A. Leonard (d. 1940)

Listed in *Long Island Society Register, 1929*: yes

Address:	Duck Pond Road, Matinecock
Acreage / map sources:	on 1927 map
	no acreage given on 1932 map
	14 acres / 1946 map

Name of estate:	
Year of construction:	c. 1927
Style of architecture:	Georgian Revival
Architect(s):	William Welles Bosworth designed the house
	(for Stone)

Landscape architect(s):
House extant: yes*
Historical notes:

The house was one of two built by Charles Augustus Stone, Sr. on the same property.
[See following entry for family information.]
*In the 1950s, the house was extensively remodeled.

Stone, Charles Augustus, Sr. (1867-1941)

Occupation(s):	industrialist - founder, Stone and Webster, Inc. (an engineering firm)
	financier - director, Federal Reserve Bank of New York, 1919-23
Civic Activism:	member, executive committee, Massachusetts Institute of
	Technology, Cambridge, MA

Marriage(s):	1902-1940 - Mary A. Leonard (d. 1940)

Listed in *Long Island Society Register, 1929*: yes

Address:	Duck Pond Road, Matinecock
Acreage / map sources:	on 1927 map
	no acreage given on 1932 map
	14 acres / 1946 map

Name of estate:	*Solana*
Year of construction:	c. 1917
Style of architecture:	Spanish Renaissance
Architect(s):	Addison Mizner designed the house (for S. H. Brown)
Landscape architect(s):	Armand J. Tibbets (for Stone)

House extant: yes
Historical notes:

The house, originally named *Solana,* was built by Stephen Howland Brown.
The estate was, subsequently, owned by Stone, who continued to call it *Solana.*
Born In Newton, MA, he was the son of Charles H. and Mary Augustus Green Stone.
Mary A. Leonard Stone was the daughter of William and Margaret Keith Leonard of Hingham, MA.
The Stones' daughter Margaret married R. Colgate Vernon Mann, the son of Samuel Vernon and Helen Colgate Mann, Sr., who resided at *Grove Point* in Kings Point. Margaret subsequently married Robert Winthrop II with whom she resided at *Groton Place* in Old Westbury.

Stone, Charles Augustus, Sr. (1867-1941)

Occupation(s):   industrialist - founder, Stone and Webster, Inc. (an engineering firm)
                                  financier - director, Federal Reserve Bank of New York, 1919-23
Civic Activism: member, executive committee, Massachusetts Institute of
                                       Technology, Cambridge, MA

Marriage(s):   1902-1940 - Mary A. Leonard (d. 1940)

Listed in *Long Island Society Register, 1929*: yes
Address: Duck Pond Road, Matinecock
Acreage / map sources: on 1927 map
                                  no acreage given on 1932 map
                                  14 acres / 1946 map

Name of estate:
Year of construction: 1928
Style of architecture: Tuscan Villa
Architect(s):   Charles Augustus Stone, Sr.
                                       designed his own house

Landscape architect(s):
House extant: yes
Historical notes:

front facade

   The house is one of two built by Charles Augustus Stone, Sr. on the same property.
   [See previous entry for family information.]

Stow, William L.

Occupation(s):   financier - president, W. L. Stow (stock brokerage firm)*

Marriage(s):

Listed in *Long Island Society Register, 1929*: no
Address: Garvan – Whitney – Phipps Road, Old Westbury
Acreage / map sources: on 1906 map; not on 1927, 1932, or 1946 maps
Name of estate:
Year of construction: c. 1902
Style of architecture: Italian Renaissance
Architect(s):   John Russell Pope designed the house
                                  Horace Trumbauer designed 1918
                                       alterations (for H. C. Phipps)
Landscape architect(s):   Olmsted, 1915-1916 (for H. C. Phipps)
Estate photographs can be found in the Nassau County Museum Collection filed under Old Westbury/Phipps.
House extant: no; demolished in 1970s
Historical notes:

   The house was built by William L. Stow.
   The *Social Register New York, 1907* lists William L. Stow as
residing at 12 West 18th Street, NYC.
   *In 1908, Stow's brokerage firm filed for bankruptcy. [*The New
York Times* April 23, 1913, p. 1.]
   The estate was owned by George Crocker and, subsequently, by
Henry Carnegie Phipps, who called it *Spring Hill*.

rear facade, c. 1910

Straight, Willard Dickerman (1880-1918)

Occupation(s):
diplomat - vice-consul general and private secretary to United States
 Ambassador to Korea;
 private secretary to United States Minister to Cuba;
 United States Consul General to Mukden, China
statesman - Acting Chief, Division of Far Eastern Affairs, Department of State
journalist - correspondent, Reuter's News Agency;
 correspondent, Associated Press
publisher - co-founder with Dorothy, *The New Republic* magazine
financier - representative in China, J. P. Morgan and Co.;
 Kuhn, Loeb and Co., First National Bank, and National City Bank
artist

Civic Activism:
a founder, Plattsburg Movement (private military training camps, 1915);
trustee, Cornell University, Ithaca, NY

Marriage(s):
1911-1918 - Dorothy Payne Whitney (1877-1968)
 - publisher - co-founder with Willard, *The New Republic* magazine
 educator - co-founder, with her second husband Leonard Knight Elmhirst
 of Dartington School in Devon, England
 Civic Activism: woman's suffrage

Listed in *Long Island Society Register, 1929*: no
Address: Post Road and Wheatley Road, Old Westbury
Acreage / map sources: on 1914 map (owned by Straight)
 on 1927 map (owned by Mrs. Elmhirst)
 71 acres / 1932 map (owned by Straight Improvement Co.)
 83 acres / 1946 map (owned by Eastern Realty Corp.)
Name of estate: *Elmhurst**
Year of construction: c. 1913
Style of architecture: Shingle
Architect(s): Delano and Aldrich designed the house, and stables (for Straight);
 later, alterations (for Elmhirst)
Landscape architect(s): Beatrix Jones Farrand, 1913-1940s (for Straight and Elmhirst);
 designed the Chinese garden and playhouse with swimming
 pool, 1913-1918 (for Straight)
Estate photographs can be found in the Nassau County Museum Collection filed under Old Westbury/Straight.
House extant: no; demolished c. 1970
Historical notes:

 The house, originally named *Elmhurst*, was built by Willard Straight.
 He was the son of Henry H. and Emma Dickerman Straight of Oswego, NY.
 Dorothy Payne Whitney was the daughter of William Collins and Flora Payne Whitney, who resided in Old Westbury.
Her brother Harry Payne Whitney also resided in Old Westbury. After the death of her husband, she married Leonard
Knight Elmhirst.
 *The original name of the Straight estate was *Elmhurst*. It was changed to *Apple Green [Applegreen]* after Dorothy
Whitney Straight's marriage to Leonard Knight Elmhirst. [Jane Brown, *Beatrix: The Gardening Life of Beatrix Jones
Farrand 1872-1959* (New York: Viking Penguin Books, 1995), p. 213.]
 The Straights' daughter Beatrice won the 1976 Academy Award for Best Supporting Actress for her role in the motion
picture *Network*.

In the 1930s their son Michael Whitney Straight became a
member of the Communist Party. After World War II, while
he was serving as an unpaid volunteer in the State Department,
he was approached by a Soviet agent to supply government
documents. According to Straight, the only documents he gave
to the Soviets were those he had written on Nazi Germany. He
later identified Guy Burgess and Anthony Blunt as Communist
spies in Great Britain resulting in the notorious British Burgess–
Blunt–Long–Maclean–Philby spy scandal.

In 1952, the estate was sold by the family's trust to Joseph
Gariano, a local developer.

Elmhurst, c. 1920

Stralem, Donald Sigmund (1903-1976)

Occupation(s):   financier - founder, Stralem and Co. (investment banking firm)
                                     capitalist - director, Screen Gems;
                                                director, FICO Corp. (a holding company for Columbia Pictures);
         director, Continental Telephone Co.;
         director, Independent Telephone Co.
         industrialist - director, Crown Central Petroleum Co.

Civic Activism: president of board, National Travelers Association;
president, George Junior Republic Association (which provided citizenship
    training for children);
president, United Community Defense Service Services (later, United
    Services Organization) during World War II;
trustee, Fog Art Museum of Harvard University, Cambridge, MA;
a founder, North Shore Community Hospital, Manhasset

Marriage(s):   1928-1959 - Jean Lehman Eckelheimer (1909-1959)
         - Civic Activism: vice president and vice chairman, The Lighthouse*;
                             board member, American Theater Wing;
                             trustee, Lenox Hill Hospital, NYC

Listed in *Long Island Society Register, 1929*: no
Address: Meadow Springs Road, Glen Cove
Acreage / map sources: not on 1927, 1932, or 1946 maps
Name of estate:
Year of construction: c. 1916
Style of architecture: Georgian Revival
Architect(s):
Landscape architect(s):
House extant: yes
Historical notes:

    The house was built by Julian Percy Fairchild, Sr.
    The estate was owned by William Rogers Coe and, subsequently, by Stralem.
    The Stralems' daughter Sharon married Ralph Albee Phraner, Jr.
    *In the 1950s Mrs. Stralem was instrumental in establishing Lighthouse nursery school.

Straus, Edward Kuhn (1909-1996)

Occupation(s):   capitalist - real estate - president, Garden–State Plaza Corp.
                                      (a subsidiary of R. H. Macy & Co.)

Marriage(s):   M/1 - 1942-1957 - Catharine Monroe
                   M/2 - 1961 - Kate F. Fraser

Listed in *Long Island Society Register, 1929*: no
Address: Mill River Road, Upper Brookville
Acreage / map sources: not on 1927, 1932, or 1946 maps
Name of estate: *Here to Yonder*
Year of construction: c. 1795
Style of architecture: Colonial
Architect(s):
Landscape architect(s):
House extant: unconfirmed
Historical notes:

    The *Social Register, Summer 1965* lists Edward K. and Kate F. Fraser Straus as residing at *Here to Yonder* on Mill River Road, Oyster Bay [Upper Brookville].
    He was the son of Herbert N. Straus of Manhattan.
    Kate F. Fraser Straus was the daughter of John C. Fraser of Montgomery, AL. She had previously been married to Frederick G. McNally.
    Edward Kuhn and Catharine Monroe Straus' daughter Susan married Richard Voorneveld of Syosset.

Straus, Jack Isidor (1900-1985)

Occupation(s):   merchant - president and chairman of board, R. H. Macy and Co.
(department store);
director, Safeway Stores Inc. (grocery store chain)
financier - director, Greenwich Savings Bank;
director, Hambro American Bank & Trust;
director, Fidelity Union Trust Co.
capitalist - director, Long Island Rail Road
industrialist - director, Continental Can Co.

Civic Activism: organizer, Public-Relief Organization, 1931;
trustee, Harvard University, Cambridge, MA;
endowed a chair at Harvard Business School;
director, Greater New York Fund;
director, Police Athletic League;
director, United Fund of Greater New York;
director, United Way of New York City;
chairman of board, Roosevelt Hospital (which became
St. Luke's–Roosevelt Hospital Center), NYC;
trustee, St. Luke's–Roosevelt Hospital Center, NYC;
member, Mayor's Business Advisory Committee, NYC;
member, New York Council of Defense;
member, New York Committee on Slum Clearance;
director, New York City World Fair Corp., 1964

Marriage(s):   M/1 - 1924-1974 - Margaret S. Hollister (d. 1974)
M/2 - 1975-1985 - Virginia Megear

Listed in *Long Island Society Register, 1929*: no
Address: Jericho Turnpike, Jericho
Acreage / map sources: not on 1927, 1932, or 1946 maps
Name of estate: *Green Pastures*
Year of construction: 1910
Style of architecture: Federal
Architect(s): Carrere and Hastings designed the house
(for W. P. Thompson, Jr.)
Landscape architect(s): Ellen Biddle Shipman designed the formal garden,
lawns, flagstone terrace, and curved driveway
(for Preston)

House extant: no
Historical notes:

The house, originally named *Longfields,* was built by William Payne Thompson, Jr.
The estate was owned by William Payne Thompson Preston, Sr., who continued to call it *Longfields.*
It was, subsequently, owned by Straus, who renamed the estate *Green Pastures.*
The *Social Register, Summer 1937* lists Jack and Margaret S. Hollister Straus as residing at *Green Pastures* in Jericho.
The Social Register, Summer 1950 lists the Strauses
as residing on Jericho Turnpike, Jericho. The *Social Register, 1988* lists only Virginia Megear Straus, then residing at 19 East 72nd Street, NYC.

Straus' father Jesse Isidor Straus was president of R. H. Macy and Co.

Margaret Hollister Straus was the daughter of Frederick Kellogg and Harriet M. Shelton Hollister, who resided in East Hampton.

Virginia Megear Straus was the daughter of Thomas Jefferson and Virginia Randolph Atkinson Megear.

rear facade, c. 1921

Straus, Jack Isidor (1900-1985)

Occupation(s):

merchant - president and chairman of board, R. H. Macy
and Co. (department store);
director, Safeway Stores Inc. (grocery store chain)

financier - director, Greenwich Savings Bank;
director, Hambro American Bank & Trust;
director, Fidelity Union Trust Co.

capitalist - director, Long Island Rail Road

industrialist - director, Continental Can Co.

Civic Activism: *[See preceding entry for detailed list.]*

Marriage(s): M/1 - 1924-1974 - Margaret S. Hollister (d. 1974)
M/2 - 1975-1985 - Virginia Megear

Listed in *Long Island Society Register, 1929*: no
Address: Cove Neck Road, Cove Neck
Acreage / map sources: not on 1927, 1932, or 1946 maps
Name of estate: *Crow's Nest*
Year of construction:
Style of architecture:
Architect(s):
Landscape architect(s):
House extant: unconfirmed
Historical notes:

The *Social Register, Summer 1961* lists Jack I. and Margaret S. Hollister Straus as residing at *Crow's Nest* on Cove Neck Road, Oyster Bay [Cove Neck], while the *Social Register, Summer 1975* and *1984* list Straus residing at *Crow's Nest* with Virginia Megear Straus.
  [See previous entry for family information.]

Strauss, Albert (1864-1929)

Occupation(s):

financier - member, J. W. Seligman (investment banking firm);
member and vice-governor, Federal Reserve Board
(appointed in 1918)

capitalist - director, Brooklyn–Manhattan Transit Corp.

diplomat - United States Department of Treasury representative
to advise President Wilson at Paris Peace
Conference, 1919

industrialist - director, Cuba Cane Sugar Corp.;
director, Manati Sugar Co.;
director, Pierce–Arrow Motor Car Co.;
director, Cuban Tobacco Co.

Marriage(s): 1896-1929 - Lucretia Mott Lord (d. 1935)

Listed in *Long Island Society Register, 1929*: yes
Address: private road, Cove Neck
Acreage / map sources: on 1927 map; 21 acres / 1932 map; not on 1946 map
Name of estate: *Brier Hill*
Year of construction:
Style of architecture:
Architect(s):
Landscape architect(s):
House extant: unconfirmed
Historical notes:

Lucretia Mott Lord Strauss was the granddaughter of philanthropist, abolitionist, and exponent of woman's suffrage Lucretia Mott.

Streeter, Edward, Sr. (1891-1976)

Occupation(s):	financier - assistant vice-president, Bankers Trust Co. of New York; partner, Blake Brothers (stock brokerage firm); vice-president, Fifth Avenue Bank (now, Bank of New York) writer* - *Dere Mabel,* 1917; *That's Me All Over Mabel,* 1918; *Same Old Bill,* 1918; *Daily Except Sunday,* 1938; *Father of the Bride,* 1949; *Skoal Scandinavia,* 1952; *Mr. Hobbs' Vacation,* 1954; *Merry Christmas Mr. Baxter,* 1956; *Mr. Robbins Rides Again,* 1957; *Window on America,* 1959
Civic Activism:	trustee, Harvard University, Cambridge, MA; trustee, Lingnan University, Canton, China
Marriage(s):	1919-1966 - Charlotte L. Warren (1894-1966)

Listed in *Long Island Society Register, 1929*: yes
Address: Cow Lane, Kings Point
Acreage / map sources: not on 1927 map; no acreage given on 1932 or 1946 maps
Name of estate:
Year of construction:
Style of architecture:
Architect(s):
Landscape architect(s):
House extant: unconfirmed
Historical notes:

Charlotte L Warren was the daughter of William C. Warren of Buffalo, NY.

The Streeters' daughter Charlotte married John Thayer Goodhue, the son of F. Abbot Goodhue of Hewlett. Their daughter Claire married John Pierpont Woods, a great-grandson of J. P. Morgan and descendant of Alexander Hamilton.

*Streeter's book *Father of the Bride* was made into the classic 1950 movie starring Spencer Tracy, Elizabeth Taylor, and Joan Bennett. A two-part remake (1991 and 1995) starred Steve Martin and Diane Keaton. *Mr. Hobbs Takes a Vacation* was also made into a successful film in 1962, starring James Stewart and Maureen O'Hara. *Daily Except Sundays* clearly reflects his commuting experiences on the Long Island Rail Road and the slim volume *Window on America* cleverly intertwines the history of the Bank of New York with a concise history of the United States from the establishment of a banking system after the departure of the British from Manhattan.

Sutton, Keith

Occupation(s):	publisher - crossword puzzles
Civic Activism:	unsuccessful independent candidate for mayor and supervisor of the City of Glen Cove
Marriage(s):	

Listed in *Long Island Society Register, 1929*: no
Address: Old Tappan Road, Glen Cove
Acreage / map sources: not on 1927, 1932, or 1946 maps
Name of estate:
Year of construction: 1934
Style of architecture: Federal
Architect(s): William Platt designed the
       house (for J. T. Pratt, Jr.)
Landscape architect(s):
House extant: yes
Historical notes:

The house, originally named *Beechwood,* was built by John Teele Pratt, Jr.

In the early 1960s, the estate was owned by Sutton.

It was owned by the Russian Orthodox Church of the Ascension for a period of time.

It is now called *Beechwood Manor* and is again a private residence.

front facade, 2003

Swan, Edward H., Sr. (1828-1903)

Occupation(s):

Marriage(s):   Julia Strong Post

Listed in *Long Island Society Register, 1929*: no
Address: Cove Neck Road, Cove Neck
Acreage / map sources: on c. 1922 map
                                 not on 1927, 1932, or 1946 maps
Name of estate: *The Evergreens*
Year of construction: 1859
Style of architecture: French Second Empire
Architect(s):   John W. Ritch designed the house (for E. H. Swan, Sr.)
Landscape architect(s):
House extant: yes
Historical notes:

   The house, originally named *The Evergreens,* was built by Edward H. Swan [Sr.]. The first Swan house was destroyed by fire in 1858. The second house was built in 1859. It was enlarged in 1872. The enlarged house was also designed by John W. Ritch.
   The Swans' daughter Caroline married Thomas Sears Young and resided at *Dunstable* in Cove Neck.
   The estate was owned by Van Santvoord Merle–Smith, Sr., who called it *The Paddocks,* by William Harris Mathers, and, in 1984, by Nicholas Ihasz.
   The house is on The National Register of Historic Places. In 1990, the house and 5.3 acres were for sale.

front facade, c. 1909

Swan, Otis D. (1821-1894)

Occupation(s):   attorney
                                financier - stockbroker;
                                       director, Bleecker Street Savings Bank

Marriage(s):

Listed in *Long Island Society Register, 1929*: no
Address: East Main Street, Oyster Bay Cove
Acreage / map sources: not on 1927, 1932, or 1946 maps
Name of estate:
Year of construction:
Style of architecture: Greek Revival
Architect(s):
Landscape architect(s):
House extant: no; demolished in mid-1930s
Historical notes:

   In 1876, Swan disappeared after embezzling money from an estate of which he was a trustee, from the building fund of the Union League Club, and from his sister's estate.
   Theodore Roosevelt, the father of President Theodore Roosevelt, rented the house in the same year. Roosevelt called it *Tranquility.*
   The house was, subsequently, owned by John Abeel Weekes, who continued to call it *Tranquility.*

front facade

Swan, William Lincoln, Sr. (1847-1925)

Occupation(s):   capitalist -   president, Oyster Bay Light & Power Co.;
                                                        a founder, Oyster Bay Water Co.;
                                                        president, Queens County Telegraph Supply Co.
                                 attorney

Marriage(s):   1881-1925 - Belle Thurston

Listed in *Long Island Society Register, 1929*: no
Address: Cove Neck Road, Cove Neck
Acreage / map sources: on 1906 map
                                          on c. 1922 map
                                          on 1927 map
                                          not on 1932 or 1946 maps

Name of estate:
Year of construction:
Style of architecture:
Architect(s):
Landscape architect(s):
House extant: unconfirmed
Historical notes:

    William Lincoln Swan, Sr. was the son of Benjamin L and Julia Strong Post Swan Sr., who resided in Oyster Bay. His sister Caroline married Thomas Sears Young and resided at *Dunstable* in Cove Neck.
    Belle Thurston Swan was the daughter of an Oyster Bay shoemaker. The Swan family did not attend the wedding. [*The New York Times* August 26, 1881, p. 8.]
    In 1928 the Swans' son William Lincoln Swan, Jr. married Frances Catherine Merryman. Her father Robert Merton Merryman resided in Rustberg, VA.

Swann, Dr. Arthur Wharton (1880-1914)

Occupation(s):   physician
                                    writer -   *A Study of the Ventricular Systole–Subclavian Interval,*
                                                        with a Discussion of the Presphymic Period, 1913;
                                               Urticaria Treated with Epinephrine, 1913;
                                               Human Serum in Urticaria, 1915
                                  educator -   instructor, College of Physicians and Surgeons

Marriage(s):   1909-1914 - Susan Ridley Sedgwick (1886-1981)
                                         - Civic Activism: president, Association of Junior Leagues
                                                 of America, Inc.

Listed in *Long Island Society Register, 1929*: yes
Address: Route 25A, Oyster Bay Cove
Acreage / map sources: on 1927 map
                                          not on 1932 or 1946 maps

Name of estate:
Year of construction:
Style of architecture:
Architect(s):   Delano and Aldrich
Landscape architect(s):
House extant: unconfirmed
Historical notes:

    The *Long Island Society Register, 1929* lists Susan R. Sedgwick Swann as residing in Syosset [Oyster Bay].
    Dr. Arthur Wharton Swann was the son of John Swann of Chattanooga, TN.
    Susan Sedgwick Swann subsequently married Paul Lyman Hammond and resided with him at *Muttontown Lodge* in Syosset.

Swope, Herbert Bayard, Sr. (1882-1958)

Occupation(s):	journalist* - executive editor, *New York World*
Civic Activism:	personal consultant to Secretary of War Stimson during World War II;
	raised over $3 million for war relief during World War II;
	board member, Beekman Street Hospital, NYC
	director, Humane Society;
	member, Committee to Control Crime in New York;
	director, Child Welfare Society;
	member, Citizens Welfare Committee;
	member, Committee to Defend America;
	treasurer, Freedom House;
	trustee, Village of Sands Point

Marriage(s): 1912-1958 - Margaret Honeyman Powell (1890-1967)

Listed in *Long Island Society Register, 1929*: no
Address: East Shore Road, Great Neck
Acreage / map sources: on 1927 map (owned by Parker)
9 acres / 1932 map (owned by Rosenberg)
7 acres / 1946 map (owned by Rosenberg)
Name of estate:
Year of construction:
Style of architecture: Victorian**
Architect(s):
Landscape architect(s):
House extant: no
Historical notes:

From 1922 to 1929, Swope rented the house from Lottie Blair Parker.
*In 1917, Swope won the Pulitzer Prize for journalism.
**It was a three-story Victorian house with a wrap-around porch.
The house was, subsequently, owned by Lee Rosenberg.

Swope, Herbert Bayard, Sr. (1882-1958)

Occupation(s):	journalist - executive editor, *New York World*
Civic Activism:	*[See preceding entry for detailed list.]*

Marriage(s): 1912-1958 - Margaret Honeyman Powell (1890-1967)

Listed in *Long Island Society Register, 1929*: no
Address: Hoffstot Lane, Sands Point
Acreage / map sources: not on 1927 map; 11 acres / 1932 and 1946 maps
Name of estate: *Keewaydin*
Year of construction: c. 1900
Style of architecture: Colonial Revival
Architect(s):
Landscape architect(s):
House extant: yes
Historical notes:

The house, originally named *Kidd's Rocks*, was built by John Scott Browning, Sr.
In 1921, Malcolm Douglas Sloane purchased the estate from Browning's widow.
After Sloane's death, his widow Elinor Lee Sloane married Albert Delmont Smith and resided with him at the former Sloane Sands Point estate, which the Smiths renamed *Keewaydin*.
In 1929, they sold the estate to Swope and moved to *Mill Pond*, in Lloyd Harbor. Swope continued to call the Sands Point estate *Keewaydin*. In 1964, Horace Richter purchased the estate from Swope's widow.. It was purchased in 1968 by Irwin Hamilton Kramer. In 1983, Charles Shipman Payson purchased the estate and renamed it *Lands End*.
In 2001, the house and fourteen acres were for sale by Mrs. Payson. The asking price was $50 million. In 2003, the asking price had been reduced to $29.5 million.

Taft, Walbridge S. (1884-1951)

Occupation(s):	attorney - partner, Cadwalader, Wickersham and Taft
	financier - trustee, Bank for Savings, NYC
Civic Activism:	chairman of board, Salvation Army*;
	director, United Service Organizations;
	director, Greater New York Fund;
	director, New York City Defense Recreation Fund
Marriage(s):	M/1 - 1917-1920 - Helen Draper
	M/2 - 1923-1951 - Elizabeth Clark

Listed in *Long Island Society Register, 1929*: yes

Address:	Cedar Swamp Road and Pound Hollow Road, Old Brookville
Acreage / map sources:	on 1927 map (owned by Taft)
	not on 1932 map
	17 acres / 1946 map (owned by E. C. Taft)
Name of estate:	*Waveland*
Year of construction:	
Style of architecture:	
Architect(s):	
Landscape architect(s):	Olmsted, 1929 (for Rentschler)
House extant: unconfirmed	
Historical notes:	

Taft purchased the estate from Gordon Sohn Rentschler, who also called it *Waveland.*

He was the son of Henry Waters and Julia Walbridge Smith Taft of NYC and the nephew of President William Howard Taft. His brother William Howard Taft II also resided in Old Brookville.

*Taft succeeded his father as chairman of the board of the Salvation Army, serving from 1940 to 1951. In 1916, Walbridge S. Taft was the unsuccessful National Progressive Party (Bull Moose Party) candidate for Congress.

Helen Draper Taft was the niece of a governor of Massachusetts.

The Tafts' daughter Elizabeth married Leon Lourie, Edward Chaplin, Peter Campbell, and, subsequently, Gerald J. Johnson II. She resided with Johnson at *Waveland Cottage,* Watch Hill, RI. The Tafts' daughter Lucie married S. Willets Meyer, with whom she resided in Glen Head, and, subsequently, Dr. Henry H. Bard, with whom she resides in Lattingtown. The Tafts' son Henry resides in Camden, ME.

Taft, William Howard, II (1888-1952)

Occupation(s):	journalist - circulation manager, *The New York Times,* 1923-1929
	financier - vice-president and secretary, Bank for Savings, NYC;
	member, White, Weld and Co. (investment banking firm);
	member, Taylor, Bates and Co. (which became James B.
	Taylor and Co.) (stock brokerage firm);
	vice-president, Central Savings Bank
Marriage(s):	

Listed in *Long Island Society Register, 1929*: yes

Address:	Cedar Swamp Road and Pound Hollow Road, Old Brookville
Acreage / map sources:	on 1927 map; not on 1932 map; 6 acres / 1946 map
Name of estate:	
Year of construction:	
Style of architecture:	
Architect(s):	
Landscape architect(s):	
House extant: unconfirmed	
Historical notes:	

The *Long Island Society Register, 1929* lists Mr. and Mrs. William Howard Taft II as residing on Cedar Swamp Road and Sea Cliff Avenue, Glen Head [Old Brookville].

[See previous entry for additional family information.]

Tailer, Thomas Suffern, Jr. (1913-1984)

Occupation(s):   sportsman -   nationally-known amateur golfer
Civic Activism: board member, Karen Horney Clinic

Marriage(s):   M/1 - 1932 - Florence Baker (1912-1933)
                            M/2 - 1942-1962 - Elizabeth Morfield Sturgis (1919-1962)
                            M/3 - Jean Sinclair

Listed in *Long Island Society Register, 1929*: yes
Address: Horse Hollow Road, Lattingtown
Acreage / map sources: on 1927 and 1932 maps; not on 1946 map
Name of estate: *Beaupre*
Year of construction: 1932
Style of architecture: French Chateau
Architect(s):   Walker and Gillette designed the house (for G. F. Baker II)
Landscape architect(s):
House extant: yes
Historical notes:

   George Fisher Baker II built the house, originally named *Beaupre,* for his daughter Florence and son-in-law Thomas Suffern Tailer, Jr. on part of the former Paul Cravath estate *Veraton.*
   Thomas Suffern Tailer, Jr. the son of Thomas Suffern and Maude Lorillard Tailer, Sr.
   Florence Baker Tailer subsequently married Stanley Martineau of Montreal, Canada. Her sister Edith married John Mortimer Schiff and resided at *Northwood* in Oyster Bay. Her brother George married Frances Drexel Munn and resided at *Ventura Point* on Centre Island.
   Thomas Suffern and Florence Tailer, Jr.'s daughter Fern married David A. Gimbel and, subsequently, Charles E. Denney, Jr. of Pinehurst, SC. Their daughter Florence married James Allen Holt, the son of John Edwin Holt of Altadena, CA.
   Elizabeth Morfield Sturgis Tailer was the daughter of Henry Sprague and Gertrude Lovett Sturgis of Cedarhurst.
   Thomas and Elizabeth Tailer's daughter True married William Dixon Wallace, the son of Thomas Wallace of Fort Worth, TX. Their daughter Toni married Kenneth Smith, the son of Kenneth E. Smith of Oceanside. Tailer's daughter Diana married David M. Pinkham.
   After Thomas and Florence Tailer divorced, the estate was owned by Polly Brooks Howe, who called it *Severn.*
   Forty acres of the estate were sold to the Locust Valley School District.
   In 1952, the estate was owned by Roderick Tower.

Tailer, Thomas Suffern, Sr. (1867-1928)

Occupation(s):   financier -   partner, Tailer and Co. (investment banking firm)

Marriage(s):   M/1 - 1893-1902 - Maude Lorillard
                            M/2 - 1909-1928 - Harriet Stewart Brown

Listed in *Long Island Society Register, 1929*: yes
Address: Locust Valley *[unable to determine exact location]*
Acreage / map sources: not on 1927, 1932 or 1946 maps
Name of estate: *Hattom*
Year of construction:
Style of architecture:
Architect(s):
Landscape architect(s):
House extant: unconfirmed
Historical notes:

   Thomas Suffern Tailer, Sr. was the son of Edward N. Tailer of Newport and Manhattan. Suffern, NY, was named for their family. [*The New York Times* May 29, 1932, p. X8.]
   Maude Lorillard Tailer was the daughter of Pierre Lorillard. She subsequently married Cecil Baring of London.
   Thomas Suffern and Maude Lorillard Tailer, Sr.'s son Lorillard resided in Rumson, NJ. Tailer's daughter Betty married Wallace Gurnee Dyer of Manhattan.
   Harriet Stewart Brown Tailer was the daughter of Alexander Brown of Baltimore.
   [See previous entry for additional family information.]

Talbott, Harold Elster, II (1888-1957)

Occupation(s):   industrialist - president and chairman of board, Dayton Wright
                                                  Airplane Co.;
                                       director and one of original investors, Chrysler Motors
                                                  (now, Daimler–Chrysler Corp.);

industrialist - president and chairman of board, Dayton Wright Airplane Co.;

director and one of original investors, Chrysler Motors (now, Daimler–Chrysler Corp.);

vice-president and general manager (later, chairman of board), The H. E. Talbott Co. (in charge of hydro-electric development & industrial construction);

chairman of board, Standard Packaging Co.;

director, North American Aviation;

director, Mead Corp.

politician - chairman, Republican National Finance Committee in East, 1934;

chairman, Republican Finance Committee for Metropolitan New York;

chairman, Republican National Finance Committee, 1948-1949

statesman - Secretary of Air Force in the Eisenhower administration

capitalist - founder and partner, Paul B. Mulligan & Co. (an engineering firm that specialized in clerical efficiency)*

Civic Activism: member, War Production Board during World War II

Marriage(s): 1925-1957 - Margaret Thayer (1900-1962)
- Civic Activism: trustee, New York Infirmary, NYC;
trustee, Sarah Lawrence College, Bronxville, NY

Listed in *Long Island Society Register, 1929*: no

Address: Store Hill Road (Long Island Expressway North Service Road), Old Westbury

Acreage / map sources: not on 1927 map
52 acres / 1932 and 1946 maps

Name of estate: *The Pillars*

Year of construction: c. 1910

Style of architecture: English Neoclassical

Architect(s): Hoppin and Koen designed the house (for G. Rose, Sr.)

Landscape architect(s):

House extant: no; demolished c. 1950

Historical notes:

The house, originally named *Overland House*, was build by George Rose, Sr.

It was subsequently owned by Talbott, who renamed it *The Pillars*.

The *Social Register, Summer 1929* and the *Social Register, Summer 1933* list Harold E. and Margaret Thayer Talbott [II] as residing in Westbury [Old Westbury]. The *Social Register, Summer 1937* lists the Talbotts as residing at *The Pillars* in Old Westbury. The *Social Register New York, 1948* lists their address as 450 East 52nd Street in NYC.

Harold E. Talbott II was the son of Harry Elstner and Katharine Hauk Talbott of Dayton, OH.

*In 1955, he resigned as Secretary of Air Force for allegedly soliciting business for Paul B. Mulligan & Co. on Secretary of Air Force stationery.

Margaret Thayer Talbott was the daughter of John B. Thayer of Philadelphia.

She committed suicide by jumping from the rear bedroom window of her twelfth floor apartment at 1133 Fifth Avenue, NYC.

The Talbotts' daughter Margaret married Blancke Noyes, the son of Jansen Noyes of Montclair, NJ and resided in Darien, CT. Their daughter Pauline married Owen Jones Toland, Jr., of Philadelphia, PA, and resided in Wynnewood, PA. Their son John Thayer Talbott married Carole Anne Parker, the daughter of William Charles Parker of Cairo, IL, and, subsequently, Ann Washington Kinsolving, the daughter of The Rev. Arthur Lee and Mrs. Kinsolving of Fisher's Island and Manhattan.

The Pillars

Taliaferro, Charles Champe, III

Occupation(s):	pilot, Eastern Airlines
Marriage(s):	M/1 - 1940-1949 - Caroline Coleman Denham
	M/2 - 1950 - Margaret Smith Salvage

Listed in *Long Island Society Regist*er, *1929*: no
Address: Shutter Lane, Oyster Bay Cove
Acreage / map sources: not on 1927, 1932, or 1946 maps
Name of estate:
Year of construction:
Style of architecture:
Architect(s):
Landscape architect(s):
House extant: unconfirmed
Historical notes:

The *Social Register New York, 1959* lists C. Champe and Margaret S. Salvage Taliaferro [III] as residing on Shutter Lane, Oyster Bay [Oyster Bay Cove]. The *Social Register New York, 1975* lists the Taliaferros as residing on Shelter Lane, Locust Valley [Lattingtown].
He was the son of Dr. Charles Champe Taliaferro II of Greenville, DE.
Margaret Smith Salvage Taliaferro was the daughter of Sir Samuel Agar and Mary Katharine Richmond Salvage, who resided at *Rynwood* in Old Brookville. She had previously been married to James Potter Polk, Sr., who resided in Lawrence. Her sister Katharine married Frank Lyon Polk II and resided in Muttontown. James Potter and Margaret Smith Savage Polk, Sr.'s daughter Margaret married Michael Howard Wells, the son of Alfred H. N. Wells of London and Hertfordshire, England.
Caroline Coleman Denham was the daughter of James Scott Denham of Greenville, DE. She subsequently married Henry Stillman Taylor, the son of Henry Calhoun and Jeannette Jennings Taylor who resided at *Cherridore* in Cold Spring Harbor. Carolina and Henry Stillman Taylor resided at *Gull's Way* on Centre Island.
Charles Champe and Caroline C. Denham Taliaferro III's son Robin married Margaret Cartwright Hooker, the daughter of Edward Gordon Hooker of Manhattan.

Taliaferro, Charles Champe, III

Occupation(s):	pilot, Eastern Airlines
Marriage(s):	M/1 - 1940-1949 - Caroline Coleman Denham
	M/2 - 1950 - Margaret Smith Salvage

Listed in *Long Island Society Regist*er, *1929*: no
Address: Shelter Lane, Lattingtown
Acreage / map sources: not on 1927, 1932, or 1946 maps
Name of estate:
Year of construction:
Style of architecture:
Architect(s):
Landscape architect(s):
House extant: unconfirmed
Historical notes:

Both the *Social Register New York, 1975* and the *Social Register, Summer 1986* list C. Champe and Margaret S. Salvage Taliaferro [III] as residing on Shelter Lane, Locust Valley [Lattingtown]. The *Social Register New York, 1999* lists the Taliaferros' residence on South Beach Road, Hobe Sound, FL.
[See previous entry for family information.]

Taliaferro, Eugene Sinclair (1895-1963)

Occupation(s):	capitalist - member, Anderson, Nichols and Co. (industrial engineering firm)*
Civic Activism:	member, executive committee, Theodore Roosevelt Memorial Association; treasurer, Berkshire Farm for Boys; director, The Nature Conservancy; **
Marriage(s):	Alice I. Blum (d. 1988)

Listed in *Long Island Society Register, 1929*: no
Address: off Laurel Cove Road, Cove Neck
Acreage / map sources: not on 1927 or 1932 maps; 11 acres / 1946 map
Name of estate: *The Wilderness*
Year of construction:
Style of architecture:
Architect(s):
Landscape architect(s):   Ellen Biddle Shipman (for Taliaferro)
House extant: unconfirmed
Historical notes:

The *Social Register, Summer 1937* lists Eugene S. and Alice I. Blum Taliaferro as residing at *The Wilderness* in Oyster Bay [Cove Neck].

His sister Elizabeth married Marjorie Merriweather Post's first husband, Edward Bennett Close, and resided at *Hermitage Farm Cottage* in Greenwich, CT. The actress Glenn Close is the daughter of Dr. William T. and Bettine Moore Close, also of Greenwich, CT.

*From 1946 to 1953, Taliaferro was an advisor to the Turkish government on railroad rehabilitation.

**He served as coordinator for the Christian Science Pavilion in New York's 1964 World's Fair.

Alice I. Blum Taliaferro was the daughter of Edward and Florence Abraham Blum, who resided at *Shore Acres* in Bay Shore. Her father was chairman of the board of Abraham & Straus department store. [Harry W. Havemeyer, *Along the Great South Bay: From Oakdale to Babylon, The Story of a Summer Spa 1840 to 1940* (Mattituck, NY: Amereon House, 1996), pp. 270-271.]

Tangeman, Cornelius Hoagland (1877-1928)

Occupation(s):	merchant - co-founder, Hollander & Tangeman (later, Hol–Tan Co.) (Fiat distributor for United States which later had rights to sale of the Lancia and other cars)
Marriage(s):	1904-1928 - Violet Lockwood Harkness (d. 1929)

Listed in *Long Island Society Register, 1929*: yes
Address: North Country Colony section (off Crescent Beach Road), Glen Cove
Acreage / map sources: on c. 1922 map (owned by George P. Tangeman);
                                          1927 map illegible; not on 1932 or 1946 maps
Name of estate:
Year of construction: c. 1896-1900
Style of architecture: Shingle
Architect(s):   Charles Pierrepont Henry Gilbert designed the house
                                          (for Hoagland)*
Landscape architect(s):
House extant: yes
Historical notes:

The house was built by Dr. Cornelius Nevius Hoagland.

The estate was owned by George Patterson Tangeman, who called it *Green Acres*.

It was owned by the Tangemans' son Cornelius Hoagland Tangeman and, subsequently, by Samuel O'Keeffe.

The *Long Island Society Register, 1929* lists Cornelius Hoagland and Violet Lockwood Harkness Tangeman as residing in Glen Cove.

*It is unconfirmed as to whether or not the farm complex, designed by Gilbert, was ever built.

Tangeman, George Patterson (1847-1919)

Occupation(s):	industrialist - officer, Royal Baking Powder Co.
Marriage(s):	Cora Hoagland (d. 1924)

Listed in *Long Island Society Register, 1929*: no

Address:	North Country Colony section (off Crescent Beach Road), Glen Cove
Acreage / map sources:	on c. 1922 map (owned by George P. Tangeman)
	1927 map illegible
	not on 1932 or 1946 maps
Name of estate:	*Green Acres*
Year of construction:	c. 1896-1900
Style of architecture:	Shingle
Architect(s):	Charles Pierrepont Henry Gilbert designed the house
	(for Hoagland)*

Landscape architect(s):
House extant: yes
Historical notes:

    The house was built by Dr. Cornelius Nevius Hoagland.
    The estate was owned by George Patterson Tangeman, who called it *Green Acres*.
    The *Brooklyn Blue Book and Long Island Society Register, 1918* lists George P. and Cora Hoagland Tangeman as residing at *Green Acres* in Glen Cove.
    It was owned by Cornelius Hoagland Tangeman and, subsequently, by Samuel O'Keeffe.
    *It is unconfirmed as to whether or not the farm complex, designed by Gilbert, was ever built.

Tanner, Frederick Chauncey, Sr. (1878-1963)

Occupation(s):	attorney -	partner, Tanner, Friend, Kinnan, and Post
	politician -	chairman, New York Republican State Committee, 1914-1917;
		member, New York State Constitutional Convention, 1915;
		delegate, Republican National Convention, 1912, 1916
	capitalist -	real estate - president, Broadway Properties
Civic Activism:	a founder and president, Piping Rock Wild Game Bird Sanctuary, Lattingtown	
Marriage(s):	1915-1963 - Jane Ogden	

Listed in *Long Island Society Register, 1929*: yes

Address:	Piping Rock Road and Wolver Hollow Road,
	Upper Brookville
Acreage / map sources:	not on 1927 map
	no acreage given on 1932 map
	3 acres / 1946 map
Name of estate:	*Normandie*

Year of construction:
Style of architecture:
Architect(s):
Landscape architect(s):
House extant: unconfirmed
Historical notes:

    The *Long Island Society Register, 1929* lists Frederick C. and Jane Ogden Tanner [Sr.] as residing in East Hampton.
    The *Social Register, Summer 1946* lists the Tanners as residing at *Normandie* on Brookville Road, Old Brookville [Piping Rock Road, Upper Brookville].
    The Tanners' son Edward married Shirley McKeever, the daughter of H. Van Brunt McKeever of Short Hills, NJ, and resided in New Canaan, CT. Their daughter Jane married K. Fenton Trimingham, Jr. and resided in Bermuda. Their son Frederick Chauncey Tanner, Jr. married Alexandra Todd, the daughter of Alexander B. Todd, Jr. of Pasadena, CA.
    The estate was, subsequently, owned by Charles J. Gallic.

Taylor, Bertrand LeRoy, Jr. (1892-1972)

Occupation(s):   financier -   member and governor, New York Stock Exchange*;
                                        chairman, New York Stock Exchange's Committee
                                        on Quotations and Commissions
Civic Activism: governor, American Hospital

Marriage(s):   M/1 - 1913 - Mary Isabel Bovee
                                        M/2 - 1935-1970 - Olive McClure (d. 1970)

Listed in *Long Island Society Register, 1929*: yes
Address: Planting Fields Road and Chicken Valley Road, Upper Brookville
Acreage / map sources: on 1927 map; not on 1932 or 1946 maps
Name of estate:
Year of construction: c. 1920
Style of architecture: French Renaissance
Architect(s):   Harrie Thomas Lindeberg designed the house (for B. L. Taylor, Jr.)
Landscape architect(s):
House extant: yes
Historical notes:

The house was built by Bertrand LeRoy Taylor, Jr.
*At the age of thirty, he was the youngest man ever elected as a governor of the New York Stock Exchange. Taylor served as a governor of the exchange from 1922 to 1939.

His sister Dorothy married Claude Grahame–White, and, subsequently, Count Carlo Dentice di Frasso of Italy.
Mary Isabel Bovee Taylor was the daughter of Christian Nestelle Bovee.
Bertrand LeRoy and Mary Isabel Bovee Taylor, Jr.'s son Bertrand LeRoy Taylor III resided in Manhattan.

Taylor, Edwin Pemberton Jr. (1879-1961)

Occupation(s):   financier -   partner, Taylor and Hoe (insurance firm)

Marriage(s):   1913-1961 - Elizabeth Williams Nichols (1888-1983)

Listed in *Long Island Society Register, 1929*: yes
Address: White Oak Tree Road, Laurel Hollow
Acreage / map sources: on 1927 map (owned by T. Taylor)
                                        no acreage given on 1932 map (owned by Taylor)
                                        not on 1946 map
Name of estate: *White Oaks*
Year of construction:
Style of architecture: Colonial Revival
Architect(s):
Landscape architect(s):
House extant: yes
Historical notes:

front facade, 2004

Elizabeth Williams Nichols Taylor was the daughter of John White Treadwell and Mary Blake Slocum Nichols, who resided at *The Kettles* in Cove Neck. Her brother George Nichols, Sr. married Jane N. Morgan and resided at *Uplands* in Cold Spring Harbor. Her sister Susan married Harold Trowbridge Pulsifer, the son of Nathan T. Pulsifer, and resided at *Cooper's Bluff* in Cove Neck.

Their son John married Joanna Russell Hadden, the daughter of Dr. David R. and Mrs. Joanna R. Jennings Hadden. Their son Benjamin married Marjorie Ellen Darling, the daughter of Harold Darling of Huntington. The Taylors' son Edwin Pemberton Taylor III was killed in action in Germany during World War II. [*The New York Times* May 19, 1945, p. 24.] Their daughter Olivia married Dr. Martin Bice Travis, Jr. and resides in Laurel Hollow. Their daughter Anna married William Low Tracy.

The estate's barn was cut into two sections with the main portion being relocated to the "Longwood" historic restoration site in Brookhaven. The smaller section is now on the Huntington Historical Society's Conklin House site. Both sites are open to the public.

Taylor, George Winship, Sr. (1884-1934)

Occupation(s):   attorney -   partner, Duer and Taylor

Marriage(s):   1921-1934 - Virginia Snowden Broomall

Listed in *Long Island Society Register, 1929*: yes
Address: Glenwood Road, Roslyn Harbor
Acreage / map sources: not on 1927 and 1946 maps
                                 5 acres / 1932 map (name misspelled as C. W. Taylor)

Name of estate:
Year of construction:
Style of architecture:
Architect(s):
Landscape architect(s):
House extant: unconfirmed
Historical notes:

    George Winship Taylor, Sr. was the son of Robert and Fannie Winship Taylor of Baltimore, MD.
    Virginia Snowden Broomall Taylor was the daughter of Henry Lewis Broomall of Manhattan.
    The Taylors' son Snowden married Alice Anne Kennedy Jones, the daughter of Russell Kennedy Jones who resided at *Hudson House* in Ardsley–on–Hudson, NY. Their son George Winship Taylor, Jr. married Caroline Stanard Laighton, the daughter of Alfred P. Laighton of Manhattan.

Taylor, Henry Calhoun (1894-1971)

Occupation(s):   merchant - president, Taylor, Pinkham & Co. (sales agents for Mohawk
                                        Cotton Mills, Inc.);
                                    director, J. P. Stevens & Co. (merged with Taylor, Pinkham & Co.)
                financier - director, Continental Insurance Co.;
                                    director, Greenwich Savings Bank;
                                    director, City Bank Farmers Trust Co.;
                                    director, First National City Bank
Civic Activism: trustee, New York Public Library, NYC;
                                  trustee, Roosevelt Hospital, NYC;
                                  chairman, John Carter Brown Library, Providence, RI;
                                  chairman, Yale Library Associates

Marriage(s):   1917-1971 - Jeannette Jennings (1898-1985)

Listed in *Long Island Society Register, 1929*: yes
Address: Snake Hill Road, Cold Spring Harbor
Acreage / map sources: not on 1929 or 1931 maps
                                   16 acres / 1944 and 1946 maps
Name of estate: *Cherridore*
Year of construction: c. 1923
Style of architecture: Colonial Revival
Architect(s):   Butler and Corse designed the
                                house (for H. C. Taylor)

Landscape architect(s):
House extant: yes
Historical notes:

rear facade, 2004

    The house, originally named *Cherridore*, was built by Henry Calhoun Taylor.
    He was the son of William Ambrose Taylor of Manhattan.
    [See following entry of additional family information.]
    Jeannette Jennings Taylor was the daughter of Walter and Jean Pollock Brown Jennings who resided at *Burrwood* in Lloyd Harbor. Her brother Oliver Burr Jennings II resided in Woodbury, and at *Burrwood* and *Dark Hollow*, both in Lloyd Harbor. Her sister Constance married Albert Heman Ely, Jr. and resided at *Elyston* in Lloyd Harbor.
    The Taylors' son Henry Stillman Taylor married Carolina Coleman Denham and resided at *Gull's Way* on Centre Island. Their son Peter Burr Taylor resided in Boulder, CO. Their son Walter Jennings Taylor resided in Busby, MT, and Aspen, CO.

Taylor, Henry Stillman (d. 1985)

Occupation(s):   capitalist - real estate
                                     industrialist - vice-president, J. P. Stevens & Co., Inc.
                                                     (textile manufacturers)

Marriage(s):   1949-1985 - Carolina C. Denham

Listed in *Long Island Society Register, 1929*: no
Address: Center Island Road, Centre Island
Acreage / map sources: not on 1927, 1932, or 1946 maps
Name of estate: *Gull's Way*
Year of construction:
Style of architecture:
Architect(s):
Landscape architect(s):
House extant: unconfirmed
Historical notes:

    Henry Stillman Taylor was the son of Henry Calhoun and Jeannette Jennings Taylor, who resided at *Cherridore* in Cold Spring Harbor.
    [See previous entry for additional family information.]
    Carolina C. Denham had previously been married to Charles Champe Taliaferro III, who resided in Oyster Bay Cove and Lattingtown.
    The Taylors' daughter Lisa married Ellis Bradley Jones of Beverly Hills, CA. Their daughter Barbara married John Drayton Cochran, the son of Drayton and Margaret L. Lawrence Cochran of Centre Island, and resided in Marian, MA.

Taylor, James Blackstone, Jr. (1897-1942)

Occupation(s):   industrialist - president, Upressit Metal Cap Corp. (manufacturers
                                             of metal caps for tin and glass containers);
                                     president, Air Associates Inc. (manufacturers of
                                             aircraft parts);
                                     director, Taylor Ainsworth, Inc. (aviation consultants)
Civic Activism: trustee, Village of Cove Neck

Marriage(s):   1919-1942 - Aileen B. Sedgwick

Listed in *Long Island Society Register, 1929*: yes
Address: Cove Neck Road, Cove Neck
Acreage / map sources: on 1927 map (owned by J. B. Taylor)
                                     14 acres / 1932 map (owned by J. B. Taylor)
                                     13 acres / 1946 map (owned by Lydia T. Taylor)
Name of estate: *Sunset House*
Year of construction: c. 1906
Style of architecture: Neo-Federal
Architect(s):   William Adams designed the house (for G. T. Maxwell)
Landscape architect(s):   Marian Coffin designed the oval garden (for J. B. Taylor, Jr.)
House extant: unconfirmed
Historical notes:

    The house, originally named *Sunset House,* was built by George Thebaud Maxwell.
    The estate was owned by James Blackstone Taylor, Sr. and, subsequently, by James Blackstone Taylor, Jr., both of whom continued to call it *Sunset House.*
    Aileen B. Sedgwick Taylor was the daughter of Harry Sedgwick of Manhattan. She subsequently married William Jackson Lippincott, Sr. of Manhattan. Her sister Adelaide married John Munroe, Jr. and, subsequently, Prince Kyril Scherbatoff of Russia.
    The Taylors' son James Blackstone III married Margaret Krout, the daughter of Ray Worrall Krout, and resided in Fairfield, CT. Their son David married Nancy Bryan, the daughter of Emery Little Bryan. Their daughter Lydia married Graeme Elliot, the son of William Elliot of East Hampton. Their daughter Aileen married Sidney Miles Gordon Butler, the son of Sidney Butler of Middleburg, the Transvaal, South Africa.
    Taylor served as a test pilot during World War II and was killed during a routine flight.

Taylor, James Blackstone, Sr. (1871-1956)

Occupation(s):	financier - partner with his brother, Talbot J. Taylor and Co. (stock brokerage firm); partner, Taylor, Bates and Co. (which became James B. Taylor and Co.) (stock brokerage firm); director, Fifth Avenue Bank and its successor, Bank of New York capitalist - real estate - president, Cove Neck Realty Corp. industrialist - president, Upressit Metal Cap Corp. (manufacturers of metal caps for tin and glass containers); founder and president, Upressit Products Corp. (manufacturers of metal caps for tin and glass containers); chairman of board, Greendale [OH] Brick Co.; president, Greendale Mineral Co.; director, American Can Co.; director, Robins Conveying Belt Co.
Marriage(s):	1896-1956 - Lilla A. Thorne (d. 1963)

Listed in *Long Island Society Register, 1929*: yes
Address: Jericho Turnpike and Kirby Lane, Jericho
Acreage / map sources: not on 1927, 1932, or 1946 maps
Name of estate:
Year of construction: c. 1904
Style of architecture: Federal
Architect(s):   Warren and Wetmore designed the house (for R. J. Preston)
Landscape architect(s):
Estate photographs can be found in the Nassau County Museum Collection filed under Jericho/Taylor.
House extant: no; demolished c. 1950
Historical notes:

   The house, originally named *Ivy Hall,* was built by Ralph Julius Preston.
   The estate was owned by Taylor from 1906 to 1920 and, subsequently, by Elbert H. Gary, who continued to call it *Ivy Hall.*
   The Taylors' son James Blackstone Taylor, Jr., who resided at *Sunset House* in Cove Neck, was married to Aileen B. Sedgwick. Their daughter Priscilla married Bruce Berwick Lanier, Jr. of Baltimore, MD. Their daughter Mildred married C. Beverly Davison, Jr.
   [See previous entry for additional family information.]

rear facade, c. 1910

Taylor, James Blackstone, Sr. (1871-1956)

Occupation(s):	financier - partner with his brother, Talbot J. Taylor and Co. (stock brokerage firm);
	partner, Taylor, Bates and Co. (which became James B. Taylor and Co.) (stock brokerage firm);
	director, Fifth Avenue Bank and its successor, Bank of New York
	capitalist - real estate - president, Cove Neck Realty Corp.
	industrialist - president, Upressit Metal Cap Corp. (manufacturers of metal caps for tin and glass containers);
	founder and president, Upressit Products Corp. (manufacturers of metal caps for tin and glass containers);
	chairman of board, Greendale [OH] Brick Co.;
	president, Greendale Mineral Co.;
	director, American Can Co.;
	director, Robins Conveying Belt Co.
Marriage(s):	1896-1956 - Lilla A. Thorne (d. 1963)

Listed in *Long Island Society Register, 1929*: yes
Address: Cove Neck Road, Cove Neck
Acreage / map sources: on 1927 map (owned by J. B. Taylor)
                                                     14 acres / 1932 map (owned by J. B. Taylor)
                                                     13 acres / 1946 map (owned by Lydia T. Taylor)
Name of estate: *Sunset House*
Year of construction: c. 1906
Style of architecture: Neo-Federal
Architect(s):   William Adams designed the house (for G. T. Maxwell)
Landscape architect(s):   Marian Coffin designed the oval garden (for J. B. Taylor, Jr.)
House extant: unconfirmed
Historical notes:

The house, originally named *Sunset House,* was built by George Thebaud Maxwell.

The estate was owned by James Blackstone Taylor, Sr. and, subsequently, by James Blackstone Taylor, Jr., both of whom continued to call it *Sunset House.*

Both the *Long Island Society Register, 1929* and the *Social Register, Summer 1951* list James Blackstone and Lilla A. Thorne Taylor [Sr.] as residing at *Sunset House* on Cove Neck Road, Oyster Bay [Cove Neck].

The *Social Register New York, 1963* lists Lilla A. Thorne Blackstone, then residing at 555 Park Avenue, NYC.

The Taylors' son James Blackstone Taylor, Jr., who resided at *Sunset House* in Cove Neck, was married to Aileen B. Sedgwick. Their daughter Priscilla married Bruce Berwick Lanier, Jr. of Baltimore, MD. Their daughter Mildred married C. Beverly Davison, Jr.

[See surname entry for James Blackstone Taylor, Jr. for additional family information.]

front facade, c. 1923

Taylor, Myron Charles (1874-1959)

Occupation(s):   attorney
                                          industrialist - chairman of the board, United States Steel (which became U S X)
                                          diplomat - personal representative, with the rank of ambassador, for
                                                            Presidents Franklin Delano Roosevelt and Harry S Truman
                                                            to His Holiness Pope Pius XII
                                          capitalist - director, American Telephone & Telegraph Co.

Civic Activism: trustee, Cornell University, Ithaca, NY;
                                          trustee, New York Public Library, NYC;
                                          trustee, Robert College, Turkey;
                                          trustee and first vice-president, Metropolitan Museum of Art, NYC;
                                          trustee, St. Luke's Hospital, NYC

Marriage(s):   1906-1958 - Anabel Stevens Mack (1880-1958)

Listed in *Long Island Society Register, 1929*: yes
Address: Locust Valley – Bayview Road, Lattingtown
Acreage / map sources: on 1927 map; no acreage given on 1932 map; 79 acres / 1946 map
Name of estate: *Killingworth*
Year of construction: c. 1922
Style of architecture: 20th-century Eclectic
Architect(s):   Harrie Thomas Lindeberg designed alterations to the
                                        pre-Civil War house (for M. C. Taylor)
Landscape architect(s):   Olmsted, 1924 (for M. C. Taylor)
                                        Ferruccio Vitale and Annette Hoyt Flanders jointly designed
                                        the meadows and woodlands, 1924 (for M. C. Taylor)
Estate photographs can be found in the Nassau County Museum Collection filed under Locust Valley/Taylor.
House extant: yes
Historical notes:

    The existing pre-Civil War house was renovated for Myron Charles Taylor, who named it *Killingworth*.
He was a descendant of Captain John Underhill.
    Since 1955, the house has been owned by the Episcopal Diocese of Long Island and used as offices.

Tenney, Daniel Gleason, Sr. (1868-1951)

Occupation(s):   financier - director, Pacific Bank;
                                                    director, American Trust Co.;
                                                    trustee, Bowery Savings Bank
                              industrialist - president, C. H. Tenney & Co. (hat manufacturing firm)

Marriage(s):   Marguerite Sedgwick Smith

Listed in *Long Island Society Register, 1929*: no
Address: Wheatley Road, Brookville
Acreage / map sources: not on 1927, 1932, or 1946 maps
Name of estate:
Year of construction: 1927-1928
Style of architecture: Georgian Revival
Architect(s):   William Lawrence Bottomley designed the house
                                        (for J. R. Robinson)

Landscape architect(s):
House extant: yes
Historical notes:

    The house was built by John Randolph Robinson after he sold his other estate to Philip Gossler.
    This estate was owned by Tenney before it became part of C. W. Post College of Long Island University.
    Born in Methuen, MA, he was the son of Charles Henry and Fanny Gleason Tenney.
    The Tenneys' son Daniel Gleason Tenney, Jr. married Constance Franchot of Baltimore, MD. Their daughter Frances married G. Morgan Brown and resided in Manhattan. Their son Charles married Joan Penfold Lusk and resided in Bay Shore.

Thatcher, John M. P., Sr. (1885-1979)

Occupation(s):	industrialist - vice-president, Iselin–Jefferson Co. (textile manufacturers)
	attorney* - partner, Thatcher, Manderen and Pullman;
	partner, Roosevelt, Kobbe and Thatcher
Marriage(s):	M/1 - Katherine S. Sands (d. 1929)
	M/2 - 1931-1966 - F. Louise Vanderhoef (d. 1966)
	M/3 - 1967-1975 - Mary Barton (d. 1975)

Listed in *Long Island Society Register, 1929*: yes
Address: Split Rock Road and Burtis Lane, Syosset
Acreage / map sources: on 1927 map; 5 acres / 1932 map; 7 acres / 1946 map
Name of estate: *Cloverfield*
Year of construction:
Style of architecture:
Architect(s):
Landscape architect(s):
House extant: unconfirmed
Historical notes:

John M. P. Thatcher, Sr. was the son of Thomas M. Thatcher of Somerset, KY.

*Thatcher served as legal council to the estate of President Theodore Roosevelt and advisor for the family's trusts and estates.

Katherine S. Sands Thatcher was the daughter of Dr. Robert A. and Mrs. Katherine Sands.

John M. P. and Katherine S. Sands Thatcher, Sr.'s daughter Katherine married Richard P. Leach and resided in Saratoga Springs, NY. Their son John M. P. Thatcher, Jr. married Dorothy Riddell and resided in Londonderry, VT.

F. Louise Vanderhoef Thatcher had previously been married to Gustav Maurice Heckscher and resided in Old Westbury.

Mary Barton Thatcher had previously been married to J. W. Fuller Potter, Henry W. Howe, and Oliver Iselin.

Thayer, Francis Kendall, Sr. (1876-1954)

Occupation(s):	attorney
Civic Activism:	a founder and trustee, Village of Sands Point
Marriage(s):	Caroline Mott (b. 1875)

Listed in *Long Island Society Register, 1929*: yes
Address: Forest Drive, Sands Point
Acreage / map sources: on 1927 map (owned by Mrs. F. M. Thayer)
                                              21 acres / 1932 and 1946 maps (owned by C. W. Thayer)
Name of estate: *Thayer House*
Year of construction: c. 1908
Style of architecture: Colonial Revival
Architect(s):   Robert Williams Gibson designed the pre-1906 barn
                                              (for K. Thayer)
Landscape architect(s):
House extant: yes
Historical notes:

The house, originally named *Thayer House,* was built by Kendall Thayer.

The estate was owned by Francis Kendall Thayer, Sr. and, subsequently, by Edward Siegel.

The *Long Island Society Register, 1929* lists Francis Kendall and Caroline Mott Thayer [Sr.] as residing at Oakwood in Sands Point. The Thayers built a house in Sands Point, presumably that house was the *Oakwood* residence.

He was the son of George Alexander and Joan Thayer.

Caroline Mott Thayer was the daughter of Thomas Mott of Sands Point.

The Thayers' daughter Margaret married Robert Lawson of Radnor, PA. He was the son of Benjamin Lawson of Richmond, VA, Their son Francis Kendall Thayer, Jr. married Marian Ball, the daughter of Wilbur Laing Ball of Locust Valley. Her sister Helen married Henry Schniewind III, whose parents resided at *Wyndhem* in Glen Cove.

The estate's former barn and gatehouse are private residences.

Thayer, Kendall

Occupation(s):	attorney
Civic Activism:	a founder, Village of Sands Point
Marriage(s):	Kanny Mott

Listed in *Long Island Society Register, 1929*: no

Address:	Forest Drive, Sands Point
Acreage / map sources:	on 1927 map; 21 acres / 1932 and 1946 maps (owned by C. W. Thayer)
Name of estate:	*Thayer House*
Year of construction:	c. 1908
Style of architecture:	Colonial Revival
Architect(s):	Robert Williams Gibson designed the pre-1906 barn (for K. Thayer)

Landscape architect(s):
House extant: yes
Historical notes:

    The house, originally named *Thayer House,* was built by Kendall Thayer.
    Kanny Mott Thayer's sister Martha married Alfred Valentine Fraser and resided at *Old House* in Sands Point.
    The estate was owned by Francis Kendall Thayer, Sr. and, subsequently, by Edward Siegel.
    The estate's former barn and gatehouse are private residences.

Thayer, Robert Helyer, Sr. (1901-1984)

Occupation(s):	attorney - member, Cadwalader, Wickersham and Taft
	diplomat - Assistant United States Ambassador to France, 1951-54; United States Minister to Romania, 1955-58; assistant to John Foster Dulles, United Nations Charter Conference, 1945
	statesman - Assistant Secretary of State, in the Eisenhower administration, 1958-61
Civic Activism:	director, Washington Performing Arts Society; trustee, St. Mark's School, Southborough, MA; trustee, National Trust for Historic Preservation
Marriage(s):	1926 - Virginia Pratt

Listed in *Long Island Society Register, 1929*: yes

Address:	Dosoris Lane, Glen Cove
Acreage / map sources:	on 1927 and 1932 maps (owned by Pratt) 12 acres / 1946 map (owned by Mrs. V. Thayer)
Name of estate:	
Year of construction:	
Style of architecture:	Neo-Colonial
Architect(s):	
Landscape architect(s):	

House extant: unconfirmed
Historical notes:

    The house was built by Robert Dunbar Pruyn with money and on land loaned to him by John Teele Pratt, Sr. Because of financial losses caused by the Depression, Pruyn realized that he would not be able to repay the loan and returned the estate to Pratt's widow Ruth Baker Pratt.
    The estate was taken over by the Pratt's daughter and son-in-law Robert Helyer and Virginia Pratt Thayer, Sr.
    Virginia Pratt Thayer's sister Sally married James Jackson, Jr. and resided in MA. Her brother John Teele Pratt, Jr. resided at *The Farm House* and at *Beechwood*, both of which were in Glen Cove. Her sister Phyllis married Paul Henry Nitze. The Nitzes subsequently owned *The Farm House*, previously owned by her brother.
    In 1956, the estate was purchased by the Glen Cove School District for use as an administration building.

Thieriot, Charles Henschel, II (1915-2000)

Occupation(s):	financier - partner, Carlisle and Jacquelin (stock brokerage firm); partner, Carlisle and De Coppet and Co. (stock brokerage firm)
Civic Activism:	trustee, New York Racing Association; trustee, The National Museum of Racing and Racing Hall of Fame, Saratoga, NY: fire commissioner, Locust Valley; trustee, Village of Matinecock; trustee, St. Mark's School, Southborough, MA; trustee, Hospital for Special Surgery, NYC
Marriage(s):	M/1 -1945 - Julia Kingsland Macy (1914-2002) M/2 - Edna H. Taylor

Listed in *Long Island Society Register, 1929*: yes
Address: Chicken Valley Road, Matinecock
Acreage / map sources: not on 1927, 1932, or 1946 maps
Name of estate:
Year of construction: c. 1929
Style of architecture: French Provincial
Architect(s):   Peabody, Wilson and Brown designed the house
                                                   (for G. Auchincloss, Sr.)
Landscape architect(s):
House extant: yes
Historical notes:

The house, originally named *Ronda*, was built by Gordon Auchincloss, Sr.

The estate was, subsequently, owned by Thieriot, who was the son of Charles Henschel and Frances Thornton Thieriot, Sr., who resided at *Cedar Hill* in Muttontown.

The *Long Island Society Register, 1929* lists Charles H. Thieriot, Jr. [II] as a minor residing with his parents at *Cedar Hill* in Oyster Bay [Muttontown]. The *Social Register, 1999* lists Charles H. and Edna H. Taylor Thieriot [II] as residing on Chicken Valley Road, Locust Valley [Matinecock].

Julia Kingsland Macy Thieriot was the daughter of William Kingsland and Julia A. Dick Macy, Sr., who resided in Islip. She had previously been married to W. Cary Potter and subsequently married William Thompson, residing with him in Tucson, AZ. W. Cary Potter was the son of Alonzo and Elsie Nicholas Potter, who resided at *Harbor House* in St. James.

Thieriot, Charles Henschel, Sr. (1880-1941)

Occupation(s):	financier - partner, Carlisle, Mellick and Co. (stock brokerage firm)
Marriage(s):	1912-1941 - Frances D. Thornton (d. 1957) - Civic Activism: committee chairman, Cancer Institute

Listed in *Long Island Society Register, 1929*: yes
Address: Mill River Road, Muttontown
Acreage / map sources: on 1927 map; 20 acres / 1932 and 1946 maps
Name of estate: *Cedar Hill*
Year of construction: c. 1919
Style of architecture: Federal
Architect(s):   James W. O'Connor designed the house (for Thieriot)
Landscape architect(s):
House extant: yes
Historical notes:

The house, originally named *Cedar Hill,* was built by Charles Henschel Thieriot, Sr.

Both the *Long Island Society Register, 1929* and the *Social Register, 1937* list Charles H. and Frances D. Thornton Thieriot [Sr.] as residing at *Cedar Hill* in Oyster Bay [Muttontown], while the *Social Register, Summer 1955* lists Mrs. Thieriot as residing at *Cedar Hill.*

The Thierots' son Charles Henschel Thieriot II resided in Matinecock. Their daughter Lucile married Elisha Walker, Jr., whose parents, Elisha and Adele D'Orn Walker, Sr., resided in Muttontown.

In 2002, the sixteen-room, 10,000-square-foot house and eight acres were for sale. The asking price was $4.25 million.

Thomas, Frederic Chichester, Sr. (1858-1920)

Occupation(s):   architect -   member, George Browne Post's firm

Marriage(s):   1899-1920 - Katharine Dobbin Brown (d. 1958)

Listed in *Long Island Society Register, 1929*: yes
Address: Woodbury Road, Cold Spring Harbor
Acreage / map sources: no acreage given on 1929 map
                              on 1931 map
                              44 acres / 1944 and 1946 maps
Name of estate: *Woodlee Farm*
Year of construction: c. 1906
Style of architecture:
Architect(s):   Frederic Chichester Thomas, Sr.
                              designed his own house

Landscape architect(s):
House extant: no; demolished in 1940
Historical notes:

    The house, originally named *Woodlee Farm*, was built by Frederic Chichester Thomas, Sr.
    The *Long Island Society Register, 1929* lists Katharine D. Brown Thomas, Sr. as residing at *Woodlee Farm* on Woodbury Road, Cold Spring Harbor.
    The *Social Register New York, 1933* lists Mrs. Thomas as residing at 10 West Read Street, Baltimore, MD, while the *Social Register New York, 1957* lists her address as 3100 St. Paul Street, Baltimore, MD.
    She was the daughter of Robert D. Brown of Baltimore, MD.
    The Thomases' son Frederic Chichester Thomas II married Roberta G. Roelker and resided at *Dogwood* in Cold Spring Harbor. Their daughter Mary married Colin Drummond Kirkpatrick of *Park Lawn*, Cheltenham, England.

Thomas, Joseph Albert (1906-1977)

Occupation(s):   financier -   partner, Lehman Brothers (investment banking firm);
                        industrialist - director, Litton Industries, Inc.;
                                      director, Halliburton Co.;
                                      director, Getty Oil Co.;
                                      director, Black & Decker Manufacturing Co.
                      capitalist - director, Pan American Airway
Civic Activism: board member, Columbia–Presbyterian Medical Center, NYC;
                        trustee, Metropolitan Museum of Art, NYC;
                        trustee, New York Zoological Society, NYC;
                        president, Robert Lehman Foundation

Marriage(s):   1949-1977 - Martha Paula Ruppanner

Listed in *Long Island Society Register, 1929*: no
Address: Piping Rock Road, Upper Brookville
Acreage / map sources: not on 1927, 1932, or 1946 maps
Name of estate: *Normandie*
Year of construction: c. 1926
Style of architecture: Tudor
Architect(s):   Polhemus and Coffin designed the house (for Blackwell)
Landscape architect(s):
House extant: yes
Historical notes:

    The house, originally named *The Cedars,* was built by Charles Addison Blackwell.
    The estate was, subsequently, owned by Thomas, who called it *Normandie.*
    The *Social Register, Summer 1950* lists Joseph A. and M. Paula Ruppanner Thomas as residing at *Normandie* in Old Brookville [Upper Brookville].

Thomas, Norman Mattoon (1884-1968)

Occupation(s):	politician - six-time unsuccessful Socialist Party candidate for
	the Presidency of the United States
	writer - twenty books and numerous articles
	journalist - associate editor, *The Nation*;
	editor, *New York Leader*
	clergy - associate pastor, Brick Presbyterian Church, NYC
Civic Activism:	co-founder, Civil Liberties Bureau, which in 1920 became American
	Civil Liberties Union;
	an advocate of democratic Socialism, civil rights, a positive peace
	policy, and world disarmament

Marriage(s): 1910-1947 - Frances Violet Stewart (1881-1947)

Listed in *Long Island Society Register, 1929*: no
Address: Goose Hill Road, Cold Spring Harbor
Acreage / map sources: not on 1929 map; on 1931 map; 4 acres / 1944 and 1946 maps
Name of estate:
Year of construction:
Style of architecture: Modified Colonial Revival
Architect(s):
Landscape architect(s):
House extant: yes
Historical notes:

front facade, 1998

The house was built by Norman Mattoon Thomas.
He was the son of Welling Evan and Emma Mattoon Thomas of Columbus, OH.
Francis Violet Stewart Thomas was the daughter of William Adams Walker and Frances Gray Stewart, Sr. Her brother William Adams Walker Stewart II resided at *Edgeover*, also in Cold Spring Harbor. Her paternal grandfather John Aikman Stewart was Assistant Secretary of the Treasury in President Abraham Lincoln's administration.

In 1934, the Thomas' son William Stewart Thomas married Mary Gabrielle Campbell, the daughter of Oliver Allen and M. Gabrielle Clarke Campbell, Sr. who resided at *The Oaces* in East Norwich. Their daughter Frances married John W. Gates, Jr. Their daughter Mary, who married Herbert C. Miller, Jr. of Columbus, OH, resided in Cold Spring Harbor as did their son Evan W. Thomas II. A third daughter, Mrs. John Friebely, resides in Plainfield, NJ.

Thomas, Ralph W., Sr.

Occupation(s):

Marriage(s): Maude P. Lindley

Listed in *Long Island Society Register, 1929*: yes
Address: Middle Neck Road, Sands Point
Acreage / map sources: on c. 1922 map; not on 1927, 1932, or 1946 maps
Name of estate:
Year of construction: c. 1910
Style of architecture: Mediterranean
Architect(s): McKim, Mead and White designed the house and garage
(for R. W. Thomas, Sr.)
Addison Mizner designed the c. 1910 tennis house
(for R. W. Thomas, Sr.)*
Landscape architect(s):
House extant: no
Historical notes:

The house was built by Ralph W. Thomas, Sr.
The estate was owned by William Averell Harriman and, subsequently, by Thomas Hitchcock, Jr.
*The tennis house is now a guest house. The garage survives and is now a private residence.

Thompson, William Payne, Jr. (1871-1922)

Occupation(s):   industrialist - executive, Standard Oil Co. (which became Exxon Corp.)

Marriage(s):   1897-1922 - Edith Blight (d. 1941)

Listed in *Long Island Society Register, 1929*: yes
Address: Jericho Turnpike, Jericho
Acreage / map sources: on 1927 map; not on 1932 or 1946 maps
Name of estate: *Longfields*
Year of construction: 1910
Style of architecture: Federal
Architect(s):   Carrere and Hastings designed the house
                                    (for W. P. Thompson, Jr.)
Landscape architect(s):   Ellen Biddle Shipman designed the formal garden
                                    lawns, flagstone terrace, and curved driveway
                                    (for W. P. T. Preston, Sr.)

House extant: no
Historical notes:

    The house, originally named *Longfields,* was built by William Payne Thompson, Jr.
    He was the son of William Payne and Evelyn Moffat Thompson, Sr., who resided in Red Bank, NJ.
    The *Long Island Society Register, 1929* lists Edith Blight Thompson as residing at *Longfields* on Jericho Turnpike, Westbury [Jericho].
    She was the daughter of Atherton Blight of Manhattan.
    The estate was, subsequently, owned by William Payne Thompson Preston, Sr., who continued to call it *Longfields,* and by Jack Isidor Straus, who renamed it *Green Pastures.*

Thurman, Steven

Occupation(s):   capitalist - builder

Marriage(s):

Listed in *Long Island Society Register, 1929*: no
Address: Feeks Lane, Lattingtown
Acreage / map sources: not on 1927, 1932, or 1946 maps
Name of estate:
Year of construction: c. 1906
Style of architecture: Federal
Architect(s):
Landscape architect(s):
House extant: yes
Historical notes:

    The house was built by H. W. Warner.
    The estate was owned by William McNair, who called it *Northway House,* and, subsequently, by his daughter Elvira McNair Fairchild, who also called it *Northway House.*

    In the 1980s, the estate was owned by Eric Ridder, Sr.

    In 1997, the estate was owned by Thurman. The house was then on 5.4 acres. The rest of the estate's property had been sold for a housing development.

    In 2000, the house and 5.4 acres were for sale. The asking price was $2.95 million; the annual taxes were $35,000.

front facade, 1994

Tiffany, Anne Cameron (d. 1961)

Civic Activism: organized the Fifth Avenue Chapter of the New York Chapter
                                       of the American Red Cross during World War I

Marriage(s):   1895 - Belmont Tiffany (1873-1952)

Listed in *Long Island Society Register, 1929*: yes
Address: Brookville – East Norwich Road, Upper Brookville
Acreage / map sources: on 1927 map; no acreage given on 1932 map; 9 acres / 1946 map
Name of estate: *Glen Nevis*
Year of construction:
Style of architecture:
Architect(s):   William Lawrence Bottomley
                                    designed 1920s alterations
                                    (for A. C. Tiffany)

Landscape architect(s):
House extant: unconfirmed
Historical notes:

dining room, 1926

    Anne Cameron Tiffany was the daughter of Sir Roderick McLeod Cameron of *Clifton Berley* in Rosebund, Staten Island, NY.
    Belmont Tiffany was a grandson of Commodore Matthew C. Perry and the son of George and Isabella Perry Tiffany. His brother Perry Tiffany resided in Old Westbury.
    The Tiffanys' son George Tiffany II married Maria Trazzi, the daughter of Alfred Trazzi of Staten Island, NY.

Tiffany, Charles Lewis, II (1878-1947)

Occupation(s):   merchant - vice-president, Tiffany & Co. (jewelers)
                              financier - director, Bankers Trust

Marriage(s):   M/1 - 1901-1927 - Katrina Brandes Ely (1875-1927)
                           - Civic Activism: woman's suffrage - recording secretary, Woman
                                                Suffrage Party of the City of New York;
                                    a founder, Woodrow Wilson Foundation;
                                    member, New York Intercollegiate Bureau;
                                    trustee, New York Infirmary for Women and Children, NYC;
                                    *
                     M/2 - 1931-1947 - Emilia de Apezteguia (1883-1961)

Listed in *Long Island Society Register, 1929*: yes
Address: Oyster Bay Cove Road, Oyster Bay Cove
Acreage / map sources: on 1927 and 1932 maps
                                24 acres / 1946 map
Name of estate: *Elmwood*
Year of construction: c. 1863

Style of architecture: Colonial Revival
Architect(s):
Landscape architect(s):
Estate photographs can be found in the Nassau County
   Museum Collection filed under Oyster Bay/Tiffany.
House extant: yes
Historical notes:

front facade, c. 1970

    The house, originally named *Elmwood*, was built by Thomas F. Young.
    The estate was, subsequently, owned by Charles Lewis Tiffany II, who continued to call it *Elmwood*.
Charles was the son of Louis Comfort Tiffany and his first wife Mary Woodbridge Goddard Tiffany.
[See following entry for additional family information.]
*A sixteen-page pamphlet entitled, *Katrina Ely Tiffany*, was published by Yale University Press in 1929.

Tiffany, Louis Comfort (1848-1933)

Occupation(s):
    artist
    interior designer
    merchant - president, Tiffany and Co., NYC (the jewelry firm
        founded by his father Charles Lewis Tiffany);
        co-founder with Samuel Colman, Lockwood de Forest,
        and Candace Wheeler, L. C. Tiffany & Associated
        Artists, 1879-1883;
        founder and president, Louis C. Tiffany & Co., 1882;
        founder and president, The Tiffany Glass Co., Inc., 1885-90;
        founder and president, Tiffany Glass & Decorating Co., 1890;
        founder and president, Tiffany Studios, 1900-32
    industrialist - founder and president, Tiffany Furnaces, 1902-24 (formed
        from the glasshouse at Corona);
        founder and president, Louis C. Tiffany Furnaces, 1920-28
    writer - *The Art Work of Louis Comfort Tiffany,* 1914
        [dictated to Charles DeKay];
        "Brittany Diary" [unpublished manuscript];
        numerous articles

Civic Activism:
    founder, Tiffany Foundation*

Marriage(s):
    M/1 - 1872-1884 - Mary Woodbridge Goddard (1846-1884)
    M/2 - 1886-1904 - Louise Wakeman Knox (1851-1904)

Listed in *Long Island Society Register, 1929*: yes
Address: off Moore's Hill Road, Laurel Hollow
Acreage / map sources: not on 1927, 1932, or 1946 maps
Name of estate: *The Briars*
Year of construction: 1890
Style of architecture: Shingle / Neo-Colonial
Architect(s):   Louis Comfort Tiffany**
Landscape architect(s):
House extant: no; the house was destroyed by fire
Historical notes:

    Louis Comfort Tiffany built *The Briars* and resided in it, with his children, before building *Laurelton Hall.* His first wife, known as May, died while *The Briars* was being built.

    The driveway to *The Briars* had an *allee* of maple trees and ground cover of daylilies. The driveway was later extended to his subsequent residence, *Laurelton Hall.*

    The *Long Island Society Register, 1929* lists Louis Comfort Tiffany as residing at *Laurelton Hall* in Laurelton [Laurel Hollow], while the *Social Register New York, 1933* lists him as summering at *Comfort Lodge,* 1865 Brickell Avenue, Miami, FL.

    Tiffany gave *The Briars* to his daughter Mary and son-in-law Dr. Graham Lusk.

    His son Charles Lewis Tiffany II, who married Katrina Brandes Ely and, subsequently, Emilia de Apezteguia, resided at *Elmwood* in Oyster Bay Cove. His daughter Julia de Forest Tiffany married Gordon Saltonstall Parker and, subsequently, Francis Minot Weld II, who resided at *Lulworth* in Lloyd Harbor and at *Hemlock House* in Glen Cove. His daughter Louise married Rodman Gilder Sr. and also resided in Laurel Hollow, as did her sister Dorothy, who married Dr. Robert Burlingham.

    *Tiffany donated his Laurelton Hall estate and eighty acres to the foundation.

    **According to Hugh F. McKean, *The "Lost" Treasures of Louis Comfort Tiffany,* Tiffany designed *The Briars.* [Hugh F. McKean, *The "Lost" Treasures of Louis Comfort Tiffany* (Garden City: Doubleday & Co., Inc., 1980), p.6.

front facade, c. 1900

Tiffany, Louis Comfort (1848-1933)

Occupation(s):
    artist

interior designer

merchant - president, Tiffany and Co., NYC (the jewelry firm
               founded by his father Charles Lewis Tiffany);
          co-founder with Samuel Colman, Lockwood de Forest,
              and Candace Wheeler, L. C. Tiffany & Associated
              Artists, 1879-1883;
          founder and president, Louis C. Tiffany & Co., 1882;
          founder and president, The Tiffany Glass Co., Inc., 1885-90;
          founder and president, Tiffany Glass & Decorating Co., 1890;
          founder and president, Tiffany Studios, 1900-32

industrialist - founder and president, Tiffany Furnaces, 1902-24 (formed
              from the glasshouse at Corona);
          founder and president, Louis C. Tiffany Furnaces, 1920-28

writer - *The Art Work of Louis Comfort Tiffany*, 1914
          [dictated to Charles DeKay];
          "Brittany Diary" [unpublished manuscript];
          numerous articles

Civic Activism:
    *

Marriage(s):
    M/1 - 1872-1884 - Mary Woodbridge Goddard (1846-1884)

    M/2 - 1886-1904 - Louise Wakeman Knox (1851-1904)

Listed in *Long Island Society Register, 1929*: yes

Address: Ridge Road, Laurel Hollow

Acreage / map sources: on 1927 map; no acreage given on 1932 map; 209 acres / 1946 map

Name of estate: *Laurelton Hall*

Year of construction: 1904

Style of architecture: Eclectic Moorish

Architect(s):   Louis Comfort Tiffany designed his own house with the
        assistance of Robert L. Pryor**

    Alfred Hopkins designed the farm complex (for Tiffany)

Landscape architect(s):   Louis Comfort Tiffany designed landscaping which included two driveways
        (one from Moore's Hill Road with *allee* of maple trees and ground cover of
        daylilies; the other from Tiffany Road, one-mile-long through woods with
        waterfall and ground cover of daffodils), daffodil field, 100-yard-long arch
        of espaliered apple trees, formal sunken garden with marble fountain and
        bronze statue, *The Boy* (Elihu Vedder, 1900-02), terraces including daffodil
        terrace, four garden fountains, pergolas, ponds, gravel paths, and "hanging"
        garden; gardens were lit by rotating colored lights***

House extant: no; demolished in 1957****

Historical notes:

    The house, originally named *Laurelton Hall*, was built by Louis Comfort Tiffany on his 580-acre estate.

    The *Long Island Society Register, 1929* lists Louis Comfort Tiffany as residing at *Laurelton Hall* in Laurelton [Laurel Hollow], while the *Social Register New York, 1933* lists him as summering at *Comfort Lodge*, 1865 Brickell Avenue, Miami, FL.

    *At Tiffany's death in 1933, a portion of the estate was donated to the Tiffany Foundation. This included the house and numerous outbuildings, where an art school was operated.

    **According to Hugh F. McKean, *The "Lost" Treasures of Louis Comfort Tiffany*, Tiffany designed *Laurelton Hall*. [Hugh F. McKean, *The "Lost" Treasures of Louis Comfort Tiffany* (Garden City: Doubleday & Co., Inc., 1980), p. 6.]

    ***The Art Institute of Chicago has Vedder's cast for the statue of *The Boy*.

    During World War II, the estate became the headquarters for the Marine Research Organization and the Nation's Research Committee. [*The North Shore Journal* 3 (March 4, 1971).]

    ****Abandoned by the art foundation and in disrepair, the eighty-four-room house was destroyed by fire in 1957. Art works of Tiffany, which could be salvaged from the ruined house, were taken to Winter Park, Florida, where they now may be viewed in the Hosmer Morse Museum of American Art. Some of the outbuildings remain and have been converted into private homes. Also surviving is the Moorish-style smoke stack from the powerhouse.

    [See previous entry for family information.]

Louis Comfort Tiffany Estate, *Laurelton Hall*

power smokestack, 1997

main house, 1907

*main house and powerhouse smokestack, upper right;
service buildings, lower left*

remnants of service building tower, 1997

smoking lounge, c. 1907

Tiffany, Perry (d. 1928)

Occupation(s):	industrialist - mining interests in Dutch Guiana
Civic Activism:	*

Marriage(s):	M/1 - 1893-1902 - Marie Havemeyer (1872-1925)
	M/2 - Olive W. Thompson (d. 1961)
	- Civic Activism: *

Listed in *Long Island Society Register, 1929*: no

Address:	I. U. Willets Road, Old Westbury
Acreage / map sources:	not on 1927, 1932, or 1946 maps
Name of estate:	
Year of construction:	1891
Style of architecture:	Georgian Revival
Architect(s):	Gage and Wallace designed the house (for P. Tiffany)
	Eliot B. Cross designed the addition of the portico to the
	stables/garage complex and additions to the house (for Cross)

Landscape architect(s):
Estate photographs can be found in the Nassau County Museum Collection filed under Westbury/Cross.
House extant: yes
Historical notes:

The house was built by Perry Tiffany.

He was a grandson of Commodore Mathew C. Perry and the son of George and Isabella Perry Tiffany. His sister-in-law Anne Cameron Tiffany resided in Upper Brookville.

Marie Havemeyer Godfrey was the daughter of Theodore Augustus and Emilie deLoosey Havemeyer, Sr. Her sister Blanche married William Butler Duncan and resided at *Park Hill* in Sands Point. Her brother Frederick Christian Havemeyer IV resided in Old Brookville. Their brother Theodore Augustus Havemeyer II resided at *Cedar Hill* in Upper Brookville. Marie Havemeyer Tiffany was, subsequently, married to Henry Fletcher Godfrey, Sr., who also resided in Old Westbury.

The *Social Register, Summer 1932* lists Olive W, Thompson Tiffany as residing at *Commodore Perry Farm* in Wakefield, RI, while the *Social Register New York, 1959* lists her residence as 320 East 53rd Street, NYC.

*During World War I, Perry and Olive W. Thompson Tiffany resided in France where they engaged in war work for the French Red Cross and the British canteens.

The estate was owned by Harry Payne Bingham, Sr., who called it *Ivycroft*, and, subsequently, by Eliot B. Cross.

Tilney, Frederick, Jr.

Occupation(s):	financier - founder, Tilney and Co. (municipal bond finance firm)

Marriage(s):	M/1 - 1937 - Francis Maitland Brown
	M/2 - 1949 - Dorothy McCabe

Listed in *Long Island Society Register, 1929*: yes

Address:	Centre Island Road, Centre Island
Acreage / map sources:	on 1927 map (owned by F. D. K. Tilney)
	5 acres / 1932 map (owned by C. Tilney)
	5 acres / 1946 map (owned by F. Tilney)
Name of estate:	
Year of construction:	
Style of architecture:	
Architect(s):	
Landscape architect(s):	
House extant: unconfirmed	
Historical notes:	

Frederick Tilney, Jr. inherited the estate originally named *Sundown* from his mother.

The *Long Island Society Register, 1929* lists Frederick Tilney, Jr. as residing with his parents on Centre Island.

Francis Maitland Brown Tilney was the daughter of J. Myron Brown of Manhattan.

Dorothy McCabe Tilney was the daughter of Charles Wesley McCabe of Tekoa, WA.

In 1980, the bank holding the estate's mortgage foreclosed because of Tilney's failure to meet the mortgage payments.

Tilney, Dr. Frederick, Sr. (1876-1938)

Occupation(s):   physician - director, Neurological Institute of Columbia–Presbyterian
                                          Medical Center, NYC
                                  writer - *The Form and Functions of the Central Nervous System,* 1921
                                          (co-authored with Henry Alsop Riley);
                                          The Brain from Ape to Man, 1928;
                                          Master of Destiny, 1930

Marriage(s):   1903-1938 - Camilla DeG. Hurley (d. 1952)

Listed in *Long Island Society Register, 1929*: yes
Address: Centre Island Road, Centre Island
Acreage / map sources: on 1927 map (owned by F. D. K. Tilney)
                                  5 acres / 1932 map (owned by C. Tilney)
                                  5 acres / 1946 map (owned by F. Tilney)
Name of estate: *Sundown*
Year of construction:
Style of architecture:
Architect(s):
Landscape architect(s):
House extant: unconfirmed
Historical notes:

   Born in Brooklyn, Dr. Frederick Tilney, Sr. was the son of Thomas J. and Katharine Hutchinson Tilney.
   The Tilneys' son Frederick Tilney, Jr. inherited the estate.
   In 1980, the bank holding the estate's mortgage foreclosed because of Tilney's failure to meet the mortgage payments.

Tinker, Edward Richmond, Jr. (1878-1959)

Occupation(s):   financier - vice-president, Chase National Bank;
                                          president, Chase Securities Corp.;
                                          president, Interstate Equities Corp.
                                  capitalist - chairman of board, Fox Film Corp.
Civic Activism: member, Commercial Bank and Trust Companies Commission
                                      during World War I;
                                  member, Liberty Loan Commission during World War I

Marriage(s):   1909-1959 - Marie Vidal Sollace (1884-1978)

Listed in *Long Island Society Register, 1929*: yes
Address: Jericho Turnpike, Syosset
Acreage / map sources: on 1927 map (name misspelled as E. H. Tinker)
                                  180 acres / 1932 map (name misspelled as E. H. Tinker)
                                  20 acres / 1946 map (owned by M. Tinker)
Name of estate: *Woodbury House*
Year of construction: c. 1915
Style of architecture: Tudor
Architect(s):   Cross and Cross designed the house (for J. W. Webb, Sr.)
                                  James W. O'Connor designed the tennis building
                                      (for J. W. Webb, Sr.)
Landscape architect(s):
House extant: yes
Historical notes:

   The house, originally named *Woodbury House,* had a partial "Tiffany Studios interior" when it was built by James Watson Webb, Sr.
   The estate was purchased by Edward Richmond Tinker, Jr., who continued to call it *Woodbury House.*
   The *Social Register, Summer 1937* lists Edward R. and Marie V. Sollace Tinker [Jr.] as residing at *Woodbury House* in Syosset.
   The estate was, subsequently, purchased by the Town of Oyster Bay and is now the Westbury–Syosset Community Park.

Tinker, Giles Knight (1856-1938)

Occupation(s):   financier - assistant manager, United States Assurance Co., Ltd.

Marriage(s):   Anna E. Hofgren

Listed in *Long Island Society Register, 1929*: yes
Address: Oyster Bay Cove Road and Yellowcote Road, Oyster Bay Cove
Acreage / map sources: on 1927 map; no acreage given on 1932 map; not on 1946 map
Name of estate: *Reknit*
Year of construction:
Style of architecture:
Architect(s):
Landscape architect(s):
House extant: unconfirmed
Historical notes:

     The *Long Island Society Register, 1929* lists Giles Knight and Anna E. Hofgren Tinker as residing at *Reknit* in Oyster Bay [Oyster Bay Cove].

Tippet, Mary Elizabeth Altemus (1905-1988)

Marriage(s):   M/1 - 1930-1940 - John Hay Whitney (1904-1982)
                                - capitalist - chairman of board, J. H. Whitney and Co.;
                                               chairman of board, Whitney Communications;
                                               chairman of board, Selznick International Pictures
                                publisher - *New York Herald Tribune;*
                                                 chairman of board, *International Herald Tribune*
                                diplomat - United States Ambassador to the Court of St. James
                                                 in the Eisenhower administration, 1956-61
                                financier - partner, Whitcom Investment Co.
                      M/2 - 1948-1952 - Dr. E. Cooper Person, Jr. (1910-1952)
                                - physician
                                educator - associate professor, clinical surgery, Cornell
                                                 University Medical College, NYC
                      M/3 - div. 1959 - Richard Dwight Lunn
                                - advertising executive
                      M/4 - 1960-1988 - Cloyce Joseph Tippet
                                - headed the Lima, Peru, office of the International Civil
                                                 Aviation Organization

Listed in *Long Island Society Register, 1929*: no
Address: Clocktower Lane, Old Westbury
Acreage / map sources: not on 1927, 1932, or 1946 maps
Name of estate:
Year of construction:
Style of architecture: Spanish Colonial
Architect(s):
Landscape architect(s):
House extant: yes
Historical notes:

front facade, 2004

     John Hay Whitney was the son of William Payne and Helen Hay Whitney, who resided at *Greentree* in Manhasset.
     In the 1950s, Mary Elizabeth Altemus Tippet converted the chapel on the Edwin Denison Morgan III estate into a home for herself.
     She owned thoroughbred stables: Llangollen of Virginia, Llangollen of Ocala, Florida; and Llangollen of California (near San Diego). At the racetrack she always dressed in her racing colors, purple and fuchsia, and traveled in her purple and fuchsia helicopter, which was piloted by her fourth husband Cloyce Joseph Tippet.
     The house, which was originally the chapel on the William Collins Whitney estate, has been extensively remodeled over the years. In 1998, it and 1.7 acres were for sale. The asking price was $1.1 million; the annual taxes were $7,752.

Tod, Robert Elliot (1867-1944)

Occupation(s):   financier - partner, J. Kennedy Tod and Co. (investment banking firm)
politician - Commissioner of Immigration for The Port of New York in
                                        the Harding administration

Civic Activism: board member, Post-Graduate Hospital and Medical College;
board member, Presbyterian Hospital (now, Columbia–Presbyterian
                                        Medical Center), NYC

Marriage(s):   1904-1944 - Katharine Alexander Chew (1883-1969)

Listed in *Long Island Society Register, 1929*: yes
Address: Burtis Lane, Syosset
Acreage / map sources: on 1927 map; no acreage given on 1932 map; 72 acres / 1946 map
Name of estate: *Thistleton*
Year of construction:
Style of architecture:
Architect(s):   Delano and Aldrich designed the swimming pool (for Tod)
Landscape architect(s):
House extant: unconfirmed
Historical notes:

    The *Long Island Society Register, 1929* lists Robert E. and Katharine A. Chew Tod as residing at *Thistleton* in Syosset, while the *Social Register, Summer 1945* lists only Mrs. Tod as residing at *Thistleton*.
    In 1911, Tod participated in the *Karina*'s defense of the America's Cup.
    During World War I, he served as navigation officer aboard J. P. Morgan's former yacht *Corsair,* gifted to the United States government for the war effort by Morgan. Subsequently, Tod became the commander in charge of the port of Brest, France.
    The Tods' daughter Katharine married Henry Bradley Martin II and resided in Oyster Bay Cove.

Toerge, Norman K., Sr. (d. 1971)

Occupation(s):   financier - partner, Toerge and Schiffer (stock brokerage firm)

Marriage(s):   M/1 - 1917 - Elinor Gates (1896-1966)
M/2 - 1934 - Katharine E. Register (d. 1978)

Listed in *Long Island Society Register, 1929*: yes
Address: Piping Rock Road, Matinecock
Acreage / map sources: on 1927 map; not on 1932 map; 8 acres / 1946 map
Name of estate: *The Hitching Post*
Year of construction: c. 1920
Style of architecture: 20th-century Eclectic
Architect(s):   Howard Major designed the house (for Toerge)
Landscape architect(s):
House extant: yes
Historical notes:

    The house, originally named *The Hitching Post,* was built by Norman K. Toerge, Sr.
    The *Long Island Society Register, 1929* lists Norman K. and Elinor Gates Toerge [Sr.] as residing in Locust Valley [Matinecock].
    He was the son of Nicholas Toerge.
    Elinor Gates Toerge was the daughter of Charles Otis and Elizabeth Hoagland Gates, who resided at *Peacock Point* and *Dormer House* in Lattingtown. She subsequently married Joseph Clendenin.
    Norman K. and Elinor Gates Toerge, Sr.'s son Norman K. Toerge, Jr. married Sally Porterfield Taylor, the daughter of Dr. Quintard Taylor of Manhattan.
    Katharine E. Register Toerge was the daughter of Albert L. Register of Boston, MA. She had previously been married to Geraldyn Livingston Redmond, Sr. and resided at *Gray House Farm* in Upper Brookville. Her sister Barbara married James Bogert Tailer, Jr. of Manhattan. Her son Geraldyn Livingston Redmond [Jr.] resides in Glen Cove. Her daughter Estelle Redmond married Cyrus Edson Manierre of Lake Forest, IL.
    The *Social Register, 1979* lists Katharine E. Register Toerge and residing in The Plains, VA, at the time of her death.

Tower, Roderick (1892-1961)

Occupation(s):   financier -   member, New York Stock Exchange

Marriage(s):   M/1 - 1920-1924 - Flora Payne Whitney (1897-1986)
                                     - Civic Activism: founder, first president, and chairman of board,
                                            Whitney Museum of American Art, NYC
                                  M/2 - 1932-1941 - Edna E. Hoyt
                                  M/3 - 1950 - Katherine W. Bonnie

Listed in *Long Island Society Register, 1929*: yes
Address: Oyster Bay Road, Syosset
Acreage / map sources: not on 1927, 1932, or 1946 maps
Name of estate: *Chestnut Vale*
Year of construction:
Style of architecture:
Architect(s):
Landscape architect(s):
House extant: unconfirmed
Historical notes:

   Roderick Tower was the son of Charlemagne Tower, Sr. of Philadelphia.
   Flora Payne Whitney Tower was the daughter of Harry Payne and Gertrude Vanderbilt Whitney, who resided in Old Westbury. *[See surname entry for Flora Payne Whitney Miller for Miller family information.]*
   Roderick and Flora Payne Whitney Tower's daughter Pamela married Jay Ketcham Secor and, subsequently, Thomas Le Boutillier III, with whom she resided in Old Westbury. Their son Whitney Tower, Sr., who married Frances Drexel Cheston, Joan Baker Spear, and, subsequently, Ludy Niblack Lyle, also resided in Old Westbury.
   Edna E. Hoyt Tower was the daughter of Walter S. Hoyt, Sr. She had previously been married to William John Warburton and Andre Lord. She subsequently married Hardwich Nevins. Roderick and Edna Tower's daughter Diana married James McMillen, Jr. of Sands Point.
   Katherine Bonnie Tower was the daughter of William M. Bonnie. She had previously been married to Carl Haynes Langenberg and resided at *Bonnie Knoll* on Fishers Island.

Tower, Roderick (1892-1961)

Occupation(s):   financier -   member, New York Stock Exchange

Marriage(s):   M/1 - 1920-1924 - Flora Payne Whitney (1897-1986)
                                     - Civic Activism: founder, first president, and chairman of board,
                                            Whitney Museum of American Art, NYC
                                  M/2 - 1932-1941 - Edna E. Hoyt
                                  M/3 - 1950 - Katherine W. Bonnie

Listed in *Long Island Society Register, 1929*: yes
Address: Horse Hollow Road, Lattingtown
Acreage / map sources: not on 1927, 1932, or 1946 maps
Name of estate:
Year of construction: 1932
Style of architecture: French Chateau
Architect(s):   Walker and Gillette designed the house (for G. F. Baker II)
Landscape architect(s):
House extant: yes
Historical notes:

   George Fisher Baker II built the house, originally named *Beaupre,* for his daughter Florence and son-in-law Thomas Suffern Tailer, Jr. on part of the former Paul Cravath estate *Veraton.*
   After the Tailers divorced, the estate was owned by Polly Brooks Howe, who called it *Severn.*
   In 1952, the estate was owned by Tower.
   Forty acres of the estate were sold to the Locust Valley School District.
   In 2003. the house and five acres were for sale; the asking price was $3.3 million.
   (See previous entry for Tower family information.)

Tower, Whitney, Sr. (1923-1999)

Occupation(s):	journalist* - *Cincinnati Enquirer;*
	Sports Illustrated
Civic Activism:	a founder, National Museum of Racing and Racing Hall of Fame,
	Saratoga, NY
Marriage(s):	M/1 - 1947 - Frances Drexel Cheston
	M/2 - 1968 - Joan Baker Krakeur
	M/3 - 1981 - Lucy Niblack Lyle

Listed in *Long Island Society Register, 1929*: no
Address: Whitney Lane, Old Westbury
Acreage / map sources: not on 1927, 1932, or 1946 maps
Name of estate:
Year of construction:
Style of architecture:
Architect(s):
Landscape architect(s):
House extant: unconfirmed
Historical notes:

Whitney Tower, Sr. was the son of Roderick and Flora Payne Whitney Tower.
[See Roderick Tower surname entries for additional family information.]
Roderick Tower had residences in Syosset and Lattingtown.
*In 1967, Whitney Tower was the recipient of the Thoroughbred Racing Association award for magazine journalism. In 1976 and 1977, he received the Eclipse Award for magazine journalism.
Frances Drexel Cheston Tower was the daughter of Radcliffe Cheston, Jr. of Oreland, PA.
Whitney and Frances Tower's daughter Alexandra married Jonathan Marshall Hornblower. Their son Whitney Tower, Jr. married Pamela Courtney Franzheim. Their daughter Frances married Thomas Day Thacher II. Their son Harry Payne Tower married Hilary Lee Harlow, the daughter of Albert L. Harlow of Southport, CT.
Joan Baker Krakeur Tower was the daughter of Richard Krakeur of Los Angeles, CA. She had previously been married to Eliot Elisofon.
Lucy Niblack Lyle Tower was the daughter of W. Gordon Lyle, Jr. of Fairfield, CT.

Townsend, Edward Mitchell II (1860-1934)

Occupation(s):	merchant - president, E. M. Townsend & Co. (dry goods firm)
	financier - trustee, New York Life Insurance & Trust Co.;
	trustee and vice-president, Union Square Savings Bank;
	director, Bank of New York and Trust Co.
Civic Activism:	trustee, Deaf and Dumb Asylum, NYC;
	member, Liberty Loan Committee during World War I
Marriage(s):	1892-1934 - Alice Greenough (d. 1938)
	- Civic Activism: trustee, Y.W.C.A

Listed in *Long Island Society Register, 1929*: yes
Address: East Main Street, Oyster Bay Cove
Acreage / map sources: on c. 1922 and 1927 maps; no acreage given on 1932 map;
                                     19 acres / 1944 map; 7 acres / 1946 map
Name of estate: *Townsend Place*
Year of construction: c. 1906
Style of architecture: Shingle
Architect(s):
Landscape architect(s):
House extant: no; demolished c. 1993
Historical notes:

Edward Mitchell Townsend II inherited the estate from his parents Edward Mitchell and Belinda Rockwell Townsend, Sr. His brother Howard Rockwell Townsend, Sr., resided at *Ramsbroke* in Oyster Bay Cove.
The Townsends' son Greenough married Rachel Maxtone Graham of Cultoquhey, Perthshire, Scotland.

Townsend, Edward Mitchell, Sr. (1829-1904)

Occupation(s):   merchant - president, E. M. Townsend & Co. (dry goods firm)
Civic Activism: board member, Deaf and Dumb Asylum, NYC;
                                       board member, DeMill Dispensary;
                                       vice-president, Institute for the Savings of Merchant's Clerks;
                                       trustee, House of Refuge

Marriage(s):   Belinda Rockwell

Listed in *Long Island Society Register, 1929*: no
Address: East Main Street, Oyster Bay Cove
Acreage / map sources: on c. 1922 and 1927 maps
                                       no acreage given on 1932 map
                                       19 acres / 1944 map
                                       7 acres / 1946 map
Name of estate: *Townsend Place*
Year of construction: c. 1906
Style of architecture: Shingle
Architect(s):
Landscape architect(s):
House extant: no; demolished c. 1993
Historical notes:

rear facade

   The estate was inherited by their son Edward Mitchell Townsend II, who continued to call it *Townsend Place*.
   [See previous and following entries for family information.]

Townsend, Howard Rockwell, Sr. (1873-1939)

Occupation(s):   industrialist - Townsend & Strickler (hosiery manufacturers)

Marriage(s):   1905-1939 - Emily Therese Firth (1882-1939)

Listed in *Long Island Society Register, 1929*: yes
Address: East Main Street, Oyster Bay Cove
Acreage / map sources: not on 1927 and 1946 maps
                                       no acreage given on 1932 map
Name of estate: *Ramsbroke*
Year of construction:
Style of architecture:
Architect(s):
Landscape architect(s):
House extant: unconfirmed
Historical notes:

   Both the *Long Island Society Register, 1929* and the *Social Register New York, 1933* list Howard R. and Therese Firth Townsend [Sr.] as residing at *Ramsbroke* in Oyster Bay [Oyster Bay Cove].
   Howard Rockwell Townsend, Sr. was the son of Edward Mitchell and Belinda Rockwell Townsend, Sr., who resided at *Townsend Place* in Oyster Bay Cove. His brother Edward Mitchell Townsend II inherited and also resided at *Townsend Place* in Oyster Bay Cove.
   Emily Therese Firth Townsend was the daughter of John Firth of Ridgewood, NJ.
   The Townsends' son Howard Rockwell Townsend, Jr. married Harriet Barton Scovil, the daughter of William Lorne Scovil of New Jersey.

Townsend, James Mulford, II (1852-1913)

Occupation(s):	attorney - partner, Townsend and Button
	educator - instructor, Yale University, School of Law, New Haven, CT
Civic Activism:	chairman of board, New York Law School, NYC
Marriage(s):	1882-1913 - Harriet Bailey Campbell

Listed in *Long Island Society Register, 1929*: no
Address: Frost Mill Road, Mill Neck
Acreage / map sources: not on 1927, 1932, or 1946 maps
Name of estate:
Year of construction:
Style of architecture:
Architect(s):   William Lawrence Bottomley designed 1915 alterations
                                                          (for J. M. Townsend II); later, alterations (for Winmill)
Landscape architect(s):
Estate photographs can be found in the Nassau County Museum Collection filed under Mill Neck/Winmill.
House extant: unconfirmed
Historical notes:

   Born in New Haven, CT, James Mulford Townsend II was the son of James Mulford and Maria Clark Townsend, Sr. Harriet Bailey Campbell Townsend was the daughter of John L. Campbell of Lexington, VA.
   The Townsends' daughter Harriet married the architect William Lawrence Bottomley and resided at *Hickory Hill* in Old Brookville.
   The estate was, subsequently, owned by Robert Campbell Winmill.

Townsend, John Allen (d. 1935)

Occupation(s):	attorney
Marriage(s):	1890-1935 - Viola S. Hawkins

Listed in *Long Island Society Register, 1929*: yes
Address: Feeks Lane, Lattingtown
Acreage / map sources: on 1927 map
                                                          no acreage given on 1932 map
                                                          not on 1946 map
Name of estate: *Forest Edge Farm*
Year of construction: c. 1914
Style of architecture:
Architect(s):
Landscape architect(s):
House extant: yes
Historical notes:

   The house, originally named *Forest Edge Farm*, was built by John Allen Townsend.
   The *Long Island Society Register, 1929* lists J. Allen and Viola S. Hawkins Townsend as residing at *Forest Edge Farm* in Locust Valley [Lattingtown].
   He was the son of Richard H. Townsend.
   Viola S. Hawkins Townsend was the daughter of Dexter Arnold and Sophie T. Meeks Hawkins, who resided in Manhattan. Her sister Estelle married Henry Wolcott Warner and resided in Syosset.
   The Townsends' daughter Viola married Robert Campbell Winmill and resided at *Borradil Farm* in Mill Neck.

Toy, Thomas Dallam, Sr. (1873-1940)

Occupation(s):   merchant - president, Thomas D. Toy & Co.
                                            (yarn merchants)

Marriage(s):   Heloise C. Kelly

Listed in *Long Island Society Register, 1929*: yes
Address: West Shore Road, Mill Neck
Acreage / map sources: not on 1927, 1932, or 1946 maps
Name of estate:
Year of construction:
Style of architecture:
Architect(s):
Landscape architect(s):
House extant: unconfirmed
Historical notes:

    The *Long Island Society Register, 1929* lists Thomas Dallam and Heloise C. Kelly Toy [Sr.] as residing on West Shore Drive [Road], Mill Neck.
    Their son Thomas Dallam Toy, Jr. died in 1929 from an accidental fall from the fifth floor window of the Pershing Square Building. [*The New York Times* August 15, 1940, p. 19.] Their son Horace married Barbara Fish, the daughter of Henry Van Courtlandt Fish of Manhattan.

Trimble, Richard, II (1904-1941)

Occupation(s):   financier - member, Shearson, Hammill & Co. (stock
                                            brokerage firm)

Marriage(s):   1930-1941 - Winifred Loew (d. 1982)

Listed in *Long Island Society Register, 1929*: yes
Address: Apple Green Drive, Old Westbury
Acreage / map sources: not on 1927, 1932, or 1946 maps
Name of estate:
Year of construction:
Style of architecture:
Architect(s):
Landscape architect(s):
House extant: yes
Historical notes:

    The *Long Island Society Register, 1929* lists Richard Trimble [II], as a youth, residing with his parents in Old Westbury.
    He was the son of Richard and Cora Randolph Trimble, Sr., who also resided in Old Westbury. His sister Countess Giovanni Revedin resided in Rome, Italy.
    Trimble was found dead on the bathroom floor by his butler. The probable cause of death was a coronary thrombosis. [*The New York Times* July 18, 1941, p. 20.]
    Winifred Loew Trimble was the daughter of William Goadby Loew, who also resided in Old Westbury, and the granddaughter of George Fisher Baker, Sr., who was known as the "Sphinx of Wall Street" because of his aversion to conversation. In 1947 she married John Parkinson Jr. and resided on Lewis Path, Old Westbury, and, later, on North Cliff Drive, Centre Island.
    The Trimbles' daughter Mary married Perry Rodgers Pease of Southampton. Pease was descendant of Commodore Mathew Perry.

Trimble, Richard, Sr. (1858-1924)

Occupation(s):

capitalist - owner, cattle ranch in Wyoming;
director, Elgin, Joliet & Eastern Railway & Co.;
director, Tennessee Coal, Iron and Railroad Co.
industrialist - secretary and treasurer, United States Steel Corp.;
director, Minnesota Steel Co.;
director and vice-president, Union Steel Co.;
director, Federated Shipbuilding;
treasurer, Federated Steel Co.;
director, Lake Superior Consolidated Iron Mines

Marriage(s): 1880-1924 - Cora Randolph (1872-1947)*

Listed in *Long Island Society Register, 1929*: yes
Address: Old Westbury Road, Old Westbury
Acreage / map sources: on 1927 map; not on 1932 or 1946 maps
Name of estate:
Year of construction:
Style of architecture:
Architect(s): William Lawrence Bottomley
Landscape architect(s):
House extant: unconfirmed
Historical notes:

The *Long Island Society Register, 1929* lists Cora Randolph Trimble as residing in Old Westbury.
He was the son of Merritt and Mary S. Underhill Trimble of NYC.
Richard Trimble, Sr. was associated with J. P. Morgan in the formation of United States Steel. Trimble was a Harvard University classmate of President Theodore Roosevelt, who resided at *Sagamore Hill* in Cove Neck, and Robert Bacon, who resided at *Old Acres* in Old Westbury. [*The New York Times* February 19, 1924, p. 15.]
*Cora Randolph was on Ward McAllister's "Four Hundred" list prior to her marriage to Trimble.
The Trimbles' son Richard Trimble II married Winifred Loew and resided in Old Westbury. Their daughter Countess Giovanni Revedin resided in Rome, Italy.

Trotter, William M.

Occupation(s):

Marriage(s): Lucy Jackson

Listed in *Long Island Society Register, 1929*: no
Address: East Main Street, Oyster Bay
Acreage / map sources: on c. 1922 map (owned by William M. Trotter)
on 1927 map (owned by William Trotter)
no acreage given on 1932 map (owned by W. M. Trotter)
4 acres / 1946 map (owned by L. Hagen)
Name of estate: *Locust Knoll*
Year of construction:
Style of architecture: Victorian
Architect(s):
Landscape architect(s):
House extant: unconfirmed
Historical notes:

front facade

William M. Trotter is listed in the June 1923 telephone directory at this address.
The *Long Island Society Register, 1928* lists Lucy Jackson Trotter as residing at *Locust Knoll* in Oyster Bay.
The estate was, subsequently, owned by Lucy Trotter Hagen, who continued to call it *Locust Knoll.*

Trowbridge, Edmund Quincy (1877-1964)

Occupation(s):   financier - member, Drysdale & Co. (investment banking firm);
                             director, The Chemical Corn Exchange Bank (which
                                 merged with New York Trust Co.; it became
                                 Chemical Bank in 1954)
Civic Activism: member, Food Administration and Fuel Administration in the
                             Wilson administration

Marriage(s):   M/1 - 1901-1939 - Gertrude Plant Harrison (d. 1939)
                             M/2 - 1941-1964 - Mary Elizabeth Elliott

Listed in *Long Island Society Register, 1929*: yes
Address: Cove Road, Oyster Bay Cove
Acreage / map sources: on 1927 map; no acreage given on 1932 map; 10 acres / 1946 map
Name of estate: *Holly Court*
Year of construction: c. 1830s
Style of architecture: Long Island Farmhouse
Architect(s):
Landscape architect(s):
House extant: yes
Historical notes:

 Both the *Long Island Society Register, 1929* and the *Social Register, Summer 1937* list Edmund Quincy and Gertrude
Plant Harrison Trowbridge as residing in Oyster Bay [Oyster Bay Cove.
 He was the son of Ezekiel Hayes and Katherine Quincy Trowbridge
of New Haven, CT, and a descendant of John Hancock.
 Edmund Quincy and Gertrude Plant Harrison Trowbridge's son
John married Frances Cole Waram, the daughter of Percy Carne
Waram of Manhattan. Their daughter Nancy married Alfred Sherman
Foote, the son of Arthur E. Foote of Englewood, NJ. Their daughter
Barbara married John Joseph Potter Murphy, the son of John J.
Murphy.
 Mary Elizabeth Elliott Trowbridge had previously been married to
Arthur E. Pew II.

rear facade, 1997

Truesdell, Dr. Edward Delavan (1879-1968)

Occupation(s):   physician - surgeon

Marriage(s):   Henrietta Norton

Listed in *Long Island Society Register, 1929*: yes
Address: Middle Hollow Road, Lloyd Harbor
Acreage / map sources: not on 1929 map; on 1931 map; 9 acres / 1944 map
Name of estate: *Gladwolden*
Year of construction:
Style of architecture:
Architect(s):
Landscape architect(s):
House extant: unconfirmed
Historical notes:

 The *Long Island Society Register, 1929* lists Dr. Edward D. and Mrs. Henrietta Norton Truesdell as residing on Cold
Spring Road, Huntington [Cold Spring Harbor]. The *Social Register, Summer 1932* lists the Truesdells as continuing to
reside in Cold Spring Harbor, while the *Social Register, Summer 1937* lists their residence as *Gladwolden* in Huntington
[Lloyd Harbor]. The *Social Register New York, 1972* lists only Mrs. Truesdell as residing at *Gladwolden*.
 The Truesdells' daughter Barbara married Dr. M. Hayne Kendrick and resided in Alexandria, VA. Their son John
married Ruth Catherine Wiebel, the daughter of Walter J. Wiebel of Dobbs Ferry, NY.

Truslow, Francis Adams, Sr. (1906-1951)

Occupation(s):   attorney -   partner, Reed, Truslow, Crane, and deGive
                                    financier   president, New York Curb Exchange
                                    diplomat -   Commissioner on U. S.–Brazil Joint Commission for Economic
                                              Development with rank of minister, 1951;
                                              United States representative at Inter-American Conference on the
                                              Problems of War and Peace, Mexico, 1945

Marriage(s):   1933-1951 - Elizabeth Auchincloss Jennings (1912-1997)
                            - Civic Activism: director, Goddard Riverside Community Center, NYC;
                                          director, Huntington Township Art League

Listed in *Long Island Society Register, 1929:* no
Address: Harbor Road, Laurel Hollow
Acreage / map sources: not on 1927, 1932 or 1946 maps
Name of estate: *The Point*
Year of construction: 1941
Style of architecture: Neo-Classical
Architect(s):
Landscape architect(s):   Elizabeth Jennings [Truslow] Howell
House extant: yes; but it has been extensively altered
Historical notes:

Francis A. Truslow Sr. was the son of Henry Adams and Jane Kent Auchincloss Truslow.

During World War II, Truslow was in charge of government procurement of wild rubber from the Peruvian upper Amazon. He would have been Secretary of State had Dewey won the presidential election in 1948. President Truman offered him the position of Ambassador-at-Large for Inter-American Economic Development which he refused.

Elizabeth Auchincloss Jennings Truslow was the daughter of Percy Hall and Elizabeth Auchincloss Jennings, Sr., who resided at *Laurel Brake* in Laurel Hollow. In 1952 she married Dr. John Taylor Howell, Jr. and continued to reside with him in Manhattan and at *The Point*.

The Truslows' son Francis Adams Truslow, Jr. married Maria Lowell Gallagher, the daughter of Rollin McCulloch Gallagher, Jr. of Manchester, MA, and resided in West Newton, MA. Their son Frederic married Aura M. Garcia. Their daughter Elizabeth married William Hamilton Russell III and resided in Huntington. Their daughter Sophia married the sculptor Bruno La Verdiere. Bruno and Sophia's son Julian, also a sculptor, was a designer of the World Trade Towers light memorial, Tribute in Light—two dramatic columns of light shining up into the sky.

Tucker, Richard Derby, Sr. (b. 1903)

Occupation(s):   artist

Marriage(s):   M/1 - 1927-1956 - Mimi Brokaw (1907-1956)
                            M/2 - 1957 - Katharine G. Aldridge

Listed in *Long Island Society Register, 1929*: yes
Address: Frost Mill Road, Mill Neck
Acreage / map sources: not on 1927 or 1932 maps; 11 acres / 1946 map
Name of estate:
Year of construction:
Style of architecture:
Architect(s):
Landscape architect(s):
House extant: unconfirmed
Historical notes:

The house was built by Richard Derby Tucker, Sr. on a portion of the former Irving Brokaw estate.

Mimi Brokaw Tucker was the daughter of Irving and Lucile Nave Brokaw, who resided at *Frost Mill Lodge* in Mill Neck and at *Goose Point* in Mill Neck. Her sister Barbara married Leonard Jarvis Cushing, Sr. and resided at *The Evergreens* in Mill Neck. Her sister Elvira was married to William McNair and resided at *Northway House* in Lattingtown.

Richard Derby and Mimi Brokaw Tucker's daughter Minnie married Stephen Kent Biggs of Cressbrook, Queensland, Australia, and resided in Washington, DC.

Tully, William John (1870-1930)

Occupation(s):   attorney
                                                  politician - senator, New York State Legislature, 1904-1908

Marriage(s):   1898-1930 - Clara Mabel Houghton (1871-1958)

Listed in *Long Island Society Register, 1929*: yes
Address: Feeks Lane and Factory Mill Pond Lane, Mill Neck
Acreage / map sources: on 1927 map
                                                no acreage given on 1932 map
                                                29 acres / 1946 map
Name of estate: *Almar*
Year of construction: c. 1916
Style of architecture: Tudor
Architect(s):   Kenneth Murchinson designed the house (for Tully)
Landscape architect(s):   Harold A. Capan (for Tully)
House extant: yes
Historical notes:

    The house, originally named *Almar,* was built by William John Tully. It was built on the site of Frank Nelson Doubleday's house, which had been destroyed by fire.
    The *Long Island Society Register, 1929* lists William J. and Clara Mabel Houghton Tully as residing at *Almar* in Locust Valley [Mill Neck]. Mrs. Tully was residing at the Savoy–Plaza Hotel, NYC, at the time of her death.
    Clara Mabel Houghton Tully's father Amory Houghton was a founder of Corning Glass Works in Corning, NY.

    The Tullys' daughter Marion married Reeve Hoover of Washington, DC. Their daughter Alice was a major contributor to the building fund for the construction of Alice Tully Hall in Lincoln Center for the Performing Arts, NYC. The actress Katherine Hepburn was a second cousin to the Tully daughters. [*The New York Times* December 11, 1993, section I, p. 30.]
    The estate was, subsequently, owned by Albert C. Winters.

Almar

Tuttle, Dr. Jason H.

Occupation(s):   physician

Marriage(s):

Listed in *Long Island Society Register, 1929*: yes
Address: Hoaglands Lane, Old Brookville
Acreage / map sources: on 1927 map
                                                  7 acres / 1932 map
                                                  not on 1946 map
Name of estate: *Tuttles Corner*
Year of construction:
Style of architecture:
Architect(s):
Landscape architect(s):
House extant: unconfirmed
Historical notes:

    The *Long Island Society Register, 1929* lists Dr. and Mrs. Jason H. Tuttle as residing at *Tuttles Corner* in Glen Head [Old Brookville].

Twohig, Dr. Daniel

Occupation(s):   physician

Marriage(s):

Listed in *Long Island Society Register, 1929*: no
Address: Old Westbury Road, Roslyn Heights
Acreage / map sources: not on 1927, 1932, or 1946 maps
Name of estate:
Year of construction: c. 1916
Style of architecture: Georgian Revival
Architect(s):   Peabody, Wilson and Brown designed c. 1925 alterations
                                              (for C. C. Auchincloss)
Landscape architect(s):   Olmsted, 1917 (for C. C. Auchincloss)
House extant: yes
Historical notes:

rear facade, 1998

   In 1946, Twohig purchased the estate from Charles C. Auchincloss, who called it *Builtover*.
   In 1966, Nellie McCory purchased the house from the estate of Twohig and renamed it *Whispered Wishes*.
   The estate is now the North Shore Child and Family Guidance Center.

Underhill, Daniel (1874-1951)

Occupation(s):   attorney -   partner, Underhill and Foster

Marriage(s):   1938-1951 - Bertha Coer (1883-1972)

Listed in *Long Island Society Register, 1929*: yes
Address: Jericho Turnpike and Route 106, Jericho
Acreage / map sources: on 1927 map (owned by Samuel J. Underhill)
                                           no acreage given on 1932 map (owned by D. Underhill)
                                           148 acres / 1946 map (owned by J. A. Underhill)
Name of estate:
Year of construction:
Style of architecture: Modified Neo-Colonial
Architect(s):
Landscape architect(s):
Estate photographs can be found in the Nassau County Museum Collection filed under Jericho/Underhill.
House extant: no; demolished in 1959*
Historical notes:

front facade, 1955

   The *Long Island Society Register, 1929* lists Daniel Underhill as residing on Jericho Turnpike, Jericho, with his mother Emma.
   Daniel Underhill was the son of Samuel Jackson and Emma A. Underhill. He inherited the estate from his mother.
   *The house was demolished when the intersection of Jericho Turnpike and Route 106 was enlarged.

Underhill, Francis T. (d. 1929)

Occupation(s):   politician - member, United States Congress
                                                             landscape architect
                                                             architect
    writer - *Driving For Pleasure,* 1897

Marriage(s):   1905-1929 - Carmelita Bibblee

Listed in *Long Island Society Register, 1929*: no
Address: Main Street, Oyster Bay
Acreage / map sources: not on 1927, 1932, or 1946 maps
Name of estate:
Year of construction: c. 1885
Style of architecture: Queen Anne
Architect(s):   Donn Barber designed c. 1920s alterations on the house transforming
                                                        it from Queen Anne to Colonial Revival, the c. 1920s Tudor garage,
                                                        stables, and boathouse (for Shonnard)
                                               George Browne Post designed c. 1888 alterations (for F. T. Underhill)
Landscape architect(s):   Donn Barber designed the formal garden, c. 1920s (for Shonnard)
House extant: no; demolished in 1950s
Historical notes:

    The house was built by Francis T. Underhill.
    The *Social Register New York, 1907* list Francis T. and
Carmelita Bibblee Underhill as residing at *La Chiquita* in Santa
Barbara, CA.
    He was the son of James W. and Margaret Varnun Underhill.
    He moved to Santa Barbara, CA, and by the early 1900s was
considered one of the three most important landscape
architects in the area, the other two being Ralph T. Stevens and
Lockwood de Forest. [Mac K. Griswold and Eleanor Weller,
*The Golden Age of American Gardens. Proud Owners, Private
Estates. 1890-1940* (New York: Harry N. Abrams, Inc., 1991),
pp. 326-27, 339, 374.]
    The estate was owned by Camille Weidenfeld and,
subsequently, by Horatio Seymour Shonnard, Sr., who called
it *Boscobel.*

front facade

Underhill, Samuel Jackson (1848-1910)

Occupation(s):   politician - supervisor, Town of Oyster Bay
                                                               dairy farmer

Marriage(s):   1872-1910 - Emma Albertson (1853-1937)

Listed in *Long Island Society Register, 1929*: yes
Address: Jericho Turnpike and Route 106, Jericho
Acreage / map sources: on 1927 map (owned by Samuel J. Underhill)
                                                 no acreage given on 1932 map (owned by D. Underhill)
                                               148 acres / 1946 map (owned by J. A. Underhill)
Name of estate:
Year of construction:
Style of architecture: Modified Neo-Colonial
Architect(s):
Landscape architect(s):
Estate photographs can be found in the Nassau County Museum Collection filed under Jericho/Underhill.
House extant: no; demolished in 1959 when the intersection of Jericho Turnpike and Route 106 was enlarged
Historical notes:

    The estate was inherited by the Underhills' son Daniel.

Uris, Percy (1899-1971)

Occupation(s):	capitalist - real estate - president and chairman of board, Uris Building Corp.
Civic Activism:	vice-chairman, board of trustees, Columbia University, NYC; trustee, Lenox Hill Hospital, NYC; trustee, Columbia University, NYC*
Marriage(s):	1935-1971 - Joanne Diotter (d. 1984)

Listed in *Long Island Society Register, 1929*: no
Address: Sands Point Road, Sands Point
Acreage / map sources: not on 1927, 1932, or 1946 maps
Name of estate: *Sandy Cay*
Year of construction: c 1930
Style of architecture: Federal
Architect(s): Ferruccio Vitale designed the the swimming pool complex (for Nast)
Landscape architect(s): Ferruccio Vitale, 1930 (for Nast)

rear facade, c. 1940

Estate photographs can be found in the Nassau County Museum Collection filed under Sands Point/Nast.
House extant: no; demolished in 1954 after fire
Historical notes:

 The house, originally named *Sandy Cay,* was built by Conde Nast.
 The estate was owned by Dorothy Schiff, Clarence Budington Kelland and, subsequently, by Uris, all of whom continued to call it *Sandy Cay.*
 Percy Uris was the son of Harris H. and Sadie Copeland Uris of NYC.
 The Urises' daughter Lynda married Alan Joel Leavitt, the son of Boris Leavitt of Hanover, PA.
 *Columbia University's Uris Hall, in which is located the Graduate School of Business, was named for Percy Uris and his brother Harold.

Uris, Percy (1899-1971)

Occupation(s):	capitalist - real estate - president and chairman of board, Uris Building Corp.
Civic Activism	vice-chairman, board of trustees, Columbia University, NYC; trustee, Lenox Hill Hospital, NYC; trustee, Columbia University, NYC
Marriage(s):	1935-1971 - Joanne Diotter (d. 1984)

Listed in *Long Island Society Register, 1929*: no
Address: Cedar Swamp Road, Brookville
Acreage / map sources: not on 1927, 1932, or 1946 maps
Name of estate: *Broadhollow*
Year of construction: c. 1926
Style of architecture: Georgian Revival
Architect(s): William Truman Aldrich [*unconfirmed*]

pool complex, 1989

Landscape architect(s):
House extant: yes
Historical notes:

 The house, originally named *Broadhollow,* was built by Winthrop Williams Aldrich.
 In 1950, the estate was sold to Alfred Gwynne Vanderbilt II.
 In 1956, Vanderbilt sold the estate to James Paul Donahue, Jr. for $400,000. In 1966, Donahue sold the estate to Uris. Vanderbilt, Donahue, and Uris continued to call the estate *Broadhollow.*
 [See previous entry for family information.]
 In 1985, the house was sold to Louis Evangelista.
 In 1990, the Cohens purchased the estate from Evangelista.

Uterhart, Henry Ayres (1875-1946)

Occupation(s):   attorney* - partner, Uterhart and Schaffer

Marriage(s):   1903-1946 - Josephine Stein (1880-1963)

Listed in *Long Island Society Register, 1929*: yes
Address: Route 25A and Oyster Bay Road, East Norwich
Acreage / map sources: on 1927 map; 7 acres / 1932 map; 14 acres / 1946 map
Name of estate: *Cross Roads Farm*
Year of construction:
Style of architecture:
Architect(s):
Landscape architect(s):
House extant: unconfirmed
Historical notes:

    Henry Ayres Uterhart was the son of Henry and Emma Jane Ayres Uterhart of NYC.
    The Uterharts' daughter Josephine married Richard T. Mayes. She was the first woman to be endorsed by a political party to run for New York's 2nd Congressional District. [*The New York Times* July 7, 1946, p. 30.]
    *Uterhart specialized in divorce law and represented many of the North Shore estate owners in their divorce cases. In 1935, he represented Marjorie Merriweather Post when she divorced E. F. Hutton. [Nancy Rubin, *American Empress: The Life and Times of Marjorie Merriweather Post* (New York: Villard Books, 1995), p. 195.]

Van Alen, James Henry (1903-1991)

Occupation(s):   publisher - vice-president, Farrar, Straus and Giroux, Inc.;
                                      owner, chain of local Long Island newspapers
                financier - director, Empire Trust Co.
Civic Activism: trustee, Village of Old Brookville

Marriage(s):   M/1 - 1929 - Eleanor Langley
                        M/2 - 1948-1991 - Candace B. Alig (d. 2002)
                             - journalist - International News Service war correspondent
                                      for Europe, during World War II;
                                      assistant editor, *The New York Herald Tribune*

Listed in *Long Island Society Register, 1929*: no
Address: Route 25A, Old Brookville
Acreage / map sources: not on 1927 map; no acreage given on 1932 map; 39 acres / 1946 map
Name of estate: *Penny Pond*
Year of construction:
Style of architecture: Colonial Revival
Architect(s):
Landscape architect(s):
Estate photographs can be found in the Nassau County Museum Collection filed under Old Westbury/Van Alen.
House extant: yes
Historical notes:

    James Henry Van Alen was the son of James Laurens Van Alen and a descendant of John Jacob Astor.
    Van Alen revolutionized the game of tennis by inventing a tie-breaking system. In 1934, he founded the International Tennis Hall of Fame in Newport, Rhode Island.
    Eleanor Langley Van Alen was the daughter of William Clark and Elida Floyd Bonnell Langley, who resided in Old Westbury. She later married Walter D. Fletcher and resided with him at *Phantom Farm* in St. James. Subsequently, she married Ray Pendleton.
    James Henry and Eleanor Van Alen's son James married Lesly Stockard. Their son Samuel, who drowned in the waters off Nassau in the Bahamas in 1970, was married to Maud L. Symington, the daughter of James Mansfield Symington of Springfield, NJ.
    Candace B. Alig Van Alen was the daughter of Otto Fidele Alig. She had previously been married to Kelvin Cox Vanderlip, the son of Frank Vanderlip.
    In 2002, the estate property was subdivided into a ten-lot housing subdivision. The eight-bedroom, eight-bath house remains on fifteen acres. [*The New York Times*, July 14, 2002, section 11, p. 7.]

Vanderbilt, Alfred Gwynne, II (1912-1999)

Occupation(s):	publisher - chairman of board, Eton Publishing Corp.
	sportsman - owner, racing thoroughbreds *Native Dancer* and *Discovery;*
	president, Belmont and Pimlico racetracks
Marriage(s):	M/1 - 1938-1942 - Manuela Hudson
	M/2 - 1945-1956 - Jeanne Lourdes Murray (b. 1923)
	- public relations executive - socialite publicity agent for Stork Club
	M/3 - 1958-1975 - Jean Harvey (b. 1936)
	- entertainers and associated professions - actress

Listed in *Long Island Society Register, 1929*: no
Address: Middle Neck Road, Sands Point
Acreage / map sources: not on 1927 or 1932 maps; 31 acres / 1946 map
Name of estate:
Year of construction: c. 1910
Style of architecture: Georgian Revival
Architect(s): Augustus N. Allen designed the house (for M. C. Fleischmann)
James W. O'Connor designed the stables (for M. C. Fleischmann)
Landscape architect(s):
House extant: yes
Historical notes:

The house, originally named *The Lindens,* was built by Max C. Fleischmann.
Fleischmann sold the estate to George Tuttle Brokaw for $250,000.
The estate was owned by Charles Schwartz and subsequently purchased in 1938 by Vanderbilt.
His mother Margaret Emerson [Vanderbilt] resided at *Cedar Knoll* in Sands Point and at *Rynwood* in Old Brookville.
[See following entry and Emerson surname entries for additional family information.]

Vanderbilt, Alfred Gwynne, II (1912-1999)

Occupation(s):	publisher - chairman of board, Eton Publishing Corp.
	sportsman - owner, racing thoroughbreds *Native Dancer* and *Discovery;*
	president, Belmont and Pimlico racetracks
Marriage(s):	M/1 - 1938-1942 - Manuela Hudson
	M/2 - 1945-1956 - Jeanne Lourdes Murray (b. 1923)
	- public relations executive - socialite publicity agent for Stork Club
	M/3 - 1958-1975 - Jean Harvey (b. 1936)
	- entertainers and associated professions - actress

Listed in *Long Island Society Register, 1929*: no
Address: West Shore Road, Mill Neck
Acreage / map sources: not on 1927, 1932, or 1946 maps
Name of estate:
Year of construction: c. 1904
Style of architecture: Colonial Revival
Architect(s): Erick Kensett Rossiter designed the house (for Peters)
Bradley Delehanty designed 1940 alterations (for Marsh)
Landscape architect(s):
House extant: yes
Historical notes:

The house, originally named *Hawirt,* was built by William Richmond Peters.
The estate was inherited by the Peters' children Thomas, Isabel, and Alice. [*The New York Times* Dec. 1, 1932, p. 14.)
In 1939, John Bigelow Marsh, Sr. purchased the estate, which he called *Nyrmah,* from Thomas and Isabel Peters.
Subsequently, it was owned by Vanderbilt.
His mother Margaret Emerson [Vanderbilt] resided at *Cedar Knoll* in Sands Point and at *Rynwood* in Old Brookville.
[See surname entries for Margaret Emerson for additional Vanderbilt family information.]
Jeanne Lourdes Murray Vanderbilt was the daughter of John Francis and Jeanne Durand Murray of Old Westbury.
In 2000, the house, with garage and guest house, on 15.9 acres was for sale. The asking price was $8.5 million.

Vanderbilt, Alfred Gwynne, II (1912-1999)

Occupation(s):   publisher - chairman of board, Eton Publishing Corp.
                                       sportsman - owner, racing thoroughbreds *Native Dancer* and *Discovery;*
                                              president, Belmont and Pimlico racetracks

Marriage(s):   M/1 - 1938-1942 - Manuela Hudson
                                       M/2 - 1945-1956 - Jeanne Lourdes Murray (b. 1923)
                                              - public relations executive - socialite publicity agent for Stork Club
                                       M/3 - 1958-1975 - Jean Harvey (b. 1936)
                                              - entertainers and associated professions - actress

Listed in *Long Island Society Register, 1929*: no
Address: Cedar Swamp Road, Brookville
Acreage / map sources: not on 1927, 1932, or 1946 maps
Name of estate: *Broadhollow*
Year of construction: c. 1926
Style of architecture: Georgian Revival
Architect(s):   William Truman Aldrich
                              [unconfirmed]

Landscape architect(s):
House extant: yes
Historical notes:

front facade, 1989

    The house, originally named *Broadhollow,* was built by Winthrop Williams Aldrich.
    In 1950, the estate was sold to Vanderbilt.
    His mother Margaret Emerson [Vanderbilt] resided at *Cedar Knoll* in Sands Point and at *Rynwood* in Old Brookville.
    [See surname entries for Margaret Emerson for additional Vanderbilt family information.]
    Jeanne Lourdes Murray Vanderbilt was the daughter of John Francis and Jeanne Durand Murray of Old Westbury.
    In 1956, Vanderbilt sold the estate to James Paul Donahue, Jr. for $400,000. In 1966, Donahue sold the estate to Percy Uris. Vanderbilt, Donahue, and Uris continued to call the estate *Broadhollow.*
    In 1985, the house was sold to Louis Evangelista. In 1990, Evangelista sold the estate to the Cohens.

Vanderbilt, Alfred Gwynne, II (1912-1999)

Occupation(s):   publisher - chairman of board, Eton Publishing Corp.
                                         sportsman - owner, racing thoroughbreds *Native Dancer* and *Discovery;*
                                              president, Belmont and Pimlico racetracks

Marriage(s):   M/1 - 1938-1942 - Manuela Hudson
                                         M/2 - 1945-1956 - Jeanne Lourdes Murray (b. 1923)
                                            - public relations executive - socialite publicity agent for Stork Club
                                       M/3 - 1958-1975 - Jean Harvey (b. 1936)
                                              - entertainers and associated professions - actress

Listed in *Long Island Society Register, 1929*: no
Address: Mill Hill Road, Mill Neck
Acreage / map sources: not on 1927, 1932, or 1946 maps
Name of estate: *Oakley Court*
Year of construction: 1936-1937
Style of architecture: Tudor
Architect(s):   Henry Corse designed the house (for Dickerman)
Landscape architect(s):
House extant: yes
Historical notes:

    The house, originally named *Hillendale,* was built by Florence Calkin Dickerman.
    Vanderbilt purchased the estate in the 1950s, renaming it *Oakley Court.*
    [See previous entry and Emerson surname entries for family information.]
    Vanderbilt sold the estate to Cornelius Vanderbilt Whitney, who gave it to the Village of Mill Neck. The village sold the estate to Mrs. Dorothy M. Fordyce. Mrs. Fordyce gradually began selling off the estate's property for development.
    Vanderbilt, Whitney, and Fordyce called the estate *Oakley Court.*

Vanderbilt, George Washington, IV (1914-1961)

Occupation(s):	scientist - paleontologist; marine biologist (self-educated)*
Civic Activism:	founder and president, George Vanderbilt Foundation, Palo Alto, CA;
	donated his yacht *Pioneer* to Stanford University for a research vessel;
	trustee, Stanford University, Stanford, CA;
	trustee, Ransom School, Coconut Grove, FL

Marriage(s):	M/1 - 1935-1946 - Lucille Merriam Parsons
	M/2 - 1946-1958 - Anita Consuelo Zabala (b. 1904)
	M/3 - 1958 - Joyce Branning
	M/4 - 1961-1961 - Louise Mitchell
	- Civic Activism: board member, Children's Cancer Fund of America;
	trustee, Association for the Relief of Respectable
	Aged and Indigent Females, NYC

rear facade, 1937

Listed in *Long Island Society Register, 1929*: no
Address: Vanderbilt Drive, Sands Point
Acreage / map sources: not on 1927 or 1932 maps
                                          31 acres / 1946 map
Name of estate:
Year of construction: c. 1937
Style of architecture: Contemporary
Architect(s):   Treanor and Fatio designed the
                                          house (for G. W. Vanderbilt IV)**
Landscape architect(s):
House extant: yes
Historical notes:

   Vanderbilt purchased the Charles William Sloane estate *The Place*, which had been owned for several years after Sloane's death by his son Charles Byron Sloane.
   *Vanderbilt led scientific expeditions to the tropics for the Philadelphia Academy of Natural Science and the California Academy of Science.
   **He built a new, Contemporary-style house in c. 1937.
   George Washington Vanderbilt IV was the son of Alfred Gwynne and Margaret Emerson Vanderbilt I. In 1915 his father drowned with the sinking of the *Lusitania*. His mother resided at *Cedar Knoll* in Sands Point and *Rynwood* in Old Brookville.
   Lucille Merriam Parsons Vanderbilt was the daughter of J. Lester Parsons of *Broadacres*, Llewellyn Park, West Orange, NJ. She subsequently married Ronald Balcom.
   Louise Mitchell Vanderbilt was the daughter of Harold E. Mitchell, Sr. of Manhattan. Her brother Harold E. Mitchell, Jr. resided in Glen Head. She had previously been married to Edward Bragg Paine of Manhattan.
   Vanderbilt's only daughter Lucille married three times. Her first marriage was to Philip H. Brady, Jr. In 1962 she married Robert Mathews Balding. She subsequently married Wallace Fennell Pate, Sr.
   George Washington Vanderbilt IV plunged to his death from the Mark Hopkins Hotel in San Francisco.
   [See surname entries for Margaret Emerson for additional Vanderbilt family information.]

Vanderbilt, Lena Thurlow (d. 1947)

Marriage(s):   Joseph White Vanderbilt

Listed in *Long Island Society Register, 1929*: yes
Address: Cedar Swamp Road and High Farms Road, Old Brookville
Acreage / map sources: not on 1927 or 1946 maps; no acreage given on 1932 map
Name of estate:
Year of construction:
Style of architecture:
Architect(s):
Landscape architect(s):
House extant: unconfirmed
Historical notes:

   Lena Thurlow Vanderbilt was residing at 152 Oxford Boulevard in Garden City at the time of her death.

Vanderbilt, Virginia Graham Fair (c. 1874-1935)

Marriage(s):   1889-1927 - William Kissam Vanderbilt, Jr. (1878-1944)
- capitalist - president, New York Central Railroad, and its subsidiaries;
director, Western Union Telegraph Co.
scientist - marine biologist (self-educated)
Civic Activism: donated Vanderbilt Motor Parkway to New York State;
donated his Centerport estate *Eagle's Nest* to Suffolk County;
donated his yacht *Alva* to the United States Navy during World War II

Listed in *Long Island Society Register, 1929*: yes
Address: 260 Country Club Road, Manhasset
Acreage / map sources: not on 1927 map
115 acres / 1932 map
not on 1946 map
Name of estate: *Fairmont*
Year of construction: c. 1915
Style of architecture: French Renaissance
Architect(s):   McKim, Mead and White designed alterations
Landscape architect(s):   Olmsted, 1924-1925 (for Munsey)
House extant: yes
Historical notes:

The house, originally named *Sherryland*, was built by Louis Sherry.

The estate was owned by Frank Andrew Munsey, who purchased it in 1922, and, subsequently, by Vanderbilt, who called it *Fairmont*.

The *Long Island Society Register, 1929* lists Virginia Graham Fair Vanderbilt as residing in Manhasset.

The *Social Register, Summer 1932* lists Virginia Fair Vanderbilt as residing at *Fairmont* in Manhasset.

[See following entry for family information.]

In 1938, the estate was sold to William Jaird Levitt, Sr., who built the Strathmore housing development on the estate property. [*The New York Times* January 16, 1938, section XII, p. 1.] The house, which is located in the Strathmore section of Manhasset, is now the Strathmore Vanderbilt Country Club of Manhasset.

front facade, 1998

Vanderbilt, Virginia Graham Fair (c. 1874-1935)

Marriage(s): 1899-1927 - William Kissam Vanderbilt, Jr. (1878-1944)
- capitalist - president, New York Central Railroad, and its subsidiaries;
        director, Western Union Telegraph Co.
    scientist - marine biologist (self-educated)
    Civic Activism: donated Vanderbilt Motor Parkway to New York State;
        donated his Centerport estate to Suffolk County;
        donated his yacht *Alva* to the U.S. Navy during World War II

side façade

Listed in *Long Island Society Register, 1929*: yes
Address: Cedar Swamp Road Brookville
Acreage / map sources: not on 1927, 1932, or 1946 maps
Name of estate:
Year of construction: c. 1911
Style of architecture: Tudor
Architect(s):   John Russell Pope designed the
                              house (for V. G. F. Vanderbilt)
Landscape architect(s):   DuChene (for V. G. F. Vanderbilt)
House extant: no
Historical notes:

The house was built by Virginia Graham Fair Vanderbilt.

Known as Birdie, she was the daughter of James Graham "Slippery Jim" and Theresa Rooney Fair of San Francisco. James Fair, James C. Flood, William S. O'Brien, and John William Mackay were called the "Silver Kings," "San Francisco's Second Big Four," and the "Irish Big Four." Their wealth was derived from the rich Comstock Silver Lode discovered in Virginia City, Nevada. Virginia's father died in 1894, estranged from his family.

After the death of her mother, Virginia moved to NYC to be with her sister Theresa, who had married Hermann Oelrichs. While summering at the Oelrichses' Newport, RI, home, she met William Kissam Vanderbilt, Jr., who was residing with his mother Alva and her second husband Oliver Hazard Perry Belmont in Alva's Newport summer home, *Marble House*. Virginia married Vanderbilt before he had finished college. They spent their wedding night at the first *Idle Hour* house of his father William Kissam Vanderbilt, Sr., in Oakdale. It burned to the ground that night.

In c. 1901 the Vanderbilts built their Long Island home, known as *Deepdale*, on Westcliff Road in Lake Success. After ten years of marriage they separated and Virginia moved to Glen Cove, Brookville, and then to her estate, *Fairmont,* in Manhasset. It wasn't until 1927 that Virginia filed for divorce. In September 1927, William Kissam Vanderbilt , Jr. married Rosamund Lancaster (Warburton), of Philadelphia, in a civil ceremony in the mayor's office in Paris, France.

William Kissam and Virginia Graham Fair Vanderbilt, Jr.'s daughter Consuelo married Earl Edward Tailer Smith, Sr., and resided at *Iradell* in Sands Point. She subsequently married Henry Gassaway Davis III, William J. Warburton III, and N. Clarkson Earl, Jr.

The estate was owned by Henry William Sage II and, subsequently, by Edouard LeRoux, who called it *Cottage Normandy*.

Vanderbilt, Virginia Graham Fair (c. 1874-1935)

Marriage(s): 1899-1927 - William Kissam Vanderbilt, Jr. (1878-1944)
              [See previous entry for additional information.]

Listed in *Long Island Society Register, 1929*: yes
Address: Ridge Road, Glen Cove
Acreage / map sources: not on 1927, 1932, or 1946 maps
Name of estate:
Year of construction:
Style of architecture: Georgian
Architect(s):   Howard Major designed c. 1918 alterations (for Beard)
Landscape architect(s):
House extant: yes
Historical notes:

The house was, subsequently owned by William Beard
William Beard is listed in the February 1918 telephone directory at this address.

Vanderbilt, William Kissam, Jr. (1878-1944)

Occupation(s):   capitalist -   president, New York Central Railroad, and its subsidiaries;
                                                  director, Western Union Telegraph Co.
                                  scientist -   marine biologist (self-educated)
Civic Activism: donated Vanderbilt Motor Parkway to New York State;
                                  donated his Centerport estate *Eagle's Nest* to Suffolk County;
                                  donated his yacht *Alva* to the United States Navy during World War II

Marriage(s):   M/1 - 1899-1927 - Virginia Graham Fair (1874-1935)
                                  M/2 - 1927-1944 - Rosamund Lancaster (1897-1947)

Listed in *Long Island Society Register, 1929*: no
Address: Westcliff Drive, Lake Success
Acreage / map sources: on 1906 map
                                  not on 1927 map
                                  21 acres / 1932 map
                                  no acreage given on 1946 map
Name of estate: *Deepdale*
Year of construction: c. 1901
Style of architecture: Federal
Architect(s):   Horace Trumbauer designed the original 1902 Federal house
                                       (for W. K. Vanderbilt, Jr.)
                                  Carrere and Hastings designed alterations
                                       (for W. K. Vanderbilt, Jr.)
                                  Warren and Wetmore designed the golf clubhouse, 1926
                                       (for W. K. Vanderbilt, Jr.)
                                  John Russell Pope designed the gatehouse, c. 1906
                                       (for W. K. Vanderbilt, Jr.)
Landscape architect(s):   Horace Trumbauer designed the formal gardens
                                       (for W. K. Vanderbilt, Jr.)
Estate photographs can be found in the Nassau County Museum Collection filed under Lake Success/Vanderbilt.
House extant: yes*
Historical notes:

    The house, originally named *Deepdale,* was built by William Kissam Vanderbilt, Jr.
    [See following entry for family information.]
    The estate's golf course and clubhouse are owned by the Village of Lake Success. The estate's gatehouse is now the rectory of St. Phillips and St. James Episcopal Church. Some of the garden statuary from *Deepdale* can be found on the grounds of Vanderbilt's Centerport estate, *Eagle's Nest*.
    *All of the house's wings were demolished in 1931. The main section of the house still exists.

gatehouse, 1992

William Kissam Vanderbilt, Jr. Estate, *Deepdale*

view from house

dining room

front facade

stting room

study

Vanderbilt, William Kissam, Jr. (1878-1944)

Occupation(s):   capitalist -   president, New York Central Railroad, and its subsidiaries;
                                                        director, Western Union Telegraph Co.
                                  scientist -   marine biologist (self-educated)
Civic Activism: donated Vanderbilt Motor Parkway to New York State;
                                  donated his Centerport estate *Eagle's Nest* to Suffolk County;
                                  donated his yacht *Alva* to the United States Navy during World War II

Marriage(s):   M/1 - 1899-1927 - Virginia Graham Fair (1874-1935)
                                  M/2 - 1927-1944 - Rosamund Lancaster (1897-1947)

Listed in *Long Island Society Register, 1929*: no
Address: Little Neck Road, Centerport
Acreage / map sources: no acreage given on 1929 map; on 1931 map; 46 acres / 1944 map
Name of estate: *Eagle's Nest*
Year of construction: 1907-1928
Style of architecture: Spanish Colonial
Architect(s):   Warren and Wetmore designed the house (for W. K. Vanderbilt, Jr.)
Landscape architect(s):
House extant: yes
Historical notes:

The thirty-eight-room house, originally known as *Eagle's Nest,* was built by William Kissam Vanderbilt, Jr.

He was the son of William Kissam and Alva Erskine Smith Vanderbilt, Sr., who resided at *Idlehour* in Oakdale, at *Marble House* in Newport, RI, and in Manhattan. In 1895 his parents divorced, after which his mother married Oliver Hazard Perry Belmont and resided with him at *Brookholt* in East Meadow, at *Marble House* in Newport, which she retained through her divorce settlement, and at *Belcourt*, Mr. Belmont's home in Newport. After the death of Belmont, his mother resided at *Beacon Towers* in Sands Point and, later, moved to France. His sister Consuelo married the Ninth Duke of Marlborough and resided at *Blenheim* near Woodstock, England. She subsequently married Louis Jacques Balsan and resided in Southampton, LI, Palm Beach, FL, and at *Old Fields* in East Norwich.

While summering at the Newport, RI, home of her sister Theresa Fair Oelrichs, Virginia Graham Fair met William Kissam Vanderbilt, Jr. They married before he had finished college and spent their wedding night at the first *Idle Hour* house of his father William Kissam Vanderbilt, Sr., in Oakdale. It burned to the ground that night.

In c. 1901 the Vanderbilts built their Long Island home, known as *Deepdale*, on Westcliff Road in Lake Success. After ten years of marriage they separated and Virginia moved to Glen Cove, Brookville, and then to her estate, *Fairmont,* in Manhasset. It wasn't until 1927 that Virginia filed for divorce.

In September 1927, William Kissam Vanderbilt, Jr. married Rosamund Lancaster (Warburton), of Philadelphia, in a civil ceremony in the mayor's office in Paris, France. They resided in the Centerport house when on Long Island.

Rosamund Lancaster Vanderbilt had previously been married to the grandson of John Wanamaker, Barclay H. Warburton, Jr. Her daughter Rosemary Warburton married William C. T. Gaynor and resided in Southampton.

William Kissam and Virginia Graham Fair Vanderbilt, Jr.'s daughter Consuelo married Earl Edward Tailer Smith, Sr., and resided at *Iradell* in Sands Point. After her divorce from Smith, Consuelo married Henry Gassaway Davis III in 1936 in Miami Beach aboard her father's yacht *Alva*. He was just recently divorced from her second cousin, the former Grace Vanderbilt. Consuelo's third marriage, in 1941, was to William J. Warburton III and her fourth, to N. Clarkson Earl, Jr.

After the death of his twenty-six-year-old son William Kissam Vanderbilt III in 1933, Vanderbilt built a addition to the house, in which a memorial to his son is still housed. It features trophies and memorabilia of his son's hunting expeditions and a mural depicting the younger Vanderbilt's 1931 expedition to Sudan.

The estate is now Suffolk County's Vanderbilt Museum and is on The National Register of Historic Places.

In 2001, plans were finalized to proceed on a $450,000 renovation of the boathouse to accommodate Cornell Cooperative Extension of Suffolk's laboratory operation, which will focus on the health of Long Island Sound as it relates to the devastation of the lobster industry. [*Newsday* May 18, 2001.]

In 2002, the county acquired the 3,315-square-foot, 9-room, French Normandy-style house that Vanderbilt had built in 1917 as a residence for the estate's superintendent. Plans are to use the house as a visitors' center. Space will be adequate to provide orientation programs as well house the museums' master gardener's program.

side facade and entrance tower

Vander Poel, William Halsted (d. 1974)

Occupation(s):	industrialist - director, foreign department, Union Carbide
Civic Activism:	trustee, Hofstra University, Hempstead
Marriage(s):	1910-1968 - Blanche P. Billings (d. 1968)

Listed in *Long Island Society Register, 1929*: yes

Address:	Route 25A and Mill River Road, Muttontown
Acreage / map sources:	on 1927 map
	29 acres / 1932 map
	29 acres / 1946 map
Name of estate:	*Woodstock*
Year of construction:	1912
Style of architecture:	Colonial Revival
Architect(s):	Henry Otis Chapman designed the house (for Provost)
Landscape architect(s):	
House extant: yes	
Historical notes:	

The house, originally named *Woodley,* was built by Cornelius W. Provost.

The estate was owned by Vander Poel, who called it *Woodstock* and, subsequently, by Camille Jean Tuorto Amato, who called it *Woodstock Manor.*

The *Long Island Society Register, 1929* lists William Halsted and Blanche P. Billing Vander Poel as residing in East Norwich, while the *Social Register, Summer 1932* and *1974* list the name of their estate as *Woodstock.*

He was the son of Dr. S. Oakley Vander Poel.

Blanche P. Billings Vander Poel was the daughter of Cornelius Kingsley Garrison and Blanche MacLeish Billings, who resided at *Farnsworth* in Upper Brookville. The Billingses' Manhattan residence was located on the present site of The Cloisters.

The Vander Poels' son Benjamin married Beverly Sartorius. Their son Halsted married Dorothy Marlatt. Their daughter Mary married G. Montagu Miller, Sinclair Hatch, and, subsequently, William Francis Russell.

During a House of Representative Ways and Means subcommittee meeting investigating tax scandals, Vander Poel testified that he had paid between $50,000 and $60,000 to obtain a favorable tax settlement for the trust of his father-in-law. [*The New York Times* May 15, 1953 pp. 1, 11.]

Vanderveer, Stephen Lott (c. 1890-1960)

Occupation(s):	financier - vice-president, Continental Bank & Trust Co.;
	president, Empire Bond & Mortgage Co.
Marriage(s):	Julia Finlay

Listed in *Long Island Society Register, 1929*: yes

Address:	Middle Neck Road, Great Neck
Acreage / map sources:	not on 1927, 1932, or 1946 maps
Name of estate:	*Kenwood*
Year of construction:	c. 1926
Style of architecture:	French Manor House
Architect(s):	Leroy P. Ward designed the house (for Vanderveer)
Landscape architect(s):	
House extant: yes	
Historical notes:	

The house, originally named *Kenwood,* was built by Stephen Lott Vanderveer.

The *Long Island Society Register, 1929* lists S. L. Vanderveer as residing at *Kenwood* on Middle Neck Road, Great Neck.

The Vanderveers' nineteen-year-old son Bruce was killed in an automobile accident.

Van Iderstine, Charles Abner

Occupation(s):   industrialist - fat and tallow business

Marriage(s):   M/1 - Adelia C. Ireland (d. 1895)
                                          M/2 - Mary Emma Mangam

Listed in *Long Island Society Register, 1929*: yes
Address: Idle Day Drive, Centerport
Acreage / map sources: no acreage given on 1929 map
                                          on 1931 map
                                          28 acres / 1944 map (family compound)

Name of estate:
Year of construction: 1897
Style of architecture: Queen Anne / Eclectic
Architect(s):
Landscape architect(s):
House extant: yes
Historical notes:

    Charles Abner Van Iderstine built this house, which still stands, south of that of his father Peter Van Iderstine.
    Adelia C. Ireland Van Iderstine was the daughter of John H. and Martha Ireland.
    The *Long Island Society Register, 1929* lists Charles Abner and Mary Emma Mangam Van Iderstine as residing in Huntington [Centerport].
    The house is on The National Register of Historic Places.

side / front facade, 1905

Van Iderstine, Peter, Jr. (1826-1893)

Occupation(s):   industrialist - fat and tallow business

Marriage(s):   Martha A. *[unable to confirm maiden name]*

Listed in *Long Island Society Register, 1929*: no
Address: Idle Day Drive, Centerport
Acreage / map sources: not on 1929, 1931, or 1944 maps
Name of estate:
Year of construction:
Style of architecture:
Architect(s):
Landscape architect(s):
House extant: no*
Historical notes:

    The house was built by Peter Van Iderstine. It was located on Spy Hill, south of the Vanderbilt estate.
    The Van Iderstines' daughter Louise was unmarried at the time of her death, as was their daughter Emma. Their daughter Hattie married Dallas T. Ward.
    *The house was destroyed by fire.

Van Iderstine, William P. M. (1866-1943)

Occupation(s):   industrialist - fat and tallow business
                                  capitalist - real estate

Marriage(s):   Kathryn Sibley (d. 1913)

Listed in *Long Island Society Register, 1929*: yes
Address: Little Neck Road, Centerport
Acreage / map sources: not listed separately on 1929, 1931, or 1946 maps
Name of estate:
Year of construction: c. 1890
Style of architecture: Shingle
Architect(s):
Landscape architect(s):
House extant: no; destroyed by fire
Historical notes:

   William P. M. Van Iderstine built his house further south than those of his father, Peter, and his brother, Charles Abner.
   The Van Iderstines' house at 270 Clinton Avenue, Brooklyn, was formerly owned by Charles Pratt. [*The New York Times* October 24, 1913, p. 11.]
   The estate was, subsequently, owned by Joseph B. Morrell, who called it *The Moorings*.

Van Ingen, Lawrence Bell, Jr. (d. 2003)

Occupation(s):   industrialist - technical analyst of supply and distribution, Mobil Oil Corp.

Marriage(s):   1958-2003 - Evelyn G. Harris

Listed in *Long Island Society Register, 1929*: no
Address: Old Tappan Road, Lattingtown
Acreage / map sources: on 1927 map (owned by H. L. Pratt)
                                  40 acres / 1932 map (owned by H. P. Van Ingen)
                                  40 acres / 1946 map (name misspelled as N. Busch)
Name of estate: *Preference*
Year of construction: 1924
Style of architecture: Georgian Revival
Architect(s):   Carrere and Hastings designed the house (for L. B. Van Ingen, Sr.)
Landscape architect(s):
Estate photographs can be found in the Nassau County Museum Collection filed under Glen Cove/Van Ingen.
House extant: yes
Historical notes:

   The house, originally named *Preference*, was built by Lawrence Bell Van Ingen, Sr.
   According to the *Social Register, Summer 1950*, Harriet Pratt Van Ingen, the wife of Lawrence Bell Van Ingen, Sr., subsequently married Donald Fairfax Bush, Jr. and resided with him at *Preference.*
   The estate was also owned by Lawrence Bell Van Ingen, Jr., who continue to call it *Preference,* and, subsequently, by Ward Wilson Woods, Jr.
   Lawrence Bell Van Ingen, Jr. was the son of Lawrence Bell and Harriet Balsdon Pratt Van Ingen, Sr., who also resided at *Preference* in Lattingtown, and the great-great-grandson of Charles Pratt.
   Evelyn G. Harris Van Ingen was the daughter of Henry Upham and Mary M. Webster Harris, Sr., who resided at *The Hameau* in Brookville. Her brother Henry Upham Harris, Jr. resided on Brookville Road, Brookville. Her sister Joan married Harold W. Hawkey, Sr. and also resided on Brookville Road, Brookville. Her brother David married Elizabeth Ann Spenker and resided in Greenwich, CT.
   Lawrence Bell and Evelyn G. Harris Van Ingen, Jr.'s daughter Evelyn married John Ruckman Fell III and resides in Haverford, PA. Their son Lawrence Bell Van Ingen III married Laurie Ann Noel, the daughter of Roland H. Noel of Fayetteville, NY, and resides in Dallas, TX. Their daughter Mary Webster Van Ingen married Robert Howard Courtemanche and resided in Bernardsville, NJ. According to *The New York Times* June 22, 1980, p. 51, Robert Howard Courtemanche and Mary Webster Van Ingen Courtemanche are cousins and both grandchildren of Henry Upham and Mary M. Webster Harris, Sr., who resided at *The Hameau* in Brookville.

Van Ingen, Lawrence Bell, Sr. (1898-1943)

Occupation(s):   financier -   stockbroker
capitalist -   real estate

Marriage(s):   1923-1938 - Harriet Balsdon Pratt (d. 1978)
- Civic Activism: first woman president, board of trustees, Roosevelt
Hospital

Listed in *Long Island Society Register, 1929*: yes
Address: Old Tappan Road, Lattingtown
Acreage / map sources: on 1927 map (owned by H. L. Pratt)
40 acres / 1932 map (owned by H. P. Van Ingen)
40 acres / 1946 map (name misspelled as N. Busch)
Name of estate: *Preference*
Year of construction: 1924
Style of architecture: Georgian Revival
Architect(s):   Carrere and Hastings designed the house (for L. B. Van Ingen, Sr.)
Landscape architect(s):
Estate photographs can be found in the Nassau County Museum Collection filed under Glen Cove/Van Ingen.
House extant: yes
Historical Notes:

The house, originally named *Preference*, was built by Lawrence Bell Van Ingen, Sr.

The *Long Island Society Register, 1929* lists Lawrence Bell and Harriet Balsdon Pratt Van Ingen [Sr.] as residing at *Preference* in Locust Valley [Lattingtown].

Harriet Pratt Van Ingen was the daughter of Herbert Lee and Florence Gibb Pratt, Sr., who resided at *The Braes* in Glen Cove. She subsequently married Donald Fairfax Bush, Jr. Her brother Herbert Lee Pratt, Jr., resided at *Whitehall* in Mill Neck. Her sister Edith also resided in Lattingtown, marrying Allan McLane, Jr., residing at *Home Wood,* and subsequently marrying Howard Washburn Maxwell, Jr. Her brother Frederic Richardson Pratt resided at *Friendfield Farm* on Skunks Misery Road, Lattingtown, having, subsequently, acquired the McLane estate. Her sister Florence married Francis Edward Powell, Jr. and resided at *Rattling Spring* in Glen Cove.

Harriet Balsdon Pratt Bush's mother Florence Gibb Pratt was the first woman president of the board of trustees of Nassau Hospital in Mineola (now, Winthrop University Hospital).

The estate was also owned by Lawrence Bell Van Ingen, Jr., who continued to call it *Preference*, and, subsequently, by Ward Wilson Woods, Jr.

Van Rensselaer, Charles Augustus, Sr. (1867-1950)

Occupation(s):   capitalist -   partner, Charles A. Van Rensselaer & Co. (importing and
merchandising firm)

Marriage(s):   1899 - Caroline Elizabeth Fitzgerald

Listed in *Long Island Society Register, 1929*: yes
Address: Muttontown Road, Muttontown
Acreage / map sources: on 1927 map; not on 1932 or 1946 maps
Name of estate: *Homewood Place*
Year of construction:
Style of architecture:
Architect(s):
Landscape architect(s):
House extant: unconfirmed
Historical notes:

The *Long Island Society Register, 1929* lists Charles A. and Caroline E. Fitzgerald Van Rensselaer [Sr.] as residing at *Homewood Place* on Muttontown Road, Syosset [Muttontown], while the *Social Register, Summer 1932* lists their residence as the Piping Rock Club in Locust Valley [Lattingtown]. The *Social Register New York, 1948* lists the Van Rensselaers as residing on Cedar Swamp Road, Jericho.

He was the son of Stephen Van Rensselaer.

Caroline Elizabeth Fitzgerald Van Rensselaer was the daughter of Desmond Fitzgerald of Boston, MA.

Van Santvoord, Alexander S., Sr. (1900-1970)

Occupation(s):   journalist - editor, Doubleday, Page & Co., Garden City
                                        (which became Doubleday & Co., Inc.)
Civic Activism: board member, for 30 years, Glen Cove Public Library, Glen Cove;
                                  headed civilian protection in Glen Cove during World War II

Marriage(s):   Wilma Wells Luster (1902-1952)
                             - journalist - editor, Doubleday, Page & Co., Garden City

Listed in *Long Island Society Register, 1929*: yes
Address: Landing Road, Glen Cove
Acreage / map sources: 1927 map illegible
                                not on 1932 or 1946 maps
Name of estate:
Year of construction:
Style of architecture:
Architect(s):
Landscape architect(s):
Estate photographs can be found in the Nassau County Museum Collection filed under Glen Cove/Van Santvoord.
House extant: unconfirmed
Historical notes:

    Both the *Long Island Society Register, 1929* and the *Social Register New York, 1952* list Alexander S. and Wilma Wells Luster Van Santvoord [Sr.] as residing on Landing Road, Glen Cove.
    Wilma Wells Luster Van Santvoord was the daughter of Nassau County treasurer William E. Luster.
    The house was inherited by the Van Santvoords' son Alexander S. Van Santvoord, Jr.

Van Strum, Kenneth Stevens (1898-1984)

Occupation(s):   financier - a founder and treasurer, Securities Corp. of America;
                                        chairman, Van Strum and Towne, Inc.
                                            (investment counselors);
                                        president, American Insurance Co.
                  writer - *Investing in Purchasing Power*, 1927;
                                      Forecasting Stock Market Trends, 1927

Marriage(s):   Anna Cecilia Zimmermann

Listed in *Long Island Society Register, 1929*: no
Address: Laurel Hollow Road, Laurel Hollow
Acreage / map sources: not on 1927 or 1932 maps
                                26 acres / 1946 map
Name of estate:
Year of construction: c. 1937
Style of architecture:
Architect(s):
Landscape architect(s):
House extant: unconfirmed
Historical notes:

    The house was built by Kenneth Stevens Van Strum.
    The *Social Register New York, 1946* lists Kenneth S. and Anna C. Zimmermann Van Strum as residing on Moore's Hill Road [Laurel Hollow Road], Syosset [Laurel Hollow].
    He was the son of Arthur Julius Van Strum of Berkeley, CA. At the time of his death, he was residing in Hillsborough, CA.
    Anna Cecilia Zimmermann Van Strum was the daughter of John Edward Zimmermann of Chestnut Hill, Philadelphia, PA.
    The Van Strums' daughter Cecilia married Walker Cowen, the son of Wilson Cowen of Bethesda, MD. Their son Stevens resided in Tidewater, OR.

Van Wart, Edwin Clark (1859-1950)

Occupation(s):   capitalist - real estate*

Marriage(s):   Maude H *[unable to confirm maiden name]*

Listed in *Long Island Society Register, 1929*: yes
Address: Harriman Drive, Sands Point
Acreage / map sources: on c. 1922 map (owned by S. I. Van Wart)
                                         on 1927 map (owned by Van Wart)
                                         28 acres / 1932 map (owned by A. Van Wart)
                                         29 acres / 1946 map (name misspelled as A. Van Wort)
Name of estate: *The Shrubbery*
Year of construction:
Style of architecture:
Architect(s):
Landscape architect(s):
House extant: no**
Historical notes:

    The *Long Island Society Register, 1929* lists E. Clark Van Wart as residing at *The Shrubbery* in Sands Point with Miss Helen Irving Van Wart and W. Irving Van Wart.
    They were the children of Henry and Abbey Irving Van Wart, who had previously resided at *The Shrubbery*.
    The estate had been in the family since the 1700s. [*The New York Times* January 15, 1950, p. 84.]
    *The Van Wart family owned the Flat Iron Building in NYC.
    **In 1963, the house, which was abandoned and boarded up, was destroyed by fire. [Joan Gay Kent, *Discovering Sands Point: Its History, Its People, Its Places* (Sands Point, NY: Village of Sands Point, 2000), p. 164.]

Van Wart, Henry

Occupation(s):   capitalist - real estate*

Marriage(s):   Abbey Irving (d. 1906)

Listed in *Long Island Society Register, 1929*: yes
Address: Harriman Drive, Sands Point
Acreage / map sources: on c. 1922 map (owned by S. I. Van Wart)
                                         on 1927 map (owned by Van Wart)
                                         28 acres / 1932 map (owned by A. Van Wart)
                                         29 acres / 1946 map (name misspelled as A. Van Wort)
Name of estate: *The Shrubbery*
Year of construction:
Style of architecture:
Architect(s):
Landscape architect(s):
House extant: no**
Historical notes:

    The estate had been in the family since the 1700s. [*The New York Times* January 15, 1950, p. 84.]
    *The Van Wart family owned the Flat Iron Building in NYC.
    Abby Irving Van Wart was the daughter of Judge John Treat Irving, Sr. of the Court of Common Pleas in NYC.
    Henry and Abbey Irving Van Wart's daughter Sarah was residing at 37 Madison Avenue, NYC, at the time of her death. [*The New York Times* March 19, 1919, p. 11.] Their twenty-year-old daughter Marian died in 1874.
    The house was, subsequently, owned by the Van Warts' son Edwin, who continued to call it *The Shrubbery*.
    **In 1963, the house, which was abandoned and boarded up, was destroyed by fire. [Joan Gay Kent, *Discovering Sands Point: Its History, Its People, Its Places* (Sands Point, NY: Village of Sands Point, 2000), p. 164.]

Vaughan, Dr. Harold Stearns (1876-1969)

Occupation(s):   physician - surgeon

                             educator - professor of clinical surgery, New York Post-Graduate
                                        Medical School

Marriage(s):   Sara M. Campbell

Listed in *Long Island Society Register, 1929*: yes
Address: Mill River Hollow Road, Upper Brookville
Acreage / map sources: not on 1927 map
                             no acreage given on 1932 map
                             11 acres / 1946 map
Name of estate: *The Catalpas*
Year of construction:
Style of architecture:
Architect(s):
Landscape architect(s):
House extant: unconfirmed
Historical notes:

    The *Long Island Society Register, 1929* lists Dr. Harold S. and Mrs. Sara M. Campbell Vaughan as residing at *Hillcote* in Oyster Bay, while the *Social Register, Summer 1932* and *1945* lists their residence as *The Catalpas* in Oyster Bay [Upper Brookville].
    The *Social Register, Summer 1946* lists the Vaughans as residing at *The Irving* in Southampton.
    The Vaughans' son Harold married Helen Katherine Wagner, the daughter of Franklin Allan Wagner of Dobbs Ferry, NY.

Verdi, Minturn de Suzzara (1888-1970)

Occupation(s):   attorney - partner, Verdi, Pierce and Van Winkle

Marriage(s):   M/1 - 1912 - Marion Lasell
                             M/2 - Hope Aspell
                             M/3 - 1943 - Thelma Given
                                - entertainers and related professions - concert violinist

Listed in *Long Island Society Register, 1929*: yes
Address: Split Rock Road, Oyster Bay Cove
Acreage / map sources: on 1927 map
                             no acreage given on 1932 map
                             3 acres / 1946 map
Name of estate:
Year of construction:
Style of architecture:
Architect(s):
Landscape architect(s):
House extant: unconfirmed
Historical notes:

    The *Long Island Society Register, 1929* lists Minturn de Suzzara and Hope Aspell Verdi as residing in Syosset [Oyster Bay Cove] while both the *Social Register, Summer 1932* and *1937* list only Mr. Verdi as residing in Syosset [Oyster Bay Cove].
    Marion Lasell Verdi was the daughter of Chester Whitin Lasell of Whitinsville, MA.
    Minturn de Suzzara and Marion Lasell Verdi's daughter Patricia married Arthur Freeborn Chace, Jr. and resided in Manhattan. Their daughter Nancy married Arthur M. Crocker and resided in Laurel Hollow.

Vermilye, H. Rowland, Sr. (d. 1931)

Occupation(s):   financier - insurance broker

Marriage(s):   1924-1931 - Ethel de Forest (d. 1955)

Listed in *Long Island Society Register, 1929*: no
Address: Wawapek Road, Cold Spring Harbor
Acreage / map sources: on 1929 map (owned by Robert de Forest)
                               on 1931 map (owned by Robert de Forest)
                               9 acres / 1944 map (owned by E. D. Vermilye)
Name of estate: *Wood Winds*
Year of construction: c. 1937
Style of architecture: Grosvenor Atterbury designed the house (for Vermilye)
Architect(s):
Landscape architect(s):
House extant: unconfirmed
Historical notes:

    The house, originally named *Wood Winds*, was built by H. Rowland Vermilye, Sr.
    The *Social Register, Summer 1950* lists Ethel de Forest Vermilye as residing at *Wood Winds* in Cold Spring Harbor.
    Ethel de Forest Vermilye had previously been married to Allen Earle Whitman, Sr., an engineer, who died in 1915. She was the daughter of Robert Weeks and Emily Johnston de Forest, who resided at *Wawapek* in Cold Spring Harbor. Her brother Johnston inherited *Wawapek*. Ethel's brother Henry Lockwood de Forest resided at *Meadowview* in Cold Spring Harbor. Her sister Frances married William Adams Walker Stewart II and resided at *Edgeover*, also in Cold Spring Harbor.

Vernam, Clarence Cottier (1873- 1937)

Occupation(s):   publisher - vice-president, Street & Street Publications;
                               partner, *The Newark Star-Eagle*;
                               partner, *The Detroit Journal*

Marriage(s):   Bessie Bovee Norris

Listed in *Long Island Society Register, 1929*: yes
Address: Park Avenue, Huntington
Acreage / map sources: no acreage given on 1929 map
                               on 1931 map
                               44 acres / 1944 map
Name of estate: *Hilaire Farm*
Year of construction:
Style of architecture:
Architect(s):
Landscape architect(s):
House extant: unconfirmed
Historical notes:

    The *Long Island Society Register, 1929* lists Clarence Cottier and Bessie B. Norris Vernam as residing at *Hilaire* in Huntington, while the *Social Register, Summer 1932* lists the name of the their estate as *Hilaire Farm*.
    The Vernams' daughter Valerie married Giraud Van Nest Foster, the son of Giraud Foster of Lenox, MA.

Vertes, Marcel Emmanuel (1895-1961)

Occupation(s):   entertainers and associated professions*
                                  writer -   *The Stronger Sex*;
                                             Art and Fashion;
                                             It's All Mental (co-authored with Bryan Holme);
                                             Amandes Vertes;
                                             But What Do You Need Me For?

Marriage(s):   1926 - Dora Hauser

Listed in *Long Island Society Register, 1929*: no
Address: Bevin Road, Asharoken
Acreage / map sources: not on 1929, 1931, or 1944 maps
Name of estate:
Year of construction: 1856
Style of architecture: Long Island Farmhouse
Architect(s):   Harry Ellingwood Donnell designed 1911 alterations
                                     (for G. H. Robinson)

Landscape architect(s):
House extant: yes
Historical notes:

   In 1862, Cornelius Henry DeLamater purchased *Walnut Farm House* from William Beebe, a farmer who had built the house. DeLamater resided in it until his house *Vermland* was completed in the latter part of 1862.

   In 1876, his daughter Lydia DeLamater Robins and her husband John moved into the house and renamed it *The Robin's Nest*.

   The house was extensively altered in 1876, 1882, 1883, and 1884.

   Upon the death of Cornelius Henry DeLamater's wife Ruth in 1894, the house was deeded to Lydia DeLamater Robins.

   In 1898, the estate was purchased by Lydia's brother-in-law George Hazard Robinson. From 1898-1902, Robinson's daughter Ruth Attmore Robinson Donnell and her husband Harry used the house as their summer home.

   In 1902, the estate became the summer home of Robinson's other daughter Laura Attmore Robinson Donnell and her husband William Ballon Donnell. After William died of appendicitis in 1905, Ruth continued to use the estate as her summer home.

   In 1911, George Hazard Robinson made extensive alterations to the house. The DeLamaters, subsequently, owned an 1876 house at 3 Bevin Road, Asharoken, named *The Point*.

   Laura Attmore Robinson Donnell inherited the estate and in 1927 began to subdivide its property.

   In 1943, Laura transferred ownership to her son-in-law Frederick Sandblom, who further subdivided the property.

   In 1946, Sandblom sold the house to Marcel Emmanuel Vertes.

   In 1954, Vertes' estate sold the house in to Lucille Borglum. The Borglums still owned the house in 1994.
[Edward A. T. Carr, Michael W. Carr, and Kari-Ann R. Carr, *Faded Laurels: The History of Eaton's Neck and Asharoken* (Interlaken, NY: Heart of the Lakes Publishing, 1994), pp. 128-31.]

   *Vertes received two Oscars from the American Academy of Motion Picture Arts and Sciences for his costume and set designs for the motion picture *Moulin Ro*uge.

front facade, 1936

Victor, Royall, Sr. (1878-1926)

Occupation(s):   attorney -   partner, Sullivan and Cromwell
                                   capitalist -   director, Detroit Edison Co.
                                   industrialist -   vice-president and director, American Agricultural
                                                    Chemical Co.;
                                                    director, Hecker–Jones–Jewell Milling Co.;
                                                    director, Manning, Maxwell & Moore, Inc.;
                                                    director, Standard Milling Co.

Marriage(s):   Anna R. V. Martin (d. 1965)

Listed in *Long Island Society Register, 1929*: yes
Address: Fox Lane, Lattingtown
Acreage / map sources: on c. 1922 map
                                     not on 1927, 1932, or 1946 maps

Name of estate:
Year of construction:
Style of architecture:
Architect(s):
Landscape architect(s):
House extant: unconfirmed
Historical notes:

     The *Long Island Society Register, 1929* lists Mrs. Royall Victor as residing in Locust Valley [Lattingtown].
[See following entry for family information.]

Victor, Royall, Sr. (1878-1926)

Occupation(s):   attorney -   partner, Sullivan and Cromwell
                                   capitalist -   director, Detroit Edison Co.
                                   industrialist -   vice-president and director, American Agricultural
                                                      Chemical Co.;
                                                    director, Hecker-Jones-Jewell Milling Co.;
                                                    director, Manning, Maxwell & Moore, Inc.;
                                                    director, Standard Milling Co.

Marriage(s):   Anna R. V. Martin (d. 1965)

Listed in *Long Island Society Register, 1929*: yes
Address: Muttontown Road, Muttontown
Acreage / map sources: not on 1927 map
                                     8 acres / 1932 map
                                     8 acres / 1946 map

Name of estate:
Year of construction:
Style of architecture:
Architect(s):
Landscape architect(s):
House extant: unconfirmed
Historical notes:

     The *Social Register New York, 1964* lists Anna R. V. Martin Victor as residing on Muttontown Road, Syosset [Muttontown].
     She was residing on Muttontown Road, Brookville [Muttontown], at the time of her death. [*The New York Times* June 21, 1965, p. 29.]
     According to the *Social Register New York, 1964,* the Victors' son Martin resided on Skunk's Misery Road, Locust Valley. Their other son Royall Victor, Jr. resided on McCoun's Lane, Glen Head.

Vietor, Dr. John Adolf, Sr. (1884-1944)

Occupation(s):   physician - surgeon
                                         educator - instructor of anatomy, College of Physicians and Surgeons,
                                                  Columbia University, NYC

Marriage(s):   M/1 - 1912-1936 - Eleanore E. Woodward (d. 1938)
                                         M/2 - 1936-1944 - Ruth Withington

Listed in *Long Island Society Register, 1929*: yes
Address: Piping Rock Road, Matinecock
Acreage / map sources: not on 1927 or 1946 maps; no acreage given on 1932 map
Name of estate: *Cherrywood*
Year of construction: c. 1910
Style of architecture: Georgian Revival
Architect(s):   James W. O'Connor designed the house,
                                         stables and swimming pool/tennis
                                         court building (for Fahys)

Landscape architect(s):   Olmsted (for Fahys)
                                         Ferruccio Vitale, 1927-1928 (for Vietor)

Estate photographs can be found in the Nassau County Museum Collection
    filed under Locust Valley/Vietor.
House extant: no; demolished c. 1980
Historical notes:

rear facade

    The house, originally named *Hilaire*, was built by George Ernest Fahys.
    The estate was owned by Vietor, who called it *Cherrywood*. It was purchased in 1936 by Edmund Calvert Lynch, Sr.
    Dr. John Adolf Vietor, Sr. was the son of George F. and Annie Achelis Vietor of Brooklyn.
    Eleanore E. Woodward Vietor was an heir to the JELL-O fortune.
    The Vietors' daughter Eleanore married Edward Nicoll Townsend, Jr. At the age of twenty-eight, she attempted
suicide. [*The New York Times* September 17, 1944, p. 44.]
    Ruth Withington Vietor was the daughter of Farley Justin Withington of Rochester, NY.
    In 1938 the Vietor Colonial homestead at 267 Broadway in Elmhurst, Queens, was demolished. It was located between
Elmhurst Avenue and Vietor Place. [*The New York Times* March 11, 1938, p. 35.]

Vilas, Guillermo (b. 1952)

Occupation(s):   professional tennis player - inducted into the Tennis Hall of Fame, 1991

Marriage(s):

Listed in *Long Island Society Register, 1929*: no
Address: Lattingtown Road, Lattingtown
Acreage / map sources: not on 1927, 1932, or 1946 maps
Name of estate: *Lockjaw Ridge*
Year of construction: c. 1916-1917
Style of architecture: Elizabethan
Architect(s):   Theodate Pope Riddle of Lamb and Rich designed the house (for E. H. Gates)
                                         James W. O'Connor designed the tennis court complex (for Sloane)
                                         William Lawrence Bottomley designed 1935 alterations to the house (for Sloane)*
Landscape architect(s):   Ferruccio Vitale, 1917 (for Mrs. Gates); 1924 (for Sloane)
House extant: yes
Historical notes:

    The seventeen-room house, originally named *Dormer House,* was built by Elizabeth Hoagland Gates.
    In 1927, it was purchased by George Sloane, who called it *Brookmeade*.
    *In 1935, the east wing of the house was added.
    The third owner was Patrice Munsel, who called it *Lockjaw Ridge*.
    In 1980, Munsel sold the estate to Vilas,.
    In 1992, it was purchased by Walter Raquet.
    Both Vilas and Raquet continued to call the estate *Lockjaw Ridge*.
    In 1999, the house and 4.07 acres were for sale. The asking price was $1.85 million; the annual taxes were $23,507.

Vivaudou, Victor (1881-1954)

Occupation(s):   industrialist - president, V. Vivaudou, Inc. (perfume manufacturer)

Marriage(s):   Rose *[unable to confirm maiden name]*

Listed in *Long Island Society Register, 1929*: no
Address: Keith Court, Centerport
Acreage / map sources: not on 1929 or 1944 maps
                                   on 1931 map [name misspelled as V. V. Vivaudau]

Name of estate:
Year of construction:
Style of architecture: Shingle
Architect(s):
Landscape architect(s):
House extant: no
Historical notes:

The house was built by D. D. Allerton, who sold it to Vivaudou.
Vivaudou was born in Cannes, France, immigrating to the United States in 1914.
In 1920, Vivaudou was fined $5,000 for violating customs regulations when he and his wife did not declare a $10,000 pearl necklace and a $500 diamond ring when returning from France on the *La Lorraine.* The items, the aggregated duties for which totaled $6,000, were concealed on their persons. Evidence collected by the United States Attorney's office verified that the items had been purchased in France by the Vivaudous during their visit and were not, as Mrs. Vivaudou claimed, family heirlooms. [*The New York Times* June 3, 1920, p. 15; November 2, 1920, p. 8; and September 20, 1924, p. 9.]

He was residing at 16 Soundview Avenue in Glen Cove at the time of his death.
The gatehouse and entrance gate have survived.

entrance gate

Von Bothmer, Dr. Dietrich Felix (b. 1918)

Occupation(s):   chairman, Department of Greek and Roman Art, Metropolitan
                                        Museum of Art, NYC
                                   educator -   professor, Institute of Fine Arts, NYC
                                   writer -   *Ancient Art From New York Private Collections*, 1960;
                                        *An Inquiry Into the Forgery of the Etruscan Terracotta
                                             Warriors,* 1961 (co-authored);
                                        Corpus Vasorum Antiquorium USA Fasicule, 1963;
                                        Greek Vase Painting, 1972;
                                        Greek Art of the Aegean Islands, 1979

Marriage(s):

Listed in *Long Island Society Register, 1929*: no
Address: Centre Island Road, Centre Island
Acreage / map sources: not on 1927, 1932, or 1946 maps
Name of estate:
Year of construction: c. 1920
Style of architecture: Federal
Architect(s):
Landscape architect(s):
House extant: yes
Historical notes:

The house, originally named *Westaways,* was built by Clifford Vail Brokaw, Sr.
The estate was owned by De LaBegassiere and, subsequently, by Von Bothmer.
In 1992 the Von Bothmer's daughter Maria married Jerome Loomis Villalba of Paris.

Von Stade, Francis Skiddy, Sr. (1884-1967)

Occupation(s):   capitalist - member, F. S. Von Stade Co. (importers of bristles)

Civic Activism: a founder and executive vice-president, National Museum of
Racing, Saratoga, NY;
mayor and trustee, Village of Old Westbury

Marriage(s):   1915-1967 - Kathryn N. Steele (d. 1981)

Listed in *Long Island Society Register, 1929*: yes

Address: Store Hill Road, Old Westbury
Acreage / map sources: on 1927 map; no acreage given on 1932 map; 84 acres / 1946 map
Name of estate:
Year of construction: c. 1914
Style of architecture: Federal
Architect(s): Cross and Cross designed the
house (for Von Stade, Sr.)
Peabody, Wilson and Brown
designed c. 1930 alterations
(for Von Stade, Sr.)
Landscape architect(s): Lewis and Valentine
(for Von Stade, Sr.)

House extant: yes
Historical notes:

front facade, c. 1922

The house was built by Francis Skiddy Von Stade, Sr.

Both the *Long Island Society Register, 1929* and the *Social Register New York, 1967* list F. Skiddy and Kathryn N. Steele Von Stade [Sr.] as residing in Westbury [Old Westbury], while the *Social Register, 1981* lists only Kathryn N. Steele Von Stade as residing on Store Hill Road, Westbury [Old Westbury].

He was a member of the Cooperstown polo team which in 1912 and 1913 won the Open Championship. [*The New York Times* February 21, 1967, p. 47.]

Kathryn Steele Von Stade's parents, Charles and Nannie French Steele, also resided in Old Westbury as did her sister Nancy, who married Devereux Milburn, Sr. and resided at *Sunridge Hall.*

The Von Stades' daughter "Dolly" married George Herbert Bostwick, Sr. and resided in Old Westbury. Their son Charles married Sara Worthington Clucas, the daughter of Edward Welch Clucas who resided at *White Oakes* in Bedminster, NJ.

Vultaggio, Donald (b. 1952)

Occupation(s):   industrialist - chairman of board and co-founder with John Ferolito,
Hornell Brewery, Brooklyn;
chairman of board and co-founder with John Ferolito,
Ferolito, Vultaggio & Sons, Lake Success
(manufacturers of Arizona Iced Tea)

Marriage(s): Ilene *[unable to confirm maiden name]*

Listed in *Long Island Society Register, 1929:* no
Address: Sands Light Road, Sands Point
Acreage / map sources: not on 1927, 1932, or 1946 maps
Name of estate:
Year of construction: c. 1995
Style of architecture: Eclectic Medieval Castle
Architect(s):
Landscape architect(s):
House extant: yes
Historical notes:

side / front facade, 2004

The house was built by Donald Vultaggio on the site of Alva Belmont's eclectic medieval castle, *Beacon Towers.*
He is the son of Joseph L. and Marion Vultaggio of Brooklyn.
The Sands Point lighthouse stands on this property.

Walbridge, Henry D. (1856-1939)

Occupation(s):   capitalist - Henry D. Walbridge & Co. (utility holding company)

Marriage(s):   M/1 - Lucy Sivey (d. 1922)
                                       M/2 - 1929-1939 - Lylian A. Wood

Listed in *Long Island Society Register, 1929*: no
Address: Willis Avenue, Roslyn
Acreage / map sources: on 1927 map; 74 acres / 1932 map; not on 1946 map
Name of estate: *Waldene*
Year of construction: c. 1900
Style of architecture: Colonial Revival
Architect(s):   Grosvenor Atterbury designed the house (for Oakman)
Landscape architect(s):
House extant: no; demolished c. 1946*
Historical notes:

     The house, originally named *Oakdene,* was built by Walter George Oakman, Sr.
     In 1912, Walbridge purchased the estate and called it *Waldene.*
     *The estate was, subsequently, owned by Samuel Rubel, who subdivided it for a housing development.

Walker, Elisha, Sr. (1879-1950)

Occupation(s):   financier -   partner, Kuhn, Loeb and Co. (investment banking firm);
                                        president, Blair and Co. (which merged into Bancamerica–
                                           Blair Corp.) (investment banking firm)
                           industrialist -   director, Standard Oil Co. (which became Exxon Corp.);
                                           director, Diamond Match Co.;
                                           director, Tidewater Assoc. Oil Co.;
                                           director, Petroleum Corp. of America;
                                           director, Rockwell Manufacturing Co.;
                                           director, Armour & Co.
                           shipping -   director, United States Lines Co.;
                           capitalist -   director, Industria Electrica de Mexico

Marriage(s):   1904-1950 - Adele D'Orn (1890-1961)

Listed in *Long Island Society Register, 1929*: yes
Address: Muttontown Road, Muttontown
Acreage / map sources: not on 1927 and 1932 maps; 24 acres / 1946 map
Name of estate: *Les Pommiers*
Year of construction: 1903-1904
Style of architecture: Federal
Architect(s):   Delano and Aldrich designed the house (for B. Winthrop)
Landscape architect(s):
Estate photographs can be found in the Nassau County Museum Collection filed under Muttontown/Winthrop
House extant: yes
Historical notes:

     The house was built by Bronson Winthrop.
     In 1911, Egerton Leigh Winthrop, Jr. took over the estate, when his brother built another house on adjoining property. Egerton called his estate *Muttontown Meadows.*
     In 1937, the estate was purchased by Walker, who renamed it *Les Pommiers,* and, subsequently in 1953, by Lansdell Kisner Christie.
     The *Social Register, Summer 1937* lists Elisha and Adele D'Orn Walker [Sr.] as residing at *Les Pommiers* in Syosset [Muttontown].
     In 1969, Nassau County acquired the estate and renamed it *Nassau Hall.* The estate is now part of Nassau County's Muttontown Preserve.

Walker, James Blaine, Jr.

Occupation(s): financier - vice-president, Goldman, Sachs and Co. (investment banking firm)

Marriage(s): 1921-1955 - Dr. Elizabeth Harrison (1897-1955)
- attorney - member of the bar in New York and Indiana
publisher - *Cues on the News* (monthly financial service for women that was distributed by banks throughout the country)
politician - secretary and only woman officer, Committee for Economic Development
Civic Activism: trustee, Town Hall, Inc., NYC

Listed in *Long Island Society Register, 1929*: yes
Address: Chicken Valley Road, Matinecock
Acreage / map sources: on 1927 map; no acreage given on 1932 map; not on 1946 map
Name of estate:
Year of construction:
Style of architecture:
Architect(s):
Landscape architect(s):
House extant: unconfirmed
Historical notes:

Both the *Long Island Society Register, 1929* and the *Social Register New York, 1933* list James Blaine and Elizabeth Harrison Walker, Jr. as residing in Locust Valley [Matinecock], while the *Social Register New York, 1966* lists only James Blaine Walker, Jr., then residing at 135 East 74th Street, NYC.

James Blaine Walker, Jr. was the great-nephew United States Secretary of State and Republican presidential candidate James G. Blaine.

Elizabeth Harrison Walker's doctorate was in jurisprudence. She was the daughter of President Benjamin Harrison. Her great-grandmother, First Lady Anna Symmes Harrison, was raised by her Tuthill grandparents in Southold and attended Clinton Academy in East Hampton, making her the first President's wife to have a formal education.

Wang, Charles B. (b. 1944)

Occupation(s): industrialist - chairman, Computer Associates International, Inc.
capitalist - co-owner, NHL Islanders (with Sanjay Kumar, who succeeded Wang as chairman of Computer Associates)
Civic Activism: chairman, Smile Train which provides surgery for children with cleft lips and palates;
financed the $40 million Charles B. Wang Center (Asian cultures)

Marriage(s):

Listed in *Long Island Society Register, 1929*: no
Address: East Main Street, Cove Neck
Acreage / map sources: not on 1927, 1932, or 1946 maps
Name of estate:
Year of construction: 18th century
Style of architecture: Long Island Farmhouse
Architect(s):
Landscape architect(s):
Estate photographs can be found in the Nassau County Museum Collection filed under Oyster Bay/Young.
House extant: yes
Historical notes:

front facade

Philip James Roosevelt, Jr., resided in the historic Young's House, to which many additions and alterations had been made since the 1700s.

In 1997, the house was purchased from Roosevelt by Wang for about $2 million. Taxes on the eight-acre estate in 1997 were approximately $14,000.

It is currently owned by Eric Best.

Wang, Charles B. (b. 1944)

Occupation(s):	industrialist - chairman, Computer Associates International, Inc.
	capitalist - co-owner, NHL Islanders (with Sanjay Kumar, who
	succeeded Wang as chairman of Computer Associates)
Civic Activism:	chairman, Smile Train which provides surgery for children with cleft
	lips and palates;
	financed the $40 million Charles B. Wang Center (Asian cultures)

Marriage(s):

Listed in *Long Island Society Register, 1929*: no
Address: off Cove Neck Road, Cove Neck
Acreage / map sources: not on 1927, 1932, or 1946 maps
Name of estate:
Year of construction: 1928
Style of architecture: Georgian Revival
Architect(s):   Hall Pleasants Pennington designed the house
                                              (for P. J. Roosevelt, Sr.)

Landscape architect(s):
House extant: yes
Historical notes:

   Philip James Roosevelt, Sr., built the house, originally named *Dolonar,* on land given to him by his father William Emlen Roosevelt.
   The estate was, subsequently, purchased by Wang, who remodeled the house.

Wang, Charles B. (b. 1944)

Occupation(s):	industrialist - chairman, Computer Associates International, Inc.
	capitalist - co-owner, NHL Islanders (with Sanjay Kumar, who
	succeeded Wang as chairman of Computer Associates)
Civic Activism:	chairman, Smile Train which provides surgery for children with cleft
	lips and palates;
	financed the $40 million Charles B. Wang Center (Asian cultures)

Marriage(s):

Listed in *Long Island Society Register, 1929*: no
Address: Cove Neck Road, Cove Neck
Acreage / map sources: not on 1927, 1932, or 1946 maps
Name of estate:
Year of construction:
Style of architecture:
Architect(s):
Landscape architect(s):
House extant: yes
Historical notes:

   The estate, called *Sakunska,* was owned by Quentin and Frances B. Webb Roosevelt II.
   In 1962, Frances Roosevelt built an artist studio on the estate.
   When Frances died in 1995, Wang purchased the 3.5-acre estate for $1.2 million.

Warburg, Gerald Felix (1901-1971)

Occupation(s):   entertainers and associated professions - concert cellist and conductor;
                                vice-president, New York City Center of Music and Drama

Civic activism: vice-president, City Center, NYC;
                                active in preventing the destruction of Carnegie Hall, NYC;
                                advisor, Metropolitan Museum of Art, NYC

Marriage(s):   M/1 - 1923-1933 - Marion Bab
                                M/2 - 1933-1971 - Natica Nast (1905-1987)
                                      - artist

Listed in *Long Island Society Register, 1929*: no
Address: Cedar Swamp Road, Brookville
Acreage / map sources: not on 1927 or 1932 maps
                                22 acres / 1946 map
Name of estate: *Box Hill Farm*
Year of construction: c. 1938
Style of architecture: Georgian Revival
Architect(s):
Landscape architect(s):
Estate photographs can be found in the Nassau County Museum
   Collection filed under Brookville/Warburg.
House extant: yes
Historical notes:

side facade, c. 1945

    The house, originally named *Box Hill Farm*, was built by Gerald Felix Warburg.
    He was the son of Felix M. and Frieda Schiff Warburg.
    Marion Bab was the daughter of F. Bab.
    Natica Nast Warburg was the daughter of Conde and Jeanne Coudert Nast, who resided at *Sandy Cay* in Sands Point.

Ward, Aaron (1851-1918)*

Occupation(s):   military - rear-admiral (1910-1913)**;
                                  served in Spanish American War;
                                  chief-of-staff of Asiatic Station, 1899-1900;
                                  commanded Atlantic Fleet, 1911-1912;
                                  supervisor of New York Harbor

Marriage(s):   1876-1918 - Ann Eliza Cairns Willis (1854-1926)

Listed in *Long Island Society Register, 1929*: no
Address: Glenwood Road, Roslyn Harbor
Acreage / map sources: on 1906 map
                                  not on 1927, 1932, or 1946 maps
Name of estate: *Willowmere*
Year of construction: 1863
Style of architecture: Colonial Revival
Architect(s):
Landscape architect(s):
Estate photographs can be found in the Nassau County Museum
   Collection filed under Roslyn/Ward.
House extant: yes
Historical notes:

front facade, 2004

    The house, originally named *Clifton*, was the ancestral home of Ann Eliza Cairns Willis Ward. Her father was Richard Storris Willis, a composer and poet. The Wards renamed the estate *Willowmere*.
    *Rear Admiral Aaron Ward's name was really Ward B. Burnett. His name was changed to Aaron Ward by his mother Emily Ward Burnett at the request of her father General Aaron Ward, who served several terms as a congressman from New York State.
    **The destroyer *USS Aaron Ward* was named in his honor.
    The estate was, subsequently, owned by James Freeman Curtis, who continued to call it *Willowmere*.

Ward, Edward Mortimer, Sr. (1873-1947)

Occupation(s):	shipping - member, Hageman and Ward (ship chandlers);
	director, Sea Train Lines (transporter of trains by ferry)
Civic Activism:	secretary and treasurer, Board of Fire Commissioners;
	treasurer, Office of Civilian Defense;
	secretary and treasurer, Locust Valley Neighborhood Association
Marriage(s):	Mary A. Post (1872-1956)

Listed in *Long Island Society Register, 1929*: yes
Address: Feeks Lane, Lattingtown
Acreage / map sources: on 1927 map; no acreage given on 1932 map; 15 acres / 1946 map
Name of estate: *Elkhurst*
Year of construction:
Style of architecture: Shingle
Architect(s):
Landscape architect(s):
House extant: yes
Historical notes:

    The house, originally named *Elkhurst*, was built by Edward Mortimer Ward, Sr.
    He was the son of George Edgar and Emily Joyce Ward. His grandfather James O. Ward was a founder of Ward Shipping Lines.

Ward, Elijah (1816-1882)

Occupation(s):	attorney - judge - New York State Judge Advocate General,
	1853-1855
	politician - member, United States Congress, 1857-1859, 1861-1865,
	and 1875-1877
Civic Activism:	president, Mercantile Library Association of NYC
Marriage(s):	1866-1882 - Ellen Eliza Cairns (1826-1893)

Listed in *Long Island Society Register, 1929*: no
Address: Glenwood Road, Roslyn Harbor
Acreage / map sources: not on 1927, 1932, or 1946 maps
Name of estate: *Locust Knoll*
Year of construction: 1855
Style of architecture: Victorian
Architect(s):
Landscape architect(s):
House extant: yes
Historical notes:

front facade, 2004

    Anna Eliza Cairns built *Locust Knoll* for her daughter Ellen Eliza and son-in-law Robert Stuart. Three years after Robert's death in 1863 Ellen married Elijah Ward. The Wards resided at *Locust Knoll* until the late 1800s.
    The estate was owned in the early 1900s by New York stockbroker Henry Herbert Hoggins.
    Renamed *Mayknoll*, it was purchased in 1948 for $50,000 by Central Intelligence Director William Joseph Casey, Jr., who was residing at *Mayknoll* at the time of his death in 1987.
    Service buildings on the estate were converted to residences for members of Mrs. Casey's family.

Ward, Sarah Donnell (d. 1962)

Marriage(s):

Listed in *Long Island Society Register, 1929*: no
Address: Locust Lane, Eaton's Neck
Acreage / map sources: not on 1929 map; on 1931 map (owned by H. E. Donnell);
                                                            106 acres / 1944 map (owned by Ruth R. Donnell)
Name of estate: *The Hill*
Year of construction: 1902
Style of architecture: Shingle / Tudor
Architect(s):   Harry Ellingwood Donnell designed his own house
Builder: Randall and Miller Construction Co.
Landscape architect(s):
House extant: yes
Historical notes:

   The house, originally named *The Hill*, was built by Harry Ellingwood Donnell.
   In 1934, Donnell, who lost his fortune in the Depression, sold some of the outbuildings and part of the estate's land.
   In 1954, he transferred ownership of the remaining portion of the estate to his daughter Sarah Donnell Ward.
   She died in 1962. In 1964, her son Nicholas sold the house to John Lang for $25,000.
   The house was owned by several more subsequent owners until it was purchased in 1987 by Robert and Marion Gerlach for $890,000. [Edward A. T. Carr, Michael W. Carr, and Kari-Ann R. Carr, *Faded Laurels: The History of Eaton's Neck and Asharoken* (Interlaken, NY: Heart of the Lakes Publishing, 1994), pp. 138-44.]
   In 1997, Edward A. T. Carr purchased the 14,4000-square-foot house and 4.8 acres at an auction from Gerlach for $373,000 and has completed the restoration of the house to the original 1902 Donnell design.
   The house is on the National Register of Historic Places.

Warner, Bradford Arnold, Sr. (1910 -1994)

Occupation(s):   financier -   vice-president, Manufacturers Trust Co.;
                                                            director, Belgian American Bank and Trust Co.;
                                                            director, European–American Bank and Trust Co.;
                                                            director, European–American Banking Corp.;
                                                            trustee, First Mortgage Investors;
                                                            trustee, Central Savings Bank;
                                                            director, John Adams Life Insurance Co.
                                                  industrialist - vice-president, Gilman Paper Co.
Civic Activism: president, board of trustees, Allen Stevenson School;
                                                  chairman of board, National Society for the Prevention of Blindness;
                                                  trustee, Woodlawn Cemetery, The Bronx;
                                                  trustee, New York Public Library, NYC

Marriage(s):   1932-1994 - Nancy Hill

Listed in *Long Island Society Register, 1929*: yes
Address: Tiffany Road, Laurel Hollow
Acreage / map sources: not on 1927, 1932, or 1946 maps
Name of estate: *La Pastura*
Year of construction:
Style of architecture: Italian Country
Architect(s):
Landscape architect(s):
House extant: yes
Historical notes:

front facade, 2004

   Bradford Arnold Warner was the son of Henry Wolcott and Estelle Emma Hawkins Warner of Syosset.
   Nancy Hill Warner was the daughter of Dr. Miner C. and Carolyn M. Pittaluga Hill, who resided at *The Terrace* on East Main Street, Oyster Bay Cove.
   The Warners' son Bradford Arnold Warner, Jr. married Pamela C. Glasier and resided in Washington, DC. Their son Miner married Ellen C. Murphy and resided in Manhattan.

Warner, Henry Wolcott (1851-1927)

Occupation(s):   financier -   partner, Warner and Co. (stock brokerage firm)

Marriage(s):   1901-1927 - Estelle Emma Hawkins

Listed in *Long Island Society Register, 1929*: yes
Address: Allen Court, Syosset
Acreage / map sources: on c. 1922 map (name misspelled as Wrarner)
                                  on 1927 map (owned by H. W. Warner)
                                  11 acres / 1932 map (owned by Mrs. H. W. Warner)
                                  10 acres /1946 map (owned by E. Warner)
Name of estate:
Year of construction:
Style of architecture:
Architect(s):
Landscape architect(s):
House extant: unconfirmed
Historical notes:

The *Long Island Society Register, 1929* lists Estelle E. Hawkins Warner as residing on Split Rock Road [Allen Court], Syosset, while the *Social Register New York, 1966* lists Mrs. Warner's residence as 1040 Fifth Avenue, NYC.

Henry Wolcott Warner was the son of Henry Scoville and Emma L. Franklin Warner, who resided in Manhattan.

Estelle Emma Hawkins Warner was the daughter of Dexter Arnold and Sophie T. Meeks Hawkins, who resided in Manhattan. Her sister Viola married John Allen Townsend and resided at *Forest Edge Farm* in Lattingtown.

The Warners' son Bradford Arnold Warner, Sr., resided at *La Pastura* in Laurel Hollow. Their son Wolcott married Nancy R. Watson, the daughter of Archibald R. Watson of Manhattan.

Watriss, Frederick N. (1872-1938)

Occupation(s):   attorney

Marriage(s):   M/1 - div. 1917 - Sarah Thompson
                                  M/2 - 1917-1922 - Helen Barney (1882-1922)
                                  M/3 - 1926 - Lady Brenda Taylor Frazier

Listed in *Long Island Society Register, 1929*: yes
Address: Route 25A and Valentine's Lane, Old Brookville
Acreage / map sources: on c. 1922 map; not on 1927, 1932, or 1946 maps
Name of estate:
Year of construction: c. 1920
Style of architecture: French Renaissance
Architect(s):   Delano and Aldrich designed the house (for Watriss)
Landscape architect(s):
House extant: no
Historical notes:

The house was built by Frederick N. Watriss.

Sarah Thompson Watriss was the daughter of Dr. William Thompson of Philadelphia, PA.

Helen Barney Watriss was the daughter of Charles Tracy and Lillian Whitney Barney, who resided in Old Westbury. She had previously been married to Archibald S. Alexander. Her sister Katharine married Courtland Dixon Barnes, Sr. and resided at *Nonesuch House* in Manhasset. Her brother Ashbel resided in Upper Brookville.

Lady Brenda Taylor Frazier Watriss was the daughter of Sir Frederick and Lady Williams Taylor Frazier, of Montreal, Canada.

The Watrisses' daughter married Sir Henry Thornton.

The estate was, subsequently, owned by Lewis Thompson Preston, Sr., who called it *Longfields*.

The estate is now Dematteis Center for Cardiac Research and Education.

Watson, John Jay, Jr. (1874-1939)

Occupation(s):	industrialist - treasurer, Joseph Banigan Rubber Co.;
	treasurer and director, United States Rubber Co.;
	president, General Rubber Co.;
	president, Rubber Goods Manufacturing Co.;
	president, International Agricultural Corp. (fertilizer manufacturers);
	founder and president, Lee Rubber Tire Co.;
	director, Prairie Phosphate Co.;
	director, Phosphate Recovery Co.
	financier - director, American Eagle Fire Insurance Co.;
	director, Fidelity–Phenix Fire Insurance Co.
	capitalist - director, Florida Mining Co.;
	director, Southern Railway Co.
	politician - member, Rhode Island House of Representatives, 1899-1904;
	member, Rhode Island State Board of Charities and Corrections
Civic Activism:	trustee, Village of Upper Brookville
Marriage(s):	1900-1939 - Eliza J. Ralph

Listed in *Long Island Society Register, 1929*: yes
Address: Ripley Road and Wolver Hollow Road, Upper Brookville
Acreage / map sources: on 1927 map
no acreage given on 1932 map
35 acres / 1946 map
Name of estate: *Cedarcroft*
Year of construction:
Style of architecture:
Architect(s):
Landscape architect(s):
House extant: unconfirmed
Historical notes:

   Born in Jamestown, RI, he was the son of John Jay and Gertrude T. Stanhope Watson, Sr. and a descendant of Caleb Carr, the governor of Colonial Rhode Island.

James Watson Webb, Sr.'s house,
Woodbury House, front facade, 2004

Webb, James Watson, Sr. (1884-1960)

Occupation(s):   financier - chairman of board, Webb and Lynch (insurance
                                                              brokerage firm)

Civic Activism: trustee, Norwich University, Northfield, VT;
trustee, New York Zoological Society, NYC;
*

Marriage(s):   1910-1960 - Electra Havemeyer (1888-1960)
                                 - Civic Activism: board member, Vermont Historical Society;
                                                       trustee, National Trust for Historic Preservation;
                                                        board member, Fletcher Hospital, Burlington, VT;
                                                        *
                                                        **

Listed in *Long Island Society Register, 1929*: yes
Address: Jericho Turnpike, Syosset
Acreage / map sources: not on 1927, 1932, or 1946 maps
Name of estate: *Woodbury House*
Year of construction: c. 1915
Style of architecture: Tudor
Architect(s):   Cross and Cross designed the house (for J. W. Webb, Sr.)
                                   James W. O'Connor designed the tennis building
                                    (for J. W. Webb, Sr.)
Landscape architect(s):
House extant: yes
Historical notes:

    The house, originally named *Woodbury House,* had a partial "Tiffany Studios interior" when it was built by James Watson Webb, Sr.

    He was the son of William Seward D. and Eliza ("Lila") Osgood Vanderbilt Webb, Sr. His brother William Seward D. Webb, Jr. resided in North Hills. His sister Frederica married Ralph Pulitzer, Sr. and resided at *Kiluna Farm* in North Hills.

    Electra Havemeyer Webb was the daughter of Henry Osborne and Louisine Waldron Elder Havemeyer, Sr. who resided at *Bayberry Point* in Islip. Her brother Horace Havemeyer resided at *Olympic Point* in Bay Shore.

    *James Watson and Electra Havemeyer Webb, Sr. founded the Shelburne Museum in Shelburne, VT.

    **Electra Havemeyer Webb was an assistant director of the Red Cross Motor Corps during World War I, director of the Civil Defense Volunteer Office's Information and War Activities Center in NYC during World War II, and director of the New York Blood Development Program during World War II.

    The Webbs resided at *Woodbury House* prior to moving to Old Westbury. Both the *Long Island Society Register, 1929* and the *Social Register, Summer 1951* list James Watson and Electra Havemeyer Webb [Sr.] as residing in Westbury [Old Westbury], while the *Social Register, Summer 1954* lists their residence as *Brick House,* Shelburne, VT.

    The Webbs' daughter Electra married Dunbar Wright Bostwick and resided in Manhattan. Their daughter Lila married John Currie Wilmerding. Their son James Watson Webb, Jr., who remained unmarried, became head of the film editing department of Twentieth-Century Fox Films and resided in Los Angeles, CA. Their son Samuel married Elizabeth Johnson and, subsequently, Martha Trinkle. Their son Harry married Kate de Forest Jennings.

    The estate was purchased by Edward Richmond Tinker, Jr., who continued to call it *Woodbury House*, and later by the Town of Oyster Bay. The estate is now the Westbury–Syosset Community Park.

Woodbury House's Tiffany interior, c. 1914

Webb, James Watson, Sr. (1884-1960)

Occupation(s):	financier - chairman of board, Webb and Lynch (insurance brokerage firm)
Civic Activism:	trustee, Norwich University, Northfield, VT;
	trustee, New York Zoological Society, NYC;
	*
Marriage(s):	1910-1960 - Electra Havemeyer (1888-1960)
	- Civic Activism: board member, Vermont Historical Society;
	trustee, National Trust for Historic Preservation;
	board member, Fletcher Hospital, Burlington, VT;
	*

[See previous entry for additional civic activism information.]

Listed in *Long Island Society Register, 1929*: yes
Address:	I. U. Willets Road and Old Westbury Road, Old Westbury
Acreage / map sources:	on 1927 map; 102 acres / 1932 map; not on 1946 map
Name of estate:	
Year of construction:	
Style of architecture:	Modified Colonial Revival
Architect(s):	
Landscape architect(s):	
House extant: unconfirmed	
Historical notes:	

The house was purchased by the Webbs in 1921, after selling their Syosset residence *Woodbury House.*

Electra Havemeyer Webb was the daughter of Henry Osborne and Louisine Waldron Elder Havemeyer, Sr. who resided at *Bayberry Point* in Islip.

*James Watson and Electra Havemeyer Webb, Sr. founded the Shelburne Museum in Shelburne, VT.

The house was constantly being enlarged to accommodate the family's ever-increasing needs. Prior to the construction of the museum at Shelburne, many of the Webbs' accumulated artifacts were stored along the perimeter of the indoor tennis court. [Lauren B. Hewes and Celia Y. Oliver. *To Collect in Earnest: The Life and Works of Electra Havemeyer Webb* (Shelburne, VT: Shelburne Museum, 1997), pp. 16, 21.]

[See previous entry for additional family information.]

Webb, William Seward D., Jr. (1887-1956)

Occupation(s):	capitalist - real estate - a founder and partner, Webb and Knapp
	financier - partner, Greer, Crane and Webb (stock brokerage firm)
Marriage(s):	1911-1956 - Gertrude Emily Gaynor (1888-c. 1970)

Listed in *Long Island Society Register, 1929*: yes
Address:	I. U. Willets Road and Old Westbury Road, Old Westbury
Acreage / map sources:	on 1927 map; 7 acres / 1932 map; not on 1946 map
Name of estate:	
Year of construction:	
Style of architecture:	
Architect(s):	Cross and Cross
Landscape architect(s):	
House extant: unconfirmed	
Historical notes:	

William Seward Webb, Jr. was the son of William Seward D. and Eliza ("Lila") Osgood Vanderbilt Webb, Sr. His brother James Watson Webb, Sr. married Electra Havemeyer and resided in Old Westbury and at *Woodbury House* in Syosset. His sister Frederica married Ralph Pulitzer, Sr. and resided at *Kiluna Farm* in North Hills.

Gertrude Emily Gaynor Webb was the daughter of New York City Mayor William Jay Gaynor, who resided at *Deepwells* in St. James. Her sister Marion married Ralph Heyward Isham and resided in Glen Head.

The Webbs' daughter Frederica married David Samuel Gamble, Jr. Their son William Seward D. Webb III married Elizabeth Barroll. Their son Jacob married Elizabeth Brann, Leonore Lemmon, and, subsequently, Mrs. Stephany Hitchcock. Their son William married Carolyn R. Ordway. Their daughter Gertrude married Harry Meades.

Weekes, Arthur Delano, Jr. (1878-1952)

Occupation(s):   attorney
                                   financier - member, Chauncey and Co. (stock brokerage firm)
Civic Activism: mayor, Village of Oyster Bay Cove

Marriage(s):   1907 - Dorothy Lee Higginson

Listed in *Long Island Society Register, 1929*: yes
Address: Oyster Bay – Cove Road, Oyster Bay Cove
Acreage / map sources: not on 1927, 1932, or 1946 maps
Name of estate: *The Anchorage*
Year of construction:
Style of architecture:
Architect(s):
Landscape architect(s):
House extant: unconfirmed
Historical notes:

    Both the *Long Island Society Register, 1929* and the *Social Register, Summer 1950* list Arthur D. and Dorothy L. Higginson Weekes [Jr.] as residing at *The Anchorage* in Oyster Bay [Oyster Bay Cove].
    He was the son of Arthur Delano and Lily Underhill Weekes, Sr. and a descendant of the Colonial Indian fighter Captain John Underhill. His brother Harold married Louisine A. Peters, the daughter of Samuel Twyford and Adaline Elder Peters who resided at *Windholme* in Islip, and, subsequently, Francis Stokes. His sister Edith married John Slade, Sr. and resided at *Underhill House* in Upper Brookville and *Berry Hill House* in Oyster Bay Cove.
    Dorothy Lee Higginson Weekes was the daughter of James J. Higginson, of Boston, MA.
    Arthur Delano and Dorothy Lee Higginson Weekes' son Arthur Delano Weekes III married Nancy Gordon Milburn, the daughter of Devereux and Nancy G. Steel Milburn, Sr. who resided at *Sunridge Hall* in Old Westbury. Their son James married Katharine Margaret Sands, the daughter of Charles Edward Sands of Manhattan. Their son Townsend married Margaret Blanchard Ranken, the daughter of David Dean Ranken of Wilmington, DE. Their daughter Dorothy married William Porter Buck and resided in Oyster Bay.

Weekes, Frances Stokes (d. 1967)

Marriage(s):   M/1 - 1915 - 1931 - Louis Crawford Clark II
                                   M/2 - 1933 -1950 - Harold H. Weekes (d. 1950)
                                        - financier - partner, Thomas, Maclay and Co. (stock brokerage firm)

Listed in *Long Island Society Register, 1929*: yes
Address: Valentine's Lane, Old Brookville
Acreage / map sources: on 1927 map (owned by Louis Clark)
                                   no acreage given on 1932 map (owned by Louis Clark)
                                   11 acres / 1946 map (owned by F. S. Weekes)
Name of estate: *Valentine Farm*
Year of construction:
Style of architecture:
Architect(s):
Landscape architect(s):
House extant: yes
Historical notes:

    The *Long Island Society Register, 1929* lists Louis C. and Frances Stokes Clark II as residing at *Valentine Farm* in Roslyn [Old Brookville].
    The *Social Register, Summer 1937* lists Harold H. and Frances Stokes Weekes as residing at *Valentine Farm* in Roslyn [Old Brookville.]
    She was the daughter of Thomas P. C. Stokes of Philadelphia, PA.
    Louis and Frances Stokes Clark's son Louis Crawford Clark III married Ann Paul Drexel of Radnor, PA. He was killed during World War II.
    [See previous entry for additional family information.]
    The estate was sold to a developer who plans to subdivide the land into three-acre lots for a housing development. [*The New York Times* January 11, 1997.] The fate of the house, as of 2000, was undetermined.

Weekes, John Abeel (1857-1939)

Occupation(s):   attorney -   partner, Weekes and Foster
                                         politician - member, New York State Legislature from 23rd
                                                                  Assembly District
Civic Activism: president of board, New York Historical Society, NYC

Marriage(s):   M/1 - Estelle Durant
                               M/2 - 1920- Elsa Adele Schreiter

Listed in *Long Island Society Register, 1929*: yes
Address: East Main Street, Oyster Bay Cove
Acreage / map sources: on 1927 map
                               no acreage given on 1932 map
                               19 acres / 1946 map
Name of estate: *Tranquility**
Year of construction:
Style of architecture: Greek Revival
Architect(s):
Landscape architect(s):
House extant: no; demolished in mid-1930s
Historical notes: *front facade*

In 1876, Theodore Roosevelt, the father of President Theodore Roosevelt, rented the house from Otis D. Swan. Roosevelt called the estate *Tranquility.*
   The house was, subsequently, owned by Weekes, who continued to call it *Tranquility.*
   *This older spelling, using a single l, was used by both Roosevelt and Weekes.
   John Abeel Weekes' sister Julia married Henry Grant de Forest and resided at *Nethermuir* in Laurel Hollow.
   Elsa Adele Schreiter Weekes was the daughter of Henry Schreiter of Manhattan.

Weidenfeld, Camille

Occupation(s):   financier -   stockbroker*

Marriage(s):   1895 - Katharine Clayton Donovan

Listed in *Long Island Society Register, 1929*: no
Address: Main Street, Oyster Bay
Acreage / map sources: on c. 1922 map
                               not on 1927, 1932, or 1946 maps
Name of estate:
Year of construction: c. 1885
Style of architecture: Queen Anne   *rear facade*
Architect(s):   Donn Barber designed c. 1920s alterations
                                  on the house transforming it from Queen Anne to Colonial
                                    Revival, Tudor garage, stables, and boathouse (for Shonnard)
                              George Browne Post designed c. 1888 alterations to the house
                                    (for Underhill)
Landscape architect(s):   Donn Barber designed the formal garden, c. 1920s (for Shonnard)
House extant: no; demolished in 1950s
Historical notes:

The house was built by Francis T. Underhill.
   The estate was owned by Weidenfeld and, subsequently, by Horatio Seymour Shonnard, Sr., who called it *Boscobel.*
   *After clashing with J. P. Morgan on a financial matter, Weidenfeld was suspended from the New York Stock Exchange for one year by the exchange's governing committee. The committee decision was rendered after a six-hour meeting during which no evidence against Weidenfeld was produced and from which Weidenfeld's attorney was prohibited. Pro-Weidenfeld witnesses were unavailable and, therefore, absent from the proceedings. [*The New York Times* February 25, 1903, pp. 1-2 and June 6, 1903, p. 14.]
   In 1917, Weidenfeld declared bankruptcy. [*The New York Times* May 13, 1917, section I, p. 16.]

Weir, Levi Candee (1842-1910)

Occupation(s):   capitalist - president and chairman of board, Adams Express Co.;
director, U. S. Express Co.;
director, Des Moines & Fort Dodge Railroad;
director, Ohio Central & Western Railway;
director, Minneapolis & St. Louis Railroad
real estate - director, Adams Land & Building Co.;
director, Matawok Land Co.;
financier - director, American National Exchange;
director, Franklin National Bank of Philadelphia;
director, Philadelphia Home Insurance Co.;
director, Mercantile Trust Co.;
director, Standard Trust Co.
shipping - director, American Mail Steamship Co.

Marriage(s):   M. Emma Weibel

Listed in *Long Island Society Register, 1929*: no
Address: Horse Hollow Road, Lattingtown
Acreage / map sources: not on 1927, 1932, or 1946 maps
Name of estate: *The Hedges*
Year of construction: c. 1905
Style of architecture: Shingle
Architect(s):
Landscape architect(s):
Estate photographs can be found in the Nassau County
Museum Collection filed under Locust Valley/Stettinius.
House extant: no
Historical notes:

front facade

The house, originally named *The Hedges,* was built Levi Candee Weir.

It was subsequently owned by Edward Reilly Stettinius, Sr. and, then, his son Edward Reilly Stettinius, Jr., both of whom called the estate *The Shelter.*

The Weirs' daughter Madelon married Oliver De Gray Vanderbilt, Jr. of Orange, NJ.

Weiss, William Erhard, Jr.

Occupation(s):   industrialist - president, Natcon Chemical Co., Inc.
statesman - chief of economic affairs division, American
High Commissioner's Office, Germany

Marriage(s):   Martha Douglas (1918-1958)

Listed in *Long Island Society Register, 1929*: no
Address: South Centre Island Road, Centre Island
Acreage / map sources: not on 1927, 1932, or 1946 maps
Name of estate:
Year of construction: c. 1920
Style of architecture: French Norman
Architect(s): Mrs. John E. McLeran designed the house (for Pettinos)
Landscape architect(s):
House extant: yes
Historical notes:

The house, originally named *Thatch Cottage,* was built by Charles E. Pettinos.

The estate was owned in 1928 by Sherman M. Fairchild and, subsequently, by Weiss.

Martha Douglas Weiss was residing on Cove Neck Road, Oyster Bay, at the time of her death. [*The New York Times* November 23, 1958, p. 88.]

The Weisses' son William married Robin Biddle Martin, the daughter of Robert Wesley Martin, Jr. of Brookville.

Welch, Charles James (1875-1959)

Occupation(s):   capitalist -   founder and president, Fairchild & Co. (raw sugar dealer);
                                                    founder and president, Cape Cruz Co. (sugar plantation
                                                        operators)

Marriage(s):   1900-1942 - Elizabeth K. Livingston (d. 1942)

Listed in *Long Island Society Register, 1929*: yes
Address: Cedar Knoll Drive, Sands Point
Acreage / map sources: on 1927 map
                                     9 acres / 1932 map
                                     7 acres / 1946 map
Name of estate: *The Glen*
Year of construction:
Style of architecture: Eclectic
Architect(s):
Landscape architect(s):
House extant: unconfirmed
Historical notes:

     Both the *Long Island Society Register, 1929* and the *Social Register, Summer 1937* list Charles James and Elizabeth K. Livingston Welch as residing at *The Glen* in Sands Point, while the *Social Register, Summer 1959* lists only Mr. Welch residing at *The Glen*.

     Elizabeth Livingston Welch was the daughter of Livingus and Eliza Young Livingston and a direct descendant of Robert Livingston, the first Lord of Livingston Manor. [*The New York Times* January 20, 1942, p. 19.]

     The Welchs' son Dr. d' Alte A. Welch married Ann Frances Goddard, the daughter of Convers Goddard of Chicago, IL. Their son Livingston married Basilia L. Hawthorne, the daughter of R. Walter Hawthorne of Manhattan, and, subsequently, Helen I. Sharp. He resided with his second wife in Manhasset.

front facade

Weld, Francis Minot, II (1875-1949)

Occupation(s):	industrialist - director, International Minerals & Chemical Co.;
	    director, Baldwin Locomotive Works
	financier - partner, White, Weld and Co. (investment banking firm);
	    director, Atlas Assurance Co.;
	    director, Greenwich Savings Bank;
	    director, Union Trust Co.

Civic Activism:	trustee, Metropolitan Museum of Art, NYC

Marriage(s):	M/1 - 1903-1925 - Margaret Low White
	M/2 - 1930-1949 - Julia de Forest Tiffany (1887-1973)
	    - scientist - research associate in pathology, College of
	        Physicians and Surgeons, Columbia
	        University, NYC
	    writer - numerous scientific articles

Listed in *Long Island Society Register, 1929*: yes

Address:	West View Drive, Lloyd Harbor
Acreage / map sources:	44.5 acres / 1929 map no acreage given on 1931 map 59 acres / 1944 and 1946 maps
Name of estate:	*Lulworth*
Year of construction:	1912-1914
Style of architecture:	Federal
Architect(s):	Charles A. Platt designed the house and stables (for Weld)*

Landscape architect(s):	Olmsted (for Weld)
	Ellen Biddle Shipman and Charles A. Platt jointly
	   designed the walled flower garden and brick terrace
	   (for Weld)

House extant: yes
Historical notes:

The seventeen-room house, with six bathrooms, originally named *Lulworth,* was built by Francis Minot Weld II.

Julia de Forest Tiffany Weld had previously been married to Gordon Saltonstall Parker. She was one of the twin daughters born to Louis Comfort Tiffany and his second wife Louise Wakeman Knox Tiffany, who resided at *The Briars* and *Laurelton Hall* in Laurel Hollow. Her sister Mary married Dr. Graham Lusk and resided at *The Briars* in Laurel Hollow after Louis Comfort Tiffany built *Laurelton Hall.* Her twin sister Louise married Rodman Gilder, Sr. and also resided in Laurel Hollow. Her brother Charles Lewis Tiffany II married Katrina Brandes Ely and, subsequently, Emilia de Apezteguia and resided at *Elmwood* in Oyster Bay Cove. Her sister Dorothy married Dr. Robert Burlingham and resided in Laurel Hollow.

Francis Minot Weld II was killed in an airplane crash in Washington, DC. He was the son of Francis Minot and Fanny E. Bartholomew Weld, Sr.

*According to Hugh F. McKean, *The "Lost" Treasures of Louis Comfort Tiffany,* Tiffany designed the 72nd St., NYC, home of his father Charles Lewis Tiffany, *The Briars, Laurelton Hall,* and "homes for his daughters as they married." He does not, however, delineate which of his daughters' homes Tiffany designed so it is, at this time, impossible to say whether there was any involvement by Louis Comfort Tiffany in the design of the Weld home. [Hugh F. McKean, *The "Lost" Treasures of Louis Comfort Tiffany* (Garden City: Doubleday & Co., Inc., 1980), p. 6.]

The house's service wing was expanded and a swimming pool and pavilion were built in the formal gardens.

The estate's property was sold for a housing development.

rear facade, 2004

Welldon, Samuel Alfred (1882-1962)

Occupation(s):   attorney - member, Byrne and Cutcheon
financier - chairman of board, First National Bank of the City of New York;
director, Equitable Life Assurance Society of the United States
capitalist - director, American Telephone and Telegraph Co.;
director, Northern Pacific Railway Co.
industrialist - director, Bigelow–Sanford Carpet Co.;
director, Chemical and Dye Co.

Civic Activism: treasurer, British War Relief Society during World War II;
member of board, Community Service Society

Marriage(s):   M/1 - 1911-1949 - Julia Marion Hoyt
M/2 - 1949-1962 - Emily Pell Coster

Listed in *Long Island Society Register, 1929*: no
Address: Wolver Hollow Road, Upper Brookville
Acreage / map sources: not on 1927, 1932, or 1946 maps
Name of estate:
Year of construction: 1928*
Style of architecture: French Chateau
Architect(s):
Landscape architect(s):
House extant: yes
Historical notes:

    *In 1928, Ashbell Hinman Barney bought an 18th-century French Chateau and reconstructed it as his home.
    The thirteen-room house was, subsequently, owned by Welldon, who was the son of John William Welldon.
    Julia Marion Hoyt Welldon was the daughter of Gerard Livingston and May Appleton Hoyt of NYC. Her brother Lydig Hoyt resided in Woodbury.
    Emily Pell Coster Welldon was the daughter of Charles Henry Coster. She had previously been married to Lewis Spencer Morris.
    In 2000, the house was for sale. The asking price for the house and twelve acres was $4.995 million.

Wellington, Herbert Galbraith, Sr. (1891-1965)

Occupation(s):   financier - partner, Redmond and Co. (investment banking firm);
founder, Wellington and Co. (investment banking firm);
governor, New York Stock Exchange, 1928-1938
capitalist - director, Greyhound Corp.;
director, Boothe Leasing Co.;
director, Greyhound Lines of Canada
industrialist - director, Eaton Manufacturing Co.;
director, Yale and Town Manufacturing Co.
merchant - director, Tiffany and Co., NYC (jewelers)

Marriage(s):   1916-1965 - Elizabeth Dutton

Listed in *Long Island Society Register, 1929*: no
Address: Duck Pond Road, Matinecock
Acreage / map sources: not on 1927, 1932, or 1946 maps
Name of estate:
Year of construction: c. 1920
Style of architecture: Colonial Revival
Architect(s):   Beers and Farley designed 1929 alterations (for J. P. Kane, Jr.)
Landscape architect(s):   Louise Payson and Ellen Biddle Shipman jointly designed
landscaping (for J. P. Kane, Jr.)*

House extant: yes
Historical notes:

    *According to Shipman records, Payson and Shipman worked together on the estate's landscaping design.
    The estate was, subsequently, owned by Wellington, who purchased the estate from John P. Kane, Jr. in 1936.

Wellman, Roderic (1882 -1948)

Occupation(s):   attorney -   partner, Wellman, Smyth and Schofield
Civic Activism: trustee, Village of Muttontown

Marriage(s):   1921-1941 - Evelyn Breese Smith (d. 1941)

Listed in *Long Island Society Register, 1929*: yes
Address: Plum Beach Point Drive, Sands Point
Acreage / map sources: on 1927 map
                                  not on 1932 or 1946 maps
Name of estate: *Soundacre*
Year of construction:
Style of architecture:
Architect(s):
Landscape architect(s):
House extant: unconfirmed
Historical notes:

The *Long Island Society Register, 1929* lists Roderic and Evelyn Smith Wellman as residing at *Soundacre* in Sands Point.

He was the son of Francis L. Wellman.

Evelyn Breese Smith was the daughter of Walker Breese and Maud Rives Smith.

The Wellmans' daughter Maud married John Owens Roche, the son of Clarence L. Roche of Houghton, MI. Their daughter Evelyn married Peter M. Jacula, the son of Michael Jacula of Rochester, NY. Their daughter Rosamund married James E. Barber and resided in Attleboro, MA.

Wellman, Roderic (1882 -1948)

Occupation(s):   attorney -   partner, Wellman, Smyth and Schofield
Civic Activism: trustee, Village of Muttontown

Marriage(s):   1921-1941 - Evelyn Breese Smith (d. 1941)

Listed in *Long Island Society Register, 1929*: yes
Address: Mill Road and Brookville – East Norwich Road, Muttontown
Acreage / map sources: not on 1927 map
                                  16 acres / 1932 map
                                  3 acres / 1946 map
Name of estate:
Year of construction: c. 1933
Style of architecture: Georgian Revival
Architect(s):
Landscape architect(s):
House extant: yes
Historical notes:

The *Social Register New York, 1933* lists Roderic and Evelyn Smith Wellman as residing in East Norwich [Muttontown].

Evelyn Breese Smith was residing on Mill Road, East Norwich [Muttontown], at the time of her death. [*The New York Times* May 9, 1948, p. 70.]

[See previous entry for family information.]

Wetmore, Charles Whitman (1854-1919)

Occupation(s):   attorney -   partner, Barlow and Wetmore
                                        capitalist -   president, Detroit Edison;
                                                        president, Montana Power Co.
                                        industrialist - director, Bethlehem Steel Co.

Marriage(s):   1891-1919 - Elizabeth Bisland (1861-1929)
                                        - journalist - *Punk*; *Cosmopolitan*; *Harper's Bazaar*
                                        writer - *A Flying Trip Around the World,* 1891

Listed in *Long Island Society Register, 1929*: no
Address: Centre Island Road, Centre Island
Acreage / map sources: not on 1927, 1932, or 1946 maps
Name of estate: *Applegarth*
Year of construction: 1892
Style of architecture: Elizabethan
Architect(s):   Renwick, Aspinwall and Owen designed the house
                                          (for C. W. Wetmore)
Landscape architect(s):
House extant: no; demolished c. 1940
Historical notes:

    The house, originally named *Applegarth*, was built by Charles Whitman Wetmore.
    Elizabeth Bisland, prior to her marriage to Wetmore, was sent out by *Cosmopolitan* to challenge Nellie Bly (formerly, Elizabeth Cochrane of Pittsburgh, PA), in Nellie's round-the-world-race with Jules Verne's fictional character Phineas T.
Fogg. Elizabeth missed a steamer connection from LeHavre, France, and returned to New York. Nellie, who was unaware of the challenge until she reached Hong Kong and unaware that it was Elizabeth who had attempted the aborted challenge until she reached the West Coast, returned to her starting point in Jersey City, NJ, in "seventy-two days, six hours, ten minutes and eleven seconds," thus beating the "round-the-world in eighty days trip of Phineas T. Fogg."

rear facade

    The estate was, subsequently, owned by William Henry Nichols, Jr., who continued to call it *Applegarth*

Wetmore, Edmund (1838-1918)

Occupation(s):   attorney -   partner, Wetmore and Jenner
Civic Activism: president, American Bar Association, 1900;
                                        president, Bar Association of New York, 1908

Marriage(s):   1860-1918 - Helen Howland (d. 1924)

Listed in *Long Island Society Register, 1929*: no
Address: Red Spring Lane, Glen Cove
Acreage / map sources: 1927 map illegible; not on 1932 or 1946 maps
Name of estate:
Year of construction: c. 1900
Style of architecture: Colonial Revival
Architect(s):
Landscape architect(s):
House extant: yes
Historical notes:

    The house was built by Edmund Wetmore.
    Helen Howland Wetmore was the daughter of Benjamin J. Howland.
    The estate was owned by John Nobel Stearns II, who called it *The Cedars,* and, subsequently, by Max Sobelman.

Whalen, Grover A., Sr. (1886-1962)

Occupation(s):   capitalist - president, 1939 World's Fair
industrialist - president, Schenley Products Co.;
head of New York City office, Coty (perfume and
cosmetics firm)
merchant - general manager, John Wanamaker Department Store
politician - New York City's official greeter*;
New York City Police Commissioner, 1928-1930 (appointed
by his close friend Mayor James J. Walker);
New York City Commissioner of Plant & Structures in
Mayor Hylan's administration;
New York City Commissioner of Purchases in Mayor
Hylan's administration

Marriage(s):   1913-1962 - Anna Dolores Kelly (1886-1968)

Listed in *Long Island Society Register, 1929*: no
Address: Searingtown Road, Roslyn Heights
Acreage / map sources: not on 1927, 1932, or 1946 maps
Name of estate:
Year of construction: c. 1926
Style of architecture: Tudor
Architect(s):   Chandler Stearns designed the house (for J. D. Ryan)
Landscape architect(s):   Noel Chamberlain prepared extensive landscape designs
(for J. D. Ryan)

House extant: yes
Historical notes:

John Dennis Ryan built the house for his son John Carlos Ryan on property adjacent to his own estate. After a heated dispute with his father, John Carlos refused to reside in the house and, indeed, never did.
    The estate was. subsequently, owned by Whalen.
    *Whalen established the tradition of New York City's ticker-tape parade.
    The house is now the clubhouse for the Renaissance Country Club.

Wheeler, Frederick Seymour (1861-1936)

Occupation(s):   industrialist - chairman of the board, American Can Co.;
secretary and treasurer, Great American Tin Plate Co.

Marriage(s):   1891 - Charlotte Putnam

Listed in *Long Island Society Register, 1929*: yes
Address: Planting Fields Road, Upper Brookville
Acreage / map sources: not on 1927 map; no acreage given on 1932 map; 24 acres / 1946 map
Name of estate: *Delwood*
Year of construction: c. 1915-1916
Style of architecture: Mediterranean Villa
Architect(s):   Hunt and Hunt designed the house (for Sanderson)
Landscape architect(s):   Olmsted, 1925 (for Sanderson)
Olmsted designed the swimming pool, 1928 (for Wheeler)
Estate photographs can be found in the Nassau County Museum Collection filed under Oyster Bay/Sanderson.
House extant: yes
Historical notes:

The house, originally named *La Selva,* was built by Henry Sanderson.
In 1928 the estate was sold to Wheeler, who called it *Delwood.*
The *Long Island Society Register, 1929* lists the name of the Wheeler estate as *Delwood.*
When Mrs. Wheeler died, she willed the estate to the Community Hospital of Glen Cove.
In 1963, the estate was owned by St. Francis Center and is now a monastery.

White, Alexander Moss, Jr. (1904-1968)

Occupation(s):	financier - partner, White, Weld and Co. (investment banking firm)
	attorney
	industrialist - director, American Cyanamid Co.
Civic Activism:	president of board (for seventeen years), American Museum of Natural History, NYC;
	overseer, Harvard University, Cambridge, MA;
	trustee, Brooklyn Children's Aid Society

Marriage(s):	1930-1968 - Mary Evelyn Lanman

Listed in *Long Island Society Register, 1929*: yes

Address:	Sunset Road, Oyster Bay Cove
Acreage / map sources:	not on 1927 or 1932 maps; 22 acres / 1946 map
Name of estate:	*Hickory Hill*
Year of construction:	
Style of architecture:	Federal
Architect(s):	Kimball and Husted designed the house (for A. M. White, Jr.)
Landscape architect(s):	Ellen Biddle Shipman (for A. M. White, Jr.)
House extant: unconfirmed	
Historical notes:	

The house, originally named *Hickory Hill*, was built by Alexander Moss White, Jr.

In 1927, White purchased the Woodbury schoolhouse in which Walt Whitman had taught for $60 and moved it to his estate. He used it to house the collection of Whitman material which he had begun collecting when he was a student at Harvard University.

Mary Evelyn Lanman White was the daughter of Jonathan Trumbull and Mary Ludlow Thoman Lanman, Sr., who resided in Lawrence.

In 2002, the Whites' son Alexander Moss White III, died at his residence *Pachelbel Farm* in Old Chatham, NY. Their daughter Sheila married T. Whitney Blake, the son of Joseph Augustus Blake of Litchfield, CT. Their daughter Elinor married George G. Montgomery, Jr. and resided in Manhattan.

[See the following entry for additional family information.]

White, Alexander Moss, Sr. (1871-1929)

Occupation(s):	financier - a founder and partner, White, Weld and Co. (investment banking firm);
	a founder, Brooklyn Trust Co.
Civic Activism:	a founder, Brooklyn Children's Aid Society;
	treasurer, Academy of Music, NYC

Marriage(s):	Elsie Helen Ogden (1874-1953)
	- Civic Activism: trustee, Perkins School, Lancaster, MA

Listed in *Long Island Society Register, 1929*: yes

Address:	Cove Neck Road, Cove Neck
Acreage / map sources:	on 1927 map; not on 1932 map; 5 acres / 1946 map
Name of estate:	*Weymouth*
Year of construction:	
Style of architecture:	
Architect(s):	
Landscape architect(s):	
House extant: yes	
Historical notes:	

The house, originally named *Weymouth*, was built by Alexander Moss White, Sr.

The Whites' son Alexander Moss White, Jr. married Mary Evelyn Lanman and resided at *Hickory Hill* in Oyster Bay Cove. Their daughter Elinor married Edward G. Janeway and resided in South Londonderry, VT, and in Cove Neck. Their son Ogden married Sally Sprague, the daughter of Phineas Warren Sprague of Boston, MA, and resided in Fall Hills, NJ.

[See previous entry for additional family information.]

White, Frederick Wheeler (1863-1937)

Occupation(s):   industrialist - president, Mutual Chemical Co.;
                                          director, Phosphate Mining Co.

Marriage(s):   M/1 - 1909-1933 - Pansy Belvin (d. 1933)
                                     M/2 - Frances Andrews

Listed in *Long Island Society Register, 1929*: yes
Address: West Shore Road, Kings Point
Acreage / map sources: on 1927 map
                                     9 acres / 1932 map
                                     not on 1946 map
Name of estate: *The Lindens*
Year of construction: c. 1900
Style of architecture: French Second Empire
Architect(s):
Landscape architect(s):
House extant: no; demolished c. 1950
Historical notes:

    The house, originally named *The Lindens*, was built by Alfred W. White.
    The estate was, subsequently, owned by Frederick Wheeler White, who continued to call it *The Lindens*.
    He was the son of George E. and Ella A. W. White of Manhattan.
    The *Long Island Society Register, 1929* lists Frederick W. and Pansy Belvin White as residing at *The Lindens* on West Shore Road, Great Neck [Kings Point], while the *Social Register, Summer 1937* lists only Frances Andrews White as residing at *The Lindens*.

White, Gardiner Winslow, Sr. (1891-1981)

Occupation(s):

Marriage(s):   1917-1961 - Sylvia Johnson Curtis (1892-1961)

Listed in *Long Island Society Register, 1929*: yes
Address: West Shore Road, Mill Neck
Acreage / map sources: on 1927 map
                                     15 acres / 1932 map
                                     8 acres / 1946 map
Name of estate: *White Lodge*
Year of construction: 1915
Style of architecture: Federal
Architect(s):   Harold Perry Erskine designed the house
                                       (for G. W. White, Sr.)
Landscape architect(s):
House extant: yes
Historical notes:

    The house, originally named *White Lodge*, was built by Gardiner Winslow White, Sr.
    The *Long Island Society Register, 1929* lists Gardiner Winslow and Sylvia Johnson Curtis White [Sr.] as residing at *White Lodge* on West Shore Drive, Oyster Bay [Mill Neck], while the *Social Register, 1981* lists Mr. White as residing at *White Lodge*.
    He was the son of Henry Winslow and Fannie S. White of Flushing, Queens, and Smithtown.
    Sylvia Johnson Curtis White was the daughter of Thomas E. H. Curtis of Plainfield, NJ.
    The Whites' daughter Sylvia married William Bradford Harwood, Jr. of Flushing, Queens, and resided in Locust Valley. Their son Gardiner Winslow White, Jr. married Elizabet N. Shontz, the daughter of Harry Blaine Shontz of Roslyn, and resided in Oyster Bay. [*The New York Times* December 23, 1961, p. 23.]

White, Leonard Dalton, Jr. (1867-1963)

Occupation(s):   financier - partner, White and Blackwell (investment banking firm);
                  member, Rutter and Co. (investment banking firm)

Civic Activism: trustee, Jennie Clarkson Home for Children

Marriage(s):   1908 - Margaret Boyd

Listed in *Long Island Society Register, 1929*: yes
Address: Station Road, Great Neck
Acreage / map sources: on 1927 map (owned by White)
              3 acres / 1932 map (owned by M. White)
              3 acres / 1945 map (owned by M. White)
Name of estate: *The Spinneys*
Year of construction:
Style of architecture:
Architect(s):
Landscape architect(s):
House extant: unconfirmed
Historical notes:

  The *Long Island Society Register, 1929* lists Leonard D. and Margaret Boyd White [Jr.] as residing on Station Road, Great Neck, while the *Social Register, Summer 1932* lists the name of their estate as *The Spinneys*. Their estate adjoined the estate of his parents. The *Social Register, Summer 1945* lists the Whites' residence as *Coy Hill Farm,* Middletown Springs, VT, while the *Social Register New York, 1951* lists only Mr. White, then residing on School House Lane, Germantown, PA.
  Born in Manhattan, he was the son of Leonard D. and Mary G. Van Dusen White, Sr.

White, Leonard Dalton, Sr. (1833-1894)

Occupation(s):   financier - partner, White and Morris (investment banking firm);
                  trustee and secretary, Greenwich Savings Bank

Marriage(s):   Mary Gilbert Van Dusen

Listed in *Long Island Society Register, 1929*: yes
Address: Station Road, Great Neck
Acreage / map sources: on 1927 map (owned by White)
              5 acres / 1932 map (owned by M. G. White)
              4 acres / 1945 map (owned by M. G. White)
Name of estate:
Year of construction:
Style of architecture:
Architect(s):
Landscape architect(s):
House extant: unconfirmed
Historical notes:

  The *Long Island Society Register, 1929* lists Mary G. Van Dusen White as residing in Great Neck.
  The White's estate was next to that of their son Leonard Dalton White, Jr.

White, Rita Kohler (d. 1970)

Marriage(s):   1921-1970 - Julius A. White (d. 1974)

Listed in *Long Island Society Register, 1929*: yes
Address: Chicken Valley Road, Mill Neck
Acreage / map sources: not on 1927 or 1932 maps
                                       32 acres / 1946 map
Name of estate: *Glenby*
Year of construction: c. 1928
Style of architecture: Federal
Architect(s):   Carrere and Hastings designed the house
                                        (for Mrs. J. A. White)

Landscape architect(s):
House extant: unconfirmed
Historical notes:

    The house, originally named *Glenby,* was built by Mrs. Julius A. White.
    The *Long Island Society Register, 1929* lists Mrs. Julius A. White as residing at *Glenby* in Brookville [Mill Neck].
    She was the daughter of Charles Kohler, who resided at *Ramapo Farm* in Mahwah, NJ. Her sister Vera married Gustav Erbe, Jr., who resided in Lattingtown and, subsequently, Carroll Booth Alker, who resided in Lattingtown, Muttontown, and at *Ca Va* in Old Brookville.
    The Whites' daughter Dr. Rita White Mathews married Sidney Mathews.

White, Robert K., Sr.

Occupation(s):

Marriage(s):   Jane Sage

Listed in *Long Island Society Register, 1929*: no
Address: Cleft Road, Mill Neck
Acreage / map sources: not on 1927 map
                                       no acreage given on 1932 map (owned by J. A. White)
                                       14 acres / 1946 map (owned by R. K. White)
Name of estate:
Year of construction: 1936
Style of architecture: Colonial Revival
Architect(s):   Fuller and Dick designed the house
                                       (for R. K. White, Sr.)*

Landscape architect(s):
House extant: yes
Historical notes:

    The house was built by Robert K. White, Sr.
    *Fuller's partner Adolph M. Dick was the son of John Henry and Julia Theodora Mollenhauer Dick, who resided at *Allen Winden Farm* in Islip.

Whitehouse, James Norman (1858-1949)

Occupation(s):   financier -   partner, Whitehouse and Co. (stock brokerage firm)

Marriage(s):   1898-1949 - Vera Boarman
                                        - Civic Activism: national president, Women's Action Committee
                                            for Lasting Peace;
                                            chairman, New York State Suffragist Association

Listed in *Long Island Society Register, 1929*: no
Address: Wheatley Road, Upper Brookville
Acreage / map sources: not on 1927 map
                              no acreage given on 1932 map
                              17 acres / 1946 map
Name of estate: *Broadwood*
Year of construction: c. 1928
Style of architecture: Georgian
Architect(s):   William Lawrence Bottomley designed the house (for Whitehouse)
Landscape architect(s):
House extant: yes
Historical notes:

rear facade, 1930

    The house, originally named *Broadwood*, was built by James Norman Whitehouse.
    The *Directory of American Society New York State and the Metropolitan District, 1929* lists James Norman and Vera Boarman Whitehouse as residing at *Broadwood* in Brookville [Upper Brookville].
    He was the son of H. Remsen Whitehouse, who served as United States *Charge d'Affairs* in Rome, Italy.
    The estate was, subsequently, owned by Julian Hart Robertson, Jr.

Whitney, Charles Morse, Sr. (1848-1920)

Occupation(s):   attorney -   corporate

Marriage(s):   Emma S. Cornwell (d. 1922)

Listed in *Long Island Society Register, 1929*: no
Address: Route 25A, Centerport
Acreage / map sources: 1929 map illegible
                              not on 1931 map
                              22 acres / 1944 map
Name of estate:
Year of construction: 1870
Style of architecture: Italianate*
Architect(s):
Landscape architect(s):
House extant: no
Historical notes:

*main residence on left;
servants residence on right, c. 1912*

    The house was purchased in 1901 by Charles Morse Whitney, Sr., who remodeled and enlarged it.
    Whitney, a founder of the Mozart Sextet of Brooklyn, was residing at 1056 Fifth Avenue, NYC, at the time of his death.
    The Whitneys' daughter May married Herman Helms and resided in Manhattan.
    The Whitney house at 728 Fifth Avenue in Manhattan was sold in 1911 to Harry Payne Whitney. [*The New York Times* May 20, 1911, p. 18.]
    *The Centerport house was greatly modified over the years, becoming, first, a boarding house and, then, a series of restaurants, obscuring its original Italianate design. It is now the site of the Original Schooner Restaurant. The building which now houses the Mill Pond Inn was the Whitney servants' quarters.

Whitney, Cornelius Vanderbilt (1899-1992)

Occupation(s):	capitalist - a founder and chairman of board, Pan-American World Airline;
	co-producer, films *Gone With the Wind, Rebecca,* and *A Star is Born*;
	producer, *The Searchers**;
	chairman of board, Whitney Industries;
	founder, Marineland of Florida
	industrialist - a founder, Hudson Bay Mining and Smelting
	statesman - Assistant Secretary of the Air Force in the Truman admin., 1947-49;
	Under Secretary of Commerce in the Truman admin., 1949-50
	writer - *Lone and Level Sand* (autobiography); *Live a Year With a Millionaire,*
	1981; *High Peaks,* 1977; *The Owl Hoots Again; First Flights*
Civic Activism:	financed, maternity wing, Community Hospital, Glen Cove;
	a founder and board member, Saratoga Performing Arts Center, Saratoga, NY;
	board member, National Museum of Dance;
	trustee, Whitney Museum of American Art, NYC;
	trustee, American Museum of Natural History, NYC;
	a founder, Whitney Gallery of Western Art, Cody, WY;
	a founder, National Museum of Racing, Saratoga, NY;
	board member, Buffalo Bill Historic Foundation, Cody, WY
Marriage(s):	M/1 - 1923-1929 - Marie Norton (1903-1970)
	- merchant - Marie Harriman Art Gallery, NYC
	M/2 - 1931-1941 - Gwladys Crosby Hopkins (b. 1905)
	M/3 - 1941-1958 - Eleanor Searle (1915-2002)
	- entertainers and associated professions - concert and opera singer
	writer - *Invitation to Joy: A Personal Story,* 1971
	Civic Activism: founded, with her second husband Leonard Franklin
	McCollum, Sr., an Annual Eleanor McCollum
	Competition for young singers at the Houston
	Grand Opera
	M/4 - 1958-1992 - Marie Louise Schroeder (b. 1925)
	- entertainers and associated professions - actress

Listed in *Long Island Society Register, 1929*: yes
Address: Garvan – Whitney – Phipps Road, Old Westbury
Acreage / map sources: not listed separately on 1927 or 1932 maps; 19 acres / 1946 map
Name of estate: *Whitney House*
Year of construction: 1941
Style of architecture: Colonial Revival
Architect(s):   Delano and Aldrich designed the house (for C. V. Whitney)
Landscape architect(s):
Estate photographs can be found in the Nassau County Museum Collection filed under Old Westbury/Whitney.
House extant: yes
Historical notes:

   The *Long Island Society Register, 1929* lists Cornelius Vanderbilt and Marie Norton Whitney as residing in Old Westbury, while the *Social Register, Summer 1937* lists Cornelius V. and Gladys Hopkins Vanderbilt as residing in Old Westbury. The *Social Register New York, 1951* lists Mr. Whitney as residing at *Whitney House* in Old Westbury with his third wife Eleanor Searle Whitney.

   The estate is now part of Old Westbury Golf and Country Club. The house, which serves as the clubhouse, was built by Cornelius Vanderbilt Whitney on the foundation of his father's house which was demolished by the Whitney family in 1941.

   [See following entry for family information.]

   *The Searchers starred John Wayne and is said to have been Wayne's favorite film.

front facade, 1948

Whitney, Cornelius Vanderbilt (1899-1992)

Occupation(s):	capitalist - a founder and chairman of board, Pan-American World Airline;
	co-producer, films *Gone With the Wind, Rebecca,* and *A Star is Born*;
	producer, *The Searchers**;
	chairman of board, Whitney Industries;
	founder, Marineland of Florida
	industrialist - a founder, Hudson Bay Mining and Smelting
	statesman - Assistant Secretary of the Air Force in the Truman admin., 1947-49;
	Under Secretary of Commerce in the Truman admin., 1949-50
	writer - *Lone and Level Sand* (autobiography); *Live a Year With a Millionaire,*
	1981; *High Peaks,* 1977; *The Owl Hoots Again; First Flights*
Civic Activism:	*[See previous entry for detailed list.]*
Marriage(s):	M/1 - 1923-1929 - Marie Norton (1903-1970)
	- merchant - Marie Harriman Art Gallery, NYC
	M/2 - 1931-1941 - Gwladys Crosby Hopkins (b. 1905)
	M/3 - 1941-1958 - Eleanor Searle (1915-2002)
	- entertainers and associated professions - concert and opera singer
	writer - *Invitation to Joy: A Personal Story,* 1971
	Civic Activism: founded, with her second husband Leonard Franklin
	McCollum, Sr., an Annual Eleanor McCollum
	Competition for young singers at the Houston
	Grand Opera
	M/4 - 1958-1992 - Marie Louise Schroeder (b. 1925)
	- entertainers and associated professions - actress

Listed in *Long Island Society Register, 1929*: yes
Address: Mill Hill Road, Mill Neck
Acreage / map sources: not on 1927, 1932, or 1946 maps
Name of estate: *Oakley Court*
Year of construction: 1936-1937
Style of architecture: Tudor
Architect(s):   Henry Corse designed the house
                                               (for Dickerman)

Landscape architect(s):
House extant: yes
Historical notes:

front facade, 2004

    The house, originally named *Hillendale,* was built by Florence Calkin Dickerman.
    Alfred Gwynne Vanderbilt II purchased the estate in the 1950s, renaming it *Oakley Court.*
    Vanderbilt sold the estate to Whitney, who gave it to the Village of Mill Neck.
    The village sold the estate to Mrs. Dorothy M. Fordyce. Mrs. Fordyce gradually began selling off the estate's property for development.
    Vanderbilt, Whitney, and Fordyce called the estate *Oakley Court.*
    Cornelius Vanderbilt Whitney, known as "Sonny," was the son of Harry Payne and Gertrude Vanderbilt Whitney, who resided in Old Westbury. His sister Barbara married Barklie McKee Henry, Samuel Anderson Peck, and, subsequently, George William Headley III. Barbara resided in Old Westbury. His sister Flora married Roderick Tower and, later, George Macculloch Miller and resided at *French House* in Old Westbury.
    In the 1920s, Evan Burrows Fontaine sued Sonny alleging that he had secretly married her while he was an undergraduate at Yale University. She was found guilty of fraud and perjury.
    Marie Norton Whitney, subsequently, married William Averell Harriman, who resided in Old Westbury and in Sands Point. Cornelius and Marie Norton Whitney's son Harry married Alexandra Ewing and, subsequently, Andrea Wyatt. Their daughter Nancy married Edward Dennison Morgan III, C. Russell Hurd, Edwin Augustus Hurd, Jr., and Pierre Lutz. Cornelius and Gwladys Whitney's daughter Gail married Richard Cromwell.
    Eleanor Searle Whitney, subsequently, married Leonard Franklin McCollum, Sr. and resided in Houston. Cornelius and Eleanor Whitney's son Cornelius Searle Whitney married Kathleen Gerard and, subsequently, Sarah W. Cross.
    *The Searchers starred John Wayne and is said to have been Wayne's favorite film.

Whitney, Edward Farley (1852-1928)

Occupation(s):   financier-   partner, J. P. Morgan and Co. (now, J. P. Morgan Chase)
                                                 (investment banking firm), 1901-1911;
                                     partner, Jacob Rogers and Co., Boston
                                               (investment banking firm), 1871-1901

Marriage(s):   bachelor

Listed in *Long Island Society Register, 1929*: no
Address: Cove Neck Road, Cove Neck
Acreage / map sources: on c. 1922 map (owned by E. Whitney)
                                  on 1927 map (owned by F. C. Whitney
                                  not on 1932 or 1946 maps
Name of estate:
Year of construction:
Style of architecture: Colonial Revival
Architect(s):
Landscape architect(s):   Beatrix Farrand executed thirty-five drawings, including
                                  designs for driveway plantings, fountains, rose trellis,
                                  seats, arbor, walled flower garden, and an informal
                                  iris garden, 1906-1914 (for E. F. Whitney)
House extant: unconfirmed
Historical notes:

    The estate was, subsequently, owned by his niece Miss Margaret Sargent Whitney.
    The *Long Island Society Register, 1929* lists Miss Margaret Sargent Whitney as residing at *Ballygurge* in Cove Neck.

rear facade

Whitney, Eleanor Searle (1915-2002)

Occupation(s):	entertainers and associated professions - concert and opera singer
	writer - *Invitation to Joy: A Personal Story,* 1971
Civic Activism:	*

Marriage(s):   M/1 - 1941-1958 - Cornelius Vanderbilt Whitney (1899-1992)
- capitalist -   a founder and chairman of board, Pan-American
World Airline;
co-producer, motion pictures *Gone With the Wind,
Rebecca,* and *A Star is Born*;
producer, *The Searchers*;
chairman of board, Whitney Industries;
founder, Marineland of Florida
industrialist -   a founder, Hudson Bay Mining and Smelting
statesman - Assistant Secretary of the Air Force in the
Truman administration, 1947-1949;
Under Secretary of Commerce in the Truman
administration, 1949-1950
writer -   *Lone and Level Sand* (autobiography); *Live a Year With
a Millionaire,* 1981; *High Peaks,* 1977; *The Owl Hoots
Again*; *First Flights*
Civic Activism: financed, maternity wing, Community Hospital,
Glen Cove;
a founder and board member, Saratoga Performing
Arts Center, Saratoga, NY;
board member, National Museum of Dance;
trustee, Whitney Museum of American Art, NYC;
trustee, American Museum of Natural History, NYC;
a founder, Whitney Gallery of Western Art, Cody, WY;
a founder, National Museum of Racing, Saratoga, NY;
board member, Buffalo Bill Historic Foundation,
Cody, WY
M/2 - 1975 - Leonard Franklin McCollum, Sr.
- industrialist - chairman, Continental Oil (1902-1993)
financier -   chairman, Capital National Bank;
chairman, Federated Capital Corp.
Civic Activism: *

Listed in *Long Island Society Register, 1929*: no
Address: Feeks Lane, Lattingtown
Acreage / map sources: not on 1927, 1932, or 1946 maps
Name of estate:
Year of construction:
Style of architecture:
Architect(s):
Landscape architect(s):
House extant: unconfirmed
Historical notes:

The *Social Register New York, 1951* lists Cornelius Vanderbilt and Eleanor Searle Whitney as residing at *Whitney House* in Old Westbury. Both the *Social Register New York, 1959* and *1975* list Eleanor Searle Whitney as residing on Feeks Lane, Locust Valley [Lattingtown].

Cornelius Vanderbilt Whitney, known as "Sonny," was the son of Harry Payne and Gertrude Vanderbilt Whitney, who resided in Old Westbury. His sister Barbara married Barklie McKee Henry, Samuel Anderson Peck, and, subsequently, George William Headley III. Barbara resided in Old Westbury. His other sister Flora married Roderick Tower and, later, George Macculloch Miller and, also, resided in Old Westbury. Cornelius had previously been married to Marie Norton, Gwladys Crosby Hopkins, and, subsequently, married Marie Louise Schroeder.

Cornelius Vanderbilt and Eleanor Searle Whitney's son Cornelius Searle Whitney married Kathleen Gerard and, subsequently, Sarah W. Cross.

*Leonard Franklin and Eleanor Searle McCollum resided in Houston where they established the annual Eleanor McCollum Competition for young singers at the Houston Grand Opera.

Whitney, George, Sr. (1885-1963)

Occupation(s):
financier - chairman of the board, J. P. Morgan and Co. (now, J. P. Morgan Chase) (investment banking firm); a founder and partner, Markoe, Morgan & Whitney;
capitalist - director, New York Central Railroad; director, Consolidated Edison Co.
industrialist - director, Continental Oil Co.; director, Johns–Manville Corp.; director, Kennecott Copper Corp.; director, Pullman Inc.; director, Texas Gulf Sulphur Co.; member, finance committee, General Motors

Civic Activism:
attended Paris Peace Conference, 1919, as an advisor to the American delegation; board member, New York Doctors Hospital, NYC; trustee, Alfred P. Sloan Foundation; trustee, Memorial Sloan–Kettering Institute for Cancer Research, NYC

Marriage(s):
1914-1963 - Martha Beatrix Bacon (1890-1967)
  - Civic Activism: *

Listed in *Long Island Society Register, 1929*: yes
Address: I. U. Willets Road and Bacon Road, Old Westbury
Acreage / map sources: not listed separately on 1927 or 1932 maps; 11 acres / 1946 map
Name of estate: *Home Acres*
Year of construction: c. 1915
Style of architecture: 20th-century Eclectic
Architect(s): Delano and Aldrich designed the house (for G. Whitney, Sr.)
Builder: E. W. Howell Co.
Landscape architect(s):
House extant: yes
Historical notes:

The house, originally named *Home Acres*, was built by George Whitney, Sr. on *Old Acres,* the estate of his father-in-law Robert Bacon.

The *Long Island Society Register, 1929* lists George and Martha B. Bacon Whitney [Sr.] as residing in Westbury [Old Westbury], while the *Social Register, Summer 1932* lists the name of their estate as *Home Acres*. The *Social Register, Summer 1955* lists the Whitneys as continuing to reside in Old Westbury, while the *Social Register New York, 1956* lists their residence as 1107 Fifth Avenue, NYC. Mrs. Whitney was residing at the Manhattan address at the time of her death.

Martha Beatrix Bacon Whitney was the daughter of Robert and Martha Waldron Cowdin Bacon, who resided at *Old Acres* in Old Westbury.

*Mrs. Whitney's philanthropic activities included the New York Public Library, the Speedwell Society, the English Speaking Union, Nassau Hospital (now, Winthrop University Hospital), Mineola, and Planned Parenthood.

The Whitneys' son George Whitney, Jr. married Phyllis Stevenson, the daughter of Philip Stevenson who resided at *Meadow Spring* in Glen Cove. Their daughter Phyllis married William S. Rowe II, the son of John J. Rowe of Cincinnati, OH. Their daughter Elizabeth married George Parkman Denny, Jr. of Boston, MA. Their son Robert Bacon Whitney, Sr. married Adelaide Weld and resided in Old Westbury. Adelaide Weld was the daughter of Philip Balch Weld of Manhattan and Wareham, MA.

The Whitney estate was, subsequently, owned by Harry Glass.

rear facade

Whitney, Harry Payne (1872-1930)*

Occupation(s):	financier/capitalist/industrialist - director of two dozen companies including banks, transportation, and utility companies

Marriage(s):   1896-1930 - Gertrude Vanderbilt (1875-1942)
                                     - artist - sculptress
                                        writer - *A Love Affair,* 1984;
                                                   Walking the Dusk, 1932 (under the pseudonym, L. J. Webb)
                                        Civic Activism: woman's suffrage;
                                                   established and maintained a 225-bed hospital in
                                                   France during World War I;
                                                   founder in 1921, Whitney Museum of American
                                                   Art, NYC

Listed in *Long Island Society Register, 1929*: yes
Address: Garvan – Whitney – Phipps Road, Old Westbury
Acreage / map sources: on 1927 map (owned by H. P. Whitney)
                                      730 acres / 1932 map (owned by H. P. Whitney)
                                      474 acres / 1946 map (owned by Gertrude Vanderbilt Whitney)
Name of estate:
Year of construction: c. 1902
Style of architecture: Tudor / Queen Anne
Architect(s):   George A. Freeman designed the gymnasium and tables,
                                      1898-1899 (for W. C. Whitney)
                                   McKim, Mead and White designed the original house
                                      (for W. C. Whitney)
                                   Delano and Aldrich designed c. 1906 alterations to the house
                                      (for H. P. Whitney); 1913 artist studio (for G. V. Whitney)
Landscape architect(s):   Olmsted, 1895-1896 (for W. C. Whitney)
                                   Leavitt and Aldrich designed the artist studio gardens
                                      (for G. V. Whitney)
Estate photographs can be found in the Nassau County Museum Collection filed under Old Westbury/Whitney.
House extant: no; demolished in 1942**
Historical notes:

The house was built by William Collins Whitney.
*The estate was inherited by the Whitneys' son Harry Payne Whitney, who was baptized Henry Payne Whitney.
In c. 1906, he remodeled the house.
The *Long Island Society Register, 1929* lists Harry Payne and Gertrude Vanderbilt Whitney as residing in Old Westbury, while the *Social Register, Summer 1937* lists only Gertrude Vanderbilt Whitney as residing in Old Westbury.
She was the daughter of Cornelius and Alice Claypoole Gwynne Vanderbilt. During a vicious and much-publicized custody trial, it was to this estate that Gertrude brought Gloria Laura Vanderbilt ("Little Gloria"), the daughter of her brother Reginald Claypoole Vanderbilt and Gloria Laura Mercedes Morgan Vanderbilt.
Harry Payne and Gertrude Whitney's daughter Barbara married Barklie McKee Henry and resided in Old Westbury. Their daughter Flora married Roderick Tower and, later, George Macculloch Miller and, also, resided in Old Westbury. Their son Cornelius Vanderbilt Whitney resided at *Whitney House* in Old Westbury and *Oakley Court* in Mill Neck.
**The house was demolished by the Whitney family. Its stained-glass window designed by John LaFarge is now in the Philadelphia Museum of Fine Art. Cornelius Vanderbilt Whitney built his house on the foundation of the William C. Whitney house.
William C. Whitney's stables and a portion of the estate property are now part of New York Institute of Technology and Old Westbury Golf and Country Club.
Gertrude Whitney's artist studio became the office of the landscape architectural firm of Innocenti and Webel, after which it was converted into a private residence and owned by Thomas E. Le Boutillier III

rear facade, c. 1910

*Harry Payne Whitney's house,
side facade, c. 1912*

Whitney, Howard Frederic, II (1874-1927)

Occupation(s):	financier - partner, H. N. Whitney and Sons (stock brokerage firm); member, board of governors, New York Stock Exchange
	industrialist - director, National Biscuit Co.; director, Pyrene Manufacturing Co.
	publisher - director, McCall Corp.
Civic Activism :	president, United States Golf Association
Marriage(s):	1903-1927 - Louise D. Maxwell (1877-1958)

Listed in *Long Island Society Register, 1929*: yes
Address: Stewart Avenue and Whitney Circle, Glen Cove
Acreage / map sources: on 1927 map
not on 1932 map
18 acres / 1946 map
Name of estate: *Craigdarroch*
Year of construction: c. 1916
Style of architecture:
Architect(s): Howard Major designed the house (for H. F. Whitney II)
Landscape architect(s): Isabella Pendleton (for H. F. Whitney II)
House extant: no; demolished c. 1962
Historical notes:

The house, originally named *Craigdarroch,* was built by Howard Frederic Whitney II.

The *Brooklyn Blue Book and Long Island Society Register, 1918* and *1921* list Howard Frederic and Louise D. Maxwell Whitney [II] as residing at *Craigdarroch.* Both the *Long Island Society Register, 1929* and the *Social Register New York, 1957* list Louise D. Maxwell Whitney's residence as *Craigdarroch.*

Born in Brooklyn, Howard Frederic Whitney II was the son of Howard Frederic and Catherine Simpson Whitney, Sr.

Louise D. Maxwell Whitney was the daughter of John Rogers and Marie Louise Washburn Maxwell, Sr., who resided at *Maxwelton* in Glen Cove. Her brother John Roger Maxwell, Jr. married Lydia Biddle Clothier and also resided at *Maxwelton* as did her other brother Howard Washburn, Sr., who married Helen S. Young.

The Whitneys' son Howard Frederic Whitney III married Hope Richardson, the daughter of Courtland Richardson.

Whitney, John Hay (1904-1982)

Occupation(s):   capitalist - chairman of board, J. H. Whitney and Co.;
                                                          chairman of board, Whitney Communications;
                                                          chairman of board, Selznick International Pictures
                                      publisher - *New York Herald Tribune;*
                                                          chairman of board, *International Herald Tribune*
                                      diplomat - United States Ambassador to the Court of St. James in the
                                                          Eisenhower administration, 1956-1961
                                      financier - partner, Whitcom Investment Co.
Civic Activism: president of board, New York Hospital, NYC;
                                      member, Commission on Foreign Economic Policy, 1954;
                                      trustee, Saratoga Performing Arts Center, Saratoga, NY;
                                      a founder and co-chairman of board, North Shore Hospital, Manhasset;
                                      chairman of board, English Speaking Union;
                                      chairman of board, Whitney Museum of American Art, NYC;
                                      trustee, National Gallery, Washington, DC;
                                      founder in 1946 and chairman of board, John Hay Whitney Foundation;
                                      bequeathed twenty-five major works of art to the Whitney Museum of
                                              American Art, NYC, the National Portrait Gallery, Washington, DC,
                                              and Yale University Art Museum;
                                      donated $15 million to Yale University for student housing

Marriage(s):   M/1 - 1930-1940 - Mary Elizabeth Altemus (1904-1982)
                                      M/2 - 1942-1982 - Betsey Cushing (1908-1998)
                                              - Civic Activism: donated $8 million to Yale University Medical School;
                                                                          member of board, Whitney Museum of American Art,
                                                                                  NYC;
                                                                          member of board, John Hay Whitney Foundation;
                                                                          member of board, Association for Homemakers Service;
                                                                          bequeathed paintings, valued at $300 million, to the
                                                                                  Whitney Museum of American Art, NYC, and the
                                                                                  National Gallery, Washington, DC

Listed in *Long Island Society Register, 1929*: no
Address: between Community Drive and Shelter Rock Road, Manhasset
Acreage / map sources: on 1927 map; 558 acres / 1932 map; 519 acres / 1946 map
Name of estate: *Greentree*
Year of construction: 1903
Style of architecture: Dutch Colonial
Architect(s):   d'Hauteville and Cooper designed the house (for W. P. Whitney)
                                      Christopher Grant LaFarge** designed the boathouse, 1929 (for J. H. Whitney)
Landscape architect(s):   Guy Lowell designed the pergola, paths, fountain, and garden (for W. P. Whitney)
Estate photographs can be found in the Nassau County Museum Collection filed under Manhasset/Whitney.
House extant: yes
Historical notes:

   The house, originally named *Greentree,* was built by William Payne Whitney.
   John Hay Whitney, known as "Jock, "subsequently, inherited the estate from his parents William Payne and Helen Hay Whitney and continued to call it *Greentree.* His maternal grandfather John Hay was President Abraham Lincoln's private secretary, U. S. Ambassador to the Court of St. James, and Secretary of State in the administrations of Presidents William McKinley and Theodore Roosevelt. His paternal grandfather William Collins Whitney, who resided in Old Westbury, was Secretary of the Navy in President Grover Cleveland's administration.
   His sister Joan, who married Charles Shipman Payson, also resided in Manhasset.
   Mary Elizabeth Altemus Whitney subsequently married Dr. E. Cooper Person, Jr. and Richard Dwight Lunn. She later married Cloyce Joseph Tippet and continued to reside in Old Westbury.
   Betsey Cushing Whitney had previously been married to James Roosevelt, the son of President Franklin Delano and Mrs. Anna Eleanor Roosevelt Roosevelt. James' brother Franklin Delano Roosevelt, Jr. married Ethel du Pont and resided in Woodbury. Her sister Barbara married Stanley Grafton Mortimer, Jr. and, subsequently William S. Paley, residing with him at *Kiluna Farm* in North Hills. Her sister Mary was married to William Vincent Astor and resided at *Cloverly Manor* in Sands Point. Mary subsequently married James Whitney Fosburgh.
   **Christopher Grant LaFarge was the son of the famed stained-glass designer John LaFarge.

Whitney, Miss Margaret Sargent (d. 1963)

Marriage(s):   unmarried

Listed in *Long Island Society Register, 1929*: yes
Address: Cove Neck Road, Cove Neck
Acreage / map sources: on c. 1922 map (owned by E. Whitney)
                                  on 1927 map (owned by F. C. Whitney)
                                  not on 1932 or 1946 maps
Name of estate: *Ballygurge*
Year of construction:
Style of architecture:
Architect(s):
Landscape architect(s):   Beatrix Farrand executed thirty-five drawings, including
                                  designs for driveway plantings, fountains, rose trellis,
                                  seats, arbor, walled flower garden, and an informal
                                  iris garden, 1906-1914 (for E. F. Whitney)
House extant: unconfirmed
Historical notes:

Margaret Sargent Whitney inherited the estate from her uncle Edward Farley Whitney.
    The *Long Island Society Register, 1929* lists Miss Margaret Sargent Whitney as residing at *Ballygurge* in Cove Neck, while both the *Social Register, Summer 1932* and the *Social Register New York, 1964* list her residence as *Findings* in Millbrook, NY.

Whitney, Robert Bacon, Sr. (1916-1952)

Occupation(s):   financier -   assistant vice-president, J. P. Morgan and Co.
                                    (now, J. P. Morgan Chase) (investment banking firm)
Civic Activism: board member, Y.M.C.A. of Nassau and Suffolk Counties (a coordinating
                                    board headquartered at the Glen Cove Y.M.C.A.);
                                trustee, Nassau County chapter, Society for the Prevention of Cruelty
                                  to Children

Marriage(s):   1939-1952 - Adelaide Weld

Listed in *Long Island Society Register, 1929*: no
Address: Bacon Road, Old Westbury
Acreage / map sources: not listed separately on 1927 or 1932 maps
                                    11 acres / 1946 map
Name of estate:
Year of construction:
Style of architecture:
Architect(s):
Landscape architect(s):
House extant: unconfirmed
Historical notes:

The *Social Register New York, 1948* and *1952* list Robert B. and Adelaide Weld Whitney [Sr.] as residing on Bacon Road, Westbury [Old Westbury].
    He was the son of George and Martha Beatrix Bacon Whitney, Sr., who resided at *Home Acres* in Old Westbury. While walking along Hillside Avenue, opposite the Wheatley Hills Golf Club, Robert was struck by a car and killed.
    Adelaide Weld Whitney was the daughter of Philip Balch and Katharine Saltonstall Weld of Bay Shore. Her brother Philip married Anne Warren, the daughter of Samuel Dennis Warren of *Rockyhill Farm* in Essex, MA. Her sister Rose married Ian Baldwin, the son of Joseph Clark Baldwin, Jr. of Mt. Kisco, NY.
    The Whitneys' son Robert Bacon Whitney, Jr. married Louise Purcell Grassi, the daughter of Ettore Howard Anthony Grassi. Their daughter Hope married John Willard Lapsley, the son of Howard Lapsley of Princeton, NJ.
    The *Social Register New York, 1957* and *1967* list Adelaide Weld Whitney as having married James Knott and continuing to reside on Bacon Road, Old Westbury. The *Social Register New York, 1969* lists the Knotts as residing on Chicken Valley Road, Locust Valley.

Whitney, William Collins (1841-1904)

Occupation(s):   attorney -   corporate council for the City of New York
                         industrialist -   partner, Standard Oil Co. (which became Exxon Corp.)
                         capitalist -   Metropolitan Street Railroad Co.
                         statesman -   Secretary of the Navy in the Cleveland and Benjamin
                                          Harrison administrations

Marriage(s):   M/1 - 1869-1893 - Flora Payne (1842-1893)
                         M/2 - 1896-1899 - Edith Sybil May (c. 1859-1899)

Listed in *Long Island Society Register, 1929*: no
Address: Garvan – Whitney – Phipps Road, Old Westbury
Acreage / map sources: on 1927 map (owned by H. P. Whitney)
                         730 acres / 1932 map (owned by H. P. Whitney)
                         474 acres / 1946 map (owned by Gertrude Vanderbilt Whitney)
Name of estate:
Year of construction: c. 1902
Style of architecture: Tudor / Queen Anne
Architect(s):   George A. Freeman designed the gymnasium and stables, 1898-1899
                             (for W. C. Whitney)
                         McKim, Mead and White designed the original house
                             (for W. C. Whitney)
                         Delano and Aldrich designed c. 1906 alterations of the house
                             (for H. P. Whitney); 1913 artists studio (for G. V. Whitney)
Landscape architect(s): Olmsted, 1895-1896 (for W. C. Whitney)
                         Leavitt and Aldrich designed the artist studio gardens (for G. V. Whitney)
Estate photographs can be found in the Nassau County Museum Collection filed under Old Westbury/Whitney.
House extant: no; demolished in 1942*
Historical notes:

   The house was built by William Collins Whitney.
   He is reported to have been the largest property owner in the Commonwealth of Massachusetts. [Jerry E. Patterson, *The First Four Hundred: Mrs. Astor's New York in the Gilded Age* (New York: Rizzoli International Publ., Inc., 2000), p. 136.]
   Born in Conway, MA, William Collins Whitney was the son of Brigadier General James Scollay and Laurenda Collins Whitney. His sister Lillian married Charles Tracy Barney and resided in Old Westbury.
   Flora Payne Whitney was the daughter of Senator Henry B. Payne of Ohio.
   William Collins and Flora Payne Whitney were on Ward McAllister's "Four Hundred" list.
   Their daughter Dorothy married William Dickerman Straight and, then, Leonard Knight Elmhirst. She resided at *Elmhurst,* later called *Applegreen*, in Old Westbury.
   Whitney's second wife was the former Edith Sybil May Randolph, who, with her first husband English Captain Arthur Randolph, had resided in Douglaston, Queens. Her husband had died when their daughter Adelaide was thirteen and their son Arthur, known as Bertie, was eleven. Edith's father Dr. J. Frederick May was the physician who identified the body of John Wilkes Booth.
   The estate was inherited by the Whitneys' son Harry Payne Whitney, who married Gertrude Vanderbilt, the daughter of Cornelius and Alice Claypoole Gwynne Vanderbilt. In c. 1906, he remodeled the house.
   During a vicious and much-publicized custody trial, it was to this estate that Gertrude brought Gloria Laura Vanderbilt ("Little Gloria"), the daughter of her brother Reginald Claypoole Vanderbilt and Gloria Laura Mercedes Morgan Vanderbilt.
   *The house was demolished by the Whitney family. Its stained-glass window designed by John LaFarge is now in the Philadelphia Museum of Fine Art. Cornelius Vanderbilt Whitney built his house on the foundation of the William C. Whitney house.
   William C. Whitney's stables and a portion of the estate property are now part of New York Institute of Technology and Old Westbury Golf and Country Club.
   Gertrude Whitney's artist studio was converted into a private residence. It was owned by Thomas E. Le Boutillier III.

*LaFarge window from
Whitney estate, 1990*

Whitney, William Payne (1867-1927)

Occupation(s):	attorney
	capitalist - real estate - vice-president, Whitney Realty Co.
	industrialist - director, Northern Paper Co.
	financier - vice-president, Northern Finance Co.
Civic Activism:	trustee, New York Public Library, NYC;
	vice-president of board, Society of New York Hospitals;
	trustee, Metropolitan Museum of Art, NYC

Marriage(s):	1902-1927 - Helen Hay (1876-1944)

- writer - *Some Verses,* 1898; *The Little Boy Book,* 1900; *The Rose of Dawn* [poetry], 1901; *Sonnets and Songs,* 1905; *Verses For Jock and Joan,* 1905; *The Punch and Judy Book,* 1906; *Gypsy Verses,* 1907; *Bed-time Book,* 1907; *Herbs and Apples,* 1910

Listed in *Long Island Society Register, 1929*: yes
Address:	between Community Drive and Shelter Rock Road, Manhasset
Acreage / map sources:	on 1927 map; 558 acres / 1932 map; 519 acres / 1946 map
Name of estate:	*Greentree*
Year of construction:	1903
Style of architecture:	Dutch Colonial
Architect(s):	d'Hauteville and Cooper designed the house (for W. P. Whitney)
	Christopher Grant LaFarge designed the boathouse, 1929 (for J. H. Whitney)*
Landscape architect(s):	Guy Lowell designed the pergola, paths, fountain, and gardens (for W. P. Whitney)

Estate photographs can be found in the Nassau County Museum Collection filed under Manhasset/Whitney.
House extant: yes
Historical notes:

The house, originally named *Greentree,* was built by William Payne Whitney [aka Payne Whitney].

The Whitneys' son John inherited the estate at his father's death and continued to call it *Greentree.* Their daughter Joan, who owned the New York Mets baseball team, was married to Charles Shipman Payson of Manhasset.

*Christopher Grant LaFarge was the son of the famed stained-glass designer John LaFarge.

The 1906 Basket Vis–A–Vis, fabricated for William Payne Whitney by Brewster and Co. of New York, is in the carriage collection of The Long Island Museum of American Art, History, & Carriages in Stony Brook.

Helen Hay Whitney's cookery collection was donated to the New York Public Library.

Widener, George Dunstan, Jr. (1889-1971)

Occupation(s):	industrialist - director, Electric Storage Battery Co.
	financier - director, Provident National Bank of Philadelphia
Civic Activism:	chairman of board, Philadelphia Museum of Fine Arts;
	established the Widener Memorial School, for training of handicapped children

Marriage(s):	1917-1968 - Jessie Sloane (1884-1968)

Listed in *Long Island Society Register, 1929*: no
Address:	Valley Road, Old Westbury
Acreage / map sources:	not on 1927 map; no acreage given on 1932 map; 39 acres / 1946 map
Name of estate:	
Year of construction:	
Style of architecture:	
Architect(s):	
Landscape architect(s):	Olmsted, 1931 (for Widener)

House extant: unconfirmed
Historical notes:

Widener's father George Dunstan Widener, Sr. and his brother Harry Elkins Widener drowned on the *Titanic.* His grandfather Peter Arrell Widener, reportedly the richest man in Philadelphia, PA, was said to have built the largest transit empire in the country. His mother established the Widener Library at Harvard University.

Jessie Sloane Widener was the daughter of Henry T. and Jessie A. Robbins Sloane. She had previously been married to William Earle Dodge of Manhattan.

Will, Harold Henry (1889-1963)

Occupation(s):   industrialist - president, Will & Baumer Candle Co.
                                   writer - (under the pseudonym, Anthony Wilson): *Cat's Eye*;
                                             All is Contradiction; *La Balau*, 1941

Marriage(s):   M/1 - 1913-1918 - Katharine Hungerford (d. 1918)
                                 M/2 - Ada M. Cowan
                                 M/3 - Ruth Holthaus

Listed in *Long Island Society Register, 1929*: yes
Address: Willis Avenue and Glen Avenue, Roslyn
Acreage / map sources: on 1927 map; 11 acres / 1932 and 1946 maps
Name of estate: *Villa Marina*
Year of construction: 1920
Style of architecture: Italian Renaissance
Architect(s):   Warren and Clark designed
                                 the house (for Henderson)

Landscape architect(s):   Hatton and DeSuarez
                                 (for Henderson)
                                 Devereux Emmet designed
                                 the estate's golf course
                                 (for Henderson)
Estate photographs can be found in the Nassau County Museum
   Collection filed under Roslyn /Henderson.
House extant: yes
Historical notes:

side facade, 1920

    The house, originally named *Villa Marina*, was built by Frank C. Henderson.
    The estate was, subsequently, owned by Will, who continued to call it *Villa Marina*.
    Both the *Long Island Society Register, 1929* and the *Social Register, Summer 1937* list Harold H. and Ada Cowan Will as residing at *Villa Marina* in Roslyn.
    The *Social Register New York, 1948* lists Harold H. and Ruth H. Holthaus Will as residing on Hunt Lane, Manhasset.
    The Wills' daughter Kay married Robert S. Salant and resided in Locust Valley. Their daughter Jane married Robert Boggs and resided in Mill Neck.
    The estate is now the Pierce Country Day Camp and the Pierce Country Day School. Established in 1918, the Pierce Country Day Camp is the oldest day camp in the United States.

Willard, George L.

Occupation(s):   capitalist - director, Long Island Rail Road

Marriage(s):

Listed in *Long Island Society Register, 1929*: no
Address: Laurel Hollow Road, Laurel Hollow
Acreage / map sources: not on 1927, 1932, or 1946 maps
Name of estate: *Airslie*
Year of construction: c. 1806
Style of architecture: Shingle Farmhouse
Architect(s):
Landscape architect(s):   Olmsted designed landscaping
                                 (for J. M. de Forest)

House extant: yes
Historical notes:

front facade, 2004

    The house was built by William Jones.
    In 1855, it was owned by Willard, who called it *Airslie*.
    It was owned by Henry Wheeler de Forest and, subsequently, by his sister Julia Mary de Forest. Both continued to call it *Airslie*.
    In 1943, the house and seven acres were sold to the Cold Spring Harbor Laboratory for $10,000.

Willetts, William Prentice (1890-1964)

Occupation(s):   industrialist - president, Airology (manufacturers of three-dimensional
                                                weather trainers)
                                    financier - partner, White and Stanley (stock brokerage firm)
Civic Activism: trustee, Village of Roslyn, 1932-1936;
                                    *

Marriage(s):   1915-1964 - Christine Newhall Clark

Listed in *Long Island Society Register, 1929*: yes
Address: 175 Warner Avenue, Roslyn**
Acreage / map sources: 1927 map illegible
                                   not on 1932 or 1946 maps

Name of estate: *Homewood*
Year of construction: 1923
Style of architecture: Colonial Revival
Architect(s):
Landscape architect(s):
House extant: yes
Historical notes:

    The house was built by Charles Willis.

rear facade, 2004

    It was, subsequently, owned by William Prentice Willets.
    He was the son of Joseph C. and Emma C. Prentice
Willetts. His sister Amie married Samuel Roosevelt
Outerbridge and resided on Centre Island. His sister Marion, who married Ernest Cuyler Brower and, subsequently,
Ernest's brother George Ellsworth Brower, resided at *Locust Hill* in Roslyn.
    *Willetts donated the Willetts Memorial Meteorological Exhibit to the New York Hayden Planetarium in memory of
his son Joseph.
    **The house is now on the property of the Shibley Day Camp

---

Williams, Arthur (1868-1937)

Occupation(s):   capitalist - vice-president, New York Edison Co.;
                                              vice-president, Yonkers Electric Light and Power Co.
                    financier - president, New York Edison Savings & Loan Association;
                                              director, Metropolitan Life Insurance Co.
Civic Activism: director, Greater New York Area, Federal Food Administration during
                                    World War I;
                         first president, American Museum of Industrial Safety;
                         member, board of appeals, Village of Roslyn Harbor, 1931-1937

Marriage(s):   bachelor

Listed in *Long Island Society Register, 1929*: yes
Address: Glenwood Road, Glen Head
Acreage / map sources: not on 1927 map
                                     no acreage given on 1932 map
                                     not on 1946 map

Name of estate: *Brook Corners*
Year of construction: c. 1920
Style of architecture: Spanish Renaissance
Architect(s):
Landscape architect(s):
House extant: yes
Historical notes:

rear facade, 2004

    The house, originally named *Brook Corners,* was built by Arthur Williams.
    The house, which has been extensively modified, is now the Swan Club.

Williams, Arthur (1868-1937)

Occupation(s):   capitalist - vice-president, New York Edison Co.;
vice-president, Yonkers Electric Light and Power Co.
financier - president, New York Edison Savings & Loan Association;
director, Metropolitan Life Insurance Co.

Civic Activism: director, Greater New York Area, Federal Food Administration during
World War I;
first president, American Museum of Industrial Safety;
member, board of appeals, Village of Roslyn Harbor, 1931-1937

Marriage(s):   bachelor

Listed in *Long Island Society Register, 1929*: yes
Address: Bryant Avenue, Roslyn Harbor
Acreage / map sources: not on 1927, 1932, or 1946 maps
Name of estate: *Greenridge*
Year of construction: 1916
Style of architecture: Tudor
Architect(s):   Harold Victor Hartman designed
the house (for A. Williams)

Landscape architect(s):
House extant: yes
Historical notes:

front facade, 2004

    The house, originally named *Greenridge,* was built by Arthur Williams.
    The estate was owned by Joseph Lionel Seligman, Sr., who continued to call it *Greenridge,* and, subsequently, by Mead L. Briggs.

Williams, Douglas

Occupation(s):
Civic Activism: vice-president of board, Society for the Preservation of Long
Island Antiquities

Marriage(s):   1941 - Priscilla M. de Forest

Listed in *Long Island Society Register, 1929*: no
Address: Shore Road, Cold Spring Harbor
Acreage / map sources: not on 1927, 1932, or 1946 maps
Name of estate: *Wawapek*
Year of construction: 1898-1900
Style of architecture: Colonial Revival
Architect(s):   Grosvenor Atterbury designed the house (for R. W. de Forest)
J. Clinton Mackenzie designed the farm complex, c. 1900
(for R. W. de Forest)
Landscape architect(s):   Olmsted, 1910-1912 (for R. W. de Forest)

Estate photographs can be found in the Nassau County Museum Collection
   filed under Cold Spring Harbor/de Forest, Robert.
House extant: yes
Historical notes:

    The house, originally named *Wawapek,* was built by Robert Weeks de Forest.
    The estate was owned by Johnston de Forest and, subsequently, by Williams. Both Johnston de Forest and Williams continued to call it *Wawapek.*
    Douglas Williams is the son of Roger H. Williams of Manhattan and Saugatuck, CT.
    Priscilla M. de Forest Williams is the daughter of Johnston and Mary E. Ogden de Forest.
    The Williamses' daughter Priscilla married Columbia University art history professor Donald Harris Dwyer.
    The house is on The National Register of Historic Places.
    In 1996, a Tiffany window was removed from the house for exhibit. It is still in the family's possession.

Williams, Harrison (1873-1953)

Occupation(s):   capitalist -   president, North American Holding Co. (the company
controlled about one-sixth of all the public utilities
in the United States)

Marriage(s):   M/1 - 1900-1915 - Katharine Gordon Breed (d. 1915)
M/2 - 1926-1953 - Mona Strader (1899-1983)
[subsequently, Countess von Bismarck]
- Civic Activism: member, central council, Community Service
Society (formed by merger of Charity
Organization Society and Association
for Improving the Condition of the Poor);
member of board, New York Zoological
Society, NYC;
financed several of the society's expeditions

Listed in *Long Island Society Register, 1929*: yes
Address: Bayville Avenue, Bayville
Acreage / map sources: on 1927 map
175 acres / 1932 map
not on 1946 map
Name of estate: *Oak Point*
Year of construction: 1903
Style of architecture: Georgian Revival
Architect(s):   Babb, Cook and Willard designed the original house
(for W. S. Pierce II)
Delano and Aldrich designed 1926 alterations (for H. Williams)
Builder: E. W. Howell Co.
Landscape architect(s):   Beatrix Jones Farrand designed the willow garden, tiered rock wall
garden with Chinese lattice fencing, Cedar-of-Lebanon garden,
long arbor, lily-pond garden, and a pool garden, 1928-1929
(for H. Williams)
Olmsted, 1933 (for H. Williams)

Estate photographs can be found in the Nassau County Museum Collection filed under Bayville/Williams.
House extant: no; demolished in 1968*
Historical notes:

    The eighty-room house, originally named *Dunstable,* was built by Winslow Shelby Pierce II.
    In 1926, Harrison Williams, the son of Everett E. Williams of Avon, OH, purchased the estate for $750,000, renaming it *Oak Point*.
    In 1925, Mrs. Laura Merriam Curtis' engagement to Harrison Williams had been formally announced. She and her former husband James Feeman Curtis had resided at *Willowmere* in Roslyn. Just days after the announcement of her engagement to Williams, she remarried her former husband and returned to *Willowmere.*
    Prior to her marriage to Williams, Mona Strader Williams had been married to Harry Schlesinger and James Bush.
Her son Robert Schlesinger married the sister of movie actor Lex Barker, of *Tarzan* fame. Mona was subsequently married to Count Albrecht Edward von Bismarck, the grandson of Germany's "Iron Chancellor," and then to Count Umberto di Martini of Italy. She was a member of the Duke and Duchess of Windsor's parallel court. [*The New York Times* October 29, 2002, p. B11.]

    In the 1960s, Mona Strader Williams [von Bismarck] sold a portion of the estate property.
    *Von Bismarck demolished the house to reduce the estate's property taxes.

front facade

Williams, Rodney W. (1893-1984)

Occupation(s):	financier - partner, Tucker, Anthony and R. L. Day, Inc. (stock brokerage firm)
Marriage(s):	M/1 - 1918-1967 - Katherine Clark Culver
	M/2 - Barbara Slatter

Listed in *Long Island Society Register, 1929*: yes
Address: Frost Mill Road, Mill Neck
Acreage / map sources: on 1927 map; no acreage given on 1932 map; 11 acres / 1946 map
Name of estate: *Boxwood*
Year of construction:
Style of architecture:
Architect(s):
Landscape architect(s):
House extant: unconfirmed
Historical notes:

Rodney W. Williams was the son of George C. Williams of Baltimore, MD.

Katherine Clark Culver Williams was the daughter of Dr. Everett Mallory and Mary C. Clark Culver. Mary, Katherine's mother, subsequently married Marius DeBrabant and resided at *Plaisance* in Centerport.

Williams' daughter Louise married Charles Robert Devine and resided in Delray Beach, FL. His daughter Edith married Constantine Jerrold MacGuire, Jr. and resided in Manhattan.

Williams, Timothy Shaler (1862-1930)

Occupation(s):	capitalist - president, Brooklyn–Manhattan Transit Co.; secretary and treasurer, Brooklyn Heights Railway Co.
	journalist - correspondent and editor, *Commercial Advertiser*
Civic Activism:	board member, Huntington Hospital, Huntington; chairman of board, Long Island Biological Association
Marriage(s):	1895-1930 - Alice Williams (d. 1936)

Listed in *Long Island Society Register, 1929*: yes
Address: Beach Road and Camel Hollow Road, Lloyd Harbor
Acreage / map sources: no acreage given on 1929 map
                                                on 1931 map
                                                72 acres / 1944 and 1946 maps
Name of estate: *Shorelands*
Year of construction: c. 1903
Style of architecture: Tudor
Architect(s):   William H. Miller designed the house (for T. S. Williams)
Landscape architect(s):
House extant: yes
Historical notes:

The house, originally named *Shorelands*, was built by Timothy Shaler Williams.

The *Brooklyn Blue Book and Long Island Society Register, 1918* lists Timothy Shaler and Alice Williams Williams as residing at *Shorelands* in Huntington [Lloyd Harbor], while the *Brooklyn Blue Book and Long Island Society Register, 1921* lists their residence as Cold Spring Harbor [Lloyd Harbor]. The *Long Island Society Register, 1929* lists the Williamses as residing at *Shorelands* on West Neck [Beach Road and Camel Hollow Road], Huntington [Lloyd Harbor].

Alice Williams Williams was the daughter of Chauncey Pratt Williams of Albany, NY. She had previously been married to James B. Kelly of Albany, NY.

In 2003, the 14,000-square-foot carriage house, which has been converted into two apartments, and 2.5 acres were for sale. The asking price was $2.295 million; the taxes were $8,651.

Willis, Harold Satterlee (1892-1958)

Occupation(s):   financier -   vice-president, Stone and Webster Securities
                                   Corp. of New York

Marriage(s):   Anita Storm (d. 1972)

Listed in *Long Island Society Register, 1929*: yes
Address: Cow Lane, Kings Point
Acreage / map sources: not on 1927 map
                                   no acreage given on 1932 map
                                   no acreage given on 1946 map

Name of estate:
Year of construction:
Style of architecture:
Architect(s):
Landscape architect(s):
House extant: unconfirmed
Historical notes:

   The *Long Island Society Register, 1929* lists Harold S. and Anita Storm Willis as residing on East Shore Road, Great Neck [Kings Point], while both the *Social Register, Summer 1932* and the *Social Register New York, 1954* list their address as Cow Lane, Great Neck [Kings Point]. The *Social Register New York, 1956* lists the Willises as then residing on Westcott Road, Princeton, NJ.
   Harold and Anita Willis' daughter Anita married Leslie Langdon Vivian, Jr. Their daughter Adele married Stanley Knowlton, the son of Hugh Gilbert and Christine Stanley Knowlton, Sr. who resided in Muttontown.

Willock, William W., Sr. (d. 1939)

Occupation(s):   industrialist - director, Jones & Laughlin Steel Co.

Marriage(s):   1889-1939 - Alice B. Jones (d. 1939)

Listed in *Long Island Society Register, 1929*: yes
Address: Muttontown Road, Muttontown
Acreage / map sources: on 1927 map
                                   no acreage given on 1932 map
                                   200 acres / 1946 map

Name of estate: *Gladwood*
Year of construction:
Style of architecture:
Architect(s):
Landscape architect(s):
House extant: unconfirmed
Historical notes:

   Both the *Long Island Society Register, 1929* and the *Social Register, Summer 1937* list William W. and Alice B. Jones Willock [Sr.] as residing at *Gladwood* in Syosset [Muttontown].
   Alice Jones Willock was the daughter of Benjamin Franklin and Mary McMasters Jones, Sr., of Pittsburgh, PA. Her father was the president of Jones & Laughlin Steel Co. Her sister Elisabeth McMasters Jones Horne resided in Upper Brookville. Her other sister married Alexander Laughlin, Jr. Her brother Benjamin Franklin Jones, Jr. married Susan Dalzell and resided in Pittsburgh, PA.
   The Willocks' son William W. Willock, Jr. married Adelaide Ingebert and resided in Manhattan.

Willys, John North (1873-1935)

Occupation(s): industrialist - founder, Willys–Overland Automobile Co.;
         founder, Elmira Arms Co., Inc. *[still extant]*
        diplomat - United States Ambassador to Poland, 1930-1932
Civic Activism: chairman, War Camp Community Recreation Fund during World War I

Marriage(s): M/1 - 1897-1934 - Isabel Van Wie (d. 1945)
      M/2 - 1934-1935 - Florence Dingler

Listed in *Long Island Society Register, 1929*: yes
Address: Centre Island Road, Centre Island
Acreage / map sources: on 1927 map
      64 acres / 1932 map
      not on 1946 map
Name of estate: *Northcliff*
Year of construction: c. 1910
Style of architecture: Federal
Architect(s): Hoppin and Koen
      designed the house
      (for O. G. Smith)
Landscape architect(s): Ralph Weinrichter
      (for O. G. Smith)

front facade

Estate photographs can be found in the Nassau County Museum
 Collection filed under Centre Island/Smith.
House extant: no; demolished c. 1940
Historical notes:

 The house, originally named *Shoremonde,* was built by Ormond Gerald Smith.
 The estate was owned by Willys, who called it *Northcliff,* and, subsequently, by E. LeRoux.
 Born in Canandaigua, NY, John North Willys was the son of David Smith and Lydia North Willys.

Wilson, Charles Porter (d. 1929)

Occupation(s): merchant - chairman, western division, Great Atlantic and Pacific
         Tea Co. (grocery store chain)

Marriage(s): Irene B. *[unable to confirm maiden name]*

Listed in *Long Island Society Register, 1929*: no
Address: Mill Hill Road, Mill Neck
Acreage / map sources: not on 1927 or 1946 maps
      no acreage given on 1932 map (name misspelled as Mrs. Proctor)
Name of estate:
Year of construction: c. 1928
Style of architecture: Tudor
Architect(s): Charles Mansfield Hart designed the house (for Wilson)
Builder: E. W. Howell Co.
Landscape architect(s):

front facade

Estate photographs can be found in the Nassau County Museum
 Collection filed under Mill Neck/Wilson.
House extant: yes
Historical notes:

 The house was built by Charles Porter Wilson.
 His brother Robert resided in Garden City. His sister Miss
Rhea Wilson resided in Great Neck as did his sister Lydia C.
Hearsey.
 The estate was owned by Chester Linwood Dane, Sr., who
called it *Linwood,* and, subsequently by Ernest P. Wanner.

Wing, S. Bryce (b. 1890)

Occupation(s):   sportsman -   prominent in steeplechase and hunting

Marriage(s):   M/1 - 1915-1930 - Marie Tailer
                                   M/2 - 1931-1937 - Maude Arden Kennedy (1893-1937)
                                   M/3 - 1939 - Frances Bonsal

Listed in *Long Island Society Register, 1929*: yes
Address: Red Ground Road, Old Westbury
Acreage / map sources: on 1927 map; 7 acres / 1932 and 1946 maps
Name of estate: *Twin Oaks*
Year of construction:
Style of architecture:
Architect(s):
Landscape architect(s):
House extant: unconfirmed
Historical notes:

    S. Bryce Wing was the son of L. Stuart Wing, Sr., who also resided at *Twin Oaks* in Old Westbury.
    Marie Tailer Wing was the daughter of J. Lee Tailer. She subsequently married H. Granger Gaither and resided in Old Westbury.
    S. Bryce and Marie Tailer Wing's daughter Margaret married Dion Kerr, Jr. of Warrenton, VA.
    Maude Arden Kennedy Wing was the daughter of Mrs. H. Van Rensselaer Kennedy, who resided at *Three Oaks* in Hempstead. She had previously been married to Frederic Winston and, then, to Malcolm Stevenson, Sr., with whom she resided at *Two Maple Farm* in Old Westbury.
    Frances Bonsal Wing was the daughter of Leigh Bonsal of Baltimore, MD. She had previously been married to Garret Ellis Winants. Her sister Mary married Frederick T. Segerman and resided in East Norwich.

Winmill, Robert Campbell (1883-1957)

Occupation(s):   financier -   partner, Gude, Winmill and Co. (stock brokerage firm);
                                                 director, American Eagle Fire Insurance Co.;
                                                 director, Fidelity–Phenix Fire Insurance Co.
                                   shipping -   director, American–Hawaiian Steamship Co.

Marriage(s):   1913-1957 - Viola Townsend (1891-1975)
                                       - Civic Activism: *

Listed in *Long Island Society Register, 1929*: yes
Address: Frost Mill Road, Mill Neck
Acreage / map sources: on 1927 map; no acreage given on 1932 map; not on 1946 map
Name of estate: *Borradil Farm*
Year of construction:
Style of architecture:
Architect(s):   William Lawrence Bottomley designed 1915 alterations
                                       (for Townsend); later, alterations (for Winmill)
Landscape architect(s):
Estate photographs can be found in the Nassau County Museum Collection filed under Mill Neck/Winmill.
House extant: unconfirmed
Historical notes:

    Robert Campbell Winmill was the subsequent owner of the James Mulford Townsend II estate.
    Both the *Long Island Society Register, 1929* and the *Social Register, Summer 1937* list Robert Campbell and Viola Townsend Winmill as residing at *Borradil Farm* in Mill Neck.
    She was the daughter of John Allen and Viola Hawkins Townsend, who resided at *Forest Edge Farm* in Lattingtown.
    *In 1968, Mrs. Winmill donated her 150 horse carriages to the Westmoreland Davis Foundation at Morven Park, Leesburg, VA. [*The New York Times* September 1, 1975, p. 18.]
    The Winmills' daughter Virginia, who married Robert H. Radsch, the son of Richard M. Radsch of Appleton, WI, resided in Mill Neck. Their daughter Viola married Randolph Gramm Duffey, the son of Harry J. Duffey of Middleburg, VA. Their daughter Josephine married John Page Austin, the son of Chellis A. Austin, and resided in Berkeley, CA. Their son Allen, a pilot killed in action in Burma during World War II, was married to Dorothy Ball of Houston, TX.

Winslow, Edward (1845-1905)

Occupation(s):   financier - partner, Winslow, Lanier and Co. (investment banking firm)
                                        industrialist - treasurer, S. John Typobar Co.
                                        capitalist - real estate - vice-president, Breevort Real Estate Co.

Marriage(s):   Emma Sweetser

Listed in *Long Island Society Register, 1929*: no
Address: West Shore Road, Kings Point
Acreage / map sources: on 1906 map
                                          not on 1927, 1932, or 1946 maps
Name of estate:
Year of construction:
Style of architecture:
Architect(s):   McKim, Mead and White designed 1887-1889 alterations
                                        (for Winslow)
Landscape architect(s):
House extant: yes
Historical notes:

    Born in Poughkeepsie, NY, Edward Winslow as the son of James Winslow, a founder of Winslow, Lanier and Co.

Winter, Keyes, Sr. (1878-1960)

Occupation(s):   attorney - judge - President Justice of the New York City
                                          Municipal Court;
                                  New York State Assistant Attorney General
                politician - Republican leader, Manhattan's "Silk Stocking"
                                  District, 1927-1933

Marriage(s):   1907-1957 - Marie Caroline Mosle (1881-1957)

Listed in *Long Island Society Register, 1929*: yes
Address: South Woods Road, Woodbury
Acreage / map sources: on 1927 map
                                            no acreage given on 1932 map
                                          12 acres / 1946 map
Name of estate: *Hiver Rough*
Year of construction:
Style of architecture:
Architect(s):
Landscape architect(s):
House extant: unconfirmed
Historical notes:

    Both the *Long Island Society Register, 1929* and the *Social Register, Summer 1951* list Keyes and Marie C. Mosle Winter [Sr.] as residing at *Hiver Rough* in Syosset [Woodbury], while the *Social Register New York, 1959* lists the address as South Woods Road, Syosset [Woodbury].
    Marie Caroline Mosle Winter was the daughter of George and Caroline D. Mosle.
    The Winters' son John married Helen Brainard Cutler, the daughter of Ralph Dennis Cutler of West Hartford, CT. Their son Henry married Liberty Dick, the daughter of Evans R. Dick of Boston, MA.

Winters, Albert C. (1921-1987)

Occupation(s):   inventor -   adjustable glass cube display lighting fixture
                                                  industrialist - president, Manhattan Store Interiors, Inc.
                                                  interior designer - designed store interiors for department stores

Marriage(s):   Sandra *[unable to confirm maiden name]*

Listed in *Long Island Society Register, 1929*: no
Address: Feeks Lane and Factory Mill Pond Lane, Mill Neck
Acreage / map sources: not on 1927, 1932, or 1946 maps
Name of estate:
Year of construction: c. 1916
Style of architecture: Tudor
Architect(s):   Kenneth Murchinson designed the house (for Tully)
Landscape architect(s):   Harold A. Capan (for Tully)
House extant: yes
Historical notes:

     The house, originally named *Almar,* was built by John William Tully.
     The estate was, subsequently, owned by Winter.

Winthrop, Beekman, II (1874-1940)

Occupation(s):   capitalist - vice-president, Cayuga & Susquehanna Railroad Co.
                                                  diplomat - private secretary to, then chairman of the Philippine Commission,
                                                                 William Howard Taft, during the Theodore Roosevelt admin.;
                                                                 Assistant Executive Secretary of the Philippines, 1901, appointed by,
                                                                 then Governor of the Philippine Islands, William Howard Taft
                                                  Governor of Puerto Rico during the Theodore Roosevelt admin.
                                                                 1904-07
                                                  financier - partner, Robert Winthrop & Co. (investment banking firm);
                                                    director, National City Bank;
                                                     director, City Bank Farmers Trust Co.;
                                                    director, International Banking Corp.
                                              attorney - judge - Court of First Instance of the Philippines, appointed in
                                                               1903 by, then Governor of the Philippine Islands
                                                               William Howard Taft
                                              statesman -   Assistant Secretary of Treasury during the Theodore Roosevelt
                                                     admin., 1907;
                                              Assistant Secretary of Navy during the Taft admin., 1909

Marriage(s):   1903-1928 - Melza Riggs Wood (d. 1928)

Listed in *Long Island Society Register, 1929*: yes
Address: Post Road, Old Westbury
Acreage / map sources: on 1927 map (owned by Beekman Winthrop)
                                 no acreage given on 1932 map (owned by Beekman Winthrop)
                                 241 acres / 1946 map (owned by G. L. Winthrop)
Name of estate: *Groton Farms*
Year of construction: 1897-1902
Style of architecture: Colonial Revival
Architect(s):   McKim, Mead and White designed the house and stables (for R. D. Winthrop)
Landscape architect(s):
House extant: no; demolished in 1948
Historical notes:

     The house, originally named *Groton Farms,* was built by Robert Dudley Winthrop.
     Beekman Winthrop II was the son of Robert and Kate Wilson Winthrop and a descendent of John Winthrop.
     Melza Riggs Wood Winthrop was the daughter of John Dunn and Alice Riggs Wood of Manhattan.
     The estate was, subsequently, owned by his brothers Beekman Winthrop II, who continued to call it *Groton Farms,*
and, then, by Grenville Lindall Winthrop. Part of the estate is now the Glen Oaks Club.

Winthrop, Bronson (1863-1911)

Occupation(s):	attorney -	partner, Winthrop and Stimson (later, Winthrop, Stimson, Putnam and Roberts)
	financier -	director, Bank of Manhattan Co.;
		director, American Surety Co.;
		director, Fiduciary Trust Co.;
		trustee, Union Square Savings Banks

Marriage(s):   bachelor

Listed in *Long Island Society Register, 1929*: yes
Address: Muttontown Road, Muttontown
Acreage / map sources: on 1927 map
                                341 acres / 1932 map
                                315 acres / 1946 map
Name of estate:
Year of construction: 1903-1904
Style of architecture: Federal
Architect(s):   Delano and Aldrich designed the house (for B. Winthrop)
Landscape architect(s):
Estate photographs can be found in the Nassau County Museum Collection filed under Muttontown/Winthrop.
House extant: yes
Historical notes:

The house was built by Bronson Winthrop.
In 1911, Egerton Leigh Winthrop, Jr. took over the estate, when his brother Bronson built another house on adjoining property. Egerton called his estate *Muttontown Meadows*.
After Winthrop's death, the estate was owned by Elisha Walker, who renamed it *Les Pommiers*, and, subsequently in 1953, by Lansdell Kisner Christie.
In 1969, Nassau County acquired the estate and renamed it *Nassau Hall*. The estate is now part of Nassau County's Muttontown Preserve.

Winthrop, Bronson (1863-1911)

Occupation(s):	attorney -	partner, Winthrop and Stimson (later, Winthrop, Stimson, Putnam and Roberts)
	financier -	director, Bank of Manhattan Co.;
		director, American Surety Co.;
		director, Fiduciary Trust Co.;
		trustee, Union Square Savings Banks

Marriage(s):   bachelor

Listed in *Long Island Society Register, 1929*: yes
Address: Jericho – Oyster Bay Road, Muttontown
Acreage / map sources: not on 1927, 1932, or 1946 maps
Name of estate:
Year of construction: c. 1920
Style of architecture: Modified Neo-Georgian
Architect(s):   Delano and Aldrich designed the house (for B. Winthrop)
Landscape architect(s):   Delano and Aldrich, Ferruccio Vitale, and Olmsted jointly
                                designed landscaping (for Griscom)
House extant: no; demolished in 1938 after a fire which destroyed the house
Historical notes:

The house was built by Bronson Winthrop.
Winthrop had previously built a house on property which adjoins the site of this c. 1920 house.
This estate was, subsequently, owned by Lloyd Carpenter Griscom, who called it *Huntover Lodge*.

Winthrop, Egerton Leigh, Jr. (1862-1926)

Occupation(s):	attorney - partner, Winthrop and Stimson (later, Winthrop, Stimson, Putnam and Roberts)*
	capitalist - real estate - director, Real Property Investing Co.; director, New York Cab Co.
Civic Activism:	Commissioner of New York City Schools, 1905; president, Board of Education, NYC, 1906-1913; president, Legal Aid Society, NYC; director, Athletic League, New York City Public Schools
Marriage(s):	1890-1926 - Emmeline D. Heckscher (1874-1948)
	- Civic Activism: woman's suffrage - third vice-president, The Equal Franchise Society; Manhattan chairman, Committee on Volunteers, Mayor's Committee of Women on National Defense during World War I; board member, Mulberry Community House

Listed in *Long Island Society Register, 1929*: yes
Address: Muttontown Road, Muttontown
Acreage / map sources: on c. 1922 map (owned by Egerton Winthrop)
                                                 on 1927 map (owned by E. Winthrop)
                                                 no acreage on 1932 map (owned by E. Winthrop)
                                                 not on 1946 map
Name of estate: *Muttontown Meadows*
Year of construction: 1903-1904
Style of architecture: Federal
Architect(s):   Delano and Aldrich designed the house (for E. L. Winthrop, Jr.)
Landscape architect(s):
Estate photographs can be found in the Nassau County Museum Collection filed under Muttontown/Winthrop.
House extant: yes
Historical notes:

The house was built by Bronson Winthrop. Egerton Leigh Winthrop, Jr. took over the estate in 1911 when his brother Bronson built another house on adjoining property. Egerton called his estate *Muttontown Meadows.*

*Egerton was appointed guardian of John Jacob Astor VI, whose father John Jacob Astor IV had drowned on the *Titanic.*

The *Long Island Society Register, 1929* lists Emmeline D. Heckscher Winthrop as residing at *Huttontown [Muttontown] Meadows* in Syosset [Muttontown]. The *Social Register New York, 1948* lists Mrs. Winthrop's residence as 1115 Fifth Avenue, NYC.

The Winthrops' daughter Muriel married Richard DeBlois Boardman of Boston, MA, and, subsequently, Harold Aymar Sands, the son of William H. Sands.

In 1937, the estate was purchased by Elisha Walker, who renamed it *Les Pommiers,* and, subsequently in 1953, by Lansdell Kisner Christie.

In 1969, Nassau County acquired the estate and renamed it *Nassau Hall.* The estate is now part of Nassau County's Muttontown Preserve.

front facade, 1998

Winthrop, Grenville Lindall (1865-1943)

Occupation(s):	attorney - partner, Ludlow, Philips and Winthrop
Civic Activism:	president, board of directors, Lenox Library Association, Lenox, MA;
	funded restoration, Congregational Church and Academy Building, Lenox, MA;
	purchased and donated top of Bald Head Mountain for preserve, Lenox, MA;
	bequeathed his art collection to Harvard University, Cambridge, MA
Marriage(s):	1892 - Mary Tallmadge Trevor

Listed in *Long Island Society Register, 1929*: no
Address: Post Road, Old Westbury
Acreage / map sources: on 1927 map (owned by Beekman Winthrop)
    no acreage given on 1932 map (owned by Beekman Winthrop)
    241 acres / 1946 map (owned by G. L. Winthrop)
Name of estate:
Year of construction: 1897-1902
Style of architecture: Colonial Revival
Architect(s): McKim, Mead and White designed the house and stables
    (for R. D. Winthrop)
Landscape architect(s):
House extant: no; demolished in 1948
Historical notes:

The house, originally named *Groton Farms,* was built by Robert Dudley Winthrop.
Grenville Lindall Winthrop was the son of Robert and Kate Wilson Winthrop and a descendent of John Winthrop.
Mary Tallmadge Trevor Winthrop was the daughter of John B. Trevor of Yonkers, NY.
Their daughters Emily and Kate eloped together. Emily married Corey Lucien Miles, the family chauffeur. Her sister Kate married Darwin Spurr Morse, a former electrician on their Lenox, MA, estate.
The Long Island estate was, subsequently, owned by Robert's brothers Beekman Winthrop II, who continued to call it *Groton Farms,* and, then, by Grenville Lindall Winthrop.
Part of the estate is now the Glen Oaks Club.

Winthrop, Henry Rogers (1876-1958)

Occupation(s):	capitalist - director, Long Island Rail Road;
	director, Loew's Inc. (holding company for MGM Studio)
	financier - director, United States and Foreign Securities Corp.;
	partner, Harris, Winthrop and Co. (stock brokerage firm);
	governor, New York Stock Exchange, 1935-1938
Civic Activism:	president of board, New York Genealogical and Biographical Society;
	director, Metropolitan Opera Association, NYC;
	director, Italy Society
Marriage(s):	1905 -1941 - Alice Woodward Babcock (d. 1941)

Listed in *Long Island Society Register, 1929*: yes
Address: Jericho Turnpike, Woodbury
Acreage / map sources: on 1927 map; no acreage given on 1932 map; 338 acres / 1946 map
Name of estate: *East Woods*
Year of construction: c. 1910
Style of architecture: Georgian Revival
Architect(s): d'Hauteville and Cooper designed the house (for H. R. Winthrop)
Landscape architect(s): Guy Lowell designed landscaping (for H. R. Winthrop)
House extant: no
Historical notes:

The house, originally named *East Woods,* was built by Henry Rogers Winthrop.
He was the son of Buchanan Winthrop.
Alice Woodward Babcock Winthrop was the daughter of Henry Dennison and Mary Woodward Babcock, Sr., who resided in Mill Neck.
The Winthrops' daughter Alice married Robert Gardiner Payne, the son of William T. Payne.

Winthrop, Robert, II (1904-1999)

Occupation(s):	financier - partner, Robert Winthrop and Co. (investment banking firm); director, First National City Bank of New York; director, National Re-insurance Co.; trustee, Seaman's Bank of Savings, NYC; industrialist - director, Austral Oil
Civic Activism:	president of board, Nassau Hospital (now, Winthrop University Hospital), Mineola*; trustee, Winthrop University Hospital, Mineola*; trustee, Presbyterian Hospital (now, Columbia–Presbyterian Medical Center), NYC; trustee, New York Hospital, NYC; trustee, Village of Old Westbury; established chair, Harvard Medical School, Harvard University, Cambridge, MA; founded Robert Winthrop Scholarship Fund, Harvard University, Cambridge, MA; trustee, Wildlife Conservation Fund; president of board, North American Wildlife Foundation; trustee, New York Zoological Society, NYC; commissioner, Long Island Parks Commission; trustee, C. W. Post College of Long Island University, Brookville; president, board of trustees, Greenvale School, Greenvale; treasurer, Cooper Union College, NYC; treasurer, Foxcroft School, Middleburg, VA; trustee, Jericho Public Library, Jericho
Marriage(s):	M/1 - 1928-1941 - Theodora Ayer (1906-1996) M/2 - 1942-1985 - Margaret Stone (d. 1985) M/3 - 1988-1999 - Floreine J. Nelson

Listed in *Long Island Society Register, 1929*: no
Address: Post Road, Old Westbury
Acreage / map sources: on 1927 map (owned by Beekman Winthrop)
                                 no acreage given on 1932 map (owned by Beekman Winthrop)
                                 45 acres / 1946 map (owned by R. Winthrop)
Name of estate: *Groton Place*
Year of construction: 1932
Style of architecture: Georgian
Architect(s):   Henry Renwick Sedgwick designed the house (for R. Winthrop II)
Landscape architect(s):
House extant: yes
Historical notes:

The house, originally named *Groton Place,* was built by Robert Winthrop II.

Born in Boston, MA, Robert Winthrop II was the son of Frederic and Dorothy Amory Winthrop. He was a descendent of John Winthrop, the first governor of the Massachusetts Bay Colony.

Theodora Ayer Winthrop was the daughter of Charles Fanning Ayer of Boston, MA. She subsequently married Dr. Archibald Cary Randolph and resided at *Oakley Farm* in Upperville, VA.

Robert and Theodora Ayer Winthrop II's daughter Cornelia married Edward S. Bonnie, the son of Sevier Bonnie of Louisville, KY. Their daughter Theodora married Thomas L. Higginson, the son of James Jackson Higginson and, subsequently, Bruce Hooton, with whom she resided in Upper Brookville. Their daughter Elizabeth married Francis Ellsworth Baker, Jr. of Cold Spring Harbor, Herbert Scott Sneed of Manhattan, and, subsequently, Malcolm Pennington Ripley, the son of Henry B. H. Ripley of Manhattan. The Ripleys resided in Upperville, VA.

Both the *Social Register, Summer 1946* and the *Social Register New York, 1964* list Robert and Margaret Stone Winthrop [II] as residing at *Groton Place* in Westbury [Old Westbury].

Margaret Stone Winthrop was the daughter of Charles Augustus and Mary A. Leonard Stone, Sr., who resided at *Solana* in Matinecock. She had previously been married to R. Colgate Vernon Mann, the son of Samuel Vernon and Helen Colgate Mann, Sr., who resided at *Grove Point* in Kings Point.

The *Social Register, 1989* and *1996* list Robert and Floreine J. Nelson Winthrop [II] as residing at *Groton Place*, Old Westbury, while the *Social Register, 1997* and *1999* list their residence as Piping Rock Road, Upper Brookville.

*In 1985, Nassau Hospital changed its name to Winthrop University Hospital in honor of Robert Winthrop II, who for many years had served on its board.

In 1997, he sold the house to Luis Emilio Rinaldini and a portion of the estate's property for a housing development.

Winthrop, Robert Dudley (1861-1912)

Occupation(s):   financier -   member, Robert Winthrop and Co. (investment banking firm);
                                                director, Nassau County Trust Co.
                       capitalist - director, Nassau Light & Power Co.;
                                                  director, Deer Range Construction Co.

Marriage(s):

Listed in *Long Island Society Register, 1929*: no
Address: Post Road, Old Westbury
Acreage / map sources: on 1927 map (owned by Beekman Winthrop)
                                 no acreage given on 1932 map (owned by Beekman Winthrop)
                                 241 acres / 1946 map (owned by G. L. Winthrop)
Name of estate: *Groton Farms*
Year of construction: 1897-1902
Style of architecture: Colonial Revival
Architect(s):   McKim, Mead and White designed
                                 the house and stables
                                 (for R. D. Winthrop)

Landscape architect(s):
House extant: no; demolished in 1948
Historical notes: *rear facade*

The house, originally named *Groton Farms,* was built by Robert Dudley Winthrop.

He was the son of Robert and Kate Wilson Winthrop and a descendent of John Winthrop, the first governor of the Massachusetts Bay Colony.

The estate was, subsequently, owned by his brothers Beekman Winthrop II, who continued to call it *Groton Farms,* and, then, by Grenville Lindall Winthrop.

Part of the estate is now the Glen Oaks Club.

Wood, Chalmers, Jr. (1883-1952)

Occupation(s):   financier -   a founder and partner, Johnson, Wood and Rogers (stock
                                                  brokerage firm)
                                           member, Board of Governors, New York Stock Exchange, 1922-29

Marriage(s):   M/1 - 1916-1924 - Katherine Benedict Turnbull
                                  M/2 - 1924-1950 - Ruby R. Pope (d. 1950)
                                      - interior designer

Listed in *Long Island Society Register, 1929*: yes
Address: South Woods Road, Woodbury
Acreage / map sources: on 1927 map
                                   no acreage given on 1932 map
                                   43 acres / 1946 map
Name of estate: *Little Ipswich*
Year of construction: 1927
Style of architecture: Classical Revival
Architect(s):   Delano and Aldrich designed the house   *front facade, 1933*
                                 (for C. Wood, Jr.)

Landscape architect(s):
Estate photographs can be found in the Nassau County Museum Collection filed under Syosset/Wood.
House extant: no; demolished c. 1995
Historical notes:

The house, originally named *Little Ipswich,* was built by Chalmers Wood, Jr.

Both the *Long Island Society Register, 1929* and the *Social Register, Summer 1946* list Chalmers and Ruby R. Pope Wood [Jr.] as residing at *Little Ipswich* in Syosset [Woodbury].

He was the son of Chalmers and Ellen Cotton Smith Wood [Sr.] of Manhattan. His brother The Rev William Lawrence Wood married Laura Cass Canfield, the daughter of Augustus Cass and Josephine Houghteling Canfield, who resided at *Cassleigh* in North Hills.

Wood, Willis Delano (1872-1957)

Occupation(s): financier - governor, New York Stock Exchange, 1910-1928;
a founder and partner, Ladd, Wood and King;
a founder and partner, Wood, Low and Co.;
a founder and partner, Wood, Walker and Co.;
trustee, Title Guaranty & Trust Co.;
director, Fidelity Casualty Co.;
director, Fidelity–Phenix Fire Insurance Co.
industrialist - director, Corn Refining Co.
capitalist - director, New York City Omnibus Corp.;
director, Western Pacific Railroad Corp.

Civic Activism: trustee, Vassar College, Poughkeepsie, NY;
trustee, Union Theological Seminary, NYC;
trustee, Y.M.C.A. of Greater New York

Marriage(s): 1905-1857 - Anna E. Matheson

Listed in *Long Island Society Register, 1929*: yes
Address: Fort Hill Lane, Lloyd Harbor
Acreage / map sources: no acreage given on 1929 map (owned by Matheson)
on 1931 map (owned by Wood)
295 acres / 1944 map (owned by Wood)
Name of estate: *Fort Hill House*
Year of construction: 1900
Style of architecture: Tudor
Architect(s): Boring and Tilton designed the 1900 Tudor house
(for Matheson)
J. Clinton Mackenzie designed the c. 1910 garage and
gatehouse (for Matheson)
Landscape architect(s): Charles Wellford Leavitt and Sons (for Alden)
J. Clinton Mackenzie designed the formal garden, terrace,
brick paths, pergola, fountain with bronze fish sculpture
by Augustus Saint-Gaudens, c. 1910 (for Matheson)
Ellen Biddle Shipman and Olmsted jointly designed
landscaping (for W. D. Wood)*

House extant: yes
Historical notes:

Anne Coleman Alden built the 1878 Queen Anne house.
In 1900, she sold the estate to William John Matheson, who immediately commissioned Boring and Tilton to transform the house into a Tudor Revival.
After his death in 1930, the estate was inherited by his daughter Anna and son-in-law Willis Delano Wood.
The *Brooklyn Blue Book and Long Island Society Register, 1918* and *1921* list Willis Delano and Anna E. Matheson Wood as residing at [Joseph] *Lloyd Manor* in Huntington [Lloyd Harbor]. The *Long Island Society Register, 1929* also lists the Woods as residing at [Joseph] *Lloyd Manor* in Huntington [Lloyd Harbor]. The *Social Register, Summer 1932* and *1958* list their residence as *Fort Hill House* in Lloyd Neck [Lloyd Harbor], while the *Social Register, 1981* lists only Mrs. Wood as continuing to reside at *Fort Hill House*.
Born in Brooklyn, Willis Delano Wood was the son of Cornelius Delano and Helen Ogden Wood.
*According to the Shipman records, she did the landscape design for Olmsted.
George W. Campbell purchased the estate in 1992 and restored the house in 1993-1994.
The house is on The National Register of Historic Places.

Fort Hill House

882

Woods, Ward Wilson, Jr. (d. 1942)

Occupation(s):   financier - managing director, Lehman Brothers, Kuhn, Loeb and Co.
                                         (investment banking firm);
                                     partner, Lazard, Freres and Co. (investment banking firm);
                                     president, Bessemer Securities Corp. [Phipps' family
                                         financial trust, now open to public investment];

Civic Activism: trustee, Boys Club of New York;
                            vice-chairman, Asia Society, NYC;
                            governor, The Nature Conservancy

Marriage(s):   Priscilla Bacon

Listed in *Long Island Society Register, 1929*: no
Address: Old Tappan Road, Lattingtown
Acreage / map sources: not on 1927, 1932, or 1946 maps
Name of estate:
Year of construction: 1924
Style of architecture: Georgian Revival
Architect(s):   Carrere and Hastings designed the house
                                (for L. B. Van Ingen, Sr.)
Landscape architect(s):
Estate photographs can be found in the Nassau County Museum Collection filed under Glen Cove/Van Ingen.
House extant: yes
Historical notes:

   The house, originally named *Preference*, was built by Lawrence Bell Van Ingen, Sr.
   According to the *Social Register, Summer 1950*, Harriet Pratt Van Ingen subsequently married Donald Fairfax Bush,
Jr. and resided with him at *Preference*.
   The estate was also owned by Lawrence Bell Van Ingen, Jr., who continued to call it *Preference*, and, subsequently, by
Woods.

Woodside, Joel David

Occupation(s):   industrialist - manufacturer

Marriage(s):   Maude Dorsey

Listed in *Long Island Society Register, 1929*: yes
Address: Red Spring Lane, Glen Cove
Acreage / map sources: 1927 map illegible
                            not on 1932 or 1946 maps
Name of estate: *Villa D'Orsay*
Year of construction:
Style of architecture:
Architect(s):
Landscape architect(s):
House extant: unconfirmed
Historical notes:

   Both the *Long Island Society Register, 1929* and the *Social Register New York, 1933* list J. David and Maude Dorsey
Woodside as residing at *Villa D'Orsay* on Red Spring Lane, Glen Cove, while the *Social Register, Summer 1937* lists the
Woodsides as residing in Highlands, NC. *The Social Register New York, 1948* and *1959* list Mrs. Woodside's address as
Cedarcliff Road, Biltmore [Asheville], NC.

Woodward, William, Jr. (1920-1955)

Occupation(s):   financier - trustee, Hanover Bank
                                                president, Turner Halsey Co.;
                                                director, Continental Insurance Co. of New York
industrialist - director, United Shoe Co.

Marriage(s):   1943-1955 - Angeline Luceil Crowell (1922-1975)
                                              (aka Ann Eden Crowell)
                            - entertainers and associated professions - radio actress;
                                                          Powers magazine model

Listed in *Long Island Society Register, 1929*: no
Address: Pond Place, Oyster Bay Cove
Acreage / map sources: not on 1927, 1932, or 1946 maps
Name of estate: *The Playhouse*
Year of construction:
Style of architecture: Norman Revival
Architect(s):   James W. O'Connor designed the addition of
                                          the pool, playhouse, and tennis court complex,
                                          c. 1928 (for McCann)
Landscape architect(s):
House extant: yes
Historical notes:

    The *Social Register, Summer 1945* lists William and Ann E. Crowell Woodward, Jr. as residing at *Taylor Cottage* on Annandale Road, Newport, RI. The *Social Register, Summer 1951* lists them as residing at *The Playhouse* in Oyster Bay.
    Their Oyster Bay Cove house was the former music conservatory of the Charles Edward Francis McCann estate.
    William Woodward, Jr., who owned the famous racing horse *Nashua*, was the son of William and Elsie Ogden Cryder Woodward II, who resided at *Enfield Chase* in Brookville. He inherited Belair stables in Maryland from his father. His sister Elizabeth married John Teele Pratt, Jr. and resided in Glen Cove.
    On October 30, 1955, Ann Eden Crowell Woodward mistook her husband William for a prowler in *The Playhouse* and shot him in the head at close range with both barrels of a twelve-gauge shotgun. Truman Capote's novel *Answered Prayers* was based on the Woodward killing as was Dominick Dunne's novel *The Two Mrs. Grenvilles*, from which the 1987 film by the same name was adapted.
    The *Social Register, Summer 1963* lists Mrs. Woodward as continuing to reside at *The Playhouse*, while the *Social Register New York, 1975* lists her residence as 1133 Fifth Avenue, NYC. She committed suicide in her Fifth Avenue, NYC, home not long after she had seen the manuscript for Capote's novel.
    The Playhouse is now owned by the religious order of the Society of Pius X.

side facade, The Playhouse, 1936

William Woodward Jr.'s, house,
The Playhouse, 2004

Woodward, William, II (1876-1953)

Occupation(s):

attorney
financier - president, Central Hanover Bank;
            director, Continental Insurance Co. of New York;
            director, Federal Reserve Board*
industrialist - director, United Shoe Co.;
            director, New Jersey Zinc Co.
diplomat - secretary to the United States Ambassador to the Court of
            St. James, Joseph H. Choate

Marriage(s):

1904-1953 - Elsie Ogden Cryder (1882-1981)
  - Civic Activism: major benefactor, New York Hospital, NYC;
            donated Woodward Wing, Baltimore Museum
            of Art, Baltimore, MD

Listed in *Long Island Society Register, 1929*: no
Address: Cedar Swamp Road, Brookville
Acreage / map sources: not on 1927 map
                              62 acres / 1932 map (owned by W. Woodward)
                              46 acres / 1946 map (owned by Elsie Woodward)
Name of estate: *Enfield Chase*
Year of construction:
Style of architecture: Georgian Revival
Architect(s):
Landscape architect(s):
House extant: unconfirmed
Historical notes:

   The fifty-three-acre estate was previously owned by Duncan Argyle Holmes. In 1930, the Holmes' estate plus additional acreage was purchased by Mrs. Woodward. The estate consisted of the main house, which had five family and guest bedrooms, six servant bedrooms, six bathrooms, a gardener's cottage, a garage with living quarters, and stables for eight horses. [*The New York Times* February 5, 1930, p. 23.]
   The *Social Register, Summer 1945* lists William and Elsie O. Cryder Woodward [II] as residing at *Enfield Chase* in Brookville. The *Social Register, Summer 1951* lists the Woodwards as continuing to reside in Brookville.
   At age thirteen, William Woodward II inherited his father's interest in the Bank of Hanover and inherited a further one-half interest in the bank at the death of his bachelor uncle James Woodward, who had become William's guardian after the early death of his father. William eventually became one of the 150 richest men in the United States. His Uncle James also bequeathed him the 3,000-acre *Belair Farm*. The oldest thoroughbred stud farm in America, it had been started by the first governor of Maryland and visited by Benjamin Franklin. It was the home of Triple Crown winners *Gallant Fox* and *Omaha*.
   *Woodward was one of the original directors of the Federal Reserve Bank. From 1927-1929 he was president of the New York Clearing House.
   Elsie Ogden Cryder Woodward was one of triplets born to Duncan and Elizabeth Callander Ogden Cryder. She was named for her Ogden ancestors, her mother, and for Elizabethtown, NJ, to which her ancestors had moved after abandoning hundreds of acres, which they had owned, in Shinnecock, saying that they did not approve of the way the Shinnecock Indians were being treated. Elsie's father was a founder of the Shinnecock Golf Club.
   The Woodwards' son William Woodward, Jr. resided at *The Playhouse* in Oyster Bay Cove. Their daughter Elizabeth married John Teel Pratt, Jr. and resided in Glen Cove.

Woolley, Daniel P. (1884-1960)

Occupation(s):	politician - New York City Commissioner of Markets in the LaGuardia administration
	advertising executive - president, Austrian Chamber of Commerce of the U. S. A., Inc.
	industrialist - vice-president and general manager, Standard Brands (food manufacturers and distributors)
Civic Activism:	regional director, Office of Price Administration, 1943-1945; vice-chairman, New York Committee, American Overseas Aid, United Nations Appeal for Children
Marriage(s):	M/1 - Miriam W. Starr
	M/2 - Ethel Yerkes (1899-1970)

Listed in *Long Island Society Register, 1929*: yes
Address: Overlook Road and Skunks Misery Road, Lattingtown
Acreage / map sources: not on 1927 map
no acreage given on 1932 map
10 acres / 1946 map
Name of estate: *Wooldon*
Year of construction: c. 1925
Style of architecture: Georgian Revival
Architect(s): Bradley Delehanty designed the house (for Woolley)
Landscape architect(s):
House extant: yes
Historical notes:

The house, originally named *Wooldon*, was built by Daniel P. Woolley.

The *Long Island Society Register, 1929* lists Daniel P. Woolley as residing on Overlook Road, Locust Valley [Lattingtown].

Miriam W. Starr Woolley was from Akron, OH. She subsequently married Bertram G. Work, Jr., whose parents resided at *Oak Knoll* in Mill Neck.

The *Social Register, Summer 1937* and *1945* list Daniel P. and Ethel Yerkes Woolley as residing at *Wooldon* on Overlook Road, Locust Valley [Lattingtown], while both the *Social Register, Summer 1946* and *1951* list their residence as *Swift Water Point* in Fineview, NY. The *Social Register, Summer 1954* lists them as residing in Edgartown, MA. The *Social Register New York, 1956* lists the Woolleys' address as Allison Road, Miami Beach, FL, while the *Social Register New York, 1967* lists only Mrs. Woolley as continuing to reside at the Miami Beach address.

Ethel Yerkes Woolley had previously been married to Robert B. Gardner, Sr.

front / side facade, 2004

Woolworth, Frank Winfield (1852-1919)

Occupation(s):	merchant - founder, president, and chairman of board, F. W. Woolworth Co. ("five and ten" stores)*
	financier - director, Irving National Bank of New York; director, Irving Trust Co.
	capitalist - real estate - president, Broadway Park Place Co. (owned Woolworth Building, NYC, and other Manhattan properties)
Civic Activism:	director, Pennsylvania Society
Marriage(s):	1878-1919 - Jennie Creighton (1853-1924)

Listed in *Long Island Society Register, 1929*: no
Address: Crescent Beach Road, Glen Cove
Acreage / map sources: on 1927 map; not on 1932 or 1946 maps
Name of estate: *Winfield Hall*
Year of construction: 1916-1917
Style of architecture: elements of Italian and French Renaissance
Architect(s):   Charles Pierrepont Henry Gilbert designed the 1899 house and stables (for Humphreys); designed the 1916 house (for Woolworth)
Landscape architect(s):   Brinley and Holbrook (for Woolworth)
Estate photographs can be found in the Nassau County Museum Collection filed under Glen Cove/Woolworth.
House extant: yes
Historical notes:

   The first house on the site, built by Dr. Alexander Crombie Humphreys, was purchased by Emmet Queen in 1907. Woolworth purchased the estate from Queen in 1914 and named it *Winfield Hall*. In 1916, the house was destroyed by fire. The present house, built in 1916-1917 by Woolworth, was also called *Winfield Hall*.
   Born in Rodman, NY, he was the son of John Hubbell and Fanny McBrier Woolworth.
   Jennie Creighton Woolworth was the daughter of Thomas Creighton of Picton, Ontario, Canada.
   The Woolworths' daughters, Helena married Charles Edward Francis McCann and resided at *Sunken Orchard* in Oyster Bay Cove; Jessie married James Paul Donahue, Sr., and resided at *Wooldon Manor* in Southampton; Edna married Franklyn Laws Hutton and resided in Bay Shore. In 1917 Edna, dressed in a white *charmeuse* evening gown, committed suicide in her room at the Hotel Plaza by taking an overdose of strychnine crystals. [C. David Heymann, *Poor Little Rich Girl: The Life and Legends of Barbara Hutton* (Secaucus, NJ: Lyle Stuart, Inc., 1984) p. 15.]
   In 1925, Charles Edward Francis McCann purchased the estate from the other Woolworth heirs for $395,000. The McCanns never resided at *Winfield Hall*; they continued to reside at their Oyster Bay Cove estate *Sunken Orchard*.
   In 1929, the estate was purchased from McCann by Richard Samuel Reynolds, Sr.
   Reynolds sold the estate to Grace Downs School, a business school for girls.
   In 1976, a group of businessmen purchased the estate and leased it to Pall Corporation, which uses it as a conference center.
   In 2003, the house, which is on The National Register of Historic Places, was for sale. The asking price was $20 million. [*Newsday* April 18, 2003, p. C2.]
   *In 1996 F. W. Woolworth Company closed all its stores.

front facade, 1991

Work, Bertram G., Sr. (1868-1927)

Occupation(s):   industrialist - president, Goodrich Rubber Co.*
                             financier - trustee, Equitable Trust Co.

Marriage(s):   Marion Sawyer (d. 1923)

Listed in *Long Island Society Register, 1929*: yes
Address: Cleft Road, Mill Neck
Acreage / map sources: on 1927 map; no acreage given on 1932 map; 17 acres / 1946 map
Name of estate: *Oak Knoll*
Year of construction: 1916
Style of architecture: Palladian
Architect(s):   Delano and Aldrich designed the house (for Work)
Landscape architect(s):   Olmsted (for Work)
Estate photographs can be found in the Nassau County Museum Collection filed under Oyster Bay/Work.
House extant: yes
Historical notes:

   The house, originally named *Oak Knoll,* was built by Bertram G. Work, Sr.
   The *Long Island Society Register, 1929* lists Bertram and Miriam W. Starr Work [Sr.] as residing at *Oak Knoll* on Cliff Road, Oyster Bay [Mill Neck].
   *His father Alanson Work was a founder of B. F. Goodrich Rubber Co.
   The Works' son Bertram G. Work, Jr. married Miriam W. Starr of Akron, OH, who had previously been married to Daniel P. Woolley and resided at *Wooldon* in Lattingtown. The younger Work subsequently married Pauline Heyward.

Wright, Boykin Cabell, Sr. (1891-1956)

Occupation(s):   attorney -   partner, Shearman, Sterling and Wright
                             industrialist - director, Georgia-Pacific Corp.;
                                              director, Corning Glass Works, Corning, NY
                             capitalist - director, City Omnibus Corp.;
                                           director, Fifth Avenue Coach Lines, Inc.;
                                           director, Gray Line Motor Tours, Inc.
                             publisher - director, Augusta Newspapers, Inc.
Civic Activism: American secretary, Supreme Economic Council, Paris Peace
                                  Conference, 1919;
                             board member, Memorial Center for Cancer and Allied Diseases, Nassau
                                  Hospital, (now, Winthrop University Hospital), Mineola;
                             board member, Beekman–Downtown Hospital (which was formed by the
                                  merger of Beekman Street Hospital and Downtown Hospital), NYC;
                             trustee, John and Mary R. Markle Foundation

Marriage(s):   1926-1947 - Marian Harriman (1894-1947)

Listed in *Long Island Society Register, 1929*: yes
Address: East Norwich Road, Jericho
Acreage / map sources: not on 1927 map; 15 acres / 1932 and 1946 maps
Name of estate: *Rolling Field*
Year of construction:
Style of architecture:
Architect(s):
Landscape architect(s):
House extant: unconfirmed
Historical notes:

   The *Social Register, Summer 1950* lists the name of Wright's estate as *Rolling Field.*
   Marian Harriman Wright was the daughter of Joseph Wright and Augusta Barney Harriman, who resided at *Avondale Farms* in Brookville.
   The Wrights' son Boykin Cabell Wright, Jr. married Nancy Runyon.

Wright, Wilkinson de Forest, Sr. (1872-1953)

Occupation(s):   industrialist - secretary and treasurer, Wright Underwear Co.
                                                         of New York

Marriage(s):   _____ Higenham

Listed in *Long Island Society Register, 1929*: yes
Address: Cedar Lane, Sands Point
Acreage / map sources: on 1906 map; not on 1927, 1932, or 1946 maps
Name of estate: *Deephaven*
Year of construction: c. 1900
Style of architecture: Neo-Tudor
Architect(s):   James Brite designed the house (for W. de F. Wright, Sr.)
Landscape architect(s):
House extant: yes
Historical notes:

   The fifteen-room house with six master bedrooms, originally named *Deephaven,* was built by Wilkinson de Forest Wright, Sr.

   The *Long Island Society Register, 1929* lists Wilkinson de Forest Wright [Sr.] as residing at *Deephaven* in Sands Point. Both the *Social Register New York, 1933* and *1953* list his residence as 277 Park Avenue, NYC.

   He was the son of Solomon Wright.

   The Wrights' daughter Emily married Robert Cunningham Myles of Manhattan.

   The estate was, subsequently, owned by K. M. Goldman.

Wyckoff, Richard Demille (b. 1873)

Occupation(s):   financier - stockbroker
                                            publisher - publisher and editor, *Magazine of Wall Street*
                                            writer - *Studies in Tape Reading,* 1909;
                                                         How I Trade and Invest in Stocks and Bonds, 1920

Marriage(s):   1913 - Cecelia Gertrude Shere (1888-1966)
                                              - publisher - director, president, and treasurer, Ticker Publications
                                                         Co. (publishers of *Magazine of Wall Street*)
                                                 journalist - regular contributor and managing editor
                                                         under the pseudonym Charles Benedict*
                                            Civic Activism: member, Child Welfare Committee of America;
                                                         board member, Academy of Political Science;
                                                         board member, American Women's Association

Listed in *Long Island Society Register, 1929*: yes
Address: West Shore Road, Kings Point
Acreage / map sources: not on 1927 map; 10 acres / 1932 and 1946 maps
Name of estate: *Twin Lindens*
Year of construction: c. 1920
Style of architecture: Mediterranean Villa
Architect(s):   Chester A. Patterson designed the house (for W. Wyckoff)
Landscape architect(s):   Clarence Fowler (for W. Wyckoff)
House extant: yes
Historical notes:

   The house, originally named *Twin Lindens,* was built by Walter Wyckoff.

   The estate was, subsequently, owned by Richard Demille Wyckoff, who continued to call it *Twin Lindens.*

   The *Long Island Society Register, 1929* lists Mrs. Richard D. Wyckoff as residing on Bayview Avenue [West Shore Road], Great Neck [Kings Point].

   *Cecelia Shere Wyckoff's pseudonym, Charles Benedict, was also the name of her father-in-law and, subsequently, of her son. Born in Detroit, MI, she was the daughter of Jacob and Anna Edelsohn Shere.

Wyckoff, Walter

Occupation(s):   publisher - financial information

Marriage(s):

Listed in *Long Island Society Register, 1929*: no
Address: West Shore Road, Kings Point
Acreage / map sources: not on 1927 map
                               10 acres / 1932 and 1946 maps
Name of estate: *Twin Lindens*
Year of construction: c. 1920
Style of architecture: Mediterranean Villa
Architect(s):   Chester A. Patterson designed the house
                               (for W. Wyckoff)
Landscape architect(s):   Clarence Fowler (for W. Wyckoff)
House extant: yes
Historical notes:

    The house, originally named *Twin Lindens*, was built by Walter Wyckoff.
    The estate was, subsequently, owned by Richard Demille Wyckoff, who continued to call it *Twin Lindens*.

Twin Lindens, front facade

Wylie, Herbert George (1867-1956)

Occupation(s):   industrialist - vice-president and general manager, Mexican
                                  Petroleum Co., Ltd. and its subsidiaries;
                                  director, British Mexican Petroleum Co., Ltd.
                     capitalist - president, Caloric Co. (distributor of petroleum in Brazil);
                                  vice-president, Pan American Petroleum & Transport Co.

Marriage(s):   1920 - Amelia Crane Brown

Listed in *Long Island Society Register, 1929*: no
Address: Kings Point Road, Kings Point
Acreage / map sources: not on 1927, 1932, or 1946 maps
Name of estate:
Year of construction: c. 1920
Style of architecture: Federal
Architect(s):
Landscape architect(s):
House extant: no
Historical notes:

    The house was built by Herbert George Wylie.
    The estate was owned by the Syosset Corporation and, subsequently, by Percy K. Hudson.

Young, Edward Lewis (1862-1940)

Occupation(s):	financier - director, First National Bank of Jersey City
	industrialist - founder, E. L. Young Coal Co.

Marriage(s):   Sibyl Eager (d. 1934)

Listed in *Long Island Society Register, 1929*: yes
Address: Duck Pond Road, Glen Cove
Acreage / map sources: on 1927 map; not on 1932 or 1946 maps
Name of estate: *Meadow Farm*
Year of construction: c. 1918
Style of architecture: Neo-Colonial
Architect(s):   Davis, McGrath, and Keissling designed the house
                                     (for E. L. Young)

Landscape architect(s):   Ferruccio Vitale (for E. L. Young)
House extant: yes
Historical notes:

The house, originally named *Meadow Farm,* was built by Edward Lewis Young.

Edward L. Young is listed in *Polk's Glen Cove Directory, 1923-1924* at this address.

The *Long Island Society Register, 1929* lists Edward L. and Sibyl Eager Young as residing on Duck Pond Road, Glen Cove, while the *Social Register New York, 1933* lists their residence as 810 Fifth Avenue, NYC.

He was the son of Edward F. C. Young of Jersey City, NJ.

Meadow Farm,
garage and farm complex, c. 1918

Young, Otto S.

Occupation(s):	financier - president, Otto S. Young Insurance Co.
	Civic Activism: mayor, Village of Lake Success

Marriage(s):

Listed in *Long Island Society Register, 1929*: no
Address: Old Field Lane, Lake Success
Acreage / map sources: on 1927 map; 10 acres / 1932 map; not on 1946 map
Name of estate:
Year of construction:
Style of architecture:
Architect(s):   Charles Mansfield Hart designed the house
                                     (for O. S. Young)

Landscape architect(s):
House extant: unconfirmed
Historical notes:

The house was built by Otto S. Young.

In 1934 the Youngs' daughter Dorothy married Guy Oakley Simons, Jr. of Great Neck.

Young, Thomas F.

Occupation(s):   merchant

Marriage(s):

Listed in *Long Island Society Register, 1929*: no
Address: Oyster Bay Cove Road, Oyster Bay Cove
Acreage / map sources: not on 1927, 1932, or 1946 maps
Name of estate: *Elmwood*
Year of construction: c. 1863
Style of architecture: Colonial Revival
Architect(s):
Landscape architect(s):
Estate photographs can be found in the Nassau County Museum
   Collection filed under Oyster Bay/Tiffany, Charles Lewis II
House extant: yes
Historical notes:

Elmwood, front facade, c. 1970

   The house, originally named *Elmwood,* was built by Thomas F. Young.
   The estate was, subsequently, owned by Charles Lewis Tiffany II, who continued to call it *Elmwood.*
   The house is on The National Register of Historic Places.

Zenz, Dr. Frederick Anton (b. 1922)

Occupation(s):   industrialist -   president, F. A. Zenz (chemical engineering firm)
                                 inventor -   held patents on fluid particle technology
                                 writer -   over 150 papers, books, and patents

Marriage(s):

Listed in *Long Island Society Register, 1929*: no
Address: Bryant Avenue, Roslyn Harbor
Acreage / map sources: on 1927 map; 13 acres / 1932 and 1946 maps
Name of estate: *Montrose*
Year of construction: c. 1830
Style of architecture: Federal
Architect(s):   Vaux, Withers and Co. designed the 1869 addition of a wing
                                (for P. Godwin)

Landscape architect(s):
House extant: yes
Historical notes:

   In 1852, William Cullen Bryant purchased *Montrose* for his daughter Fanny, who had married Parke Godwin.
   Parke Godwin deeded the house to his daughter Minna, who married Frederick M. Goddard. Minna called it *Clovercroft.*
   Their adopted son Conrad changed the estate's name back to *Montrose.*
   In 1955, the estate was sold to builders who subdivided the property for a housing development.
   The house was, subsequently owned by Zenz, who continued to call it *Montrose.*

Zinsser, William Herman, Jr. (1887-1979)

Occupation(s):   industrialist - president, William Zinsser & Co. (shellac manufacturers)
Civic Activism: mayor and trustee, Village of Kings Point

Marriage(s):   1917-1979 - Joyce Knowlton (d. 1980)

Listed in *Long Island Society Register, 1929*: no
Address: Gatsby Lane and Eagle Point Drive, Kings Point
Acreage / map sources: on 1927 map; 3 acres / 1932 and 1946 maps
Name of estate: *Windward*
Year of construction:
Style of architecture:
Architect(s):
Landscape architect(s):   Ellen Biddle Shipman (for W. Zinsser)
House extant: unconfirmed
Historical notes:

The *Social Register, Summer 1950* lists *Windward* as the name of Zinsser's estate.

The Zinssers' daughter Amy married Robert Ferreira, the son of Robert Anthony Ferreira of Seekonk, MA. Their daughter Polly married Henry Z. Steinway, the son of Theodore E. Steinway of Manhattan. He was an heir to the Steinway piano fortune. Their daughter Nancy married Edward H. Walworth, Jr. of Evanston, IL. Their daughter June married Edgar J. Applewhite and resided in Washington, DC.

Zog I, King of Albania (1895-1961)

Marriage(s):   1938-1961 - Countess Geraldine Apponyi (1915-2002)

Listed in *Long Island Society Register, 1929*: no
Address: Muttontown Lane, Muttontown
Acreage / map sources: not on 1927, 1932, or 1946 maps
Name of estate:
Year of construction: c. 1907
Style of architecture: Italian Neo-Classical
Architect(s):   Hiss and Weeks designed the house (for C. I. Hudson, Sr.)
Landscape architect(s):   Ferruccio Vitale designed the formal Italianate sunken garden,
                                descending gardens, pergola, catalpa walk, foot paths, bridle paths,
                                brick terrace, and landscaping, 1906-1920 (for C. I. Hudson, Sr.)
Estate photographs can be found in the Nassau County Museum Collection filed under East Norwich/Hudson
   and also under Muttontown/Hudson/Senff/Zog.
House extant: no; demolished in 1959**
Historical notes:

The house, originally named *Knollwood* was built by Charles I. Hudson, Sr.

After Hudson's death, the estate was owned by Gustavia Senff and, subsequently, by her nephew Charles Senff McVeigh, Sr.

In 1951, King Zog I of Albania purchased the estate from McVeigh.

Ahmed Zogu, who was the Premier of Albania from 1922 to 1924, proclaimed himself dictator in 1925 and King Zog I in 1928. He was sometimes referred to as the "Napoleon of the Balkans."

Geraldine Apponyi Zog's father was Count Gyula Apponyi de Nagy–Appony of Hungary. Her mother, the former Gladys Virginia Stewart, was a member of an old Virginia family. With the demise of the Austro–Hungarian Empire in 1919, Geraldine was eventually reduced to selling postcards in the Budapest National Museum. Despite her desperate financial position, she managed to attend social functions. A photograph taken at one of these balls was seen by Zog who then invited her to Albania. Ten days after they met their engagement was announced. In 1939, one year after their marriage, Zog's regime was toppled with Italy's invasion of Albania. In 1997 the Albanian people rejected the attempted restoration of the throne by their son Leka by a two to one vote. Geraldine returned to Albania at the invitation of the parliament just four months prior to her death. [*The New York Times* October 27, 2002, p. 45.]

After a dispute with Nassau County over property taxes, King Zog sold the estate to Lansdell Kisner Christie in 1955 without ever occupying the house.

**Christie demolished the house. His widow sold the estate to Nassau County. It is now part of Nassau County's Muttontown Preserve.

APPENDICES

Table of Contents for Appendices

Architects 897

Civic Activists 932

Estate Names 945

Golf Course on former North Shore Estates 975

Hereditary Titles 976

Landscape Architects 977

Maiden Names 1007

Motion Pictures Filmed at North Shore Estates 1060

Occupations 1066

Rehabilitative Secondary Uses of Surviving Estate Houses . . . 1102

Statesmen and Diplomats Who Resided on Long Island's North Shore . . . 1107

Village Locations of Estates 1118

America's First Age of Fortune: A Selected Bibliography 1133

Selected Bibliographic References to Individual
North Shore Estate Owners 1140

Biographical Sources Consulted 1193

Maps Consulted for Estate Locations 1194

Photographic and Map Credits 1195

See the surname entry to ascertain if more than one architect was involved in designing the various buildings on an estate. This list reflects their North Shore commissions and includes the original and subsequent owners of the estates. When the owner who contracted with the architect is known, it is indicated by an asterisk. See village entry for cross referencing of names not found as separate surname entries.

Frederick L. Ackerman

* Crary, Miner Dunham, Sr.		Asharoken

William Adams

* Maxwell, George Thebaud	*Sunset House*	Cove Neck
Taylor, James Blackstone, Jr.	*Sunset House*	Cove Neck
Taylor, James Blackstone, Sr.	*Sunset House*	Cove Neck
Meyer, George C., Sr.		Kings Point
* Meyer, J. Edward, Sr.	*Rhada*	Kings Point
* Richards, Frederick L.	*Hazelmere*	Kings Point

Adams and Prentice

Phipps, Howard, Jr.	*Erchless*	Old Westbury
* Phipps, Howard, Sr.	*Erchless*	Old Westbury

David Adler

* Field, Evelyn Marshall	*Easton*	Muttontown

Albro and Lindeberg

Batterman, Henry Lewis, Jr.	*Beaver Brook Farm*	Mill Neck
* Batterman, Henry Lewis, Sr.	*Beaver Brook Farm*	Mill Neck
Beale, Bouvier, Sr.		Glen Cove
* Rossiter, Arthur Wickes, Sr.	*Cedarcroft*	Glen Cove

William Truman Aldrich

* Aldrich, Winthrop Williams	*Broadhollow* (unconfirmed)	Brookville
Cohen	(unconfirmed)	Brookville
Donahue, James Paul, Jr.	*Broadhollow* (unconfirmed)	Brookville
Evangelista, Louis	(unconfirmed)	Brookville
* Mixter, George, Sr.		*[unable to locate - Manhasset]*
Uris, Percy	*Broadhollow* (unconfirmed)	Brookville
Vanderbilt, Alfred Gwynne, II	*Broadhollow* (unconfirmed)	Brookville

Augustus N. Allen

Brokaw, George Tuttle		Sands Point
* Fleischmann, Max C.	*The Lindens*	Sands Point
* Gould, Howard	*Castlegould* (stables)	Sands Point
Guggenheim, Daniel	*Hempstead House* (stables)	Sands Point

897

Augustus N. Allen (cont'd)

   Schwartz, Charles   Sands Point

   Vanderbilt, Alfred Gwynne, II   Sands Point

Sir Charles Carrick Allon

   Bryce, Lloyd Stephens   *Bryce House*   Roslyn Harbor
(1918-1924 alterations)

   * Frick, Childs   *Clayton*   Roslyn Harbor
(1918-1924 alterations)

Grosvenor Atterbury

   * Byrne, James   Upper Brookville

   de Forest, Johnston   *Wawapek*   Cold Spring Harbor

   * de Forest, Robert Weeks   *Wawapek*   Cold Spring Harbor

   Hadden, Arnold P.   Cold Spring Harbor

   * James, Dr. Walter Belknap   *Eagle's Beak*   Cold Spring Harbor

   * Oakman, Walter George, Sr.   *Oakdene*   Roslyn

   * Peabody, Charles Augustus, Jr.   Cold Spring Harbor

   Rubel, Samuel   Roslyn

   * Stewart, William Adams Walker, II *Edgeover*   Cold Spring Harbor

   * Vermilye, H. Rowland, Sr.   *Woodwinds*   Cold Spring Harbor

   Walbridge, Henry D.   *Waldene*   Roslyn

   Williams, Douglas   *Wawapek*   Cold Spring Harbor

Frederick Ayer II and Bradley Delehanty

   Anderson, John   *Aberfeldy*   Lattingtown
(c. 1938 alterations)

   * Shea, Edward Lane   (c 1938 alterations)   Lattingtown

Babb, Cook and Willard

   * Cravath, Paul Drennan   *Veraton* (I)   Lattingtown

   * Pierce, Winslow Shelby, II   *Dunstable*   Bayville

   * Pratt, Frederic Bayley   *Poplar Hill* (I)   Glen Cove

   * Pratt, Harold Irving, Sr.   *Welwyn*   Glen Cove

   Williams, Harrison   *Oak Point*   Bayville

Donn Barber

   * Shonnard, Horatio Seymour, Sr. *Boscobel*   Oyster Bay
(1920s alterations on house)
(garage, stables and bathhouse, 1920s)

   Underhill, Francis T.   (1920s alterations on house)   Oyster Bay
(garage, stables and bathhouse, 1920s)

   Weidenfeld, Camille   (1920s alterations on house)   Oyster Bay
(garage, stables and bathhouse, 1920s)

Barney and Chapman

   * Maxwell, Eugene Lascelles, Sr. *Maxwell Hall*   Glen Cove

John Stewart Barney

   * Emanuel, Victor   *Dorwood*   North Hills

   Kelley, Cornelius Francis   *Sunny Skies*   North Hills

Dwight James Baum

  * Murray, John Francis   Old Westbury

William Harmon Beers

  * Kane, John P., Jr.   (1929 alterations)   Matinecock

  * Lord, Franklin Butler, II   *Cottsleigh*   Syosset

  * Lord, George de Forest, Sr.   *Overfields*   Syosset

    Wellington, Herbert Galbraith, Sr.   (1929 alterations)   Matinecock

Algernon S. Bell

  * Neilson, Raymond Perry Rodgers, Sr.   Old Westbury

    Park, William Gray   *Turnpike Cottage*   Old Westbury

Charles I. Berg

  * Moore, John Chandler   *Moorelands*   Oyster Bay Cove

    Moore, Louis de Bebian   *Moorelands*   Oyster Bay Cove

Wesley Sherwood Bessell

  * Latham, Leroy   *Hemlock Hollow*   Plandome

Boring and Tilton

    Campbell, George W.   *Fort Hill House* (1900 house)   Lloyd Harbor

  * Matheson, William John   *Fort Hill House* (1900 house)   Lloyd Harbor

    Wood, Willis Delano   *Fort Hill House* (1900 house)   Lloyd Harbor

Alfred C. Bossom

  * Harriman, Joseph Wright   *Avondale Farms*   Brookville

    Smith, Albert Lawrence, Sr.   *Penllyn*   Brookville

William Welles Bosworth

  * Bliss, Cornelius Newton, Jr.   *Oak Hill*   Brookville

  * Bosworth, William Welles   *Old Trees*   Matinecock

  * Farwell, Walter   *Mallow*   Oyster Bay Cove

    Hedges, Benjamin Van Doren, II   Oyster Bay Cove

    Kohler, Calvin   Brookville

  * Stone, Charles Augustus, Sr.   Matinecock

William Lawrence Bottomley

  * Bottomley, William Lawrence   *Hickory Hill*   Old Brookville

    Burchard, Anson Wood   *Birchwood* (1930s alterations)   Lattingtown

  * Carlisle, Lloyd Leslie, Sr.   (1930s alterations)   Lattingtown

  * Fahys, George Ernest, Sr.   *Hilaire*   Matinecock

    Fremont, Julie Fay Bradley   *Lynrose*   Glen Head

    Gates, Elizabeth Hoagland   *Dormer House* (1935 alterations)   Lattingtown

  * Grosvenor, Graham Bethune   *Graymar*   Old Westbury

    Hall, Leonard Wood   (1930s alterations)   Lattingtown

  * Luckenbach, Lewis V., Sr.   Glen Cove

William Lawrence Bottomley (cont'd)

Munsel, Patrice	*Lockjaw Ridge* (1935 alterations)	Lattingtown
Powell, John		Glen Cove
Raquet, Walter	*Lockjaw Ridge* (1935 alterations)	Lattingtown
* Rathborne, Joseph Cornelius, II	*North Refuge*	Old Westbury
Robertson, Julian Hart, Jr.		Upper Brookville
* Robinson, John Randolph		Brookville
* Shipman, Julie Fay Bradley	*Lynrose*	Glen Head
* Sloane, George	*Brookmeade* (1935 alterations)	Lattingtown
Tenney, Daniel Gleason, Sr.		Brookville
* Tiffany, Anne Cameron	*Glen Nevis* (c. 1920s alterations)	Upper Brookville
* Townsend, James Mulford, II	(c. 1915 alterations)	Mill Neck
Trimble, Richard J., Sr.		Old Westbury
Vilas, Guillermo	*Lockjaw Ridge* (1935 alterations)	Lattingtown
* Whitehouse, James Norman	*Broadwood*	Upper Brookville
* Winmill, Robert Campbell	*Borradil Farm* (alterations)	Mill Neck

Franklin Nelson Breed

* Ballantine, John Herbert	*Holmdene*	Kings Point

Herbert R. Brewster

Baker, George Fisher, III	*Ventura Point*	Centre Island
* Batterman, Henry Lewis, Sr.		Glen Cove
Carey, William Francis, Jr.		Centre Island
* Maxwell, Howard Washburn, Sr.	*Maxwelton* (family compound)	Glen Cove
* Smith, Herbert Ludlam, Sr.	*Oliver's Point*	Centre Island

James Brite

* Arnold, William H.		Kings Point
Goldman, K. M.		Sands Point
* Pratt, Herbert Lee, Sr.	*The Braes* (the house and 1912 alterations)	Glen Cove
* Wright, Wilkinson de Forest, Sr.	*Deephaven*	Sands Point

Roger Harrington Bullard

* Bullard, Roger Harrington		North Hills
Cozzens, Issachar, III	*Maple Knoll* (1929 alterations)	Lattingtown
* Dimock, Edward Jordan	*Enderby*	North Hills
Emerson, Margaret	*Rynwood*	Old Brookville
* Everdell, William, Jr.		North Hills
* Harris, Henry Upham, Sr.	*The Hameau*	Brookville

Roger Harrington Bullard (cont'd)

	Lundy, Frederick William Irving	*Rynwood*	Old Brookville
*	Morgan, Henry Sturgis, Sr.	(1929 alterations)	Lattingtown
*	Morgan, Junius Spencer	*Apple Trees*	Matinecock
*	Morgan, Junius Spencer	*Salutation*	Glen Cove, West Island
	Oberlin, Abraham	(1929 alterations)	Lattingtown
*	Pennoyer, Paul Geddes, Sr.	*Round Bush*	Glen Cove
*	Richmond, L. Martin	*Sunninghill*	Old Brookville
*	Salvage, Sir Samuel Agar	*Rynwood*	Old Brookville
	Samuels, John Stockwell, III	*Salutation*	Glen Cove, West Island
*	Stevenson, Malcolm, Sr.	*Two Maple Farm*	Old Westbury

Butler and Corse

*	Taylor, Henry Calhoun	*Cherridore*	Cold Spring Harbor

Caretto and Forster

*	Hoyt, John R.		Kings Point

James Edwin Ruthven Carpenter

*	Carpenter, James Edwin Ruthven	*Keswick*	Sands Point
	Lavilla, Adolph		Sands Point

Carrere and Hastings

	Blair, James Alonzo, Jr.	*Ontare*	Oyster Bay Cove
*	Blair, James Alonzo, Sr.	*Ontare*	Oyster Bay Cove
	Bogart, Adrian T., Jr.	*Friend Field*	Lattingtown
	Bush, Donald Fairfax, Jr.	*Preference*	Lattingtown
	Diebold, Trevor		Lattingtown
*	du Pont, Alfred Irenee	*White Eagle*	Brookville
*	Duryea, Hermanes Barkula, Jr.	*Knole*	Old Westbury
	Guest, Frederick E.	*Roslyn Manor*	Brookville
	Guest, Winston Frederick Churchill	*Templeton*	Brookville
*	Hastings, Thomas	*Bagatelle*	Old Westbury
*	Howe, Richard Flint	*Linden Hill*	Brookville
*	Howe, William Deering	*Highpool*	Brookville
	Jennings, Oliver Burr, II	*Burrwood*	Lloyd Harbor
*	Jennings, Walter	*Burrwood*	Lloyd Harbor
*	Lovett, Robert Abercrombie	*Green Arbors*	Lattingtown
	Martin, Bradley, Jr.	*Knole*	Old Westbury
	Martin, Esmond Bradley, Sr.	*Knole*	Old Westbury
*	McLane, Allan, Jr.	*Home Wood*	Lattingtown
	Pratt, Frederic Richardson	*Friendfield Farm*	Lattingtown
	Preston, William Payne Thompson, Sr.	*Longfields*	Jericho
	Straus, Jack Isidor	*Green Pastures*	Jericho
*	Thompson, William Payne, Jr.	*Longfields*	Jericho

Carrere and Hastings (cont'd)

* Vanderbilt, William Kissam, Jr.	*Deepdale* (alterations)	Lake Success
Van Ingen, Herbert Terrell	*Rocky Point*	*[unable to locate - Cold Spring Harbor]*
Van Ingen, Lawrence Bell, Jr.	*Preference*	Lattingtown
* Van Ingen, Lawrence Bell, Sr.	*Preference*	Lattingtown
* White, Rita Kohler	*Glenby*	Mill Neck
Woods, Ward Wilson, Jr.		Lattingtown

Walter Boughton Chambers

* Jennings, Benjamin Brewster	*Windward*	Old Brookville

Henry Otis Chapman

Amato, Camille Jean Tuorto	*Woodstock Manor*	Muttontown
Bedford, Alfred Cotton	*Pemberton*	Muttontown
* Bendel, Henri		Kings Point
Chrysler, Walter Percy, Sr.	*Forker House*	Kings Point
Hoffman, Albert L., Sr.	*Radnor House*	Muttontown
Netter, Dr. Frank H.		Muttontown
* Provost, Cornelius W.	*Woodley*	Muttontown
* Smith, George	*Blythewood*	Muttontown
Stam, Alan		Muttontown
Vander Poel, William Halsted	*Woodstock*	Muttontown

Clinton and Russell

* Dodge, Lillian Sefton Thomas	*Sefton Manor*	Mill Neck
* Hoyt, Colgate, Jr.	*Meadow Spring*	Glen Cove

Ogden Codman, Jr.

* Bryce, Lloyd Stephens	*Bryce House*	Roslyn Harbor
Frick, Childs	*Clayton*	Roslyn Harbor
Maddocks, John L., Jr.		Brookville
* Maynard, Walter Effingham	*Haut Bois*	Brookville
Munsel, Patrice	*Malmaison*	Brookville

Frederick S. Copley

Brion, Lucille Demarest	*Sycamore Lodge*	Roslyn Harbor
Demarest, John M.	*Sycamore Lodge*	Roslyn Harbor
Emory, William Helmsley, Jr.	*Clifton*	Roslyn Harbor
Fahnestock, Frank Curry	*Sycamore Lodge*	Roslyn Harbor
Riggs, Glenn E., Sr.	*Sycamore Lodge*	Roslyn Harbor

Henry Corse

* Dickerman, Florence Calkin	*Hillendale*	Mill Neck
Fordyce, Dorothy M.	*Oakley Court*	Mill Neck
* Gould, Edwin	*Highwood* (house and outbuildings)	Oyster Bay Cove
Minicozzi, Alexander	(house and outbuildings)	Oyster Bay Cove

Henry Corse (cont'd)

Montana, Dr. Christopher	(house and outbuildings)	Oyster Bay Cove
Vanderbilt, Alfred Gwynne, II	*Oakley Court*	Mill Neck
Whitney, Cornelius Vanderbilt	*Oakley Court*	Mill Neck

George Abraham Crawley

* Phipps, John Shaffer	*Westbury House*	Old Westbury

Cross and Cross

Bingham, Harry Payne, Sr.	*Ivycroft* (alterations to house, portico, and stables/garage complex)	Old Westbury
* Cross, Eliot B.	(alterations to house, portico, and stables/garage complex)	Old Westbury
Draper, Charles Dana	*Ten Gables*	Albertson
Harkness, Edward Stephen	*Weekend*	North Hills
* Harriman, Herbert Melville	*The Lanterns*	Jericho
* Moore, Edward Small, Sr.	*Ten Gables*	Albertson
* Pyne, Percy Rivington, II	*Rivington House*	Roslyn Harbor
Tiffany, Perry	(alterations to house, portico, and stables/garage complex)	Old Westbury
Tinker, Edward Richmond, Jr.	*Woodbury House*	Syosset
* Von Stade, Francis Skiddy, Sr.		Old Westbury
* Webb, James Watson, Sr.	*Woodbury House*	Syosset
Webb, William Seward, Jr.		North Hills

Robert Crowie

* Davison, Henry Pomeroy, II	*Appledore*	Upper Brookville

Alexander Jackson Davis

Brickman, Herman	*The Point*	Kings Point
Church, Richard N. L.	*The Point*	Kings Point
* King, John Alsop, Jr.		Kings Point

Davis, McGrath and Keissling

* Young, Edward Lewis	*Meadow Farm*	Glen Cove

George B. de Gersdorff

Douglas, Barry		Oyster Bay Cove
* Ingalls, Fay	*Sunken Orchard*	Oyster Bay Cove
McCann, Charles Edward Francis	*Sunken Orchard*	Oyster Bay Cove

Delano and Aldrich

* Astor, William Vincent	*Cloverley Manor*	Sands Point
* Babcock, Richard Franklin	*Hark Away*	Woodbury
Bast, W. C.		Matinecock
Bedford, Alfred Cotton	(alterations)	Lattingtown
Belding, David, Sr.	(studio)	West Hills
Bruce, David Kirkpatrick Este	*Woodlands*	Woodbury

Delano and Aldrich (cont'd)

*	Burden, James Abercrombie, Jr.	*Woodside* (house, garage, stables and farm complex, 1916; house alterations, 1926; gatehouse, 1926)	Muttontown
	Carey, Martin F.	*Cashelmare*	Glen Cove
	Christie, Lansdell Kisner		Muttontown
*	Crane, Clinton Hoadley, Jr.		Lloyd Harbor
*	Crane, Clinton Hoadley, Jr.		Glen Cove
*	Davis, John William	*Mattapan* (alterations)	Lattingtown
	Deering, William Rogers	*Roseneath*	Laurel Hollow
	Diebold, Trevor	(alterations)	Lattingtown
*	Duer, Beverly	*Whispering Laurels*	Laurel Hollow
*	Eberstadt, Ferdinand	*Target Rock Farm*	Lloyd Harbor
*	Eldridge, Lewis Angevine, Sr.	*Redcote* (alterations)	Saddle Rock
*	Elmhirst, Leonard Knight	*Applegreen* (alterations)	Old Westbury
*	Fish, Edwin A.	*Airdrie*	Matinecock
	Glass, Harry		Old Westbury
	Griscom, Lloyd Carpenter	*Huntover Lodge*	Muttontown
*	Hammond, Paul Lyman	*Muttontown Lodge*	Syosset
*	Hoppin, Gerard Beekman	*Four Winds*	Oyster Bay Cove
*	Hoyt, Lydig		Woodbury
	Iglehart, David Stewart	*La Granja*	Old Westbury
*	Kahn, Otto Hermann	*Oheka*	Cold Spring Harbor
	Knowlton, Hugh Gilbert, Sr.		Muttontown
	Le Boutillier, Thomas III	(studio)	Old Westbury
*	Ledyard, Lewis Cass, Jr.	*Westwood* (pool & tennis court complexes)	Oyster Bay Cove
*	Lovett, Robert Abercrombie	*Green Arbors* (alterations)	Lattingtown
	Ludwig, Arthur	(studio)	West Hills
*	Lyon, John Denniston	*Wyomissing*	Matinecock
*	Mason, Julian Starkweather	*Pound Hollow Cottage*	Old Brookville
	McIntosh, Allan J.		Sands Point
	McKay, Alexandra Emery Moore	*Chelsea*	Muttontown
	Melius, Gary	*Oheka Castle*	Cold Spring Harbor
*	Merrill, Charles Edward, Jr.	*Hidden Way*	Huntington Bay
	Miller, Flora Payne Whitney	*French House*	Old Westbury
	Mondello, Joseph		Old Westbury
*	Moore, Benjamin	*Chelsea*	Muttontown
*	Morawetz, Victor	*Three Ponds*	Woodbury

Delano and Aldrich (cont'd)

* Page, Arthur Wilson, II	*County Line Farm* (alterations)	West Hills
* Page, Walter Hines, II		Cold Spring Harbor
* Payson, Charles Shipman		Manhasset
* Perkins, Robert P.		*[unable to locate - Huntington]*
* Phipps, Ogden	(alterations)	Old Westbury
Pierce, Winslow Shelby, II	*Dunstable* (1926 alterations)	Bayville
* Pratt, Harold Irving, Sr.	*Welwyn* (alterations)	Glen Cove
Preston, Lewis Thompson, Sr.	*Longfields*	Old Brookville
Price, Theodore Hazeltine, Jr.	*Ben Robyn Farm* (studio)	West Hills
* Pryibil, Helen Porter	*Bogheid*	Glen Cove
* Robbins, Francis LeBaron, Jr.	*Ben Robyn* (studio)	West Hills
* Rumbough, Stanley Maddox, Jr.	(alterations)	Old Brookville
* Sands, Miss Anna		Upper Brookville
Smith, Owen Telfair		Laurel Hollow
* Straight, Willard Dickerman	*Elmhurst* (house and stables)	Old Westbury
* Swann, Dr. Arthur Wharton		Oyster Bay Cove
* Tod, Robert Elliot	*Thistleton* (pool complex)	Syosset
Tower, Flora Payne Whitney	*French House*	Old Westbury
Walker, Elisha, Sr.	*Les Pommiers*	Muttontown
* Watriss, Frederick N.		Old Brookville
* Whitney, Cornelius Vanderbilt	*Whitney House*	Old Westbury
* Whitney, George, Sr.	*Home Acres*	Old Westbury
* Whitney, Gertrude Vanderbilt	(studio)	Old Westbury
* Whitney, Harry Payne	(alterations)	Old Westbury
Whitney, William Collins	(alterations and studio)	Old Westbury
* Williams, Harrison	*Oak Point* (1926 alterations)	Bayville
* Winthrop, Bronson	(both 1903 and 1910 houses)	Muttontown
* Winthrop, Egerton Leigh, Jr.	*Muttontown Meadows*	Muttontown
* Wood, Chalmers, Jr.	*Little Ipswich*	Woodbury
* Wood, Frank P.		*[unable to locate - Syosset]*
* Work, Bertram G., Sr.	*Oak Knoll*	Mill Neck

William Adams Delano

* Delano, William Adams	*Muttontown Corners*	Muttontown

Bradley Delehanty

* Alker, Carroll Booth		Muttontown
Andersen, Dr. Harold Willids, Sr.	*Still House*	Matinecock
* Anderson, John	*Aberfeldy* (c. 1930 alterations)	Lattingtown
Brower, Ernest Cuyler	*Locust Hill* (c. 1926 alterations)	Roslyn
* Brower, George Ellsworth	*Locust Hill* (c. 1926 alterations)	Roslyn
* Brown, Francis Gordon, Sr.	*Willow Bank*	Old Brookville
Cohn, Milton Seymour		Kings Point
* Colgate, John Kirtland , Sr.	*Oaklea*	Oyster Bay Cove
Collado, Dr. Emilio Gabriel, II		Upper Brookville
Cornell, Phebe Augusta	(c. 1926 alterations)	Roslyn
* Cravath, Paul Drennan	*Still House*	Matinecock
* Cutcheon, Franklin Warner M.	*Matinecock Farms*	Lattingtown
* Damrosch, Dr. Walter Johannes	*Monday House*	Upper Brookville
* Davey, William Nelson	*White Gates*	West Hills
Delano, Michael		Upper Brookville
* Delehanty, Bradley	*The Barn* (alterations)	Matinecock
* Dickinson, Hunt Tilford, Sr.	*Hearth Stone*	Old Brookville
* Dickson, Thomas, Sr.	*Petit Bois* (1929 alterations)	Lattingtown
* Dyer, Elisha, VII	*The Orchards* (c. 1939 alterations)	Brookville
* Dyer, George Rathbone, Sr.	*The Orchards* (c. 1939 alterations)	Brookville
Ely, Rev. Samuel Rose, Sr.	(c. 1926 alterations)	Roslyn
Erbe, Gustav, Jr.	(c. 1927 alterations)	Lattingtown
* Field, Marshall, III	*Caumsett* (1950s alterations - wing removed)	Lloyd Harbor
* Finlayson, Frank Redfern	(c. 1936 alterations)	Matinecock
* Franklin, Philip Albright Small, Sr.	*Royston*	Matinecock
* Geddes, Eugene Maxwell, Sr.	*Punkin Hill*	Matinecock
Gerry, Dr. Roger Goodman	*Locust Hill* (c. 1926 alterations)	Roslyn
* Groesbeck, Clarence Edward	*Roads End*	Matinecock
Hansen, Robert [*see* Brower]	*Locust Hill* (c. 1926 alterations)	Roslyn
* Harris, Sam Henry		Kings Point
* Hattersley, Robert Chopin, Sr.	*Cherry Leaze*	Glen Head
* Hepburn, Frederick Taylor	*Long Field*	Lattingtown
* Hepburn, George		Lattingtown
Herzog, Edwin H.		Lattingtown

Bradley Delehanty (cont'd)

Ide, George Edward	*Petit Bois* (1929 alterations)	Lattingtown
* Livingston, Miss Louise Alida		Upper Brookville
* Marsh, John Bigelow, Sr.	*Nyrmah* (1940 alterations)	Mill Neck
* Marston, Edgar Lewis, II	*Carston Hill*	Woodbury
* Ottley, Gilbert	*Wuff Woods*	Upper Brookville
Peters, William Richmond	*Hawirt* (1940 alterations)	Mill Neck
Pickett, John Olen, Jr.		Matinecock
Porter, Seton	*Still House*	Matinecock
Renard	(c. 1927 alterations)	Lattingtown
* Richards, Ira, Jr.	(c. 1927 alterations)	Lattingtown
Rothschild, Baron Eugene de	*Still House*	Matinecock
Shea, Edward Lane	(c. 1930 alterations)	Lattingtown
* Shea, Edward Lane	(c. 1938 alterations)	Lattingtown
Shutt, Edwin Holmes, Jr.		Oyster Bay Cove
Sperry, Edward G.		Upper Brookville
Stillman, F. A.	(c. 1927 alterations)	Lattingtown
Vanderbilt, Alfred Gwynne, II	(1940 alterations)	Mill Neck
Wolf, Barry	*Locust Hill* (c. 1926 alterations)	Roslyn
* Woolley, Daniel P.	*Wooldon*	Lattingtown

Henri J. de Sibour

* Dilworth, Dewees Wood	*Gloan House*	Old Westbury
Manville, Lorraine	*Les Deux Tours*	Old Westbury

d'Hauteville and Cooper

Whitney, John Hay	*Greentree*	Manhasset
* Whitney, William Payne	*Greentree*	Manhasset
* Winthrop, Henry Rogers	*East Woods*	Woodbury

Albert Frederick D'Oench

* D'Oench, Albert Frederick	*Sunset Hill*	Plandome

Harry Ellingwood Donnell

Barbolini, Guy	*The Crest*	Asharoken
Bishop Richard E.	(house and outbuildings)	Asharoken
Borglum, Lucille	(1911 alterations)	Asharoken
Carr, Edward A. T.	*The Hill*	Eaton's Neck
Cooper, Cyrus	*The Crest*	Asharoken
DeLamater, Cornelius Henry	*Walnut Farm House* (1911 alterations)	Asharoken
* DeLamater, Oakley Ramshon, Sr.	*The Crest*	Asharoken
DeWeir, Norman	*The Crest*	Asharoken

Harry Ellingwood Donnell (cont'd)

*	Donnell, Harry Ellingwood	*The Hill*	Eaton's Neck
	Donnell, Laura Attmore Robinson	(1911 alterations)	Asharoken
	Garrett, Robert Michael	*The Crest*	Asharoken
	Gerlach, Robert	*The Hill*	Eaton's Neck
	Lang, John	*The Hill*	Eaton's Neck
	Law, Reed	(house and outbuildings)	Asharoken
	Miller, John R., III	(house and outbuildings)	Asharoken
	Rice, Donald	*The Crest*	Asharoken
	Robins, Lydia DeLamater	*The Robin's Nest* (1911 alterations)	Asharoken
	Robinson, Miss Edith Attmore	*The Point* (house and outbuildings)	Asharoken
*	Robinson, George Hazard	*The Point* (house and outbuildings)	Asharoken
*	Robinson, George Hazard	(1911 alterations)	Asharoken
	Sandblom, Frederick	(1911 alterations)	Asharoken
	Vertes, Marcel Emmanuel	(1911 alterations)	Asharoken
	Ward, Sarah Donnell	*The Hill*	Eaton's Neck

Thomas Harlan Ellett

*	Alker, Carol Booth	*Ca Va* (house and outbuildings)	Old Brookville
*	Barnes, E. Mortimer	*Manana*	Old Brookville
	Breed, William Constable, Sr.	*Normandy Farms*	Old Brookville
*	Cowl, Donald Hearn	(service court)	Sands Point
	Dillon, Herbert Lowell, Sr.	*Sunninghill* (house and outbuildings)	Old Brookville
	Lewyt, Alexander Milton	(service court)	Sands Point
*	Minton, Henry Miller	*Brookwood*	North Hills
	Neelands, Thomas D., Jr.	(service court)	Sands Point

Aymar Embury II

*	Ellis, Reuben Morris		Great Neck
	Kalimian, Abi		Kings Point
*	Schieren, George Arthur, Sr.	*Beachleigh*	Kings Point

Harold Perry Erskine

*	White, Gardiner Winslow, Sr.	*White Lodge*	Mill Neck

Ewing and Chappell

	Cochran, Drayton		Centre Island
*	Remington, Franklin	*Driftwood*	Centre Island

Wilson Eyre

*	Alger, Miss Lucille	(house)	Kings Point
*	Conklin, Roland Ray	*Rosemary Farm*	Lloyd Harbor
*	Grace, Miss Louise Natalie	*Llangollen Farm* (1910 alterations)	Kings Point

Montague Flagg II

* Flagg, Montague, II	*Applewood*	Upper Brookville
Kellogg, Morris Woodruff	*Fieldston Farm*	Upper Brookville
McClintock, Harvey Childs, Jr.		Upper Brookville

Forster and Gallimore

* Fairchild, Sherman M.	*Eastfair*	Lloyd Harbor

Forster, Gade and Graham

* Lawrence, Effingham, II		Cold Spring Harbor
Nichols, George, Sr.	*Uplands*	Cold Spring Harbor

Frank J. Forster

* Kilthau, Raymond F.		Great Neck Estates

Mortimer Forster

* Hoffstot, Frank Norton	*Belcaro*	Sands Point
Rothschild, Baron Robert de	*Belcaro*	Sands Point

Paul A. Franklin

* Grumman, Leroy Randle		Plandome

George A. Freeman and Francis G. Hasselman

Holloway, William Grace, Sr.	*Foxland* (house and stables)	Old Westbury
* Keene, Foxhall Parker	*Rosemary Hall* (house and stables)	Old Westbury
Whitney, Harry Payne	(stables and gymnasium, 1898-1899)	Old Westbury
* Whitney, William Collins	(stables and gymnasium, 1898-1899)	Old Westbury

Fuller and Dick

* White, Robert K., Sr.		Mill Neck

William E. Frenayne, Jr.

Martin, Esmond Bradley, Sr.		Muttontown
* Nichols, Francis Tilden, Sr.	*Bayberry Downs*	Muttontown

Gage and Wallace

Bingham, Harry Payne, Sr.	*Ivycroft*	Old Westbury
Cross, Eliot B.	(alterations)	Old Westbury
* Tiffany, Perry		Old Westbury

Robert Williams Gibson

* Bullock, George	*Yeadon* (house, stables, farm complex, boathouse, and docks, c. 1914)	Centre Island
Deans, Robert Barr, Sr.	*Yeadon* (house, stables, farm complex, boathouse, and docks, c. 1914) (for Bullock)	Centre Island
* Gibson, Robert Williams	*North Point*	Cove Neck
Palmer, Carlton Humphreys	*Hearthstone* (house, stables, farm complex, boathouse, and docks, c. 1914) (for Bullock)	Centre Island
Siegel, Edward	(barn)	Sands Point

Robert Williams Gibson (cont'd)

	Thayer, Francis Kendall, Sr.	(barn)	Sands Point
*	Thayer, Kendall	(barn)	Sands Point

Archibald F. Gilbert

*	Cantor, Eddie		Lake Success

Bradford Lee Gilbert

*	Baldwin, William H., Jr.		Lattingtown
	Smithers, Christopher Dunkin, Sr.	*Dunrobin*	Lattingtown

Charles Pierrepont Henry Gilbert

*	Ayer, Dr. James Cook	*Shadowland*	Glen Cove
	Brewster, Samuel Dwight	*The Birches*	Glen Cove
	Brewster, Warren Dwight	*The Birches*	Glen Cove
*	Busby, Leonard J.	*Germelwyn* (house and stables)	Glen Cove
*	DeLamar, Joseph Raphael	*Pembroke*	Glen Cove
*	Fahys, George Ernest, Sr.	*Hilaire*	Glen Cove
*	Guthrie, William Dameron	*Meudon*	Lattingtown
*	Handy, Parker Douglas	*Groendak*	Glen Cove
*	Hoagland, Dr. Cornelius Nevius		Glen Cove
*	Humphreys, Dr. Alexander Crombie	(house and stables, 1899-1902)	Glen Cove
	Leeming, Thomas Lonsdale, Sr.	*Germelwyn* (house and stables, 1896-1901)	Glen Cove
	Loew, Arthur Marcus, Sr.	*Pembroke*	Glen Cove
	Lowe, Marcus	*Pembroke*	Glen Cove
*	Murdock, Harvey	*The Birches*	Glen Cove
	O'Keeffe, Samuel		Glen Cove
	Queen, Emmet		Glen Cove
	Reynolds, Richard Samuel, Sr.	*Winfield Hall*	Glen Cove
*	Rickert, Edward J.		Great Neck
	Schiff, John Mortimer	*Northwood*	Oyster Bay
*	Schiff, Mortimer L.	*Northwood*	Oyster Bay
*	Shaw, Robert Anderson		Glen Cove
	Tangeman, Cornelius Hoagland		Glen Cove
	Tangeman, George Patterson	*Green Acres*	Glen Cove
*	Woolworth, Frank Winfield	*Winfield Hall* (1916 house)	Glen Cove

Frederick A. Godley

*	Ricks, Jesse Jay		Flower Hill

William H. Gompert

	Ades, Robert		Kings Point
*	Kienle, Eugene S., Sr.	*Many Gables*	Kings Point

Bertram Grosvenor Goodhue

* Aldred, John Edward	*Ormston*	Lattingtown
Cournand, Edouard L.		Lloyd Harbor
* Lloyd–Smith, Wilton	*Kenjockety*	Lloyd Harbor
Rice, Paula		Lloyd Harbor

Philip Lippincott Goodwin

* Goodwin, Philip Lippincott	*Goodwin Place*	Woodbury
Jennings, Oliver Burr, II		Woodbury

Alexander Gorlin

DeLamar, Joseph Raphael	*Pembroke* (carriage house alteration, 2003)	Glen Cove
Loew, Arthur Marcus, Sr.	*Pembroke* (carriage house alteration, 2003)	Glen Cove
Lowe, Marcus	*Pembroke* (carriage house alteration, 2003)	Glen Cove
* Spectrum Communities	*Villa del Mar* (carriage house alteration, 2003)	Glen Cove

Julius Gregory

* O'Hara, Thomas H.		Kings Point

Howard Greenley

* Burchard, Anson Wood	*Birchwood* (house and greenhouse)	Lattingtown
Carlisle, Floyd Leslie, Sr.	(house and greenhouse)	Lattingtown
Coffin, Miss Alice	*Portledge*	Matinecock
* Coffin, Charles Albert	*Portledge*	Matinecock
Hall, Leonard Wood	(house and greenhouse)	Lattingtown
Pulsifer, George Hale	*Killibeg*	Matinecock
* Sparrow, Edward Wheeler	*Killibeg*	Matinecock

John Alexander Gurd

* L'Ecluse, Milton Albert	*Villa Amicitia*	Huntington Bay

Harrison and Abramovitz

* Dulles, Allen Welsh		Lloyd Harbor

Henry G. Harrison

* Beekman, James William, Sr.	*The Cliffs*	Mill Neck
Fritz, Dr. Albert R., Sr.	*The Cliffs*	Mill Neck

Wallace Kirkman Harrison

* Harrison, Wallace Kirkman	*Mon Souci*	West Hills

Charles Mansfield Hart

Dane, Chester Linwood, Sr.	*Linwood*	Mill Neck
Davies, Joseph Edward	*Hillwood*	Brookville
* Hutton, Edward Francis	*Hillwood*	Brookville
* Post, Marjorie Merriweather	*Hillwood*	Brookville
Wanner, Ernest P.		Mill Neck

Charles Mansfield Hart (cont'd)

   * Wilson, Charles Porter   Mill Neck

   * Young, Otto S.   Lake Success

Harold Victor Hartman

Briggs, Mead L.		Roslyn Harbor
Seligman, Joseph Lionel, Sr.	*Greenridge*	Roslyn Harbor
* Williams, Arthur	*Greenridge*	Roslyn Harbor

E. S. Hewitt

Fowler, Dr. Robert Henry		Laurel Hollow

Frederick R. Hirsh

Brightson, George Edgar	*Harbor Point*	Centre Island
Oelsner, Edward Carl William, Sr.	*Seacroft*	Centre Island
Oelsner, Warren James	*Seacroft*	Centre Island
* Shaw, Samuel T., Sr.	*The Sunnyside*	Centre Island

Hiss and Weeks

Christie, Lansdell Kisner		Muttontown
* Hudson, Charles I., Sr.	*Knollwood*	Muttontown
McVeigh, Charles Senff, Sr.		Muttontown
Senff, Gustavia		Muttontown
Zog I, King of Albania		Muttontown

F. Burrall Hoffman, Jr.

Cutting, Dr. Fulton		Brookville
* Rumsey, Charles Cary, Sr.		Brookville

Hood and Fouilhoux

Brooks, Joseph W.		Sands Point

Alfred Hopkins

* Brewster, George S.	*Fairleigh* (outbuildings, 1916)	Muttontown
Brokaw, Clifford Vail, Jr.	*The Elms* (outbuildings, 1914-1916)	Brookville
* Brokaw, Clifford Vail, Sr.	*The Elms* (outbuildings, 1914-1916)	Glen Cove
* Brokaw, Howard Crosby	*The Chimneys* (farm complex)	Muttontown
Brown, Nannie C. Inman	*The Elms* (outbuildings, 1914-1916)	Glen Cove
* Burchard, Anson Wood	(farm buildings)	Lattingtown
Carlisle, Floyd Leslie, Sr.	(farm buildings)	Lattingtown
* Davis, Joseph Edward, Sr.	*Heyday House* (farm complex)	Upper Brookville
* Field, Marshall, III	*Caumsett* (cow barns)	Lloyd Harbor
Hall, Leonard Wood	(farm buildings)	Lattingtown
Meyer, Robert J.	(outbuildings, 1916)	Muttontown

Alfred Hopkins (cont'd)

    Schiff, John Mortimer   *Northwood*   Oyster Bay
    (farm complex, c. 1914)

  * Schiff, Mortimer L.   *Northwood*   Oyster Bay
    (farm complex, c. 1914)

  * Stewart, Glenn   (farm complex)   Lattingtown

  * Tiffany, Louis Comfort   *Laurelton Hall*   Laurel Hollow
    (farm complex, 1905)

Hoppin and Koen

  * Blackton, James Stuart, Sr.   *Harbourwood*   Cove Neck
    (outbuildings, 1914)

    Bonney, Flora Macdonald   *Sunstar Hill*   Upper Brookville

    Elbert, Robert George   *Elbourne*   North Hills
    (1916 alterations)

    Grace, Joseph Peter, II   *Gracewood*   North Hills

    (1916 alterations)

    Harriman, Joseph Wright   Brookville

  * Iselin, Charles Oliver   *Wolvers Hollow*   Upper Brookville

    Leeds, William Bateman, Jr.   *Kenwood*   Cove Neck

    LeRoux, E.   Centre Island

  * Livermore, Philip Walter   *Bois Joli*   Brookville

  * Postley, Sterling   *Framewood*   Upper Brookville

  * Rose, George, Sr.   *Overland House*   Old Westbury

  * Sheehan, William Francis   *The Height*   North Hills
    (1916 alterations)

  * Smith, Ormond Gerald   *Shoremonde*   Centre Island

    Singer, William   North Hills

    Talbott, Harold Elster, II   *The Pillars*   Old Westbury

    Willys, John North   *Northcliff*   Centre Island

Howells and Stokes

    Castro, Bernard, Sr.   *Panfield*   Lloyd Harbor

    Giordano, Salvatore, Sr.   *Panfield*   Lloyd Harbor

    Guida, Bernadette Castro   *Panfield*   Lloyd Harbor

  * Hess, Harry Bellas   *The Cedars*   Huntington Station

  * Milbank, Albert Goodsell   *Panfield*   Lloyd Harbor

Hunt and Hunt

  * Gould, Howard   *Castlegould*   Sands Point

    Guggenheim, Daniel   *Hempstead House*   Sands Point

  * Horowitz, Louis Jay   Lattingtown

  * Sanderson, Henry   *La Selva*   Upper Brookville

    Wheeler, Frederick Seymour   *Delwood*   Upper Brookville

Richard Howland Hunt

  * Belmont, Alva Erskine Smith   *Beacon Towers*   Sands Point

    Hearst, William Randolph   *Saint Joan*   Sands Point

Richard Morris Hunt

    Chubb, Percy, Sr.   *Rattling Spring*   Glen Cove
                                         (house and stables)

   * Coles, Elizabeth   *Rolling Stone*   Glen Cove
                                         (house and stables)

    Hitchcock, Margaret Mellon   *Broad Hollow Farm*   Old Westbury
                                         (alterations)

   * Hitchcock, Thomas, Sr.   *Broad Hollow Farm*   Old Westbury
                                         (alterations)

    Powell, Francis Edward, Jr.   *Rattling Spring*   Glen Cove
                                         (house and stables)

Hunt and Kline

   * Hammerstein, Oscar, II   *Sunny Knoll*   Kings Point
    King, Alan   Kings Point

Allen W. Jackson

   * Ferguson, Juliana Armour   *The Monastery*   Huntington Bay

Kern and Lipper

   * Kennedy, William, Sr.   *Kennedy Villa*   Syosset

Kimball and Husted

    Bogart, Adrian T., Jr.   *Friend Field*   Lattingtown
                                 (gatehouse and farm complex)

   * Coe, Henry Eugene, Jr.   *The Beaklet*   Oyster Bay Cove

   * Lamont, Thomas Stilwell   *The Creek*   Lattingtown

   * McLane, Allan, Jr.   *Home Wood*   Lattingtown
                                 (gatehouse and farm complex)

    Pratt, Frederic Richardson   *Friendfield Farm*   Lattingtown
                                 (gatehouse and farm complex)

   * White, Alexander Moss, Jr.   *Hickory Hill*   Oyster Bay Cove

R. Barfoot King

    Lynch, Edmund Calvert, Jr.   *Floralyn*   Lattingtown
                                 (c. 1925 alterations)

   * Scott, Rufus W.   *Scottage*   Lattingtown
                                 (c. 1925 alterations)

Kirby, Petit and Green

   * Doubleday, Frank Nelson   Mill Neck

               [Doubleday had two houses in Mill Neck.]

   * Doubleday, Frank Nelson   *Effendi Hill*   Mill Neck

   * Doubleday, Frank Nelson   *New House*   Lattingtown

    Keating, Cletus, Sr.   *Holly Hill*   Mill Neck

Christopher Grant LaFarge

   * Morgan, John Pierpont, Jr.   *Matinecock Point*   Glen Cove, East Island

   * Roosevelt, Theodore   *Sagamore Hill*   Cove Neck
                              (north trophy room addition, 1905)

   * Whitney, John Hay   *Greentree*   Manhasset
                              (boathouse)

Christopher Grant LaFarge (cont'd)

    Whitney, William Payne   *Greentree*   Manhasset
                                              (boathouse)

Lamb and Rich

	Appleby, John Storm		Glen Cove
*	Babbott, Frank Lusk, Sr.		Glen Cove
*	Gates, Charles Otis	*Peacock Point*	Lattingtown
*	Gates, Elizabeth Hoagland	*Dormer House*	Lattingtown
*	Jennings, Spencer Augustus	*Ellencourt*	Glen Cove
	MacDonald, Helen Lamb Babbott		Glen Cove
	Munsel, Patrice	*Lockjaw Ridge*	Lattingtown
*	Pratt, Charles Millard	*Seamoor*	Glen Cove
	Raquet, Walter	*Lockjaw Ridge*	Lattingtown
*	Roosevelt, Theodore	*Sagamore Hill*	Cove Neck
	Sloane, George	*Brookmeade*	Lattingtown
	Vilas, Guillermo	*Lockjaw Ridge*	Lattingtown

Harrie Thomas Lindeberg

*	Ball, Wilbur Laing		Lattingtown
*	Bourne, George Galt		Lattingtown
*	Brokaw, Irving	*Frost Mill Lodge*	Mill Neck
*	Church, Charles Thomas, Sr.	*Three Brooks*	Mill Neck
	Church, Frederic Edwin	*Three Brooks*	Mill Neck
*	Doubleday, Nelson, Sr.	*Barberrys*	Mill Neck
*	Dwight, Richard Everett		Matinecock
*	Dykman, William Nelson		Glen Cove
	Fromm, Robert M.		Glen Cove
*	Gales, George M.	*Eckingston*	Lattingtown
	Gibson, Harvey Dow		Lattingtown
*	Iselin, Charles Oliver	*Wolvers Hollow* (1941 alterations)	Upper Brookville
	Kerr, Elmore Coe, Sr.		Mill Neck
*	Levison, John Jacob		Sea Cliff
*	Lindeberg, Thomas Harrie	*West Gate Lodge*	Matinecock
*	Lutz, Frederick L	*Laurel Acres*	Oyster Bay Cove
*	Martin, Henry Clifford		Glen Cove
	Milburn, Devereux, Jr.		Old Westbury
	Ohl, John Phillips		Sands Point
*	Parker, Dale M.		Sands Point
*	Reynolds, Jackson Eli		Lattingtown
	Smithers, Robert Brinkley		Mill Neck
*	Taylor, Bertrand LeRoy, Jr.		Upper Brookville
*	Taylor, Myron Charles	*Killingworth* (alterations)	Lattingtown

Electus D. Litchfield

    Outerbridge, Samuel Roosevelt   Center Island

Little and Browne

  * Adams, Horatio M.   *Appledale*   Glen Cove

  * Fowler, George   Glen Cove

    Loening, Rudolph R.   *Glimpse Water*   Glen Cove

    Miller, Nathan Lewis   *Norwich House*   Upper Brookville

  * Morse, Allon Mae Fuller   *Morse Lodge*   Old Westbury
                                     (1909-1910 alterations)

  * Page, Frank C. Bauman   *Elmcroft*   Upper Brookville

  * Proctor, Charles E.   *Shadowlane*   Kings Point

    Shepard, Rutherford Mead   Glen Cove

Little and O'Connor

  * Brokaw, William Gould   *Nirvana*   Kings Point

  * Gilbert, Harry Bramhall   *Sunshine*   Kings Point

  * Martin, James E., Sr.   *Martin Hall*   Kings Point

    Satterwhite, Dr. Preston Pope   *Preston Hall*   Kings Point

    Sinclair, Harry Ford, Sr.   Kings Point

Grover Loening

  * Loening, Grover   *Margrove*   Mill Neck

James Brown Lord

    Garvan, Francis Patrick, Sr.   *Roslyn House*   Old Westbury

  * Lanier, James Franklin Doughty   Old Westbury

  * Mortimer, Stanley, Sr.   *Roslyn Hall*   Old Westbury

    Steele, Charles   Old Westbury

Guy Lowell

  * Billings, Cornelius Kingsley Garrison   *Farnsworth*   Upper Brookville

    Bird, Wallis Clinton   *Farnsworth*   Upper Brookville

    Bryce, Lloyd Stephens   *Bryce House*   Roslyn Harbor
                                    (designed gatehouse, c. 1925)

    Byrne, James   (enlarged existing greenhouse, remodeled   Upper Brookville
                                    garden house and designed superintendent's
                                    house, 1914)

  * Coe, William Robertson   (enlarged existing greenhouse, remodeled   Upper Brookville
                                    garden house and designed superintendent's
                                    house, 1914)

    Coleman, Gregory   Muttontown

  * Cravath, Paul Drennan   *Veraton* (III)   Matinecock

  * Curran, Guernsey, Sr.   *Farlands*   Upper Brookville

  * Davis, Arthur Vining   Mill Neck

    Douglas, Josephine Hartford   Upper Brookville

  * Frick, Childs   *Clayton*   Roslyn Harbor
                                      (designed gatehouse, c. 1925)

    Heck, George Callendine, Sr.   *Linwood*   Muttontown

Guy Lowell (cont'd)

Nicastro, Louis Joseph		Mill Neck
Rentschler, Gordon Sohn		Matinecock
* Ripley, Julien Ashton, Sr.	*Three Corners Farm*	Muttontown

Clarence Sumner Luce

* Brown, George McKesson	*West Neck Farm*	Lloyd Harbor

J. Clinton Mackenzie

Blair, James Alonzo, Jr.	*Ontare* (barns)	Oyster Bay Cove
* Blair, James Alonzo, Sr.	*Ontare* (barns)	Oyster Bay Cove
Campbell, George W.	*Fort Hill House* (garage and gatehouse, c. 1910)	Lloyd Harbor
de Dampierre, Count		Centre Island
de Forest, Henry Grant	*Nethermuir* (stables, 1914)	Laurel Hollow
* de Forest, Henry Wheeler	*Nethermuir* (stables, 1914)	Laurel Hollow
de Forest, Johnston	*Wawapek* (farm complex, c. 1900)	Cold Spring Harbor
* de Forest, Robert Weeks	*Wawapek* (farm complex, c. 1900)	Cold Spring Harbor
* Inness–Brown, Hugh Alwyn, Sr.	*The Point*	Plandome Manor
Jennings, Oliver Burr, II	*Burrwood* (farm complex)	Lloyd Harbor
* Jennings, Walter	*Burrwood* (farm complex)	Lloyd Harbor
* Mackenzie, J. Clinton		Centre Island
* Matheson, William John	*Fort Hill House* (garage and gatehouse, c. 1910)	Lloyd Harbor
* Rusch, Henry Arthur, Sr.	*June Acres*	Centre Island
Williams, Douglas	*Wawapek* (farm complex, c. 1900)	Cold Spring Harbor
Wood, Willis Delano	*Fort Hill House* (garage and gatehouse, c. 1910)	Lloyd Harbor

Alexander Mackintosh

* Slade, John, Sr.	*Underhill House*	Upper Brookville

Howard Van Buren Magonigle

* Guggenheim, Isaac	*Villa Carola*	Sands Point
Guggenheim, Solomon Robert	*Trillora Court*	Sands Point

Howard Major

* Beard, William	(c. 1918 alterations)	Glen Cove
* Brewster, Samuel Dwight	*The Birches* (1915 alterations)	Glen Cove
* Carhart, Harold W., Sr.	(1920s alterations)	Lattingtown

Howard Major (cont'd)

  * Dean, Herbert Hollingshead   *Deanlea*   Lattingtown
    (1920s alterations)

  * Eldredge, Edward Irving, Jr.   (c. 1920 alterations)   Lattingtown
    Guinzburg, Harold Kleinert   (c. 1920 alterations)   Lattingtown
  * Hester, William Van Anden, Sr.   *Willada Point*   Glen Cove
    (1915 alterations)

    Hunter, Malcolm Du Bois   *Glenlo*   Glen Cove
    (c. 1920 alterations)

    Ladew, Edward R.   *Villa Louedo*   Glen Cove
    (1915 alterations)

    Murdock, Harvey   *The Birches*   Glen Cove
    (1915 alterations)

  * Ottley, James Henry, Sr.   *Oakleigh*   Glen Cove
    (1915 alterations)

  * Toerge, Norman K., Sr.   *The Hitching Post*   Matinecock
    Vanderbilt, Virginia Graham Fair   (c. 1918 alterations)   Glen Cove
    Ward, M. T.   (1915 alterations)   Glen Cove
  * Whitney, Howard Frederic, II   *Craigdarroch*   Glen Cove

Mann and MacNeille

    Devendorf, George   Lake Success
  * Jonas, Nathan Solomon   Lake Success

McKim, Mead and Bigelow

  * Alden, Anne Coleman   *Fort Hill House*   Lloyd Harbor
    (1878 house)

    Matheson, William John   *Fort Hill House*   Lloyd Harbor
    (1878 house)

McKim, Mead and White

  * Canfield, Augustus Cass   *Cassleigh*   North Hills
    (house, stables, and outbuildings)

    Choung, Terry   *Gracewood*   Cove Neck
  * Gracie, James King   *Gracewood*   Cove Neck
    Griswold, Frank Gray   (house, stables, and outbuildings)   North Hills
    Harriman, William Averell   (house and garage)   Sands Point
    Hitchcock, Thomas, Jr.   (house and garage)   Sands Point
  * Mackay, Clarence Hungerford   *Harbor Hill*   Roslyn
  * Morgan, Edwin Denison, III   *Wheatly*   Old Westbury
    Munsey, Frank Andrew   (alterations)   Manhasset
    Neilson, Raymond Perry Rodgers, Sr.   (alterations)   Old Westbury
  * Park, William Gray   *Turnpike Cottage*   Old Westbury
    (alterations)

    Roosevelt, George Emlen, Sr.   *Gracewood*   Cove Neck
  * Rumsey, Mary Harriman   Sands Point
    Ryan, John Dennis   *Derrymore*   North Hills
    (house, stables, and outbuildings)

McKim, Mead and White (cont'd)

Sherry, Louis	(alterations)	Manhasset
* Thomas, Ralph W., Sr.	(house and garage)	Sands Point
* Tuckerman, Walter C.	(house and alterations)	*[unable to locate - Oyster Bay]*
Vanderbilt, Virginia Graham Fair	*Fairmont* (alterations)	Manhasset
Whitney, Harry Payne		Old Westbury
* Whitney, William Collins		Old Westbury
* Winslow, Edward	(1887-1889 alterations)	Kings Point
Winthrop, Beekman, II	*Groton Farms* (house and stables)	Old Westbury
Winthrop, Grenville Lindall	(house and stables)	Old Westbury
* Winthrop, Robert Dudley	*Groton Farms* (house and stables)	Old Westbury

Mrs. John E. McLeran

* Cox, Irving E.	*Meadow Farm* (guest house)	Mill Neck
Fairchild, Sherman M.		Centre Island
* Pettinos, Charles E.	*Thatch Cottage*	Centre Island
Weiss, William Erhard, Jr.		Centre Island

William McMillan

* Roosevelt, Theodore, Jr.	*Old Orchard*	Cove Neck

William H. Miller

* Williams, Timothy Shaler	*Shorelands*	Lloyd Harbor

Addison Mizner

* Belmont, Alva Erskine Smith	*Beacon Towers* (tea house - unconfirmed)	Sands Point
* Brown, Stephen Howland	*Solana*	Matinecock
* Burden, Isaiah Townsend, Sr.		Brookville
De Leslie, Count Alexander Paulovitch		Sands Point
Harriman, William Averell	(c. 1910 tennis house)	Sands Point
Hearst, William Randolph	*Saint Joan* (tea house - unconfirmed)	Sands Point
Hitchcock, Thomas, Jr.	(c. 1910 tennis house)	Sands Point
Johnson, Seymour	*Driftwoods*	Sands Point
Kountze, deLancey	*Delbarton*	Brookville
* Mizner, Addison	*Old Cow Bay Manor House* (alterations)	Port Washington
* Monson, Sarah Cowen		Huntington Bay
* Parker, John Alley	*Driftwoods*	Sands Point
* Prime, William Albert, Sr.	*Warburton Hall*	Brookville
Stone, Charles Augustus, Sr.	*Solana*	Matinecock
* Thomas, Ralph W., Sr.	(c. 1910 tennis house)	Sands Point

Alexander Morgan

   * Morgan, Henry Sturgis, Sr.   Eaton's Neck

Benjamin W. Morris

Burden, James Abercrombie, III	*Woodside*	Old Brookville
* Peck, Fremont Carson, Sr.		Old Brookville

Montrose Whiting Morris

Hadley, Morris		Glen Cove
Hester, William Van Anden, Sr.	*Willada Point* (1898 stables)	Glen Cove
* Ladew, Edward R.	*Villa Louedo* (1898 stables)	Glen Cove
* Morris, Montrose Whiting		Glen Cove
Ward, M. T.	(1898 stables)	Glen Cove

Lionel Moses

Mulferrig, John B.		Lloyd Harbor
* Stafford, Jennie K.	*Broadwater*	Lloyd Harbor

Jacob Wrey Mould

Cartier		Roslyn Harbor
* Clapham, Thomas	*Stone House*	Roslyn Harbor
Hines, Ephram		Roslyn Harbor
Hughes, Dr. Wendell	*Wenlo*	Roslyn Harbor
Mott, Dr. Valentine		Roslyn Harbor
Stern, Benjamin	*Claraben Court*	Roslyn Harbor

Kenneth Murchinson

* Tully, William John	*Almar*	Mill Neck
Winters, Albert C.		Mill Neck

Daniel Murdock

Alker, Henry Alphonse, Sr.	*Hilltop*	Sands Point
Mohibu, A.		Sands Point

Francis A. Nelson

Close, Leroi		Mill Neck
* Niven, John Ballantine	*Rhuna Craig*	Mill Neck

Minerva Nichols

   * Nichols, John White Treadwell   *The Kettles*   Cove Neck

Noel and Miller

* de Milhau, Louis John de Grenon, Sr.	*Wrencroft* (1928 alterations)	Old Brookville
* Gould, Frank Miller	*Cedar Knolls*	Laurel Hollow
* Greer, William Armstrong	*Flower de Hundred*	Matinecock
Gubelmann, Walter Stanley		Laurel Hollow
* Henry, Barklie McKee		Old Westbury
Miller, Andrew Otterson, Jr.	*Ducks Landing*	Laurel Hollow
* Moffat, Douglas Maxwell	*Annandale*	Cold Spring Harbor

Noel and Miller (cont'd)

   * Noyes, David Chester, Sr.   *Netherwood*   Cold Spring Harbor

James W. O'Connor

   * Bermingham, John F.   *Midland Farm*   Muttontown

      Bono, Henry, Jr.   *The Crossroads*   Old Westbury
                               (house, stables, and tennis house)

   * Bostwick, Albert C., II   Old Westbury

   * Bostwick, George Herbert, Sr.   Old Westbury

      Bostwick, Lillian Stokes   Old Westbury

      Brokaw, George Tuttle   (stables)   Sands Point

   * Chadwick, Elbridge Gerry   *Russet*   Muttontown

      Douglas, Barry   (c. 1928 pool, playhouse and   Oyster Bay Cove
                               tennis court complex)

   * Fahys, George Ernest, Sr.   *Hilaire*   Matinecock
                               (house, stables, and pool/tennis
                               court building)

   * Fleischmann, Max C.   *The Lindens*   Sands Point
                               (stables)

      Gates, Elizabeth Hoagland   *Dormer House*   Lattingtown
                               (tennis court complex)

      Gossler, Philip Green, Sr.   *Highfield*   Brookville
                               (c. 1937 alterations)

   * Grace, Joseph Peter, Sr.   *Tullaroan*   North Hills

   * Grace, William Russell, Jr.   *The Crossroads*   Old Westbury
                               (house, stables, and tennis house)

   * Grace, William Russell, Sr.   *Gracefield*   Kings Point
                               (alterations)

   * Haggerson, Frederic H.   Plandome

   * Holmes, Artemas   *Holmestead Farm*   Old Brookville

   * Hutton, Edward Francis   *Hutfield*   Brookville
                               (c. 1937 alterations)

      Ingalls, Fay   *Sunken Orchard*   Oyster Bay Cove
                               (c. 1928 pool, playhouse and
                               tennis court complex)

   * Ladew, Harvey Smith, II   *The Box*   Old Brookville
                               (c. 1919 alterations)

      Lunning, Frederick   *Northcourt*   North Hills

      Lynch, Edmund Calvert, Sr.   (house, stables, and pool/tennis   Matinecock
                               court building)

   * Martin, Alastair Bradley   (c. 1938 alterations)   Old Brookville

   * McCann, Charles Edward Francis   *Sunken Orchard*   Oyster Bay Cove
                               (pool, playhouse, and tennis
                               court complex, c. 1928)

      Mitchell, Sidney Alexander, Sr.   *Marney*   Matinecock

   * Mitchell, Sidney Zollicoffer   Matinecock

      Munsel, Patrice   *Lockjaw Ridge*   Lattingtown
                               (tennis court complex)

James W. O'Connor (cont'd)

    Paley, William S.   *Kiluna Farms*   North Hills
                                      (tennis building)

    Park, Darragh Anderson   *Hyde Park*   Old Brookville
                                      (c. 1938 alterations)

    Patterson, Dorothy F.   Upper Brookville

* Pulitzer, Ralph, Sr.   *Kiluna Farms*   North Hills
                                      (tennis building)

    Raquet, Walter   *Lockjaw Ridge*   Lattingtown
                                      (tennis court complex)

* Redmond, Geraldyn Livingston, Sr.   *Gray Horse Farm*   Upper Brookville
    Robinson, John Randolph   (c. 1937 alterations)   Brookville
    Schwartz, Charles   (stables)   Sands Point

* Shearman, Lawrence Hobart   North Hills

* Sloane, George   *Brookmeade*   Lattingtown
                                      (tennis court complex)

* Stearns, John Noble, III   Old Brookville

* Thieriot, Charles Henschel, Sr.   *Cedar Hill*   Muttontown
    Tinker, Edward Richmond, Jr.   *Woodbury House*   Syosset
                                      (tennis building)

    Vanderbilt, Alfred, Gwynne, II   (stables)   Sands Point
    Vietor, Dr. John Adolf, Sr.   *Cherrywood*   Matinecock
                       (house, stables, and pool/tennis court building)

    Vilas, Guillermo   *Lockjaw Ridge*   Lattingtown
                                      (tennis court complex)

* Webb, James, Watson, Sr.   *Woodbury House*   Syosset
                                      (tennis building)

    Woodward, William, Jr.   *The Playhouse*   Oyster Bay Cove
                       (pool, playhouse, and tennis court complex, c. 1928)

Palmer and Hornbostel

* Dwight, Arthur Smith   Kings Point

Gordon S. Parker

* Hornblower, George Sanford   *Laurel Top*   Laurel Hollow

Chester M. Patterson

    Babcock, Henry Dennison, Sr.   Mill Neck

* Batterman, Henry Lewis, Sr.   Matinecock

* Betts, Wyllis Rossiter, Jr.   *The Pebbles*   Oyster Bay Cove

* Slade, Josephine Bissell Roe   *Pine Terrace*   Mill Neck
    Wyckoff, Richard Demille   *Twin Lindens*   Kings Point

* Wyckoff, Walter   *Twin Lindens*   Kings Point

Peabody, Wilson and Brown

    Auchincloss, Charles Crooke   *Builtover*   Roslyn Heights
                                      (c. 1925 alterations)

* Auchincloss, Gordon, Sr.   *Ronda*   Matinecock

Peabody, Wilson and Brown (cont'd)

* Barnes, Courtlandt Dixon, Sr.	*Nonesuch House*	Manhasset
* Clark, James Averell, Sr.		Old Westbury
* Cutting, Dr. Fulton	(1930s alterations)	Brookville
Cutting, Dr. Fulton		North Hills
* Dewing, Herman E.	*Appledore*	Matinecock
* Emmet, Richard Stockton, Sr.	*High Elms*	Glen Cove
Entenmann, William, Jr.	*Timber Bay Farm*	Old Westbury
* Hadden, Emily Georgina Hamilton	*Dogwood*	Jericho
Hadden, Miss Frances	*Dogwood*	Jericho
Hickox, Charles V.	*Boxwood Farm*	Old Westbury
Hoppin, William Warner, Jr.	*Friendship Hill*	Old Brookville
* Kramer, Albert Ludlow, Sr.	*Picket Farm*	Jericho
Lehman, Allan Sigmund	*Picket Farm*	Jericho
Martin, Alastair Bradley		Old Brookville
McCory, Nellie	*Whispered Wishes* (c. 1925 alterations)	Roslyn Heights
* Milburn, Devereux, Sr.	*Sunridge Hall*	Old Westbury
* Murray, Hugh A.	*Gay Gardens*	Old Westbury
* Norton, Huntington	*Notley Hill*	Oyster Bay
* Park, Darragh Anderson, Sr.	*Hyde Park*	Old Brookville
* Peabody, Julian Livingston, Sr.	*Pound Hollow Farm*	Old Westbury
* Preston, William Payne Thompson, Sr.		Jericho
Rumsey, Charles Cary, Sr.	(1930s alterations)	Brookville
* Schmidlapp, Carl Jacob, Sr.	*Rumpus House* (c. 1920 alterations)	Mill Neck
Thieriot, Charles Henschel, II		Matinecock
Twohig, Dr. Daniel	(c. 1925 alterations)	Roslyn Heights
Von Stade, Francis Skiddy, Sr.	(c. 1930 alterations)	Old Westbury

Hall Pleasants Pennington

Dick, Fairman Rogers	*Apple Tree Hill*	Old Brookville
Merrill, Joseph L.	*Chanticleer*	Matinecock
* Mixsell, Dr. Harold Ruckman	*Forest Edge*	Matinecock
* Pennington, Hall Pleasants		Matinecock
* Roosevelt, Philip James, Sr.	*Dolonar*	Cove Neck
Wang, Charles B.		Cove Neck

John H. Phillips

* Anderson, George A.		Old Brookville
* Bryan, James Taylor, Sr.		Mill Neck
Hubbs, Charles Francis		Old Brookville
* Kettles, Richard C., Jr.	*Orchard Corners*	Old Brookville

Charles A. Platt

* Bergquist, John Gosta	*Brymptonwood*	Upper Brookville
Brokaw, Clifford Vail, Jr.	*The Elms*	Glen Cove
* Brokaw, Clifford Vail, Sr.	*The Elms*	Glen Cove
Brown, Nannie C. Inman	*The Elms*	Glen Cove
Cushman, Paul, Sr.	*Tapis Vert*	Oyster Bay Cove
Dyer, Elisha, VII	*The Orchards*	Brookville
* Dyer, George Rathbone, Sr.	*The Orchards*	Brookville
* Hare, Meredith	*Pidgeon Hill*	South Huntington
Holloway, William Grace, Jr.		Upper Brookville
* Ledyard, Lewis, Cass, Jr.	*Westwood* (house, teahouse and stables)	Oyster Bay Cove
* Lloyd, Robert MacAllister, Sr.	*Tapis Vert*	Oyster Bay Cove
Nitze, Paul Henry	*The Farm House*	Glen Cove
Paley, William S.	*Kiluna Farm* (swimming pool and bathhouse, 1913)	North Hills
* Pratt, Frederic Bayley	*Poplar Hill* (II)	Glen Cove
* Pratt, John Teele, Jr.	*The Farm House*	Glen Cove
* Pratt, John Teele, Sr.	*Manor House* (house, farm complex and outbuildings)	Glen Cove
* Pulitzer, Ralph, Sr.	*Kiluna Farm* (swimming pool and bathhouse, 1913)	North Hills
* Reed, Lansing Parmelee	*Windy Hill* (house and outbuildings)	Lloyd Harbor
Sanesi, Dr. Lorenzo	*La Primavera*	Glen Cove
* Weld, Francis Minot, II	*Lulworth* (house and stables)	Lloyd Harbor

William Platt

* Pratt, John Teele, Jr.	*Beechwood*	Glen Cove
Sutton, Keith		Glen Cove

Polhemus and Coffin

* Blackwell, Charles Addison	*The Cedars*	Upper Brookville
* di Zoppola, Countess, Edith Mortimer		Mill Neck
* Ford, Nevil	*Woodford*	Lloyd Harbor
* Guggenheim, Florence Shloss	*Mille Fleurs*	Sands Point
* Guggenheim, Harry Frank	*Falaise*	Sands Point
* Gwynne, Arthur	*Mill Cove* (1929 alterations)	Lloyd Harbor
Sheeline, Paul Cushing	(1929 alterations)	Lloyd Harbor
Thomas, Joseph Albert	*Normandie*	Upper Brookville

John Russell Pope

Amari, Philippo		Dix Hills
* Bacon, Robert	*Old Acres*	Old Westbury

John Russell Pope (cont'd)

* Bacon, Robert Low	*Arlough*	Old Westbury
* Bertschmann, Louis Frederick	*Les Bouleaux*	Muttontown
* Burden, Arthur Scott		Brookville
* Burrill, Middleton Schoolbred	*Jericho Farms*	Jericho
Cary, Guy Fairfax, Sr.	*Oak Hill*	Brookville
Crocker, George		Old Westbury
* Field, Marshall, III	*Caumsett*	Lloyd Harbor
* Gavin Michael	*Greanan*	Brookville
* Gossler, Philip Green, Sr.	*Highfield* (mid-1920s alterations)	Brookville
* Gould, Charles Albert	*Chateauiver*	Dix Hills
Hutton, Edward Francis	*Hutfield* (house and mid-1920s alterations)	Brookville
Hutton, William E., II		Old Westbury
Kadish, Lawrence		Old Westbury
* Kerrigan, Joseph J.		Cove Neck
LeRoux, Eduoard	*Cottage Normandy*	Brookville
* Lowe, Henry Wheeler	*Mariemont*	Old Westbury
* Mills, Ogden Livingston		Woodbury
Phipps, Henry Carnegie	*Spring Hill*	Old Westbury
* Robinson, John Randolph		Brookville
Sage, Henry William, II		Brookville
Spiegel, Jerry		Woodbury
* Stow, William L.		Old Westbury
* Vanderbilt, Virginia Graham Fair		Brookville
* Vanderbilt, William Kissam, Jr.	*Deepdale* (gatehouse, c. 1906)	Lake Success

George Browne Post

Shonnard, Horatio Seymour, Sr.	*Boscobel* (c. 1888 alterations)	Oyster Bay
* Underhill, Francis T.	(c. 1888 alterations)	Oyster Bay
Weidenfeld, Camille	(c. 1888 alterations)	Oyster Bay

Potter and Robertson

* Adams, Sarah Sampson	*Hillside*	Oyster Bay
Derby, Dr. Richard	*Old Adam*	Oyster Bay
Dieffenbach, William		Oyster Bay

Bruce Price

Grace, Oliver Russell	*Yellowbanks*	Cove Neck
* Roosevelt, James Alfred	*Yellowbanks*	Cove Neck
Roosevelt, John Kean	*Yellowbanks*	Cove Neck
Roosevelt, William Emlen	*Yellowbanks*	Cove Neck

J. W. Von Rehling Quistgaard

    * Quistgaard, J. W. Von Rehling   *[unable to locate - Oyster Bay]*

Renwick, Aspinwall and Owen

Armsby, George Newell, Sr.		Centre Island
* Bullock, George	*The Folly* (II)	Centre Island
Gubelmann, Walter Stanley	*Southerly*	Centre Island
* Hoyt, Colgate, Sr.	*Eastover*	Centre Island
Mahana, George Shaw	*Birchlea*	Centre Island
Nichols, William Henry, Jr.	*Applegarth*	Centre Island
Smith, Albert Edward, Sr.		Centre Island
* Wetmore, Charles Whitman	*Applegarth*	Centre Island

Greville Rickard

* Barstow, William Slocum	*Elm Point*	Kings Point
* Eden, John H., II	*Topping*	Kings Point
Lundy, Frederick William Irving	*Lundy House*	Kings Point

John W. Ritch

Ihasz, Nicholas		Cove Neck
Mathers, William Harris		Cove Neck
Merle–Smith, Van Santvoord, Sr.	*The Paddocks*	Cove Neck
* Swan, Edward H., Sr.	*The Evergreens*	Cove Neck

Rogers and Zogbaum

* Clark, Frederick Ambrose	*Broad Hollow House*	Old Westbury

James Gamble Rogers

Dickson, Thomas, Sr.	*Petit Bois*	Lattingtown
* Harkness, William Lamon	(alterations)	Glen Cove, West Island
Huntington, Robert Dinsmore, Jr.	(ship room)	Mill Neck
* Huntington, Robert Dinsmore, Sr.	(ship room)	Mill Neck
* Ide, George Edward	*Petit Bois*	Lattingtown
Lehman, Ellen	(ship room)	Mill Neck
Lindsey, Christopher F.		Cove Neck
Martin, Grinnell	*Grey Cottage*	Cove Neck
Moen, A. Rene	*Renwood*	Cove Neck
* Moen, LeClanche		Cove Neck

Thomas C. Rogers

* Cooper, Kenneth F.		Kings Point
Opperman, Joseph		Kings Point

Romeyn and Stever

Hester, William Van Anden, Sr.	*Willada Point*	Glen Cove
* Ladew, Edward R.	*Villa Louedo*	Glen Cove
Ward, M. T.		Glen Cove

Erick Kensett Rossiter

	Marsh, John Bigelow, Sr.	*Nyrmah*	Mill Neck
*	Peters, William Richmond	*Hawirt*	Mill Neck
	Vanderbilt, Alfred Gwynne, II		Mill Neck

Rouse and Goldstone

	Cozzens, Issachar, III	*Maple Knoll*	Lattingtown
*	Lyon, Augusta Hay		*[unable to locate - Huntington]*
	Morgan, Henry Sturgis, Sr.		Lattingtown
	Oberlin, Abraham		Lattingtown

Henry W. Rowe

	Aldred, John Edward	*Ormston* (two gatehouses, several workers' cottages, farm complex, bathhouse, and pier)	Lattingtown

Mott B. Schmidt

*	Bateson, Edgar Farrar, Sr.	*Deramore*	Cold Spring Harbor
	Moffett, George Monroe, Sr.	*Les Bois*	Old Brookville
*	Robertson, Charles Sammis	(designed house and garage)	Lloyd Harbor
*	Runyon, Clarkson, Jr.	*The Farm House*	Glen Cove

Mott B. Schmidt and Mogen Tvede

	Appleby, Francis Storm		Old Brookville
*	Clarke, Jeremiah, Sr.		Old Brookville
*	Ely, Albert Heman, Jr.	*Elyston*	Lloyd Harbor
	Freidus, Jacob		Lloyd Harbor
*	Jennings, Oliver Burr, II	*Dark Hollow*	Lloyd Harbor
	McClure, Walter C.	*Tall Trees*	Old Brookville

Henry Renwick Sedgwick

	Lawrence, Effingham, II	(1934 alterations)	Cold Spring Harbor
	Rinaldini, Luis Emilio		Old Westbury
*	Winthrop, Robert, II	*Groton Place*	Old Westbury

Severance and Schumm

*	Anderson, John	*Aberfeldy*	Lattingtown
*	Bailey, Frank, Sr.	*Munnysunk* (1912 alterations)	Lattingtown
	Clark, John	(1912 alterations)	Lattingtown
*	O'Donohue, Charles A.		Huntington Bay
	Shea, Edward Lane		Lattingtown

Leon H. Smith

*	Ford, Hannibal Choate		Kings Point
	Seeger, Hall		Kings Point

Paul R. Smith

*	Phipps, John Shaffer	*Westbury House* (swimming pool)	Old Westbury

Chandler Stearns

* Ryan, John Carlos		Roslyn Heights
Whalen, Grover A., Sr.		Roslyn Heights

Stearns and Stanton

Emanuel, Victor	*Dorwood* (1937 tap room)	North Hills
* Kelley, Cornelius Francis	*Sunny Skies* (1937 tap room)	North Hills

Stephenson and Wheeler

* Garver, John Anson	*Wrexleigh*	Oyster Bay Cove

Stickney and Austin

* Bullock, George	*The Folly* (I)	Centre Island

Charles Augustus Stone, Sr.

* Stone, Charles Augustus, Sr.		Matinecock

Edward Durell Stone

* Goodyear, Anson Conger, Sr.		Old Westbury

Penrose V. Stout

* Doubleday, Nelson, Sr.	*Barberrys* (garage and cottage)	Mill Neck

Egbert Swartworth

* Luckenbach, Edgar Frederick, Sr.	*Elm Court*	Sands Point

Louis Comfort Tiffany

Lusk, Dr. Graham	*The Briars*	Laurel Hollow
* Tiffany, Louis Comfort	*Laurelton Hall*	Laurel Hollow
* Tiffany, Louis Comfort	*The Briars*	Laurel Hollow

Tooker and Marsh

* Carver, Amos Dow	*Amincliff*	Lattingtown
Carver, Clifford Nickels	*Amincliff*	Lattingtown
Korboth, Roland		Lattingtown

Treanor and Fatio

Balsan, Consuelo Vanderbilt	*Old Fields*	East Norwich
Bonner, Paul Hyde, Sr.		Lattingtown
Hagan, Winston Henry, II	*Fox Brae*	Lattingtown
* Schiff, Dorothy	*Old Fields*	East Norwich
* Stehli, Emil J.	*Hawk Hill Place*	Lattingtown
* Vanderbilt, George Washington, IV		Sands Point

Trowbridge and Ackerman

Cook, Walter		Lattingtown
Hirsch, Peter	*Wildbank*	Sands Point
King, Everett W.		Lattingtown
* Pratt, George du Pont, Sr.	*Killenworth* (II)	Glen Cove
* Pratt, Theodore, Sr.	*Whispering Pines*	Lattingtown
Sousa, John Philip, Sr.	*Wildbank*	Sands Point

Trowbridge and Livingston

* Brewster, George S.   *Fairleigh*   Muttontown

  Meyer, Robert J.   Muttontown

Horace Trumbauer

  Blair, Watson Keep   Muttontown

  Blair, Wolcott   Muttontown

* Brokaw, Howard Crosby   *The Chimneys*   Muttontown

  Clews, Henry, III   *La Lanterne*   Upper Brookville

* Clews, James Blanchard   *La Lanterne*   Upper Brookville

  Crocker, George   (1918 alterations)   Old Westbury

* Dows, David, Jr.   *Charlton Hall*   Muttontown

* Grace, Joseph Peter, Sr.   *Tullaroan* (1917 alterations)   North Hills

* Phipps, Henry, Jr.   *Bonnie Blink*   Lake Success

* Phipps, Henry Carnegie   *Spring Hill* (1918 alterations)   Old Westbury

* Phipps, John Shaffer   *Westbury House* (alterations)   Old Westbury

  Stow, William L.   (1918 alterations)   Old Westbury

* Vanderbilt, William Kissam, Jr.   *Deepdale*   Lake Success

William B. Tubby

  Maxwell, John Rogers, Jr.   *Maxwelton* (house and outbuildings)   Glen Cove

* Maxwell, John Rogers, Sr.   *Maxwelton* (house and outbuildings)   Glen Cove

* Pratt, George du Pont, Sr.   *Killenworth* (I)   Glen Cove

Charles A. Valentine

* Hopkins, Erustis Langdon   *Wildwood*   Matinecock

Vaux, Withers and Co.

  Goddard, Conrad Godwin   *Montrose* (addition of wing, 1869)   Roslyn Harbor

* Godwin, Parke   *Montrose* (addition of wing, 1869)   Roslyn Harbor

  Zenz, Dr. Frederick Anton   *Montrose* (addition of wing, 1869)   Roslyn Harbor

Ferruccio Vitale

* Hoppin, Gerard Beekman   *Four Winds* (swimming pool complex, 1930)   Oyster Bay Cove

  Kelland, Clarence Budington   *Sandy Cay* (swimming pool complex)   Sands Point

* Nast, Conde   *Sandy Cay* (swimming pool complex)   Sands Point

  Schiff, Dorothy   *Sandy Cay* (swimming pool complex)   Sands Point

  Uris, Percy   *Sandy Cay* (swimming pool complex)   Sands Point

Walker and Gillette

*	Aldrich, Sherwood	*Snug Harbor*	Kings Point
*	Aron, Jacob	*Hamptworth House*	Kings Point
	Astin, Dr. Sherrill	(1926 alterations)	Lattingtown
*	Baker, George Fisher, II	*Ventura Point* (alterations)	Centre Island
*	Baker, George Fisher, III	*Vikings Cove*	Lattingtown
	Barney, Charles Tracy	(1934 alterations)	Old Westbury
	Bartow, Francis Dwight, Sr.	*Belvoir* (house and outbuildings)	Glen Cove
*	Brokaw, Irving	*Goose Point*	Matinecock
	Carey, William Francis, Jr.	(alterations)	Centre Island
*	Coe, William Robertson	*Planting Fields*	Upper Brookville
*	Davison, Henry Pomeroy, Sr.	*Peacock Point* (family compound)	Lattingtown
*	Gibson, Harvey Dow	*Lands End* (1926 alterations)	Lattingtown
*	Godfrey, Henry Fletcher, Sr.		Old Westbury
*	Hill, James Norman	*Big Tree Farm*	Brookville
*	Hine, Frances Lyman	*Mayhasit* (house and outbuildings)	Glen Cove
	Howe, Polly Brooks	*Severn*	Lattingtown
	LeRoux, Edouard	(house and outbuildings)	Glen Cove
*	Loew, William Goadby	*Loewmoor* (1934 alterations)	Old Westbury
	Manice, William de Forest, Sr.	*Edgewood House*	Old Westbury
	Paley, William	*Kiluna Farm*	North Hills
*	Pulitzer, Ralph, Sr.	*Kiluna Farm*	North Hills
	Sloan, Alfred Pritchard, Jr.	*Snug Harbor*	Kings Point
	Smith, Herbert Ludlam, Sr.	(alterations)	Centre Island
	Smithers, Robert Brinkley	*Longhur*	Mill Neck
	Stevens, Charles Albert	*Annandale* (1934 alterations)	Old Westbury
	Tailer, Thomas Suffern, Jr.	*Beaupre*	Lattingtown
	Tower, Roderick		Lattingtown

Leroy P. Ward

*	Hunter, Fenley	*Porto Bello*	Kings Point
*	Schermerhorn, Alfred Coster		Matinecock
*	Vanderveer, Stephen Lott	*Kenwood* (alterations)	Great Neck

Warren and Clark

*	Henderson, Frank C.	*Villa Marina*	Roslyn
*	Osborn, Alexander Perry, Sr.	*Valley House*	Brookville
	Will, Harold Henry	*Villa Marina*	Roslyn

Architects

Warren and Wetmore

* Field, Marshall, III	*Caumsett* (indoor tennis court, 1924)	Lloyd Harbor
Gary, Elbert H.	*Ivy Hall*	Jericho
* Guggenheim, Isaac	*Villa Carola* (outbuildings)	Sands Point
Guggenheim, Solomon Robert	*Trillora Court* (outbuildings)	Sands Point
* Iselin, Charles Oliver	*Wolvers Hollow* (alterations)	Upper Brookville
* Mackay, Clarence Hungerford	*Harbor Hill* (outbuildings)	Roslyn
* Preston, Ralph Julius	*Ivy Hall*	Jericho
Stevens, Byam K., Jr.	*Kirby Hill* (house and stables)	Muttontown
* Stevens, Joseph Sampson	*Kirby Hill* (house and stables)	Muttontown
Taylor, James Blackstone, Sr.		Jericho
* Vanderbilt, William Kissam, Jr.	*Deepdale* (golf clubhouse)	Lake Success
* Vanderbilt, William Kissam, Jr.	*Eagle's Nest*	Centerport

A. Dunham Wheeler

* Anderson, Henry Burrall	*The Boulders*	*[unable to locate - Kings Point]*
Du Bois, Eugene	*Fleetwood*	Oyster Bay Cove
O'Neill, Grover, Sr.	*Fleetwood*	Oyster Bay Cove
* Sewell, Robert Van Vorst	*Fleetwood*	Oyster Bay Cove

Willauer, Sharpe and Bready

* Johnston, John Herbert	*Boatcroft*	Lloyd Harbor

Edgar Irving Williams

* Holmes, Bettie Fleischmann	*The Chimneys*	Sands Point

John Torrey Windrim

* Brady, Nicholas Frederic	*Inisfada*	North Hills

Wyeth and King

* Blagden, Linzee		Cold Spring Harbor
* Dulles, Allen Welsh		Lloyd Harbor
Folkerts, Heiko Hid		Woodbury
James, Henry	*Greenleaves*	Cold Spring Harbor
* King, Frederic Rhinelander		Woodbury
Lawrence, Effingham, II	(1951 alterations)	Cold Spring Harbor

York and Sawyer

Anderson, Henry Hill, II	*Handyhill*	Cove Neck
* Smith, D. W.		Cove Neck

See the surname entry to ascertain specific civic activism information.

Albright, Joseph Medill Patterson

Albright, Madeleine Jana Korbel

Aldred, John Edward

Aldrich, Harriet Alexander

Aldrich, Winthrop Williams

Alker, Alphonse Henry

Alker, Florence Ward

Alker, Henry Alphonse, Sr.

Alker, James Ward, Sr.

Ames, Amyas

Ames, Charles Edgar

Anderson, Henry Burrall, Sr.

Armsby, George Newell, Sr.

Aron, Jacob

Astor, Brooke Russell Marshal

Atherton, Henry Francis, Sr.

Auchincloss, Gordon

Auchincloss, Janet House

Babbott, Dr. Frank Lusk, Jr.

Babcock, Frederick Huntington

Backus, Louise Burton Laidlaw

Bacon, Martha Waldron Cowdin

Bacon, Virginia Murray

Bailey, Frank, Sr.

Baker, George Fisher, II

Baker, John C., Sr.

Baldwin, Ruth Standish Bowles

Ballantine, Arthur Atwood, Sr.

Ballantine, Helen B. Graves

Balsan, Consuelo Vanderbilt

Barstow, Francoise M. Duclos

Barstow, William Slocum

Bartow, Francis Dwight, Sr.

Baruch, Dr. Herman Benjamin

Bateson, Edgar Farrar, Sr.

Beekman, James William, Sr.

Bell, James Christy, Jr.

Belmont, Alva Erskine Smith

Belmont, Eleanor Robson

Benkard, Bertha King Bartlett

Bergquist, John Gosta

Bermingham, John F,

Bevin, Sydney

Biddle, William Canby, II

Bingham, Harry Payne, Sr.

Bishop, Richard E.

Blackstone, Henry

Blackwell, Charles Addison

Blackwell, Katherine B. Rhodes

Blagden, Dorothea Draper

Blagden, Linzee

Bleecker, Theophylact Bache, Jr.

Bliss, Zaidee C. Cobb
   [*later*, Goodyear]

Bodman, Herbert L., Sr.

Bodman, Theodora Dunham

Boegner, Margaret Helen Phipps

Bonner, Douglas Griswold, Sr.

Bonner, Paul Hyde, Sr.

Bostwick, Albert C, II

Bottomley, William Lawrence

Bowdoin, George Temple

Brady, Genevieve F. Gavan

Breed, William Constable, Sr.

Brewster, George S.

Brewster, Isabel Erskine Parks

Brion, Lester E., Sr.

Brion, Lucille Demarest

Brokaw, Clare Boothe
　[*later*, Luce] Brooks, Winthrop Holley

Brower, Marion Willetts

Brown, George McKesson

Brown, Milton D.

Bruce, David Kirkpatrick Este

Bucknall, Clara Legg

Bucknall, Henry W. J.

Bucknall, Margaret V. Powers

Bullock, George

Burchard, Allene Tew

Burchard, Anson Wood

Burden, Chester Griswold

Burden, Eleanor Cotton

Burr, Nelson Beardsley

Bush, Edith Westervelt Low

Bush, Harriet Balsdon Pratt

Byrne, James

Campbell, Oliver Allen, Sr.

Carr, Edward A. T.

Carrol, Lorraine Graves
　[*later*, Grace]

Carter, Cora Cartwright Connelly

Carver, Amos Dow

Carver, Clifford Nickels

Casey, William Joseph, Jr.

Castro, Theresa Barabas

Chadbourne, Marie Starr

Chadbourne, Thomas Lincoln, Jr.

Chadwick, Dorothy May Jordan

Chalkley, Otway Hebron

Cheney, Ward

Choate, Alice Muller
　[*later*, Gossler]

Church, Frederic Edwin

Clark, Frederick Ambrose

Clark, Grenville

Clark, James Averell, Sr.

Clark, Nancy D'Wolf Pegram

Clark, Virginia Keep

Cockran, Anne L. Ide

Coe, Henry Eugene, Jr.

Coe, William Robertson

Coe, William Rogers

Coffin, Catherine Butterfield

Coffin, Charles Albert

Coffin, William Sloane, Sr.

Colgate, Gilbert, II

Collins, Edith Derby Newcomb

Costantini, Count David A.

Coudert, Frederic Rene, Jr.

Cournand, Edouard L.

Cowl, Clarkson

Cowl, Donald Hearn

Cox, Irving E.

Cram, Edith Clare Bryce

Crane, Clinton Hoadley, Jr.

Crary, Miner Dunham, Sr.

Cravath, Paul Drennan

Crisp, Van Devanter

Cross, Martha McCook

Cudlipp, Chandler, Sr.

Curtis, James Freeman

Cushman, Cordelia S.

Cushman, Paul, Sr.

Cutcheon, Franklin Warner M.

Davey, William Nelson

Davies, Joseph Edward
 [*see* Post]

Davis, Arthur Vining

Davis, Marguerite Sawyer
 [*see* Hill]

Davis, Ellen G. Bassel

Davis, John William

Davis, Joseph Edward, Sr.

Davison, Dorothy Peabody

Davison, Frederick Trubee

Davison, Henry Pomeroy, II

Davison, Henry Pomeroy, Sr.

Davison, Kate Trubee

Davisson, Helen Porter
 [*later*, Pryibil]

Dean, Arthur Hobson

Dean, Mary Talbott Marden

DeBrabant, Mary C. Clark

de Forest, Emily Johnston

de Forest, Henry Wheeler

de Forest, Johnston

de Forest, Julia Mary

de Forest, Robert Weeks

DeGraff, Robert Fair

DeLamar, Joseph Raphael

Delehanty, Margaret E. Rowland

Demarest, John M.

de Milhau, Louis John de G., Sr.

Derby, Ethel Roosevelt

de Roulet, Vincent W.

de Seversky, Alexander Prokofieff

Dexter, Stanley Walker

Dickerman, Bradley Watson, Sr.

Diebold, Albert Henry

Dillon, Herbert Lowell, Sr.

Dilworth, Dewees Wood

Dilworth, Edith Logan

Donnell, Henry Ellingwood

Doubleday, Florence Van Wyck

Doubleday, Frank Nelson

Doubleday, Neltje Blanchan D.

Dows, David, Jr.

Draper, Charles Dana

Dresselhuys, Cornelius W
 [*see* Manville]

Du Bois, Carol Johnston Mali

Du Bois, Eugene

Duer, Beverly

Dulles, Allen Welsh

Dulles, Janet Pomeroy Avery

Dulles, John Foster

Dulles, Martha Clover Todd

Duryea, Ellen H. Winchester

Duryea, Dr. Garrett DeNyse

Dwight, Arthur Smith

Dyer, Elisha, VII

Dyer, George Rathbone, Sr.

Dykman, William Nelson

Eagle, Henry, Sr.

Earle, Henry Montague

Eberstadt, Ferdinand

Eberstadt, Mary V. A. Tongue

Eden, Bronson Beecher Tuttle, Sr.

Eden, John H., II

Eden, Muriel Seymour Tuttle

Elbert, Robert George

Eldridge, Louise Udall Skidmore

Eldridge, Roswell

Elmhirst, Dorothy Payne Whitney

Ely, Albert Heman, Jr.

Emanuel, Victor

Emmet, Helen L. Pratt

Emmet, Jesse Keena Schroeder

Emmet, Richard Stockton, Sr.

Everitt, Samuel Alexander

Fahys, George Ernest, Sr.

Fairchild, Julian Percy, Sr.

Farwell, Mildred Williams

Fates, Harold Leighton, Sr.
 [*see* M. G. Miller]

Ferry, E. Hayward

Field, Evelyn Marshall

Field, Marshal, III

Field, Ruth Pruyn
 [*see* Phipps]

Fish, Edwin A.

Fish Fleischmann, Max C.

Fisher, Joel Ellis, II

Folger, Emily Clara Jordan

Folger, Henry Clay

Ford, Nevil

Fordyce, Dorothy W.

Forrestal, Josephine Ogden

Foy, Thelma Chrysler

Francke, Jane Bush

Frank, Charles Augustus, Sr.

Frank, Louise, Clark Read

Franklin, Elizabeth Jennings

Franklin, George Small, Sr.

Franklin Philip Albright S., Sr.

Fraser, Alfred Valentine

Fraser, Martha Willets Mott

Fremont, Julie Fay Bradley
 [*see* Shipman]

Frick, Childs

Frick, Frances S. Dixon

Froessel, Charles William

Gales, George M.

Garvan, Mabel Brady

Gary, Elbert H.

Gavin, Gertrude Hill

Gerard, James Watson, III

Gerard, Mary A. Daly

Gerdes, John

Gerry, Margaret Newbauer

Gerry, Dr. Roger Goodman

Gibbs, William Frances
  [*see* Larkin]

Gibson, Harvey Dow

Gignoux, Emma Messenger

Gilder, Rodman, Sr.

Goddard, Conrad Godwin

Godwin, Elizabeth Marquand

Godwin, Parke

Goldman, Herman

Goodwin, Philip Lippincott

Goodyear, Anson Conger, Sr.

Goodyear, Zaidee C. Cobb

Gossler, Alice Muller

Gould, Edwin

Gould, Frank Miller

Grace, David R.

Grace, Joseph Peter, II

Grace, Joseph Peter, Sr.

Grace, Lorraine Graves

Grace, Louise Natalie

Grace, Morgan Hatton, Sr.

Grace, Oliver Russell

Grace, William Russell, Jr.

Grace, William Russell, Sr.

Gray, Henry Gunther

Griswold, Frank Gray

Grumman, Rose Marion Werther

Guggenheim, Daniel

Guggenheim, Florence Shloss

Guggenheim, Harry Frank

Guggenheim, Isaac

Guggenheim, Solomon Robert

Guggenheim, William, Sr.

Guthrie, Ella Elizabeth Fuller

Guthrie, William Dameron

Gwynne, Arthur

Hadley, John Wood Blodgett

Hadley, Morris

Haff, Alvah Weeks

Hagedorn, Amelia

Hagedorn, Horace

Hagen, Winston Henry, II

Halsey, Elizabeth Tower

Halsey, Richard Townley Haines

Hamersley, Louis Gordon, Sr.

Hammond, Paul Lyman

Hammond, Susan Ridley Sedgwick

Handy, Parker Douglas

Hanks, Stedman Shumway

Hare, Elizabeth Sage

Harjes, Frederica V. Berwind

Harjes, Henry Herman

Harkness, Edward Stephen

Harkness, Mary Emma Stillman

Harriman, William Averell

Harris, Henry Upham, Sr.

Harris, Mary Messinger Webster

Havemeyer, Horace, Jr.

Hawkes, Alice Sillman Belknap

Heckscher, August

Heckscher, Virginia Henry

Hedges, Benjamin Van Doren, II

Henderson, Helen Iselin

Henry, Barklie McKee

Hepburn, Frederick Taylor

Herzog, Edwin H.

Hickox, Charles V.

Hicks, Henry

Hill, Marguerite Sawyer

Hill, Dr. Miner C.

Hitchcock, Thomas, Sr.

Hoffman, William Wickham

Hoguet, Dr. Joseph Peter, Sr.

Holloway, William Grace, Sr.

Holmes, Bettie Fleischmann

Honeyman, Robert B.

Hoppin, Gerard Beekman

Hoppin, Mary Gallatin

Hoppin, William Warner, Jr.

Horowitz, Louis Jay

Houston, Herbert Sherman

Howe, Polly Brooks

Howe, Richard Flint

Howe, William Deering

Hughes, Dr. Wendell

Hull, Kenneth Duryee, Sr.

Hunter, Fenley

Huntington, Robert Dinsmore, Jr.

Hutton, Edward Francis

Ingersoll, Robert Hawley

Inness–Brown, Virginia Portia R.

Iselin Hope Goddard

James, Angeline J. Krech

James, Dorothea Draper

James, Henry

James, Oliver B., Sr.

James, Dr. Walter Belknap

Jay, DeLancey Kane

Jennings, Benjamin Brewster

Jennings, Frederic Beach

Jennings, Oliver Burr, II

Jennings, Percy Hall, Sr.

Jennings, Walter

Johaneson, Nils R.

Jonas, Nathan Soloman

Jones, Katharine Black

Jones, Rosalie Gardiner

Kahn, Addie Wolff

Kahn, Otto Hermann

Keating, Cletus, Sr.

Kefalidis, Nikos

Kelley, Cornelius Francis

Kellogg, Morris Woodruff

Kennedy, Katherine Williams

Kennedy, William Walker

Kettles, Richard C., Jr.

King, Frederic Rhinelander

Kingsbury, Alice Cary Bussing

Kingsbury, Howard Thayer, Sr.

Klein, John S.

Knowlton, Hugh Gilbert, Sr.

Kress, Claude Washington

Krim, Arthur B.

Ladew, Harvey Smith, II

Ladew, Louise Berry Wall

Laidlaw, Harriet Wright Burton

Laidlaw, James Lees

Lamont, Elinor Branscombe Miner

Lamont, Thomas Stilwell

LaMontagne, Beatrice Kinney

Langley, Jane Pickens

Langley, William Clark

Langone, Elaine Abbe

Langone, Kenneth Gerard, Sr.

Lanier, Harriet Bishop

Larkin, Vera A. H. Cravath

Lawrence, Effingham, II

L'Ecluse, Julia Manley Weeks

Ledyard, Lewis Cass, Jr.

Leeds, William Bateman, Jr.

Leeming, Thomas Lonsdale, Sr.

Leffingwell, Russell Cornell

Lehman, Allan Sigmund

Lehman, Ann Margaret Roche

Lewyt, Alexander Milton

Lindheim, Irma Levy

Lindheim, Norvin R.

Lindsay, Lady Elizabeth S. Hoyt

Livingston, Eleanor Hoffman R.

Livingston, Elisabeth Sloan Pratt

Livingston, Gerald Moncrieffe

Livingston, John Holyoke

Lloyd–Smith, Marjorie Flemming

Lloyd–Smith, Wilton

Loeb, William, Jr.

Loening, Grover

Lord, George de Forest, Sr.

Luckenbach, Edgar Frederick, Jr.

Luckenbach, John Lewis

Ludlow, Alden Rodney, Sr.

Lusk, Dr. Graham

Lutz, Lillian M. Gillett

MacDonald, Anne Hunter T.

MacDonald, Helen Lamb Babbott

MacDonald, Ranald Hugh, Jr.

Mackay, Clarence Hungerford

Mackay, Katherine Alexander

MacLaren, Archibald Waters

Manice, William de Forest, Sr.

Marsh, John Bigelow, Sr.

Marston, Edgar Lewis, II

Martin, Alastair Bradley

Martin, Bradley, Jr.

Martino, Joseph Anthony

Mathers, William Harris

Matheson, William John

Mauze, Abby Rockefeller

Maxwell, Howard Washburn, Jr.

Maxwell, Howard Washburn, Sr.

McClintock, Beatrice Kellogg

McClintock, Harvey Childs, Sr.

McCollum, Leonard Franklin, Sr.
[*see* E. S. Whitney]

McCrary, Jinx Falkenburg

McCrary, John Regan, Jr.

McKay, Alexandre Emery Moore

McKim, Lillian Stokes Bostwick
[*later*, Phipps]

McVeigh, Charles Senff, Sr.

Merle–Smith, Kate G. Fowler

Merle–Smith, Van Santvoord, Sr.

Mertz, Harold E.

Mertz, LuEsther Turner

Mestres, Ricardo Angelo, II

Meyer, Florence Augusta Ward

Milbank, Albert Goodsell

Milburn, John George, Sr.

Miller, Dorothy Randolph

Miller, Dudley Livingston, Sr.
[*see* M. G. Miller]

Miller, Elizabeth Davern

Miller, Flora Payne Whitney

Miller, George Macculloch

Miller, John Norris, Sr.

Miller, William Wilson

Mills, Ogden Livingston

Minton, Henry Miller

Mitchell, Sidney Alexander, Sr.

Mitchell, Sidney Zollicoffer

Mixsell, Charlotte Mallory

Moen, A. Rene

Moffat, Douglas Maxwell

Moffet, George Monroe, Sr.

Mooney, James David, II

Moore, Allison Douglass Pierce

Moore, Benjamin

Morawetz, Violet Westcott

Morgan, Henry Sturgis, Sr.

Morgan, John Pierpont, Jr.

Morgan, Junius Spencer

Morris, Ray, Sr.

Munsey, Frank Andrew

Munson, Carlos W.

Myers, Theodore Walter

Nichols, Acosta, Sr.

Nichols, Elizabeth Abbott Lane

Nichols, Francis Tilden, Sr.

Nichols, George, Sr.

Nichols, Jane N. Morgan

Nitze, Paul Henry

Niven, John Ballantine

Nixon, Lewis

Norton, Skeffington Sanxay, Jr.

Norton, Susan Howard King

Noyes, David Chester, Sr.

Noyes, Winchester

Ohl, John Phillips

O'Neill, Catharine Gray Porter

O'Rourke, Helen Silver

O'Rourke, Innis, Sr.

Osborn, Alexander Perry, Sr.

Ottley, Lucetta Banks Gilbert

Outerbridge, Samuel Roosevelt

Page, Arthur Wilson, II

Page, Jane N. Nichols

Page, Mollie W. Hall

Page, Walter Hines, II

Paley, Barbara Cushing

Paley, William S.

Palmer, Carlton Humphreys

Park, Darragh Anderson, Sr.

Patchin, Robert Halsey

Patterson, Alicia
  [*see* Guggenheim]

Payson, Charles Shipman

Payson, Joan Whitney

Peck, Fremont Carson, Sr.

Pell, John Howland Gibbs

Pell, Theodore Roosevelt

Pennington, Hall Pleasants

Pennoyer, Frances Tracy Morgan

Pennoyer, Paul Geddes, Sr.

Peters, William Richmond

Phelps, Georgiana L. Wilmerding

Philips, William Pyle

Phillips, Ellis Laurimore, Sr.

Phipps, Harriet Dyer Price

Phipps, Henry, Jr.

Phipps, Henry Carnegie

Phipps, Howard, Jr.

Phipps, John Shaffer

Phipps, Lillian Stokes Bostwick

Phipps, Mary N. Stone

Phipps, Ruth Pruyn
  [*later*, Field]

Pierce, Winslow Shelby, II

Pierson, Dr. Richard Norris, Sr.

Plimpton, Francis Taylor P., Sr.

Polk, Frank Lyon, Sr.

Pomeroy, Daniel Eleazer

Pool, Dr. Eugene Hillhouse

Porter, Frederica V. Berwind

Porter, Seton

Porter, William Henry

Post, Marjorie Merriweather

Potter, Clarkson

Potter, Rose Lee Saltonstall

Potter, William Chapman

Powell, Francis Edward, Jr.

Pratt, Charles Millard

Pratt, Florence Balsdon Gibb

Pratt, Frederic Bayley

Pratt, Frederic Richardson

Pratt, George du Pont, Sr.

Pratt, Harold Irving, Sr.

Pratt, Harriet L. Barnes

Pratt, Helen Deming Sherman

Pratt, Herbert Lee, Sr.

Pratt, John Teele, Jr.

Pratt, John Teele, Sr.

Pratt, Laura Cecila Parsons

Pratt, Richardson, Sr.

Pratt, Ruth Sears Baker

Pratt, Theodore, Sr.

Preston, Priscilla Baldwin

Preston, Ralph Julius

Pryibil, Helen Porter

Pulling, Thomas John Edward

Pulsifer, Harold Trowbridge

Pulsifer, Susan Farley Nichols

Pyne, Percy Rivington, II

Rathborne, Georgia Winship

Redmond, Roland Livingston

Reed, Lansing Parmelee

Remington, Franklin

Rentschler, Gordon Sohn

Reynolds, Jackson Eli

Reynolds, Marion D. Taylor

Reynolds, Richard Samuels, Sr.

Richmond. L. Martin

Ridder, Eric, Sr.

Ripley, Julien Ashton, Sr.

Robbins, Francis LeBaron, Jr.

Robertson, Charles Sammis

Robertson, Cordelia Drexel Biddle

Robertson, Julian Hart, Jr.

Robertson, Marie Louise Hoffman

Robinson, Dorothy May Jordan

Robinson, Monroe Douglas

Robinson, Thomas Linton

Roig, Harold Joseph

Roosevelt, Belle Wyatt Willard

Roosevelt, Christine Griffin Kean

Roosevelt, Eleanor B. Alexander

Roosevelt, Frances B. Webb

Roosevelt, Franklin Delano, Jr.

Roosevelt, George Emlen, Sr.

Roosevelt, James Alfred

Roosevelt, Julian Kean

Roosevelt, Laura d'Oremieulx

Roosevelt, Philip James, Jr.

Roosevelt, Philip James, Sr.

Roosevelt, Theodore

Roosevelt, Theodore, Jr.

Roosevelt, William Emlen

Rose, Bertha Benkard

Rossiter, Arthur Wickes, Sr.

Rothschild, Baron Robert de

Rousmaniere, John E.

Rubel, Dora Nachmowitz

Rumsey, Mary Harriman

Russell, Faris R.

Rutherfurd, John M. L.

Ryan, John Dennis

Sage, Henry William, II

Saltzman, Arnold Asa

Saltzman, Joan Roth

Salvage, Lady Mary K. Richmond

Salvage, Sir Samuel Agar

Samuels, John Stockwell, III

Sanders, Frank K.
  [*see* MacDonald]

Sanderson, Henry

Schenck, Pansy Wilcox

Schermerhorn, Alfred Coster

Schiff, Dorothy

Schiff, Edith Brevoort Baker

Schiff, John Mortimer

Schiff, Josephine L. Laimbeer

Schiff, Mortimer L.

Schwab, Hermann C., II

Schwartz, Bertie Grad

Sears, Anna Wentworth Caldwell

Shea, Edward Lane

Shearman, Lawrence Hobart

Sheeline, Paul Cushing

Sherman, Charles Austin, Sr.

Shipman, Julie Fay Bradley
[*later*, Fremont]

Shutt, Edwin Holmes, Jr.

Slater, Horatio Nelson, III

Sloan, Alfred Pritchard, Jr.

Sloan, Irene Jackson

Sloane, George

Sloane, Irene Jackson

Smith, Albert Lawrence, Sr.

Smith, Anna Barry Phelps

Smith, Howard Caswell, Sr.

Smithers, Christopher Dunkin, Sr.

Smithers, Robert Brinkley

Smull, Jacob Barstow

Sparks, Lady Mina Jane Roberts

Sparrow, Margaret Parish Beattie

Sperry, Edward G.

Stanley–Brown, Joseph

Sterling, Duncan, Jr.

Stern, Henry Root, Sr.

Stettinius, Edward Reilly, Jr.

Stevens, Byam K., Jr.

Stewart, Cecil Parker

Stone, Charles Augustus, Sr.

Straight, Dorothy Payne Whitney

Straight, Willard Dickerman

Stralem, Donald Sigmund

Stralem, Jean L. E.

Straus, Jack Isidor

Streeter, Edward, Sr.

Sutton, Keith

Swann, Susan Ridley Sedgwick

Swope, Herbert Bayard, Sr.

Taft, Walbridge S.

Tailer, Thomas Suffern, Jr.

Talbott, Harold Elster, II

Talbott, Margaret Thayer

Taliaferro, Eugene Sinclair

Tanner, Frederick Chauncey, Sr.

Taylor, Bertrand LeRoy, Jr.

Taylor, Henry Calhoun

Taylor, James Blackstone, Jr.

Taylor, Myron Charles

Thayer, Francis Kendall, Sr.

Thayer, Kendall

Thayer, Robert Helyer, Sr.

Thieriot, Charles Henschel, II

Thieriot, Frances D. Thornton

Thomas, Joseph Albert

Thomas, Norman Mattoon

Tiffany, Anne Cameron

Tiffany, Katrina Brandes Ely

Tiffany, Louis Comfort

Tiffany, Olive W. Thompson

Tiffany, Perry

Tinker, Edward Richmond, Jr.

Todd, Robert Elliot

Tower, Flora Payne Whitney
[*later*, Miller]

Tower, Whitney, Sr.

Townsend, Alice Greenough

Townsend, Edward Mitchell, II

Townsend, Edward Mitchell, Sr.

Townsend, James Mulford, II

Trowbridge, Edmund Quincy

Truslow, Elizabeth A. Jennings

Uris, Percy

Van Alen, James Henry

Vanderbilt, Alva Erskine Smith
  [*later*, Belmont]

Vanderbilt, George Washington, IV

Vanderbilt, Louise Mitchell

Vanderbilt, William Kissam, Jr.

Vanderbilt, William Kissam, Sr.
  [*see* Belmont]

Vander Poel, William Halsted

Van Ingen, Harriet Balsdon Pratt
  [*later*, Bush]

Van Santvoord, Alexander, Sr.

Von Stade, Francis Skiddy, Sr.

Walker, Dr. Elizabeth Harrison

Wang, Charles B.

Warburg, Gerald Felix

Ward, Edward Mortimer, Sr.

Ward, Elijah

Warner, Bradford Arnold, Sr.

Watson, John Jay, Jr.

Webb, Electra Havemeyer

Webb, James Watson, Sr.

Weekes, Arthur Delano, Jr.

Weekes, John Abeel

Weld, Francis Minot, II

Weldon, Samuel Alfred

Wellman, Roderic

Wetmore, Edmund

White, Alexander Moss, Jr.

White, Alexander Moss, Sr.

White, Elsie Helen Ogden

White, Leonard Dalton, Jr.

Whitehouse, Vera Boarman

Whitney, Betsey Cushing

Whitney, Cornelius Vanderbilt

Whitney, Eleanor Searle
  [*later*, McCollum]

Whitney, George, Sr.

Whitney, Gertrude Vanderbilt

Whitney, Howard Frederic, II

Whitney, John Hay

Whitney, Martha Beatrix Bacon

Whitney, Robert Bacon, Sr.

Whitney, William Payne

Widener, George Dunstan, Jr.

Willetts, William Prentice

Williams, Arthur

Williams, Douglas

Williams, Mona Strader

Williams, Timothy Shaler

Willys, John North

Winmill, Viola Townsend

Winthrop, Egerton Leigh Jr.

Winthrop, Emeline Heckscher

Winthrop, Grenville Lindall

Winthrop, Henry Rogers

Winthrop, Robert, II

Wood, Willis Delano

Woods, Ward Wilson, Jr.

Woodward, Elsie Ogden Cryder

Woolley, Daniel P.

Woolworth, Frank Winfield

Wright, Boykin Cabell, Sr.

Wyckoff, Cecelia Gertrude Shere

Young, Otto S.

Zinsser, William Herman, Jr.

Wealth buys you a chance to do good for your fellow man.

– Nelson W. Aldrich, Jr.
"Wall Street Week with Fortune"
December 5, 2003

When the owner who contracted for the original construction is known, it is indicated by an asterisk. Multiple owners are listed in chronological order of ownership, not alphabetically by surname. Ownership of estates is listed only for those that used that particular estate name. See the surname entry to ascertain names used by other owners of the same estate. See village entry for cross referencing of names not found as separate surname entries.

Aberfeldy	* Anderson, John	Lattingtown
The Acre	* Norris, James King	Laurel Hollow
Airdrie	* Fish, Edwin A.	Matinecock
Airslie	Willard, George L. de Forest, Henry Wheeler de Forest, Julia Mary	Laurel Hollow
Almar	* Tully, William John	Mill Neck
Aloha	Muncie, Dr. Curtis Hamilton	Kings Point
Amincliff	* Carver, Amos Dow Carver, Clifford Nickels	Lattingtown
The Anchorage	Weekes, Arthur Delano, Jr.	Oyster Bay Cove
Annandale	* Moffat, Douglas Maxwell	Cold Spring Harbor
Annandale	* Stevens, Charles Albert	Old Westbury
Appledale	* Adams, Horatio M.	Glen Cove
Appledore	* Davison, Henry Pomeroy, II	Upper Brookville
Appledore	* Dewing, Hiram E.	Matinecock
Applegarth	* Wetmore, Charles Whitman Nichols, William Henry, Jr.	Centre Island
Applegreen	Elmhirst, Leonard Knight	Old Westbury
Apple Tree Hill	Dick, Fairman Rogers	Old Brookville
Apple Trees	* Morgan, Junius Spencer	Matinecock
Apple Trees	Randall, Darley, Jr.	Woodbury
Applewood	* Flagg, Montague, II	Upper Brookville
Archway	* Chew, Philip Frederick	Muttontown
Arlough	* Bacon, Robert Low	Old Westbury
Ashcombe	* Fraser, Alfred	Sands Point
Augustina	Roesler, Edward, Sr.	Kings Point
Avondale Farms	* Harriman, Joseph Wright	Brookville
Bagatelle	* Brownsard, Mrs. D.	Dix Hills

Bagatelle	* Hastings, Thomas	Old Westbury
Ballintober Farm	Bonynge, Paul, Sr.	Lattingtown
Ballygurge	Whitney, Miss Margaret Sargent	Cove Neck
Band Box	Ames, Charles Edgar	Syosset
Barberrys	* Doubleday, Nelson, Sr.	Mill Neck
The Barn	Delehanty, Bradley	Matinecock
Bayberry Downs	* Nichols, Francis Tilden, Sr.	Muttontown
Bayberry Hill	Mestres, Ricardo Angelo, II	Upper Brookville
Beachleigh	* Schieren, George Arthur, Sr.	Kings Point
Beacon Farm	Babbott, Dr. Frank Lusk, Jr. Klein, John S. Morgan, Henry Sturgis, Sr.	Asharoken
Beacon Towers	* Belmont, Alva Erskine Smith	Sands Point
The Beaklet	* Coe, Henry Eugene, Jr.	Oyster Bay Cove
Beaupre	Tailer, Thomas Suffern, Jr.	Lattingtown
Beaver Brook Farm	* Batterman, Henry Lewis, Sr. Batterman, Henry Lewis, Jr.	Mill Neck
Beechwood	* Pratt, John Teele, Jr.	Glen Cove
Belcaro	* Hoffstot, Frank Norton Rothschild, Baron Robert de	Sands Point
Belvoir	Bartow, Francis Dwight, Sr.	Glen Cove
Ben Robyn	* Robbins, Francis LeBaron, Jr.	West Hills
Ben Robyn Farm	Price, Theodore Hazeltine, Jr.	West Hills
Bentleigh	Burnett, Vivian	Plandome Manor
Ben Trovato	Babcock, Woodward	Upper Brookville
Berry Hill Farm	* Slade, John, Sr.	Oyster Bay Cove
Bevin House	Bevin, Laura DeLamater Bevin, Sydney Froessel, Charles William Kefalidis, Nikos	Asharoken
Big Tree Farm	* Hill, James Norman	Brookville
The Bilge	Roosevelt, Miss Elizabeth E.	Cove Neck
The Birches	* Murdock, Harvey Brewster, Samuel Dwight Brewster, Warren Dwight	Glen Cove
Birchlea	Mahana, George Shaw	Centre Island

Birchwood	* Burchard, Anson Wood	Lattingtown
Blythewood	* Smith, George	Muttontown
Boatcroft	* Johnston, John Herbert	Lloyd Harbor
Bobbingsworth	Rousmaniere, John E. Rousmaniere, James Ayer	Oyster Bay Cove
Bogheid	Porter, William Henry *[different house from that of Pryibil]*	Glen Cove
Bogheid	* Pryibil, Helen Porter *[different house from that of Porter]*	Glen Cove
Bois Joli	* Livermore, Philip Walter	Brookville
Bonnie Blink	* Phipps, Henry, Jr.	Lake Success
Bonnie Brae	MacLaren, Archibald Waters Roosevelt, Julian Kean	Centre Island
Bonnieneuk	Parker, Robert Meade, Sr.	Glen Cove
Borradil Farm	Winmill, Robert Campbell	Mill Neck
Boscobel	Shonnard, Horatio Seymour, Sr.	Oyster Bay
The Box	Ladew, Harvey Smith, II	Old Brookville
Box Hill	Armstrong, Hamilton Fish	Laurel Hollow
Box Hill Farm	* Warburg, Gerald Felix	Brookville
Boxwood	Williams, Rodney W.	Mill Neck
Boxwood Farm	Hickox, Charles V.	Old Westbury
The Braes	* Pratt, Herbert Lee, Sr.	Glen Cove
The Briar Patch	Hawkes, Dr. Forbes	Sands Point
The Briars	* Tiffany, Louis Comfort Lusk, Dr. Graham	Laurel Hollow
Brick Yard Point	Phelps, Ansel	Centre Island
Brier Hill	Strauss, Albert	Cove Neck
Broadhollow	* Aldrich, Winthrop Williams Vanderbilt, Alfred Gwynne, II Donahue, James Paul, Jr. Uris, Percy	Brookville
Broad Hollow Farm	* Hitchcock, Thomas, Sr. Hitchcock, Margaret Mellon	Old Westbury
Broad Hollow House	* Clark, Frederick Ambrose	Old Westbury
Broadlawns	* Booth, Angeline Rowan	Kings Point
Broadwater	* Stafford, Jennie K.	Lloyd Harbor

Broadwood	* Whitehouse, James Norman	Upper Brookville
Brook Corners	* Williams, Arthur	Glen Head
Brookedge	Gerdes, John	Plandome
Brookmeade	Sloane, George	Lattingtown
Brookwood	* Minton, Henry Miller	North Hills
Broom Hill	Pratt, Vera Amherst Hale	Lattingtown
Bryce House	* Bryce, Lloyd Stephens	Roslyn Harbor
Brymptonwood	* Bergquist, John Gosta	Upper Brookville
Builtover	* Auchincloss, Charles Crooke	Roslyn Heights
Bunker Hill	Mott, Jordan Lawrence, IV	Oyster Bay Cove
Bunga Fields	Ellis, Ralph Nicholson, Sr.	Brookville
Burrwood	* Jennings, Walter Jennings, Oliver Burr, II	Lloyd Harbor
Callender House	* Rouss, Peter Winchester Clarkson, Robert Livingston, Sr.	Bayville
Cannon Hill	* Stewart, John Henry Jones de Roulet, Daniel Carroll, Sr.	Laurel Hollow
Cannonhill Point	Gerdes, John	Laurel Hollow
Carefree Court	* Carter, Oliver Goldsmith, Sr. Carter, George Haff, Stella Carter	Asharoken
Carston Hill	* Marston, Edgar Lewis, II	Woodbury
Cashelmare	Carey, Martin F.	Glen Cove
Cassleigh	* Canfield, Augustus Cass	North Hills
Castlegould	* Gould, Howard	Sands Point
The Catalpas	Vaughan, Dr. Harold Stearns	Upper Brookville
Caumsett	* Field, Marshall, III	Lloyd Harbor
Ca Va	* Alker, Carol Booth	Old Brookville
Cedar Cliff	* Physioc, Joseph Allen, Sr.	Bayville
Cedarcroft	* Rossiter, Arthur Wickes, Sr.	Glen Cove
Cedarcroft	Watson, John Jay, Jr.	Upper Brookville
Cedar Hill	Havemeyer, Theodore Augustus, II	Upper Brookville
Cedar Hill	* Thieriot, Charles Henschel, Sr.	Muttontown

Cedar Knoll	* MacKelvie, Neil Bruce Emerson, Margaret	Sands Point
Cedar Knolls	* Gould, Frank Miller	Laurel Hollow
Cedarmere	Bryant, William Cullen Bryant, Julia Sands Godwin, Harold Godwin, Elizabeth Love	Roslyn Harbor
Cedar Pond Farm	Alker, Edward Paul	Kings Point
The Cedars	* Blackwell, Charles Addison	Upper Brookville
The Cedars	* Cochran, William Bourke	Sands Point
The Cedars	* Hess, Harry Bellas	Huntington Station
The Cedars	Stearns, John Noble, II	Glen Cove
Chanticleer	Merrill, Joseph L.	Matinecock
Charlon House	* Frank, Charles Augustus, Sr.	Glen Cove
Charlton Hall	* Dows, David, Jr.	Muttontown
Chateauiver	* Gould, Charles Albert	Dix Hills
Chelsea	* Moore, Benjamin McKay, Alexandra Emery Moore	Muttontown
Cherridore	* Taylor, Henry Calhoun	Cold Spring Harbor
Cherry Leaze	* Hattersley, Robert Chopin, Sr.	Glen Head
Cherrywood	Vietor, Dr. John Adolf, Sr.	Matinecock
Chestnut Vale	Chanler, Lewis Stuyvesant, Jr. Tower, Roderick	Syosset
Chicken Valley Farm	Schwab, Hermann C., II	Old Brookville
The Chimneys	* Brokaw, Howard Crosby	Muttontown
The Chimneys	* Holmes, Bettie Fleischmann	Sands Point
Claraben Court	Stern, Benjamin	Roslyn Harbor
Clayton	Frick, Childs	Roslyn Harbor
Clayton	* Russell, Faris R.	Mill Neck
The Cliffs	* Beekman, James William, Sr. Fritz, Dr. Albert R., Sr.	Mill Neck
Clifton	Cairns, Anna Eliza	Roslyn Harbor
Clifton	Emory, William Helmsley, Jr.	Roslyn Harbor
Clovelly	Clowes, John Henry, Sr.	Kings Point
Cloverfield	Thatcher, John M. P., Sr.	Syosset

Cloverfields	Abbott, Paul, Sr.	Lloyd Harbor
Cloverley Manor	* Astor, William Vincent	Sands Point
Cooper's Bluff	Pulsifer, Harold Trowbridge	Cove Neck
The Corners	* Gardner, Hope Norman	Old Westbury
Cottage Normandy	Le Roux, Edouard	Brookville
Cottsleigh	* Lord, Franklin Butler, II	Syosset
Council Rock	Ballantine, Arthur Atwood, Sr.	Oyster Bay
Country Line Farm	* Page, Arthur Wilson, II	West Hills
The Cove	* Meyer, Cord, II	Kings Point
Cow Neck Farm	Schuster, Max Lincoln	Sands Point
Craigdarroch	* Whitney, Howard Frederic, II	Glen Cove
Craig Royston	Bigelow, Ernest A.	Cove Neck
The Creek	* Lamont, Thomas Stilwell	Lattingtown
The Crest	* DeLamater, Oakley Ramshon, Sr. Cooper, Cyrus Rice, Donald DeWeir, Norman Garrett, Robert Michael Barbolini, Guy	Asharoken
Cross Roads	Uterhart, Henry Ayres	East Norwich
The Crossroads	* Grace, William Russell, Jr. Bono, Henry, Jr.	Old Westbury
Crosstree	Davis, Hartley Courtland	Upper Brookville
Crow's Nest	Straus, Jack Isidor	Cove Neck
Dark Hollow	* Jennings, Oliver Burr, II	Lloyd Harbor
Deanlea	Dean, Herbert Hollingshead	Lattingtown
Deepdale	* Vanderbilt, William Kissam., Jr.	Lake Success
Deephaven	* Wright, Wilkinson de Forest, Sr.	Sands Point
Delbarton	Kountze, deLancey	Brookville
Delwood	Wheeler, Frederick Seymour	Upper Brookville
Deramore	* Bateson, Edgar Farrar, Sr.	Cold Spring Harbor
Derrymore	Ryan, John Dennis	North Hills
Dogwood	* Hadden, Emily Georgina Hamilton Hadden, Miss Frances	Jericho
Dogwood Hill	Steers, James Rich, II	Brookville

Dolonar	* Roosevelt, Philip James, Sr.	Cove Neck
Dormer House	* Gates, Elizabeth Hoagland	Lattingtown
Dorset Lodge	* Earle, Henry Montague	Old Westbury
Dorwood	* Emanuel, Victor	North Hills
Dreamwood	Daniel, Robert Williams	Old Westbury
Driftwood	* Remington, Franklin	Centre Island
Driftwoods	* Parker, John Alley Johnson, Seymour	Sands Point
Duck Hook	Gerry, Henry Averell, Sr.	Matinecock
The Duck Pond	Fish, Sidney W.	Old Brookville
Duck Puddle Farm	Guest, Winston Frederick Churchill	Oyster Bay Cove
Ducks Landing	Miller, Andrew Otterson, Jr.	Laurel Hollow
Dunrobin	Smithers, Christopher Dunkin, Sr.	Lattingtown
Dunstable	* Pierce, Winslow Shelby, II	Bayville
Eagle's Beak	* James, Walter Belknap	Cold Spring Harbor
Eagle's Nest	* Vanderbilt, William Kissam, Jr.	Centerport
Eastfair	* Fairchild, Sherman M.	Lloyd Harbor
Easton	* Field, Evelyn Marshall	Muttontown
Eastover	* Hoyt, Colgate, Sr.	Centre Island
East Woods	* Winthrop, Henry Rogers	Woodbury
Eckingston	* Gales, George M.	Lattingtown
Edenhall	* Eden, Dr. John H., Sr.	Kings Point
Edgeover	* Stewart, William Adams Walker, II	Cold Spring Harbor
Edgewood	Jones, Nicholas Ridgely	Glen Cove
Edgewood House	Manice, William de Forest, Sr.	Old Westbury
Effendi Hill	* Doubleday, Frank Nelson	Mill Neck
Elbourne	Elbert, Robert George	North Hills
Elfland	Reeve–Merritt, Edward	Cove Neck
Elkhurst	* Ward, Edward Mortimer, Sr.	Lattingtown
Ellencourt	* Jennings, Spencer Augustus	Glen Cove
Elm Court	* Luckenbach, Edgar Frederick, Sr.	Sands Point
Elmcroft	* Page, Frank C. Bauman	Upper Brookville

Elmhurst	* Straight, Willard Dickerman	Old Westbury
Elm Point	* Barstow, William Slocum	Kings Point
The Elms	* Brokaw, Clifford Vail, Sr. Brown, Nannie C. Inman Brokaw, Clifford Vail, Jr.	Glen Cove
Elmsfour	* Munson, Carlos W.	Flower Hill
Elmwood	* Young, Thomas F. Tiffany, Charles Lewis, II	Oyster Bay Cove
Elysian Hill	Morgan, William F.	Plandome Manor
Elyston	* Ely, Albert Heman, Jr.	Lloyd Harbor
Enderby	* Dimock, Edward Jordan	North Hills
Enfield Chase	Woodward, William, II	Brookville
Erchless	* Phipps, Howard, Sr. Phipps, Howard, Jr.	Old Westbury
The Evergreens	* Cushing, Leonard Jarvis, Sr.	Mill Neck
The Evergreens	* Swan, Edward H., Sr.	Cove Neck
Evermore	Livermore, Jesse Lauriston, Sr.	Kings Point
The Eyrie	Eagle, Henry, Sr.	Sands Point
Faberest	Faber, Leander B.	Lloyd Harbor
Fairleigh	* Brewster, George S.	Muttontown
Fairmont	Vanderbilt, Virginia Graham Fair	Manhasset
Fairseat	* Burnett, Frances Hodgson	Plandome Manor
Falaise	* Guggenheim, Harry Frank	Sands Point
Farlands	* Curran, Guernsey, Sr.	Upper Brookville
The Farm House	* Pratt, John Teele, Jr. Nitze, Paul Henry	Glen Cove
The Farm House	* Runyon, Clarkson, Jr.	Glen Cove
Farnsworth	* Billings, Cornelius Kingsley Garrison Bird, Wallis Clinton	Upper Brookville
Feu Follet	Heckscher, August	Kings Point
Fieldside	Gould, Aubrey Van Wyck, Sr.	Kings Point
Fieldston Farm	Kellogg, Morris Woodruff	Upper Brookville
Firth House	Patchin, Robert Halsey	East Hills

Fleetwood	* Sewell, Robert Van Vorst O'Neill, Grover, Sr. Du Bois, Eugene	Oyster Bay Cove
Floralyn	Lynch, Edmund Calvert, Jr.	Lattingtown
Flower de Hundred	* Greer, William Armstrong	Matinecock
The Folly [I] [II]	* Bullock, George	Centre Island
Forest Edge	* Mixsell, Dr. Harold Ruckman	Matinecock
Forest Edge Farm	* Townsend, John Allen	Lattingtown
Forker House	Chrysler, Walter Percy, Sr.	Kings Point
Fort Hill House (1878)	* Alden, Anne Coleman	Lloyd Harbor
Fort Hill House (1900)	* Matheson, William John Wood, Willis Delano Campbell, George W.	
Fountainhill	* Guggenheim, William, Sr.	Sands Point
Four Corners	Rose, George, Jr.	Lake Success
Four Winds	* Hoppin, Gerard Beekman	Oyster Bay Cove
Fox Brae	Hagen, Winston Henry, II	Lattingtown
Fox Hollow	Martin, John Stuart	Matinecock
Foxland	Holloway, William Grace, Sr.	Old Westbury
Foy Farm	Foy, Bryon Cecil	Matinecock
Framewood	* Postley, Sterling	Upper Brookville
French House	Tower, Flora Payne Whitney Miller, Flora Payne Whitney	Old Westbury
Friend Field	Bogart, Adrian T., Jr.	Lattingtown
Friendfield Farm	Pratt, Frederic Richardson	Lattingtown
Friendship Hill	Hoppin, William Warner, Jr.	Old Brookville
Frost Mill Lodge	* Brokaw, Irving	Mill Neck
The Gables	* Schultze, Max H. Dugmore, Cyril	Lattingtown
Gageboro	Gibb, Arthur	Glen Cove
Gay Gardens	* Murray, Hugh A.	Old Westbury
Geranium Court	Bliss, Miss Ida Evelina	Kings Point
Germelwyn	* Busby, Leonard J. Leeming, Thomas Lonsdale	Glen Cove
Gilchrist	Grace, Miss Louise Natalie	North Hills

Gladwolden	Truesdell, Dr. Edward Delavan	Lloyd Harbor
Gladwood	Willock, William W., Sr.	Muttontown
The Glen	Welch, Charles James	Sands Point
Glenby	* Francke, Luis J., Sr.	Brookville
Glenby	* White, Rita Kohler	Mill Neck
Glenlo	Hunter, Malcolm Du Bois	Glen Cove
Glen Nevis	Tiffany, Anne Cameron	Upper Brookville
Glimpse Water	Loening, Rudolph R.	Glen Cove
Gloan House	* Dilworth, Dewees Wood	Old Westbury
Goodwin Place	* Goodwin, Philip Lippincott	Woodbury
Goose Point	* Brokaw, Irving	Matinecock
Gracefield	* Grace, William Russell, Sr.	Kings Point
Gracewood	Grace, Joseph Peter, II	North Hills
Gracewood	* Gracie, James King Roosevelt, George Emlen, Sr. Choung, Terry	Cove Neck
Gray House Farm	* Redmond, Geraldyn Livingston, Sr.	Upper Brookville
Graymar	* Grosvenor, Graham Bethune	Old Westbury
Greanan	* Gavin, Michael	Brookville
Green Acres	Tangeman, George Patterson	Glen Cove
Green Arbors	* Lovett, Robert Abercrombie	Lattingtown
Green Escape	Morley, Christopher Darlington, Sr.	Roslyn Estates
Greenleaves	James, Henry	Cold Spring Harbor
Green Pastures	Straus, Jack Isidor	Jericho
Greenridge	* Williams, Arthur Seligman, Joseph Lionel, Sr.	Roslyn Harbor
Greentree	* Whitney, William Payne Whitney, John Hay	Manhasset
Grey Cottage	Martin, Grinnell	Cove Neck
Groendak	* Handy, Parker Douglas	Glen Cove
Groombridge	* Milburn, John George, Sr.	North Hills
Groton Farms	* Winthrop, Robert Dudley Winthrop, Beekman, II	Old Westbury
Groton Place	* Winthrop, Robert, II	Old Westbury

Grove Point	Mann, Samuel Vernon, Sr.	Kings Point
Guinea Hollow Farm	Robertson, Thomas Markoe	Old Westbury
Gull's Way	Taylor, Henry Stillman	Centre Island
The Hameau	* Harris, Henry Upham, Sr.	Brookville
Hamptworth House	* Aron, Jacob	Kings Point
Handyhill	Anderson, Henry Hill, II	Cove Neck
Handyhill	Anderson, Henry Hill, II	Roslyn Estates
Happy House	Mackay, John William, III	East Hills
Harbor Acres	Schreiber, Dr. George, Jr.	Port Washington
Harbor Hill	* Mackay, Clarence Hungerford	Roslyn
Harbor Point	Brightson, George Edgar	Centre Island
Harbour Lights	Hadden, Hamilton, Sr.	Cold Spring Harbor
Harbourwood	* Blackton, James Stuart, Sr.	Cove Neck
Hark Away	* Babcock, Richard Franklin	Woodbury
Harrow Hill	Lyon, Cecil T. F. B.	Muttontown
Hattom	Tailer, Thomas Suffern, Sr.	*[unable to locate]*
Haut Bois	* Maynard, Walter Effingham	Brookville
Hawirt	* Peters, William Richmond	Mill Neck
Hawk Hill Place	* Stehli, Emil J.	Lattingtown
Hawthorne House	Patchin, Robert Halsey	Roslyn Harbor
Hazeldean	* Laidlaw, James Lees Backus, Dana Converse	Sands Point
Hazelmere	* Richards, Frederick L.	Kings Point
Hearth Stone	* Dickinson, Hunt Tilford, Sr.	Old Brookville
Hearthstone	Palmer, Carlton Humphreys	Centre Island
The Hedges	Hedges, George Brown	Westbury
The Hedges	* Weir, Levi Candee	Lattingtown
The Height	Sheehan, William Francis	North Hills
Hemlock Hollow	* Latham, Leroy	Plandome
Hempstead House	Guggenheim, Daniel	Sands Point
Here to Yonder	Straus, Edward Kuhn	Upper Brookville
Heyday House	* Davis, Joseph Edward, Sr.	Upper Brookville

Hickory Hill	Bottomley, William Lawrence	Old Brookville
Hickory Hill	Clark, John Balfour	Old Westbury
Hickory Hill	* White, Alexander Moss, Jr.	Oyster Bay Cove
Hidden Way	Merrill, Charles Edward, Jr.	Huntington Bay
High Elms	* Emmet, Richard Stockton, Sr.	Glen Cove
Highfield	Gossler, Philip Green, Sr.	Brookville
Highlands	Lindsay, George Nelson, Sr.	Laurel Hollow
High Lindens	Roulston, Thomas Henry, Sr.	Huntington Bay
Highold	* Stimson, Henry Lewis	West Hills
Highpool	* Howe, William Deering	Brookville
Highwood	* Gould, Edwin	Oyster Bay Cove
Hilaire	* Fahys, George Ernest	Glen Cove and Matinecock
	[Fahys built two houses in Matinecock and one in Glen Cove with this name.]	
Hilaire Farm	Vernam, Clarence Cottier	Huntington
The Hill	* Donnell, Harry Ellingwood Ward, Sarah Donnell Lang, John Gerlach, Robert Carr, Edward A. T.	Eaton's Neck
Hillandale	Crisp, Van Devanter	Upper Brookville
Hillcrest	Kung, Hsiang-hsi Chiang, Kai-shek, Mme. Stillman, Irwin	Lattingtown
Hillendale	* Dickerman, Florence Calkin	Mill Neck
Hill House	Bodman, Herbert L., Sr.	Old Brookville
Hill House	* Hodenpyl, Anton Gysberti	Mill Neck
Hillsedge	Connfelt, Charles Maitland	Muttontown
Hillside	* Adam, Sarah Sampson	Oyster Bay
Hilltop	Alker, Henry Alphonse, Sr.	Sands Point
Hillwood	* Post, Marjorie Merriweather Hutton, Edward Francis Davies, Joseph Edward	Brookville
The Hitching Post	* Toerge, Norman K., Sr.	Matinecock
Hiver Rough	Winter, Keyes, Sr.	Woodbury
Holly Court	Trowbridge, Edmund Quincy	Oyster Bay Cove
Holly Hill	Keating, Cletus, Sr.	Mill Neck

Holly House	Miller, Margery Gerdes Howard, Alexandra C. Miller	Laurel Hollow
Holmdene	* Ballantine, John Herbert	Kings Point
Holmestead Farm	* Holmes, Artemas	Old Brookville
Home Acres	* Whitney, George, Sr.	Old Westbury
Homewood	Dean, Arthur Hobson	Upper Brookville
Home Wood	* McLane, Allan, Jr.	Lattingtown
Homewood	Willetts, William Prentice	Roslyn
Homewood Place	Van Rensselaer, Charles Augustus, Sr.	Muttontown
Honeysuckle Lodge	Burden, Chester Griswold	Cold Spring Harbor
Horse's Home Farm	Bailey, Townsend Fleet	Old Brookville
Hundred House	Franklin, Philip Albright Small, Jr.	Matinecock
Huntover Lodge	Griscom, Lloyd Carpenter	Muttontown
Hurrahs Nest	Jackson, William Eldred, II	Cold Spring Harbor
Hutfield	Hutton, Edward Francis	Brookville
Hyde Park	* Park, Darragh Anderson, Sr.	Old Brookville
Idlewilde	* Alker, Alphonse Henry	Kings Point
Inisfada	* Brady, Nicholas Frederic	North Hills
Interbaien	Kane, John Patrick	Huntington Bay
Iradell	Smith, Earl Edward Tailer, Sr.	Sands Point
Ivycroft	Bingham, Harry Payne, Sr.	Old Westbury
Ivy Hall	* Preston, Ralph Julius Gary, Elbert H.	Jericho
Jemstone	Van Rooyens Martino, Joseph Anthony	North Hills
Jericho Farms	* Burrill, Middleton Schoolbred	Jericho
Jericho House	* Kent, George Edward, Sr.	Jericho
Jones Manor [1855]	Jones, Charles Hewlett Jones, Mary Elizabeth	Laurel Hollow
Jones Manor [c. 1918]	* Jones, Mary Elizabeth Jones, Arthur Eaton Jones, Rosalie Gardiner Polsinelli, Vincent	Laurel Hollow
June Acres	* Rusch, Henry Arthur, Sr.	Centre Island
Katydid Farm	Luckenbach, John Lewis	Matinecock

Keewaydin	Smith, Albert Delmont Swope, Herbert Bayard, Sr.	Sands Point
Kenjockety	* Lloyd–Smith, Wilton	Lloyd Harbor
Kennedy Villa	* Kennedy, William, Sr.	Syosset
Kenwood	Leeds, William Bateman, Jr.	Cove Neck
Kenwood	* Vanderveer, Stephen Lott	Great Neck
Keswick	* Carpenter, James Edwin Ruthven	Sands Point
The Kettles	* Nichols, John White Treadwell	Cove Neck
Kidd's Rocks	* Browning, John Scott, Sr.	Sands Point
Killenworth [I] [II]	* Pratt, George du Pont, Sr.	Glen Cove
Killibeg	* Sparrow, Edward Wheeler Pulsifer, George Hale	Matinecock
Killingworth	Taylor, Myron Charles	Lattingtown
Kilsyth	* Livingston, Gerald Moncrieffe	Lloyd Harbor
Kiluna Farm	* Pulitzer, Ralph, Sr. Paley, William S.	North Hills
Kinross	* Simpson, Robert H.	Jericho
Kirby Hill	* Stevens, Joseph Sampson Stevens, Byam K., Jr.	Muttontown
Klotz Cottage	Chanler, Alice Remington Chamberlain Chanler, William Chamberlain	Lloyd Harbor
Knole	* Duryea, Hermanes Barkula, Jr. Martin, Bradley, Jr. Martin, Esmond Bradley, Sr.	Old Westbury
Knollwood	* Hudson, Charles I., Sr.	Muttontown
La Casita	Bacon, Daniel	Centre Island
La Chaumiere	Coudert, Frederic Rene, Jr.	Cove Neck
La Colline	* Levitt, William Jaird, Sr.	Mill Neck
La Granja	Iglehart, David Stewart	Old Westbury
La Lanterne	* Clews, James Blanchard Clews, Henry, III	Upper Brookville
Lands End	* Gibson, Harvey Dow	Lattingtown
Lands End	Payson, Charles Shipman	Sands Point
The Lanterns	* Harriman, Herbert Melville	Jericho
La Pastura	Warner, Bradford Arnold, Sr.	Laurel Hollow

La Presqu' Ile	Neelands, Thomas D., Jr.	Sands Point
La Primavera	Sanesi, Dr. Lorenzo	Glen Cove
Larch	Oeland, Isaac Raymond, Sr.	Woodbury
La Selva	* Sanderson, Henry	Upper Brookville
Laurel Acres	* Lutz, Frederick L.	Oyster Bay Cove
Laurel Brake	Jennings, Percy Hall, Sr.	Laurel Hollow
Laurelcroft	* Jelke, Ferdinand, Jr.	Bayville
Laurel Hill	* O'Brien, Henry Mauze, Abby Rockefeller	Mill Neck
Laurelton Hall	* Tiffany. Louis Comfort	Laurel Hollow
Laurel Top	* Hornblower, George Sanford	Laurel Hollow
Laurimon	* Phillips, Ellis Laurimore	Plandome Manor
Leahead	Bucknall, Henry W. J.	Glen Cove
Les Bois	Moffet, George Monroe, Sr.	Old Brookville
Les Bouleaux	* Bertschmann, Louis Frederick	Muttontown
Les Deux Tours	Manville, Lorraine	Old Westbury
Les Pommiers	Walker, Elisha, Sr.	Muttontown
Lime House	Lindsay, Lady Elizabeth Sherman Hoyt	Centre Island
Linden Farm	Pruyn, Robert Dunbar	Oyster Bay Cove
Linden Hill	Ames, Amyas	Laurel Hollow
Linden Hill	* Howe, Richard Flint	Brookville
The Lindens	* Fleischmann, Max C.	Sands Point
The Lindens	* White, Alfred W. White, Frederick Wheeler	Kings Point
Linwood	Dane, Chester Linwood, Sr.	Mill Neck
Linwood	Heck, George Callendine, Sr.	Muttontown
Lismore	Grace, Morgan Hatton, Sr.	Kings Point
Little Erchless	Phipps, Howard, Jr.	Old Westbury
Littleholme	Johaneson, Nils R.	Lattingtown
Little Ipswich	* Wood, Chalmers, Jr.	Woodbury
Little Waldingfield	Appleton, Benjamin Ward	Upper Brookville
Llangollen Farm	Grace, Miss Louise Natalie	Kings Point

Lloyd Manor	Wood, Willis Delano Lindbergh, Charles Augustus	Lloyd Harbor
Lockjaw Ridge	Munsel, Patrice Vilas, Guillermo Raquet, Walter	Lattingtown
Locust Hill	Brower, Ernest Cuyler Brower, George Ellsworth Gerry, Dr. Roger Goodman Wolf, Barry Hansen, Robert	Roslyn
Locust Knoll	Trotter, William M. Hagen, Lucy Trotter	Oyster Bay
Locust Knoll	Ward, Elijah	Roslyn Harbor
Locust Lodge	Rogers, Henry Alexander	Lattingtown
Locustmere	Lippincott, William	Sands Point
Loewmoor	Loew, William Goadby	Old Westbury
Long Field	* Hepburn, Frederick Taylor	Lattingtown
Longfields	Preston, Lewis Thompson, Sr.	Old Brookville
Longfields	* Thompson, William Payne, Jr. Preston, William Payne Thompson, Sr.	Jericho
Longford	Gray, Henry Gunther	Lattingtown
Longhur	Smithers, Robert Brinkley	Mill Neck
Long Shadows	Boyer, Philip, Sr.	North Hills
Lulworth	* Weld, Francis Minot, II	Lloyd Harbor
Lundy House	Lundy, Frederick William Irving	Kings Point
Lynrose	* Shipman, Julie Fay Bradley Fremont, Julie Fay Bradley	Glen Head
Mallow	* Farwell, Walter	Oyster Bay Cove
Malmaison	Munsel, Patrice	Brookville
Manana	* Barnes, E. Mortimer	Old Brookville
Manor House	* Jones, Walter Restored	Laurel Hollow
Manor House	* Pratt, John Teele, Sr.	Glen Cove
Many Gables	* Kienle, Eugene S., Sr.	Kings Point
Maple Knoll	* Cozzens, Issachar, III	Lattingtown
Margrove	* Loening, Grover	Mill Neck
Mariemont	* Lowe, Henry Wheeler	Old Westbury

Marlets	Houston, Herbert Sherman	Plandome Manor
Marney	Mitchell, Sidney Alexander, Sr.	Matinecock
Martin Hall	* Martin James E., Sr.	Kings Point
Matinecock Farms	* Cutcheon, Franklin Warner M.	Lattingtown
Matinecock Point	* Morgan, John Pierpont, Jr.	Glen Cove, East Island
Mattapan	Davis, John William	Lattingtown
Maxwell Hall	* Maxwell, Eugene Lascelles, Sr.	Glen Cove
Maxwelton	* Maxwell, Howard Washburn, Sr. *[family compound]* * Maxwell, John Rogers, Sr. *[family compound]* Maxwell, John Rogers, Jr. *[family compound]*	Glen Cove
Mayhasit	* Hine, Francis Lyman	Glen Cove
Mayknoll	Casey, William Joseph, Jr.	Roslyn Harbor
Meadow Cottage	Bonner, Douglas Griswold, Sr.	Matinecock
Meadow Farm	* Cox, Irving E.	Mill Neck
Meadow Farm	* Young, Edward Lewis	Glen Cove
Meadow Spring	* Hoyt, Colgate, Jr.	Glen Cove
Meadowview	de Forest, Henry Lockwood	Cold Spring Harbor
Merriefield	Miller, John Norris, Sr.	Glen Cove
Merrywitch	Miller, Margery Gerdes	Laurel Hollow
Meudon	* Guthrie, William Dameron	Lattingtown
Midland Farm	* Bermingham, John F.	Muttontown
Mill Cove	Gwynne, Arthur	Lloyd Harbor
Mille Fleurs	* Guggenheim, Florence Shloss	Sands Point
Mill Hill	Cravath, Erastus Milo, II	Matinecock
Mill Pond	Smith, Albert Delmont	Lloyd Harbor
Millstone	Hull, Kenneth Duryee, Sr.	Mill Neck
Minnamere	Gignoux, Charles Christmas Gignoux, Elise Messenger	Kings Point
Minnewawa	* Sherman, Charles Austin, Sr.	Centre Island
Mohannes	* Roosevelt, Kermit, Sr.	Cove Neck
The Monastery	* Ferguson, Juliana Armour	Huntington Bay

Monday House	* Damrosch, Dr. Walter Johannes	Upper Brookville
Monomoit	Nickerson, Hoffman	Mill Neck
Mon Souci	* Harrison, Wallace Kirkman	West Hills
Montrose	Godwin, Parke Goddard, Conrad Godwin Zenz, Dr. Frederick Anton	Roslyn Harbor
Moorelands	* Moore, John Chandler Moore, Louis de Bebian	Oyster Bay Cove
The Moorings	Hamersley, Louis Gordon, Sr.	Sands Point
The Moorings	Morrell, Joseph B.	Centerport
Morse Lodge	* Morse, Allon Mae Fuller	Old Westbury
Munnysunk	Bailey, Frank, Sr.	Lattingtown
Muttontown Corners	* Delano, William Adams	Muttontown
Muttontown Farm	Cushing, Harry Cook, III	Brookville
Muttontown Lodge	* Hammond, Paul Lyman	Syosset
Muttontown Meadows	Winthrop, Egerton Leigh, Jr.	Muttontown
Myhome	Smithers, Francis S.	Glen Cove
Naghward	Cavanaugh, Edward Francis, Jr.	Old Brookville
Nair Lane	Iselin, Adrian, II	East Williston
Nethermuir	* de Forest, Henry Grant de Forest, Henry Wheeler	Laurel Hollow
Netherwood	* Noyes, David Chester, Sr.	Cold Spring Harbor
Nevis	Bowdoin, George Temple	Oyster Bay
New House	* Doubleday, Frank Nelson	Lattingtown
The 19th Hole	* Bucknall, G. Stafford	Glen Cove
Nirvana	* Brokaw, William Gould	Kings Point
Nonesuch House	* Barnes, Courtland Dixon, Sr.	Manhasset
Normandie	Tanner, Frederick Chauncey, Sr.	Upper Brookville
Normandie	Thomas, Joseph Albert	Upper Brookville
Normandy Farms	Breed, William Constable, Sr.	Old Brookville
Northaw	Sparks, Sir Thomas Ashley	Oyster Bay Cove
Northcliff	Willys, John North	Centre Island
Northcourt	Lunning, Frederick	North Hills

Northlea	Burton, Frank V., Jr.	Westbury
North Meadow Farm	Norton, Skeffington Sanxay, Sr. Norton, Skeffington Sanxay, Jr.	Brookville
North Point	* Gibson, Robert Williams	Cove Neck
North Refuge	* Rathborne, Joseph Cornelius, II	Old Westbury
Northway House	McNair, William Fairchild, Elvira McNair	Lattingtown
Northwood	* Schiff, Mortimer L. * Schiff, John Mortimer	Oyster Bay
Norwich House	Miller, Nathan Lewis	Upper Brookville
Norwood	Sizer, Robert Ryland, Sr.	Plandome Manor
Notley Hill	* Norton, Huntington	Oyster Bay
Nyrmah	Marsh, John Bigelow, Sr.	Mill Neck
The Oaces	Campbell, Oliver Allen, Sr.	East Norwich
Oakdene	* Oakman, Walter George, Sr.	Roslyn
Oak Hill	* Bliss, Cornelius Newton, Jr.	Brookville
Oak Hill	Cary, Guy Fairfax, Sr.	Brookville
Oak Knoll	Fisher, Joel Ellis, II	Centre Island
Oak Knoll	* Work, Bertram G., Sr.	Mill Neck
Oak Lawn	Hoguet, Dr. Joseph Peter, Sr.	Matinecock
Oaklea	* Colgate, John Kirtland, Sr.	Oyster Bay Cove
Oakleigh	* Ottley, James Henry, Sr.	Glen Cove
Oakley Court	Vanderbilt, Alfred Gwynne, II Whitney, Cornelius Vanderbilt Fordyce, Dorothy W. MacElree	Mill Neck
Oak Point	Williams, Harrison	Bayville
Oakwood	* Thayer, Frances Kendall	Sands Point
Oheka	* Kahn, Otto Hermann	Cold Spring Harbor
Oheka Castle	Melius, Gary	Cold Spring Harbor
Old Acres	* Bacon, Robert	Old Westbury
Old Adam	Derby, Dr. Richard	Oyster Bay
The Old Brick	Forrestal, James Vincent Colado Gammanse Romantini, Jerry	East Hills

Old Cow Bay Manor House	Mizner, Addison	Port Washington
Old Fields	* Schiff, Dorothy Balsan, Consuelo Vanderbilt	East Norwich
Old House	Fraser, Alfred Valentine	Sands Point
Old Orchard	* Gibb, Walter	Glen Cove
Old Orchard	* Roosevelt, Theodore, Jr.	Cove Neck
Old Rectory	Stoddard, Francis Russell, Jr.	Cold Spring Harbor
Old Trees	* Bosworth, William Welles	Matinecock
Oliver's Point	* Smith, Herbert Ludlam, Sr.	Centre Island
Ontare	* Blair, James Alonzo, Sr. Blair, James Alonzo, Jr.	Oyster Bay Cove
The Orchard	* Bleecker, Theophylact Bache, Jr.	Laurel Hollow
Orchard Corners	* Kettles, Richard C., Jr.	Old Brookville
Orchard Cottage	Stewart, Cecil Parker Cardelli, Count Giovanni Guido Carlo	Centre Island
Orchard Farm	Gray, Albert Zebriskie	Old Westbury
Orchard Hill	Boegner, Margaret Helen Phipps	Old Westbury
The Orchards	* Dyer, George Rathbone, Sr. Dyer, Elisha, VII	Brookville
Ormston	* Aldred, John Edward	Lattingtown
Orolea	Dunscombe, Duncan	Muttontown
The Other House	Sears, Joseph Hamblen	Oyster Bay Cove
Overfields	* Lord, George de Forest, Sr.	Syosset
Overland Farm	Rose, George, Sr.	Glen Head
Overland House	* Rose, George, Sr.	Old Westbury
Owlscote	Hewlett, Walter Jones	Cold Spring Harbor
Oxon Hill	* Cushing, Harry Cooke, III	East Norwich
The Paddocks	Merle–Smith, Van Santvoord, Sr.	Cove Neck
Panfield	* Milbank, Albert Goodsell Giordano, Salvatore, Sr. Castro, Bernard, Sr. Guida, Bernadette Castro	Lloyd Harbor
Park Hill	* Duncan, William Butler	Sands Point

Peacock Point	* Davison, Henry Pomeroy, Sr.
	  [family compound]
	* Davison, Frederick Trubee
	  [family compound]
	* Gates, Artemus Lamb
	  [separate house on estate]
		Lattingtown

Peacock Point	* Gates, Charles Otis	Lattingtown
The Pebbles	* Betts, Wyllis Rossiter, Jr.	Oyster Bay Cove
Pelican Point	Pell, John Howland Gibbs	Centre Island
Pemberton	Bedford, Alfred Cotton	Muttontown
Pembroke	* DeLamar, Joseph Raphael Loew, Marcus Loew, Arthur Marcus, Sr.	Glen Cove
Penllyn	Smith, Albert Lawrence, Sr.	Brookville
Penny Pond	Van Alen, James Henry	Old Brookville
Penwood	Stern, Henry Root, Sr.	North Hills
Pepperidge Point	* Babcock, Frederick Huntington Gerdes, John	Mill Neck
Petit Bois	* Ide, George Edward Dickson, Thomas, Sr.	Lattingtown
Piazzola	Baehr, Irvine E. Theodore	Oyster Bay Cove
Picket Farm	* Kramer, Albert Ludlow, Sr. Lehman, Allen Sigmund	Jericho
Pidgeon Hill	* Hare, Meredith	South Huntington
The Pillars	Talbott, Harold Elster, II	Old Westbury
Pine Terrace	* Slade, Josephine Bissell Roe	Mill Neck
Pink Coat Cottage	Burton, Van Duzer, Sr.	Syosset
The Pinnacle	* Bleecker, Theophylact Bache, II Bleecker, Charles Moore	Laurel Hollow
The Place	Sloane, Charles William Sloane, Charles Bryon	Sands Point
Plaisance	* DeBrabant, Marcus	Centerport
Plandome Manor House	Littleton, Martin Wiley, Sr. Allen, Gabriel Dean, Robert, Sr. Ioannov, John	Plandome Manor
Plandome Mills	Kennedy, Louise Leeds	Plandome Manor
Planting Fields	* Coe, William Robertson	Upper Brookville
The Playhouse	Woodward, William, Jr.	Oyster Bay Cove

The Pleasantways	Fahnestock, Archer Pleasant	Plandome Manor
The Point	* Inness–Brown, Hugh Alwyn, Sr.	Plandome Manor
The Point	Church, Richard N. L. Brickman, Herman	Kings Point
The Point	* Robinson, George Hazard Robinson, Miss Edith Attmore	Asharoken
The Point	Truslow, Francis Adams, Sr. Howell, Elizabeth Auchincloss Jennings	Laurel Hollow
Pondacre	McVickar, Donald McVickar, Janet Lansing	East Norwich
Poplar Hill [I] [II]	* Pratt, Frederic Bayley	Glen Cove
Portledge	* Coffin, Charles Albert Coffin, Miss Alice	Matinecock
Porto Bello	* Hunter, Fenley	Kings Point
Pound Hollow Cottage	Mason, Julian Starkweather	Old Brookville
Pound Hollow Farm	* Peabody, Julian Livingston, Sr.	Old Westbury
Preference	* Van Ingen, Lawrence Bell, Sr. Bush, Donald Fairfax, Jr. Van Ingen, Lawrence Bell, Jr.	Lattingtown
Preston Hall	Satterwhite, Dr. Preston Pope	Kings Point
Puente Vista	Moore, William Talman, Jr.	Centre Island
Punkin Hill	* Geddes, Eugene Maxwell, Sr.	Matinecock
Radnor	Hoffman, Albert L., Sr.	Muttontown
Ramsbroke	Townsend, Howard Rockwell, Sr.	Oyster Bay Cove
Rattling Spring	Chubb, Percy, Sr. Powell, Francis Edward, Jr.	Glen Cove
Red Barns	Robinson, Thomas Linton	East Williston
Redcote	Eldridge, Lewis Angevine, Sr.	Saddle Rock
Redcote	Leffingwell, Russell Cornell Pulling, Thomas John Edward	Oyster Bay Cove
Reknit	Tinker, Giles Knight	Oyster Bay Cove
Renwood	Moen, A. Rene	Cove Neck
Rhada	* Meyer, J. Edward, Sr.	Kings Point
Rhuna Craig	* Niven, John Ballantine	Mill Neck
Ricochet	Slater, Horatio Nelson, III	Matinecock
Ridgelands	Smull, Jacob Barstow	Laurel Hollow

Rivington House	* Pyne, Percy Rivington, II	Roslyn Harbor
Roads End	* Groesbeck, Clarence Edward	Matinecock
Robinhurst Farm	Scudder, Townsend, II	Glen Head
The Robin's Nest	Robins, Lydia DeLamater	Asharoken
Rockledge	Coe, William Rogers	Mill Neck
Rocky Point	James, Oliver B., Sr.	Laurel Hollow
Rolling Field	Wright, Boykin Cabell, Sr.	Jericho
Rolling Hill Farm	Nicholas, Harry Ingersoll, II	Muttontown
Rolling Stone	* Coles, Elizabeth	Glen Cove
Ronda	* Auchincloss, Gordon, Sr.	Matinecock
Rosemary Farm	* Conklin, Roland Ray	Lloyd Harbor
Rosemary Hall	* Keene, Foxhall Parker	Old Westbury
Roseneath	Deering, William Rogers	Laurel Hollow
Roslyn Hall	* Mortimer, Stanley, Sr.	Old Westbury
Roslyn House	Garvan, Francis Patrick, Sr.	Old Westbury
Roslyn Manor	Guest, Frederick E.	Brookville
Round Bush	* Pennoyer, Paul Geddes, Sr.	Glen Cove
Royston	* Franklin, Philip Albright Small, Sr.	Matinecock
Rugby	Coudert, Frederic Rene, II	Cove Neck
Rumpus House	* Schmidlapp, Carl Jacob, Sr.	Mill Neck
Russet	* Chadwick, Elbridge Gerry	Muttontown
Rynwood	* Salvage, Sir Samuel Agar Emerson, Margaret Lundy, Frederick William Irving	Old Brookville
Sagamore Hill	* Roosevelt, Theodore	Cove Neck
Saint Joan	Hearst, William Randolph	Sands Point
Sakunska	Roosevelt, Quentin, II	Cove Neck
Salutation	* Morgan, Junius Spencer Samuels, John Stockwell, III	Glen Cove, West Island
Sands Hill	Langone, Kenneth Gerard, Sr.	Sands Point
Sandy Cay	* Nast, Conde Schiff, Dorothy Kelland, Clarence Budington Uris, Percy	Sands Point

Scottage	* Scott, Rufus W.	Lattingtown
Seacroft	Oelsner, Edward Carl William, Sr. Oelsner, Warren James	Centre Island
Seamoor	* Pratt, Charles Millard	Glen Cove
Searing Farm	D'Oench, Russell Grace, Sr.	Searingtown
Sefton Manor	* Dodge, Lillian Sefton Thomas	Mill Neck
Seven Gables	Caldwell, Robert J.	Mill Neck
Sevenoaks	Greer, Louis Morris	Bayville
Seven Springs	Savage, Rev. Theodore Fiske	Lloyd Harbor
Severn	Howe, Polly Brooks	Lattingtown
The Shack	Peck, Thomas Bloodgood, II	Syosset
Shadowland	* Ayer, Dr. James Cook	Glen Cove
Shadowlane	* Proctor, Charles E.	Kings Point
Shadow Lawn	Doubleday, Russell	Glen Cove
The Shelter	Stettinius, Edward Reilly, Sr. Stettinius, Edward Reilly, Jr.	Lattingtown
Sherryland	* Sherry, Louis	Manhasset
Shoredge	* Smith, Howard Caswell, Sr.	Cove Neck
Shorelands	* Williams, Timothy Shaler	Lloyd Harbor
Shoremonde	* Smith, Ormond Gerald	Centre Island
The Shrubbery	Van Wart, Henry Van Wart, Edwin Clark	Sands Point
Slow Tide	Reynolds, Richard Samuel, Sr.	Glen Cove
Snug Harbor	* Aldrich, Sherwood Sloane, Alfred Pritchard, Jr.	Kings Point
Solana	* Brown, Stephen Howland Stone, Charles Augustus, Sr.	Matinecock
Soundacre	Wellman, Roderic	Sands Point
Southerly	Gubelmann, Walter Stanley	Centre Island
Sparrowbush	Caesar, Charles Unger	Lattingtown
Spindrift	Lyon, Frederick Gorham Clark	Centre Island
The Spinneys	White, Leonard Dalton, Jr.	Great Neck
Spring	Morse, Daniel Parmelee, Sr.	Centerport
Spring Hill	Phipps, Henry Carnegie	Old Westbury

Steepways	* Abbott, Phillips	Mill Neck
Stepping Stones	Smith, Ormond Gerald	Brookville
Sterling	Hudson, Hans Kierstede, Sr.	Mill Neck
Still House	* Cravath, Paul Drennan Rothschild, Baron Eugene de Porter, Seton Andersen, Dr. Harold Willids, Sr.	Matinecock
Stoke Farm	Leonard, Edgar Welch	Oyster Bay Cove
Stone House	* Clapham, Thomas	Roslyn Harbor
Stramore	Bell, James Christy, Jr.	Upper Brookville
Sundown	Tilney, Dr. Frederick, Sr.	Centre Island
Sunken Orchard	* Ingalls, Fay McCann, Charles Edward Francis	Oyster Bay Cove
Sunninghill	Dillon, Herbert Lowell, Sr.	Old Brookville
Sunninghill	* Richmond, L. Martin	Old Brookville
Sunnybrook	* Brokaw, George Tuttle	Upper Brookville
Sunny Knoll	* Hammerstein, Oscar, II	Kings Point
Sunnymede	* Dexter, Stanley Walker O'Connor, John A.	Oyster Bay
The Sunnyside	* Shaw, Samuel T., Sr.	Centre Island
Sunny Skies	Kelley, Cornelius Francis	North Hills
Sunridge Hall	* Milburn, Devereux, Sr.	Old Westbury
Sunset Hill	* D'Oench, Albert Frederick	Plandome
Sunset House	* Maxwell, George Thebaud Taylor, James Blackstone, Sr. Taylor, James Blackstone, Jr.	Cove Neck
Sunshine	* Gilbert, Harry Bramhall	Kings Point
Sunstar Hill	Bonney, Flora Macdonald	Upper Brookville
Sweet Hollow	Plimpton, Francis Taylor Pearsons, Sr.	West Hills
Sycamore House	Morgan, Edwin Denison, IV	Old Westbury
Sycamore Lodge	Demarest, John M. Brion, Lucille Demarest Riggs, Glenn E., Sr. Fahnestock, Frank Curry	Roslyn Harbor
Tall Trees	McClure, Walter C.	Old Brookville
Tallwood	* Halsey, Richard Townley Haines	West Hills

Tapis Vert	* Lloyd, Robert MacAllister, Sr. Cushman, Paul, Sr.	Oyster Bay Cove
Target Rock Farm	* Eberstadt, Ferdinand	Lloyd Harbor
Target Rock Farm	* Flinsch, Rudolf E. F.	Lloyd Harbor
Templeton	Guest, Winston Frederick Churchill	Brookville
Tenacres	Noyes, Winchester	Laurel Hollow
Ten Gables	* Moore, Edward Small, Sr. Draper, Charles Dana	Albertson
The Terrace	Hill, Dr. Miner C.	Oyster Bay Cove
The Terraces	* Gelder, Irving L.	Kings Point
Thatch Cottage	* Pettinos, Charles E.	Centre Island
Thayer House	* Thayer, Kendall Thayer, Francis Kendall, Sr.	Sands Point
Thistleton	Tod, Robert Elliot	Syosset
Three Brooks	* Church, Charles Thomas, Sr. Church, Frederic Edwin	Mill Neck
Three Corners Farm	* Ripley, Julien Ashton, Sr.	Muttontown
Three Ponds	* Morawetz, Victor	Woodbury
Three Winds	Heckscher, Gustav Maurice Ceballos, Juan Manuel, Jr.	Old Westbury
Tide Hill	Everitt, Samuel Alexander	Huntington Bay
Tide Oaks	Moore, William Talman, Sr.	Centre Island
Timber Bay Farm	Entenmann, William, Jr.	Old Westbury
Topping	* Eden, John H., II	Kings Point
Topside	Clark, Bruce	Glen Head
Townsend Place	Townsend, Edward Mitchell, Sr. Townsend, Edward Mitchell, II	Oyster Bay Cove
Tranquility	Roosevelt, Theodore Weekes, John Abeel	Oyster Bay Cove
Treborcliffe	Graves, Robert, II	Lloyd Harbor
Trillora Court	Guggenheim, Solomon Robert	Sands Point
Tuckaway	Roesler, Walter, Sr.	Kings Point
Tulip Hill	Costantini, Count David A.	Lattingtown
Tullaroan	* Grace, Joseph Peter, Sr.	North Hills
Turkey Lane House	Roosevelt, Archibald Bulloch, Sr.	Cold Spring Harbor

Turnpike Cottage	Park, William Gray	Old Westbury
Tuttles Corner	Tuttle, Dr. Jason H.	Old Brookville
Twin Lindens	* Wyckoff, Walter Wyckoff, Richard Demille	Kings Point
Twin Oaks	Wing, S. Bryce	Old Westbury
Two Maple Farm	* Stevenson, Malcolm, Sr.	Old Westbury
Udalls	Eldridge, Roswell	Saddle Rock
Underhill House	* Slade, John, Sr.	Upper Brookville
Uplands	Nichols, George, Sr.	Cold Spring Harbor
Upper Field	Boardman, Kenneth	Cold Spring Harbor
Valentine Farm	Clark, Louis Crawford, II Weekes, Frances Stokes	Old Brookville
Valleybrook Farm	Alexandre, J. Henry, Jr.	Old Brookville
Valley House	Osborn, Alexander Perry, Sr.	Brookville
Van Wyck Homestead	Lockman, Myron Augustus	Lloyd Harbor
Ventura Point	Baker, George Fisher, III	Centre Island
Veraton [I]	* Cravath, Paul Drennan	Lattingtown
Veraton [II] [III]	* Cravath, Paul Drennan	Matinecock
Vermland	* DeLamater, Cornelius Henry	Asharoken
Vikings Cove	* Baker, George Fisher, II	Lattingtown
Villa Amicitia	* L'Ecluse, Milton Albert	Huntington Bay
Villa Carola	* Guggenheim, Isaac	Sands Point
Villa D'Orsay	Woodside, Joel David	Glen Cove
Villa Louedo	* Ladew, Edward R.	Glen Cove
Villa Marina	* Henderson, Frank C. Will, Harold Henry	Roslyn
Waldeck	Roosevelt, Laura d'Oremieulx	Cove Neck
Waldene	Walbridge, Henry D.	Roslyn
Walls of Jericho	Leonard, Charles Reginald, Sr.	Jericho
Walnut Farm House	DeLamater, Cornelius Henry Donnell, Laura Attmore Robinson	Asharoken
Wampage	Pell, Theodore Roosevelt	Sands Point
Warburton Hall	* Prime, William Albert, Sr.	Brookville

Waveland	Rentschler, Gordon Sohn	Old Brookville
	Taft, Walbridge S.	
Wawapek	* de Forest, Robert Weeks	Cold Spring Harbor
	de Forest, Johnston	
	Williams, Douglas	
Weekend	Harkness, Edward Stephen	North Hills
Welwyn	* Pratt, Harold Irving, Sr.	Glen Cove
Wenlo	Hughes, Dr. Wendell	Roslyn Harbor
Westacre	Hewitt, Edward Shepard	Lloyd Harbor
Westaways	* Brokaw, Clifford Vail	Centre Island
Westbury House	* Phipps, John Shaffer	Old Westbury
Westerleigh	Loeb, William, Jr.	Mill Neck
West Gate Lodge	* Lindeberg, Harrie Thomas	Matinecock
West Neck Farm	* Brown, George McKesson	Lloyd Harbor
Westwood	* Ledyard, Lewis Cass, Jr.	Oyster Bay Cove
Weymouth	* White, Alexander Moss, Sr.	Cove Neck
Wheatly	* Morgan, Edwin Dennison, III	Old Westbury
Whileaway	Ryle, Arthur, Sr.	Matinecock
Whispered Wishes	McCory, Nellie	Roslyn Heights
Whispering Laurels	* Duer, Beverly	Laurel Hollow
Whispering Pines	* Pratt, Theodore, Sr.	Lattingtown
White Eagle	* du Pont, Alfred Irenee	Brookville
White Elephant Farm	Redmond, Roland Livingston	Oyster Bay Cove
White Gates	* Davey, William Nelson	West Hills
Whitehall	Pratt, Herbert Lee, Jr.	Mill Neck
Whitehill Place	Pierson, Dr. Richard Norris, Sr.	Cold Spring Harbor
White Lodge	* White, Gardiner Winslow, Sr.	Mill Neck
White Oak Farm	Allen, Frederic Winthrop	North Hills
White Oak Farm	Stebbins, Theodore Ellis, Sr.	Syosset
White Oaks	Taylor, Edwin Pemberton, Jr.	Oyster Bay Cove
Whitewood	* Scott, Donald, Sr.	Lloyd Harbor
	Hadley, Morris	
White Wood Point	Hadley, John Wood Blodgett	Lloyd Harbor

Whitney House	* Whitney, Cornelius Vanderbilt	Old Westbury
Wildbank	Sousa, John Philip, Sr. Hirsch, Peter	Sands Point
The Wilderness	Taliaferro, Eugene Sinclair	Cove Neck
Wildwood	* Hopkins, Erustis Langdon	Matinecock
Willada Point	Hester, William Van Anden, Sr.	Glen Cove
Willow Bank	* Brown, Francis Gordon, Sr.	Old Brookville
Willowmere	Ward, Aaron Curtis, James Freeman	Roslyn Harbor
Wiltwick	Hoffman, William Wickham	Jericho
Wincoma	* Heckscher, August	Huntington Bay
Windermere House	* Perine, William DeNyse Nichols	Mill Neck
Windward	* Jennings, Benjamin Brewster	Old Brookville
Windward	Zinsser, William Herman, Jr.	Kings Point
Windy Hill	* Reed, Lansing Parmelee	Lloyd Harbor
Windy Meadow	Clark, Marshall	Centre Island
Winfield Hall	* Woolworth, Frank Winfield Reynolds, Richard Samuel, Sr.	Glen Cove
The Wings	* Dana, Charles Anderson	Glen Cove, West Island
Winthrop House	Pratt, Richardson, Sr.	Glen Cove
Wolvers Hollow	* Iselin, Charles Oliver	Upper Brookville
Woodbury House	* Webb, James Watson, Sr. Tinker, Edward Richmond, Jr.	Syosset
Woodford	* Ford, Nevil	Lloyd Harbor
Wood Hollow	DeGraff, Robert Fair	Upper Brookville
Woodlands	Bruce, David Kirkpatrick Este	Woodbury
Woodlee Farm	Thomas, Frederic Chichester, Sr.	Cold Spring Harbor
Woodley	* Provost, Cornelius W.	Muttontown
Woodside	* Burden, James Abercrombie, Jr.	Muttontown
Woodside	Burden, James Abercrombie, III	Old Brookville
Woodstock	Vander Poel, William Halsted	Muttontown
Woodstock Manor	Amato, Camille Jean Tuorto	Muttontown
Wood Winds	* Vermilye, H. Rowland, Sr.	Cold Spring Harbor

Wooldon	* Woolley, Daniel P.	Lattingtown
Wothiholme	Nichols, Acosta, Sr.	Oyster Bay Cove
Wrencroft	de Milhau, Louis John de Grenon, Sr.	Old Brookville
Wrexleigh	* Garver, John Anson	Oyster Bay Cove
Wuff Woods	* Ottley, Gilbert	Upper Brookville
Wychwood	* Milburn, John George, Jr.	North Hills
Wyndhem	Schniewind, Henry, Jr.	Glen Cove
Wyomissing	* Lyon, John Denniston	Matinecock
Yeadon	* Bullock, George Deans, Robert Barr, Sr.	Centre Island
Yellowbanks	* Roosevelt, James Alfred Roosevelt, William Emlen Roosevelt, John Kean Grace, Oliver Russell	Cove Neck
Yellowcote	Morris, Ray, Sr.	Oyster Bay Cove
Yonder House	Duncan, Eloise Stevenson	Westbury

Golf Courses

North Shore estates that are presently golf courses are identified by the original owner. For subsequent estate owners, see surname entry.

Cold Spring Country Club, East Gate Drive, Cold Spring Harbor
  —includes private golf course on the Otto Hermann Kahn estate *Oheka.*

The Creek Club, Horse Hollow Road, Lattingtown
  —remains of the Paul Drennan Cravath house *Veraton* [I] are located near the sixth hole.

Deepdale Golf Club, Community Drive, North Hills
  —located on the Joseph Peter Grace, Sr. estate, *Tullaroan.*

Glen Cove Municipal Park & Golf Course, Lattingtown Road, Glen Cove
  —located on the Helen Porter Pryibil estate *Bogheid.*

Glen Oaks Country Club, Post Road, Old Westbury
  —located on part of the Edwin Denison Morgan III estate *Wheatly.*

Incorporated Village of Lake Success Golf Course, 318 Lakeville Road, Lake Success
  —was the private golf course on the William Kissam Vanderbilt, Jr. estate *Deepdale.*

Mill River Club, Mill River Hollow Road, Upper Brookville
  —situated on properties from the Henry Pomeroy Davison II estate *Appledore;* the Nathan Lewis Miller estate *Norwich House*; and the Frank C. Bauman Page estate *Elmcroft.*

Muttontown Golf and Country Club, Northern Blvd., Muttontown
  —located on the Howard Crosby Brokaw estate *The Chimneys.*

North Hills Country Club Inc., LIE North Service Road, North Hills
  —located on part of the Edward Stephen Harkness estate *Weekend.*

Old Westbury Golf and Country Club, 270 Wheatley Road, Old Westbury
  —situated on properties from the Cornelius Vanderbilt Whitney estate, *Whitney House,* and the William Collins Whitney estate.

Pine Hollow Country Club, Northern Blvd., East Norwich
  —located on the Dorothy Schiff estate *Old Fields.*

Tom O'Shanter Country Club, Cedar Swamp Road, Brookville
  —located on the William Deering Howe estate *Highpool.*

Town of Oyster Bay Golf Course, South Woods Road, Woodbury
  —located on the Victor Morawetz estate *Three Ponds.*

Village Club of Sands Point, Middle Neck Road, Sands Point
  —located on the Isaac Guggenheim estate *Villa Carola.*

Woodcrest Country Club, Muttontown Road, Muttontown
  —located on the James Abercrombie Burden, Jr. estate *Woodside.*

Apponyi, Countess Geraldine [*see* Zog]

Balsan, Consuelo Vanderbilt [*formerly* Duchess of Marlborough]

Baruch, Anne Marie Mackay [*formerly* Baroness Mackay of the Hague]

Burchard, Allene Tew [*subsequently* Princess of Reuss and Countess de Kotzebue]

Cardelli, Count Giovanni Guido Carlo

Cardelli, Countess Jacqueline Stewart

Clews, Mary Ann Payne [*subsequently* Baroness von Wrangell]

Costantini, Count David A.

Costantini, Countess Frieda Frasch [*subsequently* Baroness von Seidlitz]

Costantini, Countess Ida Schenck

de Dampierre, Count

De Leslie, Count Alexander Paulovitch

De Leslie, Countess Florence Rice

De Leslie, Countess Lillian Campeau

di Zoppola, Count Andrea Alexsandro Mario

di Zoppola, Countess Edith Mortimer

Fairchild, Elvia McNair [*subsequently* Viscountess de Sibour]

Guest, Princess Caroline Murat

Isham, [*formerly* Viscountess] Christine Churchill

Leeds, [*formerly* Duchess] Tsenia [Xenia] Michailovitch

Lindsay, Lady Elizabeth Sherman Hoyt

Moffett, [*formerly* Countess] Odette F. Feder

Redmond, Lydia P. Bodrero [*formerly* Princess di San Faustino]

Rothschild, Baron Eugene de

Rothschild, Baron Robert de

Salvage, Lady Mary Katharine Richmond

Salvage, Sir Samuel Agar

Sparks, Lady Mina Jane Roberts

Sparks, Sir Thomas Ashley

Watriss, [*formerly* Lady] Brenda Taylor Frazier

Williams, Mona Strader [*subsequently* Countess von Bismarck]

Zog I, King of Albania

When the date of landscaping is know, it has been included in brackets. Since, in some instances, more than one landscape architect worked on an estate and, in some rare instances, the architect who designed the house also designed the estate's grounds, the surname entry should be consulted to determine if anyone else was involved in designing the estate grounds. When the estate owner who contracted for landscaping is known, it is indicated by an asterisk. Original and subsequent estate owners are included in the list. See village entry for cross referencing of names not found as separate surname entries.

William Adams

   * Richards, Frederick L.   *Hazelmere*   Kings Point

Sir Charles Carrick Allon

     Bryce, Lloyd Stephens   *Bryce House*   Roslyn Harbor
                                     (designed garden gate on south lawn, grassed in formal 1901 Italian parterre garden on east side of house)

   * Frick, Childs   *Clayton*   Roslyn Harbor
                                     (designed garden gate on south lawn, grassed in formal 1901 Italian parterre garden on east side of house)

Donn Barber

   * Shonnard, Horatio Seymour, Sr.   *Boscobel*   Oyster Bay
                                     (designed formal garden, 1920s)

     Underhill, Francis T.   (designed formal garden, 1920s)   Oyster Bay

     Weidenfeld, Camille   (designed formal garden, 1920s)   Oyster Bay

Gerard Beekman

     Beekman, James William, Sr.   *The Cliffs*   Mill Neck
                                     (designed water gardens)

     Fritz, Dr. Albert R.   *The Cliffs*   Mill Neck
                                     (designed water gardens)

Newton Bevin

     Bryce, Lloyd Stephens   *Bryce House*   Roslyn Harbor
                                     (designed teak trellis & pavilion, jointly with Henry Milliken, 1931)

   * Frick, Childs   *Clayton*   Roslyn Harbor
                                     (designed teak trellis & pavilion, jointly with Henry Milliken, 1931)

A. F. Brickeroff

   * Emanuel, Victor   *Dorwood*   North Hills

     Kelley, Cornelius Francis   *Sunny Skies*   North Hills

Brinley and Holbrook

* Guthrie, William Dameron	*Meudon* (designed stepped garden terraces descending into "horseshoe" lawn, jointly with Olmsted, 1905-1907)	Lattingtown
Humphreys, Dr. Alexander Crombie		Glen Cove
Queen, Emmet		Glen Cove
Reynolds, Richard Samuel, Sr.	*Winfield Hall*	Glen Cove
* Woolworth, Frank Winfield	*Winfield Hall*	Glen Cove

Harold A. Capan

* Tully, William John	*Almar*	Mill Neck
Winters, Albert C.		Mill Neck

Carrere and Hastings

Bryce, Lloyd Stephens	*Bryce House* (designed wrought iron gate for formal garden designed by Marian Coffin)	Roslyn Harbor
* du Pont, Alfred Irenee	*White Eagle* (designed loggia and terraces)	Brookville
* Frick Childs	*Clayton* (designed wrought iron gate for formal garden designed by Marian Coffin)	Roslyn Harbor
Guest, Frederick E.	*Roslyn Manor* (designed loggia and terraces)	Brookville
Guest, Winston Frederick Churchill	*Templeton* (designed loggia and terraces)	Brookville
Jennings, Oliver Burr, II	*Burrwood* (designed formal garden, driveway *allee* of poplar trees, and sunken garden with terraces and fountain, 1898-1900)	Lloyd Harbor
* Jennings, Walter	*Burrwood* (designed formal garden, driveway *allee* of poplar trees, and sunken garden with terraces and fountain, 1898-1900)	Lloyd Harbor

Noel Chamberlain

Lynch, Edmund Calvert, Jr.	*Floralyn*	Lattingtown
* Ryan, John Carlos	(extensive landscape designs)	Roslyn Heights
* Scott, Rufus	*Scottage* (1929)	Lattingtown
Whalen, Grover A., Sr.	(extensive landscape designs)	Roslyn Heights

Ogden Codman, Jr.

   * Bryce, Lloyd Stephens   *Bryce House*   Roslyn Harbor
                                (designed formal Italian parterre
                                garden on east side of house, c. 1901)

      Frick, Childs   *Clayton*   Roslyn Harbor
                                (designed formal Italian parterre
                                garden on east side of house, c. 1901)

Marian Coffin

   * Alexandre, J. Henry, Jr.   *Valleybrook Farm*   Old Brookville
                                (1920)

   * Benkard, Henry Horton   (designed gardens and recreated   Muttontown
                                Latimer Summer House from
                                Winterthur, 1930)

   * Brokaw, Irving   *Goose Point*   Matinecock
                                (1930)

      Bryce, Lloyd Stephens   *Bryce House*   Roslyn Harbor
                                (designed formal French garden with
                                parterre, circular reflecting pool, central
                                fountain jet and arched privet entrance
                                from adjacent polo field, 1925-early 1930s)

   * Field, Marshall, III   *Caumsett*   Lloyd Harbor
                                (designed evergreen and Pan gardens
                                and landscaping for *Winter Cottage,* 1919)

   * Flagg, W. Allston, Sr.   Old Westbury

   * Frick, Childs   *Clayton*   Roslyn Harbor
                                (designed formal French garden with
                                parterre, circular reflecting pool, central
                                fountain jet and arched privet entrance from
                                adjacent polo field, 1925-early 1930s)

      Maxwell, George Thebaud   *Sunset House*   Cove Neck
                                (designed oval garden)

   * Post, Marjorie Merriweather   *Hillwood*   Brookville
                                (designed magnolia walk and extensive
                                gardens,1922)

      Prime, William Albert, Sr.   *Warburton Hall*   Brookville
                                (designed magnolia walk and extensive
                                gardens, 1922)

      Smithers, Robert Brinkley   *Longhur*   Mill Neck
                                (1930)

   * Taylor, James Blackstone, Jr.   *Sunset House*   Cove Neck
                                (designed oval garden)

      Taylor, James Blackstone, Sr.   *Sunset House*   Cove Neck
                                (designed oval garden)

George Abraham Crawley

* Phipps, John Shaffer	*Westbury House* (designed polo field, 1905; tennis courts, 1906; rose garden, 1907; walled garden with lattice work and corner pavilions, 1907)	Old Westbury

Ruth Dean

Kalimian, Abi		Kings Point
* Phillips, Ellis Laurimore, Sr.	*Laurimore*	Plandome Manor
* Schieren, George Arthur, Sr.	*Beachleigh*	Kings Point

Delano and Aldrich

* Burden, James Abercrombie, Jr.	*Woodside* (designed extensive gardens, jointly with Olmsted, 1922-1924)	Muttontown
* Delano, William Adams	*Muttontown Corners* (designed rose garden, cutting garden and tennis court)	Muttontown
* Griscom, Lloyd Carpenter	*Huntover Lodge* (designed landscaping, jointly with Ferruccio Vitale and Olmsted)	Muttontown
McKay, Alexandra Emery Moore	*Chelsea*	Muttontown
* Moore, Benjamin	*Chelsea*	Muttontown
Winthrop, Bronson	(designed landscaping, jointly with Ferruccio Vitale and Olmsted)	Muttontown

DuChene

Cartier	(designed extensive gardens and landscaping)*[see surname entry for detailed listing]*	Roslyn Harbor
Clapham, Thomas	*Stone House* (designed extensive gardens and landscaping) *[See surname entry for detailed listing.]*	Roslyn Harbor
Hines, Ephram	(designed extensive gardens and landscaping) *[See surname entry for detailed listing.]*	Roslyn Harbor
Hughes, Dr. Wendell	*Wenlo* (designed extensive gardens and landscaping)*[See surname entry for detailed listing.]*	Roslyn Harbor
LeRoux, Eduoard	*Cottage Normandy*	Brookville
Mott, Dr. Valentine	(designed extensive gardens and landscaping) *[See surname entry for detailed listing.]*	Roslyn Harbor

DuChene (cont'd)

Sage, Henry William, II		Brookville
* Stern, Benjamin	*Claraben Court* (designed extensive gardens and landscaping)*[See surname entry for detailed listing.]*	Roslyn Harbor
* Vanderbilt, Virginia Graham Fair		Brookville

Devereaux Emmet

* Henderson, Frank C.	*Villa Marina* (designed golf course)	Roslyn
Will, Harold Henry	*Villa Marina* (designed golf course)	Roslyn

Wilson Eye

* Conklin, Roland Ray	*Rosemary Farm* (designed formal gardens)	Lloyd Harbor

Beatrix Jones Farrand

Adam, Sarah Sampson	(designed entrance, 1921)	Oyster Bay
* Ayer, Dr. James Cook	*Shadowland* (designed garden)	Glen Cove
* Chubb, Percy, Sr.	*Rattling Spring* (designed rose arbor, water rill and plantings, 1900)	Glen Cove
Coles, Elizabeth	*Rolling Stone* (designed rose arbor, water rill and plantings, 1900)	Glen Cove
* Delano, William Adams	*Muttontown Corners* (designed garden flower borders, 1921)	Muttontown
* Derby, Dr. Richard	*Old Adam* (designed entrance, 1921)	Oyster Bay
Dieffenbach, William	(designed entrance, 1921)	Oyster Bay
* Eldridge, Roswell	*Udalls* (1905-1930; designed oval enclosed garden, 1924-1930)	Saddle Rock
* Elmhirst, Leonard Knight	*Applegreen*	Old Westbury
* Harkness, Edward S.	*Weekend* (garden advice, 1921)	North Hills
Harriman, Joseph Wright	(design and planting advice, 1911)	Brookville
* Hastings, Thomas	*Bagatelle* (advise on border plantings, 1915)	Old Westbury

Beatrix Jones Farrand (cont'd)

* Iselin, Charles Oliver	*Wolvers Hollow* (designed driveway, garden and rose garden, 1914)	Upper Brookville
* Kahn Otto Hermann	*Oheka* (extensive garden designs, 1919-1928) [*See surname entry.*]	Cold Spring Harbor
* Livermore, Philip Walter	*Bois Joli* (design & planting advice, 1911)	Brookville
* Mann, Samuel Vernon, Jr.	(1929)	Kings Point
* Mann, Samuel Vernon, Sr.	*Grove Point* (extensive garden designs, 1920-1930) [*See surname entry.*]	Kings Point
Melius, Gary	*Oheka Castle* (extensive garden designs, 1919-1928) [*See surname entry.*]	Cold Spring Harbor
* Morris, Dave Hennen	(advice on screen planting estate layout, 1925)	*[unable to locate - Glen Head]*
Pierce, Winslow Shelby, II	*Dunstable* (extensive garden designs, 1928-1929) [*See surname entry.*]	Bayville
Powell, Francis Edward, Jr.	*Rattling Spring* (designed rose arbor, water rill and plantings, 1900)	Glen Cove
* Pratt, George du Pont, Sr.	*Killenworth* [II] (designed summerhouse & tennis court, 1914; 1928-1929)	Glen Cove
* Pyne, Percy Rivington, II	*Rivington House* (designed extensive gardens and model farm complex 1926-1929) [*See surname entry.*]	Roslyn Harbor
* Straight, Willard Dickerman	*Elmhurst* (designed Chinese garden and playhouse with swimming pool, 1913-1918)	Old Westbury
* Whitney, Edward Farley	(designed extensive gardens and driveway plantings 1906-1914) [*See surname entry.*]	Cove Neck
Whitney, Miss Margaret Sargent	*Ballygurge* (designed extensive gardens and driveway plantings 1906-1914) [*See surname entry.*]	Cove Neck
* Williams, Harrison	*Oak Point* (extensive garden designs, 1928-1929) [*See surname entry.*]	Bayville

Armistead Fitzhugh

Burden, James Abercrombie, III	*Woodside*	Old Brookville
* Peck, Fremont Carson, Sr.		Old Brookville

Annette Hoyt Flanders

* Astor, William Vincent	*Cloverley Manor*	Sands Point
* Barnes E. Mortimer	*Manana* (designed formal walled garden)	Old Brookville
Breed, William Constable, Sr.	*Normandy Farms* (designed formal walled garden)	Old Brookville
Douglas, Barry	(extensive garden design) *[See surname entry.]*	Oyster Bay Cove
* Flagg, Montague, II	*Applewood*	Upper Brookville
Ingalls, Fay	*Sunken Orchard* (extensive garden design) *[See surname entry.]*	Oyster Bay Cove
Kellogg, Morris Woodruff	*Fieldston Farm*	Upper Brookville
* Ledyard, Lewis Cass, Jr.	*Westwood*	Oyster Bay Cove
* McCann, Charles Edward Francis	*Sunken Orchard* (extensive garden design) *[See surname entry.]*	Oyster Bay Cove
McClintock, Harvey Childs, Jr.		Upper Brookville
McIntosh, Allan J.		Sands Point
* Taylor, Myron Charles	*Killingworth* (designed meadows and woodlands, jointly with Vitale, 1924)	Lattingtown

Clarence Fowler

Wyckoff, Richard Demille	*Twin Lindens*	Kings Point
* Wyckoff, Walter	*Twin Lindens*	Kings Point

Robert Fowler

* Redmond, Geraldyn Livingston, Sr.	*Gray House Farm*	Upper Brookville

Robert Williams Gibson

* Gibson, Robert Williams	*North Point* (designed formal gardens)	Cove Neck

James Goodwin

* Goodwin, Philip Lippincott	*Goodwin Place*	Woodbury
Jennings, Oliver Burr, II		Woodbury

Jacques Greber

* Luckenbach, Edgar Frederick, Sr.	*Elm Court*	Sands Point
* Mackay, Clarence Hungerford	*Harbor Hill* (c. 1910)	Roslyn

Jacques Greber (cont'd)

Maddocks, John L., Jr.	(designed garden, reflecting pool, and fountain)	Brookville
* Maynard, Walter Effingham	*Haut Bois* (designed garden, reflecting pool and fountain)	Brookville
Munsel, Patrice	*Malmaison* (designed garden, reflecting pool and fountain)	Brookville
* Phipps, John Shaffer	*Westbury House*	Old Westbury

James Leal Greenleaf

* Brewster, George S.	*Fairleigh*	Muttontown
* Byrne, James		Upper Brookville
Coe, William Robertson	*Planting Fields*	Upper Brookville
Meyer, Robert J.		Muttontown
* Pratt, George du Pont, Sr.	*Killenworth* [II] (designed gardens and landscaping)	Glen Cove
* Pratt, Harold Irving, Sr.	*Welwyn* (designed formal gardens and landscaping, jointly with Martha Brooks Brown Hutcheson)	Glen Cove
* Pratt, Herbert Lee, Sr.	*The Braes* (designed 2 long pergolas, formal rose garden, terraces, formal water garden, and central tier, jointly with Ellen Biddle Shipman; landscaping)	Glen Cove
* Pyne, Percy Rivington, II	*Rivington House*	Roslyn Harbor
Schiff, John Mortimer	*Northwood* (designed gardens and landscaping)	Oyster Bay
* Schiff, Mortimer L.	*Northwood* (designed gardens and landscaping)	Oyster Bay

Hatton and DeSuarez

* Henderson, Frank C.	*Villa Marina*	Roslyn
Will, Harold Henry	*Villa Marina*	Roslyn

Hicks Nurseries

Bonney, Flora Macdonald	*Sunstar Hill* (supplied plantings)	Upper Brookville
Field, Marshall, II	*Caumsett* (supplied plantings)	Lloyd Harbor

Hicks Nurseries (cont'd)

Jennings, Oliver Burr	*Burrwood* (supplied plantings)	Lloyd Harbor
* Jennings, Walter	*Burrwood* (supplied plantings)	Lloyd Harbor
* Kennedy, William, Sr.	*Kennedy Villa*	Syosset
Mitchell, Sidney Alexander, Sr.	*Marney* (supplied plantings)	Matinecock
* Mitchell, Sidney Zollicoffer	(supplied plantings)	Matinecock
* Morgan, Edwin Denison, III	*Wheatly* (supplied plantings)	Old Westbury
* Postley, Sterling	*Framewood* (supplied plantings)	Upper Brookville

Martha Brooks Brown Hutcheson

* Pratt, Frederic Bayley	*Poplar Hill* [II]	Glen Cove
* Pratt, Harold Irving, Sr.	*Welwyn* (designed gardens and landscaping, jointly with James Leal Greenleaf)	Glen Cove

Innocenti and Webel

* Babcock, Richard Franklin	*Hark Away*	Woodbury
* Baker, George Fisher, II	*Vikings Cove*	Lattingtown
Bono, Henry, Jr.	*The Crossroads*	Old Westbury
Bryce, Lloyd Stephens	*Bryce House* (designed dock, ski slope and trails; positioned *Millstone* , a research laboratory; altered driveways and entrance court, c. 1937; designed walled garden for *Leftover*, a cottage on the estate, 1941)	Roslyn Harbor
Douglas, Barry	(designed courtyard, terrace, lawns, meadows, turf walk, and enclosed evergreen garden surrounded by magnolias, c. 1936)	Oyster Bay Cove
* Field, Evelyn	*Easton* (designed lawn forecourt and rear lawn, c. 1936)	Muttontown
* Finlayson, Frank Redfern	(designed flagstone terraces, enclosed garden, shade trees, and lawn c. 1937)	Matinecock
* Frick, Childs	*Clayton* (designed dock, ski slope and trails; positioned *Millstone* , a research laboratory; altered driveways and entrance court, c. 1937; designed walled garden for *Leftover*, a cottage on the estate, 1941)	Roslyn Harbor

985

Innocenti and Webel (cont'd)

* Geddes, Eugene Maxwell, Sr.	*Punkin Hill*	Matinecock
* Gould, Edwin	*Highwood* (designed garden terrace, brick walls, seating alcove, evergreen gardens, paths, and lawns, c. 1935)	Oyster Bay Cove
* Grace, William Russell, Jr.	*The Crossroads*	Old Westbury
* Harris, Sam Henry	Kings Point	
* Ingalls, Fay	*Sunken Orchard* (designed courtyard, terrace, lawns, meadows, turf walk, and enclosed evergreen garden surrounded by magnolias, c. 1936)	Oyster Bay Cove
* McCann, Charles Edward Francis	*Sunken Orchard* (designed courtyard, terrace, lawns, meadows, turf walk, and enclosed evergreen garden surrounded by magnolias, c. 1936)	Oyster Bay Cove
McKay, Alexandra Emery Moore	*Chelsea*	Muttontown
Minicozzi, Alexander	(designed garden terrace, brick walls, seating alcove, evergreen gardens, paths, and lawns, c. 1935)	Oyster Bay Cove
Montana, Dr. Christopher	(designed garden terrace, brick walls, seating alcove, evergreen gardens, paths, and lawns, c. 1935)	Oyster Bay Cove
* Moore, Benjamin	*Chelsea*	Muttontown
* Richmond, L. Martin	*Sunninghill* (designed gardens, jointly with Ellen Biddle Shipman)	Old Brookville
* Stearns, John Noble, III		Old Brookville

Harvey Smith Ladew II

* Ladew, Harvey Smith, II	*The Box*	Old Brookville

Charles Downing Lay

Grant, Robert, Jr.		Jericho
* Simpson, Robert H.	*Kinross*	Jericho

Charles Wellford Leavitt and Sons

* Alden, Anne Coleman	*Fort Hill House*	Lloyd Harbor
Bedford, Alfred Cotton	*Pemberton*	Muttontown
Bendel, Henri	(designed terraces, paths, pergolas and driveway flower gardens)	Kings Point

Charles Wellford Leavitt and Sons (cont'd)

	Campbell, George W.	*Fort Hill House*	Lloyd Harbor
*	Chrysler, Walter Percy, Sr.	*Forker House* (designed terraces, paths, pergolas and driveway flower gardens)	Kings Point
*	Cozzens, Issachar, III	*Maple Knoll*	Lattingtown
*	Dodge, Lillian Sefton Thomas	*Sefton Manor* (designed gardens, reflecting pools and stone temples)	Mill Neck
	Hoffman, Albert L., Sr.	*Radnor House*	Muttontown
	Holloway, William Grace, Sr.	*Foxland* (designed terraces and formal garden)	Old Westbury
*	Keene, Foxhall Parker	*Rosemary Hall* (designed terraces and formal garden)	Old Westbury
	Matheson, William John	*Fort Hill House*	Lloyd Harbor
	Morgan, Henry Sturgis, Sr.		Lattingtown
	Netter, Dr. Frank H.		Muttontown
	Oberlin, Abraham		Lattingtown
*	Smith, George	*Blythewood*	Muttontown
	Stam, Alan		Muttontown
	Wood, Willis Delano	*Fort Hill House*	Lloyd Harbor

Leavitt and Aldrich

	Le Boutillier, Thomas III	(designed studio garden)	Old Westbury
*	Whitney, Gertrude Vanderbilt	(designed studio garden)	Old Westbury
	Whitney, William Collins	(designed studio garden)	Old Westbury

John Jacob Levison

*	Bailey, Frank, Sr.	*Munnysunk*	Lattingtown
	Bendel, Henri		Kings Point
	Castro, Bernard, Sr.	*Panfield*	Lloyd Harbor
*	Chrysler, Walter Percy, Sr.	*Forker House*	Kings Point
	Clark, John		Lattingtown
	Devendorf, George E.		Lake Success
*	Field, Marshall, III	*Caumsett*	Lloyd Harbor
	Giordano, Salvatore, Sr.	*Panfield*	Lloyd Harbor

John Jacob Levison (cont'd)

	Guida, Bernadette Castro	*Panfield*	Lloyd Harbor
*	Jonas, Nathan Solomon	Lake Success	
*	Kahn, Otto Hermann	*Oheka*	Cold Spring Harbor
*	Levison, John Jacob		Sea Cliff
	Melius, Gary	*Oheka Castle*	Cold Spring Harbor
*	Milbank, Albert Goodsell	*Panfield*	Lloyd Harbor

Lewis and Valentine

	Ades, Robert	(designed landscaping)	Kings Point
*	Barnes, E. Mortimer	*Manana* (supplied plantings for formal walled garden)	Brookville
	Breed, William Constable, Sr.	*Normandy Farms* (supplied plantings for formal walled garden)	Old Brookville
*	Burden, Arthur Scott		Brookville
	Cary, Guy Fairfax, Sr.	*Oak Hill*	Brookville
	Castro, Bernard, Sr.	*Panfield* (designed gardens)	Lloyd Harbor
	Coleman, Gregory		Muttontown
	Draper, Charles Dana	*Ten Gables* (designed evergreen settings)	Albertson
*	Duryea, Hermanes Barkula, Jr.	*Knole* (1917)	Old Westbury
	Giordano, Salvatore, Sr.	*Panfield* (designed gardens)	Lloyd Harbor
	Guida, Bernadette Castro	*Panfield* (designed gardens)	Lloyd Harbor
	Heck, George Callendine, Sr.	*Linwood*	Muttontown
*	Kahn, Otto Hermann	*Oheka* (1917)	Cold Spring Harbor
*	Kienle, Eugene S., Sr.	*Many Gables* (designed landscaping)	Kings Point
	Martin, Bradley, Jr.	*Knole*	Old Westbury
	Martin, Esmond Bradley, Sr.	*Knole*	Old Westbury
	Martin, James E., Sr.	*Martin Hall* (designed evergreen settings)	Kings Point
	Melius, Gary	*Oheka Castle* (1917)	Cold Spring Harbor

Lewis and Valentine (cont'd)

  * Milbank, Albert Goodsell   *Panfield*   Lloyd Harbor
(designed gardens)

  * Moore, Edward Small, Sr.   *Ten Gables*   Albertson
(designed evergreen settings)

  * Ripley, Julien Ashton, Sr.   *Three Corners Farm*   Muttontown

     Satterwhite, Dr. Preston Pope   *Preston Hall*   Kings Point
(designed evergreen settings)

     Von Stade, Francis Skiddy, Sr.   Old Westbury

Guy Lowell

  * Billings, Cornelius Kingsley Garrison   *Farnsworth*   Upper Brookville
(designed landscaping, jointly with A. R. Sargent)

     Bird, Wallis C.   *Farnsworth*   Upper Brookville
(designed landscaping, jointly with A. R. Sargent)

     Byrne, James   (designed landscaping, jointly with A. R. Sargent, 1914)   Upper Brookville

  * Coe, William Robertson   *Planting Fields*   Upper Brookville
(designed landscaping, jointly with A. R. Sargent, 1914)

  * Cravath, Paul Drennan   *Veraton* [I] [III]   Lattingtown and Matinecock

  * Curran, Guernsey, Sr.   *Farlands*   Upper Brookville
(designed formal circular terraced garden with reflecting pool, jointing with A. R. Sargent)

     Douglas, Josephine Hartford   (designed formal circular terraced garden with reflecting pool, jointing with A. R. Sargent)   Upper Brookville

  * Mackay, Clarence Hungerford   *Harbor Hill*   Roslyn
(designed location of outbuildings, approaches, connecting road, and landscaping, 1902)

     Rentschler, Gordon Sohn   Matinecock

     Whitney, John Hay   *Greentree*   Manhasset
(designed pergola, paths, fountain, and gardens)

  * Whitney, William Payne   *Greentree*   Manhasset
(designed pergola, paths, fountain, and gardens)

  * Winthrop, Henry Rogers   *East Woods*   Woodbury
(designed landscaping)

J. Clinton Mackenzie

    Alden, Anne Coleman   *Fort Hill House*   Lloyd Harbor
                                        (designed formal garden, terrace, brick
                                        paths, pergola, and fountain with bronze fish
                                        sculpture by Saint-Gaudens, c. 1910)

    Campbell, George W.   *Fort Hill House*   Lloyd Harbor
                                          (designed formal garden, terrace, brick
                                        paths, pergola, and fountain with bronze fish
                                        sculpture by Saint-Gaudens, c. 1910)

    * Matheson, William John   *Fort Hill House*   Lloyd Harbor
                                          (designed formal garden, terrace, brick
                                        paths, pergola, and fountain with bronze fish
                                        sculpture by Saint-Gaudens, c. 1910)

    Wood, Willis Delano   *Fort Hill House*   Lloyd Harbor
                                          (designed formal garden, terrace, brick
                                        paths, pergola, and fountain with bronze fish
                                        sculpture by Saint-Gaudens, c. 1910)

A. Chandler Manning

    Miller, Nathan Lewis   *Norwich House*   Upper Brookville

    * Page, Frank C. Bauman   *Elmcroft*   Upper Brookville

Warren H. Manning

    Cournand, Edouard L.   Lloyd Harbor

    * Lloyd–Smith, Wilton   *Kenjockety*   Lloyd Harbor

    Rice, Paula   Lloyd Harbor

J. R. Marsh

    * Ricks, Jesse Jay   Flower Hill

Henry Milliken

    Bryce, Lloyd Stephens   *Bryce House*   Roslyn Harbor
                                        (designed teak trellis & pavilion,
                                        jointly with Newton Bevin, 1931)

    * Frick, Childs   *Clayton*   Roslyn Harbor
                                        (designed teak trellis & pavilion,
                                        jointly with Newton Bevin,1931)

Addison Mizner

    * Cockran, William Bourke   *The Cedars*   Sands Point
                                        (designed garden and
                                        amphitheater, 1911)

    * Hitchcock, Raymond   (designed gardens, 1910)   Kings Point

Morris and Rotch

	Brokaw, Clifford Vail, Jr.	*The Elms*	Glen Cove
*	Brokaw, Clifford Vail, Sr.	*The Elms*	Glen Cove
	Brown, Nannie C. Inman	*The Elms*	Glen Cove
	Cutting, Dr. Fulton	(designed terraced garden)	Brookville
*	Rumsey, Charles Cary, Sr.	(designed terraced garden)	Brookville

Dorothy Nicholas

| | Bryce, Lloyd Stephens | *Bryce House*
(designed flower beds, 1947) | Roslyn Harbor |
| * | Frick, Childs | *Clayton*
(designed flower beds, 1947) | Roslyn Harbor |

James W. O'Connor

| | Mitchell, Sidney Alexander, Sr. | *Marney*
(designed sunken garden, terrace,
pergolas, curved settee) | Matinecock |
| * | Mitchell, Sidney Zollicoffer | (designed sunken garden, terrace,
pergolas, and curved settee) | Matinecock |

Olmsted

	Alden, Anne Coleman	*Fort Hill House* (designed landscaping, jointly with Ellen Biddle Shipman from Shipman design, c. 1938)	Lloyd Harbor
*	Aldred, John Edward	*Ormston* (designed entire landscaping, 1912-1937) [*see surname entry*]	Lattingtown
*	Aldrich, Sherwood	*Snug Harbor*	Kings Point
	Amari, Philippo		Dix Hills
*	Aron, Jacob	*Hamptworth House* (designed English country garden, 1925-1930)	Kings Point
	Astin, Dr. Sherrill		Lattingtown
*	Auchincloss, Charles Crooke	*Builtover* (1917)	Roslyn Heights
*	Babbott, Frank Lusk, Sr.		Glen Cove
*	Baker, George Fisher, II	*Vikings Cove* (1913-1933)	Lattingtown
	Barney, Charles Tracy		Old Westbury
	Bartow, Francis Dwight, Sr.	*Belvoir* (1915-1923)	Glen Cove

Olmsted (cont'd)

* Batterman, Henry Lewis, Jr.	*Beaver Brook Farm* (1926)	Mill Neck
Batterman, Henry Lewis, Sr.	*Beaver Brook Farm* (1926)	Mill Neck
* Battershall, Frederic S.	(1925-1926)	Lattingtown
* Bermingham, John F.	*Midland Farm* (1921-1923)	Muttontown
Blair, Watson Keep	(1915-1928)	Muttontown
Blair, Wolcott	(1915-1928)	Muttontown
* Bourne, George Galt		Lattingtown
* Brady, Nicholas Frederic	*Inisfada* (1919)	North Hills
Brion, Lucille Demarest	*Sycamore Lodge* (1919-1923)	Roslyn Harbor
* Brokaw, Howard Crosby	*The Chimneys* (1916-1929)	Muttontown
* Brokaw, Irving	*Frost Mill Lodge*	Mill Neck
* Brown, Dr. James		*[unable to locate - Glen Cove]*
* Bullock, George	*Yeadon*	Centre Island
* Burden, James Abercrombie, Jr.	*Woodside* (designed extensive gardens, jointly with Delano and Aldrich, 1922-1924)	Muttontown
Byrne, James	(designed extensive gardens and landscaping, 1918-1937)	Upper Brookville
Campbell, George W.	*Fort Hill House* (designed landscaping, jointly with Ellen Biddle Shipman from Shipman design, c. 1938)	Lloyd Harbor
* Campbell, Oliver Allen, Sr.	*The Oaces*	East Norwich
* Canfield, Augustus Cass	*Cassleigh* (1904-1906)	North Hills
Carey, Martin F.	*Cashelmare*	Glen Cove
* Coe, William Robertson	*Planting Fields* (designed extensive gardens and landscaping, 1918-1937)	Upper Brookville
Coleman, Gregory		Muttontown

Olmsted (cont'd)

* Conklin, Roland Ray	*Rosemary Farm* (designed amphitheater with moat and waterfall, 1912-1913)	Lloyd Harbor
* Cravath, Paul Drennan	*Veraton* [III] (designed tree *allee* entrance and formal garden)	Matinecock
Crocker, George	(1915-1916)	Old Westbury
* Dana, Charles Anderson	*The Wings* (1875)	Glen Cove, West Island
Davison, Frederick Trubee	*Peacock Point* (designed terrace, casino with pergola, reflecting pool, circular drive, and lawns, 1913-1923)	Lattingtown
* Davison, Henry Pomeroy, II	*Appledore*	Upper Brookville
* Davison, Henry Pomeroy, Sr.	*Peacock Point* (designed terrace, casino with pergola, reflecting pool, circular drive, and lawns, 1913-1923)	Lattingtown
Deans, Robert Barr, Sr.	*Yeadon*	Centre Island
Deering, William Rogers	*Roseneath* (1929-1931)	Laurel Hollow
de Forest, Henry Grant	*Nethermuir* (designed formal garden, paths, arbors, summer house, rock garden, roads, and landscaping, 1906-1927)	Laurel Hollow
de Forest, Henry Wheeler	*Airslie* (designed landscaping)	Laurel Hollow
* de Forest, Henry Wheeler	*Nethermuir* (designed formal garden, paths, arbors, summer house, rock garden, roads, and landscaping, 1906-1927)	Laurel Hollow
de Forest, Johnston	*Wawapek* (1910-1912)	Cold Spring Harbor
* de Forest, Julia Mary	*Airslie* (designed landscaping)	Laurel Hollow
* de Forest, Robert Weeks	*Wawapek* (1910-1912)	Cold Spring Harbor
* Demarest, John M.	*Sycamore Lodge* (1919-1923)	Roslyn Harbor
* Dewing, Hiram E.	*Appledore*	Matinecock
* Dickinson, Hunt Tilford, Sr.	*Hearth Stone* (1936-1937)	Old Brookville

Olmsted (cont'd)

*	Diebold, Albert Henry	(1925)	Lattingtown
*	Doubleday, Nelson, Sr.	*Barberrys* (1919-1935)	Mill Neck
	Douglas, Barry		Oyster Bay Cove
*	Dows, David, Jr.	*Charlton Hall* (1915-1928)	Muttontown
*	Draper, Dr. George		*[unable to locate - Cold Spring Harbor]*
*	Duer, Beverly	*Whispering Laurels* (1929-1931)	Laurel Hollow
	Eldridge, Lewis Angevine, Sr.	*Redcote*	Saddle Rock
*	Eldridge, Roswell	*Udalls*	Saddle Rock
	Emory, William Helmsley, Jr.	*Clifton* (1919-1923)	Roslyn Harbor
	Fahnestock, Frank Curry	*Sycamore Lodge* (1919-1923)	Roslyn Harbor
*	Fahys, George Ernest, Sr.	*Hilaire*	Matinecock
*	Field, Marshall, III	*Caumsett* (designed formal box, perennial, and rock gardens, and plantings around tennis court building, 1924-1926)	Lloyd Harbor
*	Fowler, Dr. Robert Henry		Laurel Hollow
*	Franklin, Philip Albright Small, Jr.	*Hundred House*	Matinecock
*	Franklin, Walter Simonds, Jr.		Cold Spring Harbor
*	Garvan, Francis Patrick, Sr.	*Roslyn House* (1928-1929)	Old Westbury
*	Garver, John Anson	*Wrexleigh* (1924)	Oyster Bay Cove
*	Gates, Artemus Lamb	*Peacock Point* (1929)	Lattingtown
*	Gavin, Michael	*Greanan* (1929-1930)	Brookville
*	Gibson, Harvey Dow	*Lands End*	Lattingtown
*	Gould, Charles Albert	*Chateauiver*	Dix Hills
*	Grace, Joseph Peter, Sr.	*Tullaroan* (1923)	North Hills
*	Grace, Morgan Hatton, Sr.	*Lismore* (1923)	Kings Point

Olmsted (cont'd)

Grant, Robert, Jr.		Jericho
* Gray, Henry Gunther	*Longford* (1931)	Lattingtown
* Griscom, Lloyd Carpenter	(designed landscaping, jointly with Ferruccio Vitale and Delano and Aldrich]	Muttontown
Griswold, Frank Gray		North Hills
* Groesbeck, Clarence Edward	*Roads End* (1929-1931)	Matinecock
* Guthrie, William Dameron	*Meudon* (designed stepped garden terraces descending into "horseshoe" lawn, jointly with Brinley & Holbrook, 1905-1907)	Lattingtown
Harkness, William Lamon	(1875)	Glen Cove, West Island
* Harriman, Joseph Wright	*Avondale Farms* (1918-1928)	Brookville
* Healey, A. A.		*[unable to locate - Cold Spring Harbor]*
Heck, George Callendine, Sr.	*Linwood*	Muttontown
* Henderson, Edward Cairns	(1913-1914)	Laurel Hollow
* Hill, James Norman	*Big Tree Farm* (1916-1919)	Brookville
* Hine, Francis Lyman	*Mayhasit* (1915-1923)	Glen Cove
Ingalls, Fay	*Sunken Orchard*	Oyster Bay Cove
* Iselin, Charles Oliver	*Wolvers Hollow* (1925-1946)	Upper Brookville
Jennings, Oliver Burr, II	*Burrwood* (designed rose garden, ravine garden with circular reflecting pool, paths, tea house, and fountain, 1915-1938)	Lloyd Harbor
* Jennings, Walter	*Burrwood* (designed rose garden, ravine garden with circular reflecting pool, paths, tea house, and fountain, 1915-1938)	Lloyd Harbor
* Johnston, John Herbert	*Boatcroft* (1910)	Lloyd Harbor
Jones, William	(designed landscaping)	Laurel Hollow
* Kahn, Otto Hermann	*Oheka* (1917)	Cold Spring Harbor
* Kent, George Edward, Sr.	*Jericho House* (1917-1927)	Jericho

Olmsted (cont'd)

*	Kerrigan, Joseph J.	(1929)	Cove Neck
*	La Montagne, Harry	(1946-1947)	Mill Neck
	Le Roux, Edouard	(1915-1923)	Glen Cove
*	Livermore, Jesse Lauriston, Sr.	*Evermore* (1925)	Kings Point
*	Loew, William Goadby	*Loewmoor*	Old Westbury
	Lynch, Edmund Calvert, Sr.		Matinecock
	MacDonald, Helen Lamb Babbott		Glen Cove
*	MacNutt, F. A		*[unable to locate - Port Washington]*
	Martin, James E., Sr.	*Martin Hall* (1915-1917)	Kings Point
	Matheson, William John	*Fort Hill House* (designed landscaping, jointly with Ellen Biddle Shipman from Shipman design, c. 1938)	Lloyd Harbor
*	McCann, Charles Edward Francis	*Sunken Orchard*	Oyster Bay Cove
*	McConnell, Mrs. Marion E.	(1935)	*[unable to locate - Manhasset]*
	McCory, Nellie	*Whispered Wishes* (c. 1917)	Roslyn Heights
*	McKelvey, Charles Wylie	(1916-1917)	Oyster Bay Cove
	Melius, Gary	*Oheka Castle* (1917)	Cold Spring Harbor
*	Miller, William Wilson	(1917)	Old Brookville
	Mitchell, Sidney Alexander, Sr.	*Marney* (designed cutting garden, terrace, pergolas, settee, grading, roads, and site plans for farm complex and greenhouse, 1921-1939)	Matinecock
*	Mitchell, Sidney Zollicoffer	(designed cutting garden, terrace, pergolas, settee, grading, roads, and site plans for farm complex and greenhouse, 1921-1939)	Matinecock
	Morgan, Junius Spencer	*Salutation* (1875)	Glen Cove, West Island
	Mortimer, Stanley, Sr.	*Roslyn Hall* (1928-1929)	Old Westbury
*	Munsey, Frank Andrew	(1924-1925)	Manhasset
	Palmer, Carlton Humphreys	*Hearthstone*	Centre Island
*	Pennoyer, Paul Geddes, Sr.	*Round Bush* (1926)	Glen Cove

Olmsted (cont'd)

* Phipps, Henry, Jr.	*Bonnie Blink* (1915-1916)	Lake Success
* Phipps, Henry Carnegie	*Spring Hill* (1915-1916)	Old Westbury
* Phipps, John Shaffer	*Westbury House*	Old Westbury
Pierce, Winslow Shelby, II	*Dunstable* (1933)	Bayville
* Pomeroy, Daniel Eleazer		Upper Brookville
* Poor, Henry Varnum, Sr.	(1887)	Cold Spring Harbor
* Pratt, George du Pont, Sr.	*Killenworth* [I] (1907-1909)	Glen Cove
* Pratt, Harold Irving, Sr.	*Welwyn* (c. 1906-1936)	Glen Cove
* Pratt, Richardson, Sr.	*Winthrop House*	Glen Cove
* Pryibil, Helen Porter	*Bogheid*	Glen Cove
* Rentschler, Gordon Sohn	*Waveland* (1929)	Glen Head
Rentschler, Gordon Sohn	(designed tree *allee* entrance and formal garden	Matinecock
* Ricks, Jesse Jay	(1926)	Flower Hill
Riggs, Glenn E., Sr.	*Sycamore Lodge* (1919-1923)	Roslyn Harbor
* Ripley, Julien Ashton, Sr.	*Three Corners Farm*	Muttontown
* Runyon, Clarkson, Jr.	*The Farm House* (1919)	Glen Cove
Ryan, John Dennis	*Derrymore* (1904-1906)	North Hills
Samuels, John Stockwell, III	*Salutation* (1875)	Glen Cove, West Island
* Sanderson, Henry	*La Selva* (1925)	Upper Brookville
* Satterwhite, Dr. Preston Pope	*Preston Hall* (1915-1917)	Kings Point
Sherry, Louis	*Sherryland* (1924-1925)	Manhasset
* Simpson, Robert H.	*Kinross*	Jericho
Sloan, Alfred Pritchard, Jr.	*Snug Harbor*	Kings Point

Olmsted (cont'd)

Smith, Albert Lawrence, Sr.	*Penllyn* (1918-1928)	Brookville
Smith, Owen Telfair	(1929-1931)	Laurel Hollow
Smithers, Robert Brinkley		Mill Neck
Stevens, Charles Albert	*Annandale*	Old Westbury
* Stewart, William Adams Walker, II	*Edgeover* (1910-1912)	Cold Spring Harbor
Stow, William L	(1915-1916)	Old Westbury
* Stutzer, H.		*[unable to locate - Great Neck]*
Taft, Walbridge S.	*Waveland* (1929)	Old Brookville
* Taylor, Myron Charles	*Killingworth* (designed meadows and woodlands, jointly with Annette Hoyt Flanders, 1924)	Lattingtown
Twohig, Dr. Daniel	(c. 1917)	Roslyn Heights
Vanderbilt, Virginia Graham Fair	*Fairmont* (1924-1925)	Manhasset
Vietor, Dr. John Adolf, Sr.	*Cherrywood*	Matinecock
* Weld, Francis Minot, II	*Lulworth*	Lloyd Harbor
* Wheeler, Frederick Seymour	*Delwood* (designed pool, 1928)	Upper Brookville
Whitney, Harry Payne	(1895-1896)	Old Westbury
* Whitney, William Collins	(1895-1896)	Old Westbury
* Widener, George Dunstan, Jr.	(1931)	Old Westbury
Willard, George L.	*Airslie* (designed landscaping)	Laurel Hollow
Williams, Douglas	*Wawapek* (1910-1912)	Cold Spring Harbor
* Williams, Harrison	*Oak Point* (1933)	Bayville
Winthrop, Bronson	(designed landscaping, jointly with Ferruccio Vitale and Delano and Aldrich)	Muttontown
* Wood, Willis Delano	*Fort Hill House* (designed landscaping, jointly with Ellen Biddle Shipman from Shipman design, c. 1938)	Lloyd Harbor
* Work, Bertram G., Sr.	*Oak Knoll*	Mill Neck

Samuel Parsons

    * Brady, Nicholas Frederic   *Inisfada*   North Hills

Louise Payson

    * Harris, Henry Upham, Sr.   *The Hameau*   Brookville
                                      (designed, jointly with
                                      Ellen Biddle Shipman)

    * Kane, John P., Jr.   (designed, jointly with   Matinecock
                                      Ellen Biddle Shipman)

      Wellington, Herbert Galbraith, Sr.   (designed, jointly with   Matinecock
                                      Ellen Biddle Shipman)

Isabella Pendleton

      Andersen, Dr. Harold Willids, Sr.   *Still House*   Matinecock

    * Cox, Irving E.   *Meadow Farm*   Mill Neck

    * Cravath, Paul Drennan   *Still House*   Matinecock

      Porter, Seton   *Still House*   Matinecock

    * Pratt, Harold Irving, Sr.   *Welwyn*   Glen Cove

    * Pratt, Herbert Lee, Sr.   *The Braes*   Glen Cove

      Rothschild, Baron Eugene de   *Still House*   Matinecock

    * Whitney, Howard Frederic, II   *Craigdarroch*   Glen Cove

Charles A. Platt

      Cushman, Paul, Sr.   *Tapis Vert*   Oyster Bay Cove

    * Hare, Meredith   *Pidgeon Hill*   South Huntington
                      (designed terraces, circular flower garden
                      curved driveway, and grass paths, jointly
                      with Ellen Biddle Shipman)

    * Ledyard, Lewis Cass, Jr.   *Westwood*   Oyster Bay Cove
                             (designed landscaping, jointly with
                             Ellen Biddle Shipman, 1917)

    * Lloyd, Robert MacAllister, Sr.   *Tapis Vert*   Oyster Bay Cove

      Paley, William S.   *Kiluna Farm*   North Hills
                           (designed formal garden with circular
                           lily pond and pergola)

    * Pratt, John Teele, Sr.   *Manor House*   Glen Cove
                           (designed formal gardens, reflecting pool,
                           garden pavilion, and landscaping)

    * Pulitzer, Ralph, Sr.   *Kiluna Farm*   North Hills
                           (designed formal garden with circular
                           lily pond and pergola)

Charles A. Platt (cont'd)

* Reed, Lansing Parmelee	*Windy Hill* (designed formal gardens and terraces, jointly with Ellen Biddle Shipman, 1925)	Lloyd Harbor
* Weld, Francis Minot, II	*Lulworth* (designed walled flower garden and terrace, jointly with Ellen Biddle Shipman)	Lloyd Harbor

A. R. Sargent

* Billings, Cornelius Kingsley Garrison	*Farnsworth* (designed landscaping, jointly with Guy Lowell)	Upper Brookville
Bird, Wallis Clinton	(designed landscaping, jointly with Guy Lowell)	Upper Brookville
Byrne, James	(designed landscaping, jointly with Guy Lowell)	Upper Brookville
* Coe, William Robertson	*Planting Fields* (designed landscaping, jointly with Guy Lowell, 1914)	Upper Brookville
* Curran, Guernsey, Sr.	*Farlands* (designed formal circular terraced garden with reflecting pool, jointly with Guy Lowell)	Upper Brookville
Douglas, Josephine Hartford	(designed formal circular terraced garden with reflecting pool, jointly with Guy Lowell)	Upper Brookville

Ellen Biddle Shipman

Alden, Anne Coleman	*Fort Hill House* (designed landscaping, jointly with Olmstead from Shipman design, c.1938)	Lloyd Harbor
* Bacon, Robert	*Old Acres* (1920s)	Old Westbury
Bedford, Alfred Cotton		Lattingtown
* Belmont, Eleanor Robson		Syosset
* Burchard, Anson Wood	*Birchwood*	Lattingtown
* Bushnell, Leslie E.		*[unable to locate - Mill Neck]*
Campbell, George W	*Fort Hill House* (designed landscaping, jointly with Olmsted from Shipman design, c.1938)	Lloyd Harbor
Carlisle, Floyd Leslie, Sr.		Lattingtown
* Clark, James Averell, Sr.	(1927)	Old Westbury
* Cushman, Paul, Sr.	*Tapis Vert*	Oyster Bay Cove
* Davis, Arthur Vining		Mill Neck

Ellen Biddle Shipman (cont'd)

*	Davis, John William	*Mattapan*	Lattingtown
	du Pont, Alfred Irenee	*White Eagle*	Brookville
	Dyer, Elisha, VII	*The Orchards*	Brookville
*	Dyer, George Rathbone, Sr.	*The Orchards*	Brookville
	Emerson, Margaret	*Rynwood* (designed courtyard, service courtyard, terrace, formal gardens, swimming pool, dove-cote, tea house, tennis court, and fields, 1926)	Old Brookville
*	Emmet, Richard Stockton, Sr.	*High Elms* (c. 1929)	Glen Cove
*	Gossler, Philip Green, Sr.	*Highfield* (designed gardens, courtyard, and terraces, c. 1925; 1942)	Brookville
*	Gould, Edwin	*Highwood* (1945)	Oyster Bay Cove
*	Guest, Frederick E.	*Roslyn Manor*	Brookville
	Guest, Winston Frederick Churchill	*Templeton*	Brookville
	Hall, Leonard Wood		Lattingtown
*	Handy, Parker Douglas	*Groendak*	Glen Cove
*	Hare, Meredith	*Pidgeon Hill* (designed, terraces, circular flower garden, curved driveway, and grass paths, jointly with Charles A. Platt)	South Huntington
*	Harriman, Herbert Melville	*The Lanterns*	Jericho
*	Harris, Henry Upham, Sr.	*The Hameau* (jointly with Louise Payson)	Brookville
*	Hepburn, Frederick Taylor	*Long Field*	Lattingtown
	Herzog, Edwin H.		Lattingtown
	Hickox, Charles V.	*Boxwood Farm*	Old Westbury
*	Hutton, Edward Francis	*Hutfield* (designed gardens, courtyards, and terraces, c. 1925; 1942)	Brookville
*	Iselin, Charles Oliver	*Wolvers Hollow* (1917)	Upper Brookville
*	Jackson, William H.	(1941)	West Hills
*	Jennings, Benjamin Brewster	*Windward*	Old Brookville
*	Kane, John P., Jr.	(jointly with Louise Payson)	Matinecock

Ellen Biddle Shipman (cont'd)

* Kramer, Albert Ludlow, Sr.	*Picket Farm* (1920)	Jericho
* Langley, William Clark		Old Westbury
* Ledyard, Lewis Cass, Jr.	*Westwood* (designed landscaping, jointly with Charles A. Platt, 1917)	Oyster Bay Cove
Lehman, Allan Sigmund	*Picket Farm* (1920)	Jericho
Lloyd, Robert MacAllister, Sr.	*Tapis Vert*	Oyster Bay Cove
* Lord, Franklin Butler, II	*Cottsleigh* (c. 1929)	Syosset
* Lord, George de Forest, Sr.	*Overfields* (designed gardens, c. 1930)	Syosset
Lundy, Frederick William Irving	*Rynwood* (designed courtyard, service courtyard, terrace, formal gardens, swimming pool, dove-cote, tea house, tennis court, and fields, 1926)	Old Brookville
Maddocks, John L., Jr.	(c. 1930)	Brookville
Matheson, William John	*Fort Hill House* (designed landscaping, jointly with Olmsted from Shipman design, c.1938)	Lloyd Harbor
* Maynard, Walter Effingham	*Haut Bois* (c. 1930)	Brookville
Minicozzi, Alexander	(1945)	Oyster Bay Cove
Montana, Dr. Christopher	(1945)	Oyster Bay Cove
* Morris, John B.		*[unable to locate - Roslyn]*
Munsel, Patrice	*Malmaison* (c. 1930)	Brookville
* Murray, Hugh A.	*Gay Gardens*	Old Westbury
Nicastro, Louis Joseph		Mill Neck
Peabody, Julian Livingston, Jr.	(1941)	West Hills
* Peabody, Julian Livingston, Sr.	*Pound Hollow Farm* (1924)	Old Westbury
* Pratt, Herbert Lee, Sr.	*The Braes* (designed, jointly with James Leal Greenleaf, landscaping)	Glen Cove
* Preston, William Payne Thompson, Sr.	*Longfields* (designed formal garden, lawns, flagstone terrace, and curved driveway)	Jericho

Ellen Biddle Shipman (cont'd)

    Reed, Lansing Parmelee   *Windy Hill*   Lloyd Harbor
                                  (designed formal gardens and terraces,
                                  jointly with Charles A. Platt, 1925)

  * Richmond, L. Martin   *Sunninghill*   Old Brookville
                                  (designed garden, jointly with
                                  Innocenti and Webel)

    Robinson, John Randolph   (designed gardens, courtyards, and   Brookville
                                  terraces, c. 1925; 1942)

  * Roosevelt, Kermit, Sr.   *Mohannes*   Cove Neck

  * Salvage, Sir, Samuel Agar   *Rynwood*   Old Brookville
                         (designed courtyard, service courtyard,
                         terrace, formal gardens, swimming pool,
                         dove-cote, tea house, tennis court, and fields,
                         1926)

  * Schmidlapp, Carl Jacob, Sr.   *Rumpus House*   Mill Neck
                                    (mid-1920s)

  * Smith, R. Penn   *[unable to locate - East Williston]*

  * Smithers, Francis S.   *Myhome*   Glen Cove

  * Stewart, Glenn   Lattingtown

    Straus, Jack Isidor   *Green Pastures*   Jericho
                                  (designed formal garden, lawns, flagstone
                                  terrace, and curved driveway)

  * Taliaferro, Eugene Sinclair   *The Wilderness*   Cove Neck

    Thompson, William Payne, Jr.   *Longfields*   Jericho
                                  (designed formal garden, lawns, flagstone
                                  terrace, and curved driveway)

  * Weld, Francis Minot, II   *Lulworth*   Lloyd Harbor
                                  (designed, walled flower garden and
                                  terrace, jointly with Charles A. Platt)

    Wellington, Herbert Galbraith, Sr.   (designed, jointly with Louise Payson)   Matinecock

  * White, Alexander Moss, Jr.   *Hickory Hill*   Oyster Bay Cove

  * Wood, Willis Delano   *Fort Hill House*   Lloyd Harbor
                                  (designed landscaping, jointly with
                                  Olmsted from Shipman design, c.1938)

  * Zinsser, William Herman, Jr.   *Windward*   Kings Point

Arthur Shurcliff

  * Kent, George Edward, Sr.   *Jericho House*   Jericho

Ossian C. Simmonds

  * Hodenpyl, Anton Gysberti   *Hill House*   Mill Neck

Paul Smith

    Lunning, Frederick   *Northcourt*   North Hills

   * Shearman, Lawrence Hobart   North Hills

Fletcher Steele

   * Bullock, George   *Yeadon*   Centre Island

    Deans, Robert Barr, Sr.   *Yeadon*   Centre Island

    Palmer, Carlton Humphreys   *Hearthstone*   Centre Island

Armand J. Tibbetts

    Brown, Stephen Howland   *Solana*   Matinecock

   * Stone, Charles Augustus, Sr.   *Solana*   Matinecock

Louis Comfort Tiffany

   * Tiffany, Louis Comfort   *Laurelton Hall*   Laurel Hollow
                            (designed landscaping)
                            [*see surname entry*]

Horace Trumbauer

   * Vanderbilt, William Kissam, Jr.   *Deepdale*   Lake Success
                            (designed formal gardens)

Ferruccio Vitale

   * Brady, Nicholas Frederic   *Inisfada*   North Hills
                          (1920-1924)

    Christie, Lansdell Kisner   (designed formal Italianate sunken garden,   Muttontown
                          descending gardens, pergola, catalpa walk,
                          foot paths, bridle paths, brick terrace, and
                          landscaping, 1906-1920)

   * Davis, Arthur Vining   (1922)   Mill Neck

    Fahys, George Ernest, Sr.   *Hilaire*   Matinecock
                          (1927-1928)

   * Fish, Edwin A.   *Airdrie*   Matinecock
                          (1926)

   * Gates, Elizabeth Hoagland   *Dormer House*   Lattingtown
                          (1917; 1924)

   * Geddes, Donald Grant, Sr.   (1906; designed sunken garden enclosed   Glen Cove
                          by evergreens, 1930)

   * Griscom, Lloyd Carpenter   (designed landscaping, jointly with   Muttontown
                          Olmsted and Delano and Aldrich)

   * Guggenheim, Isaac   *Villa Carola*   Sands Point
                          (designed lawns, garden terrace, brick pool,
                          terrace, rose gardens, curved driveway, and
                          perennial gardens; and later, designs, 1916-1924)

Ferruccio Vitale (cont'd)

* Guggenheim, Solomon Robert	*Trillora Court* (designed lawns, garden terrace, brick pool, terrace, rose gardens, curved driveway, and perennial gardens; and later, designs, 1916-1924)		Sands Point
* Hoppin, Gerald Beekman	*Four Winds* (designed swimming pool complex, 1930)		Oyster Bay Cove
* Hudson, Charles I., Sr.	*Knollwood* (designed formal Italianate sunken garden, descending gardens, pergola, catalpa walk, foot paths, bridle paths, brick terrace, and landscaping, 1906-1920)		Muttontown
Kelland, Clarence Budington	*Sandy Cay* (1930)		Sands Point
Lynch, Edmund Calvert., Sr.	(1927-1928)		Matinecock
Martin, Esmond Bradley, Sr.			Muttontown
* Maxwell, Howard Washburn, Sr.	*Maxwelton*		Glen Cove
McKay, Alexandra Emery Moore	*Chelsea* (1924-1932; designed pond garden, 1924)		Muttontown
McVeigh, Charles Senff, Sr.	(designed formal Italianate sunken garden descending gardens, pergola, catalpa walk, foot paths, bridle paths, brick terrace, and landscaping, 1906-1920)		Muttontown
* Moore, Benjamin	*Chelsea* (1924-1932; designed pond garden, 1924)		Muttontown
Munsel, Patrice	*Lockjaw Ridge* (1917; 1924)		Lattingtown
* Nast, Conde	*Sandy Cay* (1930)		Sands Point
Nicastro, Louis Joseph	(1922)		Mill Neck
* Nichols, Francis Tilden, Sr.	*Bayberry Downs*		Muttontown
Raquet, Walter	*Lockjaw Ridge* (1917; 1924)		Lattingtown
Schiff, Dorothy	*Sandy Cay* (1930)		Sands Point
* Schmidlapp, Carl Jacob, Sr.	*Rumpus House*		Mill Neck
Senff, Gustavia	(designed formal Italianate sunken garden, descending gardens, pergola, catalpa walk, foot paths, bridle paths, brick terrace, and landscaping, 1906-1920)		Muttontown
* Sloane, George	*Brookmeade* (1924)		Lattingtown

Ferruccio Vitale (cont'd)

*	Taylor, Myron C.	*Killingworth* (designed meadows and woodlands, jointly with Annette Hoyt Flanders, 1924)	Lattingtown
	Uris, Percy	*Sandy Cay* (1930)	Sands Point
*	Vietor, Dr. John Adolf, Sr.	*Cherrywood* (1927-1928)	Matinecock
	Vilas, Guillermo	*Lockjaw Ridge* (1917; 1924)	Lattingtown
	Winthrop, Bronson	(designed landscaping, jointly with Olmsted and Delano and Aldrich)	Muttontown
*	Young, Edward Lewis	*Meadow Farm*	Glen Cove
	Zog I, King of Albania	(designed formal Italianate sunken garden, descending gardens, pergola, catalpa walk, foot paths, bridle paths, brick terrace, and landscaping, 1906-1920)	Muttontown

Warner and White

	Fremont, Julie Fay Bradley	*Lynrose*	Glen Head
*	Shipman, Julie Fay Bradley	*Lynrose*	Glen Head

Ralph Weinrichter

*	Blackton, James Stuart, Sr.	*Harbourwood*	Cove Neck
	Leeds, William Bateman, Jr.	*Kenwood*	Cove Neck
	Le Roux, E.		Centre Island
*	Smith, Ormond Gerald	*Shoremonde*	Centre Island
	Willys, John North	*Northcliff*	Centre Island

The following list of maiden names of women associated with Long Island North Shore estates was compiled from various biographical sources, social registers, and newspaper obituaries. It should be noted that women occasionally gave surnames from previous marriages to editors, without designating them as such. If there were multiple marriages, husbands are listed in chronological order. Please note that the women included in this list were either the homeowners or spouses of homeowners. Women of subsequent generations are not included unless they assumed ownership of the house.

Abbe, Elaine	*married*	**Langone**, Kenneth Gerard, Sr.
Ackerman, Rose		**Alexander**, Harry
Adams, Catherine Quincy		**Morgan**, Henry Sturgis, Sr.
Adams, Jean Dunbar		**Gair**, Robert, Jr.
Addison, Julia Morris		**Roosevelt**, George Emlen, Sr.
Addison, Mary		**Mitchell**, Sidney Alexander, Sr.
Ahles, Lydia Lawrence		**Geddes**, Eugene Maxwell, Sr.
Albertson, Emma		**Underhill**, Samuel Jackson
Aldridge, Katharine G.		**Tucker**, Richard Derby, Sr.
Alexander, Eleanor Butler		**Roosevelt**, Theodore, Jr.
Alexander, Harriet		**Aldrich**, Winthrop Williams
Alford, Doris		**Preston**, William Payne Thompson, Sr.
Alger, Josephine		**Johaneson**, Nils R.
Alger, Miss Lucille		
Alig, Candace B.		**Vanderlip**, Kelvin Cox **Van Alen**, James Henry
Allen, Jane Peterson		**Runyon**, Clarkson, Jr.
Allen, Louise		**Dean**, Robert, Sr.
Allen, Terese		**Kramer**, Irwin Hamilton
Allilueva, Svetlana Iosifovna		**Morozov**, Gregory **Zhdanov**, Yury **Kaganovich**, Mikhail L. **Peters**, William Wesley
Almond, Jacqueline		**Martin**, Henry Bradley, II
Almy, Nathalie G.		**Battershall**, Frederic S.
Altemus, Mary Elizabeth		**Whitney**, John Hay **Person**, Dr. E. Cooper, Jr. **Lunn**, Richard Dwight **Tippett**, Cloyce Joseph
Ames, Pauline		**Plimpton**, Francis Taylor Pearsons, Sr.
Amory, Mary J.		**Cutting**, Dr. Fulton
Anderson, Erica		**Knowlton**, Hugh Gilbert, Sr.

Andrews, Frances	**White**, Frederick Wheeler
Annan, Isabel	**Dykman**, William Nelson
Appleton, Patricia	**McLane**, Allan, Jr.
Apponyi, Countess Geraldine	**Zog I**, King of Albania
Armour, Juliana	**Ferguson**, Dr. Farquhar, Sr.
Arthur, Mary Elizabeth	**Smith**, Albert Edward, Sr.
Arwild, Sara	**Hughes**, Dr. Wendell
Ashmore, Ruth	**Poor**, Henry Varnum, Sr.
Aspell, Hope	**Verdi**, Minturn de Suzzara
Atkins, Anna P.	**Heckscher**, August
Atwater, Margaret H.	**Olds**, George Daniel, Jr.
Atwell, Edwina	**Martin**, Esmond Bradley, Sr. **Stuart**, Robert Whiton, Sr.
Auchincloss, Caroline	**Fowler**, Dr. Robert Henry
Auchincloss, Elizabeth	**Jennings**, Percy Hall, Sr.
Avery, Janet Pomeroy	**Dulles**, John Foster
Ayer, Mary Farwell	**Rousmaniere**, John E.
Ayer, Theodora	**Winthrop**, Robert, II **Randolph**, Dr. Archibald Cary
Bab, Marion	**Warburg**, Gerald Felix
Babbage, Dorothy	**Deans**, Robert Barr, Sr.
Babbott, Helen Lamb	**MacDonald**, Swift Ian **Sanders**, Frank K.
Babcock, Alice Woodward	**Winthrop**, Henry Rogers
Bache, Hazel J.	**Richards**, Frederick L. **Beckman**, Frederick
Bacon, Alice Antille	**McVeigh**, Charles Senff, Sr.
Bacon, Florence A.	**Gould**, Frank Miller **Sturgeon**, John Metler, Jr.
Bacon, Martha Beatrix	**Whitney**, George, Sr.
Bacon, Priscilla	**Woods**, Ward Wilson, Jr.
Bailey, Mabel Davis	**James**, Oliver B., Sr.
Bailey, Marietta	**Provost**, Cornelius W.
Baird, Joan	**Shaw**, Samuel T., Sr.
Baker, Anne Smith	**Roesler**, Edward, Jr.
Baker, Edith Brevoort	**Schiff**, John Mortimer
Baker, Florence	**Loew**, William Goadby

Baker, Florence

Tailer, Thomas Suffern, Jr.
Martineau, Stanley

Baker, Ruth Sears

Pratt, John Teele, Sr.

Baldwin, Alice Maude

Cravath, Erastus Milo, II

Baldwin, Fanny Taylor

Preston, William Payne Thompson, Sr.
Morgan, Edwin Denison, IV

Baldwin, Mary

Goddard, Conrad Godwin

Baldwin, Priscilla

Preston, Lewis Thompson, Sr.

Ball, Alice Hughes

Groesbeck, Clarence Edward

Ball, Jessie D.

du Pont, Alfred Irenee

Bancroft, Louisa M.

Smithers, Francis S.

Banner, Rosalie

Bloomingdale, Irving Ingersoll

Bannister, Edith Marie

Ingersoll, Robert Hawley

Barabas, Theresa

Castro, Bernard

Barker, Blanche Mabelle

Schieren, George Arthur, Sr.

Barker, Catherine

Hickox, Charles V.

Barker, Lillian Lee Fordyce

Lord, Franklin Butler, II

Barnes, Carman

Armstrong, Hamilton Fish

Barnes, Harriet L.

Pratt, Harold Irving, Sr.

Barney, Augusta

Harriman, Joseph Wright

Barney, Helen

Alexander, Archibald S.
Watriss, Frederick N.

Barney, Katharine Lansing

Barnes, Courtlandt Dixon, Sr.

Bartlett, Bertha King

Benkard, Henry Horton

Barton, Mary

Potter, J. W. Fuller
Howe, Henry W.
Iselin, Oliver
Thatcher, John M. P., Sr.

Bassel, Ellen G.

Davis, John William

Baylis, Evelyn

Crawford, Edward H.

Bean, Jeannette

Perin, Charles Page

Beardsley, Jennie

Abbott, Phillips

Beare, Effie

Shearman, Lawrence Hobart

Beattie, Margaret Parish

Sparrow, Edward Wheeler

Beer, Nellie

Rothschild, Baron Robert de

Beguelin, Virginia

Clarke, Jeremiah, Sr.

Belden, Ada T.

Rogers, Henry Alexander

Belknap, Alice Silliman

Hawkes, Dr. Forbes

Belknap, Jennet Maitland	**Lloyd**, Robert MacAllister, Sr.
Bell, Alice	**Slade**, John, Sr.
Bell, Alice Pennoyer	**Mitchell**, Sidney Zollicoffer
Bell, Evangeline	**Bruce**, David Kirkpatrick Este
Bell, Helen A.	**Ripley**, Julien Ashton, Sr.
Bellis, Jane Middlesworth	**Sousa**, John Philip, Sr.
Belvin, Pansy	**White**, Frederick Wheeler
Bement, Anna	**Kramer**, Albert Ludlow, Sr.
Bemiss, Charlotte	**Christian**, Frank Palmer **Daniel**, Robert Williams
Benedict, Helen R.	**Hastings**, Thomas
Benkard, Bertha	**Rose**, Reginald Perry
Benkard, Elsie	**Sterling**, Duncan, Jr.
Bennett, Dorothy Eleanor	**Arnoult**, William W. **Heckscher**, Gustav Maurice
Bennett, Mary	**Perine**, William DeNyse Nichols
Benson, Mary L.	**Ross**, Llewellyn Gerard **Marston**, Edgar Lewis, II
Benson, Thyrza	**Flagg**, Montague, II **Fowler**, Harold
Berwind, Frederica V.	**Harjes**, Henry Herman **Porter**, Seton
Bibblee, Carmelita	**Underhill**, Francis T.
Bickford, Catherine Ellen	**Fahnestock**, Frank Curry
Biddle, Christine A.	**Fish**, Edwin A.
Biddle, Cordelia Drexel	**Duke**, Angier **Robertson**, Thomas Markoe
Bigelow, Cornelia Bartlett	**Lee**, Ivy Ledbetter, Sr.
Bigelow, Edith Evelyn	**Clark**, J. Francis A. **Davisson**, Richard L., Sr.
Billings, Blanche	**Vander Poel**, William Halsted
Bingham, Mabel	**Hess**, Harry Bellas
Birrell, Aida E. M.	**Iglehart**, David Stewart
Bishop, Alice	**Kramer**, Albert Ludlow, Sr.
Bishop, Harriet	**Lanier**, James Franklin Doughty
Bisland, Elizabeth	**Wetmore**, Charles Whitman
Bissell, Florence	**Luckenbach**, Edgar Frederick, Sr.
Bissell, Josephine H.	**Merrill**, Bradford, Jr.

Black, Katharine	**Jones**, Nicholas Ridgely
Blaine, Margaret	**Damrosch**, Dr. Walter Johannes
Blair, Lottie	**Parker**, Harry Doel
Blair, Mary M.	**Brokaw**, William Gould
Blanchard, Dorothy	**Hammerstein**, Oscar, II
Blight, Edith	**Thompson**, William Payne, Jr.
Bliss, Miss Ida E.	
Bliss, Ruth Baldwin	**Schwab**, Hermann C., II
	Bleecker, Rev. Lyman C.
Blodgett, Katherine C.	**Hadley**, Morris
Blum, Alice I.	**Taliaferro**, Eugene Sinclair
Blyth, Mary	**Craven**, Frank
Boarman, Vera	**Whitehouse**, James Norman
Bodrero, Lydia P.	**Macy**, Valentine E., Jr.
	Redmond, Roland Livingston
Boldt, Clover	**Miles**, Alfred Graham
	Johaneson, Nils R.
Boman, Dorcas Marie	**DeGraff**, Robert Fair
Bonnell, Elida Floyd	**Langley**, William Clark
Bonnell, Ysable	**Robinson**, Thomas Linton
Bonner, Marie Adele	**Beach**, William Nicholas
Bonnie, Katherine W.	**Langenberg**, Carl Haynes
	Tower, Roderick
Bonsal, Frances	**Winants**, Garret Ellis
	Wing, S. Bryce
Boothe, Claire	**Brokaw**, George Tuttle
	Luce, Henry R.
Borland, Madeline	**Pell**, Clarence Cecil, Sr.
Bosher, Eleanor G.	**Brewster**, George S.
Bostwick, Lillian Stokes	**McKim**, Robert Vandenburgh
	Phipps, Ogden
Botsford, Ruth Gardner	**Fleischmann**, Raoul Herbert
Bourne, Florence	**Deans**, Robert Barr, Sr.
	Hard, Anson Wales
	Thayer, Alexander D.
Bourne, Marian C.	**Elbert**, Robert George
Bovee, Mary Isabel	**Taylor**, Bertrand LeRoy, Jr.
Bowles, Ruth Standish	**Baldwin**, William H., Jr.
Boyd, Margaret	**White**, Leonard Dalton, Jr.
Boyden, Katrina	**Hadley**, John Wood Blodgett
Bradford, Alicia	**du Pont**, Alfred Irenee

Bradley, Julie Fay

Brady, Mabel

Brady, Mary Madeline

Branning, Joyce

Breed, Katharine Gordon

Brewster, L. A.

Brewster, Rebecca C.

Bridges, Margaret Dickson

Brigham, Miss Constance

Brinkley, Mabel Carew

Brisbane, Sara

Brokaw, Barbara

Brokaw, Elvira

Brokaw, Florence C.

Brokaw, Lilla

Brokaw, Mimi

Brooke, Helen

Brooks, Polly

Broomall, Virginia Snowden

Bronson, Elizabeth Duer

Brown, Adele Quarterley

Brown, Amelia Crane

Brown, Amy B.

Brown, Frances Maitland

Brown, Grace

Brown, Harriet Stewart

Brown, Jean Pollock

Brown, Katharine Dobbin

Brush, Jane

Brush, Marion

Brush, Mary Dobbin

Shipman, Right Rev. Herbert
Fremont, John Charles, II

Garvan, Francis Patrick, Sr.

Stevens, Charles Albert
Hall, Charles Spencer
Harriman, Herbert Melville

Vanderbilt, George Washington, IV

Williams, Harrison

Sewell, Robert Van Vorst

Garver, John Anson

Blakeslee, Dr. Albert Francis

Smithers, Christopher Dunkin, Sr.

McCrary, John ("Tex") Reagan, Jr.

Cushing, Leonard Jarvis, Sr.

Fischer–Hansen, Carl
McNair, William

Martin, James E., Sr.
Satterwhite, Dr. Preston Pope

Gilbert, H. Bramhall
Dugmore, Cyril

Tucker, Richard Derby, Sr.

Heck, John Callendine, Sr.

Howe, William Deering

Taylor, George Winship, Sr.

Griscom, Lloyd Carpenter

Lovett, Robert Abercrombie

Wylie, Herbert George

de Forest, Henry Lockwood

Tilney, Frederick, Jr.

_____, Herbert
Guggenheim, William S., Sr.

Tailer, Thomas Suffern, Sr.

Jennings, Walter

Thomas, Frederic Chichester, Sr.

Coates, Winslow Shelby, Sr.

Dean, Herbert Hollingshead

Pierce, Winslow Shelby, Jr.
Clark, Grenville, Sr.

Bryant, Frances	**Godwin**, Parke
Bryant, Miss Julia Sands	
Bryce, Edith Clare	**Cram**, John Sergeant, Sr.
Buchanan, Ellen Ewing	**Jennings**, Spencer Augustus
Buckner, Madeline	**Moffett**, George Monroe, Sr.
Budd, Beatrice	**Cram**, John Sergeant, Sr.
Buel, Constance Clough	**Burnett**, Vivian
Bullard, Constance	**Dimock**, Edward Jordan
Bulloch, Anna	**Gracie**, James King
Bulloch, Martha	**Roosevelt**, Theodore
Burden, Gwendolyn	**Dows**, David, Jr.
Burke–Roche, Cynthia	**Burden**, Arthur Scott **Cary**, Guy Fairfax, Sr.
Burnes, Marjorie	**Hedges**, George Brown
Burrows, Mary Vera	**Stetson**, James D. **Netter**, Dr. Frank H.
Burt, Daisy French	**Scott**, Rufus W.
Burton, Harriet Wright	**Laidlaw**, James Lees
Busby, Gertrude	**Leeming**, Thomas Lonsdale, Sr.
Bush, Hope	**Dillon**, Herbert Lowell, Sr.
Bush, Jane	**Francke**, Luis J., Sr.
Bushnell, Emilie	**Martin**, John Stuart **Durant**, John
Bushnell, Winthrop	**Palmer**, Carlton Humphreys
Buss, Philippa Dayrell	**Roosevelt**, Philip James, Jr.
Bussing, Alice Cary	**Kingsbury**, Howard Thayer, Sr.
Butterfield, Catherine	**Coffin**, William Sloane, Sr.
Byers, Maude Fleming	**Lyon**, John Denniston
Byron, Nina	**Sloane**, Charles William
Cacace, Lenore	**Belding**, David, Sr.
Cairns, Ellen Eliza	**Stuart**, Robert **Ward**, Elijah
Calderon, Carmen Torres	**Houston**, Herbert Sherman
Caldwell, Anna Wentworth	**Sears**, Joseph Hamblen
Calkin, Florence	**Dickerman**, Bradley Watson, Sr.
Callender, Ruth	**Fairchild**, Julian Percy, Sr.
Caller, Ruth Oakley	**DeLamater**, Cornelius Henry

Callery, Mary K.

Coudert, Frederic Rene, Jr.
Dangeli, Carlo Frua

Cameron, Anne

Tiffany, Belmont

Cameron, Margaret

Crary, Miner Dunham, Sr.

Cameron, Rhoda

Clark, John Balfour
Wichfeld, Ivan Henning

Campbell, Carina

Murdock, Lewis Chapen

Campbell, Harriet Bailey

Townsend, James Mulford, II

Campbell, Jean Fisher

Moore, William Talman, Sr.

Campbell, Nanette C.

Miller, William Wilson

Campbell, Sara M.

Vaughan, Dr. Harold Stearns

Campeau, Lillian

Johnson, Seymour
De Leslie, Count Alexander Paulovitch

Cannon, Elizabeth A.

Leonard, Edgar Welch

Cantrell, Marie

Osborn, Alexander Perry, Sr.

Carnegie, Margaret

Miller, Roswell, Jr.

Carow, Edith Kermit

Roosevelt, Theodore

Carr, Florence S.

Marston, Edgar Lewis, II

Carrington, Judith

Stettinius, Edward Reilly, Sr.

Carter, Mary Hartwell

Adams, Horatio M.

Carter, Mary Custis Lee

Patchin, Robert Halsey

Carter, Stella

Haff, Alvah Weeks

Case, Anna

Mackay, Clarence Hungerford

Casey, Bernadette

Smith, Owen Telfair

Castro, Bernadette

Austin, David F.
Guida, Dr. Peter Matthew

Catlin, Charlotte deGrasse

Graves, Robert, II

Catlin, Irene

Allen, Frederic Winthrop

Chalmers, Theresa

Barnes, E. Mortimer
Baker, Cecil

Chamberlain, Alice Remington

Chanler, Lewis Stuyvesant, Sr.

Chapin, Joan K.

Hutton, William E., II

Chapman, Joy

Pettinos, Charles E.

Chardin, Jessie Maud

Stewart, Glenn

Chauncey, Grace

Babcock, Woodward

Cheney, Louise

Collins, Dr. Burnet Charles

Cheston, Frances Drexel

Tower, Whitney, Sr.

Chew, Katharine Alexander

Tod, Robert Elliot

Chidsey, Mary Daggett

Chrysler, Thelma

Church, Helen Dwight

Churchill, Viscountess Christine

Claflin, Mary

Clark, Anna Josephine

Clark, Christine Newhall

Clark, Elizabeth

Clark, Mary C.

Clarke, Edith Kinsman

Clarke, Mary Gabrielle

Clemmons, Viola

Close, Marjorie

Clothier, Lydia Biddle

Coates, Elise

Cobb, Mildred

Cobb, Zaidee C.

Cochrane, Lucy (aka "Cee Zee"; later, "C. Z.")

Coe, Mary L.

Coer, Bertha

Coffin, Natalie

Coleman, Anne

Colgate, Alice Riggs

Colgate, Helen

Combs, Lycia

Comstock, Ruth Constance

Conkling, Elizabeth

Converse, Louise

Connelly, Cora Cartwright

Cook, Ethel

Cookman, Frances P.

Coolidge, Mary S.

Eden, Dr. John H., Sr.

Foy, Bryon Cecil

Minton, Henry Miller

Isham, Ralph Heyward
Oliphant, Sir Lancelot

Gossler, Philip Green, Sr.

De Selding, Hermann

Willetts, William Prentice

Taft, Walbridge S.

Culver, Dr. Everett Mallory
King, Charles Potter
DeBrabant, Marius

Bedford, Alfred Cotton

Campbell, Oliver Allen, Sr.

Gould, Howard

Ryan, John Carlos

Maxwell, John Rogers, Jr.

Alsop, Dr. Reese Fell

Rich, Dudley, Sr.
Roosevelt, George Emlen, Sr.

Bliss, Cornelius Newton, Jr.
Goodyear, Anson Conger, Sr.

Guest, Winston Frederick Churchill

Earle, Henry Montague

Underhill, Daniel

de Forest, Johnston

Alden, Bradley Ripley

Rossiter, Arthur Wickes, Sr.

Mann, Samuel Vernon, Sr.

Hepburn, George

Nickerson, Hoffman

Oakman, Walter George, Sr.

Morgan, Junius Spencer

Carter, Oliver Goldsmith, Sr.

Postley, Sterling

Baehr, Irvine E. Theodore

Atkins, _____
Rentschler, Gordon Sohn

Cooper, Gretchen Riefer	**Colgate**, John Kirtland , Jr. **Sesnon**, Porter, Jr.
Cooper, Edith	**Bryce**, Lloyd Stephens
Cooper, Frances	**Schmidlapp**, Carl Jacob, Sr.
Corigliano, Letizia A. L.	**Bogart**, Adrian T., Jr.
Cornwell, Emma S.	**Whitney**, Charles Morse, Sr.
Cory, Jane	**Chew**, Philip Frederick
Coster, Emily Pell	**Morris**, Lewis Spencer **Weldon**, Samuel Alfred
Cotton, Eleanor	**Burden**, Chester Griswold
Couch, Treva M.	**Diebold**, Albert Henry
Coudert, Coralie	**Brokaw**, William Gould
	Roelker, William **Erskine**, Harold Perry
Coudert, Jeanne Clarisse	**Nast**, Conde **Onativia**, Jose Victor, Jr.
Covert, Cornelia M.	**Meyer**, Cord, II
Cowan, Ada M.	**Will**, Harold Henry
Cowdin, Martha Waldron	**Bacon**, Robert
Cramp, Florence	**Pell**, Theodore Roosevelt
Crane, Emily	**Chadbourne**, Thomas Lincoln, Jr.
Cravath, Vera Agnes Huntington	**Larkin**, James Satterthwaite **Gibbs**, William Francis
Creighton, Jennie	**Woolworth**, Frank Winfield
Crocker, Mary	**Fraser**, Alfred
Crosse, Audrey Margaret Elizabeth	**Griscom**, Lloyd Carpenter
Crotty, Gertrude	**Davenport**, Dr. Charles Benedict, Sr.
Crowell, Angeline Luceil (aka Ann Eden Crowell)	**Woodward**, William, Jr.
Crozer, Florence	**Rutherfurd**, John M. L.
Cryder, Elsie Ogden	**Woodward**, William, II
Cudahy, Alice	**McCormick**, Leander James **Stearns**, John Nobel, III
Culver, Katherine Clark	**Williams**, Rodney W.
Cummings, Grace C.	**Bergquist**, John Gosta
Cunoss, Elizabeth	**Hudson**, Percy Kierstede
Curtis, Carrie Hastings	**Gibson**, Harvey Dow
Curtis, Kathleen H.	**Wagstaff**, Alfred, III **Bonner**, Douglas Griswold, Sr. **Moffett**, James A., II

Curtis, Laura Elizabeth	**Bostwick**, George Herbert, Sr.
Curtis, Marjorie A.	**Chadbourne**, Thomas Lincoln, Jr.
Curtis, Sylvia Johnson	**White**, Gardiner Winslow, Sr.
Cushing, Barbara	**Mortimer**, Stanley G., Jr. **Paley**, William S.
Cushing, Betsey	**Roosevelt**, James **Whitney**, John Hay
Cushing, Mary Benedict	**Astor**, William Vincent **Fosburgh**, James Whitney
Cushman, Kathleen	**Merrill**, Joseph L.
Cutting, Mary Josephine	**McFadden**, Alexander Bloomfield **Blair**, Watson Keep
Cutting, Olivia Bayard	**James**, Henry
Daily, Ocean K.	**Carey**, William Francis, Jr.
Dallas, Trevania	**Blair–Smith**, Hugh **Pomeroy**, Daniel Eleazer
Dalumi, Amalia	**Shaw**, Samuel T., Sr.
Daly, Mary A.	**Gerard**, James Watson, III
Damon, Charlotte	**Peabody**, Charles Augustus, Jr.
Damrosch, Alice	**Pennington**, Hall Pleasants **Wolfe**, Dudley Francis **Kiaer**, Herman S.
Dana, Winifred L.	**Gould**, Aubrey Van Wyck, Sr.
Darlington, Eleanor Townsend	**Fisher**, Joel Ellis, II
Darrah, Marion M.	**Brewster**, Warren Dwight
Davern, Elizabeth	**Miller**, Nathan Lewis
Davies, Augusta	**Clark**, Frederick Ambrose
Davies, Florence	**Roulston**, Thomas Henry, Sr.
Davison, Alice Trubee	**Gates**, Artemus Lamb
Davison, Barbara Virginia	**Blackstone**, Henry
Davison, Frances Pomeroy	**Cheney**, Ward
Deacon, Edith	**Gray**, Henry Gunther
Deacon, Mary	**Mann**, Dr. John, Sr.
Dean, Pauline	**Fiske**, Dr. E. Rodney
Deans, Elizabeth	**Howell**, J. Taylor
Dear, Dorothy	**Hutton**, Edward Francis
de Apezteguia, Emilia	**Tiffany**, Charles Lewis, II
de Bebian, Corinne	**Moore**, John Chandler

Decker, Mary E.

Deering, Abby

de Forest, Ethel

de Forest, Frances E.

de Forest, Miss Julia

de Forest, Julia Mary

de Forest, Priscilla M.

Degener, Eleanor Belmont

DeGraff, Neltje Blanchan

deKoven, Ethel LeRoy

DeLamater, Laura

DeLamater, Lydia

DeLamater, Sarah

Delano, Sara

Delano, Susan Adams

de Lopez, Maria Elvira Tanco

Demarest, Lucille

de Montauzan, Rose

Denham, Carolina Coleman

de Rippetau, Evangeline Russell
  (aka Evangeline Russell)

de Rivas, Isabel

DeVol, Jeanne

de Zerman, Denyze

Digby, Pamela

Dingler, Florence

Diotter, Joanne

Dixon, Frances S.

Dodge, Isabel C.

Dodge, Pauline

Dolliver, Eda Florence

Horowitz, Louis Jay

Howe, Richard Flint

Whitman, Allen Earle
Vermilye, H. Rowland, Sr.

Stewart, William Adams Walker, II

Duer, Beverly

Williams, Douglas

Graham, Philip Sands
Brown, Francis Gordon, Sr.

Doubleday, Frank Nelson

Hudson, Hans Kierstede, Sr.

Ramshon, Curt
Bevin, Leander Augustus

Robins, John

Robinson, George Hazard

Redmond, Roland Livingston

McKelvey, Charles Wylie

Collado, Dr. Emilio Gabriel, II

Brion, Lester E., Sr.

Register, Henry Bartol
Pennington, Hall Pleasants

Taliaferro, Charles Champe, III
Taylor, Henry Stillman

Blackton, James Stuart, Sr.

Jennings, Oliver Burr, II

Grace, Oliver Russell

Whitman, Allen
Mott, Jordan Lawrence, IV

Churchill, Randolph
Hayward, Leland
Harriman, William Averell

Willys, John North

Uris, Percy

Frick, Childs

Sloane, George

Pratt, Frederic Richardson
Webel, Richard

Rusch, Henry Arthur, Sr.

Donovan, Katharine Clayton	**Weidenfeld**, Camille
Dore, Oroville	**Spreckels**, Claus August
d'Oremieulx, Laura	**Roosevelt**, Dr. James West
D'Orn, Adele	**Walker**, Elisha, Sr.
Dorr, Katherine W.	**Loeb**, William, Jr.
Dorsey, Maude	**Woodside**, Joel David
Doubleday, Dorothy V.	**Babcock**, Frederick Huntington
Douglas, Martha	**Weiss**, William Erhard, Jr.
Dowdney, Louise	**Deering**, William Rogers
Dowsey, Gladys	**Hall**, Leonard Wood
Drake, Gertrude W.	**Ballantine**, John Herbert
Draper, Dorothea	**Blagden**, Linzee
	James, Henry
Draper, Helen	**Taft**, Walbridge S.
Du Bois, Michele Diane	**Neff**, Walter Perry
Duclos, Francoise M.	**Barstow**, William Slocum
Duer, Katherine Alexander	**Mackay**, Clarence Hungerford
	Blake, Dr. Joseph
Dunham, Theodora	**Bodman**, Herbert L., Sr.
Dunn, Evelyn	**Ceballos**, Juan Manuel, Jr.
Dunn, Kathleen	**Dunning**, Clifford A.
	Lowe, Henry Wheeler
du Pont, Ethel	**Roosevelt**, Franklin Delano, Jr.
	Warren, Benjamin S., Jr.
Durand, Georgia	**Clapham**, Thomas
Durand, Jeanne	**Murray**, John Francis
Durant, Estelle	**Weekes**, John Abeel
Durant, Margery	**Daniel**, Robert Williams
Dutton, Elizabeth	**Wellington**, Herbert Galbraith, Sr.
Dutton, Marion	**Prime**, William Albert, Sr.
du Vivier, Nathalie	**O'Connor**, John A.
Dwight, Fanny Pickman	**Clark**, Grenville, Sr.
Eager, Sibyl	**Young**, Edward Lewis
Eckelheimer, Jean Lehman	**Stralem**, Donald Sigmund
Eckstein, Harriet H.	**Jelki**, Ferdinand, Jr.
Eckstein, Jane	**Cox**, Irving E.
Eckstein, Janet	**Bullock**, George

Eddy, Grace	**Willis**, Charles F., II **Peabody**, Julian Livingston, Jr.
Eden, Ruth Agnes	**Grace**, Morgan Hatton, Sr.
Eginton, Grace	**Auchincloss**, John
Eldredge, Katherine	**Ford**, Hannibal Choate
Eliott, Beatrice Boswell	**Burton**, Frank V., Jr.
Elliott, Mary Elizabeth	**Pew**, Arthur E., II **Trowbridge**, Edmund Quincy
Ellis, Dorothy	**Mahana**, George Shaw
Ely, Katrina Brandes	**Tiffany**, Charles Lewis, II
Emerson, Margaret	**McKim**, Dr. Smith Hollins **Vanderbilt**, Alfred Gwynne, I **Baker**, Raymond Thomas **Amory**, Charles Minot
Emery, Alexandra	**Moore**, Benjamin **McKay**, Robert Gordon
Emery, Ruth Langdon	**Ledyard**, Lewis Cass, Jr.
Emetaz, Rosemary	**Baruch**, Dr. Herman Benjamin
Emlen, Elizabeth Norris	**Roosevelt**, James Alfred
Emmet, Elizabeth Winthrop	**Morgan**, Edwin Denison, IV
Equen, Florence Augusta	**Moore**, William Talman, Sr.
Erskine, Nancy Major	**Grace**, David R. **Hussey**, George, Jr.
Eskridge, Jessica	**Physioc**, Joseph Allen, Sr.
Etzgold, Elsie	**Martino**, Joseph Anthony
Eustis, Louise	**Hitchcock**, Thomas, Sr.
Eustis, Mary Channing	**Scott**, Donald, Sr.
Evans, Marjorie	**Betts**, Wyllis Rossiter, Jr.
Everdell, Rosalind	**Havemeyer**, Horace, Jr.
Fahnestock, Ruth	**Schermerhorn**, Alfred Coster **de Marigney**, Marie Alfred Fouqueroux
Fair, Anne K.	**Gray**, Albert Zebriskie
Fair, Virginia Graham	**Vanderbilt**, William Kissam, Jr.
Fairchild, Elizabeth	**Howard**, _____ **Sanderson**, Henry
Fairchild, Frances	**Bryant**, William Cullen
Fairchild, Helen	**Morley**, Christopher Darlington, Sr.
Falkenburg, Jinx	**McCrary**, John ("Tex") Reagan, Jr.
Falligant, Jeanie H.	**Coe**, William Robertson

Farrell, Elizabeth	**Sinclair**, Harry Ford, Sr.
Faulkner, Elizabeth	**Chapman**, T. Irvin
	Pierce, Roy E.
	Henderson, Frank C.
Fearing, Laura	**Hagen**, Winston Henry, Sr.
Feder, Countess Odette Fuller	**de Bozas**, Count Guy du Burg
	Moffett, George Monroe, Sr.
Feigenbaum, Claire F.	**Freidus**, Jacob
Fennelly, Margaret M.	**Grace**, Joseph Peter, II
Fenno, Neva	**Palmer**, George S.
	Mitchell, Sidney Zollicoffer
Fenwick, Andrea Marie	**Luckenbach**, Edgar Frederick, Sr.
Ferguson, Martha Munro	**Breasted**, Charles
Fernstrom, Karin	**McKelvey**, Charles Wylie
Ferry, Harriet	**Manice**, William de Forest, Sr.
Field, Olive	**Shea**, Edward Lane
Finlay, Julia	**Vanderveer**, Stephen Lott
Finn, Myra	**Hammerstein**, Oscar, II
Finucane, M. Gertrude	**Smithers**, Robert Brinkley
Firth, Emily Therese	**Townsend**, Howard Rockwell, Sr.
Fish, Marian A.	**Gray**, Albert Zebriskie
Fisher, Caroline E.	**Ryle**, Arthur, Sr.
Fitch, Helen Louise	**Fairchild**, Julian Percy, Sr.
Fitzgerald, Caroline Elizabeth	**Van Rensselaer**, Charles Augustus, Sr.
Flagg, Josephine Bond	**Boyer**, Philip, Sr.
Flandrau, Sarah Gibson	**Cutcheon**, Franklin Warner M.
Fleischmann, Bettie	**Holmes**, Dr. Christian R.
Flemming, Marjorie	**Lloyd–Smith**, Wilton
Flood, Mary Emma	**Stebbins**, Theodore Ellis, Sr.
Floris, Agnetta	**Peck**, Thomas Bloodgood, II
Forker, Della V.	**Chrysler**, Walter Percy, Sr.
Forman, Diana M.	**Colgate**, John Kirtland, Jr.
Forman, Mary Martha	**Goodyear**, Anson Conger, Sr.
	Ames, John W.
Fornaris, Signa	**Lynch**, Edmund Calvert, Sr.
	McDonald, Stewart
Fosheim, Margarete	**Homolka**, Oscar
	Gould, Howard

Foss, Esther	**Moore**, George Gordon **Fish**, Sidney W.
Foster, Ann R.	**Le Boutillier**, Thomas, III **Duryea**, Wright
Foster, Leslie	**Nast**, Conde **Benson**, Rex
Foster, Mary Isabel	**Peck**, Fremont Carson, Sr.
Fowler, Kate Grosvenor	**Merle-Smith**, Van Santvoord, Sr.
Fowler, Mary Eleanor	**Hewitt**, Edward Shephard
Fox, Dorothea	**Livermore**, Jesse Lauriston, Sr. **Longcope**, Walter
Fox, Mary Lindley	**Devereux**, Walter Bourchier, Jr.
Frank, Louise Tiffany	**Taylor**, Talbot J., II **Bell**, James Christy, Jr.
Franklin, Susan Latimer	**Dewing**, Hiram E.
Frasch, Frieda	**Whiton**, Henry Devereux **Costantini**, Count David A. **von Seidlitz**, Baron Carl Gottleib
Fraser, Kate F.	**McNally**, Frederick G. **Straus**, Edward Kuhn
Frazer, Myra Tutt	**Martin**, Grinnell
Frazier, Lady Brenda Taylor	**Watriss**, Frederick N.
French, Elizabeth Basset	**Babbott**, Dr. Frank Lusk, Jr.
French, Nannie	**Steele**, Charles
Friedman, Sadie Cecilia	**Annenberg**, Moses Louis
Frost, Louise	**Cozzens**, Issachar, III
Frowert, Dorothy	**Fleischmann**, Raoul Herbert
Fuller, Allon Mae	**Black**, Harry S. **Morse**, Tyler
Fuller, Ella Elizabeth	**Guthrie**, William Dameron
Galland, Dr. Mathilde	**Krim**, Arthur B.
Gallatin, Mary	**Hoppin**, William Warner, Jr.
Gamble, Alicia	**Ludlow**, Alden Rodney, Sr.
Gardiner, Bessie	**du Pont**, Aldred Irenee
Gardiner, Eliza Gracie	**Jones**, Charles Hewlett
Gardner, Nettie M.	**Ryan**, John Dennis
Garfield, Mary	**Stanley–Brown**, Joseph
Garner, Frances	**Iselin**, Charles Oliver
Garrison, Lydia Knight	**Auchincloss**, Samuel Sloan, II

Garvan, Genevieve F.

Brady, Nicholas Frederic
Macaulay, William J.

Garvin, Mary Elizabeth

Sperry, Edward G.

Gates, Elinor

Toerge, Norman K., Sr.
Clendenin, Joseph

Gaynor, Gertrude Emily

Webb, William Seward D., Jr.

Gaynor, Marion

Isham, Ralph Heyward

Gear, Luella

Chandler, Byron
Heckscher, Gustav Maurice

Geekie, Agnes G.

Knott, David Hurst, Sr.

Gent, Jane

Robertson, Charles Sammis

Gerard, Carol

McCann, David Anthony

Gerdes, Margery

Miller, Dudley Livingston, Sr.
Twining, Edmund S., Jr.
Fates, Harold Leighton, Sr.

Gerhard, Bertha

Davey, William Nelson

Gibb, Ada Louise

Hester, William Van Anden, Sr.

Gibb, Althea

Eldredge, Edward Irving, Jr.
Hunter, Malcolm Du Bois

Gibb, Florence Balsdon

Pratt, Herbert Lee, Sr.

Gibb, Ruth

Carhart, Harold W., Sr.
Addinsell, Harry Messiter

Gignoux, Miss Elise Messenger

Gilbert, Elizabeth Ward

Dickinson, Hunt Tilford, Sr.

Gilbert, Gertrude

Loening, Rudolph R.

Gilbert, Janet

Collado, Dr. Emilio Gabriel, II

Gilbert, Lucetta Banks

Ottley, James Henry, Sr.

Gilbert, Mary Mitchell

Martin, John Stuart

Gilchrist, Dalsy

Knott, David Hurst, Sr.

Gilchrist, Lillius

Grace, William Russell, Sr.

Gillett, Lillian M.

Lutz, Frederick L.

Gilmore, Gladys L.

Johnston, Douglas Turner

Given, Thelma

Verdi, Minturn de Suzzara

Givney, Ethel J.

Jones, Arthur Eaton

Gleason, Elizabeth F.

Peck, Fremont Carson, Sr.

Goddard, Hope

Iselin, Charles Oliver

Goddard, Mary Woodbridge

Tiffany, Louis Comfort

Godfrey, Dorothy

Dillon, Herbert Lowell, Sr.

Godwin, Miss Elizabeth Love

Gooch, Linnor Irene	**Brooks**, Winthrop Holley
Gookin, Dorothy Quincy	**Lawrence**, Effingham, II
Gordon, Susan Wallace Ogden	**Niven**, John Ballantine
Gourd, Helen Noel	**Hoguet**, Dr. Joseph Peter, Sr.
Gourd, Renee Noel	**de Milhau**, Louis John de Grenon, Sr.
Gowen, Allison	**Harrison**, William Frazer **Clark**, Louis Crawford, II
Gowen, Harriet	**Bingham**, Harry Payne, Sr. **Miller**, Harlan
Grace, Alice Gertrude	**Holloway**, William E. **D'Oench**, Albert Frederick
Grace, Gertrude	**Dwight**, Richard Everett
Grace, Lillias Juanita	**Kent**, George Edward, Sr.
Grace, Margarita Celia	**Phipps**, John Shaffer
Grad, Bertie	**Schwartz**, Charles
Graham, Caroline	**Coe**, William Roberston
Graham, Gladys Howland	**Ottley**, Gilbert **Magnuson**, Paul Budd, Jr.
Graham, Florence Madeleine	**Roosevelt**, Julian Kean **Ridder**, Eric, Sr.
Grandy, Melvina	**Busby**, Leonard J.
Grant, Eleanor	**Sheridan**, Frank J., Jr.
Grant, Helen Therese	**Sparrow**, Edward Wheeler
Grauwiller, Helen L.	**Christie**, Lansdell Kisner
Graves, Helen Bailey	**Ballantine**, Arthur Atwood, Sr.
Graves, Julia	**Preston**, Ralph Julius
Graves, Julia E.	**Gary**, Elbert H.
Graves, Lorraine	**Carroll**, David Donald **Grace**, Oliver Russell
Graves, Marie Robertine	**Harjes**, Henry Herman
Greeff, G. Helen D.	**Schniewind**, Henry, Jr.
Greeley, Margaret	**Pell**, Howland Haggerty, Sr.
Green, Anne Barton	**Gubelmann**, Walter Stanley
Greenough, Alice	**Townsend**, Edward Mitchell II
Grew, Elsie	**Lyon**, Cecil T. F. B.
Grew, Jane Norton	**Morgan**, John Pierpont, Jr.
Grey, Florence	**Mason**, Julian Starkweather
Griffith, Katharine M.	**Kane**, John Patrick

Griffith, Mary T.	**Kane**, John Patrick
Grigorcea, Eugenia S.	**Breed**, William Constable, Sr.
Grinnell, Katharine	**Morris**, Ray, Sr.
Griswold, Inglis	**Neilson**, Raymond Perry Rodgers, Sr.
Guillaudeau, Eleanor	**Lyon**, Frederick Gorham Clark
Guillaudeau, Eva	**Humphreys**, Dr. Alexander Crombie
Guthrie, Elinor	**McVickar**, Donald
Guthrie, Ella Fuller	**Kimball**, W. Eugene **Rossiter**, Arthur Wickes, Sr.
Gwynne, Anita McKim	**Mestres**, Ricardo Angelo, II
Hale, Edith	**Harkness**, William Lamon
Hale, Vera Amherst	**Pratt**, George du Pont, Sr.
Hall, Elizabeth Livingston	**Mortimer**, Stanley, Sr.
Hall, Mollie W.	**Page**, Arthur Wilson, II
Hallowell, Ellen Rice	**Pratt**, Harold Irving, Jr.
Hamilton, Emily Georgina	**Hadden**, J. E. Smith
Hamilton, Dr. Elizabeth	**Muncie**, Dr. Edward Henry
Hamilton, Olive	**Leeds**, William Bateman, Jr.
Hammill, Maude Elizabeth	**Ceballos**, Juan Manuel, Jr.
Hammond, Caroline	**Gibson**, Robert Williams
Hancock, Margery	**Hanks**, Stedman Shumway
Hancock, May Candee	**Boyd**, ____ **Ayer**, Dr. James Cook
Hansen, Maren Andrea	**Frank**, Charles Augustus, Sr.
Hardenberg, Hildegarde	**Eagle**, Henry, Sr.
Harkness, Violet Lockwood	**Tangeman**, Cornelius Hoagland
Harmon, Marie Burr	**Curran**, Guernsey, Sr.
Harriman, Marian	**Wright**, Boykin Cabell, Sr.
Harriman, Mary	**Rumsey**, Charles Cary, Sr.
Harris, Evelyn G.	**Van Ingen**, Lawrence Bell, Jr.
Harris, Joan	**Hawkey**, Harold W., Sr.
Harrison, Dr. Elizabeth	**Walker**, James Blaine, Jr.
Harrison, Gertrude Plant	**Trowbridge**, Edmund Quincy
Harrison, Virginia Norris	**Smith**, Albert Lawrence, Sr.
Hart, Dorothy	**Hearst**, John Randolph, Sr. **Paley**, William S.
Hart, Rosalie	**Myers**, Theodore Walter
Hartford, Josephine	**O'Donnell**, Charles Oliver **Makaroff**, Vadim **Douglas**, Barclay K. **Bryce**, John Felix Charles

Hartshorne, Louise

Harvey, Jean

Hasbrouk, Elizabeth Lawrence

Haskell, Rae B.

Hauser, Dora

Havemeyer, Blanche

Havemeyer, Carlotta

Havemeyer, Electra

Havemeyer, Emily Blanche

Havemeyer, Marie

Hawes, Eppes

Hawkins, Elizabeth

Hawkins, Estelle Emma

Hawkins, Viola S.

Hay, Helen

Hayens, Henrietta B.

Hays, Ethel Sanders

Hayward, Sybil

Hazard, Mary Pelton

Hazzard, Jessie A.

Hearn, Caroline Lancaster

Hearons, Charlotte

Heckscher, Emmeline D.

Heckscher, Nancy A.

Heim, Helen Louise

Heister, Helen

Henderson, Keokee Monroe

Henry, Isabelle

Henry, Virginia

Hepburn, Cordelia S.

Hepburn, Mary McClellan

Moore, John G.
Leeds, Warner Mifflin, II

Vanderbilt, Alfred Gwynne, II

DeLamater, Oakley Ramshon, Sr.

Levison, John Jacob
Schuster, Max Lincoln

Vertes, Marcel, Emmanuel

Duncan, William Butler

Bigelow, Anson Alexander

Webb, James Watson, Sr.

Potter, Edward Clarkson, Sr.

Tiffany, Perry
Godfrey, Henry Fletcher, Sr.

Preston, Lewis Thompson, Sr.
Moore, Lloyd
Fahnestock, William, Jr.
Berdeau, LeRoy

Davis, Arthur Vining

Warner, Henry Wolcott

Townsend, John Allen

Whitney, William Payne

Roig, Harold Joseph

Bonner, Douglas Griswold, Sr.

Ricks, Jesse Jay

Holmes, Duncan Argyle

Leonard, Charles Reginald, Sr.

Cowl, Clarkson

Godfrey, Henry Fletcher, Sr.

Winthrop, Egerton Leigh, Jr.

Price, Theodore Hazeltine, Jr.

Herzog, Edwin H.

Peters, William Richmond

Perin, Charles Page

Black, Harry S.

Curtis, Edwin Burr
Heckscher, August

Cushman, Paul, Sr.

Lazo, Carlos
Gillies, George J.

Herlow, Janna	**Rumbough**, Stanley Maddox, Jr.
Hering, Julia	**Kienle**, Eugene S., Sr.
Herring, Katherine Chamber	**Rutherfurd**, John M. L.
Hester, Carrie W.	**Ide**, George Edward
Hewitt, Lucy	**Leffingwell**, Russell Cornell
Hickox, Lesly Stockard	**Smith**, Earl Edward Tailer, Sr.
Higenbotham, Emily	**Dwight**, Richard Everett
Higenham, _____	**Wright**, Wilkinson de Forest, Sr.
Higginson, Dorothy Lee	**Weekes**, Arthur Delano, Jr.
Hilburn, Paula (aka Paula Dean)	**Blackton**, James Stuart, Sr.
Hill, Gertrude	**Gavin**, Michael
Hill, Nancy	**Warner**, Bradford Arnold, Sr.
Hillis, Marjorie	**Roulston**, Thomas Henry, Sr.
Hinckley, Elizabeth C.	**Milburn**, Devereux, Jr.
Hinckley, Francesca	**Pell**, Clarence Cecil, Jr.
Hinz, Edith Elizabeth	**Fox**, Fontaine Talbot, Jr.
Hitchcock, Celestine E.	**Peabody**, Julian Livingston, Sr.
Hitchcock, Helen	**Clark**, James Averell, Sr.
Hoadley, Helen	**Hoyt**, Lydig
Hoagland, Cora	**Tangeman**, George Patterson
Hoagland, Elizabeth	**Gates**, Charles Otis
Hodgson, Edith	**Fahnestock**, Pleasant Andrew **Jordan**, Frank
Hodgson, Frances Eliza	**Burnett**, Dr. Swan Moses **Townesend**, Dr. Stephen
Hoffman, Josephine	**McIntosh**, Allan J.
Hoffman, Marie Louise	**Robertson**, Charles Sammis
Hofgren, Anna E.	**Tinker**, Giles Knight
Hoguet, Christine Ramsay	**Hagen**, Winston Henry, II
Holland, Amy	**Potter**, Clarkson
Hollister, Margaret S.	**Straus**, Jack Isidor
Holmes, Hilda	**Holloway**, William Grace, Sr.
Holmes, Jean Beatrice	**Caldwell**, Robert J.
Holthaus, Ruth	**Will**, Harold Henry
Homes, Rachel Connwell	**Ingalls**, Fay
Hopkins, Gwladys Crosby	**Whitney**, Cornelius Vanderbilt

Hoppin, Esther Phillips

Hornblower, Rosilla

Horton, Blanche

Hostetter, Greta

Houghteling, Josephine

Houghton, Clara Mabel

Houghton, Florence Preston

Houghton, Helen Seymour

House, Janet

Howard, Anne

Howard, Eunice

Howard, Maude

Howe, Mollie Richards

Howe, Rosemary, D.

Howland, Helen

Hoyt, Edna E.

Hoyt, Elizabeth S.

Hoyt, Elizabeth Sherman

Hoyt, Julia Marion

Hoyt, Rosina Sherman

Hubbs, Dorothy

Hubbs, Marjorie

Hudson, Caroline

Hudson, Manuela

Hughes, Eloise

Hull, Lucia

Hume, Jane

Humpstone, Helen

Hungerford, Katharine

Pool, Dr. Eugene Hillhouse

Breed, Alan R.
Hawes, Alexander B.

Hutton, Edward Francis

Stewart, Glen

Canfield, Augustus Cass
Griswold, Frank Gray

Tully, William John

Ellis, Reuben Morris
Baker, Edwin Howard

Gales, George M.

Auchincloss, Gordon, Sr.

Chapin, Thomas Christy
Dwight, Arthur Smith

Dane, Chester Linwood, Sr.

Remington, Franklin

Hubbs, Charles Francis

Fish, Edwin A.
Crocker, Frank Longfellow

Wetmore, Edmund

Warburton, William John
Lord, Andre
Tower, Roderick
Nevins, Hardwick

Stewart, William Adams Walker, II
Philbin, Stephen H.

Lindsay, Sir Ronald

Welldon, Samuel Alfred

Hoppin, Gerard Beekman

Kettles, Richard C., Jr.

Anderson, George A.

Lynch, Edmund Calvert, Jr.

Vanderbilt, Alfred Gwynne, II

Smith, Lucien P.
Daniel, Robert Williams

Lindeberg, Harrie Thomas

Parker, John Alley

Noyes, Winchester

Will, Harold Henry

Hunnewell, Isabella	**Harriman**, Herbert Melville **Barclay**, J. Searle
Hunter, Sarah Jane	**Harriman**, Herbert Melville
Huntington, Agnes	**Cravath**, Paul Drennan
Huntington, Helen Dinsmore	**Astor**, William Vincent **Hull**, Lytle
Hurley, Camilla deG.	**Tilney**, Dr. Frederick, Sr.
Hurt, Margaret Dorothy	**Isham**, Ralph Heyward
Hutton, Nedenia M. (aka Dina Merrill)	**Rumbough**, Stanley Maddox, Jr. **Roberston**, Cliff
Huyck, Elizabeth M.	**Eldridge**, Lewis Angevine, Sr.
Hyde, Dorothy	**Park**, Darragh Anderson, Sr. **Iselin**, Oliver
Ide, Anne Louisa	**Cochran**, William Bourke
Ingalls, Katherine Elizabeth	**Alker**, Carroll Booth **Sloane**, George **Graves**, Edward Darius, Jr.
Inglis, Emily L.	**D'Oench**, Russell Grace, Sr.
Ingraham, Edith	**Crary**, Miner Dunham, Sr.
Inman, Nannie C.	**Brokaw**, Clifford Vail, Sr. **Brown**, Milton D.
Innis, Katharine B.	**O'Rourke**, John Francis, Sr.
Inslee, Grace	**Hepburn**, Leonard F.
Ireland, Adelia C.	**Van Iderstine**, Charles Abner
Irving, Abbey	**Van Wart**, Henry
Iselin, Fannie Garner	**Livermore**, Philip Walter
Iselin, Helen	**Henderson**, Edward Cairns
Israel, Hortense	**Aron**, Jacob
Ives, Eunice	**Maynard**, Walter Effingham
Jackson, Caroline U.	**Hicks**, Henry
Jackson, Esther	**Porter**, William Henry
Jackson, Henrietta	**Page**, Frank C. Bauman
Jackson, Irene	**Sloane**, Alfred Pritchard, Jr.
Jackson, Lucy	**Trotter**, William H.
Jackson, Mary	**Cochran**, William Bourke
James, Audrey	**Field**, Marshall, III
James, Eunice	**Coe**, Henry Eugene, Jr.
James, Helen Belknap	**Anderson**, Henry Hill, II

Jamison, Glee C.	**Smith**, Albert Lawrence, Sr.
Jaques, Hallie	**Schreiber**, Dr. George, Jr.
Jennings, Constance	**Ely**, Albert Heman, Jr.
Jennings, Elizabeth	**Franklin**, George Small, Sr.
Jennings, Elizabeth Auchincloss	**Truslow**, Francis Adams, Sr. **Howell**, Dr. John Taylor, Jr.
Jennings, Helen Goodsell	**James**, Dr. Walter Belknap
Jennings, Jeannette	**Taylor**, Henry Calhoun
Jennings, Louise Bell	**Muncie**, Dr. Curtis Hamilton
Joel, Audrey S.	**Brokaw**, Clifford Vail, Jr.
Johnson, Antoinette	**Palmer**, Carlton Humphreys
Johnson, Martha	**Kountze**, deLancey
Johnston, Emily	**de Forest**, Robert Weeks
Johnston, Mary Jeanne	**Harris**, Henry Upham, Jr.
Johnston, Mary Mathilde	**Shea**, Edward Lane
Jones, Alice B.	**Willock**, William W., Sr.
Jones, Joyce Augusta	**Alker**, James Ward, Sr.
Jones, Katharine R.	**Beale**, Bouvier, Sr.
Jones, Margaret	**Moen**, LeClanche
Jones, Mary Elizabeth	**Jones**, Dr. Oliver Livingston, Sr.
Jones, Nina Gregory	**Proctor**, Charles E.
Jones, Rosalie Gardiner	**Dill**, Clarence C.
Jordan, Dorothy May	**Robinson**, Monroe Douglas **Chadwick**, Elbridge Gerry
Jordan, Emily Clara	**Folger**, Henry Clay
Jordan, Nettie	**Livermore**, Jesse Lauriston, Sr.
Joyce, Elizabeth	**Shonnard**, Horatio Seymour, Sr.
Kalley, Beatrice Sherman	**Bedford**, Alfred Clarke, Sr.
Kane, Edith Brevoort	**Baker**, George Fisher, II
Kane, H. Dorothea	**Johnston**, Seymour
Kay, Winifred Prentiss	**Shepard**, Rutherford Mead
Kean, Christine, Griffin	**Roosevelt**, William Emlen
Keegan, Grace	**MacLaren**, Archibald Waters
Keep, Virginia	**Clark**, Marshall
Kelley, Cornelia	**Hepburn**, George
Kelley, Mary P.	**Doubleday**, George Chester

Kellogg, Beatrice	**McClintock**, Harvey Childs, Sr.
Kelly, Anna Dolores	**Whalen**, Grover A., Sr.
Kelly, Heloise C.	**Toy**, Thomas Dallam, Sr.
Kemper, Helen W.	**Ahles**, _____ **Stearns**, John Noble, II
Kendall, Marjorie Winifred	**Bishop**, Maitland Lathrop **Wainwright**, Howard **Bird**, Wallis Clinton
Kennedy, Maude Arden	**Winston**, Frederick **Stevenson**, Malcolm, Sr. **Wing**, S. Bryce
Kent, Katherine	**Erhart**, Charles Huntington, Sr. **Chapin**, C. Merrill, Jr.
Kerr, Frances E.	**Marshall**, Richard H. **Roesler**, Edward, Jr.
Kierstede, Sara E.	**Hudson**, Charles I., Sr.
King, Eleanor Erving	**Ames**, Charles Edgar
King, Nina Haven	**Colgate**, Gilbert, II **Heiner**, R. Graham
King, Susan Howard	**Norton**, Skeffington Sanxay, Sr.
Kinney, Beatrice	**La Montagne**, Harry
Kirlin, Elizabeth L.	**Keating**, Cletus, Sr.
Kirshner, Rhoda	**Levitt**, William Jaird, Sr.
Knapp, Maude E.	**Cox**, Dr. Gerard Hutchison, Sr.
Kniffen, Mary	**Huntington**, Robert Dinsmore, Jr. **Snyder**, John Anthony
Knight, Emlen	**Davies**, Joseph Edward
Knight, Kathryn	**Dunscombe**, Duncan **Baker**, Carl F.
Knight, Rose Alexis	**Myers**, Theodore Walter
Knowles, Josephine	**Seligman**, Joseph Lionel, Sr.
Knowles, Kathryn	**Jandorf**, Louis C.
Knowlton, Joyce	**Zinsser**, William Herman, Jr.
Knox, Louise Wakeman	**Tiffany**, Louis Comfort
Kobbe, Carol	**Morgan**, Robert Woodward **Snow**, George Palen
Kohler, Rita	**White**, Julius A.
Kohler, Vera	**Erbe**, Gustav, Jr. **Alker**, Carroll Booth **Bell**, William Henry
Korbel, Dr. Madeleine Jana	**Albright**, Joseph Medill Patterson

Kountze, Natalie B. — **Sterling**, Duncan, Jr.

Kouwenhoven, Joanna — **Ball**, Wilbur Laing

Kraft, Virginia — **Payson**, Charles Shipman

Krakeur, Joan Baker — **Elisofon**, Eliot / **Tower**, Whitney

Kramer, Marleigh — **Gerry**, Robert Livingston, Jr. / **Bingham**, Harry Payne, Jr.

Krech, Angeline J. — **James**, Oliver B., Sr. / **Lindeberg**, Harrie Thomas

Krech, Helen — **Holmes**, Duncan Argyle

Kroehle, Mary — **Chanler**, Lewis Stuyvesant, Jr.

Kurz, Sophia — **Casey**, William Joseph, Jr.

Ladd, Caroline Ames — **Pratt**, Frederic Bayley

Ladew, Elise W. — **Grace**, William Russell, Jr.

Lafrentz, Hazel Rosalind — **Bryan**, James Taylor, Sr.

Laidlaw, Jessie Onderdonk — **Roesler**, Edward, Sr.

Laidlaw, Louise Burton — **Backus**, Dana Converse

Laimbeer, Josephine L. — **Fell**, John Randolph, Jr. / **Schiff**, John Mortimer

Laird, Elizabeth Ann — **Riggs**, Glenn E., Sr.

Lamb, Gwendoline — **Steers**, James Rich, II

Lambert, Helen — **Norton**, Huntington

Lambert, Marie Louise — **Bailey**, Frank, Sr.

Lamont, Frances Cleveland — **Robbins**, Francis LeBaron, Jr.

Lamorere, Mona — **Rickert**, Edward J.

Lancaster, Rosamund — **Warburton**, Barclay H., Jr. / **Vanderbilt**, William Kissam, Jr.

Lane, Elizabeth Abbott — **Nichols**, Acosta, Sr.

Langdon, Emily — **Mott**, Dr. Valentine

Langley, Eleanor — **Van Alen**, James Henry / **Fletcher**, Walter D. / **Pendleton**, Ray

Langley, Marjorie S. — **Ryan**, Byford

Lanman, Evelyn Mary — **White**, Alexander Moss, Jr.

Lansing, Janet S. — **McVickar**, Henry Goelet

La Pierre, Pauline Meyer — **Lathan**, Leroy

Larocque, Marie Whittemore — **Anderson**, Henry Burrall, Sr.

Larson, Eleanor — **Garrett**, Robert Michael

Lasell, Marion	**Verdi**, Minturn de Suzzara
Lathrop, Sylvia Alexander	**Maxwell**, Eugene Lascelles, Sr.
Lawrance, Katharine Lanier	**Harriman**, William Averell **Pool**, Dr. Eugene Hillhouse **Mortimer**, Stanley G.
Lawrance, Margaret L.	**Cochran**, Drayton **Frost**, Winston H.
Lawrence, Mary	**White**, Frank Worth **Keene**, Foxhall Parker
Lawrence, Ruth	**Reed**, Lansing Parmelee
Lazarus, Elsie Weston	**Stern**, Henry Root, Sr.
Lea, Margorie Vaughn	**Hudson**, Percy Kierstede
Leake, Elizabeth H.	**Walker**, Bradford H. **Burden**, James Abercrombie, III
Learmonth, Patricia	**Fleischmann**, Raoul Herbert
Leary, Marie C.	**Lowe**, Henry Wheeler
Lee, Alice	**Roosevelt**, Theodore
Lee, Alice Bigelow	**Cudlipp**, Chandler, Sr.
Lee, Elinor	**Sloane**, Malcolm Douglas **Smith**, Albert Delmont
Lee, Eva	**Appleby**, Francis Storm
Leech, Margaret K.	**Pulitzer**, Ralph, Sr.
Leeds, Louise	**Kennedy**, William Walker **Shafer**, Judson Bell
Leffingwell, Lucy	**Pulling**, [Thomas John] Edward
Lehman, Ellen	**McCluskey**, Richard **Long**, Preston
Leighton, Donrue	**Phipps**, Thomas Wilton **Marston**, Edgar Lewis, II
L'Engle, Madeleine	**Iselin**, Adrian, II
Legg, Clara	**Bucknall**, Henry W. J.
Leonard, Mary A.	**Stone**, Charles Augustus, Sr.
Levy, Ethel	**Cohan**, George Michael
Levy, Irma	**Lindheim**, Norvin R.
Lewis, Grace A.	**Crawford**, Edward H.
Lewis, Elinor Parke Custis	**Peck**, Thomas Bloodgood, II
Lewis, Helen M.	**Roesler**, Walter, Sr. **Renner**, Edward P.
Lewis, Laura B. F.	**Norris**, James King

Ligon, Emily Castleton	**Bowdoin**, George Temple **Foley**, Edward H., Jr.
Lindley, Maude P.	**Thomas**, Ralph W., Sr.
Lines, Jessie	**Hunter**, Fenley
Linnard, Frances C.	**Fahnestock**, Archer Pleasant
Livingston, Miss Alida	
Livingston, Eleanor Moncrieffe	**Briggs**, Lloyd Cabot **Deering**, William Rogers
Livingston, Elizabeth K.	**Welch**, Charles James
Lockman, Jenat DeWitt	**Appleby**, John Storm
Lockwood, Emma	**Dole**, Edward E.
Lockwood, Grace Stackpole	**Roosevelt**, Archibald Bulloch, Sr.
Lockwood, Harriet Masters	**Pirie**, Samuel Carson, Sr.
Loew, Edna Goadby	**Brokaw**, Howard Crosby
Loew, Winifred	**Trimble**, Richard, II **Parkinson**, John, Jr.
Logan, Edith	**Dilworth**, Dewees Wood
Loney, Virginia B.	**Abbott**, Paul, Sr.
Loomis, Anne	**Alexandre**, J. Henry, Jr.
Lord, Lucretia Mott	**Strauss**, Albert
Lorett, Hilda	**Fritz**, Dr. Albert R., Sr.
Lorillard, Maude	**Tailer**, Thomas Suffern, Sr. **Baring**, Cecil
Low, Edith Westervelt	**Bush**, Donald Fairfax, Sr.
Low, Helen	**Chubb**, Percy, Sr.
Low, Mary Ide	**Hine**, Francis Lyman
Lowrie, Marjorie	**Sage**, Henry William, II
Lucas, Priscilla Gilpin	**Stevens**, Byam K., Jr.
Luckenbach, Dorothy N.	**Hull**, Kenneth Duryee, Sr.
Luke, Virginia	**Tew**, J. Dinsmore, II **Hattersley**, Robert Chopin, Sr.
Lundbeck, Lillian	**Luckenbach**, Lewis, II
Luster, Wilma Wells	**Van Santvoord**, Alexander S., Sr.
Lyle, Lucy Niblack	**Tower**, Whitney, Sr.
Lynch, Alice	**Powell**, John
Lynch, Doreen	**Caesar**, Charles Unger **Van der Straeten**, Roger A.
Lyon, Martha Byers	**Slater**, Horatio Nelson, III

MacArthur, Isabelle Mabel	**Blackton**, James Stuart, Sr.
Macdaniel, Eunice	**Dana**, Charles Anderson
Macdonald, Flora	**Bonney**, Leonard Warden
MacDonald, Ida May	**Mooney**, James David, II
Macdonald, Janet	**Grace**, Joseph Peter, Sr.
MacDonald, Janet M.	**Doubleday**, Russell
MacDougall, Rachel	**Parker**, Robert Meade, Sr.
MacElree, Dorothy W.	**Fordyce**, Robert Dinwall
MacFadden, Mary	**Conklin**, Roland Ray
MacGregor, Helen	**Armstrong**, Hamilton Fish
	Lippmann, Walter
MacGregor, Helen	**Byrne**, James
Mack, Anabel Stevens	**Taylor**, Myron Charles
Mack, Rhoda	**Cochran**, William Bourke
Mackay, Baroness Anna Marie	**Eschauzier**, George
	Baruch, Dr. Herman Benjamin
MacLeish, Blanche	**Billings**, Cornelius Kingsley Garrison
Macy, Julia Kingsland	**Potter**, W. Cary
	Thieriot, Charles Henschel, II
	Thompson, William
Maginnis, Josephine M.	**Rose**, George, Sr.
Maguire, Megan Elizabeth	**de Roulet**, Daniel Carroll, Sr.
Maiello, Amelia (aka Amy Maiello)	**Valentine**, Joseph P.
	Hagedorn, Horace
Maken, Florence	**Catacosinos**, William James, Sr.
Mali, Carol Johnston	**Du Bois**, Eugene
Mali, Eva	**Noyes**, David Chester, Sr.
Mali, Gertrude	**Moffat**, Douglas Maxwell
Mallory, Charlotte	**Mixsell**, Dr. Harold Ruckman
Mangan, Camille	**Lefpla**, Louis J.
	Bloomingdale, Hiram Collenberger
Mangan, Mary Emma	**Van Iderstine**, Charles Abner
Manger, Mary	**Mayo**, Dr. Woodward B.
	Barnes, E. Mortimer
Mann, Laura E.	**Piquet**, Dr. Samuel D.
Manuel, Florence	**Colgate**, John Kirtland, Sr.
Manville, Lorraine	**Gould**, Clarence
	Aldao, Camillo
	Dresselhuys, Cornelius W.

Marden, Mary Talbott	**Dean**, Arthur Hobson
Marquand, Elizabeth L	**Godwin**, Harold
Marshall, Dorothy	**Hornblower**, George Sanford
Marshall, Evelyn	**Field**, Marshall, III **DeSuarez**, Diego (aka Diego Suraez)
Martin, Anna R. V.	**Victor**, Royall, Sr.
Martin, Jeanne Buckley	**Postley**, Sterling
Martin, Mary Clayton	**Russell**, Faris R.
Martin, Mary Doran	**Nixon**, Lewis
Martin, Myra Tutt	**Mathers**, William Harris
Martin, Sabina Redmond	**Bartow**, Francis Dwight, Sr.
Matheson, Anna E.	**Wood**, Willis Delano
Mathews, Emily	**Gibb**, Arthur **Gibb**, John Richmond, Sr.
Matz, Claire H.	**Anderson**, Harry B., Jr.
Maxwell, Grace Lester	**Geddes**, Donald Grant, Sr.
Maxwell, Helena Philae	**Carver**, Clifford Nickels
Maxwell, Louise D.	**Whitney**, Howard Frederic, II
Maxwell, Mary Carleton	**Davis**, Joseph Edward, Sr.
May, Edith Sybil	**Randolph**, Arthur **Whitney**, William Collins
Maynard, Pauline	**Pratt**, Theodore, Sr.
McAdoo, Nona Gibbs	**Park**, Darragh Anderson, Sr.
McAllister, Gabrielle Manigault	**Dexter**, Stanley Walker
McAllister, Louise	**Ford**, Nevil
McCabe, Dorothy	**Tilney**, Frederick, Jr.
McCann, Constance W.	**Betts**, Wyllis Rossiter, Jr. **McMullan**, Joseph
McCann, Helena Woolworth	**Guest**, Winston Frederick Churchill **Tassel**, George Maurice Tassel **Charlton**, Richard Charlton
McCaren, Theodora	**Gerdes**, John
McCarter, Ellen G.	**Doubleday**, Nelson, Sr.
McClelland, Mary	**Hepburn**, Frederick Taylor
McClure, Olive	**Taylor**, Bertrand LeRoy, Jr.
McClurg, Frances Moffat	**McClure**, Walter C.
McCook, Martha	**Cross**, Eliot B.
McCormick, Eleanor	**Sloane**, Charles Byron

McCutchen, Alice Booth	**Scudder**, Townsend, II
McDonald, Eva	**Hopkins**, Arthur
McDonald, Julia	**Davis**, John William
McDonnell, Ann Chilton	**Grace**, Oliver Russell **Kendall**, Donald McIntosh
McGinley, Jean R.	**Moore**, Edward Small, Sr. **Draper**, Charles Dana
McGowen, Elizabeth	**Bonner**, Paul Hyde, Sr.
McGregor, Kate Isabel	**Luckenbach**, John Lewis
McHugh, Elaine Nash	**Rinaldini**, Luis Emilio
McKay, Craigie	**Schwartz**, Alexander Charles, Sr.
McNair, Elvira	**Hutchinson**, Reginald L **Fairchild**, William Samuel **de Sibour**, Jacques Jean
McVicar, Charlotte Ronaldson	**MacLaren**, Archibald Waters
Megear, Virginia	**Straus**, Jack Isidor
Meldrim, Sophie	**Coy**, Edward H. **Shonnard**, Horatio Seymour, Sr.
Mellick, Elizabeth	**Baker**, John C., Sr.
Mellon, Ailsa	**Bruce**, David Kirkpatrick Este
Mellon, Margaret	**Laughlin**, Alexander, II **Hitchcock**, Thomas, Jr.
Menz, Annemarie D.	**Cochran**, Drayton
Merriam, Laura Beatrice	**Curtis**, James Freeman **Gross**, John Messick
Merrick, Laura	**Pratt**, Theodore, Sr. **Sarre**, Gordon
Merrill, Dina (aka Nedenia M. Hutton)	**Rumbough**, Stanley Maddox, Jr. **Robertson**, Cliff
Merryman, Laura	**Franklin**, Philip Albright Small, Sr.
Messenger, Emma	**Gignoux**, Charles Christmas
Metcalf, Betty	**Pruyn**, Robert Dunbar
Metcalf, Mary Fletcher	**Robinson**, John Randolph
Metz, Harriet	**Noble**, A. Warren **Livermore**, Jesse Lauriston, Sr.
Meurer, Grace M.	**Richards**, Ira, Jr. **Sarre**, Gordon
Michailovitch, Duchess Tsenia [Xenia]	**Leeds**, William Bateman, Jr. **Jud**, Herman
Micolino, Dorothy	**Gucker**, Henry John, Sr.

Milburn, Dorothy	**Auchincloss**, Samuel Sloan, II **Russell**, Frank Ford
Milburn, Patty	**Auchincloss**, Edgar Sterling, III
Milledoler, Abian S.	**Beekman**, James William, Sr.
Miller, Alexandra C.	**Howard**, George H., III
Miller, Bessie Catherine	**Appleton**, Benjamin Ward
Miller, Katharine C.	**Hoffman**, William Wickham
Miller, Lorraine	**Swan**, Kingsley **Graves**, Robert, II **Wood**, Benjamin **Van Rensselaer**, Kiliaen **Granary**, Henry Aldrich
Miller, Mary C.	**Peabody**, Richard A. **Moen**, A. Rene
Miller, Mildred	**Cooper**, Kenneth F.
Miller, Nancy	**Cavanaugh**, Edward Francis, Jr.
Mills, Gladys	**Phipps**, Henry Carnegie
Milton, Abby Rockefeller	**O'Neill**, George Dorr, Sr.
Milton, Ellen Hunt	**Harrison**, Wallace Kirkman
Miner, Elinor Branscombe	**Lamont**, Thomas Stilwell
Mitchell, Dorothy	**Sloane**, Charles Bryon
Mitchell, L. Virginia	**Prince**, Frederick Henry, Jr.
Mitchell, Louise	**Paine**, Edward Bragg **Vanderbilt**, George Washington, IV
Moen, Katherine Lyall	**Smith**, Howard Caswell, Sr.
Moffat, Harriet	**Sheeline**, Paul Cushing
Momand, Grace Lucille	**Breese**, James Lawrence **Bingham**, Harry Payne, Sr.
Monroe, Catharine	**Straus**, Edward Kuhn
Montant, Marie Adele	**Norton**, Huntington
Moore, Agnes	**Bermingham**, John F.
Moore, Caroline	**Bleecker**, Theophylact Bache, II
Moore, Grace A.	**LeRoy**, Robert
Moran, Elizabeth	**Morgan**, Edwin Denison, III
Morgan, Edith Percy	**King**, Frederic Rhinelander
Morgan, Elizabeth Hamilton	**Belmont**, August, II
Morgan, Elizabeth S.	**Jay**, DeLancey Kane
Morgan, Frances Tracy	**Pennoyer**, Paul Geddes, Sr.
Morgan, Jane N.	**Nichols**, George, Sr.

Morgau Leone	**Havemeyer**, Frederick Christian, IV
Morley, Susan	**Queen**, Emmet
Morris, Eliza Ellen	**Hoagland**, Dr. Cornelius Nevius
Morris, Helen Van Courtland	**Burr**, Nelson Beardsley
Morris, Hilles	**Hamersley**, Louis Gordon, Sr. **Bartlett**, George Leslie
Morris, Mary Seymour	**Pratt**, Charles Millard
Morrison, Violet Mary	**Brokaw**, Clifford Vail, Sr.
Morrow, Anne Spencer	**Lindbergh**, Charles Augustus, Jr.
Morse, Frances	**Pomeroy**, Daniel Eleazer
Mortimer, Edith	**di Zoppola**, Count
Mortimer, Eve	**Pell**, Clarence Cecil, Jr. **Ledyard**, Lewis Cass, III
Mortimer, Wilfreda	**Rutherfurd**, John M. L.
Morton, Caroline	**Potter**, William Chapman **Guggenheim**, Harry Frank
Moses, Ethel Revere	**Merrill**, Charles Edward, Jr.
Mosle, Marie C.	**Winter**, Keyes, Sr.
Mott, Caroline	**Thayer**, Francis Kendall, Sr.
Mott, Kanny	**Thayer**, Kendall
Mott, Martha Willets	**Fraser**, Alfred Valentine
Moyer, Katherine	**Ford**, Hannibal Choate
Muller, Alice	**Choate**, Joseph K. **Gossler**, Philip Green, Sr.
Munn, Frances Drexel	**Baker**, George Fisher, III
Munroe, Eleanor	**Curtis**, James Freeman
Munsel, Patrice	**Schuler**, Robert
Murphy, Helen	**Miller**, John Norris, Sr.
Murray, Jeanne Lourdes	**Vanderbilt**, Alfred Gwynne, II
Murray, Paula	**Coudert**, Frederic Rene, Jr.
Murray, Leslie	**Chanler**, Lewis Stuyvesant, Jr.
Murray, Virginia	**Bacon**, Robert Low
Myers, Jeannette	**Hoyt**, Colgate, Jr.
Myers, Jessie Isabel	**Blair**, James Alonzo, Sr.
Nast, Natica	**Warburg**, Gerald Felix
Nave, Lucile	**Brokaw**, Irving
Neason, Hazel	**Smith**, Albert Edward, Sr.

1039

Nebrbas, Jeanne	**Carter**, George
Neilson, Emilie	**Burrill**, Middleton Schoolbred
Nellany, Blanche Cecilia	**Sheehan**, William Francis
Nelson, Floreine J.	**Winthrop**, Robert, II
Neustadt, Adele G.	**Schiff**, Mortimer L.
Newbauer, Margaret	**Gerry**, Dr. Roger Goodman
Newcomb, Edith Derby	**Collins**, Dr. Burnet Charles
Nichols, Alice Slocum	**Church**, Frederic Edwin
Nichols, Charlotte Slocum	**Church**, Charles Thomas, Sr.
Nichols, Elizabeth Williams	**Taylor**, Edwin Pemberton, Jr.
Nichols, Jane N.	**Page**, Walter Hines, II
Nichols, Leta	**Clews**, James Blanchard
Nichols, Susan Farley	**Pulsifer**, Harold Trowbridge
Nicholson, Martha J.	**Doubleday**, Nelson, Sr.
Nickels, Evelyn	**Moore**, Edward Small, Sr.
Nickels, Inez	**Carver**, Amos Dow
Noel, Louise	**Greer**, William Armstrong
Noel, Teenie	**Johnston**, John Herbert
Nolan, Agnes	**Cohan**, George Michael
Nolan, Alice	**Harris**, Sam Henry
Nolan, Ann Elizabeth	**Cowl**, Donald Hearn
Norman, Hope	**Bacon**, Elliot Cowdin **Gardner**, Paul Edgerton
Norris, Bessie Bovee	**Vernam**, Clarence Cottier
Norton, Frances	**Lord**, William Galey
Norton, Henrietta	**Truesdell**, Dr. Edward Delavan
Norton, Marie	**Whitney**, Cornelius Vanderbilt **Harriman**, William Averell
Nott, Marjorie	**Morawetz**, Victor
Noyes, Julia Gilman	**de Forest**, Henry Wheeler
Oakes, Patricia Luisa	**Roosevelt**, Franklin Delano, Jr.
Oakley, Elaine Sargent	**Bleecker**, Charles Moore
Oberle, Renee	**Bosworth**, William Welles
Ogden, Elsie Helen	**White**, Alexander Moss, Sr.
Ogden, Jane	**Tanner**, Frederick Chauncey, Sr.
Ogden, Josephine	**Forrestal**, James Vincent

Ogden, Mary E.	**de Forest**, Johnston
O'Hair, Lucile Beatrice	**Smith**, Albert Edward, Sr.
Oliver, Grace Little	**Dane**, Chester Linwood, Sr.
Olliphant, Evelyn	**de Seversky**, Alexander Prokofieff
Ono, Yoko	**Lennon**, John
Otis, Ethel	**Simpson**, Robert H.
Otis, Rosina H.	**Bateson**, Edgar Farrar, Sr.
Ottley, Martha M.	**Crisp**, Van Devanter
Parham, Julia Louise	**Reynolds**, Richard Samuel, Sr.
Park, Edith G.	**Martin**, Alastair Bradley
Park, Laura Hall	**Jennings**, Frederic Beach
Park, Mary Stevenson	**Neilson**, Raymond Perry Rodgers, Sr.
Parks, Isabel Erskine	**Brewster**, Samuel Dwight
Parson, Amelia	**Ferry**, E. Hayward
Parsons, Laura Cecila	**Pratt**, Richardson, Sr.
Parsons, Lucille Merriam	**Vanderbilt**, George Washington, IV **Balcom**, Ronald
Patterson, Alicia	**Simpson**, James, Jr. **Brooks**, Joseph W. **Guggenheim**, Harry Frank
Payne, Flora	**Whitney**, William Collins
Payne, Mary Ann	**Clews**, James Blanchard **Blumenthal**, George **Robertson**, Ralph Kenyon **von Wrangell**, Baron Carl
Payson, Lorinda	**de Roulet**, Vincent W.
Peabody, Anita L.	**Hadden**, Hamilton, Sr.
Peabody, Dorothy	**Davison**, Frederick Trubee
Pearl, Eva	**Oelsner**, Edward Carl William, Sr.
Pegram, Nancy D'Wolf	**Clark**, Bruce
Peine, Virginia	**Reynolds**, Quentin **Foy**, Bryon Cecil
Peirce, Evelyn	**Baehr**, Irvine E. Theodore
Pellet, Grace Hewitt	**Smith**, Ormond Gerald
Penniman, Mary	**Morgan**, Edwin Denison, III
Percival, Constance	**Bertschmann**, Louis Frederick
Perkins, Carol	**Oelsner**, Warren James
Perkins, Evelyn I.	**Ames**, Amyas

Perkins, Lucy Fairfield	**Ripley**, Paul Morton
Perrin, Suzanne	**Roosevelt**, Franklin Delano, Jr.
Peters, Frances Sarah	**Cushing**, Harry Cooke, III
Petrova, Mme. Olga	**Stewart**, Dr. John Dillon **Willoughby**, Louis
Phelps, Anna Barry	**Smith**, Howard Caswell, Sr.
Phelps, Mary Fitch	**Smith**, Howard Caswell, Sr.
Phipps, Amy T.	**Guest**, Frederick E.
Phipps, Helen Margaret	**Martin**, Bradley, Jr.
Phipps, Margaret Helen	**Douglas**, James Gordon, II **Boegner**, Etienne
Pickens, Jane	**Clark**, Russell **Langley**, William Clark **Hoving**, Walter
Pierce, Allison Douglass	**Moore**, Louis de Bebian
Pierce, Jessie Broadus	**Rousmaniere**, James Ayer
Pink, Lucia	**Ames**, Amyas
Pittaluga, Carolyn M.	**Hill**, Dr. Miner C.
Polley, Myra	**Tolley**, Albert E. **Kilthau**, Raymond F.
Pomeroy, Lucy	**Deans**, Robert Barr, Sr.
Ponvert, Natalie	**Brown**, Francis Gordon, Sr.
Pope, Minga	**Duryea**, Harry H. **Patchin**, Robert Halsey
Pope, Ruby R.	**Wood**, Chalmers, Jr.
Porter, Catharine Gray	**O'Neill**, Grover, Sr.
Porter, Helen	**Davisson**, Richard L., Sr. **Pryibil**, Paul
Post, Julia Strong	**Swan**, Edward H., Sr.
Post, Marjorie Merriweather	**Close**, Edward Bennett **Hutton**, Edward Francis **Davies**, Joseph Edward **May**, Herbert Arthur
Post, Mary A.	**Ward**, Edward Mortimer, Sr.
Postley, Elise	**Curran**, Guernsey, Sr.
Potter, Louisa	**Delano**, William Adams
Potter, Elizabeth Sturgis	**Polk**, Frank Lyon, Sr.
Potter, Nancy Atterbury	**Bourne**, George Galt **Vandenburgh**, Robert McKim
Powell, Margaret Honeyman	**Swope**, Herbert Bayard, Sr.

1042

Powell, Myrtle

Levison, John Jacob

Powers, Margaret Van Vorst

Bucknall, G. Stafford

Prall, Anne

Fahnestock, Archer Pleasant

Pratt, Edith Gibb

McLane, Allan, Jr.
Maxwell, Howard Washburn, Jr.

Pratt, Elisabeth Sloan

Livingston, John Holyoke

Pratt, Florence Gibb

Powell, Francis E., Jr.

Pratt, Harriet Balsdon

Van Ingen,, Lawrence Bell, Sr.
Bush, Donald Fairfax Jr.

Pratt, Helen L.

Emmet, Richard Stockton, Sr.
Philbin, Jessie Holladay A.

Pratt, Lydia Richardson

Babbott, Frank Lusk, Sr.

Pratt, Phyllis

Nitze, Paul Henry

Pratt, Virginia

Thayer, Robert Helyer, Sr.

Prentice, Kate de Forest

Jennings, Benjamin Brewster

Preusser, Anne E.

Hodenpyl, Anton Gysberti

Price, Harriet Dyer

Phipps, Howard, Sr.

Prindeville, Cora

Potter, Edwin A., Jr.

Pritchett, Florence

Smith, Earl Edward Tailer, Sr.

Pruyn, Ruth

Phipps, Ogden
Field, Marshall, III

Purviance, Eleanor

Sage, Henry William, II
Bostwick, Albert C., II

Putnam, Charlotte

Wheeler, Frederick Seymour

Quartley, Grace V.

Brown, Stephen Howland

Quinn, Eugenie Lee

Lindeberg, Harrie Thomas

Quortrup, Emma Ruth

Farber, Leander B.

Ralph, Eliza J.

Watson, John Jay, Jr.

Ramsey, Margaret Guion

Herzog, Edwin H.

Randolph, Cora

Trimble, Richard, Sr.

Randolph, Dorothy

Fell, John R., Sr.
Mills, Ogden Livingston
Austin, James Madison

Randolph, Ellen

Havemeyer, Charles Frederick, Jr.

Rasmusson, Judith Ann

Parker, Valentine Fraser

Raymond, Marie

Maxwell, George Thebaud
Cullen, Dorsey

Read, Ada B.

Hicks, Gilbert
Muncie, Curtis Hamilton

Read, Louise Clark

Reed, Jane Earl

Register, Katharine E.

Reizenstein, Alice

Remsen, Lillian Livingston

Rennex, Jane May

Rhinelander, Mary Colden

Rhodes, Charlotte

Rhodes, Katherine B.

Rice, Florence

Rice, Helen

Richards, Ellen

Richardson, Mimi E.

Richmond, Mary Katharine

Riggs, Rebecca

Riley, Rachel Florence

Ripley, Lesley H.

Ritchie, Mary Alice

Robbins, Julia Wainwright

Robbins, Marjorie E.

Robenne, Anna

Roberts, Lady Mina Jane

Robinette, E. May

Robinson, Anne Cambreieng

Robinson, Celia Randolph

Robinson, Cynthia

Robinson, Miss Edith Attmore

Robinson, Laura Attmore

Robinson, Ruth Attmore

Robson, Eleanor

Roche, Ann Margaret

Frank, Charles Augustus, Sr.

Dwight, Arthur Smith

Redmond, Geraldyn Livingston, Sr.
Toerge, Norman K., Sr.

Guinzburg, Harold Kleinert

Franklin, Philip Albright Small, Jr.

Aldred, John Edward

King, John Alsop, Jr.

Burton, Van Duzer
Pearce, Gordon

Blackwell, Charles Addison

De Leslie, Count Alexander Paulovitch

Watts, Dr. Robert, Jr.
Morgan, Townsend
Sanderson, Henry

Samuels, John Stockwell, III

Smith, Earl Edward Tailer, Sr.

Salvage, Sr. Samuel Agar

Crane, Clinton Hoadley, Jr.

Chalkley, Otway Hebron

Schwab, Lesley R.
Deering, William Rogers

Grosvenor, Graham Bethune

Hoyt, Lydig
Calhern, Louis

Milbank, Albert Goodsell

Robbins, Francis LeBaron, Jr.

Sparks, Sir Thomas Ashley

Alexander, Harry

Bonynge, Paul, Sr.

Peabody, Julian Livingston, Jr.

Chapin, C. Merrill, Jr.

Donnell, William Ballon

Donnell, Harry Ellingwood

August, Belmont, II

Lehman, Allan Sigmund

Rockefeller, Abby	**Milton**, David **Pardee**, Dr. Irving Hotchkiss **Mauze**, Jean
Rockwell, Belinda	**Townsend**, Edward Mitchell, Sr.
Rodewald, Eleanor Hoffman	**Livingston**, Gerald Moncrieffe
Roe, Josephine Bissell	**Slade**, Prescott
Rogers, Edna	**Carlisle**, Floyd Leslie, Sr.
Rogers, Mai Huttleston	**Coe**, William Robertson
Romeyn, Rosalind	**Everdell**, William, Jr.
Roosen, Helen	**Curran**, William Greathead **Gould**, Frank Miller
Roosevelt, Caroline	**Moore**, William Talman, Jr.
Roosevelt, Ethel Carow	**Derby**, Dr. Richard
Roosevelt, Gladys	**Dick**, Fairman Rogers
Roosevelt, Jean Schermerhorn	**Roosevelt**, Philip James, Sr.
Roosevelt, Leila	**Schuyler**, Montgomery Roosevelt **Reeve–Merritt**, Edward
Roosevelt, Nancy Dabney	**Jackson**, William Eldred, II
Rose, Charity Margarite	**Alker**, Henry Alphonse, Sr.
Rose, Josephine Gwendolyn	**Mackay**, John William, III
Roseberg, Helen	**Guggenheim**, Harry Frank **Matzinger**, Harold S.
Rosenheim, Carrie	**Loew**, Marcus
Ross, Jeannette T.	**Vogel**, James P.
Roth, Joan	**Saltzman**, Arnold Asa
Rothschild, Irene	**Guggenheim**, Solomon Robert **Rose**, George, Jr.
Rowan, Angeline	**Booth**, Henry Prosper
Rowe, Betty	**Bowdoin**, George Temple
Rowland, Margaret E.	**Delehanty**, Bradley
Royall, Virginia Portia	**Inness–Brown**, Hugh Alwyn, Sr.
Ruppanner, Martha Paula	**Thomas**, Joseph Albert
Russell, Brooke	**Kuser**, J. Dryden **Marshall**, Charles H. **Astor**, William Vincent
Russell, Caroline Louise	**Coffin**, Charles Albert
Rutherford, Emma	**Crocker**, George

Rutherfurd, Margaret Stuyvesant

Mills, Ogden Livingston
Dukes, Sir Paul
Murat, Prince Charles
Sprague, Frederick Leybourne

Ryder, Emma

Breed, William Constable, Sr.

Saffold, Georgia W.

Gossler, Philip Green, Sr.

Sage, Elizabeth M.

Goodwin, Walter L., Sr.
Hare, Meredith

Sage, Jane

White, Robert K., Sr.

Sage, Marjorie Lowrie

Flagg, W. Allston, Sr.

Sala, Aurora

Regan, Thomas J.

Saltonstall, Frances

Meyer, George von L., Sr.
Pool, Dr. Eugene Hillhouse

Saltonstall, Rosamond

Auchincloss, Charles Crooke

Saltonstall, Rose Lee

Potter, William Chapman

Salvage, Katharine Hoppin

Polk, Frank Lyon, II
Wilmerding, John C.

Romeyn, Rosalind

Everdell, William, Jr.

Roosen, Helen

Curran, William Greathead
Gould, Frank Miller

Roosevelt, Caroline

Moore, William Talman, Jr.

Roosevelt, Ethel Carow

Derby, Dr. Richard

Roosevelt, Gladys

Dick, Fairman Rogers

Roosevelt, Jean Schermerhorn

Roosevelt, Philip James, Sr.

Roosevelt, Leila

Schuyler, Montgomery Roosevelt
Reeve–Merritt, Edward

Roosevelt, Nancy Dabney

Jackson, William Eldred, II

Rose, Charity Margarite

Alker, Henry Alphonse, Sr.

Rose, Josephine Gwendolyn

Mackay, John William, III

Roseberg, Helen

Guggenheim, Harry Frank
Matzinger, Harold S.

Rosenheim, Carrie

Loew, Marcus

Ross, Jeannette T.

Vogel, James P.

Roth, Joan

Saltzman, Arnold Asa

Rothschild, Irene

Guggenheim, Solomon Robert
Rose, George, Jr.

Rowan, Angeline

Booth, Henry Prosper

Rowe, Betty

Bowdoin, George Temple

Rowland, Margaret E.

Delehanty, Bradley

Royall, Virginia Portia

Inness–Brown, Hugh Alwyn, Sr.

Ruppanner, Martha Paula	**Thomas**, Joseph Albert
Russell, Brooke	**Kuser**, J. Dryden **Marshall**, Charles H. **Astor**, William Vincent
Russell, Caroline Louise	**Coffin**, Charles Albert
Rutherford, Emma	**Crocker**, George
Rutherfurd, Margaret Stuyvesant	**Mills**, Ogden Livingston **Dukes**, Sir Paul **Murat**, Prince Charles **Sprague**, Frederick Leybourne
Ryder, Emma	**Breed**, William Constable, Sr.
Saffold, Georgia W.	**Gossler**, Philip Green, Sr.
Sage, Elizabeth M.	**Goodwin**, Walter L., Sr. **Hare**, Meredith
Sage, Jane	**White**, Robert K., Sr.
Sage, Marjorie Lowrie	**Flagg**, W. Allston, Sr.
Sala, Aurora	**Regan**, Thomas J.
Saltonstall, Frances	**Meyer**, George von L., Sr. **Pool**, Dr. Eugene Hillhouse
Saltonstall, Rosamond	**Auchincloss**, Charles Crooke
Saltonstall, Rose Lee	**Potter**, William Chapman
Salvage, Katharine Hoppin	**Polk**, Frank Lyon, II **Wilmerding**, John C.
Salvage, Margaret Smith	**Polk**, James Potter, Sr. **Taliaferro**, Dr. Charles Champe, III
Sameborn, Carrie	**Guggenheim**, Isaac
Sampson, Sarah	**Adam**, John Henry
Sands, Miss Anna	
Sanders, Lucille	**Cohn**, Milton Seymour
Sands, Katherine S.	**Thatcher**, John M. P., Sr.
Sands, Katherine Aymar	**Havemeyer**, Theodore Augustus, II
Sands, Nellie Virginia	**DeLamar**, Joseph Raphael
Sawyer, Marguerite	**Fahnestock**, Dr. Clarence **Hill**, James Norman **Neal**, Herbert **Davis**, Charles Blevins
Sawyer, Marion	**Work**, Bertram G., Sr.
Scatcherd, Madeline	**Milburn**, John George, Jr.
Schaefer, Elois	**Pryibil**, Paul
Schafer, Madeline	**Stern**, Benjamin
Schaffer, Adelaide	**Hoffstot**, Frank Norton
Schantz, Cornelia Graham	**Mackenzie**, J. Clinton

Schantz, Margaret Fay	**Scholle**, Donald William
Schenck, Ida	**Costantini**, Count David A. **Roosevelt**, Julian Kean
Schiff, Dorothy	**Hall**, Richard B. W. **Backer**, George **Thackrey**, Theodore O. **Sonneborn**, Rudolf Goldschmid
Schiffer, Evelyn	**Lehman**, Allan Sigmund
Schiffer, Rosalind C.	**Bloomingdale**, Hiram Collenberger **Cowen**, Arthur
Schmertz, Anne K.	**Smith**, George Campbell, Sr.
Schmid, Pauline	**Rhodes**, John **Murray**, Hugh A.
Schmitt, Melita J.	**Loew**, Arthur Marcus, Sr.
Schneider, Martha	**Entenmann**, William, Jr.
Schoonmaker, Marie	**Smith**, Herbert Ludlam, Sr.
Schreiner, Marie Germaine	**Miller**, Roswell, Jr.
Schreiter, Elsa Adele	**Weekes**, John Abeel
Schroeder, Jessie Keena	**Emmett**, Richard Stockton, Sr.
Schroeder, Marie Louise	**Whitney**, Cornelius Vanderbilt
Schutt, Kyra	**Hickox**, Charles V.
Scott, Barbara Ellen	**Roosevelt**, Philip James, Jr. **deKay**, Ormond, Jr.
Scott, Elizabeth	**Nitze**, Paul Henry
Scott, Grace	**Dyer**, George Rathbone, Sr.
Scott, Maude	**Keating**, Cletus, Sr.
Scott, Susan	**Norton**, Skeffington Sanxay, Jr.
Scoville, Olive A.	**O'Donohue**, Charles A.
Seaman, Marilyn	**Pickett**, John Olen, Jr. **Hollingsworth**, William Irving, III
Searle, Eleanor	**Whitney**, Cornelius Vanderbilt **McCollum**, Leonard Franklin, Sr.
Sedgwick, Aileen B.	**Taylor**, James Blackstone, Jr. **Lippincott**, William Jackson, Sr.
Sedgwick, Susan Ridley	**Swann**, Dr. Arthur Wharton **Hammond**, Paul Lyman
Sefton, Lillian	**Thomas**, Vincent Benjamin **Dodge**, Robert Leftwich
Serrano, Maria	**Polsinelli**, Vincent
Seymour, Frances F.	**Brokaw**, George Tuttle **Fonda**, Henry

Seymour, Mabel A.

Shaffer, Adelaide Whitier

Shaffer, Anne Childs

Sharp, Dorothy N.

Sharp, Katharine

Shaw, Katharine

Sheedy, Florence E.

Sheehan, Agatha F.

Sheldon, Cecily I.

Shere, Cecelia Gertrude

Sherlock, Sarah Hamilton

Sherman, Helen Deming

Sherman, Lida

Sherwood, Clara

Shevlin, Elizabeth

Shields, Cora G.

Shloss, Florence

Short, Julie Sayre

Showker, Selwa Carman

Shrady, Sarah Cantine

Sibley, Kathryn

Sierck, Ernestine Josephine

Silver, Helen

Simonton, Clover

Sims, Nell

Sinclair, Jean

Sisson, Kathryn F.

Sivey, Lucy

Sizer, Elizabeth Standish

Skidmore, Louise Udall

Slade, Katherine

Slater, Esther

Slatter, Barbara

Greer, Louis Morris

Hoffstot, Frank Norton

Phipps, Henry, Jr.

D'Oench, Russell Grace, Sr.

Hoyt, Colgate, Sr.
Perin, Charles Page

Dickson, Thomas, Sr.

Burden, Isaiah Townsend, Sr.

Kress, Claude Washington

Work, John Clinton
Satterlee, Dr. Henry Suydam, Sr.

Wyckoff, Richard Demille

Fleischmann, Max C.

Pratt, George du Pont, Sr.

Hoyt, Colgate, Sr.

Stevens, Joseph Sampson

Howe, William Deering

Clarkson, Robert Livingston, Sr.

Guggenheim, Daniel

Rinaldini, Luis Emilio

Roosevelt, Archibald Bulloch, Jr.

Gould, Edwin

Van Iderstine, William P. M.

Alker, Edward Paul

Foster, Stephen M.
O'Rourke, Innis, Sr.

Coe, William Rogers

Erbe, Gustav, Jr.
Dobbs, Samuel Candler, Jr.

Tailer, Thomas Suffern, Jr.

Phillips, Ellis Laurimore, Sr.

Walbridge, Henry D.

Mann, Samuel Vernon, Jr.

Eldridge, Roswell

Babcock, Henry Dennison, Sr.

Welles, Sumner
Kerrigan, Joseph J.

Williams, Rodney W.

Sloane, Florence Adele	**Burden**, James Abercrombie, Jr.
	Tobin, Richard Montgomery
Sloane, Jessie	**Dodge**, William Earle
	Widener, George Dunstan, Jr.
Slocum, Mary Blake	**Nichols**, John White Treadwell
Small, Cassandra Morris	**Franklin** Walter Simonds, Jr.
Smith, Alice L.	**Provost**, Cornelius W.
Smith, Alva Erskine	**Vanderbilt**, William Kissam, Sr.
	Belmont, Oliver Hazard Perry
Smith, Anne	**Bevin**, Sydney
Smith, Barbara	**Levant**, Oscar
	Loew, Arthur Marcus
Smith, Betty Carolina	**Kelland**, Clarence Budington
Smith, Dorothy F.	**Holmes**, Artemas
Smith, Evelyn Breese	**Wellman**, Roderic
Smith, Marguerite Sedgwick	**Tenney**, Daniel Gleason, Sr.
Smith, Marjorie Young	**Cowl**, Donald Hearn
Smith, Mary Louise	**Scott**, Donald, Sr.
Smith, Maude M.	**Bertschmann**, Louis Frederick
Smyth, Marian Lyman	**Kerr**, Elmore Coe, Sr.
Snow, Dorothy	**Nicholas**, Harry Ingersoll, II
Soames, Jane	**Nickerson**, Hoffman
Sokolowska, Leokadja Gruzindski	**Moen**, A. Rene
Soley, Una F.	**Connfelt**, Charles Maitland
Sollace, Marie Vidal	**Tinker**, Edward Richmond, Jr.
Soong, Ailing	**Kung**, Hsiang-hsi
Soong, Mei-ling	**Chiang**, Kai-shek
Sparks, Amy F. A.	**Burton**, Van Duzer, Sr.
	Sim, Edward William Boyd
	Seggerman, Frederick T.
Sparks, Eleanor M. A.	**Mott**, Jordan Lawrence, IV
	Martin, John Stuart
	Davison, Henry Pomeroy, II
Sparrow, Margaret A.	**Pulsifer**, George Hale
Spinetti, Adelina	**Devendorf**, George E.
Sprung, Jeannette	**King**, Alan
Stackpole, Priscilla Cresson	**Grant**, Robert, Jr.
Stahle, Dr. Helen R.	**Blackton**, James Stuart, Sr.
Stalin (*see* Allilueva, Svetlana)	

Stanley, Christine	**Knowlton**, Hugh Gilbert, Sr.
Stanton, Priscilla Dixon	**Auchincloss**, Joseph Howland, Sr.
Starr, Marie	**Chadbourne**, Humphrey Wallingford
Starr, Miriam W.	**Woolley**, Daniel P. **Work**, Bertram, Jr.
Steel, Anne M.	**Osborn**, Alexander Perry, Sr. **Nash**, Edmund W.
Steele, Kathryn N.	**Von Stade**, Francis Skiddy, Sr.
Steele, Nancy G.	**Milburn**, Devereux, Sr.
Stehli, Lilly M.	**Bonner**, Paul Hyde, Sr.
Stein, Josephine	**Uterhart**, Henry Ayres
Steinberg, Aimee Lillian	**Guggenheim**, William, Sr.
Stephenson, Ethel	**Haggerson**, Frederic H.
Stettinius, Isabel	**Marsh**, John Bigelow, Sr.
Stevens, Mabel	**Smithers**, Francis S.
Stevens, Marie C.	**Hicks**, Frederick Cocks
Stevens, Marjorie	**Finlayson**, Frank Redfern
Stevenson, Augusta Carolotta	**Anderson**, John
Stevenson, Eloise	**Kernochan**, James Lorillard **Duncan**, Alexander Butler
Stevenson, Florence	**Le Boutillier**, Thomas, II
Stevenson, Linda	**Roosevelt**, Franklin Delano, Jr.
Stewart, Frances Dorothy	**Pierson**, Dr. Richard Norris, Sr.
Stewart, Frances Violet	**Thomas**, Norman Mattoon
Stewart, Jacqueline	**Cardelli**, Count Giovanni Guido Carlo
Stewart, Marian	**Honeyman**, Robert B., Jr.
Stier, Elsie	**Froessel**, Charles William
Stillman, Anne	**Davison**, Henry Pomeroy, II
Stillman, Mary Emma	**Harkness**, Edward Stephen
Stilwell, Ethel	**Smull**, Jacob Barstow
Stires, Marion Van Rensselaer	**Carpenter**, James Edwin Ruthven
Stocking, Patty	**Milburn**, John George, Sr.
Stockwell, Ethel Sweet	**Jadwin**, Stanley Palmer
Stokes, Frances	**Clark**, Louis Crawford, II **Weekes**, Harold H.
Stokes, Florence L.	**Clark**, Frederick Ambrose
Stone, Margaret	**Mann**, R. Colgate Vernon **Winthrop**, Robert, II

Stone, Mary N.	**Phipps**, Howard, Jr.
Storm, Anita	**Willis**, Harold Satterlee
Strader, Mona	**Schlesinger**, Harry
	Bush, James
	Williams, Harrison
	Von Bismarck, Count Albrecht Edward
	di Martini, Count Umberto
Stratton, Jennifer	**Neelands**, Thomas D., Jr.
Strauss, Jennie	**Jonas**, Nathan Solomon
Strong, Clara Louise	**Ketcham**, Francis I.
Strong, Georgina	**Hicks**, Frederick Cocks
Stuart, Jeanne	**Rothschild**, Baron Eugene de
Sturges, Anne A.	**Bullard**, Roger Harrington
Sturgis, Elizabeth Morfield	**Tailer**, Thomas Suffern, Jr.
Sullivan, Elaine S.	**Hoffman**, Albert L., Sr.
Sullivan, Leta	**Hoffman**, Albert L., Sr.
Sullivan, Rita	**Cournand**, Edouard L.
Swan, Ellen	**Rouss**, Peter Winchester
Swan, Florence Althea	**Gibb**, Walter
Sweetser, Emma	**Winslow**, Edward
Sweitzer, Elizabeth	**Park**, William Gray
Swift, Martha E.	**Dickerman**, Bradley Watson, Sr.
Symington, Hazel	**Lord**, George de Forest, Sr.
Tailer, Marie	**Wing**, S. Bryce
	Gaither, H. Granger
Talbot, Grace Helen	**Randall**, Darley, Jr.
Talman, Helen	**Bigelow**, Ernest A.
Tamara, Catherine	**Brokaw**, William Gould
Tapscott, Gustavia A.	**Senff**, Charles H.
Taylor, Edith	**Huntington**, Robert Dinsmore, Sr.
Taylor, Edna H.	**Thieriot**, Charles Henschel, II
Taylor, Marion D.	**Reynolds**, Jackson Eli
Terhune, Adelia Z.	**Morse**, Daniel Parmelee, Sr.
Terry, May Halsted	**Savage**, Rev. Theodore Fiske
Tew, Allene	**Hostetter**, Theodore H.
	Nichols, Morton Colton
	Burchard, Anson Wood
	Henry XXXIII, Prince of Reuss
	Paul de Kotzebue, Count of Russia

Thacher, Sarah	**Richmond**, L. Martin
Thayer, Louise	**Nichols**, Francis Tilden, Sr.
Thayer, Margaret	**Talbott**, Harold Elster, II
Thayer, Marjorie	**Clark**, Bruce
Thayer, Mary Dannat	**Scudder**, Townsend, II
Thomas, Jeannette	**Root**, Walstein **Aldrich**, Sherwood
Thompson, Anne Hunter	**MacDonald**, Ranald Hugh, Jr.
Thompson, Elizabeth	**Preston**, Ralph Julius
Thompson, Elizabeth Steenrod	**Babcock**, Richard Franklin
Thompson, Lillian Margaret	**Ohl**, John Phillips
Thompson, Mary Noyes	**Dwyer**, Martin, Jr.
Thompson, Nina Cornelia	**Prime**, William Albert, Sr.
Thompson, Olive W.	**Tiffany**, Perry
Thompson, Sarah	**Watriss**, Frederick N.
Thomsen, Mary Theodora	**Sizer**, Robert Ryland, Sr.
Thorne, Lilla A.	**Taylor**, James Blackstone, Sr.
Thornton, Eddie Elizabeth	**Baylis**, Lester Yates
Thornton, Frances D.	**Thieriot**, Charles Henschel, Sr.
Thurlow, Lena	**Vanderbilt**, Joseph White
Thurston, Belle	**Swan**, William Lincoln, Sr.
Tian, Lynn	**Riggs**, Glenn E., Sr.
Tieken, Robin	**Hadley**, John Wood Blodgett
Tiffany, Dorothy Trimble	**Burlingham**, Dr. Robert
Tiffany, Julia de Forest	**Parker**, Gordon Saltonstall **Weld**, Francis Minot, II
Tiffany, Louise Comfort	**Gilder**, Rodman, Sr.
Tiffany, Mary Christy	**Pratt**, John Teele, Jr. **Knight**, Harry **Nickerson**, William Gifford
Tiffany, Mary Woodbridge	**Lusk**, Dr. Graham
Tilden, Rose	**Nichols**, William Henry, Jr.
Tilton, Pyma Daphne	**Pell**, John Howland Gibbs
Tobias, Ida	**Cantor**, Eddie
Tod, Katharine Kennedy	**Martin**, Henry Bradley, II
Todd, Martha Clover	**Dulles**, Allen Welsh
Tongue, Mary Van Arsdale	**Eberstadt**, Ferdinand

Torrey, Harriet	**Matheson**, William John
Touzeau, Colette	**Armsby**, George Newell, Sr.
Tower, Elizabeth	**Halsey**. Richard Townley Haines
Tower, Pamela	**Secor**, Jay Ketcham **Le Boutillier**, Thomas, III
Towne, Marjorie R.	**Hull**, Kenneth Duryee, Sr.
Townsend, Emma	**Gary**, Elbert H.
Townsend, Harriet. B. C.	**Bottomley**, William Lawrence
Townsend, Viola	**Winmill**, Robert Campbell
Tracy, Reine Marie	**Stewart**, Cecil Parker
Travers, Augusta L.	**O'Rourke**, Innis, Sr.
Travers, Lily Harriman	**Havemeyer**, Frederick Christian, IV
Treibick, Alice	**Lynch**, Edmund Calvert, Jr.
Tremblay, Mary	**Kelley**, Cornelius Francis
Trevor, Mary Tallmadge	**Winthrop**, Grenville Lindall
Trotter, Lucy	**Hagen**, Winston Henry, Sr.
Trowbridge, Margaret	**Henry**, Barklie McKee **Setton**, Dr. Kenneth M.
Trubee, Kate	**Davison**, Henry Pomeroy, Sr.
True, Agnes Louise	**Houston**, Herbert Sherman
Truesdale, Margaret L.	**Loening**, Grover **Carroll**, Hanson T. **du Pont**, Alexis Felix, Jr.
Truesdale, Mary	**Shutt**, Edwin Holmes, Jr.
Tucker, Ethelette French	**Ridder**, Eric, Sr.
Tucker, Josephine Vance	**Robertson**, Julian Hart, Jr.
Tull, Jacqueline Gebhard	**Loew**, Arthur Marcus, Sr.
Turnbull, Katherine Benedict	**Wood**, Chalmers, Jr.
Turner, LuEsther	**Mertz**, Harold E.
Tuorto, Camille Jean	**Amato**, Thomas
Tuttle, Minnie	**Beard**, William
Tuttle, Muriel Seymour	**Eden**, John H., II
Tweed, Katherine Winthrop	**Roosevelt**, Archibald Bulloch, Jr. **Robertson**, Dr. Robert Blackwood
Tweedy, Alice	**Cox**, Gerard Hutchison, Sr.
Urquhart, Elise	**Duggan**, Philip Richard **Dick**, Fairman Rogers

Vanderbilt, Cathleen	**Cushing**, Harry Cooke, III **Lowman**, Lawrence Wise
Vanderbilt, Consuelo	**Marlborough**, Ninth Duke of **Balsan**, Louis Jacques
Vanderbilt, Consuelo	**Smith**, Earl Edward Tailer, Sr. **Davis**, Henry Gassaway, III **Warburton**, William J., III **Earl**, N. Clarkson, Jr.
Vanderbilt, Gertrude	**Whitney**, Harry Payne
Vanderhoef, F. Louise	**Heckscher**, Gustav Maurice **Thatcher**, John M. P., Sr.
Van Dusen, Mary Gilbert	**White**, Leonard Dalton, Sr.
Van Gilder, Mary	**Ely**, Rev. Samuel Rose, Sr.
Van Hodenpyl, Antoinette G.	**Fahys**, George Ernest, Sr.
Van Nostrand, Helen	**Meyer**, George C., Sr.
Van Schaick, Mildred	**Gwynne**, Arthur
Vanson, Rosalie Laura	**Nicastro**, Louis Joseph
Van Wie, Isabel	**Willys**, John North
Van Wyck, Florence	**Doubleday**, Frank Nelson
Van Wyck, Helen	**Lockman**, Myron Augustus
Varet, Leila Alice	**Appleby**, Charles Herbert, Sr. **Crawford**, Robert Leighton
Verplanck, Virginia Darby	**Bleecker**, Theophylact Bache, Jr.
Vickers, Susan G.	**Luckenbach**, Edgar Frederick, Sr.
Vliet, Eleanor	**Lindsay**, George Nelson, Sr.
Von Neufville, Olga	**Flinsch**, Rudolf E. F.
Von Stade, G. H. ("Dolly")	**Bostwick**, George Herbert, Sr.
Von Tippelskirch, Christa	**Armstrong**, Hamilton Fish
Wagstrom, Margaretha	**Rumbough**, Stanley Maddox, Jr.
Wahl, Sandra	**Sheeline**, Paul Cushing
Wall, Louise Berry	**Ladew**, Edward R.
Wallace, Dorothy Kimball	**Stewart**, Cecil Parker
Wallace, Virginia Gordon	**Stettinius**, Edward Reilly, Jr.
Walser, Violet Elizabeth	**Goodrich**, Donald Wells, Sr.
Walter, Beatrice	**Sanderson**, Henry
Warburg, Felicia Schiff	**Sarnoff**, Robert **Roosevelt**, Franklin Delano, Jr.
Ward, Dorothy	**Eden**, Bronson Beecher Tuttle, Sr.

Ward, Florence Augusta

Ward, Marjorie

Warder, Elizabeth

Warner, Anne Kissam

Warren, Charlotte L.

Washburn, Marie Louise

Wassall, Grace

Watson, Kathleen Brent

Watson, Leonora Jane

Waver, Minnie Christina

Webb, Frances Blanche

Webb, Frederica Vanderbilt

Weber, Elfrieda A.

Webster, Mary Messinger

Weekes, Edith B.

Weekes, Julia Mary

Weeks, Julia Manley

Weibel, M. Emma

Weinacht, Elise Annette

Weld, Adelaide

Weld, Anne

Weller, Emily

Wells, Harriet Boynton

Wesselhoeft, Susan

Wesson, Madeline Burt

Werther, Rose Marion

Westcott, Violet

Wheeler, Hannah

Wheeler, Lucy Dunham

Wheeler, Olivia D.

Whipple, Eleanor Sherburne

Alker, Alphonse Henry
Meyer, J. Edward, Sr.

Wing, L. Stuart
Clark, John Balfour

Ellis, Ralph Nicholson, Sr.

Handy, Parker Douglas

Streeter, Edward, Sr.

Maxwell, John Rogers, Sr.

Chadbourne, Thomas Lincoln, Jr.

Harris, Sam Henry

Mooney, James David, II
Thomas, Reginald

Allen, Gabriel

Roosevelt, Quentin, II

Pulitzer, Ralph, Sr.
Jones, Hamlen

Martin, Henry Clifford

Harris, Henry Upham, Sr.

Slade, John, Sr.

de Forest, Henry Grant

L'Ecluse, Milton Albert

Weir, Levi Candee

Roosevelt, John Kean

Whitney, Robert Bacon, Sr.
Knott, James

Crawford, William, Jr.
McLane, Allan, Jr.

Dows, David, Jr.

Gardner, Davis F.
Gerry, Robert Livingston, Jr.

Pell, Clarence Cecil, Sr.

Atherton, Henry Francis, Sr.

Grumman, Leroy Randle

Morawetz, Victor

Corbin, Austin

Riggs, George

Sturgis, Thomas R.
Post, George B., Jr.
Alexandre, J. Henry, Jr.

Stoddard, Francis Russell, Jr.

1056

Whitaker, Katharine Rusling	**Dyer**, Elisha, VII
White, Carmel	**Snow**, George Palen
White, Jeanne L.	**Miller**, Andrew Otterson, Jr.
White, Mabel Wellington	**Stimson**, Henry Lewis
White, Margaret Low	**Weld**, Francis Minot, II
White, Margaret O.	**Bacon**, Daniel
Whitehouse, Julia Christina	**Boardman**, Kenneth
Whiting, Hattie	**Morrell**, Joseph B.
Whitmore, Vida	**Hudson**, Percy Kierstede
Whitney, Barbara	**Henry**, Barklie McKee **Peck**, Samuel Anderson **Headley**, George William, III
Whitney, Dorothy Payne	**Straight**, Willard Dickerman **Elmhirst**, Leonard Knight
Whitney, Edith	**Batterman**, Henry Lewis, Sr.
Whitney, Ethel A.	**Satterlee**, Dr. Henry Suydam, Sr.
Whitney, Flora Payne	**Tower**, Roderick **Miller**, George Macculloch
Whitney, Helen C.	**Bourne**, George Galt **Gibson**, Harvey Dow
Whitney, Joan	**Payson**, Charles Shipman
Whitney, Lillian	**Barney**, Charles Tracy
Whitney, Miss Margaret Sargent	
Whitney, Nancy	**Gerry**, Henry Averell, Sr.
Whitney, Sarah Swan	**Belmont**, Oliver Hazard Perry
Whiton, Angeline	**Davis**, Hartley Courtland
Whittemore, Beatrice	**Bevin**, Sydney
Wiborg, Oga	**Fish**, Sidney W.
Widener, Josephine P.	**Leidy**, Carter **Holden**, Milton W. **Wichfeld**, Aksel C. P. **Bigelow**, Anson Alexander
Wilckes, Estelle	**Cushing**, Leonard Jarvis, Sr.
Wilcox, Constance Devereux	**O'Keeffe**, Samuel
Wilcox, Marjory	**Atwater**, John Jacob, Sr.
Wilcox, Pansy	**Schenck**, Nicholas Michael
Wilgus, Lois N.	**Ballantine**, John Herbert
Wilhelm, Myrtle Grace	**Shaw**, Robert Anderson
Willard, Anne	**Hoffstot**, Frank Norton

Willard, Belle Wyatt — **Roosevelt**, Kermit, Sr.

Willets, Mary Wilson — **Pell**, Howland Haggerty, Sr.

Willetts, Amie W. — **Outerbridge**, Samuel Roosevelt

Willetts, Marion — **Brower**, Ernest Cuyler
Brower, George Ellsworth

Williams, Alice — **Kelly**, James B.
Williams, Timothy Shaler

Williams, Elizabeth — **Potter**, Dr. Gilbert

Williams, Frances Randall — **Rogers**, John S., Jr.
Chanler, William Chamberlain

Williams, Grace Douglass — **Pierce**, Winslow Shelby, II

Williams, Mabel — **Munson**, Carlos W.

Williams, Mildred — **Farwell**, Walter

Williams, Muriel — **Hoyt**, Colgate, Jr.

Williamson, Katherine — **Kennedy**, William, Sr.

Willis, Ann Eliza Cairns — **Ward**, Aaron

Willis, Blanche — **Emory**, William Helmsley, Jr.

Willis, Caroline Skidmore — **Hewlett**, Walter Jones

Willis, Leila Morse — **Sherman**, Charles Austin, Sr.

Wills, Nevada L. — **Demarest**, John M.

Wilmerding, Alice Tracy — **Coudert**, Frederic Rene, II

Wilmerding, Georgiana L. — **Phelps**, Ansel

Wilson, Beverly — **Davisson**, Richard L., Sr.

Wilson, Elizabeth — **Linkletter**, George Onderdonk, Sr.

Wilson, Maude E. — **Littleton**, Martin Wiley, Sr.

Wilson, Millicent — **Hearst**, William Randolph

Winchester, Ellen H. — **Weld**, William
Duryea, Hermanes Barkulo, Jr.

Winchester, Hope G. — **Pratt**, Herbert Lee, Jr.

Wing, Marion — **Flint**, Dr. Austin, Jr.

Winship, Georgia — **Rathborne**, Joseph Cornelius, II

Winslow, Anne C. — **Brown**, Francis Gordon, Sr.

Winston, Eugenia — **Graham**, Raymond Austin, Sr.

Winthrop, Marie — **Kellogg**, Morris Woodruff

Wiswell, Dorothy — **Clowes**, John Henry, Sr.

Withers, Anne — **Oeland**, Isaac Raymond, Sr.

Withington, Ruth — **Vietor**, Dr. John Adolf, Sr.

Wolff, Adelaide — **Kahn**, Otto Hermann

Wolff, Katherine — **Rothschild**, Baron Eugene de

Wolkonsky, Maria

Wood, Alice

Wood, Katharine

Wood, Leonora

Wood, Lylian A.

Wood, Melza Riggs

Wood, Sally Lewis

Woodruff, Dorothy Elizabeth

Woodward, Eleanore E.

Woodward, Elizabeth

Woodward, Gabrielle

Woodward, Mary

Woolman, Edna

Woolworth, Helena Maud

Yauch, Margaret A.

Yerkes, Ethel

Yost, Audrey Jean

Young, Helen S.

Young, Kari-Ann R.

Youngs, Carrie

Youngs, Keziah

Yuille, Ellen D.

Yuille, Melissa W.

Zabala, Anita Consuelo

Zabelle, Flora

Zimmermann, Anna Cecilia

Zukor, Mildred

Zweifel, Marguerite J.

Luckenbach, Lewis V., Sr.
de Peyster, George Livingston

Simpson, Robert H.

Crocker, Frank Longfellow

Armsby, George Newell, Sr.

Walbridge, Henry D.

Winthrop, Beekman, II

Nixon, Lewis

Emanuel, Victor

Vietor, Dr. John Adolf, Sr.

Pratt, John Teele, Jr.

Murdock, Harvey

Babcock, Henry Dennison, Sr.

Chase, Francis Dane
Newton, Richard T.

McCann, Charles Edward Francis

Kane, John P., Jr.

Gardner, Robert B., Sr.
Woolley, Daniel P.

Hammer, Frederick O.
Luckenbach, Edgar Frederick, Jr.

Maxwell, Howard Washburn, Sr.

Carr, Edward A. T.

Bailey, Townsend Fleet

Jones, William

Sturgis, William J.
Blair, Wolcott

Bingham, Harry Payne, Sr.

Vanderbilt, George Washington, IV

Hitchcock, Raymond

Van Strum, Kenneth Stevens

Loew, Arthur Marcus, Sr.

Stehli, Emil J.

The estates mentioned in this compilation of motion pictures, filmed at North Shore estate sites, are identified by the original owner of the estate. For subsequent estate owners, see surname entry.

AN AFFAIR TO REMEMBER (1957) - The driveway and front exterior of the house scene was filmed at the George Smith estate, *Blythewood,* in Muttontown.

>
> starring: Cary Grant, Deborah Kerr, Richard Denning, Neva Patterson, Cathleen Nesbitt, Robert Q. Lewis, Charles Watts, Fortunio Bonanova
> directed by Leo McCarey

AGE OF INNOCENCE (1993) - The Floridian garden scene was filmed at the John Shaffer Phipps estate, *Westbury House*, in Old Westbury (now, Old Westbury Gardens). Note the damaged left arm of the statue and the Long Island, not Florida, floral display. The ladies archery contest scene, with the house in the background, and the river scene were filmed at the William Bayard Cutting estate, *Westbrook*, in Great River (now, Bayard Cutting Arboretum). Scenes were also filmed at the Harold Irving Pratt, Sr. estate, *Welwyn*, in Glen Cove (now, Welwyn Preserve).

>
> starring: Daniel Day–Lewis, Michelle Pfieffer, Winona Ryder
> directed by Martin Scorsese

AMERICAN CUISINE (1997) was filmed at the Herbert Lee Pratt, Sr. estate, *The Braes*, in Glen Cove (now, Webb Institute of Naval Architecture).
> Cast list unavailable

AMERICA'S CASTLES (1996) - Part of the Arts and Entertainment Network's series was devoted to Long Island's North Shore estates. The hour episode was filmed at the John Shaffer Phipps estate, *Westbury House*, in Old Westbury (now, Old Westbury Gardens); the William Kissam Vanderbilt, Jr. estate, *Eagle's Nest*, in Centerport (now, Suffolk County Vanderbilt Museum and Planetarium); the Daniel Guggenheim estate, *Hempstead House*, and the Harry Guggenheim estate, *Falaise*, (both of which are now part of the Sands Point Country Park and Preserve) in Sands Point.

ANNA ASCENDS (1922) was filmed at the John William Matheson estate, *Fort Hill*, in Lloyd Harbor.
> starring: Alice Brady, Robert Ellis, David Powell, Neta Naldi, Charles Gerrard, Edward Durrand
> directed by Victor Fleming

ANOTHER WORLD (1998) - A television series episode was filmed at the John Edward Aldred estate, *Ormston,* in Lattingtown (now, Saint Josaphat's Monastery).

ARTHUR (1981) - Stable scenes were filmed at the Marshall Field III estate, *Caumsett*, in Lloyd Harbor (now, Caumsett State Park). The exterior of the Alfred Irenee du Pont house, *White Eagle*, in Brookville (now, the DeSeversky Conference Center) and the estate's driveway are seen in the film. Filming was also done at the Hermanes Barkulo Duryea, Jr. estate, *Knole*, in Old Westbury, and at the William Robertson Coe estate, *Planting Fields,* in Upper Brookville (now, Planting Fields Arboretum).
> starring: Dudley Moore, Liza Minnelli, John Gielgud, Jill Eikenberry, Geraldine Fitzgerald
> directed by Steve Gordon

THE ASSOCIATE (1996) - Interior reception and dance scene was filmed at the Hermanes Barkulo Duryea, Jr. estate, *Knole*, in Old Westbury. Exterior scenes were filmed at the John Shaffer Phipps estate, *Westbury House*, in Old Westbury (now, Old Westbury Gardens).
> starring: Whoopi Goldberg, Babe Neuwirth, Tim Daly, Lainie Kazin
> directed by Donald Pretrie

BARE ESSENCE (1982), a made-for-television movie, was filmed at an unnamed Glen Cove estate.
> starring: Genie Francis, Bruce Borleitner, Linda Evans, Lee Grant, Joel Higgins, Donna Mills, Tim Thomerson, Belinda Montgomery
> directed by Walter Grauman

BATMAN FOREVER (1995) - Both interior and exterior scenes depicting Bruce Wayne's home were filmed at the Herbert Lee Pratt, Sr. estate, *The Braes*, in Glen Cove (now, Webb Institute of Naval Architecture).
> starring: Val Kilmer, Tommy Lee Jones, Jim Carrey, Nicole Kidman, Chris O'Donnell, Michael Gough, Drew Barrymore
> directed by Joel Schumacher

BELLY (1998) - was filmed at the Hermanes Barkulo Duryea, Jr. estate, *Knole*, in Old Westbury.
> starring: Taral Hicks, Tionne "T-Boz" Watkins, Method Man
> directed by Hype Williams

BRIDE OF VIOLENCE was filmed at the John Shaffer Phipps estate, *Westbury House*, in Old Westbury (now, Old Westbury Gardens). *[It is questionable as to whether this film was ever released.]*
> Cast list unavailable

BRIGHT LIGHTS, BIG CITY (1988) was filmed at an unnamed Old Westbury estate. The fashion show scene was filmed at the estate.
> starring: Michael J. Fox, Kiefer Sutherland, Phoebe Cates, Swoosie Kurtz, Frances Sternhagen, Dianne Wiest, Jason Robards, John Housemann
> directed by James Bridges

CAT ON A HOT TIN ROOF (1958) was filmed at the Julien Ashton Ripley, Sr. estate, *Three Corners Farm*, in Muttontown. The porch on second floor of the house was used in the film.
> starring: Elizabeth Taylor, Paul Newman, Burl Ives, Judith Anderson, Madeleine Sherwood
> directed by Richard Brooks

CHARLES AND DIANA: A ROYAL LOVE STORY (1982) was filmed at the Daniel Guggenheim estate, *Hempstead House*, in Sands Point (now, part of Sands Point County Park and Preserve).
> starring: David Robb, Caroline Bliss
> directed by James Goldstone

CITIZEN KANE (1941) was filmed at the Otto Hermann Kahn estate, *Oheka*, in Cold Spring Harbor. The opening aerial view of the house and the garden scene were filmed at the estate.
> starring: Orson Wells, Joseph Cotten, Dorothy Comingore, Ruth Warrick, Everett Sloane, Agnes Moorehead
> written and directed by Orson Wells

COMPROMISING POSITIONS (1985) - In addition to filming at an unnamed Great Neck estate, the skating rink in Great Neck's Steppingstone Park and Woodbury Common Shopping Center in Woodbury were used as locations.
> starring: Susan Saradon, Edward Herrmann, Raul Julia, Judith Ivey, Mary Beth Hurt, Ann De Salvo, Joe Mantegna, John Mostel
> directed by Frank Perry

CROCODILE DUNDEE II (1988) - Both interior and exterior scenes, depicting the drug dealer's estate, were filmed at the William Kissam Vanderbilt, Jr. estate, *Eagle's Nest*, in Centerport (now, Suffolk County Vanderbilt Museum and Planetarium).
> starring: Paul Hogan, Linda Kozlowski, Charles Dutton
> directed by Frank Perry

CRUEL INTENTIONS (1998) was filmed at the John Shaffer Phipps estate, *Westbury House*, in Old Westbury (now, Old Westbury Gardens).
> starring: Sarah Michelle Gellar, Ryan Phillippe, Reese Witherspoon
> directed by Roger Kumble

DEATH WISH (1974) was filmed at the Lillian Sefton Thomas Dodge estate, *Sefton Manor*, in Mill Neck (now, Mill Neck Manor School for Deaf Children). Both the interior and exterior of the house were used for the sanitarium scenes. The Shakespearean-themed stained glass windows at the foot of the stairs are very recognizable. *[Note: These were not fabricated by Tiffany Studios.]*
> starring: Charles Bronson, Hope Lange, Vincent Gardenia, Stuart Margolin, William Redfield
> directed by Michael Winner

THE DELI (1996) was filmed at the Alex Nichol Horse Farm in Laurel Hollow.
> starring: Jerry Stiller, Iman, Debbie Mazur, Heather Matarazzo, Bert Young, Michael Imperioli

DEVIL'S ADVOCATE (1997) - Interior scenes were filmed at the Hermanes Barkulo Duryea, Jr. estate, *Knole*, in Old Westbury.
> starring: Al Pacino, Keanu Reeves, Jeffrey Jones, Charlize Theron
> directed by Taylor Hackford

DOLLY PARTON AND JULIO IGLESIAS VIDEO (1994) - This music video was filmed at the Otto Hermann Kahn estate, *Oheka*, in Cold Spring Harbor.

EIGHT MILLIMETER (1998) - was filmed at the John Shaffer Phipps estate, *Westbury House*, in Old Westbury (now, Old Westbury Gardens).
        starring: Nicholas Cage, Joaquin Phoenix, James Gandolfini, Peter Stormare
        directed by Joel Schumacher

THE EMPEROR'S CLUB (2002) - was filmed at the Howard Crosby Brokaw estate, *The Chimneys*, in Muttontown (now, Muttontown Golf and Country Club) and at the Otto Hermann Kahn estate, *Oheka*, in Cold Spring Harbor.
        starring: Kevin Kline, Steven Culp, Embeth Davidtz
        directed by Michael Hoffman

FAMILY REUNION (1981) was filmed at the Harold Irving Pratt, Sr. estate, *Welwyn* , in Glen Cove (now, Welwyn Preserve). The estate, as well as the Village of Locust Valley, were used in this made-for-television movie.
        starring: Bette Davis, David Huddleston, John Shea, J. Ashley Hyman
        directed by Field Cook

FOREVER YOURS (1991) - This music video was filmed at the Guggenheim estate in Sands Point (now, Sands Point County Park and Preserve).
        starring: Toshi

FROM THE TERRACE (1960) was filmed at the George Smith estate, *Blythewood,* in Muttontown. Based on book by John O'Hara.
        starring: Paul Newman, Joanne Woodward, Ina Balin, Leon Ames, Myrna Loy
        directed by Mark Robson

THE GODFATHER (1972) - The horse's head scene was filmed in the Harry Guggenheim/Alicia Patterson house, *Falaise*, in Sands Point (now, part of Sands Point County Park and Preserve). The toll booth scene was filmed at Michel Field, Garden City.
        starring: Marlon Brando, Al Pacino, James Caan, Richard Castellano, Robert Duvall,
                  Diane Keaton, Sterling Hayden, Richard Conti
        directed by Francis Ford Coppola

THE GODFATHER, PART III (1990) was filmed at an unnamed Mill Neck estate.
        starring: Al Pacino, Diane Keaton, Talia Shire, Eli Wallach, Bridget Fonda, Joe Mantegna,
                  George Hamilton
        directed by Francis Ford Coppola

GREAT EXPECTATIONS (1997) - Interior scenes were filmed at the Daniel Guggenheim estate, *Hempstead House,* in Sands Point (now, Sands Point County Park and Preserve). An exterior scene was filmed at the Herbert Lee Pratt, Sr. estate, *The Braes*, in Glen Cove (now, Webb Institute of Naval Architecture).
        starring: Ethan Hawke, Gwyneth Paltrow, Robert DeNiro, Anne Bancroft
        directed by Alfonso Cuaron

HAIR (1979) was filmed at the Florence Calkin Dickerman estate, *Hillendale,* in Mill Neck.
        starring: John Savage, Treat Williams, Beverly D'Angelo, Annie Golden, Dorsey Wright,
                  Don Dacus, Cheryl Barnes, Richard Bright, Nicholas Ray
        directed by Milos Forman

HELLO AGAIN (1987) was filmed at *The Willow* in Oyster Bay Cove.
        starring: Shelley Long, Judith Ivey, Gabriel Byrne, Corbin Bernsen, Austin Pendleton
        directed by Frank Perry

IN AND OUT (1997) was filmed at the William Russell Grace, Jr. estate, *The Crossroads*, in Old Westbury. Exterior scenes include many Long Island buildings and landscapes including several which include St. Johns Episcopal Church, Cold Spring Harbor, and Main Street, Northport.
        starring: Kevin Kline, Tom Selleck, Matt Dillon, Joan Cusack, Wilford Brimley, Debbie Reynolds,
                  Bob Newhart
        directed by Frank Oz

INFINITY (1996) was filmed at the John Shaffer Phipps estate, *Westbury House*, (now, Old Westbury Gardens) in Old Westbury.
>   starring: Matthew Broderick, Patricia Arquette
>   directed by Matthew Broderick

I, THE JURY (1982) was filmed at the Hermanes Barkulo Duryea, Jr. estate, *Knole*, in Old Westbury.
>   starring: Armand Assante, Barbara Carrera, Alan King, Geoffrey Lewis
>   directed by Richard T. Heffron

I THINK I DO (1997) was filmed at the Helen Porter Pryibil estate, *Bogheid,* in Glen Cove.
>   starring: Alexis Arquette, Christian Maelen, Maddie Corman
>   directed by Brian Sloan

KOJACK (1990) - The made-for-television movie was filmed at the John Shaffer Phipps estate, *Westbury House*, in Old Westbury (now, Old Westbury Gardens). The Hermanes Barkulo Duryea, Jr. estate, *Knole*, in Old Westbury was also used. A second Kojak made-for-television movie was also made in Nassau County.
>   starring: Telly Savalas, Kevin Dobson, Darin Mc Gavin

LOOK AT ME (1996) was filmed at the Hermanes Barkulo Duryea, Jr. estate, *Knole*, in Old Westbury and at the William Robertson Coe estate, *Planting Fields*, in Upper Brookville (now, Planting Fields Arboretum).
>   Cast list unavailable

LOVE STORY (1970) was filmed at the John Shaffer Phipps estate, *Westbury House*, in Old Westbury (now, Old Westbury Gardens). According to the guides at *Westbury House*, the entrance roads and the library were used in the movie. Based on book by Erich Segal.
>   starring: Ali Mc Graw, Ryan O'Neil, Ray Milland, John Marley, Katherine Balfour
>   directed by Arthur Hiller

MALCOLM X (1992) was filmed at the Guggenheim estate in Sands Point (now, Sands Point County Park and Preserve).
>   starring: Denzel Washington, Angela Bassett, Albert Hall, Al Freeman, Jr., Spike Lee, Theresa Randle
>   directed by Spike Lee

MARCY PLAYGROUND music video was filmed at the Otto Hermann Kahn estate, *Oheka*, in Cold Spring Harbor.

MICKEY BLUE EYES (1999) - was filmed at the Hermanes Barkulo Duryea, Jr. estate, *Knole*, in Old Westbury.
>   starring: Hugh Grant, James Caan, Jeanne Tripplehorn, James Fox, Burt Young
>   directed by Kelly Makin

MICK JONES VIDEO - This video was filmed at the Hermanes Barkulo Duryea, Jr. estate, *Knole*, in Old Westbury in August of 1989.

THE MONEY PIT (1986) - The house scenes were filmed at the H. W. Warner estate in Lattingtown.
>   starring: Tom Hanks, Shelley Long, Alexander Godunov, Maureen Stapleton, Joe Mantegna, Philip Bosco, Josh Mostel
>   directed by Richard Benjamin

NEW JACK CITY (1991) - The house scenes were as filmed at the Daniel Guggenheim estate, *Hempstead House*, in Sands Point (now, part of Sands Point County Park and Preserve).
>   starring: Ice T; Wesley Snipes, Judd Nelson
>   directed by Mario Van Pebbles

A NEW LEAF (1971) was filmed at the Harold Irving Pratt, Sr. estate, *Welwyn*, in Glen Cove (now, Welwyn Preserve). The driveway, the gardens, and both the exterior and the interior of the house are seen in the film. Portions of this movie were also filmed at the Julien Ashton Ripley estate, *Three Corners Farm*, in Muttontown.
>   starring: Walter Matthau, Elaine May, James Coco, George Rose, Jack Weston
>   directed by Elaine May

THE NIGHT WE NEVER MET (1993) was filmed at the Hermanes Barkulo Duryea, Jr. estate, *Knole*, in Old Westbury.

    starring: Matthew Broderick, Annabella Sciorra, Justin Bateman, Louise Lasser, Doris Roberts
    directed by Warren Light

NORTH BY NORTHWEST (1959) - The exterior of *Manor House*, the John Teele Pratt, Sr. estate in Glen Cove (now, Harrison House Conference Center), was used in this film. In addition, the interior of the John Shaffer Phipps estate, *Westbury House*, in Old Westbury (now, Old Westbury Gardens) was used in several scenes.

    starring: Cary Grant, Eva Marie Saint, James Mason, Martin Landau, Leo G. Carroll
    directed by Alfred Hitchcock

PAPER DOLLS (1984) - Portions of this television mini-series were filmed at the John Shaffer Phipps estate, *Westbury House*, in Old Westbury (now, Old Westbury Gardens).

    starring: Lloyd Bridges, Morgan Fairchild, Mimi Rogers, Dack Rambo, Jennifer Warren
    directed by Leonard Goldberg

A PERFECT MURDER (1998) was filmed at the Junius Spencer Morgan estate, *Salutation,* on West Island, Glen Cove.

    starring: Michael Douglas, Gwyneth Paltrow, Viggo Mortensen
    directed by Andrew Davis

RAGE OF ANGELS: THE STORY CONTINUES (1986) - This made-for-television movie was filmed at an unnamed Old Westbury estate.

    starring: Jaclyn Smith, Ken Howard, Angela Lansbury, Susan Sullivan, Michael Nouri, Mason Adams, Brad Dourrif
    directed by Paul Wendkos

RAIN WITHOUT THUNDER (1992) was filmed at the Guggenheim estate in Sands Point (now, Sands Point County Park and Preserve).

    starring: Betty Buckley, Jeff Daniels, Frederic Forrest, Graham Greene, Linda Hunt, Robert Earl Jones
    directed by Gary Bennett

REVERSAL OF FORTUNE (1990) - The Claus Von Bulow story was filmed at the Hermanes Barkulo Duryea, Jr. estate, *Knole*, in Old Westbury.

    starring: Glen Close, Jeremy Irons, Ron Silver
    directed by Barbet Schroeder

RUNNING ON EMPTY (1988) - The beach scenes were filmed at the Daniel Guggenheim estate, *Hempstead House*, in Sands Point (now, part of Sands Point County Park and Preserve).

    starring: Christine Lahti, Judd Hirsch, River Phoenix, Jonas Abry, Martha Plimpton
    directed by Sidney Lumet

SABRINA (1954) - This movie, based on the play *Sabrina Fair*, was filmed in the house and on the grounds of the John Teele Pratt, Sr. estate, *Manor House*, in Glen Cove (now, Harrison House Conference Center). The Glen Cove Railroad Station was also used as a filming site.

    starring: Audrey Hepburn, Humphrey Bogart, William Holden
    directed by Billy Wilder

SABRINA (1997) was filmed at the Junius Spencer Morgan estate, *Salutation,* on West Island, Glen Cove.

    starring: Harrison Ford, Julia Ormond, Greg Kinnear, Nancy Marchand, Richard Crenna, Angie Dickinson
    directed by Sydney Pollack

SCENES FROM THE PLAGUE YEAR (1991) - This film short was filmed at the Benjamin Moore estate, *Chelsea*, in Muttontown (now, part of Muttontown Preserve).

SCENT OF A WOMAN (1992) was filmed at the Daniel Guggenheim estate, *Hempstead House*, in Sands Point (now, part of Sands Point County Park and Preserve).

    starring: Al Pacino, Chris O'Donnell
    directed by Martin Brest

SECRET GARDEN MUSIC VIDEO (1996) was filmed at the Benjamin Moore estate, *Chelsea*, in Muttontown (now, part of Muttontown Preserve).

SERENITY (1998) was filmed at the Otto Hermann Kahn estate, *Oheka*, in Cold Spring Harbor.
   Cast list unavailable

SIX DAYS AT OTTO KAHN (1997) was filmed at the Otto Hermann Kahn estate, *Oheka*, in Cold Spring Harbor.
   Cast list unavailable

STRANGER IN THE HOUSE was filmed at the Grace estate in Muttontown and at the Flagg estate in Oyster Bay Cove. Filming began in June 1990 but the production was canceled during the second week of filming. *(It is not known whether this film was ever completed.)*
      It was to star Terrance Stamp, Lorraise Bracco, Harry Dean Stanton
      and to be directed by Terrance Stamp.

TAKE A CHANCE (1933) was filmed at the Charles E. Proctor estate, *Shadowlane*, in Kings Point.
   starring: Monte Brice, James Dunn, Cliff Edwards, June Knight, Charles "Buddy" Rogers,
                  Lillian Roth, Dorothy Lee
   directed by Laurence Schwab

TO WONG FOO, THANKS FOR EVERYTHING, JULIE NEWMAR (1995) - The final awards scene was filmed on the terrace at the John Shaffer Phipps estate, *Westbury House*, in Old Westbury (now, Old Westbury Gardens).
   starring: Wesley Snipes, Patrick Swayze
   director by Beeban Kidron

TRADING PLACES (1983) was filmed at the Lillian Sefton Thomas Dodge estate, *Sefton Manor*, in Mill Neck (now, Mill Neck Manor School for Deaf Children).
   starring: Dan Aykroyd, Eddie Murphy, Ralph Bellany, Don Ameche, Denholm Elliot,
                  Jamie Lee Curtis, Paul Gleason
   directed by John Landis

VENDETTA: SECRETS OF A MAFIA BRIDE (1989) was filmed at the at the John Shaffer Phipps estate, *Westbury House*, in Old Westbury (now, Old Westbury Gardens).
   starring: Eli Wallach, Eric Roberts, Crol Alt, Nick Mancuso

WHERE'S POPPA (1970) was filmed at the John Teele Pratt, Sr. estate, *Manor House*, in Glen Cove (now, Harrison House Conference Center).
   starring: George Segal, Ruth Gordon, Vincent Gardenia, Barnard Hughes, Rob Reiner
   directed by Carl Reiner

WOLF (1994) - Both interior and exterior scenes were filmed at the John Shaffer Phipps estate, *Westbury House*, in Old Westbury (now, Old Westbury Gardens).
   starring: Jack Nicholson, Michelle Pfeiffer, James Spader, Kate Nelligan, Christopher Plummer
   directed by Mike Nichols

WOMAN'S WORLD (1954) was filmed at the Lillian Sefton Thomas Dodge estate, *Sefton Manor*, in Mill Neck (now, Mill Neck Manor School for Deaf Children).
   starring: June Allison, Clifton Webb, Van Heflin, Lauren Bacall, Fred Mac Murray, Arlene Dahl,
                  Cornel Wilde
   directed by Jean Negulesco

Occupations

See the surname entry to ascertain if an individual is listed under several occupational headings

ADVERTISING EXECUTIVES

Abbott, Paul, Sr.

Carey, Martin F.

Clark, Marshall

de Roulet, Daniel Carroll

de Roulet, Vincent W.

Hagen, Winston Henry, II

Hattersley, Robert Chopin, Sr.

Ludlow, Alden Rodney, Sr.

Lunn, Richard Dwight
  [see Tippet]

McVickar, Donald

Sheridan, Frank J., Jr.

Woolley, Daniel P.

ARCHITECTS

Bosworth, William Welles

Bottomley, William Lawrence

Bullard, Roger Harrington

Carpenter, James Edwin Ruthven

Cross, Eliot B.

Delano, William Adams

Delehanty, Bradley

D'Oench, Albert Frederick

Donnell, Harry Ellingwood

Flagg, Montague, II

Folkerts, Heiko Hid

Gibson, Robert Williams

Goodwin, Philip Lippincott

Harrison, Wallace Kirkman

Hastings, Thomas

Hewitt, Edward Shepard

King, Frederic Rhinelander

Lindeberg, Harrie Thomas

Mackenzie, J. Clinton

Miller, George Macculloch

Mizner, Addison

Morris, Montrose Whiting

Peabody, Julian Livingston, Sr.

Pennington, Hall Pleasants

Peters, William Wesley
  [see Allilueva]

Rinaldini, Luis Emilio

Robertson, Thomas Markoe

Underhill, Francis T.

ARTISTS

Babcock, Elizabeth Steenrod T.

Brokaw, Irving

Church, Frederic Edwin

Clark, Virginia Keep

Coudert, Mary K. Callery

de Forest, Julia Mary

De Leslie, Count Alexander Paulovitch

Dodge, Robert Leftwich

Duryea, Minga Pope
  [later, Patchin]

Eden, Muriel Seymour Tuttle

Fox, Fontaine Talbot, Jr.

Godwin, Harold

Grace, Louise Natalie

Hagen, Lucy Trotter

Hewitt, Mary Eleanor Fowler

Hornblower, Dorothy Marshall

Ladew, Harvey Smith, II

La Montagne, Harry

McNair, William

Miller, George Macculloch

Morgan, Elizabeth W. Emmet

Mortimer, Stanley, Sr.

Neilson, Raymond Perry R., Sr.

Netter, Dr. Frank H.

O'Connor, John A.

Ono, Yoko

Peabody, Grace Eddy

Physioc, Joseph Allen, Sr.

Proctor, Charles E.

Randall, Grace Helen Talbot

ARTISTS (cont'd)

Ripley, Lucy Fairfield Perkins

Roosevelt, Frances B. Webb

Rumsey, Charles Cary, Sr.

Sewell, Robert Van Vorst

Smith, Albert Delmont

Stebbins, Mary Emma Flood

Straight, Willard Dickerman

Tiffany, Louis Comfort

Tucker, Richard Derby, Sr.

Warburg, Natica Nast

Whitney, Gertrude Vanderbilt

ATTORNEYS

Abbott, Phillips

Aldrich, Sherwood

Aldrich, Winthrop Williams

Alker, Alphonse Henry

Anderson, Henry Burrall, Sr.

Anderson, Henry Hill, II

Appleby, Francis Storm

Atherton, Henry Francis, Sr.

Auchincloss, Charles Crooke

Auchincloss, Gordon, Sr.

Auchincloss, Joseph Howland, Sr.

Backus, Dana Converse

Bacon, Robert Low

Bailey, Frank, Sr.

Ball, Wilbur Laing

Ballantine, Arthur Atwood, Sr.

Bateson, Edgar Farrar, Sr.

Batterman, Henry Lewis, Sr.

Baylis, Lester Yates

Beale, Bouvier, Sr.

Beekman, James William, Sr.

Berritt, Harold

Bigelow, Ernest A.

Blagden, Linzee

Bonynge, Paul

Breed, William Constable, Sr.

Brickman, Herman

Brokaw, George Tuttle

Brokaw, Irving

Brower, Ernest Cuyler

Brower, George Ellsworth

Bryant, William Cullen

Burden, Isaiah Townsend, Sr.

Burr, Nelson Beardsley

Burrill, Middleton Schoolbred

Byrne, James

Carlisle, Floyd Leslie, Sr.

Cary, Guy Fairfax, Sr.

Casey, William Joseph, Jr.

Cavanaugh, Edward Francis, Jr.

Chadbourne, Thomas Lincoln, Jr.

Chanler, Lewis Stuyvesant, Sr.

Chanler, William Chamberlain

Clark, Grenville, Sr.

Close, Edward Bennett
  [*see* Post]

Coates, Winslow Shelby, Sr.

Cochran, William Bourke

Coffin, Charles Albert

Cohn, Milton Seymour

Corbin, Austin

Coudert, Frederic Rene, Jr.

Coudert, Frederic Rene, II

Cram, John Sergeant, Sr.

Cravath, Paul Drennan

Crocker, Frank Longfellow

Curtis, James Freeman

Cutcheon, Franklin Warner M.

Dane, Chester Linwood, Sr.

Davies, Joseph Edward
  [see Post]

Davis, John William

Davison, Frederick Trubee

Davisson, Richard L., Sr.

Dean, Arthur Hobson

de Forest, Henry Grant

de Forest, Henry Lockwood

de Forest, Henry Wheeler

de Forest, Johnston

ATTORNEYS (cont'd)

de Forest, Robert Weeks

de Milhau, Louis John de G., Sr.

Dexter, Stanley Walker

Dilworth, Dewees Wood

Dimock, Edward Jordan

Dulles, Allen Welsh

Dulles, John Foster

Dwight, Richard Everett

Dwyer, Martin, Jr.

Dykman, William Nelson

Earle, Henry Montague

Eberstadt, Ferdinand

Eden, Bronson Beecher Tuttle, Sr.

Ellis, Ralph Nicholson, Sr.

Ely, Albert Heman, Jr.

Emanuel, Victor

Emmet, Richard Stockton, Sr.

Everdell, William, Jr.

Faber, Leander B.

Fates, Harold Leighton, Sr.
  [*see* M. G. Miller]

Fish, Sidney W.

Folger, Henry Clay

Fordyce, Dorothy W. MacElree

Franklin, George Small, Sr.

Franklin, Walter Simonds, Jr.

Froessel, Charles William

Garvan, Francis Patrick, Sr.

Garver, John Anson

Gary, Elbert H.

Gavin, Michael

Gerard, James Watson, III

Gerdes, John

Geula, Rachel

Gibbs, William Francis
  [*see* Larkin]

Godwin, Parke

Goldman, Herman

Grace, Joseph Peter, Sr.

Gray, Henry Gunther

Griscom, Lloyd Carpenter

Gucker, Henry John, Sr.

Guest, Winston Frederick Churchill

Guthrie, William Dameron

Hadley, Morris

Hagen, Winston Henry, Sr.

Hall, Leonard Wood

Hammerstein, Oscar, II

Hare, Meredith

Hedges, George Brown

Henderson, Edward Cairns

Hitchcock, Thomas, Sr.

Hoffman, William Wickham

Honeyman, Robert B., Jr.

Hoppin, William Warner, Jr.

Hornblower, George Sanford

Howe, William Deering

Hoyt, Lydig

Ingalls, Fay

Ioannou, John

Iselin, Charles Oliver

Jackson, William Eldred, II

James, Henry

James, Oliver B., Sr.

Jay, DeLancey Kane

Jelke, Ferdinand, Jr.

Jennings, Frederic Beach

Jennings, Walter

Jones, Nicholas Ridgely

Jones, Rosalie Gardiner

Keating, Cletus, Sr.

Kelland, Clarence Budington

Kelley, Cornelius Francis

Kent, George Edward, Sr.

King, John Alsop, Jr.

Kingsbury, Howard Thayer, Sr.

Knowlton, Hugh Gilbert, Sr.

Kramer, Albert Ludlow, Sr.

Krim, Arthur B.

Lazo, Carlos

Ledyard, Lewis Cass, Jr.

Leffingwell, Russell Cornell

LeRoy, Robert

ATTORNEYS (cont'd)

Lindheim, Norvin R.

Lindsay, George Nelson, Sr.

Linkletter, George Onderdonk, Sr.

Littleton, Martin Wiley, Sr.

Livingston, John Holyoke

Lloyd–Smith, Wilton

Loening, Rudolph R.

Lord, Franklin Butler, II

Lord, George de Forest, Sr.

Lovett, Robert Abercrombie

Lusk, Dr. Graham

MacLaren, Archibald Waters

Manice, William de Forest, Sr.

Marsh, John Bigelow, Sr.

Martin, Bradley, Jr.

Mathers, William Harris

Matheson, John William

McCann, Charles Edward Francis

McKelvey, Charles Wylie

McVeigh, Charles Senff, Sr.

McVickar, Henry Goelet

Merle-Smith, Van Santvoord, Sr.

Mestres, Ricardo Angelo, II

Milbank, Albert Goodsell

Milburn, Devereux, Jr.

Milburn, Devereux, Sr.

Milburn, John George, Jr.

Milburn, John George, Sr.

Miller, Andrew Otterson, Jr.

Miller, Dudley Livingston, Sr.
[*see* M. G. Miller]

Miller, John Norris, Sr.

Miller, Margery Gerdes
[*later*, Twining and Fates]

Miller, Nathan Lewis

Miller, William Wilson

Mills, Ogden Livingston

Milton, David
[*see* Mauze]

Mitchell, Sidney Alexander, Sr.

Moffat, Douglas Maxwell

Mondello, Joseph

Moore, Benjamin

Morawetz, Victor

Morse, Tyler

Mortimer, Stanley, Sr.

Nast, Conde

Neff, Walter Perry

Oeland, Isaac Raymond, Sr.

Ohl, John Phillips

Osborn, Alexander Perry, Sr.

Parker, Dale M.

Parker, Valentine Fraser

Payson, Charles Shipman

Peabody, Charles Augustus, Jr.

Peabody, Julian Livingston, Jr.

Pennoyer, Paul Geddes, Sr.

Philips, William Pyle

Phipps, John Shaffer

Pierce, Winslow Shelby, II

Plimpton, Francis Taylor P., Sr.

Polk, Frank Lyon, II

Polk, Frank Lyon, Sr.

Poor, Henry Varnum, Sr.

Potter, Edwin A., Jr.

Pratt, Frederic Bayley

Pratt, Harold Irving, Jr.

Pratt, John Teele, Sr.

Preston, Ralph Julius

Price, Theodore Hazeltine, Jr.

Redmond, Roland Livingston

Reed, Lansing Parmelee

Regan, Thomas J.

Reynolds, Jackson Eli

Ricks, Jesse Jay

Robbins, Francis LeBaron, Jr.

Robinson, Thomas Linton

Roig, Harold Joseph

Roosevelt, Franklin Delano, Jr.

Rousmaniere, John E.

Ryan, Marjorie S. Langley

Samuels, John Stockwell, III

Schwartz, Bertie Grad

Schwartz, Charles

ATTORNEYS (cont'd)

Scudder, Townsend, II

Shaw, Robert Anderson

Sheehan, William Francis

Sheeline, Paul Cushing

Sloane, Charles William

Smith, Owen Telfair

Snow, George Palen

Steele, Charles

Stern, Henry Root, Sr.

Stewart, William Adams Walker, II

Stimson, Henry Lewis

Stoddard, Francis Russell, Jr.

Swan, Otis D.

Swan, William Lincoln, Sr.

Taft, Walbridge S.

Tanner, Frederick Chauncey, Sr.

Taylor, George Winship, Sr.

Taylor, Myron Charles

Thatcher, John M. P., Sr.

Thayer, Francis Kendall, Sr.

Thayer, Kendall

Thayer, Robert Helyer, Sr.

Townsend, James Mulford, II

Townsend, John Allen

Truslow, Francis Adams, Sr.

Tully, William John

Underhill, Daniel

Uterhart, Henry Ayres

Verdi, Minturn de Suzzara

Victor, Royall, Sr.

Walker, Dr. Elizabeth Harrison

Ward, Elijah

Watriss, Frederick N.

Weekes, Arthur Delano, Jr.

Weekes, John Abeel

Weldon, Samuel Alfred

Wellman, Roderic

Wetmore, Charles Whitman

Wetmore, Edmund

White, Alexander Moss, Jr.

Whitney, Charles Morse, Sr.

Whitney, William Collins

Whitney, William Payne

Winter, Keyes, Sr.

Winthrop, Beekman, II

Winthrop, Bronson

Winthrop, Egerton Leigh, Jr.

Winthrop, Grenville Lindall

Woodward, William, II

Wright, Boykin Cabell, Sr.

CAPITALISTS

Adam, John, Henry

Aldred, John Edward

Alker, Henry Alphonse, Sr.

Allen, Gabriel

Amato, Camille Jean Tuorto

Ames, Charles Edgar

Anderson, George A.

Appleby, Charles Herbert, Sr.

Appleby, John Storm

Armsby, George Newell, Sr.

Aron, Jacob

Astor, William Vincent

Auchincloss, Gordon, Sr.

Auchincloss, John

Auchincloss, Samuel Sloan, II

Austin, David F.
 [*see* Guida]

Avedon, Peter M.

Babcock, Richard Franklin

Bailey, Frank, Sr.

Baker, George Fisher, II

Baldwin, William H., Jr.

Ball, Wilbur Laing

Barney, Ashbel Hinman

Barney, Charles Tracy

Barstow, William Slocum

Baruch, Dr. Herman Benjamin

Batterman, Henry Lewis, Jr.

Batterman, Henry Lewis, Sr.

Baylis, Lester Yates

CAPITALISTS (cont'd)

Beard, William

Belding, David, Sr.

Belmont, August, II

Bergquist, John Gosta

Bigelow, Ernest A.

Billings, Cornelius Kingsley G.

Black, Harry S.

Blackton, James Stuart, Sr.

Blair, James Alonzo, Jr.

Bleecker, Theophylact Bache, Jr.

Bliss, Cornelius Newton, Jr.

Bloomingdale, Hiram Collenberger

Bodman, Herbert L., Sr.

Bono, Henry, Jr.

Booth, Henry Prosper

Brady, Nicholas Frederic

Brewster, George S.

Brightson, George Edgar

Brooks, Winthrop Holley

Brown, George McKesson

Bucknall, Henry W. J.

Bullock, George

Burchard, Anson Wood

Burden, Chester Griswold

Burr, Nelson Beardsley

Burton, Frank V., Jr.

Burton, Van Duzer, Sr.

Campbell, George W.

Carey, William Francis, Jr.

Carlisle, Floyd Leslie, Sr.

Cary, Guy Fairfax, Sr.

Casey, William Joseph, Jr.

Catacosinos, William James, Sr.

Cavanaugh, Edward Francis, Jr.

Chadbourne, Humphrey W.

Chadbourne, Thomas Lincoln, Jr.

Chadwick, Elbridge Gerry

Christie, Lansdell Kisner

Clarkson, Robert Livingston, Sr.

Clews, James Blanchard

Cochran, Drayton

Cocks, William Hall, Sr.

Coe, Henry Eugene, Jr.

Coe, William Robertson

Coe, William Rogers

Coffin, Charles Albert

Coffin, William Sloane, Sr.

Cohan, George Michael

Cohn, Milton Seymour

Conklin, Roland Ray

Cook, Walter

Corbin, Austin

Coudert, Frederic Rene, II

Crane, Clinton, Hoadley, Jr.

Crawford, Edward H.

Crocker, George

Cross, Eliot B.

Curran, Guernsey, Sr.

Dane, Chester Linwood, Sr.

Davis, Arthur Vining

Davison, Henry Pomeroy, II

Davison, Henry Pomeroy, Sr.

Dean, Arthur Hobson

DeBrabant, Marius

Deering,, William Rogers

de Forest, Henry Lockwood

de Forest, Henry Wheeler

de Forest, Johnston

de Forest, Robert Weeks

DeLamar, Joseph Raphael

Demarest, John M.

de Roulet, Vincent W.

De Selding, Hermann

de Sibour, Jacques Jean
   [*see* Fairchild]

Devendorf, George E.

Dickson, Thomas, Sr.

Dilworth, Dewees Wood

Dresselhuys, Cornelius W.
   [*see* Manville]

Duncan, William Butler

Dwyer, Martin, Jr.

Dykman, William Nelson

CAPITALISTS (cont'd)

Elbert, Robert George

Elmhirst, Leonard Knight

Emanuel, Victor

Evangelista, Louis

Farwell, Walter

Fates, Harold Leighton, Sr.
 [*see* M. G. Miller]

Ferry, E. Hayward

Fisher, Carl Graham

Fisher, Joel Ellis, II

Ford, Hannibal Choate

Forrestal, Josephine Ogden

Fowler, Dr. Robert Henry

Foy, Bryon Cecil

Francke, Luis J.

Franklin, Walter Simonds, Jr.

Freidus, Jacob

Fritz, Dr. Albert R. Sr.

Frost, Henry R.

Gair, Robert, Jr.

Garrett, Robert Michael

Garver, John Anson

Gates, Artemus Lamb

Geddes, Donald Grant, Sr.

Geddes, Eugene Maxwell, Sr.

Gelder, Irving L.

Gerard, James Watson, III

Gerdes, John

Gerlach, Robert

Gerry, Robert Livingston, Jr.

Gibson, Harvey Dow

Giordano, Salvatore, Sr.

Goodyear, Anson Conger, Sr.

Gossler, Philip Green, Sr.

Gould, Edwin

Gould, Frank Miller

Grace, David R.

Grace, Joseph Peter, II

Grace, Morgan Hatton, Sr.

Grace, William Russell, Jr.

Grace, William Russell, Sr.

Gracie, James King

Greer, Louis Morris

Greer, William Armstrong

Groesbeck, Clarence Edward

Grosvenor, Graham Bethune

Gubelmann, Walter Stanley

Gucker, Henry John, Sr.

Guest, Winston Frederick Churchill

Guggenheim, Daniel

Guggenheim, Isaac

Guggenheim, Solomon Robert

Gwynne, Arthur

Hadden, J. E. Smith

Hall, Leonard Wood

Hamersley, Louis Gordon, Sr.

Hammerstein, Oscar, II

Hammond, Paul Lyman

Hanks, Stedman Shumway

Harkness, Edward Stephen

Harriman, William Averell

Harris, Henry Upham, Sr.

Harris, Sam Henry

Heckscher, Gustav Maurice

Hedges, George Brown

Henry, Barklie McKee

Hepburn, Frederick Taylor

Hester, William Van Anden, Sr.

Hicks, Frederick Cocks

Hill, James Norman

Hoagland, Dr. Cornelius Nevius

Hodenpyl, Anton Gysberti

Holmes, Artemas

Hopkins, Arthur

Hoppin, Gerard Beekman

Horowitz, Louis Jay

Houston, Herbert Sherman

Howard, Alexandra C. Miller

Howe, William Deering

Hoyt, Colgate, Sr.

Hoyt, John R.

Ide, George Edward

Ingalls, Fay

CAPITALISTS (cont'd)

Iselin, Adrian, II

Isham, Ralph Heyward

Jadwin, Stanley Palmer

James, Henry

Jennings, Frederic Beach

Jennings, Percy Hall, Sr.

Johaneson, Nile R.

Johnston, John Herbert

Jones, Mary Elizabeth

Jones, Dr. Oliver Livingston, Sr.

Jones, Walter Restored

Kadish, Lawrence

Kahn, Otto Hermann

Kalimian, Abi

Kane, John P., Jr.

Kefalidis, Nikos

Kelley, Cornelius Francis

Kennedy, William, Sr.

Kettles, Richard C., Jr.

King, Alan

Knott, David Hurst, Sr.

Kramer, Albert Ludlow, Sr.

Kramer, Irwin Hamilton

Kramer, Terry Allen

Krim, Arthur B.

Langone, Kenneth Gerard, Sr.

L'Ecluse, Milton Albert

Leeming, Thomas Lonsdale, Sr.

Lehman, Allan Sigmund

LeRoux, Edward

LeRoy, Robert

Levitt, William Jaird, Sr.

Lindbergh, Charles Augustus, Jr.

Lindheim, Norvin R.

Lloyd–Smith, Wilton

Loeb, William, Jr.

Loew, Arthur Marcus, Sr.

Loew, Marcus

Lovett, Robert Abercrombie

Luckenbach, Edgar Frederick, Sr.

Lynch, Edmund Calvert, Sr.

Lyon, John Denniston

Mackay, Clarence Hungerford

MacKelvie, Neil Bruce

MacLaren, Archibald Waters

Manice, William de Forest

Martino, Joseph Anthony

Maxwell, Howard Washburn, Sr.

Maxwell, John Rogers, Sr.

Maynard, Walter Effingham

McCann, Charles Edward Francis

McNair, William

Melius, Gary

Merle–Smith, Van Santvoord, Sr.

Meyer, Cord, II

Meyer, George C., Sr.

Meyer, J. Edward, Sr.

Meyer, Robert J.

Milburn, John George, Sr.

Miller, Dudley Livingston, Sr.
   [*see* M. G. Miller]

Miller, Roswell, Jr.

Miller, William Wilson

Mitchell, Sidney Alexander, Sr.

Mitchell, Sidney Zollicoffer

Moen, A. Rene

Moore, Benjamin

Moore, Edward Small, Sr.

Moore, William Talman, Jr.

Moore, William Talman, Sr.

Morgan, Edwin Denison, III

Munsey, Frank Andrew

Murdock, Harvey

Murray, Hugh A.

Nast, Conde

Neelands, Thomas D., Jr.

Nichols, Acosta, Sr.

Nichols, George, Sr.

Nichols, John White Treadwell

Norton, Helen Lambert

Noyes, David Chester, Sr.

Oakman, Walter George, Sr.

O'Rourke, Innis, Sr.

CAPITALISTS (cont'd)

O'Rourke, John Francis Sr.

Osborn, Alexander Perry, Sr.

Page, Arthur Wilson, II

Paley, William S.

Palmer, Carlton Humphreys

Park, William Gray

Parker, Dale M.

Parker, Robert Meade, Sr.

Patchin, Robert Halsey

Payson, Charles Shipman

Payson, Joan Whitney

Peabody, Charles Augustus, Jr.

Pell, Theodore Roosevelt

Philips, William Pyle

Phillips, Ellis Laurimore, Sr.

Phipps, Henry Carnegie

Phipps, Howard, Sr.

Phipps, John Shaffer

Pickett, John Olen, Jr.

Pierce, Winslow Shelby, II

Pirie, Samuel Carson, Sr.

Polk, Frank Lyon, Sr.

Polsinelli, Vincent

Porter, Seton

Potter, Clarkson

Potter, Edwin A., Jr.

Potter, William Chapman

Powell, Frances Edward, Jr.

Pratt, Charles Millard

Pratt, Frederic Bayley

Pratt, George du Pont, Sr.

Pratt, Harold Irving, Sr.

Pratt, John Teele, Jr.

Price, Theodore Hazeltine, Jr.

Prime, William Albert, Sr.

Pyne, Percy Rivington, II

Queen, Emmet

Redmond, Roland Livingston

Reed, Lansing Parmelee

Regan, Thomas J.

Rentschler, Gordon Sohn

Reynolds, Jackson Eli

Rickert, Edward J.

Ripley, Julien Ashton, Sr.

Ripley, Paul Morton

Rogers, Henry Alexander

Roig, Harold Joseph

Roosevelt, George Emlen, Sr.

Roosevelt, John Kean

Roosevelt, Julian Kean

Roosevelt, Kermit, Sr.

Roosevelt, Philip James, Sr.

Roosevelt, Quentin, II

Roosevelt, Theodore, Jr.

Roosevelt, William Emlen

Rose, Reginald Perry

Ryan, John Carlos

Ryan, John Dennis

Saltzman, Arnold Asa

Sanderson, Henry

Schenck, Nicholas Michael

Schieren, George Arthur, Sr.

Schiff, John Mortimer

Schiff, Mortimer L.

Schuler, Robert
  [*see* Munsel]

Schwartz, Alexander Charles, Sr.

Schwartz, Charles

Shaw, Samuel T., Sr.

Shea, Edward Lane

Sheehan, William Francis

Sheeline, Paul Cushing

Sherman, Charles Austin, Sr.

Shutt, Edwin Holmes, Jr.

Smith, Albert Edward, Sr.

Smith, Albert Lawrence, Sr.

Smith, Ormond Gerald

Smithers, Francis S.

Sparrow, Edward Wheeler

Sperry, Edward G.

Spiegel, Jerry

Stafford, Jennie K.

Stafford, Robert

CAPITALISTS (cont'd)

Stam, Alan

Stanley–Brown, Joseph

Steele, Charles

Steers, James Rich, II

Stettinius, Edward Reilly, Jr.

Stewart, Cecil Parker

Stillman, Irwin

Stralem, Donald Sigmund

Straus, Edward Kuhn

Straus, Jack Isidor

Strauss, Albert

Swan, William Lincoln, Sr.

Talbott, Harold Elster, II

Taliaferro, Eugene Sinclair

Tanner, Frederick Chauncey, Sr.

Taylor, Henry Stillman

Taylor, James Blackstone, Sr.

Taylor, Myron Charles

Thomas, Joseph Albert

Thurman, Steven

Tinker, Edward Richmond, Jr.

Trimble, Richard, Sr.

Uris, Percy

Vanderbilt, William Kissam, Jr.

Vanderbilt, William Kissam, Sr.
  [*see* Belmont]

Van Iderstine, William P. M.

Van Ingen, Lawrence Bell, Sr.

Van Rensselaer, Charles A., Sr.

Van Wart, Edwin Clark

Van Wart, Henry

Victor, Royall, Sr.

Von Stade, Francis Skiddy, Sr.

Walbridge, Henry D.

Walker, Elisha, Sr.

Wang, Charles B.

Watson, John Jay, Jr.

Webb, William Seward D., Jr.

Weir, Levi Candee

Welch, Charles, James

Welldon, Samuel Alfred

Wellington, Herbert Galbraith, Sr.

Wetmore, Charles Whitman

Whalen, Grover A., Sr.

Whitney, Cornelius Vanderbilt

Whitney, George, Sr.

Whitney, Harry Payne

Whitney, John Hay

Whitney, William Collins

Whitney, William Payne

Willard, George L.

Williams, Arthur

Williams, Harrison

Williams, Timothy Shaler

Winslow, Edward

Winthrop, Beekman, II

Winthrop, Egerton Leigh, Jr.

Winthrop, Henry Rogers

Winthrop, Robert Dudley

Wood, Willis Delano

Woolworth, Frank Winfield

Wright, Boykin Cabell, Sr.

Wylie, Herbert George

CLERGY

Ely, Samuel Rose, Sr.

Salvage, Theodore Fiske

Shipman, Herbert

Thomas, Norman Mattoon

COMPOSERS

Burnett, Vivian

Cohan, George Michael

Damrosch, Dr. Walter Johannes

Hammerstein, Oscar, II

Lennon, John
  [*see* Ono]

Sousa, John Philip, Sr.

DIPLOMATS

Albright, Dr. Madeleine J. Korbel

Aldrich, Winthrop Williams

Armstrong, Hamilton Fish

Auchincloss, Gordon, Sr.

Bacon, Robert

Baker, Raymond Thomas
  [*see* Emerson]

Balsan, Louis Jacques

Baruch, Dr. Herman Benjamin

Bonner, Paul Hyde, Sr.

Brokaw, Clare Boothe
  [*later*, Luce]

Bruce, David Kirkpatrick Este

Bryce, Lloyd Stephens

Burden, Chester, Griswold

Carver, Clifford Nickels

Collado, Dr. Emilio Gabriel, II

Costantini, Count David A.

Cravath, Paul Drennan

Davies, Joseph Edward
  [*see* Post]

Davis, John William

Dean, Arthur Hobson

de Roulet, Vincent W.

DeSuarez, Diego
  aka Diego Suarez
  [*see* Field]

Dresselhuys, Cornelius W.
  [*see* Manville]

Dulles, Allen Welsh

Dulles, John Foster

Emmet, Richard Stockton, Sr.

Emory, William Helmsley, Jr.

Gerard, James Watson, III

Griscom, Lloyd Carpenter

Guggenheim, Harry Frank

Hanks, Stedman Shumway

Harriman, Pamela Digby Churchill

Harriman, William Averell

Hoffman, Albert L., Sr.

Hoffman, William Wickham

Hoyt, Lydig

Kerrigan, Joseph J.

Lindsay, Sir Ronald

Lyon, Cecil T. F. B.

Merle–Smith, Van Santvoord, Sr.

Mitchell, Sidney Alexander, Sr.

Moffat, Douglas Maxwell

Mooney, James David, II

Nitze, Paul Henry

Nixon, Lewis

Pennoyer, Paul Geddes, Sr.

Plimpton, Francis Taylor P., Sr.

Polk, Frank Lyon, Sr.

Robinson, Monroe Douglas

Roosevelt, Archibald Bulloch, Jr.

Saltzman, Arnold Asa

Smith, Earl Edward Tailer, Sr.

Stettinius, Edward Reilly, Jr.

Stewart, Glenn

Stimson, Henry Lewis

Straight, Willard Dickerman

Strauss, Albert

Taylor, Myron Charles

Thayer, Robert Helyer, Sr.

Truslow, Francis Adams, Sr.

Whitney, John Hay

Willys, John North

Winthrop, Beekman, II

Woodward, William, II

EDUCATORS

Albright, Dr. Madeleine J. Korbel

Alden, Bradley Ripley

Alsop, Dr. Reese Fell

Babbott, Dr. Frank Lusk, Jr.

Carey, Ocean K. Daily

Davenport, Gertrude Crotty

Davis, John William

Dean, Mary Talbott Marden

de Roulet, Megan E. Maguire

Dieffenbach, William

Elmhirst, Dorothy Payne Whitney

Elmhirst, Leonard Knight

EDUCATORS (cont'd)

Ferguson, Dr. Farquhar, Sr.

Froessel, Charles William

Gates, Charles Otis

Gerdes, John

Gerry, Dr. Roger Goodman

Goodrich, Donald Wells, Sr.

Guida, Dr. Peter Matthew

Hines, Ephram

Hoguet, Dr. Joseph Peter, Sr.

Holmes, Dr. Christian R.

Humphreys, Dr. Alexander C.

Langone, Kenneth Gerard, Sr.

Lockman, Myron Augustus

Lusk, Dr. Graham

Miller, Roswell, Jr.

Neilson, Raymond Perry R., Sr.

Netter, Dr. Frank H.

O'Rourke, John Francis, Sr.

Palmer, Antoinette Johnson

Pell, John Howland Gibbs

Person, Dr. E. Cooper, Jr.
  [*see* Tippet]

Phillips, Kathryn F. Sisson

Pool, Dr. Eugene Hillhouse

Pulling, Thomas John Edward

Roig, Harold Joseph

Roosevelt, Frances B. Webb

Ryan, Marjorie S. Langley

Scott, Donald, Sr.

Sloane, Charles Byron

Smith, Owen Telfair

Swann, Dr. Arthur Wharton

Townsend, James Mulford, II

Vaughan, Dr. Harold Stearns

Vietor, Dr. John Adolf, Sr.

von Bothmer, Dr. Dietrich Felix

ENTERTAINERS AND

ASSOCIATED PROFESSIONS

Armsby, Colette Touzeau

Baehr, Irvine E. Theodore
  aka Robert Allen

Belmont, Eleanor Robson

Blackton, James Stuart, Sr.

Brigham, Constance

Cantor, Eddie

Cantor, Ida Tobias

Cohan, Agnes Nolan

Cohan, George Michael

Cravath, Agnes Huntington

Craven, Frank

Craven, Mary Blyth

Damrosch, Dr. Walter Johannes

Dane, Eunice Howard

de Rippeteau, Evangeline Russell
  aka Evangeline Russell
  [*see* Blackton]

Falkenburg, Jinx
  [*see* McCrary]

Foy, Virginia Peine

Gould, Margarete Fosheim

Gould, Clarence
  [*see* Manville]

Gould, Viola Clemmons

Guest, Lucy Cochrane
  aka ."Cee Zee"; *later*, C. Z. Guest

Hammerstein, Dorothy Blanchard

Harris, Alice Nolan

Hearst, Millicent Wilson

Heckscher, Eleanor Bennett

Heckscher, Luella Gear

Hilburn, Paula
  aka Paula Dean
  [*see* Blackton]

Hitchcock, Flora Zabelle

Hitchcock, Raymond

Hopkins, Arthur

Hoyt, Julia Wainwright Robbins

King, Alan

Langley, Jane Pickens

Lennon, John
  [*see* Ono]

ENTERTAINERS AND
ASSOCIATED PROFESSIONS (cont'd)

Livermore, Harriet Metz

Loew, Barbara Smith

Mackay, Anna Case

Marston, Florence S. Carr

McCrary, John ("Tex") Reagan, Jr.

Merrill, Dina
  aka Nedenia Hutton Rumbough

Miller, Nanette C. Campbell

Munsel, Patrice

Ono, Yoko

Parker, Harry Doel

Parker, Lottie Blair

Petrova, Mme. Olga

Physioc, Jessica Eskridge

Physioc, Joseph Allen, Sr.

Provost, Marietta Bailey

Riggs, Glenn E., Sr.

Rothschild, Jeanne Stuart de

Rumbough, Nedenia Hutton
  aka Dina Merrill

Ryan, Byford

Schiff, Josephine L. Laimbeer

Schuler, Robert
  [see Munsel]

Sinclair, Elizabeth Farrell

Smith, Florence Pritchett

Sousa, John Philip, Sr.

Townesend, Dr. Stephen
  [see Burnett]

Vanderbilt, Jean Harvey

Verdi, Thelma Given

Vertes, Marcel Emmanuel

Warburg, Gerald Felix

Whitney, Eleanor Searle

Whitney, Marie Louise Schroeder

Willoughby, Louis
  [see Petrova]

Woodward, Angeline L. Crowell
  aka Ann Eden Crowell Woodward

FINANCIERS

Aldrich, Sherwood

Aldrich, Winthrop Williams

Alexandre, J. Henry, Jr.

Alker, Carroll Booth

Alker, Edward Paul

Alker, Henry Alphonse, Sr.

Allen, Frederic Winthrop

Ames, Amyas

Ames, Charles Edgar

Anderson, George A.

Anderson, Harry B., Jr.

Anderson, John

Armsby, George Newell, Sr.

Arnold, William H.

Aron, Jacob

Auchincloss, Charles Crooke

Auchincloss, Gordon, Sr.

Auchincloss, John

Auchincloss, Joseph Howland, Sr.

Babbott, Frank Lusk, Sr.

Babcock, Henry Dennison, Sr.

Babcock, Richard Franklin

Babcock, Woodward

Bacon, Elliot
  [see Gardner]

Bacon, Robert

Bacon, Robert Low

Bailey, Frank, Sr.

Bailey, Townsend Fleet

Baker, George Fisher, II

Baker, George Fisher, III

Baker, John C., Sr.

Baker, Raymond Thomas
  [see Emerson]

Ball, Wilbur Laing

Ballantine, Arthur Atwood, Sr.

Barnes, Courtlandt Dixon, Sr.

Barnes, E. Mortimer

Barney, Charles Tracy

Bartow, Francis Dwight, Sr.

Baruch, Dr. Herman Benjamin

FINANCIERS (cont'd)

Batterman, Henry Lewis, Sr.

Battershall, Frederic S.

Baylis, Lester Yates

Bell, James Christy, Jr.

Belmont, August, II

Belmont, Oliver Hazard Perry

Benkard, Henry Horton

Bermingham, John F.

Bertschmann, Louis Frederick

Betts, Wyllis Rossiter, Jr.

Bingham, Harry Payne, Sr.

Black, Harry S.

Blackwell, Charles Addison

Blagden, Linzee

Blair, James Alonzo, Jr.

Blair, James Alonzo, Sr.

Blair, Watson Keep

Blair, Wolcott

Bleecker, Charles Moore

Bleecker, Theophylact Bache, II

Bliss, Cornelius Newton, Jr.

Boardman, Kenneth

Bodman, Herbert L., Sr.

Bonner, Douglas Griswold, Sr.

Booth, Henry Prosper

Bostwick, Albert C., II

Bostwick, George Herbert, Sr.

Bourne, George Galt

Bowdoin, George Temple

Boyer, Philip, Sr.

Brewster, George S.

Briggs, Mead L.

Brokaw, Clifford Vail, Jr.

Brokaw, Clifford Vail, Sr.

Brokaw, Howard Crosby

Brooks, Joseph W.

Brown, Francis Gordon, Sr.

Brown, Stephen Howland

Bryan, James Taylor, Sr.

Bucknall, G. Stafford

Burden, Arthur Scott

Burden, James Abercrombie, Jr.

Burton, Frank V., Jr.

Busby, Leonard J.

Caesar, Charles Unger

Caldwell, Robert J.

Carhart, Harold W., Sr.

Carlisle, Floyd Leslie, Sr.

Cary, Guy Fairfax, Sr.

Casey, William Joseph, Jr.

Ceballos, Juan Manuel, Jr.

Chadwick, Elbridge Gerry

Chanler, Lewis Stuyvesant, Jr.

Cheney, Ward

Chew, Philip Frederick

Chubb, Percy, Sr.

Clark, Bruce

Clark, James Averell, Sr.

Clark, Louis Crawford, II

Clarkson, Robert Livingston, Sr.

Clews, James Blanchard

Clowes, John Henry, Sr.

Coates, Winslow Shelby, Sr.

Coe, Henry Eugene, Jr.

Coe, William Robertson

Coe, William Rogers

Coleman, Gregory

Collado, Dr. Emilio Gabriel, II

Conklin, Roland Ray

Connfelt, Charles Maitland

Corbin, Austin

Coudert, Frederic Rene, II

Cowl, Clarkson

Crary, Miner Dunham, Sr.

Cravath, Erastus Milo, II

Crawford, Edward H.

Crisp, Van Devanter

Crocker, George

Cross, Eliot B.

Crossman, William H.

Curran, Guernsey, Sr.

Curtis, James Freeman

Cushing, Harry Cooke, III

FINANCIERS (cont'd)

Cushing, Leonard Jarvis, Sr.

Cushman, Paul, Sr.

Daniel, Robert Williams

Davey, William Nelson

Davis, Arthur Vining

Davison, Frederic Trubee

Davison, Henry Pomeroy, II

Davison, Henry Pomeroy, Sr.

Dean, Arthur Hobson

Dean, Herbert Hollingshead

Deans, Robert Barr, Sr.

de Forest, Henry Lockwood

de Forest, Henry Wheeler

de Forest, Johnston

DeLamar, Joseph Raphael

de Roulet, Vincent W.

Devendorf, George E.

Dewing, Hiram E.

Dick, Fairman Rogers

Dickerman, Bradley Watson, Sr.

Dickinson, Hunt Tilford, Sr.

Dickson, Thomas, Sr.

Dillon, Herbert Lowell, Sr.

Dilworth, Dewees Wood

D'Oench, Russell Grace, Sr.

Douglas, James Gordon, II
  [see Boegner]

Dows, David, Jr.

Draper, Charles Dana

Dresselhuys, Cornelius W.
  [see Manville]

Duer, Beverly

Duncan, William Butler

Dunscombe, Duncan

du Pont, Alfred Irenee

du Pont, Jessie Ball

Dyer, George Rathbone, Sr.

Dykman, William Nelson

Eberstadt, Ferdinand

Elbert, Robert George

Eldredge, Edward Irving, Jr.

Eldridge, Roswell

Emanuel, Victor

Fairchild, Julian Percy, Sr.

Fairchild, William Samuel

Fates, Harold Leighton, Sr.
  [see M. G. Miller]

Ferry, E. Hayward

Fish, Edwin A.

Flagg, W. Allston, Sr.

Fleischmann, Max C.

Flinsch, Rudolf E. F.

Ford, Hannibal Choate

Ford, Nevil

Forrestal, James Vincent

Frank, Charles Augustus, Sr.

Franklin, Philip Albright Small, Jr.

Franklin Walter Simonds, Jr.

Fraser, Alfred Valentine

Frick, Childs

Fritz, Dr. Albert R., Sr.

Gales, George M.

Gallic, Charles J.

Gardner, Paul Edgerton

Garver, John Anson

Gates. Artemus Lamb

Gavin, Michael

Geddes, Donald Grant, Sr.

Geddes, Eugene Maxwell, Sr.

Gerry, Henry Averell, Sr.

Gibb, Arthur

Gibson, Harvey Dow

Godfrey, Henry Fletcher, Sr.

Goodyear, Anson Conger, Sr.

Gossler, Philip Green, Sr.

Gould, Aubrey Van Wyck, Sr.

Gould, Edwin

Gould, Howard

Grace, David R.

Grace, Joseph Peter, II

Grace, Oliver Russell

Grace, William Russell, Sr.

Grant, Robert, Jr.

FINANCIERS (cont'd)

Gray, Albert Zebriskie

Greer, Louis Morris

Greer, William Armstrong

Guggenheim, Daniel

Guggenheim, Isaac

Gwynne, Arthur

Hadden, Hamilton, Sr.

Haggerson, Frederic H.

Hall, Leonard Wood

Halsey, Richard Townley Haines

Hamersley, Louis Gordon, Sr.

Hammond, Paul Lyman

Handy, Parker Douglas

Harjes, Henry Herman

Harriman, Herbert Melville

Harriman, Joseph Wright

Harriman, William Averell

Harris, Henry Upham, Jr.

Harris, Henry Upham, Sr.

Havemeyer, Charles Frederick, Jr.

Hedges, Benjamin Van Doren, II

Henry, Barklie McKee

Hepburn, Frederick Taylor

Hepburn, George

Hepburn, Leonard F.

Herzog, Edwin H.

Hester, William Van Anden, Sr.

Hewlett, Walter Jones

Hickox, Charles V.

Hicks, Frederick Cocks

Hill, James Norman

Hine, Francis Lyman

Hirsch, Peter

Hitchcock, Thomas, Jr.

Hoagland, Dr. Cornelius Nevius

Hodenpyl, Anton Gysberti

Hoffman, William Wickham

Hoffstot, Frank Norton

Hoguet, Dr. Joseph Peter, Sr.

Holloway, William Grace, Sr.

Holmes, Duncan Argyle

Hopkins, Erustis Langdon

Hoppin, Gerard Beekman

Howard, George H., III

Howe, Richard Flint

Howe, William Deering

Hoyt, Colgate, Jr.

Hoyt, Colgate, Sr.

Hubbs, Charles Francis

Hudson, Charles I., Sr.

Hudson, Hans Kierstede, Sr.

Hudson, Percy Kierstede

Hunter, Malcolm Du Bois

Huntington, Robert Dinsmore, Jr.

Hutton, Edward Francis

Hutton, William E., II

Ide, George Edward

Iglehart, David Stewart

Ihasz, Nicholas

Ingalls, Fay

Iselin, Charles Oliver

Isham, Ralph Heyward

Jadwin, Stanley Palmer

James, Henry

Jay, DeLancey Kane

Jelke, Ferdinand, Jr.

Jennings, Benjamin Brewster

Jennings, Frederic Beach

Jennings, Percy Hall, Sr.

Jennings, Walter

Johnson, Seymour

Johnston, Douglas Turner

Johnston, John Herbert

Jonas, Nathan Solomon

Jones, Walter Restored

Kahn, Otto Hermann

Keating, Cletus, Sr.

Kellogg, Morris Woodruff

Kennedy, William Walker

Kerr, Elmore Coe, Sr.

Kerrigan, Joseph J.

Ketcham, Francis

Kilthau, Raymond F.

FINANCIERS (cont'd)

Knowlton, Hugh Gilbert, Sr.

Kramer, Albert Ludlow, Sr.

Kramer, Irwin Hamilton

Kung, Hsiang-hsi

Ladew, Edward R.

Laidlaw, Harriet Wright Burton

Laidlaw, James Lees

Lamont, Thomas Stilwell

Langley, William Clark

Langone, Kenneth Gerard, Sr.

Lanier, James Franklin Doughty

Lawrence, Effingham, II

Ledyard, Lewis Cass, Jr.

Leeming, Thomas Lonsdale, Sr.

Leffingwell, Russell Cornell

Lehman, Allan Sigmund

Leonard, Charles Reginald, Sr.

Leonard, Edgar Welch

LeRoy, Robert

Lindsay, George Nelson, Sr.

Livermore, Jesse Lauriston, Sr.

Livermore, Philip Walter

Livingston, Gerald Moncrieffe

Lloyd–Smith, Wilton

Loeb, William, Jr.

Loew, William Goadby

Lord, George de Forest, Sr.

Lovett, Robert Abercrombie

Lowe, Henry Wheeler

Luckenbach, Edgar Frederick, Jr.

Lynch, Edmund Calvert, Jr.

Lynch, Edmund Calvert, Sr.

Lyon, Cecil T. F. B.

Lyon, Frederick Gorham Clark

Lyon, John Denniston

MacDonald, Ranald Hugh, Jr.

MacDonald, Swift Ian

MacKelvie, Neil Bruce

Mann, Samuel Vernon, Sr.

Martin, Alastair Bradley

Martin, Bradley, Jr.

Martin, Esmond Bradley, Sr.

Martin, Grinnell

Martin, Henry Bradley, II

Martino, Joseph Anthony

Matheson, William John

Mauze, Jean

Maxwell, Eugene Lascelles, Sr.

Maxwell, George Thebaud

Maxwell, Howard Washburn, Sr.

Maxwell, John Rogers, Sr.

May, Herbert Arthur
  [*see* Post]

Maynard, Walter Effingham

McClintock, Harvey Childs, Jr.

McClure, Walter C.

McCullum, Leonard Franklin, Sr.
  [*see* E. S. Whitney]

McIntosh, Allan J.

McKay, Robert Gordon

McLane, Allan, Jr.

McVeigh, Charles Senff, Sr.

McVickar, Donald

Merle-Smith, Van Santvoord, Sr.

Merrill, Charles Edward, Jr.

Merrill, Joseph L.

Mestres, Ricardo Angelo, II

Meyer, Cord, II

Meyer, George C., Sr.

Meyer, J. Edward, Sr.

Milbank, Albert Goodsell

Milburn, John George, Sr.

Mills, Ogden Livingston

Mitchell, Sidney Alexander, Sr.

Mitchell, Sidney Zollicoffer

Moen, LeClanche

Moffett, George Monroe, Sr.

Moore, Edward Small, Sr.

Moore, John Chandler

Moore, William Talman, Jr.

Moore, William Talman, Sr.

Morgan, Edwin Denison, III

Morgan, Edwin Denison, IV

FINANCIERS (cont'd)

Morgan, Henry Sturgis, Sr.

Morgan, John Pierpont, Jr.

Morgan, Junius Spencer

Morell, Joseph B.

Morris, Ray, Sr.

Murray, Hugh A.

Murray, John Francis

Myers, Theodore Walter

Neelands, Thomas D., Jr.

Neff, Walter Perry

Nicastro, Louis Joseph

Nicholas, Harry Ingersoll, II

Nichols, Acosta, Sr.

Nitze, Paul Henry

Niven, John Ballantine

Norton, Huntington

Noyes, David Chester, Sr.

Oakman, Walter George, Sr.

O'Donohue, Charles A.

O'Hara, Thomas H.

O'Neill, George Dorr, Sr.

O'Neill, Grover, Sr.

Osborn, Alexander Perry, Sr.

Ottley, Gilbert

Ottley, James Henry, Sr.

Outerbridge, Samuel Roosevelt

Page, Walter Hines, II

Paley, William S.

Park, Darragh Anderson, Sr.

Park, William Gray

Parker, Dale M.

Parker, John Alley

Peabody, Charles Augustus, Jr.

Peck, Thomas Bloodgood, II

Pell, Clarence Cecil, Jr.

Pell, Clarence Cecil, Sr.

Pell, Howland Haggerty, Sr.

Pell, John Howland Gibbs

Perine, William DeNyse Nichols

Peters, William Richmond

Phelps, Ansel

Philips, William Pyle

Phillips, Ellis Laurimore, Sr.

Phipps, Howard, Jr.

Phipps, John Shaffer

Phipps, Ogden

Pierce, Winslow Shelby, II

Pirie, Samuel Carson, Sr.

Plimpton, Francis Taylor P., Sr.

Polk, Frank Lyon, Sr.

Polsinelli, Vincent

Pomeroy, Daniel Eleazer

Porter, William Henry

Postley, Sterling

Potter, Clarkson

Potter, Edward Clarkson, Sr.

Potter, Edwin A., Jr.

Potter, William Chapman

Pratt, Charles Millard

Pratt, Frederic Bayley

Pratt, Frederic Richardson

Pratt, George du Pont, Sr.

Pratt, Harold Irving, Jr.

Pratt, Harold Irving, Sr.

Pratt, Herbert Lee, Jr.

Pratt, Herbert Lee, Sr.

Pratt, John Teele, Jr.

Pratt, John Teele, Sr.

Pratt, Richardson, Sr.

Pratt, Theodore, Sr.

Preston, William Payne T., Sr.

Price, Theodore Hazeltine, Jr.

Prime, William Albert, Sr.

Provost, Cornelius W.

Pruyn, Robert Dunbar

Pryibil, Paul

Pulsifer, George Hale

Pyne, Percy Rivington, II

Randall, Darley, Jr.

Raquet, Walter

Reeve–Merritt, Edward

Remington, Franklin

Rentschler, Gordon Sohn

FINANCIERS (cont'd)

Reynolds, Jackson Eli

Reynolds, Richard Samuel, Sr.

Richards, Frederick L.

Richards, Ira, Jr.

Richmond, L. Martin

Rinaldini, Luis Emilio

Robertson, Charles Sammis

Robertson, Julian Hart, Jr.

Robinson, George Hazard

Robinson, Thomas Linton

Roesler, Edward, Jr.

Roesler, Edward, Sr.

Roesler, Walter, Sr.

Roig, Harold Joseph

Roosevelt, Archibald Bulloch, Jr.

Roosevelt, Archibald Bulloch, Sr.

Roosevelt, George Emlen, Sr.

Roosevelt, James Alfred

Roosevelt, John Kean

Roosevelt, Julian Kean

Roosevelt, Philip James, Jr.

Roosevelt, Philip James, Sr.

Roosevelt, Theodore

Roosevelt, William Emlen

Rose, George, Jr.

Rose, Reginald Perry

Rosenberg, Lee

Rossiter, Arthur Wickes, Sr.

Rothschild, Baron Eugene de

Rothschild, Baron Robert de

Roulston, Thomas Henry, Sr.

Rousmaniere, James Ayer

Rousmaniere, John E.

Rumbough, Nedenia Hutton
   aka Dina Merrill

Rumbough, Stanley Maddox, Jr.

Runyon, Clarkson, Jr.

Rusch, Henry Arthur, Sr.

Russell, Faris R.

Ryan, John Dennis

Ryle, Arthur, Sr.

Samuels, John Stockwell, III

Sanderson, Henry

Schenck, Nicholas Michael

Schermerhorn, Alfred Coster

Schiff, John Mortimer

Schiff, Mortimer L.

Schmidlapp, Carl Jacob, Sr.

Schultze, Max H.

Schwab, Hermann C., II

Schwartz, Alexander Charles, Sr.

Seligman, Joseph Lionel, Sr.

Sheeline, Paul Cushing

Shephard, Rutherford Mead

Shonnard, Horatio Seymour, Sr.

Shutt, Edwin Holmes, Jr.

Simpson, Robert H.

Slade, John, Sr.

Slade, Prescott
   [*see* J. B. R. Slade]

Sloane, George

Smith, Albert Lawrence, Sr.

Smith, Earl Edward Tailer, Sr.

Smith, Herbert Ludlam, Sr.

Smith, Howard Caswell, Sr.

Smithers, Christopher Dunkin, Sr.

Smithers, Francis S.

Smithers, Robert Brinkley

Smull, Jacob Barstow

Snow, George Palen

Sparrow, Edward Wheeler

Sperry, Edward G.

Stanley–Brown, Joseph

Steele, Charles

Sterling, Duncan, Jr.

Stettinius, Edward Reilly, Jr.

Stettinius, Edward Reilly, Sr.

Stevens, Byam K., Jr.

Stevens, Joseph Sampson

Stewart, John Henry Jones

Stewart, William Adams Walker, II

Stone, Charles Augustus, Sr.

Stow, William L.

FINANCIERS (cont'd)

Straight, Willard Dickerman

Stralem, Donald Sigmund

Straus, Jack Isidor

Strauss, Albert

Streeter, Edward, Sr.

Swan, Otis D.

Taft, Walbridge S.

Taft, William Howard, II

Tailer, Thomas Suffern, Sr.

Taylor, Bertrand LeRoy, Jr.

Taylor Edwin Pemberton, Jr.

Taylor, Henry Calhoun

Taylor, James Blackstone, Sr.

Tenney, Daniel Gleason, Sr.

Thieriot, Charles Henschel, II

Thieriot, Charles Henschel, Sr.

Thomas, Joseph Albert

Tiffany, Charles Lewis, II

Tilney, Frederick, Jr.

Tinker, Edward Richmond, Jr.

Tinker, Giles Knight

Tod, Robert Elliot

Toerge, Norman K., Sr.

Tower, Roderick

Townsend, Edward Mitchell II

Trimble, Richard, II

Trowbridge, Edmund Quincy

Truslow, Francis Adams, Sr.

Van Alen, James Henry

Vanderveer, Stephen Lott

Van Ingen, Lawrence Bell, Sr.

Van Strum, Kenneth Stevens

Vermilye, H. Rowland, Sr.

Walker, Elisha, Sr.

Walker, James Blaine, Jr.

Warner, Bradford Arnold, Sr.

Warner, Henry Wolcott

Watson, John Jay, Jr.

Webb, James Watson, Sr.

Webb, William Seward D., Jr.

Weekes, Arthur Delano, Jr.

Weekes, Harold H.

Weidenfeld, Camille

Weir, Levi Candee

Weld, Francis Minot, II

Welldon, Samuel Alfred

Wellington, Herbert Galbraith, Sr.

White, Alexander Moss, Jr.

White, Alexander Moss, Sr.

White, Leonard Dalton, Jr.

White, Leonard Dalton, Sr.

Whitehouse, James Norman

Whitney, Edward Farley

Whitney, George, Sr.

Whitney, Harry Payne

Whitney, Howard Frederic, II

Whitney, John Hay

Whitney, Robert Bacon, Sr.

Whitney, William Payne

Widener, George Dunstan, Jr.

Willets, William Prentice

Williams, Arthur

Williams, Rodney W.

Willis, Harold Satterlee

Winmill, Robert Campbell

Winslow, Edward

Winthrop, Beekman, II

Winthrop, Bronson

Winthrop, Henry Rogers

Winthrop, Robert, II

Winthrop, Robert Dudley

Wood, Chalmers, Jr.

Wood, Willis Delano

Woods, Ward Wilson, Jr.

Woodward, William, Jr.

Woodward, William, II

Woolworth, Frank Winfield

Work, Bertram G., Sr.

Wyckoff, Richard Demille

Young, Edward Lewis

Young, Otto S.

FIRST LADIES

Chiang Kai-shek, Mme.

Roosevelt, Edith Kermit Carow

INDUSTRIALISTS

Abbott, Paul, Sr.

Adams, Horatio M.

Aldrich, Sherwood

Alexander, Harry

Alker, Alphonse Henry

Alker, Edward Paul

Alker, James Ward, Sr.

Allen, Frederic Winthrop

Allen, Gabriel

Amato, Camille Jean Tuorto

Anderson, George A.

Anderson, John

Appleton, Benjamin Ward

Armsby, George Newell, Sr.

Atherton, Henry Francis, Sr.

Atwater, John Jacob, Sr.

Auchincloss, Charles Crooke

Auchincloss, Gordon, Sr.

Auchincloss, Samuel Sloan, II

Babbott, Frank Lusk, Sr.

Babcock, Frederick Huntington

Babcock, Richard Franklin

Bailey, Frank, Sr.

Baker, George Fisher, II

Baker, Raymond Thomas
  [*see* Emerson]

Ball, Wilbur Laing

Ballantine, John Herbert

Balsan, Louis Jacques

Bancroft, John Jr.

Baruch, Dr. Herman Benjamin

Battershall, Frederic S.

Beach, William Nicholas

Bedford, Alfred Clarke, Sr.

Bedford, Alfred Cotton

Bermingham, John F.

Bevin, Leander Augustus

Biddle, William Canby, II

Billings, Cornelius Kingsley G.

Bishop, Richard E.

Blackstone, Henry

Bliss, Cornelius Newton, Jr.

Bonner, Paul Hyde, Sr.

Booth, Henry Prosper

Bourne, George Galt

Breed, William Constable, Sr.

Brewster, George S.

Bucknall, Henry W. J.

Bullock, George

Burchard, Anson Wood

Burden, Arthur Scott

Burden, Isaiah Townsend, Sr.

Burden, James Abercrombie, Jr.

Burden, James Abercrombie, III

Burr, Nelson Beardsley

Busby, Leonard J.

Caldwell, Robert J.

Carey, William Francis, Jr.

Carlisle, Floyd Leslie, Sr.

Carter, Oliver Goldsmith, Sr.

Carver, Amos Dow

Carver, Clifford Nickels

Cary, Guy Fairfax, Sr.

Castro, Bernard, Sr.

Castro, Theresa Barabas

Catacosinos, William James, Sr.

Cavanaugh, Edward Francis, Jr.

Ceballos, Juan Manuel, Jr.

Chadbourne, Thomas Lincoln, Jr.

Chalkley, Otway Hebron

Chapin, C. Merrill, Jr.

Cheney, Ward

Christie, Lansdell Kisner

Chrysler, Walter Percy, Sr.

Chubb, Percy, Sr.

Church, Charles Thomas, Sr.

Church, Richard N. L.

Clark, Frederick Ambrose

INDUSTRIALISTS (cont'd)

Clark, John Balfour

Clarke, Jeremiah, Sr.

Clarkson, Robert Livingston, Sr.

Clews, James Blanchard

Cochran, Drayton

Coe, Henry Eugene, Jr.

Coffin, Charles Albert

Coffin, William Sloane, Sr.

Cohn, Milton Seymour

Colgate, Gilbert, II

Colgate, John Kirtland, Sr.

Collado, Dr. Emilio Gabriel, II

Conklin, Roland Ray

Cooper, Kenneth F.

Corbin, Austin

Cournand, Edouard L.

Cournand, Rita

Cozzens, Issachar, III

Crane, Clinton Hoadley, Jr.

Crawford, Edward H.

Crisp, Van Devanter

Cushing, Harry Cooke, III

Cutting, Dr. Fulton

Davis, Arthur Vining

Davis, Joseph Edward, Sr.

Davison, Henry Pomeroy, II

Davison, Henry Pomeroy, Sr.

de Forest, Henry Lockwood

de Forest, Johnston

de Forest, Robert Weeks

DeLamar, Joseph Raphael

DeLamater, Cornelius Henry

de Seversky, Alexander Prokofieff

Dickinson, Hunt Tilford, Sr.

Dickson, Thomas, Sr.

Diebold, Albert Henry

Dodge, Lillian Sefton Thomas

Donnell, Harry Ellingwood

Donnell, William Ballon

Doubleday, George Chester

Dows, David

Duncan, William Butler

du Pont, Alfred Irenee

du Pont, Jessie D. Ball

Duryea, Harry H.

Duryea, Hendrick Vanderbilt

Dwight, Arthur Smith

Eagle, Henry, Sr.

Elbert, Robert George

Ellis, Reuben Morris

Emanuel, Victor

Entenmann, William, Jr.

Evangelista, Louis

Fahnestock, Archer Pleasant

Fahys, George Ernest, Sr.

Fairchild, Sherman M.

Fates, Harold Leighton, Sr.
  [*see* M. G. Miller]

Ferry, E. Hayward

Fisher, Joel Ellis, II.

Fleischmann, Max C.

Fleischmann, Raoul Herbert

Folger, Henry Clay

Ford, Hannibal Choate

Foy, Bryon Cecil

Gair, Robert, Jr.

Gales, George M.

Gary, Elbert H.

Gates, Artemus Lamb

Gates, Charles Otis

Geddes, Donald Grant, Sr.

Gerdes, John

Gibson, Harvey Dow

Gilder, Rodman, Sr.

Giordano, Salvatore

Goldman, Herman

Goodyear, Anson Conger, Sr.

Gould, Edwin

Grace, Joseph Peter, II

Grace, Oliver Russell

Grace, William Russell, Jr.

Graham, Raymond Austin, Sr.

Graves, Robert, II

INDUSTRIALISTS (cont'd)

Gray, Henry Gunther

Griswold, Frank Gray

Grosvenor, Graham Bethune

Grumman, Leroy Randle

Guggenheim, Daniel

Guggenheim, Harry Frank

Guggenheim, Isaac

Guggenheim, Solomon Robert

Guggenheim, William, Sr.

Guida, Bernadette Castro

Haar, Herbert

Hadley, John Wood Blodgett

Hagedorn, Horace

Hagen, Winston Henry, II

Haggerson, Frederic H.

Hall, Leonard Wood

Hamersley, Louis Gordon, Sr.

Handy, Parker Douglas

Harkness, William Lamon

Harris, Henry Upham, Sr.

Havemeyer, Frederick Christian, IV

Havemeyer, Horace, Jr.

Havemeyer, Theodore Augustus, II

Hawkey, Harold W., Sr.

Heckscher, August

Henderson, Frank C.

Henry, Barklie McKee

Hepburn, Frederick Taylor

Hine, Francis Lyman

Hoagland, Dr. Cornelius Nevius

Hodenpyl, Anton Gysberti

Hoffstot, Frank Norton

Howe, Richard Flint

Howe, William Deering

Hoyt, Colgate, Jr.

Hoyt, Colgate, Sr.

Hubbs, Charles Francis

Hunter, Fenley

Hutton, Edward Francis

Iglehart, David Stewart

Ingersoll, Robert Hawley

Jadwin, Stanley Palmer

Jandorf, Louis C.

Jennings, Benjamin Brewster

Jennings, Frederic Beach

Jennings, Percy Hall, Sr.

Jennings, Walter

Johnston, Douglas Turner

Johnston, John Herbert

Jones, Charles Hewlett

Jones, Walter Restored

Kane, John P., Jr.

Kane, John Patrick

Keating, Cletus, Sr.

Kefalidis, Nikos

Kelley, Cornelius Francis

Kellogg, Morris Woodruff

Kienle, Eugene S.

Kountze, deLancey

Krim, Arthur B.

Ladew, Edward R.

Ladew, Louise Berry Wall

Lamont, Thomas Stilwell

Langley, William Clark

Langone, Kenneth Gerard, Sr.

Latham, Leroy

Laughlin, Alexander, II
 [*see* Hitchcock]

Le Boutillier, Thomas, II

Ledyard, Lewis Cass, Jr.

Leeds, Warner Mifflin, II

Leeming, Thomas Lonsdale, Sr.

Lehman, Allan Sigmund

Leonard, Edgar Welch

Lewyt, Alexander Milton

Lloyd, Robert MacAllister, Sr.

Lloyd–Smith, Wilton

Loeb, William, Jr.

Loening, Grover

Lord, William Galey

Lyon, Frederick Gorham Clark

Lyon, John Denniston

Mackay, Clarence Hungerford

INDUSTRIALISTS (cont'd)

MacKelvie, Neil Bruce

MacLaren, Archibald Waters

Mahana, George Shaw

Manice, William de Forest, Sr.

Mann, Samuel Vernon, Jr.

Martin, Henry Clifford

Martin, James E., Sr.

Martino, Joseph Anthony

Mathers, William Harris

Matheson, William John

Maxwell, Howard Washburn, Jr.

Maxwell, Howard Washburn, Sr.

Maxwell, John Rogers, Jr.

Maxwell, John Rogers, Sr.

May, Herbert Arthur
  [*see* Post]

McCulllum, Leonard Franklin, Sr.
  [*see* E. S. Whitney]

McVickar, Elinor Guthrie

Merrill, Joseph L.

Meyer, Cord, II

Middlemark, Marvin P.

Milbank, Albert Goodsell

Miller, Andrew Otterson, Jr.

Miller, Dudley Livingston, Sr.
  [*see* M. G. Miller]

Miller, William Wilson

Mills, Ogden Livingston

Minton, Henry Miller

Moen, A. Rene

Moffett, George Monroe, Sr.

Mooney, James David, II

Moore, Edward Small, Sr.

Morgan, Henry Sturgis, Sr.

Morgan, John Pierpont, Jr.

Morgan, Junius Spencer

Morris, Ray, Sr.

Morse, Daniel Parmelee, Sr.

Mott, Jordan Lawrence, III

Murray, Hugh A.

Murray, John Francis

Neelands, Thomas D., Jr.

Nicastro, Louis Joseph

Nichols, Acosta, Sr.

Nichols, William Henry, Jr.

Nixon, Lewis

Norris, James King

Oakman, Walter George, Sr.

Oberlin, Abraham

Oeland, Isaac Raymond, Sr.

Olds, George Daniel, Jr.

O'Rourke, Innis, Sr.

Osborn, Alexander Perry, Sr.

Outerbridge, Samuel Roosevelt

Page, Arthur Wilson, II

Page, Frank C. Bauman

Page, Walter Hines, II

Paley, William S.

Palmer, Carlton Humphreys

Park, William Gray

Parker, Robert Meade, Sr.

Perin, Charles Page

Peters, William Richmond

Pettinos, Charles E.

Philips, William Pyle

Phipps, Henry, Jr.

Phipps, John Shaffer

Phipps, Ogden

Pierce, Winslow Shelby, Jr.

Polsinelli, Vincent

Pomeroy, Daniel Eleazer

Porter, Seton

Post, Marjorie Merriweather

Potter, Clarkson

Potter, William Chapman

Powell, Francis Edward, Jr.

Powell, John

Pratt, Charles Millard

Pratt, Frederic Richardson

Pratt, Harold Irving, Sr.

Pratt, Herbert Lee, Sr.

Pratt, John Teele, Jr.

Prime, William Albert, Sr.

Queen, Emmet

INDUSTRIALISTS (cont'd)

Rathborne, Joseph Cornelius, II

Reed, Lansing Parmelee

Remington, Franklin

Rentschler, Gordon Sohn

Reynolds, Jackson Eli

Reynolds, Richard Samuel, Sr.

Richter, Horace

Ricks, Jesse Jay

Ripley, Paul Morton

Robertson, Josephine Vance T.

Robinson, George Hazard

Robinson, John Randolph

Robinson, Thomas Linton

Roig, Harold Joseph

Roosevelt, Philip James, Sr.

Rousmaniere, John E.

Rumbough, Nedenia M. Hutton
  aka Dina Merrill

Rumbough, Stanley Maddox, Jr.

Russell, Faris R.

Ryan, John Dennis

Ryle, Arthur, Sr.

Sage, Henry William, II

Saltzman, Arnold Asa

Salvage, Sir Samuel Agar

Samuels, John Stockwell, III

Schieren, George Arthur, Sr.

Schiff, John Mortimer

Schiff, Mortimer L.

Schmidlapp, Carl Jacob, Sr.

Schniewind, Henry, Jr.

Scott, Rufus W.

Senff, Charles H.

Shaffer, Judson Bell
  [*see* Kennedy]

Shea, Edward Lane

Shutt, Edwin Holmes, Jr.

Sinclair, Harry Ford, Sr.

Slater, Horatio Nelson, III

Sloan, Alfred Pritchard, Jr.

Smith, Albert Lawrence, Sr.

Smith, Earl Edward Tailer, Sr.

Smith, Howard Caswell, Sr.

Smithers, Christopher Dunkin, Sr.

Sobelman, Max

Sonneborn, Rudolf Goldschmid
  [*see* Schiff]

Sperry, Edward G.

Spreckels, Claus August

Stearns, John Noble, II

Stearns, John Noble, III

Steele, Charles

Stehli, Emil J.

Stettinius, Edward Reilly, Jr.

Stettinius, Edward Reilly, Sr.

Stevenson, Malcolm, Sr.

Stewart, Cecil Parker

Stewart, John K.

Stone, Charles Augustus, Sr.

Stralem, Donald Sigmund

Straus, Jack Isidor

Strauss, Albert

Talbott, Harold Elster, II

Tangeman, George Patterson

Taylor, Henry Stillman

Taylor, James Blackstone, Jr.

Taylor, James Blackstone, Sr.

Taylor, Myron Charles

Tenney, Daniel Gleason, Sr.

Thatcher, John M. P., Sr.

Thomas, Joseph Albert

Thomas, Vincent Benjamin
  [*see* Dodge]

Thompson, William Payne, Jr.

Tiffany, Louis Comfort

Tiffany, Perry

Townsend, Howard Rockwell, Sr.

Trimble, Richard, Sr.

Twining, Edmund S., Jr.
  [*see* M. G. Miller]

Vander Poel, William Halsted

Van Iderstine, Charles Abner

Van Iderstine, Peter, Jr.

Van Iderstine, William P. M.

INDUSTRIALISTS (cont'd)

Van Ingen, Lawrence Bell, Jr.

Victor, Royall, Sr.

Vivaudou, Victor

Vultaggio, Donald

Walker, Elisha, Sr.

Wang. Charles

Warner, Bradford Arnold, Sr.

Watson, John Jay, Jr.

Weiss, William Erhard, Jr.

Weld, Francis Minot, II

Welldon, Samuel Alfred

Wellington, Herbert Galbraith, Sr.

Wetmore, Charles Whitman

Whalen, Grover A., Sr.

Wheeler, Frederick Seymour

White, Alexander Moss, Jr.

White, Frederick Wheeler

Whitney, Cornelius Vanderbilt

Whitney, George, Sr.

Whitney, Harry Payne

Whitney, Howard, Frederic, II

Whitney, William Collins

Whitney, William Payne

Widener, George Dunstan, Jr.

Will, Harold Henry

Willetts, William Prentice

Willock, William W., Sr.

Willys, John North

Winslow, Edward

Winters, Albert C.

Winthrop, Robert, II

Wood, Willis Delano

Woodside, Joel David

Woodward, William, Jr.

Woodward, William, II

Woolley, Daniel P.

Work, Bertram G., Sr.

Wright, Boykin Cabell, Sr.

Wright, Wilkinson de Forest, Sr.

Wylie, Herbert George

Young, Edward Lewis

Zens, Dr. Frederick Anton

Zinsser, William Herman, Jr.

INTELLIGENCE AGENTS

Auchincloss, Gordon, Sr.

Brown, Francis Gordon, Sr.

Bruce, David Kirkpatrick Este

Casey, William Joseph, Jr.

Davison, Frederick Trubee

Dulles, Allen Welsh

O'Donnell, Charles Oliver
[*see* Douglas]

Polk, Frank Lyon, Sr.

Roosevelt, Archibald Bulloch, Jr.

Roosevelt, Frances

Roosevelt, Quentin, II

INTERIOR DESIGNERS

Boyer, Josephine Bond Flagg

Cardelli, Jacqueline Stewart

Coe, Clover Simonton

Cudlipp, Chandler, Sr.

Hammerstein, Dorothy Blanchard

Hitchcock, Flora Zabelle

Lehman, Ellen

Tiffany, Louis Comfort

Winters, Albert C.

Wood, Ruby R. Pope

INVENTORS

Alexander, Harry

Allen, Gabriel

Barstow, William Slocum

Bergquist, John Gosta

Bonney, Leonard Warden

Castro, Bernard, Sr.

Clapham, Thomas

Cochran, Drayton

Cutting, Dr. Fulton

INVENTORS (cont'd)

du Pont, Alfred Irenee

Dwight, Arthur Smith

Fahnestock, Archer Pleasant

Fahnestock, Frank Curry

Fairchild, Sherman M.

Felix, Numa J.

Ford, Hannibal Choate

Grosvenor, Graham Bethune

Grumman, Leroy Randle

Hammond, Paul Lyman

Hanks, Stedman Shumway

Lewyt, Alexander Milton

Lindbergh, Charles Augustus, Jr.

Lloyd, Robert MacAllister, Sr.

Loening, Grover

Middlemark, Marvin P.

Morgan, William F.

Murray, John Francis

Newton, Richard T.
  [*see* Chase]

Pierce, Winslow Shelby, Jr.

Reynolds, Richard Samuel, Sr.

Riggs, George

Smith, Albert Edward, Sr.

Sperry, Edward G.

Winters, Albert C.

Zenz, Dr. Frederick Anton

JOURNALISTS

Albright, Joseph Medill Patterson

Aldao, Camillo
  [*see* Manville]

Armstrong, Hamilton Fish

Backus, Louise Burton Laidlaw

Belmont, Alva Erskine Smith

Breasted, Charles

Brokaw, Clare Boothe
  [*later*, Luce]

Brooks, Joseph W., Jr.

Chase, Edna Woolman

Davenport, Dr. Charles B., Sr.

Doubleday, Neltje Blanchan D.

Du Bois, Eugene

Fahnestock, Archer Pleasant

Falkenburg, Jinx
  [*see* McCrary]

Farwell, Mildred Williams

Forrestal, Josephine Ogden

Gilder, Rodman, Sr.

Godwin, Harold

Godwin, Parke

Guest, Lucy Cochrane

Hall, Gladys Dowsey

Harriman, Pamela Digby Churchill

Hitchcock, Thomas, Sr.

Houston, Carmen Torres Calderon

Ingalls, Fay

Kelland, Clarence Budington

Kingsbury, Alice Cary Bussing

Krim, Arthur B.

Martin, John Stuart

Mason, Julian Starkweather

McCrary, John ("Tex") Reagan, Jr.

McVickar, Elinor Guthrie

Mixsell, Dr. Harold Ruckman

Morley, Christopher D., Sr.

Paley, Barbara Cushing

Palmer, Winthrop Bushnell

Patchin, Robert Halsey

Payson, Virginia Kraft

Robinson, Monroe Douglas

Roosevelt, Selwa Carman Showker

Roulston, Marjorie Hillis

Schuster, Max Lincoln

Sears, Joseph Hamblen

Smith, Florence Pritchett

Snow, Carmel White

Straight, Willard Dickerman

Swope, Herbert Bayard, Sr.

Taft, William Howard, II

Thomas, Norman Mattoon

Tower, Whitney, Sr.

Van Alen, Candace B. Alig

JOURNALISTS (cont'd)

Van Santvoord, Alexander, Sr.

Van Santvoord, Wilma Wells L.

Wetmore, Elizabeth Bisland

Williams, Timothy Shaler

Wyckoff, Cecelia Gertrude Shere

LANDSCAPE ARCHITECTS

DeSuarez, Diego
aka Diego Suarez
[*see* Field]

Duryea, Minga Pope
[*later*, Patchin]

Ladew, Harvey Smith, II

Levison, John Jacob

Levison, Rae B. Haskell
[*later*, Schuster]

Lindsay, Lady Elizabeth Sherman

Nicholas, Dorothy Snow

Underhill, Francis T.

MERCHANTS

Andersen, Dr. Harold Willids, Sr.

Atwater, John Jacob, Sr.

Baruch, Dr. Herman Benjamin

Bast, W. C.

Batterman, Henry Lewis, Sr.

Belding, David, Sr.

Bendel, Henri

Biddle, William Canby, II

Bliss, Cornelius Newton, Jr.

Bloomingdale, Hiram Collenberger

Bloomingdale, Irving Ingersoll

Bogart, Adrian, T., Jr.

Brewster, Samuel Dwight

Brightson, George Edgar

Brokaw, Clifford Vail, Sr.

Brokaw, Howard Crosby

Brooks, Winthrop Holley

Busby, Leonard J.

Bush, Donald Fairfax, Sr.

Castro, Bernard, Sr.

Castro, Theresa Barabas

Coffin, William Sloane, Sr.

Colgate, John Kirtland, Jr.

Connfelt, Charles Maitland

Cowl, Clarkson

Cowl, Donald Hearn

Cudlipp, Chandler, Sr.

Davison, Henry Pomeroy, II

Dole, Edward E.

Eldredge, Edward Irving, Jr.

Evangelista, Louis

Farwell, Walter

Foy, Bryon Cecil

Fraser, Alfred

Fraser, Alfred Valentine

Gales, George M.

Gates, Artemus Lamb

Geula, Kiumarz

Gibb, Arthur

Gibb, Florence Althea Swan

Gibb, Walter

Gould, Charles Albert

Gross, John J.

Guest, Lucy Cochrane

Guida, Bernadette Castro

Harriman, Marie Norton

Hess, Harry Bellas

Hicks, Henry

Horowitz, Louis Jay

Howard, Alexandra C. Miller

Hunter, Malcolm Du Bois

Jones, Walter Restored

Kane, John P., Jr.

Kress, Claude Washington

Langone, Kenneth Gerard, Sr.

Lunning, Frederick

Lutz, Frederick L.

Merrill, Joseph L.

Mertz, Harold E.

Mertz, LuEsther Turner

Moore, John Chandler

MERCHANTS (cont'd)

Moore, Louis de Bebian

Morrell, Joseph B.

Munsey, Frank Andrew

Peck, Fremont Carson, Sr.

Pirie, Samuel Carson, Sr.

Polsinelli, Maria Serrano

Polsinelli, Vincent

Potter, Edwin A., Jr.

Roosevelt, Franklin Delano, Jr.

Roulston, Thomas Henry, Sr.

Rouss, Peter Winchester

Schiff, John Mortimer

Sizer, Robert Ryland, Sr.

Stern, Benjamin

Straus, Jack Isidor

Tangeman, Cornelius Hoagland

Taylor, Henry Calhoun

Tiffany, Charles Lewis, II

Tiffany, Louis Comfort

Townsend, Edward Mitchell II

Townsend, Edward Mitchell, Sr.

Toy, Thomas Dallam, Sr.

Wellington, Herbert Galbraith, Sr.

Whalen, Grover A. Sr.

Wilson, Charles Porter

Woolworth, Frank Winfield

Young, Thomas F

MILITARY

Bigelow, Anson Alexander

Davison, Frederick Trubee

Dugmore, Cyril

Dyer, George Rathbone, Sr.

Emory, William Helmsley, Jr.

Fremont, John Charles, II
   [*see* Shipman]

Goodyear, Anson Conger, Sr.

Hoffman, Albert L., Sr.

Hoffman, William Wickham

Huntington, Robert Dinsmore, Sr.

Jones, William

Merle–Smith, Van Santvoord, Sr.

O'Donnell, Charles Oliver
   [*see* Douglas]

Roosevelt, Theodore, Jr.

Ward, Aaron

NAVAL ARCHITECTS

Canfield, Augustus Cass

Cardelli, Count Giovanni Guido C.

Clapham, Thomas

Cox, Irving E.

Crane, Clinton Hoadley, Jr.

Gibbs, William Francis
   [*see* Larkin]

Nixon, Lewis

PHYSICIANS

Alsop, Dr. Reese Fell

Andersen, Dr. Harold Willids, Sr.

Andersen, Dr. Shirley R. P.

Astin, Dr. Sherrill
   [*see* H. D. Gibson]

Ayer, Dr. James Cook

Babbott, Dr. Frank Lusk, Jr.

Baruch, Dr. Herman Benjamin

Burlingham, Dr. Robert

Burnett, Dr. Swan Moses

Collins, Dr. Burnet Charles

Cox, Dr. Gerard Hutchison, Sr.

Derby, Dr. Richard

Duryea, Dr. Garrette DeNyse

Eden, Dr. John H., Sr.

Ferguson, Dr. Farquhar, Sr.

Fiske, Dr. E. Rodney

Flint, Dr. Austin, Jr.

Fowler, Dr. Robert Henry

Fritz, Dr. Albert R., Sr.

Gerry, Dr. Roger Goodman

Guida, Dr. Peter Matthew

Hawkes, Dr. Forbes

PHYSICIANS (cont'd)

Hill, Dr. Miner C.

Hoguet, Dr. Joseph Peter, Sr.

Holmes, Dr. Christian R.

Howell, Dr. John Taylor, Jr.

Hughes, Dr. Wendell

James, Dr. Walter Belknap

Jones, Dr. Oliver Livingston, Sr.

Mann, Dr. John, Sr.

McKim, Dr. Smith Hollins
  [*see* Emerson]

Mixsell, Dr. Harold Ruckman

Montana, Dr. Christopher

Mott, Dr. Valentine

Muncie, Dr. Curtis Hamilton

Muncie, Dr. Edward Henry

Muncie, Dr. Elizabeth Hamilton

Netter, Dr. Frank H.

Pardee, Dr. Irving Hotchkiss
  [*see* Mauze]

Person, Dr. E. Cooper, Jr.
  [*see* Tippet]

Pierson, Dr. Richard Norris, Sr.

Piquet, Dr. Samuel D.

Pool, Dr. Eugene Hillhouse

Potter, Dr. Gilbert

Roosevelt, Dr. James West
  [*see* Laura d'Oremieulx Roosevelt]

Sanesi, Dr. Lorenzo

Satterlee, Dr. Henry Suydam, Sr.

Satterwhite, Dr. Preston Pope

Schreiber, Dr. George, Jr.

Stahle, Dr. Helen R.
  [*see* Blackton]

Sterling, Dr. G.

Stewart, Dr. John Dillon
  [*see* Petrova]

Swann, Dr. Arthur Wharton

Tilney, Dr. Frederick, Sr.

Townesend, Dr. Stephen
  [*see* Burnett]

Truesdell, Dr. Edward Delavan

Tuttle, Dr. Jason H.

Twohig, Dr. Daniel

Vaughan, Dr. Harold Stearns

Vietor, Dr. John Adolf, Sr.

POLITICIANS

Auchincloss, Gordon, Sr.

Bacon, Robert Low

Beekman, James William, Sr.

Belmont, Oliver Hazard Perry

Breed, William Constable, Sr.

Brokaw, Clare Boothe
  [*later*, Luce]

Brown, Milton D.

Bruce, David Kirkpatrick Este

Bryce, Cornelia

Bryce, Lloyd Stephens

Carey, William Francis, Jr.

Casey, William Joseph, Jr.

Cavanaugh, Edward Francis, Jr.

Chadbourne, Thomas Lincoln, Jr.

Chanler, Lewis Stuyvesant, Sr.

Chiang Kai-Shek, Mme.

Christie, Lansdell Kisner

Clark, John

Cochran, William Bourke

Coudert, Frederic Rene, Jr.

Cram, John Sergeant, Sr.

Cutcheon, Franklin Warner M.

Daniel, Robert Williams

Davies, Joseph Edward
  [*see* Post]

Davis, John William

Davis, Joseph Edward, Sr.

Davison, Frederick Trubee

DeLamar, Joseph Raphael

de Roulet, Vincent W.

Dill, Clarence C.
  [*see* R. G. Jones]

Dulles, John Foster

Dyer, George Rathbone, Sr.

Dykman, William Nelson

Gary, Elbert H.

Gerard, James Watson, III

POLITICIANS (cont'd)

Gerdes, John

Godwin, Parke

Goodyear, Anson Conger, Sr.

Grace, William Russell, Sr.

Guest, Frederick E.

Guida, Bernadette Castro

Hall, Leonard Wood

Harriman, Pamela Digby Churchill

Harriman, William Averell

Hicks, Frederick Cocks

Kelland, Clarence Budington

King, John Alsop, Jr.

Knott, David Hurst, Sr.

Krim, Arthur B.

Littleton, Martin Wiley, Sr.

Loeb, William, Jr.

Martino, Joseph Anthony

Meyer, Cord, II

Miller, Nathan Lewis

Mills, Ogden Livingston

Mondello, Joseph

Murray, John Francis

Myers, Theodore Walter

Nickerson, Hoffman

Nixon, Lewis

Norton, Helen Lambert

Polk, Frank Lyon, Sr.

Pomeroy, Daniel Eleazer

Pratt, Ruth Sears Baker

Roosevelt, Franklin Delano, Jr.

Roosevelt, Theodore

Roosevelt, Theodore, Jr.

Rousmaniere, John E.

Scudder, Townsend, II

Sheehan, William Francis

Smith, Earl Edward Tailer, Sr.

Smith, Owen Telfair

Stanley–Brown, Joseph

Stern, Henry Root, Sr.

Stoddard, Francis Russell, Jr.

Talbott, Harold Elster, II

Tanner, Frederick Chauncey, Sr.

Thomas, Norman Mattoon

Tod, Robert Elliot

Tully, William John

Underhill, Francis T.

Underhill, Samuel Jackson

Walker, Dr. Elizabeth Harrison

Ward, Elijah

Watson, John Jay, Jr.

Weekes, John Abeel

Whalen, Grover A., Sr.

Winter, Keyes, Sr.

Woolley, Daniel P.

PUBLIC RELATIONS EXECUTIVES

Du Bois, Eugene

Lee, Ivy Ledbetter, Sr.

McCrary, John Reagan, Jr.

Vanderbilt, Jeanne L. Murray

PUBLISHERS

Abbott, Paul, Sr.

Annenberg, Moses Louis

Babcock, Frederick Huntington

Backer, George
  [*see* Schiff]

Backus, Dana Converse

Barnes, Courtlandt Dixon, Sr.

Baylis, Lester Yates

Belmont, Oliver Hazard Perry

Bryant, William Cullen

Bryce, Lloyd Stephens

Carter, George

Cooper, Cyrus

Dana, Charles Anderson

Davis, Hartley Courtland

DeGraff, Robert Fair

Dickinson, Hunt Tilford, Sr.

Doubleday, Frank Nelson

Doubleday, Nelson, Sr.

PUBLISHERS (cont'd)

Doubleday, Russell

du Pont, Alfred Irenee

Everitt, Samuel Alexander

Field, Marshall, III

Fleischmann, Raoul Herbert

Gates, Artemus Lamb

Godwin, Harold

Godwin, Parke

Griscom, Lloyd Carpenter

Guggenheim, Alicia Patterson

Guggenheim, Harry Frank

Guinzburg, Harold Kleinert

Hearst, William Randolph

Henry, Barklie McKee

Hitchcock, Thomas, Sr.

Holmes, Artemas

Houston, Herbert Sherman

Inness–Brown, Hugh Alwyn, Sr.

Lippincott, William

Maynard, Walter Effingham

McCann, David A.

Mertz, LuEsther Turner

Miller, John R., III

Mills, Ogden Livingston

Moore, Edward Small, Sr.

Moore, William Talman, Jr.

Morley, Christopher D., Sr.

Munsey, Frank Andrew

Nast, Conde

Ottley, James Henry, Sr.

Page, Arthur Wilson, II

Paley, William S.

Patterson, Alicia
  [*see* Guggenheim]

Peck, Fremont Carson, Sr.

Pell, John Howland Gibbs

Poor, Henry Varnum, Sr.

Powell, John

Pratt, John Teele, Sr.

Pulitzer, Ralph, Sr.

Pulsifer, Harold Trowbridge

Ridder, Eric, Sr.

Roosevelt, Theodore, Jr.

Rumsey, Mary Harriman

Schiff, Dorothy

Schuster, Max Lincoln

Schuster, Rae B. Haskell

Scott, Donald, Sr.

Sears, Joseph Hamblen

Smith, George Campbell, Sr.

Smith, Howard Caswell, Sr.

Smith, Ormond Gerald

Stewart, Cecil Parker

Straight, Dorothy Payne Whitney

Straight, Willard Dickerman

Sutton, Keith

Thackrey, Theodore O.
  [*see* Schiff]

Van Alen, James Henry

Vanderbilt, Alfred Gwynne, II

Vernam, Clarence Cottier

Walker, Dr. Elizabeth Harrison

Whitney, Howard Frederic, II

Whitney, John Hay

Wright, Boykin Cabell, Sr.

Wyckoff, Cecelia Gertrude Shere

Wyckoff, Richard Demille

Wyckoff, Walter

RESTAURATEURS

Derby, Dr. Richard

Langone, Kenneth Gerard, Sr.

Lundy, Frederick William Irving

Melius, Gary

Robinson, Monroe Douglas

Roosevelt, Archibald Bulloch, Sr.

Roosevelt, Kermit, Sr.

Roosevelt, Philip James, Sr.

Roosevelt, Theodore, Jr.

Sherry, Louis

Smith, Owen Telfair

SCIENTISTS

Blakeslee, Dr. Albert Francis
Davenport, Dr. Charles B., Sr.
Davenport, Gertrude Crotty
Frick, Childs
Krim, Dr. Mathilde Galland
Lusk, Dr. Graham
Vanderbilt, William Kissam, Jr.
Weld, Julia de Forest Tiffany

SHIPPING

Alker, Carroll Booth
Atwater, John Jacob, Sr.
Bacon, Daniel
Booth, Henry Prosper
Carver, Amos Dow
Carver, Clifford Nickels
Dickinson, Hunt Tilford, Sr.
D'Oench, Russell Grace, Sr.
Eldridge, Lewis Angevine, Sr.
Eldridge, Roswell
Franklin, Philip Albright Small, Sr.
Gibson, Harvey Dow
Goldman, Herman
Grace, Joseph Peter, II
Grace, Joseph Peter, Sr.
Grace, Oliver Russell
Grace, William Russell, Jr.
Grace, William Russell, Sr.
Holloway, William Grace, Sr.
Hull, Kenneth Duryea, Sr.
Iglehart, David Stewart
Jones, John Divine
Jones, Walter Restored
Keating, Cletus, Sr.
Luckenbach, Edgar Frederick, Jr.
Luckenbach, Edgar Frederick, Sr.
Luckenbach, John Lewis
Luckenbach, Lewis, II
Luckenbach, Lewis V., Sr.
Lyon, John Denniston

MacLaren, Archibald Water
Merrill, Bradford, Jr.
Moore, William Talman, Jr.
Moore, William Talman, Sr.
Morris, Ray, Sr.
Munson, Carlos W.
Norton, Skeffington Sanxay, Jr.
Norton, Skeffington Sanxay, Sr.
Noyes, Winchester
Oelsner, Edward Carl William, Sr.
Oelsner, Warren James
Outerbridge, Samuel Roosevelt
Patchin, Robert Halsey
Peters, William Richmond
Phipps, John Shaffer
Ripley, Paul Morton
Roig, Harold Joseph
Roosevelt, Kermit, Sr.
Shearman, Lawrence Hobart
Smull, Jacob Barstow
Sparks, Sir Thomas Ashley
Stewart, Cecil Parker
Walker, Elisha, Sr.
Ward, Edward Mortimer, Sr.
Weir, Levi Candee
Winmill, Robert Campbell

STATESMEN

Albright, Dr. Madeleine J. Korbel
Bacon, Robert
Ballantine, Arthur Atwood, Sr.
Bruce, David Kirkpatrick Este
Casey, William Joseph, Jr.
Chiang, Kai-shek
Collado, Dr. Emilio Gabriel, II
Curtis, James Freeman
Cutcheon, Franklin Warner M.
Dana, Charles Anderson
Davies, Joseph Edward
  [*see* Post]
Davison, Frederick Trubee

STATESMEN (cont'd)

Dulles, John Foster

Forrestal, James Vincent

Gates, Artemus Lamb

Guest, Frederick E.

Harriman, William Averell

Kung, Hsiang-hsi

Leffingwell, Russell Cornell

Lovett, Robert Abercrombie

Merle–Smith, Van Santvoord, Sr.

Mills, Ogden Livingston

Nitze, Paul Henry

Pennoyer, Paul Geddes, Sr.

Polk, Frank Lyon, Sr.

Roosevelt, Franklin Delano, Jr.

Roosevelt, Theodore

Roosevelt, Theodore, Jr.

Rumbough, Stanley Maddox, Jr.

Ryan, John Dennis

Stettinius, Edward Reilly, Jr.

Stettinius, Edward Reilly, Sr.

Stimson, Henry Lewis

Straight, Willard Dickerman

Talbott, Harold Elster, II

Thayer, Robert Helyer, Sr.

Weiss, William Erhard, Jr.

Whitney, Cornelius Vanderbilt

Whitney, William Collins

Winthrop, Beekman, II

WRITERS

Albright, Joseph Medill Patterson

Albright, Dr. Madeleine J. Korbel

Allilueva, Svetlana Iosifovna

Alsop, Dr. Reese Fell

Ames, Evelyn I. Perkins

Ames, Charles Edgar

Armstrong, Carman Barnes

Armstrong, Hamilton Fish

Babbott, Frank Lusk, Sr.

Babcock, Elizabeth Steenrod T.

Backus, Louise Burton Laidlaw

Bailey, Frank, Sr.

Ballantine, Arthur Atwood, Sr.

Baruch, Dr. Herman Benjamin

Beach, William Nicholas

Belmont, Alva Erskine Smith

Belmont, Eleanor Robson

Blackton, James Stuart, Sr.

Bloomingdale, Hiram Collenberger

Boegner, Margaret Helen Phipps

Bonner, Paul Hyde, Sr.

Bottomley, William Lawrence

Boyer, Josephine Bond Flagg

Breasted, Charles

Brokaw, Clare Boothe
  [*later*, Luce]

Brokaw, Irving

Brooks, Joseph W., Jr.

Bryant, William Cullen

Bryce, Lloyd Stephens

Burnett, Constance Clough Buell

Burnett, Frances Hodgson

Burnett, Vivian

Caldwell, Robert J.

Carr, Edward A. T.

Carr, Kari-Ann R. Young

Carver, Clifford Nickels

Casey, William Joseph, Jr.

Chase, Edna Woolman

Chiang Kai-shek, Mme.

Clark, Grenville, Sr.

Coudert, Frederic Rene, II

Crane, Clinton Hoadley, Jr.

Craven, Frank

Cushing, Harry Cooke, III

Dana, Charles Anderson

Davenport, Dr. Charles B. Sr.

Davenport, Gertrude Crotty

Davison, Dorothy Peabody

Dean, Arthur Hobson

de Forest, Julia Mary

de Milhau, Louis John de G., Sr.

WRITERS (cont'd)

DeSuarez, Diego
  aka Diego Suarez
  [*see* Field]

Doubleday, Neltje B. DeGraff

Doubleday, Russell

Dulles, Allen Welsh

Dulles, John Foster

du Pont, Bessie Gardner

Duryea, Minga Pope
  [*later,* Patchin]

Eberstadt, Ferdinand

Elbert, Robert George

Flint, Dr. Austin, Jr.

Fordyce, Dorothy W. MacElree

Fowler, Dr. Robert Henry

Fox, Fontaine Talbot, Jr.

Frick, Childs

Gerard, James Watson, III

Gerdes, John

Gerry, Dr. Roger Goodman

Gilder, Rodman, Sr.

Godwin, Harold

Godwin, Parke

Goodwin, Philip Lippincott

Goodyear, Anson Conger, Sr.

Griscom, Lloyd Carpenter

Griswold, Frank Gray

Guest, Lucy Cochrane

Guggenheim, Harry Frank

Guggenheim, William, Sr.

Guthrie, William Dameron

Hadley, Morris

Hall, Gladys Dowsey

Halsey, Elizabeth Tower

Halsey, Richard Townley Haines

Hanks, Stedman Shumway

Harriman, William Averell

Herzog, Margaret Guion Ramsey

Hicks, Henry

Hitchcock, Thomas, Sr.

Hopkins, Arthur

Houston, Herbert Sherman

Humpreys, Dr. Alexander Crombie

Ingalls, Fay

James, Henry

Jones, Rosalie Gardiner

Keene, Foxhall Parker

Kelland, Clarence Budington

King, Alan

Kingsbury, Alice Cary Bussing

Knowlton, Hugh Gilbert, Sr.

Kramer, Albert Ludlow, Sr.

Kramer, Alice Bishop

Kress, Claude Washington

Ladew, Harvey Smith, II

Lee, Ivy Ledbetter, Sr.

Levison, John Jacob

Lindbergh, Anne Spencer Morrow

Lindbergh, Charles Augustus, Sr.

Lindheim, Irma Levy

Livermore, Jesse Lauriston, Sr.

Loening, Grover

Lusk, Dr. Graham

Mackay, John William, III

Martin, Bradley, Jr.

Martin, John Stuart

McVickar, Henry Goelet

Mitchell, Sidney Alexander, Sr.

Mizner, Addison

Mooney, James David, II

Morawetz, Victor

Morley, Christopher D., Sr.

Muncie, Dr. Curtis Hamilton

Munsey, Frank Andrew

Nicholas, Dorothy Snow

Nickerson, Hoffman

Nickerson, Jane Soames

Palmer, Winthrop Bushnell

Parker, Lottie Blair

Patchin, Minga Pope
  [*see* Duryea]

Patchin, Robert Halsey

Pell, John Howland Gibbs

Perin, Charles Page

WRITERS (cont'd)

Petrova, Mme. Olga

Phillips, Kathryn F. Sisson

Pierson, Frances Dorothy Stewart

Plimpton, Francis Taylor P., Sr.

Pool, Dr. Eugene Hillhouse

Pulitzer, Margaret K. Leech

Pulling, Thomas John Edward

Pulsifer, Harold Trowbridge

Remington, Franklin

Reynolds, Richard Samuel, Sr.

Robertson, Cordelia Drexel Biddle

Roosevelt, Archibald Bulloch, Jr.

Roosevelt, Kermit, Sr.

Roosevelt, Theodore

Roosevelt, Theodore, Jr.

Roulston, Marjorie Hillis

Saltzman, Arnold Asa

Savage, Theodore Fiske

Schuster, Max Lincoln

Schwartz, Bertie Grad

Schwartz, Charles

Sears, Anna Wentworth Caldwell

Sears, Joseph Hamblen

Smith. Albert Edward, Sr.

Smith, Earl Edward Tailer, Sr.

Smith, Owen Telfair

Streeter, Edward, Sr.

Stettinius, Edward Reilly, Jr.

Stimson, Henry Lewis

Stoddard, Francis Russell, Jr.

Swann, Dr. Arthur Wharton

Thomas, Norman Mattoon

Tiffany, Louis Comfort

Tilney, Dr. Frederic, Sr.

Townesend, Dr. Stephen
  [*see* Burnett]

Underhill, Francis T.

Van Strum, Kenneth Stevens

Vertes, Marcel Emmanuel

Von Bothmer, Dr. Dietrich Felix

Weld, Julia de Forest Tiffany

Wetmore, Elizabeth Bisland

Whitney, Cornelius Vanderbilt

Whitney, Eleanor Searle

Whitney, Gertrude Vanderbilt

Whitney, Helen Hay

Will, Harold Henry

Wyckoff, Richard Demille

Zenz, Dr. Frederick Anton

Rehabilitative Uses

Non-residential rehabilitative secondary uses of surviving estate houses
listed are current as of 2006. Estates are identified by the original owner.
For subsequent estate owners, see surname entry.

American Merchant Marine Museum

William Slocum Barstow estate,
Elm Point, Kings Point

Association for the Help of Retarded Children

James Norman Hill estate,
Big Tree Farm, Brookville

Bailey Arboretum

John Clark estate,
Lattingtown

Banfi Vintners

Sir Samuel Agar Salvage estate,
Rynwood, Old Brookville

Benevolent and Protective Order of Elks

Spencer Augustus Jennings estate,
Ellencourt, Glen Cove

Buckley Country Day School

Lawrence Hobart Shearman estate,
North Hills

Caumsett State Park

Marshall Field III estate,
Caumsett, Lloyd Harbor

Centerport Yacht Club

Daniel Parmelee Morse, Sr. estate,
Spring, Centerport

Christian Fellowship House

Franklin Butler Lord II estate,
Cottsleigh, Syosset

Clark Botanic Garden

Grenville Clark, Sr. estate,
Albertson

Cold Spring Country Club

Otto Hermann Kahn estate,
Oheka, Cold Spring Harbor
(incorporates Kahn's private golf course)

Cold Spring Harbor Laboratory

Julia Mary de Forest estate,
Airslie, Laurel Hollow

Dr. Charles Benedict Davenport, Sr. estate,
Laurel Hollow

Charles Sammis Robertson estate,
Lloyd Harbor

Deepdale Golf Club

Joseph Peter Grace, Sr. estate,
Tullaroan, North Hills

East Woods School

Walter Farwell estate,
Mallow, Oyster Bay Cove

The Episcopal Diocese of Long Island

Myron Charles Taylor estate,
Killingworth, Lattingtown

Glen Cove School District, administrative building

Robert Dunbar Pruyn estate,
Glen Cove

Glengariff Nursing Home

Frederic Bayley Pratt estate,
Poplar Hill [II], Glen Cove

Gracewood Clubhouse	William Singer estate, North Hills
Great Neck Village Hall	John C. Baker estate, Great Neck
Great Neck Estates Village Hall	John Jacob Atwater, Sr. estate, Great Neck Estates
Great Neck School District, administration building	Henry Phipps, Jr. estate, *Bonnie Blink*, Lake Success
Harmony Heights Residency for Girls	John Anson Garver estate, *Wrexleigh*, Oyster Bay Cove
Harrison House Conference Center of Glen Cove	John Teele Pratt, Sr. estate, *Manor House*, Glen Cove
Hoffman Center	George S. Brewster estate, *Fairleigh*, Muttontown
The Holocaust Memorial and Educational Center of Nassau County	Harold Irving Pratt, Sr., estate, *Welwyn*, Glen Cove
Incorporated Village of Lake Success Golf Club	William Kissam Vanderbilt, Jr. estate, *Deepdale,* Lake Success (includes Vanderbilt's golf clubhouse)
Jones Manor on the Sound	Peter Winchester Rouss estate, *Callender House*, Bayville
Lin Yun Temple, an Eastern religious order	William Russell Grace, Jr. estate, *The Crossroads,* Old Westbury
Long Island University, C. W. Post College	Marjorie Merriweather Post estate, *Hillwood,* Brookville
	John Randolph Robinson estate, Brookville
	John Randolph Robinson estate, (second estate, also unnamed), Brookville
Lutheran High School Association	William Deering Howe estate, *Highpool*, Brookville
Madonna Heights Crisis Residence for Young Women	Mrs. D. Brownsard estate, *Bagatelle*, Dix Hills
Meadow Brook Polo Club	Middleton Schoolbred Burrill estate, *Jericho Farms*, Jericho
Mill Neck Manor School for Deaf Children	Lillian Sefton Thomas Dodge estate, *Sefton Manor*, Mill Neck
Mill River Club	Henry Pomeroy Davison II estate, *Appledore*, Upper Brookville
Muttontown Golf and Country Club	Howard Crosby Brokaw estate, *The Chimneys*, Muttontown

Nassau County Art Museum	Lloyd Stephens Bryce estate, *Bryce House*, Roslyn Harbor
Nassau County, Muttontown Preserve	Benjamin Moore estate, *Chelsea*, Muttontown
	Bronson Winthrop estate, (now called *Nassau Hall)*, Muttontown
Nassau County Museum, *Cedarmere*	William Cullen Bryant estate, *Cedarmere*, Roslyn Harbor
Nassau County, Sands Point Preserve	Howard Gould estate, *Castlegould,* Sands Point
Nassau County, Sands Point Preserve	Florence Shloss Guggenheim estate, *Mille Fleurs*, Sands Point
	Harry Frank Guggenheim estate, *Falaise,* Sands Point
Nassau County, Welwyn Preserve	Harold Irving Pratt, Sr. estate, *Welwyn*, Glen Cove
New York Institute of Technology	Isaiah Townsend Burden Sr. estate, Brookville
	Alfred Irenee du Pont estate, *White Eagle*, Brookville
North Shore Child and Family Guidance Center	Charles C. Auchincloss estate, *Builtover,* Roslyn Heights
North Shore Day School and Camp	Leonard J. Busby estate, Glen Cove
North Shore Reform Temple	Henry Lewis Batterman, Sr. estate, Glen Cove
Oheka Castle Catering	Otto Hermann Kahn estate, *Oheka,* Cold Spring Harbor
Old Westbury Gardens	John Shaffer Phipps estate, *Westbury House*, Old Westbury
Old Westbury Golf and Country Club	Cornelius Vanderbilt Whitney estate, *Whitney House,* Old Westbury
Orthodox Church in America	Lewis Cass Ledyard, Jr. estate, *Westwood*, Oyster Bay Cove
Our Lady of Grace Center	Victor Emanuel estate, *Dorwood*, North Hills
Pall Corporation	Frank Winfield Woolworth estate, *Winfield Hall*, Glen Cove
Pierce Country Day School and Camp	Frank C. Henderson estate, *Villa Marina,* Roslyn
Pine Hollow Country Club	Dorothy Schiff estate, *Old Fields*, East Norwich

Planting Fields Arboretum	William Robertson Coe estate, *Planting Fields*, Upper Brookville
Portledge School	Charles Albert Coffin estate, *Portledge*, Matinecock
Renaissance Country Club	John Carlos Ryan estate, Roslyn Heights
Republic of the Ivory Coast	John Herbert Johnston estate, *Boatcroft*, Lloyd Harbor
The Roman Catholic Diocese of Rockville Centre	Thomas Hitchcock, Sr. estate, *Broad Hollow Farm*, Old Westbury
Saint Francis Center	Henry Sanderson estate, *La Selva*, Upper Brookville
Saint Ignatius Retreat House	Nicholas Frederic Brady estate, *Inisfada*, North Hills
Saint Josaphat's Monastery	John Edward Aldred estate, *Ormston*, Lattingtown
Saint Phillips and St. James Episcopal Church Rectory	William Kissam Vanderbilt, Jr. estate, *Deepdale*, Lake Success (rectory is located in the gatehouse of the former estate)
Sands Point Community Synagogue	Bettie Fleischmann Holmes estate, *The Chimneys*, Sands Point
Science Museum of Long Island	Herman Goldman estate, Plandome Manor
Seventh Day Adventists	John George Milburn, Sr. estate, *Groombridge*, North Hills
Shibley Day Camp	Charles Willis estate, Roslyn
Sikh Forum, Inc.	Edward Irving Eldredge, Jr. estate, Lattingtown
Society of Pius X	Charles Edward Francis McCann estate, *Sunken Orchard*, Oyster Bay Cove (utilizing the playhouse of the estate)
Soviet, and later Russian, Mission to the United Nations	Frank C. Bauman Page estate, *Elmcroft*, Upper Brookville
Soviet, and later Russian, Mission to the United Nations	George du Pont Pratt, Sr. estate, *Killenworth* [II], Glen Cove
Strathmore Vanderbilt Country Club of Manhasset	Louis Sherry estate, *Sherryland*, Manhasset
Suffolk County, Gold Coast Museum of Long Island	George McKesson Brown estate, *West Neck Farm*, Lloyd Harbor
Suffolk County Vanderbilt Museum	William Kissam Vanderbilt, Jr. estate, *Eagle's Nest*, Centerport

Swan Club	Arthur Williams estate, Brook Corners, Glen Head
Town of Oyster Bay Golf Course	Victor Morawetz estate, *Three Ponds*, Woodbury
The Unitarian Church	Charles Shipman Payson estate, Manhasset
United States Merchant Marine Academy	Henri Bendel estate, Kings Point
Village Club of Sands Point	Isaac Guggenheim estate, *Villa Carola*, Sands Point
Webb Institute of Naval Architecture	Herbert Lee Pratt, Sr. estate, *The Braes,* Glen Cove
Westbury – Syosset Community Park	James Watson Webb, Sr. estate, *Woodbury House,* Syosset
West Hills Day Camp	Richard Townley Haines Halsey estate, *Tallwood,* West Hills
Woodcrest Country Club	James Abercrombie Burden, Jr. estate, *Woodside*, Muttontown

Listed are only those statesmen and diplomats who resided on Long Island's North Shore.

Statesmen

Premier of Nationalist China, 1939–1945
    Kung, Hsiang–hsi
        Hillcrest, Lattingtown

President of the United States, 1901–1909
    Roosevelt, Theodore
        Sagamore Hill, Cove Neck

Vice President of the United States, 1901
    Roosevelt, Theodore – McKinley administration
        Sagamore Hill, Cove Neck

Department of State

    Secretaries of State –

    Albright, Dr. Madeleine Jana Korbel – Clinton administration
        Upper Brookville
    Bacon, Robert – Theodore Roosevelt and Taft administrations
        Old Acres, Old Westbury
    Dulles, John Foster – Eisenhower administration
        Lloyd Harbor
    Lovett, Robert Abercrombie – (Acting) – Truman administration
        Green Arbors, Lattingtown
    Polk, Frank Lyon, Sr. – (Acting) – Wilson administration
        Muttontown
    Stettinius, Edward Reilly, Jr. – FDR administration
        Lattingtown
    Stimson, Henry Lewis – Hoover administration
        Highold, West Hills

    Under Secretaries, and Assistant Secretaries, and Deputy Secretaries of State –

    Bruce, David Kirkpatrick Este
        – Under Secretary of State (Truman administration)
        Woodlands, Woodbury

    Casey, William Joseph, Jr.
        – Under Secretary of State (Nixon administration)
        Mayknoll, Roslyn Harbor

    Collado, Dr. Emilio Gabriel, II
        – Deputy Secretary of State for Financial Affairs (Truman administration)
        Upper Brookville

    Davies, Joseph Edward [*see* Post]
        – Special Assistant to the Secretary of State (FDR administration)
        Hillwood, Brookville

Harriman, William Averell
> – Under Secretary of State for Political Affairs (Kennedy administration)
> – Under Secretary of State for Far Eastern Affairs (Kennedy administration)
Sands Point and Old Westbury

Lovett, Robert Abercrombie
> – Deputy Secretary of State (Truman administration)
> – Under Secretary of State (Truman administration)
Green Arbors, Lattingtown

Lyon, Cecil T. F. B
> – Deputy Assistant Secretary of State for Inter–American Affairs
Harrow Hill, Muttontown

Merle–Smith, Van Santvoord, Sr.
> – Assistant Secretary of State (Wilson administration)
The Paddocks, Cove Neck

Polk, Frank Lyon, Sr.
> – Under Secretary of State (Wilson administration)
Muttontown

Stettinius, Edward Reilly, Jr.
> – Under Secretary of State (FDR administration)
Lattingtown

Thayer, Robert Helyer, Sr.
> – Assistant Secretary of State (Eisenhower administration)
Glen Cove

Department of the Treasury

Secretaries of the Treasury –

Mills, Ogden Livingston – Hoover administration
Woodbury

Under Secretaries and Assistant Secretaries of the Treasury –

Ballantine, Arthur Atwood, Sr.
> – Assistant Secretary of Treasury (Hoover administration)
> – Under Secretary of Treasury (FDR administration)
Council Rock, Oyster Bay

Curtis, James Freeman
> – Assistant Secretary of Treasury (Taft and Wilson administrations)
Willowmere, Roslyn Harbor

Leffingwell, Russell Cornell
> – Fiscal Assistant Secretary of Treasury (Wilson administration)
Redcote, Oyster Bay Cove

Mills, Ogden Livingston
> – Under Secretary of Treasury (Coolidge and Hoover administrations)
Woodbury

Winthrop, Beekman, II
> – Assistant Secretary of Treasury (Theodore Roosevelt administration)
Groton Farms, Old Westbury

Director of the Mint –

Baker, Raymond Thomas Livingston [*see* Emerson] – Wilson and Harding administrations
Rynwood, Old Brookville and *Cedar Knoll*, Sands Point

Department of Commerce

Secretaries of Commerce

Harriman, William Averell – Truman administration
Sands Point and Old Westbury

Under Secretaries and Assistant Secretaries of Commerce –

Bruce, David Kirkpatrick Este
– Assistant Secretary of Commerce (Truman administration)
Woodlands, Woodbury

Roosevelt, Franklin Delano, Jr.
– Under Secretary of Commerce (Kennedy administration)
Woodbury

Rumbough, Stanley Maddox, Jr.
– Special assistant to Secretary of Commerce (Eisenhower administration)
Old Brookville

Whitney, Cornelius Vanderbilt
– Under Secretary of Commerce (Truman administration)
Whitney House, Old Westbury and *Oakley Court,* Mill Neck

Department of War (became the Department of the Army and a branch of Department of Defense in 1947)

Secretaries of War –

Stimson, Henry Lewis – Taft, FDR, and Truman administrations
Highold, West Hills

Under Secretaries and Assistant Secretaries of War –

Dana, Charles Anderson
– Assistant Secretary of War (Lincoln administration)
The Wings, West Island, Glen Cove

Davison, Frederick Trubee
– Assistant Secretary of War for Air (Coolidge and Hoover administrations)
Peacock Point, Lattingtown

Lovett, Robert Abercrombie
– Assistant Secretary of War for Air (FDR administration)
Green Arbors, Lattingtown

Ryan, John Dennis
– Assistant Secretary of War and Director of Air Service (Wilson administration)
Derrymore, North Hills

Stettinius, Edward Reilly, Sr.
– Assistant Secretary of War (Wilson administration)
The Shelter, Lattingtown

Department of Navy (became part of Department of Defense in 1947)

Secretaries of Navy (see also Department of Defense for more recent secretaries) –

Forrestal, James Vincent – FDR and Truman administrations
The Old Brick, East Hills
Whitney, William Collins – Cleveland and Benjamin Harrison administrations
Old Westbury

Under Secretaries and Assistant Secretaries of Navy –

Forrestal, James Vincent
– Under Secretary of Navy (FDR administration)
The Old Brick, East Hills

Gates, Artemus Lamb
– Assistant Secretary of Navy (FDR administration)
– Under Secretary of Navy (Truman administration)
Peacock Point, Lattingtown

Roosevelt, Theodore
– Assistant Secretary of Navy (McKinley administration)
Sagamore Hill, Cove Neck

Roosevelt, Theodore, Jr.
– Assistant Secretary of Navy (Harding and Coolidge administrations)
Old Orchard, Cove Neck

Winthrop, Beekman, II
– Assistant Secretary of Navy (Taft administration)
Groton Farms, Old Westbury

Department of Defense

Secretaries of Defense –

Forrestal, James Vincent – Truman administration
The Old Brick, East Hills
Lovett, Robert Abercrombie – Truman administration
Green Harbors, Lattingtown

Under Secretaries and Assistant Secretaries of Defense –

Nitze, Paul Henry
– Deputy Secretary of Defense (Lyndon B. Johnson administration)
The Farmhouse, Glen Cove

Secretaries of Air Force –

Talbott, Harold Elster, II
– Secretary of Air Force (Eisenhower administration)
The Pillars, Old Westbury

Whitney, Cornelius Vanderbilt
– Assistant Secretary of Air Force (Truman administration)
Whitney House, Old Westbury and *Oakley Court,* Mill Neck

Secretaries of Navy –

> **Nitze**, Paul Henry
>> – Secretary of Navy (Lyndon B. Johnson administration)
>> *The Farmhouse,* Glen Cove

also – **Guest**, Frederick E.
>> – British Secretary of State for Air (Lloyd George administration)
>> *Roslyn Manor*, Brookville

Diplomats

Albright, Dr. Madeleine Korbel
>> – United States Permanent Representative to the United Nations, with rank of cabinet officer, ambassador extraordinary, and plenipotentiary, 1993-1997
>> Upper Brookville

Aldrich, Winthrop Williams
>> – Ambassador to the Court of Saint James, 1953–1957
>> *Broadhollow,* Brookville

Armstrong, Hamilton Fish
>> – Special Assistant to the United States Ambassador in London, with rank of minister, 1944
>> *Box Hill,* Laurel Hollow

Bacon, Daniel
>> – Ambassador to France, 1909-1912
>> *Old Acres*, Old Westbury

Balsan, Louis Jacques
>> – Member of French Aeronautical Mission to London during World War II
>> *Old Fields*, East Norwich

Baruch, Dr. Herman Benjamin
>> – Ambassador Extraordinary and Plenipotentiary to Portugal, 1945–1947
>> – Ambassador Extraordinary and Plenipotentiary to The Netherlands, 1947–1949
>> Dix Hills

Bonner, Paul Hyde, Sr.
>> – Ambassador Extraordinary, 1962
>> Lattingtown

Brokaw, Clare Boothe [*later*, Luce]
>> – Ambassador to Italy, 1953–1957
>> Sands Point and Upper Brookville

Bruce, David Kirkpatrick Este
>> – Ambassador to France, 1949–1952
>> – Ambassador to Federal Republic of Germany, 1957–1959
>> – Ambassador to the Court of Saint James, 1961–1969
>> – United States Representative to Vietnam Peace Talks, Paris, 1970–1971
>> – Chief United States Liaison Officer to Peoples' Republic of China, 1972–1974
>> – United States Ambassador to NATO, 1974–1975
>> *Woodlands,* Woodbury

Diplomats (cont'd)

Bryce, Lloyd Stephens
> – Minister to The Netherlands and Luxembourg, 1911–1913
> *Bryce House*, Roslyn Harbor

Burden, Chester Griswold
> – Member of International Secretariat at the Paris Peace Conference, 1919
> *Honeysuckle Lodge*, Cold Spring Harbor

Collado, Dr. Emilio Gabriel, II
> – Member of United States negotiating team at Bretton Woods Conference, 1944
> Upper Brookville

Costantini, Count David A.
> – Member of Italian Delegation to Washington Arms Conference, 1921
> – Counselor attached to Italian Embassy in Washington during World War I
> *Tulip Hill,* Lattingtown

Cravath, Paul Drennan
> – United States Treasury Representative at Inter-Allied War Conference, Paris, 1917
> *Veraton* and *Still House*, Matinecock

Cutcheon, Franklin Warner M.
> – Member of World War I Reparation Committee, 1927–1929
> *Matinecock Farms,* Lattingtown

Davies, Joseph Edward [*see* Post]
> – Ambassador to the Soviet Union, 1936–1938
> – Ambassador to Belgium and Diplomatic Minister to Luxembourg [concurrent posts], 1938–1939
> – Advisor to President Wilson at Paris Peace Conference, 1918
> – Advisor with rank of ambassador, Marshall – Stalin Conference, May–June, 1943
> – Advisor with rank of ambassador, Potsdam Conference, 1945
> *Hillwood*, Brookville

Davis, John William
> – Ambassador Extraordinary to the Court of St. James, 1918-1921
> *Mattapan*, Lattingtown

Dean, Arthur Hobson
> – Ambassador to South Korea, 1953–1954
> – Chairman of United Sates Delegation to Geneva Conference on Discontinuance of Nuclear Weapons Tests, 1961–1962
> *Homewood,* Upper Brookville

de Roulet, Vincent W.
> – Ambassador to Jamaica, 1969–1973
> North Hills

De Suarez, Diego (aka. Diego Suarez) [*see* Field]
> – Colombian Press Attaché and Minister Council to the United States, 1948-1952
> *Easton,* Muttontown

Dresselhuys, Cornelius [*see* Manville]
> – Liberian Minister to the Court of St. James
> *Les Deux Tours*, Old Westbury

Diplomats (cont'd)

Dulles, Allen Welsh
- Secretary to United States Delegation, Vienna, 1916
- Member of American Committee at Paris Peace Conference, 1918
- Member of United States Commission, Constantinople, 1920
- Chief of Near Eastern Division, Department of States, 1922–1926
- Delegate to Arms Traffic Commission, 1925
- Member of United States Delegation to Preparatory Disarmament Commission, 1926

Lloyd Harbor

Dulles, John Foster
- Secretary, The Hague Peace Conference, 1907
- Special Agent to Central America, United States State Department, 1917
- Member of Reparation Committee and Supreme Economic Council, 1919
- Representative to Berlin Debt Conference, 1933
- Member of United States Delegation to San Francisco Conference, 1945
- Acting Chairman of United States Delegation to United Nations General Assembly, Paris, 1948
- Special Representative of the President, with rank of ambassador, at the Japanese Peace Treaty, 1951

Lloyd Harbor

Emmet, Richard Stockton, Sr.
- Minister to The Netherlands, 1933

High Elms, Glen Cove

Emory, William Helmsley, Jr.
- Naval Attaché to Court of Saint James
- Representative to Queen Victoria's Jubilee, 1897

Clifton, Roslyn Harbor

Gerard, James Watson, III
- Ambassador Extraordinary and Minister Plenipotentiary to Germany, 1913–1917

Lloyd Harbor

Griscom, Lloyd Carpenter
- Charge d' affairs, Constantinople, 1899–1901
- E. E. and M. P. to Persia, 1901–1902
- E. E. and M. P. to Japan, 1902–1906
- Ambassador to Brazil, 1906–1907
- Ambassador to Italy, 1907–1909

Huntover Lodge, Muttontown

Guggenheim, Harry Frank
- Ambassador to Cuba, 1929–1933

Falaise, Sands Point

Hanks, Stedman Shumway
- Special Representative of the Secretary of State on three confidential foreign assignments

Old Brookville

Harriman, Pamela Digby Churchill Hayward
- Ambassador to France, 1993–1997

Sands Point and Old Westbury

Harriman, William Averell
- Ambassador to the Soviet Union, 1943–1946
- Ambassador to the Court of Saint James, 1946

Sands Point and Old Westbury

Diplomats (cont'd)

Hoffman, Albert L., Sr.
– Military attaché to Spain and Luxembourg
Radnor House, Muttontown

Hoffman, William Wickham
– Military attaché in Brussels after World War I
Wiltwick, Jericho

Lindsay, Sir Ronald
– Ambassador from the Court of Saint James to the United States, 1930s
Lime House, Centre Island

Lyon, Cecil T. F. B
– Ambassador to Chile, 1956–1958
– Minister in Paris, 1958–1964
– Ambassador to Ceylon, 1964–1967
– Ambassador to Maldives, 1965–1967
Harrow Hill, Muttontown

Merle–Smith, Van Santvoord, Sr.
– Special Attaché to United States Legation at The Hague
– Member of Secretariat at Paris Peace Conference, 1919
– Military Attaché at Melbourne during World War II
The Paddocks, Cove Neck

Mitchell, Sidney Alexander, Sr.
– special attaché to Court of St. James
Marney, Matinecock

Moffat, Douglas Maxwell
– Ambassador to Australia, 1956
Annandale, Cold Spring Harbor

Mooney, James David, II
– As unofficial envoy of Franklin Delano Roosevelt, Mooney held secret talks with
Nazi leaders. He tried to prevent the "phony war" from erupting into a World War.
Centre Island

Nitze, Paul Henry
– Member of United States delegation to Strategic Arms Limitation Talks, 1969–1974
– Chief United States Delegate to International Nuclear Forces Talks, 1981–1984
– Ambassador–at–Large, 1986
The Farmhouse, Glen Cove

Nixon, Lewis
– Delegate to Fourth Pan-American Conference, 1910
– E. E. and M. P. to Chilean Centenary, 1910
Sands Point

Pennoyer, Paul Geddes, Sr.
– Delegate to United Nations San Francisco Conference, 1945
Round Bush, Glen Cove

Plimpton, Francis Taylor Pearsons, Sr.
– Deputy Representative to the United Nations, 1961–1965
Sweet Hollow, West Hills

Diplomats (cont'd)

Polk, Frank Lyon, Sr.
> – United States Plenipotentiary to negotiate peace, 1919;
> – Chairman, United States delegation to Paris Peace Conference, 1919
>
> Muttontown

Robinson, Monroe Douglas
> – Goodwill Ambassador to Peru
>
> Muttontown

Roosevelt, Theodore, Jr.
> – Governor of Puerto Rico, 1929–1932
> – Governor of The Philippines, 1932–1933
>
> *Old Orchard,* Cove Neck

Saltzman, Arnold Asa
> – Ambassador to Czechoslovakia
> – Ambassador to Austria
> – Ambassador to Soviet Union
> – Ambassador to South America
> – Ambassador to Central America
>
> Sands Point

Smith, Earl Edward Tailer, Sr.
> – Ambassador to Cuba, 1957–1959
>
> *Iradell,* Sands Point

Stettinius, Edward Reilly, Jr.
> – Chairman of the United States Delegation to the first session of the United Nations, 1946
>
> Lattingtown

Stewart, Glen
> – First Secretary, United States Embassy in Vienna in the Wilson administration
> – Second Secretary, United States Embassy in Havana in the Wilson administration
>
> Lattingtown

Stimson, Henry Lewis
> – Special Representative of the President to Nicaragua, 1927
> – Chairman of the United States Delegation to London Naval Conference, 1930
> – Chairman of the United States Delegation to Disarmament Conference, 1932
>
> *Highold,* West Hills

Straight, Willard Dickerman
> – Vice-Consul General and Private Secretary to United Sates Ambassador to Korea, 1905
> – Secretary to United States Minister to Cuba, 1906
> – Consul General to Mukden, China, 1906–1908
>
> *Elmhurst,* Old Westbury

Taylor, Myron Charles
> – Personal Representative of the President, with rank of ambassador, to The Vatican,
>   1939–1950
>
> *Killingworth,* Lattingtown

Thayer, Robert Helyer, Sr.
> – Assistant Ambassador to France, 1951–1954
> – Minister to Romania, 1955–1958
>
> Glen Cove

Diplomats (cont'd)

Tobin, Richard Montgomery [*see* J. A. Burden, Jr.]
  – E. E. and M. P. to The Netherlands, 1923-1929
  Woodside, Muttontown

Truslow, Francis Adams, Sr.
  – Commissioner on United States–Brazil Joint Commission for Economic Development,
      with rank of minister, 1951
  – Representative to Inter–American Conference on the Problems of War and Peace,
      Mexico, 1945
  The Point, Laurel Hollow

Weiss, William Erhard, Jr.
  – Chief of Economic Affairs Division, American High Commissioner's Office, Germany
  Centre Island

Whitney, John Hay
  – Ambassador to the Court of Saint James, 1956–1961
  Greentree, Manhasset

Willys, John North
  – Ambassador to Poland, 1930–1932
  Northcliff, Centre Island

Winthrop, Beekman, II
  – Governor of Puerto Rico, 1904–1907
  Groton Farms, Old Westbury

Advisors and Personal Secretaries

Armstrong, Hamilton Fish
  – Advisor, United States delegation to the United Nations Charter Conference, 1945
  – Special Advisor to Secretary of State, 1945
  Box Hill, Laurel Hollow

Auchincloss, Gordon, Sr.
  – Secretary to United States War Mission to Great Britain and France, 1917
  – Secretary to Colonel Edward M. House during Paris Peace Conference, 1919
  Glen Cove and *Ronda,* Matinecock

Baker, Raymond Thomas [*see* Emerson]
  – Secretary to United States Ambassador to Petrograd, Russia, 1914–1916
  Rynwood, Old Brookville

Bonner, Paul Hyde, Sr.
  – Special Advisor for Economics to United States Ambassador to Italy, 1947–1951
  Lattingtown

Carver, Clifford Nickels
  – Secretary to United States Ambassador to the Court of Saint James
  – Secretary to Colonel Edward M. House's mission to Europe, 1915-1916
  Amincliff, Lattingtown

Hanks, Stedman Shumway
  – Secretary to United States Ambassador to Court of Saint James, 1912
  Old Brookville

Advisors and Personal Secretaries (cont'd)

Hoyt, Lydig
– Secretary to United States Ambassador to Court of Saint James, 1908-1909
Woodbury

Kerrigan, Joseph J.
– Assistant to United States Ambassador to Russia
Cove Neck

Roosevelt, Archibald Bullock, Jr.
– Special Assistant to United States Ambassador to Court of Saint James
– Special Assistant to United States Ambassador to Spain
Turkey Lane House, Cold Spring Harbor

Rumbough, Stanley Maddox, Jr.
– Special Assistant to Secretary of Commerce (Eisenhower administration)
– Special Assistant of White House in charge of executive board liaison
(Eisenhower administration)
Old Brookville

Winthrop, Beekman, II
– Assistant Executive Secretary of the Philippines, 1901
– Private Secretary to the chairman of the Philippine Commission
Groton Farms, Old Westbury

Woodward, William, II
– Secretary to the United States Ambassador to the Court of St. James
Enfield Chase, Brookville

The village references used in this compilation are the current (2006) village or hamlet boundaries and should not be confused with zip code designations. When the owner who contracted for the original construction of the house is known, it is indicated by an asterisk.

ALBERTSON

Clark, Grenville, Sr.
Draper, Charles Dana, *Ten Gables*
* Moore, Edward Small, Sr., *Ten Gables*

ASHAROKEN

Babbott, Dr. Frank Lusk, Jr., *Beacon Farm*
Barbolini, Guy, *The Crest* [*see* O. R. DeLamater, Sr.]
Bevin, Laura DeLamater, *Bevin House*
Bevin, Sydney, *Bevin House*
Bishop, Richard E.
Borglum, Lucille [*see* C. H. DeLamater]
Carter, George, *Carefree Court*
* Carter, Oliver Goldsmith, Sr., *Carefree Court*
Cooper, Cyrus, *The Crest*
* Crary, Miner Dunham, Sr.
DeLamater, Cornelius Henry, *Walnut Farm House*
* DeLamater, Cornelius Henry, *Vermland*
* DeLamater, Oakley Ramshon, Sr., *The Crest*
* de Seversky, Alexander Prokofieff
DeWeir, Norman, *The Crest*
[*see* O. R. DeLamater, Sr.]
Donnell, Laura Attmore Robinson, *Walnut Farm House*
* Felix, Numa J.
Froessel, Charles William, *Bevin House*
Garrett, Robert Michael, *The Crest*
Haff, Stella Carter, *Carefree Court*
Kefalidis, Nikos, *Bevin House*
Klein, John S., *Beacon Farm*
Law, Reed [*see* Robinson]
Miller, John R., III
Morgan, Henry Sturgis, Sr., *Beacon Farm*
Rice, Donald, *The Crest*
[*see* O. R. DeLamater, Sr.]
Robins, Lydia DeLamater, *The Robin's Nest*
Robinson, Miss Edith Attmore, *The Point*
* Robinson, George Hazard, *The Point*
[*Robinson owned two houses in Asharoken.*]
Sandblom, Frederick [*see* C. H. DeLamater]
Vertes, Marcel Emmanuel

BAYVILLE

Clarkson, Robert Livingston, Sr., *Callender House*
Coates, Winslow Shelby, Sr., *Dunstable*
Greer, Louis Morris, *Sevenoaks*
* Jelke, Ferdinand, Jr., *Laurelcroft*
Jelke, Minot ("Mickey") Frazier, III [*see* F. Jelke, Jr.]
* Physioc, Joseph Allen, Sr., *Cedar Cliff*
Pierce, Winslow Shelby, Jr., *Dunstable*
* Pierce, Winslow Shelby, II, *Dunstable*
* Rouss, Peter Winchester, *Callender House*
Sterling, Duncan, Jr.
Williams, Harrison, *Oak Point*

BROOKVILLE

* Aldrich, Winthrop Williams, *Broadhollow*
* Bliss, Cornelius Newton, Jr., *Oak Hill*
* Burden, Arthur Scott
* Burden, Isaiah Townsend, Sr.
Cary, Guy Fairfax, Sr., *Oak Hill*
Chadbourne, Thomas Lincoln, Jr.
Cohen [*see* Aldrich]
Cushing, Harry Cooke, III, *Muttontown Farm*
Cutting, Dr. Fulton
Davies, Joseph Edward, *Hillwood* [*see* Post]
Donahue, James Paul, Jr., *Broadhollow*
* du Pont, Alfred Irenee, *White Eagle*
Dyer, Elisha, VII, *The Orchards*
* Dyer, George Rathbone, Sr., *The Orchards*
Ellis, Ralph Nicholson, Sr., *Bunga Fields*
Evangelista, Louis
* Francke, Luis J., Sr., *Glenby*
* Gavin, Michael, *Greanan*
Gossler, Philip Green, Sr., *Highfield*
Guest, Frederick E., *Roslyn Manor*
Guest, Winston Frederick Churchill, *Templeton*
* Harriman, Joseph Wright, *Avondale Farms*
(Harriman owned two houses in Brookville.)
Harris, Henry Upham, Jr.
* Harris, Henry Upham, Sr., *The Hameau*
Hawkey, Harold W., Sr.
* Hill, James Norman, *Big Tree Farm*
Holmes, Duncan Argyle
* Howe, Richard Flint, *Linden Hill*
* Howe, William Deering, *Highpool*
* Hutton, Edward Francis, *Hillwood* and *Hutfield*
[*Hutton and his wife built Hillwood*])
Kohler, Calvin [*see* Bliss]
Kountze, deLancey, *Delbarton*
LeRoux, Eduoard, *Cottage Normandy*
* Livermore, Philip Walter, *Bois Joli*
Maddocks, John L., Jr. [*see* Maynard]
* Maynard, Walter Effingham, *Haut Bois*
Munsel, Patrice, *Malmaison*
Norton, Skeffington Sanxay, Jr., *North Meadow Farm*
Norton, Skeffington Sanxay, Sr., *North Meadow Farm*
Osborn, Alexander Perry, Sr., *Valley House*
* Post, Marjorie Merriweather, *Hillwood*
[*Post and her husband build Hillwood.*]
* Prime, William Albert, Sr., *Warburton Hall*
* Robinson, John Randolph
[*Robinson built two houses in Brookville.*]
* Rumsey, Charles Cary, Sr.
Sage, Henry William, II
Smith, Albert Lawrence, Sr., *Penllyn*
Smith, Ormond Gerald, *Stepping Stones*
Steers, James Rich, II, *Dogwood Hill*
Tenney, Daniel Gleason, Sr.

BROOKVILLE (cont'd)
  Uris, Percy, *Broadhollow*
  Vanderbilt, Alfred Gwynne, II, *Broadhollow*
* Vanderbilt, Virginia Graham Fair
  Vitrol, H. A. [*see* Francke]
* Warburg, Gerald Felix, *Box Hill Farm*
  Woodward, William, II, *Enfield Chase*

CENTERPORT
* Allerton, D. D. [*see* Vivaudou]
* Corbin, Austin
* DeBrabant, Marius, *Plaisance*
* Gucker, Henry John, Sr.
  Honeyman, Robert B., Jr.
  Morrell, Joseph B., *The Moorings*
  Morse, Daniel Parmelee, Sr., *Spring*
  Stewart, John K.
* Vanderbilt, William Kissam, Jr., *Eagle's Nest*
* Van Idestine, Charles Abner
* Van Iderstine, Peter, Jr.
* Van Iderstine, William P. M.
  Vivaudou, Victor
* Whitney, Charles Morse, Sr.

CENTRE ISLAND
  Armsby, George Newell, Sr.
  Bacon, Daniel, *La Casita*
  Baker, George Fisher, III, *Ventura Point*
  Brightson, George Edgar, *Harbor Point*
* Brokaw, Clifford Vail, Sr., *Westaways*
* Bullock, George, *The Folly* [I] [II]
* Bullock, George, *Yeadon*
  Burr, Nelson Beardsley
  Cardelli, Count Giovanni Guido C., *Orchard Cottage*
  Carey, William Francis, Jr.
  Clark, Marshall, *Windy Meadow*
  Cochran, Drayton
  Deans, Robert Barr, Sr., *Yeadon*
  de Dampierre, Count [*see* Mackenzie]
  De LaBegassiere [*see* C. V. Brokaw, Jr.]
  Fairchild, Sherman M.
  Fisher, Joel Ellis, II, *Oak Knoll*
  Gubelmann, Walter Stanley, *Southerly*
* Hoyt, Colgate, Sr., *Eastover*
  LeRoux, E. [*see* O. G. Smith]
  Lindsay, Lady Elizabeth Sherman Hoyt, *Lime House*
  Lyon, Frederick Gorham Clark, *Spindrift*
* Mackenzie, J. Clinton
  MacLaren, Archibald Waters, *Bonnie Brae*
  Mahana, George Shaw, *Birchlea*
  Mooney, James David, II
  Moore, William Talman, Jr., *Puente Vista*
  Moore, William Talman, Sr., *Tide Oaks*
  Neff, Walter Perry
  Nichols, William Henry, Jr., *Applegarth*
  Oelsner, Edward Carl William, Sr.
  Oelsner, Warren James, *Seacroft*
  Outerbridge, Samuel Roosevelt
  Palmer, Carlton Humphreys, *Hearthstone*
  Pell, John Howland Gibbs, *Pelican Point*

  Perin, Charles Page
* Pettinos, Charles E., *Thatch Cottage*
  Phelps, Ansel, *Brick Yard Point*
* Remington, Franklin, *Driftwood*
  Roosevelt, Julian Kean, *Bonnie Brae*
* Rusch, Henry Arthur, Sr., *June Acres*
* Shaw, Samuel T., Sr., *The Sunnyside*
* Sherman, Charles Austin, Sr., *Minnewawa*
  Smith, Albert Edward, Sr.
* Smith, Herbert Ludlam, Sr., *Oliver's Point*
* Smith, Ormond Gerald, *Shoremonde*
  Stewart, Cecil Parker, *Orchard Cottage*
  Taylor, Henry Stillman, *Gull's Way*
  Tilney, Frederick, Jr.
  Tilney, Dr. Frederick, Sr., *Sundown*
  Von Bothmer, Dr. Dietrich Felix
  Weiss, William Erhard, Jr.
* Wetmore, Charles Whitman, *Applegarth*
  Willys, John North, *Northcliff*

COLD SPRING HARBOR
* Bateson, Edgar Farrar, Sr., *Deramore*
* Blagden, Linzee
  Blakeslee, Dr. Albert Francis
  Boardman, Kenneth, *Upper Field*
  Burden, Chester Griswold, *Honeysuckle Lodge*
  de Forest, Henry Lockwood, *Meadowview*
  de Forest, Johnston, *Wawapek*
* de Forest, Robert Weeks, *Wawapek*
  Dole, Edward E.
  Franklin Walter Simonds, Jr.
  Hadden, Arnold P. [*see* C. A. Peabody, Jr.]
  Hadden, Hamilton, Sr., *Harbour Lights*
  Hewlett, Walter Jones, *Owlscote*
  Jackson, William Eldred, II, *Hurrahs Nest*
  James, Henry, *Greenleaves*
* James, Dr. Walter Belknap, *Eagle's Beak*
* Kahn, Otto Hermann, *Oheka*
* Lawrence, Effingham, II
  Melius, Gary, *Oheka Castle*
* Moffat, Douglas Maxwell, *Annandale*
  Nichols, George, Sr., *Uplands*
* Noyes, David Chester, Sr., *Netherwood*
* Page, Walter Hines, II
* Peabody, Charles Augustus, Jr.
  Pierson, Dr. Richard Norris, Sr., *Whitehill Place*
  Poor, Henry Varnum, Sr.
  Roosevelt, Archibald Bulloch, Jr.,
    Turkey Lane House
  Roosevelt, Archibald Bulloch, Sr.,
    Turkey Lane House
* Stewart, William Adams Walker, II, *Edgeover*
  Stoddard, Francis Russell, Jr., *Old Rectory*
* Taylor, Henry Calhoun, *Cherridore*
  Thomas, Frederic Chichester, Sr., *Woodlee Farm*
* Thomas, Norman Mattoon
* Vermilye, H. Rowland, Sr., *Wood Winds*
  Williams, Douglas, *Wawapek*

1119

COVE NECK
   Anderson, Henry Hill, II, *Handyhill*
   Best, Eric
   Bigelow, Ernest A., *Craig Royston*
* Blackton, James Stuart, Sr., *Harbourwood*
   Choung, Terry, *Gracewood* [*see* Gracie]
   Coudert, Frederic Rene, Jr., *La Chaumiere*
   Coudert, Frederic Rene, II, *Rugby*
* Gibson, Robert Williams, *North Point*
   Grace, Oliver Russell, *Yellowbanks*
* Gracie, James King, *Gracewood*
   Ihasz, Nicholas
   Ingersoll, Robert Hawley
* Kerrigan, Joseph J.
   Leeds, William Bateman, Jr., *Kenwood*
   Lindsey, Christopher F. [*see* L. Moen]
   Martin, Grinnell, *Grey Cottage*
   Mathers, William Harris
* Maxwell, George Thebaud, *Sunset House*
   Merle–Smith, Van Santvoord, Sr., *The Paddocks*
   Moen, A. Rene, *Renwood*
* Moen, LeClanche
* Nichols, John White Treadwell, *The Kettles*
   Pulsifer, Harold Trowbridge, *Cooper's Bluff*
   Reeve–Merritt, Edward, *Elfland*
   Roosevelt, George Emlen, Sr., *Gracewood*
* Roosevelt, James Alfred, *Yellowbanks*
   Roosevelt, John Kean, *Yellowbanks*
* Roosevelt, Kermit, Sr., *Mohannes*
   Roosevelt, Laura d'Oremieulx, *Waldeck*
   Roosevelt, Philip James, Jr.
* Roosevelt, Philip James, Sr., *Dolonar*
   Roosevelt, Quentin, II, *Sakunska*
* Roosevelt, Theodore, *Sagamore Hill*
* Roosevelt, Theodore, Jr., *Old Orchard*
   Roosevelt. William Emlen, *Yellowbanks*
   Satterlee, Dr. Henry Suydam, Sr.
* Smith, D. W. [*see* H. H. Anderson II]
* Smith, Howard Caswell, Sr., *Shoredge*
   Straus, Jack Isidor, *Crow's Nest*
   Strauss, Albert, *Brier Hill*
* Swan, Edward H., Sr., *The Evergreens*
   Swan, William Lincoln, Sr.
   Taliaferro, Eugene Sinclair, *The Wilderness*
   Taylor, James Blackstone, Jr., *Sunset House*
   Taylor, James Blackstone, Sr., *Sunset House*
   Wang, Charles B.
     [Wang owns three Roosevelt houses in Cove Neck.]
* White, Alexander Moss, Sr., *Weymouth*
   Whitney, Edward Farley
   Whitney, Miss Margaret Sargent, *Ballygurge*

DIX HILLS
   Amari, Philippo [*see* C. A. Gould]
   Baruch, Dr. Herman Benjamin
* Brownsard, Mrs. D., *Bagatelle* [*see* Baruch]
* Gould, Charles Albert, *Chateauiver*
   Havemeyer, Horace, Jr.

DOSORIS ISLAND
(*see* **GLEN COVE, WEST ISLAND**)

EAST HILLS
   Colado, *The Old Brick* [*see* Forrestal]
   Forrestal, James Vincent, *The Old Brick*
   Gammanse, *The Old Brick* [*see* Forrestal]
   Mackay, John William, III, *Happy House*
   Patchin, Robert Halsey, *Firth House*
   Romantini, Jerry, *The Old Brick*

EAST ISLAND
(*see* **GLEN COVE, EAST ISLAND**)

EAST NORWICH
   Balsan, Consuelo Vanderbilt, *Old Fields*
   Campbell, Oliver Allen, Sr., *The Oaces*
* Cushing, Harry Cooke, III, *Oxon Hill*
   McVickar, Donald, *Pondacre*
   McVickar, Janet S. Lansing, *Pondacre*
* Schiff, Dorothy, *Old Fields*
   Uterhart, Henry Ayres, *Cross Roads Farm*

EAST WILLISTON
   Iselin, Adrian, II, *Nair Lane*
   Robinson, Thomas Linton, *Red Barns*

EATON'S NECK
   Carr, Edward A. T., *The Hill*
* Donnell, Harry Ellingwood, *The Hill*
   Gerlach, Robert, *The Hill*
* Jones, Charles Hewlett
   Jones, Mary Elizabeth
   Jones, Miss Rosalie Gardiner
   Lang, John, *The Hill* [*see* Donnell]
* Morgan, Henry Sturgis, Sr.
   Ward, Sarah Donnell, *The Hill*

FLOWER HILL
* Munson, Carlos W., *Elmsfour*
* Ricks, Jesse Jay

GLEN COVE
* Adams, Horatio M., *Appledale*
   Appleby, Charles Herbert, Sr.
   Appleby, John Storm
   Auchincloss, Gordon, Sr.
* Ayer, Dr. James Cook, *Shadowland*
* Babbott, Frank Lusk, Sr.
   Bartow, Francis Dwight, Sr., *Belvoir*
* Batterman, Henry Lewis, Sr.
   Beale, Bouvier, Sr.
   Beard, William
   Brewster, Samuel Dwight, *The Birches*
   Brewster, Warren Dwight, *The Birches*

GLEN COVE (cont'd)
  Brokaw, Clifford Vail, Jr., *The Elms*
* Brokaw, Clifford Vail, Sr., *The Elms*
  Brown, Nannie C. Inman
* Bucknall, G. Stafford, *The 19th Hole*
  Bucknall, Henry W. J., *Leahead*
* Busby, Leonard J.
* Bush, Donald Fairfax, Sr.
  Carey, Martin F., *Cashelmare*
  Chubb, Percy, Sr., *Rattling Spring*
  Coe, William Rogers
* Coles, Elizabeth, *Rolling Stone*
  Cox, Dr. Gerard Hutchison, Sr.
* Crane, Clinton Hoadley, Jr.
  Crawford, Edward H.
  Cudlipp, Chandler, Sr.
  Davisson, Richard L., Sr.
* DeLamar, Joseph Raphael, *Pembroke*
  Doubleday, Russell, *Shadow Lawn*
  Duryea, Dr. Garrett DeNyse
  Duryea, Hendrick Vanderbilt
* Dykman, William Nelson
* Emmet, Richard Stockton, Sr., *High Elms*
* Fahys, George Ernest, Sr., *Hilaire*
* Fairchild, Julian Percy, Sr.
  Folger, Henry Clay
* Fowler, George [*see* Loening]
* Frank, Charles Augustus, Sr., *Charlon House*
  Fromm, Robert M. [*see* H. C. Martin]
* Geddes, Donald Grant, Sr.
  Gibb, Arthur, *Gageboro*
* Gibb, Walter, *Old Orchard*
  Hadley, Morris
* Handy, Parker Douglas, *Groendak*
  Hester, William Van Anden, Sr., *Willada Point*
* Hine, Francis Lyman, *Mayhasit*
* Hoagland, Dr. Cornelius Nevius
* Hoyt, Colgate, Jr., *Meadow Spring*
* Humphreys, Dr. Alexander Crombie
  Hunter, Malcolm Du Bois, *Glenlo*
* Jennings, Spencer Augustus, *Ellencourt*
  Jones, Nicholas Ridgely, *Edgewood*
  Knott, David Hurst, Sr.
  Kress, Claude Washington
* Ladew, Edward R., *Villa Louedo*
  Lee, Ivy Ledbetter, Sr.
  Leeming, Thomas Lonsdale, Sr., *Germelwyn*
  LeRoux, Edward
  Lindheim, Norvin R.
  Loening, Rudolph R., *Glimpse Water*
  Loew, Arthur Marcus, Sr., *Pembroke*
  Loew, Marcus, *Pembroke*
* Luckenbach, Lewis V., Sr.
  MacDonald, Helen Lamb Babbott
* Martin, Henry Clifford
* Maxwell, Eugene Lascelles, Sr., *Maxwell Hall*
* Maxwell, Howard Washburn, Sr., *Maxwelton*
    [*family compound*]
  Maxwell, John Rogers, Jr., *Maxwelton*
    [*family compound*]
* Maxwell, John Rogers, Sr., *Maxwelton*
    [*family compound*]

  Miller, John Norris, Sr., *Merriefield*
* Morris, Montrose Whitney
* Murdock, Harvey, *The Birches*
  Nitze, Paul Henry, *The Farm House*
  O'Keeffe, Samuel
* Ottley, James Henry, Sr., *Oakleigh*
  Parker, Robert Meade, Sr., *Bonnieneuk*
* Pennoyer, Paul Geddes, Sr., *Round Bush*
  Porter, William Henry, *Bogheid*
    [*different house from that of Pryibil*]
  Potter, Edward Clarkson, Sr.
  Powell, Francis Edward, Jr., *Rattling Spring*
  Powell, John
* Pratt, Charles Millard, *Seamoor*
* Pratt, Frederic Bayley, *Poplar Hill* [I] [II]
* Pratt, George du Pont, Sr., *Killenworth* [I] [II]
  Pratt, Harold Irving, Jr.
* Pratt, Harold Irving, Sr., *Welwyn*
* Pratt, Herbert Lee, Sr., *The Braes*
* Pratt, John Teele, Jr., *The Farm House*
* Pratt, John Teele, Jr., *Beechwood*
* Pratt, John Teele, Sr., *Manor House*
  Pratt, Richardson, Sr., *Winthrop House*
* Pruyn, Robert Dunbar
* Pryibil, Helen Porter, *Bogheid*
    [*different house from that of Porter*]
  Queen, Emmet
  Reynolds, Richard Samuel, Sr., *Slow Tide*
  Reynolds, Richard Samuel, Sr., *Winfield Hall*
  Roosevelt, John Kean
* Rossiter, Arthur Wickes, Sr., *Cedarcroft*
* Runyon, Clarkson, Jr., *The Farm House*
  Sanesi, Dr. Lorenzo, *La Primavera*
  Schniewind, Henry, Jr., *Wyndhem*
* Shaw, Robert Anderson
  Shepard, Rutherford Mead
  Smithers, Francis S., *Myhome*
  Sobelman, Max
  Stearns, John Noble, II, *The Cedars*
  Stralem, Donald Sigmund
  Sutton, Keith
  Tangeman, Cornelius Hoagland
  Tangeman, George Patterson, *Green Acres*
  Thayer, Robert Helyer, Sr.
  Vanderbilt, Virginia Graham Fair
  Van Santvoord, Alexander S., Sr.
  Ward, M. T. [*see* Hester]
* Wetmore, Edmund
* Whitney, Howard Frederic, II, *Craigdarroch*
  Woodside, Joel David, *Villa D'Orsay*
* Woolworth, Frank Winfield, *Winfield Hall*
* Young, Edward Lewis, *Meadow Farm*

GLEN COVE, WEST ISLAND
* Dana, Charles Anderson, *The Wings*
  Harkness, William Lamon
* Morgan, Junius Spencer, *Salutation*
  Samuels, John Stockwell, III, *Salutation*

1121

GLEN COVE, EAST ISLAND
* Morgan, John Pierpont, Jr., *Matinecock Point*

GLEN HEAD
Chapin, C. Merrill, Jr.
Clark, Bruce, *Topside*
Fremont, Julie Fay Bradley, *Lynrose* [*see* Shipman]
* Hattersley, Robert Chopin, Sr., *Cherry Leaze*
Isham, Ralph Hayward
Miller, Roswell, Jr.
Rose, George, Sr., *Overland Farm*
Scudder, Townsend, II, *Robinhurst Farm*
* Shipman, Julie Fay Bradley, *Lynrose*
* Williams, Arthur, *Brook Corners*

GREAT NECK
Baker, John C., Sr.
* Ellis, Reuben Morris
Parker, Lottie Blair
* Rickert, Edward J.
Rosenberg, Lee
Swope, Herbert Bayard, Sr.
* Vanderveer, Stephen Lott, *Kenwood*
White, Leonard Dalton, Jr., *The Spinneys*
White, Leonard Dalton, Sr.

GREAT NECK ESTATES
Atwater, John Jacob, Sr.
Hopkins, Arthur
* Kilthau, Raymond F.

HUNTINGTON
Baylis, Lester Yates
Potter, Dr. Gilbert
Vernam, Clarence Cottier, *Hilaire Farm*

HUNTINGTON BAY
Everitt, Samuel Alexander, *Tide Hill*
* Ferguson, Juliana Armour, *The Monastery*
Frost, Henry R.
* Heckscher, August, *Wincoma*
Jadwin, Stanley Palmer
Kane, John Patrick, *Interbaien*
* L'Ecluse, Milton Albert, *Villa Amicitia*
Merrill, Charles Edward, Jr., *Hidden Way*
* Monson, Sarah Cowen
* O'Donohue, Charles A.
Parker, Valentine Fraser
* Robb, John [*see* Jadwin]
Roulston, Thomas Henry, Sr., *High Lindens*

HUNTINGTON STATION
* Hess, Harry Bellas, *The Cedars*

JERICHO
Beard, Minnie Tuttle
* Burrill, Middleton Schoolbred, *Jericho Farms*
Gary, Elbert H., *Ivy Hall*
Grant, Robert, Jr.
* Hadden, Emily Georgina Hamilton, *Dogwood*
Hadden, Miss Frances, *Dogwood* [*see* E. Hadden]
* Harriman, Herbert Melville, *The Lanterns*
Hoffman, William Wickham, *Wiltwick*
* Kent, George Edward, Sr., *Jericho House*
* Kramer, Albert Ludlow, Sr., *Picket Farm*
Lehman, Allan Sigmund, *Picket Farm*
Leonard, Charles Reginald, Sr., *Walls of Jericho*
* Preston, Ralph Julius, *Ivy Hall*
Preston, William Payne Thompson, Sr., *Longfields*
    [Preston owned two houses in Jericho.]
* Simpson, Robert H., *Kinross*
Straus, Jack Isidor, *Green Pastures*
Taylor, James Blackstone, Sr.
* Thompson, William Payne, Jr., *Longfields*
Underhill, Daniel
Underhill, Samuel Jackson
Wright, Boykin Cabell, Sr., *Rolling Field*

KINGS POINT
Ades, Robert [*see* Kienle]
* Aldrich, Sherwood, *Snug Harbor*
Alexander, Harry
* Alger, Miss Lucille
* Alker, Alphonse Henry, *Idlewilde*
Alker, Edward Paul, *Cedar Pond Farm*
Alker, James Ward, Sr.
Annenberg, Moses Louis
* Arnold, William H.
* Aron, Jacob, *Hamptworth House*
Atwater, John Jacob, Sr.
Auchincloss, John
* Ballantine, John Herbert, *Holmdene*
Bancroft, John, Jr.
* Barstow, William Slocum, *Elm Point*
* Beach, William Nicholas
* Bendel, Henri
Bliss, Miss Ida Evelina, *Geranium Court*
Bloomingdale, Hiram Collenberger
Bloomingdale, Rosalie Banner
* Booth, Angeline Rowan, *Broadlawns*
Brickman, Herman, *The Point*
* Brokaw, William Gould, *Nirvana*
Chrysler, Walter Percy, Sr., *Forker House*
Church, Richard N. L., *The Point*
Clowes, John Henry, Sr., *Clovelly*
Cohan, George Michael
Cohn, Milton Seymour
* Cooper, Kenneth F.
Cowl, Clarkson
Craven, Frank
* Crossman, William H.
* Dwight, Arthur Smith
* Eden, John H., II, *Topping*
* Eden, Dr. John H., Sr., *Edenhall*
* Ford, Hannibal Choate

KINGS POINT (cont'd)
* Gelder, Irving L., *The Terraces*
  Geula, Kiumarz
  Gignoux, Miss Elise Messenger, *Minnamere*
  Gignoux, Charles Christmas, *Minnamere*
* Gilbert, Harry Bramhall, *Sunshine*
  Goodrich, Donald Wells, Sr.
  Gould, Aubrey Van Wyck, Sr., *Fieldside*
  Grace, David R.
  Grace, Miss Louise Natalie, *Llangollen Farm*
  Grace, Morgan Hatton, Sr., *Lismore*
* Grace, William Russell, Sr., *Gracefield*
  Gross, John J.
  Haar, Herbert
* Hammerstein, Oscar, II, *Sunny Knoll*
* Harris, Sam Henry
  Heckscher, August, *Feu Follet*
  Hitchcock, Raymond
* Houston, William S.
* Hoyt, John R.
  Hudson, Percy Kierstede
* Hunter, Fenley, *Porto Bello*
  Kalimian, Abi
* Kienle, Eugene S., Sr., *Many Gables*
  King, Alan
* King, John Alsop, Jr.
  Krim, Arthur B.
  Leigh, Samuel [*see* Gelder]
  Livermore, Jesse Lauriston, Sr., *Evermore*
  Lundy, Frederick William Irving, *Lundy House*
  Mann, Samuel Vernon, Jr.
  Mann, Samuel Vernon, Sr., *Grove Point*
* Martin, James E., Sr., *Martin Hall*
* Meyer, Cord, II, *The Cove*
  Meyer, George C., Sr.
* Meyer, J. Edward, Sr., *Rhada*
* Mitchell, Willard H. [*see* Haar]
  Muncie, Dr. Curtis Hamilton, *Aloha*
  Muncie, Dr. Elizabeth Hamilton
* O'Hara, Thomas H.
  Olds, George Daniel, Jr.
  Opperman, Joseph [*see* K. Cooper]
  O'Rourke, Innis, Sr.
* O'Rourke, John Francis, Sr.
  Petrova, Mme. Olga
* Proctor, Charles E., *Shadowlane*
* Richards, Frederick L., *Hazelmere*
  Roesler, Edward, Sr., *Augustina*
  Roesler, Walter, Sr., *Tuckaway*
* Roig, Harold Joseph
  Satterwhite, Dr. Preston Pope, *Preston Hall*
  Schenck, Nicholas Michael
* Schieren, George Arthur, Sr., *Beachleigh*
  Seeger, Hal [*see* H. C. Ford]
  Sinclair, Harry Ford, Sr.
  Sloan, Alfred Pritchard, Jr., *Snug Harbor*
  Streeter, Edward, Sr.
* White, Alfred W., *The Lindens* [*see* F. W. White]
  White, Frederick Wheeler, *The Lindens*
  Willis, Harold Satterlee
  Wilson, George B. [*see* Crossman]
  Winslow, Edward

  Wyckoff, Richard Demille, *Twin Lindens*
* Wyckoff, Walter, *Twin Lindens*
* Wylie, Herbert George
  Zinsser, William Herman, Jr., *Windward*

LAKE SUCCESS
* Cantor, Eddie
  Devendorf, George E.
* Jonas, Nathan Solomon
* Phipps, Henry, Jr., *Bonnie Blink*
  Rose, George, Jr., *Four Corners*
* Vanderbilt, William Kissam, Jr., *Deepdale*
* Young, Otto S.

LATTINGTOWN
* Aldred, John Edward, *Ormston*
  Alker, Carroll Booth
  Allilueva, Svetlana Iosifovna
* Anderson, John, *Aberfeldy*
  Astin, Dr. Sherrill [*see* H. D. Gibson]
  Bailey, Frank, Sr., *Munnysunk*
* Baker, George Fisher, II, *Vikings Cove*
* Baldwin, William H., Jr.
* Ball, Wilbur Laing
  Battershall, Frederic S.
* Bedford, Alfred Cotton
  Bogart, Adrian T., Jr., *Friend Field*
  Bonner, Paul Hyde, Sr.
  Bonynge, Paul, Sr., *Ballintober Farm*
* Bourne, George Galt
  Breasted, Charles
  Brigham, Constance
* Burchard, Anson Wood, *Birchwood*
  Bush, Donald Fairfax, Jr., *Preference*
  Caesar, Charles Unger, *Sparrowbush*
  Carhart, Harold W., Sr.
  Carlisle, Floyd Leslie, Sr.
* Carver, Amos Dow, *Amincliff*
  Carver, Clifford Nickels, *Amincliff*
* Cheney, Ward
  Chiang Kai-shek, Mme., *Hillcrest*
  Clark, John
  Clews, James Blanchard
  Cook, Walter
  Costantini, Count David A., *Tulip Hill*
* Cozzens, Issachar, III, *Maple Knoll*
* Cravath, Paul Drennan, *Veraton* [I]
* Cutcheon, Franklin Warner M., *Matinecock Farms*
  Davis, John William, *Mattapan*
* Davison, Frederick Trubee, *Peacock Point*
  [family compound]
* Davison, Henry Pomeroy, Sr., *Peacock Point*
  [family compound]
  Dean, Herbert Hollingshead, *Deanlea*
  Dick, Fairman Rogers
  Dickson, Thomas, Sr., *Petit Bois*
  Diebold, Albert Henry
  Diebold, Trevor [*see* Lovett]
* Doubleday, Frank Nelson, *New House*
  Dugmore, Cyril, *The Gables*

LATTINGTOWN (cont'd)
  Eldredge, Edward Irving, Jr.
  Erbe, Gustav, Jr.
  Fairchild, Elvira McNair, *Northway House*
* Gales, George M., *Eckingston*
* Gates, Artemus Lamb, *Peacock Point*
* Gates, Charles Otis, *Peacock Point*
* Gates, Elizabeth Hoagland, *Dormer House*
  Gibson, Harvey Dow, *Lands End*
    [*Gibson owned two houses in Lattingtown.*]
  Gray, Henry Gunther, *Longford*
  Guinzburg, Harold Kleinert
* Guthrie, William Dameron, *Meudon*
  Hagan, Winston Henry, II, *Fox Brae*
  Hall, Leonard Wood
* Hepburn, Frederick Taylor, *Long Field*
* Hepburn, George
  Herzog, Edwin H.
* Horowitz, Louis Jay
  Howe, Polly Brooks, *Severn*
* Ide, George Edward, *Petit Bois*
  Johaneson, Nils R., *Littleholme*
  King, Everett W.
  Korboth, Roland [*see* A. D. Carver]
  Kung, Hsiang-hsi, *Hillcrest*
* Lamont, Thomas Stilwell, *The Creek*
  Lazo, Carlos
* Lovett, Robert Abercrombie, *Green Arbors*
  Lynch, Edmund Calvert, Jr., *Floralyn*
  Mackay, John William, III
  Maxwell, Howard Washburn, Jr.
* McLane, Allan, Jr., *Home Wood*
  McNair, William, *Northway House*
  Morgan, Henry Sturgis, Sr.
  Munsel, Patrice, *Lockjaw Ridge*
  Oberlin, Abraham
  Pool, Dr. Eugene Hillhouse
  Pratt, Frederic Richardson, *Friendfield Farm*
* Pratt, Theodore, Sr., *Whispering Pines*
  Pratt, Vera Amherst Hale, *Broom Hill*
  Raquet, Walter, *Lockjaw Ridge*
  Renard [*see* Erbe]
* Reynolds, Jackson Eli
  Richards, Ira, Jr.
  Ridder, Eric, Sr.
  Rogers, Henry Alexander, *Locust Lodge*
  Ryan, Byford
* Schultze, Max H., *The Gables*
* Scott, Rufus W., *Scottage*
  Shea, Edward Lane
  Sloane, George, *Brookmeade*
  Smithers, Christopher Dunkin, Sr., *Dunrobin*
* Stehli, Emil J., *Hawk Hill Place*
  Stettinius, Edward Reilly, Jr., *The Shelter*
  Stettinius, Edward Reilly, Sr., *The Shelter*
  Stewart, Glenn
  Stillman, F. A. [*see* Erbe]
  Stillman, Irwin, *Hillcrest*
  Tailer, Thomas Suffern, Jr., *Beaupre*
  Taliaferro, Charles Champe, III
  Taylor, Myron Charles, *Killingworth*
  Thurman, Steven

  Tower, Roderick
* Townsend, John Allen, *Forest Edge Farm*
  Van Ingen, Lawrence Bell, Jr., *Preference*
* Van Ingen, Lawrence Bell, Sr., *Preference*
  Victor, Royall, Sr.
  Vilas, Guillermo, *Lockjaw Ridge*
* Ward, Edward Mortimer, Sr., *Elkhurst*
* Warner, H. W. [*see* McNair]
* Weir, Levi Candee, *The Hedges*
  Whitney, Eleanor Searle
  Woods, Ward Wilson, Jr.
* Woolley, Daniel P., *Wooldon*

LAUREL HOLLOW
  Ames, Amyas, *Linden Hill*
  Ames, Charles Edgar
  Armstrong, Hamilton Fish, *Box Hill*
  Blackstone, Henry
  Bleecker, Charles Moore, *The Pinnacle*
* Bleecker, Theophylact Bache, Jr., *The Orchard*
* Bleecker, Theophylact Bache, II, *The Pinnacle*
  Burlingham, Dr. Robert
  Davenport, Dr. Charles Benedict, Sr.
  Davenport, Joseph [*see* C. B. Davenport]
  Deering, William Rogers, *Roseneath*
  Deesposito, Frank [*see* M. E. Jones]
* de Forest, Henry Grant, *Nethermuir*
  de Forest, Henry Wheeler, *Airslie*
  de Forest, Henry Wheeler, *Nethermuir*
  de Forest, Miss Julia Mary, *Airslie*
  de Roulet, Daniel Carroll, Sr., *Cannon Hill*
* Duer, Beverly, *Whispering Laurels*
  Dwyer, Martin, Jr.
  Fowler, Dr. Robert Henry
  Franklin, George Small, Sr.
  Gerdes, John, *Cannonhill Point*
  Gilder, Rodman, Sr.
* Gould, Frank Miller, *Cedar Knolls*
  Gubelmann, Walter Stanley
  Havemeyer, Charles Frederick, Jr.
  Henderson, Edward Cairns
* Hornblower, George Sanford, *Laurel Top*
  Howard, Alexandra C. Miller, *Holly House*
  Howell, Elizabeth Auchincloss Jennings, *The Point*
  James, Oliver B., Sr., *Rocky Point*
  Jennings, Frederic Beach
  Jennings, Percy Hall, Sr., *Laurel Brake*
  Jones, Arthur Eaton, *Jones Manor* [*see* M. E. Jones]
  Jones, Charles Hewlett, *Jones Manor*
* Jones, John Divine
* Jones, Mary Elizabeth, *Jones Manor*
    [*c. 1918 - one of two houses called Jones Manor
    which she owned in Laurel Hollow*]
  Jones, Rosalie Gardiner, *Jones Manor*
* Jones, Walter Restored, *Manor House*
* Jones, William
  Lindsay, George Nelson, Sr., *Highlands*
  Lusk, Dr. Graham, *The Briars*
  Miller, Andrew Otterson, Jr., *Ducks Landing*
  Miller, Margery Gerdes [*later,* Twining and Fates],
    Merrywitch and *Holly House*

LAUREL HOLLOW (cont'd)
* Norris, James King, *The Acre*
  Noyes, Winchester, *Tenacres*
  Ono, Yoko
  Polsinelli, Vincent, *Jones Manor*
  Smith, Owen Telfair
  Smull, Jacob Barstow, *Ridgelands*
* Stanley–Brown, Joseph
* Stewart, John Henry Jones, *Canon Hill*
    [*Stewart owned two houses in Laurel Hollow.*]
* Tiffany, Louis Comfort, *The Briars*
* Tiffany, Louis Comfort, *Laurelton Hall*
  Truslow, Francis Adams, Sr., *The Point*
* Van Strum, Kenneth Stevens
  Warner, Bradford Arnold, Sr., *La Pastura*
  Willard, George L., *Airslie*

LLOYD HARBOR
  Abbott, Paul, Sr., *Cloverfields*
* Alden, Anne Coleman, *Fort Hill House*
  Alsop, Dr. Reese Fell
  Black, Harry S.
* Brown, George McKesson, *West Neck Farm*
  Campbell, George W., *Fort Hill House*
    (1900 house)
  Castro, Bernard, Sr., *Panfield*
  Chanler, Alice Remington Chamberlain,
    Klotz Cottage
  Chanler, William Chamberlain, *Klotz Cottage*
  Colgate, Gilbert, II
* Conklin, Roland Ray, *Rosemary Farm*
  Cournand, Edouard L.
  Crane, Clinton Hoadley, Jr.
* Dulles, Allen Welsh
  Dulles, John Foster
* Eberstadt, Ferdinand, *Target Rock Farm*
* Ely, Albert Heman, Jr., *Elyston*
  Faber, Leander B., *Faberest*
* Fairchild, Sherman M., *Eastfair*
* Field, Marshall, III, *Caumsett*
  Fiske, Dr. E. Rodney
* Flinsch, Rudolf E. F., *Target Rock Farm*
* Ford, Nevil, *Woodford*
  Freidus, Jacob
  Gerard, James Watson, III
  Giordano, Salvatore, Sr., *Panfield*
  Graves, Robert, II, *Treborcliffe*
  Guida, Bernadette Castro, *Panfield*
  Gwynne, Arthur, *Mill Cove*
  Hadley, John Wood Blodgett, *White Wood Point*
  Hadley, Morris, *Whitewood*
  Hewitt, Edward Shepard, *Westacre*
  Jennings, Oliver Burr, II, *Burrwood*
* Jennings, Oliver Burr, II, *Dark Hollow*
* Jennings, Walter, *Burrwood*
* Johnston, John Herbert, *Boatcroft*
  Lindbergh, Charles Augustus, Jr., *Lloyd Manor*
* Livingston, Gerald Moncrieffe, *Kilsyth*
* Lloyd–Smith, Wilton, *Kenjockety*
  Lockman, Myron Augustus, *Van Wyck Homestead*

* Matheson, William John, *Fort Hill House*
    [*1900 house*]
  McCann, David Anthony
* Milbank, Albert Goodsell, *Panfield*
  Mulferrig, John B. [*see* Stafford]
* Reed, Lansing Parmelee, *Windy Hill*
  Rice, Paula [*see* Lloyd–Smith]
* Robertson, Charles Sammis
  Savage, Rev. Theodore Fiske, *Seven Springs*
* Scott, Donald, Sr., *Whitewood*
  Sheeline, Paul Cushing
  Smith, Albert Delmont, *Mill Pond*
* Stafford, Jennie K., *Broadwater*
  Steers, James Rich, II
  Truesdell, Dr. Edward Delavan, *Gladwolden*
* Weld, Francis Minot, II, *Lulworth*
* Williams, Timothy Shaler, *Shorelands*
  Wood, Willis Delano, *Fort Hill House* [*1900 house*]
    and *Lloyd Manor*

MANHASSET
* Barnes, Courtlandt Dixon, Sr., *Nonesuch House*
  Linkletter, George Onderdonk, Sr.
  McCrary, John ("Tex") Reagan, Jr.
  Munsey, Frank Andrew
* Payson, Charles Shipman
* Sherry, Louis, *Sherryland*
  Vanderbilt, Virginia Graham Fair, *Fairmont*
  Whitney, John Hay, *Greentree*
* Whitney, William Payne, *Greentree*

MATINECOCK
  Andersen, Dr. Harold Willids, Sr., *Still House*
* Auchincloss, Gordon, Sr., *Ronda*
  Auchincloss, Joseph Howland, Sr.
  Bast, W. C.
* Batterman, Henry Lewis, Sr.
  Bedford, Alfred Clarke, Sr.
  Bonner, Douglas Griswold, Sr., *Meadow Cottage*
* Bosworth, William Welles, *Old Trees*
* Brown, Stephen Howland, *Solana*
  Coffin, Miss Alice, *Portledge*
* Coffin, Charles Albert, *Portledge*
  Cravath, Erastus Milo, II, *Mill Hill*
* Cravath, Paul Drennan, *Still House*
* Cravath, Paul Drennan, *Veraton* [II] [III]
  Delehanty, Bradley, *The Barn*
* Dewing, Hiram E., *Appledore*
* Dwight, Richard Everett
* Fahys, George Ernest, Sr., *Hilaire*
    [*Fahys built two houses, named Hilaire, in Matinecock.*]
  Finlayson, Frank Redfern
* Fish, Edwin A., *Airdrie*
  Foy, Bryon Cecil, *Foy Farm*
  Franklin, Philip Albright Small, Jr., *Hundred House*
* Franklin, Philip Albright Small, Sr., *Royston*
* Geddes, Eugene Maxwell, Sr., *Punkin Hill*
  Gerry, Henry Averell, Sr., *Duck Hook*
* Greer, William Armstrong, *Flower de Hundred*
* Groesbeck, Clarence Edward, *Roads End*

MATINECOCK cont'd)
Hoguet, Dr. Joseph Peter, Sr., *Oak Lawn*
* Hopkins, Erustis Langdon, *Wildwood*
Kane, John P., Jr.
Larkin, Vera Agnes Huntington Cravath
* Lindeberg, Harrie Thomas, *West Gate Lodge*
Luckenbach, John Lewis, *Katydid Farm*
Lynch, Edmund Calvert, Sr.
* Lyon, John Denniston, *Wyomissing*
Martin, John Stuart, *Fox Hollow*
Merrill, Joseph L., *Chanticleer*
Mitchell, Sidney Alexander, Sr., *Marney*
* Mitchell, Sidney Zollicoffer
* Mixsell, Dr. Harold Ruckman, *Forest Edge*
* Morgan, Junius Spencer, *Apple Trees*
* Pennington, Hall Pleasants
Pickett, John Olen, Jr.
Porter, Seton, *Still House*
Pulsifer, George Hale, *Killibeg*
Rentschler, Gordon Sohn
Rothschild, Baron Eugene de, *Still House*
Ryle, Arthur, Sr., *Whileaway*
* Schermerhorn, Alfred Coster
Slater, Horatio Nelson, III, *Ricochet*
Smith, George Campbell, Sr.
* Sparrow, Edward Wheeler, *Killibeg*
Stone, Charles Augustus, Sr., *Solana*
[*Stone owned three houses in Matinecock, two of which he built.*]
Thieriot, Charles Henschel, II
* Toerge, Norman K., Sr., *The Hitching Post*
Vietor, Dr. John Adolf, Sr., *Cherrywood*
Walker, James Blaine, Jr.
Wellington, Herbert Galbraith, Sr.

MILL NECK
* Abbott, Phillips, *Steepways*
Avedon, Peter M.
* Babcock, Frederick Huntington, *Pepperidge Point*
Babcock, Henry Dennison, Sr.
Batterman, Henry Lewis, Jr., *Beaver Brook Farm*
* Batterman, Henry Lewis, Sr., *Beaver Brook Farm*
* Beekman, James William, Sr., *The Cliffs*
* Brokaw, Irving, *Frost Mill Lodge* and *Goose Point*
* Bryan, James Taylor, Sr.
Caldwell, Robert J., *Seven Gables*
Catacosinos, William James, Sr.
Chadbourne, Humphrey Wallingford
* Church, Charles Thomas, Sr., *Three Brooks*
Church, Frederic Edwin, *Three Brooks*
Close, Leroi
Coe, William Rogers, *Rockledge*
* Cox, Irving E., *Meadow Farm*
* Cushing, Leonard Jarvis, Sr., *The Evergreens*
Dane, Chester Linwood, Sr., *Linwood*
* Davis, Arthur Vining
* De Selding, Hermann
* Dickerman, Florence Calkin, *Hillendale*
* di Zoppola, Countess Edith Mortimer
* Dodge, Lillian Sefton Thomas, *Sefton Manor*

* Doubleday, Frank Nelson, *Effendi Hill*
[*Doubleday owned two houses in Mill Neck.*]
* Doubleday, Nelson, Sr., *Barberrys*
Eden, Bronson Beecher Tuttle, Sr.
Fordyce, Mrs. Dorothy MacElree, *Oakley Court*
Fritz, Dr. Albert R., Sr., *The Cliffs*
Gerdes, John, *Pepperidge Point*
* Hepburn, Leonard F.
* Hodenpyl, Anton Gysberti, *Hill House*
Hollander, Mrs.
Hudson, Hans Kierstede, Sr., *Sterling*
Hull, Kenneth Duryee, Sr., *Millstone*
Huntington, Robert Dinsmore, Jr.
* Huntington, Robert Dinsmore, Sr.
Keating, Cletus, Sr., *Holly Hill*
Kerr, Elmore Coe, Sr.
La Montagne, Harry
Lehman, Ellen
* Levitt, William Jaird, Sr., *La Colline*
Loeb, William, Jr., *Westerleigh*
* Loening, Grover, *Margrove*
Ludlow, Alden Rodney, Sr.
Marsh, John Bigelow, Sr., *Nyrmah*
Martin, Mrs. William
Mauze, Abby Rockefeller, *Laurel Hill*
Murdock, Lewis Chapen
Nicastro, Louis Joseph
Nickerson, Hoffman, *Monomoit*
* Niven, John Ballantine, *Rhuna Craig*
* O'Brien, Henry, *Laurel Hill*
* Perine, William DeNyse Nichols, *Windermere House*
* Peters, William Richmond, *Hawirt*
Pratt, Herbert Lee, Jr., *Whitehall*
Proctor, Charles E.
Russell, Faris R., *Clayton*
* Schmidlapp, Carl Jacob, Sr., *Rumpus House*
* Slade, Josephine Bissell Roe, *Pine Terrace*
Smithers, Robert Brinkley, *Longhur*
[*Smithers owned two houses in Mill Neck.*]
Sterling, Dr. G.
Townsend, James Mulford, II
Toy, Thomas Dallam, Sr.
* Tucker, Richard Derby, Sr.
* Tully, William John, *Almar*
Vanderbilt, Alfred Gwynne, II
[*Vanderbilt owned two houses in Mill Neck.*]
Vanderbilt, Alfred Gwynne, II, *Oakley Court*
Wanner, Ernest P. [*see C. P. Wilson*]
* White, Gardiner Winslow, Sr., *White Lodge*
* White, Rita Kohler, *Glenby*
* White, Robert K., Sr.
Whitney, Cornelius Vanderbilt, *Oakley Court*
Williams, Rodney W., *Boxwood*
* Wilson, Charles Porter
Winmill, Robert Campbell, *Borradil Farm*
Winters, Albert C.
* Work, Bertram G., Sr., *Oak Knoll*

MUTTONTOWN

* Alker, Carroll Booth
  Amato, Camille Jean Tuorto, *Woodstock Manor*
  Bedford, Alfred Cotton, *Pemberton*
  Benkard, Henry Horton
* Bermingham, John F., *Midland Farm*
* Bertschmann, Louis Frederick, *Les Bouleaux*
  Blair, Watson Keep
  Blair, Wolcott
* Brewster, George S., *Fairleigh*
* Brokaw, Howard Crosby, *The Chimneys*
* Burden, James Abercrombie, Jr., *Woodside*
* Chadwick, Elbridge Gerry, *Russet*
* Chew, Philip Frederick, *Archway*
  Christie, Lansdell Kisner
      [Christie owned two houses in Muttontown.]
  Coleman, Gregory
  Connfelt, Charles Maitland, *Hillsedge*
* Delano, William Adams, *Muttontown Corners*
* Dows, David, Jr., *Charlton Hall*
  Dunscombe, Duncan, *Orolea*
* Field, Evelyn Marshall, *Easton*
  Flint, Dr. Austin, Jr.
  Griscom, Lloyd Carpenter, *Huntover Lodge*
  Heck, George Callendine, Sr., *Linwood*
  Hoffman, Albert L., Sr., *Radnor House*
* Hudson, Charles I., Sr., *Knollwood*
  Hudson, Percy Kierstede
  Knowlton, Hugh Gilbert, Sr.
  Lyon, Cecil T. F. B., *Harrow Hill*
  Martin, Esmund Bradley, Sr.
  McKay, Alexandra Emery Moore, *Chelsea*
  McVeigh, Charles Senff, Sr.
  Meyer, Robert J.
* Moore, Benjamin, *Chelsea*
  Netter, Dr. Frank H.
  Nicholas, Harry Ingersoll, II, *Rolling Hill Farm*
* Nichols, Francis Tilden, Sr., *Bayberry Downs*
  Polk, Frank Lyon, II
  Polk, Frank Lyon, Sr.
* Provost, Cornelius W., *Woodley*
* Ripley, Julien Ashton, Sr., *Three Corners Farm*
  Ripley, Lucy Fairfield Perkins
  Robinson, Monroe Douglas
  Senff, Gustavia
* Smith, George, *Blythewood*
  Stam, Alan
  Stevens, Byam K., Jr., *Kirby Hill*
* Stevens, Joseph Sampson, *Kirby Hill*
* Thieriot, Charles Henschel, Sr., *Cedar Hill*
  Vander Poel, William Halsted, *Woodstock*
  Van Rensselaer, Charles Augustus, Sr.,
      Homewood Place
  Victor, Royall, Sr.
  Walker, Elisha, Sr., *Les Pommiers*
  Wellman, Roderic
  Willock, William W., Sr., *Gladwood*
* Winthrop, Bronson
      [Bronson Winthrop built two houses in Muttontown.]
  Winthrop, Egerton Leigh, Jr., *Muttontown Meadows*
  Zog I - King of Albania

NORTH HILLS

  Allen, Frederic Winthrop, *White Oak Farm*
  Auchincloss, Patty Milburn
  Boyer, Philip, Sr., *Long Shadows*
* Brady, Nicholas Frederic, *Inisfada*
* Bullard, Roger Harrington
* Canfield, Augustus Cass, *Cassleigh*
  Cutting, Dr. Fulton
  de Roulet, Vincent W.
* Dimock, Edward Jordan, *Enderby*
  Elbert, Robert George, *Elbourne*
* Emanuel, Victor, *Dorwood*
* Everdell, William, Jr.
  Grace, Joseph Peter, II, *Gracewood*
* Grace, Joseph Peter, Sr., *Tullaroan*
  Grace, Miss Louise Natalie, *Gilchrist*
  Griswold, Frank Gray
  Harkness, Edward Stephen, *Weekend*
  Kelley, Cornelius Francis, *Sunny Skies*
  Lunning, Frederick, *Northcourt*
  Martino, Joseph Anthony, *Jemstone*
  Merrill, Bradford, Jr.
* Milburn, John George, Jr., *Wychwood*
* Milburn, John George, Sr., *Groombridge*
* Minton, Henry Miller, *Brookwood*
  Paley, William S., *Kiluna Farm*
* Pulitzer, Ralph, Sr., *Kiluna Farm*
  Ryan, John Dennis, *Derrymore*
* Shearman, Lawrence Hobart
  Sheehan, William Francis, *The Height*
* Singer, William
  Spreckels, Claus August
  Stern, Henry Root, Sr., *Penwood*
  Van Rooyens, *Jemstone* [*see* Martino]
  Webb, William Seward D., Jr.

OLD BROOKVILLE

  Alexandre, J. Henry, Jr., *Valleybrook Farm*
* Alker, Carrol Booth, *Ca Va*
* Anderson, George A.
  Appleby, Francis Storm
  Bailey, Townsend Fleet, *Horse's Home Farm*
* Barnes, E. Mortimer, *Manana*
  Bodman, Herbert L., Sr., *Hill House*
  Bottomley, William Lawrence, *Hickory Hill*
  Breed, William Constable, Sr., *Normandy Farms*
  Brooks, Winthrop Holley
* Brown, Francis Gordon, Sr., *Willow Bank*
  Burden, James Abercrombie, III, *Woodside*
  Cavanaugh, Edward Francis, Jr., *Naghward*
  Clark, Louis Crawford, II, *Valentine Farm*
* Clarke, Jeremiah, Sr.
  de Milhau, Louis John de Grenon, Sr., *Wrencroft*
  Dick, Fairman Rogers, *Apple Tree Hill*
* Dickinson, Hunt Tilford, Sr., *Hearth Stone*
  Dillon, Herbert Lowell, Sr., *Sunninghill*
  Duryea, Harry H.
  Emerson, Margaret, *Rynwood*
  Fish, Sidney W., *The Duck Pond*
  Graham, Raymond Austin, Sr.
  Hanks, Stedman Shumway

OLD BROOKVILLE (cont'd)

Havemeyer, Frederick Christian, IV
* Holmes, Artemas, *Holmestead Farm*
Hoppin, William Warner, Jr., *Friendship Hill*
Hubbs, Charles Francis
* Jennings, Benjamin Brewster, *Windward*
Keating, Cletus, Sr.
Ketcham, Francis I.
* Kettles, Richard C., Jr., *Orchard Corners*
Ladew, Harvey Smith, II., *The Box*
LeRoy, Robert
Luckenbach, Edgar Frederick, Jr.
Lundy, Frederick William Irving, *Rynwood*
Martin, Alastair Bradley
Mason, Julian Starkweather, *Pound Hollow Cottage*
McClure, Walter C., *Tall Trees*
Miller, William Wilson
Moffett, George Monroe, Sr., *Les Bois*
* Park, Darragh Anderson, Sr., *Hyde Park*
* Peck, Fremont Carson, Sr.
Philips, William Pyle
Potter, Clarkson
Preston, Lewis Thompson, Sr., *Longfields*
Rentschler, Gordon Sohn, *Waveland*
* Richmond, L. Martin, *Sunninghill*
Rumbough, Stanley Maddox, Jr.
Salvage, Sir. Samuel Agar, *Rynwood*
Schwab, Hermann C., II, *Chicken Valley Farm*
* Stearns, John Noble, III
Taft, Walbridge S., *Waveland*
Taft, William Howard, II
Tuttle, Dr. Jason H., *Tuttles Corner*
Van Alen, James Henry, *Penny Pond*
Vanderbilt, Lena Thurlow
* Watriss, Frederick N.
Weekes, Frances Stokes, *Valentine Farm*

OLD WESTBURY
* Bacon, Robert, *Old Acres*
* Bacon, Robert Low, *Arlough*
Barney, Charles Tracy
Bingham, Harry Payne, Sr., *Ivycroft*
Boegner, Margaret Helen Phipps, *Orchard Hill*
Bono, Henry, Jr., *The Crossroads*
* Bostwick, Albert C., II
* Bostwick, George Herbert, Sr.
Bostwick, Lillian Stokes
Ceballos, Juan Manuel, Jr., *Three Winds*
* Clark, Frederick Ambrose, *Broad Hollow House*
* Clark, James Averell, Sr.
Clark, John Balfour, *Hickory Hill*
Cram, John Sergeant, Sr.
Crocker, George
Cross, Eliot B.
Daniel, Robert Williams, *Dreamwood*
* Dilworth, Dewees Wood, *Gloan House*
* Duryea, Hermanes Barkula, Jr., *Knole*
* Earle, Henry Montague, *Dorset Lodge*
Elmhirst, Leonard Knight, *Applegreen*
Entenmann, William, Jr., *Timber Bay Farm*
Ferry, E. Hayward

Flagg, W. Allston, Sr.
* Gardner, Hope Norman, *The Corners*
Garvan, Francis Patrick, Sr., *Roslyn House*
Gerry, Robert Livingston, Jr.
Glass, Harry [*see* Geo. Whitney, Sr.]
* Godfrey, Henry Fletcher, Sr.
* Goodyear, Anson Conger, Sr.
* Grace, William Russell, Jr., *The Crossroads*
Gray, Albert Zebriskie, *Orchard Farm*
* Grosvenor, Graham Bethune, *Graymar*
Harriman, William Averell
* Hastings, Thomas, *Bagatelle*
Heckscher, Gustav Maurice, *Three Winds*
* Henry, Barklie McKee
Hickox, Charles V., *Boxwood Farm*
Hitchcock, Margaret Mellon, *Broad Hollow Farm*
Hitchcock, Thomas, Sr., *Broad Hollow Farm*
Holloway, William Grace, Sr., *Foxland*
Hutton, William E., II
Iglehart, David Stewart, *La Granja*
Jay, De Lancey Kane
Kadish, Lawrence
* Keene, Foxhall Parker, *Rosemary Hall*
Langley, William Clark
* Lanier, James Franklin Doughty
Le Boutillier, Thomas, II
Le Boutillier, Thomas, III
Loew, William Goadby, *Loewmoor*
Lord, William Galey
* Lowe, Henry Wheeler, *Mariemont*
Manice, William de Forest, Sr., *Edgewood House*
Mann, Dr. John, Sr.
Manville, Lorraine, *Les Deux Tours*
Martin, Bradley, Jr., *Knole*
Martin, Esmond Bradley, Sr., *Knole*
Middlemark, Marvin P.
Milburn, Devereux, Jr.
* Milburn, Devereux, Sr., *Sunridge Hall*
Miller, Flora Payne Whitney, *French House*
Mondello, Joseph
Morgan, Edwin Denison, IV, *Sycamore House*
* Morgan, Edwin Denison, III, *Wheatly*
* Morse, Allon Mae Fuller, *Morse Lodge*
* Mortimer, Stanley, Sr., *Roslyn Hall*
* Murray, Hugh A., *Gay Gardens*
* Murray, John Francis
* Neilson, Raymond Perry Rodgers, Sr.
Park, William Gray, *Turnpike Cottage*
* Peabody, Julian Livingston, Sr., *Pound Hollow Farm*
Pell, Clarence Cecil, Jr.
Pell, Clarence Cecil, Sr.
* Pell, Howland Haggerty, Sr.
Phipps, Henry Carnegie, *Spring Hill*
Phipps, Howard, Jr., *Erchless* and *Little Erchless*
* Phipps, Howard, Sr., *Erchless*
* Phipps, John Shaffer, *Westbury House*
Phipps, Ogden
Potter, William Chapman
Prince, Frederick Henry, Jr.
* Rathborne, Joseph Cornelius, II, *North Refuge*
Regan, Thomas J.
Rinaldini, Luis Emilio

1128

OLD WESTBURY (cont'd)

Robertson, Thomas Markoe, *Guinea Hollow Farm*
* Rose, George, Sr., *Overland House*
Steele, Charles
* Stevens, Charles Albert, *Annandale*
* Stevenson, Malcolm, Sr., *Two Maple Farm*
* Stow, William L.
* Straight, Willard Dickerman, *Elmhurst*
Talbott, Harold Elster, II, *The Pillars*
* Tiffany, Perry
Tippett, Mary Elizabeth Altemus
Tower, Flora Payne Whitney, *French House*
  [*see* F. P. W. Miller)
Tower, Whitney, Sr.
Trimble, Richard, II
Trimble, Richard, Sr.
* Von Stade, Francis Skiddy, Sr.
Webb, James Watson, Sr.
Webb, William Seward D., Jr.
* Whitney, Cornelius Vanderbilt, *Whitney House*
* Whitney, George, Sr., *Home Acres*
Whitney, Harry Payne
Whitney, Robert Bacon, Sr.
* Whitney, William Collins
Widener, George Dunstan, Jr.
Wing, S. Bryce, *Twin Oaks*
Winthrop, Beekman, II, *Groton Farms*
Winthrop, Grenville Lindall
* Winthrop, Robert, II, *Groton Place*
* Winthrop, Robert Dudley, *Groton Farms*

OYSTER BAY
* Adam, Sarah Sampson, *Hillside*
Ballantine, Arthur Atwood, Sr., *Council Rock*
Bowdoin, George Temple, *Nevis*
Derby, Dr. Richard, *Old Adam*
* Dexter, Stanley Walker, *Sunnymede*
Dieffenbach, William
Hagen, Lucy Trotter, *Locust Knoll*
* Norton, Huntington, *Notley Hill*
O'Connor, John A., *Sunnymede*
* Schiff, John Mortimer, *Northwood*
* Schiff, Mortimer L., *Northwood*
Shonnard, Horatio Seymour, Sr., *Boscobel*
Trotter, William M., *Locust Knoll*
* Underhill, Francis T.
Weidenfeld, Camille

OYSTER BAY COVE
Baehr, Irvine E. Theodore, *Piazzola*
* Betts, Wyllis Rossiter, Jr., *The Pebbles*
Blair, James Alonzo, Jr., *Ontare*
* Blair, James Alonzo, Sr., *Ontare*
* Coe, Henry Eugene, Jr., *The Beaklet*
Coffin, William Sloane, Sr.
* Colgate, John Kirtland, Sr., *Oaklea*
Cushman, Paul, Sr., *Tapis Vert*
Devereux, Walter Bourchier, Jr.
Douglas, Barry [*see* Ingalls]
Du Bois, Eugene, *Fleetwood*

* Farwell, Walter, *Mallow*
Gair, Robert, Jr.
* Garver, John Anson, *Wrexleigh*
* Gould, Edwin, *Highwood*
Guest, Winston Frederick Churchill,
  Duck Puddle Farm
* Harjes, Henry Herman
Hedges, Benjamin Van Doren, II
Hill, Dr. Miner C., *The Terrace*
* Hoppin, Gerard Beekman, *Four Winds*
* Ingalls, Fay, *Sunken Orchard*
* Ledyard, Lewis Cass, Jr., *Westwood*
Leffingwell, Russell Cornell, *Redcote*
Leonard, Edgar Welch, *Stoke Farm*
Livingston, John Holyoke
* Lloyd, Robert MacAllister, Sr., *Tapis Vert*
* Lutz, Frederick L., *Laurel Acres*
Martin, Henry Bradley, II
McCann, Charles Edward Francis, *Sunken Orchard*
McKelvey, Charles Wylie
Minicozzi, Alexander [*see* E. Gould]
Montana, Dr. Christopher
* Moore, John Chandler, *Moorelands*
Moore, Louis de Bebian, *Moorelands*
Morris, Ray, Sr., *Yellowcote*
Mott, Jordan Lawrence, IV, *Bunker Hill*
Nichols, Acosta, Sr., *Wothiholme*
O'Neill, George Dorr, Sr.
O'Neill, Grover, Sr., *Fleetwood*
Pruyn, Robert Dunbar, *Linden Farm*
Pulling, Thomas John Edward, *Redcote*
Redmond, Roland Livingston, *White Elephant Farm*
Roosevelt, Theodore, *Tranquility*
Rousmaniere, James Ayer, *Bobbingsworth*
Rousmaniere, John E., *Bobbingsworth*
Sears, Joseph Hamblen, *The Other House*
* Sewell, Robert Van Vorst, *Fleetwood*
Shutt, Edwin Holmes, Jr.
* Slade, John, Sr., *Berry Hill Farm*
Sparks, Sr. Thomas Ashley, *Northaw*
Swan, Otis D.
Swann, Dr. Arthur Wharton
Taliaferro, Charles Champe, III
Taylor, Edwin Pemberton, Jr., *White Oaks*
Tiffany, Charles Lewis, II, *Elmwood*
Tinker, Giles Knight, *Reknit*
Townsend, Edward Mitchell II, *Townsend Place*
Townsend, Edward Mitchell, Sr., *Townsend Place*
Townsend, Howard Rockwell, Sr., *Ramsbroke*
Trowbridge, Edmund Quincy, *Holly Court*
Verdi, Minturn de Suzzara
Weekes, Arthur Delano, Jr., *The Anchorage*
Weekes, John Abeel, *Tranquility*
* White, Alexander Moss, Jr., *Hickory Hill*
Woodward, William, Jr., *The Playhouse*
* Young, Thomas F., *Elmwood*

PLANDOME

D'Oench, Albert Frederic, *Sunset Hill*
Gerdes, John, *Brookedge*
* Haggerson, Frederic H.
* Latham, Leroy, *Hemlock Hollow*
Ricks, Jesse Jay
Roesler, Edward, Jr.

PLANDOME MANOR

Allen, Gabriel, *Plandome Manor House*
* Burnett, Frances Hodgson, *Fairseat*
Burnett, Vivian, *Bentleigh*
Dean, Robert Sr., *Plandome Manor House*
Fahnestock, Archer Pleasant, *The Pleasantways*
Fleischmann, Raoul Herbert
* Goldman, Herman
* Grumman, Leroy Randle
Houston, Herbert Sherman, *Marlets*
* Inness–Brown, Hugh Alwyn, Sr., *The Point*
Ioannou, John, *Plandome Manor House*
Jordan, Edith Hodgson
Kennedy, Louise Leeds, *Plandome Mills*
Leeds, Warner Mifflin, II
Littleton, Martin Wiley, Sr., *Plandome Manor House*
Morgan, William F., *Elysian Hill*
* Phillips, Ellis Laurimore, Sr., *Laurimon*
Riggs, George
Sizer, Robert Ryland, Sr., *Norwood*

PORT WASHINGTON

Bigelow, Anson Alexander
Chalkley, Otway Hebron
Cocks, William Hall, Sr.
Fisher, Carl Graham
Fox, Fontaine Talbot, Jr.
Kelland, Clarence Budington
Mertz, LuEsther Turner
Mizner, Addison, *Old Cow Bay Manor House*
Schreiber, Dr. George, Jr., *Harbor Acres*

ROSLYN

Brower, Ernest Cuyler, *Locust Hill*
Brower, George Ellsworth, *Locust Hill*
Cornell, Phebe Augusta
Ely, Rev. Samuel Rose, Sr.
Gerry, Dr. Roger Goodman, *Locust Hill*
Hansen, Robert, *Locust Hill* [see Brower]
* Henderson, Frank C., *Villa Marina*
* Mackay, Clarence Hungerford, *Harbor Hill*
* Oakman, Walter George, Sr., *Oakdene*
Rubel, Samuel
Walbridge, Henry D., *Waldene*
Will, Harold Henry, *Villa Marina*
Willetts, William Prentice, *Homewood*
Willis, Charles
Wolf, Barry, *Locust Hill*

ROSLYN ESTATES

Anderson, Henry Hill, II, *Handyhill*
Fox, Fontaine Talbot, Jr.
Morley, Christopher Darlington, Sr., *Green Escape*

ROSLYN HARBOR

Briggs, Mead L.
Brion, Lucille Demarest, *Sycamore Lodge*
Bryant, Miss Julia Sands, *Cedarmere*
Bryant, William Cullen, *Cedarmere*
* Bryce, Lloyd Stephens, *Bryce House*
Cairns, Anna Eliza, *Clifton*
Cartier [*see* Clapham]
Casey, William Joseph, Jr., *Mayknoll*
* Clapham, Thomas, *Stone House*
Curtis, James Freeman, *Willowmere*
Demarest, John M., *Sycamore Lodge*
Emory, William Helmsley, Jr., *Clifton*
Fahnestock, Frank Curry, *Sycamore Lodge*
Frick, Childs, *Clayton*
Goddard, Conrad Godwin, *Montrose*
Godwin, Miss Elizabeth Love, *Cedarmere*
Godwin, Harold, *Cedarmere*
Godwin, Parke, *Montrose*
Hines, Ephram
Hughes, Dr. Wendell, *Wenlo*
Mott, Dr. Valentine
Patchin, Robert Halsey, *Hawthorne House*
* Pyne, Percy Rivington, II, *Rivington House*
Reed, Stanley, Jr. [*see* Patchin]
Riggs, Glenn E., Sr., *Sycamore Lodge*
Seligman, Joseph Lionel, Sr., *Greenridge*
Stern, Benjamin, *Claraben Court*
Taylor, George Winship, Sr.
Ward, Aaron, *Willowmere*
Ward, Elijah, *Locust Knoll*
* Williams, Arthur, *Greenridge*
Zenz, Dr. Frederick Anton, *Montrose*

ROSLYN HEIGHTS

Auchincloss, Charles Crooke, *Builtover*
McCory, Nellie, *Whispered Wishes*
Potter, Edwin A., Jr.
Ryan, John Carlos
Twohig, Dr. Daniel
Whalen, Grover A., Sr.

SADDLE ROCK

Eldridge, Lewis Angevine, Sr., *Redcote*
Eldridge, Roswell, *Udalls*

SANDS POINT

Alker, Henry Alphonse, Sr., *Hilltop*
Anderson, Harry B., Jr.
Anderson, Henry Burrall, Sr.
* Astor, William Vincent, *Cloverley Manor*
Auchincloss, Samuel Sloan, II
Backus, Dana Converse, *Hazeldean*

SANDS POINT (cont'd)

* Belmont, Alva Erskine Smith, *Beacon Towers*
  Berritt, Harold
  Biddle, William Canby, II
  Brokaw, George Tuttle
  Brooks, Joseph W.
* Browning, J. S., *Kidd's Rocks* [see Sloane]
* Carpenter, James Edwin Ruthven, *Keswick*
* Cockran, William Bourke, *The Cedars*
* Cowl, Donald Hearn
  De Leslie, Count Alexander Paulovitch
* Duncan, William Butler, *Park Hill*
  Eagle, Henry, Sr., *The Eyrie*
  Emerson, Margaret, *Cedar Knoll*
  Fisher, Carl Graham
* Fleischmann, Max C., *The Lindens*
* Fraser, Alfred, *Ashcombe*
  Fraser, Alfred Valentine, *Old House*
  Goldman, K. M. [see W. de F. Wright, Sr.]
* Gould, Howard, *Castlegould*
  Guggenheim, Daniel, *Hempstead House*
* Guggenheim, Florence Shloss, *Mille Fleurs*
* Guggenheim, Harry Frank, *Falaise*
* Guggenheim, Isaac, *Villa Carola*
  Guggenheim, Solomon Robert, *Trillora Court*
* Guggenheim, William, Sr., *Fountainhill*
  Hagedorn, Horace
  Hamersley, Louis Gordon, Sr., *The Moorings*
  Harriman, William Averell
  Hawkes, Dr. Forbes, *The Briar Patch*
  Hearst, William Randolph, *Saint Joan*
  Hicks, Frederick Cocks
  Hirsch, Peter, *Wildbank*
  Hitchcock, Thomas, Jr.
* Hoffstot, Frank Norton, *Belcaro*
* Holmes, Bettie Fleischmann, *The Chimneys*
  Jandorf, Louis C.
  Johnson, Seymour, *Driftwoods*
  Johnston, Douglas Turner
  Kelland, Clarence Budington, *Sandy Cay*
  Kingsbury, Howard Thayer, Sr.
  Kramer, Irwin Hamilton
* Laidlaw, James Lees, *Hazeldean*
  Langone, Kenneth Gerard, Sr., *Sands Hill*
  Lavilla, Adolph [see Carpenter]
  Lewyt, Alexander Milton
  Lippincott, William, *Locustmere*
* Luckenbach, Edgar Frederick, Sr., *Elm Court*
  Luckenbach, Lewis, II
* MacKelvie, Neil Bruce, *Cedar Knoll*
  McIntosh, Allan J.
  Mohibu, A. [see H. A. Alker, Sr.]
  Myers, Theodore Walter
* Nast, Conde, *Sandy Cay*
  Neelands, Thomas D., Jr.
  Nixon, Lewis
  Ohl, John Phillips
* Parker, Dale M.
* Parker, John Alley, *Driftwoods*
  Payson, Charles Shipman, *Lands End*
    [see M. D. Sloane)
  Pell, Theodore Roosevelt, *Wampage*

  Richter, Horace
  Rothschild, Baron Robert de, *Belcaro*
* Rumsey, Mary Harriman
  Rutherfurd, John M. L.
  Saltzman, Arnold Asa
  Schenck, Nicholas Michael
  Schiff, Dorothy, *Sandy Cay*
  Schuster, Max Lincoln, *Cow Neck Farm*
  Schwartz, Alexander Charles, Sr.
  Schwartz, Charles
  Sheridan, Frank J., Jr.
  Siegel, Edward [see F. K. Thayer, Sr.]
  Sizer, Robert Ryland, Jr.
  Sloane, Charles Byron, *The Place*
  Sloane, Charles William, *The Place*
  Sloane, Malcolm Douglas
  Smith, Albert Delmont, *Keewaydin*
  Smith, Earl Edward Tailer, Sr., *Iradell*
  Sousa, John Philip, Sr., *Wildbank*
  Swope, Herbert Bayard, Sr., *Keewaydin*
* Thayer, Francis Kendall, Sr., *Oakwood*
    and *Thayer House*
* Thayer, Kendall, *Thayer House*
* Thomas, Ralph W., Sr.
  Uris, Percy, *Sandy Cay*
* Vanderbilt, Alfred Gwynne, II
* Vanderbilt, George Washington, IV
  Van Wart, Edwin Clark, *The Shrubbery*
  Van Wart, Henry, *The Shrubbery*
  Vultaggio, Donald
  Weaver, Sylvester [see A. V. Fraser]
  Welch, Charles James, *The Glen*
  Wellman, Roderic, *Soundacre*
* Wright, Wilkinson de Forest, Sr., *Deephaven*

SEA CLIFF
* Levison, John Jacob
* Pirie, Samuel Carson, Sr.

SEARINGTOWN
  Crocker, Frank Longfellow
  D'Oench, Russell Grace, Sr., *Searing Farm*

SOUTH HUNTINGTON
* Hare, Meredith, *Pidgeon Hill*

SYOSSET
  Ames, Charles Edgar, *Band Box*
  Belmont, Eleanor Robson
  Burton, Van Duzer, Sr., *Pink Coat Cottage*
  Chanler, Lewis Stuyvesant, Jr., *Chestnut Vale*
* Hammond, Paul Lyman, *Muttontown Lodge*
* Kennedy, William, Sr., *Kennedy Villa*
* Lord, Franklin Butler, II, *Cottsleigh*
* Lord, George de Forest, Sr., *Overfields*
  Peck, Thomas Bloodgood, II, *The Shack*
  Snow, George Palen
  Stebbins, Theodore Ellis, Sr., *White Oak Farm*

SYOSSET (cont'd)
Thatcher, John M. P., Sr., *Cloverfield*
Tinker, Edward Richmond, Jr., *Woodbury House*
Tod, Robert Elliot, *Thistleton*
Tower, Roderick, *Chestnut Vale*
Warner, Henry Wolcott
* Webb, James Watson, Sr., *Woodbury House*

UPPER BROOKVILLE
Albright, Dr. Madeleine Korbel
Appleton, Benjamin Ward, *Little Waldingfield*
Atherton, Henry Francis, Sr.
Babcock, Woodward, *Ben Trovato*
* Barney, Ashbel Hinman
Bell, James Christy, Jr., *Stramore*
* Bergquist, John Gosta, *Brymptonwood*
* Billings, Cornelius Kingsley G., *Farnsworth*
Bird, Wallis Clinton, *Farnsworth*
* Blackwell, Charles Addison, *The Cedars*
Bonney, Flora Macdonald, *Sunstar Hill*
* Brokaw, George Tuttle, *Sunnybrook*
* Byrne, James
Chase, Richard Newton
Clews, Henry, III, *La Lanterne*
* Clews, James Blanchard, *La Lanterne*
* Coe, William Robertson, *Planting Fields*
Colgate, John Kirtland, Jr.
    [Colgate owned two houses in Upper Brookville.]
Collado, Dr. Emilo Gabriel, II
Collins, Dr. Burnet Charles
Crisp, Van Devanter, *Hillandale*
* Curran, Guernsey, Sr., *Farlands*
* Damrosch, Dr. Walter Johannes, *Monday House*
Davis, Hartley Courtland, *Crosstree*
* Davis, Joseph Edward, Sr., *Heyday House*
* Davison, Henry Pomeroy, II, *Appledore*
Dean, Arthur Hobson, *Homewood*
DeGraff, Robert Fair, *Wood Hollow*
Delano, Michael *[see L. A. Livingston]*
Doubleday, George Chester
Douglas, Josephine Hartford
* Flagg, Montague, II, *Applewood*
Gallic, Charles J.
Havemeyer, Theodore Augustus, II, *Cedar Hill*
Holloway, William Grace, Jr. *[see Bergquist]*
Horne, Elizabeth McMasters Jones
* Iselin, Charles Oliver, *Wolvers Hollow*
Kellogg, Morris Woodruff, *Fieldston Farm*
* Livingston, Miss Louise Alida
MacDonald, Ranald Hugh, Jr.
McClintock, Harvey Childs, Jr.
Mestres, Ricardo Angelo, II, *Bayberry Hill*
Miller, Nathan Lewis, *Norwich House*
* Ottley, Gilbert, *Wuff Woods*
* Page, Frank C. Bauman, *Elmcroft*
Pomeroy, Daniel Eleazer
* Postley, Sterling, *Framewood*
* Redmond, Geraldyn Livingston, Sr.,
    Gray House Farm
Robertson, Julian Hart, Jr.
Rose, Reginald Perry

* Sanderson, Henry, *La Selva*
Sands, Miss Anna
* Slade, John, Sr., *Underhill House*
Sperry, Edward G.
Straus, Edward Kuhn, *Here to Yonder*
Tanner, Frederick Chauncey, Sr., *Normandie*
* Taylor, Bertrand LeRoy, Jr.
Thomas, Joseph Albert, *Normandie*
Tiffany, Anne Cameron, *Glen Nevis*
Vaughan, Dr. Harold Stearns, *The Catalpas*
Watson, John Jay, Jr., *Cedarcroft*
Welldon, Samuel Alfred
Wheeler, Frederick Seymour, *Delwood*
* Whitehouse, James Norman, *Broadwood*

WESTBURY
Burton, Frank V., Jr., *Northlea*
Duncan, Eloise Stevenson, *Yonder House*
Hedges, George Brown, *The Hedges*
Hicks, Henry

WEST HILLS
Belding, David, Sr.
* Davey, William Nelson, *White Gates*
* Halsey, Richard Townley Haines, *Tallwood*
* Harrison, Wallace Kirkman, *Mon Souci*
Jackson, William H.
Ludwig, Arthur *[see Robbins]*
Page, Arthur Wilson, II, *Country Line Farm*
Peabody, Julian Livingston, Jr.
Plimpton, Francis Taylor Pearsons, Sr.,
    Sweet Hollow
Price, Theodore Hazeltine, Jr., *Ben Robyn Farm*
* Robbins, Francis LeBaron, Jr., *Ben Robyn*
* Stimson, Henry Lewis, *Highold*

WEST ISLAND
(*see* **GLEN COVE, WEST ISLAND**)

WOODBURY
* Babcock, Richard Franklin, *Hark Away*
Bruce, David Kirkpatrick Este, *Woodlands*
Folkerts, Heiko Hid
* Goodwin, Philip Lippincott, *Goodwin Place*
* Hoyt, Lydig
Jennings, Oliver Burr, II
* King, Frederic Rhinelander
* Marston, Edgar Lewis, II, *Carston Hill*
* Mills, Ogden Livingston
* Morawetz, Victor, *Three Ponds*
Oeland, Isaac Raymond, Sr., *Larch*
Piquet, Dr. Samuel D.
Randall, Darley, Jr., *Apple Trees*
Roosevelt, Franklin Delano, Jr.
Spiegel, Jerry
Winter, Keyes, Sr., *Hiver Rough*
* Winthrop, Henry Rogers, *East Woods*
* Wood, Chalmers, Jr., *Little Ipswich*

America's First Age of Fortune:
A Selected Bibliography

Books listed in this section are, in most instances, different from the listings in the section entitled Selected Bibliographic References to Individual North Shore Estate Owners. Both sections should, therefore, be consulted.

AIA Architectural Guide to Nassau and Suffolk Counties, Long Island. New York: Dover Publications, Inc., 1992.

Aldrich, Nelson W., Jr. *Old Money: The Mythology of America's Upper Class.* New York: Alfred A. Knopf, 1988.

Aldrich, Nelson W., IV. "The Upper Class, Up for Grabs." *Wilson Quarterly* 17:3 (Summer 1993).

Allen, Michael Patrick. *The Founding Fortunes: A New Anatomy of the Super–Rich Families in America.* New York: E. P. Dutton, 1987.

Alsop, Joseph W. *"I've Seen the Best of It: Memoirs"* New York: W. W. Norton & Co., 1992.

Amory, Cleveland. *Celebrity Register: An Irreverent Compendium of American Quotable Notables.* New York: Harper & Row Publishers, 1959. [Published intermittently. Since 1973 it has been edited by Earl Blackwell.]

Amory, Cleveland. *The Last Resorts.* New York: Harper & Brothers, 1952.

Amory, Cleveland. *Who Killed Society?* New York: Harper & Brothers, 1960.

Armour, Lawrence A. *The Young Millionaires.* Chicago: Playboy Press, 1973.

Armstrong, Hamilton Fish. *Those Days.* New York: Harper & Brothers, 1963.

Armstrong, Margaret. *Five Generations.* New York: Harper & Brothers, 1930.

Ashburn, Frank D. *Peabody of Groton.* New York: Coward, McCann & Co., 1944.

Aslet, Clive. *The American Country Home.* New Haven: Yale University Press, 1990.

Auchincloss, Louis. *The Rector of Justin.* Boston: Houghton, Mifflin & Co., 1964.

Auchincloss, Louis. *The Vanderbilt Era: Profiles of a Gilded Age.* New York: The Macmillan Co., 1989.

Bahn, Jacqueline K. and George L. Williams. *The Sketchbook of Historic Homes on Cow Neck Peninsula.* Port Washington, NY: Cow Neck Peninsula Historical Society, 1982.

Baker, John C. *American Country Homes and Their Gardens.* Philadelphia: C. Winston, 1906.

Baker, Paul R. *Richard Morris Hunt.* New York: MIT Press, 1980.

Baker, Paul R. *Stanny: The Gilded Life of Stanford White.* New York: The Free Press, 1989.

Baldwin, Charles. *Stanford White.* New York: DaCapo Press, 1931.

Balmori, Diana, Diana McGuire Kostial, and Eleanor M. McPeck. *Beatrix Farrand's American Landscapes: Her Gardens and Campuses.* Sagaponack, NY: Sagapress, 1985.

Baltzel, E. Digby. *The Protestant Establishment: Aristocracy and Caste in America.* New York: Random House, 1964.

Baltzel, E. Digby. *The Protestant Establishment Revisited.* New Brunswick, NJ: New Jersey Transaction Publishers, 1991.

Barrett, Richmond. *Good Old Summer Days.* Boston: Houghton, Mifflin & Co., 1952.

Batterberry, Michael and Ariane Batterberry. *Mirror, Mirror.* New York: Holt, Rinehart & Winston, 1977.

Beach, Moses Yale. *Wealth and Biography of the Wealthy Citizens of New York City.* New York: The Sun Office, 1845.

Bedford, Stephen and Richard Guy Wilson. *The Long Island Country House, 1870–1930.* Southampton, NY: Parrish Art Museum, 1988.

Beebee, Lucius Morris. *The Big Spenders.* Garden City: Doubleday & Co., Inc., 1966.

Beebee, Lucius. *Mansion On Rails: The Folklore of the Private Railway Car.* Berkeley: Howell–North, 1959.

Beer, Thomas. *The Mauve Decade: American Life at the End of the 19th Century.* New York: Alfred A. Knopf, Inc., 1926.

"Behind the Gates of the Last Estates," *Newsday* September 25, 1986.

Bender, Marilyn. *The Beautiful People.* New York: Coward–McCann, Inc., 1967.

Bendix, Reinhard and Seymour Martin Lipset, ed. *Class, Status and Power.* New York: The Free Press, 1966.

Biddle, Francis. *A Casual Past.* Garden City: Doubleday & Co., Inc., 1961.

Biddle, Francis. *The Llanfear Pattern.* New York: Charles Scribner's Sons, 1927.

Bigelow, Poultney. *Seventy Summers: New York.* 2 vols. Longmans, Green & Co., 1925.

Birmingham, Stephen. *America's Secret Aristocracy.* Boston: Little, Brown & Co., 1987.

Birmingham, Stephen. *The Grandees: America's Sephardic Elite.* New York: Harper & Row Publishers, 1971.

Birmingham, Stephen. *The Grandes Dames.* New York: Simon & Schuster, Inc., 1982.

Birmingham, Stephen. *Our Crowd: The Great Jewish Families of New York.* New York: Harper & Row Publishers, 1967.

Birmingham, Stephen. *Real Lace: America's Irish Rich.* New York: Harper & Row Publishers, 1973.

Birmingham, Stephen. *The Right People: A Portrait of the American Social Establishment.* Boston: Little, Brown & Co., 1968.

Birmingham, Stephen. *The Right Places for the Right People.* Boston: Little, Brown & Co., 1973.

Bloom, Murray Teigh. *Rogues To Riches: The Trouble With Wall Street.* New York: G. P. Putnam's Sons, 1971.

Bolton, Sarah. *Famous Givers and Their Gifts.* New York: T. Y. Crowell & Co., 1896.

Bradley, Hugh. *Such Was Saratoga.* Garden City: Doubleday, Doran & Co., 1940.

Brandon, Ruth. *The Dollar Princesses: Sagas of Upward Nobility, 1870–1914.* New York: Alfred A. Knopf, 1980.

Bremner, Robert H. *American Philanthropy.* Chicago: The University of Chicago Press, 1960.

Bremner, Robert H. *American Social History Since 1860.* New York, 1971.

Brooklyn Blue Book. Brooklyn, NY: Rugby Press, Inc., annual.

Brooklyn Blue Book and Long Island Society Register. Brooklyn, NY: Brooklyn Life Publishing Co., annual.

Brooklyn Blue Book and Long Island Society Register. Brooklyn, NY: Rugby Press, Inc., annual.

Brooks, John. *Once In Galconda. A True Drama of Wall Street 1920–1938.* New York: Harper & Row Publishers, 1969.

Brooks, John. *Showing Off in America.* Boston: Little, Brown & Co., 1981.

Browder, Clifford. *The Money Game In Old New York: Daniel Drew and His Times.* Lexington, KY: University Press of Kentucky, 1986.

Brown, Jane. *Beatrix: The Gardening Life of Beatrix Jones Farrand 1872–1959.* New York: Viking Penguin Books, 1995.

Browne, Irving. *Our Best Society.* New York: Samuel French, 1875.

Burr, Anna Robeson. *The Portrait of a Banker: James Stillman, 1850–1918.* New York: Duffield & Co., 1927.

Burt, Nathaniel. *First Families.* Boston: Little, Brown & Co., 1970.

Byrnes, Rev. Horace W. *Pictorial Bay Shore and Vicinity: A Souvenir.* Bay Shore, NY: privately printed, 1903.

Cable, Mary. *Top Drawer: American Society from Gilded Age to the Roaring Twenties.* New York: Atheneum, 1984.

Cantacuzene, Princess. *My Life Here and There.* New York: Charles Scribner's Sons, 1921.

Capen, Oliver Bronson. *Country Homes of Famous Americans.* Garden City: Doubleday, Page & Co., 1905.

Caro, Robert A. *The Power Broker: Robert Moses and the Fall of New York.* New York: Alfred A. Knopf, 1989.

Carr, Edward A. T., Michael W. Carr, and Kari–Ann R. Carr. *Faded Laurels: The History of Eaton's Neck and Asharoken.* Interlaken, NY: Heart of the Lakes Publishing, 1994.

Carson, Gerald. *The Polite Americans.* New York: William Morrow & Co., 1966.

Chanler, Mrs. Winthrop [Margaret]. *Autumn in the Valley.* Boston: Little, Brown & Co., 1936.

Chanler, Mrs. Winthrop [Margaret]. *Roman Spring.* Boston: Little, Brown & Co., 1934.

Chase, Edna Woolman and Ilka Chase. *Always in Vogue.* Garden City: Doubleday & Co., Inc., 1954.

Churchill, Allen. *The Splendor Seekers: An Informal Glimpse of America's Multimillionaire Spenders – Members of the $50,000,000 Club.* New York: Grosset & Dunlop, 1974.

Churchill, Allen. *The Upper Crust: An Informal History of New York's Highest Society.* Englewood Cliffs, NJ: Prentice Hall, 1970.

Clark, Herma. *The Elegant Eighties.* Chicago: A. C. McClurg & Co., 1941.

Clews, Henry. *Fifty Years in Wall Street.* New York: Irving Publishing Co., 1908.

Close, Leslie Rose. *Portrait of an Era in Landscape Architecture: The Photographs of Mattie Edwards Hewitt.* The Bronx, NY: Wave Hill, 1983.

Crockett, Albert Stevens. *Peacocks On Parade.* New York: Sears Publishing, 1931.

Crofutt, William A. *The Leisure Class in America.* New York: Arno Press, 1975.

Curtis, George W. *Our Best Society.* New York: G. P. Putnam's Sons, 1899.

Curwen, Henry Darcey, ed. *Exeter Remembered.* Exeter, NH: Phillips–Exeter Academy, 1965.

Darby, Edwin. *The Fortune Builders.* Garden City: Doubleday & Co., Inc. 1986.

Dayton, Abram C. *The Last Days of Knickerbocker Life in New York.* New York: G. P. Putnam's Sons, 1897.

Delano & Aldrich. *Portraits of Ten Country Houses.* Garden City: Doubleday, Page & Co., 1924.

Depew, Chauncey M. *My Memories of Eighty Years.* New York: Charles Scribner's Sons, 1924.

Directory of American Society New York State and the Metropolitan District, 1929. New York: Town Topics, 1928.

Directory of Directors in the City of New York and the Tri–State Area. Southport, CT: Directory of Directors Co., Inc., annual.

Directory Port Washington and Plandome. Hempstead, NY: Nassau Advertising Service, 1931.

Domestic Architecture of H. T. Lindeberg. New York: William Helburn, Inc., 1940.

Domhoff, G. William. *The Bohemian Grove and Other Retreats.* New York: Harper & Row Publishers, 1974.

Domhoff, G. William. *Fat Cats and Democrats.* Englewood, NJ: Prentice–Hall, 1972.

Domhoff, G. William. *The Higher Circles: The Governing Class in America.* New York: Random House, 1970.

Domhoff, G. William. *The Powers That Be: Process of Ruling Class Domination in America.* New York: Random House, 1978.

Downey, Fairfax. *Portrait of an Era.* New York: Charles Scribner's Sons, 1936.

Drury, Roger W. *Drury and St. Paul's: The Scars of a Schoolmaster.* Boston: Little, Brown & Co., 1964.

Ellet, Elizabeth. *The Queens of American Society.* Philadelphia: Porter & Coates, 1867.

Eliot, Elizabeth [Lady Elizabeth Kinnaird]. *Heiresses and Coronets.* New York: McDowell, Obolensky, 1959.

Elliott, Maude Howe. *This Was My Newport.* Cambridge, MA: The Mythology Co., 1944.

Elliott, Maude Howe. *Three Generations.* Boston: Little, Brown & Co., 1923.

Elliott, Osborne. *Men at the Top.* New York: Harper & Brothers, 1959.

"Estates and Their Story," *Newsday* December 1, 1965.

Faucigny–Lucinge, Prince Jean–Louis de. *Legendary Parties 1922–1972*. New York: The Vendome Press, 1987.

Ferrell, Merri McIntyre. "Fox Hunting on Long Island." *The Nassau County Historical Society Journal* 54 (2001):1–10.

Ferry, John William. *A History of the Department Store*. New York: The Macmillan Co., 1960.

Ferree, Barr. *American Estates & Gardens*. New York: Munn & Co., 1904.

Finkle, Orin Z. "Society Weddings at the Turn of the Century." *North Shore* February/March 1985:44.

Fisher, Kenneth L. *100 Minds That Made the Market*. Woodside, CA: Business Classics, 1993.

Fiske, Stephen. *Offhand Portraits of Prominent New Yorkers*. New York: George Lockwood & Sons, 1884.

Fleming, Nancy. *Money, Manure & Maintenance: Ingredients for Successful Gardens of Marian Coffin, Pioneer Landscape Architect 1876–1957*. Weston, MA: Country Place Books, 1995.

Forbes, Malcolm and Jeffery Block. *What Happened to Their Children?* New York: Simon & Schuster, Inc., 1990.

Fowler, Marian. *In a Gilded Cage: From Heiress to Duchess*. New York: St. Martin's Press, 1993.

Frelinhuysen, Alice Cooning, et al. *Splendid Legacy: The Havemeyer Collection*. New York: The Metropolitan Museum of Art, 1993.

Fuller, Henry B. *The Cliff Dwellers*. New York: Harper & Brothers, 1893.

Gerard, James W. *My First Eighty–Three Years in America*. Garden City: Doubleday & Co., Inc., 1951.

Geus, Averill Dayton. *The Maidstone Club: The Second Fifty Years 1941 to 1991*. East Hampton, NY: Maidstone Club, 1991.

Gordon, Panmure. *Land of the Almighty Dollar*. London: Frederick Warne & Co., 1892.

Goulden, Joseph, C. *The Money Givers*. New York: Random House Publishers, 1971.

Gouverneur, Marion. *As I Remember: Recollections of American Society During the Nineteenth Century*. New York: D. Appleton & Co., 1911.

Graham, Sheila. *How to Marry Super Rich or Love, Money and the Morning After*. New York: Grosset & Dunlap Publishers, 1974.

Greene, Bert and Philip Stephen Schulz. *Pity the Poor Rich: It's a Losing Battle to Stay on Top But See How They Try*. Chicago: Contemporary Books, 1978.

Gregory, Alexis. *Families of Fortune: Life in the Gilded Age*. New York: Rizzoli International Publications, Inc., 1993.

Griswold, Mac K. and Eleanor Weller. *The Golden Age of American Gardens . Proud Owners . Private Estates . 1890–1940*. New York: Harry N. Abrams, Inc., Publishers, 1991.

Gunther, Max. *The Very Rich and How They Got That Way*. New York: Playboy Press, 1972.

Halberstam, David. *The Powers That Be*. New York: Alfred A. Knopf, 1979.

Hall, Edward Tuck. *Saint Mark's School: A Centennial History*. Southborough, MA: Saint Mark's Alumni Association, 1967.

Hamm, Margherita Arlina. *Famous Families of New York*. New York: G. P. Putnam's Sons, 1901.

Harmond, Richard and Vincitorio Gaetano. "Working on the Great Estates." *Long Island Forum* Spring 1988.

Harriman, E. Roland. *I Reminisce*. Garden City: Doubleday & Co., Inc., 1975.

Harriman, Mrs. J. Borden. *From Pinafores to Politics*. New York: Henry Holt & Co., 1923.

Harriman, Margaret Chase. *The Vicious Circle*. New York: Rinehart & Co., 1951.

Harris, Leon. *Merchant Princes: An Intimate History of Jewish Families Who Built Great Department Stores*. New York: Harper & Row Publishers, 1979.

Harrison, Constance Cary. *Recollections Grave and Gay*. New York: Charles Scribner's Sons, 1911.

Harrison, Constance Cary. *The Well–Bred Girl in Society*. Garden City: Doubleday, Page & Co., 1904.

Havemeyer, Harry W. *Along the Great South Bay From Oakdale to Babylon, the Story of a Summer Spa, 1840 to 1940*. Mattituck, NY: Amereon House, 1996.

Havemeyer, Harry W. *East on the Great South Bay: Sayville and Bellport 1860–1960*. Mattituck, NY: Amereon House, 2001.

Havemeyer, Harry W., "The Story of Saxton Avenue." *Long Island Forum* Winter, February 1, 1990 and Spring, May 1, 1990.

Havemeyer, Harry W. *Merchants of Williamsburg: Frederick C. Havemeyer, Jr., William Dick, John Mollenhauer, Henry O. Havemeyer*. New York: privately printed, 1989.

Havemeyer, Louisine W. *Sixteen to Sixty: Memoirs of a Collector*. New York: Ursus Press, 1993.

Hersh, Burton. *The Old Boys: The American Elite and the Origins of the CIA*. New York: Charles Scribner's Sons, 1992.

Hess, Stephen. *America's Political Dynasties from Adams to Kennedy*. Garden City: Doubleday & Co., Inc., 1966.

Hewitt, Mark Alan. *The Architect & the Country House, 1890–1940*. New Haven: Yale University Press, 1990.

Hoff, Henry B., ed. *Long Island Source Records: From the New York Genealogical and Biographical Record*. Baltimore: Genealogical Publishing, 1987.

Holbrook, Stewart H. *The Age of Moguls*. London: Victor Gollancz, Ltd., 1954.

Holloway, Laura C. *Famous American Fortunes and the Men Who Have Made Them*. New York: J. A. Hill, 1889.

Homberger, Eric. *Mrs. Astor's New York: Money and Social Power in a Gilded Age*. New Haven: Yale University Press, 2002.

Hoogenboom, Ari and Olive Hoogenboom, eds. *The Gilded Age*. Englewood, NJ: Prentice–Hall, 1967.

Hopkins, Alfred. *Modern Farm Buildings*. New York: McBride, Nast & Co., 1913.

Hopkins, Alfred. *Planning for Sunshine and Fresh Air.* New York: Architectural Book Publishing, 1931.

Howath, Susan. *The Rich Are Different.* New York: Simon & Schuster, Inc., 1977.

Howe, Samuel. *American Country Houses of To–Day.* New York: Architectural Book Publishing Co., 1915.

Howell, E. W. *Noted Long Island Homes.* Babylon, NY: E. W. Howell Co., 1933.

Hunt, Freeman. *Lives of the American Merchants.* New York: Hunts' Merchants' Magazine, 1895.

Hunter, Floyd. *The Big Rich and the Little Rich.* Garden City: Doubleday & Co., Inc., 1965.

Ingham, John. *Biographical Dictionary of American Business Leaders.* New York: Greenwood Press, 1983.

Ingham, John and Lynne B. Feldman. *Contemporary Business Leaders: A Biographical Dictionary.* New York: Greenwood Press, 1990.

International Celebrity Register. New York: Celebrity Register Ltd., annual.

Irwin, William Henry, et al. *A History of the Union League Club of New York City.* New York: Dodd, Mead & Co., 1952.

Jaher, Frederic Cople. *The Gilded Elite: American Multimillionaires, 1865 to the Present.* London: Croom Helm, 1980.

Jaher, Frederic Cople, ed. *The Rich, The Wellborn, and The Powerful: Elite and Upper Classes in History.* Secaucus: Citadel Press, 1975.

Jenkins, Alan. *The Rich Rich: The Story of the Big Spenders.* New York: G. P. Putnam's Sons, 1978.

Jennings, Walter Wilson. *20 Giants of American Business.* New York: Exposition Press, 1953.

Josephson, Matthew. *The Money Lords: The Great Finance Capitalists 1925–1950.* New York: Weybright & Talley Publishers, 1972.

Josephson, Matthew. *The Robber Barons…,1861–1901.* New York: Harcourt, Brace, Jovanovich, Publishers, 1934.

Kahn, E. J., III. "The Brahmin Mystique." *Boston Magazine* 75 (May 1983):119–161.

Kaiser, Harvey. *Great Camps of the Adirondacks.* Boston: David R. Godine, Publisher, Inc., 1982.

Kamisher, Lawrence, ed. *One Hundred Years of Knickerbocker History.* Port Washington, NY: Knickerbocker Yacht Club, 1974.

Kavaler, Lucy. *The Private World of High Society: Its Rules and Rituals.* New York: David McKay Co., Inc., 1960.

Kent, Joan Gay. *Discovering Sands Point: Its History, Its People, Its Places.* Sands Point, NY: Village of Sands Point, 2000.

Kirstein, George G. *The Rich: Are They Different?* Boston: Houghton Mifflin & Co., 1968.

Klepper, Michael. *The Wealthy 100: From Benjamin Franklin to Bill Gates – A Ranking of the Richest Americans Past and Present.* Secaucus, NJ: The Citadel Press, 1996.

Knapp, Edward Spring, Jr. *We Knapps Thought It Was Nice.* New York: privately printed, 1940.

Knox, Thomas W. "Summer Clubs on the Great South Bay." *Harper's New Monthly Magazine* July 1880.

Konolige, Kit. *The Richest Women in the World.* New York: The Macmillan Co., 1985.

Konolige, Kit and Frederica Konolige. *The Power of Their Glory: America's Ruling Class: The Episcopalians.* New York: Wyden Books, 1978.

Kouwenhoven, John A. *Partners in Banking: An Historical Portrait of a Great Private Bank, Brown Brothers Harriman & Co., 1818–1968.* Garden City: Doubleday & Co., Inc., 1968.

Kowet, Don. *The Rich Who Own Sports.* New York: Random House, 1977.

Krieg, Joann P., ed. *Long Island Architecture.* Interlaken, NY: Heart of the Lakes Publishing, 1991.

Krieg, Joann P., ed. *Robert Moses: Single–Minded Genius.* Interlaken, NY: Heart of the Lakes Publishing, 1989.

Lamont, Kenneth Church. *The Moneymakers: The Great Big New Rich in America.* Boston: Little, Brown & Co., 1969.

Lampman, Robert J. *The Share of Top Wealth–Holders in National Wealth 1922–1956.* Princeton, NJ: Princeton University Press, 1962.

Lapham, Lewis. *Money and Class in America.* New York: Weidenfeld & Nicolson, 1988.

Lee, Henry J., ed. *The Long Island Almanac and Year Book.* New York: Eagle Library Publications, 1931, 1934.

Lehr, Elizabeth Drexel. *"King Lehr" and the Gilded Age.* Philadelphia: J. B. Lippincott Co., 1935.

Lehr, Elizabeth Drexel. *Turn of the World.* Philadelphia: J. B. Lippincott Co., 1937.

Lewis & Valentine Nursery. New York: Lewis & Valentine Co., 1916.

Lewis, Arnold, et al. *The Opulent Interiors of the Golden Age.* New York: Dover Publications, Inc., 1987.

Libby, Valencia. "Marian Cruger Coffin, the Landscape Architect and the Lady." The House and Garden Exhibition Catalog. Roslyn, NY: Nassau County Museum of Fine Art, 1986.

Lindeman, Eduard C. *Wealth and Culture.* New York: Harcourt, Brace & Co., Inc., 1936.

Livingston, Bernard. *Their Turf: America's Horsey Set and Its Princely Dynasties.* New York: Arbor House Publishers, 1973.

Logan, Andy. *The Man Who Robbed the Robber Barons.* New York: W. W. Norton & Co., 1965.

Long Island Society Register 1929. Brooklyn, NY: Rugby Press, Inc., 1929.

Lowe, Corinne. *Confessions of a Social Secretary.* New York: Harper & Brothers, 1916.

Lowe, David Garrard. *Stanford White and New York in the Gilded Age.* Garden City: Doubleday and Co., Inc., 1992.

Lucas, Nora. "The Historic Resource Survey for the Period 1900–1940 of the Unincorporated Sections of the Town of North Hempstead." Preservation Computer Services, 1991.

Lucie–Smith, Edward and Celestine Dars. *How the Rich Lived.* New York: Two Continents Publishing Group, 1976.

Lundberg, Ferdinand. *America's 60 Families.* New York: The Vanguard Press, 1937.

Lundberg, Ferdinand. *The Rich and the Super–Rich: A Study in the Power of Money Today.* New York: Lyle Stuart & Co., 1968.

Lundberg, Ferdinand. *"Who Controls Industry?* [pamphlet concerning Richard Whitney case], c. 1938.

Lynes, Russell. *The Domesticated Americans.* New York: Harper & Row Publishers, 1963.

MacColl, Gail and Carol McD. Wallace. *To Marry an English Lord.* New York: Workman Publishing, 1989.

Mackay, Robert B., Anthony K. Baker, and Carol A. Traynor. *Long Island Country Houses and Their Architects 1860–1940.* New York: W. W. Norton & Co., 1997.

Maher, James T. *The Twilight of Splendor: Chronicles of the Age of American Palaces.* Boston: Little Brown & Co., 1975.

Maher, Matthew. "A Study of the Effects of Accelerated Suburbanization [in Nassau–Suffolk] Upon the Social Structure." M. A. thesis, St. John's University, 1982.

Mahoney, Tom and Leonard Stone. *The Great Merchants: America's Foremost Retail Institutions and People Who Made Them Great.* New York: Harper & Row Publishers, 1974.

Marcus, George E. *Lives In Trust: The Fortunes of Dynastic Families in Late Twentieth–Century America.* Boulder, CO: Westview Press, 1992.

Martin, Frederick Townsend. *Things I Remember.* New York: John Lane Co., 1913.

Martin, Frederick Townsend. *The Passing of the Idle Rich.* Garden City: Doubleday, Page, & Co., 1911.

Mathews, Jane. "A Case Study of the Tactical Differences Between Two Prominent Long Island Suffragists: Mrs. Ida Bunce Sammis and Miss Rosalie Jones, The Woman's Suffrage Movement in Suffolk County, New York, 1911–1917." M. A. thesis, Adelphi University, 1987.

Maxwell, Elsa. *The Celebrity Circus.* London: Allen, 1964.

Maxwell, Elsa. *R. S. V. P.: Elsa Maxwell's Own Story.* Boston: Little, Brown & Co., 1954.

Mayer, Martin. *The Bankers.* New York: Weybright & Talley Publishers, 1974.

Mazzola, Anthony T. and Frank Zachary, ed. *The Best Families: The Town and Country Social Directory, 1846–1996.* New York: Harry N. Abrams, Inc., Publishers, 1996.

McAllister, Ward. *Society As I Have Found It.* New York: Cassell Publishing Co., 1890.

McCash, June Hall. *The Jekyll Island Cottage Colony.* Athens, GA: The University of Georgia Press, 1998.

McCash, William Barton and June Hall McCash. *The Jekyll Island Club: Southern Haven for America's Millionaires.* Athens, GA: The University of Georgia Press, 1989.

McCusker, John J. *How Much Is That in Real Money? A Historical Price Index for Use as a Deflator of Money Values in the Economy of the United States.* Worcester, MA: American Antiquarian Society, 1992.

McKim, Mead, & White. *A Monograph of the Work of McKim, Mead & White 1879–1915.* New York: DaCapo Press, 1985.

McVickar, Harry Whitney. *The Greatest Show on Earth: Society.* New York: Harper & Brothers, 1892.

Metcalf, Pauline C. and Libby Valencia. *The House and Garden.* Roslyn, NY: Nassau County Museum of Fine Art, 1986.

Miller, Frances [Breese]. *More About Tanty.* Southampton, NY: Sandbox Press, 1980.

Miller, Frances [Breese]. *Tanty: Encounter With the Past.* Southampton, NY: Sandbox Press, 1979.

Mills, C. Wright. *The Power Elite.* New York: Oxford University Press, 1956.

Milne, Gordon. *The Sense of Society.* Cranbury, NJ: Fairleigh Dickinson University Press, 1977.

Minnigerode, Meade. *Certain Rich Men.* New York: G. P. Putnam's Sons, 1927.

Montgomery, Maureen E. *Gilded Prostitution: Status, Money and Transatlantic Marriage 1870–1914.* London: Routledge Press, 1989.

Moody, John. *The Masters of Capital: A Chronicle of Wall Street.* New Haven: Yale University Press, 1919.

Morris, Lloyd. *Incredible New York: High Life and Low Life of the Last Hundred Years.* New York: Random House, 1951.

Moses, Robert. *Working For the People.* New York: Harper and Brothers, 1956.

Mountfield, David. *The Railway Barons.* New York: W. W. Norton & Co., 1979.

Myers, Gustavus. *The Ending of Hereditary American Fortunes.* New York: Julian Messner, Inc., 1939.

Myers, Gustavus. *History of the Great American Fortunes.* New York: Random House, 1937.

Noyes, Dorothy McBurney. *The World Is So Full.* Islip, NY: privately printed, 1953.

Obolensky, Serge. *One Man in His Time: The Memoirs of Serge Obolensky.* New York: privately printed, 1958.

O'Connor, Harvey. *The Empire of Oil.* New York: Monthly Review Press, 1955.

O'Connor, Richard. *The Oil Barons: Men of Greed and Grandeur.* Boston: Little, Brown & Co., 1971.

Orr, Christina. *Addison Mizner: Architect of Dreams and Realities (1872–1933).* Palm Beach, FL: Norton School of Art, 1977.

Ostrander, Susan A. *Women of the Upper Class.* Philadelphia: Temple University Press, 1984.

Packard, Vance. *The Status Seekers.* New York: David McKay Co., Inc., 1959.

Parsons, Schuyler Livingston. *Untold Friendships.* Boston: Houghton Mifflin Co., 1955.

Patterson, Augusta Owen. *American Homes of Today.* New York: The Macmillan Co., 1924.

Patterson, Jerry E. *Fifth Avenue: The Best Addresses.* New York: Rizzoli International Publications, Inc., 1998.

Patterson, Jerry E. *The First Four Hundred: Mrs. Astor's New York in the Gilded Age.* New York: Rizzoli International Publications, Inc., 2000.

Pearson, Hesketh. *The Marrying Americans.* New York: Coward McCann, Inc., 1961.

Pendrell, Nan and Ernest Pendrell. *How the Rich Live and Whom to Tax.* New York: Workers Library Publishers, Inc., May 1939.

Persons, Stow. *The Decline of American Gentility.* New York: Columbia University Press, 1973.

Phillips, David. *The Reign of Gilt.* New York: James Pott & Co., 1905.

Pless, Princess Mary. *Better Left Unsaid.* New York: E. P. Dutton & Co., 1931.

Pless, Princess Mary. *What I Left Unsaid.* New York: E. P. Dutton & Co., 1936.

Polk's Glen Cove Directory. New York: R. L. Polk & Co., Inc., annual. [includes Lattingtown and Locust Valley]

Porzelt, Paul. *The Metropolitan Club of New York.* New York: Rizzoli International Publications, Inc., 1982.

Prominent Residents of Long Island and Their Clubs. New York: Edward C. Watson, c. 1916.

Pulitzer, Ralph. *New York Society on Parade.* New York: Harper & Brothers, 1910.

Randall, Monica. *The Mansions of Long Island's Gold Coast.* New York: Rizzoli International Publications, Inc., 1987.

Rattray, Jeannette Edwards. *Fifty Years of the Maidstone Club: 1891–1941.* East Hampton, NY: privately printed, 1941.

Residences Designed by Bradley Delehanty. New York: Architectural Catalogue Co., Inc., 1939.

Robinson's Port Washington and Roslyn 1934 Red Book Resident Directory. Hempstead, NY: Nassau Resident Directories, Publ., 1934.

Robinson's Port Washington Householder's and Street Directory. Great Neck, NY: Robinson's Directory Service, annual.

Rodgers, Cleveland. *Robert Moses, Builder of Democracy.* New York: Henry Holt and Co., 1952.

Roosevelt, Felicia Warburg. *Doers and Dowagers.* Garden City: Doubleday & Co., Inc., 1975.

Roosevelt, Robert Barnwell. *Love and Luck: The Story of a Summer's Loitering on the Great South Bay.* New York: Harper, 1886.

Sands Point. Sands Point, NY: Sands Point Civic Association 1979.

Sands Point Historic Inventory. Sands Point, NY: Sands Point Historic Landmark Preservation Commission, 1991.

Schnadelbach, R. Terry. *Ferruccio Vitale: Landscape Architect of the Country Place Era.* New York: Princeton Architectural Press, 2001.

Schrag, Peter. *The Decline of the Wasp.* New York: Simon & Schuster, Inc., 1970.

Sclare, Liisa and Donald Sclare. *Beaux–Arts Estates: A Guide to the Architecture of Long Island.* New York: The Viking Press, 1980.

Sedgwick, Henry Dwight. *In Praise of Gentlemen.* Boston: Little, Brown & Co., 1935.

Sedgwick, John. *Rich Kids.* New York: William Morrow & Co., 1985.

Shodell, Elly. *In The Service: Workers on the Grand Estates of Long Island 1890s – 1940s.* Port Washington, NY: Port Washington Public Library, 1991.

Shopsin, William C. and Grania Bolton Marcus. *Saving Large Estates: Conservation, Historic Preservation, Adaptive Re–Use.* Setauket, NY: Society for the Preservation of Long Island Antiquities, 1977.

Simon, Kate. *Fifth Avenue: A Very Social History.* New York: Harcourt, Brace, Jovanovich Publishers, 1978.

Slater, Philip. *Wealth Addiction.* New York: E. P. Dutton & Co., 1980.

Smith, Arthur D. Howden. *Men Who Run America.* New York: Bobbs–Merrill Co., 1936.

Soben, Dennis P. *Dynamics of Community Change; the Case of Long Island's Declining "Gold Coast."* Port Washington, NY: Ira J. Friedman, 1968.

Social Register. New York: The Social Register Association, annual.

Social Register New York. New York: Social Register Association, annual.

Social Register Summer. New York: Social Register Association, annual.

Spinzia, Raymond E. "Society Chameleons:' Long Island's Gentlemen Spies." *The Nassau County Historical Society Journal* 55 (2000): 27–38.

Spinzia, Raymond E. and Judith A. Spinzia. *"Gatsby:* Myths and Realities of Long Island's North Shore Gold Coast." *The Nassau County Historical Society Journal* 52 (1997):16–26.

Stein, Susan R. *The Architecture of Richard Morris Hunt.* Chicago: University of Chicago, 1986.

Stephens, W. P. *The Seawanhaka Corinthian Yacht Club: Origins and Early History, 1871–1896.* New York: privately printed, 1963.

Studenroth, Zachary. *Historic Resources Inventory: Reconnaissance Level Survey for the City of Glen Cove, Nassau County, New York.* Glen Cove: Glen Cove Landmarks Preservation Commission, 1992.

Swaine, Robert T. *The Cravath Firm and Its Predecessors, 1819–1948.* vols. 1, 2. New York: Ad Press, Ltd., 1946, 1948.

Talese, Gay. *The Kingdom and the Power.* New York: World Publishers, 1969.

Tankard, Judith B. *The Gardens of Ellen Biddle Shipman.* Sagaponack, NY: Sagapress, Inc., 1996.

Tarbell, Ida. *History of Standard Oil Company.* New York: The Macmillan Co., 1925.

Tebbel, John William. *The Inheritors: A Study of America's Great Fortunes and What Happened to Them.* New York: Putnam, 1962.

Teutonico, Jeanne Marie. "Marian Cruger Coffin: The Long Island Estates; a Study of the Early Work of a Pioneering Woman in American Landscape Architecture." M. S. thesis, Columbia University, 1983.

Thompson, Jacqueline. *The Very Rich Book: America's Supermillionaires and Their Money – Where They Got It, How They Spend It.* New York: William Morrow & Co., Inc., 1981.

Thorndike, Joseph J., Jr. *The Very Rich: A History of Wealth.* New York: American Heritage, 1976.

Tishler, William, ed. *American Landscape Architecture: Designers and Places.* Washington, DC: Preservation Press, 1989.

Townsend, Reginald T. *God Pack My Picnic Basket: Reminiscences of the Golden Age of Newport and New York.* New York: Hastings House, 1970.

Townsend, Reginald T. *Mother of Clubs.* New York: Union Club, 1936.

Ulman, Albert. *New Yorkers from Stuyvesant to Roosevelt.* Port Washington, NY: Ira J. Friedman, 1969.

Updike, D. P. *Hunt Clubs and Country Clubs in America.* Cambridge, MA: The Merrymount Press, 1928.

Vanderbilt, Cornelius, Jr. *Farewell to Fifth Avenue.* New York: Simon & Schuster, Inc., 1935.

Vanderbilt, Cornelius, Jr. *Man of the World: My Life on Five Continents.* New York: Crown Publishers, Inc., 1959.

Vanderbilt, Cornelius, Jr. *Palm Beach.* New York: Macaulay, 1931.

Vanderbilt, Cornelius, Jr. *Reno.* New York: Macaulay, 1929.

Vanderbilt, Cornelius, Jr. *Queen of the Golden Age: The Fabulous Story of Grace Wilson Vanderbilt.* New York: McGraw–Hill Book, Co., Inc., 1956.

Van Liew, Barbara and Kurt E. Kahofer. "Intensive Level Survey of Historic Resources in the Town of North Hempstead." Setauket, NY: Society for the Preservation of Long Island Antiquities, 1989.

Van Rensselaer, Mrs. John King. *Newport: Our Social Capital.* Philadelphia: J. B. Lippincott Co., 1905.

Van Rensselaer, Mrs. John King. *New Yorkers of the XIX Century.* New York: F. T. Neely, 1897.

Van Rensselaer, Mrs. John King and Frederic Van De Water. *The Social Ladder.* New York: Henry Holt & Co., 1924.

Van Rensselaer, Peter. *Rich Was Better.* New York: Wynwood Press, 1990.

VanWagner, Judith, et al. *Long Island Estate Gardens.* Greenvale, NY: Hillwood Art Gallery, 1985.

Van Wyck, Frederick. *Recollections of an Old New Yorker.* New York: Liveright, Inc., Publishers, 1932.

Veblen, Thorstein. *The Theory of the Leisure Class: An Economic Study of Institutions.* New York: New Modern Library, 1934.

Views From the Circle: Seventy–Five Years of Groton School. Groton, MA: The Trustees of Groton Schools, 1960.

Wall Street Journal, ed. *American Dynasties Today.* Homewood, IL, c. 1980.

Walker, Stanley. *Mrs. Astor's Horse.* New York: Frederick A. Stokes Co., 1935.

Wecter, Dixon. *The Saga of American Society: A Record of Social Aspiration, 1607–1937.* New York: Charles Scribner's Sons, 1937.

Weigold, Marilyn. *The American Mediterranean: An Environmental, Economic, and Social History of Long Island Sound.* Port Washington, NY: Kennikat Press, 1974.

Weitzenhoffer, Frances. *The Havemeyers: Impressionism Comes to America.* New York: Harry N. Abrams, Inc., Publishers, 1986.

Wells, Richard A. *Manners, Culture and Dress of the Best American Society.* Springfield, MA: King Richardson & Co., 1894.

White, Samuel G. *The Houses of McKim, Mead, and White.* New York: Rizzoli International Publications, Inc., 1998.

Who's Who In New York State. New York: Lewis Historical Publishing Co., annual.

Williams, George L. *Port Washington in the Twentieth Century: Places and People–Part I. Eastern Port Washington (From Beacon Hill to the Salems).* Port Washington, NY: Cow Neck Peninsula Historical Society, 1995.

Williamson, Ellen. *When We Went First Class.* Garden City: Doubleday & Co., Inc., 1977.

Winsche, Richard A. *The History of Nassau County Community Place–Names.* Interlaken, NY: Empire State Books, 1999.

Woolson, Abba G. *Woman in American Society.* Cambridge, MA: Roberts Brothers, 1873.

Worden, Helen. *Society Circus: From Ring to Ring With a Large Cast.* New York: Covici, Friede, Publishers, 1936.

Zerbe, Jerome. *The Art of Social Climbing.* Garden City: Doubleday & Co., Inc., 1965.

Selected Bibliographic References
to Individual North Shore Estate Owners

This portion of the bibliography contains references not only to the North Shore estate owners, but also to their families and their estates. Since books listed in this section are, in most instances, different from the listings in the general bibliography, America's First Age Of Fortune: A Selected Bibliography, both sections should be consulted.

Adam, Sarah Sampson – Oyster Bay – *Hillside*
　　American Architect and Building News November 3, 1878.

Albright, Dr. Madeleine Jana Korbel – Upper Brookville
　　Blood, Thomas. *Madam Secretary: A Biography of Madeleine Albright.* New York: St. Martin's Press, 1997.
　　Dobbs, Michael. *Madeleine Albright: A Twentieth–Century Odyssey.* New York: Henry Holt and Co., 1999.

Alden, Anne Coleman – Lloyd Harbor – *Fort Hill House*
　　"House for Mrs. A. C. Alden on Fort Hill, Lloyd's Neck, Long Island." *American Architect and Building News* August 30, 1879.

Aldred, John Edward – Lattingtown – *Ormston*
Frederic Law Olmsted National Historic Site, Brookline, MA, has 730 Olmsted drawings of the estate's landscape.
　　"The Fabled Past: A Tale of Bygone Days." *The North Shore Journal* 5 (July 15, 1971) n.p.
　　Landscape Architecture 28 (July 1938):191.
　　Worden, Helen. "Aldred Lost $3,000,000 L. I. Estate." *New York World Telegram,* October 20, 1942:17.

Aldrich, Sherwood – Kings Point – *Snug Harbor*
　　Patterson, Augusta Owen. *American Homes of Today.* New York: The Macmillan Co., 1924.

Alexandre, J. Henry, Jr. – Old Brookville – *Valleybrook Farm*
　　Fleming, Nancy. *Money, Manure & Maintenance: Ingredients for Successful Gardens of Marian Coffin, Pioneer Landscape Architect 1876–1957.* Weston, MA: Country Place Books, 1995.

Anderson, George A. – Old Brookville
　　Howell, E. W. *Noted Long Island Homes.* Babylon, NY: E. W. Howell Co., 1933.

Annenberg, Moses Louis – Kings Point
　　Bailey, Colin B., et al. *The Annenberg Collection.* Philadelphia: Philadelphia Museum of Art, 1989.
　　Cooney, John. *The Annenbergs: The Salvaging of a Tainted Dynasty.* New York: Simon and Schuster, 1982.
　　Dimitman, E. Z. *The Philadelphia Inquirer and the Annenbergs.* 1971. [unpublished ms]
　　Fonzi, Gaeton. *Annenberg: A Biography of Power.* New York: Weybright and Talley, 1970.
　　Ogden, Christopher. *Legacy: A Biography of Moses and Walter Annenberg.* Boston: Little Brown and Co., 1999.

Astor, William Vincent – Sands Point – *Cloverly Manor*
The Nassau County Museum Collection includes photographs of the estate.
The New York Public Library, NYC, has William Vincent Astor's papers.
　　Astor, Brooke. *Footprints: An Autobiography by Brooke Astor.* Garden City: Doubleday & Co., Inc., 1980.
　　Cowles, Virginia. *The Astors.* New York: Alfred A. Knopf, 1979.
　　Gates, John D. *The Astor Family.* Garden City: Doubleday & Co., Inc., 1981.
　　Grafton, David. *The Sisters: The Lives and Times of the Fabulous Cushing Sisters.* New York: Villard Books, 1992.
　　Kavaler, Lucy. *The Astors: A Family Chronicle of Pomp and Power.* New York: Dodd, Mead & Co., 1966.
　　New York Sun August 10, 1928.
　　O'Connor, Harvey. *The Astors.* New York: Alfred A. Knopf, 1941.
　　Sinclair, David. *Dynasty: The Astors and Their Times.* New York: Beuford Books, Inc., 1984.
　　The Spur March 15, 1927.
　　Vogue January 1926.
　　Wilson, Derek. *The Astors 1763–1992: Landscape With Millionaires.* New York: St. Martin's Press, 1993.

Individual Bibliographic References

Atherton, Henry Francis, Sr. – Upper Brookville
Architectural Review 11 (September 1920):69–72.

Auchincloss, Gordon, Sr. – Glen Cove;
                 and Matinecock – *Ronda*
Sterling Memorial Library, Yale University, New Haven, CT, has Gordon Auchincloss, Sr.'s papers.
    Hersh, Burton. *The Old Boys: The American Elite and the Origins of the CIA.* New York: Charles Scribner's
        Sons, 1992.
    Jeffreys–Jones, Rhodi. *American Espionage from Secret Service to CIA.* New York: The Free Press, 1977.

Auchincloss, Joseph Howland, Sr. – Matinecock
Alterman Library, University of Virginia, Charlottesville, VA, has papers of Louis Auchincloss. [the son of Joseph, Sr.]
    Gelderman, Carol. *Louis Auchincloss: A Writer's Life.* New York: Crown Publishers, Inc., 1993.

Ayer, Dr. James Cook – Glen Cove – *Shadowland*
Architectural Record 36 (October 1914):286–93.

Babcock, Frederick Huntington – Mill Neck – *Pepperidge Point*
Architecture 34 (November 1916):242.

Babcock, Richard Franklin – Woodbury – *Hark Away*
    "*Hark Away*: The Estate of Elizabeth Babcock of Woodbury, Long Island." Boston: Robert W. Skinner, Inc.,
        1985. auction catalog
    Jennings, Liz. "Funny Things Happened On the Way to the Fox." *Newsday* April 18, 1982, magazine section,
        pp. 23–39.

Bacon, Robert – Old Westbury – *Old Acres*
Foreign Relations Documents of the United States, 1906–1912, and the Manuscript Archives of the United States State
    Department, Washington, DC, have Robert Bacon's Secretary of State and ambassadorial papers.
    Patterson, Augusta Owen. "Mr. Robert Bacon's Westbury Garden." *Town and Country* August 1926:44–7.
    Scott, James Brown. *Robert Bacon: Life and Letters.* Garden City: Doubleday & Co., Inc., 1923.

Bacon, Robert Low – Old Westbury – *Arlough*
    Bedford, Stephen and Richard Guy Wilson. *The Long Island Country House, 1870–1930.* Southampton, NY:
        The Parrish Art Museum, 1988.
    Cortissoz, Royal, ed. *The Architecture of John Russell Pope.* vol. 1. New York: W. Helbrun, Inc., 1930.
    Patterson, Augusta Owen. *American Homes of Today.* New York: The Macmillan Co., 1924.

Bailey, Frank, Sr. – Lattingtown – *Munnysunk*
    Bailey, Frank. *It Can't Happen Here Again.* New York: Alfred A. Knopf, 1944.
    "The Fabled Past: A Tale of Bygone Days." *The North Shore Journal* 11 (May 29, 1980) n.p.

Baker, George Fisher, II – Lattingtown – *Vikings Cove*
    "Property of the Late Edith Kane Baker 'Viking Cove,' Locust Valley, New York and New York City." New
        York: Sotheby Parke–Bernet, Inc., 1977. auction catalog

Ballantine, John Herbert – Kings Point – *Holmdene*
The Nassau County Museum Collection includes photographs of the estate.

Balsan, Consuelo Vanderbilt – East Norwich – *Old Fields*
[*see also* General References to Vanderbilt Family]
Biltmore Estate, Asheville, NC, has material collected from all Vanderbilt families in their archives.
Dowling College Library, Historical Collection, Oakdale, LI, has photographs of the family.
Sewall–Belmont House [National Woman's Party Headquarters], Washington, DC, has scrapbooks pertaining to Alva
    Belmont and photographs of the family
Suffolk County Vanderbilt Museum and Planetarium archives, Centerport, LI, has photographs of the family.
Suffolk County Surrogate Court, Riverhead, LI, has Consuelo Vanderbilt Balsan's will on file. It was filed 12/11/1965 and
    submitted for probate on 1/25/1966.
    Balsan, Consuelo Vanderbilt. *The Glitter and the Gold.* New York: Harper & Brothers, 1952.
    Brough, James. *Consuelo: Portrait of an American Heiress.* New York: Coward, McCann & Geoghegan, Inc.,
        1979.
    Fowler, Marian. *In a Gilded Cage: From Heiress to Duchess.* New York: St. Martin's Press, 1994.

Balsan, Consuelo Vanderbilt – East Norwich – *Old Fields* (cont'd)
> MacColl, Gail and Carol McD. Wallace. *To Marry an English Lord: Or, How Anglomania Really Got Started.* New York: Workman Publishing, 1989.
>
> Marlborough, Duchess of [Consuelo Vanderbilt Balsan]. "Hostels for Women." *The Nineteenth Century and After* 1911:858–66.
>
> Marlborough, Duchess of [Consuelo Vanderbilt Balsan]. "The Position of Woman," Parts 2, 3, 10. *North American Review* 89(1909):180–93, 351–59, 11–24.

Barnes, Courtlandt Dixon, Sr. – Manhasset – *Nonesuch House*
> *Architectural Forum* 30 (February 1919):47–50.
>
> *Architectural Record* 50 (October 1921):320.
>
> *Architectural Review* 9 (October 1919):117.
>
> Howell, E. W. *Noted Long Island Homes.* Babylon, NY: E. W. Howell Co., 1933.
>
> Patterson, Augusta Owen. *American Homes of Today.* New York: The Macmillan Co., 1924.

Barnes, E. Mortimer – Old Brookville – *Manana*
The Nassau County Museum Collection includes photographs of the estate.
> *House and Garden* November 1931.
>
> *Town and Country* July 1930.
>
> *Vogue* February 15, 1930.
>
> *Vogue* April 12, 1930.

Barstow, William Slocum – Kings Point – *Elm Point*
> Sclare, Liisa and Donald. *Beaux–Arts Estates: A Guide to the Architecture of Long Island.* New York: The Viking Press, 1980.

Batterman, Henry Lewis, Sr. – Matinecock
The Nassau County Museum Collection includes photographs of the estate.

Baylis, Lester Yates – Huntington
The Nassau County Museum Collection includes photographs of the estate.

Belmont, Alva Erskine Smith – Sands Point – *Beacon Towers*
[*see also* General References to Vanderbilt Family]
Biltmore Estate, Asheville, NC, has material collected from all Vanderbilt families in their archives.
Dowling College Library, Historical Collection, Oakdale, LI, has photographs of the family.
Melville Library, SUNY Stony Brook, LI, has the National Woman's Party papers on microfilm.
The Nassau County Museum Collection includes photographs of the estate.
Nassau County Museum of Art, Roslyn, LI, has photographs of the estate.
Newport Historical Society, Newport, RI, has material relating to Woman Suffrage events held in Newport by Alva Belmont.
Octagon Museum of American Architectural Foundation, Prints and Drawings Collection, Washington, DC, has photographs and sketches of *Beacon Towers.*
Port Washington Public Library, Port Washington, NY, has local newspaper clippings mentioning Alva Belmont, *Beacon Towers*, and suffrage.
The Preservation Society of Newport County, Newport, RI, has Alva Belmont's personal scrapbook of newspaper clippings about the March 26, 1883, Masque Ball held at 660 Fifth Avenue, New York City.
Queens College Library, Historical Collection, Flushing, NY, has Vanderbilt family records, including 1699 tax rolls and a deposit of 1790–1840 material.
Mrs. Consuelo [Mimi] Russell, Alva Belmont's great-great-granddaughter has a scrapbook about Woman's Suffrage events held July 8–9, 1914, at Marble House, Newport, RI.
Sewall–Belmont House [National Woman's Party Headquarters], Washington, DC, has scrapbooks pertaining to Alva Belmont and photographs of the family.
Suffolk County Vanderbilt Museum and Planetarium archives, Centerport, LI, has photographs of the family and an album of photographs of the house taken by Samuel H. Gottscho whose collection is also in the Avery Architectural and Fine Arts Library, Columbia University, NYC, and in Library of Congress, Washington, DC. The photographs at *Eagles Nest* of *Beacon Towers* show the mansion from all sides. They also have one interior photograph of *Beacon Towers* and an album with Alva Belmont's funeral photographs and newspaper clippings.
> Bedford, Stephen and Richard Guy Wilson. *The Long Island Country House, 1870–1930.* Southampton, NY: The Parrish Art Museum, 1988.
>
> Belmont, Alva Vanderbilt. "Are Women Really Citizens?" *Good Housekeeping* September 1931.

Belmont, Alva Erskine Smith – Sands Point – *Beacon Towers* (cont'd)
Belmont, Alva Vanderbilt. Foreword to article by Christable Pankhurst, "Story of the Woman's War." *Good Housekeeping* November 1913.
Belmont, Alva Vanderbilt. *Harper's Bazaar* March 1910.
Belmont, Alva Vanderbilt. "How Can Woman Get the Suffrage?" *The Independent* 31 (March 1910).
Belmont, Alva. *One Month's Log of the Seminole*. New York: privately printed, 1916.
Belmont, Alva. "Unpublished 1917 Autobiography of Alva Vanderbilt Belmont." In Wood Collection, Huntington Library, San Marino, California.
Belmont, Alva. "Unpublished 1933 Autobiography of Alva Vanderbilt Belmont." In Matilda Young Papers, Special Collections Department, William R. Perkins Library, Duke University, Durham, North Carolina.
Belmont, Alva Vanderbilt. "What the Woman's Party Wants." *Collier's* 23 (December 1922).
Belmont, Alva Vanderbilt. "Why I Am a Suffragist." *The World To–Day* October 1911.
Belmont, Alva Vanderbilt. "Woman's Right to Govern Herself." *North American Review* 190 (November 1909).
Belmont, Alva Vanderbilt. "Woman Suffrage as It Looks To–Day." *The Forum* March 1910.
Belmont, Alva Vanderbilt. "Women as Dictators." *Ladies Home Journal* September 1922.
"Belmont to Sell Belcourt." *New York Herald Tribune* December 30, 1908. [Newport estate]
"Brookholt on the Market." *The New York Times* January 6, 1909:1. [Uniondale estate]
"Buys Chateau in France: Mrs. O. H. P. Belmont Plans to Live Abroad, Newport Hears." *The New York Times* September 4, 1926:5.
Geidel, Peter. "Alva E. Belmont: A Forgotten Feminist." Ph.D. dissertation, Columbia University, 1993.
Keeler, Rebecca T. "Alva Belmont: Exacting Benefactor for Women's Rights." Ph.D. dissertation, University of South Alabama, 1987.
"Mrs. Belmont's Funeral." *The New York Times* January 27, 1933.
"Mrs. O. H. P. Belmont Buys a Lighthouse." *The New York Times* February 1, 1924:19.
"Mrs. O. H. P. Belmont Dies at Paris Home." *The New York Times* January 26, 1933.
Patterson, Augusta Owen. *American Homes of Today*. New York: The Macmillan Co., 1924.
Rector, Margaret. *Alva, That Vanderbilt–Belmont Woman: Her Story as She Might Have Told It*. Wickford, RI: The Dutch Island Press, 1992.
Spinzia, Raymond E. "In Her Wake: The Story of Alva Smith Vanderbilt Belmont." *The Long Island Historical Journal* 6 (Fall 1993):96–105.
Stasz, Clarice. *The Vanderbilt Women: Dynasty of Wealth, Glamour, and Tragedy*. New York: St. Martin's Press, 1991.
"To Build Belmont Hospital: Mrs. O. H. P. Belmont the Sponsor for One as a Memorial." *The New York Times* September 17, 1909:1.
Town and Country October 15, 1928.
"Want Wall Removed: Hempstead Board Denies Mrs. Belmont's Right to Fence Beach." *The New York Times* September 20, 1918:15.
"What the Woman's Party Wants." *Collier's* December 23, 1922.

Belmont, Eleanor Robson – Syosset
Avery Architectural and Fine Arts Library, Columbia University, NYC, has Eleanor Robson Belmont's papers.
Belmont, Eleanor Robson. *The Fabric of Memory*. New York: Farrar & Straus, & Co., 1957.
Birmingham, Stephen. *The Grandees Dames*. New York: Simon & Schuster, Inc., 1982.
Gottheil, Richard James Horatio. *Belmont–Belmonte Family: A Record of Four Hundred Years, Put Together From the Original Documents in the Archives and Libraries of Spain, Portugal, Holland, England and Germany*. 1917.
Opera News December 9, 1978.

Bendel, Henri – Kings Point
Sclare, Liisa and Donald. *Beaux–Arts Estates: A Guide to the Architecture of Long Island*. New York: The Viking Press, 1980.

Benkard, Henry Horton – Muttontown
Fleming, Nancy. *Money, Manure & Maintenance: Ingredients for Successful Gardens of Marian Coffin, Pioneer Landscape Architect 1876–1957*. Weston, MA: Country Place Books, 1995.

Betts, Wyllis Rossiter, Jr. – Oyster Bay Cove – *The Pebbles*
The Nassau County Museum Collection includes photographs of the estate.
Antiques June 1934.
House and Garden March 1933.
Howell, E. W. *Noted Long Island Homes*. Babylon, NY: E. W. Howell Co., 1933.
The Spur October 15, 1931.

Billings, Cornelius Kingsley Garrison – Upper Brookville – *Farnsworth*
   Architecture 34 (August 1916):xxx.

Blackton, James Stuart, Sr. – Cove Neck – *Harbourwood*
Mystic Seaport, Mystic, CT, has a picture of Blackton's yacht, *Baby Reliance II*, in its Rosenfeld Collection.
   Smith, Albert E. and Phil A. Koury. *Two Reels and a Crank.* Garden City: Doubleday & Co., Inc., 1952.

Blair, James Alonzo, Sr. – Oyster Bay Cove – *Ontare*
   "The Country Home of Mr. James A. Blair." *Town and Country* 65 (November 5, 1910):34.

Bliss, Cornelius Newton, Jr. – Brookville – *Oak Hill*
The Nassau County Museum Collection includes photographs of the estate.
   Howell, E. W. *Noted Long Island Homes.* Babylon, NY: E. W. Howell Co., 1933.

Bliss, Miss Ida Evelina – Kings Point – *Geranium Court*
   "Estate of Ida Evelina Bliss, Great Neck; and Property of Mrs. M. Tipping, New Orleans." New York: Parke–
    Bernet Galleries, Inc., 1943. auction catalog

Bottomley, William Lawrence – Old Brookville – *Hickory Hill*
   Bottomley, William Lawrence. "The American Country House." *Architectural Record* 48 (October 1920):
    258–368.
   Bottomley, William Lawrence. The Design of the Country House." *Architectural Record* 49 (October1921):
    243–73.
   Bottomley, William Lawrence. *Great Georgian Houses of America.* 2 vols., 1933, 1937.
   Bottomley, William Lawrence. "A Selection from the Works of Delano and Aldrich." *Architectural Record* 54
    (July 1923):3–71.
   Bottomley, William Lawrence. *Spanish Details.* New York: W. Helbrun, Inc., 1924.
   Colton, Arthur Willis. "The Works of William Lawrence Bottomley." *Architectural Review* 50 (November
    1921):338–57.
   Colton, Arthur Willis. "The Works of William Lawrence Bottomley." *Architectural Review* 50 (December
    1921):418–41.

Boyer, Philip, Sr. – North Hills – *Long Shadows*
The Nassau County Museum Collection includes photographs of the estate.
   Vogue May 24, 1930.

Brady, Nicholas Frederic – North Hills – *Inisfada*
The Nassau County Museum Collection includes photographs of the estate.
   Architectural Record 56 (December 1924):499.
   Inisfada. Manhasset, NY: St. Ignatius Retreat House, n.d.
   Kaufman, Peter. "Inisfada: The Story Behind the Estate." *Long Island Forum* 49 (July 1986):134–40.
   Patterson, Augusta Owen. *American Homes of Today.* New York: The Macmillan Co., 1924.

Brewster, George S. – Muttontown – *Fairleigh*
The Nassau County Museum Collection includes photographs of the estate.
   Architectural Review 8 (January 1919):6–7.

Brokaw, Clare Boothe – Sands Point;
     and Upper Brookville – *Sunnybrook [see George Tuttle Brokaw]*
Library of Congress, Washington, DC, has Clare Boothe's [Luce] papers. They include material on her early life.
   Martin, Ralph G. *Henry and Clare: An Intimate Portrait of the Luces.* New York: G. P. Putnam's Sons, 1991.
   Morris, Sylvia Jukes. *Rage for Fame: The Ascent of Clare Boothe Luce.* New York: Random House, 1997.
   Shadegg, Stephen. *Clare Boothe Luce: A Biography.* New York: Simon & Schuster, Inc., 1970.
   Sheed, Wilfrid. *Clare Boothe Luce.* New York: E. P. Dutton, 1982.

Brokaw, Clifford Vail, Sr. – Centre Island – *Westaways;*
     and Glen Cove – *The Elms*
   Architectural Review 11 (November 1920):149.
   Architecture 34 (August 1916):xxx.
   "House of Clifford V. Brokaw." *Architectural Record* 40 (October 1916):383–85.

Brokaw, George Tuttle – Sands Point;
and Upper Brookville – *Sunnybrook*

Collier, Peter. *The Fondas: A Hollywood Dynasty*. New York: Berkeley Books, 1992.
"The Jewels and Objects of *Vertu* of the Honorable Clare Booth Luce." New York: Sotheby, 1998. auction catalog
Martin, Ralph G. *Henry and Clare: An Intimate Portrait of the Luces*. New York: G. P. Putnam's Sons, 1991.
Morris, Sylvia Jukes. *Rage for Fame: The Ascent of Clare Boothe Luce*. New York: Random House, 1997.
Shadegg, Stephen. *Clare Boothe Luce: A Biography*. New York: Simon & Schuster, Inc., 1970.
Sheed, Wilfrid. *Clare Boothe Luce*. New York: E. P. Dutton, 1982.

Brokaw, William Gould – Kings Point – *Nirvana*

"Property of Mrs. William Gould Brokaw – Summerville, S. C." New York: Sotheby Parke–Bernet, Inc., 1950. auction catalog

Brown, George McKesson – Lloyd Harbor – *West Neck Farm*

Sclare, Liisa and Donald. *Beaux–Arts Estates: A Guide to the Architecture of Long Island*. New York: The Viking Press, 1980.

Bruce, David Kirkpatrick Este – Woodbury – *Woodlands*
Central Intelligence Agency, Langley, VA, has declassified information on David Bruce.
Federal Bureau of Investigation, Washington, DC, has declassified information on David Bruce.
The Nassau County Museum Collection includes photographs of the estate.
The National Archives, Washington, DC, has Bruce's Office of Strategic Services papers.
Office of the Surrogate Court, New York County, has Ailsa Mellon Bruce's will in File No. 5183/1969.
Virginia Historical Society, Richmond, VA, has the bulk of David Bruce's papers.

The Architectural Forum 34:6 (June 1921):plate 94.
The Architectural Forum 36:6 (June 1922):247–52.
The Architectural Review 26 (October 1919):97–104.
Brown, Anthony Cave. *The Last Hero: Wild Bill Donovan*. New York: Time Books, 1982.
Bruce, John Goodall. *The Bruce Family: Descending from George Bruce (1650–1715)*. Parsons, West Virginia: McClain, 1977.
Casey, William. *The Secret War Against Hitler*. Washington, DC: Regnery Gateway, 1988.
Conner, Jane Stuart. "David K. E. Bruce's Gift of County Libraries to Rural Virginia." M. S. thesis, University of North Carolina, Chapel Hill, 1984.
Croly, Herbert. "The Lay–Out of a Large Estate." *The Architectural Record* 16 (December 1940):537.
Delano and Aldrich. *Portraits of Ten Country Houses Designed by Delano and Aldrich*. Drawn by Chester Price. Garden City: Doubleday, Page & Co., 1924.
Harmond, Richard and Gaetano Vincitorio. "A Quiet Estate 1915–1969." *Long Island Forum* 50 (January 1987):4–11.
Hersh, Burton. *The Mellon Family: A Fortune in History*. New York: William Morrow & Co., Inc., 1978.
Hewitt, Mark Alan. "Domestic Portraits: The Early Long Island Country Houses of Delano and Aldrich." In *Long Island Architecture*, Joann P. Krieg, ed. (Interlaken, NY: Heart of the Lakes Publishing, 1991).
Lankford, Nelson Douglas. *The Last American Aristocrat: The Biography of David K. E. Bruce, 1898–1977*. Boston: Little, Brown & Co., 1996.
Lankford, Nelson Douglas, ed. *OSS Against the Reich: The World War II Diaries of Colonel David K. E. Bruce*. Kent, OH: The Kent State University Press, 1991.
Persico, Joseph E. *Piercing the Reich*. New York: The Viking Press, 1979.
Rothschild, Baronne Philippe de. "The Amazing Bruces: The Life in London of the American Ambassador and Mrs. David K. E. Bruce at Winfield House." *Vogue* September 15, 1964.
Town and Country April 15, 1931.

Bryant, William Cullen – Roslyn Harbor – *Cedarmere*
The Bryant Library, Roslyn, LI, has elevation sketches of the house.
Bureau County Historical Society, Princeton, IL, has the Bryant Family Association Papers.
The Nassau County Museum Collection includes photographs, vertical file material, historical research reports, and inventories of the estate. Nassau County also has blueprints of the house and Bryant's manuscripts.
The New York Public Library, NYC, has William Cullen Bryant papers on microfilm.

Bennett, Diane Tarleton. *William Cullen Bryant in Roslyn*. Roslyn, NY: The Bryant Library, 1978.
Brown, Charles H. *William Cullen Bryant*. New York: Charles Scribner's Sons, 1971.
Bryant, William Cullen, II, and Thomas G. Voss. *The Letters of William Cullen Bryant*. 6 vols. 1809–1878. New York: Fordham University Press, 1975–1992.

Bryant, William Cullen – Roslyn Harbor – *Cedarmere* (cont'd)
    Godwin, Parke. *A Biography of William Cullen Bryant, with Extracts from His Private Correspondence.* 2 vols. 1883. Reprint. New York: Russell & Russell, [1967].
    Peckham, Harry Houston. *Gotham Yankee: A Biography of William Cullen Bryant.* New York: Russell and Russell, 1971.

Bryce, Lloyd Stephens – Roslyn Harbor – *Bryce House*
Cooper–Hewitt Museum, The Smithsonian National Museum of Design, NYC, has a model of the garden treillage.
Library of Congress, Washington, DC, has Cornelia Bryce Pinchot's papers which consists of over 250,000 items.
The Nassau County Museum Collection includes photographs of the estate.
    Ferree, Barr. *American Estates & Gardens.* New York: Munn & Co., 1904.
    Platt, Frederick. *America's Gilded Age: Its Architecture and Decoration.* New York: A. S. Barnes & Co., 1976.
    Sclare, Liisa and Donald. *Beaux–Arts Estates: A Guide to the Architecture of Long Island.* New York: The Viking Press, 1980.
    Sanger, Martha Frick Symington. *The Henry Clay Frick Houses: Architecture . Interiors . Landscapes in the Golden Era.* New York: The Monacelli Press, 2001

Bucknall, G. Stafford – Glen Cove – *The 19th Hole*
The Nassau County Museum Collection includes photographs of the estate.

Bullock, George – Centre Island – *The Folly* [I], [II] and *Yeadon*
The Nassau County Museum Collection includes photographs of *Yeadon*.
Society for the Preservation of Long Island Antiquities, Cold Spring Harbor, LI, has a watercolor sketch of *The Folly* [II].
    House Beautiful July 1937.
    The Spur March 1934.

Burden, Arthur Scott – Brookville
    Architectural Review 8 (May 1919):130.
    Architecture 34 (October 1916):226, 228.

Burden, James Abercrombie, Jr. – Muttontown – *Woodside*
The Nassau County Museum Collection includes photographs of the estate.
New York State Library, Albany, NY, has the papers of the Burden Iron Manufacturing firm of Troy, NY. [It also contains information on the family.]
    Architectural Forum 34:6 (June 1921):plate 94.
    Architectural Forum 36:6 (June 1922):247–52.
    Architectural Record 50 (October 1921):294, 309.
    Architectural Review 1917.
    Architectural Review October 1919, 97–104.
    Bedford, Stephen and Richard Guy Wilson. *The Long Island Country House, 1870–1930.* Southampton, NY: The Parrish Art Museum, 1988.
    Burden, Shirley. *The Vanderbilts in My Life: A Personal Memoir.* New Haven: Ticknor & Fields, 1981.
    Delano and Aldrich. *Portraits of Ten Country Houses Designed by Delano and Aldrich.* Drawn by Chester Price. Garden City: Doubleday, Page & Co., 1924. (Plates 1–7)
    Forecast September 1927.
    Garden Magazine December 1924.
    Hewitt, Mark Alan. "Domestic Portraits: The Early Long Island Country Houses of Delano and Aldrich." In *Long Island Architecture*, Joann P. Krieg, ed. (Interlaken, NY: Heart of the Lakes Publishing, 1991).
    House and Garden October 1924.
    House and Garden February 1925.
    House and Garden August 1925.
    House and Garden January 1926.
    Logan, Andy. *The Man Who Robbed the Robber Barons.* New York: W. W. Norton & Co., 1965.
    Mendel, Mesick, Cohen, architects. "The Burden Iron Company Office Building: A Historic Structure Report." Albany, *The Architects*, 1976.
    The New York Times Magazine July 19, 1931.
    Patterson, Augusta Owen. *American Homes of Today.* New York: The Macmillan Co., 1924.
    Sloane, Florence Adele. *Maverick in Mauve: The Diary of a Romantic Age.* New York: Doubleday & Co., Inc., 1983.

Burnett, Frances Hodgson – Plandome Manor – *Fairseat*

Bixler, Phyllis. *Frances Hodgson Burnett*. Boston: Twayne Publishers, 1984.

Burnett, Frances Hodgson. *The One I Knew Best of All*. New York: Charles Scribner's Sons, 1893.

Burnett, Constance Buel. *Happy Ever After*. New York: Vanguard Press, 1969.

Burnett, Vivian. *The Romantick Lady* [Frances Hodgson Burnett]: *The Life Story of an Imagination*. New York: Charles Scribner's Sons, 1927.

"Famous Woman Author Leaves $150,000 Estate." *Nassau Daily Review* November 15, 1924.

Jefferson, Miles Matthew. "Frances Hodgson Burnett, Novelist, as a Factor in the Life of Her Times." M. A. thesis, Columbia University, 1930.

Thwaite, Ann. *Waiting For the Party: The Life of Frances Hodgson Burnett 1849–1924*. Boston: David R. Godine, Publisher, 1991.

Tusiani, Beatrice A. "Last Stop Plandome: Frances Hodgson Burnett." In *Long Island Women Activists and Innovators,* Natalie A. Naylor and Maureen O. Murphy, eds. (Interlaken, NY: Empire State Books, 1998).

Tusiani, Beatrice A. "A Complete History of Plandome Manor." *The Long Island Forum* 44 (July 1981): 132–41.

Burnett, Vivian – Plandome Manor – *Bentleigh*

Burnett, Vivian. *The Romantick Lady* [Frances Hodgson Burnett]: *The Life Story of an Imagination*. New York: Charles Scribner's Sons, 1927.

Handler, F. J. "The Real Fauntleroy – Lived in Plandome." *Great Neck News Magazine* February 1977.

McCarthy, Tom. "The Real Lord Fauntleroy." *American Heritage* February 1970.

"Original Fauntleroy Dies in Boat After Helping Rescue 4 in Sound." *The New York Times* July 26, 1937:1–2.

Burrill, Middleton Schoolbred – Jericho – *Jericho Farms*

Patterson, Augusta Owen. *American Homes of Today*. New York: The Macmillan Co., 1924.

Busby, Leonard J. – Glen Cove – *Germelwyn*

Architecture May 15, 1901:122.

Byrne, James – Upper Brookville

The American Architect and Brickbuilders News April 22, 1908.

Cairns, Anna Eliza – Roslyn Harbor – *Clifton*

The Nassau County Museum Collection includes photographs of the estate.

Society for the Preservation of Long Island Antiquities, Cold Spring Harbor, LI, has a cast iron birdhouse modeled after the house.

Campbell, Oliver Allen, Sr. – East Norwich – *The Oaces*

Architectural Review 10 (April 1920):98, 101–4.

Canfield, Augustus Cass – North Hills – *Cassleigh*

The Nassau County Museum Collection includes photographs of the estate.

Platt, Frederick. *America's Gilded Age: Its Architecture and Decoration*. New York: A. S. Barnes & Co., 1976.

Cary, Guy Fairfax, Sr. – Brookville – *Oak Hill*

Patterson, Augusta Owen. *American Homes of Today*. New York: The Macmillan Co., 1924.

Casey, William Joseph, Jr. – Roslyn Harbor – *Mayknoll*

Hoover Institution on War Revolution and Peace, Stanford University, Stanford, CA, has William Joseph Casey's Jr.'s papers.

Cline, Ray S. *The CIA Under Reagan, Bush and Casey*. Washington, DC: Acropolis Books, 1981.

Persico, Joseph E. *Casey from OSS to CIA*. New York: The Viking Press, 1991.

Persico, Joseph E. *Piercing the Reich*. New York: The Viking Press, 1979.

Walsh, Lawrence E. *Firewall: The Iran–Contra Conspiracy and Cover–up*. New York: W. W. Norton & Co., 1997.

Chanler, Alice Remington Chamberlain – Lloyd Harbor – *Klotz Cottage*

Aldrich, Margaret Chanler. *Family Vista*. privately printed pamphlet, 1958.

Gates, John D. *The Astor Family*. Garden City: Doubleday & Co., Inc., 1981.

Thomas, Lately. *The Astor Orphans, a Pride of Lions: The Chanler Chronicle*. New York: William Morrow & Co., Inc., 1971.

Chanler, Lewis Stuyvesant, Jr. – Syosset – *Chestnut Vale*
Aldrich, Margaret Chanler. *Family Vista.* privately printed pamphlet, 1958.
Gates, John D. *The Astor Family.* Garden City: Doubleday & Co., Inc., 1981.
Thomas, Lately. *The Astor Orphans, a Pride of Lions: The Chanler Chronicle.* New York: William Morrow & Co., Inc., 1971.

Chase, Edna Woolman – Upper Brookville
The Nassau County Museum Collection includes photographs of the estate.

Chrysler, Walter Percy, Sr. – Kings Point – *Forker House*
Office of the County Clerk, Nassau County, Mineola, LI, has Walter Chrysler's will on file.
Architectural Record January 1901:3.
Chrysler, Walter P. *Life of an American Workman.* New York: Dodd, Mead & Co., 1950.
Curcio, Vincent. *Chrysler: The Life and Times of an Automotive Genius.* New York: Oxford University Press, 2000.
Moritz, Michael. *Going for Broke: The Chrysler Story.* Garden City: Doubleday & Co., Inc., 1981.
Sclare, Liisa and Donald. *Beaux–Arts Estates: A Guide to the Architecture of Long Island.* New York: The Viking Press, 1980.
Zeder, Fred Morrell. *Leadership: A Message to America.* New York: The Newcomen Society of England, American Branch, 1947.

Clark, Frederick Ambrose – Old Westbury – *Broad Hollow House*
The Nassau County Museum Collection includes photographs of the estate.
Architecture April 1918:106.
Country Life June 1934.
Sclare, Liisa and Donald. *Beaux–Arts Estates: A Guide to the Architecture of Long Island.* New York: The Viking Press, 1980.

Clark, Grenville, Sr. – Albertson
Baker Library, Dartmouth College, White River Junction, VT, has Grenville Clark Sr.'s papers.
Cousins, Norman and J. Garry Clifford, eds. *Memoirs of a Man, Grenville Clark.* New York: W. W. Norton, 1975.
Dunne, Gerald T. *Grenville Clark Public Citizen.* New York: Farrar, Straus & Giroux, 1986.
Ellis, Francis M. and Edward F. Clark, Jr. *A Brief History of Carter, Ledyard and Milburn from 1854 to 1988.* Portsmouth, NH: Peter Randall Publisher, 1988.
"Grenville Clark; Statesman Incognito." *Fortune* February 1946.

Clark, James Averell, Sr. – Old Westbury
Architectural Forum 39 (December 1923):315.
Howell, E. W. *Noted Long Island Homes.* Babylon, NY: E. W. Howell Co., 1933.

Clarkson, Robert Livingston, Sr. – Bayville – *Callender House*
The Nassau County Museum Collection includes photographs of the estate.

Coates, Winslow Shelby, Sr. – Bayville – *Dunstable*
The Nassau County Museum Collection includes photographs of the estate.

Cockran, William Bourke – Sands Point – *The Cedars*
The Nassau County Museum Collection includes photographs of the estate.
Chernow, Ron. *The House of Morgan: An American Banking Dynasty and The Rise of Modern Finance.* New York: Atlantic Monthly Press, 1990.
McCurran, James. *Bourke Cockran: A Free Lance in American Politics.* New York: Charles Scribner's Sons, 1948.

Coe, William Robertson – Upper Brookville – *Planting Fields*
Frederic Law Olmsted National Historic Site, Brookline, MA, has over 300 Olmsted landscape drawings of the estate.
The Nassau County Museum Collection includes photographs of the estate.
Planting Fields Arboretum, Upper Brookville, LI, has extensive material on the Coe family and the estate.
Arts and Decoration April 1936.
Arts and Decoration May 1936.
Boyd, John Taylor, Jr. "The Residence of William R. Coe, Esq., Oyster Bay, Long Island: Walker and Gillette, Architects." *Architectural Record* March 1921:195.

Coe, William Robertson – Upper Brookville – *Planting Fields* (cont'd)
    Charm November 1924.
    Charm January 1925.
    Charm August 1926.
    Country Life January 1930.
    Country Life February 1931.
    Country Life October 1932.
    Country Life June 1934.
    The Field August 1922.
    Garden Magazine February 1922.
    Garden Magazine August 1922.
    Garden Magazine April 1923.
    Garden Magazine August 1923.
    Golf Illustrated July 1932.
    Griswold, Mac and Eleanor Weller. *The Golden Age of American Gardens . Proud Owners . Private Estates . 1890–1940.* New York: Harry N. Abrams, Inc., Publishers, 1991.
    Harper's Bazaar July 1923.
    House and Garden August 1921.
    House and Garden August 1922.
    House and Garden December 1922.
    House Beautiful June 1922.
    New York Herald Tribune June 2, 1921.
    New York Herald Tribune May 26, 1929.
    New York Herald Tribune June 16, 1929.
    New York Herald Tribune April 13, 1930.
    New York Herald Tribune June 21, 1931.
    New York Herald Tribune November 15, 1931.
    New York Sun October 18, 1929.
    New York Sun April 5, 1930.
    New York Sun September 19, 1931.
    Patterson, Augusta Owen. *American Homes of Today.* New York: The Macmillan Co., 1924.
    Planting Fields – Past and Present: A Brief History of the Arboretum Beginning with the Glacial Formation of Long Island. New York: Planting Fields Arboretum, 1976.
    "Planting Fields: The Residence of William R. Coe, Esq., at Oyster Bay, Long Island." *Country Life in America* 53 (February 1928):49–53.
    Sclare, Liisa and Donald. *Beaux–Arts Estates: A Guide to the Architecture of Long Island.* New York: The Viking Press, 1980.
    The Spur April 1, 1924.
    The Spur May 1, 1927.
    Town and Country May 1, 1922.
    Town and Country June 15, 1931.

Cohn, Milton Seymour – Kings Point
The Nassau County Museum Collection includes photographs of the estate.

Coleman, Gregory – Muttontown
The Nassau County Museum Collection includes photographs of the estate.

Conklin, Roland Ray – Lloyd Harbor – *Rosemary Farm*
Architectural Archives, University of Pennsylvania, Philadelphia, PA, has Wilson Eyre's architectural designs for the house.
Avery Library, Columbia University, NYC, has Wilson Eyre's architectural designs for the house.
Frederic Law Olmsted National Historic Site, Brookline, MA, has twenty-four of Olmsted's landscape drawings and photographs of the estate.
    Bedford, Stephen and Richard Guy Wilson. *The Long Island Country House, 1870–1930.* Southampton, NY: The Parrish Art Museum, 1988.
    "Rosemary Farm: The Residence of Ronald R. Conklin, Esq., Wilson Eyre, Architect." *Architectural Record* 28 (October 1910):238.

Cooper, Kenneth F. – Kings Point
The Nassau County Museum Collection includes photographs of the estate.
> *Home and Field* July 1932.
> *House Beautiful* January 1931.
> *Successful Farming* February 1, 1937.

Cox, Irving E. – Mill Neck – *Meadow Farm*
The Nassau County Museum Collection includes photographs of the estate.
> *Arts and Decoration* August 1932.
> *Christian Science Monitor* December 31, 1934.

Cozzens, Issachar, III – Lattingtown – *Maple Knoll*
The Nassau County Museum Collection includes photographs of the estate.

Crary, Miner Dunham, Sr. – Asharoken
> Howell, E. W. *Noted Long Island Homes*. Babylon, NY: E. W. Howell Co., 1933.

Cravath, Paul Drennan – Lattingtown – *Veraton* **[I];**
> > **and Matinecock –** *Veraton* **[II], [III], and** *Still House*
> Cravath, Paul D. "Preserving Country Lanes." *Country Life In America* January 1913:27.
> "The Fabled Past: House and Garden." *The North Shore Journal* 9 (May 25, 1978) n.p.
> Swaine, Robert T. *The Cravath Firm and Its Predecessors, 1819–1948*. vols. 1, 2. New York: Ad Press, Ltd.,
> > 1946, 1948.

Crocker, George – Old Westbury
The Nassau County Museum Collection includes photographs of the estate.

Cross, Eliot B. – Old Westbury
The Nassau County Museum Collection includes photographs of the estate.

Curran, Guernsey, Sr. – Upper Brookville – *Farlands*
The Nassau County Museum Collection includes photographs of the estate.
> Patterson, Augusta Owen. *American Homes of Today*. New York: The Macmillan Co., 1924.

Curtis, James Freeman – Roslyn Harbor – *Willowmere*
The Nassau County Museum Collection includes photographs of the estate.
> *Canadian Saturday Night* April 26, 1949.

Cutting, Dr. Fulton –   North Hills;
> > **and Brookville**
> Howell, E. W. *Noted Long Island Homes*. Babylon, NY: E. W. Howell Co., 1933.

Dana, Charles Anderson – West Island, Glen Cove – *The Wings*
> DeRiggi, Mildred Murphy. "Glen Cove's Most Famous Resident." *Long Island Forum* 43 (July 1980):132–35.
> Rosebault, Charles J. *When Dana Was The Sun: Story of Personal Journalism*. New York: Robert M. McBride
> > & Co., 1931.
> Steele, Janet E. *The Sun Shines for All: Journalism and Ideology in the Life of Charles A. Dana*. Syracuse:
> > Syracuse University Press, 1993.
> Stone, Candace. *Dana and The Sun*. New York: Dodd, Mead & Co., 1938.
> Wilson, James Harrison. *The Life of Charles A. Dana*. New York: Harper & Brothers, 1907.

Dane, Chester Linwood, Sr. – Mill Neck – *Linwood*
The Nassau County Museum Collection includes photographs of the estate.

Davis, John William – Lattingtown – *Mattapan*
Avery Architectural and Fine Arts Library, Columbia University, NYC, has a transcript of John W. Davis' Oral Memoir.
Sterling Memorial Library, Yale University, New Haven, CT, has John William Davis' papers.
West Virginia University Library, Morgantown, WV, has a collection of John William and Julia McDonald Davis' papers.
> Harbaugh, William H. *Lawyer's Lawyer: The Life of John W. Davis*. New York: Oxford University Press, 1973.
> Huntley, Theodore A. *The Life of John W. Davis*. New York: Duffield, 1924.

Davison, Frederick Trubee – Lattingtown – *Peacock Point*
Glen Cove Public Library, Glen Cove, LI, has seven microfilm reels of Frederick Trubee Davison's family scrapbook
    covering the years 1921–1931.

Davison, Henry Pomeroy, Sr. – Lattingtown – *Peacock Point*
The Nassau County Museum Collection includes photographs of the estate.
       Architectural Review 11 (November 1920):150.
         Boyd, John Taylor, Jr. "Peacock Point – The Residence of Henry P. Davison, Esq." *Architectural Record* July
           1917:249–51.
         Davison. *Sketches of Mother at Peacock Point*, privately printed, n.d.
         "The Fabled Past: House and Garden." *The North Shore Journal* 9 (May 25, 1978) n.p.
         Lamont, Thomas W. *Henry P. Davison: The Record of a Useful Life.* New York: Harper & Brothers, 1933.
         Patterson, Augusta Owen. *American Homes of Today.* New York: The Macmillan Co., 1924.

Deans, Robert Barr, Sr. – Centre Island – *Yeadon*
The Nassau County Museum Collection includes photographs of the estate.

de Forest, Henry Wheeler – Laurel Hollow – *Nethermuir*
Frederic Law Olmsted National Historic Site, Brookline, MA, has 250 Olmsted drawings of the estate's landscaping.
         Watson, Elizabeth. *Houses For Science: A Pictorial History of the Cold Spring Harbor Laboratory.* Cold
           Spring Harbor, NY: Cold Spring Harbor Press, 1991.

de Forest, Johnston – Cold Spring Harbor – *Wawapek*
The Nassau County Museum Collection includes photographs of the estate.

de Forest, Miss Julia Mary – Laurel Hollow – *Airslie*
Frederic Law Olmsted National Historic Site, Brookline, MA, has Olmsted's landscape drawings of the estate.
         Watson, Elizabeth. *Houses For Science: A Pictorial History of the Cold Spring Harbor Laboratory.* Cold
           Spring Harbor, NY: Cold Spring Harbor Press, 1991.

de Forest, Robert Weeks – Cold Spring Harbor – *Wawapek*
The Nassau County Museum Collection includes photographs of the estate.
         Charm August 1926.
         New York Herald Tribune March 22, 1931.

DeLamar, Joseph Raphael – Glen Cove – *Pembroke*
The Nassau County Museum Collection includes photographs of the estate.
         The American Architect 116 (1919):367.
         Arts and Decoration 16 (April 1922):430.
         Lewis & Valentine Nursery. New York: Lewis & Valentine Co., 1916.
         The Spur 31 (April 1916):22.
         Town & Country December 1921:37.
         Town & Country November 1926:64.

Delano, William Adams – Muttontown – *Muttontown Corners*
Avery Architectural and Fine Arts Library, Columbia University, NYC, has photographs of the estate.
The McIlwaine Collection, Avery Architectural and Fine Arts Library, Columbia University, NYC, contains the office
    files of Delano and Aldrich.
         The American Architect 107 (May 12, 1915):2055.
         Delano and Aldrich. *Portraits of Ten Country Houses Designed by Delano and Aldrich.* Drawn by Chester
           Price. Garden City: Doubleday, Page & Co., 1924.
         "A House in an Apple Orchard: The Home of William Adams Delano at Syosset, Long Island." *Country Life*
           May 1918:68–9.
          Hewitt, Mark Alan. *The Architect & the Country House 1890–1940.* New Haven: Yale University Press, 1990.
         Hewitt, Mark Alan. "Domestic Portraits: The Early Long Island Country Houses of Delano and Aldrich." In
           Long Island Architecture, Joann P. Krieg, ed. (Interlaken, NY: Heart of the Lakes Publishing, 1991).
         Hewitt, Mark Alan. "William Adams Delano and the Muttontown Enclave." *Antiques* 132 (August 1987):
           316–27.
         Nevins, Allan and Dean Albertson, eds. "The Reminiscences of William Adams Delano." Unpublished
           manuscript. Columbia University Oral History Project, 1972.
         "Residence of W. A. Delano, Syosset, L. I., Owner and Architect." *Architectural Record* 47 (April 1920):
           319–20.

Derby, Dr. Richard – Oyster Bay – *Old Adam*
    American Architect and Building News November 3, 1878.
    Caroli, Betty Boyd. *The Roosevelt Women.* New York: Basic Books, 1998.

Dick, Fairman Rogers – Lattingtown;
               and Old Brookville – *Apple Tree Hill*
    Howell, E. W. *Noted Long Island Homes.* Babylon, NY: E. W. Howell Co., 1933.

Dilworth, Dewees Wood – Old Westbury – *Gloan*
The Nassau County Museum Collection includes photographs of the estate.

Dodge, Lillian Sefton Thomas – Mill Neck – *Sefton Manor*
The Nassau County Museum Collection includes photographs of the estate.
Society for the Preservation of Long Island Antiquities, Cold Spring Harbor, LI, has c. 1925 Lenox dinnerware depicting
    scenes on the estate. The service was made as a birthday present for Lillian Sefton Dodge.

Donahue, James Paul, Jr. – Brookville – *Broadhollow*
    Wilson, Christopher. *Dancing With the Devil: The Windsors and Jimmy Donahue.* New York: St. Martin's
        Press, 2001.

Doubleday, Frank Nelson – Mill Neck – *Effendi Hall*;
             and Lattingtown – *New House*
    Doubleday, Frank Nelson. *He's Done It Again: More Indiscreet Recollections.* privately printed, n.d.

Douglas, Josephine Hartford – Upper Brookville
The Nassau County Museum Collection includes photographs of the estate.
    Town and Country December 1, 1929.

Draper, Charles Dana – Albertson – *Ten Gables*
The Nassau County Museum Collection includes photographs of the estate.

Dulles, Allen Welsh – Lloyd Harbor
Butler Library, Columbia University, NYC, has the oral history recorded by Allen Welsh and John Foster Dulles' sister
    Eleanor Lansing Dulles.
Central Intelligence Agency, Langley, VA, declassified Allen Dulles' CIA papers in 1994.
Franklin D. Roosevelt Presidential Library, Hyde Park, NY, has Allen Dulles' OSS war dispatches.
Library of Congress, Washington, DC, has numerous letters from Allen Dulles in the Robert Lansing Collection.
The National Archives, Washington, DC, has Allen Dulles' papers relating to OSS operations in World War II. These are
    included in the files of the Office of Strategic Services.
Seeley G. Mudd Library, Princeton University, Princeton, NJ, has Allen Dulles' personal papers and those of his wife
    Clover Todd Dulles.
Truman, Eisenhower, Kennedy, and Johnson Presidential Libraries also have documents pertaining to Allen Dulles.
    Bancroft, Mary. *Autobiography of a Spy.* New York: William Morrow & Co., 1983.
    Brown, Anthony Cave. *The Last Hero: Wild Bill Donovan.* New York: Times Books, 1982.
    Carvo, Max. *The OSS in Italy.* New York: Praeger, 1990.
    Dean, Arthur H. *William Nelson Cromwell, 1854–1948: An American Pioneer in Corporation, Comparative
        and International Law.* New York: privately printed, 1957.
    Grose, Peter. *Gentleman Spy: The Life of Allen Dulles.* New York: Richard Todd/Houghton Mifflin, 1995.
    Hersh, Burton. *The Old Boys: The American Elite and the Origins of the CIA.* New York: Charles Scribner's
        Sons, 1992.
    Lankford, Nelson Douglas, ed. *OSS Against the Reich: The World War II Diaries of Colonel David K. E. Bruce.*
        Kent, OH: The Kent State University Press, 1991.
    Mosley, Leonard. *Dulles: A Biography of Eleanor, Allen, and John Foster Dulles and Their Family Network.*
        New York: The Dial Press, 1978.
    Persico, Joseph E. *Piercing The Reich.* New York: The Viking Press, 1979.
    Smith, Bradley F. and Elena Agarossi. *Operation Sunrise.* New York: Basic Books, 1979.
    Smith, Bradley F. *The Shadow Warriors.* New York: Basic Books, 1983.
    Strodes, James. *Allen Dulles Master of Spies.* Washington, DC: Regnery Publishing, Inc., 1999.

Dulles, John Foster – Lloyd Harbor
Butler Library, Columbia University, NYC, has the oral history recorded by John Foster and Allen Welsh Dulles' sister
    Eleanor Lansing Dulles.

Dulles, John Foster – Lloyd Harbor (cont'd)
Seeley G. Mudd Library, Princeton University, Princeton, NJ, has John Foster Dulles' papers.
    Dean, Arthur H. *William Nelson Cromwell, 1854–1948: An American Pioneer in Corporation, Comparative and International Law.* New York: privately printed, 1957.
    Dulles, Eleanor Lansing. *John Foster Dulles: The Last Years.* New York: Harcourt, Brace, 1963.
    Hersh, Burton. *The Old Boys: The American Elite and the Origins of the CIA.* New York: Charles Scribner's Sons, 1992.
    Hoopes, Townsend. *The Devil and John Foster Dulles.* Boston: Little, Brown & Co., 1973.
    Martin, James Stewart. *All Honorable Men.* Boston: Little, Brown & Co., 1950.
    Mosley, Leonard. *Dulles: A Biography of Eleanor, Allen, and John Foster Dulles and Their Family Network.* New York: The Dial Press, 1978.
    Pruessen, Ronald W. *John Foster Dulles: The Road to Power.* New York: Free Press, 1982.

du Pont, Alfred Irenee – Brookville – *White Eagle*
Avery Architectural and Fine Arts Library, Columbia University, NYC, has photographs and sketches of the estate.
    Bedford, Stephen and Richard Guy Wilson. *The Long Island Country House, 1870–1930.* Southampton, NY: The Parrish Art Museum, 1988.
    Sclare, Liisa and Donald. *Beaux–Arts Estates: A Guide to the Architecture of Long Island.* New York: The Viking Press, 1980.

Duryea, Harry H. – Old Brookville
The Nassau County Museum Collection includes photographs of the estate.

Duryea, Hermanes Barkulo, Jr. – Old Westbury – *Knole*
    Ferree, Barr. "Notable American Houses, The House of Herman B. Duryea, Esq., Old Westbury, N. Y." *Scientific American Building Monthly* November 1904:93.

Eberstadt, Ferdinand – Lloyd Harbor – *Target Rock Farm*
Seeley G. Mudd Library, Princeton University, Princeton, NJ, has Ferdinand Eberstadt's papers.
Surrogate's Court of Suffolk County, Suffolk County, Riverhead, LI, has Ferdinand Eberstadt's will in file number 1677, p. 1969.
    Christman, Calvin Lee. "Charles A. Beard, Ferdinand Eberstadt, and America's Postwar Security." *Mid–America* 54 (July 1972):187–94.
    Christman, Calvin Lee. "Ferdinand Eberstadt and Economic Mobilization for War, 1941–1943." Ph.D. dissertation, Ohio State University, 1971.
    Cuff, Robert D. "Ferdinand Eberstadt, the National Security Resources Board, and the Search for Integrated Mobilization Planning, 1947–1948." *Public Historian* 7 (Fall 1985):37–52.
    Dowart, Jeffrey M. *Eberstadt and Forrestal: The National Security Partnership 1909–1949.* College Station, TX: Texas A & M University Press, 1991.
    "Ferdinand Eberstadt." *Fortune* April 1939:72–5.
    Perez, Robert C. and Edward F. Willet. *The Will to Win: A Biography of Ferdinand Eberstadt.* Westport: Greenwood Press, 1989.

Eldridge, Lewis Angevine, Sr. – Saddle Rock – *Redcote*
    Howell, E. W. *Noted Long Island Homes.* Babylon, NY: E. W. Howell Co., 1933.

Eldridge, Roswell – Saddle Rock – *Udalls*
Architectural Archives, University of Pennsylvania, Philadelphia, PA, has Wilson Eyre's architectural designs for the house.

Elmhirst, Leonard Knight – Old Westbury – *Applegreen* [see also Straight, Willard Dickerman]
The Department of Landscape Architecture Documents Collection, University of California, Berkeley, CA, has Beatrix Farrand's papers which include her sketches for the Straight estate landscaping.
The Elmhirst Centre Archive, Dartington Hall, Totnes, Devon, England, has correspondence between Beatrix Jones Farrand, the Straights, and the Elmhirsts concerning the landscaping of both their Old Westbury estate and Dartington Hall. The Elmhirst Centre Archive also has Dorothy Whitney [Straight] Elmhirst's English papers.
The Nassau County Museum Collection includes photographs of the estate.
Olin Library, Cornell University, Ithaca, NY, has the American papers of Dorothy Whitney [Straight] Elmhirst.
    Balmori, Diana, Diane Kostial McGuire, and Eleanor M. McPeck. *Beatrix Farrand's American Landscapes: Her Gardens and Campuses.* Sagaponack, NY: Sagapress, Inc., 1985.
    Brown, Jane. *Beatrix: The Gardening Life of Beatrix Jones Farrand 1872–1959.* New York: Viking Penguin Books, 1995.

Elmhirst, Leonard Knight – Old Westbury – *Applegreen* [*see also* Straight, Willard Dickerman] (cont'd)
    Elmhirst, Leonard Knight. *The Straight and Its Origin*. Ithaca, NY: Willard Straight Hall, n.d.
    Emery, Anthony. *Dartington Hall*. New York: Oxford University Press, 1970.
    Snell, Reginald. *From the Bare Stem: The Making of Dorothy Elmhirst's Garden at Dartington Hall*. Exeter, Devon: Devon Books, 1989.
    Spinzia, Raymond E. "Michael Straight and the Cambridge Spy Ring." *The Freeholder* 5 (Winter 2001):3–5
    Straight, Michael. *After Long Silence*. New York: W. W. Norton & Co., 1983.
    Straight, Michael. *Make This the Last War*. New York: Harcourt Brace & Co., 1943.
    Straight, Michael. *Trial By Television*. Boston: The Beacon Press, 1954.
    Young, Michael. *The Elmhirsts of Dartington: The Creation of an Utopian Community*. Boston: Routledge & Kegan Paul, 1982.

Emerson, Margaret – Old Brookville – *Rynwood*;
                 and Sands Point – *Cedar Knoll*
The Nassau County Museum Collection includes photographs of *Rynwood*.
    Kaiser, Harvey H. *Great Camps of the Adirondacks*. Boston: David R. Godine, 1982.

Erbe, Gustav, Jr. – Lattingtown
The Nassau County Museum Collection includes photographs of the estate.
    Country Life December 1927.

Everitt, Samuel Alexander – Huntington Bay – *Tide Hill*
The Nassau County Museum Collection includes photographs of the estate.

Fahnestock, Archer Pleasant – Plandome Manor – *The Pleasantways*
    "Fahnestock Blaze Damage $100,000." *Manhasset Mail* January 2, 1935.
    Pitman, H. Minot. *The Fahnestock Genealogy*. Concord, NH: The Rumford Press, 1945.
    "Relics Rescued as Fauntleroy Building Burns." *New York Herald Tribune* December 30, 1935.

Fahys, George Ernest, Sr. – Glen Cove – *Hilaire*;
                 and Matinecock – *Hilaire*
The Nassau County Museum Collection includes photographs of the Matinecock estate.
    Architecture 3 (January 1901):14.

Fairchild, Sherman M. – Lloyd Harbor – *Eastfair*
Library of Congress, Washington, DC, has Sherman M. Fairchild's papers.
    Howell, E. W. *Noted Long Island Homes*. Babylon, NY: E. W. Howell Co., 1933.

Farwell, Walter – Oyster Bay Cove – *Mallow*
The Nassau County Museum Collection includes photographs of the estate.
    Vogue December 1929.

Ferguson, Dr. Farquhar – Huntington Bay – *The Monastery*
Huntington Historical Society, Huntington, LI, has photographs of the estate.
    King, Robert B. *Ferguson's Castle*. New York: Exposition Press, 1978.

Field, Marshall, III – Lloyd Harbor – *Caumsett*
Frederick Law Olmsted National Historic Site, Brookline, MA, has twenty-eight Olmsted landscape drawings of the estate.
Lloyd Harbor Historical Society, Lloyd Harbor, LI, has a Structure Inventory form that was compiled on the estate as well as circa 1977 photographs of the estate.
    American Architect and Builders Monthly 1928.
    American Artist 1928.
    Becker, Stephen. *Marshall Field III: A Biography*. New York: Simon & Schuster, Inc., 1964.
    Bedford, Stephen and Richard Guy Wilson. *The Long Island Country House, 1870–1930*. Southampton, NY: The Parrish Art Museum, 1988.
    Benziger, Barbara Field. *The Prison of My Mind*. New York: Walker & Co., 1969.
    Bessell, Matthew. *Caumsett: The Home of Marshall Field III in Lloyd Harbor, New York*. Huntington, NY: Huntington Town Board, 1991.
    Coffin, Marian Cruger. *Trees and Shrubs for Landscape Effects*. New York: Charles Scribner's Sons, 1940.
    Country Life in America 52 (August 1927):49.
    Field, Marshall, III. *Freedom Is More Than a Word*. Chicago: University of Chicago Press, 1945.

Individual Bibliographic References

Field, Marshall, III – Lloyd Harbor – *Caumsett* (cont'd)

Fleming, Nancy. *Money, Manure & Maintenance: Ingredients for Successful Gardens of Marian Coffin, Pioneer Landscape Architect 1876–1957.* Weston, MA: Country Place Books, 1995.

Hellman, Geoffrey T. "Full–Length Portrait of a Country Gentleman–Marshall Field." *Country Life in America* 65 (April 1934):42.

Hewitt, Mark Alan. *The Architect & the Country House 1890–1940.* New Haven: Yale University Press, 1990.

Madsen, Axel. *The Marshall Fields.* Hoboken, NJ: John Wiley & Sons, Inc., 2002.

Monograph of the Works of John Russell Pope. 3 vols. New York: W. Helbrun, Inc., 1937.

Patterson, Augusta Owen. *American Homes of Today.* New York: The Macmillan Co., 1924.

Sclare, Liisa and Donald. *Beaux–Arts Estates: A Guide to the Architecture of Long Island.* New York: The Viking Press, 1980.

Tebbel, John. *The Marshall Fields: A Study in Wealth.* New York: E. P. Dutton, 1947.

Fisher, Carl Graham – Sands Point;
                and Port Washington

Fisher, Jane. *Fabulous Hoosier.* New York: Robert M. McBride and Co., 1947.

Fisher, Jerry M. *The Pacesetter, the Untold Story of Carl G. Fisher.* Fort Bragg, CA: Lost Coast, Press, n.d.

Williams, George L. "Bayview Colony: Carl Fisher's Contribution to Cow Neck." *Journal of Cow Neck Peninsula Historical Society* Fall 1999:23–33.

Folger, Emily Clara Jordan – Glen Cove

Vassar College Library, Schenectady, NY, has material on the Folgers in its college archives.

"Edward Jordan Diary." Unpublished manuscript. In the possession of the Honorable Jordan Dimock, New York City.

Folger Shakespeare Library. Annual Report, 1935–1936. Washington, DC.

Harrison, Robert L. " The Folgers and Shakespeare: A Long Island Story." *The Nassau County Society Journal* 54 (2001):11–18.

Henry C. Folger. privately printed, 1931.

James, Edward T., ed. *Notable American Women: A Biographical Dictionary, 1607–1950. s.v.,* "Folger, Emily Clara Jordan," vol. I:637–38.

King, Stanley. *Recollections of the Folger Shakespeare Library.* Ithaca, NY: Cornell University Press, 1950.

McManaway, James G. "The Folger Shakespeare Library." In *Shakespeare Survey,* Allardyce Nicoll, ed. vol. I. (1948).

Woman's Who's Who in America, 1914–1915. s. v., "Folger, Emily Jordan."

Forrestal, James Vincent – East Hills – *The Old Brick*

The Nassau County Museum Collection includes photographs of the estate.

Naval Historical Division, Operational Archives, Washington, DC, has papers relating to James Vincent Forrestal as Secretary of the Navy.

Office of the Secretary of Defense Historical Office, Pentagon, Arlington, VA, has some of James Vincent Forrestal's unpublished diaries.

Seeley G. Mudd Library, Princeton University, Princeton, NY, also has some of James Vincent Forrestal's unpublished diaries.

Albion, Robert G. and Robert H. Connery. *Forrestal and the Navy.* New York: Columbia University Press, 1962.

American Agriculturist January 1934.

Better Homes and Gardens September 1936.

Forrestal, James. *The Forrestal Diaries.* New York: The Viking Press, 1951.

Hoopes, Townsend. *Driven Patriot: The Life and Times of James Forrestal.* New York: Alfred A. Knopf, 1992.

Huie, William Bradford. *"Untold Facts in the Forrestal Case." New American Mercury* 71 (December 1950): 643–52.

Philips, Evelyn. "The Old Brick Mansion: A New Family in an Old Home." *The North Shore Community* September 26, 1974, 12(B)–13(B).

Rogow, Arnold A. *James Forrestal: A Study of Personality, Politics, and Policy.* New York: The Macmillan Co., 1963.

Vogue August 2, 1930.

Vogue September 15, 1930.

Fowler, Dr. Robert H. – Laurel Hollow
The Nassau County Museum Collection includes photographs of the estate.
    House and Garden May 1922.
    House Beautiful April 1922.
    The Small Home June 1929.

Fox, Fontaine Talbot, Jr. – Roslyn Estates;
               and Port Washington
The Nassau County Museum Collection includes photographs of the Roslyn Estates house.

Foy, Thelma Chrysler – Matinecock – *Foy Farm*
    "French Modern Paintings, XVIII Century French Furniture, Objects of Art Collected by the Late Thelma
        Chrysler Foy." New York: Parke–Bernet Galleries, Inc., 1959. auction catalog

Frick, Childs – Roslyn Harbor – *Clayton*
Cooper–Hewitt Museum, The Smithsonian National Museum of Design, NYC, has a model of the garden treillage.
David C. Duniway Archives, Salem, Oregon, has photographs of the family in their collection.
Frick Art and Historical Center, Pittsburgh, PA, has photographs of the family in their collection.
The Nassau County Museum Collection includes photographs of the estate.
    Ferree, Barr. *American Estates & Gardens.* New York: Munn & Co., 1904.
    Fleming, Nancy. *Money, Manure & Maintenance: Ingredients for Successful Gardens of Marian Coffin,*
        Pioneer Landscape Architect 1876–1957. Weston, MA: Country Place Books, 1995.
    Griswold, Mac and Eleanor Weller. *The Golden Age of American Gardens . Proud Owners . Private Estates .*
        1890–1940. New York: Harry N. Abrams, Inc., Publishers, 1991.
    Harvey, George. *Henry Clay Frick.* privately printed, 1936.
    Sanger, Martha Frick Symington. *Henry Clay Frick: An Intimate Portrait.* New York: Abbeville Press, 1998.
    Sanger, Martha Frick Symington. *The Henry Clay Frick Houses: Architecture . Interiors . Landscapes in the*
        Golden Era. New York: The Monacelli Press, 2001
    Sclare, Liisa and Donald. *Beaux–Arts Estates: A Guide to the Architecture of Long Island.* New York: The
        Viking Press, 1980.

Garvan, Francis Patrick, Sr. – Old Westbury – *Roslyn House*
    "Important Silver from the Estates of Mabel Brady Garvan, Donald S. Morrison, Pearl D. Morrison, June 6,
        1980." New York: Sotheby, 1980. auction catalog

Garver, John Anson – Oyster Bay Cove – *Wrexleigh*
The Nassau County Museum Collection includes photographs of the estate.
    Architectural Record 35 (March 1914):180, 202.

Gary, Elbert H. – Jericho – *Ivy Hall*
The Nassau County Museum Collection includes photographs of the estate.
    Tarbell, Ida M. *The Life of Elbert H. Gary: The Story of Steel.* New York: D. Appleton–Century Co., 1933.

Gavin Michael– Brookville – *Greanan*
    "French and English Furniture and Silver Together with Gothic and Renaissance Sculptures, Furniture and
        Tapestries from the Estate of the Late Gertrude Hill Gavin." New York: Sotheby Park–Bernet, Inc., 1977.
        auction catalog

Geddes, Donald Grant, Sr. – Glen Cove
The Nassau County Museum Collection includes photographs of the estate.

Gerard, James Watson, III – Lloyd Harbor
    Gerard, James W. *My First Eighty–Three Years in America: The Memoirs of James W. Gerard.* Garden City:
        Doubleday & Co., Inc., 1951.

Giordano, Salvatore, Sr. – Lloyd Harbor – *Panfield*
The Nassau County Museum Collection includes photographs of the estate.

Godwin, Miss Elizabeth Love – Roslyn Harbor – *Cedarmere*
The Nassau County Museum Collection includes photographs of the estate.

Godwin, Harold – Roslyn Harbor – *Cedarmere*
The Bryant Library, Roslyn, LI, has elevation sketches of the house.
Bureau County Historical Society, Princeton, IL, has the Bryant Family Association Papers.
The Nassau County Museum Collection includes photographs, vertical file material, historical research reports, and
    inventories of the estate. Nassau County also has blueprints of the house.
        Garden Magazine August and September 1926.
        House and Garden July 1930.

Goldman, Herman – Plandome Manor
The Nassau County Museum Collection includes photographs of the estate.

Gossler, Philip Green, Sr. – Brookville – *Highfield*
The Nassau County Museum Collection includes photographs of the estate.
Olin Library, Cornell University, Ithaca, NY, has Ellen Shipman's landscape designs for the estate.
        New York Herald Tribune October 20, 1929.
        The New York Times April 26, 1931.
        "House of Philip Gossler, Wheatley Hills, Long Island." *Architecture* 54 (December 1926):383–88.
        Sclare, Liisa and Donald. *Beaux–Arts Estates: A Guide to the Architecture of Long Island.* New York: The
           Viking Press, 1980.
        The Spur October 1, 1927.
        The Spur March 15, 1928.

Gould, Charles Albert – Dix Hills – *Chateauiver*
        Patterson, Augusta Owen. *American Homes of Today.* New York: The Macmillan Co., 1924.

Gould, Howard – Sands Point – *Castlegould*
The Nassau County Museum Collection includes vertical file material, historical research reports, and photographs of the
    estate, as well as blueprints of the house and stables.
        Bedford, Stephen and Richard Guy Wilson. *The Long Island Country House, 1870–1930.* Southampton, NY:
           The Parrish Art Museum, 1988.
        O'Connor, Richard. *Gould's Millions.* Garden City: Doubleday & Co., Inc., 1962.
        Sclare, Liisa and Donald. *Beaux–Arts Estates: A Guide to the Architecture of Long Island.* New York: The
           Viking Press, 1980.
        Winsche, Richard A. and Gary P. Hammond. "The Evolution of the Gould/Guggenheim Estate at Sands Point."
           In *Long Island: The Suburban Experience*, Barbara M. Kelly, ed. (Interlaken, NY: Heart of the Lakes
           Publishing, 1990).

Grace, Joseph Peter, Sr. – North Hills – *Tullaroan*
        Architectural Review 10 (April 1920):97, 99–101.

Grace, William Russell, Sr. – Kings Point – *Gracefield*
        Architectural Review 9 (December 1919):plates 81–91.
        Grace, J. P. "W. R. Grace (1832–1904) and the Empires He Created." American Newcomer Society Collection,
           New York Historical Society.

Greer, Louis Morris – Bayville – *Sevenoaks*
The Nassau County Museum Collection includes photographs of the estate.

Griswold, Frank Gray – North Hills
The Nassau County Museum Collection includes photographs of the estate.
        Griswold, Frank Gray. *After Thoughts: Recollections of Frank Gray Griswold.* New York: Harper & Brothers,
           1936.

Guest, Frederick E. – Brookville – *Roslyn Manor*
Avery Architectural and Fine Arts Library, Columbia University, NYC, has photographs and sketches of the estate.
        American Architect and Architectural Review 124 (December 5–23, 1923):528.
        American Architect and Architectural Review 125 (January 16, 1924):82.
        American Architect and Architectural Review 126 (August 13, 1924):146–47.
        Sclare, Liisa and Donald. *Beaux–Arts Estates: A Guide to the Architecture of Long Island.* New York: The
           Viking Press, 1980.

Guggenheim, Daniel – Sands Point – *Hempstead House*
The Nassau County Museum Collection includes vertical file material, historical research reports, and photographs of the estate, as well as blueprints of the house and stables. The Collection also includes photographs of the family.
> *Architecture* September 1912.
>> Davis, John Hagg. *The Guggenheims: An American Epic.* New York: William Morrow & Co., Inc., 1978.
>> Howell, E. W. *Noted Long Island Homes.* Babylon, NY: E. W. Howell Co., 1933.
>> Hoyt, Edwin P. *The Guggenheims and the American Dream.* New York: Funk & Wagnalls, 1967.
>> Lomask, Milton. *Seed Money: The Guggenheim Story.* New York: Farrar, Straus & Co., 1964.
>> O'Connor, Richard. *The Guggenheims: The Making of an American Dynasty.* New York: Covici Friede Publishers, 1937.
>> Sclare, Liisa and Donald. *Beaux–Arts Estates: A Guide to the Architecture of Long Island.* New York: The Viking Press, 1980.
>> Unger, Irwin and Debi Unger. *The Guggenheims: A Family.* New York: Harper Collins Publishers, 2005.
>> Winsche, Richard A. and Gary P. Hammond. "The Evolution of the Gould/Guggenheim Estate at Sands Point." In *Long Island: The Suburban Experience,* Barbara M. Kelly, ed. (Interlaken, NY: Heart of the Lakes Publishing, 1990).

Guggenheim, Florence Shloss – Sands Point – *Mille Fleurs*
The Nassau County Museum Collection includes vertical file material, historical research reports, a ledger of maintenance expenses, and photographs of the estate. The Collection also includes photographs of the family.
>> Sclare, Liisa and Donald. *Beaux–Arts Estates: A Guide to the Architecture of Long Island.* New York: The Viking Press, 1980.

Guggenheim, Harry Frank – Sands Point – *Falaise*
The Nassau County Museum Collection includes vertical file material, historical research reports, a ledger of maintenance expenses, and photographs of the estate. The Collection also includes photographs of the family and newspaper clippings of Guggenheim's aeronautical activity.
>> Davis, John Hagg. *The Guggenheims: An American Epic.* New York: William Morrow & Co., Inc., 1978.
>> Hallion, Richard. *Legacy of Flight: The Guggenheim Contribution to American Aviation.* Seattle: University of Washington Press, 1977.
>> Howell, E. W. *Noted Long Island Homes.* Babylon, NY: E. W. Howell Co., 1933.
>> Hoyt, Edwin P. *The Guggenheims and the American Dream.* New York: Funk & Wagnalls, 1967.
>> Lomask, Milton. *Seed Money: The Guggenheim Story.* New York: Farrar, Straus & Co., 1964.
>> O'Connor, Richard. *The Guggenheims: The Making of an American Dynasty.* New York: Covici Friede Publishers, 1937.
>> Sclare, Liisa and Donald. *Beaux–Arts Estates: A Guide to the Architecture of Long Island.* New York: The Viking Press, 1980.
>> Tebbel, John. *An American Dynasty: The Story of the McCormicks, Medills and Pattersons.* New York: Greenwood Press, 1968.
>> Winsche, Richard A. and Gary P. Hammond. "The Evolution of the Gould/Guggenheim Estate at Sands Point." In *Long Island: The Suburban Experience,* Barbara M. Kelly, ed. (Interlaken, NY: Heart of the Lakes Publishing, 1990).

Guggenheim, Isaac – Sands Point – *Villa Carola*
The Nassau County Museum Collection includes photographs of the estate.
>> *Arts and Decoration* 12 (February 1920):244.
>> *Architectural Forum* 32 (April 1920):143.
>> *Architectural League of New York* 35 (1920).
>> Davis, John Hagg. *The Guggenheims: An American Epic.* New York: William Morrow & Co., Inc., 1978.
>> "Fountain in Faience: The Isaac Guggenheim Estate." *Country Life* May 1918.
>> *House Beautiful* November 1921, 371.
>> Hoyt, Edwin P. *The Guggenheims and the American Dream.* New York: Funk & Wagnalls, 1967.
>> O'Connor, Richard. *The Guggenheims: The Making of an American Dynasty.* New York: Covici Friede Publishers, 1937.
>> Patterson, Augusta Owen. *American Homes of Today.* New York: The Macmillan Co., 1924.

Guggenheim, Solomon Robert – Sands Point – *Trillora Court*
The Nassau County Museum Collection includes photographs of the estate.
>> *American Hebrew* July 1, 1927.
>> *American Hebrew* February 17, 1928.
>> Davis, John Hagg. *The Guggenheims: An American Epic.* New York: William Morrow & Co. Inc., 1978.
> Hoyt, Edwin P. *The Guggenheims and the American Dream.* New York: Funk & Wagnalls, 1967.

Guggenheim, Solomon Robert – Sands Point – *Trillora Court* (cont'd)

O'Connor, Harvey. *The Guggenheims: The Making of an American Dynasty.* New York: Covici Friede Publishers, 1937.

Patterson, Augusta Owen. *American Homes of Today.* New York: The Macmillan Co., 1924.

Town and Country February 15, 1927.

Town and Country September 1, 1928.

Guggenheim, William, Sr. – Sands Point – *Fountainhill*

Davis, John Hagg. *The Guggenheims: An American Epic.* New York: William Morrow & Co., Inc., 1978.

Hoyt, Edwin P. *The Guggenheims and the American Dream.* New York: Funk & Wagnalls, 1967.

O'Connor, Richard. *The Guggenheims: The Making of an American Dynasty.* New York: Covici Friede Publishers, 1937.

Williams, Gatenby. *William Guggenheim: The Story of an Adventurous Career.* New York: Lone Voice Publishing Co., n.d. [pseudonym for William Guggenheim; address of publisher, 3 Riverside Drive, was his New York City address]

Guida, Bernadette Castro – Lloyd Harbor – *Panfield*

The Nassau County Museum Collection includes photographs of the estate.

Guthrie, William Dameron – Lattingtown – *Meudon*

Architectural Forum 41 (July 1924):7.

Swaine, Robert T. *The Cravath Firm and Its Predecessors, 1819–1948.* vols. 1, 2. New York: Ad Press, Ltd., 1946, 1948.

Haar, Herbert – Kings Point

The Nassau County Museum Collection includes photographs of the estate.

Hadden, Emily Georgina Hamilton – Jericho – *Dogwood*

Architectural Forum 30 (February 1919):45, 47–50.

Hall, Leonard Wood – Lattingtown

Avery Architectural and Fine Arts Library, Columbia University, NYC, has Leonard Wood Hall's reminiscences in their oral history collection.

The Nassau County Museum Collection has Leonard Wood Hall's unpublished memoirs.

Hammerstein, Oscar, II – Kings Point – *Sunny Knoll*

House Beautiful 117 (April 1975):54–7.

Hammond, Paul Lyman – Syosset – *Muttontown Lodge*

The Nassau County Museum Collection includes photographs of the estate.

New York Herald Tribune July 28, 1935.

Vogue August 1, 1931.

Handy, Parker Douglas – Glen Cove – *Groendak*

Architecture 3 (January 1901):14.

Hare, Meredith – South Huntington – *Pidgeon Hill*

Croly, Herbert. "Pidgeon Hill, Residence of Meredith Hare, Huntington, Long Island." *Architectural Record* 48 (September 1920):178–91.

Harkness, Edward Stephen – North Hills – *Weekend*

The Nassau County Museum Collection includes photographs of the estate.

Good Housekeeping April 1927.

Good Housekeeping June 1928.

House and Garden January 1926.

House and Garden May 1926.

Howell, E. W. *Noted Long Island Homes.* Babylon, NY: E. W. Howell Co., 1933.

Klepper, Michael. *The Wealthy 100: From Benjamin Franklin to Bill Gates – A Ranking of the Richest Americans Past and Present.* Secaucus, NJ: The Citadel Press, 1996.

Ladies Home Journal May 1932.

The New York Times July 5, 1936.

Parents May 1931.

Harkness, Edward Stephen – North Hills – *Weekend* (cont'd)
> *Pictorial Review* March 1928.
> *Pictorial Review* April 1928.
> *The Small Home* January 1928.
> *The Small Home* November 1930.
> *Your Home* July 1927.

Harriman, Mrs. Herbert Melville – Jericho – *The Lanterns*
The Nassau County Museum Collection includes photographs of the estate.
> *Good Housekeeping* January 1921.
> *Town and Country* September 20, 1918.

Harriman, William Averell – Sands Point;
and Old Westbury
Brown Brothers, Harriman and Company, NYC, has clippings of the Harriman family history.
George Arents Research Library, Syracuse University, Syracuse, NY, has William Averell Harriman's gubernatorial papers.
Library of Congress, Washington, DC, has a large portion of William Averell Harriman's papers.
Katharine Lanier Lawrence Harriman's papers were destroyed for lack of space in the depository.
> Abramson, Rudy. *Spanning the Century: The Life of W. Averell Harriman, 1891–1986.* New York: William Morrow & Co., Inc., 1992.
> Harriman, W. Averell and Elie Abel. *Special Envoy to Churchill and Stalin, 1941–1946.* New York: Random House, 1975.
> Kouwenhoven, John A. *Partners in Banking: An Historical Portrait of a Great Private Bank, Brothers Harriman & Company, 1818–1968.* Garden City: Doubleday & Co., Inc., 1968.
> Ogden, Christopher. *Life of the Party: The Biography of Pamela Digby Churchill Hayward Harriman.* Boston: Little, Brown & Co., 1994.
> Smith, Sally Bedell. *Reflected Glory: The Life of Pamela Churchill Harriman.* New York: Simon & Schuster, Inc., 1996.

Harris, Sam Henry – Great Neck
The Nassau County Museum Collection includes photographs of the estate.
> *Good Housekeeping* July 1922.
> *The World* April 8, 1923.
> *The World* April 15, 1923.
> *The World* May 27, 1923.
> *The World* September 23, 1923.
> *The World* February 17, 1924.
> *Your Own Home* May 1926.
> *Your Own Home* September 1926.
> *Your Own Home* June 1927.

Harris, Sam Henry – Kings Point
The Nassau County Museum Collection includes photographs of the estate.
> *The American Hebrew* July 4, 1924.
> *Canadian Home Journal* February 1924.
> *Canadian Home Journal* March 1924.
> *Delineator* March 1925.
> *House and Garden* September and December 1923.
> *Theatre Magazine* January 1923.

Hastings, Thomas – Old Westbury – *Bagatelle*
Avery Architectural and Fine Arts Library, Columbia University, NYC, has the Samuel Gottscho Collection of photographs. The collection includes homes designed by Thomas Hastings.
The Nassau County Museum Collection includes photographs of the estate.
> *American Country Houses of To–Day,* 8 vols. 1915.
> Blake, Channing C. "The Architecture of Carrere and Hastings." Ph.D. dissertation, Columbia University, 1976.
> Gray, David. *Thomas Hastings, Architect.* Cambridge, MA: Houghton Mifflin & Co., 1933.
> Hastings, Thomas, et al. "The Work of Messrs. Carrere & Hastings," *Architectural Record* 27 (January 1910):60.

Hastings, Thomas – Old Westbury – *Bagatelle* (cont'd)
> Howe, Samuel. "Mr. Hastings House at Roslyn Reveals a Sincere Reverence for Italy's Renaissance." *Town and Country* 69 (August 22, 1914):18–9.
> "Mr. Thomas Hastings' Home at Roslyn." *American Country Homes of Today* 1 (1912):203–4.
> Patterson, Augusta Owen. *American Homes of Today.* New York: The Macmillan Co., 1924.
> "Thomas Hastings, 1860–1929." *Architectural Record* 66 (December 1929):596.

Havemeyer, Theodore Augustus, II – Upper Brookville – *Cedar Hill*
The Nassau County Museum Collection includes photographs of the estate.
> *Country Life* June 1923.
> *Delineator* September 1923.
> *Good Housekeeping* January 1925.
> Havemeyer, Horace, Sr. *Biographical Record of the Havemeyer Family 1600–1945.* New York: privately printed by Scribner's Press, 1945.
> *House and Garden* March 1923.
> *The New York Times* August 7, 1927.

Hearst, William Randolph – Sands Point – *Saint Joan*
Bancroft Library, University of California, Berkeley, CA, has the Hearst family archives.
The Nassau County Museum Collection includes photographs of the estate.
New York Lincoln Library, Lincoln Center, NYC, has clipping files which document Millicent Hearst's stage career.
> Chaney, Lindsay and Michael Cieply. *The Hearsts: Family and Empire.* New York: Simon & Schuster, Inc., 1981.
> Hearst, William Randolph, Jr. and Jack Casserly. *The Hearsts: Father and Son.* Niwot, CO: Roberts Rinehart Publishers, 1991.
> Nasaw, David. *The Chief: The Life of William Randolph Hearst.* Boston: Houghton Mifflin Co., 2000.
> Proctor, Ben. *William Randolph Hearst: The Early Years, 1863–1910.* New York: Oxford University Press, 1998.
> Robinson, Judith. *The Hearsts: An American Dynasty.* New York: Avon Books, 1991.
> Swanberg, W. A. *Citizen Hearst: A Biography of William Randolph Hearst.* New York: Charles Scribner's Sons, 1961.
> Tebbel, John. *The Life and Good Times of William Randolph Hearst.* New York: E. P. Dutton, 1952.

Heck, George Callendine, Sr. – Muttontown – *Linwood*
The Nassau County Museum Collection includes photographs of the estate.

Heckscher, August – Kings Point – *Feu Follet*;
> **and Huntington Bay – *Wincoma***
The Nassau County Museum Collection includes photographs of the Kings Point estate.

Heckscher, Gustav Maurice – Old Westbury – *Three Winds*
> *Town and Country* July 19, 1913.

Hedges, Benjamin Van Doren, II – Oyster Bay Cove
The Nassau County Museum Collection includes photographs of the estate.

Hedges, George Brown – Westbury – *The Hedges*
The Nassau County Museum Collection includes photographs of the estate.
> *Arts and Decoration* June 1926.
> *Arts and Decoration* April 1927.
> *Garden and Home Builder* May 1928.
> *Garden Architecture* December 1934.
> *House and Garden* September 1925.
> *House and Garden* October 1925.
> *House and Garden* November 1925.
> *House and Garden* February 1926.
> *House and Garden* March 1928.
> *The Small Home* November 1930.

Henderson, Frank C. – Roslyn – *Villa Marina*
The Nassau County Museum Collection includes photographs of the estate.
> *Country Life* January 1934.
> *Garden Magazine* October 1922.
> *Harper's Bazaar* August 1922.
> *Le Bon Ton* November 1922.
> *Own Your Own Home* July 1926.
> *Physical Culture* November 1923.
> *Tavern Topics* August 1931.
> *Vogue* April 1921.
> *The World* February 11, 1923.
> *The World* July 1, 1923.
> *The World* November 25, 1923.
> *The World* February 17, 1924.

Hill, James Norman – Brookville – *Big Tree Farm*
> Patterson, Augusta Owen. *American Homes of Today.* New York: The Macmillan Co., 1924.

Hine, Francis Lyman – Glen Cove – *Mayhasit*
The Nassau County Museum Collection includes photographs of the estate.
> Cornelius, Charles Oliver. "The Country House of Francis L. Hine, Esq." *Architectural Record* July 1918:20.
> *New York Herald Tribune* March 3, 1929.
> Patterson, Augusta Owen. *American Homes of Today.* New York: The Macmillan Co., 1924.
> Ruhling, Nancy. "Manors for the Masses." *Historic Preservation* February 1986:55.
> *The Spur* August 1, 1925.

Hines, Ephram – Roslyn Harbor
The Nassau County Museum Collection includes photographs of the estate.

Hitchcock, Thomas, Jr. – Sands Point;
> **and Old Westbury – *Broad Hollow Farm***
The Nassau County Museum Collection includes photographs of *Broad Hollow Farm.*
> Aldrich, Nelson, Jr. *Old Money: The Mythology of America's Upper Class.* New York: Alfred A. Knopf, 1988.
> Aldrich, Nelson, Jr. *Tommy Hitchcock: An American Hero.* Gaithersburg: Fleet Street Corp., 1984.
> Hersh, Burton. *The Mellon Family: A Fortune in History.* New York: William Morrow & Co., Inc., 1978.
> Ruther, Frederick. *Long Island Today*, 1909. (featured *Broad Hollow Farm*)

Hoguet, Dr. Joseph Peter, Sr. – Matinecock – *Oak Lawn*
The Nassau County Museum Collection includes photographs of the estate.

Holloway, William Grace, Sr. – Old Westbury – *Foxland*
The Nassau County Museum Collection includes photographs of the estate.
> Sclare, Liisa and Donald. *Beaux–Arts Estates: A Guide to the Architecture of Long Island.* New York: The Viking Press, 1980.

Holmes, Artemas – Old Brookville – *Holmestead Farm*
The Nassau County Museum Collection includes photographs of the estate.
> *The American Home* September 1929.
> *Arts and Decoration* October 1925.
> *Charm* July 1926.
> *The Small Home* March and June 1930.
> *Your Home* January 1930.

Holmes, Bettie Fleischmann – Sands Point – *The Chimneys*
The Nassau County Museum Collection includes photographs of the estate.
> Sclare, Liisa and Donald. *Beaux–Arts Estates: A Guide to the Architecture of Long Island.* New York: The Viking Press, 1980.

Hoppin, William Warner, Jr. – Old Brookville – *Friendship Hill*
> Howell, E. W. *Noted Long Island Homes.* Babylon, NY: E. W. Howell Co., 1933.

Howe, William Deering – Brookville – *Highpool*;
        and Lattingtown – *Severn*
Avery Architectural and Fine Arts Library, Columbia University, NYC, has elevation sketches of *Highpool*.
        Bedford, Stephen and Richard Guy Wilson. *The Long Island Country House, 1870–1930.* Southampton, NY:
            The Parrish Art Museum, 1988.

Hoyt, John R. – Kings Point
        Architectural Review 12 (March 1921):81.
        Architecture 30 (September 1914): 205.

Hubbs, Charles Francis – Old Brookville
        Howell, E. W. *Noted Long Island Homes.* Babylon, NY: E. W. Howell Co., 1933.

Hudson, Charles I., Sr. – Muttontown – *Knollwood*
The Nassau County Museum Collection includes vertical file material, historical research reports, and photographs of the
        estate.

Hughes, Dr. Wendell – Roslyn Harbor – *Wenlo*
The Nassau County Museum Collection includes photographs of the estate.

Humphreys, Dr. Alexander Crombie – Glen Cove
        Architecture 3 (June 1, 1900):227.

Huntington, Robert Dinsmore, Sr. – Mill Neck
        Howell, E. W. *Noted Long Island Homes.* Babylon, NY: E. W. Howell Co., 1933.

Hutton, Edward Francis – Brookville – *Hillwood*;
        and Brookville – *Hutfield*
The Nassau County Museum Collection includes photographs of *Hillwood* and *Hutfield*.
        Carpenter, Donna Sammons and John Feloni. *The Fall of the House of Hutton.* New York: Henry Holt, 1989.
        Howell, E. W. *Noted Long Island Homes.* Babylon, NY: E. W. Howell Co., 1933.
        "The Property of Mrs. Edward Hutton of Westbury, Long Island: French Nineteenth and Twentieth Century
            Paintings and Drawings." London: Sotheby, 1964. auction catalog
        Sclare, Liisa and Donald. *Beaux–Arts Estates: A Guide to the Architecture of Long Island.* New York: The
            Viking Press, 1980.
        Steven, Mark. *Sudden Death: The Rise and Fall of E. F. Hutton.* New York: New American Library, 1989.

Ide, George Edward – Lattingtown – *Petit Bois*
        Architectural Record 41 (May 1917):458–62.

Ingalls, Fay – Oyster Bay Cove – *Sunken Orchard*
The Nassau County Museum Collection includes photographs of the estate.

Jennings, Oliver Burr, II – Lloyd Harbor – *Burrwood*
Frederick Law Olmsted National Historic Site, Brookline, MA, has Olmsted's landscape designs for the estate.
The Nassau County Museum Collection includes photographs of the estate.

Jennings, Walter – Lloyd Harbor – *Burrwood*
Frederick Law Olmsted National Historic Site, Brookline, MA, has Olmsted's landscape designs for the estate.
The Nassau County Museum Collection includes photographs of the estate.
        Arts and Decor July 1924.
        New York Herald Tribune March 1, 1931.
        New York Herald Tribune February 2, 1936.
        Tarbell, Ida. *History of Standard Oil.* New York: The Macmillan Co., 1925.

Johaneson, Nils R. – Lattingtown – *Littleholme*
The Nassau County Museum Collection includes photographs of the estate.

Jones, Rosalie Gardiner – Laurel Hollow – *Jones Manor*;
        and Eaton's Neck
Suffolk County Historical Society, Riverhead, LI, has vertical file material on Rosalie Gardiner Jones.
        Funnell, Walter S. "General Jones, a Real Fighter." *Nassau Daily Review* April 10, 1936.

Jones, Rosalie Gardiner – Laurel Hollow – *Jones Manor*;
and Eaton's Neck (cont'd)

Matthews, Jane. "General Rosalie Jones, Long Island Suffragist." *The Nassau County Historical Journal* 47 (1992):23–34.

Matthews, Jane. "The Woman Suffrage Movement in Suffolk County, New York: 1911–1917; A Case Study of the Tactical Differences Between Two Prominent Long Island Suffragists: Mrs. Ida Bunce Sammis and Miss Rosalie Jones." M. A. thesis, Adelphi University, 1987.

Jones, Walter Restored – Laurel Hollow – *Manor House*

Albion, Robert. *The Rise of the New York Port.* New York: Charles Scribner's Sons, 1970.

Atlantic Mutual Company. *Atlantic Log. November 1974.* New York: Atlantic Mutual Co., 1974.

Atlantic Mutual Company. *The Atlantic Story.* New York: Atlantic Mutual Co., 1970.

Barbuto, Domenica M. "Economic Opportunities in New York and its Vicinity, 1800–1850: A Study of the Career of Walter Restored Jones 1793–1855, a Businessman from Cold Spring Harbor." M. A. thesis, Hofstra University, 1975.

Barbuto, Domenica M. "Walter Restored Jones, Long Island Merchant Capitalist." *The Nassau County Historical Society Journal* 46 (1991):19–26.

Jones, John H. *The Jones Family of Long Island: Descendants of Major Thomas Jones (1665–1726) and Allied Families.* New York: Tobias A. Wright, 1907.

Jones, William A. "Walter Restored Jones." In *Lives of American Merchants,* Freeman Hunt, ed. (New York: Derby and Jackson, 1858).

Watson, Elizabeth. *Houses for Science: A Pictorial History of the Cold Spring Harbor Laboratory.* Cold Spring Harbor, NY: Cold Spring Harbor Press, 1991.

Kahn, Otto Hermann – Cold Spring Harbor – *Oheka*

Firestone Library, Princeton University, Princeton, NJ, has Otto Hermann Kahn's papers.

Library of Congress, Washington, DC, has correspondence between Otto Kahn and Delano and Aldrich and between Otto Kahn and the Olmsted Brothers.

The Nassau County Museum Collection includes photographs of the estate.

American Homes Today 1924.

Architectural Forum 41 (July 1924):2.

Architectural Record August 1919. [article about Kahn's New York City house]

Collins, Theresa M. "A Life of Otto H. Kahn, 1867–1934: Finance, Art, and Questions of Modernity." Ph.D. dissertation, New York University, 1998.

Country Life December 1920.

Die Dame [Germany] July 1929.

Griswold, Mac and Eleanor Weller. *The Golden Age of American Gardens . Proud Owners . Private Estates . 1890–1940.* New York: Harry N. Abrams, Inc., Publishers, 1991.

Hewitt, Mark Alan. *The Architect & the American Country House 1890–1940.* New Haven: Yale University Press, 1990.

Kahn, Otto [Hermann]. *Reflections of a Financier.* New York: Gordon Press, 1972.

Kaiser, Harvey H. *Great Camps of the Adirondacks.* Boston: David R. Godine, 1982.

King, Robert B. *Raising a Fallen Treasure: The Otto Kahn Home, Huntington, Long Island.* privately printed, 1985.

Kobler, John. *Otto the Magnificent.* New York: Charles Scribner's Sons, 1988.

Matz, Mary Jane. *The Many Lives of Otto Kahn.* New York: The Macmillan Co., 1963.

New York Herald Tribune January 11, 1931.

New York Herald Tribune July 12, 1931.

Patterson, Augusta Owen. *American Homes of Today.* New York: The Macmillan Co., 1924.

The Spur September 15, 1928.

Kane, John P., Jr. – Matinecock

The Nassau County Museum Collection includes photographs of the estate.

Keene, Foxhall Parker – Old Westbury – *Rosemary Hall*

The Nassau County Museum Collection includes photographs of the estate.

Keene, Foxhall Parker. *Full Tilt: The Sporting Memoirs of Foxhall Keene.* New York: The Derrydale Press, 1938.

Sclare, Liisa and Donald. *Beaux–Arts Estates: A Guide to the Architecture of Long Island.* New York: The Viking Press, 1980.

Kelland, Clarence Budington – Sands Point – *Sandy Cay*
The Nassau County Museum Collection includes photographs of the estate.

Kent, George Edward, Sr. – Jericho – *Jericho House*
Architectural Archives, University of Pennsylvania, Philadelphia, PA, has Wilson Eyre's architectural sketches of the house.
> Patterson, Augusta Owen. *American Homes of Today.* New York: The Macmillan Co., 1924.

Kerrigan, Joseph J. – Cove Neck
The Nassau County Museum Collection includes photographs of the estate.
> *Country Life* February 1934.
> *Country Life* August 1933.
> *Country Life* April 1934.

Kettles, Richard C., Jr. – Old Brookville – *Orchard Corners*
> Howell, E. W. *Noted Long Island Homes.* Babylon, NY: E. W. Howell Co., 1933.

Kramer, Albert Ludlow, Sr. – Jericho – *Picket Farm*
The Nassau County Museum Collection includes photographs of the estate.
> *Architectural Forum* 30 (February 1919):47–50.
> *Canadian Home Journal* September 1924.
> *Garden Magazine* October 1923.
> *Garden Magazine* January 1925.
> "The Garden of A. L. Kramer, Esq., Westbury, Long Island." *House Beautiful* March 1924:255.
> "The Garden of Mrs. A. L. Kramer at Westbury, L. I." *Garden Magazine* April 1924:128–29.
> Tankard, Judith B. *The Gardens of Ellen Biddle Shipman.* Sagaponack, NY: Sagapress, Inc., 1996.
> Van Horn, Henry. "Mr. A. L. Kramer's Residence at Westbury." *Town and Country* May 1, 1920:53–6.

Ladew, Edward R. – Glen Cove – *Villa Louedo*
Glen Cove Public Library, Glen Cove, LI, has Edward R. Ladew's papers on microfilm.

Ladew, Harvey Smith, II – Old Brookville – *The Box*
Pleasant Valley Topiary Gardens, Towson, MD, has family papers.
> *Architecture* 34 (October 1916):216–22.
> "Around the World in Eighty Years" (uncompleted autobiography)

Laidlaw, Harriet Wright Burton – Sands Point – *Hazeldean*
Joan and Donald E. Axinn Library, Special Collections, Hofstra University, Hempstead, LI, has Harriet Wright Burton Laidlaw's papers on microfilm.
The New York Historical Society has Harriet Wright Burton Laidlaw's scrapbooks.
Schlesinger Library, Radcliffe College, Cambridge, MA, has Harriet Wright Burton Laidlaw's papers.
Sophia Smith Collection, Smith College, Northampton, MA, includes Harriet Wright Burton Laidlaw's correspondence.
> *The History of Woman Suffrage,* vols. V, VI.
> James, Edward T., ed. *Notable American Women: A Biographical Dictionary.* Cambridge, MA: The Belknap Press of Harvard University Press, vol. II:358–60.
> *The National Cyclopaedia of American Biography.* Clifton, NJ: James T. White & Co., 38 (1953):21–2.
> *Woman's Who's Who of America, 1914–15, s.v.* "Laidlaw, Harriet Burton."
> *Who Was Who in America.* II (1950), *s.v.* "Laidlaw, Harriet Burton"

Laidlaw, James Lees – Sands Point – *Hazeldean*
> Laidlaw, Harriet Burton. *James Lees Laidlaw, 1868–1932.* privately printed, 1932.

Lamont, Thomas Stillwell – Lattingtown – *The Creek*
Baker Library, Harvard Business School, Cambridge, MA, has Thomas Stillwell Lamont's papers.
> Lamont, Corliss. *The Thomas Lamonts in America.* New York: A. S. Barnes, 1962.

Langley, William Clark – Old Westbury
The Nassau County Museum Collection includes photographs of the estate.
> *Canadian Home Journal* December 1925.
> *Charm* July 1924.
> *Country Life* July 1925.
> *Country Life* August 1937.

Langley, William Clark – Old Westbury (cont'd)
>*Good Housekeeping* October 1924.
>*House and Garden* January 1924.
>*New York Herald Tribune* September 8, 1936.
>*The New York Times Magazine* April 26, 1939.
>*The Small Home* December 1926.

Le Boutillier, Thomas, III – Old Westbury
The Nassau County Museum Collection includes photographs of the estate.

Ledyard, Lewis Cass, Jr. – Oyster Bay Cove – *Westwood*
>Ellis, Francis M. and Edward F. Clark, Jr. *A Brief History of Carter, Ledyard and Milburn from 1854 to 1988.* Portsmouth, NH: Peter Randall Publishers, 1988.

Leffingwell, Russell Cornell – Oyster Bay Cove – *Redcote*
Baker Library, Harvard Business School, Cambridge, MA, has Russell Cornell Leffingwell's correspondence in the Thomas Lamont Papers.
J. P. Morgan and Co., New York, NY, has Russell Cornell Leffingwell's business papers.
Library of Congress, Washington, DC, has Russell Cornell Leffingwell's papers dealing with his tenure at the United States Department of the Treasury.
Sterling Memorial Library, Yale University, New Haven, CT, has Russell Cornell Leffingwell's papers, Yale memorabilia, and family photograph album.
>Pulling, [Thomas John] Edward. *Random Reminiscences.* Oyster Bay, NY: privately printed, 1973.
>Pulling, [Thomas John] Edward, ed. *Selected Letters of R. C. Leffingwell.* Hicksville, NY: Exposition Press, 1980.
>Swaine, Robert T. *The Cravath Firm and Its Predecessors, 1819–1948.* vols. 1, 2. New York: Ad Press, Ltd., 1946, 1948.

Lehman, Allan Sigmund – Jericho – *Picket Farm*
The Nassau County Museum Collection includes photographs of the estate.

Leonard, Edgar Welch – Oyster Bay Cove – *Stoke Farm*
The Nassau County Museum Collection includes photographs of the estate.
>*Vogue* October 13, 1930.

LeRoux, Edouard – Glen Cove
The Nassau County Museum Collection includes photographs of the estate.

Levison, John Jacob – Sea Cliff
The Nassau County Museum Collection includes photographs of the estate.

Lindbergh, Anne Morrow – Lloyd Harbor – *[Joseph] Lloyd Manor*
The Nassau County Museum Collection includes photographs of the house.
>Herrmann, Dorothy. *Anne Morrow Lindbergh: A Gift for Life.* New York: Ticknor & Fields, 1992.
>Lindbergh, Anne Morrow. *Bring Me a Unicorn: Diaries and Letters of Anne Morrow Lindbergh.* New York: Harcourt, Brace, Jovanovich, 1972.
>Lindbergh, Anne Morrow. *Dearly Beloved: A Theme and Variations.* New York: Harcourt, Brace & World, Inc., 1962.
>Lindbergh, Anne Morrow. *Earth Shine.* New York: Harcourt, Brace, Jovanovich, 1969.
>Lindbergh, Anne Morrow. *Gift From the Sea.* New York: Pantheon Books, 1955.
>Lindbergh, Anne Morrow. *Hour of Gold, Hour of Lead: Diaries and Letters of Anne Morrow Lindbergh 1929–1932.* New York: Harcourt, Brace, Jovanovich, 1973.
>Lindbergh, Anne Morrow. *Locked Rooms and Open Doors: Diaries and Letters of Anne Morrow Lindbergh.* New York: Harcourt, Brace, Jovanovich, 1974.
>Lindbergh, Anne Morrow. *North To the Orient.* New York: Harcourt, Brace & Co., 1935.
>Lindbergh, Anne Morrow. *War Within and Without: Diaries and Letters of Anne Morrow Lindbergh 1939–1944.* New York: Harcourt, Brace, Jovanovich, 1980.
>Milton, Joyce. *Loss of Eden: A Biography of Charles and Anne Morrow Lindbergh.* New York: Harper–Collins Publ., 1993.

Lindbergh, Charles Augustus, Jr. – Lloyd Harbor – *[Joseph] Lloyd Manor*
The Nassau County Museum Collection includes photographs of the house.
Yale University, Dept. of Manuscripts & Archives, New Haven, CT, has Charles Augustus Lindbergh Jr.'s photograph
    collection.

> Lindbergh, Charles. *Autobiography of Values.* New York: Harcourt, Brace, Jovanovich, 1978.
> Lindbergh, Charles. *The Spirit of St. Louis.* New York: Charles Scribner's Sons, 1953.
> Lindbergh, Charles. *"We."* New York: G. P. Putnam's Sons, 1927.
> Milton, Joyce. *Loss of Eden: A Biography of Charles and Anne Morrow Lindbergh.* New York: Harper–Collins
>   Publ., 1993.
> Mosley, Leonard. *Dulles: A Biography of Eleanor, Allen, and John Foster Dulles and Their Family Network.*
>   New York: The Dial Press, 1978.

Lindsay, Lady Elizabeth Sherman Hoyt – Centre Island – *Lime House*

> James, Olivia, ed. *The Letters of Elizabeth Sherman Lindsay 1911–1954.* New York; privately printed, 1960

Lloyd–Smith, Wilton – Lloyd Harbor – *Kenjockety*
Society for the Preservation of Long Island Antiquities, Cold Spring Harbor, LI, has the records of Barrow, Wade,
    Goodhue and Company, Accountants and Auditors, which include the construction accounts of the estate. The
    Society also has an oil painting of the house.

> Whitaker, Charles Harris. *Bertram Grosvenor Goodhue: Architect and Master of Many Arts.* New York: Press
>   of the American Institute of Architects, Inc., 1925.

Loening, Grover – Mill Neck – *Margrove*
The Nassau County Museum Collection includes photographs of the estate.

> Aslet, Clive. *The American Country House.* New Haven: Yale University Press, 1990.
> Howell, E. W. *Noted Long Island Homes.* Babylon, NY: E. W. Howell Co., 1933.
> "Margrove: An Aviator's Home at Mill Neck, Long Island." *Country Life in America* 60 (April 1932):57–60.
> *Vogue* November 1, 1931.

Lord, Franklin Butler, II – Syosset – *Cottsleigh*
The Nassau County Museum Collection includes photographs of the estate.

> *Vogue* October 1, 1931.

Lord, George de Forest, Sr. – Syosset – *Overfields*
The Nassau County Museum Collection includes photographs of the estate.

Lovett, Robert Abercrombie – Lattingtown – *Green Arbors*
The National Archives, Washington, DC, has Robert Abercrombie Lovett's papers.

> Fanton, Jonathan F. "Robert A, Lovett, the War Years." Ph.D. dissertation, Yale University, 1978.
> Isacson, Walter and Evan Thomas. *The Wise Men: Architects of the American Century.* New York: Simon &
>   Schuster, Inc., 1986.
> Paine, Ralph. *The First Yale Unit.* Cambridge, MA: Riverside Press, 1925.

Lowe, Arthur Marcus, Sr. – Glen Cove – *Pembroke*
The Nassau County Museum Collection includes photographs of the estate.

Lowe, Marcus – Glen Cove – *Pembroke*
The Nassau County Museum Collection includes photographs of the estate.

Luckenbach, Edgar Frederick, Sr. – Sands Point – *Elm Court*
The Nassau County Museum Collection includes photographs of the estate.

> *The Forecast* September 1928.
> *House and Garden* April 1924.
> *New York Herald Tribune* September 6, 1925.
> *The New York Times* November 18, 1928.
> *The Spur* May 15, 1924.

Lundy, Frederick William Irving – Old Brookville – *Rynwood*
The Nassau County Museum Collection includes photographs of the estate.

Lynch, Edmund Calvert, Jr. – Lattingtown – *Floralyn*
The Nassau County Museum Collection includes photographs of the estate.

Lynch, Edmund Calvert, Sr. – Matinecock
The Nassau County Museum Collection includes photographs of the estate.

Mackay, Clarence Hungerford – Roslyn – *Harbor Hill*
Brooklyn Historical Society, Brooklyn, NY, has some of the Mackay family papers.
The Bryant Library, Roslyn, LI, has fifty volumes of the Mackay family newspaper clipping service 1898–1924 on
    microfilm and indexed as well as an extensive photograph collection of the estate. The library's vertical file
    collection on the estate and family is also extensive.
Museum of the City of New York, Byron Photograph Collection, NYC, has photographs of the estate plans.
The Nassau County Museum Collection includes photographs of the estate and the indexed Mackay family newspaper
    clipping service 1898–1924 on microfilm.
The New York Historical Society, NYC, has some of Katherine Duer Mackay's correspondence, photographs of *Harbor
    Hill*, and architectural drawings of Trinity Episcopal Church, Roslyn.
> Baker, Paul R. *Stanny: The Gilded Life of Stanford White.* New York: Free Press, 1989.
> Barrett, Mary Ellin. *Irving Berlin: A Daughter's Memoir.* New York: Simon & Schuster, Inc., 1994.
> Bergreen, Laurence. *As Thousands Cheer: The Life of Irving Berlin.* New York: The Viking Press, 1990.
> Berlin, Ellin. *The Best of Families.* Garden City: Doubleday & Co., Inc., 1970.
> Berlin, Ellin. *Lace Curtain.* Garden City: Doubleday & Co., Inc., 1948. [fictionalized, but autobiographical]
> Berlin, Ellin. *Land I Have Chosen.* Garden City: Doubleday & Co., Inc., 1944. [fictionalized account of her
>   mother's half–sister Mary Blake's marriage to Nazi diplomat, Ruprecht von Boeklin]
> Berlin, Ellin. *Silver Platter.* Garden City: Doubleday & Co., Inc., 1957. [fictionalized story of her maternal
>   grandmother, Marie Louise Hungerford Mackay]
> Croly, Herbert. "The Lay-out of a Large Estate 'Harbor Hill,' The Country Seat of Mr. Clarence Mackay at
>   Roslyn, L. I." *Architectural Record* 16 (December 1904):535.
> Ferree, Barr. *American Estates and Gardens.* New York: Munn & Co., 1904.
> Griswold, Mac and Eleanor Weller. *The Golden Age of American Gardens . Proud Owners . Private Estates .
>   1890–1940.* New York: Harry N. Abrams, Inc., Publishers, 1991.
> Hewitt, Mark Alan. *The Architect & the American Country House 1890–1940.* New Haven: Yale University
>   Press, 1990.
> Lewis, Oscar. *Silver Kings.* New York: Alfred A. Knopf, 1947.
> Mackay, John W. *Mark.* New York: Coward–McCann, Inc., 1956.
> McKim, Mead & White. *A Monograph of the Work of McKim, Mead & White 1879–1915.* New York: DaCapo
>   Press, 1985.
> Patterson, Augusta Owen. *American Homes of Today.* New York: The Macmillan Co., 1924.
> Platt, Frederick. *America's Gilded Age: Its Architecture and Decoration.* New York: A. S. Barnes & Co., 1976.
> Whalen, Grover A. *Mr. New York: The Autobiography of Grover A. Whalen.* New York: G. P. Putnam's Sons,
>   1955.
> Wodehouse, Lawrence. "Stanford White and the Mackays: A Case Study in Architect–Client Relationships."
>   *Winterthur Portfolio* 11 (1976):229.

Martin, Bradley, Jr. – Old Westbury – *Knole*
> Locke, Kate Greenleaf. "Mr. Bradley Martin, Jr.'s House at Westbury." *Town and Country* 67 (September 21,
>   1912):37.

Martin, James E., Sr. – Kings Point – *Martin Hall*
The Nassau County Museum Collection includes photographs of the estate.

Matheson, William John – Lloyd Harbor – *Fort Hill House*
Society for the Preservation of Long Island Antiquities, Cold Spring Harbor, LI, has dinner china embossed with the
    Matheson family crest. The Society also has a c. 1900 watercolor sketch by Robert W. Gipson of the estate's
    boathouse.
> "House for Mrs. A. C. Alden on Fort Hill, Lloyd's Neck, Long Island." *American Architect and Building News*
>   August 30, 1878. [relevant to the original 1878 shingle Queen Anne house]
> *The Brickbuilder* August 1903.
> Matheson, John W. *An Historic Sketch of Fort Hill, Lloyd Harbor, Long Island.* New York: privately printed,
>   n.d.

Mauze, Abby Rockefeller – Mill Neck – *Laurel Hill*
Rockefeller Archive Center, Rockefeller University, Pocantico Hills, North Tarrytown, NY, has Abby Rockefeller
    Mauze's papers.
> Chase, Mary Ellen. *Abby Aldrich Rockefeller.* New York: The Macmillan Co., 1950.

Mauze, Abby Rockefeller – Mill Neck – *Laurel Hill* (cont'd)
> Collier, Peter and Horowitz. *The Rockefellers: An American Dynasty*. New York: Holt, Rinehart & Winston, 1976.
> Harr, John Ensor and Peter J. Johnson. *The Rockefeller Century: Three Generations of America's Greatest Family*. New York: Scribner's Sons, 1988.
> Kert, Bernice. *Abby Aldrich Rockefeller: The Woman in the Family*. New York: Random House, 1993.
> Morris, Joe Alex. *Nelson Rockefeller: A Biography*. New York: Harper & Brothers, 1960.
> Morris, Joe Alex. *Those Rockefeller Brothers*. New York: Harper & Brothers, 1953.
> Moscow, Alvin. *The Rockefeller Inheritance*. Garden City: Doubleday & Co., Inc., 1977.
> Persico, Joseph E. *The Imperial Rockefeller: A Biography of Nelson Rockefeller*. New York: Washington Square Press, 1982.
> Stasz, Clarice. *The Rockefeller Women: Dynasty of Piety, Privacy and Service*. New York: St. Martin's Press, 1995.

Maxwell, John Rogers, Sr. – Glen Cove – *Maxwelton*
The Nassau County Museum Collection includes photographs of the estate.

Maynard, Walter Effingham – Brookville – *Haut Bois*
The Nassau County Museum Collection includes photographs of the estate.
> *Vogue* July 1930.
> *Vogue* October 1930.

McCann, Charles Edward Francis – Oyster Bay Cove – *Sunken Orchard*;
> **and Glen Cove – *Winfield Hall***

The Nassau County Museum Collection includes photographs of both estates.
> Griswold, Mac and Eleanor Weller. *The Golden Age of American Gardens . Proud Owners . Private Estates . 1890–1940*. New York: Harry N. Abrams, Inc., Publishers, 1991.
> *House and Garden* January 1926.
> *House and Garden* April 1926.
> *House and Garden* May 1926.
> LeCorbeiller, Clare. *China Trade Porcelain; Patterns of Exchange; additions to the Helena Woolworth McCann Collection in the Metropolitan Museum of Art*. New York: Metropolitan Museum of Art, 1974.

McClure, Walter C. – Old Brookville – *Tall Trees*
The Nassau County Museum Collection includes photographs of the estate.
> *Home and Field* August 1931.

McLane, Allan, Jr. – Lattingtown – *Home Wood*
The Nassau County Museum Collection includes photographs of the estate.
> *The Spur* October 15, 1927.

McVeigh, Charles Senff, Sr. – Muttontown
The Nassau County Museum Collection includes vertical file material, historical research reports, and photographs of the estate.

Melius, Gary – Cold Spring Harbor – *Oheka Castle*
The Nassau County Museum Collection includes photographs of the estate.

Meyer, George C., Sr. – Kings Point
The Nassau County Museum Collection includes photographs of the estate.
> *Architecture* 29 (April 1914):86, 89.
> *Delineator* February 1925.

Meyer, J. Edward, Sr. – Kings Point – *Rhada*
The Nassau County Museum Collection includes photographs of the estate.

Meyer, Robert J. – Muttontown
The Nassau County Museum Collection includes photographs of the estate.

Milbank, Albert Goodsell – Lloyd Harbor – *Panfield*
The Nassau County Museum Collection includes photographs of the estate.
> *Architecture* 1918.
> *American Architect & Building News* 1920.

Milburn, Devereux, Jr. – Old Westbury
> Ellis, Francis M. and Edward F. Clark, Jr. *A Brief History of Carter, Ledyard and Milburn from 1854 to 1988.* Portsmouth, NH: Peter Randall Publishers, 1988.

Milburn, Devereux, Sr. – Old Westbury – *Sunridge Hall*
> Ellis, Francis M. and Edward F. Clark, Jr. *A Brief History of Carter, Ledyard and Milburn from 1854 to 1988.* Portsmouth, NH: Peter Randall Publishers, 1988.
> Patterson, Augusta Owen. *American Homes of Today.* New York: The Macmillan Co., 1924.

Milburn, John George, Jr. – North Hills – *Wychwood*
> Ellis, Francis M. and Edward F. Clark, Jr. *A Brief History of Carter, Ledyard and Milburn from 1854 to 1988.* Portsmouth, NH: Peter Randall Publishers, 1988.
> Goodyear, Anson Conger. *A Memoir: John George Milburn, Jr.* Angola, NY: privately printed, 1938.

Milburn, John George, Sr. – North Hills – *Groombridge*
> Ellis, Francis M. and Edward F. Clark, Jr. *A Brief History of Carter, Ledyard and Milburn from 1854 to 1988.* Portsmouth, NH: Peter Randall Publishers, 1988.

Miller, Flora Payne Whitney – Old Westbury – *French House*
> Howell, E. W. *Noted Long Island Homes.* Babylon, NY: E. W. Howell Co., 1933.
> Whitney Museum of Art, ed. *Flora Whitney Miller: Her Life – Her World.* New York: Whitney Museum of Art, 1987.

Mills, Ogden Livingston – Woodbury
Avery Architectural and Fine Arts Library, Columbia University, NYC, has photographs of the estate in their Samuel Gottscho Collection of photographs.
Library of Congress, Washington, DC, has Ogden Livingston Mills' papers. [They are described in *Mississippi Valley Review,* December 1954.]
> Bedford, Stephen and Richard Guy Wilson. *The Long Island Country House, 1870–1930.* Southampton, NY: The Parrish Art Museum, 1988.
> Hewitt, Mark Alan. *The Architect & the American Country Home 1890–1940.* New Haven: Yale University Press, 1990.
> *Monograph of the Works of John Russell Pope.* 3 vols. New York: William Helburn, Inc., 1937.
> Patterson, Augusta Owen. *American Homes of Today.* New York: The Macmillan Co., 1924.

Minton, Henry Miller – North Hills – *Brookwood*
> Howell, E. W. *Noted Long Island Homes.* Babylon, NY: E. W. Howell Co., 1933.

Mitchell, Sidney Zollicoffer – Matinecock
> Bonbright, J. C. and Gardiner C. Means. *The Holding Company.* New York: McGraw Hill & Co., 1932.
> "The Curb and Its Own EBS." *Fortune* June 1932.
> Curtis, E. Calder. *S. Z: Sidney Z. Mitchell (1862–1949), Electrical Pioneer.* New York: Newcomen Society in North America, 1950.
> Mitchell, Alexander Sidney. *S. Z. Mitchell and the Electrical Industry.* New York: Straus & Cudahy, 1960.
> Mitchell, Sidney Zollicoffer. "Conservation of Water Powers and their Development for the Public Good." Address delivered before a public hearing under the auspices of the transmission section of the National Light Assoc., New York City, April 8, 1911.
> Mitchell, Sidney Zollicoffer. Statement before Committee on Public Lands, United States Senate, on Ferris bill providing for the use of public lands in connection with the development of water power. December 23, 1914.
> Mitchell, Sidney Zollicoffer. "Superpower – the Name and the Facts." Address delivered before the Bond Club of New York, March 26, 1926.
> Mitchell, Sidney Zollicoffer. "Today's Problems in Public Utility Finance." Address delivered before the thirty-ninth convention of the Association of Edison Illuminating Companies, New London, Connecticut, September 13–16, 1920.
> Waterman, Merwin Howe. *Economic Implications of Public Utility Holding Company Operations.* Ann Arbor: University of Michigan Business Administration, 1941.

Mizner, Addison – Port Washington – *Old Cow Bay Manor House*
Mizner, Addison. *The Many Mizners.* New York: Sears Publishing Co., 1932.
Orr, Christina. *Addison Mizner: Architect of Dreams and Realities (1872–1933).* Palm Beach, FL: Norton School of Art, 1977.

Moffett, George Monroe, Sr. – Old Brookville – *Les Bois*
Arts and Decoration April 1937.
The New York Times Magazine February 16, 1930.
Town and Country March 1, 1929.

Moore, Benjamin – Muttontown – *Chelsea*
The Nassau County Museum Collection includes vertical file material, historical research reports, and photographs of the estate.
Howell, E. W. *Noted Long Island Homes.* Babylon, NY: E. W. Howell Co., 1933.

Moore, Edward Small, Sr. – Albertson – *Ten Gables*
The Nassau County Museum Collection includes photographs of the estate.
The American Home September 1929.
Garden Magazine October 1927.
Good Housekeeping May 1927.
Home and Field March 1933.
House and Garden August 1925.
House and Garden September 1925.
House and Garden January 1926.
House and Garden February 1926.
House and Garden April 1926.
House and Garden May 1926.
Ladies Home Journal May 1929.
New York Sun January 31, 1931.
The Small Home January 1930.

Moore, John Chandler – Oyster Bay Cove – *Moorelands*
Architecture 38 (November 1918):plates 182–85.

Morawetz, Victor – Woodbury – *Three Ponds*
The Nassau County Museum Collection includes photographs of the estate.
Architectural Forum 29:1 (July 1918):plates 5–7.
"Gold Medal of the Architectural League." *The Architectural Review* 26 (October 1919):97–104.
Delano and Aldrich. *Portraits of Ten Country Houses Designed by Delano and Aldrich.* Drawn by Chester Price. Garden City: Doubleday, Page & Co., 1924.
Harmond, Richard and Gaetano Vincitorio. "A Quiet Estate 1915–1969." *Long Island Forum* 50 (January 1987):4–11.
Hewitt, Mark Alan. "Domestic Portraits: The Early Long Island Country Houses of Delano and Aldrich." In *Long Island Architecture*, Joann P. Krieg, ed. (Interlaken, NY: Heart of the Lakes Publishing, 1991).
Patterson, Augusta Owen. *American Homes of Today.* New York: The Macmillan Co., 1924.
Swaine, Robert T. *The Cravath Firm and Its Predecessors, 1819–1948.* vols. 1, 2. New York: Ad Press, Ltd., 1946, 1948.

Morgan, Edwin Dennison, III – Old Westbury – *Wheatly*
Bedford, Stephen and Richard Guy Wilson. *The Long Island Country House, 1870–1930.* Southampton, NY: The Parrish Art Museum, 1988.
McKim, Mead & White. *A Monograph of the Work of McKim, Mead & White 1879–1915.* New York: DaCapo Press, 1985.
Morgan, Edwin D. *Recollections for My Family.* New York: Charles Scribner's Sons, 1938.

Morgan, Henry Sturgis, Sr. – Asharoken – *Beacon Farm;*
                Eaton's Neck;
                and Lattingtown
Carr, Edward A. T., Michael W. and Kari–Ann. *Faded Laurels: The History of Eaton's Neck and Asharoken.* Interlaken, NY: Heart of the Lakes Publishing, 1994.
Chernow, Ron. *The House of Morgan: An American Banking Dynasty and The Rise of Modern Finance.* New York: Atlantic Monthly Press, 1990.

Morgan, Henry Sturgis, Sr. – Asharoken – *Beacon Farm*;
Eaton's Neck;
and Lattingtown (cont'd)
Hoyt, Edwin P., Jr. *The House of Morgan.* New York: Dodd, Mead & Co., 1966.
Kneisel, William J. *Morgan Stanley & Co., Inc.: A Brief History.* New York: Morgan Stanley, 1977.
Morgan Stanley Fiftieth Anniversary Review. New York: Morgan Stanley, 1985.
Persico, Joseph E. *Casey from OSS to CIA.* New York: The Viking Press, 1991.
Persico, Joseph E. *Piercing the Reich.* New York: The Viking Press, 1979.

Morgan, John Pierpont, Jr. – East Island, Glen Cove – *Matinecock Point*
The Nassau County Museum Collection includes photographs of the estate.
Pierpont Morgan Library, NYC, has both John Pierpont Sr. & Jr.'s papers.
Chernow, Ron. *The House of Morgan: An American Banking Dynasty and The Rise of Modern Finance.* New York: Atlantic Monthly Press, 1990.
Forbes, John Douglas. *J. P. Morgan, Jr. 1867–1943.* Charlottesville: University of Virginia, 1981.
Hoyt, Edwin P., Jr. *The House of Morgan.* New York: Dodd, Mead & Co., 1966.
Patterson, Augusta Owen. *American Homes of Today.* New York: The Macmillan Co., 1924.

Morgan, Junius Spencer –   Matinecock – *Apple Trees*;
and West Island, Glen Cove – *Salutation*
Casey, William. *The Secret War Against Hitler.* Washington, DC: Regnery Gateway, 1988.
Chernow, Ron. *The House of Morgan: An American Banking Dynasty and The Rise of Modern Finance.* New York: Atlantic Monthly Press, 1990.
Hoyt, Edwin P., Jr. *The House of Morgan.* New York: Dodd, Mead & Co., 1966.
"Louise C. Morgan: At *Salutation*, West Island, Glen Cove, Long Island, New York." New York: Sotheby Parke–Bernet, Inc., 1974. auction catalog
Persico, Joseph E. *Casey from OSS to CIA.* New York: The Viking Press, 1991.
Persico, Joseph E. *Piercing the Reich.* New York: The Viking Press, 1979.

Morley, Christopher Darlington, Sr. – Roslyn Estates – *Green Escape*
The Nassau County Museum Collection includes photographs of Morley's cabin *The Knothole.*

Morse, Allon Mae Fuller – Old Westbury – *Morse Lodge*
The Nassau County Museum Collection includes photographs of the estate.
Canadian Home Journal May 1924.
Garden Magazine September 1920.

Mott, Dr. Valentine – Roslyn Harbor
The Nassau County Museum Collection includes photographs of the estate.

Munsel, Patrice – Brookville – *Malmaison*;
and Lattingtown – *Lockjaw Ridge*
The Nassau County Museum Collection includes photographs of *Malmaison.*

Munsey, Frank Andrew – Manhasset
Britt, George. *Forty Years – Forty Millions: The Career of Frank A. Munsey.* New York: Farrar & Rinehart, 1935.
Churchill, Allen. *Park Row.* New York: Farrar & Rinehart, 1935.
Duffus, Robert L. "Mr. Munsey." *American Mercury* 2 (July 1924):297–304.
Lowell, D. O. S. *A Munsey – Hopkins Genealogy: Being the Ancestry of Andrew Chauncey Munsey and Mary Jane Merritt Hopkins.* Boston: privately printed, 1920.
Ridgeway, E. J. *Frank A. Munsey: An Appreciation.* Chula Vista, CA: privately printed, 1926.
Villard, Oswald Garrison. *Some Newspapers and Newspaper–Men.* New York: Alfred A. Knopf, 1923.

Murdock, Harvey – Glen Cove – *The Birches*
The Nassau County Museum Collection includes photographs of the estate.

Murray, John Francis – Old Westbury
Howell, E. W. *Noted Long Island Homes.* Babylon, NY: E. W. Howell Co., 1933.

Nast, Conde – Sands Point – *Sandy Cay*
The Nassau County Museum Collection includes photographs of the estate.
      Chase, Edna Woolman and Ilka Chase. *Always in Vogue.* Garden City: Doubleday and Co., Inc., 1954.
      Chase, Edna Woolman. "Fifty Years of Vogue." *Vogue* 15 (November 1943):33.
      Howell, E. W. *Noted Long Island Homes.* Babylon, NY: E. W. Howell Co., 1933.
      Pringle, Henry. "High Hat." *Scribner's Magazine* July 1938:19.
      Robinson, Walter G. "With the Makers of Vogue." *Vogue* January 1, 1923:74.
      Seebohm, Caroline. *The Man Who Was Vogue: The Life and Times of Conde Nast.* New York: The Viking
         Press, 1982.

Nitze, Paul Henry – Glen Cove – *The Farm House*
      Talbott, Strobe. *The Master of the Game: Paul Nitze and the Nuclear Peace.* New York: Alfred A. Knopf, 1988.

Norton, Huntington – Oyster Bay – *Notley Hill*
      Architectural Forum 30 (February 1919):47–50.

Oberlin, Abraham – Lattingtown
The Nassau County Museum Collection includes photographs of the estate.

Outerbridge, Samuel Roosevelt – Centre Island
      Architectural Forum 33 (October 1920):plates 55–57.
      Architectural Review 12 (January 1921):31.

Paley, William S. – North Hills – *Kiluna Farm*
The Nassau County Museum Collection includes photographs of the estate.
      Grafton, David. *The Sisters: The Lives and Times of the Fabulous Cushing Sisters.* New York: Villard Books,
         1992.
      Halberstam, David. *The Powers That Be.* New York: Alfred A. Knopf, 1979.
      Paley, William S. *As It Happened: A Memoir.* Garden City: Doubleday & Co., Inc. 1979.
      Smith, Sally Bedell. *In All His Glory: The Life of William S. Paley. The Legendary Tycoon and His Brilliant
         Circle.* New York: Simon & Schuster, Inc., 1990.

Palmer, Carlton Humphreys – Centre Island – *Hearthstone*
The Nassau County Museum Collection includes photographs of the estate.

Payson, Charles Shipman – Manhasset
      Aronson, Steven M. L. *House and Garden* 157 (June 1985):140.
      Howell, E. W. *Noted Long Island Homes.* Babylon, NY: E. W. Howell Co., 1933.

Phillips, Ellis Laurimore, Sr. – Plandome Manor – *Laurimon*
The Nassau County Museum Collection includes photographs of the estate.

Phipps, Henry, Jr. – Lake Success – *Bonnie Blink*
Carnegie Library, Pittsburgh, PA, has photographs of Henry Phipps, Jr.
      Boegner, Peggie Phipps and Richard Gachot. *Halcyon Days: An American Family Through Three Generations.*
         New York: Harry N. Abrams, Inc., Publishers, 1986.

Phipps, Henry Carnegie – Old Westbury – *Spring Hill*
The Nassau County Museum Collection includes photographs of the estate.

Phipps, John Shaffer – Old Westbury – *Westbury House*
The Nassau County Museum Collection includes photographs of the estate.
Westbury Gardens Archives, Old Westbury, LI, has photographs of the estate and family.
      Architectural Forum 30 (February 1919):47–50.
      Architectural Review 12 (January 1921):plates II, III.
      Architectural Review 12 (March 1921):88.
      Bedford, Stephen and Richard Guy Wilson. *The Long Island Country House, 1870–1930.* Southampton, NY:
         The Parrish Art Museum, 1988.
      Boegner, Peggie Phipps and Richard Gachot. *Halcyon Days: An American Family Through Three Generations.*
         New York: Harry N. Abrams, Inc., Publishers, 1986.
      Cuthbert, Headlam. *George Abraham Crawley: A Short Memoir.* London: privately printed, 1929.
      "The Fabled Past: The Phipps Family." *The North Shore Journal* 14 (May 26, 1983) n.p.

Phipps, John Shaffer – Old Westbury – *Westbury House* (cont'd)
Finkle, Orin Z. "Westbury House," *Gold Coast* Fall 1982.
Home and Field February 1931.
House Beautiful March 1925.
Modes and Manners Summer 1929.
New York Herald Tribune August 10, 1930.
New York Herald Tribune October 26, 1930.
Patterson, Augusta Owen. *American Homes of Today.* New York: The Macmillan Co., 1924.
Town and Country May 1, 1925.
Sclare, Liisa and Donald. *Beaux–Arts Estates: A Guide to the Architecture of Long Island.* New York: The Viking Press, 1980.
Old Westbury Gardens. Old Westbury, NY: Old Westbury Gardens, 1985.

Pierce, Winslow Shelby, II – Bayville – *Dunstable*
The Nassau County Museum Collection includes photographs of the estate.

Polk, Frank Lyon, Sr. – Muttontown
Sterling Memorial Library, Yale University, New Haven, CT, has Frank Lyon Polk, Sr.'s papers.
Jeffreys–Jones, Rhodi. *American Espionage from Secret Service to CIA.* New York: The Free Press, 1977.
Polk, William R. *Polk's Folly: An American Family History.* New York: Doubleday & Co., Inc., 2000.

Post, Marjorie Merriweather – Brookville – *Hillwood*
The Bentley Historical Library of the University of Michigan, Ann Arbor, MI, has Marjorie Merriweather Post's papers.
Hillwood Museum, Washington, DC, has photographs of Post's Long Island estate. Both Post's Long Island estate and her DC home were named *Hillwood.*
The Nassau County Museum Collection includes photographs of the estate.
Arts and Decoration July 1926.
Coffin, Marian. "Garden of Edward F. Hutton." *House and Garden* May 1924:82.
Coffin, Marian. *Trees and Shrubs for Landscape Effects.* New York: Charles Scribner's Sons, 1940.
Country Life August 1933.
Country Life October 1933.
Country Life April 1934.
Country Life June 1934.
"The Fabled Past: A Tale of Bygone Days." *The North Shore Journal* 11 (May 29, 1980) n.p.
Fortune July 1934.
Griswold, Mac and Eleanor Weller. *The Golden Age of American Gardens . Proud Owners . Private Estates . 1890–1940.* New York: Harry N. Abrams, Inc., Publishers, 1991.
Hewitt, Mark Alan. *The Architect & the American Country Home 1890–1940.* New Haven: Yale University Press, 1990.
House Beautiful June 1926.
House Beautiful May 1934.
Kaiser, Harvey H. *Great Camps of the Adirondacks.* Boston: David R. Godine, 1982.
Major, Nettie Leitch. *C. W. Post: The Hour and the Man.* Washington, DC: Press of Judd & Detweiler, Inc., 1963.
New York Herald Tribune March 19, 1933.
Rubin, Nancy. *American Empress: The Life and Times of Marjorie Merriweather Post.* New York: Villard Books, 1995.
The Spur March 15, 1926.
Sclare, Liisa and Donald. *Beaux–Arts Estates: A Guide to the Architecture of Long Island.* New York: The Viking Press, 1980.
Town and Country June 1, 1926.
Wright, William. *Heiress: The Rich Life of Marjorie Merriweather Post.* Washington, DC: New Republic Books, 1978.

Pratt, Charles Millard – Glen Cove – *Seamoor*
The Nassau County Museum Collection includes photographs of the estate.
Pratt Institute, Brooklyn, NY, has an unpublished photograph album with text catalogued as, "Pratt, Frederic B. 'The Pratt Family at Dosoris 1889–1939."
Arts and Decoration April 1926.
Country Life June 1927
House and Garden April 1923.
In Memoriam: Charles Pratt, 1830–1891. New York: The DeVinne Press, 1891.

Pratt, Charles Millard – Glen Cove – *Seamoor* (cont'd)
      Piccano, Darlene. "The Pratt Family of Glen Cove." *Long Island Forum* 54 (Fall 1992):4–12.
      Tarbell, Ida M. *The History of the Standard Oil Company.* New York: Peter Smith & Co., 1950.

Pratt, Frederic Bayley – Glen Cove – *Poplar Hill* [I], [II]
The Nassau County Museum Collection includes photographs of *Poplar Hill* [II].
Pratt Institute, Brooklyn, NY, has an unpublished photograph album with text catalogued as, "Pratt, Frederic B. 'The Pratt
    Family at Dosoris 1889–1939."
      Home and Field December 1933.
      New York Herald Tribune May 5, 1929.
      New York Herald Tribune May 11, 1930.
      The Spur July 1, 1927.
      Tarbell, Ida M. *The History of the Standard Oil Company.* New York: Peter Smith & Co., 1950.

Pratt, Frederic Richardson – Lattingtown – *Friendfield Farm*
The Nassau County Museum Collection includes photographs of the estate.

Pratt, George du Pont, Sr. – Glen Cove – *Killenworth* [I], [II]
The Nassau County Museum Collection includes photographs of *Killenworth II].*
Pratt Institute, Brooklyn, NY, has an unpublished photograph album with text catalogued as, "Pratt, Frederic B. 'The Pratt
    Family at Dosoris 1889–1939."
      Architectural Record 35 (June 1914):558–73.
      Country Life March 1924.
      Finkle, Orin Z. "Lifting the Veil on Killenworth." *Community Newspapers* October 25, 1984:16A.
      Garden Magazine May 1921.
      House and Garden April 1921.
      House and Garden December 1922.
      New York Herald Tribune November 17, 1929.
      New York Herald Tribune January 5, 1930.
      Patterson, Augusta Owen. *American Homes of Today.* New York: The Macmillan Co., 1924.
      Tarbell, Ida M. *The History of the Standard Oil Company.* New York: Peter Smith & Co., 1950.
      Town and Country August 15, 1925.
      Vogue August 15, 1923.

Pratt, Harold Irving, Sr. – Glen Cove – *Welwyn*
The Nassau County Museum Collection includes photographs of the estate.
Pratt Institute, Brooklyn, NY, has an unpublished photograph album with text catalogued as, "Pratt, Frederic B. 'The Pratt
    Family at Dosoris 1889–1939."
      Griswold, Mac and Eleanor Weller. *The Golden Age of American Gardens . Proud Owners . Private Estates .*
        1890–1940. New York: Harry N. Abrams, Inc., Publishers, 1991.
      Ottusch–Kianka, Donna and Michael Petraglia. "A History of the Welwyn Preserve." *Long Island Forum* 46
        (August 1983):150–57.
      Patterson, Augusta Owen. *American Homes of Today.* New York: The Macmillan Co., 1924.
      Tarbell, Ida M. *The History of the Standard Oil Company.* New York: Peter Smith & Co., 1950.

Pratt, Herbert Lee, Sr. – Glen Cove – *The Braes*
The Nassau County Museum Collection includes photographs of the estate.
Pratt Institute, Brooklyn, NY, has an unpublished photograph album with text catalogued as, "Pratt, Frederic B. 'The Pratt
    Family at Dosoris 1889–1939."
      Architectural Review 11 (November 1920):149.
      Architecture 30 (November 1914):252–53, 257–59.
      Arts and Decoration April 1926.
      "Country House, H. L. Pratt, Glen Cove, Long Island." *Architecture* 29 (1914):257–59.
      Country Life June–July 1932.
      Griswold, Mac and Eleanor Weller. *The Golden Age of American Gardens . Proud Owners . Private Estates .*
        1890–1940. New York: Harry N. Abrams, Inc., Publishers, 1991.
      Sclare, Liisa and Donald. *Beaux–Arts Estates: A Guide to the Architecture of Long Island.* New York: The
        Viking Press, 1980.
      "Study and Executed Plan for House of H. L. Pratt, Esq., Glen Cove, Long Island, N. Y." *American Architect*
        and Building News 70 (1900):31.
      Tarbell, Ida M. *The History of the Standard Oil Company.* New York: Peter Smith & Co., 1950.

Pratt, Herbert Lee, Sr. – Glen Cove – *The Braes* (cont'd)
> *Town and Country* October 1, 1925.
> *Town and Country* January 15, 1926.

Pratt, John Teele, Sr. – Glen Cove – *Manor House*
Pratt Institute, Brooklyn, NY, has an unpublished photograph album with text catalogued as, "Pratt, Frederic B. 'The Pratt Family at Dosoris 1889–1939."
> Bedford, Stephen and Richard Guy Wilson. *The Long Island Country House, 1870–1930.* Southampton, NY: The Parrish Art Museum, 1988.
> Howell, E. W. *Noted Long Island Homes.* Babylon, NY: E. W. Howell Co., 1933.
> "The Manor House: Estate of John T. Pratt." *Architectural Record* 46 (October 1919):296–97.
> Tarbell, Ida M. *The History of the Standard Oil Company.* New York: Peter Smith & Co., 1950.

Preston, Ralph Julius – Jericho – *Ivy Hall*
The Nassau County Museum Collection includes photographs of the estate.

Preston, William Payne Thompson, Sr. – Jericho – *Longfields*
> "The Country Work of Peabody, Wilson and Brown." *Architecture* 30 (October 1914):214.
> Eberlein, Harold Donald. "Individuality in Architectural Vernacular, a Study in Materials and Detail as Revealed in the Interesting Home of W. P. T. Preston, Esq., Long Island." *Architectural Forum* 30 (February 1919):47.

Proctor, Charles E. –   Kings Point – *Shadowlane*;
                          and Mill Neck
> *Architectural Record* 36 (October 1914):272–85.

Pryibil, Helen Porter – Glen Cove – *Bogheid*
> "Furniture, Porcelain, Silver and Other Decorations of the Estate of the Late Helen Porter Pryibil, Glen Cove, Long Island to be Exhibited and Sold on the Premises." New York: Parke–Bernet Galleries, Inc., 1969. auction catalog

Pulitzer, Ralph, Sr. – North Hills – *Kiluna Farm*
The Nassau County Museum Collection includes photographs of the estate.
> *Architectural Forum* 29 (August 1918):53.
> *Architectural Record* 25 (April 1914):310–11.
> Patterson, Augusta Owen. *American Homes of Today.* New York: The Macmillan Co., 1924.
> Pulitzer, Ralph. *New York Society on Parade.* New York: Harper & Brothers, 1910.
> *Town and Country* October 1, 1926.

Pyne, Percy Rivington, II – Roslyn Harbor – *Rivington House*
The Nassau County Museum Collection includes photographs of the estate.
> Brown, Jane. *Beatrix: The Gardening Life of Beatrix Jones Farrand 1872–1959.* New York: Viking Penguin Books, 1995.
> *The Field* September 1929.
> *Home and Field* April 1930.
> *Home and Field* February 1931.
> *Home and Field* May 1931.
> *International Studio* December 1929.
> *The Small Home* July 1930.
> *Town and Country* October 15, 1929.

Redmond, Roland Livingston – Oyster Bay Cove – *White Elephant Farm*
> Ellis, Francis M. and Edward F. Clark, Jr. *A Brief History of Carter, Ledyard and Milburn from 1854 to 1988.* Portsmouth, NH: Peter Randall Publishers, 1988.

Reed, Lansing Parmelee – Lloyd Harbor – *Windy Hill*
Olin Library, Cornell University, Ithaca, NY, has Ellen Shipman's landscape designs for the estate.

Reynolds, Richard Samuel, Sr. – Glen Cove – *Slow Tide* and *Winfield Hall*
The Nassau County Museum Collection includes photographs of *Winfield Hall.*
> Reynolds, Patrick and Tom Shachtman. *The Gilded Leaf, Triumph, Tragedy, and Tobacco: Three Generations of the R. J. Reynolds Family and Fortune.* Boston: Little, Brown & Co., 1989.

Reynolds, Richard Samuel, Sr. – Glen Cove – *Slow Tide* and *Winfield Hall* (cont'd)
> Reynolds, Richard S., Jr. "Opportunity in Crisis." In *The Reynolds Metal Story.* New York: Newcomen Society in North America, 1956.
> Reynolds, Richard S., Jr. *Stories About the Reynolds Family.* privately printed, 1970.
> Reynolds, Richard S., Sr. *The Marble King of Bristol.* privately printed, 1981. [an autobiography]

Richards, Ira, Jr. – Lattingtown
The Nassau County Museum Collection includes photographs of the estate.
> *Home and Garden* February 1927.

Ricks, Jessie Jay – Flower Hill;
> **and Plandome**
Octagon Museum of American Architectural Foundation, Prints and Drawings Collection, Washington, DC, has photographs of the Flower Hill house.
Society for the Preservation of Long Island Antiquities, Cold Spring Harbor, LI, has a model of the Flower Hill house.

Ripley, Julien Ashton, Sr. – Muttontown – *Three Corners Farm*
The Nassau County Museum Collection includes photographs of the estate.

Robinson, John Randolph – Brookville
The Nassau County Museum Collection includes photographs of the estate.
> *Architectural Forum* 28 (January 1918):plates 6–10.
> Sclare, Liisa and Donald. *Beaux–Arts Estates: A Guide to the Architecture of Long Island.* New York: The Viking Press, 1980.

Robinson, Thomas Linton – East Williston – *Red Barns*
The Nassau County Museum Collection includes photographs of the estate.

Roosevelt, Archibald Bulloch, Jr. – Cold Spring Harbor – *Turkey Lane House*
Houghton and Widner Library, Harvard University, Cambridge, MA, has the Theodore Roosevelt Collection which consists of over 12,000 printed items, 3,500 cartoons, 10,000 photographs, manuscripts, and the Roosevelt family papers.
> Roosevelt, Archibald, Jr. *For Lust of Knowing: Memoirs of an Intelligence Officer.* Boston: Little, Brown & Co., 1988.

Roosevelt, Archibald Bulloch, Sr. – Cold Spring Harbor – *Turkey Lane House*
Houghton and Widner Library, Harvard University, Cambridge, MA, has the Theodore Roosevelt Collection which consists of over 12,000 printed items, 3,500 cartoons, 10,000 photographs, manuscripts, and the Roosevelt family papers.
> Roosevelt, Archibald, Jr. *For Lust of Knowing: Memoirs of an Intelligence Officer.* Boston: Little, Brown & Co., 1988.

Roosevelt, Kermit, Sr. – Cove Neck – *Mohannes*
Houghton and Widner Library, Harvard University, Cambridge, MA, has the Theodore Roosevelt Collection which consists of over 12,000 printed items, 3,500 cartoons, 10,000 photographs, manuscripts, and the Roosevelt family papers.
> Gasiorowski, Mark J. "The 1953 Coup d' Etat in Iran." *International Journal of Middle East Studies* 19 (1987):261–89.
> Mosley, Leonard. *Dulles: A Biography of Eleanor, Allen, and John Foster Dulles and Their Family Network.* New York: The Dial Press, 1978.
> Naylor, Natalie A., Douglas Brinkley, and John Allen Gable, eds. *Theodore Roosevelt: Many–Sided American.* Interlaken, NY: Heart of the Lakes Publishing, 1992.
> Persico, Joseph E. *Piercing the Reich.* New York: The Viking Press, 1979.
> Roosevelt, Kermit. *Countercoup: The Struggle for Control of Iran.* New York: McGraw–Hill, 1981.
> Roosevelt, Kermit. *The Overseas Targets.* vol. 2. New York: Walter and Co., 1976.

Roosevelt, Philip James, Jr. – Cove Neck
The Nassau County Museum Collection includes photographs of the estate.

Roosevelt, Theodore – Oyster Bay Cove – *Tranquility*
Houghton and Widner Library, Harvard University, Cambridge, MA, has the Theodore Roosevelt Collection which consists of over 12,000 printed items, 3,500 cartoons, 10,000 photographs, manuscripts, and the Roosevelt family papers.

Caroli, Betty Boyd. *The Roosevelt Women.* New York: Basic Books, 1998.
Dodge, William E. Jr., et al. "Theodore Roosevelt, Senior, a Tribute." In *The Proceedings at a Meeting of the Union Club, New York City, February 14, 1878.* New York: privately printed, 1902.
Naylor, Natalie A., Douglas Brinkley, and John Allen Gable, eds. *Theodore Roosevelt: Many–Sided American.* Interlaken, NY: Heart of the Lakes Publishing, 1992.

Roosevelt, Theodore – Cove Neck – *Sagamore Hill*
Houghton and Widner Library, Harvard University, Cambridge, MA, has the Theodore Roosevelt Collection which consists of over 12,000 printed items, 3,500 cartoons, 10,000 photographs, manuscripts, and the Roosevelt family papers.
Library of Congress, Washington, DC, has Theodore Roosevelt's papers.
The Nassau County Museum Collection includes photographs of the estate.

Caroli, Betty Boyd. *The Roosevelt Women.* New York: Basic Books, 1998.
Cobb, William T. *The Strenuous Life: The Oyster Bay Roosevelts in Business and Finance.* New York: William E. Rudge's Sons, 1946.
Collier, Peter and David Horowitz. *The Roosevelts: An American Saga.* New York: Simon & Schuster, Inc., 1994.
Donn, Linda. *The Roosevelt Cousins: Growing Up Together, 1882–1924.* New York: Alfred A. Knopf, 2001.
Gluck, Sherwin. *TR's Summer White House.* privately printed, 1999.
Hagedorn, Hermann. *The Roosevelt Family of Sagamore Hill.* New York: The Macmillan Co., 1954.
Morris, Edmund. *The Rise of Theodore Roosevelt.* New York: G. P. Putnam's Sons, 1979.
Morris, Edmund. *Theodore Rex.* New York: Random House, 2001.
Naylor, Natalie A., Douglas Brinkley, and John Allen Gable, eds. *Theodore Roosevelt: Many–Sided American.* Interlaken, NY: Heart of the Lakes Publishing, 1992. [Dr. Naylor, *et al,* have included an extensive bibliography about and by Theodore Roosevelt.]
Robinson, Corinne Roosevelt. *My Brother Theodore Roosevelt.* New York: Charles Scribner's Sons, 1921.
Roth, George G. "The Roosevelt Memorial Association and the Preservation of Sagamore Hill, 1919–1953." M. A. thesis, Wake Forest University, 1980.
Sclare, Liisa and Donald. *Beaux–Arts Estates: A Guide to the Architecture of Long Island.* New York: The Viking Press, 1980.

Roosevelt, Theodore, Jr. – Cove Neck – *Old Orchard*
Houghton and Widner Library, Harvard University, Cambridge, MA, has the Theodore Roosevelt Collection which consists of over 12,000 printed items, 3,500 cartoons, 10,000 photographs, manuscripts, and the Roosevelt family papers.
Manuscript Division, Library of Congress, Washington, DC, has Theodore Roosevelt, Jr.'s papers.

Roosevelt, Eleanor B. *Day Before Yesterday: The Reminiscences of Mrs. Theodore Roosevelt, Jr.* Garden City: Doubleday & Co., Inc., 1959.

Roulston, Thomas Henry, Sr. – Huntington Bay – *High Lindens*
The Nassau County Museum Collection includes photographs of the estate.

The Small Home July 1931.
The Small Home March 1932.
World January 27, 1924.

Rouss, Peter Winchester – Bayville – *Callender House*
The Nassau County Museum Collection includes photographs of the estate.

"The Fabled Past: A Tale of Bygone Days." *The North Shore Journal* 5 (July 15, 1971) n.p.

Rumsey, Mary Harriman – Brookville;
and Sands Point
Documents pertaining to William Averell Harriman's early business career were stored in a Brooklyn warehouse. Also included was an inventory of documents which had been destroyed, for lack of space, which included the personal papers of his sister Mary Harriman Rumsey and those of his first wife Katharine Lanier Lawrence Harriman. The surviving material from the Brooklyn warehouse, presumably including the inventory of missing documents, is now in Library of Congress, Washington, DC.
The Nassau County Museum Collection includes photographs of the Sands Point estate.

Rumsey, Mary Harriman – Brookville;
               and Sands Point (cont'd)

Abramson, Rudy. *Spanning the Century: The Life of W. Averell Harriman, 1891–1986.* New York: William Morrow, 1992.

Architectural Record 41 (June 1917):554.

Architecture 22 (July 1910):105.

The Brickbuilder 25 (June 1916):152.

Campbell, Persia Crawford. *Consumer Representation in the New Deal.* New York, 1940.

James, Edward T., ed. *Notable American Women: A Biographical Dictionary.* Cambridge, MA: The Belknap Press of Harvard University Press. vol. III:208–9.

The National Cyclopaedia of American Biography. Clifton, NJ: James T. White & Co., 25 (1980):27.

The New York Times December 19, 1934. [extensive obituary]

Patterson, Augusta Owen. *American Homes of Today.* New York: The Macmillan Co., 1924.

Perkins, Frances. *The Roosevelt I Knew.* New York: The Viking Press, 1946.

Schlesinger, Arthur, Jr. *The Coming of the New Deal.* Boston: Houghton Mifflin, 1958.

Tugwell, Rexford G. *The Democratic Roosevelt: A Biography of Franklin D. Roosevelt.* Garden City: Doubleday & Co., 1957.

White, Shelton. "The County Consumer Councils and Their Service." *National Consumer News* August 25, 1935:5.

Russell, Faris R. – Mill Neck – *Clayton*

Architectural Record 50 (December 1921):435–38.

Ryan, John Dennis – North Hills – *Derrymore*

The Nassau County Museum Collection includes photographs of the estate.

Salvage, Sir Samuel Agar – Old Brookville – *Rynwood*

The Nassau County Museum Collection includes photographs of the estate.

American Architect and Building News 133 (1928).

American Architect and Building News 135 (May 1929):593.

American Architect and Building News 136 (1929):52–4.

American Home September 1934.

Architectural Forum 53 (July 1930):51–85.

Architectural Annual, 1929, New York: Architectural League of New York, 1929.

Architectural League of New York 1928.

Country Homes 8 (May 1930):4.

Country Life in America 1930.

Country Life in America 65 (April 1934):59.

Country Life in America 73 (March 1938):41.

"House of Samuel A. Salvage, Glen Head, Long Island." *Architecture* 59 (June 1929):359–66.

Life Magazine July 1946:73.

"Long Island Shows a Varied Garden." *House and Garden* October 1936:89.

Patterson, Augusta Owen. "The Residence of Mr. Samuel A. Salvage." *Town and Country* May 1, 1929:59.

"Rynwood, House of Samuel A. Salvage, Esq." *Architectural Forum* 53 (July 1930):51–85.

Van Wagner, Judith, et. al. *Long Island Estate Gardens.* Greenvale, NY: Hillwood Art Gallery, 1985.

Sanderson, Henry – Upper Brookville – *La Selva*

The Nassau County Museum Collection includes photographs of the estate.

St. Francis Center, Upper Brookville, LI, has an extensive collection of drawings, photographs, and watercolors of the estate.

Charm August 1926.

Country Life October 1922.

Home and Field February 1931.

House and Garden March 1922.

House and Garden February 1931.

House Beautiful March 1922.

New York Herald Tribune March 25, 1928.

New York Herald Tribune July 28, 1929.

New York Herald Tribune November 25, 1929.

New York Herald Tribune May 25, 1930.

Satterwhite, Dr. Preston Pope – Kings Point – *Preston Hall*
The Nassau County Museum Collection includes photographs of the estate.
> *Arts and Decoration* July 1931.
> *New York Herald Tribune* June 1, 1930.
> *New York Herald Tribune* February 22, 1931.
> *New York Herald Tribune* July 26, 1931.
> *New York Sun* March 15, 1930.

Schieren, George Arthur, Sr. – Kings Point – *Beachleigh*
> *Architectural Review* 11 (September 1920):89.

Schiff, Dorothy – East Norwich – *Old Fields*;
and Sands Point – *Sandy Cay*
The Nassau County Museum Collection includes photographs of *Sandy Cay*.
> Potter, Jeffrey. *Men, Money and Magic: The Story of Dorothy Schiff.* New York: Coward, McCann & Geoghegan, Inc., 1976.

Schiff, Mortimer L. – Oyster Bay – *Northwood*
The Nassau County Museum Collection includes photographs of the estate.
> Adler, Cyrus. *Jacob H. Schiff: His Life and Letters.* Garden City: Doubleday, Doran & Co., 1928.
> Cohen, Naomi W. *Jacob H. Schiff: A Study in American Jewish Leadership.* Hanover, NH: Brandeis University Press, 1999.
> Hopkins, Alfred. *Modern Farm Buildings.* New York: McBride, Nast & Company, 1913.

Schmidlapp, Carl Jacob, Sr. – Mill Neck – *Rumpus House*
> Howell, E. W. *Noted Long Island Homes.* Babylon, NY: E. W. Howell Co., 1933.
> "In a Long Island Garden." *House and Garden* October 1926:129.

Scott, Rufus W. – Lattingtown – *Scottage*
The Nassau County Museum Collection includes photographs of the estate.

Senff, Gustava A. Tapscott – Muttontown
The Nassau County Museum Collection includes vertical file material, historical research reports, and photographs of the estate.

Shaw, Samuel T., Sr. – Centre Island – *The Sunnyside*
Society for the Preservation of Long Island Antiquities, Cold Spring Harbor, LI, as a water color sketch of the house.

Sherry, Louis – Manhasset – *Sherryland*
> Hungerford, Edward. *The Story of Louis Sherry and the Business He Built.* New York: William E. Rudge's Sons, 1929.

Shipman, Julie Fay Bradley – Glen Head – *Lynrose*
The Nassau County Museum Collection includes photographs of the estate.
> *Printers Magazine* January 1938.
> *The Spur* March 1933.

Sinclair, Harry Ford, Sr. – Kings Point
> Bates, James Leonard. *The Origins of Teapot Dome; Progressives, Parties and Petroleum, 1909–1921.* Urbana: University of Illinois Press, 1963.
> Connelly, William. *Oil Business As I Saw It.* Tulsa, OK: University of Oklahoma Press, 1954.
> "The Fabled Past: Gambling Man." *The North Shore Journal* 11 (November 27, 1980) n.p.
> Ise, John. *The United States Oil Policy.* New Haven: Yale University Press, 1928.
> Noggle, Burl. *Teapot Dome: Oil and Politics in the 1920s.* Baton Rouge: Louisiana State University Press, 1962.
> Ravage, Marcus E. *The Story of Teapot Dome.* New York: The New Republic, 1924.
> Starr, John. *Teapot Dome.* New York: Viking, 1959.
> Swaine, Robert T. *The Cravath Firm and Its Predecessors, 1819–1948.* vols. 1, 2. New York: Ad Press, Ltd., 1946, 1948.
> Werner, Morris Robert. *Teapot Dome.* New York: The Viking Press, 1959.

Sloan, Alfred Pritchard, Jr. – Kings Point – *Snug Harbor*
      Sloan, Alfred Pritchard. *My Years with General Motors.* Garden City: Doubleday & Co., Inc., 1964.

Smith, Albert Edward, Sr. – Centre Island
      Smith, Albert E. and Phil A. Koury. *Two Reels and a Crank.* Garden City: Doubleday & Co., Inc., 1952.

Smith, George – Muttontown – *Blythewood* [*see Bedford, Alfred Cotton*]
The Nassau County Museum Collection includes photographs of the estate.

Smith, Ormond Gerald – Brookville – *Stepping Stones*;
                  and Centre Island – *Shoremonde*
The Nassau County Museum Collection includes photographs of the Centre Island estate.
      Reynolds, Quentin. *The Fiction Factory: The Story of 100 years of Publishing at Street and Smith.* New York:
          Random House, 1955.

Snow, George Palen – Syosset
The Nassau County Museum Collection includes photographs of the estate.
      Better Homes and Gardens June 1936.

Steele, Charles – Old Westbury
      Hopkins, Alfred. *Modern Farm Buildings.* New York: McBride, Nast & Company, 1913.
      Leffingwell, Russell C. *Memorial of Charles Steele.* New York: Association of the Bar of New York, 1940.
      Swaine, Robert T. *The Cravath Firm and Its Predecessors, 1819–1948.* vols. 1, 2. New York: Ad Press, Ltd.,
          1946, 1948.

Stern, Benjamin – Roslyn Harbor – *Claraben Court*
The Nassau County Museum Collection includes photographs of the estate.
      Country Life October 1925.
      Ferry, John William. *A History of the Department Store.* New York: The Macmillan Co., 1960.
      House and Garden September 1921.
      House and Garden July 1932.

Stettinius, Edward Reilly, Jr. – Lattingtown – *The Shelter*
Aldenham Library, University of Virginia, Charlottesville, VA, has Edward Reilly Stettinius, Jr.'s papers.
The Nassau County Museum Collection includes photographs of the estate.
      Stettinius, Edward R. *The Diaries of Edward R. Stettinius, 1943–1946.* New York: New Viewpoints, 1975.
      Stettinius, Edward R., Jr. *Roosevelt and the Russians.* Westport, CT: Greenwood Press, 1949.
      Stettinius, Edward R., Jr. *Lend Lease: Weapon For Victory.* New York: The Macmillan Co., 1944.

Stettinius, Edward Reilly, Sr. – Lattingtown – *The Shelter*
The Nassau County Museum Collection includes photographs of the estate.
      Forbes, John Douglas. *Stettinius Sr.: Portrait of a Morgan Partner.* Charlottesville: University of Virginia
          Press, 1974.
      Town and Country March 15, 1930.

Stevens, Byam K., Jr. – Muttontown – *Kirby Hill*
The Nassau County Museum Collection includes photographs of the estate.

Stevens, Joseph Sampson – Muttontown – *Kirby Hill*
The Nassau County Museum Collection includes photographs of the estate.

Stewart, Glen – Lattingtown
      Architectural Review 9 (October 1919):106–8.

Stewart, William Adams Walker, II – Cold Spring Harbor – *Edgeover*
      Ellis, Francis M. and Edward F. Clark, Jr. *A Brief History of Carter, Ledyard and Milburn from 1854 to 1988.*
          Portsmouth, NH: Peter Randall Publishers, 1988.

Stimson, Henry Lewis – West Hills – *Highold*
Sterling Memorial Library, Yale University, New Haven, CT, has Henry Lewis Stimson's diaries and papers.
      Hodgson, Godfrey. *The Colonel: The Life and Times of Henry Stimson, 1867–1950.* New York: Alfred A.
          Knopf, 1990.

Stimson, Henry Lewis – West Hills – *Highold* (cont'd)

Morison, Elting E. *Turmoil and Tradition: A Study of the Life and Times of Henry L. Stimson.* Boston: Houghton Mifflin, 1960.

Stimson, Henry L. and McGeorge Bundy. *On Active Service in Peace and War.* New York: Harper & Brothers, 1948.

Stimson, Henry Lewis. *My Vacations.* privately printed, 1949. [discusses *Highold*]

Stow, William L. – Old Westbury

The Nassau County Museum Collection includes photographs of the estate.

Straight, Willard Dickerman – Old Westbury – *Elmhurst* [*see also* Elmhirst, Leonard Knight]

Avery Architectural and Fine Arts Library, Columbia University, NYC, has material on Straight in their Oral History Collection.

The Department of Landscape Architecture Documents Collection, University of California, Berkeley, CA, has Beatrix Farrand's papers which include her sketches for the Straight estate landscape.

The Elmhirst Centre Archive, Dartington Hall, Totnes, Devon, England, has correspondence between Beatrix Jones Farrand, the Straights, and the Elmhirsts concerning the landscaping of both their Old Westbury estate and Dartington Hall. The Elmhirst Centre Archive also has the English papers of Dorothy Whitney Straight [Elmhirst].

The Nassau County Museum Collection includes photographs of the estate.

Office of the County Clerk, Nassau County, Mineola, LI, has Willard Straight's will on file.

Olin Library, Cornell University, Ithaca, NY, has the American papers of Dorothy Whitney Straight [Elmhirst].

Balmori, Diana, Diane Kostial McGuire, and Eleanor M. McPeck. *Beatrix Farrand's American Landscapes: Her Gardens and Campuses.* Sagaponack, NY: Sagapress, Inc., 1985.

Brown, Jane. *Beatrix: The Gardening Life of Beatrix Jones Farrand 1872–1959.* New York: Viking Penguin Books, 1995.

Croly, Herbert. *Willard Straight.* New York: The Macmillan Co., 1924.

"The Fabled Past: The Whitneys of Westbury." *The North Shore Journal* 13 (May 27, 1982) n.p.

Graves. Louis. *Willard Straight in the Orient.* New York: Asia Publishing Co., 1922.

Hirsh, Mark D. *William C. Whitney: Modern Warwick.* New York: Dodd, Mead & Co., 1948.

Spinzia, Raymond E. "Michael Straight and the Cambridge Spy Ring." *The Freeholder* 5 (Winter 2001):3–5.

Straight, Michael. *After Long Silence.* New York: W. W. Norton & Co., 1983.

Straight, Michael. *Make This the Last War.* New York: Harcourt Brace & Co., 1943.

Straight, Michael. *Trial By Television.* Boston: The Beacon Press, 1954.

Swanberg, W. A. *Whitney Father, Whitney Heiress.* New York: Charles Scribner's Sons, 1980.

Swope, Herbert Bayard, Sr. – Great Neck;
and Sands Point – *Keewaydin*

Avery Architectural and Fine Arts Library, Columbia University, NYC, has photographs of the estate.

Avery Architectural and Fine Arts Library, Columbia University, NYC, has material on Herbert Bayard Swope, Sr. in their Oral History Collection.

Manuscript Division, Library of Congress, Washington, DC, has some of Herbert Bayard Swope, Sr.'s papers.

FDR Library, Hyde Park, NY, also has some of Herbert Bayard Swope, Sr.'s papers.

Amato, Dennis J. "Croquet on Long Island." *Long Island Forum* 55 (Spring 1993):17–21.

Kahn, E. J., Jr. *The World of Swope: A Biography of Herbert Bayard Swope.* New York: Simon & Schuster, Inc., 1965.

Kirk, Donald. "Herbert Bayard Swope." B. A. thesis, Princeton University, 1959.

Lewis, Alfred Allen. *Man of the World, Herbert Bayard Swope: A Charmed Life of Pulitzer Prizes, Poker, and Politics.* Indianapolis: The Bobbs-Merrill Co., Inc., 1978.

Taylor, James Blackstone, Jr. – Cove Neck – *Sunset House*

Fleming, Nancy. *Money, Manure & Maintenance: Ingredients for Successful Gardens of Marian Coffin, Pioneer Landscape Architect 1876–1957.* Weston, MA: Country Place Books, 1995.

Taylor, James Blackstone, Sr. – Cove Neck – *Sunset House*;
and Jericho

The Nassau County Museum Collection includes photographs of the estate.

Taylor, Myron Charles – Lattingtown – *Killingworth*

The Nassau County Museum Collection includes photographs of the estate.

Architectural Forum 41 (October 1924):161–68.

House and Garden September 1923.

New York Herald Tribune February 9, 1930.

Thierot, Charles Henschel, Sr. – Matinecock;
and Muttontown – *Cedar Hill*

   The Charles H. Thierot Collection of Sporting Paintings, Cedar Hill, Oyster Bay, Long Island, NY. privately printed, 1940.

Thomas, Norman Mattoon – Cold Spring Harbor
The New York Public Library, NYC, has Norman Thomas' papers.

   Fleishman, Harry. *Norman Thomas: A Biography.* New York: W. W. Norton & Co., 1969.
   Gorham, Charles. *Leader At Large.* New York: Farrar, Straus & Giroux, 1970.
   Johnpoll, Bernard K. *Pacifist's Progress.* New York: Quadrangle, 1970.
   Seidler, Murray B. *Norman Thomas: Respectable Rebel.* Syracuse: Syracuse University Press, 1961.
   Swanberg, W. A. *Norman Thomas: The Last Idealist.* New York: Charles Scribner's Sons, 1976.

Tiffany, Charles Lewis, II – Oyster Bay Cove – *Elmwood*
The Nassau County Museum Collection includes photographs of the estate.

   Burlingham, Michael John. *'The Last Tiffany' A Biography of Dorothy Tiffany Burlingham.* New York: Atheneum, 1989.

Tiffany, Katrina Brandes Ely – Oyster Bay Cove – *Elmwood*
The Nassau County Museum Collection includes photographs of the estate.

   Burlingham, Michael John. *'The Last Tiffany' A Biography of Dorothy Tiffany Burlingham.* New York: Atheneum, 1989.
   The History of Woman Suffrage. vol. 6. New York: New York Source Book Press, 1970.
   Katrina Ely Tiffany. New Haven: Yale University Press, 1929.

Tiffany, Louis Comfort – Laurel Hollow – *The Briars* **and** *Laurelton Hall*
Harvard Law School, Manuscripts Division, Harvard University, Cambridge, MA, has the Charles Culp Burlingham papers.
The Charles Hosmer Morse Museum, Winter Park, FL, has photographs of Laurelton Hall.
The Nassau County Museum Collection includes Frederick M. Savage's 1919 *Laurelton Hall Inventory.*
Sterling Library, Yale University, New Haven, CT, has Tiffany papers and correspondence filed under the Mitchell–Tiffany papers.
Schlesinger Library, Radcliffe College, Cambridge, MA, has Edith Banfield Jackson papers.
Tiffany & Company archives are in Parsippany, NJ.

   "American Country House of Louis Comfort Tiffany." *International Studio* 33 (February 1908):294–96.
   "Artists Heaven; Long Island Estate of Louis Tiffany To Be an Artists' Home." *Review* 1 (November 1, 1919):533.
   Bedford, Stephen and Richard Guy Wilson. *The Long Island Country House, 1870–1930.* Southampton, NY: The Parrish Art Museum, 1988.
   Bing, Siegfried. *Artistic America, Tiffany Glass, and Art Nouveau.* reprint. Robert Koch, ed. Cambridge, Mass: MIT Press, [1895–1903] 1970.
   Bingham, Alfred Mitchell. *The Tiffany Fortune and Other Chronicles of a Connecticut Family.* Chestnut Hill, MA: Abeel and Leet Publishers, 1996.
   Brownell, William C. "The Younger Painters of America." *Scribner's Monthly* July 1881:321–24.
   Burke, Doreen Bolger. "Louis C. Tiffany and His Early Training at Eagleswood, 1862–1865." *The American Art Journal* 19 (1987):29–39.
   Burlingham, Michael John. *'The Last Tiffany' A Biography of Dorothy Tiffany Burlingham.* New York: Atheneum, 1989.
   Catalogue Of the Officers and Students of the Eagleswood Military Academy. 1863.
   Conway, Edward Harold. "Mr. Louis C. Tiffany, Laurelton Hall at Cold Spring, Long Island." *The Spur* 15 (August 15, 1914):24–9.
   Couldrey, Vivienne. *The Art of Louis Comfort Tiffany.* Secaucus, NJ: The Wellfleet Press, 1989.
   DeKay, Charles. "Laurelton Studios." *International Studio* 7 (October 1920):78–81.
   Desmond, Harry W. and Herbert Croly. *Stately Homes in America.* New York: D. Appleton, 1903.
   Duncan, Alastair. *Louis Comfort Tiffany.* New York: Harry N. Abrams, Inc., Publishers, 1992.
   Duncan, Alastair. *Masterworks of Louis Comfort Tiffany.* New York: Harry N. Abrams, Inc., Publishers, 1989.
   Duncan, Alastair. *Tiffany Windows.* New York: Simon and Schuster, Inc., 1980.
   Eidelberg, Martin and Nancy A. McClelland. *Behind the Scenes of Tiffany Glassmaking: The Nash Notebooks.* New York: St. Martin's Press, 2001.
   "The End of a Dream." *Newsday* March 8, 1957:7.
   Faude, Wilson H. "Associated Artists and the American Renaissance in Decorative Arts." *Winterthur Portfolio* 10 (1975):101–30.

Tiffany, Louis Comfort – Laurel Hollow – *The Briars* and *Laurelton Hall* (cont'd)

Frelinghuysen, Alice Cooney. "Louis Comfort Tiffany at the Metropolitan Museum." *The Metropolitan Museum of Art Bulletin* Summer 1998.

Grant, Marena. "Treasures From Laurelton Hall; Collection of Tiffany Glass of the Hugh F. McKeans." *Antiques* 111 (April 1977):752–59.

Harrison, Mrs. Burton. "Some Work of the Associated Artists." *Household Art* 1893:56–73.

Harrison, Constance C. "Some Work of the Associated Artists." *Harper's Magazine* 69 (1884):343–51.

Hopkins, Alfred. *Modern Farm Buildings.* New York: McBride, Nast and Co., 1913.

Howe, Samuel. "American Country House of Louis Comfort Tiffany." *International Studio* 33 (February 1908):294–96.

Howe, Samuel. "The Garden of Mr. Louis Comfort Tiffany." *House Beautiful* 35 (January 1914):40–2.

Howe, Samuel. "The Long Island Home of Mr. Louis C. Tiffany." *Town and Country* September 6, 1913: 24–26, 42.

Howe, Samuel. "One Source of Color Values [Louis C. Tiffany Gardens]." *House & Garden* 10 (September 1906):105–13.

Howe, Samuel. "The Silent Fountains of Laurelton Hall." *Arts and Decoration* September 1913:377–79.

Kaufmann, Edgar. "At Home with Louis C. Tiffany." *Interiors* 117 (December 1957):112–25, 183.

Kaufmann, Edgar. "Tiffany, Then and Now." *Interiors* February 1955:82–5.

Kellogg, Cynthia. "Designs by Mr. Tiffany." *The New York Times Magazine* January 26, 1958:50–1.

Koch, Robert. "Hidden Treasures in the McKean Tiffany Collection." In *Revolt in the Parlor: Five Essays Given at Rollins College.* (Winter Park, FL: The Parlor Press, 1969):79–84.

Koch, Robert. *Louis Comfort Tiffany.* New York: Museum of Contemporary Crafts, 1958.

Koch, Robert. *Louis C. Tiffany, Rebel In Glass.* New York: Crown Publishers, Inc., 1982.

Koch, Robert. *Louis C. Tiffany's Art Glass.* New York: Crown Publishers, Inc., 1977.

Koch, Robert. *Louis C. Tiffany's Glass – Bronzes – Lamps: A Complete Collector's Guide.* New York: Crown Publishers, Inc., 1971.

Koch, Robert. "The Stained Glass Decades: A Study of Louis Comfort Tiffany (1848–1933) and the Art Nouveau in America. " Ph.D. dissertation. Yale University, 1957.

"The Long Island Home of Mr. Louis C. Tiffany." *Town and Country* 6 (September 1913):24–6, 42.

"Long Island Landmark Burns." *The New York Herald Tribune* March 6, 1957.

Lothrop, Stanley. "Louis Comfort Tiffany Foundation." *American Magazine of Art* 14 (1923):615–17.

"Louis C. Tiffany." *Art Digest* 1 (February 1933).

"Louis C. Tiffany Enjoined." *The New York Times* June 9, 1916:21.

"Louis C. Tiffany Wins." *The New York Times* May 22, 1904.

Louis Comfort Tiffany and Stanford White and Their Circle. Roslyn Harbor, NY: Nassau County Museum of Art. 1999.

Louis Comfort Tiffany: The Laurelton Hall Years. Roslyn, NY: Fine Arts Museum, 1986.

Louis Comfort Tiffany: The Paintings. New York: Grey Gallery and Study Center, New York University, 1979. exhibition catalog

"A Many–Sided Creator of the Beautiful." *Arts and Decoration* 17 (1922):176–77.

McKean, Hugh F. "Looking at the World Through Colored Favrile Glass." In *Revolt in the Parlor: Five Essays Given at Rollins College.* (Winter Park, FL: The Parlor Press, 1969):17–32.

McKean, Hugh F. *The 'Lost' Treasures of Louis Comfort Tiffany,* Garden City: Doubleday & Co., Inc., 1980.

"Mr. Louis C. Tiffany, Famous Artist in Stained Glass," *New York Herald Magazine* 23 (April 1916).

Mumford, J. K. "A Year at the Tiffany Foundation." *Arts and Decoration* 14 (1921):272–73.

Neustadt, Egon. *The Lamps of Tiffany.* New York: The Fairfield Press, 1970.

"Old Tiffany Mansion Burns on NY North Shore." *The New York Times* March 8, 1957:27.

"On the Exhibit of Stained Glass at the Fair." *American Architect and Building News* 11 (November 1893): 74–5.

Paul, Tessa. *The Art of Louis Comfort Tiffany.* New York: Exeter Books, 1987.

Pierson, Dorothy Stewart. *Uncle Louis and Laurelton Hall.* privately printed, 1981.

"Portrait of Louis C. Tiffany." *Arts and Decoration* December 1921.

Potter, Norman. *Tiffany Glassware.* New York: Crown Publishers, Inc., 1988.

Price, Joan Elliot. *Louis Comfort Tiffany: The Painting Career of a Colorist.* New York: Peter Lang Publishing, 1996.

Purtell, Joseph. *The Tiffany Touch.* New York: Random House, 1972.

Ralph, Julian. *Chicago and the World's Fair.* New York: Harper & Brothers, 1892.

"Revival of the Fanciest: Tiffany Glass." *Harper's Magazine* 213 (September 1956):80.

Saarinen, Aline B. "Famous, Derided and Revived." *The New York Times* March 13, 1955:9.

Saylor, Henry H. "The Country Home of Mr. Louis C. Tiffany." *Country Life in America* 15 (December 1908):157–62.

Saylor, Henry H. "Indoor Fountains." *Country Life in America* August 1908:366.

Tiffany, Louis Comfort – Laurel Hollow – *The Briars* **and** *Laurelton Hall* (cont'd)

Shiel, John B. "Louis Comfort Tiffany." *Long Island Forum* February 1983:26–31.

Smith, Minna Caroline. "Louis C. Tiffany – The Celestial Hierarchy." *International Studio* 33 (February 1908):96–9.

Speenburgh, Gertrude. *The Arts of the Tiffanys.* Chicago: Lightner Publishing Corp., 1956.

Spinzia, Judith A. "Artistry In Glass: Louis Comfort Tiffany's Legacy in Nassau County." *The Nassau County Historical Society Journal* 1991:8–17.

Spinzia, Judith A. "Artistry In Glass: The Queens Ecclesiastical Windows of Louis Comfort Tiffany." *Newsletter of the Queens Historical Society* July/August 1989:8–10.

Spinzia, Judith A. "Artistry In Glass: The Undisputed Master, Our Oyster Bay Neighbor." *The Freeholder* 2 (Winter 1998):3–5; and 2 (Spring 1998):3–5, 24.

Spinzia, Raymond, Judith, and Kathryn. *Long Island: A Guide to New York's Suffolk and Nassau Counties.* New York: Hippocrene Books, Inc., second edition, 1991. [Please note that subsequent research by the authors has proven that the stained–glass windows in Saint John the Baptist Episcopal Church, Center Moriches, were not created by Tiffany but, most probably, by the firm of Duffner and Kimberly.]

"Tiffany Home and Art Works Will Go On Sale." *The New York Herald Tribune* September 8, 1946.

Tiffany, Louis Comfort. "American Art Supreme in Colored Glass." *The Forum* 15 (1893):621–28.

Tiffany, Louis Comfort [as dictated to Charles DeKay]. *The Art Work of Louis Comfort Tiffany.* Garden City: Doubleday, Page & Co., 1914. [Reprinted with a new forward by J. Alastair Duncan (Poughkeepsie, NY: Apollo), 1987.]

Tiffany, Louis Comfort. "Brittany Diary," Unpublished manuscript [in family possession], 1907.

Tiffany, Louis Comfort. "Color and Its Kinship to Sound." *The Art World* 2 (1917):142–43.

Tiffany, Louis Comfort. *The Dream Garden.* Philadelphia: Curtis Publishing Co., 1915. [booklet]

Tiffany, Louis Comfort. "The Gospel of Good Taste." *Country Life in America* 14 (November 1910):105.

Tiffany, Louis Comfort. "The Quest of Beauty." *Harper's Bazaar* December 1917:43–4.

Tiffany, Louis Comfort. "The Tasteful Use of Light and Color in Artificial Illumination." *Scientific American* 104 (April 15, 1911):373.

Tiffany, Louis Comfort. "What Is the Quest of Beauty?" *The International Studio* 58 (April 1916):lxiii.

"Tiffany Mansion Fire Continues to Flame." *Newsday* March 9, 1957:10.

Tiffany, Nelson Otis. *The Tiffanys of America, History and Genealogy.* Buffalo, NY: privately printed, 1901.

"Tiffany's Home." *Architectural Record* 10 (October 1900):191–202.

"Tiffany Sues Oyster Bay." *The New York Times* June 25, 1916.

"A Tribute to Mr. Louis Comfort Tiffany." *Bulletin of the Stained Glass Association of America* December 1928:8–12.

Triennial Catalog Of the Eagleswood Military Academy, and Prospectus For 1864–1865. 1864.

VanWagner, Judith, et al. *Long Island Estate Gardens.* Greenvale, NY: Hillwood Art Gallery, 1985.

Waern, Ceclia. "The Industrial Arts of America: The Tiffany Glass & Decorating Company." *International Studio* 2 (1897):156–65.

Waern, Ceclia. "The Industrial Arts of America: The Tiffany Glass & Decorating Company." *International Studio* 5 (1898):16–21.

Wallach, Amei. "New Setting for Old Treasures of American Art." *Newsday, Long Island Magazine* August 3, 1980:21.

"Watercolors by Louis C. Tiffany." *American Magazine of Art* 13 (1922):258–59.

Weir, Hugh. "Through the Looking Glass – An Interview with Louis Comfort Tiffany." *Collier's* 23 (May 1925).

Winter, Henry J. Francis. *The Dynasty of Louis Comfort Tiffany.* Boston: privately printed, 1971.

Winter, Henry J. Francis. *The Louis Comfort Tiffany Commemorative Edition.* Boston: privately printed, 1972.

Tiffany, Perry – Old Westbury

The Nassau County Museum Collection includes photographs of the estate.

Tower, Roderick – Lattingtown; Syosset – *Chestnut Vale***;**
      and Old Westbury – *French House*

The Nassau County Museum Collection includes photographs of the Old Westbury estate.

Sclare, Liisa and Donald. *Beaux–Arts Estates: A Guide to the Architecture of Long Island.* New York: The Viking Press, 1980.

Townsend, James Mulford, II – Mill Neck

The Nassau County Museum Collection includes photographs of the estate.

Underhill, Daniel – Jericho

The Nassau County Museum Collection includes photographs of the estate.

Underhill, Samuel Jackson – Jericho
The Nassau County Museum Collection includes photographs of the estate.

Uris, Percy – Brookville – *Broadhollow*;
          and Sands Point – *Sandy Cay*
The Nassau County Museum Collection includes photographs of the Sands Point estate.
     "The Contents of *Broadhollow,* Oyster Bay, Long Island, NY: The Property of the Estate of Mrs. Percy Uris."
        New York: Christie, Manson & Woods International, Inc., 1985. auction catalog

Van Alen, James H. – Old Brookville – *Penny Pond*
The Nassau County Museum Collection includes photographs of the estate.

General References to Vanderbilt Family

[*see also* references to individual Vanderbilt family members]

Biltmore Estate, Asheville, NC, has material collected from all Vanderbilt families in their archives.
New York State Library, Albany, NY, has Cornelius Vanderbilt's six–volume will.
Queens College Library, Historical Collection, Flushing, NY, has Vanderbilt family records, including 1699 tax rolls and
    a deposit of 1790–1840 material.
Suffolk County Vanderbilt Museum and Planetarium archives, Centerport, LI, has photographs of the family.
    Allen, Armin Brand. *The Cornelius Vanderbilts of the Breakers: A Family Retrospective May 27 – October 1,*
        1995. Newport: The Preservation Society of Newport County, 1995.
    Andrews, Wayne. *The Vanderbilt Legend: The Story of the Vanderbilt Family, 1794–1940.* New York:
        Harcourt, Brace and Co., 1941.
    Auchincloss, Louis. *The Vanderbilt Era: Profile of a Gilded Age.* New York: Charles Scribner's Sons, 1989.
    Baker, Paul. *Richard Morris Hunt.* Cambridge: The MIT Press, 1980.
    Balsan, Consuelo Vanderbilt. *The Glitter and the Gold.* New York: Harper & Brothers, 1952.
    Beebee, Lucius. *The Big Spenders.* Garden City: Doubleday & Co., Inc., 1966.
    Belmont, Alva. "Unpublished 1917 Autobiography of Alva Vanderbilt Belmont." In Wood Collection,
        Huntington Library, San Marino, California.
    Belmont, Alva. "Unpublished 1933 Autobiography of Alva Vanderbilt Belmont." In Matilda Young Papers,
        Special Collections Department, William R. Perkins Library, Duke University, Durham, North Carolina.
    Brough, James. *Consuelo: Portrait of an American Heiress.* New York: Coward, McCann & Geoghegan, Inc.,
        1979.
    Burden, Shirley. *The Vanderbilts in My Life: A Personal Memoir.* New Haven: Ticknor & Fields, 1981.
    Field, Frederick Vanderbilt. *From Right to Left: An Autobiography.* Westport, CT: L. Hill, 1983.
    Foreman, John and Robbe Pierce Stimson. *The Vanderbilts and the Gilded Age: Architectural Aspirations,*
        1879–1901. New York: St. Martin's Press, 1991.
    Fowler, Marian. *In a Gilded Cage: From Heiress to Duchess.* New York: St. Martin's Press, 1994.
    Gavan, Terrence. *The Newport Barons.* Newport: Pineapple Publications, 1988.
    Goldsmith, Barbara. *Little Gloria . . . Happy At Last.* New York: Alfred A. Knopf, 1980.
    Kaiser, Harvey H. *Great Camps of the Adirondacks.* Boston: David R. Godine, 1982.
    King, Robert B. *The Vanderbilt Homes.* New York: Rizzoli International Publications, Inc., 1989.
    Lane, Wheaton. *Commodore Vanderbilt: An Epic of the Steam Age.* New York: Alfred A. Knopf, 1942.
    MacColl, Gail and Carol McD. Wallace. *To Marry an English Lord: Or, How Anglomania Really Got Started.*
        New York: Workman Publishing, 1989.
    MacDowell, Dorothy K. *Commodore Vanderbilt and His Family: A Biographical Account of the Descendants*
        of Cornelius and Sophia Johnson Vanderbilt. privately printed by Dorothy K. MacDowell, 1700 Fifth
        Avenue W., Hendersonville, NC., 1989.
    Marlborough, Duchess of [Consuelo Vanderbilt Balsan]. "Hostels for Women." *The Nineteenth Century and*
        After 1911:858–66.
    Marlborough, Duchess of [Consuelo Vanderbilt Balsan]. "The Position of Woman," Parts 2, 3, 10. *North*
        American Review 89 (1909):180–93, 351–59, 11–24.
    The Old Oakdale History, Volume I. Oakdale, NY: William K. Vanderbilt Historical Society of Dowling
        College, 1983.
    The Old Oakdale History, Volume II: Era of Elegance, Part I. Oakdale, NY: William K. Vanderbilt Historical
        Society of Dowling College, 1993.
    Patterson, Jerry E. *The Vanderbilts.* New York: Harry N. Abrams, Inc., Publishers, 1989.
    Rector, Margaret Hayden. *Alva, That Vanderbilt–Belmont Woman.* Wickford, RI: The Dutch Island Press, 1992.

General References to Vanderbilt Family (cont'd)

Sloane, Florence Adele. *Maverick In Mauve.* Garden City: Doubleday & Co., Inc., 1983.

Smith, Arthur D. *Commodore Vanderbilt: An Epic of American Achievement.* New York: Robert M. McBride & Co., 1927.

Spinzia, Raymond E. "In Her Wake: The Story of Alva Smith Vanderbilt Belmont." *The Long Island Historical Journal* 6 (Fall 1993):96–105.

Stasz, Clarice. *The Vanderbilt Women: Dynasty of Wealth, Glamour and Tragedy.* New York: St. Martin's Press, 1991.

Stein, Susan R. *The Architecture of Richard Morris Hunt.* Chicago: The University of Chicago Press, 1986.

Swanberg, W. A. *Whitney Father, Whitney Heiress.* New York: Charles Scribner's Sons, 1980.

Vanderbilt, Arthur T. *Fortune's Children: The Fall of the House of Vanderbilt.* New York: William Morrow & Co., Inc., 1989.

Vanderbilt, Cornelius, Jr. *Farewell to Fifth Avenue.* New York: Simon & Schuster, Inc., 1935.

Vanderbilt, Cornelius, Jr. *Man of the World: My Life on Five Continents.* New York: Crown Publishers, Inc., 1959.

Vanderbilt, Cornelius, Jr. *Queen of the Golden Age: The Fabulous Story of Grace Wilson Vanderbilt.* New York: McGraw–Hill Book Co., Inc., 1956.

Vanderbilt, Gloria. *Black Knight, White Knight.* New York: Alfred A. Knopf, 1987.

Vanderbilt, Gloria. *Once Upon a Time.* New York: Alfred A. Knopf, 1985.

Vanderbilt, Gloria Morgan and Lady Thelma Furness. *Double Exposure: A Twin Autobiography.* New York: David McKay Co., Inc., 1958.

Vanderbilt, Gloria Morgan. *Without Prejudice.* New York: E. P. Dutton, 1936.

Van Rensselaer, Philip. *The Vanderbilt Women.* Chicago: Playboy Press, 1978.

Vichers, Hugo. *Gladys: Duchess of Marlborough.* New York: Holt, Rinehart & Winston, 1979

References to individual estate owners continue alphabetically

Vanderbilt, Virginia Graham Fair – Brookville; Glen Cove;
Lake Success – *Deepdale*;
and Manhasset – *Fairmont*

The Nassau County Museum Collection includes photographs of *Deepdale.*
Architectural Forum 29 (December 1918):plates 95, 96.
Architectural Forum 41 (July 1924):6.
Patterson, Augusta Owen. *American Homes of Today.* New York: The Macmillan Co., 1924.

Vanderbilt, William Kissam, Jr. – Centerport – *Eagle's Nest*;
and Lake Success – *Deepdale*

Avery Architectural and Fine Arts Library, Columbia University, NYC, has photographs of *Deepdale* in their Samuel Gottscho Collection of photographs.

The Long Island Division, Queens Borough Public Library, Jamaica, NY, has the 1949 sales brochure for *Deepdale.*

The Nassau County Museum Collection includes photographs of *Deepdale.*

Office of the County Clerk, Suffolk County, Riverhead, LI, has William Kissam Vanderbilt, Jr.'s will on file.

Suffolk County Vanderbilt Museum and Planetarium archives, Centerport, LI, has photographs of the family, an album of photographs showing building of Motor Parkway, an album on *Deepdale,* photographs of Vanderbilt's yacht *Tarantula,* and film clips of Vanderbilt's plane.
"Alva." *Country Life in America* 1934.
"The *Alva*." *Illustrated American* August 6, 1892.
American Homes and Gardens 2 (April 1906):229–35.
"The Baronial Parks of Long Island: Mr. W. K. Vanderbilt, Jr. and His Lake Success Purchase and Plans." *New York Herald* January 25, 1903. *[Deepdale]*
Fashionable Dress December 1923. *[Deepdale]*
Ferree, Barr. "Notable American Homes, *Deepdale*, the Estate of W. K. Vanderbilt, Jr., Great Neck, Long Island." *American Homes and Gardens,* 2 (April 1906):229–30.
Good Housekeeping August 1923. *[Deepdale]*
McKim, Mead & White. *A Monograph of the Work of McKim, Mead & White 1879–1915.* New York: DaCapo Press, 1985.
Patterson, Augusta Owen. "A Rambling Spanish House on Long Island." *Town and Country* October 15, 1928.
Pearce, Ronald H. "The Deepdale Golf and Country Club, Great Neck, Long Island." *Architectural Record* 60 (December 1926):524.

Vanderbilt, William Kissam, Jr. – Centerport – *Eagle's Nest*;
and Lake Success – *Deepdale* (cont'd)

Sclare, Liisa and Donald. *Beaux–Arts Estates: A Guide to the Architecture of Long Island.* New York: The Viking Press, 1980.

"Tudor Manor Style is Adapted to Modern Life in the Long Island Home of Mrs. William K. Vanderbilt." *Vogue* September 1917.*[Deepdale]*

Vanderbilt, William Kissam., Jr. *West Made East with Loss of a Day: A Chronicle of Motor Ship Alva on the First Circumnavigation of the Globe Under the United States Naval Reserve Yacht Pennant.* New York: privately printed, 1933.

"The William K. Vanderbilt, Jr. Place at Deepdale, Long Island." *The Spur* 13 (January 15, 1914):27.

The William Kissam Vanderbilt II Library at the Vanderbilt Museum, Centerport, Long Island, New York: A Catalog of Selected Materials. Centerport, NY: Vanderbilt Museum, 1981.

"W. K. Vanderbilt Gives Yacht *Alva* to Navy. $3,000,000 Craft Thrice circled Globe." *New York Herald Tribune* December 28, 1942.

Your Home July 1928. *[Deepdale]*

Van Ingen, Lawrence Bell, Jr. – Lattingtown – *Preference*

The Nassau County Museum Collection includes photographs of the estate.

Van Ingen, Lawrence Bell, Sr. – Lattingtown – *Preference*

The Nassau County Museum Collection includes photographs of the estate.

Van Santvoord, Alexander S. – Glen Cove

The Nassau County Museum Collection includes photographs of the estate.
Home and Field May 1933.

Vietor, Dr. John Adolf, Sr. – Matinecock – *Cherrywood*

The Nassau County Museum Collection includes photographs of the estate.
Town and Country April 1, 1930.

Von Stade, Francis Skiddy, Sr. – Old Westbury

Howell, E. W. *Noted Long Island Homes.* Babylon, NY: E. W. Howell Co., 1933.

Walker, Elisha, Sr. – Muttontown – *Les Pommiers*

The Nassau County Museum Collection includes photographs of the estate.

Wang, Charles B. – Cove Neck

The Nassau County Museum Collection includes photographs of the Youngs House.

Warburg, Gerald Felix – Brookville – *Box Hill Farm*

The Nassau County Museum Collection includes photographs of the estate and family, blueprints of the house, and Gerald Felix Warburg's papers.

Ward, Aaron – Roslyn Harbor – *Willowmere*

The Nassau County Museum Collection includes photographs of the estate.

Watriss, Frederick N. – Old Brookville

Country Life in America 46 (September 1924):38.

Webb, James Watson., Sr., and Electra Havemeyer Webb – Old Westbury;
and Syosset – *Woodbury House*

Shelburne Museum, Shelburne, VT. has the Webb papers.

Hewes, Lauren B. and Celia Y. Oliver. *To Collect in Earnest: The Life and Work of Electra Havemeyer Webb.* Shelburne, VT: Shelburne Museum, 1997.

Sherman, Joe. *The House at Shelburne Farms: The Story of One of America's Great Country Estates.* Middlebury, VT: Ericksson, 1985.

Webb, William Seward D., Jr. – Old Westbury

Architecture 36 (September 1917):178–9.

Weld, Francis Minot, II – Lloyd Harbor – *Lulworth*
    Architectural Record 50 (October 1921):255–57.
    "Country House of F. M. Weld, Esquire, Huntington, Long Island." *American Architect* 108 (July 7, 1915):263.

Wetmore, Elizabeth Bisland – Centre Island – *Applegarth*
    Bisland, Elizabeth. "The Building of *Applegarth.*" *Country Life in America* 18 (October 1910):657–60.
    Bisland, Elizabeth. "The Abdication of Man." *North American Review* 167 (August 1898):191–99.
    Marks, Jason. *Around the World in 72 Days.* Pittsburgh: Sterlinghouse Publisher, Inc., 1999.
    (Wetmore) Bisland, Elizabeth. *A Flying Trip Around the World.* New York: Harper & Brothers, 1891.

Whalen, Grover A., Sr. – Roslyn Heights
    Whalen, Grover A. *Mr. New York: The Autobiography of Grover A. Whalen.* New York: G. P. Putnam's Sons, 1955.

Wheeler, Frederick Seymour – Brookville – *Delwood*
The Nassau County Museum Collection includes photographs of the estate.

Whitney, Cornelius Vanderbilt – Mill Neck – *Oakley Court*;
              and Old Westbury – *Whitney House*
The Nassau County Museum Collection includes photographs of the estate.
    "The Fabled Past: The Whitneys of Westbury." *The North Shore Journal* 13 (May 27, 1982) n.p.
    Howell, E. W. *Noted Long Island Homes.* Babylon, NY: E. W. Howell Co., 1933.
    Hoyt, Edwin P. *The Whitneys: An Informal Portrait, 1635–1975.* New York: Weybright & Talley Publishers, 1976.
    Rodengen, Jeffrey L. *The Legend of Cornelius Vanderbilt Whitney.* Fort Lauderdale, FL: Write Stuff Enterprises, Inc., 2000.
    Whitney, Cornelius Vanderbilt. *High Peaks.* Lexington, KY: The University Press of Kentucky, 1977. [an autobiography]
    Whitney, Cornelius Vanderbilt. *Lone and Level Sand.* [an autobiography]
    Whitney, Cornelius Vanderbilt. *Live a Year With a Millionaire.* Lexington, KY: Maple Hill Press, 1981.
    Whitney, Cornelius Vanderbilt. *The Owl Hoots Again.*
    Whitney, Cornelius Vanderbilt. *First Flights.*
    Whitney, Eleanor Searle. *Invitation to Joy: A Personal Story.* New York: Harper & Row Publishers, 1971.

Whitney, Edward Farley – Cove Neck
The Department of Landscape Architecture Documents Collection, University of California, Berkeley, CA, has Beatrix Farrand's landscape plans for the estate.
    Brown, Jane. *Beatrix: The Gardening Life of Beatrix Jones Farrand 1872–1959.* New York: Viking Penguin Books, 1995.

Whitney, George, Sr. – Old Westbury – *Home Acres*
    Howell, E. W. *Noted Long Island Homes.* Babylon, NY: E. W. Howell Co., 1933.

Whitney, Gertrude Vanderbilt – Old Westbury
Archive of American Art, Whitney Museum of American Art, NYC, has Gertrude Vanderbilt Whitney's personal papers and those of the Whitney Studio Gallery.
The Nassau County Museum Collection includes photographs of the estate.
Smithsonian Museum, Washington, DC, has Gertrude Vanderbilt Whitney's papers, c. 1850–1946 and the papers of her grandmother, Flora Miller Irving, which include information on Gertrude Vanderbilt Whitney.
    Architectural Record 21 (February 1907).
    Architectural Review 8 (January 1919):4–5.
    Bedford, Stephen and Richard Guy Wilson. *The Long Island Country House, 1870–1930.* Southampton, NY: The Parrish Art Museum, 1988.
    Berman, Avis. *Rebels on Eighth Street: Juliana Force and Whitney Museum of American Art.* New York: Atheneum, 1990.
    Bottomley, William Lawrence. "A Selection from the Works of Delano and Aldrich." *Architectural Record* 54 (1923):3–71.
    Breuning, Margaret. "Gertrude Whitney's Sculpture." *Magazine of Art* February 19, 1943:62–5.
    "*Chateau des Beaux Arts*, Huntington, Long Island, NY." *The American Architect* 91:1636 (May 4, 1907).
    "The Fabled Past: The Whitneys of Westbury." *The North Shore Journal* 13 (May 27, 1982) n.p.
    Friedman, B. H. *Gertrude Vanderbilt Whitney.* Garden City: Doubleday & Co., Inc., 1978.

Whitney, Gertrude Vanderbilt – Old Westbury (cont'd)

Hewitt, Mark Alan. "Domestic Portraits: The Early Long Island Country Houses of Delano and Aldrich." In *Long Island Architecture*, Joann P. Krieg, ed. (Interlaken, NY: Heart of the Lakes Publishing, 1991).

Hoyt, Edwin P. *The Whitneys: An Informal Portrait, 1635–1975*. New York: Weybright & Talley Publishers, 1976.

McCarthy, Kathleen D. *Women's Culture: American Philanthropy and Art, 1830–1930*. Chicago: The University of Chicago Press, 1991.

Nochlin, Linda and Karen Radkai. "High Bohemia; Sculptor . . . Studio Evokes the American Artistic Taste of the Twenties." *House and Garden* 157 (September 1985):180.

Patterson, Augusta Owen. *American Homes of Today*. New York: The Macmillan Co., 1924.

Stasz, Clarice. *The Vanderbilt Women: Dynasty of Wealth, Glamour and Tragedy*. New York: St. Martin's Press, 1991.

Vanderbilt, Gloria. *Once Upon a Time: A True Story by Gloria Vanderbilt*. New York: Alfred A. Knopf, 1985.

Vanderbilt, Gloria Morgan. *Without Prejudice*. New York: E. P. Dutton, 1936.

Vanderbilt, Gloria Morgan and Lady Thelma Furness. *Double Exposure: A Twin Autobiography*. New York: David McKay Co., Inc., 1958.

Webb, L. J. *Walking the Dusk*. New York: Coward, McCann, 1932. [written by Gertrude Vanderbilt Whitney under pseudonym]

Whitney, Gertrude Capen. *Roses from My Garden*. Boston: Sherman French & Co., 1912.

Whitney, Gertrude Vanderbilt. *A Love Affair*. New York: Richardson & Snyder, 1984. [a novel]

Whitney, John Hay – Manhasset – *Greentree*

The Nassau County Museum Collection includes photographs of the estate.

Grafton, David. *The Sisters: The Lives and Times of the Fabulous Cushing Sisters*. New York: Villard Books, 1992.

Hoyt, Edwin P. *The Whitneys: An Informal Portrait, 1635–1975*. New York: Weybright & Talley Publishers, 1976.

Kahn, Ely Jacques, Jr. *Jock: The Life and Times of John Hay Whitney*. Garden City: Doubleday & Co., 1981.

Whitney, William Collins – Old Westbury

Library of Congress, Washington, DC, has William Collins Whitney's papers.

The Nassau County Museum Collection includes photographs of the estate.

"The Fabled Past: The Whitneys of Westbury." *The North Shore Journal* 13 (May 27, 1982) n.p.

"Furniture & Works of Art – Architectural Elements of the Residence of the Late Helen Hay Whitney, 972 Fifth Avenue, New York." New York: Parke–Bernet Galleries, Inc., 1946. auction catalog [New York City house]

Hirsh, Mark D. *William C. Whitney: Modern Warwick*. New York: Dodd, Mead & Co., 1948.

Hoyt, Edwin P. *The Whitneys: An Informal Portrait, 1635–1975*. New York: Weybright & Talley Publishers, 1976.

Klepper, Michael. *The Wealthy 100: From Benjamin Franklin to Bill Gates – A Ranking of the Richest Americans Past and Present*. Secaucus, NJ: The Citadel Press, 1996.

McKim, Mead & White. *A Monograph of the Work of McKim, Mead & White 1879–1915*. New York: DaCapo Press, 1985. [New York City house]

Swanberg, W. A. *Whitney Father, Whitney Heiress*. New York: Charles Scribner's Sons, 1980.

Whitney, William Payne – Manhasset – *Greentree*

The Nassau County Museum Collection includes photographs of the estate.

Architecture 30 (December 1914):282, 284.

Hoyt, Edwin P. *The Whitneys: An Informal Portrait, 1635–1975*. New York: Weybright & Talley Publishers, 1976.

McKim, Mead & White. *A Monograph of the Work of McKim, Mead & White 1879–1915*. New York: DaCapo Press, 1985.

"Mr. Payne Whitney's Home at Manhasset." *Town and Country* 70 (February 1, 1915):30.

New York Herald Tribune August 18, 1929.

Town and Country April 1, 1929.

Will, Harold Henry – Roslyn – *Villa Marina*

The Nassau County Museum Collection includes photographs of the estate.

Williams, Douglas – Cold Spring Harbor – *Wawapek*

The Nassau County Museum Collection includes photographs of the estate.

Williams, Harrison – Bayville – *Oak Point*
The Nassau County Museum Collection includes photographs of the estate.
> Brown, Jane. *Beatrix: The Gardening Life of Beatrix Jones Farrand 1872–1959.* New York: Viking Penguin
> > Books, 1995.
> "The Fabled Past: A Tale of Bygone Days." *The North Shore Journal* 3 (September 30, 1971) n.p.
> Howell, E. W. *Noted Long Island Homes.* Babylon, NY: E. W. Howell Co., 1933.

Wilson, Charles Porter – Mill Neck
The Nassau County Museum Collection includes photographs of the estate.

Wing, S. Bryce – Old Westbury – *Twin Oaks*
> *Architectural Review* 10 (April 1920):99, 101, 104.

Winmill, Robert Campbell – Mill Neck – *Borradil Farm*
The Nassau County Museum Collection includes photographs of the estate.
> *House and Garden* July 1927.

Winthrop, Bronson – Muttontown
The Nassau County Museum Collection includes photographs of the estate.

Winthrop, Egerton Leigh, Jr. – Muttontown – *Muttontown Meadows*
The Nassau County Museum Collection includes photographs of the estate.
> *The American Architect* July 28, 1915.
> Delano & Aldrich. *Portraits of Ten Country Houses.* Garden City: Doubleday & Page, 1924.
> *Garden Magazine* February 1922.
> *Garden Magazine* March 1922.
> *Garden Magazine* August 1923.
> *Good Housekeeping* August 1921.
> Hewitt, Mark Alan. *The Architect & the American Country Home 1890–1940.* New Haven: Yale University
> > Press, 1990.
> *House and Garden* February 1925.
> *House Beautiful* 1922.
> Howe, Samuel. "The Country House of Mr. E. L. Winthrop, Jr." *Town and Country* 14 (November 1914).
> Patterson, Augusta Owen. *American Homes of Today.* New York: The Macmillan Co., 1924.
> Sclare, Liisa and Donald. *Beaux–Arts Estates: A Guide to the Architecture of Long Island.* New York: The
> > Viking Press, 1980.
> *The Sun* June 28, 1930.
> *Town and Country* May 20, 1921.
> *Vogue* September 15, 1919.

Wood, Chalmers, Jr. – Woodbury – *Little Ipswich*
The Nassau County Museum Collection includes photographs of the estate.
Octagon Museum of American Architectural Foundation, Prints and Drawings Collection, Washington, DC, has
> photographs of the estate.
> > *Arts and Decoration* April 1937.
> > *Arts and Decoration* April 1938.
> > Bedford, Stephen and Richard Guy Wilson. *The Long Island Country House, 1870–1930.* Southampton, NY:
> > > The Parrish Art Museum, 1988.
> > Howell, E. W. *Noted Long Island Homes.* Babylon, NY: E. W. Howell Co., 1933.
> > *The New York Times* April 13, 1941.
> > *The Spur* March 1936.

Woods, Ward Wilson, Jr. – Lattingtown
The Nassau County Museum Collection includes photographs of the estate.

Woodward, William, Jr. – Oyster Bay Cove – *The Playhouse*
> Braudy, Susan. *This Crazy Thing Called Love: The Golden World and Fatal Marriage of Ann and Billy
> > Woodward.* New York: Alfred A. Knopf, 1992.

Woodward, William, II – Brookville – *Enfield Chase*
Braudy, Susan. *This Crazy Thing Called Love: The Golden World and Fatal Marriage of Ann and Billy Woodward.* New York: Alfred A. Knopf, 1992.

"The Residence of William Woodward, Esq. New York City, Delano & Aldrich Architects, New York" *The Architectural Record* April 1919.

Woolworth, Frank Winfield – Glen Cove – *Winfield Hall*
The Nassau County Museum Collection includes photographs of the estate.
Nassau County Surrogate's Court, Mineola, LI, Probate Department file #7966 and Box #22 have papers relating to the construction costs and payment dates for *Winfield Hall.*
Architecture 3 (June 1, 1900):227. [1899 house]

Brough, James. *The Woolworths.* New York: McGraw–Hill Book Co., 1982.

Croly, Herbert. "Residence of the Late F. W. Woolworth." *Architectural Record* 47 (March 1920):194.

Klepper, Michael. *The Wealthy 100: From Benjamin Franklin to Bill Gates – A Ranking of the Richest Americans Past and Present.* Secaucus, NJ: The Citadel Press, 1996.

Nichols, John P. *Skyline Queen and the Merchant Prince: The Woolworth Story.* New York: Trident Press, 1973.

Sclare, Liisa and Donald. *Beaux–Arts Estates: A Guide to the Architecture of Long Island.* New York: The Viking Press, 1980.

Winkler, John K. *Five and Dime: The Fabulous Life of F. W. Woolworth.* New York: Robert McBride & Co., 1940.

Work, Bertram G., Sr. – Mill Neck – *Oak Knoll*
The Nassau County Museum Collection includes photographs of the estate.
Architectural Forum 41 (July 1924):8.

Architectural Record 50 (October 1921):296, 329.

Arts and Decoration July 1922.

Arts and Decoration September 1922.

Charm April 1925.

Country Life October 1924.

Country Life in America 1918.

Delano & Aldrich. Portraits of Ten Country Houses. Garden City: Doubleday, Page & Co., 1924.

Garden Magazine August 1927.

Hewitt, Mark Alan. *The Architect & the American Country Home 1890–1940.* New Haven: Yale University Press, 1990.

Hewitt, Mark Alan. "Domestic Portraits: The Early Long Island Country Houses of Delano and Aldrich." In *Long Island Architecture*, Joann P. Krieg, ed. (Interlaken, NY: Heart of the Lakes Publishing, 1991).

House and Garden July 1921.

House and Garden June 1922.

House and Garden October 1922.

Patterson, Augusta Owen. *American Homes Today.* New York: The Macmillan Co., 1924.

Vogue August 1, 1923.

Young, Edward Lewis – Glen Cove – *Meadow Farm*
Architectural Record 23 (January 1918).

Young, Thomas F. – Oyster Bay Cove – *Elmwood*
The Nassau County Museum Collection includes photographs of the estate.

Zog I, King of Albania – Muttontown
The Nassau County Museum Collection includes vertical file material, historical research reports, and photographs of the estate.

Biographical Dictionaries Master Index 1975–1976. Detroit: Gale Research Co., 1975.

Biography and Genealogy Master Index 1981–1985. Detroit: Gale Research Co., 1985.

Biography and Genealogy Master Index 1986–1990. Detroit: Gale Research Co., 1990.

Biography and Genealogy Master Index 1991–1995. Detroit: Gale Research Co., 1995.

Current Biography Yearbook. New York: The H. W. Wilson Co. [selected volumes]

Dow Jones News Internet Retrieval.

The Eagle and Brooklyn: The Record of the Progress of the Brooklyn Daily Eagle. 2 vols. Brooklyn, NY: The Brooklyn Eagle, 1893.

Levy, Felice, ed. *Obituaries on File.* New York: Facts on File, 1979.

Lexis Nexis Academic Universe, Internet.

Malone, Dumas, ed. *Dictionary of American Biography.* NY: Charles Scribner's Sons, 1935.

The National Cyclopaedia of American Biography. Clifton, NJ: James T. White & Co., 1984.

Newsday Internet Retrieval.

New York State's Prominent and Progressive Men. 2 vols. New York: New York Tribune, 1900.

The New York Times Index. New York: The New York Times. [annual obituaries from 1979–1997]

The New York Times Obituaries Index, vol. 1, 1858–1968. New York: The New York Times, 1970.

The New York Times Obituaries Index, vol. 2, 1969–1978. New York: The New York Times, 1980.

Polk's Glen Cove Directory. New York: R. L. Polk & Co., Inc., 1924.

Prominent Families of New York. New York: The Historical Co., 1898.

Standard and Poor's Register of Corporations, Directors and Executives. Charlottesville, VA: Standard and Poors, Inc. [selected volumes]

Who's Who in America. Chicago: Marquis Who's Who, Inc. [selected volumes]

Who's Who in Finance and Industry. Chicago: Marquis Who's Who, Inc. [selected volumes]

Who's Who in New York. New York: Lewis Historical Publishing Co. [selected volumes]

Who's Who in New York City and State. New York: L. R. Hamersly Co., 1904–1960 [selected volumes]

Who's Who in the East. Chicago: Marquis Who's Who, Inc. [selected volumes]

Who's Who of American Women. Chicago: Marquis Who's Who, Inc. [selected volumes]

Who Was Who in America with World Notables. New Providence, NJ: Marquis Who's Who, Inc. [selected volumes]

Nassau County

Atlas of Nassau County, Long Island, N. Y. Brooklyn: E. Belcher Hyde, Inc., 1906.

Atlas of Nassau County, Long Island, N. Y. Brooklyn: E. Belcher Hyde, Inc., 1914.

Map of Nassau County. Great Neck, NY: Baker Crowell, Inc., c. 1922.

Hagstrom's Street, Road and Property Ownership Map of Nassau County, Long Island, New York. New York: Hagstrom Co., Inc., 1932.

Hagstrom's Street, Road and Property Ownership Map of Nassau County, Long Island, New York. New York: Hagstrom Co., Inc., 1946.

Hagstrom Map of Nassau County. Maspeth, NY: Hagstrom Map Co., Inc., 1995.

Real Estate Map of Nassau County, New York. New York: E. Belcher Hyde, Inc., 1927.

Suffolk County

Dolph's Street, Road and Land Ownership Map of Suffolk County. New York: Dolph & Stewart, 1929.

Hagstrom's Street, Road and Property Ownership Map of Nassau County, Long Island, New York. New York: Hagstrom Co., Inc., 1946. [includes Suffolk County villages located in the western section of the Town of Huntington]

Hagstrom Map of Western Suffolk County. Maspeth, NY: Hagstrom Map Co., Inc., 1996.

Hagstrom's Street, Road and Landownership Atlas of Suffolk County, Long Island, Western Half. New York: Hagstrom Co., Inc., 1944.

Real Estate Reference Map of a Part of Suffolk County, Long Island, N.Y.: Comprising of the Townships [Towns] of Huntington, Smithtown, Babylon and Islip. New York: E. Belcher Hyde, Inc. Engineers & Publishers, 1931.

American Architect and Building News, 106

American Homes and Gardens, 720

The Architect, 78

Architect and Builders Journal, 48

Architectural League of New York, 301, 491, 793 top and bottom right, 891

Architectural Record, 29, 639

The Architectural Review, 315

Architecture, 107 top, 739

The Brickbuilder, 109, 530, 531

Edward A. T. Carr, 30, 61 bottom, 124, 162, 170, 204, 205 top and bottom, 221, 222, 260, 282, 417, 423, 546, 664, 665, 666, 667, 827

Robert R. Coles Long Island History Collection, Glen Cove Public Library, 92, 202 all, 203, 623

Country Life, 316

Country Life in America, 732

Mrs. Margery Gerdes Fates, 31, 241 bottom, 293, 294

Damon Friesocin, 418, 419

Greenlawn – Centerport Historical Association, 163 bottom, 195, 381, 550 bottom, 552 bottom, 759, 818, 820, 830, 855 bottom

Oswald C. Hering. *Concrete and Stucco Houses,* 747

Hicks Nursery, 242, 616

Alfred P. Hopkins. *Modern Farm Buildings,* 189

House and Garden, 782

E. W. Howell. *Noted Long Island Homes,* 42 top, 143 top, 213, 244, 383, 396, 472, 695, 713, 860, 870, 873 bottom, 881 bottom

Innocenti and Webel, 262

Gary Lawrance, 7 34, 43, 52, 60, 69 top, 114, 127, 146 bottom, 153, 161, 169, 171, 188, 229, 233, 236 bottom, 261, 298, 300, 303 top, 334, 351, 376, 384, 387 top, 389, 393, 407, 451, 494, 500, 506, 520 top, 552 top, 553, 572, 575, 596, 624 top, 636, 642, 645, 651, 688, 714, 721, 741, 750, 753, 754, 755, 756 top, 763 top, 766, 769, 774, 806, 831 top, 861, 862, 873 top, 881, top, 890

Library of Congress, 150, 159, 179, 182, 201, 226, 230 all, 239, 259 all except middle, 264 all except middle, 265, 272, 290, 309, 310 top, 369, 439, 508, 532, 539, 576, 584, 585 all, 619, 631, 647, 705, 751, 790 top, 813, 855 top, 856, 882, 884

Locust Valley Leader, 15, 490

Munsey Magazine, 103, 303 bottom

Nassau County Division of Museum Services, 42 bottom, 47, 54, 56 top left, lower right, 61 top, 73, 84 all except middle, 86, 88, 101, 102, 105 top, 107 bottom, 108, 118, 120, 129, 137, 141, 151, middle, bottom right and left, 156, 163 top, 175, 194 bottom, 199, 217, 235, 252 top, 274 top and bottom, 275, 281, 287, 289, 302, 329 all, 330, 333, 348, 360, 362 both, 372 bottom, 391, 412, 414, 427 all, 430, 432, 443 both, 474, 489 top left, middle, bottom right, 507 both, 511, 520 bottom, 521, 540 top, 544, 547 both, 556, 558, 561, 573, 604, 606, 609, 618 top and bottom left, 625, 627, 628, 629, 644, 661, 681, 693, 706, 710, 712, 719, 740, 763 bottom, 764, 781, 790 bottom, 807 bottom, 809 top, 817 all, 829, 835 top, 867 top, 892

New York State Office of Parks, Recreation, and Historic Preservation, 1, 567, 599, 673

The Oyster Bay Historical Society, 21, 53, 214, 314, 483, 540 bottom, 543, 618 top right, 650, 657, 677, 684, 729, 756 bottom, 769 top, 791, 793 middle, 800, 803, 808, 833, 840, 843 both, 849, 857, 858

Private Collection, 5, 220, 252 bottom, 288, 555 bottom, 733, 809 bottom, 812, 815

Mrs. Margaret Fay Schantz Roosevelt, 679

Raymond E. Spinzia, xiii, xiv, xv, 2, 10, 12, 18, 20, 24, 25, 37, 38, 45, 56 top right, lower left, 58, 69 bottom, 79, 84 middle, 89, 90, 93, 94, 95, 99 all, 105 bottom, 110, 113, 115, 121, 123, 126, 128, 132, 138, 142, 143 bottom, 146 top, 151 top right and left, 155, 158, 160 all, 184, 185, 186, 191, 197, 198, 200, 207, 218, 234, 236 top, 241 top, 243, 245, 246 top, 248, 249, 255, 257, 259 middle, 264 middle, 269, 271, 277, 286, 292, 297, 304, 305 top and bottom, 308, 310, 311, 322, 325, 326, 331, 332, 336 both, 337, 343, 345, 353, 358, 361, 365, 371, 372 top, 373, 374, 375 both, 378, 380, 387 bottom, 395, 399, 400, 403, 404, 413, 420, 422, 424, 429, 438 both, 447, 450, 455, 457 bottom, 463, 467, 475, 476, 481, 482, 489 top right, bottom left, 501, 502, 503, 509, 510, 512, 514, 516, 519, 524, 525, 527, 528, 536, 538, 542, 550 top, 557, 565, 574, 579, 583, 591, 592, 597, 600, 603, 618 middle, bottom right, 624 bottom, 630, 632, 633, 640, 641, 648, 652, 653, 654, 658, 659, 662, 663, 669, 670, 676, 682, 683, 685, 696, 702, 703, 704, 709, 722, 725, 728, 744, 758, 768, 778, 779, 785, 788, 789, 793 top and bottom left, 796, 804, 807 top, 814, 816, 831 bottom, 835 bottom, 836, 837, 839, 844, 845, 846, 865, 867 bottom, 868 both, 869, 878, 885, 886, 887

The Spur, 67, 457 top

John Williams Taylor, 72 top and bottom, 611

Vanderbilt Museum, 56 middle

Charles Harris Whitaker. *Bertram Grosvenor Goodhue: Architect and Master of Many Arts*, 470

Dr. George L. Williams, 194 top, 402, 466

About the Authors

Judith and Raymond Spinzia are former Long Island residents, now residing in central Pennsylvania. Their first book, *Long Island: A Guide to New York's Suffolk and Nassau Counties* (New York: Hippocrene Books, 1988; 1991 (revised), is a standard reference book which has been used as a textbook for teaching Long Island history and can still be found in almost all public libraries and schools on Long Island. A third (revised) edition of the guidebook is scheduled to be published in 2007.

The Spinzias write and speak, jointly and separately, on a variety of Long Island-related subjects including the North and South Shore estates, Tiffany stained-glass windows, and the Vanderbilts of Long Island. On several occasions their lectures have been chosen by the radio station of *The New York Times*, WQXR, as the cultural event of the day in the New York Metropolitan area. Additionally, they have been featured on local television and radio programs and in articles published by *The New York Times, Newsday*, and other regional newspapers.

The Spinzias served as Long Island history consultants for a local cable television channel that, in an effort to encourage local interest, aired material from their guidebook twice daily. They also were consultants for a Japanese television network for a documentary on Louis Comfort Tiffany and contributed material to the Arts and Entertainment Network's "Biography" series for its presentations on the Vanderbilt and Tiffany families.

Their companion volume to this North Shore work entitled *Long Island's Prominent South Shore Familes: Their Estates and Their Country Homes in the Towns of Babylon and Islip* was also published in 2006.